Handbook of Spirituality, Health, and Well-Being

A Psychological Perspective

Edited by Jon R. Webb

Routledge
Taylor & Francis Group
NEW YORK AND LONDON

Designed cover image: Getty Images

First published 2026
by Routledge
605 Third Avenue, New York, NY 10158

and by Routledge
4 Park Square, Milton Park, Abingdon, Oxon, OX14 4RN

Routledge is an imprint of the Taylor & Francis Group, an informa business

ISBN: 978-1-032-57591-9 (hbk)
ISBN: 978-1-032-57590-2 (pbk)
ISBN: 978-1-003-44004-8 (ebk)

DOI: 10.4324/9781003440048

Typeset in Times New Roman
by SPi Technologies India Pvt Ltd (Straive)

"A landmark contribution. This handbook signals the coming-of-age of the psychological study of spirituality. It moves spiritual study from the background to the foreground of theory, research, and practice. This large volume brings together over 100 researchers who describe the wide-ranging implications of spirituality for topics including health, positive psychology, mental health treatment, neuroscience, struggles, gender, race, and culture. Webb has done a masterful job organizing and integrating these diverse contributions in ways that honor the multi-dimensional, multi-level, and multi-valent character of spiritual life. This is an essential volume for researchers and professionals interested in understanding the deepest dimension of our lives."

Kenneth I. Pargament, PhD, *Professor Emeritus, Department of Psychology, Bowling Green State University, Bowling Green, Ohio, USA, Chief Editor of 2-Volume:* APA Handbook of Psychology, Religion, and Spirituality *(2013), Author of* Spiritually Integrated Psychotherapy: Understanding and Addressing the Sacred *(2007), Author (with Julie J. Exline) of* Spiritual Struggles in Psychotherapy: From Research to Practice *(2022) and Former President of Division 36 of the American Psychological Association, the Society for the Psychology of Religion and Spirituality (1996–1997)*

"Dr. Jon Webb has brought together an amazing array of gifted scholars to produce an engaging and informative volume. This well-designed, up-to-date, and wide-ranging handbook is a must-have for scientists, practitioners, scholars, and educators seeking a deep dive into the topics of spirituality, well-being, and health."

Julie J. Exline, PhD, *Bonner-Lowry Professor of Psychiatry and Neurobehavioral Sciences and Director, Division of Perceptual Studies, University of Virginia Health Systems, Charlottesville, Virginia, USA, Co-Associate Editor:* APA Handbook of Psychology, Religion, and Spirituality *(Volume 1, 2013) and Former President of Division 36 of the American Psychological Association, the Society for the Psychology of Religion and Spirituality (2012–2013)*

"The *Handbook of Spirituality, Health, and Well-Being: A Psychological Perspective* is a landmark contribution to the field of healthcare. Edited and authored by distinguished scholars and researchers who are leaders in psychology, religion, spirituality, and healthcare, this compelling volume features over 40 in-depth chapters that explore groundbreaking theories, insightful research findings, and practical applications concerning the significant influence of religion and spirituality in human health and well-being. It is a comprehensive and authoritative resource for researchers, medical and mental health providers, clergy, and the media. Its wealth of knowledge makes it essential for all healthcare professionals and researchers."

P. Scott Richards, PhD, *Co-Founder and President, Bridges Institute for Spiritually Integrated Psychotherapies, Saint George, Utah, USA, Editor of* Handbook of Spiritually Integrated Psychotherapies *(2023), Former President of Division 36 of the American Psychological Association, the Society for the Psychology of Religion and Spirituality (2004–2005), Fellow of the Society for the Psychology of Religion and Spirituality and Fellow of Division 29 of the American Psychological Association, the Society for the Advancement of Psychotherapy*

"Authoritative, relevant, and comprehensive, this Handbook will stand as a beacon for current and future generations of scholars and practitioners in spirituality and health, directing the way toward deep knowledge and effective practice. This volume reflects the combined expertise and genius of a diverse set of scholars well versed in spirituality and health. This is the sort of work that consolidates and advances fields of study. Dr. Webb and his collaborators have done us all a great service."

Nathaniel G. Wade, PhD, *Professor and Associate Chair of Psychology, Iowa State University, Ames, Iowa, USA, Co-Editor of* Handbook of Forgiveness *(2nd Edition, 2020)*

"In the face of an already vast and expanding literature on spirituality, health and well-being, it is natural to question the need for another book. Yet here expert chapter authors show the value of conceptual and empirical exploration of multiple sectors of this landscape, including psychology, culture, well-being, neuroscience, secular spirituality, interventions, competencies, spiritual struggles and future directions. The result is a comprehensive resource providing uniquely helpful context and content for both new students and experienced scholars."

John R. Peteet, MD, *Associate Professor of Psychiatry, Harvard Medical School, Boston, Massachusetts, USA, Co-Author of* Handbook of Religion and Health *(3rd Edition, 2024)*

"This volume is a monumental achievement, with chapters authored by the leading experts in their fields and a scope encompassing both empirical research and sophisticated theoretical contributions. A particular strength is the focus, not just on physical health, but on well-being in its many facets, recognizing the importance of religion and spirituality to human flourishing when facing difficulties such as those associated with health challenges. Chapters on psychological foundations of the spirituality-health/well-being connection make this volume accessible to newcomers to the field, while comprehensive chapters on specific health conditions as well as specific spiritual practices and interventions make this the go-to volume for state-of-the-art knowledge in this vital and rapidly evolving field."

M. Elizabeth Lewis Hall, PhD, *Professor of Psychology, Rosemead School of Psychology, Biola University, La Mirada, California, USA, Former President of Division 36 of the American Psychological Association, the Society for the Psychology of Religion and Spirituality (2013–2014)*

"Webb's *Handbook of Spirituality, Health, and Well-Being* covers an amazing breadth of pioneering topics - suicidology, gender, sexuality, culture, neuroscience - all the while grounded within the RiTE model of spirituality and written by experts in their fields. The *Handbook* offers the reader a state-of-the-science review of research on the intricate connections between spirituality, health, and well-being from a psychological perspective and paves the way for the work yet to be done to further illuminate our understanding of human spirituality. This volume is a rich resource with a myriad of applications for students, practitioners, and scholars alike…a real gift to anyone intellectually curious about spirituality."

Gina Magyar-Russell, PhD, *Professor of Psychology, Loyola University Maryland, Baltimore, Maryland, USA*

"This groundbreaking volume is a tour de force in the integration of spirituality, health, and psychological science. Combining contributions from respected scholars and practitioners, it offers a comprehensive exploration from conceptual frameworks to hands-on therapeutic strategies. The book does not shy away from difficult questions or emerging frontiers, including spiritual struggles, moral injury, and secular spirituality. Drawing on my background in the field, I found it to be an invaluable resource that thoughtfully integrates empirical rigor with the complex, often overlooked dimensions of spirituality and well-being. A must-read for clinicians, researchers, and anyone seeking to understand the role of spirituality in human flourishing."

Edyta Charzyńska, PhD, *Institute of Applied Psychology, Faculty of Management and Social Communication, Jagiellonian University, Kraków, Poland; Institute of Psychology, Institute of Pedagogy, Faculty of Social Sciences, University of Silesia in Katowice, Katowice, Poland*

"Webb has brought together an impressive range of contributions for this Handbook from both established and up-and-coming scholars from the fields of spirituality and health that is as diverse as it is informative. From positive psychology to cultural contexts to neuroscience, the *Handbook of Spirituality, Health, and Well-Being* offers the full spectrum of psychological perspectives on the value and relevance of spirituality for health and well-being. With its comprehensive coverage of theory and practice related to issues in understanding and addressing physical health and mental well-being from a spiritual perspective across diverse populations, this Handbook is sure to become the quintessential resource for those interested in the role of spirituality in health and well-being."

Fuschia M. Sirois, PhD, *Professor of Social and Health Psychology, Durham University, Durham, England, Co-Editor-in-Chief of* British Journal of Health Psychology, *Editor of* The Palgrave Handbook of Positive Psychology and Health *(2025)*

"Social science in general - and psychology in particular - has long eschewed the spiritual domain, despite its clear sociological, personal, and even clinical importance. This comprehensive volume boldly closes that gap. It is rigorously empirical and deeply relevant to contemporary psychological science."

David H. Rosmarin, PhD, *Associate Professor of Psychology, Harvard Medical School, Director, Spirituality & Mental Health Program, McLean Hospital, Belmont, Massachusetts, USA and President of Division 36 of the American Psychological Association, the Society for the Psychology of Religion and Spirituality (2025-2026)*

Handbook of Spirituality, Health, and Well-Being

This edited volume is a one-stop repository of the most current research on the relevance and application of the broad construct of spirituality to health and well-being, including mental, physical, and social aspects.

This book brings together foundational material (e.g., definitions, neuroscience, and culture/diversity), a focus on particular health and well-being related outcomes impacted by spiritual factors (e.g., chronic medical conditions, depression, and trauma), a focus on particular manifestations of spirituality and their relationship to health and well-being (e.g., forgiveness, meditation, and gratitude), clinical interventions and perspectives (e.g., mindfulness, compassion, and hope), and inclusive contextual considerations (e.g., sexual and gender minorities, racial and ethnic minorities, and persons with intellectual and developmental disabilities and their families). Additionally, given the international-level public health crisis of addiction, each of these broad sections of the book includes a chapter focused on addiction recovery.

This book is the go-to resource for scholars, researchers, clinicians, and lay people who are interested in understanding, developing, and/or providing ethically comprehensive and inclusive spiritually attuned healthcare.

This edited volume concludes with a call for increased funding in both the public and private sectors for intentional initiatives focused on not only additional research, but active dissemination and implementation of the science related to spirituality, health, and well-being.

Jon R. Webb is a licensed clinical psychologist and a tenured associate professor in the Department of Community, Family, and Addiction Sciences at Texas Tech University.

To all those who have gone before – both personally and professionally. For building the foundation for something like this to happen. That is, the publication of a scholarly volume focused on spirituality, health, and well-being, and enabling me to play a part in bringing it to pass. Especially to my mother. I love you and I miss you terribly.

Contents

Figures

Tables

About the Editor

Jon R. Webb, Ph.D., is a licensed psychologist and a tenured associate professor in the Department of Community, Family, and Addiction Sciences at Texas Tech University. He received his American Psychological Association accredited doctorate in Clinical Psychology from the California School of Professional Psychology, Los Angeles (under the mentorship of Seymour L. Zelen, Ph.D.), and completed two Research Postdoctoral Fellowships at the University of Michigan Medical School – one in the Department of Psychiatry (Substance Abuse Section, Addiction Research Center) and one in the Department of Physical Medicine and Rehabilitation (Division of Rehabilitation Psychology and Neuropsychology). Dr. Webb also completed a Clinical Postdoctoral Fellowship at the Kaiser Permanente Medical Center in San Rafael, California in the Department of Psychiatry, Chemical Dependency Services. Dr. Webb's primary professional interests are in the area of spirituality and health, including ritualistic, theistic, and existential spirituality, forgiveness, temptation, psychache, existangst, addiction recovery, suicidal behavior, and medical rehabilitation. He has published more than 65 peer-reviewed journal articles and edited-book chapters on these topics. And, with Routledge in 2021, released a sole-authored book entitled, *Understanding Forgiveness and Addiction: Theory, Research, and Clinical Application*. Lastly, two developing areas of scholarly interest for Dr. Webb are (1) the identification and illumination of a *transcendent thread* tying all of humanity together (see the corresponding entry in the Index for this volume) and (2) addressing the reluctance of therapeutic psychology (and related fields) to R.A.I.S.E. particular issues with our clients; that is, religiousness/spirituality, addictive behavior, interpersonal violence, suicidal behavior, and ethical behavior.

Contributors

Hisham Abu-Raiya
Bob Shapell School of Social Work
Tel Aviv University
Tel Aviv, Israel

Eric Y. Aglozo
Department of Psychology
Arizona State University
Tempe, Arizona, USA

Ernestina Aidoo
Department of Community, Family, and Addiction Sciences
Texas Tech University
Lubbock, Texas, USA

Micheline R. Anderson
Department of Psychiatry & Human Behavior
Warren Alpert Medical School of Brown University
Providence, Rhode Island, USA

Heather Austin-Robillard
Department of Community, Family, and Addiction Sciences
Texas Tech University
Lubbock, Texas, USA

Greta Bivins
School of Psychology, Counseling, and Family Therapy
Wheaton College
Wheaton, Illinois, USA

Comfort M. Boye
Department of Psychology
Indiana University South Bend
South Bend, Indiana, USA

Matilda K. Boye
College of Media and Communication
Texas Tech University
Lubbock, Texas, USA

Craig S. Cashwell
Department of Education and Human Development
Clemson University
Clemson, South Carolina, USA

Amy L. Chapman
Mary Lou Fulton College for Teaching and Learning Innovation
Arizona State University
Tempe, Arizona, USA

Zhuo Job Chen
School of Nursing
University of North Carolina at Charlotte
Charlotte, North Carolina, USA

Adam B. Cohen
Department of Psychology
Arizona State University
Tempe, Arizona, USA

Jamian Coleman
Department of Counseling, Human Development, and Family Science
The University of Tennessee, Knoxville
Knoxville, Tennessee, USA

George E. Comiskey
Department of Community, Family, and Addiction Sciences
Center for Students in Addiction Recovery
Texas Tech University
Lubbock, Texas, USA

Carla Nikki Cook
Counseling and Testing Services
University of North Texas
Denton, Texas, USA

Richard G. Cowden
Human Flourishing Program, Institute for Quantitative Social Science
Department of Epidemiology, Harvard T.H. Chan School of Public Health
Harvard University
Cambridge, Massachusetts, USA

Abigail A. Crete
Spirituality Mind Body Institute
Department of Counseling and Clinical Psychology
Teachers College, Columbia University
New York, New York, USA

Joseph M. Currier
Psychology Department
University of South Alabama
Mobile, Alabama, USA

Trever Dangel
Department of Psychology, Addiction, and Trauma Recovery Services
Springfield Hospital Center
Sykesville, Maryland, USA

Don E. Davis
Department of Counseling and Psychological Services
Georgia State University
Atlanta, Georgia, USA

Edward (Ward) B. Davis
School of Psychology, Counseling, and Family Therapy
Wheaton College
Wheaton, Illinois, USA

Janet B. Dean
School of Counseling
Asbury Theological Seminary
Wilmore, Kentucky, USA

Maya Joshi Delity
Department of Psychology
University of Colorado Denver
Denver, Colorado, USA

Frederick A. DiBlasio
School of Social Work
University of Maryland
Baltimore, Maryland, USA

David C. Dollahite
School of Family Life
Brigham Young University
Provo, Utah, USA

Mariel Emrich
Department of Psychological Sciences
University of Connecticut
Storrs, Connecticut, USA

George Fitchett
Department of Religion, Health, and Human Values
Rush University Medical Center
Chicago, Illinois, USA

Jesse Fox
Department of Counselor Education
Stetson University
DeLand, Florida, USA

William F. Gerber
Department of Community, Family, and Addiction Sciences
Center for Students in Addiction Recovery
Texas Tech University
Lubbock, Texas, USA

Brandon J. Griffin
Department of Psychiatry
University of Arkansas for Medical Sciences
Little Rock, Arkansas, USA

Benjamin B. Hall
Department of Behavioral Sciences
Harding University
Searcy, Arkansas, USA

J. Irene Harris
Mental and Behavioral Health
VA Maine Healthcare System
Augusta, Maine, USA, and
Institute of Medicine
University of Maine
Orono, Maine, USA

William L. Hathaway
Academic Affairs
Regent University
Virginia Beach, Virginia, USA

Alyssa Hill
Department of Community, Family, and Addiction Sciences
Texas Tech University
Lubbock, Texas, USA

Jameson K. Hirsch
Department of Psychiatry and Behavioral Sciences
Quillen College of Medicine
East Tennessee State University
Johnson City, Tennessee, USA

Joshua N. Hook
Department of Psychology
University of North Texas
Denton, Texas, USA

Anthony Isacco
Clinical Psychology Programs
Saint Mary's University of Minnesota
Minneapolis, Minnesota, USA

Kate Fiona Jones
Institute for Ethics and Society
University of Notre Dame Australia
Sydney, NSW, Australia

Nicholas D. Kellar
Department of Psychology
University of Colorado Denver
Denver, Colorado, USA

Elizabeth Palmer Kelly
The Ohio State University Comprehensive Cancer Center
Columbus, Ohio, USA

Harold G. Koenig
Department of Psychiatry & Behavioral Sciences
Department of Medicine
Duke University Medical Center
Durham, North Carolina, USA

Karol Konaszewski
Faculty of Education
University of Białystok
Białystok, Poland

Jacob Kranendonk
Department of Psychology
University of North Texas
Denton, Texas, USA

Jean L. Kristeller
Department of Psychology
Indiana State University
Terre Haute, Indiana, USA

Yejin Lee
Department of Counseling and Psychological Services
Georgia State University
Atlanta, Georgia, USA

Loren D. Marks
School of Family Life
Brigham Young University
Provo, Utah, USA

Kevin S. Masters
Department of Psychology | Anschutz Health and Wellness Center
University of Colorado Denver | Anschutz Medical Campus
Denver, Colorado, USA

Ashnita S. Maxton
Department of Community, Family, and Addiction Sciences
Texas Tech University
Lubbock, Texas, USA

Jessica McCleese
Department of Psychology
Regent University
Virginia Beach, Virginia, USA

Julia A. McGee
Tulane University School of Medicine
New Orleans, Louisiana, USA

Aaron T. McLaughlin
Department of Psychology and Counseling
University of Central Arkansas
Conway, Arkansas, USA

Lisa Miller
Spirituality Mind Body Institute
Columbia University
New York, New York, USA

Elisabeth J. Mistur
New York Anxiety Treatment
New York, New York, USA

Declan P. Murphy
Department of Community, Family, and Addiction Sciences
Texas Tech University
Lubbock, Texas, USA

James M. Nelson
Department of Psychology
Valparaiso University
Valparaiso, Indiana, USA

Jenae M. Nelson
Department of Psychology
Brigham Young University
Provo, Utah, USA

Andrew Newberg
Department of Integrative Medicine and Nutritional Sciences
Department of Radiology
Thomas Jefferson University
Philadelphia, Pennsylvania, USA

Cate Newcity
School of Psychology, Counseling, and Family Therapy
Wheaton College
Wheaton, Illinois, USA

Michael E. Nielsen
Department of Psychology
Georgia Southern University
Statesboro, Georgia, USA

Steve Oberg
Wheaton College Library
Wheaton College
Wheaton, Illinois, USA

David A. O'Connor
School of Psychology, Counseling, and Family Therapy
Wheaton College
Wheaton, Illinois, USA

Doug Oman
School of Public Health
University of California
Berkeley, California, USA

Crystal L. Park
Department of Psychological Sciences
University of Connecticut
Storrs, Connecticut, USA

Timothy M. Pawlik
Department of Surgery
The Ohio State University Wexner Medical Center
Columbus, Ohio, USA

Ralph L. Piedmont
Center for Professional Studies
Timonium, Maryland, USA

Nicole Piland
Department of Community, Family, and Addiction Sciences
Texas Tech University
Lubbock, Texas, USA

Thomas G. Plante
Department of Psychology
Department of Religious Studies
Jesuit School of Theology
Santa Clara University
Santa Clara, California, USA, and
Department of Psychiatry and Behavioral Sciences
Stanford University School of Medicine
Palo Alto, California, USA

Sharon E. Prager
Department of Community, Family, and Addiction Sciences
Texas Tech University
Lubbock, Texas, USA

Jeffrey M. Pyne
Center for Mental Health Outcome Research
Central Arkansas Veterans Healthcare System

Little Rock, Arkansas, USA, and
Department of Psychiatry
University of Arkansas for Medical Sciences
Little Rock, Arkansas, USA

Kristin E. Rabil
Department of Psychology
University of Colorado Denver
Denver, Colorado, USA

Jennifer S. Ripley
Department of Psychology
Regent University
Virginia Beach, Virginia, USA

Seyma N. Saritoprak
City of Hope Orange County
Lennar Foundation Cancer Center
Department of Supportive Care Medicine
Irvine, California, USA

Suza C. Scalora
Department of Psychiatry
Weill Cornell Medicine
New York, New York, USA

Sarah A. Schnitker
Department of Psychology and Neuroscience
Baylor University
Waco, Texas, USA

Anthony Scioli
Department of Psychology
Keene State College
Keene, New Hampshire, USA

Anna L. Scott
Department of Counseling and Psychological Services
Georgia State University
Atlanta, Georgia, USA

Edward P. Shafranske
Graduate School of Education and Psychology
Pepperdine University
Irvine, California, USA

Sebastian Binyamin Skalski-Bednarz
Institute of Psychology
Humanitas University
Sosnowiec, Poland, and
Faculty of Philosophy and Education
Katholische Universität Eichstätt-Ingolstadt
Eichstätt, Germany

Andrew J. Smith
Department of Psychiatry
Geisel School of Medicine at Dartmouth
Hanover, New Hampshire, USA

Eden Song
School of Psychology, Counseling, and Family Therapy
Wheaton College
Wheaton, Illinois, USA

Peta Stapleton
School of Psychology
Bond University
Robina, QLD, Australia

Jill D. Stinson
Department of Psychology
East Tennessee State University
Johnson City, Tennessee, USA

Stephen P. Stratton
School of Counseling
Asbury Theological Seminary
Wilmore, Kentucky, USA

Lauren A. Stutts
Department of Public Health
Davidson College
Davidson, North Carolina, USA

Janusz Surzykiewicz
Faculty of Philosophy and Education
Katholische Universität Eichstätt-Ingolstadt
Eichstätt, Germany
and
Faculty of Education
Cardinal Stefan Wyszyński University in Warsaw
Warsaw, Poland

Loren L. Toussaint
Department of Psychology
Luther College
Decorah, Iowa, USA

Jo-Ann C. Tsang
Department of Psychology and Neuroscience
Baylor University
Waco, Texas, USA

Timothy J. Usset
Division of Health Policy & Management
University of Minnesota
Minneapolis, Minnesota, USA

Daryl R. Van Tongeren
Department of Psychology
Frost Center for Social Science Research
Hope College
Holland, Michigan, USA

Tyler J. VanderWeele
Human Flourishing Program, Institute for Quantitative Social Science
Department of Epidemiology, Harvard T.H. Chan School of Public Health
Department of Biostatistics, Harvard T.H. Chan School of Public Health
Harvard University
Cambridge, Massachusetts, USA

Tehya A. Vassar
School of Family Life
Brigham Young University
Provo, Utah, USA

Vivian S. Vigliotti
Department of Social and Behavioral Sciences
Yale School of Public Health
New Haven, Connecticut, USA

Carley Vornlocher
Department of Psychology
Arizona State University
Tempe, Arizona, USA

Amy Wachholtz
Department of Psychology
University of Colorado Denver
Denver, Colorado, USA
and
Department of Psychiatry, Division of Addiction
Department of Hematology, Division of Oncology
University of Colorado Medical School/CU Medicine
Aurora, Colorado, USA,
and
Department of Psychiatry and Behavioral Sciences
University of Massachusetts Medical School
Worcester, Massachusetts, USA

Jon R. Webb
Department of Community, Family, and Addiction Sciences
Texas Tech University
Lubbock, Texas, USA

Noah Wilmoth
Department of Psychology
Georgia Southern University
Statesboro, Georgia, USA

Abigail G. Wiser
Department of Psychology
East Tennessee State University
Johnson City, Tennessee, USA

Hee Chan Woo
Department of Counseling and Psychological Services
Georgia State University
Atlanta, Georgia, USA

Alexandra S. Wormley
Department of Psychology
University of Michigan
Ann Arbor, Michigan, USA

Everett L. Worthington, Jr.
Department of Psychology
Virginia Commonwealth University
Richmond, Virginia, USA

Mark A. Yarhouse
School of Psychology, Counseling, and Family Therapy
Wheaton College
Wheaton, Illinois, USA

Sabrina G. Zuniga
Department of Psychology
University of North Texas
Denton, Texas, USA

Acknowledgments

This book project has been on my mind for a long time. At least since August 5, 2012 – the first time I purposefully added a date to a note file in my phone, after having already updated a couple/few times an initial outline of my ideas for what was to become this edited book. But, knowing myself, I'm sure I was thinking about it even before creating that initial note file, because I usually wind up making a note in my phone under only two circumstances. First, quick thoughts or pending tasks that I don't want to forget about. And, second, when I have – what seem to *me* to be – good ideas accumulating about a topic or project and I start getting concerned that I won't be able to remember everything when the time comes, so to speak. Once again, I'm grateful to Amanda Savage at Routledge for agreeing with me that this book project was a good idea! I truly appreciate the support I have received from Amanda, Ayushi Awasthi, and Sreevas Mangattumana, including those who work behind the scenes to make something like this happen.

After the contract was finalized for this project and everything was beginning to take shape in reality (as opposed to just in my mind!), it quickly became very clear to me that this project would never come to fruition without all of the wonderful colleagues that agreed to be contributors. Some I consider mentors, others I have known and worked with over the years, and still others I had never met, but knew of and admired their work from afar. I have had some incredible conversations and experiences over the course of inviting participation in and reviewing contributions to this project. As I mention in Chapter 1, when introducing the aims for this *Handbook*, I am truly amazed that I have the opportunity to explore and empirically examine topics related to spirituality, a topic of never-ending fascination for me! And, getting to talk through ideas with others, including in the context of bringing this project to completion has been and always is an incredible experience that I will always cherish. I am most grateful to each of you – the contributors to this project – for the time, effort, and excellence reflected in your work in the chapters that comprise this edited volume. Thank you! Likewise, I truly appreciate your support and encouraging words throughout this entire process. Also, I want to express my appreciation to those who served as reviewers of my book proposal to Routledge, for their expertise and time spent early in this process providing valuable feedback and suggestions. Thank you to colleagues who provided suggestions for authors for a couple of the chapters and facilitated introductions. And, last, but certainly not least, I am grateful to my wife, Jana, for your patience and support during this entire project, including assisting with data transfer and accuracy when creating the Tables in Chapter 1, and for your willingness to lend a helping hand whenever needed. I love you!

In the dedication section above, I mentioned those who have gone before – both personally and professionally. For brevity purposes both there and here, there are too many to mention.

Nevertheless, there, in the personal category, I felt compelled to mention my mother. Here, in the professional category, I feel compelled to mention Allen E. Bergin (1934-2024). Though I only corresponded very briefly with him in the late 1990s through the mail, his work and vision have had a profound impact on my career. His pioneering work in the context of values, religion/spirituality, and psychotherapy have played a large role in shaping the state-of-the-science – as we know it today – of counseling and psychotherapy, and the psychology of religion and spirituality.

Even though projects like this are what dreams are made of for an academic like me, time spent away from loved ones can be challenging. Truly, none of this would be possible without the love and support of both my immediate family and my family of origin. Each member of my family is inspiring to me. Earlier this year, my mother would have celebrated her 100th birthday, and of course another Mother's Day has come and gone without her. One of the reasons I am so fascinated by spirituality, professionally and personally, is because of my mother. She was exactly the mother I needed, in every way, including instilling in me a fervent desire to know more, based on the life of faith that she lived. Approaching two years ago, I was looking through some old LPs from my teenage years and I found a note from my mother, written to me during my wayward years. It was in pristine condition after having sat tucked away between album covers, untouched in a box for at least 40 years. It was a simple note, really, but I have framed it and look at it pretty much every day now.

Given my endless fascination with spirituality, and my abiding belief in and deep desire to know God, I must acknowledge that anything good and decent that I may do is a result of my pursuit of Him. Indeed, I know what my life would be like otherwise, and though I have a long way to go, I am no longer interested in that other life. For me, the principle discussed in *John* 7:17 is an anchor to my soul, and in a very real way, in part, an impetus for this book project.

Lubbock, Texas
September 2025

Part I

Relevance and Historical Development

Chapter 1

The Empirical Examination of the Association of Spirituality with Health and Well-Being

An Introduction

*Jon R. Webb**

On the wall to the left of me – as I am sitting at my computer beginning to write this introductory chapter – is a framed poster of a comment made in the spring of 1925 by Albert Einstein (b. 1879) in conversation with and as recalled by Esther Salaman (1955, p. 371): "I want to know [God's] thoughts, the rest are details." As an academic clinical psychologist, I occasionally tell my students (and others) how excited and privileged I am to make a living thinking about and studying such an endlessly fascinating topic to me – spirituality. Related to this, Einstein also argued in 1941 that "science without religion is lame, religion without science is blind" (Einstein 1954, p. 49). Although these are the opinions of one person from about 85 to 100 years ago (and some might argue, an appeal to authority), this person continues to be world-renowned for his commonly accepted genius-level stature in the context of modern science. As such, to me, it is important to consider his views on a matter,[1] still so hotly contested in both the scientific community and popular culture; that is, the compatibility of science and religion. The first portion of this chapter will provide brief discussions of (1) the presence of religion and spirituality in the world, (2) the relevance of religion and spirituality to health and well-being, and (3) the recently developed RiTE Model of Spirituality (including a very brief overview of circumstances spurring its development). The RiTE Model somewhat serves as a guiding framework for this project, including as a catalyst for discussion of definitional issues related to conceptualizing religion and spirituality.[2] This first portion is intended to provide a justification for a book focused on, in very simple terms, the compatibility of science and religion, or the need to understand religion and spirituality from a scientific perspective. The second portion of this chapter will provide an overview of the remainder of this edited volume focused on understanding the empirical association of spirituality with health and well-being, largely from a psychological perspective.

The Presence of Religion and Spirituality in the World

Simply put, religion (cf. religiousness) and spirituality are ubiquitous in the human population; to be clear, across the globe. For example, in their most recently available data from 2018 (i.e., Religion I-IV Cumulation; 1991, 1998, 2008, and 2018), the International Social Survey Programme (ISSP) Research Group (2025; see also, GESIS, 2024)[3] reports an estimated 75.34% and 88.71% of the world's population and the United States' population, respectively, believe in deity[4] or a higher power of some sort (see Table 1.7, v21). Likewise, 73.96% and 86.98%, respectively, are religious and/or spiritual (see Table 1.8, v49). Also, from their 2018 – Religion IV Report, an estimated 35.26% and 58.90%, respectively, have read scripture

* Corresponding Author: jon.r.webb@ttu.edu.

DOI: 10.4324/9781003440048-2

(outside of a worship service) during the past 12 months (GESIS, 2020).[5] From these few data points, three things are evident: (1) the vast majority of the world's population believes in deity, or a higher power of some sort; (2) at least 1 in 3 adults has read scripture during the past year; and (3) the United States' population appears to be more religious/spiritual than the rest of the world as a whole.[6] For more details regarding religion/spirituality among both the global population and the United States' population, including year-to-year fluctuation across 1991, 1998, 2008, and 2018, see Tables 1.1–1.8 and their corresponding Figures 1.1–1.4. Data reported therein are in the context of (1) science versus religion, (2) additional beliefs about God, (3) life after death, (4) heaven, (5) religious miracles, (6) God's concern for humans at a personal level, (7) meaning in life derived from belief in God, (8) connecting with God without formal worship services, (9) frequency of prayer, (10) levels of religiousness, and (11) whether respondents consider themselves to be (a) religious and spiritual, (b) religious, but not spiritual, (c) spiritual, but not religious, or (d) not spiritual and not religious.

Whether one is a believer (as I am), a non-believer, a disbeliever, or a former believer; indeed, whether one embraces, acknowledges, accepts, or rejects the data-driven reality that the vast majority of the human population is inclined toward religious and/or spiritual beliefs, values, and/or practices, the reasonable, indeed, ethical minimum is for scientists (i.e., the practitioners of science) to seek to maximize any salubrious effects and minimize any deleterious effects thereof.[7] And, in a non-biased manner, without seeking to impose personal perspectives, for or against. That is, disseminating empirical or otherwise objective findings to the consumer public.

The Relevance of Spirituality to Health and Well-Being

Engaging with religion/spirituality can play an important contributing role in human health, whether with respect to salubrious or deleterious effects. Indeed, important authored and edited books have brought together wide and varied empirical evidence largely in support of a salubrious[8] effect (see Koenig et al., 2024; Rosmarin & Koenig, 2020). However, though of great worth and value, much of this work has been in the context of religious activity and commitment (e.g., attending formal worship services), as opposed to particular spiritual principles such as gratitude, hope, and humility, among others.[9] Likewise, much of the previous, otherwise compiled work has been in the context of medical diagnosis. Importantly, the World Health Organization (WHO), in the first principle of its Constitution, defines health as "a state of complete physical, mental and social well-being and not merely the absence of disease or infirmity" (WHO, 2025, p. 1). One of the implications of this definition is that health (and related considerations regarding severity) is more than the presence or absence of one or more symptoms or diagnoses. For example, a reduction in symptoms does not necessarily address the problem, its implications, or the originating cause. To this end, an important guiding principle for this edited volume is that the notion of health is in reference to physical, mental, *and* social indicators of health *and* well-being (each of which is broadly construed).

Given the broad relevance of religiousness and spirituality to health and well-being, the largely salubrious effect thereof, and the ubiquitous presence of religion and spirituality in the human population, it is imperative to understand the associations of *particular* aspects of religiousness and spirituality with health and well-being (as opposed to focusing primarily on religious activity and commitment as more generalized constructs[10]). However, what exactly does religiousness and spirituality refer to? A distinction between religious activity and commitment versus engaging in particular spiritual principles was implied in the brief statement immediately above. Is there more to understanding what is meant by the constructs of *religiousness* and *spirituality*, how they relate to each other, and/or how they are thought about in the context of each other?

Table 1.1 Spirituality Related Estimates for the Year: 1991[a,b] – Part 1

Survey Item	*Response Options*								*Respondents*[c]		*Spirituality*[d]	
v63. Science v. Religion[e]	(SA)	(A)	(NAND)	(D)	(SD)	—	(CC)	(NA)	N	Nv	% +	% –
- Global	—	—	—	—	—	—	—	—	—	—	—	—
- United States	—	—	—	—	—	—	—	—	—	—	—	—
v21. Belief about God[f]	(1)	(2)	(3)	(4)	(5)	(6)						
- Global	3015	2617	3743	2193	4510	8418	161	313	24970	24496	77.01	22.99
- United States	31	60	92	69	241	834	1	31	1359	1327	93.14	6.86
v22. Beliefs about God[g]	(1)	(2)	(3)	(4)	—	—						
- Global	4079	2587	1588	13059	—	—	2865	792	24970	21313	68.72	31.28
- United States	24	47	63	1074	—	—	127	24	1359	1208	94.12	5.88
v23. Life After Death[h]	(1)	(2)	(3)	(4)	—	—						
- Global	5953	5806	4273	5941	—	—	2645	352	24970	21973	53.52	46.48
- United States	674	278	150	123	—	—	94	40	1359	1225	77.71	22.29
v24. Heaven[h]	(1)	(2)	(3)	(4)	—	—						
- Global	5807	5623	3622	6840	—	—	2515	563	24970	21892	52.21	47.79
- United States	776	275	115	63	—	—	38	62	1359	1229	85.52	14.48
v26. Religious Miracles[hy]	(1)	(2)	(3)	(4)	—	—						
- Global	4736	6464	4424	6205	—	—	2534	607	24970	21829	51.31	48.69
- United States	543	331	193	123	—	—	95	74	1359	1190	73.45	26.55

[a] GESIS (2024), ISSP (2025).
[b] For 1991, 1998, 2008, and 2018, the number of participating countries was 18, 31, 40, and 33, respectively.
[c] N = overall sample size; Nv = valid sample size (i.e., not including CC and NA). Note: If N - CC - NA ≠ Nv, it is likely that a particular country was not included on said item.
[d] Spirituality: % + = Spiritual (i.e., religious and/or spiritual responses / Nv); % – = Non-Spiritual (i.e., non-religious and/or non-spiritual responses / Nv).
[e] v63: “We trust too much in science and not enough in religious faith.” SA = strongly agree; A = agree; NAND = neither agree nor disagree; D = disagree; SD = strongly disagree; CC = can’t choose; NA = no answer. Note: % + = SA + A; % - = D + SD.
[f] 1 = no belief; 2 = no belief and no way to find out; 3 = not a personal God, but a Higher Power of some kind; 4 = belief in God, at times; 5 = have doubts, but believe; 6 = believe and have no doubts; CC = can’t choose; NA = no answer.
[g] 1 = no belief now and never have; 2 = no belief now, but used to; 3 = believe now, but didn’t used to; 4 = believe now and always have; CC = can’t choose; NA = no answer.
[h] 1 = yes, definitely; 2 = yes, probably; 3 = no, probably not; 4 = no, definitely not; CC = can’t choose; NA = no answer.

Table 1.2 Spirituality Related Estimates for the Year: 1991[a,b] – Part 2

Survey Item	*Response Options*													*Respondents*[c]		*Spirituality*[d]	
v31. God Concerned with Every Human Being Personally[e]	(SA)	(A)		(NAND)		(D)		(SD)		—		(CC)	(NA)	N	Nv	% +	% –
- Global	4215	5626		3977		4114		4290		—		2175	573	24970	22222	44.28	55.72
- United States	585	333		199		72		55		—		65	50	1359	1244	73.79	26.21
v33. Life is Meaningful, only because God Exists[e]	(SA)	(A)		(NAND)		(D)		(SD)		—							
- Global	2389	4161		4216		6035		6018		—		1526	625	24970	22819	28.70	71.30
- United States	298	305		312		190		133		—		58	63	1359	1238	48.71	51.29
v36. Connect with God without Church/Religious Services[e]	(SA)	(A)		(NAND)		(D)		(SD)		—							
- Global	—	—		—		—		—		—		—	—	—	—	—	—
- United States	—	—		—		—		—		—		—	—	—	—	—	—
v46. How Often Pray[f]	(1)	(2)	(3)	(4)	(5)	(6)	(7)	(8)	(9)	(10)	(11)						
- Global	8303	999	1364	2212	732	850	936	1118	1764	3618	2359	322	393	24970	24255	46.91	53.09
- United States	105	37	73	110	65	71	77	61	166	289	271	1	33	1359	1325	75.47	24.53
v48. Religiousness[g]	(1)	(2)		(3)		(4)		(5)	(6)	(7)							
- Global	558	2235		8021		4862		2016		2193	3083	732	270	24970	22968	47.08	52.92
- United States	61	284		620		219		52		38	32	28	25	1359	1306	73.89	26.11
v49. Religious and/or Spiritual[h]	(1)	(2)		(3)		(4)		—		—							
- Global	—	—		—		—		—		—		—	—	—	—	—	—
- United States	—	—		—		—		—		—		—	—	—	—	—	—

[a] GESIS (2024), ISSP (2025).
[b] For 1991, 1998, 2008, and 2018, the number of participating countries was 18, 31, 40, and 33, respectively.
[c] N = overall sample size; Nv = valid sample size (i.e., not including CC and NA). Note: If N - CC - NA ≠ Nv, it is likely that a particular country was not included on said item.
[d] Spirituality: % + = Spiritual (i.e., religious and/or spiritual responses / Nv); % – = Non-Spiritual (i.e., non-religious and/or non-spiritual responses / Nv).
[e] SA = strongly agree; A = agree; NAND = neither agree nor disagree; D = disagree; SD = strongly disagree; CC = can't choose; NA = no answer.
[f] 1 = never; 2 = less than once a year; 3 = about once or twice a year; 4 = several times a year; 5 = about once a month; 6 = 2–3 times a month; 7 = nearly every week; 8 = every week; 9 = several times a week; 10 = once a day; 11 = several times a day; CC = can't choose; NA = no answer.
[g] 1 = extremely religious; 2 = very religious; 3 = somewhat religious; 4 = neither religious nor non-religious; 5 = somewhat non-religious; 6 = very non-religious; 7 = extremely non-religious; CC = can't choose; NA = no answer.
[h] 1 = follow a religion and spiritual; 2 = follow a religion, but not spiritual; 3 = don't follow a religion, but spiritual; 4 = don't follow a religion and not spiritual; CC = can't choose; NA = no answer.

Table 1.3 Spirituality Related Estimates for the Year: 1998 – Part 1[a]

Survey Item	*Response Options*								*Respondents*[c]		*Spirituality*[d]	
v63. Science v. Religion[e]	(SA)	(A)	(NAND)	(D)	(SD)	—	(CC)	(NA)	N	Nv	% +	% –
- Global	2481	7748	9268	10173	5214	—	2683	352	37919	34884	29.32	44.11
- United States	106	270	329	347	155	—	42	35	1284	1207	31.15	41.59
v21. Belief about God[f]	(1)	(2)	(3)	(4)	(5)	(6)						
- Global	4092	3592	6158	3543	6334	13675	74	451	37919	37394	79.45	20.55
- United States	40	60	121	58	181	775	1	48	1284	1235	91.90	8.10
v22. Beliefs about God[g]	(1)	(2)	(3)	(4)	—	—						
- Global	5759	3343	2725	20389	—	—	5165	538	37919	32216	71.75	28.25
- United States	33	59	69	960	—	—	118	45	1284	1121	91.79	8.21
v23. Life After Death[h]	(1)	(2)	(3)	(4)	—	—						
- Global	9873	9211	5717	7591	—	—	3883	334	37919	32392	58.92	41.08
- United States	660	247	110	110	—	—	110	47	1284	1127	80.48	19.52
v24. Heaven[h]	(1)	(2)	(3)	(4)	—	—						
- Global	9155	7948	6029	8922	—	—	3927	628	37919	32054	53.36	46.64
- United States	770	223	90	75	—	—	71	55	1284	1158	85.75	14.25
v26. Religious Miracles[h]	(1)	(2)	(3)	(4)	—	—						
- Global	8022	8623	6441	9074	—	—	3812	637	37919	32160	51.76	48.24
- United States	577	304	142	99	—	—	102	60	1284	1122	78.52	21.48

[a] See notes for Table 1.1.

Table 1.4 Spirituality Related Estimates for the Year: 1998 – Part 2[a]

Survey Item	*Response Options*											*Respondents*[c]				*Spirituality*[d]	
v31. God Concerned with Every Human Being Personally[e]	(SA)	(A)	(NAND)	(D)	(SD)	—						(CC)	(NA)	N	Nv	% +	% –
- Global	7648	8480	6091	6096	5848	—						3246	510	37919	34163	47.21	52.79
- United States	493	370	142	107	67	—						50	55	1284	1179	73.20	26.80
v33. Life is Meaningful, only because God Exists[e]	(SA)	(A)	(NAND)	(D)	(SD)	—											
- Global	4004	5641	6618	9852	9167	—						2050	587	37919	35282	27.34	72.66
- United States	242	282	285	240	120	—						50	65	1284	1169	44.82	55.18
v36. Connect with God without Church/ Religious Services[e]	(SA)	(A)	(NAND)	(D)	(SD)	—											
- Global	—	—	—	—	—	—						—	—	—	—	—	—
- United States	—	—	—	—	—	—						—	—	—	—	—	—
v46. How Often Pray[f]	(1)	(2)	(3)	(4)	(5)	(6)	(7)	(8)	(9)	(10)	(11)						
- Global	11088	1739	2389	3765	1303	1515	1646	1824	3281	5748	2865	428	328	37919	37163	48.93	51.07
- United States	132	41	41	54	49	57	62	63	164	306	275	—	40	1284	1244	78.46	21.54
v48. Religiousness[g]	(1)	(2)	(3)	(4)	(5)	(6)	(7)										
- Global	957	4217	12967	7940	3985	3625	3111					927	190	37919	36802	49.29	50.71
- United States	83	234	603	121	59	46	56					40	42	1284	1202	76.54	23.46
v49. Religious and/or Spiritual[h]	(1)	(2)	(3)	(4)	—	—											
- Global	—	—	—	—	—	—						—	—	—	—	—	—
- United States	—	—	—	—	—	—						—	—	—	—	—	—

[a] See notes for Table 1.2.

Table 1.5 Spirituality Related Estimates for the Year: 2008 – Part 1[a]

Survey Item	*Response Options*								*Respondents*[c]		*Spirituality*[d]	
v63. Science v. Religion[e]	(SA)	(A)	(NAND)	(D)	(SD)	—	(CC)	(NA)	N	Nv	% +	% –
- Global	3366	11056	12918	15877	9635	—	2846	517	56215	52852	27.29	48.27
- United States	100	321	343	406	162	—	26	7	1365	1332	31.61	42.64
v21. Belief about God[f]	(1)	(2)	(3)	(4)	(5)	(6)						
- Global	6013	4854	7136	5109	9123	23343	230	407	56215	55578	80.45	19.55
- United States	38	68	140	48	229	830	5	7	1365	1353	92.17	7.83
v22. Beliefs about God[g]	(1)	(2)	(3)	(4)	—	—						
- Global	7693	4659	3531	32224	—	—	6348	740	56215	48107	74.32	25.68
- United States	56	72	96	1099	—	—	30	12	1365	1323	90.33	9.67
v23. Life After Death[h]	(1)	(2)	(3)	(4)	—	—						
- Global	17532	13556	9401	10349	—	—	4817	560	56215	50838	61.15	38.85
- United States	745	279	152	127	—	—	54	8	1365	1303	78.59	21.41
v24. Heaven[h]	(1)	(2)	(3)	(4)	—	—						
- Global	17698	12620	9101	11342	—	—	4715	739	56215	50761	59.73	40.27
- United States	853	276	117	80	—	—	33	6	1365	1326	85.14	14.86
v26. Religious Miracles[h]	(1)	(2)	(3)	(4)	—	—						
- Global	14398	14200	10868	11719	—	—	4063	967	56215	51185	55.87	44.13
- United States	738	311	183	101	—	—	29	3	1365	1333	78.69	21.31

[a] See notes for Table 1.1.

Table 1.6 Spirituality Related Estimates for the Year: 2008 – Part 2[a]

Survey Item	*Response Options*													*Respondents*[c]		*Spirituality*[d]	
v31. God Concerned with Every Human Being Personally[e]	(SA)	(A)		(NAND)		(D)		(SD)			—	(CC)	(NA)	N	Nv	% +	% –
- Global	13465	14046		8466		7853		8112			—	3551	722	56215	51942	52.96	47.04
- United States	578	368		185		136		76			—	16	6	1365	1343	70.44	29.56
v33. Life is Meaningful, only because God Exists[e]	(SA)	(A)		(NAND)		(D)		(SD)			—						
- Global	7853	10226		9420		12682		13009			—	2221	804	56215	53190	33.99	66.01
- United States	268	352		278		298		151			—	13	5	1365	1347	46.03	53.97
v36. Connect with God without Church/Religious Services[e]	(SA)	(A)		(NAND)		(D)		(SD)			—						
- Global	9672	16050		8921		8571		8369			—	3634	998	56215	51583	49.87	50.13
- United States	339	543		155		194		118			—	9	7	1365	1349	65.38	34.62
v46. How Often Pray[f]	(1)	(2)	(3)	(4)	(5)	(6)	(7)	(8)	(9)	(10)	(11)						
- Global	14432	2343	2833	5048	1900	2355	2326	2792	5054	7672	7232	431	782	56215	53987	54.33	45.67
- United States	138	28	25	68	38	63	27	66	149	356	391	6	10	1365	1349	80.80	19.20
v48. Religiousness[g]	(1)	(2)		(3)	(4)		(5)	(6)			(7)						
- Global	2466	7785		19794	10659		5414	4532			4052	1121	392	56215	54702	54.92	45.08
- United States	91	271		678	96		97	52			70	4	6	1365	1355	76.75	23.25
v49. Religious and/or Spiritual[h]	(1)	(2)		(3)		(4)		—			—						
- Global	13252	18507		8127		10702		—			—	4887	740	56215	50588	78.84	21.16
- United States	528	304		312		154		—			—	48	19	1365	1298	88.14	11.86

[a] See notes for Table 1.2.

Table 1.7 Spirituality Related Estimates for the Year: 2018 – Part 1[a]

Survey Item	*Response Options*								*Respondents*[c]		*Spirituality*[d]	
v63. Science v. Religion[e]	(SA)	(A)	(NAND)	(D)	(SD)	—	(CC)	(NA)	N	Nv	% +	% –
- Global	3443	9497	10275	10145	8419	—	2035	445	44259	41779	30.97	44.43
- United States	127	295	357	221	145	—	18	12	1175	1145	36.86	31.97
v21. Belief about God[f]	(1)	(2)	(3)	(4)	(5)	(6)						
- Global	6291	4472	6479	4185	6232	15993	308	299	44259	43652	75.34	24.66
- United States	55	75	144	36	217	624	15	9	1175	1151	88.71	11.29
v22. Beliefs about God[g]	(1)	(2)	(3)	(4)	—	—						
- Global	8256	4627	3139	22692	—	—	5007	538	44259	38714	66.72	33.28
- United States	73	105	120	826	—	—	41	10	1175	1124	84.16	15.84
v23. Life After Death[h]	(1)	(2)	(3)	(4)	—	—						
- Global	12837	10503	8433	8668	—	—	3417	401	44259	40441	57.71	42.29
- United States	662	242	126	99	—	—	36	10	1175	1129	80.07	19.93
v24. Heaven[h]	(1)	(2)	(3)	(4)	—	—						
- Global	12948	9036	8175	10229	—	—	3411	460	44259	40388	54.43	45.57
- United States	698	224	118	101	—	—	26	8	1175	1141	80.81	19.19
v26. Religious Miracles[h]	(1)	(2)	(3)	(4)	—	—						
- Global	10621	10396	9007	10777	—	—	2907	551	44259	40801	51.51	48.49
- United States	591	277	159	114	—	—	25	9	1175	1141	76.07	23.93

[a] See notes for Table 1.1.

Table 1.8 Spirituality Related Estimates for the Year: 2018 – Part 2[a]

Survey Item	*Response Options*													*Respondents*[c]		*Spirituality*[d]	
v31. God Concerned with Every Human Being Personally[e]	(SA)	(A)		(NAND)		(D)		(SD)		—		(CC)	(NA)	N	Nv	% +	% –
- Global	8278	10285		7178		7228		8167		—		2606	517	44259	41136	45.13	54.87
- United States	481	298		175		99		100		—		13	9	1175	1153	67.56	32.44
v33. Life is Meaningful, only because God Exists[e]	(SA)	(A)		(NAND)		(D)		(SD)		—							
- Global	5427	7571		6675		9473		12956		—		1646	511	44259	42102	30.87	69.13
- United States	253	264		226		240		174		—		7	11	1175	1157	44.68	55.32
v36. Connect with God without Church/Religious Services[e]	(SA)	(A)		(NAND)		(D)		(SD)		—							
- Global	7298	11829		7263		6687		7451		—		3060	671	44259	40528	47.19	52.81
- United States	299	443		144		158		114		—		8	9	1175	1158	64.08	35.92
v46. How Often Pray[f]	(1)	(2)	(3)	(4)	(5)	(6)	(7)	(8)	(9)	(10)	(11)						
- Global	13328	2195	2643	3871	1621	1853	1683	1960	3991	5355	5048	172	539	44259	43548	49.40	50.60
- United States	168	11	28	35	28	30	31	83	730	—	—	20	11	1175	1144	78.85	21.15
v48. Religiousness[g]	(1)	(2)		(3)	(4)		(5)	(6)		(7)							
- Global	2058	5941		13186	7597		4526	4819			4864	927	341	44259	42991	49.28	50.72
- United States	73	249		451	136		82	92			73	8	11	1175	1156	66.87	33.13
v49. Religious and/or Spiritual[h]	(1)	(2)		(3)		(4)		—		—							
- Global	10913	12310		6727		10545		—		—		3197	567	44259	40495	73.96	26.04
- United States	495	231		243		145		—		—		44	17	1175	1114	86.98	13.02

[a] See notes for Table 1.2.

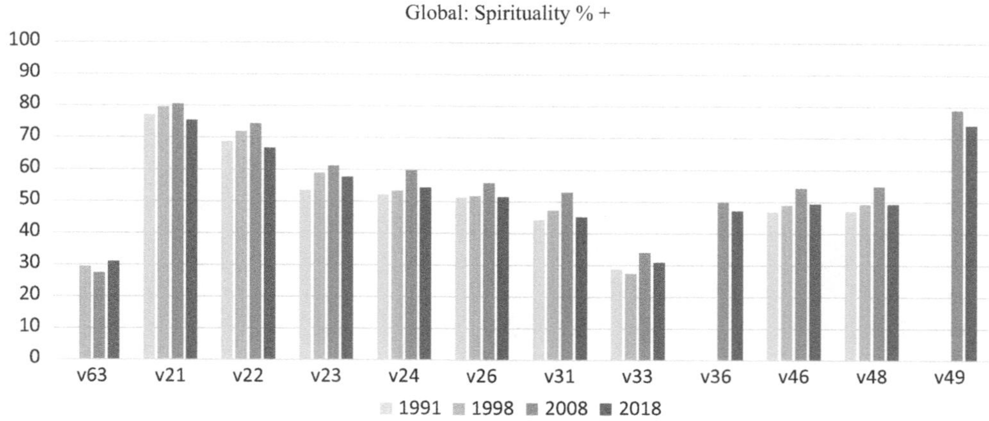

Figure 1.1 Global: Positive Spirituality Percentages.

Spirituality % +: Spiritual (i.e., religious and/or spiritual responses). Spirituality % –: Non-Spiritual (i.e., non-religious and/or non-spiritual responses). The following items are taken verbatim, and the answer options are paraphrased from GESIS (2024; see pp. 33–36, 38, 43, 45, 48, 62, 64, 65, 79). Also, missing years reflect a lack of item inclusion.

v63: We trust too much in science and not enough in religious faith.

Answer options are based on the level of agreement versus disagreement.

v21: Please indicate which statement below comes closest to expressing what you believe about God.

Answer options are based on (dis)belief and doubt(less).

v22: Which best describes your beliefs about God?

Answer options are based on current versus past beliefs.

v23: Do you believe in: Life after death?

Answer options are: yes (definitely or probably), or no (definitely or probably).

v24: Do you believe in: Heaven?

Answer options are: yes (definitely or probably), or no (definitely or probably).

v26: Do you believe in: Religious miracles?

Answer options are: yes (definitely or probably), or no (definitely or probably).

v31: There is a God who concerns Himself with every human being personally.

Answer options are based on the level of agreement versus disagreement.

v33: To me, life is meaningful only because God exists.

Answer options are based on the level of agreement versus disagreement.

v36: I have my own way of connecting with God without churches or religious services.

Answer options are based on the level of agreement versus disagreement.

v46: About how often do you pray?

Answer options range from (1) never to (11) several times a day.

v48: Would you describe yourself as ...

Answer options range from (1) extremely religious to (7) extremely non-religious.

v49: What best describes you: [R = Religious; S = Spiritual]

Answer options: (1) R & S, (2) R, not S, (3) S, not R, (4) not S, not R.

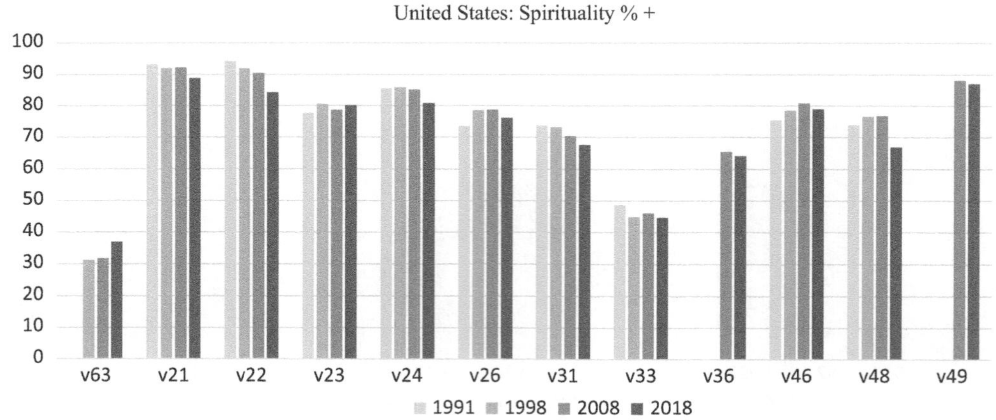

Figure 1.2 United States: Positive Spirituality Percentages (See notes for Figure 1.1).

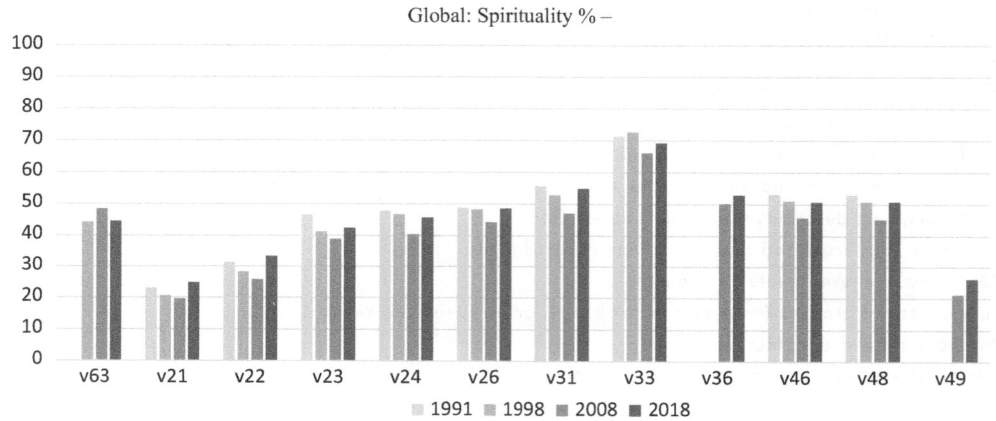

Figure 1.3 Global: Negative Spirituality Percentages (See notes for Figure 1.1).

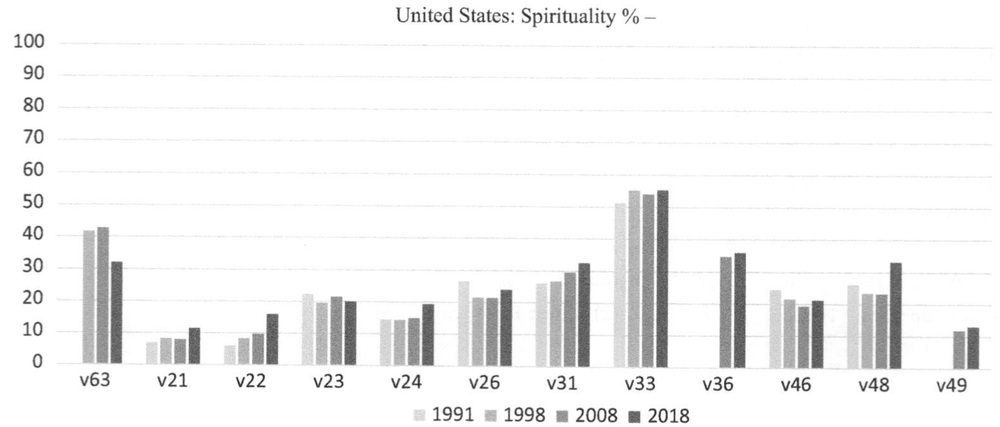

Figure 1.4 United States: Negative Spirituality Percentages (See notes for Figure 1.1).

The RiTE Model of Spirituality

The RiTE Model of Spirituality (see Figure 1.5) has been consistently included in scientific publications (i.e., peer-reviewed articles, edited book chapters, and an authored book) for over 20 years, whether with respect to the conceptual model itself (Webb, 2007/2003, 2021; Webb et al., 2014) or work including all or part of the RiTE Measure of Spirituality[11] (Webb et al., 2014; see below). The RiTE Model defines spirituality as "the salient, searching pursuit of the transcendently sacred ritualistic, theistic, and/or existential aspects of the human condition" (Webb et al., 2014, p. 974). It was developed in an effort to be cross-culturally inclusive (i.e., traditions derived from diverse monotheistic, polytheistic, non-theistic, Eastern, and Western belief systems) and to address the developing dichotomy between religion and spirituality present (and rising) in some segments of (1) the scientific community and (2) popular culture. Indeed, there can be meaningful, if not profound, tension between religion and spirituality (see Hood, 2003; Pargament et al., 2013; Webb et al., 2014); that is, it is not unusual for religion (especially *organized* religion) to be considered largely "bad" and spirituality to be considered otherwise "good." In this regard, the pre-existing notions of religiousness and spirituality were collapsed into an all-encompassing term, *Spirituality*, and then broken into three inter-related, rather than trichotomous, dimensions. That is, Ritualistic Spirituality (a structured connection with deity; formerly otherwise known as religiousness, or the intrinsic and extrinsic largely nomothetic practice of religion), Theistic Spirituality (a *non*-structured connection with deity; formerly otherwise known as spirituality, or the notion of a largely individual, idiosyncratic, and/or personalized relationship with deity), and Existential Spirituality (a non-theistic, yet transcendent search for meaning and purpose; to potentially include individuals otherwise known as formally agnostic[12] or atheist). Additionally, this model argues that generally constructive spirituality (i.e., good, healthy relationships with the self and others) is a relatively balanced mix of the three dimensions, with counterproductive effects (e.g., unreasonable bias, hostility, and aggression) associated with unbalanced spirituality, or beliefs and practices overly concentrated in one of the three dimensions (i.e., approaching the arrowed corners of the triangular component of the diagram in Figure 1.5) *and* without respect for the other dimensions.

Importantly, the RiTE Model of Spirituality (see Webb, 2021) is a conceptual model and focused on definitional issues, with some initial, though growing empirical examination and support in the context of its association with other constructs and variables (see Cameron et al., 2023; Chang et al., 2016; Chang, Jilani, et al., 2015a; Chang, Yu, et al., 2015b; Dangel & Webb, 2017; Fernandez & Walker, 2021; Hall et al., 2020; Stauber & Stutts, 2023). The RiTE conceptualization of spirituality holds that spirituality is an aspect of culture and diversity (consistent with Chapter 2 of this volume) *and* a component of human nature (consistent with Chapter 5 of this volume). Indeed, the RiTE Model conceptualizes spirituality as a cross-culturally unifying thread, yet it is also respectful and honoring of diversity through intentional and deliberate inclusion of varied manifestations of spirituality. The categories of Ritualistic Spirituality, Theistic Spirituality, and Existential Spirituality are not intended to constrict the conceptualization of spirituality; rather, they are intended to acknowledge and provide a sufficiently distinct, yet broad and overlapping, categorization of the myriad possibilities of the human capacity and drive for seeking and experiencing the transcendent aspect of what it means to be human. To be clear, the RiTE Model – and its three inter-related dimensions – is not intended to argue that all human beings actually believe in deity and that they may not realize, accept, or admit it yet. Rather (and consistent with Piedmont's work; see Chapter 5), all human beings are in pursuit of a connection to something transcendent,

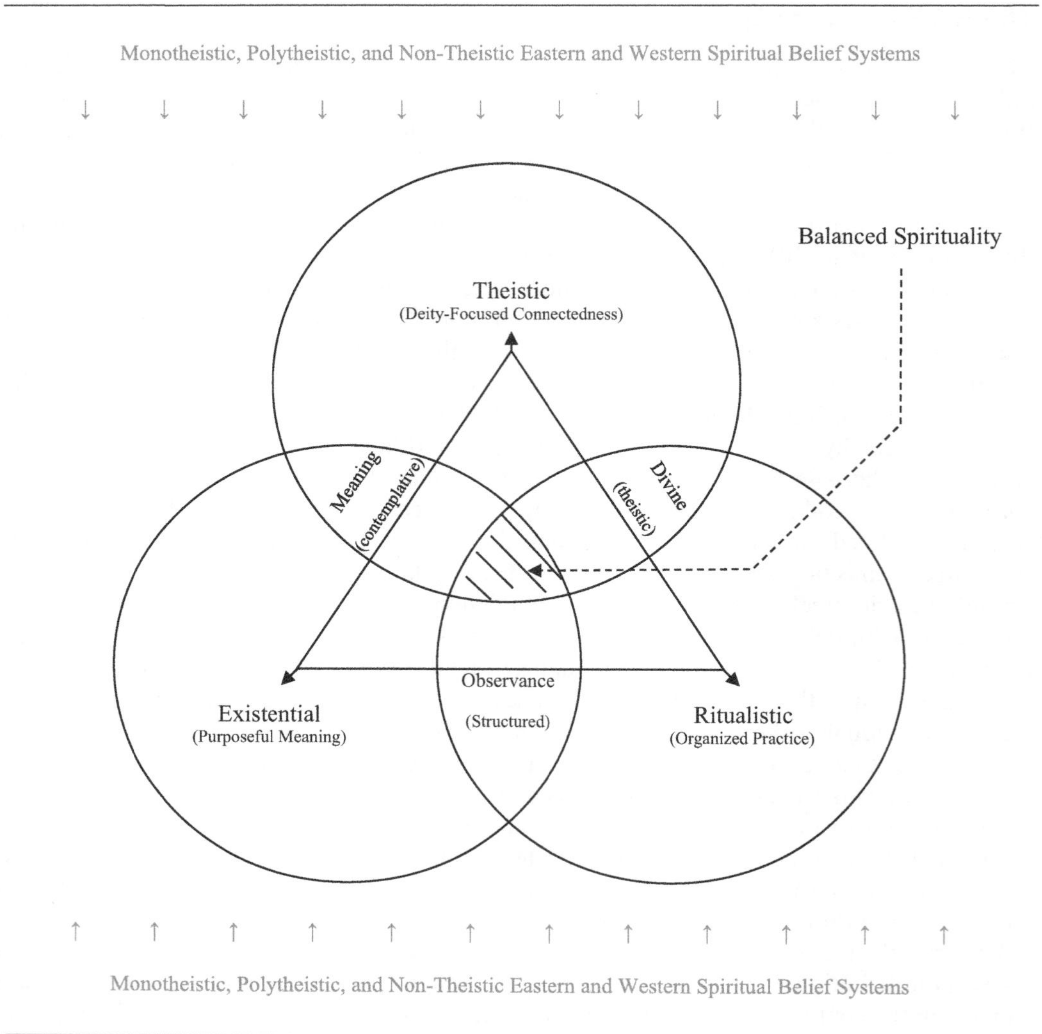

Figure 1.5 The RiTE Model of Spirituality Adapted from Webb (2021). See also Webb et al. (2014) and Webb (2007/2003).

whether (1) external to and greater than the self, (2) within the self, or (3) aside from the self. For many, the primary target of this sacred pursuit may be deity or the divine, but not necessarily so, as many may engage in secular spirituality (see Chapter 6 of this volume), of which the target may be nature, the universe, knowledge, etc. Indeed, and with respect not only to the RiTE Model, but also to the material presented in the rest of this edited volume, "the pathway from spirituality to [health and well-being] is likely complex, yet comprised of much and varied opportunity for success" (Webb, in press, p. 4; see also Chapter 9 of this volume for a comprehensive discussion of models and mechanisms related to the association of spirituality with health and well-being). See Chapter 44 of this volume for more discussion of the RiTE Model of Spirituality.

In sum, and as briefly outlined above, (1) over 4 of 5 adults believe in God or a higher power of some sort and over 3 of 4 adults are religious and/or spiritual (GESIS, 2024; ISSP Research Group, 2025), and (2) spirituality (broadly construed) appears to be a fundamental component of human nature, or what it means to be human, regardless of whether or not one believes in deity (Pargament, 2013; Piedmont & Wilkins, 2013; Webb et al., 2014). As such, understanding the relationship between spirituality and better outcomes related to health and well-being is relevant to all humans across the globe. And, likely of interest to scholars, scientists, healthcare professionals (e.g., clinicians, technicians, administrators, etc.), and policy-makers invested in comprehensively and inclusively understanding and promoting health and well-being in terms consistent with the internationally accepted definition of health; that is (and to reiterate with emphasis), "a state of complete physical, mental and social well-being and not merely the absence of disease or infirmity" (WHO, 2025, p. 1).

Spirituality, Health, and Well-Being: A Psychological Perspective

The **mission** of this edited volume is to address the relevance and application of the broad construct of spirituality to health and well-being, including the physical, mental, and social aspects thereof. The first section or part of the book (i.e., Part I) will cover *relevance*; that is, justification of need, importance of spirituality as culture and diversity, and historical perspectives (including definitions and measurement). Part II will be focused on *foundations* for understanding the science of spirituality, health, and well-being; that is, the psychology of faith, personality, secular spirituality, positive psychology, neuroscience, and models and mechanisms of the association of spirituality with health and well-being. Part III will be focused on *outcomes*; that is, how various aspects of spirituality are related to chronic medical conditions, chronic pain, cardiovascular issues, cancer-related outcomes, living with HIV, medical rehabilitation, psychological disstress, suicidal behavior, addictive behavior, and trauma. Part IV will be focused on *predictors, interventions, and clinical perspectives*; that is, both broad and specific issues, principles, and interventions. Example broad-based topics include issues governing the implementation of spiritually oriented interventions (e.g., developing competence in addressing spirituality in treatment-related settings and ethics) and integrating or incorporating spirituality into psychological care. Specific, more narrowly focused predictors and interventions include religiousness, meditation, forgiveness, mindfulness, compassion, gratitude, hope, and humility. Particular clinical perspectives include collegiate addiction recovery and sex offender treatment, as well as a tribute to a scientist-practitioner with over 50 years of clinical experience. Part V will be focused on spirituality and health *in context*. That is, among children and adolescents, couples, women in addiction recovery, minority populations (e.g., sexual, gender, ethnic, and racial), and clergy. Part VI will be focused on *emerging areas*; that is, topics that have recently begun to receive focused attention from psychological science. That is, spiritual struggle, temptation, moral injury, spiritual bypass, persons living with intellectual and developmental disabilities and their families, and forgiveness *education*. The concluding chapter (Part VII) will address important considerations *moving forward*, including broad themes distilled from the chapters regarding defining spirituality, limitations to the research, and future directions for the psychological science of spirituality, health, and well-being.

The **overall aim** of this effort is to create an authoritative repository of the state-of-the-science regarding the largely salubrious association of spirituality with health and well-being (broadly construed) and to make this material readily available and otherwise easily accessible to academics, researchers, students, clinicians, and any other consumer with interest. Moreover, to foster the inclusive recognition and consideration of the diverse yet unifying aspects of spirituality (broadly speaking) and its association with health and well-being.

Part I: Relevance and Historical Development

The first portion of this *chapter* outlines (1) the ubiquitous presence and common value of spirituality among the world's population and (2) the basic association of spirituality with health and well-being. Also, the additional chapters of Part I provide (3) important perspectives regarding spirituality as an expression of culture and diversity and (4) an overview of the historical development of the scientific field of spirituality, health, and well-being.

Part II: A Foundation for Understanding Spirituality, Health, and Well-Being

The *Foundations* section is designed to provide fundamental information and perspective to facilitate the understanding of basic issues relevant to the psychological science of spirituality as it is related to health and well-being. For example, Chapter 4 is focused on the notion of faith, including what it means to have faith *in* something (e.g., deity).[13] And, thus, in the context of spirituality – in broad terms – believing and trusting in an enabling power (1) external to and greater than the self (e.g., the Abrahamic faith traditions; Fatemi, 2020; Knabb & Bates, 2020; Pirutinsky, 2020), (2) within the self (e.g., Hinduism; Oman & Paranjpe, 2020), or (3) derived from transcending the self (e.g., Buddhism; Lee & Ng, 2020).[14] Chapter 4 draws on philosophical assumptions and theological underpinnings that impact the understanding of the notion of faith and its association with spirituality, health, and well-being.

Part III: Health and Well-Being Related Outcomes

The *Outcomes* section is formatted to focus the presentation of the material on a particular health- and well-being-related outcome. That is, for example, how spirituality is related to chronic medical conditions, or what aspects of spirituality are related to better[8] health and well-being among people struggling with persistent health concerns such as diabetes, fibromyalgia, or neurological disorders (see Chapter 10). In a very practical sense, this section of the book will allow a reader to focus on or select a particular aspect of health and well-being and understand how spirituality, in its potentially various manifestations, is related to it.

Part IV: Predictors, Interventions, and Clinical Perspectives

This section is formatted to focus the presentation of the material on particular manifestations of spirituality in association with health and well-being. For each manifestation of spirituality, a discussion will be provided regarding (1) the empirical evidence in support[8] of its basic association with health and well-being and (2) as applicable, the procedure of and empirical support for attendant interventions. That is, for example, what is the nature of the research supporting the basic association of forgiveness with health and well-being, what do forgiveness interventions look like, and what is the nature of the research supporting the use of said forgiveness intervention(s) (see Chapter 23)? In a very practical sense, this format will allow a reader to focus on or select a particular manifestation of spirituality and understand how it is related to various aspects of health and well-being. Importantly, Part IV will start with a chapter discussing big-picture topics related to addressing spirituality in treatment-related settings, for example, issues regarding ethics and religious/spiritual diversity, and an overview of particular approaches to spirituality-informed healthcare-related services.

Part V: Spirituality, Health, and Well-Being in Context

The *In Context* section presents information related to spirituality, health, and well-being with a focus on diversity and inclusivity. Contextual information is provided so as to facilitate understanding of the application of spirituality to health and well-being among non-dominant populations in society. Indeed, what are particular issues to deliberately pay attention to (and/ or not overlook) in the context of otherwise alternative and/or unique circumstances and situations?

Part VI: Emerging Areas in the Science of Spirituality, Health, and Well-Being

The *Emerging Areas* section provides a platform for newer fields of focused inquiry in the empirical examination of the association of spirituality with health and well-being. Each of these areas is not new to humanity's awareness. Rather, they are areas of otherwise long-standing interest, which only relatively recently have begun to receive deliberate and/or sustained attention from psychological science.

Part VII: Moving the Science of Spirituality, Health, and Well-Being Forward

The concluding *Moving Forward* chapter serves to bring together the common themes drawn from the chapters regarding (1) defining spirituality, (2) limitations to the current state-of-the-science and directions for future research and development to pursue, and (3) a broad summary of the empirical evidence in support of the association of spirituality with health and well-being; indeed, the bottom line.

A Word about Addiction Recovery as a Component of Health and Well-Being

In addition to much data-driven material regarding many aspects of religiousness and spirituality in association with health and well-being, a minor thematic thread regarding addiction recovery is noticeably present and serves as another distinguishing component of this edited volume. Given the compounding nature of (1) addiction as a global public health crisis, (2) the stigma experienced by those struggling with addiction, and also (3) the relevance of spirituality to addiction recovery (see Webb, 2021; Webb & Boye, 2024), 5 of the 44 chapters comprising this book are included to deliberately provide a platform to help increase awareness of, attention to, and – ultimately – address the societal-level problem of addiction. The association of substance use *disorders* with death, disability, and economic burden – annually, worldwide – is over 300,000 deaths, over 40 million years lost due to poor health and early death (i.e., disability-adjusted life-years lost; DALYs), and at least a $500 billion economic impact (see Webb, 2021). Also, in terms of the worldwide impact of the mere consumption of alcohol (i.e., problems associated with alcohol use, but not necessarily misuse), there are about 3 million deaths each year and about 133 million DALYs each year (WHO, 2018). Indeed, "the harmful use of alcohol is one of the leading risk factors for population health worldwide and has a direct impact on many health-related targets"; such that the current state-of-the-science is that there is no safe level of alcohol consumption (WHO, 2018, p. xii; see also Burton & Sheron, 2018; GBD, 2018; US Department of Health and Human Services, 2025; WHO, 2023).

Accordingly, the *Foundations* section (Part II) includes a chapter (#7) dedicated to a discussion of the Twelve-Step Model of addiction recovery as another example of the parallels between positive psychology and spirituality. The *Outcomes* section (Part III) includes a chapter (#18) dedicated to a discussion of the empirical association of various aspects of spirituality with outcomes related to addictive behavior, including as related to substance use and behavioral or process addictions. As well as a chapter (#17) dedicated to suicidal behavior, which is highly comorbid[15] with addictive behavior (e.g., Amiri & Behnezhad, 2020; Yuodelis-Flores & Ries, 2015) and is sometimes viewed as consistent therewith, if not a form thereof (e.g., Blasco-Fontecilla et al., 2016; Firestone, 2006; Hatteschweiler et al., 2015; see also www.suicideanonymous.net). The *Predictors, Interventions, and Perspectives* section (Part IV) includes a chapter (#30) focused on the influence of spirituality on college student recovery, as supported by collegiate recovery programs. And, lastly, the *In Context* section (Part V) includes a chapter (#34) focused on particular issues related to spirituality among women struggling with addiction and recovery.

Notes

1 It is important to note that Einstein's opinions related to the compatibility of science and religion, as expressed in 1925 and 1941, may have changed before he died in 1955.

2 At the very least, for the reader as a backdrop when considering the discussion of spirituality throughout the remainder of this edited volume. That is, when the nature of (1) religion/spirituality itself is discussed, or (2) particular spiritual principles are discussed, how are these discussions of principles and practices informed by the RiTE Model and its conceptualization of spirituality, and its three broad dimensions? That is, for example, when (1) religious activity, (2) religious commitment, (3) meditation, (4) prayer, (5) gratitude, or (6) hope, etc. are discussed in the context of any given chapter, does its conceptualization fit best (or not at all) with ritualistic, theistic, and/or existential spirituality?

3 The GESIS – Leibniz Institute for the Social Sciences (www.gesis.org) conducts global research on various topics, and provides access to their data and reports free of charge. Many thanks! The GESIS data reported in this chapter is drawn from a larger project collecting much more information related to religion among the world's population.

4 Here, I am referring to the *notion* of deity; that is, to divine entities, rather than to *a* deity (i.e., a particular deity). Elsewhere in this chapter, I will use related terms in this manner.

5 v45, q26: "During the last 12 months, have you read or listened to the reading of any holy scripture such as the Bible, Buddhist sutra, Koran, Sruti, Torah, or other religious scripture, not counting any reading that happened during a worship service?" (yes/no; GESIS, 2020, pp. 226–227).

6 To be clear, the United States is not ranked first in the world based on the reported percentages for these three measures (i.e., with all other individual countries ranked lower). Rather, in comparison to the world's population considered together as a whole, the United States' percentages are higher. A similar pattern is observed in the additional measures outlined in Tables 1.1–1.8.

7 Related questions include: Does empirical evidence of an association between religiousness/spirituality and health and well-being provide support for the veracity claims of any given religious/spiritual belief system? Or, more broadly, the existence of deity, or an existence (a) before this life or (b) after death? The short answer to all of these types of questions is a friendly, but resounding, No, of course not! Nor are these questions included in the aims of this edited volume. Why? Because these

are not scientific questions. That is, these questions are not conducive to the scientific method.* Does this mean that questions not conducive to the scientific method are not important? Again, the answer is a friendly, No. Fortunately, we *can* ask empirical questions about how religious and spiritual principles and activities may or may not be related to better health and well-being. An example empirical question in this regard is: Are higher levels of forgiveness associated with lower levels of depression? The short answer is, Yes (see Chapters 23 and 43). Why is this an empirical question? Because forgiveness can be measured, as can depression.

* The American Psychological Association (APA, p. 941) defines the *scientific method* as: "a set of procedures, guidelines, assumptions, and attitudes required for the organized and systematic collection, interpretation, and verification of data and the discovery of reproducible evidence, enabling laws and principles to be stated or modified. See also science; scientific explanation." See Chapter 4 for more discussion of the philosophy of science and its interface with the psychology of faith and spirituality.

8 There are deleterious effects, of course. An example is positive versus negative religious coping (cf. spiritual struggle; see Chapter 38 of this volume). For the seminal, pioneering work regarding religious coping from a psychological perspective, see *The Psychology of Religious Coping: Theory, Research, Practice* (Pargament, 1997). Importantly, many of the chapters in this volume provide examples of particular deleterious effects.

9 Some may pause and question whether examples of character strengths and virtues (see Davis et al., 2023; Peterson & Seligman, 2004; Snyder et al., 2021) were just given as examples of spirituality. The short answer is: kind of. :) For a more in-depth answer, see Chapter 7 for a discussion of the relationship between spirituality and positive psychology.

10 As opposed to specific constructs. The APA (2015, p. 239) defines *construct* as: "a complex idea or concept formed from a synthesis of simpler ideas. See higher order construct." Of note, though religious activity often refers to frequency related behavioral data (e.g., how often does one (a) attend worship services, (b) pray, or (c) read scripture), religious commitment is not necessarily always employed in a generalized fashion. That is, Worthington and colleagues (2003) have operationally defined *religious commitment* as a formal construct and have developed a psychometrically sound measure thereof.

11 This measure was originally developed as a 30-item measure of the three dimensions of the RiTE Model; that is, 10 items per dimension. With colleagues, based on 4 additional datasets, we are preparing a manuscript for peer-review publication describing a shortened 12-item version (i.e., the RiTE-S), drawn from the original 30-item measure. Within the RiTE-S, we also identify a single item to represent each dimension; such that, a 3-item measure could be used (e.g., in large-scale, public health oriented research). Each measure is freely available for public use. The original 30-item version is in the public domain (see Webb et al., 2014) and the RiTE-S will be in the public domain upon peer-reviewed publication. Also, interested parties can email me at: jon.r.webb@ttu.edu.

12 Aside from any/all theological-level claims of any/all past, current, or future religious/spiritual belief systems (and persons) in the world, in my view, all human beings have been, are, and forever will be agnostic,** or as literally translated from Greek, *without knowledge*; in *this* case, regarding the existence of deity, and related potentialities. That is, and more precisely, without *empirical* knowledge of such matters. No doubt there are other ways of knowing (cf. epistemology), but such ways are not necessarily conducive to empiricism and the scientific method (see above). The APA (2015, p. 366) defines *empiricism* as: "1. an approach to epistemology holding that all knowledge of matters of fact either arises from experience or requires experience for its validation. In particular, empiricism denies the possibility of innate ideas, arguing that the mind at birth is like a blank sheet of paper (see tabula rasa). .... 2. the view that experimentation is the most important, if not the only, foundation of scientific knowledge and the means by which individuals evaluate truth claims or the adequacy of theories and models. 3. in philosophy, the position that all linguistic expressions that are not tautologous must be empirically verifiable if they are to be deemed valid or meaningful. This principle was essential to the philosophy of logical positivism. See also positivism." Hence, my use of the phrase *formally agnostic* in reference to those who otherwise select agnostic when presented with the question of whether to identify as religious, spiritual, agnostic, or atheist. See Chapter 4 for more discussion of the philosophy of science and its interface with the psychology of faith and spirituality.

** That is, unless and until empirical (experiential) evidence is discovered (gained). Which evidence ostensibly will only come in some other realm of existence, if there is such a thing. As noted above, I am a believer, but only because I am without *empirical* knowledge.

13 I have been thinking about the notion of faith in the context of the compatibility of science and religion for over 20 years. Also, I have been thinking about this book project for well over 10 years. One of the first chapters to crystalize as important to include was a chapter (#4) on faith. My original thought was not to capitalize the word in the chapter title (i.e., The Psychology of faith). My intent was to emphasize that the chapter would be about the noun,*** and not its colloquial use as a proper noun – when used in reference to the espousal of a religious belief system (e.g., a person of Faith). My purpose for this chapter was not to discuss the psychology of having *a* Faith, but the psychology of *having* faith. Why do I think about these things? Often times in society or popular culture when something tragic happens – whether as reported in the news or at a personal level – people *of* Faith who are *expressing* faith, will say that their thoughts and prayers are with those suffering. And, it is not uncommon for a segment of society to become frustrated with this sentiment and criticize others for embracing it – arguing that it does nothing in terms of actually helping. Related to this, during the aftermath of Hurricane Ian (Florida, USA; September 2022), by chance, I overheard a news clip that my wife was watching in her office near our kitchen. One of the first phrases I heard immediately caught my attention, and has stayed with me ever since. Casey DeSantis was speaking at a press conference with her husband, the Governor of Florida, Ron DeSantis. She remarked that "our hearts and our prayers are with so many people who are suffering, which is why about 24 hours ago we launched the Disaster Relief Fund …" (starting at minute 22:10; https://www.youtube.com/live/P5hwzxeJeuU?si=9_KhgXmVIFsqHvlV). Whatever one may think of the DeSantis' politics (for or against), to me this statement encapsulates the notion of faith. *Because* of their faith (expressed through prayer), they were proactive. Presumably operating under the assumption that if they were going to ask God to do something, it was important for them to do what they could as well. All of this to say, it may be that, part (or all) of why "prayers go along way" – as the saying goes – is that in situations like these, offering support in times of need through thoughts and prayers, may be more than simple wishful thinking. Rather, it may lead those expressing said faith to take further action [while also trusting God to answer their heart-felt supplication (which answer may be through inspiring others to behave in helpful ways, etc.); see also, *James* 2:14–18 (King James Version, 1983)]. Of note, such is an empirical question: Do persons who offer thoughts and prayers in times of need, also do other, more tangible things to help?

*** The APA (2015, p. 408) defines *faith* as: "unwavering loyalty, belief, and trust. See also religious faith." As a side note, as I was referencing the definition of faith provided by Merriam-Webster (online; i.e., 2b(1): firm belief in something for which there is no proof), I decided to check if APA provides a definition thereof. While the humorous irony of science defining faith does not escape me, I will leave it up to the reader to contemplate and decide upon the consistency between the two definitions. :).

14 In addition to these chapters discussing broad emic perspectives on the interface between psychology and spirituality in the context of Judaism, Christianity, Islam, Hinduism, and Buddhism, Sisemore and Knabb (2020) also includes chapters focused on North American indigenous spirituality (Gray, 2020), Chinese traditional religions (Ting et al., 2020), and African traditional religion (Okozi, 2020).

15 When teaching courses on clinically oriented topics (and training clinical students), due to the high comorbidity between addictive behavior and suicidal behavior, I emphasize that during the intake process – as well as throughout treatment, as clinically indicated – it is essential to be mindful of, pay attention to, query and, if need be, address both issues. Moreover, the critical necessity that, if one of the topics is disclosed or arises, a healthcare provider *must* follow-up regarding the other.

References

American Psychological Association. (2015). *APA dictionary of psychology* (Second ed.). Author.https://dictionary.apa.org/

Amiri, S., & Behnezhad, S. (2020). Alcohol use and risk of suicide: A systematic review and meta-analysis. *Journal of Addictive Diseases*, *38*(2), 200–213. https://doi.org/10.1080/10550887.2020.1736757

Blasco-Fontecilla, H., Fernández-Fernández, R., Colino, L., Fajardo, L., Perteguer-Barrio, R., & de Leon, J. (2016). The addictive model of self-harming (non-suicidal and suicidal) behavior. *Frontiers in Psychiatry*, *7*. https://doi.org/10.3389/fpsyt.2016.00008

Burton, R., & Sheron, N. (2018). No level of alcohol consumption improves health. *The Lancet*, *392*(10152), 987–988. https://doi.org/10.1016/S0140-6736(18)31571-X

Cameron, E. C., Toussaint, L., Baffour Adjei, S., Crawford, J. N., Mounet, O., Trend-Cunningham, F. J., & Jacquin, K. M. (2023). Finding meaning in crisis: Gender, spiritual practice, and trauma symptomology impact posttraumatic growth in COVID-19 Ghana. *Journal of Research in Psychology*, *1*(2), 1–20.

Chang, E. C., Jilani, Z., Fowler, E. E., Yu, T., Chia, S. W., Yu, E. A., McCabe, H. K., & Hirsch, J. K. (2016). The relationship between multidimensional spirituality and depressive symptoms in college students: Examining hope agency and pathways as potential mediators. *The Journal of Positive Psychology*, *11*(2), 189–198. https://doi.org/10.1080/17439760.2015.1037859

Chang, E. C., Jilani, Z., Yu, T., Fowler, E. E., Lin, J., Webb, J. R., & Hirsch, J. K. (2015a). Fundamental dimensions of personality underlying spirituality: Further evidence for the construct validity of the RiTE measure of spirituality. *Personality and Individual Differences*, *75*, 175–178. https://doi.org/10.1016/j.paid.2014.11.027

Chang, E. C., Yu, T., Jilani, Z., Muyan, M., Lin, J., & Hirsch, J. K. (2015b). The pursuit of perfection in spiritual engagements: The centrality of parental expectations as a positive and unique predictor. *Personality and Individual Differences*, *79*, 162–165. https://doi.org/10.1016/j.paid.2015.02.009

Dangel, T., & Webb, J. R. (2017). Spirituality and psychological pain: The mediating role of social support. *Mental Health, Religion & Culture*, *20*(3), 246–259. https://doi.org/10.1080/13674676.2017.1345880

Davis, E. B., Worthington, E. L., Jr., & Schnitker, S. A. (Eds.). (2023). *Handbook of positive psychology, religion, and spirituality*. Springer.

Einstein, A. (1954). *Ideas and opinions* (1994 Modern Library ed.). Random House, Inc.

Fatemi, S. M. (2020). An overview of an Islam-based psychology. In T. A. Sisemore & J. J. Knabb (Eds.), *The psychology of world religions and spiritualities: An indigenous perspective* (pp. 117–135). Templeton Press.

Fernandez, M., & Walker, B. R. (2021). Spirituality in the stands: Sports spectatorship, spirituality, wellbeing and personality. *Journal of Spirituality in Mental Health*, *23*(2), 122–154. https://doi.org/10.1080/19349637.2019.1654427

Firestone, L. (2006). Suicide and the Inner Voice. In T. E. Ellis (Ed.), *Cognition and suicide: Theory, research, and therapy* (pp. 119–147). American Psychological Association. https://doi.org/10.1037/11377-006

GBD. (2018). [GBD 2016 Alcohol Collaborators] Alcohol use and burden for 195 countries and territories, 1990–2016: A systematic analysis for the Global Burden of Disease Study 2016. *The Lancet*, *392*(10152), 1015–1035. https://doi.org/10.1016/S0140-6736(18)31310-2

GESIS. (2020). ed. 2020. ISSP 2018 – Religion IV, Variable Report: Documentation release 2020/12/01 related to the international dataset Archive-Study-No. ZA7570 Version 2.1.0. Variable Reports 2020|14. Cologne: Author.

GESIS. (2024). ed. 2024. International Social Survey Programme: Religion I-IV Cumulation, Variable Report: Documentation release 2025/02 related to the international dataset GESIS Study-No. Z8792 Version 2.0.0. Variable Reports 2025|03. Cologne: Author.

Gray, J. S. (2020). Psychology of North American indigenous spirituality. In T. A. Sisemore & J. J. Knabb (Eds.), *The psychology of world religions and spiritualities: An indigenous perspective* (pp. 197–236). Templeton Press.

Hall, B. B., Webb, J. R., & Hirsch, J. K. (2020). Spirituality and suicidal behavior: The mediating role of self-forgiveness and psychache. *Psychology of Religion and Spirituality*, *12*(1), 36–44. https://doi.org/10.1037/rel0000182

Hatteschweiler, C., Graziani, P., Bon, M., & Charbonnier, E. (2015). Addiction et passage à l'acte suicidaire: Des processus cognitifs similaires? = Addiction and passage to the suicidal act: Similar cognitive processes? *Revue Francophone de Clinique Comportementale et Cognitive*, *20*(3), 35–44.

Hood, R. W., Jr. (2003). The relationship between religion and spirituality. In A. L. Greil & D. G. Bromley (Eds.), *Defining religion: Investigating the boundaries between the sacred and secular* (pp. 241–264). Elsevier Science. https://doi.org/10.1016/S1061-5210(03)10014-X

ISSP Research Group. (2025). International Social Survey Programme: Religion I-IV Cumulation. *GESIS, Cologne. Z8792 Data file Version 2.0.0*, http://dx.doi.org/10.4232/1.14482

King James Version. (1983). *Holy Bible*. Church of Jesus Christ of Latter-day Saints.

Knabb, J. J., & Bates, M. T. (2020). Walking home with God: Toward an indigenous Christian psychology. In T. A. Sisemore & J. J. Knabb (Eds.), *The psychology of world religions and spiritualities: An indigenous perspective* (pp. 85–115). Templeton Press.

Koenig, H. G., VanderWeele, T. J., & Peteet, J. R. (2024). *Handbook of religion and health* (3rd ed.). Oxford University Press.

Lee, K. C., & Ng, C. F. (2020). An indigenous perspective on Buddhism. In T. A. Sisemore & J. J. Knabb (Eds.), *The psychology of world religions and spiritualities: An indigenous perspective* (pp. 137–164). Templeton Press.

Okozi, I. F. (2020). African traditional religion and psychology of religion. In T. A. Sisemore & J. J. Knabb (Eds.), *The psychology of world religions and spiritualities: An indigenous perspective* (pp. 263–284). Templeton Press.

Oman, D., & Paranjpe, A. C. (2020). Psychology of Hinduism from the inside out. In T. A. Sisemore & J. J. Knabb (Eds.), *The psychology of world religions and spiritualities: An indigenous perspective* (pp. 165–196). Templeton Press.

Pargament, K. I. (1997). *The psychology of religious coping: Theory, research, practice*. Guilford Press.

Pargament, K. I., Mahoney, A., Exline, J. J., Jones, J. W., & Shafranske, E. P. (2013). Envisioning an integrative paradigm for the psychology of religion and spirituality. In K. I. Pargament, J. J. Exline, & J. W. Jones (Eds.), *APA handbook of psychology, religion, and spirituality (Vol 1): Context, theory, and research* (pp. 3–19). American Psychological Association. https://doi.org/10.1037/14045-001

Peterson, C., & Seligman, M. E. P. (2004). *Character strengths and virtues: A handbook and classification*. American Psychological Association / Oxford University Press.

Piedmont, R. L., & Wilkins, T. A. (2013). Spirituality, religiousness, and personality: Theoretical foundations and empirical applications. In K. I. Pargament, J. J. Exline, & J. W. Jones (Eds.), *APA handbook of psychology, religion, and spirituality (Vol 1): Context, theory, and research*. (pp. 173–186). American Psychological Association. https://doi.org/10.1037/14045-009

Pirutinsky, S. (2020). I created the evil inclination and I created Torah its antidote: An indigenous Jewish psychology. In T. A. Sisemore & J. J. Knabb (Eds.), *The psychology of world religions and spiritualities: An indigenous perspective* (pp. 59–84). Templeton Press.

Rippentrop, E. A., Altmaier, E. M., Chen, J. J., Found, E. M., & Keffala, V. J. (2005). The relationship between religion/spirituality and physical health, mental health, and pain in a chronic pain population. *Pain*, *116*(3), 311–321. https://doi.org/10.1016/j.pain.2005.05.008

Rosmarin, D. H., & Koenig, H. G. (Eds.). (2020). *Handbook of spirituality, religion, and mental health* (2nd ed.). Elsevier Academic Press.

Salaman, E. (1955). A talk with Einstein. *The Listener*, *54*(1384), 370–371.

Sisemore, T. A., & Knabb, J. J. (Eds.). (2020). *The psychology of world religions and spiritualities: An indigenous perspective*. Templeton Press.

Snyder, C. R., Lopez, S. J., Edwards, L. M., & Marques, S. C. (Eds.). (2021). *The Oxford handbook of positive psychology* (3rd ed.). Oxford University Press. https://doi.org/10.1093/oxfordhb/9780199396511.001.0001

Stauber, L. G., & Stutts, L. A. (2023). The relationship among spirituality, self-compassion, and body satisfaction in college students. *Spirituality in Clinical Practice*, *10*(4), 326–336. https://doi.org/10.1037/scp0000284

Ting, R. S.-K., Mah, S.-C., & Zhang, K. (2020). Chinese traditional religions and mental health: An indigenous psychology perspective. In T. A. Sisemore & J. J. Knabb (Eds.), *The psychology of world religions and spiritualities: An indigenous perspective* (pp. 237–262). Templeton Press.

U. S. Department of Health and Human Services. (2025). *Alcohol and cancer risk: The U.S. Surgeon General's advisory*. U. S. Department of Health and Human Services, Office of the Surgeon General. Retrieved April 29, 2025, from https://www.hhs.gov/surgeongeneral/reports-and-publications/alcohol-cancer/index.html

Webb, J. R. (2007/2003). Spiritual factors and adjustment in medical rehabilitation: Understanding forgiveness as a means of coping. In A. E. DellOrto & P. W. Power (Eds.), *The psychological and social impact of illness and disability* (5th ed., pp. 455–471). Springer. (Reprinted from *Journal of Applied Rehabilitation Counseling*, 34(3), 16–24: 2003.)

Webb, J. R. (2021). *Understanding forgiveness and addiction: Theory, research, and clinical application*. Routledge.

Webb, J. R. (In Press). Spirituality and addictions. In J. M. Currier, J. Fox, & C. Vieten (Eds.), *Handbook of training in spiritual and religious competencies in mental health professions*. Oxford University Press.

Webb, J. R., & Boye, C. M. (2024). Self-forgiveness and self-condemnation in the context of addictive behavior and suicidal behavior. *Substance Abuse and Rehabilitation, 15*, 21–30. https://doi.org/10.2147/sar.S396964

Webb, J. R., Toussaint, L., & Dula, C. S. (2014). Ritualistic, theistic, and existential spirituality: Initial psychometric qualities of the RiTE measure of spirituality. *Journal of Religion and Health*, *53*(4), 972–985. https://doi.org/10.1007/s10943-013-9697-y

World Health Organization. (2018). *Global status report on alcohol and health (2018)*. Executive Summary. Geneva: Author. Retrieved April 29, 2025, from https://www.who.int/publications/i/item/9789241565639

World Health Organization. (2023). *No level of alcohol consumption is safe for our health*. News Release. Geneva: Author. Retrieved April 29, 2025, from https://www.who.int/europe/news/item/04-01-2023-no-level-of-alcohol-consumption-is-safe-for-our-health

World Health Organization. (2025). *Constitution of the World Health Organization*. Geneva: Author. Retrieved April 29, 2025, from https://www.who.int/about/governance/constitution

Worthington, E. L., Jr., Wade, N. G., Hight, T. L., Ripley, J. S., McCullough, M. E., Berry, J. W., Schmitt, M. M., Berry, J. T., Bursley, K. H., & O'Connor, L. (2003). The religious commitment inventory-10: Development, refinement, and validation of a brief scale for research and counseling. *Journal of Counseling Psychology*, *50*(1), 84–96. https://doi.org/10.1037/0022-0167.50.1.84

Yuodelis-Flores, C., & Ries, R. K. (2015). Addiction and suicide: A review. *The American Journal on Addictions*, *24*(2), 98–104. https://doi.org/10.1111/ajad.12185

Chapter 2

Spirituality as a Manifestation of Culture and Diversity

Alexandra S. Wormley, Carley Vornlocher, Eric Y. Aglozo, and Adam B. Cohen*

A patient enters the emergency room after a major motor vehicle accident. A massive loss of blood has put the patient in serious danger. The patient's odds of survival would greatly increase if they could receive a blood transfusion. The blood bank has its type available, and the necessary personnel and equipment are present, but the transfusion does not occur. Why? The patient is a Jehovah's Witness, a religious group based in Christian theology that believes that one's life comes from their blood; to accept blood from another person would be a critical sin even if it meant saving their own life (Effa-Heap, 2009; Gohel et al., 2005; Ott, 1977).

Our cultural identities undeniably play an important role in health. In a myriad of ways, culture dictates what it means to be healthy (e.g., ideal weight), what it means to be sick (e.g., culture-bound syndromes like *ataque de nervios*; Guarnaccia & Rogler, 1999), and how to promote health (e.g., "Western" vs. "Eastern" medicine). It does so via norms, practices, and communication networks. Importantly, we now also understand culture to be more than just one's race or nationality, including one's spiritual identities and commitments (Cohen, 2009). Many of our group memberships constitute some sense of culture – your favorite sports team prescribes what color you should wear on game days; your hometown shapes your verbal accent; your workplace has norms about working on weekends or after 5:00 pm. In this sense, culture is far more diverse than we might immediately consider.

Spirituality represents a core, yet unique, part of one's cultural identity: Do you believe in a higher power? Do you pray? What is your purpose in life? As with more traditional conceptions of culture, spirituality is as diverse as are humans themselves. The goal of this chapter is to explore how spirituality is one of a multitude of forms of culture. If spirituality, as a form of culture, is diverse, then we should also expect that the effects of spirituality on health will be diverse as well. We begin by defining spirituality and differentiating it from religiousness. From this definition, we argue that spirituality meets the definition of a form of culture. Briefly, we describe how the diversity of spiritual experiences has a varying effect on health before closing with limitations and future directions for understanding spirituality as a diverse manifestation of culture.

Defining and Differentiating Spirituality

Defining spirituality is complicated – a definition accepted by all has evaded researchers since the dawn of psychology with William James' work on culture and religion (James, 1902/1997). The RiTE model proposes three domains of spirituality: ritualistic spirituality (how do I practice?), theistic spirituality (how do I understand the Divine?), and existential spirituality

* Corresponding Author: awormley@umich.edu.

DOI: 10.4324/9781003440048-3

(how do I perceive meaning in life?; Webb et al., 2014; see also Chapters 1 and 44 of this volume). While we concur with this definition, our functional definition of spirituality also includes the social component of spirituality, as its relationship with health relies heavily on the social support model (see Michaelson et al., 2021 for empirical support for a community dimension of spirituality).

Differentiating spirituality from religiousness is even more complicated. Here, we resonate with this quote from Zinnbauer et al. (1997, p. 551):

> Whereas religiousness historically included both individual and institutional elements, spirituality is now commonly regarded as an individual phenomenon and identified with such things as personal transcendence, supraconscious sensitivity, and meaningfulness … [r]eligiousness, in contrast, is now often described narrowly as formally structured and identified with religious institutions and prescribed theology and rituals.

In this vein, religiousness refers to the structural, organized, and formalized components of faith, whereas spirituality refers to the more intrinsic and emotional component of faith. That said, while religion and spirituality are often (perhaps overly) dichotomized, spirituality is not always an individual phenomenon, but can often involve group processes, identities, and commitments.

Individuals may be any combination of spiritual and/or religious. One might be both spiritual and religious; these individuals likely adhere to behaviors and practices of a formal religious tradition, like Jehovah's Witnesses or Jainism, and hold the corresponding doctrinal beliefs. However, one can also be spiritual but not religious; the practice of yoga is often deeply spiritual but may not be formally affiliated with a religious tradition. Finally, it is possible to be religious but not spiritual by engaging in religious traditions and rituals while not maintaining any spiritual connection to the teachings and practices. Even within these categories, we should expect some variety, as spirituality and religiousness exist along a continuum.

Spirituality as a Form of Culture

This definition of spirituality lends itself to the idea that spirituality is a form of culture. Here, we work from Fiske's (2002) definition that culture is a "constellation" of practices, norms, ideas, goals, and institutions. Indeed, spirituality contributes to each of these components. While it has previously been argued that religion is a form of culture (Cohen, 2009), we argue here that spirituality is too. The ritualistic component of spirituality prescribes practices and norms for adherents to follow (e.g., yoga and religious diets). The theistic component provides followers with an idea about how the world came to be and how the world works (e.g., creationism and deism). The existential component provides followers with goals to achieve in life (e.g., charity and transcendence). Finally, the social component we have proposed here may create formal or informal institutions for socializing (e.g., prayer groups and interfaith chapels).

People come by their spiritual identities in different ways. Some are born into families and/or broader social contexts that encourage them to develop certain spiritual outlooks and identities. Others discover them on their own, either in a slow process of discovery or in more sudden, epiphany moments, reminiscent of the kinds of born-again experiences that James (1902/1997) discussed in *Varieties of Religious Experience*. Whatever combination of these occurs for a given individual, we must resist the temptation to think that people just happen to hold certain spiritual identities. For many people, their spiritual identities are both profoundly important and foundational to their self-concepts and, moreover, critically shape many areas of psychological function, such as their moral outlooks, how they view themselves, and their interpersonal and intergroup relations (Cohen, 2015), and, what we focus on here, can have profound implications for their physical and mental health. For many people, spirituality is a sacred part of their identity and performs functions (such as answering deep questions about meaning and purpose) that no singular cultural identity can do; nevertheless, we do resonate with arguments regarding the need to rigorously research this and provide reasonable comparison groups or processes (Moon et al., 2023).

Thus, from our definition of spirituality, we can conclude that spirituality has all the defining characteristics of culture. Just as with other forms of culture, there is a wide diversity in spiritual identities and experiences. The diversity between spiritual identities is paired with diversity within these groups as well. Some individuals will resonate with some aspects of spirituality (e.g., theistic component) more than others (e.g., social component) even within the same spiritual identity. Some social contexts emphasize spirituality more than others (e.g., being in a mosque will likely elicit more spiritual experiences than being in a grocery store).

Spirituality and Health

Importantly, the effects of spirituality on health will be diverse as well. So, how might the four components of spirituality – ritualistic, theistic, existential, and social – impact our health? In regard to rituals, consider the previous example of yoga. Yoga practices often emphasize spiritual components like peace and profound connection with nature. There is some evidence to suggest that yoga benefits health by downregulating the hypothalamic-pituitary-adrenal (HPA) axis and the sympathetic nervous system (Ross & Thomas, 2010). Alternatively, consider a more religious practice like religious dietary prescriptions and proscriptions. Many religions dictate what foods adherents should and should not eat. The Church of Jesus Christ of Latter-day Saints emphasizes healthy diets and explicitly bans coffee, tea, tobacco, alcohol, and illegal drugs. Rituals around food could be a key pathway from spirituality to health, but at the same time, they reflect deeper, not-of-this-world spiritual commitments (Cohen, 2021).

In fairness, rituals may be deleterious to health. Extreme spiritual stress or obsession can cause harm to an individual's overall well-being. Religious scrupulosity is characterized by intense fears of religious and moral failing (Cefalu, 2010; Huppert & Siev, 2010; Taylor, 2002), which can cause distress in an individual and those around them. This may be evidenced by excessive prayer or seeking frequent reassurances from religious leaders. While religious individuals are not necessarily more prone to religious obsessions, among individuals with obsessive-compulsive disorder (OCD), the prevalence of religious OCD in one clinical population was 42% (Tek & Ulug, 2001), suggesting that it is quite prominent in individuals with OCD.

Consider also the role that a Divine Being plays in the desire to be healthy. Individuals who identify with theistic spirituality often have some belief in a God or a Supreme Being (Richards & Bergin, 2005). These beliefs can be incorporated into spiritual psychotherapies to treat psychopathologies through spiritually guided cognitive-behavioral therapy, meditation, discussions with God or a Supreme Being, and the promotion of positive psychology (Richards & Bergin, 2005). While many of these therapies might only be *as* effective as their secular equivalents, they may be more appealing to spiritual individuals who may oppose treatment otherwise (Richards & Worthington, 2010).

In times of distress, spiritual individuals may turn to the Divine for emotional relief or guidance and/or their religious community for emotional and structural support (Pargament et al., 2000). For example, belief in Divine control provides a beneficial buffer when dealing with health issues in certain populations (Pargament et al., 1998; Umezawa et al., 2012; Upenieks, 2022). These forms of coping are important resources that may be afforded by one's sense of spirituality and have been linked to better psychological adjustment (Ano & Vasconcelles, 2005).

Though religious coping is generally viewed as a resource afforded to those who are spiritual, use of negative religious coping strategies (e.g., appraising God as punishing), in contrast to positive religious coping (e.g., appraising God as benevolent), has been shown to negatively influence mental health outcomes. Those who implement negative religious coping strategies tend to experience greater depression over time, especially when these strategies are used to cope with chronic stressors or traumatic events (Gerber et al., 2011; Pargament et al., 2004; Wijngaards-de Meij et al., 2005; Zwingmann et al., 2006). These processes could be occurring because of the critical importance of spiritual outlooks in how people view their lives and their relationships to their spiritual communities and beliefs.

One's spiritual identity may also provide meaning in life and guiding values that promote healthful practices. Intrinsic religiousness, service attendance, spiritual satisfaction, spiritual commitment, and daily spiritual practice have all been positively linked to meaning in life (Ardelt, 2003; Bauer-Wu & Farran, 2005; Chamberlain & Zika, 1992; Harris & Standard, 2001; Kashdan & Nezlek, 2012). Extensive work has identified a positive effect of religiousness and spirituality on one's health and well-being. Often, this work emphasizes the role that meaning in life plays in creating health benefits (Chamberlain & Zika, 1992; Krok, 2015; Nelson et al., 2021; Steger & Frazier, 2005). Individuals may be more motivated to tend to their health and have the resilience to overcome challenges when they identify with existential spirituality.

Finally – and perhaps most importantly – spiritual communities convey social support that can bolster one's health. Extensive evidence has identified how the social support provided by one's religious group can provide health benefits (Chatters, 2000; Fredrickson, 2002; Krok, 2015; McCullough et al., 2009; Wallace et al., 2019). Meta-analyses have found that religious participation in the form of service attendance was associated with a 1.29 times lower risk for mortality, with an even stronger effect for women than men (Chida et al., 2009; McCullough et al., 2000). Broadly, these effects have been replicated outside of the United States in Christian populations in Denmark (la Cour et al., 2006) and Finland (Teinonen et al., 2005), Taoist and Buddhist populations in Taiwan (Yeager et al., 2006), and Jews in Israel (Litwin, 2007). Thus, regardless of the surrounding cultural context, participation in religious or spiritual activities is positively related to health outcomes. Of course, it should be noted that while social support plays a critical role in the relationship between spirituality and health, in its absence, spirituality can become deleterious to one's health. For example, negative interactions at church can lead to higher levels of psychological distress (Ellison & Lee, 2010; Krause et al., 1998).

However, as previously mentioned, it is possible to be spiritual without being religious. Still, interfaith communities, meditation centers, and the loose community of "Spiritual but Not Religious" individuals all confer social and spiritual benefits without an organized religious dogma. One of the noted benefits of the spiritual practice of yoga is the sense of community it provides with other practitioners (Kinser et al., 2013; Lacasse et al., 2019). Thus, we understand that social support plays a critical role in the relationship between spirituality and health (Holt et al., 2018; Jarvis & Northcott, 1987; Li et al., 2016). This work makes the critical point that acceptance or rejection from our spiritual communities can be as profoundly important to us as other aspects of spirituality (e.g., personal beliefs) and can have important effects on health and well-being as a result.

Limitations

Certainly, a wealth of time and resources has been dedicated to understanding the vital roles of diverse spiritualities in physical and mental health. It is, however, difficult to assess the relative importance of the religious (ritualistic), theistic, and existential spirituality from the available evidence. It also remains unclear how the social component of spirituality, in the absence of a formal religious affiliation, may play a role in health; this is all the more critical given the rising number of individuals who identify as spiritual, but not religious (SBNRs). Similarly, these dimensions are involved in the sometimes-detrimental impacts of spirituality on health and well-being, with some evidence emanating from the religious coping literature (e.g., Pirutinsky et al., 2011). Negative religious coping, such as blaming God for misfortune, reflects an insecure relationship with the Divine. Therefore, it is our provocative hypothesis that the current evidence falls more within the social dimension of spirituality than the other dimensions of spirituality. However, the other dimensions of spirituality certainly play an important role in health processes, underscoring the need for more research on these dimensions.

Further, the four components of spirituality do not work in isolation. Lim and Putnam (2010) proposed a comprehensive theoretical model of these processes, highlighting that ritualistic spirituality may provide opportunities for positive, nurturing interactions. For example, service attendance and friendships within one's congregation may enhance life satisfaction. Moreover, they propose that one's religious identity and religious social network are salubrious when they mutually reinforce one another. Meeting regularly with close others in religious contexts is believed to connect individuals to their religious communities more concretely, which in turn enhances the salience of one's spirituality. Overall, relationships with like-minded others should reinforce one's choices, values, and goals in a way that is rewarding and beneficial to health and well-being. Additionally, these social bonds may serve as a resource in times of need, such that people can seek instrumental or emotional support from close religious community members. This support, in turn, can reinforce not only one's social bonds but also one's spirituality. Relatedly, religious social networks may also improve health and well-being by establishing social norms related to health behaviors (e.g., strict norms against smoking, drinking, and risky sexual behavior and in support of healthy eating and physical activity). While we might be accustomed to thinking about how one or another dimension of spirituality might be acting on health outcomes or paying disproportionate attention to one dimension (e.g., personal identity, more so than social aspects), our review reminds us that many aspects of spirituality can be important to people and have impacts on health and well-being.

Many of the past studies have been conducted in the United States and Europe. Although the United States and Europe have various religious traditions, participants from Catholic, Protestant, and Jewish traditions are predominantly represented in these studies, including those that have investigated religious differences and well-being (Cohen, 2002; Shiah et al., 2016). Islam is a rapidly growing religion worldwide, and it is projected to become the second-largest religion in the United States by 2040 (Lipka, 2017). Yet, there is little research that has investigated spirituality, health, and well-being among Muslims in the United States (e.g., Abu-Raiya et al., 2011). Even less common are studies that have investigated religious differences and health and well-being among Muslim and non-Muslim samples within or outside of the United States. One such study examined the association between religious coping and life satisfaction and depression among Muslims and Jews in Israel, finding that the benefits of religious coping vary according to religious affiliation (Abu-Raiya et al., 2020).

A major critique of religion/spirituality and health research is the use of inadequate control of confounding variables, and the presence of adequate controls leads to the weakening or disappearance of the salubrious effects of religion and spirituality (Sloan et al., 1999). However, this area of research has improved methodologically over time and is actively addressing this concern (VanderWeele, 2017). Another critique is that measures of spirituality contain items that are similar to items on well-being measures such as optimism, meaning and purpose, and harmony (Koenig, 2008). Studies that use such contaminated measures lead to tautological findings (Koenig, 2008; Visser et al., 2017).

The context of spiritual involvement is also a critical moderating factor. For unwed mothers whose situation may conflict with the traditional family values present in Christian churches, religious participation is associated with higher depression rates (Koenig, 2009; Sorenson et al., 1995). In a study of the effects of religious affiliation on longevity (derived from gravestones), the religiousness of the surrounding city moderated the positive effect of religious affiliation on longevity, such that there was a stronger effect in more religious cities (Wallace et al., 2019).

Finally, much of this work presumes a 2 × 2 matrix where individuals are religious or not and spiritual or not. However, the reality is far more complicated than this – religiousness and spirituality exist on multiple continuums (e.g., intrinsic religiousness, extrinsic religiousness, and fundamentalism). At times, this is an inescapable limitation of the design. In graveyard mortality studies, religiousness is indicated by a binary variable: the presence of religious imagery or not on gravestones (Wallace et al., 2019). Still, ideally, researchers can be more thoughtful and intentional about their measures of religiousness and spirituality by forming concrete research questions (i.e., is it being spiritual, or is it the degree to which one is spiritual), working with scales that are inclusive of a diversity of spiritual experiences, and using caution when titling and summarizing their research.

Future Directions

A rich body of literature on the role of spirituality in health and well-being has accumulated over time, with some evidence coming from non-Christian and non-Western samples (e.g., Kim, 2003; Tiliouine & Belgoumidi, 2009). Despite the growth in this research area, more work is needed in other cultural contexts. One under-explored issue is the health and well-being of religious minorities and the impact of spirituality on these outcomes (Wallace et al., 2019). Religious groups can possess minority status in certain societies while not in others, and within minority religious groups, there can be variations in the challenges and limitations they face. These differences may consequently influence the manner in which spirituality affects the health and well-being of minority group members. Gaining an understanding of these implications can provide valuable insights. As cultural identities are often intersectional, it will be critical for future research to look at how spiritual identities in different cultural contexts affect health.

Religious minorities may experience struggles in their relationships with people outside their religion, perhaps due to perceived distinctiveness or even incompatibility of their spiritual behavior, practices, or beliefs (Marks et al., 2019); such differences may lead to feelings of isolation and distress among members of minority religious groups. Moreover, spiritual notions are often construed as sacred values on which no kind of compromise is possible (Atran & Axelrod, 2008). However, belief certainty and a positive construction of their religious identity (e.g., as being chosen by God or the Divine) may buffer against the impact of negative social experiences and conflict.

Just as there are multiple dimensions of religion and spirituality, there are multiple dimensions of well-being (Cohen & Johnson, 2017), and certain dimensions of well-being may be more suitable for certain cultural contexts than others, as is the case for religion and spirituality (Cohen et al., 2017). However, studies on spirituality and well-being, which are mainly conducted in the United States, commonly use individualism-themed measures of well-being that emphasize hedonic and eudaimonic concepts of well-being, such as personal satisfaction and positive emotions. The values of certain religions may not match well with these aspects of well-being. For example, socially oriented subjective well-being, measured as fulfillment of obligations and dialectical balance, was greater among Buddhist than Christian participants in Taiwan (Shiah et al., 2016). In the same vein, it would be important to consider how well-being is conceptualized in underrepresented religions and societies in such research. Scholars have argued that the emergence of Pentecostal Charismatic Christianity in West Africa since the 1980s has led to the introduction of individualistic values, including those that emphasize autonomy and personal growth (Asamoah-Gyadu, 2020). These individualist values are less emphasized among members of traditional, Western mission churches (TWMCS), who emphasize family obligation and social harmony more (Osei-Tutu et al., 2022). Differences in value orientations may manifest in differences in religious groups and the aspect of well-being relevant to these groups.

Cultural competency is a major issue in contemporary discussions about mental health. It refers to the possession of cultural knowledge and skills of a particular culture to provide effective interventions to clients of that culture (Sue, 1998). Religious and spiritual identity are forms of culture (Cohen, 2009) and an important consideration in therapy. Often, cultural competency is interpreted as solely understanding what religion means to a client or patient, rather than having a basic knowledge of different faith systems. While understanding the individual's interpretation of their own faith is certainly important, clinicians must understand the broader spiritual, religious, and cultural contexts in which a client is operating. Clinical training programs should strive to strike a balance between understanding both the individual's role within their spirituality and the system of belief writ large. Handbooks, such as the *Handbook on Religious Diversity* (Keller, 2014), and similar resources serve to give one a working knowledge of different spiritual and religious contexts that people might be bringing into the room.

Additionally, further work is needed on the part of the clinician to understand how to differentiate components of spirituality from psychological disorders. This differentiation may look different across the wide array of spiritual contexts. For example, take the role of religious scrupulosity in OCD across Judaism and Christianity. Jewish theology pays more attention to behavior than thoughts, whereas Christian theology treats them much more similarly (Cohen & Rozin, 2001). Siev and Cohen (2007) looked at Jewish individuals and Christians in a non-OCD sample. They found that Christians had highly elevated scores on thought-action fusion, a tendency among individuals with OCD to see thoughts as being as morally important as actions, higher even than the norms for OCD patients. Thus, a normative component of Christianity – seeing thoughts and actions as morally relevant – appeared similar to a component of psychopathology, underscoring the need for clinicians to understand the contextual role of religion in diagnosis and treatment.

Conclusion

Overall, the literature documents a mostly positive impact of spirituality on health and well-being. Looking at the available evidence from the perspective of the RiTE model of spirituality (Webb et al., 2014), much of the evidence about the association between religion and spirituality and physical health, particularly mortality, stems from the influence of social involvement, which aligns strongly with ritualistic spirituality. The three dimensions of spirituality per the RiTE model are reflected in findings about spirituality and mental health and well-being, which have been studied in a variety of ways, including depression, anxiety, life satisfaction, positive emotion, meaning, optimism, and psychological well-being. Going forward, researchers and practitioners should be intentional about expanding their definitions of spirituality to include the social components and be mindful of the diversity of spiritual experiences. Further, it is false to assume that spirituality will always benefit health; therefore, we should also attend to the boundary conditions of when spirituality is not salubrious for one's health.

References

Abu-Raiya, H., Pargament, K. I., & Mahoney, A. (2011). Examining coping methods with stressful interpersonal events experienced by Muslims living in the United States following the 9/11 attacks. *Psychology of Religion and Spirituality*, *3*(1), 1–14. https://doi.org/10.1037/a0020034

Abu-Raiya, H., Sasson, T., Pargament, K. I., & Rosmarin, D. H. (2020). Religious coping and health and well-being among Jews and Muslims in Israel. *The International Journal for the Psychology of Religion*, *30*(3), 202–215. https://doi.org/10.1080/10508619.2020.1727692

Ano, G. G., & Vasconcelles, E. B. (2005). Religious coping and psychological adjustment to stress: A meta-analysis. *Journal of Clinical Psychology*, *61*(4), 461–480.

Ardelt, M. (2003). Effects of religion and purpose in life on elders' subjective well-being and attitudes toward death. *Journal of Religious Gerontology*, *14*(4), 55–77.

Asamoah-Gyadu, J. K. (2020). *Pentecostalism in Africa: Experiences from Ghana's Charismatic Ministries*. Augsburg Fortress Publishers. https://muse.jhu.edu/pub/261/monograph/book/85402

Atran, S., & Axelrod, R. (2008). Reframing sacred values. *Negotiation Journal*, *24*, 221–246.

Bauer-Wu, S., & Farran, C. J. (2005). Meaning in life and psycho-spiritual functioning: A comparison of breast cancer survivors and healthy women. *Journal of Holistic Nursing*, *23*(2), 172–190.

Cefalu, P. (2010). The doubting disease: Religious scrupulosity and obsessive-compulsive disorder in historical context. *Journal of Medical Humanities*, *31*(2), 111–125. https://doi.org/10.1007/s10912-010-9107-3

Chamberlain, K., & Zika, S. (1992). Religiosity, meaning in life, and psychological well-being. In J. F. Schumaker (Ed.), *Religion and Mental Health* (pp. 138–148). Oxford University Press. https://doi.org/10.1093/oso/9780195069853.003.0011

Chatters, L. M. (2000). Religion and health: Public health research and practice. *Annual Review of Public Health*, *21*, 335–367. https://doi.org/10.1146/annurev.publhealth.21.1.335

Chida, Y., Steptoe, A., & Powell, L. H. (2009). Religiosity/spirituality and mortality: A systematic quantitative review. *Psychotherapy and Psychosomatics*, *78*(2), 81–90.

Cohen, A. B. (2002). The importance of spirituality in well-being for Jews and Christians. *Journal of Happiness Studies*, *3*, 287–310.

Cohen, A. B. (2009). Many forms of culture. *American Psychologist*, *64*(3), 194–204. https://doi.org/10.1037/a0015308

Cohen, A. B. (2015). Religion's profound influences on psychology: Morality, intergroup relations, self-construal, and enculturation. *Current Directions in Psychological Science*, *24*, 77–82.

Cohen, A. B. (2021). You can learn a lot about religion from food. *Current Opinion in Psychology*, *40*, 1–5. https://doi.org/10.1016/j.copsyc.2020.07.032

Cohen, A. B., & Johnson, K. A. (2017). The relation between religion and well-being. *Applied Research in Quality of Life*, *12*, 533–547.

Cohen, A. B., Mazza, G. L., Johnson, K. A., Enders, C. K., Warner, C. M., Pasek, M. H., & Cook, J. E. (2017). Theorizing and measuring religiosity across cultures. *Personality and Social Psychology Bulletin*, *43*(12), 1724–1736. https://doi.org/10.1177/0146167217727732

Cohen, A. B., & Rozin, P. (2001). Religion and the morality of mentality. *Journal of Personality and Social Psychology*, *81*, 697–710. https://doi.org/10.1037/0022-3514.81.4.697

Effa-Heap, G. (2009). Blood transfusion: Implications of treating a Jehovah's Witness patient. *British Journal of Nursing*, *18*(3), 174–177.

Ellison, C. G., & Lee, J. (2010). Spiritual struggles and psychological distress: Is there a dark side of religion? *Social Indicators Research*, *98*, 501–517.

Fiske, A. P. (2002). Using individualism and collectivism to compare cultures—A critique of the validity and measurement of the constructs: Comment on Oyserman et al. (2002). *Psychological Bulletin*, *128*(1), 78–88. http://doi.org/10.1037/0033-2909.128.1.78

Fredrickson, B. L. (2002). How does religion benefit health and well-being? Are positive emotions active ingredients? *Psychological Inquiry*, *13*(3), 209–213.

Gerber, M. M., Boals, A., & Schuettler, D. (2011). The unique contributions of positive and negative religious coping to posttraumatic growth and PTSD. *Psychology of Religion and Spirituality*, *3*(4), 298–307. https://doi.org/10.1037/a0023016

Gohel, M. S., Bulbulia, R. A., Slim, F. J., Poskitt, K. R., & Whyman, M. R. (2005). How to approach major surgery where patients refuse blood transfusion (including Jehovah's Witnesses). *Annals of The Royal College of Surgeons of England*, *87*(1), 3–14.

Guarnaccia, P. J., & Rogler, L. H. (1999). Research on culture-bound syndromes: New directions. *American Journal of Psychiatry*, *156*(9), 1322–1327. https://doi.org/10.1176/ajp.156.9.1322

Harris, A. H., & Standard, S. (2001). Psychometric properties of the life regard index–revised: A validation study of a measure of personal meaning. *Psychological Reports*, *89*(3), 759–773.

Holt, C. L., Roth, D. L., Huang, J., & Clark, E. M. (2018). Role of religious social support in longitudinal relationships between religiosity and health-related outcomes in African Americans. *Journal of Behavioral Medicine*, *41*(1), 62–73. https://doi.org/10.1007/s10865-017-9877-4

Huppert, J. D., & Siev, J. (2010). Treating Scrupulosity in Religious Individuals Using Cognitive-Behavioral Therapy. *Cognitive and Behavioral Practice*, *17*(4), 382–392. https://doi.org/10.1016/j.cbpra.2009.07.003

James, W. (1902/1997). *The varieties of religious experience*. Harvard University Press.

Jarvis, G. K., & Northcott, H. C. (1987). Religion and differences in morbidity and mortality. *Social Science & Medicine*, *25*(7), 813–824. https://doi.org/10.1016/0277-9536(87)90039-6

Kashdan, T. B., & Nezlek, J. B. (2012). Whether, when, and how is spirituality related to well-being? Moving beyond single occasion questionnaires to understanding daily process. *Personality and Social Psychology Bulletin*, *38*(11), 1523–1535.

Keller, R. R. (2014). Religious diversity in North America. In *Handbook of psychotherapy and religious diversity*, *2nd* ed (pp. 21–50). American Psychological Association. https://doi.org/10.1037/14371-002

Kim, A. E. (2003). Religious influences on personal and societal well-being. *Social Indicators Research*, *62*(1), 149–170. https://doi.org/10.1023/A:1022641100109

Kinser, P. A., Bourguignon, C., Taylor, A. G., & Steeves, R. (2013). "A feeling of connectedness": Perspectives on a gentle yoga intervention for women with major depression. *Issues in Mental Health Nursing*, *34*(6), 402–411. https://doi.org/10.3109/01612840.2012.762959

Koenig, H. G. (2008). Concerns About Measuring "Spirituality" in Research. *The Journal of Nervous and Mental Disease*, *196*(5), 349–355. https://doi.org/10.1097/NMD.0b013e31816ff796

Koenig, H. G. (2009). Research on religion, spirituality, and mental health: A review. *The Canadian Journal of Psychiatry*, *54*(5), 283–291.

Krause, N., Ellison, C. G., & Wulff, K. M. (1998). Church-based emotional support, negative interaction, and psychological well-being: Findings from a national sample of Presbyterians. *Journal for the Scientific Study of Religion*, *37*(4), 725–741.

Krok, D. (2015). The role of meaning in life within the relations of religious coping and psychological well-being. *Journal of Religion and Health*, *54*(6), 2292–2308. https://doi.org/10.1007/s10943-014-9983-3

la Cour, P., Avlund, K., & Schultz-Larsen, K. (2006). Religion and survival in a secular region. A twenty year follow-up of 734 Danish adults born in 1914. *Social Science & Medicine*, *62*(1), 157–164. https://doi.org/10.1016/j.socscimed.2005.05.029

Lacasse, J., Santarossa, S., & Woodruff, S. J. (2019). #Yoga on Instagram: Understanding the nature of yoga in the online conversation and community. *International Journal of Yoga*, *12*(2), 153–157. https://doi.org/10.4103/ijoy.IJOY_50_18

Li, S., Stampfer, M. J., Williams, D. R., & VanderWeele, T. J. (2016). Association of religious service attendance with mortality among women. *JAMA Internal Medicine*, *176*(6), 777–785. https://doi.org/10.1001/jamainternmed.2016.1615

Lim, C., & Putnam, R. D. (2010). Religion, social networks, and life satisfaction. *American Sociological Review*, *75*(6), 914–933. https://doi.org/10.1177/0003122410386686

Lipka, M. (2017, August 9). Muslims and Islam: Key findings in the U.S. and around the world. *Pew Research Center*. https://www.pewresearch.org/short-reads/2017/08/09/muslims-and-islam-key-findings-in-the-u-s-and-around-the-world/

Litwin, H. (2007). What really matters in the social network–mortality association? A multivariate examination among older Jewish-Israelis. *European Journal of Ageing*, *4*(2), 71–82. https://doi.org/10.1007/s10433-007-0048-2

Marks, L. D., Dollahite, D. C., & Young, K. P. (2019). Struggles experienced by religious minority families in the United States. *Psychology of Religion and Spirituality*, *11*(3), 247–256. https://doi.org/10.1037/rel0000214

McCullough, M. E., Friedman, H. S., Enders, C. K., Martin, L. R., Hoyt, W. T., & Larson, D. B. (2009). Does devoutness delay death? Psychological investment in religion and its association with longevity in the Terman sample. *Journal of Personality and Social Psychology*, *97*(5), 866–882. https://doi.org/10.1037/a0016366

McCullough, M. E., Hoyt, W. T., Larson, D. B., Koenig, H. G., & Thoresen, C. (2000). Religious involvement and mortality: A meta-analytic review. *Health Psychology*, *19*(3), 211–222. https://doi.org/10.1037/0278-6133.19.3.211

Michaelson, V., Šmigelskas, K., King, N., Inchley, J., Malinowska-Cieślik, M., Pickett, W., & HBSC Spiritual Health Writing Group. (2021). Domains of spirituality and their importance to the health of 75 533 adolescents in 12 countries. *Health Promotion International*, daab185. https://doi.org/10.1093/heapro/daab185

Moon, J. W., Cohen, A. B., Laurin, K., & MacKinnon, D. P. (2023). Is religion special?. *Perspectives on Psychological Science*, *18*(2), 340–357.

Nelson, T. A., Abeyta, A. A., & Routledge, C. (2021). What makes life meaningful for theists and atheists? *Psychology of Religion and Spirituality*, *13*(1), 111–118. https://doi.org/10.1037/rel0000282

Osei-Tutu, A., Adams, G., Dzokoto, V., Affram, A. A., Kenin, A., Vural, N., & Omar, S. M. (2022). Conception and experience of well-being in two Ghanaian samples: Implications for Positive Psychology. *International Journal of Wellbeing*, *12*(4), 51–64. https://doi.org/10.5502/ijw.v12i4.2123

Ott, D. A. (1977). Cardiovascular surgery in Jehovah's witnesses: Report of 542 operations without blood transfusion. *JAMA*, *238*(12), 1256–1258. https://doi.org/10.1001/jama.1977.03280130038011

Pargament, K. I., Koenig, H. G., & Perez, L. M. (2000). The many methods of religious coping: Development and initial validation of the RCOPE. *Journal of Clinical Psychology*, *56*(4), 519–543. https://doi.org/10.1002/(sici)1097-4679(200004)56:4<519::aid-jclp6>3.0.co;2-1

Pargament, K. I., Koenig, H. G., Tarakeshwar, N., & Hahn, J. (2004). Religious coping methods as predictors of psychological, physical and spiritual outcomes among medically ill elderly patients: A two-year longitudinal study. *Journal of Health Psychology*, *9*(6), 713–730.

Pargament, K. I., Smith, B. W., Koenig, H. G., & Perez, L. (1998). Patterns of positive and negative religious coping with major life stressors. *Journal for the Scientific Study of Religion*, *37*(4), 710–724. https://doi.org/10.2307/1388152

Pirutinsky, S., Rosmarin, D. H., Pargament, K. I., & Midlarsky, E. (2011). Does negative religious coping accompany, precede, or follow depression among Orthodox Jews? *Journal of Affective Disorders*, *132*(3), 401–405.

Richards, P. S., & Bergin, A. (2005). *A spiritual strategy for counseling and psychotherapy*. (2nd ed.). American Psychological Association. https://doi.org/10.1037/11214-000

Richards, P. S., & Worthington Jr., E. L. (2010). The need for evidence-based, spiritually oriented psychotherapies. *Professional Psychology: Research and Practice*, *41*(5), 363. https://doi.org/10.1037/a0019469

Ross, A., & Thomas, S. (2010). The health benefits of yoga and exercise: A review of comparison studies. *The Journal of Alternative and Complementary Medicine*, *16*(1), 3–12. https://doi.org/10.1089/acm.2009.0044

Shiah, Y.-J., Chang, F., Chiang, S.-K., & Tam, W.-C. C. (2016). Religion and subjective well-being: Western and Eastern religious groups achieved subjective well-being in different ways. *Journal of Religion and Health*, *55*, 1263–1269.

Siev, J., & Cohen, A. B. (2007). Is thought–action fusion related to religiosity? Differences between Christians and Jews. *Behaviour Research and Therapy*, *45*(4), 829–837. https://doi.org/10.1016/j.brat.2006.05.001

Sloan, R. P., Bagiella, E., & Powell, T. (1999). Religion, spirituality, and medicine. *The Lancet*, *353*(9153), 664–667. https://doi.org/10.1016/S0140-6736(98)07376-0

Sorenson, A. M., Grindstaff, C. F., & Turner, R. J. (1995). Religious involvement among unmarried adolescent mothers: A source of emotional support? *Sociology of Religion*, *56*(1), 71–81.

Steger, M. F., & Frazier, P. (2005). Meaning in life: One link in the chain from religiousness to well-being. *Journal of Counseling Psychology*, *52*(4), 574.

Sue, S. (1998). In search of cultural competence in psychotherapy and counseling. *American Psychologist*, *53*(4), 440–448. https://doi.org/10.1037/0003-066X.53.4.440

Taylor, C. Z. (2002). Religious addiction: Obsession with spirituality. *Pastoral Psychology*, *50*(4), 291–315.

Teinonen, T., Vahlberg, T., Isoaho, R., & Kivelä, S.-L. (2005). Religious attendance and 12-year survival in older persons. *Age and Ageing*, *34*(4), 406–409. https://doi.org/10.1093/ageing/afi107

Tek, C., & Ulug, B. (2001). Religiosity and religious obsessions in obsessive-compulsive disorder. *Psychiatry Research*, *104*(2), 99–108. https://doi.org/10.1016/s0165-1781(01)00310-9

Tiliouine, H., & Belgoumidi, A. (2009). An exploratory study of religiosity, meaning in life and subjective wellbeing in Muslim students from Algeria. *Applied Research in Quality of Life*, *4*, 109–127.

Umezawa, Y., Lu, Q., You, J., Kagawa-Singer, M., Leake, B., & Maly, R. C. (2012). Belief in divine control, coping, and race/ethnicity among older women with breast cancer. *Annals of Behavioral Medicine*, *44*(1), 21–32. https://doi.org/10.1007/s12160-012-9358-5

Upenieks, L. (2022). Religious/spiritual struggles and suicidal ideation in the COVID-19 era: Does the belief in divine control and religious attendance matter? *Psychology of Religion and Spirituality*, *14*(3), 338–350. https://doi.org/10.1037/rel0000467

VanderWeele, T. J. (2017). Religious communities and human flourishing. *Current Directions in Psychological Science*, *26*(5), 476–481. https://doi.org/10.1177/0963721417721526

Visser, A., Garssen, B., & Vingerhoets, A. J. (2017). Existential well-being: Spirituality or well-being? *Journal of Nervous & Mental Disease*, *205*(3), 234–241. https://doi.org/10.1097/NMD.0000000000000617

Wallace, L. E., Anthony, R., End, C. M., & Way, B. M. (2019). Does religion stave off the grave? Religious affiliation in one's obituary and longevity. *Social Psychological and Personality Science*, *10*(5), 662–670. https://doi.org/10.1177/1948550618779820

Webb, J. R., Toussaint, L., & Dula, C. S. (2014). Ritualistic, theistic, and existential spirituality: Initial psychometric qualities of the RiTE measure of spirituality. *Journal of Religion and Health*, *53*, 972–985.

Wijngaards-de Meij, L., Stroebe, M., Schut, H., Stroebe, W., van den Bout, J., van der Heijden, P., & Dijkstra, I. (2005). Couples at risk following the death of their child: Predictors of grief versus depression. *Journal of Consulting and Clinical Psychology*, *73*(4), 617–623. https://doi.org/10.1037/0022-006X.73.4.617

Yeager, D. M., Glei, D. A., Au, M., Lin, H.-S., Sloan, R. P., & Weinstein, M. (2006). Religious involvement and health outcomes among older persons in Taiwan. *Social Science & Medicine*, *63*(8), 2228–2241. https://doi.org/10.1016/j.socscimed.2006.05.007

Zinnbauer, B. J., Pargament, K. I., Cole, B., Rye, M. S., Butter, E. M., Belavich, T. G., Hipp, K. M., Scott, A. B., & Kadar, J. L. (1997). Religion and spirituality: Unfuzzying the fuzzy. *Journal for the Scientific Study of Religion*, *36*(4), 549–564. https://doi.org/10.2307/1387689

Zwingmann, C., Wirtz, M., Müller, C., Körber, J., & Murken, S. (2006). Positive and negative religious coping in German breast cancer patients. *Journal of Behavioral Medicine*, *29*, 533–547.

Chapter 3

Spirituality, Health, and Well-Being

Field Overview and Emerging Frontiers

*Doug Oman**

The scientific study of spirituality, religion, and health has expanded enormously in recent decades. Spirituality and religion (S/R) now draw sustained attention as health factors in clinical fields such as psychology, medicine, nursing, and allied fields that include public health, social work, and gerontology (Cobb et al., 2012; Cockell & Mcsherry, 2012; George et al., 2013; Hodge, 2018; Koenig et al., 2023; Oman, 2018b; Pargament, 2013). Well over 100 systematic reviews and more than 30 meta-analyses have linked S/R to health, usually to better health (Oman & Syme, 2018). In psychological research, too, the quality, absolute number, and relative number of empirical studies have grown enormously: the proportion of refereed publications with titles that mention "spirituality" has expanded 36-fold from 1970 to the 21st century, and the proportion mentioning "religion" has nearly doubled (1.78-fold; see Figure 3.1). Moreover, sets of obligatory professional competencies in S/R have been proposed, and ever more resources now support psychologists in addressing client spirituality and religiousness in clinical practice (Richards & Bergin, 2014; Salcone et al., 2023; Vieten & Lukoff, 2022).

The field's evidence base, resources, and proposed competencies did not spring up overnight, of course. As sketched in this chapter, the literature on these vital topics has emerged from many compelling empirical findings and from conceptual and methodological ferment and development. For example, nationally representative samples have empirically linked religious engagement to longevity differentials of more than 7 years in the US general population and nearly 14 years in African Americans (Hummer et al., 1999; see also Chida et al., 2009). Regarding therapies, a meta-analysis of 46 published reports of spiritually infused psychotherapy has reported that S/R psychotherapies outperform both no-treatment controls (Cohen's $d = 0.45$ in 22 studies) and alternate secular psychotherapies ($d = 0.26$ in 29 studies) (Worthington et al., 2011). As detailed later in this chapter, advances have also occurred in conceptualizing S/R by attending to both substantive and functional features (Hill & Pargament, 2003). Religion is now commonly affirmed as a social determinant of health alongside factors such as age, gender, ethnicity, and socioeconomic status (Idler, 2014; Oman, 2018b). Nonetheless, for optimal treatment, prevention, and health promotion, we still need better comprehension of many issues, such as understanding who benefits most from spirituality, which aspects of spirituality are more/less beneficial and when, how benefits occur, and implications for professional training and practice in diverse fields.

Building on past research and responding to emerging opportunities and needs, the present chapter – alongside many other chapters in this volume – foregrounds *spirituality*, in contrast to most previous overviews that have foregrounded religion (e.g., Koenig et al., 2023). The two

* Corresponding Author: docnid@berkeley.edu.

DOI: 10.4324/9781003440048-4

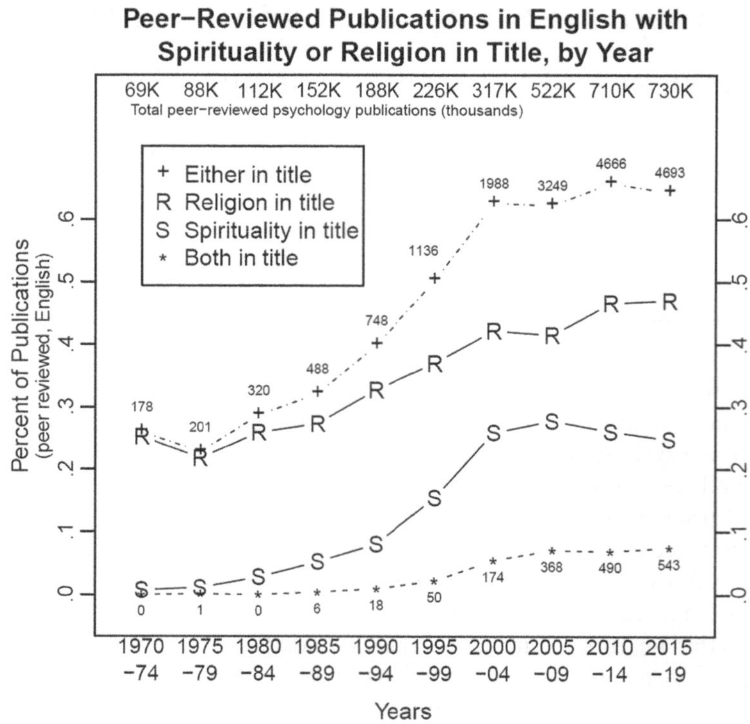

Figure 3.1 Growth of Attention to "Spirituality" and "Religion" in Professional Psychology Literature. Based on peer-reviewed English-language publications indexed in PsycINFO on May 8, 2023. Title search terms were spirituality or spiritual (for spirituality), and religion, religious, religiousness or religiosity (for religion). Pooled across all years, about 9% of all titles that included spirituality or religion had both (1650/17,667). The proportion of peer-reviewed publications containing spirituality grew 36-fold from the 1970 to 1974 value of 0.007%, to a pooled average of 0.260% from 2000 to 2019.

constructs of S/R are deeply interrelated and overlapping (see section below on definitions). Yet, perspectives from spirituality are distinct from perspectives from religion, and each perspective offers unique insights, even as the two perspectives are arguably *complementary* as guides for future work. At least four specific contemporary concerns benefit from foregrounding spirituality.

First, people self-identifying as "spiritual but not religious" (SBNR) now constitute double-digit percentages of adults in the United States (22%), Western Europe (median 11%), and Australia (17%) (Bouma & Halafoff, 2017; Pew Research Center, 2023, 2018, May 29). Such self-identified spiritual engagement *apart* from religion is comparatively new as a widespread phenomenon in Western culture, and it was only in 2023 that the Pew Foundation began monitoring US trends by periodically surveying US adults using a battery of spirituality-focused questions (Pew Research Center, 2023). Foregrounding spirituality supports directing needed theoretical and practical attention to SBNRs and to the spiritual facets of religious engagement.

Second, key gaps remain in our understanding of the health impacts of various forms of "spirituality" as compared to impacts from engaging in "religion" (Ransome, 2020). More research is needed to guide psychologists and other clinicians in accommodating and/or supporting spirituality. Importantly, such understanding is needed not only in the clinic, but also in the expanding array of contexts in which psychological or interdisciplinary health promotion activities may occur, including "partnership with multiple public sectors such as health, education, employment, judicial, housing, social and other relevant sectors as well as the private sector" (World Health Organization, 2013, p. 10; see also Oman, 2025a, 2025b).

Third, in the clinic as well as in other contexts, best-practice health promotion efforts are now multi-level, seeking to beneficially influence not only individuals but also sociocultural *environments* (Institute of Medicine, 2000; Schensul & Trickett, 2009). Across various sociocultural and institutional environments, the constructs of S/R offer partly overlapping yet distinct conceptual bases and *affordances* for developing socio-environmentally focused health-promotion interventions that are legal, ethical, and feasible. In particular, the vocabulary of spirituality appears increasingly accepted – among both scientific and religious communities – for referring to families of practices and purposes that are shared across religious traditions, possess a mutual "coherent resemblance" (Peterson & Seligman, 2004, p. 35), and sometimes possess variants *outside* of formalized religious traditions. For supporting such practices and purposes, "spirituality" thus merits exploration in its affordances for both conceptualizing and administering sound and acceptable interventions and also for its affordances as a "magnet" for mobilizing broad-based coalitions to develop and implement such interventions (Béland & Cox, 2016; Swinkels, 2020; espoused by Balboni & Balboni, 2018, p. 261, as a need for "alliance"). For such coalition-building purposes, the flexibility and partial ambiguity of the term spirituality is a positive asset, enabling it to function akin to what sociologists have called "boundary objects [that] act as cooperation facilitators among heterogeneous actors" (Cino Pagliarello, 2022, p. 889) and are "both plastic enough to adapt to local needs and constraints of the several parties employing them, yet robust enough to maintain a common identity" (Star & Griesemer, 1989, p. 393).

Finally, on a global scale, the emergence of spirituality as a common factor that major religious traditions increasingly acknowledge they share (despite operationalizing in diverse ways) is relevant to navigating cultural, institutional, and worldview diversity. It is now widely acknowledged that the world is evolving "multiple modernities," without any straightforward global convergence on what has been called "Euro-American modernity" (Eisenstadt, 2000; Geltner & Coomans, 2023). Societies and modernities worldwide also vary substantially in the degree to which religion – and many forms of spirituality along with it – have been privatized and excluded from other social sectors that operate on their own "logics," such as education, medicine, law, and the economy (Beyer, 1990). Ironically, however, because of its potential to function as a coalition magnet, the construct of spirituality, sometimes criticized for exacerbating individualism (Carrette & King, 2004), could *also* become pivotal for *deprivatizing* how people in contemporary societies engage with transcendent values and ultimate concerns. Moreover, the recent joint privatization of religion and spirituality has led some to argue that "secular privilege" operates in many sectors of modern society (Hodge, 2009), with privilege having been rather blatant in psychiatry until the 1990s, when religion ceased being classified as inherently pathological (Lukoff et al., 1998).

Importantly, overall relations between S/R and health are cross-culturally robust, despite enormous global cultural and religious diversity. On every continent, and in cultures shaped by each of the world's major religious traditions, empirical studies have replicated findings of favorable fundamental relations between S/R and many health factors, such as better health behaviors, less depression and anxiety, less risk of hypertension, better self-rated health, and/or better adult and youth well-being (Grant & Oman, 2018). A caveat is that the largest bulk of the evidence base remains predominantly Western, so we lack clarity on which of the more nuanced findings, such as findings pertaining to specific dimensions of spirituality or religiousness, or particular health outcomes, will reliably generalize beyond Western populations. Also unclear are what might be the implications for *practice* in non-Western settings, including how best to tailor interventions, the needed professional skill sets, and the optimal conduct of community partnerships for public mental health (e.g., Oman, 2025a, 2025b).

Progress on such questions is important not only for fostering human betterment, but also because "the right to health, like other economic and social rights, is now recognized as an inalienable international human right along with traditional civil and political rights" (Tobin, 2012, p. 15); such a right to health is affirmed in the Universal Declaration of Human Rights, adopted by the United Nations in 1948, as well as in the constitutions of about two-thirds of nations worldwide ("67.5%" – see Kinney & Clark, 2004, p. 287). Moreover, globally, the proportion of people self-identifying as religious has been projected to *increase* in the next several decades (Pew Research Center, 2015, April 2). For such reasons, the need has never been greater for developing strong toolkits to proactively accommodate diverse and committed forms of engagement with S/R (Kitayama et al., 2022; Nissen et al., 2021).

How best to understand connections between spirituality/religion and health depends in part, of course, upon each profession's specific concerns, responsibilities, and needs.[1] To support psychologically oriented and other readers in navigating this complex field, the following seven sections begin by recounting the S/R and health field's emergence through 2003; its evolving concern for positive, salutogenic factors and outcomes; definitions; measurement instruments; multifaith inclusiveness; availability of systematic reviews and meta-analyses; and attention to causality.

Readers already somewhat familiar with the R/S-health field may be especially interested in the final two sections, which emphasize the field's increasing relevance to public health, focusing on (i) settings for application, followed by (ii) application to the *collective levels* of social environments and policies. An overall timeline that includes selected key events from many of these histories is presented in Table 3.1.

Table 3.1 Timeline of Major Events in Empirical Research on Spirituality/Religion (S/R) and Health, Selected

Year	*Event*
1907	Sigmund Freud (1907/1989, p. 435) characterizes religion as a "universal obsessional neurosis"
1910	William Osler (1910) publishes *The Faith That Heals*
1926	*Journal of the American Medical Association* publishes a report on religious healing (Paulsen, 1926)
1962	First issue of *Journal of Religion and Health*
1967	Allport's (1967) first empirical study of intrinsic and extrinsic religiousness
1983	First meta-analysis of religion and health (Bergin, 1983)
1987	First attempted comprehensive review of empirical studies (Levin & Schiller, 1987)
1988	First coverage in *Annual Review of Psychology* (Gorsuch, 1988)
1988	Byrd's (1988) controversial study of intercessory prayer
1994	DSM-IV reconceptualizes religion as *not* inherently pathological (Lukoff et al., 1998)
1994	First systematic analysis of evidence for causal effects (Levin, 1994)
1996	American Psychological Association publishes its first book on religion (Shafranske, 1996)
1997	First well-controlled population study focused on religion (Strawbridge et al., 1997)

(Continued)

Table 3.1 (Continued)

Year	*Event*
1997	Comprehensive volume on religion and coping published (Pargament, 1997)
1998	World Health Organization (1998) publishes instrument on S/R in quality of life
1999	Comprehensive volume of religiousness measures published (Hill & Hood, 1999)
1999	National Institute of Aging in collaboration with Fetzer Institute publishes a collection of short measures for inclusion in health studies (Fetzer Institute, 1999)
2000	First coverage in *Annual Review of Public Health* (Chatters, 2000)
2001	*Handbook of Religion and Health* published (Koenig et al., 2001)
2003	Special section in *American Psychologist* (Miller & Thoresen, 2003)
2005	First randomized trial of "spiritual" versus "secular" foci for sitting meditation (Wachholtz & Pargament, 2005)
2006	Null findings in largest randomized trial of intercessory prayer (Benson et al., 2006)
2007-8	Key edited volumes on integration of psychology with specific traditions (Rao et al., 2008; Stevenson et al., 2007)
2013	First systematic study of proposed S/R competencies for psychologists (Vieten et al., 2013)
2013	*APA Handbook of Psychology, Religion, and Spirituality* (Pargament, 2013)
2014	First book published on religion and public health (Idler, 2014)
2014	American Psychological Association begins publishing *Spirituality in Clinical Practice*
2016	Developmental model of interreligious competencies (Morgan & Sandage, 2016)
2022	First history of spiritual interest in World Health Organization (Peng-Keller et al., 2022)
2022	*JAMA* evidence-based review recommends spiritual care training for all members of multidisciplinary care teams (Balboni et al., 2022)
2023	Pew Research Center (2023) begins regular surveys of spirituality among Americans

Early Beginnings and Emergence

Founding figures of the psychology field in the late 19th and early 20th centuries, such as William James, G. Stanley Hall, and James Leuba, possessed much interest in religious phenomena. However, many of their early- and mid-20th-century successors sought to distance the field from anything related to religion and from related phenomena such as superstition and magic. Freud, for example, dismissed religion as a "universal obsessional neurosis" (Freud, 1907/1989, p. 435), and other major figures such as Watson and Skinner were similarly dismissive (see Pargament, 2023). Scientific medicine also generally shied away from religious phenomena, although some major figures, such as Osler (1910), expressed favorable views about the healing powers of faith. In the 1920s, the *Journal of the American Medical Association* reviewed psychological factors in faith healing, concluding that "the medical problem is to… recognize the true function of the mental and the spiritual as well as the material in the alleviation of human ills" (Paulsen, 1926). These, however, were exceptions, and most well-established health fields gave little attention to religion in the middle of the 20th century (nursing retained its interest, as described by Narayanasamy, 1999).

Psychological interest in religion began to return in the 1950s, with investigations of racial prejudice by psychologist Gordon Allport. His influential distinction between intrinsic and extrinsic religion not only helped renew psychological interest in religion but also highlighted the importance of attending to both internal (psychological) and external (collective/institutional; worship services) facets of religious engagement (Donahue, 1985). Thereafter, interest in S/R gradually accelerated in psychology and other health-related fields. The 1960s and

1970s saw the beginnings of attention by epidemiologists to religious variables in large community cohort studies (e.g., Comstock & Partridge, 1972). In the early 1980s, psychologist Allen Bergin (1983) conducted the first meta-analysis of religious engagement and psychological outcomes, reporting that 24 meta-analyzed studies revealed a small favorable association between religion and mental health, contrary to earlier disparaging assumptions. Later that decade, Levin and Schiller (1987) undertook the first comprehensive review of epidemiologic studies of religion and health, identifying over 200 studies from 9 health-related areas. In the 1990s, Levin, an epidemiologist, published several additional papers that helped to theorize the importance of religion from an epidemiologic and public health perspective (Levin, 1994, 1996). The mid-1990s also saw further reopening by psychology toward religion: Stanton Jones (1994) proposed a "constructive relationship" between religion and professional psychology in the pages of the American Psychological Association's (APA's) flagship journal, *American Psychologist*. Soon after, Ed Shafranske (1996) published the APA's first edited book on religion and mental health, and Kenneth Pargament published his *Psychology of Religion and Coping* (1997), synthesizing decades of work on how religion informs and supports the highly health-relevant processes of coping with stress.

Last but not least, two landmark events punctuated the beginning of the 21st century: first, Harold Koenig and his colleagues definitively consolidated religion and health as an interdisciplinary field by publishing the first edition of the *Handbook of Religion and Health* (Koenig et al., 2001), systematically indexing more than 1200 extant empirical studies of mental and physical health, while describing implications for medical practice. Soon after, the *American Psychologist* published a special section on "Spirituality, Religion, and Health," comprising 4 key papers from an expert working group convened by the NIH's Office of Behavioral and Social Sciences Research. To a much greater degree than most key work in the 1990s, this section foregrounded spirituality alongside religion, viewing them as "distinguishable yet overlapping constructs" (Miller & Thoresen, 2003, p. 29).

Loss and Recovery of Positive Health and Flourishing

Modern psychology as a field has consistently studied and attempted to reverse pathological outcomes (illness). In contrast, psychology's interest in positive health and flourishing, present at its inception, has fluctuated over time. Corresponding trends are found in psychological studies of S/R. Early psychologist William James, for example, contrasted a "healthy-minded" religious orientation versus that of a "sick soul" (James, 1902/1961, p. 114). Positive and salutogenic approaches to human psychology were also encouraged by the 1946 Constitution of the World Health Organization (2020, p. 1), which defined health as "a state of complete physical, mental and social well-being and not merely the absence of disease or infirmity."

But in the post-WWII United States, influenced by the new National Institute of Mental Health and an enlarged Veterans Administration, US psychology emphasized a narrow focus on healing pathology and mental illness (Linley et al., 2006; Seligman & Csikszentmihalyi, 2000). Similarly, the first wave of empirical studies of religion focused on pathologies such as depression and anxiety (Bergin, 1983). Such a pathological focus dominated the immediate post-war psychology of S/R, although the trend was resisted by a few leading investigators of positive processes, such as Rogers, Maslow, and Bandura, who on rare occasions examined religion (e.g., Bandura, 2003; Maslow, 1964).

But the situation has changed radically in the new millennium. Supported by the modern positive psychology movement that was launched in 1998, there has been a corresponding growth of study of S/R in relation to positive outcomes such as well-being and flourishing (e.g., Davis et al., 2023). And an important recent related development has been salutogenic approaches to spiritual and religious *diversity*. For example, concerned that institutional discourses too often "reify difference," Beaman (2017, p. 24), holder of the Canada Research Chair in Religious Diversity and Social Change, has instead examined success stories of everyday living with religious difference, a phenomenon sometimes called "street-level ecumenism" (Davie et al., 2018, p. 642). The viability of such successes is supported by documentation, even among children, of pluralistic understandings of religious norms (e.g., Srinivasan et al., 2019; see also Singh et al., 2023b).

Strengthening Definitions of Spirituality and Religion

Definitions of key terms are important in most scientific fields and are necessary for purposes such as aggregating research findings through systematic reviews, constructing theories, specifying the limits of a theory's applicability, and communicating findings to the public. Yet, as noted by many scholars, no definitions of spirituality or religion have ever become uniformly accepted, nor are any candidates on the horizon (for definitions of both S/R from diverse academic fields, see Oman, 2013).

However, a few definitions have emerged as especially influential. Table 3.2 shows three recent definitions from psychology and medicine. With scholars potentially able to choose from multiple definitions, Molendijk (1999) has argued that "from a modern point of view, definitions of religion are not expected to describe its 'essence' as such, but are considered as proposals to use the term within a specific context" (p. 9).

Table 3.2 Definitions of Spirituality and Religion, selected

Core concepts	*Definition and source(s)*
Searching, the sacred	Spirituality and religion are each defined as search processes related to the sacred (Hill et al., 2000; Pargament, 1997; Zinnbauer & Pargament, 2005) • Spirituality and religion are each *search* processes, where "search" means "attempts to identify, articulate, maintain, or transform" the object of search (Hill et al., 2000, p. 66) • Each search involves the *sacred*, most prototypically referring to "a divine being, divine object, Ultimate Reality, or Ultimate Truth as perceived by the individual" (Hill et al., 2000, p. 66) • Spirituality is defined as a "search for the sacred" and religion (or religiousness) is defined more broadly as a "search for significance in ways related to the sacred" (Pargament, 1997, p. 32) • Religion is defined as a "search for significance that occurs within the context of established institutions that are designed to facilitate spirituality" (Pargament and colleagues, quoted in, Oman & Paranjpe, 2018, p. 141)
Meaning, connection	"Spirituality is the aspect of humanity that refers to the way individuals seek and express meaning and purpose and the way they experience their connectedness to the moment, to self, to others, to nature, and to the significant or sacred" (Puchalski et al., 2009, p. 887)
Ritual, theism, the existential	Spirituality is "the salient, searching pursuit of the transcendently sacred ritualistic, theistic, and/or existential aspects of the human condition" (Webb et al., 2014, p. 974), expressed through engagement in one or more of "(1) *Ritualistic Spirituality*, a structured connection with deity; (2) *Theistic Spirituality*, a non-structured connection with deity; and (3) *Existential Spirituality*, a transcendent, yet non-theistic search for meaning and purpose" (Webb, 2021, p. 61)

Lack of a single universal definition need not be viewed as necessarily disadvantageous, as the benefits of definitions, while real, are sometimes overstated. Philosopher of science Karl Popper, for example, argued that "we reach precision not by reducing [our terms'] penumbra of vagueness, but… by carefully phrasing our sentences in such a way that the possible shades of meaning of our terms do not matter" (Popper, quoted in Oman, 2013, p. 23). From a different perspective, Saler (2000) viewed the conceptual status of religion as being "analogous" to the familiar notion of a "family resemblance" (p. 170). He argued for approaches to defining religion through its prototypical features, "without supposing that any one element is necessary for the existence of a religion. These elements, or 'typicality features' [such as theism]… are formally predicated of 'religion,' [but] not all of them will be found in all 'religions.'" (p. xi) (see also Oman, 2013).

Through much of the 20th century, many definitions of religion (and, more recently, spirituality) have reflected and sometimes combined two major approaches: substantive and functional. Substantive approaches define religion and/or spirituality through what is viewed as distinctive about their substance, such as a belief in an ultimate controller of destiny, a divine or superhuman power, or something else deemed sacred. Wholly substantive definitions are often criticized for failing to capture the dynamism of religion and spirituality. In contrast, functional approaches emphasize the *purposes* served in an individual's life by religiousness (or spirituality), such as providing existential meaning or fostering social cohesion, but have been criticized for a lack of specificity (e.g., social cohesion may arise from many sources). Definitions that combine substantive and functional approaches are often now advocated as most robust (e.g., Table 3.2) (Oman, 2013; Zinnbauer & Pargament, 2005). A combined substantive/functional approach pioneered by Pargament has been especially influential in psychology and has been argued to be relevant to both Eastern and Western traditions (see Table 3.2; Oman & Paranjpe, 2018).

Contemporary definitions also reflect changes over time in the perceived relationship *between* spirituality and religion. Terms related to each construct can be traced back at least two millennia in European languages, since approximately the beginning of the common era, and their connotations have changed and evolved (Oman, 2013). In particular, when modern psychology was founded in the late 19th century, "spiritual", tended to connote the most essential or serious side of religion. For example, in *Varieties of Religious Experience*, although William James (1902/1961) did not employ the term "spirituality," he repeatedly used phrases such as "spiritual judgment," "spiritual problem," "spiritual value," and "spiritual sagacity and capacity." As the 20th century progressed, "spirituality" gained increasing use in religious scholarship in titles for textbooks, scholarly societies, and journals, even as the construct was largely neglected by mid-century social scientists.

Late in the 20th century, scholars began noting increasing proportions of adults in the United States and some European countries who self-identified as "spiritual but not religious," with the US adult proportion of such SBNRs recently measured as 22% (Pew Research Center, 2023). Even though near-majorities of adults in the United States have continued to identify as both spiritual and religious, such cultural trends highlight the need to distinguish spirituality and religion as separate constructs. Tendencies toward polarization have also arisen in popular discourse as well as some scholarly fields. In such polarization, religion has often been treated as substantive, institutional, and often negative, whereas spirituality has been viewed as functional and positive.

Commentators have argued that this polarizing discourse is not only misleading but also poses dangers. To Zinnbauer and Pargament (2005), the "most egregious examples [of polarization] are those that place a substantive, static, institutional, objective, belief-based, 'bad' religiousness in opposition to a functional, dynamic, personal, subjective, experience-based, 'good' spirituality" (p. 24). They criticize such polarization as being "likely to hinder inquiry" (p. 27), "unnecessarily constrictive" (p. 27), and oblivious to relevant terms that reverse some polarity facets (e.g., personal religiousness, collective spirituality). They also criticize polarization as an approach in which "evaluation has been confounded with description" in a way that "may reflect simple prejudice" (p. 28) and "does not reflect the perspectives of all [survey] respondents" (p. 28). Such polarization also runs counter to the many empirically documented favorable health associations of religion and the fact, noted by sociologists, that spiritual practices, both among the religiously engaged and among the SBNR, are "facilitated by institutions [such as] congregations and religious orders… retreat centers… publishing companies, internet sites" that provide resources, and that "because of this embeddedness in institutions, spiritual practices are inevitably *social*" (Wuthnow, 1998, p. 181; see also Hill & Pargament, 2003).

Nonetheless, personalized definitions of "spirituality," and an increased prevalence of SBNR identities appear to be stable features in popular culture in the United States and some other Western countries. In response, Koenig (2008) has influentially argued for using distinct definitions of spirituality in (i) research versus (ii) clinical practice. He argued that research should avoid definitions and measures of spirituality that are confounded with positive outcomes (e.g., "I feel peaceful," p. 252). In contrast, in clinical work, "health professionals must communicate in a language that is welcoming and supportive" (p. 353), and spirituality is acceptable as a "vague term that patients can define for themselves" (p. 354).

Also in response to spirituality's increased prominence have been efforts to enunciate broader definitions of spirituality that resonate both with SBNRs and with people engaged in conventional religion. For example, Webb et al. (2014) have identified three major and non-mutually exclusive ways that people may search for and express spiritual dimensions of the human condition, which they call ritualistic, theistic, and existential (see Table 3.2; see also Chapters 1 and 44, this volume).

Another influential, although infrequently analyzed, approach to broaden the construct of spirituality involves *inherent human capacities*. For example, Myers and Williard (2003) define spirituality as "the capacity and tendency present in all human beings to find and construct meaning about life and existence and to move toward personal growth, responsibility, and relationship with others" (p. 149). In its solely functional reliance on meaning-making, the foregoing definition, along with many other inherent-capacity definitions, may be criticized as lacking specificity, failing to distinguish spirituality from related constructs such as meaning-making (Pargament et al., 2017).

Also questionable is whether the word "spiritual" should be applied to various practices that have been extracted from S/R traditions and have been widely disseminated in secularized forms and contexts, such as modern "mindfulness" meditation and modern forms of "yoga" that emphasize physical postures and exercises. Such systems of practice retain some characteristics that are commonly used to define S/R, but they generally drop many other defining S/R characteristics, such as references to the sacred or higher powers. Do such systems of practice still qualify as possessing a "family resemblance" with more prototypical forms of spirituality? Like in Koenig's (2008) approach to defining spirituality, the answer may depend on context and details. Elsewhere, modernized mindfulness and yoga have been called "borderline spiritual constructs" (Oman, 2018b). Here, for brevity, we shall refer to them simply as quasi-spiritual practices.

Importantly, the term "spirituality" is used, perhaps increasingly, by adherents to different religious traditions *themselves* for affirming an ostensible common feature that exists – albeit in varying forms – within multiple traditions. As a term that is robustly amenable to inclusive definitions (e.g., Table 3.2), yet sufficiently plastic that in specific communities it easily acquires a "taken-for-grantedness" of specific meanings through a "naturalisation process" (Cino Pagliarello, 2022, p. 889; Star, 2010, p. 611), the term "spirituality" can facilitate coalition-building across diverse religious traditions, and perhaps beyond to include SBNR, potentially enhancing coalitions' ability to address issues of common concern (e.g., sustainability, Beaman & Stacey, 2021; Deal & Magyar-Russell, 2022). And while contemporary scholars readily concede the lack of cross-culturally universal religious doctrines, debate continues on the implications of striking commonalities across diverse traditions in key aspects of spiritual experience, especially mystical experience (Rose, 2016; Hood et al., 2001).

In this regard, contemporary definitions of S/R possess advantages over earlier definitions, still sometimes present in the literature, which too often privileged some traditions while marginalizing or excluding others. For example, definitions of religion as "theistic" can exclude Buddhism, and viewing all meditation as "mindfulness" marginalizes non-Buddhist traditions (Oman, 2013, 2023). There is now a large and growing body of resources for pursuing work that is more cross-culturally and cross-worldview valid and sensitive (e.g., Oman & Paranjpe, 2018; Sisemore & Knabb, 2020).

Evolving Measurement Toolkits

As cultural and psychosocial phenomena, S/R have been investigated through a variety of empirically oriented fields, each of which has brought its own measurement toolkits, ranging from anthropological participant observation to neuroimaging to behavioral observation. Yet by far the most commonly employed measures have been self-report questionnaires, utilized in fields that include psychology, sociology, demography, medicine, and public health.

For many years, in fact, self-report scale development was a preoccupation in the psychology of religion. As the field re-awoke in the 1960s, Allport developed one of the first and most influential religion measures, a 20-item two-dimensional measure of intrinsic and extrinsic religiosity (Allport & Ross, 1967). Other efforts were contemporaneous or followed, and by the late 1990s, Hill and Hood (1999) were able to catalogue more than one hundred self-report measures on various religiousness facets, sorted into more than a dozen categories ranging from religious beliefs and practices, attitudes, experience, development, and fundamentalism to concepts of God, spirituality and mysticism, and religious coping and problem-solving. Also in the 1990s, through a remarkably broad cross-cultural collaboration, the World Health Organization (1998) published an instrument on S/R in quality of life, now translated into dozens of languages (Peng-Keller et al., 2022). In the midst of this surge, Gorsuch (1984) characterized questionnaire measurement as having become a "paradigm" in the study of religion, serving as both a "boon and bane" – a boon that enables substantive study, but a bane if it becomes an end in itself or eclipses non-questionnaire approaches.

Over time, although questionnaire scales have remained a mainstay, several efforts have been made to make measures for specific purposes more readily available. One key challenge is that many originally developed S/R questionnaire scales were rather lengthy, rendering them cumbersome to include in much ongoing research, such as large community-based epidemiologic studies (e.g., Strawbridge et al., 1997). Therefore, the National Institute of Aging, in collaboration with the Fetzer Institute, assembled a working group that published a volume of brief religion/spirituality measures "for use in health research" (Fetzer Institute, 1999). Normative data were obtained by embedding these measures in the 1998 US General Social Survey (Idler et al., 2003).

More recently, the questionnaire measurement toolkit has been further expanded and refined through programs to develop measurement instruments for previously neglected religious traditions such as Hinduism and Islam (e.g., Abu-Raiya & Pargament, 2015; Singh et al., 2023a; Singh & Saxena, 2023). Review articles and volumes have also been published to evaluate or make available measures of spirituality and constructs usable across traditions or otherwise especially relevant to diverse modern societies (e.g., 19 measures in Ai et al., 2021; 24 measures in Kapuscinski & Masters, 2010).

Importantly, methodological alternatives to S/R questionnaire measures have long been utilized, albeit not as widely. Examples of alternative approaches include qualitative interviews, laboratory measures, studies of organizational statements and cultures, experiments, natural experiments, field research, experience sampling, and psychoanalysis (Finke & Bader, 2017; Hood & Belzen, 2013). For example, using news databases and organizational position statements, Idler and her colleagues (2022) recently examined trends in media coverage of how religious communities were responding to the COVID-19 pandemic and the resulting public health guidance. Although multimethod investigations are only intermittently implemented in practice, perhaps due to feasibility constraints, these diverse methods, like philosophical, historical, and theological scholarship, are generally viewed as complementary, consistent with the favorably received "multilevel interdisciplinary paradigm" advocated by Emmons and Paloutzian (2003) for the psychology of religion.

Expanding Multifaith Inclusion

In recent decades, especially since the turn of the 21st century, the empirical study of S/R and health has expanded to better include non-Judeo-Christian religious traditions, as well as additional forms of spirituality that are pursued outside of religion. In the previous section, we noted the expanding toolkit of S/R measurement instruments. As shown in Table 3.3, this has been accompanied by increasing overall numbers of empirical studies on major faith traditions, for which health studies have been a major driver. Beginning in the mid-1980s (i.e., 1984), in Judaism, Christianity, and all traditions combined, each decade saw the publication of a substantial proportion of studies (i.e., about 10% of the 2023 total), with the total number of publications approximately doubling on average each decade thereafter. Hinduism studies show this same trajectory, although its total number of publications remains small in comparison to the global Hindu population. Buddhism, Islam, and atheism began similar trajectories slightly later, with increased numbers clearly visible in the early 21st century (i.e., beginning 2004). Such increased attention may be driven by a variety of causes, including the persistence of religious adherence in many parts of the world, the fading of the secularization expectation and paradigm in academia, and increased migration and religious diversity in many societies.

Importantly, atheism is now being studied not merely as a belief, but also as an *identity* (Brewster et al., 2014), and "atheist spirituality" is now a topic of popular self-identification and scholarly discussion (Comte-Sponville, 2008; Schnell & Keenan, 2013). As an emerging subfield, ideas remain in flux on how best to conceptualize and measure varieties of atheism and other forms of non-belief (Coleman & Jong, 2021). In the United States, some evidence suggests that the mental health of atheists is somewhat better than that of adherents to several conventional

Table 3.3 Numbers of Empirical Studies Indexed in PsycINFO with Specific Traditions Mentioned in Title or Abstract

	Number of publications ([column] percent within tradition)						
Years	*Judaism*	*Christianity*	*Hinduism*	*Buddhism*	*Islam*	*Atheism*	*Total*[a]
1919–1973	103 (2)	86 (1)	5 (1)	5 (1)	3 (0)	4 (1)	186 (1)
1974–1983	50 (1)	84 (1)	13 (2)	1 (0)	18 (0)	1 (0)	148 (1)
1984–1993	483 (11)	812 (10)	89 (11)	40 (4)	124 (2)	14 (3)	1404 (8)
1994–2003	699 (16)	1142 (14)	115 (14)	65 (7)	322 (6)	25 (6)	2150 (12)
2004–2013	1304 (30)	2493 (31)	257 (31)	297 (32)	1698 (30)	98 (22)	5399 (30)
2014–2023	1775 (40)	3333 (42)	342 (41)	510 (56)	3404 (61)	298 (68)	8434 (48)
TOTAL[b]	4414	7950	821	918	5569	440	17721

Note. Restricted to peer reviewed empirical studies. Searches queried whether title or the abstract included: (juda* OR jew*); (christ* OR catholic* OR protestant*); (hindu*); (buddhis*); (islam* OR muslim); (atheis*); totals queried presence of any of the foregoing terms. All searches conducted in PsycINFO on 24 April 2024.

[a] For each period, the sum of tradition-specific studies exceeds the total by 10 to 15 percent due to some studies mentioning multiple traditions.

[b] Percents may not sum to 100% because of rounding.

religious traditions (e.g., Baker et al., 2018). Some evidence also suggests that atheists are subject to social discrimination, although a case has also been made for the existence of a "secular privilege" experienced by nonreligious individuals (Cragun et al., 2012; Hodge, 2009); it seems highly likely that the privileging implications of atheist versus religious identities can vary considerably across contexts and settings (e.g., political candidacy versus academics in materialist scientific fields; see Chapter 6 of this volume for a more detailed discussion of secular spirituality).

"Spiritual but not religious" identities are also receiving much greater study in the 21st century, with evidence suggesting they are "heterogeneous… not necessarily reducible to one disposition" (Wixwat & Saucier, 2021, p. 121). Some have presented evidence suggesting that SBNR identities "do not necessarily represent a prevalent new form of religiosity, so much as a prevalent form of cultural rhetoric" (Ammerman, 2013, p. 275). Regardless of their precise meanings, such identities, while showing mixed trends in Europe (Kasselstrand, 2022), are increasing in prevalence in the United States (Chaves & Chaves, 2017), leading the Pew Research Center (2023) to embark on systematic longitudinal surveys to study the prevalence and correlates of spirituality, as distinct from religion.

A Flood of Systematic Reviews and Meta-Analyses

As noted earlier, Bergin (1983) published the first meta-analysis of studies on S/R and health – in this case, mental health – and soon thereafter, Levin and Schiller's (1987) review began making clearer the large number of extant studies. As the volume of empirical studies increased (Figure 3.1), more systematic reviews and meta-analyses began to appear.

In a recent review of reviews, Oman and Syme (2018) identified 118 systematic reviews, sometimes involving a meta-analysis or meta-synthesis, that they sorted into more than a dozen categories. Only 6 systematic reviews appeared in the 20th century, with 37 appearing in the 2000s and 75 in the 2010s. The reviews addressed topics that included mental health (addressed by n = 17 systematic reviews or meta-analyses), patient psychosocial well-being (n = 10), health behaviors (n = 9), patient sources of spiritual well-being (n = 8), stress and coping (n = 6), psychological well-being in healthy populations (n = 4), substance misuse (n = 3), dementia (n = 2), prayer (n = 7), mortality (n = 3), physical health (n = 2), crime and delinquency (n = 3), discrimination (n = 1), environmental health (n = 1), infectious diseases (n = 4), nutrition (n = 7), family, youth, and reproductive outcomes (n = 8), training or well-being of health professionals or religious leaders (n = 6), spiritual well-being interventions at end of life (n = 6), referrals and adherence (n = 4), programs for prevention or treatment (n = 8), organizational factors (n = 1), individual treatments/interventions (n = 16), doctor-patient conversations (n = 2), perspectives on end of life (n = 1), and issues relevant to specific religions (n = 9). Of these systematic reviews, 33 were quantitative meta-analyses, published less often in the 1980s (n = 2) and 1990s (n = 2) than in the 2000s (n = 13) and 2010s (n = 16). We know of no updated listing, but dozens of additional systematic reviews have likely been published since 2018 (see Chapter 21 of this volume for a recent scoping review of the association of R/S with health and well-being).

Evolving Attention to Roles in Causality

A question of recurring interest in studies of S/R is the strength of the evidence supporting effects on health that are *causal*. Randomized trials are typically regarded as the most compelling form of evidence for causality, but randomizing people to engage in religion or spirituality is ethically unacceptable and practically infeasible. For evaluating the causal effects from non-randomizable variables, epidemiologists led by Bradford Hill (1965) developed what has become known as the Hill criteria: a collection of 9 perspectives or guidelines from which to evaluate evidence relevant to causality. Hill and his colleagues were tasked with evaluating causal effects from smoking, especially long-term smoking, a variable that could not be randomized. Examples of Hill's listed perspectives include *consistency* (is the relation seen in diverse places, circumstances, times, and populations?), coherence (e.g., no conflict with well-established facts?), temporality (not fully attributable to reverse causality?; relation seen in longitudinal studies?), and strength (e.g., clinically consequential?). Hill's perspectives continue to be advocated, in comparison to meta-analysis, as "a superior strategy for assessing a large volume and diversity of evidence" (Stegenga, 2011, p. 497; see also Kaplan, 1986).

In the 1990s, Levin (1994) used Hill's perspectives to evaluate evidence that religion has a causal effect on health, concluding that the evidence for consistency was strongly "yes," for coherence was "probably yes," for temporality was "insufficient," and for strength was "inconclusive" (p. 1480). His overall conclusion was that "examining the evidence in light of Hill's guidelines is inconclusive, but promising" (p. 1480). Nearly 25 years later, Oman and Syme (2018) revisited the topic, noting that the evidence base had expanded dramatically, and "what in 1994 could be addressed through only a small handful or a single study, can [now] in many cases be addressed through one or more meta-analyses or systematic reviews" (p. 276). In particular, for the perspectives of consistency, coherence, temporality, and strength, Table 3 in Oman and Syme (2018) lists multiple meta-analyses and systematic reviews that support causality. While not advocating that such findings provided evidence for "spooky action at a distance" (Leder, 2005), because such relations could be mediated by well-established processes such as health behaviors, social relations, and coping processes, they concluded (p. 278) that:

> From the standpoint of the Hill guidelines, the case for a causative relation between religion/spirituality and health has been enormously strengthened. On balance, we believe the case is compelling. Can anyone sincerely maintain that religion and spirituality are entirely non-causal epiphenomenal byproducts of other variables, and that all of the R/S-health relationships documented in ... systematic reviews... are purely due to confounding?

In recent years, the case for causality has also been strengthened by innovative statistical methods, sometimes termed "E-values," that permit better appraisals of whether findings are robust against threats to validity from unmeasured confounding (VanderWeele et al., 2016). For example, a pioneering study by Li et al. (2016) reported evidence for bidirectional effects between religious service attendance and depression, observing that "for an unmeasured confounder to fully explain away the association… it would have to both increase the likelihood of service attendance and decrease the likelihood of depression by 2.1-fold, above and beyond the measured covariates, which may not be likely" (pp. 881–882). E-values have also been employed by Chen et al. (2020), who provided evidence from three longitudinal cohorts in support of causal effects of religious service attendance on subsequent mortality, health behaviors, and psychosocial well-being.

A closely related question of interest concerns the *causal pathways*, often called "mediating factors," through which S/R factors can or do operate to foster health. Such questions have been widely discussed in the literature for decades. Strong theoretical and empirical support exists for pathways that include social connections, health behaviors, and improved mental health (Oman, 2018a). Varying levels of theoretical or empirical support are also available for so-called "added value" pathways that arise from S/R engagement, but "lack clear analogues outside of S/R traditions," such as sanctification, S/R methods of coping, secure relational attachment to divinity, and engagement with spiritual strivings (Oman, 2025c, p. 1037).

"Spirituality," as distinct from religion, has not, to our knowledge, been the focus of causal analyses based on either E-values or Hill's criteria. However, evidence for causal effects of some facets of spirituality has been provided by randomized trials of spiritually infused forms of psychotherapy (Worthington et al., 2011) and of certain specific spiritual practices such as repetition of a mantra (Hulett et al., 2023; Oman, 2025c). Randomized trials have also supported causal benefits from some explicitly spiritual forms of meditation (e.g., Oman et al., 2006), as well as from quasi-spiritual mindfulness-based interventions (Oman, 2025a). The most recent meta-analyses have also offered evidence for some "psi" phenomena of complex and debatable relation to spirituality. Yet meta-analyses remain divided about causal benefits for recipients of intercessory prayer, investigated since the 1980s in randomized trials and sometimes conceptualized as a form of "distant intentionality" (Cardeña, 2018; Radin et al., 2015).

Last but not least, from the perspective of most S/R traditions, undergirded by a decolonizing perspective (Nye, 2019; Walsh, 2015), one could expect that gains in *wisdom* would likely be an overarching causally efficacious mediating factor between S/R and health. And indeed, some initial empirical evidence does support a positive relation between spirituality and wisdom (e.g., Jeste & Lee, 2019). However, such evidence remains weak and preliminary, perhaps because neither wisdom nor spirituality is easily conceptualized or measured, perhaps especially in the context of cultural flux.

In sum, evidence is now compelling that religious engagement, as well as certain types of spiritual practices, such as meditation, can causally affect health. Many of these relations may plausibly occur through well-established pathways such as social support, coping, and health behavior improvement, although causal roles cannot be ruled out for key cross-culturally resonant constructs such as wisdom or for controversial and poorly understood processes such as distant intentionality, where the evidence for causality remains more debatable.

Expanding Settings for Application

Application of the practice of research on S/R and health has been expanding in recent decades, illustrating what Levin (2022) has called the "translational epidemiology of religion." Perhaps most prominent has been what Levin called *clinical translation*: taking S/R into account in clinical practice. Also important has been *public health translation*, in which "the target of translation is not… an individual patient – but rather the community or population" (p. 28) – for example, by partnering with faith-based organizations for intervention delivery or policy development. Importantly, international interest in S/R and health is widespread, and relations between spirituality and health have for many decades been intermittently discussed at the World Health Organization (Peng-Keller et al., 2022).

Importantly, efforts at health promotion are common outside of clinics, in other settings such as workplaces and schools, which have long been recognized as relevant to promoting physical health and are now also recognized as settings for fostering mental health (Amri et al., 2022; Hinrichsen et al., 2022; Wahlbeck, 2015). Promoting health through such diverse settings reflects a "socio-ecological" approach, which affirms the "importance of supportive environments and endorses the role of schools, workplaces, neighbourhoods, and communities as providing key contexts or settings for promoting mental health" (Barry, 2019, p. 27; Eriksson et al., 2018).

Multiple Sectors, Each with Multiple Levels

Socio-ecological and other contemporary best practices in health promotion, besides being multisectoral, are also *multi-level* (Institute of Medicine, 2000; Schensul & Trickett, 2009). Multilevel health promotion involves interventions not only for individuals, but also for "families, and communities and 'upstream' policy interventions" (Barry, 2019, p. 27). Such multilevel integration of promising health promotion approaches is sometimes called "vertical scale-up" to distinguish it from "horizontal scale-up… across multiple settings" (Leeman et al., 2022, p. 156; see also Dodge et al., 2024; World Health Organization, 2010). One internationally influential example is the "Health in All Policies" (HiAP) approach, which "across sectors… systematically takes into account the health implications of decisions [and] seeks synergies… in order to improve population health" (World Health Organization & Finland Ministry of Social Affairs and Health, 2014, p. 7).

Spiritually oriented components of health interventions have therefore become potentially relevant across many diverse settings (horizontal expansion) and levels (vertical expansion), wherever treatments are implemented, health is promoted, or spirituality is deemed relevant in other ways. Indeed, interventions with spiritual *components* – or sometimes full interventions that are primarily spiritually focused – have been developed or tested in a growing range of settings and levels. Many *observational* studies have also been conducted in an even wider range of settings at various levels, shedding light on whether and how such settings might become host to interventions or become maximally health-supportive. These spiritual interventions and observational studies have employed a wide range of social and biomedical sciences, but almost always build on explicit or implicit understandings of the psychology of S/R.

The status and promise of such work are briefly explored in this and the following section. The present section describes a range of primarily *individually* oriented interventions and observational studies that have been explored across social settings that include schools, clinics, and workplaces. We note interventions delivered individually as well as those delivered through groups assembled for the primary purpose of intervention delivery. The next section ("Expanding Levels") then shifts to emphasize the levels of *policy* and of study and intervention at a *collective* level, such as interventions to modify public spaces or other ongoing social environments. Table 3.4 offers an overview of interventions and contexts discussed in these two sections.

Table 3.4 Health-Relevant Interventions and Contexts from a Multilevel Perspective, Selected Examples

Setting	*Description*	*Level*[a]	*Reference(s)*[b]
Religion	Faith/health collaborative health interventions[c]	I	(Campbell et al., 2007; Tuggle, 2000)
Religion	Strengthening health-supportiveness of religious social environments[d]	C	(Ayling et al., 2023; Derose et al., 2019)
Many sectors	Chaplains present	C	(Wolf & Feldbauer-Durstmüller, 2023)
Many sectors	"Rooms of silence" as set-aside spaces for prayer, reflection, meditation, or personal ritual	C	(Christensen et al., 2019)
Education	Education in spiritual meditation[e] or in addressing spiritual struggles	I[f]	(Dworsky et al., 2013; Oman et al., 2008)
Education	Fostering spiritually supportive campus social environments	C	(Barton et al., 2020; Goodman et al., 2015)
Workplace	Foster meaningful work and work/life balance	C	(Peccoud, 2004; Pfeffer, 2003)
Workplace	Training in nonsectarian spiritual or quasi-spiritual practices (e.g., mantra/holy name repetition; postural yoga)	I[f]	(Buttner et al., 2016; de Diego-Cordero et al., 2021; Michaelsen et al., 2023)
Clinic, medicine	Spiritual history or spiritual needs assessment	I	(Koenig, 2000; Kristeller et al., 2005)
Clinic, medicine	All care team members receive training in spiritual care provision	C	(Balboni et al., 2022)
Clinic, psychology	Spiritually infused and spiritually responsive psychotherapy delivered individually or to ad-hoc groups	I	(Vieten & Lukoff, 2022; Worthington et al., 2011) (Cornish & Wade, 2010)
Clinic	Mantra repetition or spiritual meditation for focus or stress management	I[f]	(Gonçalves et al., 2015; Hulett et al., 2023)
Clinic, psychiatry	Supporting spiritually infused activities in county mental health and wellness centers	P	(Yamada et al., 2014)

[a] I=Individual, C=Collective, P=Policy
[b] See text for additional references.
[c] Such interventions are often time-limited.
[d] Alterations to religious social environments emphasize integration of *pre-existing* S/R factors with positive health practices.
[e] As explained in text, modernized mindfulness and postural yoga interventions are categorized in the present discussion as quasi-spiritual.
[f] Depending on the level of publicity, backing by leadership, and participation by employees, individual trainings may also affect the collective social environment.

Clinical, Educational, Congregational, Workplace, and Other Settings

Within *clinical* settings, physicians in their interactions with individual patients may signal concern for adequate spiritual support in brief conversations, sometimes followed by referrals to chaplains or other resources (e.g., Koenig, 2000; Kristeller et al., 2005; see also Nissen et al., 2021). In clinical psychology and counseling, abundant literature now describes how attending to spirituality may be integrated into individual psychological treatment through modalities such as spiritually infused psychotherapy, in which psychotherapists can individually tailor content and support or make referrals when issues arise outside their scope of practice (Vieten & Lukoff, 2022; Worthington et al., 2011). Psychologists have also developed scientific frameworks and therapies that integrate psychological insights with specific traditions (e.g., Stevenson et al., 2007). S/R factors are also being addressed in multiple ways in psychiatry (Moreira-Almeida et al., 2014; Rosmarin & Koenig, 2020). In medicine and psychology, solid progress is evident in developing interventions and training for individual clinicians to give appropriate attention to S/R factors (e.g., Cobb et al., 2012; Currier et al., in press; Puchalski et al., 2014; Salcone et al., 2023; Vieten & Lukoff, 2022; Worthington et al., 2011).

Guidance also exists for addressing S/R factors in patient or client groups convened for therapeutic or counseling purposes. Such guidance has long existed for working with homogeneous groups that share ethnicity or particular presenting concerns (Cornish & Wade, 2010). Attending to S/R in therapy or counseling with *heterogeneous* groups has received less attention, but suggested guidelines include initially "setting the norm that spirituality and religion are appropriate topics by asking… general questions," and ensuring "respect for others' beliefs [with] an explicit sanction against proselytizing" (Cornish & Wade, 2010, p. 402). Group delivery has also been used in some spiritually oriented psychological and psychiatric programs that serve stress management functions, such as portable mantra repetition and various forms of spiritual meditation (Gonçalves et al., 2015; Hulett et al., 2023; Oman et al., 2008). Such programs may accommodate spiritual and cultural diversity by supporting recipients in choosing mantras (also known as holy names) or foci for meditation from their own spiritual background (Oman, 2025c; see also appendix in Oman, 2025b).

In the *educational* sector, spiritual interventions for youth, and occasionally children, have been conducted in settings ranging from private religious colleges and public universities in the United States to Iranian and Israeli secondary schools (Aggarwal et al., 2023; Hardy et al., 2019). For example, a program to address spiritual struggles has shown promising results among non-clinical samples of college students at a state university in the United States (Dworsky et al., 2013). Other programs for college students have employed nonsectarian, spiritually oriented meditation (Oman et al., 2008). Interest in youth-focused S/R interventions, such as spiritual meditation or cultivating spiritual intelligence, is globally widespread, with a recent meta-analysis identifying 29 intervention studies that examined effects on symptoms of depression or anxiety, many involving healthy populations, conducted in countries ranging from the United States and Canada to India, Pakistan, Iran, Indonesia, Taiwan, Kenya, Nepal, and South Africa (Aggarwal et al., 2023). At least in the United States, however, S/R-focused programs have seldom been implemented on a large scale, apart from two quasi-spiritual approaches: Transcendental Meditation and mindfulness meditation (Oman, 2025a, 2025c; Wendt et al., 2015).

In the *religious* sector, congregations and other faith-based organizations have commonly been sites for so-called "faith-placed" interventions that are wholly secular in nature (Campbell et al., 2007, p. 217). Increasingly, however, contemporary interventions conducted through faith-based organizations may include spiritual elements, either emanating from within the organizations ("faith-based") or emerging in *collaborations* between health professionals and religious organizations. Such faith-based and collaborative interventions commonly employ S/R cultural adaptation or tailoring – for example, providing motivational support by citing scriptural verses that emphasize the "body as a temple of God and the need to keep it holy by refraining from unhealthy behaviors" (Campbell et al., 2007, p. 217; Tuggle, 2000).

Additional societal sectors in which S/R interventions have been employed include sports, adult criminal rehabilitation, and programs for juvenile delinquency (e.g., Kermen, 2018; Noh & Shahdan, 2020; Schaefer et al., 2016; Waller et al., 2016). Spiritually oriented interventions have also been implemented for homeless youth and adults (Aggarwal et al., 2023; Hardy et al., 2019).

Last but not least, in recent decades, the *workplace* has been the focus of a large conceptual and empirical literature on spirituality (e.g., Benefiel et al., 2014; de Diego-Cordero et al., 2021; Giacalone & Jurkiewicz, 2010; Pawar, 2009a). Empirical findings are consistent across diverse countries and suggest that spirituality and religion at work are positively related to an individual's organizational commitment, job satisfaction, altruism, and a variety of other positive outcomes (Benefiel et al., 2014). In this literature, workplace spirituality is commonly understood, or sometimes even *defined*, as fostering employee well-being (e.g., "promote employees'... sense of being connected to others in a way that provides... completeness and joy" Benefiel et al., 2014, p. 182; see also Pawar, 2009a). Perhaps because the workplace spirituality field "emerged through theoretical advocacy and organizational case study rather than by data sets compiled from individual respondents" (Benefiel et al., 2014, p. 178), the large body of existing empirical research, although employing a rich mix of qualitative and quantitative methods, remains overwhelmingly observational. Two partial exceptions are experimental studies of individually focused workplace quasi-spiritual interventions involving mindfulness and postural yoga (de Diego-Cordero et al., 2021; Michaelsen et al., 2023).

The preceding paragraphs recount how S/R factors have been perceived as relevant to health promotion or treatment across numerous major social sectors that include health, education, religion, the workplace, and other settings such as sports, criminal rehabilitation, and homelessness. Despite such widespread multisectoral interest, large-scale public health utilization of spirituality as a health-promotion factor has to date been infrequent, at least in the United States. One impediment may be uncertainties about the appropriate scope and legal bases for recognizing S/R in operations by civic organizations and government, for which norms and procedures vary considerably between countries (Burchardt, 2020; Triandafyllidou & Magazzini, 2021; Witte, 2010; see also Hill, 2011).

Another challenge in developing spiritually oriented health promotion efforts concerns tradeoffs between *scalability* to multiple traditions versus *tailoring* to individual spiritual traditions. Outside of the religious sector, the most widely implemented quasi-spiritually oriented health-promotion approaches, such as mindfulness, have tended to lack proactive inclusiveness of religious diversity, sometimes eliciting strong criticism or determined opposition (Brown, 2019; Carsley et al., 2018; Oman, 2025a). Such neglect is arguably at best analogous to a purely "colorblind" approach to ethnicity, commonly now complemented and sometimes supplanted by approaches that intentionally support the "identity safety" of demographically diverse groups (Brannon & Lin, 2021, p. 489; Markus et al., 2000, p. 256). At their best, identity safety approaches encourage "practices that promote inclusion and a sense that one's group identity will not be a source of devaluation" (Markus et al., 2000, p. 256) and involve "leveraging and supporting culture and strengths tied to marginalized identities" (Brannon & Lin, 2021, p. 498), which can sometimes be regarded as including even numerically majoritarian religious identities (Hodge, 2009; Taylor, 2007). Yet it is also desirable that identity safety be conveyed in a manner that does not "reify difference… through a language of diversity that can exacerbate essentialisms" (Beaman, 2017, p. 24) and recognizes that "'street-level ecumenism' (pragmatic cooperative activity)" can be a way in which "religiously diverse people learn to flourish in each other's company" (Davie et al., 2018, p. 642).

Some scalable spiritual interventions, such as mantra repetition, do appear generally, perhaps intrinsically, supportive of identity safety by directly synergizing with diverse pre-existing forms of spiritual or religious commitment (e.g., Buttner et al., 2016; Oman, 2025c). At present, however, interventions that integrate multifaith-compatible and non-reified support for identity safety with non-problematic scalability are not abundant, suggesting their development and testing should be prioritized.

Expanding Levels

Contemporary best practices in health promotion, besides being multisectoral, are also *multilevel* (Institute of Medicine, 2000; Schensul & Trickett, 2009). This recognition has helped drive a corresponding interest in the health-relevant societal dynamics of S/R and a nascent, slowly emerging interest in multilevel spiritual interventions. As noted earlier, such multilevel integration is sometimes called "vertical scale-up," and involves applying the socio-ecological model at the collective and policy levels (Eriksson et al., 2018). In this way, the conscientious application of a population health approach to the social determinants of health points to a partial and circumscribed reversal of the modern privatization of S/R (Beyer, 1990).

Such relinking and partial deprivatization of S/R is not out of step with the myriad of other cross-sectoral interfaces and collaborations in society (e.g., Hutter, 2001; Knudsen, 2007). Ongoing and episodic interactions between institutions in different societal sectors are commonplace, especially in what sociologists and system theorists call a partially autonomous or "loosely coupled" form (Thornton et al., 2012, p. 58; Vanderstraeten, 2023, p. 101). Moreover, the operative logics of various institutions within major societal sectors, such as government, professions, corporations, religion, and community, are continually adapting and evolving through diverse processes (see typology in Thornton et al., 2012, Table 7.1; see also Gümüsay, 2020, on religious logics; Reay & Hinings, 2009, on managing competing logics). Such institutional logics, which may vary within sectors as well as across sectors, are grounded in socially constructed institutional features such as sources of legitimacy, authority, identity, bases of norms, and root metaphors (see Thornton et al., 2012, Table 3.2). The ongoing cross-sectoral relevance of S/R will mainly seem surprising if viewed from the perspective of the now largely rejected secularization thesis (Gorski & Altınordu, 2008) or from some other perspective that presumes an end of cultural evolution in what philosopher Charles Taylor (2007) has called the "immanent frame" (p. 542), in which all facets of life are uncritically presumed likely or proven able to proceed indefinitely without reference to any transcendent or nonmaterial order.

Many S/R integration initiatives have occurred without the involvement of health professionals or the field, but all hold potential implications for the public's health. The following five subsections examine multilevel integration in various sectoral and policy contexts, concluding with a sketch of the corresponding emergent field and some of its likely driving research questions.

Within the Religion Sector

In the religious sector, spiritual constructs are pervasive in congregations and many faith-based schools and other social environments, but all too often fail to be integrated with *health*. That is, congregational cultures often give inadequate support to congregants for translating their health-relevant spiritual engagements into health practice. Faith-based organizations such as congregations and schools have therefore sought to improve the health alignment of their own internal cultures in various ways, such as by spiritually integrated health education or sermons on the importance of healthy eating and physical activity (Ayling et al., 2023; Derose et al., 2019). Such activities may sometimes be conducted through or catalyzed by partnerships with health professionals or agencies (Campbell et al., 2007; Barnes & Curtis, 2009). Levin (2022) has characterized such efforts as the *pastoral* translation of epidemiologic findings on S/R.

Recurring Themes Across Sectors

Outside of the religious sector, a social ecological approach also suggests collective-level interventions on social environments within education, the workplace, and healthcare. Such social environments are, in turn, affected by various tiers of government policy, often referred to as another "level." Thus, at least three overall levels are typically recognized in social-ecological models: individual, collective, and policy. Within the policy level, Levin (2016) noted interventions that include the 1996 "charitable choice" legislation that enabled US federal funding of health service delivery by faith-based organizations, as well as successful work by faith and public health advocacy coalitions (e.g., the Affordable Care Act). Other policy-level work, such as the 2009 California Mental Health and Spirituality Initiative, has also facilitated mental health integration efforts, such as the integration of spiritually infused activities into 98% of Los Angeles County Department of Mental Health wellness and recovery centers (Yamada et al., 2014). Most socio-ecological model "levels," however, concern social environments of various sizes and compositions.

Some types of spiritually relevant interventions have occurred in analogous forms in multiple sectors. Perhaps the oldest and most prominent cross-sectoral spiritual presence has been chaplaincy, now commonly enacted as interfaith chaplaincy. Chaplains have long been employed in settings such as healthcare, universities, the police, the military, legislative bodies, and increasingly in recent decades, in other workplaces such as factories (Cadge, 2023; Paget & McCormack, 2006; Plummer, 1996). To a much greater extent than secular counselors, chaplains proactively engage and mingle with the communities they serve – for example, in a workplace, "the chaplain often walks the assembly line providing availability and a ministry of presence" (Plummer, 1996, p. 6). Other common activities by chaplains include providing spiritual care (e.g., discerning needs and offering counsel), being a liaison or an advocate, providing referrals, crisis intervention, and officiating at weddings or other celebrations (Paget & McCormack, 2006). Chaplaincy and its effects have received much empirical study, especially in healthcare, where it has been linked with positive quality of life, spiritual well-being, and satisfaction with clinical care (Poncin et al., 2020; Wolf & Feldbauer-Durstmüller, 2023).

Second, and arguably complementary to the social presence of the chaplain, has been the establishment of "rooms of silence," also called by numerous other names such as "multi-faith room" and "prayer space," that have been defined as rooms "in a public (institutional) space, generally accessible for anyone and set apart primarily to offer space for prayer, reflection, meditation and personal ritual" (Holsappel-Brons, quoted in Christensen et al., 2019, p. 300). In recent decades, in a "massive proliferation," such rooms have been established in institutions that range from hospitals, schools, and prisons to public places such as airports, train stations, shopping malls, and sports arenas (Burchardt, 2023, p. 103). Such rooms are "open for use by adherents of different religions and intentionally established to address diverse religious or spiritual needs" (Christensen et al., 2019, p. 300). Almost all related research to date has been ethnographic descriptions of the motivation, nature, public experience, and design strategies, challenges, and accomplishments of these rooms (e.g., Gilliat-Ray, 2005).

Third, individually focused interventions may exert *spillover effects* on the collective-level social environment, especially if their proportional uptake is significant or their publicized availability sends an impactful signal (Francetic et al., 2022; see also Chaney et al., 2016). For example, in schools, hospitals, or workplaces, posters on official bulletin boards that advertise the availability of spiritual or quasi-spiritual activities or interventions (chaplain-led activities, spiritual fellowship groups, workshops on mantra, mindfulness, or yoga) may be perceived as signaling the organization's support for spiritual engagement and receptiveness to relevant spiritual identities.

Education, the Workplace, and Elsewhere

Besides such cross-cutting phenomena as pastors, rooms, and individual-level spillover, many interventions also pertain to specific sectors. In education, for example, college campuses in the United States are grappling with what is often called a student "mental health crisis" (Oswalt et al., 2020). Two widespread sources of distress are perceived lack of meaning and social connection, each of which is often otherwise received through S/R. Driven by such concerns in the last two decades, campus student affairs professionals are increasingly fostering students' abilities to draw upon spirituality, religion, and other sources of meaning and connection (Goodman et al., 2015). Even in the United States, "there is no legal reason student affairs professionals cannot attend to the spiritual and religious needs of the students they serve, as long as they are providing equal opportunity for all religious groups rather than promoting a single perspective," leading to calls to "stop using the public institution defense" (Goodman et al., 2015, pp. 132, 133, because "to cite separation of church and state… is faulty logic," p. 131). Thus, partly driven by perceived benefits to health and well-being, a rich empirical and applied literature has emerged in the past two decades on S/R on campus. Many functions in supporting campus spirituality have long been served by campus chaplains, who are also increasingly involved in "interreligious bridge-building" (Barton et al., 2020, p. 80). Other campus initiatives, often supported or launched by student service divisions, include supporting spirituality-related courses and pedagogy, cocurricular practices, interfaith initiatives, and partnerships between campus student organizations and S/R organizations in the community (Goodman et al., 2015; see also Sarath, 2003; Simmer-Brown & Grace, 2011). Such work has sometimes been supported by federal policy initiatives, such as the White House Interfaith and Community Service Campus Challenge, which supported students from diverse backgrounds engaging together in community service (Patel & Giess, 2016). Also, collegiate recovery programs and centers – designed to provide safety and support for college students in recovery from addictive behavior(s) – are often founded on spirituality (see Chapter 30, this volume).

In the workplace, the workplace spirituality literature has long recognized that spirituality manifests not only through individual workers but also may operate at the level of work units or groups and in the organization as a whole (Benefiel et al., 2014; Milliman et al., 2003). For example, high organizational-level workplace spirituality has been characterized as "alignment with organizational values," as when an organization has "a high sense of ethics or integrity and [contributes] to the welfare of employees, customers, and society" (Milliman et al., 2003, pp. 429–430). A key force that may empower or impede worker spirituality is thus an organization's purpose, as expressed in its organizational culture, legal structure, and managerial choices (Bart, 2007; Foster & Wall, 2019; Lips-Wiersma & Morris, 2009; van Ingen et al., 2021). Governments vary in how their policies mandate that for-profit as well as non-profit corporations must pursue various purposes, such as sustainability versus maximization of shareholder return (Mélon, 2019; Stout, 2012). Major religious and spiritual traditions join in recognizing a "need to embrace the spiritual dimension of the human being in formulating and implementing international public policies" related to work – for example, "a person works not only for the self, but also for others: for his or her family, society and country, and for the family of humanity" (Peccoud, 2004, pp. 21, 37). Implications of related policy choices for employee spiritual well-being and health seem potentially large, but to date have seldom been considered in the S/R and health literature.

Studies of collective-level workplace spirituality, like those conducted at the individual level, remain overwhelmingly observational rather than experimental (Benefiel et al., 2014; Dubey & Bedi, 2024). Nonetheless, scholars in this field have given much attention to how to facilitate workplace spirituality at levels ranging from the individual to the organization (Pawar, 2009b). Other organizational practices to encourage workplace spirituality include fostering meaningful work and supporting employee work/life balance (Pfeffer, 2003). Spiritually supportive interior design may be undertaken in workspaces as well as rooms of silence (Kluver & Wicks, 2014; Petersson & Sandin, 2020). Organizational leaders may also affect the social environment through spiritual leadership (e.g., promulgating "a transcendent vision that contributes to the greater good," Vedula & Agrawal, 2024, p. 323). Dik et al. (2024, p. 291) reported a paucity of experimental studies in workplace spirituality, but cited a "rare experimental [studies which] showed that spiritual well-being and spiritual integrity improved after participation in a spirituality training program" an adaptation of a well-studied program for portable repetition of a mantra or holy name (Buttner et al., 2016; Hulett et al., 2023; Oman, 2025c).

Chaplains have also been present in many workplaces. While some of these chaplains have been employed by organizations, it is significant that some have been supported by labor unions, such as the United Auto Workers, which has trained hundreds of chaplains, implementing programs in numerous factories nationwide (Plummer, 1996; Waller, 2012). Moreover, in many countries, "a critical role in highlighting injustices" in the workplace, aiming for their redress, may be played by chaplains (Wolf & Feldbauer-Durstmüller, 2023, p. 1151).

Clinical Medicine

Clinical medicine has recently emerged as a proposed focal point for integrating attention to spirituality at the level of the social environment. Contemporary medical care in the United States has long been criticized for its excessively physical and impersonal orientation, resulting in many calls for improving the spiritual sensitivity and "care" that is embedded – or too often omitted – in clinical practice, especially for patients with serious or life-threatening illness (Balboni et al., 2022; Doehring, 2019; Oman & Brown, 2018). Chaplains have long had key responsibilities for spiritual care in hospital settings (Timmins et al., 2018). But the work of chaplains *alone*, as traditionally understood, no longer seems sufficient for ensuring adequate spiritual support, which takes place not solely within single interpersonal relationships, but also in a "healing milieu," a "social and institutional healing context" (Balboni & Balboni, 2018, p. 186). Evidence suggests that the sociospiritual milieus of hospitals and many other clinical settings are deficient and may even be experienced as imposing an "alien" worldview, a "spirituality of immanence that is centered on the body" (Balboni & Balboni, 2018, pp. 198, 239), as opposed to or at the expense of the spirit or other conceptions of ultimate concern. Can improved spiritual support and care be better integrated into hospital and clinical practice, taking into account the influence not only of individual or specialized professionals, but of the clinical social milieu?

Recent evidence-based reviews in *JAMA* concluded that medical care for patients with serious illness should include "specialty practitioners of spiritual care (e.g., chaplains)," and also that "all members of the multidisciplinary care team should receive training in spiritual care provision" (Balboni et al., 2022, p. 194). Thus, as part of "person-centered, value-sensitive care" (p. 184), evidence supports key and complementary functions played by the spiritual care specialist and the clinical (e.g., care team) social environment. The authors also noted that "research and ethical reflection is needed to determine... practical application in clinical and other health settings... [and] care should be individualized, patient-centered, and respectful of beliefs and preferences" (p. 195). Indeed, healthcare providers must not impose their personal S/R belief systems – whether present or absent, or positive or negative in connotation – on their patients. A healthcare provider's

> role is not to absolve sin or adjudicate doctrine, but to provide a safe, professional, and empirical ... environment to facilitate ... health and ... healing, while also ethically, competently, and appropriately incorporating the religiousness and spirituality of the client.
>
> (Toussaint et al., 2012, p. 344)

See Chapter 20 in this volume for a more detailed discussion of ethics and competencies related to healthcare provider/client interactions.

For spiritual care to be adequately patient-centered, how *fully* and *tightly*, and in what *manner*, should a clinical social environment be structured to precisely match a patient's own spiritual orientation? A discussion on such implementation issues was recently sparked by Balboni and Balboni (2018), two professors at Harvard Medical School, who advocated circumscribed spaces for full tradition-specific integrations of medicine with major religious traditions, arguing for what they called a "structural pluralism for medicine and religion" (p. 268). They proposed that modern medical systems should provide larger "spaces" (p. 287) – primarily sociocultural, but perhaps partly "architectural" (p. 281) – to nurture the development of multiple independent partnerships between scientifically informed medicine and specific traditions, such as "Catholic, Protestant, Hindu, Muslim, Humanist" (p. 299), in which "each community would have access to organizational and professional structures to incrementally develop its unique, tradition-dependent spiritual viewpoints and practices for the sake of serving and caring for the seriously ill who identify with each tradition" (p. 299), allowing each tradition to "express itself within its own natural, thick way of life" (p. 272), thereby providing a range of more spiritually supportive healing milieus that patients can "opt into" (p. 299). The Balbonis proposal represents one of the higher levels of faith/health integration on a 6-step "continuum" recently articulated by Idler and Kellehear (2017).

Commentators (e.g., symposia in *Society*, 2019; *Spiritual Care*, 2020) were generally sympathetic to the Balbonis' critique of medical dehumanization and deficiencies in spiritual care, but many were skeptical about the structural modularity proposed by the Balbonis, instead pointing to various alternative ways that greater spiritual care can be or is already being integrated into the clinical social environment (e.g., see Frank, 2019; Sprik, 2019). All commentators agreed, however, that spiritually supportive clinical environments are important, and most agreed that more work was required.

An Emergent Frontier and Field

The preceding subsections have described how spiritually supportive social environments and policies are increasingly recognized, but often understudied as generally beneficial for outcomes of interest in societal sectors that, among others, include education, the workplace, mental healthcare, and medical clinics and hospitals (Table 3.4). But approaches for systematically strengthening and cultivating such spiritually supportive environments have drawn comparatively little systematic scholarship, despite the wide embrace by public health of multilevel interventions as best practices. In some environments, such as education and the workplace, such spiritual integration has emerged *in vivo* largely or entirely without direct support from health professionals, public health systems, and health policies. How might such multilevel spiritually oriented practices and supports become more prevalent, effective, and beneficially impactful? Could their integration be viewed as a form of intentional culture change to be implemented by reforming predominant ideas, institutions, modes of interaction, and individual practices and understandings (Hamedani et al., 2024)?

Cross-sector spiritual integration questions, like S/R themselves, are relevant to every nation (Grant & Oman, 2018). Although the needs, challenges, and constraints on appropriate integration vary tremendously between societies and sectors, the challenges are often parallel, suggesting much potential for cross-sectoral and cross-national dissemination of effective tools and strategies. A new public health translational field – a sort of translational epidemiology of spirituality, or of transcendence, or of the sacred – is therefore seemingly needed to theorize, explore, collate, and develop successful approaches in this area. Whereas Levin (2022) emphasized policy levels and collaborations with faith-based organizations in characterizing a public health translation of the epidemiology of religion, here we have highlighted the complementary translational need for action by and collaboration with a much wider range of sectors, organizations, and actors.

Decades ago, psychologist Allen Bergin and his colleagues explicated tools for a "spiritual strategy" in counseling, psychotherapy, and behavior change (Richards & Bergin, 1997). This was a key step beyond a "modernist academic gaze [in] which... the agency and salience of the sacred" is "ignored or suppressed" (Dwyer, 2016, pp. 758–759). The needed new field could be viewed as elevating such strategies from an individual to a collective level, while maintaining necessary cultural and legal sensitivity, humility, and inclusiveness.

How might one begin to implement such a public health strategy? In some social environments, such as healthcare clinics, a first step could be offering individually focused opt-in interventions, which could yield spillover effects on sociospiritual climate through their presence, such as by setting a tone or exemplifying an inclusive orientation (Schensul & Trickett, 2009). For example, healthcare clinics have begun by offering spiritually infused therapies, and universities have offered trainings not only on quasi-spiritual contemplative practices such as mindfulness, but on forms that more readily synergize with multiple religious traditions beyond Buddhism (e.g., Oman, 2025a).

Next, an organization or community could seek to integrate additional novel spiritually supportive features into its social environments, such as a nonsectarian room of silence or a

Table 3.5 Questions for an Emerging Field of Cross-Sectoral Multi-Level Spiritual Support Intervention

#	*Question*
Q1	How can existing practices and interventions, such as chaplains, rooms of silence, or opt-in group-delivery of spiritual practice instruction in meditation or mantra repetition, be refined or improved?
Q2	Can existing practices be horizontally disseminated to additional sites and sectors?
Q3	What is the optimal collective-level use of quasi-spiritual practices such as mindfulness and yoga (e.g., what spiritual or religious adaptations are needed Oman, 2025a, 2025b)?
Q4	What is the role of improved professional training in fostering spiritually supportive social environments in healthcare and other sectors (Balboni et al., 2022; Vieten & Lukoff, 2022; Wolf & Feldbauer-Durstmüller, 2023)?
Q5	What are the best ways to administratively support and disseminate various types of spiritual interventions, practices, or social environmental support?[a]
Q6	What is the role of approaches such as structural pluralism that create larger spaces to allow deeper integration of non-religious institutional logics with one or more specific S/R traditions?[b]
Q7	What legal clarifications, protections, precautions, or changes are needed in various societies and localities?[c]
Q8	What are optimal conditions for an organization to align its culture and formally stated purpose with inclusive spiritual goals (e.g., sustainability)?
Q9	What combination of adaptation, opt-in, opt-out, and/or other functional alternatives can ensure that non-spiritual individuals are optimally respected and supported in each environment?

[a] For larger changes, for example, Balboni and Balboni (2018) have suggested a "gradual unfolding through scientific testing, trial, and public evaluation toward the common good" (pp. 287–288).

[b] Idler and Kellehear (2017) have described a 6-step "continuum" of degrees of relationship or integration, ranging from episodic "faith-secular partnerships" to "faith saturated" activities reflecting a "merged identity" (pp. 235, 236).

[c] Despite great diversity in national law codifications, the post-WWII era has seen the emergence of a considerable and widely accepted body of internal law – a set of "international norms" – on freedom of religion (Witte, 2010, p. 406). Not all US citizens may be aware, however, that "conspicuously absent from international human rights instruments ... are the more radical demands for separationism, rooted in the popular American metaphor of a 'wall of separation between church and state'" (p. 412). Views such as that "only the secular state can guarantee religious liberty... which still pervade popular opinion in America, are not reflected in international human rights instruments nor, indeed, widely shared by other nation-states around the world" (p. 412).

proactive, worldview-inclusive chaplain (sometimes called by titles such as director of spiritual life, Cadge, 2023). Table 3.5 shows a range of questions that are likely to emerge during these phases of implementation and that could benefit from reflection and research.

Finally, policies, training, or other appropriate efforts could be undertaken to ensure the sustainability of achievements in spiritual integration. Such integration may often be achieved through the joint efforts of diverse stakeholders. Efforts to ensure that such integration is sustained may benefit from relevant professional expertise as well as findings from translational sciences and other relevant literature (e.g., Helsper et al., 2023; Lobb & Colditz, 2013; Quilling et al., 2020; Schensul & Trickett, 2009; Super et al., 2020).

Policy and intervention development efforts must also correct any mistakes in groundwork or implementation and learn from them. One likely need would be to refine and fine-tune interventions that were initially insufficiently adapted to the needs of adherents to specific S/R traditions or worldviews. Large literatures are often available to support such refinements (e.g., Oman, 2025a; see also Oman, 2025b). Some other problems may be harder to correct. For example, features of US law have allowed the proliferation of "zombie religious institutions" that are perpetually legally *obligated* to observe certain religious restrictions in the services they offer, even though these institutions no longer possess any living connection to any authentic religious community (Sepper, 2017).

Summary and Conclusion

In this chapter, we have sketched the history and current status of nine intertwined facets of the rapidly expanding field of spirituality, religion, and health. After sketching the field's 19th- and 20th-century history, we noted contemporary psychology of S/R's renewed interest in positive health and flourishing, evolution and refinement in how S/R are defined, and the expansion and refinement of measurement tools. Beginning slowly in the 1980s, there has now been a flood of over 100 systematic reviews and, in the 21st century, dozens of meta-analyses, which have greatly strengthened the case, now arguably compelling, that religious engagement can causally affect health, usually but not always favorably. Expanding from origins that especially emphasized individual interventions and clinical outcomes in Judeo-Christian populations, the S/R and health field is now giving more attention to studying S/R in diverse social sectors, to diverse spiritual and religious traditions that include atheists and the "spiritual but not religious," and to studying or intervening in social environments, which holds promise as an emerging field of international and global relevance.

This overview has revealed a field of steadily increasing breadth, depth, sophistication, and ability to translate its findings into effective action. The field is also steadily growing in cross-cultural, interfaith, and inter-worldview inclusiveness (including atheists), which is greatly needed at a time when psychology and many other fields are prioritizing internationalization of curricula and research (e.g., Kitayama et al., 2022; Leask, 2015; Shealy et al., 2023; Takooshian et al., 2016). But there is still much progress needed for this field to make its fullest contribution to guiding a world beset by climate change and other existential challenges, and where novel spiritual phenomena, such as "spiritual but not religious" identities, are becoming common in some localities, even as worldwide per capita religious belief is projected to increase. Can a troubled world and the individuals that comprise it learn to live harmoniously with our diverse spiritualities and draw strength and inner peace from them for facing our many challenges (Beaman, 2017)? We hope that this chapter, and the other chapters in this volume, will assist each reader in making a maximal contribution in relation to S/R and their ever-evolving relation to individual and collective health and well-being.

Note

1 Various histories of S/R and health research are available, reflecting a range of disciplinary emphases and levels of detail (see, for example, Koenig et al., 2001, pp. 24–49, for histories of Western religious concern for health since ancient times; Koenig et al., 2012, pp. 7–9, for history since 1980; Levin & Chatters, 2008, for gerontology; Levin, 2009, for the 20th century; Oman & Thoresen, 2005, for psychology; Pargament, 2023, for psychology since 1970; Puchalski et al., 2014, for medicine).

References

Abu-Raiya, H., & Pargament, K. I. (2015). Religious coping among diverse religions: Commonalities and divergences. *Psychology of Religion and Spirituality*, *7*(1), 24–33. https://doi.org/10.1037/a0037652

Aggarwal, S., Wright, J., Morgan, A., Patton, G., & Reavley, N. (2023). Religiosity and spirituality in the prevention and management of depression and anxiety in young people: A systematic review and meta-analysis. *BMC Psychiatry*, *23*(1), 729. https://doi.org/10.1186/s12888-023-05091-2

Ai, A. L., Wink, P., Paloutzian, R. F., & Harris, K. A. (Eds.). (2021). *Assessing spirituality in a diverse world*. Cham, Switzerland: Springer International. https://doi.org/10.1007/978-3-030-52140-0

Allport, G. W., & Ross, M. J. (1967). Personal religious orientation and prejudice. *Journal of Personality and Social Psychology*, *5*(4), 432–443. https://doi.org/10.1037/h0021212

Ammerman, N. T. (2013). Spiritual but not religious? Beyond binary choices in the study of religion. *Journal for the Scientific Study of Religion*, *52*(2), 258–278. https://doi.org/10.1111/jssr.12024

Amri, M., Chatur, A., & O'Campo, P. (2022). An umbrella review of intersectoral and multisectoral approaches to health policy. *Social Science and Medicine*, *315*, 115469. https://doi.org/10.1016/j.socscimed.2022.115469

Ayling, D., Whatman, S., Williams, B., & Main, K. (2023). Health education in Christian faith-based primary schools: A scoping study. *Curriculum Studies in Health and Physical Education*. https://doi.org/10.1080/25742981.2023.2253207

Baker, J. O., Stroope, S., & Walker, M. H. (2018). Secularity, religiosity, and health: Physical and mental health differences between atheists, agnostics, and nonaffiliated theists compared to religiously affiliated individuals. *Social Science Research*, *75*, 44–57. https://doi.org/10.1016/j.ssresearch.2018.07.003

Balboni, M. J., & Balboni, T. A. (2018). *Hostility to hospitality: Spirituality and professional socialization within medicine*. New York: Oxford University Press.

Balboni, T. A., VanderWeele, T. J., Doan-Soares, S. D., Long, K. N. G., Ferrell, B. R., Fitchett, G., Koenig, H. G., Bain, P. A., Puchalski, C., Steinhauser, K. E., Sulmasy, D. P., & Koh, H. K. (2022). Spirituality in serious illness and health. *Journal of the American Medical Association*, *328*(2), 184–197. https://doi.org/10.1001/jama.2022.11086

Bandura, A. (2003). On the psychosocial impact and mechanisms of spiritual modeling. *The International Journal for the Psychology of Religion*, *13*(3), 167–173. https://doi.org/10.1207/S15327582IJPR1303_02

Barnes, P. A., & Curtis, A. B. (2009). A national examination of partnerships among local health departments and faith communities in the United States. *Journal of Public Health Management and Practice*, *15*(3), 253–263. https://doi.org/10.1097/01.PHH.0000349740.19361.ac

Barry, M. M. (2019). Concepts and principles of mental health promotion. In M. M. Barry, A. M. Clarke, I. Petersen, & R. Jenkins (Eds.), *Implementing mental health promotion* (pp. 3–34). Cham: Springer International Publishing. https://doi.org/10.1007/978-3-030-23455-3_1

Bart, C. (2007). A comparative analysis of mission statement content in secular and faith-based hospitals. *Journal of Intellectual Capital*, *8*(4), 682–694. https://doi.org/10.1108/14691930710830837

Barton, R., Cadge, W., & van Stee, E. G. (2020). Caring for the whole student: How do chaplains contribute to campus life? *Journal of College and Character*, *21*(2), 67–85. https://doi.org/10.1080/2194587X.2020.1741392

Beaman, L. G. (2017). *Deep equality in an era of religious diversity*. Oxford University Press. https://doi.org/10.1093/oso/9780198803485.001.0001

Beaman, L. G., & Stacey, T. (2021). *Nonreligious imaginaries of world repairing*. Cham, Switzerland: Palgrave Macmillan. https://doi.org/10.1007/978-3-030-72881-6

Béland, D., & Cox, R. H. (2016). Ideas as coalition magnets: Coalition building, policy entrepreneurs, and power relations. *Journal of European Public Policy*, *23*(3), 428–445. https://doi.org/10.1080/13501763.2015.1115533

Benefiel, M., Fry, L. W., & Geigle, D. (2014). Spirituality and religion in the workplace: History, theory, and research. *Psychology of Religion and Spirituality*, *6*(3), 175–187. https://doi.org/10.1037/a0036597

Benson, H., Dusek, J. A., Sherwood, J. B., Lam, P., Bethea, C. F., Carpenter, W., Levitsky, S., Hill, P. C., Clem, D. W., Jr., Jain, M. K., Drumel, D., Kopecky, S. L., Mueller, P. S., Marek, D., Rollins, S., & Hibberd, P. L. (2006). Study of the therapeutic effects of intercessory prayer (step) in cardiac bypass patients: A multicenter randomized trial of uncertainty and certainty of receiving intercessory prayer. *American Heart Journal*, *151*(4), 934–942. https://doi.org/10.1016/j.ahj.2005.05.028

Bergin, A. E. (1983). Religiosity and mental health: A critical reevaluation and meta-analysis. *Professional Psychology: Research & Practice*, *14*(2), 170–184. https://doi.org/10.1037/0735-7028.14.2.170

Beyer, P. F. (1990). Privatization and the public influence of religion in global society. *Theory, Culture & Society*, *7*(2-3), 373–395. https://doi.org/10.1177/026327690007002022

Bouma, G. D., & Halafoff, A. (2017). Australia's changing religious profile—rising nones and Pentecostals, declining British Protestants in superdiversity: Views from the 2016 census. *Journal for the Academic Study of Religion*, *30*(2), 129–143. https://doi.org/10.1558/jasr.34826

Brannon, T. N., & Lin, A. (2021). "Pride and prejudice" pathways to belonging: Implications for inclusive diversity practices within mainstream institutions. *American Psychologist*, *76*(3), 488–501. https://doi.org/10.1037/amp0000643

Brewster, M. E., Robinson, M. A., Sandil, R., Esposito, J., & Geiger, E. (2014). Arrantly absent: Atheism in psychological science from 2001 to 2012 ψ. *The Counseling Psychologist*, *42*(5), 628–663. https://doi.org/10.1177/0011000014528051

Brown, C. G. (2019). *Debating yoga and mindfulness in public schools: Reforming secular education or reestablishing religion?* Chapel Hill, NC: University of North Carolina Press.

Burchardt, M. (2020). *Regulating difference: Religious diversity and nationhood in the secular west*. New Brunswick, NJ: Rutgers University Press. https://doi.org/10.2307/j.ctvxhrhx3

Burchardt, M. (2023). Designing interreligious encounters: Space, materiality, and media in berlin's house of one. *Material Religion*, *19*(2), 101–125. https://doi.org/10.1080/17432200.2023.2196655

Buttner, M. M., Bormann, J. E., Weingart, K., Andrews, T., Ferguson, M., & Afari, N. (2016). Multi-site evaluation of a complementary, spiritually-based intervention for veterans: The mantram repetition program. *Complementary Therapies in Clinical Practice*, *22*, 74–79. https://doi.org/10.1016/j.ctcp.2015.12.008

Byrd, R. C. (1988). Positive therapeutic effects of intercessory prayer in a coronary care unit population. *Southern Medical Journal*, *81*(7), 826–829.

Cadge, W. (2023). *Spiritual care: The everyday work of chaplains*. New York, NY: Oxford University Press. https://doi.org/10.1093/oso/9780197647813.001.0001

Campbell, M. K., Hudson, M. A., Resnicow, K., Blakeney, N., Paxton, A., & Baskin, M. (2007). Church-based health promotion interventions: Evidence and lessons learned. *Annual Review of Public Health*, *28*, 213–234. https://doi.org/10.1146/annurev.publhealth.28.021406.144016

Cardeña, E. (2018). The experimental evidence for parapsychological phenomena: A review. *American Psychologist*, *73*(5), 663–677. https://doi.org/10.1037/amp0000236

Carrette, J., & King, R. (2004). *Selling spirituality: The silent takeover of religion*. New York: Routledge.

Carsley, D., Khoury, B., & Heath, N. L. (2018). Effectiveness of mindfulness interventions for mental health in schools: A comprehensive meta-analysis. *Mindfulness*, *9*(3), 693–707. https://doi.org/10.1007/s12671-017-0839-2

Chaney, K. E., Sanchez, D. T., & Remedios, J. D. (2016). Organizational identity safety cue transfers. *Personality & Social Psychology Bulletin*, *42*(11), 1564–1576. https://doi.org/10.1177/0146167216665096

Chatters, L. M. (2000). Religion and health: Public health research and practice. *Annual Review of Public Health*, *21*, 335–367. https://doi.org/10.1146/annurev.publhealth.21.1.335

Chaves, M., & Chaves, M. (2017). *American religion: Contemporary trends* (2 ed.). Princeton, NJ: Princeton University Press. https://doi.org/10.1515/9781400888375

Chen, Y., Kim, E. S., & VanderWeele, T. J. (2020). Religious-service attendance and subsequent health and well-being throughout adulthood: Evidence from three prospective cohorts. *International Journal of Epidemiology*, *49*(6), 2030–2040. https://doi.org/10.1093/ije/dyaa120

Chida, Y., Steptoe, A., & Powell, L. H. (2009). Religiosity/spirituality and mortality. *Psychotherapy and Psychosomatics*, *78*(2), 81–90. https://doi.org/10.1159/000190791

Christensen, H. R., Høeg, I. M., Kühle, L., & Nordin, M. (2019). Rooms of silence at three universities in Scandinavia. *Sociology of Religion*, *80*(3), 299–322. https://doi.org/10.1093/socrel/sry040

Cino Pagliarello, M. (2022). Unpacking ambiguity in ideational change: The polysemy of the 'Europe of knowledge'. *West European Politics*, *45*(4), 884–905. https://doi.org/10.1080/01402382.2021.1918429

Cobb, M., Puchalski, C. M., & Rumbold, B. (Eds.). (2012). *Oxford textbook of spirituality in healthcare*. New York, NY: Oxford University Press.

Cockell, N., & Mcsherry, W. (2012). Spiritual care in nursing: An overview of published international research. *Journal of Nursing Management*, *20*(8), 958–969. https://doi.org/10.1111/j.1365-2834.2012.01450.x

Coleman, T. J., & Jong, J. (2021). Counting the nonreligious: A critical review of new measures. In A. L. Ai, P. Wink, R. F. Paloutzian, & K. A. Harris (Eds.), *Assessing spirituality in a diverse world* (pp. 87–116). Cham: Springer International Publishing. https://doi.org/10.1007/978-3-030-52140-0_5

Comstock, G. W., & Partridge, K. B. (1972). Church attendance and health. *Journal of Chronic Disease*, *25*(12), 665–672. https://doi.org/10.1016/0021-9681(72)90002-1

Comte-Sponville, A. (2008). *The book of atheist spirituality*. London: Bantam.

Cornish, M. A., & Wade, N. G. (2010). Spirituality and religion in group counseling: A literature review with practice guidelines. *Professional Psychology: Research and Practice*. September, *41*(5), 398–404. https://doi.org/10.1037/a0020179

Cragun, R. T., Kosmin, B., Keysar, A., Hammer, J. H., & Nielsen, M. (2012). On the receiving end: Discrimination toward the non-religious in the United States. *Journal of Contemporary Religion*, *27*(1), 105–127. https://doi.org/10.1080/13537903.2012.642741

Currier, J. M., Fox, J., & Vieten, C. (Eds.). (in press). *Handbook of training in spiritual and religious competencies in mental health professions*. New York, NY: Oxford University Press.

Davie, G. T., Ammerman, N., Huq, S., Leustean, L. N., Masoud, T., Moon, S., Olupona, J. K., Sinha, V., Smilde, D. A., Woodhead, L., Yang, F., & Zurlo, G. (2018). Religions and social progress: Critical assessments and creative partnerships. In International Panel on Social Progress (Ed.), *Rethinking society for the 21st century: Report of the International Panel on Social Progress: Volume 3: Transformations in values, norms, cultures* (Vol. 3, pp. 641–676). Cambridge: Cambridge University Press.

Davis, E. B., Worthington, E. L. Jr., & Schnitker, S. A. (Eds.). (2023). *Handbook of positive psychology, religion, and spirituality*. Cham: Springer International. https://doi.org/10.1007/978-3-031-10274-5

de Diego-Cordero, R., Zurrón Pérez, M. P., Vargas-Martínez, A. M., Lucchetti, G., & Vega-Escaño, J. (2021). The effectiveness of spiritual interventions in the workplace for work-related health outcomes: A systematic review and meta-analysis. *Journal of Nursing Management*, *29*(6), 1703–1712. https://doi.org/10.1111/jonm.13315

Deal, P. J., & Magyar-Russell, G. M. (2022). A qualitative study of sanctification: How nature becomes sacred for nontheistic environmental activists. *Spirituality in Clinical Practice*, *9*(1), 40–54. https://doi.org/10.1037/scp0000285

Derose, K. P., Williams, M. V., Branch, C. A., Flórez, K. R., Hawes-Dawson, J., Mata, M. A., Oden, C. W., & Wong, E. C. (2019). A community-partnered approach to developing church-based interventions to reduce health disparities among African-Americans and latinos. *Journal of Racial and Ethnic Health Disparities*, *6*(2), 254–264. https://doi.org/10.1007/s40615-018-0520-z

Dik, B. J., Daniels, D., & Alayan, A. J. (2024). Religion, spirituality, and the workplace: A review and critique. *Annual Review of Organizational Psychology and Organizational Behavior*, *11*, 279–305. https://doi.org/10.1146/annurev-orgpsych-110721-041458

Dodge, K. A., Prinstein, M. J., Evans, A. C., Ahuvia, I. L., Alvarez, K., Beidas, R. S., Brown, A. J., Cuijpers, P., Denton, E.-G., Hoagwood, K. E., Johnson, C., Kazdin, A. E., McDanal, R., Metzger, I. W., Rowley, S. N., Schleider, J., & Shaw, D. S. (2024). Population mental health science: Guiding principles and initial agenda. *American Psychologist*, *79*(6), 805–823. https://doi.org/10.1037/amp0001334

Doehring, C. (2019). Using spiritual care to alleviate religious, spiritual, and moral struggles arising from acute health crises. *Ethics, Medicine and Public Health, 9*, 68–74. https://doi.org/10.1016/j.jemep.2019.05.003

Donahue, M. J. (1985). Intrinsic and extrinsic religiousness: Review and meta-analysis. *Journal of Personality and Social Psychology, 48*(2), 400–419. https://doi.org/10.1037/0022-3514.48.2.400

Dubey, S., & Bedi, S. S. (2024). Workplace spirituality: A systematic review and future research agenda. *Journal of Management, Spirituality & Religion, 21*(1), 83–128. https://doi.org/10.51327/CQER6430

Dworsky, C. K. O., Pargament, K. I., Gibbel, M. R., Krumrei, E. J., Faigin, C. A., Gear Haugen, M. R., Desai, K. M., Lauricella, S. K., Lynn, Q., & Warner, H. L. (2013). Winding road: Preliminary support for a spiritually integrated intervention addressing college students' spiritual struggles. *Research in the Social Scientific Study of Religion, 24*, 309–339. https://doi.org/10.1163/9789004252073_013

Dwyer, C. (2016). Why does religion matter for cultural geographers? *Social & Cultural Geography, 17*(6), 758–762. https://doi.org/10.1080/14649365.2016.1163728

Eisenstadt, S. N. (2000). Multiple modernities. *Daedalus, 129*, 1–29.

Emmons, R. A., & Paloutzian, R. F. (2003). The psychology of religion. *Annual Review of Psychology, 54*, 377–402.

Eriksson, M., Ghazinour, M., & Hammarström, A. (2018). Different uses of bronfenbrenner's ecological theory in public mental health research: What is their value for guiding public mental health policy and practice? *Social Theory & Health, 16*(4), 414–433. https://doi.org/10.1057/s41285-018-0065-6

Fetzer Institute (1999). *Multidimensional measurement of religiousness / spirituality for use in health research*. Kalamazoo, MI: Fetzer Institute.

Finke, R., & Bader, C. (Eds.). (2017). *Faithful measures: New methods in the measurement of religion*. New York University Press. https://doi.org/10.18574/nyu/9781479875214.001.0001

Foster, S., & Wall, T. (2019). Organizational initiatives for spiritual well-being. In W. Leal Filho, T. Wall, A. M. Azul, L. Brandli, & P. G. Özuyar (Eds.), *Good health and well-being* (pp. 527–539): Springer.

Francetic, I., Meacock, R., Elliott, J., Kristensen, S. R., Britteon, P., Lugo-Palacios, D. G., Wilson, P., & Sutton, M. (2022). Framework for identification and measurement of spillover effects in policy implementation: Intended non-intended targeted non-targeted spillovers (intents). *Implementation Science Communications, 3*(1), 30. https://doi.org/10.1186/s43058-022-00280-8

Frank, A. W. (2019). Does medicine need ultimate values? *Society, 56*(2), 123–129. https://doi.org/10.1007/s12115-019-00338-9

Freud, S. (1907/1989). Obsessive actions and religious practices (originally published 1907). In P. Gay (Ed.), *The Freud reader* (pp. 429–436). New York: W.W. Norton.

Geltner, G., & Coomans, J. (2023). The healthscaping approach: Toward a global history of early public health. *Historical Methods: A Journal of Quantitative and Interdisciplinary History, 56*(1), 18–33. https://doi.org/10.1080/01615440.2022.2128487

George, L. K., Kinghorn, W. A., Koenig, H. G., Gammon, P., & Blazer, D. G. (2013). Why gerontologists should care about empirical research on religion and health: Transdisciplinary perspectives. *The Gerontologist, 53*(6), 898–906. https://doi.org/10.1093/geront/gnt002

Giacalone, R. A., & Jurkiewicz, C. L. (2010). *Handbook of workplace spirituality and organizational performance* (2nd ed.). Armonk, NY: M.E. Sharpe.

Gilliat-Ray, S. (2005). From 'chapel' to 'prayer room': The production, use, and politics of sacred space in public institutions. *Culture and Religion, 6*(2), 287–308. https://doi.org/10.1080/01438300500226448

Gonçalves, J. P. B., Lucchetti, G., Menezes, P. R., & Vallada, H. (2015). Religious and spiritual interventions in mental health care: A systematic review and meta-analysis of randomized controlled clinical trials. *Psychological Medicine, 45*(14), 2937–2949. https://doi.org/10.1017/S0033291715001166

Goodman, K. M., Wilson, K., & Nicolazzo, Z. (2015). Campus practice in support of spirituality, faith, religion, and life purpose: What has been accomplished and where do we go next? In J. L. Small (Ed.), *Making meaning: Embracing spirituality, faith, religion, and life purpose in student affairs* (pp. 118–140). Sterling, VA: Stylus. https://doi.org/10.4324/9781003445838-10

Gorski, P. S., & Altınordu, A. (2008). After secularization? *Annual Review of Sociology, 34*(Volume 34, 2008), 55–85. https://doi.org/10.1146/annurev.soc.34.040507.134740

Gorsuch, R. L. (1984). Measurement: The boon and bane of investigating religion. *American Psychologist*, *39*(3), 228–236.

Gorsuch, R. L. (1988). Psychology of religion. *Annual Review of Psychology*, *39*, 201–221.

Grant, L., & Oman, D. (2018). International and global perspectives on spirituality, religion, and public health. In D. Oman (Ed.), *Why religion and spirituality matter for public health: Evidence, implications, and resources* (pp. 447–462). Cham, Switzerland: Springer International. https://doi.org/10.1007/978-3-319-73966-3_27

Gümüsay, A. A. (2020). The potential for plurality and prevalence of the religious institutional logic. *Business & Society*, *59*(5), 855–880. https://doi.org/10.1177/0007650317745634

Hamedani, M. G., Markus, H. R., Hetey, R. C., & Eberhardt, J. L. (2024). We built this culture (so we can change it): Seven principles for intentional culture change. *American Psychologist*, *79*(3), 384–402. https://doi.org/10.1037/amp0001209

Hardy, S. A., Nelson, J. M., Moore, J. P., & King, P. E. (2019). Processes of religious and spiritual influence in adolescence: A systematic review of 30 years of research. *Journal of Research on Adolescence*, *29*(2), 254–275. https://doi.org/10.1111/jora.12486

Helsper, N., Dippon, L., Birkholz, L., Rütten, A., Kohler, S., Weber, P., Pfeifer, K., & Semrau, J. (2023). What makes community-based, multilevel physical activity promotion last? A systematic review with narrative synthesis on factors for sustainable implementation. *Perspectives in Public Health*. https://doi.org/10.1177/17579139231186693

Hill, A. B. (1965). The environment and disease: Association or causation? *Proceedings of the Royal Society of Medicine*, *58*, 1217–1219.

Hill, P. C., & Hood, R. W., Jr. (Eds.). (1999). *Measures of religiosity*. Birmingham, AL: Religious Education Press.

Hill, P. C., & Pargament, K. I. (2003). Advances in the conceptualization and measurement of religion and spirituality: Implications for physical and mental health research. *American Psychologist*, *58*(1), 64–74. https://doi.org/10.1037/0003-066X.58.1.64

Hill, P. C., Pargament, K. I., Hood, R. W., Jr., McCullough, M. E., Swyers, J. P., Larson, D. B., & Zinnbauer, B. J. (2000). Conceptualizing religion and spirituality: Points of commonality, points of departure. *Journal for the Theory of Social Behaviour*, *30*(1), 51–77. https://doi.org/10.1111/1468-5914.00119

Hill, P. S. (2011). Understanding global health governance as a complex adaptive system. *Global Public Health*, *6*(6), 593–605. https://doi.org/10.1080/17441691003762108

Hinrichsen, C., Nielsen, L., Tamminen, N., Nelausen, M. K., Kusier, A. O., Santini, Z. I., Schou-Juul, F., Meilstrup, C., Rod, M. H., Koushede, V., & Lauridsen, S. (2022). Intersectoral mental health promotion – a practice-oriented taxonomy of roles and a study of intersectoral dynamics. *SSM - Mental Health*, *2*, 100136. https://doi.org/10.1016/j.ssmmh.2022.100136

Hodge, D. R. (2009). Secular privilege: Deconstructing the invisible rose-tinted sunglasses. *Journal of Religion & Spirituality in Social Work: Social Thought*, *28*(1-2), 8–34. https://doi.org/10.1080/15426430802643281

Hodge, D. R. (2018). The evolution of spirituality and religion in international social work discourse: Strengths and limitations of the contemporary understanding. *Journal of Religion & Spirituality in Social Work: Social Thought*, *37*(1), 3–23. https://doi.org/10.1080/15426432.2017.1350125

Hood, R. W., Jr., & Belzen, J. A. (2013). Research methods in the psychology of religion and spirituality. In R. F. Paloutzian, & C. L. Park (Eds.), *Handbook of the psychology of religion and spirituality* (2nd ed., pp. 75–93). New York: Guilford.

Hood, R. W., Jr., Ghorbani, N., Watson, P. J., Ghramaleki, A. F., Bing, M. N., Davison, H. K., Morris, R. J., & Williamson, W. P. (2001). Dimensions of the mysticism scale: Confirming the three-factor structure in the United States and Iran. *Journal for the Scientific Study of Religion*, *40*(4), 691–705. https://doi.org/10.1111/0021-8294.00085

Hulett, J. M., Corona, M., Hartman, B. M., & Bormann, J. E. (2023). A systematic review of interventional trials reporting relationships between silent mantram repetition and health in adults. *Complementary Therapies in Clinical Practice*, *50*, 101709. https://doi.org/10.1016/j.ctcp.2022.101709

Hummer, R. A., Rogers, R. G., Nam, C. B., & Ellison, C. G. (1999). Religious involvement and U.S. Adult mortality. *Demography*, *36*(2), 273–285. https://doi.org/10.2307/2648114

Hutter, M. (2001). Structural coupling between social systems: Art and the economy as mutual sources of growth. *Soziale Systeme*, *7*(2), 290–312. https://doi.org/10.1515/sosys-2001-0207

Idler, E., Bernau, J. A., & Zaras, D. (2022). Narratives and counter-narratives in religious responses to COVID-19: A computational text analysis. *PLoS ONE*, *17*(2), e0262905. https://doi.org/10.1371/journal.pone.0262905

Idler, E., & Kellehear, A. (2017). Religion in public health-care institutions: U.S. And U.K. Perspectives. *Journal for the Scientific Study of Religion*, *56*(2), 234–240. https://doi.org/10.1111/jssr.12349

Idler, E. L. (Ed.). (2014). *Religion as a social determinant of public health*. New York, NY: Oxford University Press. https://doi.org/10.1093/acprof:oso/9780199362202.001.0001

Idler, E. L., Musick, M. A., Ellison, C. G., George, L. K., Krause, N., Ory, M. G., Pargament, K. I., Powell, L. H., Underwood, L. G., & Williams, D. R. (2003). Measuring multiple dimensions of religion and spirituality for health research: Conceptual background and findings from the 1998 general social survey. *Research on Aging*, *25*(4), 327–365. https://doi.org/10.1177/0164027503025004001

Institute of Medicine (2000). *Promoting health: Intervention strategies from social and behavioral research*. Washington, DC: National Academy Press. https://doi.org/10.17226/9939

James, W. (1902/1961). *The varieties of religious experience: A study in human nature*. New York: Collier.

Jeste, D. V., & Lee, E. E. (2019). The emerging empirical science of wisdom: Definition, measurement, neurobiology, longevity, and interventions. *Harvard Review of Psychiatry*, *27*(3), 127–140. https://doi.org/10.1097/hrp.0000000000000205

Jones, S. L. (1994). A constructive relationship for religion with the science and profession of psychology: Perhaps the boldest model yet. *American Psychologist*, *49*(3), 184–199. https://doi.org/10.1037/0003-066X.49.3.184

Kaplan, T. J. (1986). The narrative structure of policy analysis. *Journal of Policy Analysis and Management*, *5*(4), 761–778. https://doi.org/10.1002/pam.4050050406

Kapuscinski, A. N., & Masters, K. S. (2010). The current status of measures of spirituality: A critical review of scale development. *Psychology of Religion and Spirituality*, *2*(4), 191–205. https://doi.org/10.1037/a0020498; Supplemental.

Kasselstrand, I. (2022). Secularization or alternative faith?: Trends and conceptions of spirituality in northern Europe. *Journal of Religion in Europe*, *15*(1-4), 27–55. https://doi.org/10.1163/18748929-bja10049

Kermen, U. (2018). Spiritual interventions in juvenile delinquency. *Spiritual Psychology and Counseling*, *3*(1), 61–84.

Kinney, E. D., & Clark, B. A. (2004). Provisions for health and health care in the constitutions of the countries of the world. *Cornell International Law Journal*, *37*(2), 285–355.

Kitayama, S., Salvador, C. E., Nanakdewa, K., Rossmaier, A., San Martin, A., & Savani, K. (2022). Varieties of interdependence and the emergence of the modern west: Toward the globalizing of psychology. *American Psychologist*, *77*, 991–1006. https://doi.org/10.1037/amp0001073

Kluver, J. R., & Wicks, A. C. (2014). Decoration, self-transcendence, and spiritual expression: Stakeholder cooperation and the creation of joint value in the workplace. *Journal of Management, Spirituality & Religion*, *11*(4), 357–382. https://doi.org/10.1080/14766086.2014.913495

Knudsen, M. (2007). Structural couplings between organizations and function systems: Looking at standards in health care. *Cybernetics & Human Knowing*, *14*(2-3), 111–131.

Koenig, H. G. (2000). Religion, spirituality, and medicine: Application to clinical practice. *Journal of the American Medical Association*, *284*(13), 1708. https://doi.org/10.1001/jama.284.13.1708-JMS1004-5-1

Koenig, H. G. (2008). Concerns about measuring "spirituality" in research. *Journal of Nervous and Mental Disease*, *196*(5), 349–355. https://doi.org/10.1097/NMD.0b013e31816ff796

Koenig, H. G., King, D. E., & Carson, V. B. (2012). *Handbook of religion and health* (2nd ed.). Oxford; New York: Oxford University Press.

Koenig, H. G., McCullough, M. E., & Larson, D. B. (2001). *Handbook of religion and health*. New York: Oxford University Press.

Koenig, H. G., VanderWeele, T. J., & Peteet, J. R. (2023). *Handbook of religion and health* (3rd ed.). Oxford; New York: Oxford University Press.

Kristeller, J. L., Rhodes, M., Cripe, L. D., & Sheets, V. (2005). Oncologist assisted spiritual intervention study (OASIS): Patient acceptability and initial evidence of effects. *International Journal of Psychiatry in Medicine*, *35*(4), 329–347. https://doi.org/10.2190/8AE4-F01C-60M0-85C8

Leask, B. (2015). *Internationalizing the curriculum (Internationalization in higher education series)*. New York: Taylor and Francis. https://doi.org/10.4324/9781315716954

Leder, D. (2005). "Spooky actions at a distance": Physics, psi, and distant healing. *The Journal of Alternative and Complementary Medicine*, *11*(5), 923–930. https://doi.org/10.1089/acm.2005.11.923

Leeman, J., Boisson, A., & Go, V. (2022). Scaling up public health interventions: Engaging partners across multiple levels. *Annual Review of Public Health, 43*(Volume 43, 2022), 155–171. https://doi.org/10.1146/annurev-publhealth-052020-113438

Levin, J. (2009). "And let us make us a name": Reflections on the future of the religion and health field. *Journal of Religion and Health*, *48*(2), 125–145. https://doi.org/10.1007/s10943-009-9243-0

Levin, J. (2016). Partnerships between the faith-based and medical sectors: Implications for preventive medicine and public health. *Preventive Medicine Reports*, *4*, 344–350. https://doi.org/10.1016/j.pmedr.2016.07.009

Levin, J. (2022). Toward a translational epidemiology of religion: Challenges and applications. *Annals of Epidemiology*, *75*, 25–31. https://doi.org/10.1016/j.annepidem.2022.08.053

Levin, J., & Chatters, L. M. (2008). Religion, aging, and health: Historical perspectives, current trends, and future directions. *Journal of Religion, Spirituality & Aging*, *20*(1-2), 153–172. https://doi.org/10.1080/15528030801922103

Levin, J. S. (1994). Religion and health: Is there an association, is it valid, and is it causal? *Social Science and Medicine*, *38*(11), 1475–1482. https://doi.org/10.1016/0277-9536(94)90109-0

Levin, J. S. (1996). How religion influences morbidity and health: Reflections on natural history, salutogenesis and host resistance. *Social Science and Medicine*, *43*(5), 849–864. https://doi.org/10.1016/0277-9536(96)00150-5

Levin, J. S., & Schiller, P. L. (1987). Is there a religious factor in health? *Journal of Religion and Health*, *26*(1), 9–36. https://doi.org/10.1007/BF01533291

Li, S., Okereke, O. I., Chang, S.-C., Kawachi, I., & VanderWeele, T. J. (2016). Religious service attendance and lower depression among women—a prospective cohort study. *Annals of Behavioral Medicine*, *50*(6), 876–884. https://doi.org/10.1007/s12160-016-9813-9

Linley, P. A., Joseph, S., Harrington, S., & Wood, A. M. (2006). Positive psychology: Past, present, and (possible)future. *The Journal of Positive Psychology*, *1*(1), 3–16. https://doi.org/10.1080/17439760500372796

Lips-Wiersma, M., & Morris, L. (2009). Discriminating between 'meaningful work' and the 'management of meaning'. *Journal of Business Ethics*, *88*(3), 491–511. https://doi.org/10.1007/s10551-009-0118-9

Lobb, R., & Colditz, G. A. (2013). Implementation science and its application to population health. *Annual Review of Public Health*, *34*(1), 235–251. https://doi.org/10.1146/annurev-publhealth-031912-114444

Lukoff, D., Lu, F., & Turner, R. (1998). From spiritual emergency to spiritual problem: The transpersonal roots of the new DSM-IV category. *Journal of Humanistic Psychology*, *38*(2), 21–50. https://doi.org/10.1177/00221678980382003

Markus, H. R., Steele, C. M., & Steele, D. M. (2000). Colorblindness as a barrier to inclusion: Assimilation and nonimmigrant minorities. *Daedalus*, *129*(4), 233–259.

Maslow, A. H. (1964). *Religions, values and peak-experiences*.

Mélon, L. (2019). *Shareholder primacy and global business: Re-clothing the eu corporate law*. New York, NY: Routledge. https://doi.org/10.4324/9780429061349

Michaelsen, M. M., Graser, J., Onescheit, M., Tuma, M. P., Werdecker, L., Pieper, D., & Esch, T. (2023). Mindfulness-based and mindfulness-informed interventions at the workplace: A systematic review and meta-regression analysis of rcts. *Mindfulness*, *14*(6), 1271–1304. https://doi.org/10.1007/s12671-023-02130-7

Miller, W. R., & Thoresen, C. E. (2003). Spirituality, religion, and health: An emerging research field. *American Psychologist*, *58*(1), 24–35. https://doi.org/10.1037/0003-066X.58.1.24

Milliman, J., Czaplewski, A. J., & Ferguson, J. (2003). Workplace spirituality and employee work attitudes: An exploratory empirical assessment. *Journal of Organizational Change Management*, *16*(4), 426–447. https://doi.org/10.1108/09534810310484172

Molendijk, A. L. (1999). In defense of pragmatism. In J. Platvoet, & A. L. Molendijk (Eds.), *The pragmatics of defining religion: Contexts, concepts, and contests* (pp. 3–19). Leiden; Boston: Brill.

Moreira-Almeida, A., Koenig, H. G., & Lucchetti, G. (2014). Clinical implications of spirituality to mental health: Review of evidence and practical guidelines. *Brazilian Journal of Psychiatry*, *36*, 176–182. https://doi.org/10.1590/1516-4446-2013-1255

Morgan, J., & Sandage, S. J. (2016). A developmental model of interreligious competence. *Archive for the Psychology of Religion*, *38*(2), 129–158. https://doi.org/10.1163/15736121-12341325

Myers, J. E., & Williard, K. (2003). Integrating spirituality into counselor preparation: A developmental, wellness approach. *Counseling and Values*, *47*(2), 142–155. https://doi.org/10.1002/j.2161-007X.2003.tb00231.x

Narayanasamy, A. (1999). Learning spiritual dimensions of care from a historical perspective. *Nurse Education Today*, *19*(5), 386–395. https://doi.org/10.1054/nedt.1999.0325

Nissen, R. D., Falkø, E., Stripp, T. K., & Hvidt, N. C. (2021). Spiritual needs assessment in post-secular contexts: An integrative review of questionnaires. *International Journal of Environmental Research and Public Health*, *18*(24), 12898. https://doi.org/10.3390/ijerph182412898

Noh, Y.-E., & Shahdan, S. (2020). A systematic review of religion/spirituality and sport: A psychological perspective. *Psychology of Sport and Exercise*, *46*, 101603. https://doi.org/10.1016/j.psychsport.2019.101603

Nye, M. (2019). Decolonizing the study of religion. *Open Library of Humanities*, *5*(1). https://doi.org/10.16995/olh.421

Oman, D. (2013). Defining religion and spirituality. In R. F. Paloutzian, & C. L. Park (Eds.), *Handbook of the psychology of religion and spirituality* (2nd ed., pp. 23–47). New York: Guilford.

Oman, D. (2018a). Model of individual health effects from religion/spirituality: Supporting evidence. In D. Oman (Ed.), *Why religion and spirituality matter for public health: Evidence, implications, and resources* (pp. 27–63). Cham, Switzerland: Springer International. https://doi.org/10.1007/978-3-319-73966-3_3

Oman, D. (Ed.). (2018b). *Why religion and spirituality matter for public health: Evidence, implications, and resources*. Cham, Switzerland: Springer International. https://doi.org/10.1007/978-3-319-73966-3

Oman, D. (2025a). Mindfulness for global public health: Critical analysis and agenda. *Mindfulness*, *16*(3), 573–612. https://doi.org/10.1007/s12671-023-02089-5

Oman, D. (2025b). Reply: The PHIOMM framework for implementing mindfulness in public health, with groundwork. *Mindfulness*, *16*(3), 752–782. https://doi.org/10.1007/s12671-025-02553-4

Oman, D. (2025c). What is a mantra? Guidance for practitioners, researchers, and editors. *American Psychologist*. https://doi.org/10.1037/amp0001368

Oman, D., & Brown, T. T. (2018). Health policy and management, religion, and spirituality. In D. Oman (Ed.), *Why religion and spirituality matter for public health: Evidence, implications, and resources* (pp. 191–210). Cham, Switzerland: Springer International. https://doi.org/10.1007/978-3-319-73966-3_11

Oman, D., Flinders, T., & Thoresen, C. E. (2008). Integrating spiritual modeling into education: A college course for stress management and spiritual growth. *The International Journal for the Psychology of Religion*, *18*(2), 79–107. https://doi.org/10.1080/10508610701879316

Oman, D., Hedberg, J., & Thoresen, C. E. (2006). Passage meditation reduces perceived stress in health professionals: A randomized, controlled trial. *Journal of Consulting and Clinical Psychology*, *74*(4), 714–719. https://doi.org/10.1037/0022-006X.74.4.714

Oman, D., & Paranjpe, A. C. (2018). Indian spirituality: How relevant is Pargament's framework? *Psychological Studies*, *63*(2), 140–152. https://doi.org/10.1007/s12646-017-0412-z

Oman, D., & Syme, S. L. (2018). Weighing the evidence: What is revealed by 100+ meta-analyses and systematic reviews of religion/spirituality and health? In D. Oman (Ed.), *Why religion and spirituality matter for public health: Evidence, implications, and resources* (pp. 261–281). Cham, Switzerland: Springer International. https://doi.org/10.1007/978-3-319-73966-3_15

Oman, D., & Thoresen, C. E. (2005). Do religion and spirituality influence health? In R. F. Paloutzian, & C. L. Park (Eds.), *Handbook of the psychology of religion and spirituality* (pp. 435–459). New York: Guilford.

Osler, W. (1910). The faith that heals. *British Medical Journal, 1*(2581, June 18), 1470–1472. https://doi.org/10.1136/bmj.1.2581.1470

Oswalt, S. B., Lederer, A. M., Chestnut-Steich, K., Day, C., Halbritter, A., & Ortiz, D. (2020). Trends in college students' mental health diagnoses and utilization of services, 2009–2015. *Journal of American College Health, 68*(1), 41–51. https://doi.org/10.1080/07448481.2018.1515748

Paget, N. K., & McCormack, J. R. (2006). *The work of the chaplain*. Valley Forge, PA: Judson.

Pargament, K. I. (1997). *The psychology of religion and coping: Theory, research, practice*. New York: Guilford.

Pargament, K. I. (2013). *APA handbook of psychology, religion, and spirituality (2 vol.) (vol. 1: Context, theory, and research; vol. 2: An applied psychology of religion and spirituality)*. Washington, DC: American Psychological Association.

Pargament, K. I. (2023). From research to practice: Three waves in the evolution of the psychology of religion and spirituality. *Spiritual Psychology and Counseling, 8*(3), 207–225.

Pargament, K. I., Oman, D., Pomerleau, J., & Mahoney, A. (2017). Some contributions of a psychological approach to the study of the sacred. *Religion, 47*(4), 718–744. https://doi.org/10.1080/0048721X.2017.1333205

Patel, E., & Giess, M. E. (2016). Engaging religious diversity on campus: The role of student affairs. *About Campus, 20*(6), 8–15. https://doi.org/10.1002/abc.21223

Paulsen, A. E. (1926). Religious healing: Preliminary report [series]. *Journal of the American Medical Association, 86*(20), 1519–1524, 1617–1623, 1692–1697.

Pawar, B. S. (2009a). Individual spirituality, workplace spirituality and work attitudes: An empirical test of direct and interaction effects. *Leadership & Organization Development Journal, 30*(8), 759–777. https://doi.org/10.1108/01437730911003911

Pawar, B. S. (2009b). Workplace spirituality facilitation: A comprehensive model. *Journal of Business Ethics, 90*(3), 375–386. https://doi.org/10.1007/s10551-009-0047-7

Peccoud, D. (Ed.). (2004). *Philosophical and spiritual perspectives on decent work*. Geneva: International Labour Office.

Peng-Keller, S., Winiger, F., & Rauch, R. (2022). *The spirit of global health: The World Health Organization and the 'spiritual dimension' of health, 1946-2021*. Oxford: Oxford University Press. https://doi.org/10.1093/oso/9780192865502.001.0001

Peterson, C., & Seligman, M. E. P. (2004). *Character strengths and virtues: A handbook and classification*. Washington, DC: American Psychological Association.

Petersson, A., & Sandin, G. (2020). Interior design dilemmas in a shared room of silence. *Material Religion, 16*(2), 213–235. https://doi.org/10.1080/17432200.2020.1722899

Pew Research Center (2015, April 2). *The future of world religions: Population growth projections, 2010-2050; why Muslims are rising fastest and the unaffiliated are shrinking as a share of the world's population*. Washington, DC: Pew Research Center.

Pew Research Center (2018, May 29). *Being Christian in western Europe*. Washington, DC: Pew Research Center.

Pew Research Center (2023). *Spirituality among Americans*. Washington, DC: Pew Research Center.

Pfeffer, J. (2003). Business and the spirit: Management practices that sustain values. In R. A. Giacalone, & C. L. Jurkiewicz (Eds.), *Handbook of workplace spirituality and organizational performance* (pp. 29–45). Armonk, NY: M.E. Sharpe.

Plummer, D. B. (1996). Chaplaincy: The greatest story never told. *Journal of Pastoral Care, 50*(1), 1–11. https://doi.org/10.1177/002234099605000101

Poncin, E., Brandt, P.-Y., Rouiller, F., Drouin, M., & Dandarova Robert, Z. (2020). Mapping the healthcare chaplaincy literature: An analytical review of publications authored by chaplains and theologians between 2000 and 2018. *Journal of Health Care Chaplaincy, 26*(1), 16–44. https://doi.org/10.1080/08854726.2019.1593722

Puchalski, C., Ferrell, B., Virani, R., Otis-Green, S., Baird, P., Bull, J., Chochinov, H., Handzo, G., Nelson-Becker, H., Prince-Paul, M., Pugliese, K., & Sulmasy, D. (2009). Improving the quality of spiritual care as a dimension of palliative care: The report of the consensus conference. *Journal of Palliative Medicine*, *12*(10), 885–904. https://doi.org/10.1089/jpm.2009.0142

Puchalski, C. M., Blatt, B., Kogan, M., & Butler, A. (2014). Spirituality and health: The development of a field. *Academic Medicine*, *89*(1), 10–16. https://doi.org/10.1097/acm.0000000000000083

Quilling, E., Kruse, S., Kuchler, M., Leimann, J., & Walter, U. (2020). Models of intersectoral cooperation in municipal health promotion and prevention: Findings from a scoping review. *Sustainability*, *12*(16), 6544. https://doi.org/10.3390/su12166544

Radin, D., Schlitz, M., & Baur, C. (2015). Distant healing intention therapies: An overview of the scientific evidence. *Global Advances in Health and Medicine*, *4*(1_suppl), gahmj.2015.2012.suppl. https://doi.org/10.7453/gahmj.2015.012.suppl

Ransome, Y. (2020). Religion, spirituality, and health: New considerations for epidemiology. *American Journal of Epidemiology*, *189*(8), 755–758. https://doi.org/10.1093/aje/kwaa022

Rao, K. R., Paranjpe, A. C., & Dalal, A. K. (Eds.). (2008). *Handbook of Indian psychology*. New Delhi: Cambridge University Press India. https://doi.org/10.1017/UPO9788175968448

Reay, T., & Hinings, C. R. (2009). Managing the rivalry of competing institutional logics. *Organization studies*, *30*(6), 629–652. https://doi.org/10.1177/0170840609104803

Richards, P. S., & Bergin, A. E. (1997). *A spiritual strategy for counseling and psychotherapy*. Washington, DC: American Psychological Association.

Richards, P. S., & Bergin, A. E. (2014). *Handbook of psychotherapy and religious diversity* (2nd ed.). Washington, DC: American Psychological Association.

Rose, K. (2016). *Yoga, meditation, and mysticism: Contemplative universals and meditative landmarks* (1 ed.). London: Bloomsbury. https://doi.org/10.5040/9781474297837

Rosmarin, D. H., & Koenig, H. G. (Eds.). (2020). *Handbook of spirituality, religion, and mental health* (2nd ed.). San Diego. https://doi.org/10.1016/B978-0-12-816766-3.00012-4

Salcone, S. G., Currier, J. M., Hinkel, H. M., Pearce, M. J., Wong, S., & Pargament, K. I. (2023). Evaluation of spiritual competency training in mental health (sct-mh): A replication study with mental health professionals. *Professional Psychology: Research and Practice*, *54*(5), 336–341. https://doi.org/10.1037/pro0000525

Saler, B. (2000). *Conceptualizing religion: Immanent anthropologists, transcendent natives, and unbounded categories*. New York / Oxford: Berghahn.

Sarath, E. (2003). Meditation in higher education: The next wave? *Innovative Higher Education*, *27*(4), 215–233. https://doi.org/10.1023/A:1024072313202

Schaefer, L., Sams, T., & Lux, J. (2016). Saved, salvaged, or sunk:A meta-analysis of the effects of faith-based interventions on inmate adjustment. *The Prison Journal*, *96*(4), 600–622. https://doi.org/10.1177/0032885516650883

Schensul, J. J., & Trickett, E. (2009). Introduction to multi-level community based culturally situated interventions. *American Journal of Community Psychology*, *43*(3-4), 232–240. https://doi.org/10.1007/s10464-009-9238-8

Schnell, T., & Keenan, W. J. F. (2013). The construction of atheist spirituality: A survey-based study. In H. Westerink (Ed.), *Constructs of meaning and religious transformation current issues in the psychology of religion* (pp. 101–118). Göttingen, Germany: Vienna University Press.

Seligman, M. E. P., & Csikszentmihalyi, M. (2000). Positive psychology: An introduction. *American Psychologist*, *55*(1), 5–14. https://doi.org/10.1037//0003-066X.55.1.5

Sepper, E. (2017). Zombie religious institutions. *Northwestern University Law Review*, *112*(5), 929–988.

Shafranske, E. P. (Ed.). (1996). *Religion and the clinical practice of psychology*. Washington, DC: American Psychological Association.

Shealy, C., Bullock, M., & Kapadia, S. (Eds.). (2023). *Going global: How psychologists can meet a world of need*. Washington: American Psychological Association. https://doi.org/10.1037/0000311-000

Simmer-Brown, J., & Grace, F. (Eds.). (2011). *Meditation and the classroom: Contemplative pedagogy for religious studies*. Albany, NY: SUNY Press.

Singh, K., Raina, M., & Oman, D. (2023a). Positive psychology and Hinduism. In E. B. Davis, E. L. Worthington, & S. Schnitker (Eds.), *Handbook of positive psychology, religion, and spirituality* (pp. 195–209): Springer. https://doi.org/10.1007/978-3-031-10274-5_13

Singh, K., & Saxena, G. (Eds.). (2023). *Religious and spiritual practices in India: A positive psychological perspective*. Singapore: Springer. https://doi.org/10.1007/978-981-99-2397-7

Singh, P., Misra, G., Kapur, P., Mishra, A. K., & Siddiqui, R. (2023b). Towards deciphering shared spaces among religious groups in contemporary Indian society: Some illustrations and challenges. *Social Change*, *53*(4), 469–485. https://doi.org/10.1177/00490857231203413

Sisemore, T. A., & Knabb, J. J. (Eds.). (2020). *The psychology of world religions and spiritualities: An indigenous perspective* West Conshohocken, PA: Templeton Press.

Sprik, P. J. (2019). The depersonalization of medicine, and the promises of spiritual care. *Society*, *56*(2), 147–152. https://doi.org/10.1007/s12115-019-00342-z

Srinivasan, M., Kaplan, E., & Dahl, A. (2019). Reasoning about the scope of religious norms: Evidence from Hindu and Muslim children in India. *Child Development*, *90*(6), e783–e802. https://doi.org/10.1111/cdev.13102

Star, S. L. (2010). This is not a boundary object: Reflections on the origin of a concept. *Science, Technology, & Human Values*, *35*(5), 601–617. https://doi.org/10.1177/0162243910377624

Star, S. L., & Griesemer, J. R. (1989). Institutional ecology, 'translations' and boundary objects: Amateurs and professionals in berkeley's museum of vertebrate zoology, 1907-39. *Social Studies of Science*, *19*(3), 387–420. https://doi.org/10.1177/030631289019003001

Stegenga, J. (2011). Is meta-analysis the platinum standard of evidence? *Studies in History and Philosophy of Science Part C: Studies in History and Philosophy of Biological and Biomedical Sciences*, *42*(4), 497–507. https://doi.org/10.1016/j.shpsc.2011.07.003

Stevenson, D. H., Eck, B. E., & Hill, P. C. (Eds.). (2007). *Psychology & Christianity integration: Seminal works that shaped the movement*. Batavia, IL: Christian Association for Psychological Studies.

Stout, L. A. (2012). *The shareholder value myth: How putting shareholders first harms investors, corporations, and the public* (1st ed. ed.). San Francisco: Berrett-Koehler.

Strawbridge, W. J., Cohen, R. D., Shema, S. J., & Kaplan, G. A. (1997). Frequent attendance at religious services and mortality over 28 years. *American Journal of Public Health*, *87*(6), 957–961. https://doi.org/10.2105/AJPH.87.6.957

Super, S., Klerkx, L. W. A., Hermens, N., & Koelen, M. A. (2020). A multilevel transition perspective on embedding intersectoral action in local health policies. *Health Promotion International*, *36*(4), 1050–1061. https://doi.org/10.1093/heapro/daaa131

Swinkels, M. (2020). How ideas matter in public policy: A review of concepts, mechanisms, and methods. *International Review of Public Policy*, *2*(3), 281–316. https://doi.org/10.4000/irpp.1343

Takooshian, H., Gielen, U. P., Plous, S., Rich, G. J., & Velayo, R. S. (2016). Internationalizing undergraduate psychology education: Trends, techniques, and technologies. *American Psychologist*, *71*(2), 136–147. https://doi.org/10.1037/a0039977

Taylor, C. (2007). *A secular age*. Cambridge, MA: Belknap Press of Harvard University Press. https://doi.org/10.4159/9780674044289

Thornton, P. H., Ocasio, W., & Lounsbury, M. (2012). *The institutional logics perspective foundations, research, and theoretical elaboration*. Oxford: Oxford University Press.

Timmins, F., Caldeira, S., Murphy, M., Pujol, N., Sheaf, G., Weathers, E., Whelan, J., & Flanagan, B. (2018). The role of the healthcare chaplain: A literature review. *Journal of Health Care Chaplaincy*, *24*(3), 87–106. https://doi.org/10.1080/08854726.2017.1338048

Tobin, J. (2012). *The right to health in international law*. Oxford: Oxford University Press. https://doi.org/10.1093/acprof:oso/9780199603299.001.0001

Toussaint, L., Webb, J. R., & Keltner, W. (2012). Religion, spirituality, and mental health. In J. Aten, K. O'Grady, & E. L. Worthington (Eds.), *The psychology of religion and spirituality for clinicians: Using research in your practice* (pp. 331–356). New York, NY: Routledge.

Triandafyllidou, A., & Magazzini, T. (Eds.). (2021). *Routledge handbook on the governance of religious diversity*. Routledge. https://doi.org/10.4324/9781003083405

Tuggle, M. B. (2000). *It is well with my soul: Churches and institutions collaborating for public health*. Washington, DC: American Public Health Association.

van Ingen, R., Peters, P., De Ruiter, M., & Robben, H. (2021). Exploring the meaning of organizational purpose at a new dawn: The development of a conceptual model through expert interviews. *Frontiers in Psychology*, *12*. https://doi.org/10.3389/fpsyg.2021.675543

Vanderstraeten, R. (2023). Niklas luhmann on religion and secularisation. In R. Rogowski (Ed.), *The anthem companion to Niklas Luhmann* (pp. 93–110). London: Anthem Press. https://doi.org/10.2307/jj.766968.9

VanderWeele, T. J., Jackson, J. W., & Li, S. (2016). Causal inference and longitudinal data: A case study of religion and mental health. *Social Psychiatry and Psychiatric Epidemiology*, *51*(11), 1457–1466. https://doi.org/10.1007/s00127-016-1281-9

Vedula, S. B., & Agrawal, R. K. (2024). Mapping spiritual leadership: A bibliometric analysis and synthesis of past milestones and future research agenda. *Journal of Business Ethics*, *189*(2), 301–328. https://doi.org/10.1007/s10551-023-05346-8

Vieten, C., & Lukoff, D. (2022). Spiritual and religious competencies in psychology. *American Psychologist*, *77*(1), 26–38. https://doi.org/10.1037/amp0000821

Vieten, C., Scammell, S., Pilato, R., Ammondson, I., Pargament, K. I., & Lukoff, D. (2013). Spiritual and religious competencies for psychologists. *Psychology of Religion and Spirituality*, *5*(3), 129–144. https://doi.org/10.1037/a0032699

Wachholtz, A. B., & Pargament, K. I. (2005). Is spirituality a critical ingredient of meditation? Comparing the effects of spiritual meditation, secular meditation, and relaxation on spiritual, psychological, cardiac, and pain outcomes. *Journal of Behavioral Medicine*, *28*(4), 369–384. https://doi.org/10.1007/s10865-005-9008-5

Wahlbeck, K. (2015). Public mental health: The time is ripe for translation of evidence into practice. *World Psychiatry*, *14*(1), 36–42. https://doi.org/10.1002/wps.20178

Waller, S. N. (2012). Workplace chaplaincy. In W. J. Rothwell, & R. K. Prescott (Eds.), *The encyclopedia of human resource management* (pp. 443–447). San Francisco, CA: Pfeiffer. https://doi.org/10.1002/9781118364741.ch83

Waller, S. N., Huffman, L. T., & Hardin, R. L. (2016). The sport chaplain's role in the holistic care model for collegiate athletes in the United States. *Practical Theology*, *9*(3), 226–241. https://doi.org/10.1080/1756073X.2016.1221642

Walsh, R. (2015). What is wisdom? Cross-cultural and cross-disciplinary syntheses. *Review of General Psychology*, *19*(3), 278–293. https://doi.org/10.1037/gpr0000045

Webb, J. R. (2021). *Understanding forgiveness and addiction: Theory, research, and clinical application*. Milton: Taylor and Francis. https://doi.org/10.4324/9780429200274

Webb, J. R., Toussaint, L., & Dula, C. S. (2014). Ritualistic, theistic, and existential spirituality: Initial psychometric qualities of the RiTE measure of spirituality. *Journal of Religion and Health*, *53*(4), 972–985. https://doi.org/10.1007/s10943-013-9697-y

Wendt, S., Hipps, J., Abrams, A., Grant, J., Valosek, L., & Nidich, S. (2015). Practicing transcendental meditation in high schools: Relationship to well-being and academic achievement among students. *Contemporary School Psychology*, *19*(4), 312–319. https://doi.org/10.1007/s40688-015-0066-6

Witte, J., Jr. (2010). American religious liberty in international perspective. In D. Davis (Ed.), *The Oxford handbook of church and state in the United States* (pp. 404–422). New York, NY: Oxford University Press. https://doi.org/10.1093/oxfordhb/9780195326246.003.0016

Wixwat, M., & Saucier, G. (2021). Being spiritual but not religious. *Current Opinion in Psychology*, *40*, 121–125. https://doi.org/10.1016/j.copsyc.2020.09.003

Wolf, T., & Feldbauer-Durstmüller, B. (2023). New insights into workplace chaplaincy. *Review of Managerial Science*, *17*(4), 1147–1173. https://doi.org/10.1007/s11846-022-00553-5

World Health Organization (1998). *WHOQOL and spirituality, religiousness and personal beliefs (SRPB)*. Geneva, Switzerland: World Health Organization, Social Change and Mental Health Cluster.

World Health Organization (2013). *Mental health action plan 2013-2020*. Geneva: World Health Organization. https://www.who.int/publications/i/item/9789241506021

World Health Organization (2020). *Basic documents: Forty-ninth edition (including amendments adopted up to 31 May 2019)*. Geneva: World Health Organization. https://apps.who.int/gb/bd/

World Health Organization & ExpandNet (2010). *Nine steps for developing a scaling-up strategy*. Geneva, Switzerland: World Health Organization. https://iris.who.int/handle/10665/44432

World Health Organization & Finland Ministry of Social Affairs and Health (2014). *Health in all policies: Helsinki statement. Framework for country action*. Geneva: World Health Organization. https://iris.who.int/handle/10665/112636

Worthington, E. L., Hook, J. N., Davis, D. E., & McDaniel, M. A. (2011). Religion and spirituality. *Journal of Clinical Psychology*, *67*(2), 204–214. https://doi.org/10.1002/jclp.20760

Wuthnow, R. (1998). *After heaven: Spirituality in America since the 1950s*. Berkeley, CA: University of California Press.

Yamada, A.-M., Subica, A. M., Kim, M. A., Van Nguyen, K., Lim, C. S., & Mancuso, L. L. (2014). State of spirituality-infused mental health services in Los Angeles county wellness and client-run centers. *Administration and Policy in Mental Health and Mental Health Services Research*, *41*(6), 835–844. https://doi.org/10.1007/s10488-014-0536-6

Zinnbauer, B. J., & Pargament, K. I. (2005). Religiousness and spirituality. In R. F. Paloutzian, & C. L. Park (Eds.), *The handbook of the psychology of religion and spirituality* (pp. 21–42). New York: Guilford.

Part II

A Foundation for Understanding the Science of Spirituality, Health, and Well-Being

Chapter 4

The Psychology of Faith

James M. Nelson[*]

Faith is an endemic word in our culture, particularly for individuals who adhere to religious traditions. It is also an important concept for psychologists. A quick literature search using the PsycINFO and MEDLINE databases reveals hundreds of articles, book chapters, monographs, and dissertations on faith, particularly as it relates to other concepts of importance to psychologists like health or well-being. However, little has been written about what a psychology of faith *is* and how it ought to be conducted. Ultimately, what we mean by "psychology of faith" depends on what we mean by the terms "psychology" and "faith." A deconstruction of these terms using concepts from the philosophy of science can provide a good theoretical basis and practical suggestions for building a psychology of faith.

The Meaning of Psychology as a Science

In most of the Western tradition, psychology has been understood to refer to the systematic study of the psyche (Greek *psuche*) or soul (Latin *anima* or *animus*) and its powers, development, and characteristics. However, since the mid-19th century, this traditional definition has been abandoned in favor of newer, narrower understandings. While articles seldom, if ever, are explicit about their definition of psychology, most use versions of the following, often seen in introductory psychology textbooks: *psychology is the scientific study of human behavior*. This narrowing of methodological approach was a response to epistemological skepticism that became prominent after Descartes, as well as a desire to emulate the successful advance of knowledge taking place in the natural sciences. With this new definition, the meaning of "psychology" in a "psychology of faith" is heavily dependent on our understanding of what it means to have a "scientific" study of faith.

An immediate issue that comes to the fore when considering a scientific study of faith is that scientific inquiry, whether narrowly or broadly constituted, depends upon a set of assumptions made by the investigator. These assumptions are of four types (Nelson & Slife, 2024). *Ontological and metaphysical assumptions* are especially important and deal with our understanding of the nature of the world and how it works. In contemporary psychology, a fundamental assumption made by investigators is that of naturalism, that is, that the things we study behave in a lawlike manner similar to things we examine in the natural sciences, and that they can be understood mechanistically, that is, processes can be broken down into their constituent parts and studied (cf. Rea, 2002). The emphasis is on the nomothetic over the idiographic (Gorsuch, 2002).

* Corresponding Author: Jim.Nelson@valpo.edu.

DOI: 10.4324/9781003440048-6

Other types of assumptions are also important. *Ethical assumptions* touch on the values underlying the research; for instance, who is the research for, and who should benefit from it? In typical psychological research, quite a bit of attention is paid to avoiding harm, but relatively little attention is given to how research will benefit the persons being studied. Often, it is the investigator or the scholarly community that is the primary beneficiary. *Epistemological and methodological assumptions* cover pre-understandings of the investigator about what we can learn about something and how we can do it. For instance, psychologists typically assume that our methods are very adaptable, so that the same kind of quantitative confirmatory approach used to study memory problems in traumatic brain injury can be applied to the study of faith or well-being with a simple change of instruments. A final important assumption in this area is that scientific psychology, like the rest of science, is a cumulative enterprise, continuously acquiring better knowledge through an epistemological cycle of discovery and confirmation. All of these assumptions have deep impacts on research but are seldom made explicit by investigators; in fact, many researchers may be unaware of these assumptions and their effects.

These assumptions pose a series of dilemmas for an investigator attempting to study faith, because the typically accepted assumptions in psychology can create conflicts. The *ontological assumptions* of naturalism and mechanism, with their emphasis on the nomothetic, raise issues because many individuals and communities for whom faith is important have views of strong transcendence, holism, and particularity of effect that are inescapably idiographic and thereby in direct conflict with the assumptions of researchers. Very understandably, researchers want to draw general conclusions from their work, but their rejection of the basic worldview of the people they study introduces the potential for bias (Slife & Reber, 2009; Slife & Whoolery, 2006). This problem also becomes part of broader *ethical assumption* issues. If researchers reject fundamental beliefs of the people being studied, how can these people be expected to benefit from the research, other than by requiring them to set aside their core ideals? How can participants as well as researchers benefit from the work? In terms of *epistemological and methodological assumptions*, investigators understandably would like to use methods and concepts that are familiar to them and other psychologists. Commonly, researchers combine a naturalistic agenda with assumptions based on positivism that call for a psychology based on universal definitions and quantitative methods reminiscent of those used in the natural sciences. However, is this kind of positivistic naturalism (PN) appropriate for a psychology of faith? Are there important aspects of the topic that cannot be captured by quantitative studies? Does the use of well-used psychological concepts (e.g., well-being) inhibit the use of new concepts and the discovery phase of the scientific epistemological cycle (Nelson & Slife, 2024)? In-depth and open discussions of these questions are needed.

Meanings of Faith

As with the term "psychology," the term "faith" is largely undefined in the literature that seeks to study it. Out of the hundreds of articles reviewed for this study, perhaps one in fifty attempts a clear definition of what they mean by faith. Sometimes the study has no obvious meaning for the term as it is used, and the reader is left guessing at its sense from its common meanings or the article context (e.g., Arnold, 2021), while other times it is used in a generic sense as an expression of confidence in something (e.g., Hirshbein, 2020). Frequently, authors will use terms and phrases like "faith traditions" (e.g., Koenig et al., 2020; Johnstone et al., 2012), "faith practices" (e.g., Boehm & Carter, 2019), "faith communities" (e.g., Wang, 2021), or "faith-based" programs (e.g., Connerton & Theuri, 2023), where the term faith appears to be a cipher for religion. Sometimes the link to religion is made explicit in expressions like "religious faith," but the specific meaning of faith is left undefined (e.g., Li et al., 2022). Often, faith is used in a kind of cognitive sense as an assent to the truth value of certain ways of thinking (e.g., Saide et al., 2021), which facilitates an understanding of "faith" that goes beyond religious or spiritual contexts. Also common are articles that appear to use faith in multiple senses at different points. Furthermore, attempts made to define faith are not always successful. For instance, Colenda & Blazer (2022) offer an excellent discussion of the components that might go into a construct, but never offer a firm definition of it, so it is difficult to evaluate the appropriateness of the measurement areas they suggest. In an exhaustive survey of the terms faith, religion, and spirituality *as used in the literature*, Harris and his colleagues (2018) appear to conclude that faith is simply a term that encompasses religion and spirituality but has no separate meaning. However, an examination of the essential characteristics of these terms found in their literature survey reveals that there are a number of characteristics of faith that are not included as part of religion and spirituality, and vice versa, calling into question their definition and understanding of the concepts. When studies differ in their definition of the concept, their results cannot be compared with each other, derailing the scientific epistemological cycle that allows for cumulative progress toward understanding a topic.

The Nature of Definition

In order to correct this problem, it is helpful to start at the beginning and pose the question: What does it mean to define and name something? This is an issue productively explored in the philosophy of science and language. How we think about definition will depend on whether or not we believe the thing in question is a *natural kind*, that is, an object, grouping, or category of things that has a mind-independent reality (Nelson, 2022). These are the sorts of things that we presumably deal with in science. There are two approaches to natural kind definitions. In *essentialist* groupings or categories, the items in the group are thought to possess similar essential properties. For example, hydrogen as an element might be considered a natural kind with mind-independent boundaries, but "courage" is perhaps not so mind-independent and is much more an interpretive judgment. Presumably, for these mind-independent categories, it is possible to develop "rigid designators" that provide stable references to the thing being described (Kripke, 1980). Thus, language can be developed by a community (e.g., of researchers) to refer to these universal, mind-independent realities (LaPorte, 2004, 2010). *Structuralist* definitions define objects based on their relationship to other objects, an approach that is fruitful in an established field with knowledge of these relationships but inappropriate for new areas of investigation, such as a psychology of faith. Related to this approach, complex factor analytic and structural equation procedures can be used to "prove" the reliability and validity of certain concepts and measurement procedures. These are certainly a step forward from our current situation. However, here we run into the philosophy of science issue of *underdetermination* (Nelson & Slife, 2024), which points out that such analyses can only tell us if particular conceptual structures and measurement procedures are *possible* because they are internally consistent, but not if they are the *only or best way* of viewing the topic. Such analyses can thus serve to obscure conceptual problems and our ignorance of a topic.

The traditional approach in psychology, based on a PN philosophy of science, attempts to provide universal definitions of terms that can lead to clear measurement procedures. A well-thought-out universal definition is certainly superior to the present state of affairs. However, the dilemma here is that universal definitions contain their own limitations. Many authors in the philosophy of science and language (e.g., Quine, 1969; Hacking, 1991) have pointed out difficulties in defining natural kinds based on the supposed essential similarity of items in a group. Any time we attempt to make this kind of definition, we find unusual cases that don't fit a standard definition. This leads us to broaden our definition, making it so thin and vague that it has no practical meaning, or we can treat the category as a description of an exemplar that may be difficult or impossible to find. Another issue is that the meaning of supposedly rigid designators varies by degrees and is, in fact, not consistent but varies by context (Besson, 2010; cf. Mumford, 2005). For example, the phrase "good faith" has a certain set of meanings in a religious context and a different set of meanings in a legal matter or business contract. The more universal we make our definition, the more it can become overly thin or unable to capture contextual usages.

Definition and Authority

As noted above, definitions and references are decisions that are typically made by a community. So, with reference to a psychology of faith, what is the community that should do the defining and naming? In psychological research, typically, the researcher or a research community does the defining. Presumably, this allows for agreement on the nature of a term, a prerequisite for generating a research program with comparable studies leading to cumulative gains in knowledge. However, this approach carries with it its own dilemmas.

The Researcher-Centric Definition

The classic positivist statement justifying researcher-centric definitions of terms related to religion was made by James Leuba, the early 20th-century psychologist of religion. Leuba (1925) argued that religion can be explained on a completely naturalistic basis as a psychological phenomenon, and that as a result, research should depend upon the judgment of psychological experts, not "ignorant" religious practitioners or theologians. Any research depending on individuals with religious convictions would be "hopelessly biased and blind," so research needed to be conducted by those who were free of religious convictions (Leuba, 1912, p. 275).

While presumably unbiased and operating from a justifiably privileged position, the dilemma is that researcher-centric definitions can carry with them their own kinds of bias and limitations. Certainly, if the definition of the investigator varies considerably from its meaning to the people being studied, the usefulness of the research becomes questionable.

The Participant-Centric Definition

Thick, specific definitions based on the views of the community being studied offer an interesting alternative. They provide an opportunity to expand our thinking to a more diverse point of view that encompasses concepts from a variety of groups and traditions. The participant-centric definition has long been championed by qualitative researchers (e.g., Hennink et al., 2020). Qualitative procedures like grounded theory are particularly valuable as they help generate new ideas about constructs, which can later be tested in confirmatory research. Fortunately, there is an increasing tradition within faith research toward the use of qualitative methods (e.g., Ochieng et al., 2021). As scientists, we are interested in studying *natural kinds*, things that have a mind-independent reality. Following the understandings of the people we study helps ensure that our research has some degree of mind-independence from the investigator.

How would individuals in religious traditions define faith? A full discussion is beyond the scope of this essay, but we can sketch out some ideas from two influential religious traditions: Christianity and Buddhism.

Faith in Christianity

When we consider the Christian concept of faith, we can begin by focusing on the meaning of the words "faith" or to "have faith" (Greek *pistis*, *pisteuo*) as they first appear in the Koine Greek of the Bible's New Testament. These terms have a rich linguistic and cultural background. The complexity of the Christian faith concept revolves around four predominant themes. It is (1) part of a holistic package, (2) a way of life, (3) intensely relational in nature, and (4) individually particular.

Holistic

In the New Testament, faith (*pistis*) is viewed as "the constitution of the Christian life" (Bultmann, 1968, p. 222). Because it is so foundational, it is impossible to separate the concept of faith from other aspects of Christianity, such as hope and love (Augustine, 2014, 1.15, 1.37–1.39). In Eastern Christianity, the first comprehensive summary of Christian beliefs and practices written by John of Damascus (1958) was simply titled *An exact exposition of the orthodox faith* (*ekdosis akribas tas orthodoxou pisteos*). In the Catholic tradition, Thomas Aquinas held to a deep holism, arguing, for instance, that charity as love in practice is simply the form of faith (*forma fidei*) by which we are helped on our journey toward the enjoyment of God (Aquinas, 2018, II-II Q1A1, Q4A3). Given this holism, attempts to separate variables like faith-based beliefs and virtues (e.g., Schuurmans-Stekhoven, 2011) seem misguided and unlikely to be meaningfully fruitful in examinations of Christian faith.

Way of Life

Given this holistic understanding of faith, it is not surprising that faith was viewed not as merely a set of isolated beliefs but as a way or manner of life (Augustine, 2014, 2.9): Christians "will live by faith" (*ek pisteos zasetai*; Heb 10:38; Rom 1:17). It is a constantly changing "radical re-orientation to God which governs the whole of life and changes how we live it" (Bultmann, 1968, p. 216), a "basic attitude of life which determines all detailed conduct" (p. 220), and a renunciation of the world and acceptance of a new life that is more real than the old one (pp. 223–224). This way of life includes a belief or attitudinal component, a confidence (*hypostasis*) or assurance (*elegchos*) in what is hoped for but unseen (Heb 11:1). A living faith then goes beyond this into action, for "faith without works is worthless" (*pistis chorus ton ergon arge estin*; Jam 2:20). Although faith is more than intellectual belief, there is a reciprocal relationship between faith and knowledge, where knowledge of what God has done for us begins with faith, and faith becomes knowledge as it builds us toward a new self-understanding: a life – and subsequently self – characterized by the same motives, actions, and priorities as Christ (cf. Bultmann, 1968, pp. 218, 227).

Relationship

Faith is not an abstract quality but involves a relationship. It is a faith in Christ Jesus (*pistin … en Christo Iasou*; Col 1:4) that is a gift from God (*theou to doron*; Eph 2:8). Or as Aquinas (2018, I-II Q62A2) puts it, the object of faith is God himself (*ipse Deus*), who by nature is our final end (*ultimus rerum finis*). In this relationship, faith is required to please God, and we can trust that God will, in turn, reward us (Heb 11:1, 6). Faith means that God is *my God* in a personal sense.

Particularity

Faith is not a unitary concept that looks the same in everyone; rather, it is particular to the individual in their life. Faith is distributed by God (Rom 12:3), and each Christian has their own unique function (Rom 12:4) and set of gifts (Rom 12:6). Thus, while there is a nomothetic quality to Christian faith, there is also an inherently idiographic aspect of it. This parallels a point made by Gordon Allport: "Individuality is not the residual ragbag left over after the nomothetic sciences have had their say. The organization of the individual life is first, last, and all the time a primary fact of human nature" (Allport, 1961, p. 15).

Faith in Buddhism

A convenient scientific hope would be that we could find a definition for faith that would cut across religious traditions, allowing for a universal category that could be used in research. However, this does not seem likely. For instance, looking at the Buddhist tradition, it is clear that some important meanings of faith differ substantially from those in Christianity, and that even within Buddhism, one finds significant divergences (Brankhorst, 2010).

Faith is also important in Buddhism, although its meaning is often subtly different from the Christian concept. Early Theravada Buddhism tends to treat faith as belief in a set of teachings that will lead to salvation, like the Four Noble Truths. In early Buddhist texts (e.g., Nanamoli & Bodhi, 1995), faith (Pali *saddhā*) is a realization, belief, and trust in the Buddha and his teachings that allows one to become a faith follower (*saddhanusari*) who can then progress on the first stages of the Buddhist path (McKeon, 1989). The emphasis in this understanding of faith is more about belief or confidence in doctrine with subjective power (Gokhale, 1980) and less about a way of life or relationship, contrary to the Christian view. Faith is a tool that can be discarded when one has grown past the point of needing it (Burford, 1990). However, relationality is not totally absent in some Buddhist groups and aspects of the tradition. Buddhists, particularly in the Theravada tradition, will have faith in the Three Jewels of *Buddha*, *dharma* (truth or doctrine), and *sangha* (community). Varieties of Mahayana Buddhism introduce the concept of the *bodhisattva*, an individual who has achieved enlightenment but retains a connection to our level of existence in order to help others. In later Buddhism, the theme recurs that faith involves right belief and is an entry into the Buddhist path (Dogen, 2002). However, there is sometimes an increasing emphasis on a relational component to faith. Some Buddhists can speak of a "Pure Land faith devoted to Amitabha" Buddha (Ingram, 2019, p. 175; Inagaki & Stewart, 2006). However, the non-theistic and non-Christological nature of Buddhism means that the relationships described have a somewhat different character than those envisioned by Christian understandings of faith.

Compounding the Problem: Faith and Spirituality, Health, or Well-Being

Ultimately, many psychologists will be interested in faith as a way of exploring its relationship with other interesting constructs and desirable goals such as health and well-being. Many of the scientific and definitional issues encountered with regard to the concept of faith are also important for the use and understanding of other key concepts like "spirituality," "health," or "well-being."

Spirituality

Spirituality is an important construct in modern culture that has a huge influence in some branches of psychology. In the psychological literature, it is often defined as "*the experiential and personal side of our relationship to the transcendent or sacred*," or in the context of religious communities as "*the living reality of religion as experienced by an adherent of the tradition*" (Nelson, 2009, p. 8; cf. Dykstra, 1986). However, there are dilemmas to its use.

The first dilemma has to do with the thinness of the definition and the lack of consensus about its exact meaning. Harris and colleagues found a total of 20 discernible characteristics of "spirituality" as the concept was used in the research literature, which they then condensed down into the following definition: "*a faith concept referring to a search for the sacred involving a relationship with an ultimate concern that is in some way meaningful*" (Harris et al., 2018, p. 14) – a somewhat thin and vague definition for a rich concept (cf. Ellor & McGregor, 2011). Not surprisingly, the variety of conceptual features has led to a multiplicity of measurement procedures. Over 10 years ago, Monod et al. (2011) found 35 different instruments being used to measure spirituality in relation to health outcomes! Given the breadth of the concept and how it is measured, it is not surprising that in the current literature, there does not appear to be a consistent understanding of how faith relates to spirituality. For instance, Byron and Miller-Perrin (2009) refer to spirituality as an aspect of faith, but Papaleontiou-Louca and colleagues (Papaleontiou-Louca et al., 2023) see faith as an expression of spirituality. Still others would distinguish the two, with spirituality relating to a particular kind of experience and faith as a type of belief.

A second dilemma is that since spirituality is not a native concept in traditions like Christianity or Buddhism, the relevance of a researcher-centric definition may be limited. Consider, for instance, the RiTE definition and model of spirituality considered in this current volume (see Chapters 1 and 44; see also Webb et al., 2014). Webb and his colleagues divide spirituality into three basic types: Ritualistic, Theistic, and Existential. How would a Christian understanding of faith fit within this framework? While aspects of Christian faith fit within the "Ritualistic" category, faith in this tradition is much more than "structured connection with a deity." However, at times it does involve structure and so is more than a Theistic "non-structured connection with deity." The Existential issues of "meaning and purpose" are surely of interest to faith in the Christian context, but consideration of these things as "transcendent" but "non-theistic" would not make sense within a faith context. Nor would faith necessarily fit within a general category of spirituality when defined as "the salient, searching pursuit of the transcendently sacred ritualistic, theistic, and/or existential aspects of the human condition" (pp. 973–974), for faith is about a relationship more than the pursuit of particular goals. This is not to say that people of faith do not find such pursuits important or even necessary, or that the idea of spirituality cannot be recognized in religious communities as important to them, just that important aspects of faith cannot be reduced to them.

Health and Well-Being

A vast, longstanding, and interesting literature in the philosophy of medicine exists that points out divergences and difficulties in definitions of health. Most scholars have negative definitions of health as the absence of illness or a departure from natural function causing life decline (Boorse, 2011), while others offer positive definitions like a state that allows us to pursue vital goals (Nordenfelt, 2007, 2014). Many scholars reject the idea of a universal definition of health because the concept is inherently value-laden (Engelhardt, 1974; Fulford, 2004; Fulford & Colombo, 2004). Ereshefsky (2009; Ereshefsky & Reydon, 2015) argues that at a minimum, investigators should be explicit about the values that underlie their understandings of concepts and the motivating principles that lie behind any classificatory schedule used in a research study.

The concept of well-being is a powerful and useful construct in research, but unfortunately, like health, there is no single agreed-upon meaning to the concept, and it is rarely explicitly defined in the literature (Anderson et al., 2011). Almost ten years ago, Linton and colleagues (2016) found 99 different measures of well-being in use, covering some 196 different dimensions! Traditionally, definitions of well-being have been of two types: a *hedonic* approach often focused on feelings, and a *eudaemonic* approach that sees well-being as related to virtue. The feeling approach to well-being is often taken in the faith literature, as in the study by Sharma & Singh (2019), even though the purpose of the study was to focus on positive virtues, not feelings. Historically, the concept of well-being traces back to the Aristotelian idea of *eudaimonia*, often translated as "happiness" but actually referring to a particular way of life, not a feeling (Nelson & Canty, 2023). The distinction between health and well-being is also fuzzy, as the term well-being is often used in some contemporary definitions of health, although the meaning of well-being is left undefined (Larsen, 2022).

A Circular Firing Squad

From a philosophy of science standpoint, the task of defining faith so that it can be studied presents a series of problems and dilemmas, which in the past have been solved by investigators in different ways. Studies on "faith" done by Researcher A and Researcher B may not be directly comparable, depending on how they define terms and approach the topic. Unfortunately, the same situation seems to hold with concepts like spirituality, health, and well-being. When we attempt to carry out studies involving several of these constructs, it is likely that we have multiple terms with varying meanings. This produces compounding effects that make it impossible to compare research findings and accumulate them in a way that allows science to progress. Instead of a cumulative scientific enterprise, one has a circular firing squad kind of effect where theoretical differences between investigators lead to divergent findings, undermining each other's work. It is entirely likely that frequently commented upon differences in studies relating faith or spirituality to health or well-being may be due in part to this circular firing squad effect.

Implications and Future Directions

A look at the current status of the psychology of faith reveals a gloomy current situation with exciting possibilities. Researchers obviously hold important assumptions that underlie their work, but seldom articulate and justify them to their readers. Especially concerning, the meanings of fundamental concepts in their work largely remain mysterious. When combined with equally undefined or vague concepts, a research program loses its progressive character and becomes a circular firing squad. Faith is an exciting concept with important relationships to health and wellness. We can and should do better than this.

Broad definitions are surely an improvement over this rather embarrassing state of affairs. The RiTE model (Webb et al., 2014) offers a view of what this might look like for the concept of spirituality. Presumably, such a definition could also be written for the concept of faith. There are certainly benefits from broad, all-encompassing definitions of terms. But no one should be under any illusions that such definitions do not also have their drawbacks and limitations. Broad definitions can be so broad that they lose the specific meaning necessary for a concept that can support the progressive nature of science. Also at issue is the ethical concern that the concept defined by us may have no meaningful benefit or relevance to the people we study.

What is essential in the way forward? At a minimum, researchers need to embrace the epistemic virtues of openness and humility. In the traditional positivist-naturalist philosophy of science, researchers pretend that they offer a superior "view from nowhere" à la Leuba, but in fact, we are deeply constrained by the presuppositions that underlie our work. It is customary in the psychology academic empirical literature to include reflections on the limitations of a study in the discussion section of the paper. Papers looking at the intersection between faith, spirituality, health, and well-being should do no less and can use that opportunity to discuss their framework and how it affects their work. Humility calls us to the possibility that we can learn from the people we study and that our conceptual structures should be informed by their wisdom, experience, and points of view. Conducting research using concepts that benefit the people we study should be a moral and ethical priority for us.

In a psychology of faith, researchers must engage the theoretical and conceptual issues discussed in this paper in their thinking and writing so that their readers can understand the presuppositions, limitations, and possibilities of their research. Otherwise, a true psychology of faith will never develop.

References

Allport, G. (1961). *Pattern and growth in personality*. Holt, Rinehart & Winston.

Anderson, P., Jane-Llopis, E., & Cooper, C. (2011). The imperative of well-being. *Stress and Health*, *27*(5), 353–355. https://doi.org/10.1002/smi.1433

Aquinas, T. (2018). *Summa theologiae* (L. Shapcote, Trans.). Aquinas Institute. (Original work written c. 165–1273 CE)

Arnold, P. (2021). The value of grounded faith in mental illness. *Journal of Psychiatric Mental Health Nursing*, *28*(2), 261–263. https://doi.org/10.1111/jpm.12636

Augustine. (2014). *Teaching Christianity (De Doctrina Christiana)* (E. Hill, Trans.). New City. (Original work written 296–426 CE)

Besson, C. (2010). Rigidity, natural kind terms, and metasemantics. In H. Beebee & N. Sabbarton-Leary (Eds.), *The semantics and metaphysics of natural kinds* (pp. 25–45). Routledge.

Boehm, T. & Carter, E. (2019). Facets of faith: Spirituality, religiosity, and parents of individuals with intellectual disability. *Intellectual and Developmental Disabilities*, *57*(6), 512–526. https://doi.org/10.1352/1934-9556-57.6.512

Boorse, C. (2011). Concepts of health and disease. In F. Gifford (Ed.), *Handbook of philosophy of science, Volume 16: Philosophy of medicine* (pp. 13–64). North Holland. https://doi.org/10.1016/B978-0-444-51787-6.50002-7

Brankhorst, J. (2010). On the genesis of Buddhism in its historical context: Proprium and definition vis-à-vis Hindu traditions and Jainism. In J. Brankhorst & A. Bsteh (Eds.), *Buddhism questioning Christianity: Lectures, questions, interventions* (pp. 151–196). St. Gabriel Publications.

Bultmann, R. (1968). The πίστις group in the New Testament. In G. Kittel & G. Friedrich (Eds.) & G. Bromiley (Ed. & Trans.), *Theological dictionary of the New Testament*, Vol. 6 (pp. 203–228). Wm. B. Eerdmans.

Burford, G. (1990). Believing and seeing: The roles of faith, reason, and experience in Theravada Buddhism. *Horizons*, *17*(2), 217–227. https://doi.org/10.1017/S036096690002017X

Byron, K. & Miller-Perrin, C. (2009). The value of life purpose: Purpose as a mediator of faith and well-being. *The Journal of Positive Psychology*, *4*(1), 64–70. https://doi.org/10.1080/17439760802357867

Colenda, C. & Blazer, D. (2022). Review of religious variables in advance care planning for end-of- life care: Consideration of faith as a new construct. *American Journal of Geriatric Psychiatry*, *30*(7), 747−758. https://doi.org/10.1016/j.jagp.2021.11.014

Connerton, C. & Theuri, S. (2023). NEWSTART: An 8-week faith-based health promotion program to reduce chronic disease risk factors in the US. *Journal of Religion and Health*, *62*, 3175–3187. https://doi.org/10.1007/s10943-023-01849-w

Dogen. (2002). Bendowa. In N. Waddell & M. Abe (Trans.), *The heart of Dogen's* Shobogenzo.(pp. 7–30). State University of New York. (Original work written 1231 CE)

Dykstra, C. (1986). Youth and the language of faith. *Religious Education*, *81*:163–184. https://doi.org/10.1080/0034408600810202

Ellor, J., & McGregor, J. (2011). Reflections on the words "religion," "spiritual well-being," and "spirituality". *Journal of Religion, Spirituality & Aging*, 23:275–278. https://doi.org/10.1080/15528030.2011.603074

Engelhardt, Jr., H. T. (1974). Explanatory models in medicine: facts, theories, and values. *Texas Reports on Biology and Medicine*, *32*(1), 225–239.

Ereshefsky, M. (2009). Defining 'health' and 'disease.' *Studies in History and Philosophy of Biological and Biomedical Sciences*, *40*(2), 221–227. https://doi.org/10.1016/j.shpsc.2009.06.005

Ereshefsky, M. & Reydon, T. (2015). Scientific kinds. *Philosophical Studies*, *172*(4), 969–986. https://doi.org/10.1007/s11098-014-0301-4

Fulford, K. W. M. (2004). Facts/values: Ten principles of values-based medicine. In J. Radden (Ed.), *The philosophy of psychiatry: A companion* (pp. 205–234). Oxford. https://doi.org/10.1093/acprof:oso/9780195149531.003.0017

Fulford, K. W. M., & Colombo, A. (2004). Six models of mental disorder: A study combining linguistic-analytic and empirical methods. *Philosophy, Psychiatry, and Psychology*, *11*(2), 129–144. https://doi.org/10.1353/ppp.2004.0051

Gokhale, B. (1980). *Bhakti* in early Buddhism. *Journal of Asian and African Studies*, *15*(1–2), 16–28. https://doi.org/10.1177/002190968001500102

Gorsuch, R. L. (2002). The pyramid of sciences and of humanities. *American Behavioral Scientist*, *45*(12), 1822–1838. https://doi.org/10.1177/0002764202045012005

Hacking, I. (1991). A tradition of natural kinds. *Philosophical Studies*, *61*(1–2), 109–126. https://doi.org/10.1007/BF00385836

Harris, K., Howell, D., & Spurgeon, D. (2018). Faith concepts in psychology: Three 30-year definitional content analyses. *Psychology of Religion and Spirituality*, *10*(1), 1–29. https://doi.org/10.1037/rel0000134

Hennink, M., Hutter, I., & Bailey, A. (2020). *Qualitative research methods* (2nd ed.). Sage.

Hirshbein, L. (2020). Religion and spirituality, meaning, and faith in American psychiatry from the 19th to the 21st Century. *Journal of Nervous and Mental Disease*, *208*(8), 582–586. https://doi.org/10.1097/NMD.0000000000001191

Inagaki, H., & Stewart, H. (Trans.). (2006). *The three Pure Land sutras* (2nd Rev. Ed.). BDK. (Original work written 2nd-5th cent. CE)

Ingram, E. (2019). Chogens vision of Todaijis Great Buddha as both Mahavairocana and Amitabha. *Japanese Journal of Religious Studies*, *46*(2), 173–192. https://doi.org/10.18874/jjrs.46.2.2019.173-192

John of Damascus. (1958). The orthodox faith. In F. Chase Jr. (Trans.), *Writings* (pp. 165–406). Catholic University of America. (Original work written c. 8th cent. CE)

Johnstone, B., Yoon, D. P., Cohen, D., Schopp, L. H., McCormack, G., Campbell, J. & Smith, M. (2012). Relationships among spirituality, religious practices, personality factors, and health for five different faith traditions. *Journal of Religion and Health*, *51*(4), 1017–1041. https://doi.org/10.1007/s10943-012-9615-8

Koenig, H., Al-Zaben, F. & VanderWeele, T. (2020). Religion and psychiatry: recent developments in research. *BJPsych Advances*, *26*(5), 262–272. https://doi.org/10.1192/bja.2019.81

Kripke, S. (1980). *Naming and necessity*. Harvard.

LaPorte, J. (2004). *Natural kinds and conceptual change*. Cambridge.

LaPorte, J. (2010). Theoretical identity statements, their truth, and their discovery. In H. Beebee & N. Sabbarton-Leary (Eds.), *The semantics and metaphysics of natural kinds* (pp. 104–124). Routledge.

Larsen, L. (2022). Not merely the absence of disease: A genealogy of the WHO's positive health definition. *History of the Human Sciences*, *35*(1), 111–131. https://doi.org/10.1177/0952695121995355

Leuba, J. (1912). *A psychological study of religion: Its origin, function and future*. Macmillan.

Leuba, J. (1925). *The psychology of religious mysticism*. Harcourt, Brace.

Li, L., Lou, X., & Bond, M. H. (2022). Societal emphasis on religious faith as a cultural context for shaping the social-psychological relationships between personal religiosity and well-being. *Journal of Cross-Cultural Psychology*, *53*(3–4), 306–326. https://doi.org/10.1177/00220221221079875

Linton, M.-J., Dieppe, P., & Medina-Lara, A. (2016). Review of 99 self-report measures for assessing well- being in adults: exploring dimensions of well-being and developments over time. *BMJ Open*, *6*(7), e010641. https://doi.org/10.1136/bmjopen-2015-010641

McKeon, J. (1989). Faith-content of Theravada: The national religion of Ceylon (Sri Lanka). *Journal of Dharma*, *14*(1), 37–47.

Monod, S., Brennan, M., Rochat, E., Martin, E., Rochat, S. & Bula, C. (2011). Instruments measuring spirituality in clinical research: A systematic review. *Journal of General Internal Medicine*, *26*(11), 1345–1357. https://doi.org/10.1007/s11606-011-1973-5

Mumford, S. (2005). Kinds, essences, powers. *Ratio: An International Journal of Analytic Philosophy*, *18*(4), 420–436. https://doi.org/10.1111/j.1467-9329.2005.00303.x

Nanamoli, B. & Bodhi, B. (Trans.). (1995). *The middle-length discourses of the Buddha: A new translation of the Majjhima Nikaya*. Wisdom Publications. (Original work written c. 5th-6th cent. CE)

Nelson, J. (2009). *Psychology, Religion, and Spirituality*. Springer.

Nelson, J. (2022). Carving the joints: The ontology and epistemology of natural kinds in psychology. In B. Slife, S. Yanchar, and F. Richardson (Eds.), *The Routledge international handbook of theoretical and philosophical psychology* (pp. 130–148). Routledge. https://doi.org/10.4324/9781003036517-9

Nelson, J. & Canty, N. (2023). Positive psychology and the psychology of religion and spirituality in historical perspective. In W. Davis, E. Worthington, & S. Schnitker (Eds.), *Handbook of positive psychology, religion, and spirituality* (pp. 21–36). Springer. https://doi.org/10.1007/978-3-031-10274-5_2

Nelson, J. & Slife, B. (2024). Theoretical and epistemological foundations. In L. Miller (Ed.), *Oxford handbook of psychology and spirituality* (2nd ed., pp. 22-48). Oxford.

Nordenfelt, L. (2007). The concepts of health and illness revisited. *Medicine, Health Care and Philosophy*, *10*(1), 5–10. https://doi.org/10.1007/s11019-006-9017-3

Nordenfelt, L. (2014). On the notion of health as ability. *Scandinavian Journal of Occupational Therapy*, *21*(1), 48–52. https://doi.org/10.3109/11038128.2014.952902

Ochieng, C., Minion, J., Turner, A., Blell, M., & Murtagh, M. (2021). What does engagement mean to participants in longitudinal cohort studies? A qualitative study *BMC Medical Ethics*, *22*, 77. https://doi.org/10.1186/s12910-021-00648-w

Papaleontiou-Louca, E., Esmailnia, S., & Thoma, N. (2023). Spirituality of the developing person according to Maslow. *New Ideas in Psychology*, 69:1–13. https://doi.org/10.1016/j.newideapsych.2022.100994

Quine, W. (1969). Natural kinds. In W. V. Quine, *Ontological relativity and other essays* (pp. 114–138). https://doi.org/10.7312/quin92204-006

Rea, M. (2002). *World without design: The ontological consequences of naturalism*. Oxford.

Saide, A., McCaffree, K. & Richert, R. (2021). Does "faith" in science correlate with indicators of well-being? Journal of Cognition and Culture, 21(1-2), 178–199. https://doi.org/10.1163/15685373-12340102

Schuurmans-Stekhoven, J. (2011). Is it God or just the data that moves in mysterious ways? How well-being research may be mistaking faith for virtue. *Social Indicators Research*, *100*(2), 313–330. https://doi.org/10.1007/s11205-010-9630-7

Sharma, S., & Singh, K. (2019). Religion and well-Being: The mediating role of positive virtues. *Journal of Religion and Health*, *58*(1), 119–131. https://doi.org/10.1007/s10943-018-0559-5

Slife, B., & Reber, J. (2009). Is there a pervasive implicit bias against theism in psychology? *Journal of Theoretical and Philosophical Psychology*, *29*(2), 63–79. https://doi.org/10.1037/a0016985

Slife, B., & Whoolery, M. (2006). Are psychology's main methods biased against the worldview of many religious people? *Journal of Psychology and Theology*, 34(3), 217 – 231. https://doi.org/10.1177/009164710603400304

Wang, D. (2021). Where do we go from here? A call to the Christian mental health community to leverage the resources of science and faith for social action and community renewal. *Journal of Psychology and Christianity*, *40*(1), 78–83.

Webb, J., Toussaint, L., & Dula, C. (2014). Ritualistic, theistic, and existential spirituality: Initial psychometric qualities of the RiTE measure of spirituality. *Journal of Religion and Health*, 53, 972–985. https://doi.org/10.1007/s10943-013-9697-y

Chapter 5

An Introduction to the Sixth Major Dimension of Personality

The Numinous

Ralph L. Piedmont[*]

The psychology of religion and spirituality (PRS) is a vibrant field of endeavor that has been gaining in popularity for over 30 years with little apparent abatement in interest (e.g., Emmons & Paloutzian, 2003). Professionals from across the scientific disciplines are recognizing the value of religious and spiritual (R/S) constructs for addressing key psychological issues in the psychological lives of people. R/S qualities represent important aspects of who we are as people; in fact, some consider these qualities to be defining aspects of our species (Albright & Ashbrook, 2001). No doubt R/S constructs are important because they reflect important questions concerning existential ultimacy, such as "What happens to us after we die?" and "Does life carry an intrinsic meaning or is it all chaos?" Answers to these questions, and those like it, carry important implications for how individuals engage life and the issues they confront (e.g., Boyd & Zimbardo, 1997). Nonetheless, the field is stymied by a number of conceptual and empirical issues related to the definition of its constructs, inclusivity, and generalizability of findings. While some may believe that the field is unable to provide satisfying answers to these issues (e.g., Buss, 2002; Paloutzian & Park, 2021; Sloan, Bagiella, & Powell, 2001), I believe that science does have the tools to address these concerns and to empirically develop those processes that underlie humans' strong interest in religion and spirituality into a more relevant, universal psychological dimension. At the heart of this approach is the Five-Factor Model (FFM) of personality. Its inherent taxonomic structure can be useful for identifying potentially new, universal personality domains and for providing empirically explicit definitions for them. The purpose of this report is to outline the empirical criteria for developing such a construct and to present evidence supporting the existence of a new dimension of personality, termed *the Numinous*.

The Big Five and Beyond

Perhaps the most important empirical development in personality psychology has been the emergence of the FFM (Digman, 1990; McCrae & Costa, 2010). This model has shown itself to be quite robust, subsuming constructs from other personality models (see Piedmont, 1998),

* *Author Note*: The author would like to thank Drs. Martin Sherman, Jesse Fox, John Johnson, and Magda Żemojtel-Piotrowska for their comments on an earlier draft of this paper. Address correspondence regarding this paper to the author at The Center for Professional Studies, 9603 Deereco Road, #5334, Timonium, MD 21094, or via email at drralph@thecfps.com. None of the research studies cited here have, to the knowledge of this author, been preregistered in an independent, institutional registry. Conflict of Interest Statement: Dr. Piedmont receives royalties on the sale of the *Assessment of Spirituality and Religious Sentiments* (ASPIRES) scale and the *Numinous Motivation Inventory*.

DOI: 10.4324/9781003440048-7

generalizing across languages and cultures, being recoverable across information sources, predicting a wide array of salient psycho-social-clinical outcomes, and providing a rather comprehensive taxonomy of individual difference traits that have been traditionally viewed in psychology as personality dimensions (de Raad & Mlačić, 2017; McCrae et al., 2004; Miller, 1991; Penley & Tomaka, 2002; Piedmont, 1994; Piedmont, McCrae, & Costa, 1991). The FFM provided a powerful rebuttal to the many criticisms that had emerged concerning the value of trait psychology (e.g., Mischel, 1968). One strength of this model is that it is open-ended: what constitutes a dimension of personality is determined by empirical criteria. Because the FFM is not theory-driven, the potential exists for the model to evolve as new data become available.

The five dimensions comprising the FFM are a) *Neuroticism*, the tendency to experience negative emotions such as anxiety, depression, and hostility; b) *Extraversion*, the quantity and intensity of one's interpersonal interactions; c) *Openness*, the proactive seeking and appreciation of new experiences; d) *Agreeableness*, the quality of one's interpersonal interactions along a continuum from compassion to antagonism; and e) *Conscientiousness*, the persistence, organization, and motivation exhibited in goal-directed behaviors (Costa & McCrae, 1992). These dimensions have also been found to be extremely stable over the adult lifespan (Costa & McCrae, 1994) and have been shown to possess a strong genetic basis (Heath, Neale, Kessler, Eaves, & Kendler, 1992).

While these five personality domains are well-established, one question continues to remain: "Are there other dimensions of personality yet to be discovered?" (Becker, 1999; Saucier & Goldberg, 1998). In a series of studies by Goldberg and colleagues (e.g., Ashton, Lee, & Goldberg, 2004; Saucier & Goldberg, 1998), when looking beyond the five factors, other dimensions were found, including a factor labelled *Religiousness* (Ashton et al., 2004). Ashton et al. (2004, p. 719) concluded, "Religiosity can now be added to the diverse array of seventh factors that have emerged, additional to the six widely replicated dimensions, within seven-factor solutions derived from personality-descriptive terms." While these authors noted that religiousness was considered a personality domain in other models (e.g., Clonninger, Svrakic, & Przybeck, 1993; Piedmont, 1999), they believed religiosity to be different from the other FFM domains, and thus to fall outside of the domain of personality proper. Their reasons were that religiousness is based on a system of beliefs and social attitudes and that it is influenced by environmental forces to a greater extent than is found for the FFM domains. Nonetheless, Ashton et al. also noted (p. 719), "Most researchers would probably agree that Religiosity is a very important dimension of individual differences."

The Case for Religiousness as a Personality Dimension

Unlike the other individual-difference variables that have turned up in the various lexical analyses, R/S issues are potentially more valuable. R/S represents the varying efforts of people to address the most important issues of life, including ontology (why are we here? Where have we come from?), epistemology (Is there intrinsic meaning to life?), and eschatology (Where are we going? What is our ultimate purpose and goal?). These are important questions that psychology needs to address systematically in its work. The ultimate success of research in this area will depend on the social science's ability to create empirically satisfying constructs that provide nonredundant insights into functioning that are falsifiable.

A large literature has developed outlining the role and relevance of R/S constructs for understanding a truly varied number of outcomes, including coping, mental health/well-being, life satisfaction, interpersonal style, vocational interests, physical health, and many more (see Koenig, McCullough, & Larson, 2001; Miller, 2012; Paloutzian & Park, 2013; Pargament, 2013). The value of these constructs for psychotherapy has long been noted, and numerous volumes have appeared that outline methods and techniques for including R/S constructs in treatment (Pargament, 2007; Richards & Bergin, 1997; Worthington, Johnson, Hook, & Aten, 2013). It is unusual to find a single construct that has such broad predictive breadth.

Nonetheless, the mainstream field tends to view this area in a monolithic manner, using the term "religiosity" to refer to all things R/S. While this term was an accepted perspective, the avalanche of research in this area has allowed for a greater parsing of the term. Today, it is more common to recognize that there is a difference between religiosity (the preferred term in the field is now religiousness) and spirituality. The data seem to indicate that these terms capture different types of phenomena, and it has been argued that disaggregating the two terms will provide more precision to the research (Seeman, Dubin, & Seeman, 2003).

Based on a series of studies, Piedmont and colleagues (e.g., Piedmont, Mapa, & Williams, 2006; Piedmont, Hassinger et al., 2007) have demonstrated that spirituality and religiousness, while overlapping, represent distinct psychological processes. Spirituality was seen to represent a personality trait that captured individuals' efforts at creating a broad sense of personal meaning within an eschatological context. In other words, knowing that we are eventually going to die, spirituality represents our motivations to create a viable sense of meaning and purpose for the lives we are leading (Piedmont, Ciarrocchi, Dy-Liacco, & Williams, 2009). Religiousness, on the other hand, is conceptualized as a "sentiment," which reflects emotional tendencies that develop out of social traditions and educational experiences (Woodworth, 1940). Sentiments, like love, gratitude, and patriotism, do not represent innate, genotypic qualities like spirituality. That is why the expression of sentiments can and does vary across cultures and time periods.

Using Structural Equation Modeling (SEM) analyses, Piedmont et al. (2009) demonstrated that Religiousness and Spirituality are best conceptualized as correlated constructs (the latent disattenuated correlation between them was $\Phi = .71$). Other SEM analyses in this study also demonstrated that the model that postulated spirituality as being the causal precedent over religiousness was the best-fitting model. These structural findings were replicated in both self and observer data and in the United States and Filipino samples. Hierarchical multiple regression analyses, controlling for the FFM personality domains and each of these constructs, indicated that religiousness was a better predictor of scores on scales related to sexual and moral attitudes (e.g., erotophilia vs. erotophobia; attitudes toward abortion), while spirituality did not uniquely correlate with these outcomes. Further, religiousness was found to be a significant negative predictor of negative affect, while spirituality was independent. Spirituality was significantly positively related to positive affect, while religiousness was orthogonal. These findings indicate that there is empirical value to disaggregating these two terms by separating those aspects of belief that are based on personal ideologies (religiousness) from those that are hypothesized to be organismically motivated (spirituality). The psychological distinctiveness between these two constructs has been replicated across studies using international samples and experimental designs (e.g., Piotrowski & Żemojtel-Piotrowska, 2024; Żemojtel-Piotrowska, Piotrowski, & Sawicki, 2021).

Wilson (1978) outlined the evolutionary significance of religiousness as a mechanism that enables survival by encouraging people to subordinate their own needs to the larger interests of the group. There is growing evidence of the genetic basis of spirituality and religiousness. Steger, Hicks, Krueger, and Bouchard (2011) have shown that there is a substantial genetic component to one's spiritual beliefs and behaviors, suggesting that our spirituality arises from needs hard-wired into our genetic makeup (see also Bouchard, McGue, Lykken & Tellegen, 1999; Kirk, Eaves, & Martin, 1999). Newberg, D'Aquili, and Rause (2001) have detailed the neurological mechanisms and structures that appear to be the supporting foundation for the Numinous. Griffiths, Richards, McCann, and Jesse (2006) have demonstrated how specific pharmacological agents (i.e., psilocybin) can directly affect and enhance spiritual experiences. Clearly, there are specific evolutionary-based, neuro-anatomical, and physiological systems that have been identified as foundational to our existential experiences.

Allport (1950) has argued that religiousness represents a "master motive" that organizes all other aspects of personality because it represents our longest-ranged intentions. Building on this idea, Frankl made it clear that the heart of spirituality represents our ultimate sense of meaning and purpose, which provides an all-encompassing understanding of self in relation to all things understood. As Frankl (1959, pp. 102–103) noted, "Man is the only being which is able to transcend himself, to emerge above the level of his own psychic and physical conditions. By this very fact man enters, nay he even creates a new dimension, the dimension of noetic processes—call them spiritual groping or moral decisions—*in contrast to psychic processes in general*" [italics added]. There is a long psychological tradition for viewing the Numinous as an essential element of psychological functioning (e.g., James, 1994; Jung, 1963; Maslow, 1971). More than just a learned set of values and beliefs, these existential dynamics have been viewed as representing core aspects of psychological growth and maturity.

Perhaps the most compelling reason to include R/S constructs is that they represent psychological qualities that are unique to the human experience (Albright & Ashbrook, 2001). Religion and spirituality are qualities that are essential parts of every culture, across all time periods. These qualities play a significant role in defining cultural identities, and they inform all aspects of a civilization, including laws, science, philosophy, and worldview. Unlike the FFM domains, which can be assessed in various animal species (e.g., Gosling & John, 1999; King & Figueredo, 1997), R/S issues are unique to the human species and are defining of it. There are no animal models for R/S processes, and no other species evidence these qualities (Piedmont & Wilkins, 2020). Examining our spiritual and religious selves is, therefore, a process of understanding the most intimate aspects of our own humanity. To not include or consider these constructs in any psychological model would render the model incomplete and leave a significant vacuum in our understanding of the key forces that shape and direct our species through time.

It is not surprising, then, to learn that the study of spirituality in general and of transcendence in particular has taken a major role in the area of positive psychology (Peterson & Seligman, 2004). This approach moves counterintuitively to traditional psychology and its focus on dysfunction. As Peterson and Seligman noted (2004, p. 4),

> When psychiatrists and psychologists talk about mental health, wellness, or well-being, they mean little more than the absence of disease, distress, and disorder…This handbook focuses on what is right about people and specifically about the strengths of character that make the good life possible.

Understanding what is "right" about humanity is itself a universal good and can offer hope and encouragement to all people. This perspective ought to be sufficient for investing more in this area.

Nonetheless, there are several structural and technical problems in this field that hamper its ability to demonstrate the tremendous value and power of R/S constructs. The lack of developed conceptual models, reliance on simple research designs, and an inability to consensually define its constructs all conspire to keep R/S research from a more central role in the field (Batson, 1997; Funder, 2002; Hill et al., 2000; Koenig, 2008; Piedmont, 2014; Paloutzian & Park, 2021). It would also be essential that any new personality dimension derived from R/S constructs be untethered from explicit theological/religious content and represent universal, human qualities. The value and relevance of these constructs would need to apply for use with all types of people, not just believers or people of faith. The goal would be to identify those basic motivations that make religion and spirituality so important to us as a species.

Fortunately, these problems are, ultimately, fixable issues. Science does have the methods and tools necessary to provide rigorous examinations of R/S constructs, identify their universal elements, and detail their value for both understanding people and for intervening in their lives. The FFM of personality offers a conceptual and empirical tool that can help develop, define, and validate Numinous constructs in a manner that makes them relevant and important for all people regardless of their religious affiliations (or lack of them) and cultural perspective. The remainder of this paper will focus on two issues. First, an overview of the Numinous and its associated psychological qualities will be provided. Second, the assumptions and methods that were used to bootstrap measures of spirituality into a sixth dimension of personality that meets the field's standards for psychometric rigor and psychological salience will be overviewed.

A Note on Terminology

The perspective being taken here represents a shift from the traditional R/S approach. Rather than creating a new R/S construct, the goal here is to bootstrap off this literature to create a new organismic variable that explains our interest in, and need for, concepts such as the sacred, God(s), religion, spirituality, and metaphysical ultimacy. This variable would be completely psychological in nature and focus on our ultimate, existential engagement with life. While existential issues are not new to psychology, the identification of an empirically robust construct would help to articulate and clarify better the types of motivations and their effects that individuals use to create coherence, depth, and wholeness for their lives. As a new motivational concept, it is necessary to have a new term that represents these dynamics. I prefer to use the term "*the Numinous.*" It is a useful term that has many advantages over current usage.

First, the term has clear existential value. It was used by Otto (1958) to reflect aspects of the mystical experience: the awe, wonder, emotional integration, and essential ineffability of encountering a transcendent reality. The term reflects the noetic qualities associated with ultimate meaning. Second, it is a term that has been used psychologically by Erik Erikson. The Numinous represents one of the positive outcomes experienced at the first stage of psychosocial development: trust versus mistrust. For Erikson, a child develops feelings of the Numinous (awesome, hallowed) as a result of a mother's care and reliable concern for the needs of her child. She promotes and supports her child's beginning sense of self-identity while also supporting the child's ability to transcend his/her fears of aloneness and separateness (Erikson, 1977). This usage of the term reveals that the Numinous has its roots in the very beginning of our psychological lives and its presence influences all future development. Social Axiom theory (Leung & Bond, 2004) has shown empirically the universal, fundamental importance of religiousness for how people interpret and make sense of their personal and social worlds. As will be outlined below, these qualities will become hypothesized essential features of the Numinous as outlined in its ontological model.

Finally, the term includes many different elements and underscores the reality that there are diverse parts to our existential perspective. Therefore, the Numinous represents a useful descriptive domain for organizing various aspects of spiritual functioning: there are elements of transcendence, spirituality, religiousness (e.g., the prayers we say and the rituals we perform), wonderment, and mysticism, among others (e.g., Harris et al., 2018). Yet, the Numinous represents a deeper, more fundamental dynamic that is based on our need to create a comprehensive, personally meaningful paradigm that can provide direction and personal value for the life being led. Ultimately, the Numinous allows us to become enmeshed in the fabric of life, creating profound connections with others that both actualize our abilities and can help us to transform the communities of which we are part. Ultimately, developing this construct within the FFM will identify three basic, correlated motivations that are understood to be at the core of the Numinous (e.g., Infinitude, Meaning, and Worthiness, defined below). The psychological pedigree of the term makes it more amenable to social scientists and does not involve any specific theological or metaphysical concepts. As such, this term will be used to refer to the new personality dimension.

Describing and Defining the Numinous in Personality

The Numinous enables individuals to create a broad understanding of the universe that includes an eternal psychological time perspective and a belief that one's life is only one stage in a larger ontological process. Boyd and Zimbardo (1997) demonstrated that this transcendental time perspective has a significant impact on psychological functioning and represents a unique quality not contained in the FFM. Psychological time is an essential element of the Numinous. Having a transcendent time perspective carries with it an understanding of a larger set of values and standards that supersede more common, secular models. This is what Frankl (1997; p. 68) has referred to as the *transcendent unconscious*. The ultimate values that flow from this perspective are understood to inspire our best capacities. Freed from perceived temporal constraints, individuals find the personal freedom to completely invest themselves in these larger concerns, such concerns being most centrally community-oriented. Thus, the Numinous individual understands personal fulfillment within a larger social context: care for community and the need to improve/transform community. Such individuals can go "all in" with these ultimate values, committing their lives to their work, without counting the personal costs of these efforts (examples of people with this perspective include Mother Theresa, Martin Luther King Jr., and Gandhi, among others).

It is the assumption of this model that the Numinous is a psychological quality that uniquely defines our species. It is a consequence of the exceptional cognitive powers that our species has (Baumeister, Bauer, & Lloyd, 2010). Our ability to think abstractly, broadly, and creatively on complex topics and ideas provides the neurological substrate to this motivation (Newberg et al., 2001). Our consciousness, which includes being self-aware as active agents, creates its own psychological space, encumbered with its own unique set of needs. These needs include 1) *Infinitude*: a desire to find durability for our actions, to know that despite being mortal our efforts will continue to bear fruit after we are gone; 2) *Meaning*: a demand to find purpose and cohesiveness to life. There need to be justifications for things that we do, the goals that we pursue, and the ultimate endings we seek; and, 3) *Worthiness*: a belief that while we may individually be imperfect, our involvement in life and our contribution to the human endeavor was "good enough." These three needs are the constituent elements of the Numinous drive (they are also the components of the *Numinous Motivation Inventory* [NMI; Piedmont,

2017], which is a validated measure of the Numinous). They work together synergistically, leading us to fully engage life and to put new value into it for the benefit of those both present and yet to come (Tillich, 2000). These are the qualities that arise from our powerful brains, which enable humans to be a species that is the least tied to instinctual scripts of any animal. The Numinous fills this void and allows us to deploy an almost limitless capacity to act in a manner that is directed toward, and of ultimate value for, the survivability of the species.

As individual differences constructs, the dimensions of Infinitude, Meaning, and Worthiness are essential existential concerns for all people. We all address and deal with these issues to various degrees in our lives. The Numinous motivates us to take broader perspectives on life's processes and to identify more connections with others and communities. Ultimately, a fully expressed Numinous motive impels us to consider our lives and actions within an eternal time frame. This perspective does not necessarily include a belief in a life after death (e.g., Comte-Sponville, 2008). Rather, it is a perspective that understands that our current actions carry consequences that may reverberate in life long after we have died. Levels of the Numinous are defined below.

Individuals with the lowest levels of the Numinous reflect an orientation toward life that Hart (2019, p. 20) referred to as hyparxeolatry (hī – PARKS – ē – ah – la – trē), "the worship of subsistence in and of itself, or the sort that misers and thieves and those who would never give their lives for others." Such individuals are not necessarily materialistic or narcissistic; rather, they value their lives as of ultimate importance and as such are not willing to risk harming or losing them under any circumstances. There is a strong self-focus here, as the object of concern is for personal safety and security. Such individuals move toward acquiring physical objects and/or organizations to provide the necessary material support and protection. There is also a recognition of the need to invest resources into personal growth and development in order to acquire additional material support for personal security.

As Numinous levels increase, the attention to external individuals and groups grows. There is a burgeoning sense of *social interest* that begins to develop. As the Numinous grows, people's attention begins to broaden from a strictly solipsistic perspective to include other people. These "others" can be caregivers or family members, individuals who can provide not only material, but also emotional support and succorance. There is a capacity to extend oneself in order to address the needs and issues of these other people/groups/communities because of the acknowledged value they have to the individual. Further, increases in the Numinous can motivate individuals to become more socially conscious and involved in larger civic groups, because these organizations are seen as providing useful resources and support for individuals in the community. This may involve taking social action in response to perceived community needs or financially supporting groups whose mission is seen as personally important. With higher levels of the Numinous, individuals may become donors who wish to provide levels of support to the community that may continue after they have died (see also McFarland, Brown, & Webb, 2013 and their psycho-moral construct, "Identification with all Humanity").

Still higher levels of the Numinous begin to support a more value-centered orientation to the world. Such individuals develop a commitment to larger ideals and values that have the potential for improving the perceived worlds of these people. These values begin to give a sense of personal definition and meaning. Emerging at this level is a *transpersonal perspective*, which includes developing a broad perspective on the patterns operating in nature through time. There is an appreciation of how human activities grow, develop, and become more complex. There is the recognition that this developed complexity exerts its own inertia through time. Acknowledging this underlying structure to the flow of life engenders a personal desire to know it, connect with it, and facilitate its unfolding. This view allows for an identification of a larger, transcendent moral/value system that these individuals come to align themselves with and in which they desire to participate. Their perspectives and understandings are holistic and inclusive, and their engagements with life reflect a universal acceptance and commitment to humanity. However, the goal of this involvement is to bring the individual closer to the ultimate reality they perceive.

At the highest level of Numinous motivation, individuals come to align themselves with the ultimate values and morals of the eternal perspective they take. These values become most salient in guiding the direction and content of their lives. Their moral conscience, based on these perceived eternal realities, becomes defining values for them and compels them to act in ways to provide goodness and compassion to those communities, however they define them, that are of most importance to them. These values de-emphasize personal needs for safety and security and boldly thrust them to care for the perceived needs of the world, wherever they may find it. This level is referred to as the *transformative* level because these individuals renounce the self-serving secular models in favor of those values that define their existence in the broadest possible terms. It is here that those high on the Numinous become agents of social transformation, putting all their energies into caring for and nurturing people and communities, articulating higher principles of collaboration and interpersonal engagement. Because these individuals believe that their current lives are merely one stage in a larger, ontological process, they can unreservedly commit themselves, and their lives, to reaching goals that may, at least in the span of their own lives, never be met. From this perspective, there is no need to count any personal costs to these commitments, because there is the belief that there will be other opportunities after the current life to acquire more things of value. The most salient feature of those who are high on the Numinous is the transformative sense of meaning they bring to life. There is a care and compassion for their community as well as a strong urge to work to move this group to a higher level of functioning that is characterized by greater inclusiveness, enhanced social justice, and more harmonious interpersonal dynamics.

The ultimate fruits of the Numinous include *dignity*, the belief in the unique value and importance of human life; *hope*, an underlying trust in the innate goodness of life; *justice*, the need for fairness and consistency in interpersonal relations; *abundance*, a feeling that one has sufficient personal resources to fulfill one's needs as well as to provide value and support to others; and *fulfillment (eudaimonia)*, an intrinsic experience of completeness that arises from a full engagement with life. The Numinous calls on people to give their very best to life and to be productive agents in the development of both personal and social potentials.

Empirical Criteria for Using the FFM to Develop the Numinous Domain

There are six empirical criteria that were identified as essential for determining whether the Numinous can be considered a useful sixth personality domain. Each will be discussed in turn.

The first, and most fundamental, criterion was that the Numinous represented an empirically distinct dimension from the domains of the FFM. What is most potentially valuable about a Numinous dimension is that it represents a new quality and not simply a combination of other Big 5 dimensions. This requirement is seen as one of the two key features that define a measure as being Numinous. The lack of orthogonality would indicate that a scale is merely a repackaged assessment of the extant FFM domains. As noted earlier, religiousness has repeatedly emerged as being independent of the FFM (Ashton et al., 2004). MacDonald

(2000) and Piedmont (1999) have also examined spiritual and religious constructs in relation to the FFM and found that they represented a distinct dimension. Webb and colleagues (e.g., Chang et al., 2015; Webb, Toussaint, & Dula, 2014) have provided data that support spirituality as a distinct element of psychological functioning independent of the FFM. They have shown that their three-dimensional model of spirituality was empirically separate from the FFM domains. Working from a biological approach to personality, Clonninger, Svrakic, and Przybeck (1993) have identified Self-Transcendence as an additional aspect of character distinct from other motivational constructs.

The second quality of a Numinous scale is that it evidences significant, incremental, predictive validity over the FFM. This is the second essential quality of a Numinous scale. It must be able to *add to* our understanding of important psycho-social-spiritual outcomes. Demonstrating incremental validity is conceptually essential for documenting the usefulness of a Numinous scale to show that the new scale provides nonredundant insights into important outcomes. Typically, in conducting incremental validity analyses, hierarchical multiple regression is used. On the first step of the analysis, all five personality domains are entered simultaneously, and then on step 2, the Numinous scales are added using a forward entry approach. Partial *F*-tests are then calculated to determine whether the Numinous scale(s) added significant additional explanatory variance in the outcome. Failure to demonstrate incremental validity would be conclusive evidence that a measure is not a Numinous variable. Typically, Numinous measures add between 3% and 8% additional variance (e.g., the *Assessment of Spirituality and Religious Sentiments* [ASPIRES; Piedmont, 2020] scale and the NMI [Piedmont, 2017]). Given that Numinous variables are being entered on the *sixth and later steps* (after the Big 5 domains), the magnitude of these values is quite a robust contribution (Nunnally & Bernstein, 1994; Hunsley & Meyer, 2003).

The third criterion concerns the breadth of the Numinous dimension. Like the other five personality domains, the Numinous ought to be sufficiently broad as to contain multiple facets. The Numinous is a distinct dimension of psychological functioning that incorporates a few linked qualities (e.g., Meaning-Making, Worthiness, and Transcendence) and is related to an array of outcomes (e.g., well-being, purpose in life, and mental health) that provide it with an extensive range of interpretive and predictive abilities. Allport (1950) considered the Numinous to be a master motive, a dynamic that organized and directed all other aspects of functioning. As such, it represents an aspect of functioning that has a pervasive impact on the mental system. Both the ASPIRES and NMI noted above contain three facet scales that assess various elements of this broad dimension (these facets were described above). Piedmont and Wilkins (2020) provided a detailed review of the development of both these instruments and illustrated how these facets, while all cohering on a single dimension, do have differential correlations with various outcomes.

The fourth criterion concerns the overall robustness of the construct, in that as a substantive aspect of functioning, it ought to be recoverable across multiple information sources (e.g., life outcome, observer ratings, self-reports, and test data). R/S constructs are frequently described as unique qualities of the individual, often stemming from personal experiences that are considered mystical or noetic (e.g., Hood & Chen, 2013; James, 1994). Such unique and personal experiences may give rise to solipsistic interpretations and understandings that may not necessarily find expression in behavior. Such personalized experiences defy categorization and assessment, given that the form, quality, and value of these transcendent experiences are different from person to person. If we assume that the Numinous represents a broad dimension of personality, then there must be some demonstration of the construct's consensual validity. In other words, it needs to be shown that self-reported scores on a scale agree with scores obtained from other information sources, such as knowledgeable observers. This cross-observer convergence provides assurance that the Numinous: a) is not a solipsistic construct but does find expression in behavior; b) the expression of Numinous qualities in behavior can be systematically identified by others; and c) such identification by others indicates that there is a general understanding of what constitutes Numinous functioning that is shared by a community or culture. Such broad consensus demonstrates the value of the construct as well as its importance for understanding people. The ASPIRES and NMI are the only R/S-type scales that have validated observer rater forms, and each scale has demonstrated cross-observer validity with the level of convergence as high as or higher than that typically found for the FFM domains (Piedmont & Wilkins, 2020). For example, the mean cross-observer agreement correlation (after z transformation) for the three ASPIRES Spiritual Transcendence facet scales is $r(981) = 0.45$ (Piedmont, 2020), while similar agreement for the FFM personality domains on the NEO PI-3 (after z transformation) is $r(250) = 0.43$ (McCrae & Costa, 2010).

The fifth criterion is concerned with the generalizability of the construct. If the Numinous is a universal aspect of psychological functioning, then it should be relevant for both describing people and predicting their behavior everywhere. This capacity is the antithesis of R/S constructs, which are limited to those for whom religious belief is important. As a dimension of personality, and one that is considered to be unique to humans, the Numinous needs to be shown as relevant to people across cultures, languages, and religious affiliations (or the lack of them). The ASPIRES has been found psychometrically robust across many languages, including Hungarian (Rican & Janosova, 2010), Polish (Piotrowski, Żemojtel-Piotrowska, Piedmont, & Baran, 2021), and Filipino (Tagalog; Pargament, 2007). It has also been found valid across faith groups, including various Christian, Jewish, Hindu, and Muslim faiths (Josanloo, 2012; Piedmont & Leach, 2002; Piedmont, Werdel, & Fernando, 2009). The NMI has been found useful in working with nontheists (Piedmont, Fox, & Toscano, 2020) and with economically marginalized people (Piedmont, Fox, & Copello, 2021).

The sixth, and final, criterion concerns the ultimate causal role that the Numinous plays in the mental lives of people. While Numinous constructs relate to a wide array of outcomes, the question to be answered is, "why these associations?" There are two possible answers. The least interesting answer is that Numinous variables represent outcomes from existing psychological processes. For example, an individual who is depressed may consequently have a negative view of God, believing that God is punishing him or her, or that God is just uninterested in the person. If the depression is remediated, the person feels happier and consequently has a more positive view of God. The second answer to this question has greater importance: Numinous variables serve as *inputs* into our psychological system. Our ultimate existential engagement has direct consequences for our psychological status. There is a growing literature demonstrating the causal precedence of the Numinous on levels of emotional and characterological adjustment (e.g., Piedmont, Fox, & Toscano, 2020; Piedmont, Town, & Hollwitz, 2023).

Using various causal modeling techniques (e.g., structural equation modeling [SEM] and cross-lagged panel analyses [CLPA]), evidence has been consistently accruing demonstrating that scores on Numinous scales uniquely and incrementally predict psychological outcomes. In a longitudinal study examining psychotherapeutic outcome among outpatient clients, Cheston, Piedmont, Eanes, and Lavin (2003) demonstrated using CLPA that changes in clients' images of God were more predictive of counselor ratings of symptom experience than the reverse. Using SEM analyses, Piedmont (2007) demonstrated the causal precedence of the Numinous on emotional well-being in both United States and Filipino samples. Most interestingly, Piedmont, Fox, and Toscano (2020) demonstrated that aspects of the Numinous were independent of the FFM (especially Neuroticism) and incrementally predictive of both emotional dysphoria and characterological impairment. These findings suggest that there is a second pathway mediating psychological distress in addition to Neuroticism (see also Fox & Piedmont, 2020). The value of these findings is that they open the door to an entirely new, universally relevant personality dimension that plays an important causal role in a number of key psychological processes, some of which have proven therapeutically challenging (e.g., substance misuse, Piedmont, 2004a), and may suggest new intervention strategies that can effectively resolve these issues.

The six criteria presented here offer a clear, methodological route for developing a new construct that contains important, nonredundant information from the FFM. Taken as a whole, the data support viewing the Numinous as an important sixth personality dimension and contains qualities that have been traditionally considered as personality. As a motivational construct, the Numinous unlocks new insights into functioning that carry the promise of a fuller understanding of our humanity and the potential for identifying new strategies for treatment.

Convergence with the RiTE Model of Spirituality

As was noted earlier in this chapter, the PRS is plagued by several critical conceptual and empirical issues that keep it from wider acceptance and involvement in the larger scientific community (e.g., Piedmont, 2014). It was for these reasons that the development of the Numinous model began with an appeal to the FFM. Its empirical structure allows for the identification of important, new personological motivations. It also stipulates specific empirical criteria for validly capturing these qualities. Yet while the field may be experiencing difficulties, it is exciting to note that there are more recent R/S models, being developed from different perspectives, that appear to be converging with the Numinous model presented here. One such model is the RiTE Model of Spirituality (Webb, Toussaint, & Dula, 2014; see also Chapters 1 and 44 of this volume). The RiTE model contains three measures of spirituality: Ritualistic, Theistic, and Existential. Nominally, these scales align with the three facets of the Numinous: Infinitude (similar to Theistic, which has items such as "I feel connected to a deity or deities" and "A deity or deities is/are at some time going to judge the rightness or wrongness of the actions of individuals"), Meaning (similar to Existential, contains items such as " I see life as a journey toward fulfillment" and "I believe that finding meaning and purpose in life is very important") and Worthiness (similar to Ritualistic and includes items such as, "I feel good after I attend organized worship services" and "I would not be good in the judgment of a deity or deities if I did not practice my faith as prescribed"). Thus, taking different conceptual approaches to understanding spirituality, both models appear to have identified similar content.

This approach makes some assumptions that are similar to those of the Numinous model. For example, the RiTE model identifies three scales because spirituality represents a diverse array of phenomena that cannot be contained by a single construct. Rather, a broader domain seems necessary. While Webb et al. interpret their RiTE scale to be multidimensional, it may be more efficacious to see it as multifaceted. The former indicates the presence of multiple, *independent* dimensions, while the latter indicates the presence of multiple, *correlated* facets that cohere on a single dimension. There are significant associations among the three scales that make it more likely to be a multifaceted scale. Further, the authors also recognized that there are nontheistic approaches to spirituality that also need to be included in any comprehensive spiritual model (e.g., Comte-Sponville, 2008). This is an implicit recognition that there may be more basic, universal motivational dynamics that impel people to address ultimate existential issues. In support of the assumption of uniqueness, Chang et al. (2015) demonstrated that the RiTE scales were distinguishable from the domains of the FFM. While there was some modest correlational overlap, regression analyses indicated that FFM scores were mostly orthogonal. Of the 48 obtained beta weights linking FFM scores to the three RiTE scales (12 beta weights for each analysis), only three of them were greater than 30! Dangel and Webb (2017) demonstrated that the RiTE scales' relationships to psychological pain were not mediated by social support, a variable frequently found to be a complete mediator of this effect (e.g., Salsman, Brown, Brechting, & Carlson, 2005). These findings support these scales as capturing a unique, broad psychological domain not overlapping with the FFM.

It is exciting to see how two models, moving from different perspectives, converge on a similar set of assumptions and findings. Because replication is the standard for determining sound scientific information, this alignment of ideas and data needs to be taken seriously. I contend that any effort at uncovering the underlying existential strivings of R/S constructs will lead to an uncovering of the Numinous, especially when there is an appeal to the taxonomical features of the FFM. Of course, more work needs to be done. The RiTE scales ought to be directly correlated with measures of the Numinous to assess their true overlap. Further, future research with the RiTE scales would benefit from addressing the six empirical criteria noted above. Clearly, meeting those standards would go a long way in supporting the RiTE scales as being useful indicators of the Numinous. Potentially, they may also represent new facets to be added to the domain! Such a possibility underscores the value of working with empirical models rather than ones that are rationally or theologically determined, which leave little room for empirical innovation and development.

Conclusions

The PRS is an exciting and active area of investigation because it deals with the ultimate existential aspects of living, the "why" of our existence. These concerns are at the heart of who we are: issues relating to mortality, meaning, and worth are essential defining qualities of our humanity. Termed the Numinous, this secular construct is hypothesized to represent a universal, defining quality of our species that explains why religion and spirituality are so important to us. Empirically, the Numinous has been shown to exert a causal influence on several important psychosocial qualities, such as well-being, purpose in life, psychological distress, characterological dysfunction, and mental health. The Numinous represents a motivational drive important for understanding all people, regardless of culture, language, and religious status. The Numinous also helps to better understand the predictive value of R/S constructs: their associations with mental and physical health outcomes are not so much a function of the specialness of a religious or spiritual perspective. Rather, their predictiveness is derived from the fact that R/S constructs are themselves products of these underlying Numinous motivations.

Understanding the Numinous as a personality domain opens the door for creating more comprehensive and predictive psychological models. The Numinous domain can be helpful in organizing a wide array of research dealing with issues such as Terror Management Theory (Solomon, Greenberg, & Pyszcznski, 1991) and its focus on finitude and mortality. The Numinous outlines those psychological motivations that help individuals cope with the certainty of death and enable them to live lives of value, depth, and coherence (e.g., Piotrowski & Żemojtel-Piotrowska, 2018). Meaning and purpose have long been recognized as being important aspects of resilience and well-being (Frankl, 1997). What the Numinous adds is a better delineation of the different types of meaning and their psychological significance (e.g., Piedmont, 2004b; Piedmont & Fox, 2023). Most importantly, the Numinous adds a new dimension to the Meaning-Making process, specifically the transformative aspects of meaning. Individuals high on the Numinous find not only meaning and direction for their own lives, but also include goals for enhancing and extending the value of communities to which these individuals belong (Piedmont, 2004b; Piedmont & Fox, 2023). Finally, the Numinous provides new insights into understanding existential crises, where individuals believe that they are unworthy and unaccepted by life (e.g. Exline & Rose, 2005; Piedmont, Hassinger et al., 2007). More than just feeling a rejection by the God of one's understanding, low levels of Worthiness (that component of the Numinous related to ultimate feelings of acceptance) have been demonstrated to represent a second, independent pathway to mental illness and maladaptiveness (Piedmont et al., 2020).

What makes the Numinous such an important construct is that it represents a uniquely human quality. As such, its examination in people opens a conversation on the most intimate and personal aspects of our humanity. Engaging with this content with clients can both provide a process for their reframing of distressing aspects of their lives and offer the potential to transform how individuals understand themselves and their style of overall engagement with life.

From a professional perspective, the scientific and secular (yet transcendent) nature of the Numinous can be easily accepted by all clinicians, regardless of their training backgrounds or religious status. It has important clinical value, both interpretively and predictively. More than just a cultural variable, the Numinous captures important human motivations that are at the highest level of personal organization. The Numinous provides a useful psychological template that therapists can use to better understand and to address effectively the concerns of their religiously oriented clients when they speak of faith-related issues. Rather than engaging with denominationally specific content (with which a clinician may not be familiar or comfortable), therapists can now reframe these issues into the larger context of existential strivings.

It is hoped that this report has provided sufficient justification for the importance of our Existential/Numinous nature and to consider the motivations that flow from this capacity as a basic sixth dimension of our personality. Engaging the Numinous opens the door to an entirely new dimension of functioning that will generate additional understandings of our psychology and suggest innovative treatment modalities that may offer the potential for truly transformative therapeutic experiences.

References

Albright, C. R., & Ashbrook, J. B. (2001). *Where God lives in the human brain*. Naperville, IL: Sourcebooks.

Allport, G. W. (1950). *The individual and his religion*. New York, NY: MacMillan.

Ashton, M. C., Lee, K., & Goldberg, L. R. (2004). A hierarchical analysis of 1,710 English personality-descriptive adjectives. *Journal of Personality and Social Psychology*, *87*, 707–721. https://doi.org/10.1037/0022-3514.87.5.707

Batson, C. D. (1997). An agenda item for the psychology of religion: Getting respect. In B. Spilka & D. N. McIntosh (Eds.), *The psychology of religion: Theoretical approaches* (pp. 3–10). Boulder, CO: Westview Press.

Baumeister, R. F., Bauer, I. M., & Lloyd, S. A. (2010). Choice, free will, and religion, *Psychology of Religion and Spirituality*, *2*, 67–82. https://doi.org/10.1037/a0018455

Becker, P. (1999). Beyond the Big Five. *Personality and Individual Differences*, *26*, 511–530. https://doi.org/10.1016/S0191-8869(98)00168-8

Bouchard, T. J., McGue, M. Lykken, D., & Tellegen, A. (1999). Intrinsic and extrinsic religiousness, genetic and environmental influences and personality correlates. *Twin Research*, *2*, 88–98. https://doi.org/10.1375/twin.2.2.88

Boyd, J. N., & Zimbardo, P. G. (1997). Constructing time after death: The transcendental-future time perspective. *Time and Society*, *6*, 35–56. https://doi.org/10.1177/0961463X97006001002

Buss, D. M. (2002). Sex, marriage, and religion: What adaptive problems do religious phenome3na solve? *Psychological Inquiry*, *13*, 201–203. http://www.jstor.org/stable/1449329

Chang, E. C., Jilani, Z, Yu, T., Fowler, E. E., Lin, J., Webb, J. R., & Hirsch, J. K. (2015). Fundamental dimensions of personality underlying spirituality: Further evidence for the construct validity of the RiTE measure of spirituality. *Personality and Individual Differences*, *75*, 175–178. https://doi.org/10.1016/j.paid.2014.11.027

Cheston, S. E., Piedmont, R. L., Eanes, B., & Lavin, L. P. (2003). Changes in clients' images of God over the course of outpatient therapy. *Counseling and Values*, *47*, 96–108. http://dx.doi.org/10.1002/j.2161-007X.2003.tb00227.x

Clonninger, C. R., Svrakic, D. M., & Przybeck, T. R. (1993). A psychobiological measure of temperament and character. *Archives of General Psychiatry*, *50*,975–990. http://doi.org/10.1001/archpsyc.1993.01820240059008

Comte-Sponville, A. (2008). *The little book of atheist spirituality*. London, England: Penguin Group.

Costa, P. T., Jr., & McCrae, R. R. (1992). *The NEO-PI-R professional manual*. Odessa, FL: Psychological Assessment Resources.

Costa, P. T., Jr., & McCrae, R. R. (1994). Set like plaster? Evidence for the stability of adult personality. In T. F. Heatherton & J. L. Weinberger (Eds.), *Can personality change?* (pp. 21.40). Washington, DC: American Psychological Association.

Dangel, T. & Webb, J. R. (2017). Spirituality and psychological pain: The mediating role of social support. *Mental Health, Religion, & Culture*, *20*, 246–259. https://doi.org/10.1080/13674676.2017.1345880

de Raad, B, & Mlačić, B. (2017). The lexical foundation of the Big Five Factor Model. In T. A. Widiger (Ed.), *The Oxford Handbook of the five factor model* (pp. 191–216). New York, NY: Oxford University Press.

Digman, J. M. (1990). Personality structure: Emergence of the five-factor model. *Annual Review of Psychology*, *41*, 417–440. https://doi.org/10.1146/annurev.ps.41.020190.002221

Emmons, R. A., & Paloutzian, R. F. (2003). The psychology of religion. *Annual Review of Psychology*, *54*, 377–402. https://doi.org/10.1146/annurev.psych.54.101601.145024

Erikson, E. H. (1977). *Toys and reasons*. New York, NY: Norton.

Exline, J. J., & Rose, E. (2005). Religious and spiritual struggles. In R. Paloutzian & C. Park (Eds.), *Handbook of the psychology of religion and spirituality* (pp. 315–330). New York, NY: The Guilford Press.

Fox, J., & Piedmont, R. L. (2020). Religious crisis as an independent causal predictor of psychological distress: Understanding the unique role of the Numinous for intrapsychic functioning. *Religions*, *11*. https://doi.org/10.3390/rel11070329

Frankl, V. E. (1959). *From death camp to existentialism*. Boston, MA: Beacon Press.

Frankl, V. E. (1997). *Man's search for ultimate meaning*. New York, NY: Plenum Press.

Funder, D. C. (2002). Why study religion? *Psychological Inquiry*, *13*, 213–214. https://www.jstor.org/stable/1449329

Gosling, S. D., & John, O. P. (1999). Personality dimensions in nonhuman animals: A cross-species review. *Current Directions in Psychological Science*, *8*(3), 69–75. https://doi.org/10.1111/1467-8721.00017

Griffiths, R. R., Richards, W. A., McCann, U., & Jesse, R. (2006). Psilocybin can occasion mystical-type experiences having substantial and sustained personal meaning and spiritual significance. *Psychopharmacology*, *187*, 268–283. https://doi.org/10.1007/s00213-006-0457-5

Harris, K. A., Howell, D. S., & Spurgeon, D. W. (2018). Faith concepts in psychology: Three 30-year definitional content analyses. *Psychology of Religion and Spirituality*, *10*, 1–29. https://doi.org/10.1037/rel0000134

Hart, D. B. (2019). *That all shall be saved: Heaven, hell and universal salvation*. New Haven, CT: Yale University Press.

Heath, A. C., Neale, M. C., Kessler, R. C., Eaves, L. J., & Kendler, K. S. (1992). Evidence for genetic influences on personality from self-reports and informant ratings. *Journal of Personality and Social Psychology*, *63*, 85–96.

Hill, P. C., Pargament, K. I., Hood, R. W., Jr., McCullough, M. E., Swyers, J. P., Larson, D. B., & Zinnbauer, B. J. (2000). Conceptualizing religion and spirituality: Points of commonality, points of departure. *Journal for the Theory of Social Behavior*, *30*, 51–77. https://doi.org/10.1111/1468-5914.00119

Hood, R. W., Jr., & Chen, Z. (2013). Mystical, spiritual, and religious experiences. In R. F. Paloutzian and C. L. Park (Eds.). *Handbook of the psychology of religion and spirituality* (2nd ed., pp. 422–440). New York, NY: The Guilford Press.

Hunsley, J., & Meyer, G. J. (2003). The incremental validity of psychological testing and assessment: Conceptual, methodological, and statistical issues. *Psychological Assessment*, *15*, 446–455.

James, W. (1994). *Varieties of religious experience*. New York, NY: Random House. (Original work published 1902).

Josanloo, M. (2012). Investigation of the factor structure of spirituality and religiosity in Iranian Shiite university students. *International Journal of Psychology*, *47*, 211–221. https://doi.org/10.1080/00207594.2011.617372

Jung, C. G. (1963). *Memories, dreams, reflections*. New York, NY: Knopf Doubleday Publishing Group.

King, J. E., & Figueredo, A. J. (1997). The five factor model plus dominance in chimpanzee personality. *Journal of Research in Personality*, *31*, 257–271. https://doi.org/10.1006/jrpe.1997.2179

Kirk, K. M., Eaves, L. J., & Martin, N. G. (1999). Self-transcendence as a measure of spirituality in a sample of older Australian twins. *Twin Research*, *2*, 81–87. https://doi.org/10.1375/136905299320565942

Koenig, H. G. (2008). Concerns about measuring spirituality in research. *Journal of Nervous and Mental Disease*, *196*, 349–355. https://doi.org/10.1097/NMD.0b013e31816ff796

Koenig, H. G., McCullough, M. E., & Larson, D. B. (2001). *Handbook of religion and health*. New York, NY: Oxford University Press.

Leung, K., & Bond, M. H. (2004). Social axioms: A model for social beliefs in multicultural perspective. In M. P. Zanna (Ed.), *Advances in experimental social psychology, Vol. 36*, (pp. 119–197). Elsevier Academic Press. https://doi.org/10.1016/S0065-2601(04)36003-X

MacDonald, D. A. (2000). Spirituality: Description, measurement and relation to the five-factor model of personality. *Journal of Personality*, *68*(1), 153–197. https://doi.org/10.1111/1467-6494.t01-1-00094

Maslow, A. H. (1971). *The farther reaches of human nature*. New York, NY: Viking Press.

McCrae, R. R., & Costa, P. T., Jr. (2010). *NEO inventories professional manual*. Lutz, FL: Psychological Assessment Resources.

McCrae, R. R., et al. (2004). Consensual validation of personality traits across cultures. *Journal of Research in Personality*, *38*, 178–201. https://doi.org/10.1016/S0092-6566(03)00056-4

McFarland, S., Brown, D., & Webb, M. (2013). Identification with all humanity as a moral concept and psychological construct. *Current Directions in Psychological Science*, *22*(3), 194–198. https://doi.org/10.1177/0963721412471346

Miller, L. J. (2012). *The Oxford handbook of psychology and spirituality*. Oxford, UK: Oxford University Press.

Miller, T. (1991). The psychotherapeutic value of the five-factor model of personality: A clinician's experience. *Personality Assessment*, *57*,415–433. https://doi.org/10.1207/s15327752jpa5703_3

Mischel, W. (1968). *Personality assessment*. New York, NY: Wiley.

Newberg, A., D'Aquili, E., & Rause, V. (2001). *Why God won't go away*. New York, NY: Ballantine Publishing Group.

Nunnally, J. C., & Bernstein, I. H. (1994). *Psychometric theory* (3rd ed.). New York, NY: McGraw-Hill.

Otto, R. (1958). *The idea of the holy* (J. W. Harvey, Trans.). Oxford, England: Oxford University Press.

Paloutzian, R. F., & Park, C. L. (2013). *Handbook of the psychology of religion and spirituality* (2nd ed). New York, NY: Guilford.

Paloutzian, R. F., & Park, C. L. (2021). The psychology of religion and spirituality: How big the tent? *Psychology of Religion and Spirituality*, *13*, 3–13. https://doi.org/10.1037/rel0000218

Pargament, K. I. (2007). *Spiritually integrated psychotherapy: Understanding and addressing the sacred*. New York, NY: Guilford.

Pargament, K. I. (2013). *APA handbook of psychology, religion, and spirituality*. Washington, DC: American Psychological Association.

Penley, J. A., & Tomaka, J. (2002). Associations among the Big 5, emotional responses, and coping with acute stress. *Personality and Individual Differences*, *32*, 1215–1228. https://doi.org/10.1016/S0191-8869(01)00087-3

Peterson, C., & Seligman, M. E. P. (2004). *Character strengths and virtues: A handbook of classification*. Washington, DC and New York, NY: American Psychological Association and Oxford University Press.

Piedmont, R. L. (1994). Validation of the NEO-PIR observer form for college students: Toward a paradigm for studying personality development. *Assessment*, *1*, 259–268. https://doi.org/10.1037/0022-3514.78.3.582

Piedmont, R. L. (1998). *The Revised NEO Personality Inventory: Clinical and research applications*. New York, NY: Plenum.

Piedmont, R. L. (1999). Does spirituality represent the sixth factor of personality? Spiritual Transcendence and the five-factor model. *Journal of Personality*, *67*, 985–1013. https://doi.org/10.1111/1467-6494.00080

Piedmont, R. L. (2004a). Spiritual Transcendence as a predictor of psychosocial outcome from an outpatient substance abuse program. *Psychology of Addictive Behaviors*, *18*, 213–222. https://doi.org/10.1037/0893-164X.18.3.213

Piedmont, R. L. (2004b). The logoplex as a paradigm for understanding spiritual transcendence. *Research in the Social Scientific Study of Religion*, *15*, 263–284.

Piedmont, R. L. (2007). Cross-cultural generalizability of the Spiritual Transcendence Scale to the Philippines: Spirituality as a human universal. *Mental Health, Religion, & Culture*, *10*, 89–107. https://doi.org/10.1080/13694670500275494

Piedmont, R. L. (2014). Looking back and finding our way forward: An editorial call to action. *Psychology of Religion and Spirituality*, *4*, 265–267. https://doi.org/10.1037/rel0000014

Piedmont, R. L. (2017). *Numinous Motivation Inventory: Preliminary technical manual*. Timonium, MD: Author.

Piedmont, R. L., (2020). *Assessment of Spirituality and Religious Sentiments: Technical manual* (3rd ed.). Timonium, MD: Author.

Piedmont, R. L., Ciarrocchi, J. W., Dy-Liacco, G., & Williams, J. E. G. (2009). The empirical and conceptual value of the Spiritual Transcendence and Religious Involvement scales for personality research. *Psychology of Religion and Spirituality*, *1*, 162–179. https://doi.org/10.1037/a0015883

Piedmont, R. L., & Fox, J. (2023). Hope and the Numinous: Psychological concepts for promoting wellness in a medical context. *Medical Research Archives*, *11*(11). https://doi.org/10.18103/mra.v11i11.4667

Piedmont, R. L., Fox, J., & Copello, E. (2021). "Whatsoever you do unto the least of my brethren, you do unto me:" Using the *Assessment of Spirituality and Religious Sentiments Scale* (ASPIRES) in a socially and economically marginalized rescue mission sample. *Religions*, *12*, 474. https://doi.org/10.3390/rel12070474

Piedmont, R. L., Fox, J., & Toscano, M. E. (2020). Spiritual crisis as a unique causal predictor of emotional and characterological impairment in atheists and agnostics: Numinous motivations as universal psychological qualities. *Religions*, *11*, 551–570. https://doi.org/10.3390/rel11110551

Piedmont, R. L., Hassinger, C. J., Rhorer, J., Sherman, M. F., Sherman, N. C., & Williams, J. E. G. (2007). The relations among spirituality and religiosity and Axis II functioning in two college samples. *Research in the Social Scientific Study of Religion*, *18*, 53–73.

Piedmont, R.L., & Leach, M.M. (2002). Cross-cultural generalizability of the Spiritual Transcendence Scale in India: Spirituality as a universal aspect of human experience. *American Behavioral Scientist, 45*, 1886–1899. https://doi.org/10.1177/0002764202045012011

Piedmont, R. L., Mapa, A. T., & Williams, J. E. G. (2006). A factor analysis of the Fetzer/NIA Brief Multidimensional Measure of Religiousness/Spirituality (MMRS). *Research in the Social Scientific Study of Religion, 17*, 177–196.

Piedmont, R. L., McCrae, R. R., & Costa, P. T., Jr. (1991) Adjective check list scales and the five-factor model. *Journal of Personality and Social Psychology, 60*, 630–637. https://doi.org/10.1037/0022-3514.60.4.630

Piedmont, R. L., Town, S., & Hollwitz, J. (2023). Undergraduate management course that promotes existential development for business. *Journal of Management, Spirituality & Religion, 20*(2), 182–205. https://doi.org/10.51327/vxrm7190

Piedmont, R.L., Werdel, M. B., & Fernando, M. (2009). The utility of the Assessment of Spirituality and Religious Sentiments (ASPIRES) scale with Christians and Buddhists in Sri Lanka. *Research in the Social Scientific Study of Religion, 20*, 131–146.

Piedmont, R. L., & Wilkins, T. A. (2020). *Understanding the psychological soul of spirituality: A guidebook for research and practice*. New York, NY: Routledge.

Piotrowski, J. P., & Żemojtel-Piotrowska, M. (2018). Spiritual Transcendence as a buffer against death anxiety. *Current psychology*. Online Publication. https://doi.org/10.1007/s12144-018-9810-1

Piotrowski, J. P., Żemojtel-Piotrowska, M., Piedmont, R. L., & Baran, T. (2021). Polish adaptation of the Assessment of Spirituality and Religious Sentiments (ASPIRES) scale and examining a spiritual transcendence nomological net. *Psychology of Religion and Spirituality, 13*, 36–45. http://doi.org/10.1037/rel0000273

Piotrowski, J. P., & Żemojtel-Piotrowska, M. (2024). Relationship between Numinous constructs and values. *Psychology of Religion and Spirituality, 16*(2), 133–141. https://doi.org/10.1037/rel0000306

Rican, P., & Janosova, P. (2010) Spirituality as a basic aspect of personality: A cross-cultural verification of Piedmont's model. *The International Journal for the Psychology of Religion, 20*, 2–13. https://doi.org/10.1080/10508610903418053

Richards, P. S., & Bergin, A. E. (1997). *A spiritual strategy for counseling and psychotherapy*. Washington, DC: American Psychological Association.

Salsman, J. M., Brown, T. L., Brechting, E. H., & Carlson, C. R. (2005). The link between religion and spirituality and psychological adjustment: The mediating role of optimism and social support. Personality and Social Psychology Bulletin, 31(4), 522–535. https://doi.org/10.1177/0146167204271563

Saucier, G., & Goldberg, L. R. (1998). What is beyond the big five? *Journal of Personality, 66*, 495–524. https://doi.org/10.1111/1467-6494.00022

Seeman, T. E., Dubin, L. F., & Seeman, M. (2003). Religiosity/spirituality and health: A critical review of the evidence for biological pathways. *American Psychologist, 58*, 53–63. https://doi.org/10.1037/0003-066X.58.1.53

Sloan, R. P., Bagiella, E., & Powell, T. (2001). Without a prayer: Methodological problems, ethical challenges, and misrepresentations in the study of religion, spirituality, and medicine. In T. G. Plante & A. C. Sherman (Eds.), *Faith and health: Psychological perspectives* (pp. 339–354). New York, NY: The Guilford Press.

Solomon, S., Greenberg, J., & Pyszcznski, T. (1991). A terror management theory of self-esteem. In C. R. Snyder & F. R. Donelson (Eds.). *Handbook of social and clinical psychology: The health perspective* (pp. 21–40). Elmsford, NY: Pergamon Press.

Steger, M. F., Hicks, B. M., Krueger, R. F., & Bouchard, T. J. (2011). Genetic and environmental influences and covariance among meaning in life, religiousness, and spirituality. *The Journal of Positive Psychology, 6*, 181–191. https://doi.org/10.1080/17439760.2011.569172

Tillich, P. (2000). *The courage to be* (2nd ed.). New Haven, CT: Yale University Press.

Webb, J. R., Toussaint, L., & Dula, C. S. (2014). Ritualistic, theistic, and existential spirituality: Initial psychometric qualities of the RiTE measure of spirituality. *Journal of Religion and Health*, *53*, 972–985. https://doi.org/10.1007/s10943-013-9697-y

Wilson, E. O. (1978). *On human nature*. Cambridge, MA: Harvard University Press.

Woodworth, R. S. (1940). *Psychology* (4th ed.). New York, NY: Henry Holt & Co.

Worthington, E. L., Jr., Johnson, E. L., Hook, J. N., & Aten, J. D. (2013). *Evidence-based practices for Christian counseling and psychotherapy*. Dowers Grove, IL: InterVarsity Press.

Żemojtel-Piotrowska, M., Piotrowski, J., & Sawicki, A. (2021). Religiosity, spirituality, national narcissism, and prejudice toward refugees and sexual minorities in Poland. *Psychology of religion and spirituality*. Advanced online publication. https://doi.org/10.1037/rel0000430

Chapter 6

Secular Spirituality

Michael E. Nielsen and Noah Wilmoth*

What role does spirituality play in the lives of atheists, agnostics, and the religious "nones"? At first, such a question may seem oxymoronic; is not spirituality synonymous with religion? Of course, readers of this book will know this is not the case, that religiosity and spirituality are not synonymous. And yet, a common characterization of nonreligious individuals is that they also lack a sense of spirituality. In this chapter, we examine spirituality's role in secular people's lives. First, we note the trends in demographic research regarding secular individuals. Next, we consider how the concepts of spirituality as presented in the RiTE model (Webb et al., 2014) apply to the nonreligious. Research suggesting that spirituality is healthy or unhealthy for secular individuals is examined. Finally, we note limitations in the existing research and future directions scholars may wish to pursue.

In recent years, the "rise of the nones" has been a common headline. Pew (2012) reports that during the five years from 2007 to 2012, atheist, agnostic, and "nothing in particular" respondents in their periodic surveys on religion grew from just over 15% to nearly 20% of all US adults. Particularly relevant for our purposes, Pew found that a substantial percentage of nonreligious individuals also consider themselves to be spiritual. Among the US populace as a whole, 65% indicated they were religious, 18% declared themselves spiritual but not religious, and 15% neither religious nor spiritual. Among atheist and agnostic respondents, 34% considered themselves spiritual, a figure that rose to 39% among the "nothing in particular" respondents. Pew collected additional data in 2023, which showed the number of US adults who consider themselves atheists, agnostics, or "nothing in particular" had increased to 28%. "Nothing in particular" was endorsed most frequently (63% of atheist, agnostic, and nonreligious respondents), and there were slightly more agnostics (20%) than atheists (17%) in the sample (Smith et al., 2024).

Efforts to define and categorize spirituality for research can be traced back to the late 1960s when Glenn Vernon (1968) made arguments that religious "nones" neglected the nuance of individuals who do not identify with standard religious terminology. This led to *nones* being considered *independents*, a term allowing for a greater variety of beliefs regarding personal morality without necessarily invoking the supernatural. The labels *atheist* and *agnostic* have become more common and begin to reflect the heterogeneity found among secular people. These terms also have some value; for example, atheists show higher levels of scientism and less skepticism, while agnostics show more skepticism and lower dogmatism (Schnell et al., 2021, 2023). Some researchers have further distinguished among secular individuals. Focusing specifically on atheists, Schnell and Keenan (2011) report three types: those with low commitment, a second group who show broad commitment, and a third who emphasize self-actualization. Schnell and Keenan found that, compared with religious

* Corresponding Author: mnielsen@georgiasouthern.edu.

DOI: 10.4324/9781003440048-8

people, atheists generally showed lower levels of meaning in life, but they did not differ in terms of having crises of meaning.

Another framework for categorizing atheists distinguishes among six different types of nonbelievers (Silver et al., 2014). Most common were *intellectual atheists* (37.6%) who seek out intellectual discussion on religion as part of the search for truth. *Activist atheists* (23%) are highly engaged in socio-political issues. *Anti-theists* (14.8%) consider religion to be a net negative on society, and they seek to persuade others to agree. *Ritual atheist/agnostic* (12.5%) individuals identify symbolically with a religious or spiritual tradition, but they nevertheless do not believe. *Seeker-agnostic* (7.6%) individuals engage in an open-minded search for meaning. *Non-theists* (4.4%) are generally apathetic and disinterested.

Whether known as *religious nones*, *independents*, or by another term, it is clear that substantial diversity exists among the nonreligious. Unless a more specific term, such as atheist or agnostic, is needed, we prefer the terms *worldview* (Taves et al., 2018) or *lifestance* (Stephenson & Cragun, 2022) to reflect a person's outlook on life and its ultimate questions. Saying one has a secular worldview or a theistic lifestance, for example, allows researchers to refer to people by what they are, rather than by what they are not.

Spirituality Among the Secular

Researchers have taken a variety of approaches to defining spirituality among the nonreligious, or secular spirituality (Cimino & Smith, 2014). Our operational definition of spirituality must be flexible in light of the diversity of positions taken by atheists, agnostics, and other secular people. The multidimensionality of the RiTE model of spirituality is useful in this regard. To summarize the model, spirituality consists of ritualistic, theological, and existential dimensions. Webb (2021, p. 61; see also Chapters 1 and 44 of this volume) defines ritualistic spirituality as having a "structured relationship with a deity" or higher power. Theistic spirituality features an unstructured relationship with deity. Existential spirituality involves a transcendent, "non-theistic search for meaning and purpose" (p. 61). These three dimensions overlap, such that an individual may experience each of these forms of spirituality, with the balanced position having nearly equal portions of all three dimensions present in their spiritual lives. We focus on the sense of meaning and purpose found in existential spirituality.

As discussed above, research by Pew finds that a minority of secular individuals attend services, which implies some degree of ritualistic spirituality. Somewhat more secular individuals indicate a belief in God or a higher power, suggesting that theistic spirituality would be somewhat more relevant to them. Existential spirituality, reflecting a search for meaning and purpose, is much more likely to be valued by secular people as a group and was the focus of our review of the literature. The pursuit of meaning and purpose in life, often expressed as a sense of awe, wonder, or a deep feeling of connection with nature or the universe, is key to understanding spirituality among secular individuals. This can come through many different avenues, such as feelings of awe at nature (Ahmadi et al., 2022) or inspirational music (Ji et al., 2021). When polled, 71% of atheists claimed to have feelings of awe and wonderment when taking part in something bigger than themselves, and of this 71%, more than half of these participants attributed such feelings to nature; science and music also were frequently cited as contributing to awe (Caldwell-Harris et al., 2011). Engaging in nature was also found to be the most common coping method among academics in Sweden during the COVID-19 pandemic (Ahmadi et al., 2022). A growing body of literature reinforces the notion that self-transcendent music and media also can stimulate a sense of awe, inspiration, and purpose (Ji et al., 2021).

A good starting point for understanding spirituality as a sense of connection or awe is found in the Pew (2012) survey, which asked respondents, "How often, if at all, do you feel a deep connection with nature and the earth?" The great majority of atheist and agnostic respondents affirmed they experience such feelings often (56%) or sometimes (27%), as did their "nothing in particular" respondents (59% often and 25% sometimes). These figures mirror those of religiously affiliated respondents (59% often and 26% sometimes).

Pew (2012) also asked how often respondents thought about the meaning of life, and respondents showed high engagement with existential questions. Such thoughts were common among atheist/agnostic individuals, 45% of whom entertained such questions often, and 37% sometimes. "Nothing in particular" participants considered them more frequently, with 56% indicating "often" and 26% thinking of them sometimes. These numbers are lower than comparable statistics for religiously affiliated people, 70% of whom often and 22% of whom sometimes think about the meaning of life, but nevertheless indicate that the great majority of secular individuals engage with existential questions.

Atheist and agnostic refer to one's lack of belief in deity, and yet, people do not always respond to surveys in a manner one might expect. For example, Pew's (2012) data showed that 38% of atheist/agnostic respondents (reported jointly) and 81% of "nothing in particular" respondents were fairly or absolutely certain they believe in God or a Universal Spirit. A little over a decade later, Pew's data reflected a decrease, with 23% of atheists, 67% of agnostics, and 83% of "nothing in particular" believing in God or a higher power (Smith et al., 2024). The recent data also indicated some level of worship attendance, with 16% of atheist/agnostic individuals and 32% of "nothing in particular" attending services at least annually. The number of secular people who attended services at least a few times a year had dropped to 10% (Smith et al., 2024). Data such as these may reflect shifting demographic trends, changes in methodology, or both. More broadly, such a pattern of results may be consistent with the notion that persons who indicate they are spiritual but not religious are on a path toward agnosticism, as suggested by Perez and Vallières' (2019) qualitative study of people who deconverted from Christianity. It is worth noting, however, that Perez and Vallières use spirituality as a contrast to nonbelief, rendering invalid the notion of spirituality among secular people.

In an ambitious study of nonbelievers, van Mulukom et al. (2023) asked 996 people from 10 different countries to respond to open-ended questions regarding their worldviews. Participants indicated whether they considered themselves to be agnostic, atheist, humanist, indifferent, no religion, spiritual-but-not-religious (SBNR), or other. Analyses of responses showed that these formed three different clusters: spiritual, humanistic, and scientific and logical beliefs. Participants were then asked to "list the worldviews, beliefs, or understandings of the world that are particularly meaningful to you" (p. 145). Responses resulted in 51 categories, which were then grouped into "supercategories" reflecting general worldviews or beliefs. The most commonly mentioned were science (35.1%), humanism (25.5%), critical skepticism (17.4%), natural laws (15.6%), equality (14.0%), kindness and caring (13.6%), care for the earth (11.5%), left-wing political causes (10.1%), atheism (9.9%), and individualism and freedom (9.8%). Findings such as these broaden our understanding of what was once deemed a "none" and let us see the once-generalized group as what they are: a group of individuals who share the sentiment of having nonreligious beliefs but have diverse worldviews.

As operational definitions of spirituality vary, so does the percentage of people claiming spiritual experiences. For example, Smith et al. (2024) report that 38% of religious *nones* indicate they have experienced a "sudden sense of connection with something beyond this world" (n.p.). Somewhat fewer (35%) report having had a sense that a person who is deceased is communicating with them, and a quarter (25%) say they have felt the presence of "something from beyond this world at least several times a year." Consistently, atheists are less likely to report these experiences than agnostics, and people who are *nothing in particular* are more likely to report these experiences. Those who are *nothing in particular* show a similarity with religious people on each of these measures and even indicate that they have felt as though they are communicating with someone who is deceased more than do religious people (44% vs. 38%).

Beneficial Correlates of Spirituality

If a substantial portion of secular people experience a sense of spirituality, as Smith et al. (2024) report, what is known about the effects of such experiences? From an existentialist perspective, we humans must create a sense of purpose and direction. Whether this occurs in a religious or a secular form, "meaning-making is a dynamic, fluid process and can be reconfigured" (Smith & Halligan, 2020, p. 87). Whether in a secular or a religious setting, shared practices of community and culture contribute to a sense of meaning. This strikes us as consistent with the ritualistic dimension in the RiTE model. Examples of this in secular contexts can be seen in Sunday Assembly or other mass gatherings of like-minded people, which are associated with positive social bonds and positive affect (Carles et al., 2021; Frost, 2023) that, in at least one study, persisted months afterwards (Yudkin et al., 2022). Rave experiences that invoke "the 4Ds: dance, drums, sleep deprivation, and drugs" (Newson et al., 2021, n.p.) are another instance of ritualistic spirituality.

As intriguing as the possibility of a ritualistic secular spirituality may be, much more common are examples of existential spirituality among secular people. How does existential spirituality benefit secular people?

In their review of 43 studies, Rew and Wong (2006) found that 84% demonstrated that religious or spiritual practices had a favorable impact on adolescent health behaviors or attitudes. Most of those studies defined religiosity or spirituality in simplistic terms, such as religious service attendance or self-rated importance of religion. Importantly, 11 of the 43 studies used unique measures of spirituality, suggesting that idiosyncratic understandings of spirituality may also have positive effects on adolescent health. Rew and Wong did not analyze secular individuals separately from others, but the results of their analysis are intriguing. Many of the studies measured spirituality and found that spiritual practices tend to be associated with positive health effects. This finding, in conjunction with the literature indicating that many religious "nones" score highly on measures of spirituality (e.g., Pew, 2012), implies that spirituality may offer health benefits to at least some secular individuals.

Given that the study of secular worldviews began in earnest only recently (Schnell, 2021), relatively few studies have pursued the role of spirituality among secular people. More common are studies that examine spirituality in a general sample. Examples of this research might nevertheless imply something about the effects of spirituality among secular people. For example, consider a series of four experiments demonstrating that inducing feelings of awe resulted in increased generosity, ethical decision-making, and prosocial values (Piff et al., 2015). These results were demonstrated via three general, online samples (Knowledge Networks and Mechanical Turk) and one college student sample and did not specifically mention participants' religious or spiritual beliefs. But, in light of research (Lewis et al., 2015) demonstrating that Mechanical Turk generates samples with twice as many nonbelievers as are found in the General Social Survey or in large samples of students, the results suggest that these effects may be found in secular people.

In a similar vein, experiment participants who listened to music that invoked a sense of "vastness and a need for accommodation" (Ji et al., 2021, p. 309), conveyed by such techniques as crescendos and sudden tempo or harmony changes, experienced increased positive affect. Again, although participants' religious beliefs were not reported, we are aware of nothing in the literature to suggest that the effect of music is different for religious versus secular people.

One avenue for understanding spirituality among atheist, agnostic, or nonreligious people is through their involvement with 12-Step programs. Spirituality is integral to Alcoholics Anonymous and Narcotics Anonymous and is represented in 5 of the 12 steps. In fact, 73% of programs in the United States that address addiction treatment are spirituality-based in a manner consistent with 12-Step programs (Grim & Grim, 2019). Moreover, the role of spirituality in these programs has been a focus of several interesting studies.

Twelve-Step groups featuring God or a higher power as an integral part of recovery work may appear to be at odds with the belief systems of atheist, agnostic, and nonreligious individuals. A natural question, therefore, is whether such groups are helpful to secular individuals. Relatively few studies bear on this question, but we can glean some useful information from the literature. One such study (Kelly et al., 2011) found that successful participation in Alcoholics Anonymous was most strongly predicted by changes in their social networks and that spirituality facilitated change among people who were more severely alcohol-impaired. Spirituality did not, however, have the same effect among more modestly impaired individuals.

A more direct examination of God in a 12-Step program gives firmer evidence on this question. Galanter et al. (2020) investigated the role that God and a higher power may play in the efficacy of 12-Step programs. They found no difference between atheists, agnostics, and religious believers' cravings for narcotics or depression, even though 12-Step programs include explicit mention of "God" or a higher power. Moreover, whether individuals labeled their higher power as God or as something else, the majority agreed that "God determines what happens to me," and that "God talks to me."

Recognizing that AA might be difficult for atheist or agnostic participants, the Making AA Easier (MAAEZ) project is designed to promote social connectedness with like-minded individuals in AA and thereby increase the effectiveness of the 12 steps (Kaskutas et al., 2009). Important for the current focus, one of the four core MAAEZ sessions focused on spirituality and gave participants a variety of ways to define and implement it, including engaging in spirituality without religion. After 12 months in this program, atheist/agnostic and nonreligious participants showed a significantly increased likelihood of avoiding alcohol or drugs, even beyond that of religious participants.

Although most research on spirituality does not directly address secular people, this is not universally the case. In a sample of atheist and agnostic people, Hall et al. (2020) found that existential spirituality was associated with higher levels of self-forgiveness. Existential spirituality also reduced a construct known as "psychache," or an intense psychological pain (see Shneidman, 1993). In turn, this was associated with lower levels of suicidal behavior. It is difficult to imagine a more important effect than this.

In a large project designed to examine secular spirituality, Schnell and Keenan (2013) arrived at a construction of spirituality that includes five elements: immanence or transcendence, an ethic of compassion, acceptance toward oneself and the world, spiritual practice, and experiences of transcendence. Drawing on data from the European Values Survey (N = 67,786), they found that spirituality is not associated with happiness, satisfaction with life, or trust in other people. Although spirituality was associated positively with tolerance toward minorities and with values of responsibility, tolerance and respect, and unselfishness, the large sample size and relatively small magnitude of the correlations reduce the importance of this finding.

Engagement with science has also been associated with awe. Perhaps one of the most interesting examples of this is found in a series of six studies that showed awe facilitated scientific thinking (Gottlieb et al., 2018). Moreover, awe was not associated with scientism, a dogmatic promotion of science above other human activities.

Challenges to the Role of Spirituality

Although the research above indicates some beneficial effects for spirituality among secular people, other studies present evidence to the contrary. One important reason for this may be that definitions of health and wellness often include a spiritual element (Trombley, 2023). For example, Alcoholics Anonymous has its origin in psychology via connections with Carl Jung and William James (White, 2014). Rowland Hazard sought out Jung's help in dealing with problematic alcohol use. Hazard subsequently participated in the Oxford Group, which focused on spirituality through a set of shared Christian ideals, and through that group, met a man known as Ebby Thatcher, who had another friend who dealt with alcoholism. Their meetings at the Oxford Group led Thatcher to give that friend, Bill Wilson, a copy of William James' *Varieties of Religious Experience* to help him understand a religious experience Wilson had while hospitalized. Wilson cited James' *Varieties* and the Oxford Group as pivotal in shaping the establishment of Alcoholics Anonymous (White, 2014).

With religious undertones in the establishment of AA, it may not be surprising that belief in God can be an important factor in the effectiveness of Alcoholics Anonymous. Tonigan et al. (2002) categorized AA affiliates as religious, spiritual, unsure, agnostic, or atheist and tracked how long participants continued to attend AA meetings. The effectiveness of AA did not differ among those who continued to attend, but atheist and agnostic persons were far less likely to continue with AA. Tonigan et al. conclude that although atheist and agnostic individuals can benefit from AA through the social support it provides, the program's emphasis on spirituality leads most atheist and agnostic individuals to discontinue attending.

Interviews with AA participants reveal that the spiritual undertones of the program can be a barrier to nonreligious participants (Trombley, 2023). Although religious and nonreligious participants in AA did not differ in terms of the resources available in their recovery efforts, nonreligious participants expressed anxiety over religious elements of the program, the use of prayer, and "God talk" during meetings. They also described instances of prejudice directed toward them by other program participants. In order to cope with these challenges, they tended either to speak up about their beliefs regarding religion or seek out more secular AA groups.

The role of religion or spirituality in AA extends to other 12-Step programs, as illustrated by a comparison of cognitive-behavioral therapy and a 12-Step program for treating crack cocaine users (Maude-Griffin et al., 1998). Among participants who were high in religiosity (operationalized as scoring high on a measure of intrinsic religious orientation), 40% demonstrated successful abstinence from cocaine, compared with 35% who received cognitive-behavioral therapy. In contrast, among participants low in religiosity, only 12% abstained from cocaine use with the 12-Step program, but 48% abstained when receiving cognitive-behavioral therapy.

In an oft-cited review of AA, Kelly et al. (2020) reviewed 27 studies, most of which were randomized or quasi-randomized control studies comparing AA with other interventions.

They distinguished between manualized AA, non-manualized AA, and cognitive behavior therapy, concluding that manualized AA is more effective than CBT and other interventions in facilitating abstinence, and that non-manualized AA is at least as effective. Kelly et al., however, did not focus on the role of spirituality in attaining these outcomes. Trombley (2023) notes that by focusing on abstinence and by not considering participants' drop-out rate, which is greater among nonreligious people, Kelly et al.'s methods may have affected the results they obtained, particularly in light of their reliance on abstinence as the primary indicator of success. Including other measures of success, such as physical or mental well-being, social support, etc., is likely to give a more complete understanding of AA's efficacy.

Beyond the work done with 12-Step programs, there are relatively few examples of spirituality failing to have a positive effect among people whose worldview excludes the supernatural. A study of patients with multiple sclerosis and mental illness found that gratitude and awe were unrelated to meaning in life (Büssing et al., 2014). Perhaps one of the most intriguing is a series of studies by Burris (2020), who found that atheists are less emotionally expressive than theists. In one of those studies, observers viewed a videotaped interview played with no volume. Observers who rated the person in the video noted lower levels of positive emotional expression among atheists than among theists. Of course, this is not to say that atheists do not experience positive emotions, including those of awe or other aspects of existential spirituality. It does, however, lead one naturally to consider the extent to which people experience various forms of spirituality. Further research in this area is warranted. This is particularly true in light of Burris's findings that emotional suppression reduced the experience of positive emotions among atheists, but that negative emotions did not appear to be affected in the same manner.

The degree of certitude in one's worldview is also important. In response to a stressful social situation, religious and atheist students showed lower stress responses (blood pressure, heart rate, and salivary cortisol) than did agnostic and spiritual students (Schnell et al., 2020). This type of pattern appears in other studies (e.g., Abbott & Franks, 2021) and is an important predictor of health outcomes (Speed & Fowler, 2021). Certainty in one's worldview carries beneficial effects.

Limitations

The literature we have examined is constrained by several limitations. At a conceptual level, much of the relevant scholarship relies on notions of spirituality that align, either explicitly or implicitly, with ideas associated with supernatural beliefs more than with a sensitivity to natural awe and wonder. Our position is that natural awe and wonder offer a rich avenue for spiritual life, regardless of one's worldview or lifestance regarding the supernatural. This is consistent with the existential dimension of the RiTE model.

This translates to a second important limitation in the current literature. Too frequently, spirituality is measured in a manner reflecting a theistic worldview that constrains the options for people who hold secular worldviews (e.g., Büssing et al., 2021; Speed & Fowler, 2016). For example, an otherwise interesting comparison of coping among cancer patients in Sweden and South Korea assessed spirituality by combining religious and spiritual coping methods in an interview question asking how patients' faith or spirituality was affected (Ahmadi et al., 2017). Developing measures of spirituality and existential concerns that reflect a variety of worldviews will provide a more complete understanding of people and their experiences. Placing those measures in nationally representative surveys will be an important step toward better understanding the distinctions between theistic and secular worldviews or lifestance, and hold the potential for us to see the variety of forms spirituality takes.

In a related vein, the samples used in the great majority of studies are limited in their generalizability. Small convenience samples are common and tend to feature white, educated participants from Western industrialized countries. The extent to which their responses reflect secular responses from other countries is uncertain.

Another avenue for further research concerns the effect of labeling life concerns as existential versus spiritual. Based on their data from largely secular Denmark, Hvidt et al. (2022) argue that *existential* should be used in place of *spiritual* because the former generates less reactance than the latter does among secular individuals. *Existential* invoked more cognitive and practical aspects, whereas *spiritual* suggested a transcendent source of existence. At a minimum, researchers in the future would be wise to consider carefully which term is best suited for their needs and the population they are studying.

Finally, and most importantly, the primary limitation we see in this research is one of scale: there are simply too few studies examining the notion of spirituality in people whose worldview or lifestance is based more on secularity than on religion. Additional research is sorely needed.

Future Directions

With this area of study in its infancy, researchers have many opportunities to contribute to a better understanding of spirituality in secular individuals. Here, we list several possibilities for interested researchers to pursue.

The effect of shared existential spirituality on committed relationships deserves attention. A small, qualitative study suggests that spirituality can be helpful in marriages in which one partner is religious and the other is not (Williams, 2021). This is worth further exploration; do religious, theological, and existential spiritual experiences improve couples equally? Can shared experiences invoking awe help maintain or even improve relationship quality? Or does the effect depend on the nature of the individuals' worldviews?

Exploring further the effects of engagement with science has the potential to enlighten our understanding of awe and existential spirituality. Research indicates that science can both promote and hinder theistic beliefs (Johnson et al., 2019) and that it can play an important role in generating a sense of awe (Gottlieb et al., 2018). More fundamentally, the mechanisms involved in experiencing awe are beginning to be understood (Monroy & Keltner, 2023), but this rich area of study merits further attention.

Another potentially productive direction for future efforts is found in the Netherlands, a predominantly secular country where spiritual caregivers provide care to patients with terminal illness (Koper et al., 2019). Spiritual caregivers themselves may be Christian, but they may also be secular. In either case, they discuss with the patient and with their family spiritual issues, life, death, euthanasia, and other difficult end-of-life topics. More research directed to ways that secular spirituality can help people is needed.

Finally, it is worth exploring the possibility that, to the extent that atheists show poorer outcomes, this may be due to internalized stereotypes (Bergstrom & Chasteen, 2022). Such a finding would be consistent with other research showing that atheists, particularly those who make their views known publicly, experience discrimination (Cragun et al., 2012); it is also consistent with the well-established literature on stereotype threat (Steele & Aronson, 1995).

References

Abbott, D. M., & Franks, A. S. (2021). Coping with COVID-19: An examination of the role of (non) religiousness/(non)spirituality. *Journal of Religion and Health*, *60*, 2395–2410. https://doi.org/10.1007/s10943-021-01284-9

Ahmadi, F., Cetrez, Ö., Akhavan, S., & Zandi, S. (2022). Meaning-making coping with COVID-19 in academic settings: The case of Sweden. *Illness, Crisis & Loss*, *30*(4), 770–794. https://doi.org/10.1177/10541373211022002

Ahmadi, F., Park, J., Kim, K. M., & Ahmadi, N. (2017). Meaning-making coping among cancer patients in Sweden and South Korea: A comparative perspective. *Journal of Religion and Health*, *56*, 1794–1811. https://doi.org/10.1007/s10943-017-0383-3

Bergstrom, V. N. Z., & Chasteen, A. L. (2022, October 31). Are agnostics associated with immorality to the same degree as atheists? *Psychology of religion and spirituality*. Advance online publication. https://doi.org/10.1037/rel0000491

Burris, C. T. (2020). Poker-faced and Godless: Expressive suppression and atheism. *Psychology of Religion and Spirituality*, *14*(3), 351–361. http://dx.doi.org/10.1037/rel0000361

Büssing, A., Recchia, D. R., Dienberg, T., Surzykiewicz, J., & Baumann, K. (2021). Awe-gratitude as an experiential aspect of spirituality and its association to perceived positive changes during the COVID-19 pandemic. *Frontiers in Psychiatry*, *12*, 642716. https://doi.org/10.3389/fpsyt.2021.642716

Büssing, A., Wirth, A. G., Reiser, F., Zahn, A., Humbroich, K, Gerbershagen, K., Schimrigk, S., Haupts, M., Hvidt, N. C., & Baumann, K. (2014). Experience of gratitude, awe and beauty in life among patients with multiple sclerosis and psychiatric disorders. *Health and Quality of Life Outcomes*, *12*, https://doi.org/10.1186/1477-7525-12-63

Caldwell-Harris, C. L., Wilson, A. L., LoTempio, E., & Beit-Hallahmi, B. (2011). Exploring the atheist personality: Well-being, awe, and magical thinking in atheists, Buddhists, and Christians. *Mental Health, Religion & Culture*, *14*(7), 659–672. https://doi.org/10.1080/13674676.2010.509847

Charles, S. J., van Mulukom, V., Brown, J. E., Watts, F., Dunbar, R. I. M., & Farias, J. (2021). United on Sunday: The effects of secular rituals on social bonding and affect. *PLoS One*, *16*(1): e0242546. https://doi.org/10.1371/journal.pone.0242546

Cimino, R., & Smith, C. (2014). *Atheist awakening: Secular activism and community in America*. New York: Oxford University Press.

Cragun, R. T., Kosmin, B., Keysar, A., Hammer, J. H., & Nielsen, M. (2012). On the receiving end: Discrimination toward the non-religious in the United States. *Journal of Contemporary Religion*, *27*(1), 105–127. https://doi.org/10.1080/13537903.2012.642741

Frost, J. (2023). Ritualizing Nonreligion: Cultivating rational rituals in secular spaces. *Social Forces*, *101*(4), 2013–2033. https://doi.org/10.1093/sf/soac042

Glanter, M., White, W. L., Ziegler, P. P., & Hunter, B. (2020). An empirical study on the construct of "God" in the twelve step process. *The American Journal of Drug and Alcohol Abuse*, *46*(6), 731–739. https://doi.org/10.1080/00952990.2020.1789870

Gottlieb, S., Keltner, D., & Lombrozo, T. (2018). Awe as a scientific emotion. *Cognitive Science*, *42*(6), 2081–2094. http://doi.org/10.1111/cogs.12648

Grim, B. J., & Grim, M. E. (2019). Belief, behavior, and belonging: How faith is indispensable in preventing and recovering from substance abuse. *Journal of Religion and Health*, *58*, 1713–1750. https://doi.org/10.1007/s10943-019-00876-w

Hall, B. B., Webb, J. R., & Hirsch, J. K. (2020). Spirituality and suicidal behavior: The mediating role of self-forgiveness and psychache. *Psychology of Religion and Spirituality*, *12*(1), 36–44. https://doi.org/10.1037/rel0000182

Hvidt, N. C., Assing Hvidt, E., & la Cour, P. (2022). Meanings of "the existential" in a secular country: A survey study. *Journal of Religion and Health*, *61*(4), 3276–3301. https://doi.org/10.1007/s10943-021-01253-2

Ji, Q., Janicke-Bowles, S. H., De Leeuw, R. N. H., & Oliver, M. B. (2021). The melody to inspiration: The effects of awe-eliciting music on approach motivation and positive well-being. *Media Psychology*, *24*(3), 305–331. https://doi.org/10.1080/15213269.2019.1693402

Johnson, K. A., Moon, J. W., Okun, M. A., Scott, M. J., O'Rourke, H. P., Hook, J. N., & Cohen, A. B. (2019). Science, God, and the cosmos: Science both erodes (via logic) and promotes (via awe) belief in God. *Journal of Experimental Social Psychology*, *84*. Published online 17 July 2019. https://doi.org/10.1016/j.jesp.2019.103826

Kaskutas, L. A., Subbaraman, M., Witbrodt, J., & Zemore, S. E. (2009). Effectiveness of making alcoholics anonymous easier (MAAEZ), a group format 12-step facilitation approach. *Journal of Substance Abuse Treatment*, *37*(3), 228–239. https://doi.org/10.1016/j.jsat.2009.01.004

Kelly, J. F., Hoeppner, B., Stout, R. L., & Pagano, M. (2011). Determining the relative importance of mechanisms of behavior change within Alcoholics Anonymous: A multiple mediator analysis. *Addiction*, *107*, 289–299. https://doi.org/10.1111/j.1360-0443.2011.03593.x

Kelly, J. F., Humphreys, K., & Ferri, M. (2020). Alcoholics anonymous and other 12-step programs for alcohol use disorder (review). *Cochrane Database of Systematic Reviews* 2020, Issue 3, Art. No.: CD012880. https://doi.org/10.1002/14651858.CD012880.pub2

Koper, I., Pasman, H. R. W., Schweitzer, B. P. M., Kuin, A., & Onwuteaka-Philipsen, B. D. (2019). Spiritual care at the end of life in the primary care setting: Experiences from spiritual caregivers – a mixed methods study. *BMC Palliative Care*, *18*, 98 https://doi.org/10.1186/s12904-019-0484-8

Lewis, A. R., Mockabee, S. T., Djupe, P. A., & Su-Ya Wu, J. (2015). The (non) religion of mechanical turk workers. *Journal for the Scientific Study of Religion*, *54*(2), 419–429. https://doi.org/10.1111/jssr.12184

Maude-Griffin, P. M., Hohenstein, J. M., Humbleet, G. L., Beilly, P. M., Tussle, D. J., & Hall, S. M. (1998). Superior efficacy of cognitive-behavioral therapy for urban crack cocaine abusers: Main and matching effects. *Journal of Consulting and Clinical Psychology*, *66*(5), 832–837.

Monroy, M., & Keltner, D. (2023). Awe as a pathway to mental and physical health. *Perspectives on Psychological Science*, *18*(2), 309–320. https://doi.org/10.1177/17456916221094856

Newson, M., Khurana, R., Cazorla, F., & van Mulukom, V. (2021). 'I get high with a little help from my friends' – How raves can invoke identity fusion and lasting cooperation via transformative experiences. *Frontiers in Psychology*, *12*: 719596. https://doi.org/10.3389/fpsyg.2021.719596

Perez, S., & Vallières, F. (2019). How do religious people become atheists? Applying a grounded theory approach to propose a model of deconversion. *Secularism & Nonreligion*, *8* (3), 1–14. https://doi.org/10.5334/snr.108

Pew Research Center. (2012, October 9). "Nones" on the rise. https://www.pewresearch.org/religion/2012/10/09/nones-on-the-rise/

Piff, P. K., Dietze, P., Feinberg, M., Stancato, D. M., & Keltner, D. (2015). Awe, the small self, and prosocial behavior. *Journal of Personality and Social Psychology*, *108*(6), 883–899. https://doi.org/10.1037/pspi0000018

Rew, L., & Wong, Y. J. (2006). A systematic review of associations among religiosity/spirituality and adolescent health attitudes and behaviors. *Journal of Adolescent Health*, 433–442. https://doi.org/10.1016/j.jadohealth.2005.02.004

Schnell, T. (2021). *The psychology of meaning in life*. Routledge.

Schnell, T., de Boer, E., & Alma, H. (2023). Worlds Apart? Atheist, agnostic, and humanist worldviews in three European countries. *Psychology of Religion and Spirituality*, *15*(1), 83–93. https://doi.org/10.1037/rel0000446

Schnell, T., Fuchs, D., & Hefti, R. (2020). Worldview under stress: Preliminary findings on cardiovascular and cortisol stress responses predicted by secularity, religiosity, spirituality, and existential search. *Journal of Religion and Health*, *59*(6), 2969–2989. https://doi.org/10.1007/s10943-020-01008-5

Schnell, T., & Keenan, W. (2011). Meaning-Making in an Atheist World. *Archive for the Psychology of Religion*, *33*, 55–78.

Schnell, T., & Keenan, W. J. F. (2013). The construction of atheist spirituality: A survey-based study. In Westerink, H. (Ed.), *Constructs of meaning and transformation: Current issues in the psychology of religion* (pp. 101–118). Vienna University Press.

Shneidman, E. S. (1993). *Suicide as psychache: A clinical approach to self-destructive behavior*. Jason Aronson, Inc.

Silver, C. F., Coleman, T. J. III, Hood, R. W. Jr., & Holcombe, J. M. (2014). The six types of nonbelief: A qualitative and quantitative study of type and narrative. *Mental Health, Religion & Culture*, *17*(10), 990–1001. http://dx.doi.org/10.1080/13674676.2014.987743

Smith, G. A., Tevington, P., Nortey, J., Rotolo, M., Kallo, A., & Alper, B. A. (2024, January 24). *Religious 'nones' in America: Who they are and what they believe*. Pew Research Center. https://www.pewresearch.org/religion/2024/01/24/religious-nones-in-america-who-they-are-and-what-they-believe/

Smith, J. M., & Halligan, C. L. (2020). Making meaning without a maker: Secular consciousness through narrative and cultural practice. *Sociology of Religion*, *82*(1), 85–110. https://doi.org/10.1093/socrel/sraa016

Speed, D., & Fowler, K. (2016). What's god got to do with it? How religiosity predicts atheists' health. *Journal of Religion and Health*, *55*(1), 296–308. https://doi.org/10.1007/s10943-015-0083-9

Speed, D., & Fowler, K. (2021). One size doesn't fit all: Religious/spiritual identities moderate salutary effects of religion. *Mental Health, Religion, & Culture*, *24*(2), 117–124. https://doi.org/10.1080/13674676.2020.1863934

Steele, C. M., & Aronson, J. (1995). Stereotype threat and the intellectual test performance of African Americans. *Journal of Personality and Social Psychology*, *69*(5), 797–811. https://doi.org/10.1037/0022-3514.69.5.797

Stephenson, K., & Cragun, R. T. (2022, August 8). Digging for Worldviews in Community Gardens. In *Paper presented at the Association for the Sociology of Religion Annual Conference*, Los Angeles, CA.

Taves, A., Asprem, E., & Ihm, E. (2018). Psychology, meaning making, and the study of Worldviews: Beyond Religion and non-religion. *Psychology of Religion and Spirituality*, *10*(3), 207–217. https://doi.org/10.1037/rel0000201

Tonigan, J. S., Miller, W. R., & Schermer, C. (2002). Atheists, agnostics and alcoholics anonymous. *Journal of Studies on Alcohol*, *63*(5), 534–541. https://doi.org/10.15288/jsa.2002.63.534

Trombley, C. (2023). Side-Stepping God: How the Nonreligious Find Success in Alcoholics Anonymous. [Doctoral dissertation, Western Michigan University. Western Michigan Digital Archive. https://scholarworks.wmich.edu/dissertations/3971

van Mulukom, V., Turpin, H., Haimila, R., Purzycki, B. G., Bendixen, T., Kundtová Klocová, E., Řezníček, D., Coleman, T. J., III, Sevinç, K., Maraldi, E., Schjoedt, U., Rutjens, B. T., & Farias, M. (2023). What do nonreligious nonbelievers believe in? Secular worldviews around the world. *Psychology of Religion and Spirituality*, *15*(1), 143–156. https://doi.org/10.1037/rel0000480

Vernon, G. M. (1968). The religious "Nones": A neglected category. *Journal for the Scientific Study of Religion*, *7*(2), 219. https://doi.org/10.2307/1384629

Webb, J. R. (2021). *Understanding forgiveness and addiction: Theory, research, and clinical application*. Routledge.

Webb, J. R., Toussaint, L., & Dula, C. S. (2014). Ritualistic, theistic, and existential spirituality: Initial psychometric qualities of the RiTE measure of spirituality. *Journal of Religion and Health*, *53*, 972–985. https://doi.org/10.1007/s10943-013-9697-y

White, W. (2014). *Slaying the dragon: The history of addiction treatment and recovery in America* (2nd ed.). Chestnut Health Systems/Lighthouse Institute.

Williams, L. M. (2021). Unequally yoked? Religion and spirituality in couples in which one believes in God and the other does not. *Pastoral Psychology*, *70*(3), 225–238. https://doi.org/10.1007/s11089-021-00948-3

Yudkin, D. A., Prosser, A. M. B., Heller, S. M., McRae, K., Chakroff, A., & Crockett, M. J. (2022). Prosocial correlates of transformative experiences at secular multi-day mass gatherings. *Nature Communications*, *13*:2600. https://doi.org/10.1038/s41467-022-29600-1

Chapter 7

Parallels between Positive Psychology and Spirituality

The Twelve-Step Model as Another Example

Jon R. Webb, Seyma N. Saritoprak, George E. Comiskey, James M. Nelson, and Doug Oman*

The field of scientific psychology, especially therapeutic psychology (e.g., clinical psychology and counseling psychology), has been described as the *secular priesthood* (see Reisner & Lawson, 1992). The implication here is that there are meaningful similarities between psychology and religion/spirituality. Indeed, both psychology and religion/spirituality are immersed in understanding and explaining the human condition, including "the nature of the soul and … the proper ends of human action and life, [as well as] in more practical ways, such as disciplines of character formation" (Kugelmann & Belzen, 2009, p. 126). In this regard, scholars are beginning to examine the association of positive psychology (PP) (i.e., human strengths and virtues) with religion and spirituality (Davis et al., 2023; Pargament & Mahoney, 2021), including the identification of many parallels or shared constructs between PP and religion/spirituality (e.g., empathy, compassion, and courage; Webb, 2021), and the relevance of such to health and well-being (see Part V of Davis et al., 2023). Of note, work in the specific context of addictive behavior has begun to describe the ties between PP and addiction recovery (Krentzman, 2013). This chapter will provide (1) brief discussions of (a) the definitions of spirituality and (b) PP, and (2) a larger discussion of the parallels between PP and (a) Judaism, Christianity, Islam, Hinduism, and Buddhism, and (b) the spirituality of the Twelve-Step Model (TSM) of Addiction Recovery.

Definition of Spirituality

There are many scholarly definitions of religion (cf. religiousness) and spirituality (e.g., Oman, 2013; Zinnbauer & Pargament, 2005; see also Chapter 3 of this volume), each of which, ostensibly, is seeking to bring clarity to topics arguably with nearly as many scholarly *and* lay definitions as persons thinking on or discussing the subject matter. In an effort to bring parsimony and consensus, Webb and colleagues have developed the RiTE Model of Spirituality (Webb, 2007/2003, 2021; Webb & Boye, 2024; Webb et al., 2014; see also Chapters 1 and 44 of this volume). In short, the common notions referenced by the largely dichotomous terms *religiousness* and *spirituality* were collapsed into an all-encompassing, overarching term *Spirituality*, which contains three *inter-related* dimensions. Accordingly, the RiTE definition of spirituality addresses "the salient, searching pursuit of the transcendently sacred [1] *ritualistic*, [2] *theistic*, and/or [3] *existential* aspects of the human condition" (Webb et al., 2014, p. 974; emphasis added). As religiousness and spirituality are subsumed under this expanded

* Corresponding Author: jon.r.webb@ttu.edu.

DOI: 10.4324/9781003440048-9

conceptualization and definition, hereafter, only the term spirituality will be used in reference thereto, unless otherwise indicated.

Definition of Positive Psychology

The American Psychological Association (APA) defines PP as "a field of psychological theory and research that focuses on the psychological states (e.g., contentment, joy), individual traits or CHARACTER STRENGTHS (e.g., intimacy, integrity, altruism, wisdom), and social institutions that enhance SUBJECTIVE WELL-BEING and make life most worth living" (APA, 2015, p. 810; emphasis in original). Related to this, the *Handbook of Positive Psychology, Religion, and Spirituality*, edited by Davis, Worthington, and Schnitker (2023), includes much material incorporating the conceptualization of *virtue* into the discussion of principles shared between PP and spirituality.

In sum, PP comprises the study of the constructive states, traits, strengths, and virtues (and related institutions) underlying and facilitating well-being. Importantly, the principles of PP are consistent with spirituality, whether ritualistic, theistic, and/or existential in its manifestation.

Parallels Between Positive Psychology and Spiritual Belief Systems

Given their shared priority of understanding and improving the human condition (see Davis et al., 2023; Kugelmann & Belzen, 2009), it would be fair to expect that PP and spirituality would value, espouse, and promote similar principles, practices, and interventions in their respective pursuit of such. It goes without saying that spirituality historically precedes not only PP but the *field* of psychology as a whole. Indeed, modern psychology can trace its emergence to the late 1800s when seeking to distinguish itself from philosophy, ground itself in empiricism, and establish its independence from spiritual teachings (see Levin & Vanderpool, 1991). Though spirituality has continually held near-matchless sway, for better or worse, in the context of the human condition (see Pincus, 1998), the grounding of psychology in empiricism ostensibly serves to maximize psychology's beneficence and minimize its malfeasance. Notwithstanding the intentional separation of psychology from spirituality, the fundamental principles of PP derive from, if not originate in, the major religious/spiritual belief systems of the world (see Hodge et al., 2023; Saritoprak & Abu-Raiya, 2023; Schiffman et al., 2023; Segall & Kristeller, 2023; Singh et al., 2023; see also Webb, in press). As such, the discussion of positive psychological principles as spiritual principles *first* (as is the case throughout this volume) is warranted.

As an example of a principle common to both PP and spirituality, consider the construct of forgiveness, defined "at a minimum, [as] an absence of ill will toward an offender" (Webb et al., 2017, p. 220). The basic notion of forgiveness is valued by all mainstream, worldwide religious/spiritual belief systems, whether Eastern, Western, monotheistic, polytheistic, or non-theistic (i.e., Judaism, Christianity, Islam, Hinduism, and Buddhism), as evidenced by both sacred (i.e., scripture) and scholarly (i.e., academic) writings (Webb, Toussaint, et al., 2012b). Likewise, forgiveness is a core construct in the PP movement, as evidenced, for example, by its inclusion in (1) the seminal work, *Character Strengths and Virtues: A Handbook and Classification* (Peterson & Seligman, 2004), (2) each of the three editions of the *Oxford Handbook of Positive Psychology* (McCullough et al., 2009; McCullough & Witvliet, 2002; Tsang & Martin, 2021), and (3) the more recently released first edition of the open-access

Handbook of Positive Psychology, Religion, and Spirituality (Washington-Nortey et al., 2023; see also Chapters 23 and 43 of this volume).

In addition to forgiveness, there are many constructs shared by PP and spirituality, for example, compassion, gratitude, hope, love, optimism, and wisdom. In Tables 7.1–7.5, we build upon an outline of 28 similarities between Judeo-Christian and positive psychological and positive psychotherapeutic principles previously provided by Webb (2021), by including references to Islamic scripture, references to the foundational literature of the TSM of addiction recovery, as well as corresponding references to the scientific literature.

Before turning our focus to understanding the TSM as another example of the interface between spirituality and PP, we will provide a brief overview of some areas of consistency of PP with Hinduism and Buddhism. Although Hinduism and Buddhism have each developed with reference to a rich corpus of ancient, sacred, scriptural texts, neither possesses a single widely utilized scripture that is regarded as fully authoritative. This can make it difficult to quote sacred text in the same manner as with respect to the Judeo-Christian and Islamic scriptures. As such, the tables do not include columns for Hindu and Buddhist scripture; instead, brief overviews of shared principles will be provided in the next two subsections of this chapter. Of note, each of the principles discussed in Tables 7.1–7.5 and the remainder of this chapter is not simply in the context of a particular positive psychological principle matched with a particular spiritual principle found in a particular spiritual belief system. Rather, said principles are largely shared across each approach to understanding the human condition, with regard to strengths and virtues and their association with health and well-being. That is, such principles are common to Judaism, Christianity, Islam, Hinduism, Buddhism, the TSM, and PP, though not necessarily in terms of exact meaning and/or application. That is, there can be nuanced differences in some cases, and even profound differences in other cases when considering potential implications related to underlying philosophy (e.g., conceptualization of the self[1]). Notwithstanding such potential differences, consistent with Peterson and Seligman (2004, p. 35), these common principles show "coherent resemblance" across the seven belief systems featured in this chapter.

Positive Psychology and Hinduism

Hinduism is the world's oldest and third-largest major religious tradition, although comparatively understudied in modern psychology (Oman, 2019). Nonetheless, Hinduism clearly possesses significant alignments with PP. With an eye to these alignments, a sampling of which will be noted in relation to Tables 7.1–7.5, this section presents a brief, albeit incomplete, sketch of some of Hinduism's key concepts and practices (for a fuller sketch, see Oman & Paranjpe, 2020). Hinduism shares many conceptual alignments with other Indic traditions (e.g., Sikhism, Jainism, and Buddhism), but differs from them in grounding itself in the *Vedas*, orally transmitted since the 2nd millennium BCE, which are regarded as authoritative and Hinduism's most sacred scriptures. Often, more directly influential in daily practice, however, are Hinduism's many "auxiliary" sacred texts, which include the *Bhagavad Gītā*, epics such as the *Rāmāyaṇa* and *Mahābhārata*, and too many others to list here. Also influential are Hinduism's six classic schools of philosophy, such as *Vedanta*, *Samkhya*, and *Yoga*, which present many nuanced psychological ideas. These sources collectively view the highest reality, or God, as simultaneously possessing both impersonal and personal aspects – an approach that has been described as *transimpersonal* because it goes "beyond the perspective… that the world is ultimately governed solely by laws that are impersonal, rather than by something that surpasses the impersonal by being both impersonal and personal" (Oman, 2025, p. 766).

Table 7.1 Parallels[a] between Positive Psychology, Spirituality[b], and the Twelve-Step Model – Part 1

Principle[c]	*Judeo-Christian*[d]	*Islam*[e]	*Twelve-Step*[f]	*Positive Psychology*
1. Action-oriented; Goal-directed; Commitment; Dedication	Isaiah 1:19 Zechariah 6:15 John 7:17 James 1:22 Deuteronomy 10:12 Joshua 22:5 Luke 9:62 Job 2:3 Job 27:5 2 Timothy 4:7	2:82 4:122 6:160 28:67	Big Book, pp. 72, 93–94 12 & 12, p. 106 Living Sober, p. 13 Came to Believe, p. 4	Locke (2002)
2. Altruism; Empathy	Luke 10:25–37 John 9:1-3	59:9 90:12–18	Big Book, pp. 74, 84 Came to Believe, p. 3 New Glasses, pp. 181–182	Duan and Sager (2021) Preston (2021)
3. Awareness of Feelings; Awareness of Thoughts (cf. Being Mindful)	Genesis 3:5 John 8:9 Acts 2:37 Ephesians 4:19 1 Timothy 4:2 1 Peter 1:13 1 Peter 5:8	4:1 5:93 59:18	12 & 12, p. 124 Living Sober, pp. 30, 46 Came to Believe, p. 4	Langer and Ngnoumen (2021)
4. Communal Reliance; Social Support	Leviticus 19:18, 34 Luke 22:32 2 Corinthians 8:4 Ephesians 4:11–16	4:36	12 & 12, pp. 57, 130 Came to Believe, p. 3	Hooker et al. (2021)
5. Compassion	Zechariah 7:9 Luke 10:33 1 Peter 3:8	24:20 90:17	Big Book; pp. 67, 115 Came to Believe, p. 4	Cassell (2021)

[a] This table builds upon Table 4 from Webb (2021), which builds upon Appendix B from Webb (1999).

[b] For a chapter-level scholarly discussion regarding positive psychology in the context of: (1) Hinduism, see Singh et al. (2023) and (2) Buddhism, see Segall and Kristeller (2023).

[c] Importantly, the references included in the columns of this table are but a sampling of material supporting these principles.

[d] References are taken from the King James Version (KJV, 1983) of *The Bible*. Also, see Schiffman et al. (2023) and Hodge et al. (2023) for chapter-level scholarly discussions regarding positive psychology in the context of Judaism and Christianity, respectively.

[e] References are taken from *The Qur'an* (quran.com); Surah : Ayah (chapter : verse). Also, see Saritoprak and Abu-Raiya (2023) for a chapter-level scholarly discussion regarding positive psychology in the context of Islam.

[f] References taken from various fundamental resource literature of the Twelve-Step Model of addiction recovery:
Big Book: AA (2001)
12 & 12: AA (1981)
Living Sober: AA (2019)
As Bill Sees It: W (1986; 1967)
Came to Believe: AA (1973)
Comes of Age: Co-Founder and W (1957)
New Glasses: Chuck (1984)

Table 7.2 Parallels[a] between Positive Psychology, Spirituality[b], and the Twelve-Step Model – Part 2[*]

Principle[c]	*Judeo-Christian*[d]	*Islam*[e]	*Twelve-Step*[f]	*Positive Psychology*
6. Courage	Deuteronomy 31:6 Joshua 1:7 2 Timothy 1:7	3:152	Big Book, p. 68 12 & 12, pp. 40–41, 83 Came to Believe, p. 4	Pury et al. (2021)
7. Forgiveness	Leviticus 19:18 Matthew 18:21–22 Luke 6:37	4:106 24:22 28:16 42:43	Big Book, pp. 77, 86 12 & 12, pp. 57–58 As Bill Sees It, p. 268	Tsang and Martin (2021) Washington-Nortey et al. (2023)
8. Gratitude	Psalms 100:4 Colossians 3:15	2:152 16:114 31:12 34:1 39:7	12 & 12, p. 95 Living Sober, p. 57 As Bill Sees It, p. 30 Came to Believe, p. 4	Watkins and McCurrach (2021) Cauble et al. (2023)
9. Happiness	Proverbs 16:20 John 16:33	36:54–55 41:30	Big Book, pp. 86–87 12 & 12, pp. 15, 16 Living Sober, p. 12	Oishi et al. (2021) Mancuso and Lorona (2023)
10. Hope	Jeremiah 17:7 Hebrews 3:6 Hebrews 6:19	4:104 12:87 68:32	Big Book, pp. xxii, xxiv, 17 12 & 12, p. 76 Living Sober, p. 86	Rand and Touza (2021) Washington-Nortey et al. (2023)
11. Humility	Proverbs 15:33 Proverbs 18:12 Proverbs 27:2 Matthew 23:12 Colossians 3:12	2:45 6:42-43 7:94 11:23 20:111-112	Big Book, pp. 60, 62, 75 12 & 12, p. 124 As Bill Sees It, p. 11	Worthington et al. (2021) Cauble et al. (2023)
12. Integrity; Non-Hypocrisy; Honesty	Job 13:16 Luke 11:39 Exodus 20:16 Matthew 19:18	2:204 9:77–78 14:38 17:35 26:89 26:181 29:11	Big Book, p. 58 12 & 12, p. 72 Came to Believe, p. 4	Harter (2002)
13. Knowledge	Proverbs 14:18 Proverbs 15:14 Proverbs 24:5 Romans 15:14 2 Peter 1:5	41:47 96:1–3	Big Book, pp. 7, 17, 25 12 & 12, p. 125 Living Sober, p. 43 As Bill Sees It, p. 202	Schulman (2002a)

[*] See notes a, b, c, d, e, and f in Table 7.1

Table 7.3 Parallels[a] between Positive Psychology, Spirituality[b], and the Twelve-Step Model – Part 3*

Principle[c]	*Judeo-Christian*[d]	*Islam*[e]	*Twelve-Step*[f]	*Positive Psychology*
14. Meaning; Purpose	Proverbs 3:13, 18 Proverbs 21:21	23:115 51:56	Big Book, pp. 10, 84 Living Sober, p. 18	Steger (2021) Park and Van Tongeren (2023)
	Matthew 10:39 John 6:35 Romans 8:6 Philippians 2:16 Ecclesiastes 3:1 Daniel 1:8 Acts 11:23 2 Corinthians 9:7	64:3	As Bill Sees It, p. 294	
15. Meditation	Psalms 19:14 1 Timothy 4:15	15:75 23:68 47:24	Big Book, pp. 86–87 12 & 12, p. 96 Living Sober, p. 44	Shapiro et al. (2021)
16. Moderate Behavior; Personal Control	Psalms 119:101 Proverbs 15:1 Proverbs 25:28 1 Corinthians 9:25 1 Corinthians 13:5 Philippians 4:5 Mark 8:34	2:168–169 3:134 5:91 5:105 90:11	Big Book, p. xxix 12 & 12, pp. 40–41, 52, 91 Living Sober, p. 33	Thompson (2021)
17. Morality; Ethics	Leviticus 19:18 Matthew 22:39	2:168 4:135	Big Book, p. 59 12 & 12, p. 72	Schulman (2002b) Handelsman et al. (2009)
		17:31-35 93:9-10	Living Sober, p. 41 Came to Believe, p. 119	
18. Other-oriented Love	Leviticus 19:18	2:177	Big Book, pp. 86, 95	Gable and Maisel (2021)
	Matthew 22:39 John 13:34–35	4:36 14:37 19:96 30:21 49:10	12 & 12, pp. 72, 106 Living Sober, p. 57 As Bill Sees It, p. 294 Came to Believe, p. 4	
19. Optimism	Proverbs 15:13 Proverbs 17:22	3:148 12:87 28:67 94:7–8	Big Book, p. 84 Living Sober, p. 86	Mens et al. (2021)
20. Self-Aware Love;	Leviticus 19:18	82:6-7	12 & 12, p. 124	North and Swann (2021)
Self-Regard; Self-Esteem	Deuteronomy 15:12–15 Matthew 7:12 Matthew 22:39	91:9	Living Sober, pp. 17, 41, 68 Came to Believe, p. 57	Hewitt (2021)

* See notes a, b, c, d, e, and f in Table 7.1

Table 7.4 Parallels[a] between Positive Psychology, Spirituality[b], and the Twelve-Step Model – Part 4*

Principle[c]	*Judeo-Christian*[d]	*Islam*[e]	*Twelve-Step*[f]	*Positive Psychology*
21. Self-Reliance; Self-Efficacy; Self-Determination (cf. Resilience; Personal Growth)	Proverbs 24:27 Luke 14:28–30 Philippians 4:13	2:153 8:46 16:41–42 76:11–12	Big Book, pp. 89–103 12 & 12, pp. 106–125 Came to Believe, p. 4	Maddux and Kleiman (2021) Wehmeyer et al. (2021) Cutuli et al. (2021) Anderson and Melo (2021) Captari et al. (2023)
22. Spirituality (including God, love of God); Faith	Romans 8:6 Deuteronomy 6:5 Matthew 22:37 Deuteronomy 32:20 Matthew 9:29	2:165 2:177 3:31	Big Book, pp. xxix, 45, 52 As Bill Sees It, p. 52 Came to Believe, p. 3	Pargament and Mahoney (2021)
23. Wisdom	Psalms 37:30 Proverbs 4:7 Ephesians 1:17 Colossians 4:5	26:83 33:70 43:3–4	12 & 12, pp. 40–41 As Bill Sees It, p. 14 Came to Believe, p. 4	Scheibe and Kunzmann (2021)
24. Addressing Personal Issues before Others'	Matthew 7:1–5		Big Book, p. 417	
25. Non-Judgmental; Righteous Judgment	Leviticus 19:15 Psalms 58:1 Isaiah 11:3–5 Matthew 7:1–5 Luke 6:37 John 7:24	5:49-50 40:20	12 & 12, pp. 82, 134 Living Sober, pp. 23, 48 As Bill Sees It, p. 80	

* See notes a, b, c, d, e, and f in Table 7.1

Like PP, Hinduism recognizes that people find diverse sources of meaning. Hinduism recognizes four overarching classes of legitimate human goals (*puruṣārthas*), roughly translatable as (1) duty (*dharma*), (2) success (*artha*), (3) gratification (*kāma*), and (4) the attainment of liberation/salvation, or self-realization, through a spiritually elevated and transformed state of consciousness (note parallels with Table 7.4, row 22). This last goal has been designated by numerous names that include God-realization, *mokṣa*, *apavarga*, *niḥśreyasa*, *kaivalya*, and *nirvāṇa* (Maharaj, 2017; Rao & Paranjpe, 2016).

People's pursuit of each of these classes of goals is acknowledged as an inevitable fact of life, and also affirmed as, in many cases, appropriate from a spiritual development

Table 7.5 Parallels[a] between Positive Psychology, Spirituality[b], and the Twelve-Step Model – Part 5[*]

Principle[c]	*Judeo-Christian*[d]	*Islam*[e]	*Twelve-Step*[f]	*Positive Psychology*
26. Organization; Order	Psalms 37:23 Psalms 119:133 Isaiah 9:7 1 Corinthians 14:40 Ephesians 4:11–16 Titus 1:5	10:3 82:6–7	Big Book, p. 164 Living Sober, p. 33 As Bill Sees It, p. 52 Comes of Age, pp. 224–225	
27. Rational Perfectionism (cf. self-capability)	Isaiah 5:27 Isaiah 40:31 1 Corinthians 9:24		Big Book, p. xxix Came to Believe, p. 4	
28. Responsibility	Joshua 7:19 Luke 16:2 Romans 2:6	10:41 17:26–27 76:7–9	12 & 12, p. 87 As Bill Sees It, p. 115 As Bill Sees It, p. 271	
29. Service; Volunteerism (cf. Charity)	Exodus 23: 4–5 Leviticus 19:18 Isaiah 1:17 Matthew 5:43–44 Matthew 7:12 Luke 10:33–35 Romans 12:1	2:177 2:280 3:134 3:92	Big Book, pp. 93–94, 97 (89–103) 12 & 12, pp. 106–125 Came to Believe, p. 119 New Glasses, pp. 181–182	

[*] See notes a, b, c, d, e, and f in Table 7.1

perspective (compare Table 7.3, row 14). Yet, like some strands of PP, Hinduism recognizes that "all goals are not created equal" (Ryan et al., 1996, p. 7; Waterman, 2008). Rather, Hinduism teaches that pursuing different goals leads to diverging long-term consequences. Hinduism views the material world as a site of ceaseless change, and regards the pursuit of desires directed to changeable objects as incapable of leading to *lasting* human joy or peace (e.g., *Mahābhārata* 1.75.50; *Manu Smṛti* 2.94). As expressed by Rao and Paranjpe (2016, p. 59): "Human desires can never be completely sated by means of objects of pleasure; instead they get stronger like fire flared by fuel." In the Hindu view, only through self-realization/liberation – the fourth major goal category (*puruṣārtha*) – will an individual's personal suffering come to an end.

Such liberation from suffering involves freeing oneself from the "separate" ego – that is, from egoistic desires for prestige, power, pleasure, profit, or other materially – or externally oriented goals or objects (for similar concepts in PP, see Leary & Guadagno, 2011). Becoming liberated involves breaking through one's conditioned identification with one's separate individual circumstances, body, and persona (the embodied individual, called *jīva*), a conditioned identification viewed as rooted in ignorance (*avidyā*). Breaking through such self-misunderstanding allows one to realize one's abiding and true self (*ātman*), usually understood[2] as a principle of *consciousness* that "unlike in Descartes [is] neither the thinker nor thoughts, but an experiencer beyond thoughts" (Rao & Paranjpe, 2016, p. 130). This true self is often said to be the same in all beings, so that a liberated individual "sees all beings in his own self and his own self in all beings" (*Īśa Upaniṣad* 6; Radhakrishnan, 1994, p. 572), leading to selflessness and altruism (compare Table rows 2, 18, and 29). This true self – experienced both internally and externally (within both oneself and others) – may also be experienced as *united* with the supreme divine reality.[3] A self-realized and liberated individual will experience abiding bliss, but may continue to function in the world as a so-called *īśvarakoṭi*, analogous to a Buddhist *bodhisattva*. Such a liberated individual possesses a "ripe ego" (*paka ami*) in which his or her sense of individual separateness can drop away easily – as needed – to serve the good of the whole, as a ripe fruit easily falls from a tree (Oman, 2023-).

For attaining such self-realization/liberation, Hinduism recognizes several different pathways, or *yogas*, especially the four so-called classical *yogas* that emphasize meditation (*dhyāna yoga*; see row 15), work and action (*karma yoga*), love and devotion (*bhakti yoga*), and wisdom (*jñāna yoga*; see row 23). Corresponding to each classic yoga are frequent or prototypical practices, such as selfless action (*niṣkāma karma*) in the yoga of work and action, discrimination between the changing and the changeless (*nitya-anitya viveka*) in the yoga of wisdom, and earnest-hearted calling of God's name (*nāma-japa, nāma-kīrtana*) in the yoga of love and devotion (Oman, 2024).[4] Contemporary approaches to yoga often emphasize an integrated combination of these practices (Oman & Paranjpe, 2020). This yoga-based pathway/destination structure renders many features of Hinduism coherently understandable with reference to Pargament's (2013) influential framework for conceptualizing religion and spirituality as involving a "search for the sacred" (Oman & Paranjpe, 2018, p. 142). Moreover, attaining the goal of such yogas – by whatever name the goal is called – is also generally recognized as beyond human self-effort alone, and thus requiring grace (*deva-prasāda* or *kṛpā*; Oman & Paranjpe, 2018, 2020). Such acknowledgement of a need for grace may be one reason why Indian participants in Alcoholics Anonymous (AA) have experienced the program as compatible with Indic religions (Kuruvilla et al., 2004).

Hinduism's understandings of life's ultimate and legitimate goals and pathways provide context for its resonance with PP. Singh et al. (2023) note that "Hinduism and positive psychology… share the common goal of enhancing human well-being" (p. 205), and that both encourage the cultivation of character strengths and virtues, such as temperance, humility, forgiveness, and self-regulation (see Peterson & Seligman, 2004; see also *Bhagavad Gītā* 16.1– 3, and compare Table rows 1–2, 5–8, 10–13, and 16). Such virtues are viewed as indispensable for pursuing self-realization and also helpful for attaining other legitimate life goals (Prabhavananda, 1963).

Importantly, only a small fraction of relevant scholarship on similarities between PP and Hinduism uses "Hinduism" in its title. Instead, a significant portion of such scholarship uses "Indian" in its title, or "Indian Psychology," reflecting a broader recent movement among psychologists in India to identify psychological teachings embedded within Hinduism and other Indic traditions that include Sikhism, Jainism, and Buddhism, which are viewed as largely mutually aligned in their psychological implications (Cornelissen, 2002; Rao & Paranjpe, 2016). Thus, for example, Rao and Paranjpe (2016) affirm a "convergence of positive psychology's focus on meaningful life with Indian ethos as depicted in Indian epics and puranas…. Providing guidelines for proper and meaningful behavior… [and] pointers for cultivating habits of mind conducive to making life meaningful" (p. 226). Sometimes, attention focuses on specific sacred texts – for example, Dabas and Singh (2018) observe "many similarities between Positive psychology and the teachings of the ancient Indian Scriptures… ideas like … flow and Seligman's happiness model can be traced to similar ideas in the

Bhagavad Gita and other Indian scriptures. Seligman's model of Happiness that has components of pleasure; meaning; and engagement, is very similar to the concept of *Purusharth* as described in the ancient Indian texts of the *Upanishads* and the *Mahabharata*" (p. 4).

It should also be noted that very commonly, scholars also assert *differences* between PP and the ideas common across Hinduism and other Indic traditions. Several scholars suggest that the resulting combination of similarities and differences with PP could support mutual learning or even "mutual reinforcement" (Rao, 2014, p. 94; see also Bhawuk, 2011; Ghosh & Deb, 2016; Lahiri, 2024; Singh et al., 2023). For example, a PP special issue target article by Rao (2014) commended PP's growing empirical base, but viewed it as "weak in theory" (p. 102), overemphasizing forms of hedonic happiness that are "inconsistent with the true purport of PP [positive psychology]" (p. 102), and that Indian psychology could provide "the necessary theoretical underpinning for many of the concepts that are prominently but loosely used in PP, such as positive emotion, happiness, suffering, flow, subjective wellbeing, spirituality, wisdom and so on" (p. 96).

In sum, Hinduism resonates in numerous ways with PP, many of which roughly correspond to ideas in the rows of Tables 7.1–7.5. However, Indian psychologists also have noted nontrivial differences between Hinduism and PP, such as the latter's greater emphasis on hedonic well-being.

Positive Psychology and Buddhism

Some useful comparisons can be made that illustrate potential similarities and differences of viewpoint between PP and Buddhism about important human issues. However, it is not realistic to make a definitive statement about the relationship between Buddhism and PP. This is because both PP and Buddhism are not monolithic entities, allowing for a diversity of comparisons, any one of which will have exceptions. Similarly, though shared principles may otherwise be identified, nuance and alternate interpretations can play a role.

Buddhism is one of the world's great religions, dating to the life of Gautama Buddha in the sixth to fifth century BCE. Since its founding, Buddhism has evolved into a family of Buddhist traditions with important differences in practices and beliefs. Details of any comparison of Buddhism and PP will thus depend to some extent on the specific Buddhist group considered in the analysis. Mahayana Pure Land Buddhism is not equivalent to Rinzai Zen or Nyingma Vajrayana. A reasonable approach to a first approximation is to focus on Buddhism in terms of its practice and belief as outlined in the earliest Buddhist documents, such as parts of the Pali canon, such as the *Majjhima Nikaya*, and early practice manuals like the *Visuddhimagga*.

PP has historically also been a diverse movement attempting to find an alternative to the perceived negative and psychopathological focus of twentieth-century psychology (Nelson & Canty, 2023). The fundamental presupposition of the movement is that an analysis of the human condition should focus on strengths, virtues, human potential, and positive outcomes. Classically, this has taken two approaches: a hedonic emphasis focusing on the development of positive emotions and a eudaemonic approach that focuses on the living of a good life.

From the Buddhist perspective, both the overall presupposition of PP and its hedonic or eudaemonic conceptualizations contain wisdom but have important limitations. In critique of the overall view of PP, Buddhists would certainly agree that any psychology lacking an understanding of human potential is deficient, but they would also ask, is it possible to have an understanding of human well-being without analysis and focus on the nature and causes of suffering? Classical Buddhism, based on the Four Noble Truths, argues that any understanding of the human condition must begin with an acknowledgement of suffering and an analysis of its causes (Nanamoli & Bodhi, 2001). Nevertheless, concepts such as compassion, gratitude, forgiveness, humility, and others included in Tables 7.1–7.5 arise from the Buddhist understanding of and approach to addressing suffering (i.e., the Four Noble Truths, including the Eightfold Path). Thus, it is fair to say that important basic principles and practices (though not necessarily all) are shared between Buddhism and PP. Even still, there can be important differences, in some cases nuanced and in other cases more obvious and profound.

Some PP writers have recognized this problem and attempted to broaden their analysis by including suffering in the picture (e.g., Ivtzan et al., 2016; Wong, 2011). Typically, this has taken an existential-type approach, arguing that suffering has a positive benefit and thus has an appropriate place in positive conceptions of human life. In contrast, Buddhism sees suffering (*dukkha*) as a sign of deep problems rather than a necessary or desirable part of life. Thus, while early Buddhism is sympathetic with the concerns of PP, it takes a significantly divergent path to exploring human potential.

The hedonic approach of PP has the most significant divergences from Buddhism. Both agree that an analysis of emotion is essential to understanding human life and development, and that personal development should go beyond the elimination of negative emotions and involve some kind of positive mental state. However, there are differing perspectives on the nature and importance of this mental state. For hedonic PP, this state is often described in terms of happiness, which is thought of as a state of pleasure, joy, and/or contentment. In contrast, for Buddhism, a state of tranquility (*passaddhi*) is seen as the end result. More importantly, the two approaches differ dramatically on the role and importance of this feeling state. As is typical in Western culture, especially since Descartes and the Early Modern period (Dixon, 2003), hedonic PP holds that positive emotions are highly desirable and should be sought as an end goal. Buddhism has a much more critical view of emotions because they can become objects of attachment, so that we desire or crave a particular emotional state, destroying the possibility for free personal development. Feeling states like tranquility will occur, but they are signs of advances toward enlightenment rather than ends to be pursued for their own sake.

The eudaemonic approach in PP generally has more in common with Buddhism than its hedonic alternative. Eudaemonic PP sees human flourishing as a way of life rather than an emotional state (cf. Nelson & Canty, 2023), and most Buddhists would strongly agree that the way one lives their life in practices and ethical conduct is incredibly important. In early Buddhism, right ethical conduct (as a component of the Eightfold Path) is a necessary precursor to any kind of genuine spiritual practice and advancement (Buddhaghosa, 1999). Eudaemonic PP is similarly attuned to ethical concerns, perhaps because of its historic link with Aristotelian philosophy in the *Nicomachean Ethics*.

However, there are also important differences. Ultimately, a comparison must also address the question: Are the PP concepts of the good life equivalent to those in Buddhism, or are there important differences? It is impossible to give a categorical answer to the question, since PP does not have a consensus definition of the meaning of these terms. However, many differences are apparent. On a superficial level, Buddhist devotional practices and community life are strikingly different from those described in PP. On a deeper level, there are also more fundamental differences. It is common for psychologists in the PP tradition to have a view of the good life that includes and supports the development of a strong personal identity and sense of self. In contrast, Buddhism from its earliest incarnations generally rejects this and holds a doctrine of no-self (*anatta*) that sees the self as an impermanent illusion, and that focus on maintaining or strengthening the self actually impedes our progress toward enlightenment.

The Twelve Steps

Each of the 12 steps of the TSM (aa.org/the-twelve-steps) is considered critical for full addiction recovery to occur, take hold, and endure (see AA, 2001; see also Webb, 2021, in press). The first and foremost task of the TSM (i.e., Step 1) is for the person struggling with addiction to develop a clear understanding of where they do and do not have control in their day-to-day life, including the ostensible reality of being powerless over their addictive behavior. Step 2 involves the careful identification and deliberate choice of a personally congruent Higher Power. Step 3 involves a voluntary decision to commit one's will and life to this entity. Step 4 is the personal development of a candid and comprehensive accounting of one's life experiences – for better or worse – and Step 5 entails an appropriately open, genuine, and full disclosure of this personal accounting to one's chosen and trusted sponsor, or other trusted confidant (religious leader, therapist, healthcare worker, etc.). Next, one is to engage in active (Step 6) and humble (Step 7) submission to one's Higher Power, thereby effectuating an intentional and collaborative relationship therewith. Hart (1999) has described Steps 8 and 9 as the forgiveness steps of the TSM. While Step 8 involves becoming willing to make amends, Step 9 requires following through with such when possible and appropriate (i.e., one is not to cause *more* pain and suffering when seeking to make amends). Step 10 is the unwavering commitment to a continual and deliberate process of examining and applying the principles of Steps 4 through 9 to any and all matters (a) arising moving forward and (b) missed from the past. Step 11 entails the intentional and consistent return to Steps 2 and 3 in a genuine and forthright effort to maintain, strengthen, and deepen one's connection with their Higher Power, including the full recognition that recovery cannot emerge, take shape, and flourish without this whole-hearted relationship. Step 12 is a two-fold process involving the determined (a) provision of service to those still struggling with active addiction and (b) application of the TSM to all aspects of one's life. In sum, TSM-based addiction recovery is not simply a question of reducing or eliminating one's addictive behavior (i.e., Step 1 through Step 11). Steadfast service to others and durable lifestyle change (i.e., Step 12) are critical and necessary components of ongoing and persistent addiction recovery, from a TSM point of view.

Three Fundamental Processes Embedded in the Twelve Steps

Although each of the steps in the TSM is of singular importance, the individual steps can be grouped together into three critical processes designed to further generate and evoke practicable and viable addiction recovery (see AA, 2001; see also Webb, 2021, in press). The initial, first three steps facilitate the process commonly known as acceptance and surrender. That is, recognizing one's problem and struggle with addictive behavior, conceding the need for help, and submitting to an enabling power external to and greater than the self. This process allows a person struggling with addictive behavior to admit the need for and start on the path to recovery. Without acceptance and surrender, a person struggling with addictive behavior – per the TSM – will likely continue to wrestle against the unmanageable nature of their addictive behavior and their powerlessness over it. The middle six steps (i.e., 4 through 9) are designed to "develop the necessary tools for addressing the past, stabilizing the present, and instilling hope for a different future" (Webb, in press, p. 9). The initial process of acceptance and surrender and the middle process of "clear[ing] away the wreckage of [the] past" (AA, 2001, p. 164), together facilitate early recovery and lay the groundwork for lasting recovery. The final three steps (i.e., 10 through 12) serve to broaden, deepen, and strengthen the progress made in the first nine steps through the process of methodical, comprehensive lifestyle change. That is, in a consistent and continual manner, one is to intentionally, deliberately, and explicitly (a) revisit and engage with the principles and procedures of Steps 1 through 9, (b) serve others, and (c) integrate the TSM into all aspects of one's life *and* day-to-day living. Of note, "sustainable long-term addiction recovery – per the TSM – is not an event, but a life-long pursuit of ever-increasing self-improvement and refinement, as a function of renewal and a newfound meaning and purpose in life derived from a spiritual awakening" (Webb, in press, p. 9).

Forgiveness as a Parallel Between Positive Psychology and TSM-Oriented Spirituality

In keeping with forgiveness as an example of a principle shared by PP and the mainstream spiritual belief systems of the world (i.e., Judaism, Christianity, Islam, Hinduism, and Buddhism; see above), it is also a fundamental principle in the TSM of addiction recovery. The word forgive and its variants are found only 29 times in the combined 884 pages of the following books (i.e., 10, 19, and 0 times, respectively): the so-called *Big Book* (AA, 2001), *Twelve Steps and Twelve Traditions* (AA, 1981), and *Living Sober* (AA, 2019); arguably, the three most foundational sources of authoritative literature for the TSM as a whole (i.e., regardless of the substance or target behavior the TSM is applied to). Nevertheless, the notion of forgiveness is implicit to the TSM, given the central, organizing concern of resentments to the development, maintenance, and resolution of addictive behavior, and the role of forgiveness as a natural antidote to resentment.

Indeed, in the *Big Book* of AA and its equivalents in the context of other substances and targeted behaviors that the TSM has been applied to, the fundamental relevance of resentment is emphasized. For example, with regard to Alcoholics Anonymous (2001, p. 64), "Resentment is the 'number one' offender. It destroys more alcoholics than anything else." Narcotics Anonymous (2008, p. 4), "Hostile, resentful, self-centered and self-seeking, we cut ourselves off from the outside world," Cocaine Anonymous (ca.org/literature/guide-to-the-12-steps/), "[Identify] any [and all] resentments, fears, or persons we have harmed," Marijuana Anonymous (2017, p. 16), "We held on to resentments about the past, which prohibited us from embracing the present and living our lives to the fullest." Nicotine Anonymous (2015, p. 84), "That process of exploration involved looking at the people and events that led to past fears, resentments, self-loathing …," Gamblers Anonymous (1989, p. 44), "Anger could lead you back to a bet via the hatred and resentment created," Overeaters Anonymous (2018, p. 78), "Our energies are no longer bound up in our worries and resentments, and we are free to move forward again." Sex Addicts Anonymous (2005, p. 34), "[R]esentment is one of the most stubborn obstacles to our spiritual growth." Suicide Anonymous (2015, p. 35), "Often victims of emotional deprivation in childhood, we had learned to survive on anger and resentment," and Codependents Anonymous (2012, p. 18), "For many of us, fear is our guardian; it helps protect us from harm. … Our fear may be cloaked in anger or resentment, rage, pain, or loneliness."

Moreover, the *comprising nature* of forgiveness is consistent with the entire TSM of addiction recovery. Not only have Steps 8 and 9 been described as the forgiveness steps of the TSM (Hart, 1999), given their focus on making amends (see above), but Webb and colleagues have also identified and provided extensive, detailed discussion of the fundamental components of forgiveness within each of the steps of the TSM (esp. Webb, 2021; see also Webb et al., 2015; Webb & Trautman, 2010).

Models of Forgiveness

Worthington and colleagues (see Worthington, 1998, 2003, 2006; Worthington & Sandage, 2016) and Enright and colleagues (Enright, 2001; Enright & Fitzgibbons, 2015; Enright et al., 1998; Enright & The Human Development Study Group, 1991) have each developed comprehensive models of the psychology of forgiveness, including with regard to how to *engage* in forgiveness. Although other models have been developed (e.g., Cornish & Wade, 2015; Luskin, 2002), the pioneering models developed by Worthington and Enright have received the most empirical attention (Wade et al., 2014; Worthington & Wade, 2020), both in terms of their capacity to increase levels of forgiveness *and* as interventions in the context of health and well-being – whether largely employed as a (1) self-directed resource (i.e., Worthington's REACH Model; see Worthington, 2020) or (2) clinician-directed resource (i.e., Enright's Process Model; see Freedman & Enright, 2020). Of note, both Worthington and Enright developed their initial models in the context of forgiveness of others, but have since adapted their models to incorporate the additional, specific context of forgiveness of self (e.g., Enright & The Human Development Study Group, 1996; Worthington, 2006). Importantly, forgiveness of self is meaningfully different from forgiveness of others; for example, as one cannot avoid the self, forgiveness of self requires reconciliation, whereas forgiveness of others does not (Enright & The Human Development Study Group, 1996; Hall & Fincham, 2005; Tangney et al., 2005). Nevertheless, the fundamental principles and aims of forgiveness – in its multiple dimensions – are largely the same regardless of the target (e.g., self, other, deity) *or* method thereof (e.g., offering, seeking, feeling) (Toussaint & Webb, 2005; Webb, 2021; Webb et al., 2017).

The REACH Model of Forgiveness

Worthington's REACH Model of Forgiveness is a psychoeducational intervention that was intentionally designed to be implementable by the lay public through the utilization of freely available workbooks (see Worthington, 2025) by individuals and otherwise untrained facilitators. The REACH Model is meant to assist persons seeking to forgive to engage in a five-part procedure (see, e.g., Worthington, 2006, 2020; see also Webb, 2021). That is (and very briefly), to (1) *recall* an offense or transgression and its associated pain and justifiable negative emotional responses in a forthright, genuine, and objective manner – with eyes wide open and without minimizing or overlooking anything at all; (2) develop *empathy* for the offender (or emotional reprocessing) – not to justify the offense or somehow view the offense as now a good or inconsequential experience, but to understand context, circumstance, and common humanity; (3) thoughtfully, voluntarily, and freely offer forgiveness as an *altruistic gift* – indeed, to an undeserving offender that committed a wholly unjustifiable and unnecessary offense; (4) thoroughly and, of necessity, publicly *commit* to the procedure of forgiveness – for example, write a letter, even if it will never be delivered; that is, it is critical to get the task and work of forgiveness out of one's mind; and (5) *hold on* to progress made, not if, but when doubts (and their associated pain, fear, and frustration) arise – as they so invariably and inevitably will. Indeed, in the words of Mohandas Karamchand Gandhi, "The weak can never forgive. Forgiveness is the attribute of the strong" (1931, p. 59).[5]

The Process Model of Forgiveness

Enright's Process Model of Forgiveness is a psychotherapeutic intervention that was designed to be implemented by professionally trained clinicians in counseling-oriented settings.

The Process Model is a four-phase method, consisting of 20 steps or units of forgiveness (see, e.g., Enright & Fitzgibbons, 2015; Freedman & Enright, 2020; see also Webb, 2021).

Very briefly, the initial phase is termed *uncovering* and includes eight units designed to address (1) defense mechanisms, (2) anger, (3) shame and/or guilt, dysfunctional (4) emotions and (5) cognitions, (6) offender versus offended transgression-related, outcome-based experiential discrepancies, and lastly to help the offended understand that the (7) arduous nature of the offense sensibly is enduring, as is (8) its consequent, negative impact on their worldview. The second phase is termed *decision*, and includes three units designed to facilitate (9) the personal recognition that an alternate, more constructive response to offensive experiences is needed, (10) an accurate and reasoned understanding of and freely determined choice to consider forgiveness as an option, and (11) a commitment to and trust in the prospect of forgiveness.

The third phase is termed *work*, and includes four units designed to help the offended (12) reframe and re-envision the offense and/or offender based on any relevant context, (13) not to justify or explain away, but to develop perspective, empathy, and compassion for the offender, so that (14) the pain, through full acknowledgement and acceptance – not denial – can begin to heal rather than fester due to rumination, all of which is intended (15) to catalyze the undeserved, but moral gift of forgiveness. The ending phase is termed *deepening*, and includes five units designed to empower the offended to (16) derive meaning from their suffering, (17) recognize that all humans need and struggle for, but do not deserve forgiveness, and (18) embrace (a) the universality of the pain and suffering associated with the struggle for forgiveness and thus (b) the opportunity and *need* for reciprocal social support. All of which further develops a sense of meaning and purpose, which serves to (19) reinforce, stabilize, and sustain progress, such that (20) the heretofore negative – yet, largely justifiable – responses to offensive experiences dissipate, thereby enabling the end product of forgiveness to crystallize.

Shared Principles Between the Twelve-Step Model and Models of Forgiveness

The fundamental principles of the TSM of addiction recovery and the fundamental principles of forgiveness are consistent with each other (see Webb, 2021; see also Webb et al., 2015; Webb & Trautman, 2010). As outlined in Table 9 (and the corresponding body of text) in Webb (2021), the first component of Worthington's REACH Model (i.e., Recall) and the first component of Enright's Process Model (i.e., Uncovering) are consistent with Step 1 of the TSM, or Acceptance. The second, third, and fourth components of the REACH Model (i.e., Empathy, Altruistic Gift, and Commit, respectively) and the second and third components of the Process Model (i.e., Decision and Work, respectively) are consistent with Step 2 and Step 3 of the TSM, or Surrender. The fourth component of the REACH Model and the third component of the Process Model are consistent with Steps 4 through 9 of the TSM, or the means of laying the groundwork for lasting recovery. And, the fifth component of the REACH Model (i.e., Hold On) and the fourth component of the Process Model (i.e., Deepening) are consistent with Steps 10 through 12 of the TSM, or the means of maintaining progress and creating comprehensive lifestyle change.

In addition to forgiveness, there are many constructs common to PP and spirituality found in the TSM of addiction recovery (see Tables 7.1–7.5). Related to this, example strengths and virtues with explicit scientific support in the context of addiction recovery include forgiveness (Webb, 2021), gratitude (Chen, 2017), hope (Kimball et al., 2017), altruism, meaning and purpose in life, and spirituality itself (see Krentzman, 2013). Chapters 18 and 17 of this volume provide a more in-depth discussion of spirituality and addictive behavior, including suicidal behavior. In sum, when considering the parallels between spirituality and PP, including forgiveness, in the context of the TSM of addiction recovery, there are many similarities in principle and practice. Indeed, "the pathway from spirituality to addiction recovery [*and* health and well-being, more broadly] is likely complex, yet comprised of much and varied opportunity for success" (Webb, in press, p. 4).

The Twelve-Step Model, Health, and Well-Being

The TSM can play a powerful role in facilitating recovery for persons struggling with addictive behavior, which is a component of their overall health and well-being as well. However, it is critical also to said persons' *general* health and well-being. In this regard, the culminating aspect of the TSM is its 12th step. Step 12 is the unfaltering resolve to provide selfless service and aid to others, especially those mired in active addiction, including sharing the message of recovery – in word and in deed – as embodied by the TSM. That is, "the only way we can keep what was given to us is by sharing this new gift of life [with those still suffering from addiction]" (Narcotics Anonymous, 2008, p. 50). The notion of service (i.e., helping others, volunteerism, charity – broadly construed) is a fundamental component of spirituality and spiritual health and well-being (see Tables 7.1–7.5), and likely health and well-being, more broadly. Related to this is the multicultural truism that serving others is an antidote to the pitfalls associated with personal struggle and self-rumination.

Of equal importance in Step 12 is to continually and explicitly work to incorporate the TSM in *all* aspects of one's life, not just with regard to addictive behavior (see above). That is, not only is comprehensive lifestyle change critical for long-term, sustainable addiction recovery (per the TSM), but also the power of the TSM to enable such lifestyle change is thought to have the capacity also to facilitate health and well-being in the context of many psychological and mental health-related difficulties. Both in the context of its formal application to negative emotions (e.g., depressedanon.com; emotionsanonymous.org), and with respect to informal personal grounding in and application of the TSM, in general. Indeed, the implication of the assumed relevance of the general principles of the TSM to health and well-being (broadly construed) is that they are effective in facilitating emotional stability, behavior change, and adaptive living, whether in terms of prevention or intervention. As such, adherence to the TSM has relevance not only to addiction recovery but also to health promotion in general. Said another way, the TSM may very well facilitate health and well-being whether a person struggles with addictive behavior or not (see AA, 1981, p. 16). A common caution to prevent relapse[6] in the context of the TSM is to self-monitor one's levels of hunger, anger, loneliness, and tiredness (HALT; see AA, 2019; Nowinski et al., 1994). Excessive levels of such can lead to difficulties with thinking clearly and thus, problem-solving effectively and efficiently, thereby increasing one's vulnerability and risk for relapse, or returning to addictive behavior. While the utility of HALT enjoys much anecdotal evidence among adherents to the TSM, it is also beginning to find empirical support in the context of better outcomes related to addiction recovery (Webb et al., 2024; Webb & Brewer, 2010; Webb, Hill, et al., 2012a; Webb et al., 2013). And, evidence is beginning to emerge regarding the utility of HALT in the context of health and well-being more broadly (Ragau et al., 2018; see also Cornes et al., 2023; Fonseka et al., 2021).

Conclusion

Spirituality and PP share many similar constructs in their common pursuit of understanding and improving the human condition. Indeed, these similarities are reflected in the sacred texts of the Abrahamic faith traditions (i.e., Judaism, Christianity, and Islam), the organizing principles and fundamental values of Hinduism and Buddhism, and in empirically supported, scholarly work as contained, for example, in (1) the seminal work, *Character Strengths and Virtues: A Handbook and Classification* (Peterson & Seligman, 2004), (2) the *Oxford Handbook of Positive Psychology* (Snyder et al., 2021), and (3) the *Handbook of Positive Psychology, Religion, and Spirituality* (Davis et al., 2023). Importantly, the TSM (e.g., AA, 2001) provides another example of the interface between PP and spirituality in service of health and well-being, both in the specific context of addiction recovery and health and well-being more broadly construed. Although empirical evidence is beginning to emerge in support of the relevance of the TSM to health and well-being in general (i.e., the HALT principle), much more work needs to be done, including with respect to (1) expanding beyond HALT and (2) the assumptions regarding the salubrious effect of the TSM on emotional stability, behavior change, and adaptive living.

Notes

1 Hinduism and Buddhism are typically thought of as having different concepts of the self, as compared to Western psychology and the Abrahamic faith traditions. However, the TSM, though grounded in the Judeo-Christian beliefs of its founders (see section: The TSM as Spirituality), also values moving away from self (though, not necessarily entirely), in terms of its facilitative effect for spiritual awakening and self-transformation. Along these lines is the common TSM theme of the ubiquitous presence and role of self-centeredness in active addiction (see Webb & Toussaint, 2018). Indeed, consider the following two quotes from the *Big Book* of Alcoholics Anonymous (AA, 2001). "Being convinced that self, manifested in various ways, was what had defeated us, we considered its common manifestations" (p. 64), and "Selfishness – self-centeredness! That, we think, is the root of our troubles. Driven by a hundred forms of fear, self-delusion, self-seeking, and self-pity .... Above everything, we [persons struggling with addiction] must be rid of this selfishness. We must, or it kills us!" (p. 62).

2 Rao and Paranjpe (2016) note that in contrast to Hinduism's other classic philosophical schools, the Nyāya and Vaiśeṣika schools conceptualize the self as also encompassing "the agent of action" (p. 139).

3 Oman and Paranjpe (2020, p. 180) describe how Hinduism offers varying narratives for the ontological bases of such experiences of unity – differing narratives for "*what* is merged" – noting that narratives by some schools of *Vedānta* offer significant parallels to Abrahamic mystical narratives of union.

4 Note that these classic *yogas* do *not* include the sets of physical exercises known in the West as "yoga." For thousands of years, most Hindu understandings of *yoga* gave minimal or no attention to the physical postures and stretching exercises now disseminated widely in what Singleton (2013, p. 38) has called "transnational anglophone yoga." For example, posture (*āsana*) is mentioned in only two of the 196 aphorisms that comprise Patañjali's *Yoga Sūtras*, the foundational text of Hinduism's *Yoga* school of philosophy, which focuses on explicating the *yoga* (or pathway to liberation) of meditation (*dhyāna yoga*; for further discussion, see Oman & Paranjpe, 2020, Appendix, pp. 191–192).

5 Of note, the fuller quote – including its context – is: "Q. 'Do not you think it impolitic to forgive a government which has been guilty of a thousand murders?' A. 'I do not know a single instance where forgiveness has been found so wanting as to be impolitic.' Q. But no country has ever shown such forgiveness as India is showing to Britain?' A. 'That does not affect my reply. What is true of individuals is true of nations. One cannot forgive too much. The week can never forgive. Forgiveness is the attribute of the strong' " (Gandhi, 1931, p. 59).

6 The field of Addiction-Recovery is moving away from using the term *relapse*. Much of society associates this term with failure because of an antiquated and baseless condemnation of individuals with substance use disorder or addiction who do not become "cured" with their first treatment. Most people in the field now use the less stigmatized term *return to use* (or, *return to addictive behavior*), which is consistent with the term *recurrence* used for other chronic diseases that, just like with addiction, have varying degrees of success or adherence after treatment.

References

Alcoholics Anonymous. (1973). *Came to believe*. Author.

Alcoholics Anonymous. (1981). *Twelve steps and twelve traditions*. Author. See https://www.aa.org/pages/en_US/twelve-steps-and-twelve-traditions

Alcoholics Anonymous. (2001). *Alcoholics Anonymous: The story of how many thousands of men and women have recovered from alcoholism* (Fourth ed.). Author. See https://www.aa.org/pages/en_US/alcoholics-anonymous

Alcoholics Anonymous. (2019). *Living sober*. Author. See https://www.aa.org/living-sober-book

Alcoholics Anonymous. (2023). Understanding Alcoholics Anonymous and Spirituality. Retrieved August 29, 2024, from https://www.aa.org/sites/default/files/literature/AA%20and%20Spirituality%20Press%20Release%20-%20EN_0.pdf

American Psychological Association. (2015). *APA dictionary of psychology* (Second ed.). Author.

Anderson, A., & Melo, H. (2021). Neurogenetics of resilience. In C. R. Snyder, S. J. Lopez, L. M. Edwards, & S. C. Marques (Eds.), *Oxford handbook of positive psychology* (3rd ed., pp. 718–733). Oxford University Press.

Bhawuk, D. P. S. (2011). *Spirituality and Indian psychology: Lessons from the Bhagavad Gita*. Springer. https://doi.org/10.1007/978-1-4419-8110-3

Buddhaghosa, B. (1999). *The path of purification (Visuddhimagga)*. (B. Nanamoli, Trans.). BPS Pariyatti.

Captari, L. E., Shannonhouse, L., Aten, J. D., & Snyder, J. D. (2023). Building spiritual fortitude and resilience following disaster: Synthesizing the contributions of positive psychology and religion/spirituality. In E. B. Davis, E. L. Worthington, Jr., & S. A. Schnitker (Eds.), *Handbook of positive psychology, religion, and spirituality* (pp. 475–490). Springer Nature Switzerland AG. https://doi.org/10.1007/978-3-031-10274-5_30

Cassell, E. J. (2021). Compassion. In C. R. Snyder, S. J. Lopez, L. M. Edwards, & S. C. Marques (Eds.), *Oxford handbook of positive psychology* (3rd ed., pp. 507–518). Oxford University Press. https://doi.org/10.1093/oxfordhb/9780199396511.013.31

Cauble, M. R., Said, I. A., McLaughlin, A. T., Gazaway, S., Van Tongeren, D. R., Hook, J. N., Lacey, E. K., Davis, E. B., & Davis, D. E. (2023). Religion/spirituality and the twin virtues of humility and gratitude. In E. B. Davis, E. L. Worthington, Jr., & S. A. Schnitker (Eds.), *Handbook of positive psychology, religion, and spirituality* (pp. 379–393). Springer Nature Switzerland AG. https://doi.org/10.1007/978-3-031-10274-5_24

Chen, G. (2017). Does gratitude promote recovery from substance misuse? *Addiction Research & Theory*, *25*(2), 121–128. https://doi.org/10.1080/16066359.2016.1212337

Chuck, C. (1984). *A new pair of glasses*. New Look Publishing Company.

Co-Founder, C., & W, B. (1957). *Alcoholics Anonymous comes of age* (1st ed.). Harper.

Codependents Anonymous. (2012). *Co-dependents anonymous* (3rd ed.). Codependents Anonymous, Inc.

Cornelissen, M. (2002). Pondicherry Manifesto of Indian Psychology. *Psychological Studies*, *47*(1-3), 168–169.

Cornes, S., Dario, T. B. F. T., Sandra, O., Arianne, T., & and Chen, H. C. (2023). When students' words hurt: 12 tips for helping faculty receive and respond constructively to student evaluations of teaching. *Medical Education Online*, *28*(1), 2154768. https://doi.org/10.1080/10872981.2022.2154768

Cornish, M. A., & Wade, N. G. (2015). A therapeutic model of self-forgiveness with intervention strategies for counselors. *Journal of Counseling & Development*, *93*(1), 96–104. https://doi.org/10.1002/j.1556-6676.2015.00185.x

Cutuli, J. J., Herbers, J. E., Masten, A. S., & Reed, M.-G. J. (2021). Resilience in development. In C. R. Snyder, S. J. Lopez, L. M. Edwards, & S. C. Marques (Eds.), *Oxford handbook of positive psychology* (3rd ed., pp. 171–188). Oxford University Press.

Dabas, P., & Singh, A. (2018). Bhagavad Gita teachings and positive psychology: Efficacy for semi-urban Indian students of ncr. *Cogent Psychology*, *5*(1), Article 1467255. https://doi.org/10.1080/23311908.2018.1467255

Davis, E. B., Worthington, E. L., Jr., & Schnitker, S. A. (Eds.). (2023). *Handbook of positive psychology, religion, and spirituality*. Springer.

Dixon, T. (2003). *From passions to emotions: The creation of a secular psychological category*. Cambridge University Press.

Duan, C., & Sager, K. (2021). Understanding empathy: Current state and future research challenges. In C. R. Snyder, S. J. Lopez, L. M. Edwards, & S. C. Marques (Eds.), *Oxford handbook of positive psychology* (3rd ed., pp. 533–550). Oxford University Press.

Enright, R. D. (2001). *Forgiveness is a choice: A step-by-step process for resolving anger and restoring hope*. American Psychological Association.

Enright, R. D., & Fitzgibbons, R. P. (2015). *Forgiveness therapy: An empirical guide for resolving anger and restoring hope* (2nd ed.). American Psychological Association.

Enright, R. D., Freedman, S., & Rique, J. (1998). The psychology of interpersonal forgiveness. In R. D. Enright & J. North (Eds.), *Exploring forgiveness* (pp. 46–62). University of Wisconsin Press.

Enright, R. D., & The Human Development Study Group. (1991). The moral development of forgiveness. In W. Kurtines & J. Gewirtz (Eds.), *Handbook of moral behavior and development* (Vol. 1, pp. 123–152). Lawrence Erlbaum.

Enright, R. D., & The Human Development Study Group. (1996). Counseling within the forgiveness triad: On forgiving, receiving forgiveness, and self-forgiveness. *Counseling and Values*, *40*(2), 107–126. https://doi.org/10.1002/j.2161-007X.1996.tb00844.x

Fonseka, T., Ellis, R., Salem, H., Brennan, P., & Terry, T. (2021). The effects of COVID-19 on training within urology: Lessons learned in virtual learning, human factors, non-technical skills and reflective practice. *Journal of Clinical Urology*, *14*(1), 29–35. https://doi.org/10.1177/2051415820950109

Freedman, S., & Enright, R. D. (2020). A review of the empirical research using Enright's Process Model of interpersonal forgiveness. In E. L. Worthington, Jr. & N. G. Wade (Eds.), *Handbook of forgiveness* (Second ed., pp. 266–276). Routledge.

Gable, S. L., & Maisel, N. C. (2021). Positive processes in close relationships. In C. R. Snyder, S. J. Lopez, L. M. Edwards, & S. C. Marques (Eds.), *Oxford handbook of positive psychology* (3rd ed., pp. 599–610). Oxford University Press. https://doi.org/10.1093/oxfordhb/9780199396511.013.35

Gamblers Anonymous. (1989). *A new beginning*. Author.

Gandhi, M. K. (1931). The test of faith. *Young India*, *13*(14), 58–59. https://archive.org/details/HindSwaraj.YoungIndia.Portal.vol13/page/n51/mode/2up

Ghosh, A., & Deb, A. (2016). Positive psychology progress in India: Accomplishments and pathways ahead. *Psychological Studies*, *61*(3), 113–125. https://doi.org/10.1007/s12646-016-0367-5

Hall, J. H., & Fincham, F. D. (2005). Self-forgiveness: The stepchild of forgiveness research. *Journal of Social and Clinical Psychology*, *24*(5), 621–637. https://doi.org/10.1521/jscp.2005.24.5.621

Handelsman, M. M., Knapp, S., & Gottlieb, M. C. (2009). Positive ethics: Themes and variations. In S. J. Lopez & C. R. Snyder (Eds.), *Oxford handbook of positive psychology* (2nd ed.). Oxford University Press. https://doi.org/10.1093/oxfordhb/9780195187243.013.0011

Hart, K. E. (1999). A spiritual interpretation of the 12-steps of Alcoholics Anonymous: From resentment to forgiveness to love. *Journal of Ministry in Addiction & Recovery*, *6*(2), 25–39. https://doi.org/10.1300/J048v06n02_03

Harter, S. (2002). Authenticity. In C. R. Snyder & S. J. Lopez (Eds.), *Handbook of positive psychology* (pp. 382–394). Oxford University Press.

Hewitt, J. P. (2021). The social construction of self-esteem. In C. R. Snyder, S. J. Lopez, L. M. Edwards, & S. C. Marques (Eds.), *Oxford handbook of positive psychology* (3rd ed., pp. 309–318). Oxford University Press. https://doi.org/10.1093/oxfordhb/9780199396511.013.18

Hodge, A. S., Hook, J. N., Kim, J. J., Mosher, D. K., McLaughlin, A. T., Davis, D. E., & Van Tongeren, D. R. (2023). Positive psychology and Christianity. In E. B. Davis, E. L. Worthington, Jr., & S. A. Schnitker (Eds.), *Handbook of positive psychology, religion, and spirituality* (pp. 147–161). Springer Nature Switzerland AG. https://doi.org/10.1007/978-3-031-10274-5_10

Hooker, E. D., Zoccola, P. M., & Dickerson, S. S. (2021). Toward a biology of social support. In C. R. Snyder, S. J. Lopez, L. M. Edwards, & S. C. Marques (Eds.), *Oxford handbook of positive psychology* (3rd ed., pp. 659–668). Oxford University Press. https://doi.org/10.1093/oxfordhb/9780199396511.013.41

Ivtzan, I., Lomas, T., Hefferon, K., & Worth, P. (2016). *Second wave positive psychology*. Routledge.

Kelly, J. F., Humphreys, K., & Ferri, M. (2020). Alcoholics Anonymous and other 12-step programs for alcohol use disorder. *Cochrane Database of Systematic Reviews*, (3), Article CD012880. https://doi.org/10.1002/14651858.CD012880.pub2

Kimball, T. G., Shumway, S. T., Austin-Robillard, H., & Harris-Wilkes, K. S. (2017). Hoping and coping in recovery: A phenomenology of emerging adults in a collegiate recovery program. *Alcoholism Treatment Quarterly*, *35*(1), 46–62. https://doi.org/10.1080/07347324.2016.1256714

King James Version. (1983). *Holy Bible*. Church of Jesus Christ of Latter-day Saints.

Krentzman, A. R. (2013). Review of the application of positive psychology to substance use, addiction, and recovery research. *Psychology of Addictive Behaviors*, *27*(1), 151–165. https://doi.org/10.1037/a0029897

Kugelmann, R., & Belzen, J. A. (2009). Historical intersections of psychology, religion, and politics in national contexts. *History of Psychology*, *12*(3), 125–131. https://doi.org/10.1037/a0016855

Kuruvilla, P. K., Vijayakumar, N., & Jacob, K. S. (2004). A cohort study of male subjects attending an alcoholics anonymous program in India: One-year follow-up for sobriety. *Journal of Studies on Alcohol*, *65*(4), 546–549. https://doi.org/10.15288/jsa.2004.65.546

Lahiri, A. (2024). What does positive psychology mean to the people of India? In A. Sathiyaseelan & S. Balasundaram (Eds.), *Promoting mindfulness and well-being with Indian psychology* (pp. 182–202). IGI Global Scientific Publishing.

Langer, E. J., & Ngnoumen, C. (2021). Well-being: Mindfulness versus positive evaluation. In C. R. Snyder, S. J. Lopez, L. M. Edwards, & S. C. Marques (Eds.), *Oxford handbook of positive psychology* (3rd ed., pp. 379–395). Oxford University Press. https://doi.org/10.1093/oxfordhb/9780199396511.013.23

Leary, M. R., & Guadagno, J. (2011). The role of hypo-egoic self-processes in optimal functioning and subjective well-being. In K. M. Sheldon, T. B. Kashdan, & M. F. Steger (Eds.), *Designing positive psychology: Taking stock and moving forward* (pp. 135–146). Oxford University Press. https://doi.org/10.1093/acprof:oso/9780195373585.003.0009

Lembke, A., & Humphreys, K. (2012). What self-help organizations tell us about the syndrome model of addiction. In H. Shaffer, D. A. LaPlante, & S. E. Nelson (Eds.), *APA addiction syndrome handbook, Vol. 2: Recovery, prevention, and other issues* (pp. 157–168). American Psychological Association. https://doi.org/10.1037/13750-007

Levin, J. S., & Vanderpool, H. Y. (1991). Religious factors in physical health and the prevention of illness. *Prevention in Human Services*, *9*(2), 41–64. https://doi.org/10.1300/J293v09n02_03

Locke, E. A. (2002). Setting goals for life and happiness. In C. R. Snyder & S. J. Lopez (Eds.), *Handbook of positive psychology* (pp. 299–312). Oxford University Press.

Longabaugh, R., & Wirtz, P. W. (Eds.). (2001). *Project MATCH: Hypotheses, results, and causal chain analyses*. National Institute on Alcohol Abuse and Alcoholism.

Luskin, F. (2002). *Forgive for good: A proven prescription for health and happiness*. HarperOne.

Maddux, J. E., & Kleiman, E. M. (2021). Self-efficacy: The power of believing you can. In C. R. Snyder, S. J. Lopez, L. M. Edwards, & S. C. Marques (Eds.), *Oxford handbook of positive psychology* (3rd ed., pp. 443–452). Oxford University Press. https://doi.org/10.1093/oxfordhb/9780199396511.013.26

Maharaj, A. (2017). 'God is infinite, and the paths to God are infinite': A reconstruction and defense of Sri Ramakrishna's vijñāna-based model of religious pluralism. *Journal of Religion*, *97*(2), 181–213. https://doi.org/10.1086/690478

Mancuso, E. K., & Lorona, R. T. (2023). The scientific study of life satisfaction and religion/spirituality. In E. B. Davis, E. L. Worthington, Jr., & S. A. Schnitker (Eds.), *Handbook of positive psychology, religion, and spirituality* (pp. 299–313). Springer Nature Switzerland AG. https://doi.org/10.1007/978-3-031-10274-5_19

Marijuana Anonymous World Services. (2017). *Life with hope: A return to living through the 12 steps and 12 traditions of marijuana anonymous* (Third ed.). A New Leaf Publications.

McCullough, M. E., Root, L. M., Tabak, B. A., & Witvliet, C. V. (2009). Forgiveness. In S. J. Lopez & C. R. Snyder (Eds.), *Oxford handbook of positive psychology* (2nd ed., pp. 427–435). Oxford University Press.

McCullough, M. E., & Witvliet, C. V. (2002). The psychology of forgiveness. In C. R. Snyder & S. J. Lopez (Eds.). In *Handbook of positive psychology* (pp. 446–458). Oxford University Press.

Mens, M. G., Scheier, M. F., & Carver, C. S. (2021). Optimism. In C. R. Snyder, S. J. Lopez, L. M. Edwards, & S. C. Marques (Eds.), *Oxford handbook of positive psychology* (3rd ed., pp. 396–412). Oxford University Press. https://doi.org/10.1093/oxfordhb/9780199396511.013.24

Miller, W. R. (Ed.). (2004). *COMBINE Monograph Series, Volume 1. Combined behavioral intervention manual: A clinical research guide for therapists treating people with alcohol abuse and dependence.* National Institute on Alcohol Abuse and Alcoholism.

Nanamoli, B., & Bodhi, B. (Trans.). (2001). *The middle length discourses of the Buddha: A translation of the Majjhima Nikaya* (2nd ed.). Wisdom.

Narcotics Anonymous. (2008). *Narcotics Anonymous* (Sixth ed.). Author.

Nelson, J. M., & Canty, N. (2023). Positive psychology and the psychology of religion and spirituality in historical perspective. In E. B. Davis, E. L. Worthington, Jr., & S. A. Schnitker (Eds.), *Handbook of positive psychology, religion, and spirituality* (pp. 21–35). Springer Nature Switzerland AG. https://doi.org/10.1007/978-3-031-10274-5_2

Nicotine Anonymous World Services. (2015). *Nicotine Anonymous: The book* (Fifth ed.). Author.

North, R. J., & Swann, W. B., Jr. (2021). What's positive about self-verification. In C. R. Snyder, S. J. Lopez, L. M. Edwards, & S. C. Marques (Eds.), *Oxford handbook of positive psychology* (3rd ed., pp. 623–634). Oxford University Press. https://doi.org/10.1093/oxfordhb/9780199396511.013.37

Nowinski, J., Baker, S., & Carroll, K. M. (1994). *Twelve step facilitation therapy manual: A clinical research guide for therapists treating individuals with alcohol abuse and dependence*. National Institute on Alcohol Abuse and Alcoholism.

Oishi, S., Diener, E., & Lucas, R. E. (2021). Subjective well-being: The science of happiness and life satisfaction. In C. R. Snyder, S. J. Lopez, L. M. Edwards, & S. C. Marques (Eds.), *Oxford handbook of positive psychology* (3rd ed., pp. 255–264). Oxford University Press. https://doi.org/10.1093/oxfordhb/9780199396511.013.14

Oman, D. (2013). Defining religion and spirituality. In R. F. Paloutzian & C. L. Park (Eds.), *Handbook of the psychology of religion and spirituality* (Second ed., pp. 23–47). Guilford.

Oman, D. (2019). Introduction to the special section: Psychology of Indian spirituality and religion, emerging perspectives. *Psychology of Religion and Spirituality*, *11*(2), 87–90. https://doi.org/10.1037/rel0000256

Oman, D. (2023-). Hinduism and happiness In L. Bormans (Ed.), *The new world book of happiness: The essence*. (By Feb. 2025, had been published in Dutch, French, and German; English edition scheduled for release in August, 2025). https://www.lannoo.be/nl/world-book-happiness-en

Oman, D. (2024). What is a mantra? Guidance for practitioners, researchers, and editors. *American Psychologist*. https://doi.org/10.1037/amp0001368

Oman, D. (2025). Reply: The PHIOMM framework for implementing mindfulness in public health, with groundwork. *Mindfulness*, *16*(3), 752–782. https://doi.org/10.1007/s12671-025-02553-4

Oman, D., & Paranjpe, A. C. (2018). Indian spirituality: How relevant is Pargament's framework? *Psychological Studies*, *63*(2), 140–152. https://doi.org/10.1007/s12646-017-0412-z

Oman, D., & Paranjpe, A. C. (2020). Psychology of Hinduism from the inside out. In T. A. Sisemore & J. J. Knabb (Eds.), *The psychology of world religions and spiritualities: An indigenous perspective* pp. 165–196). Templeton Press.

Overeaters Anonymous. (2018). *The twelve steps and twelve traditions of overeaters anonymous* (Second ed.). Author.

Pargament, K. I. (2013). Searching for the sacred: Toward a nonreductionistic theory of spirituality. In K. I. Pargament, J. J. Exline, & J. W. Jones (Eds.), *APA handbook of psychology, religion, and spirituality (Vol 1): Context, theory, and research.* (pp. 257–273). American Psychological Association. https://doi.org/10.1037/14045-014

Pargament, K. I., & Mahoney, A. (2021). Spirituality: The search for the sacred. In C. R. Snyder, S. J. Lopez, L. M. Edwards, & S. C. Marques (Eds.), *Oxford handbook of positive psychology* (3rd ed., pp. 878–891). Oxford University Press. https://doi.org/10.1093/oxfordhb/9780199396511.013.51

Park, C. L., & Van Tongeren, D. R. (2023). Meaning as a framework for integrating positive psychology and the psychology of religiousness and spirituality. In E. B. Davis, E. L. Worthington, Jr., & S. A. Schnitker (Eds.), *Handbook of positive psychology, religion, and spirituality* (pp. 83–96). Springer Nature Switzerland AG. https://doi.org/10.1007/978-3-031-10274-5_6

Peterson, C., & Seligman, M. E. P. (2004). *Character strengths and virtues: A handbook and classification.* American Psychological Association / Oxford University Press.

Pettinati, H. M., Weiss, R. D., Miller, W. R., Donovan, D., Ernst, D. B., & Rounsaville, B. J. (2004). *COMBINE Monograph Series, Volume 2. Medical management treatment manual: A clinical research guide for medically trained clinicians providing pharmacotherapy as part of the treatment for alcohol dependence.* National Institute on Alcohol Abuse and Alcoholism.

Pincus, H. A. (1998). Preface. In H. G. Koenig (Ed.), *Handbook of religion and mental health* (pp. xxv–xxvi). Academic Press.

Prabhavananda. (1963). *The spiritual heritage of India.* Doubleday.

Preston, S. D. (2021). Neural and physiological mechanisms of altruism and empathy. In *Oxford handbook of positive psychology* (3rd ed., pp. 754–772). Oxford University Press.

Pury, C. L. S., Brawley Newlin, A. M., Burnett, E. A., & Lopez, S. J. (2021). Courage. In C. R. Snyder, S. J. Lopez, L. M. Edwards, & S. C. Marques (Eds.), *Oxford handbook of positive psychology* (3rd ed., pp. 493–504). Oxford University Press. https://doi.org/10.1093/oxfordhb/9780199396511.013.30

Radhakrishnan, S. (1994). *The principal Upaniṣads.* HarperCollins India. (Original work published Great Britain, 1953)

Ragau, S., Hitchcock, R., Craft, J., & Christensen, M. (2018). Using the HALT model in an exploratory quality improvement initiative to reduce medication errors. *British Journal of Nursing, 27*(22), 1330–1335. https://doi.org/10.12968/bjon.2018.27.22.1330

Rand, K. L., & Touza, K. K. (2021). Hope theory. In C. R. Snyder, S. J. Lopez, L. M. Edwards, & S. C. Marques (Eds.), *Oxford handbook of positive psychology* (3rd ed., pp. 425–442). Oxford Uiversity Press. https://doi.org/10.1093/oxfordhb/9780199396511.013.25

Rao, K. R. (2014). Positive psychology and Indian psychology in need of mutual reinforcement. *Psychological Studies, 59*(2), 94–102. https://doi.org/10.1007/s12646-013-0228-4

Rao, K. R., & Paranjpe, A. C. (2016). *Psychology in the Indian tradition.* Springer. https://doi.org/10.1007/978-81-322-2440-2

Reisner, A. D., & Lawson, P. (1992). Psychotherapy, sin, and mental health. *Pastoral Psychology, 40*(5), 303–311. https://doi.org/10.1007/BF01042291

Ryan, R. M., Sheldon, K. M., Kasser, T., & Deci, E. L. (1996). All goals are not created equal: An organismic perspective on the nature of goals and their regulation. In P. M. Gollwitzer & J. A. Bargh (Eds.), *The psychology of action: Linking cognition and motivation to behavior* (pp. 7–26). Guilford.

Saritoprak, S. N., & Abu-Raiya, H. (2023). Living the good life: An Islamic perspective on positive psychology. In E. B. Davis, E. L. Worthington, Jr., & S. A. Schnitker (Eds.), *Handbook of positive psychology, religion, and spirituality* (pp. 179–193). Springer Nature Switzerland AG. https://doi.org/10.1007/978-3-031-10274-5_12

Scheibe, S., & Kunzmann, U. (2021). Territories of positive life span development: Wisdom and *Sehnsucht* (life longings). In C. R. Snyder, S. J. Lopez, L. M. Edwards, & S. C. Marques (Eds.), *Oxford handbook of positive psychology* (3rd ed., pp. 238–252). Oxford University Press. https://doi.org/10.1093/oxfordhb/9780199396511.013.13

Schenker, M. D. (2009). *A clinician's guide to 12-Step recovery*. W. W. Norton & Co.

Schiffman, M., Cherniak, A., Schnall, E., Brooks, S., Pirutinsky, S., & Shabtai, D. (2023). Positive psychology and Judaism. In E. B. Davis, E. L. Worthington, Jr., & S. A. Schnitker (Eds.), *Handbook of positive psychology, religion, and spirituality* (pp. 163–177). Springer Nature Switzerland AG. https://doi.org/10.1007/978-3-031-10274-5_11

Schulman, M. (2002a). How we become moral: The sources of moral motivation. In C. R. Snyder & S. J. Lopez (Eds.), *Handbook of positive psychology* (pp. 499–512). Oxford University Press.

Schulman, M. (2002b). The passion to know: A developmental perspective. In C. R. Snyder & S. J. Lopez (Eds.), *Handbook of positive psychology* (pp. 313–326). Oxford University Press.

Segall, S. Z., & Kristeller, J. L. (2023). Positive psychology and Buddhism. In E. B. Davis, E. L. Worthington, Jr., & S. A. Schnitker (Eds.), *Handbook of positive psychology, religion, and spirituality* (pp. 211–225). Springer Nature Switzerland AG. https://doi.org/10.1007/978-3-031-10274-5_14

Sex Addicts Anonymous. (2005). *Sex addicts anonymous* (Third ed.). International Service Organization of SAA, Inc.

Shapiro, S. L., Jazaieri, H., & de Sousa, S. (2021). Meditation and positive psychology. In C. R. Snyder, S. J. Lopez, L. M. Edwards, & S. C. Marques (Eds.), *Oxford handbook of positive psychology* (3rd ed., pp. 863–877). Oxford University Press. https://doi.org/10.1093/oxfordhb/9780199396511.013.50

Singh, K., Raina, M., & Oman, D. (2023). Positive psychology and Hinduism. In E. B. Davis, E. L. Worthington, Jr., & S. A. Schnitker (Eds.), *Handbook of positive psychology, religion, and spirituality* (pp. 195–209). Springer Nature Switzerland AG. https://doi.org/10.1007/978-3-031-10274-5_13

Singleton, M. (2013). Transnational exchange and the genesis of modern postural yoga. In B. Hauser (Ed.), *Yoga traveling: Bodily practice in transcultural perspective* (pp. 37–56). Springer International Publishing. https://doi.org/10.1007/978-3-319-00315-3_2

Snyder, C. R., Lopez, S. J., Edwards, L. M., & Marques, S. C. (Eds.). (2021). *The Oxford handbook of positive psychology* (3rd ed.). Oxford University Press. https://doi.org/10.1093/oxfordhb/9780199396511.001.0001

Steger, M. F. (2021). Meaning in life: A unified model. In C. R. Snyder, S. J. Lopez, L. M. Edwards, & S. C. Marques (Eds.), *Oxford handbook of positive psychology* (3rd ed., pp. 959–967). Oxford University Press. https://doi.org/10.1093/oxfordhb/9780199396511.013.56

Suicide Anonymous. (2015). *Suicide Anonymous, The Little Book* (Revised Edition). Memphis, TN: Author. Retrieved January 10, 2023, from https://suicideanonymous.net/readings-and-downloads

Tangney, J. P., Boone, A. L., & Dearing, R. (2005). Forgiving the self: Conceptual issues and empirical findings. In E. L. Worthington, Jr. (Ed.), *Handbook of forgiveness* (pp. 143–158). Routledge.

Thompson, S. C. (2021). The role of personal control in adaptive functioning. In C. R. Snyder, S. J. Lopez, L. M. Edwards, & S. C. Marques (Eds.), *Oxford handbook of positive psychology* (3rd ed., pp. 368–378). Oxford University Press. https://doi.org/10.1093/oxfordhb/9780199396511.013.22

Toussaint, L. L., & Webb, J. R. (2005). Theoretical and empirical connections between forgiveness, mental health, and well-being. In E. L. Worthington, Jr. (Ed.), *Handbook of forgiveness* (pp. 349–362). Routledge.

Tsang, J.-A., & Martin, S. R. (2021). Forgiveness. In C. R. Snyder, S. J. Lopez, L. M. Edwards, & S. C. Marques (Eds.), *Oxford handbook of positive psychology* (3rd ed., pp. 551–570). Oxford University Press. https://doi.org/10.1093/oxfordhb/9780199396511.013.32

W, B. (1986/1967). *As Bill sees it: the BIG BOOK way of life: Selected writings of BIG BOOK's co-founder*. Alcoholics Anonymous.

Wade, N. G., Hoyt, W. T., Kidwell, J. E. M., & Worthington, E. L., Jr. (2014). Efficacy of psychotherapeutic interventions to promote forgiveness: A meta-analysis. *Journal of Consulting and Clinical Psychology*, *82*(1), 154–170. https://doi.org/10.1037/a0035268

While comparisons between PP and Buddhism are difficult, they are certainly valuable. A comparison of Buddhist conceptions with either hedonic or eudaemonic views helps us understand the specific presuppositions and claims present in PP thought, which, if thoughtfully considered, can lead us to improve PP understandings of human flourishing. A beginning point may be the Buddhist perspective on understanding the nature and causes of suffering, and the principles and practices underlying its alleviation (i.e., the Four Noble Truths). Indeed, the Eightfold Path (i.e., the Fourth Noble Truth) points to many fundamental principles and practices, some of which are represented in Tables 7.1–7.5. However, nuanced and/or profound differences in the understanding and application of any given otherwise shared principle or practice may be warranted (e.g., the concept of self).

The Twelve-Step Model as Spirituality

The TSM of addiction recovery is the default, or otherwise de facto, approach to the interface between spirituality and addictive behavior (see AA, 2001; see also Webb, 2021, in press). Given its highly structured nature and its grounding in the Judeo-Christian beliefs of its founders, the TSM is often misunderstood to be a religiously oriented program (arguably a manifestation of Ritualistic Spirituality; see above). Nevertheless, the TSM is typically described by its adherents as "a spiritual program, not a religious one" (AA, 2001, p. 346; see also AA, 2023), given its primary value of intentional, voluntary, and *collaborative* reliance upon a self-determined, -selected, and -congruent *higher* power to facilitate one's journey toward self-transformation and addiction recovery through a profound spiritual (re)connection with said Higher Power. The TSM originated in the 1930s in the United States and arose in the context of alcohol misuse. It is a grass-roots, community-based, mutual-help program that is now accessible across the globe (aa.org/find-aa), and with respect to many substances and targeted behaviors. For example, opiates (narcotics.com), cocaine (ca.org), cannabis (marijuana-anonymous.org), nicotine (nicotine-anonymous.org), gambling (gamblersanonymous.org), overeating (oa.org), sexual activity (e.g., saa-recovery.org), suicidal behavior (suicideanonymous.net), and codependency (e.g., coda.org), among many others (see Schenker, 2009). In the context of AA alone, not only does the TSM have a worldwide presence with over 2 million members in more than 123,000 local and online groups spread across some 180 nations and 100 languages (aa.org/aa-around-the-world), it also enjoys a critical mass of empirical support, both in the context of its original mutual-help format *and* as a more formal, structured, and/or standardized treatment modality (see Kelly et al., 2020; Lembke & Humphreys, 2012; Zemore et al., 2018; see also Longabaugh & Wirtz, 2001; Miller, 2004; Pettinati et al., 2004).

Fundamental Assumptions of the Twelve-Step Model

The TSM of addiction recovery rests upon five fundamental, underlying assumptions (see AA, 2001; see also Webb, 2021, in press): (1) addiction is a disease, not a moral weakness, and (2) once addiction develops, it is a constant, ever-present struggle without a cure, such that (3) abstinence-based sobriety is necessary, and can only come through (4) the genuine, heartfelt, and focused attention to, full embrace, and thorough completion of 12 explicit, sequential steps, which requires (5) the close guidance and tutelage of a mentor or sponsor who is actively engaged in their own long-term, TSM-based addiction recovery.

Washington-Nortey, M., Worthington, E. L., Jr., & Ahmed, R. (2023). The scientific study of religion/spirituality, forgiveness, and hope. In E. B. Davis, E. L. Worthington, Jr., & S. A. Schnitker (Eds.), *Handbook of positive psychology, religion, and spirituality* (pp. 361–377). Springer Nature Switzerland AG. https://doi.org/10.1007/978-3-031-10274-5_23

Waterman, A. S. (2008). Reconsidering happiness: A eudaimonist's perspective. *The Journal of Positive Psychology*, *3*(4), 234–252. https://doi.org/10.1080/17439760802303002

Watkins, P. C., & McCurrach, D. (2021). Progress in the science of gratitude. In C. R. Snyder, S. J. Lopez, L. M. Edwards, & S. C. Marques (Eds.), *Oxford handbook of positive psychology* (3rd ed., pp. 571–585). Oxford University Press. https://doi.org/10.1093/oxfordhb/9780199396511.013.33

Webb, J. R. (1999). Forgiveness and control: Toward an understanding of the dynamics of forgiveness (Doctoral dissertation, California School of Professional Psychology, Los Angeles, 1998). *Dissertation Abstracts International*, *60*(1-B), 0379.

Webb, J. R. (2007/2003). Spiritual factors and adjustment in medical rehabilitation: Understanding forgiveness as a means of coping. In A. E. DellOrto & P. W. Power (Eds.), *The psychological and social impact of illness and disability* (5th ed., pp. 455–471). Springer. (Reprinted from *Journal of Applied Rehabilitation Counseling*, 34(3), 16-24: 2003)

Webb, J. R. (2021). *Understanding forgiveness and addiction: Theory, research, and clinical application*. Routledge.

Webb, J. R. (in press). Spirituality and addictions. In J. M. Currier, J. Fox, & C. Vieten (Eds.), *Handbook of training in spiritual and religious competencies in mental health professions*. Oxford University Press.

Webb, J. R., & Boye, C. M. (2024). Self-forgiveness and self-condemnation in the context of addictive behavior and suicidal behavior. *Substance Abuse and Rehabilitation*, *15*, 21–30. https://doi.org/10.2147/sar.S396964

Webb, J. R., Boye, C. M., Maxton, A. S., Mills, M. E., Murphy, D. P., & Brewer, K. G. (2024). Forgiveness, resentment, well-being, and college student substance use in Southern Appalachia and West Texas. *Alcoholism Treatment Quarterly*, *42*(3), 303–321. https://doi.org/10.1080/07347324.2024.2322117

Webb, J. R., & Brewer, K. (2010). Forgiveness and college student drinking in Southern Appalachia. *Journal of Substance Use*, *15*(6), 417–433. https://doi.org/10.3109/14659891003706373

Webb, J. R., Bumgarner, D. J., Conway-Williams, E., Dangel, T., & Hall, B. B. (2017). A consensus definition of self-forgiveness: Implications for assessment and treatment. *Spirituality in Clinical Practice*, *4*(3), 216–227. https://doi.org/10.1037/scp0000138

Webb, J. R., Hill, S. K., & Brewer, K. G. (2012a). Dimensions of social support as mediators of the forgiveness-alcohol outcome relationship. *Addictive Disorders & Their Treatment*, *11*(2), 64–75. https://doi.org/10.1097/ADT.0b013e31822dcd56

Webb, J. R., Hirsch, J. K., Conway-Williams, E., & Brewer, K. G. (2013). Forgiveness and alcohol problems: Indirect associations involving mental health and social support. *Addiction Research & Theory*, *21*(2), 141–153. https://doi.org/10.3109/16066359.2012.703267

Webb, J. R., Hirsch, J. K., & Toussaint, L. L. (2015). Forgiveness as a positive psychotherapy for addiction and suicide: Theory, research, and practice. *Spirituality in Clinical Practice*, *2*(1), 48–60. https://doi.org/10.1037/scp0000054 (Suicide and Spirituality in the Military)

Webb, J. R., Toussaint, L., & Dula, C. S. (2014). Ritualistic, theistic, and existential spirituality: Initial psychometric qualities of the RiTE measure of spirituality. *Journal of Religion and Health*, *53*(4), 972–985. https://doi.org/10.1007/s10943-013-9697-y

Webb, J. R., & Toussaint, L. L. (2018). Self-forgiveness as a critical factor in addiction and recovery: A 12-step model perspective. *Alcoholism Treatment Quarterly*, *36*(1), 15–31. https://doi.org/10.1080/07347324.2017.1391057

Webb, J. R., Toussaint, L. L., & Conway-Williams, E. (2012b). Forgiveness and health: Psycho-spiritual integration and the promotion of better healthcare. *Journal of Health Care Chaplaincy*, *18*(1-2), 57–73. https://doi.org/10.1080/08854726.2012.667317

Webb, J. R., & Trautman, R. P. (2010). Forgiveness and alcohol use: Applying a specific spiritual principle to substance abuse problems. *Addictive Disorders & Their Treatment*, *9*(1), 8–17. https://doi.org/10.1097/ADT.0b013e318195000d

Wehmeyer, M. L., Shogren, K. A., Little, T. D., & Adams, N. (2021). Self-determination. In C. R. Snyder, S. J. Lopez, L. M. Edwards, & S. C. Marques (Eds.), *Oxford handbook of positive psychology* (3rd ed., pp. 471–481). Oxford University Press. https://doi.org/10.1093/oxfordhb/9780199396511.013.28

Wong, P. T. P. (2011). Positive psychology 2.0: Towards a balanced interactive model of the good life. *Canadian Psychology / Psychologie canadienne*, *52*(2), 69–81. https://doi.org/10.1037/a0022511

Worthington, E. L., Jr. (1998). The pyramid model of forgiveness: Some interdisciplinary speculations about unforgiveness and the promotion of forgiveness. In E. L. Worthington, Jr. (Ed.), *Dimensions of forgiveness: Psychological research and theological perspectives* (pp. 107–137). Templeton Foundation Press.

Worthington, E. L., Jr. (2003). *Forgiving and reconciling: Bridges to wholeness and hope* (Revised ed.). InterVarsity Press.

Worthington, E. L., Jr. (2006). *Forgiveness and reconciliation: Theory and application*. Routledge.

Worthington, E. L., Jr. (2020). An update of the REACH Forgiveness Model: Psychoeducation in groups, do-it-yourself formats, couple enrichment, religious congregations, and as an adjunct to psychotherapy. In E. L. Worthington, Jr. & N. G. Wade (Eds.), *Handbook of forgiveness* (Second ed., pp. 277–287). Routledge.

Worthington, E. L., Jr. (2025). Forgiveness intervention manuals. Accessed May 16, 2025 from: http://www.evworthington-forgiveness.com/

Worthington, E. L., Jr., Goldstein, L., Hammock, B., Griffin, B. J., Garthe, R. C., Lavelock, C., Davis, D. E., Hook, J. N., & Van Tongeren, D. R. (2021). Humility: A qualitative review. In C. R. Snyder, S. J. Lopez, L. M. Edwards, & S. C. Marques (Eds.), *Oxford handbook of positive psychology* (3rd ed., pp. 643–656). Oxford University Press. https://doi.org/10.1093/oxfordhb/9780199396511.013.39

Worthington, E. L., Jr., & Sandage, S. J. (2016). *Forgiveness and spirituality in psychotherapy: A relational approach*. American Psychological Association.

Worthington, E. L., Jr., & Wade, N. G. (2020). How you can benefit from this handbook. In E. L. Worthington, Jr. & N. G. Wade (Eds.), *Handbook of forgiveness* (Second ed., pp. 1–8). Routledge.

Zemore, S. E., Lui, C., Mericle, A., Hemberg, J., & Kaskutas, L. A. (2018). A longitudinal study of the comparative efficacy of Women for Sobriety, LifeRing, SMART Recovery, and 12-step groups for those with AUD. *Journal of Substance Abuse Treatment*, *88*, 18–26. https://doi.org/10.1016/j.jsat.2018.02.004

Zinnbauer, B. J., & Pargament, K. I. (2005). Religiousness and spirituality. In R. F. Paloutzian & C. L. Park (Eds.), *Handbook of the psychology of religion and spirituality* (pp. 21–42). Guilford Press.

Chapter 8

The Neuroscience of Spirituality

*Andrew Newberg**

Introduction and Definitions

In the late 18th century, a shift occurred in the understanding of religions, particularly in the Western context, moving away from a focus on sacred texts and dogma, and toward a more experiential conception. Friedrich Schleiermacher (1999) was among the pioneers who sought to redefine "religion" by emphasizing cognitive, visceral, or intuitive aspects rather than doctrinal ones. He characterized religion as a "feeling of absolute dependence," marking a departure from previous doctrinal or theological definitions. Subsequent attempts at defining religion have continued to prioritize these intuitive and emotional elements over doctrinal aspects, which have significant implications for applying a neuroscientific approach to the study of spirituality. Furthermore, as definitions evolve, the distinction between spirituality and religiousness becomes increasingly intricate.

Emile Durkheim's perspective, presented in "The Elementary Forms of the Religious Life" (1926/1915), posits religion as a societal phenomenon emerging from communal dynamics. Conversely, Sigmund Freud interpreted religious behaviors and spiritual feelings as manifestations of intrapsychic processes, often from a psychopathological viewpoint. For Freud, religion served as a means of addressing psychological deficiencies (Gay, 1995). B. F. Skinner (1953) approached religious beliefs as products of past experiences shaping hopes and expectations.

At the turn of the 20th century, scholars began exploring religious and spiritual experiences phenomenologically, independent of doctrinal frameworks. William James (1902), in *The Varieties of Religious Experience*, adopted a scientific lens to classify and analyze a wide array of experiences, ranging from ordinary to pathological. However, much of his work was based on anecdotal evidence and descriptions of religious experiences rather than true scientific evaluations. Rudolf Otto, in "The Idea of the Holy" (1923/1917), characterized religious awareness as awe, a blend of fear and fascination in the presence of the divine, though this framework primarily pertained to Western mysticism.

A more recent effort to define religion and spirituality emerged from a consensus conference among scientists studying their physical, psychological, and neuroscientific aspects (Larson et al., 1998). These definitions were formulated as criteria rather than strict definitions. Spirituality was delineated as subjective feelings, thoughts, experiences, and behaviors arising from a search or quest for the sacred, with "search" referring to attempts to identify, articulate, maintain, or transform, and "sacred" encompassing perceptions of a divine being, ultimate reality, or truth. Religion encompassed these criteria and added a search for

* Corresponding Author: andrew.newberg@jefferson.edu.

DOI: 10.4324/9781003440048-10

non-sacred goals within a spiritual context, requiring validation and support from an identifiable group. Perhaps one of the more common elements that differentiate religiousness from spirituality is that religiousness is determined by a group of people who share the same doctrinal beliefs. Thus, being a Catholic requires a belief in Jesus and partaking in various Catholic rituals such as baptism or communion. These elements differentiate Catholicism from other traditions, such as Islam or Judaism. However, various spiritual groups are also identified by their participants. Hence, as with many elements of religiousness and spirituality, there is a great deal of overlap.

Definitions of spirituality and religiousness draw from various disciplines, including religious studies, anthropology, sociology, neuroscience, and medicine. The effectiveness of these definitions hinges on their alignment with religious perspectives and their suitability for scientific analysis. However, constructs relying on cognitive, emotional, and perceptual elements may inherently overlook the true nature of spirituality. Thus, if spirituality involves a connection with the supernatural, scientific approaches may only capture its effects rather than its essence.

Investigating the Neurological and Psychiatric Dimensions of Spiritual Experiences

In adopting a neurocognitive perspective to explore religious and spiritual phenomena, it is imperative to recognize the diverse pathways individuals traverse to encounter such experiences (d'Aquili & Newberg, 1999). These avenues encompass adherence to sacred texts, participation in rituals, engagement in practices like meditation or prayer, encounters with altered states induced by various psychoactive substances, near-death experiences, and certain medical, neurological, or psychiatric conditions. It is essential to discern the cognitive, emotional, and experiential components of these encounters. Many of these experiences involve a diminished sense of self-boundaries and a heightened sense of interconnectedness with others, fostering a profound sense of communal unity. Ultimately, unitary experiences may culminate in the dissolution of discrete boundaries of the self and other objects in the universe, leading to a state of absolute unity.

Group rituals and individual meditation or prayer practices exhibit a degree of overlap, with each potentially influencing the other. Ceremonial rituals may afford the average individual access to spiritual or mystical types of experiences, but are potentially distinct from those who engage in intensive contemplation, such as highly religious monks or nuns.

Descriptions of religious and spiritual experiences associated with meditation, prayer, and spiritual rituals span biomedical, psychological, anthropological, and religious literature, with some accounts dating back millennia. In recent years, there has been a surge in studies examining the neurophysiological and physiological correlates of spiritual experiences. This has helped form the basis of a field of scholarship and research often referred to as neurotheology (Newberg, 2018). Neurotheology seeks to understand the relationship between the brain and religious and spiritual phenomena. One important focus of neurotheology is the study of spiritual experiences. From an evolutionary perspective, the emergence of complex brain structures in early primates and Homo sapiens likely facilitated the advent of these experiences. This neurological evolution coincided with the proliferation of religious traditions throughout human history. Neurobiological and neuropsychological correlates of religious and spiritual experiences have begun to be identified, offering insights into a spectrum of spiritual encounters, from profound awe to intense mystical states (Yaden & Newberg, 2022).

The use of hallucinogenic agents by some individuals to induce intensive spiritual experiences has long been observed (Yaden et al., 2016). Careful studies of drug-induced spiritual experiences, possibly utilizing modern imaging techniques, may elucidate the neurobiological mechanisms involved in such experiences. Comparing drug-induced phenomena to naturally occurring spiritual encounters may facilitate a better distinction between pathological and non-pathological experiences. Of course, determining "normal" from "abnormal" spiritual experiences is also quite challenging, as such denotations can arise from a psychological or spiritual perspective. Ethical and legal considerations notwithstanding, studying individuals who have undergone pharmacologically induced spiritual experiences using radioactive analogues of these agents may provide insights into receptor concentration and agonist activity. Additionally, studying the effects of drug withdrawal on spiritual experience could yield valuable information.

Neuropathological conditions, including seizure disorders, brain tumors, stroke, schizophrenia, and mania, have been associated with alterations in religious beliefs and spiritual experiences (Saver & Rabin, 1997; Yaden & Newberg, 2022). Understanding the type and location of pathology can aid in identifying the neurobiological substrate of spiritual encounters. Neuropsychiatric disorders serve as a valuable tool for investigating the neuroscience of spiritual experience, shedding light on both normal and pathological manifestations.

Research on pathological conditions has traditionally informed our understanding of normal biological functioning. Spiritual experiences in psychiatric and neurological disorders may reveal nascent neurobiological systems underlying typical spiritual encounters. This underscores the importance of distinguishing normal spiritual experience from pathological manifestations. For example, is it possible that a spiritual experience arising in someone with a brain tumor is actually a "normal" rather than "pathological" experience, even if there is an underlying pathology? Furthermore, scholars and researchers should be careful about reductionist interpretations that solely attribute spiritual experiences to neurophysiological mechanisms.

Neuroscience and the RiTE Model

Neuroscience offers a promising avenue for deepening our understanding of the RiTE multidimensional model of spirituality. The RiTE model, proposed by Webb et al. (2014; see also Chapters 1 and 44 of this volume), conceptualizes spirituality as a multifaceted construct consisting of three dimensions: religious (ritualistic), theistic, and existential. By leveraging neuroscientific techniques such as functional magnetic resonance imaging (fMRI) and electroencephalography (EEG), researchers can explore how each dimension of spirituality is instantiated in the brain. For instance, studies have shown that engaging in religious practices activates brain regions associated with reward processing and social bonding, such as the ventral striatum and anterior cingulate cortex (Bulbulia & Schjoedt, 2011). By examining the neural correlates of each dimension of spirituality, neuroscience can provide insights into the underlying mechanisms through which spirituality influences cognition, emotion, and behavior, and vice versa.

Furthermore, neuroscience can help elucidate the interplay between spirituality and various psychological processes, shedding light on how spirituality contributes to mental health and well-being. For example, neuroimaging studies have demonstrated that religious beliefs and practices are associated with alterations in brain structure and function, including increased cerebral function and gray matter density in regions implicated in emotion regulation and self-awareness (Newberg et al., 2010; Holzel et al., 2011). By mapping the neural circuits underlying spirituality, researchers can identify biomarkers of spiritual well-being and develop targeted interventions to enhance spiritual resilience and coping mechanisms. Overall, integrating neuroscience with the RiTE multidimensional model of spirituality holds promise for advancing our understanding of the complex interrelationships between spirituality, brain function, and psychological health.

Developing a Neurophysiological Model of Religious and Spiritual Experiences

Incorporating recent advancements in neuroimaging, neurochemistry, neuropathology, hormonal studies, and physiology, the model outlined below serves as an updated framework for understanding various religious experiences and practices (Newberg & Iversen, 2003). Figure 8.1 illustrates the model's components, starting with the prefrontal cortex (PFC) and highlighting intricate interactions with the inferior frontal region, thalamus, posterior superior parietal lobe, limbic system, and autonomic nervous system. Many of these structures are integral to other neural networks, such as the default mode network and the reward system, suggesting their involvement in spiritual experiences within this broader context. Furthermore, multiple excitatory and inhibitory neurotransmitters, including dopamine, serotonin (ST), and acetylcholine, are implicated in different facets of spiritual experiences, as reflected in the model. Depending on the specific spiritual tradition, practice, and individual, variations in activation patterns within this network are anticipated. Thus, the model accommodates diverse experiences, encompassing sensory, cognitive, and affective dimensions. While initially informed by studies on meditative practices due to data availability (e.g., d'Aquili & Newberg, 1993; Newberg et al., 2001; Newberg & Iversen, 2003), the model's applicability extends to various spiritual practices and experiences.

Activation of the Prefrontal and Cingulate Cortex

Engagement in spiritual practices such as meditation or prayer often involves sustained attention directed toward a visualized object, mantra, prayer, or other spiritual focus. Brain imaging studies indicate that tasks requiring sustained attention are initiated by activity in the PFC, particularly in the right hemisphere and also in conjunction with the inferior frontal region (Ingvar, 1994; Frith et al., 1991; Posner & Petersen, 1990; Pardo, Fox, & Raichle, 1991; Hernández et al., 2020). Additionally, the cingulate gyrus is implicated in attentional focus, likely in conjunction with the PFC (Vogt, Finch, & Olson, 1992; Fox et al., 2016). Spiritual practices demanding intense attention likely commence with activation of the PFC (particularly the right hemisphere) and the cingulate gyrus. This hypothesis finds support in brain imaging studies of volitional meditation types, revealing heightened activity in the PFC and anterior cingulate (Newberg et al., 2001; Fox et al., 2016; Gotink et al., 2016). Investigations further demonstrate increased functional connectivity between the frontal lobe and temporal regions within the default mode network (Panda et al., 2016; Devaney et al., 2021). Consequently, it appears that many spiritual practices initiate by activating the prefrontal and cingulate cortex, indicative of the individual's will or intent to focus on a sacred object. Notably, frontal lobe activity may fluctuate throughout the practice, particularly during peak experiences, a phenomenon we will explore later. In addition, the cingulate cortex appears to be substantially affected by spiritual practices, which might also be related to potential mental health benefits (Brewer et al., 2013).

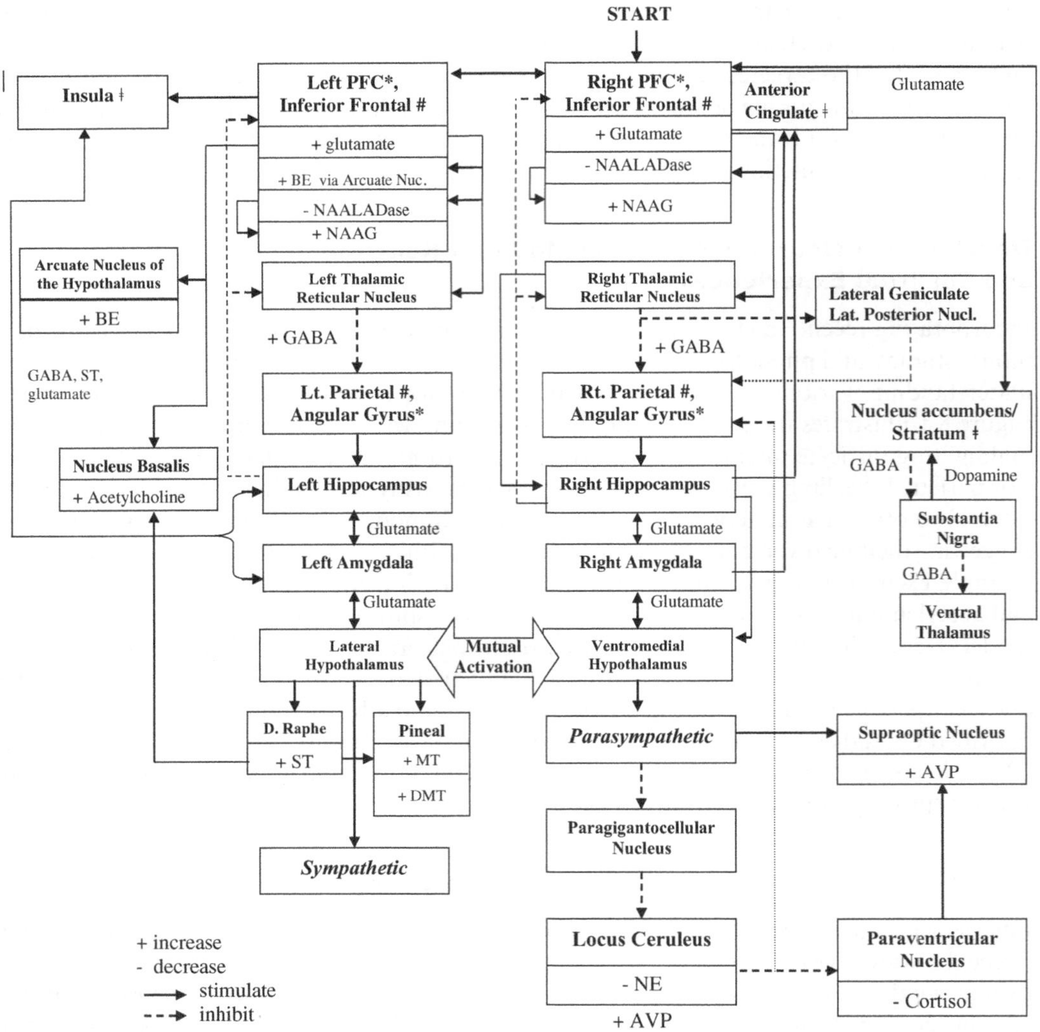

Figure 8.1 Schematic Diagram of Neurophysiological Processes Associated with Spiritual Practices. Please note that not all interactions and connections between the brain structures are shown, just those that are likely involved in spiritual practices and experiences. Networks that are represented by these structures are denoted as follows: ǂ Salience network; * Default mode network; # Attention network.

Thalamic Activity in Spiritual Practices

The thalamus plays a pivotal role in relaying sensory information and regulating attentional processes within the brain (Cornwall & Phillipson, 1988). Activation of the PFC is known to influence the reticular nucleus of the thalamus, primarily via glutamatergic pathways (Zikopoulos & Barbas. 2006). This activation modulates sensory input to the cortex, particularly to regions like the superior parietal lobe involved in spatial orientation (Bucci, Conley, & Gallagher, 1999). During meditation, increased PFC activity, particularly on the right, likely results in heightened thalamic activity, leading to decreased sensory input to the superior parietal lobe (Newberg et al., 2001).

The reticular nucleus releases GABA, an inhibitory neurotransmitter, onto thalamic nuclei, reducing sensory input in line with reticular activation (Destexhe, Contreras, & Steriade, 1998). This functional deafferentation, supported by studies showing increased GABA levels during meditation, enhances focus by limiting distracting stimuli (Streeter et al., 2007; Guglietti et al., 2013). Thalamic involvement in spiritual experiences may alter the sense of reality, given its role in consciousness and sensory processing (Newberg & Waldman, 2016).

Moreover, the dopaminergic system, linked to the reward system, likely modulates thalamic activity during spiritual practices (Kjaer et al., 2002). Studies suggest increased dopamine release during meditation, associated with positive emotions and potentially priming the brain for spiritual experiences (Ferguson et al., 2018). Our recent findings from a spiritual retreat also indicate dopaminergic changes, underscoring the importance of dopamine in meditative states (Newberg et al., 2017).

Thus, thalamic activity, influenced by both glutamatergic and dopaminergic pathways, plays a crucial role in mediating sensory processing and attentional focus during spiritual practices. Further research is needed to elucidate the intricate interplay between neurotransmitter systems and their impact on spiritual experiences.

Functional Role of the Superior Parietal Lobe

The parietal lobe is integral to processing higher-order sensory information and spatial orientation (Adair et al., 1995). It functions within an attentional network involving the PFC and thalamus (Fernandez-Duque & Posner, 2001). By receiving input from the thalamus, it constructs a three-dimensional body image and aids in spatial coordination.

Recent studies have also suggested the involvement of the superior temporal lobe in spatial representation, although its relationship with the parietal lobe remains unclear (Karnath, Ferber, & Himmelbach, 2001). Moreover, alterations in the default mode network, including the posterior subnet, have been linked to meditation-induced changes in self-perception (Fingelkurts, Fingelkurts, & Kallio-Tamminen, 2016).

Deafferentation of the parietal lobe during spiritual practices may decrease the perception of the self, or the boundary between the self and other objects in the world. Neuroimaging studies have consistently shown decreased activity in this region during intense spiritual experiences (Newberg et al., 2001; Herzog et al., 1990–1991). Our earlier SPECT study also demonstrated a correlation between increased thalamic activity and decreased superior parietal lobe activity, suggesting a link between focused attention and altered self-perception (Newberg et al., 2001, 2003). Thus, deeper focus during spiritual practices may facilitate the attainment of unitary states and the loss of the sense of self.

Hippocampal and Amygdala Activation During Spiritual Practices

Spiritual practices, particularly when they include strong emotional intensity, are likely associated with activity in the limbic structures. The hippocampus modulates cortical responsiveness and arousal, partly through the glutamate and GABA neurotransmitters (Tao et al., 2016). Studies suggest that spiritual practices induce hippocampal activation, potentially enhancing prefrontal-thalamic interactions via the nucleus accumbens, a key dopamine area of the brain (Newman & Grace, 1999).

The hippocampus and amygdala interact to regulate attention, emotion, and memory (Kreiman, Koch, & Fried, 2000). Increased activity in these regions during meditation has been reported (Lazar et al., 2000; Engström et al., 2010). These findings support the involvement of limbic structures in spiritual experiences.

Hypothalamic and Autonomic Nervous System Changes

The hypothalamus, interconnected with the limbic system, influences autonomic function. Stimulation of the lateral amygdala can activate the ventromedial hypothalamus, leading to parasympathetic activation (Davis, 1992). Spiritual practices often induce parasympathetic dominance, observed through reduced heart rate and respiratory rate (Jevning, Wallace & Beidebach, 1992).

Decreased norepinephrine levels during a variety of meditation practices may result from reduced locus coeruleus activity, impacting cortical areas such as the parietal lobe (Foote, 1987). This reduction in norepinephrine contributes to sensory deafferentation during meditation.

Decreased cortisol levels during meditation, supported by urine and plasma studies, indicate a reduced stress response (Jevning, Wilson, & Davidson, 1978). Hippocampal modulation may play a role in this cortisol reduction as well (Lau et al., 2015).

Increased arginine vasopressin (AVP) during meditation might enhance arousal and memory consolidation (Pietrowsky et al., 1991). Plasma AVP levels have been reported to rise during meditation (O'Halloran et al., 1985), potentially influencing subjective experiences of fatigue and arousal.

Prefrontal Cortex Effects on Other Neurochemical Systems

Sustained PFC activity during spiritual practices increases glutamate levels, potentially stimulating beta-endorphin release from the hypothalamic arcuate nucleus (Kiss et al., 1997). Beta-endorphin's effects include pain reduction and euphoria, which align with experiences during meditation.

Excitotoxic glutamate levels during meditation may lead to an increase in N-acetylaspartylglutamate (NAAG), protecting neurons from damage (Thomas et al., 2000). However, excess NAAG, acting as an NMDAr inhibitor, may induce hallucinogenic states akin to mystical experiences (Jevtovic-Todorovic et al., 2001).

Autonomic Nervous System Dynamics

Although the relationship between the autonomic nervous system and spiritual experiences has been discussed above, it is important to expand upon this relationship. Gellhorn and Kiely's early 1970s model focused on autonomic nervous system activity during meditation, emphasizing its significance (Gellhorn & Kiely, 1972). They proposed that intense sympathetic or parasympathetic stimulation could lead to simultaneous activation of both systems, reflecting a breakthrough phenomenon. Studies have shown predominantly parasympathetic activity during meditation, indicated by reduced heart rate, blood pressure, respiratory rate, and oxygen metabolism (Travis, 2001). However, research suggests mutual activation of sympathetic and parasympathetic systems during meditation, evidenced by increased heart rate variability (Peng et al., 1999; Libby et al., 2012), aligning with the calmness-alertness dichotomy of meditative states (Amihai & Kozhevnikov, 2015; Buttle, 2015). These findings could have important implications for mental and physical health. If spiritual practices and experiences affect the autonomic nervous system in complex ways, the results could be reduced heart rate, blood pressure, and stress response in the context of parasympathetic activity. Alternatively, when such experiences are associated with increased sympathetic activity, the result would be increased heart rate and blood pressure. Interestingly, increased heart rate variability has been associated with improved overall health (Kemp & Quintana, 2013; Thayer et al., 2012).

Serotonergic Modulation

Autonomic activation can stimulate the lateral hypothalamus and median forebrain bundle, inducing ecstatic and blissful feelings (Olds & Forbes, 1981). Lateral hypothalamic stimulation also affects ST activity, supported by increased ST breakdown products post-meditation (Walton et al., 1995). ST, influencing visual association flow in the temporal lobes, originates from the dorsal raphe when stimulated by the lateral hypothalamus or PFC (Juckel et al., 1999). Elevated ST correlates with positive affect, suggesting its role in mood regulation and the antidepressant effects of spiritual practices (Van Praag & De Hann, 1980; Newberg et al., 2005).

Cortical ST receptor activation, especially in the temporal lobes, can induce hallucinogenic effects, similar to tryptamine psychedelics (Aghajanian & Marek, 1999). This is why psychedelic experiences associated with LSD or psilocybin can be particularly important both in terms of understanding the biological underpinnings of spiritual experiences, and for trying to discern potential benefits for mental health. If psychedelic experiences can provide benefits for people with depression or post-traumatic stress disorder (PTSD), perhaps it is related to the acute and strong effects of these substances on the ST system. Elevated ST levels may modulate other neurotransmitter systems, enhancing euphoria and attention via dopamine modulation and acetylcholine release (Vollenweider et al., 1997, 1999; Manfridi et al., 1999). Melatonin production may rise due to increased ST and lateral hypothalamic innervation of the pineal gland, contributing to calmness and pain reduction during meditation (Tooley et al., 2000; Shaji & Kulkarni, 1998).

Under intense activation, pineal enzymes can synthesize the hallucinogen N, N-dimethyltryptamine (DMT), which primarily binds to ST receptors, and is associated with mystical experiences (Barker, Monti, & Christian, 1981; Strassman et al., 1996). Hyperstimulation of the pineal gland may lead to DMT production, inducing various mystical-type experiences.

Frontal Lobe Inhibition in Spiritual States

Extended meditation or prayer practices may lead to reduced frontal lobe activity, observed in Pentecostal speaking in tongues and Brazilian mediums in trance (Newberg et al., 2006; Peres et al., 2012). This hypofrontality may result from either sustained attentional depletion or reciprocal modulation by other brain regions such as the hippocampus, thalamus, or limbic system. Alternatively, meditation practices may initially augment frontal lobe activity before subsequent decreases, priming the brain for spiritual experiences. Such shifts in neuronal activity may underlie mystical or enlightenment states, leading to permanent cognitive and emotional transformations (Newberg & Waldman, 2016).

Neuroscience of the Beneficial Effects of Spirituality on Mental Health

Studying the beneficial aspects of spirituality on mental health through the lens of neuroscience offers profound insights into the potential therapeutic effects of spiritual beliefs and practices. Spirituality is often associated with positive outcomes such as improved well-being, resilience, and coping mechanisms in the face of adversity (Koenig, 2012). Neuroscience research has begun to unravel the neurobiological mechanisms underlying these beneficial effects, shedding light on how spiritual experiences modulate brain function and promote psychological resilience.

Neuroimaging studies have revealed that engaging in spiritual practices such as prayer, meditation, or mindfulness induces neuroplastic changes in the brain associated with improved emotional regulation, stress reduction, and enhanced cognitive function (Newberg et al., 2010). For example, meditation practices have been shown to increase gray matter density in brain regions involved in attention, emotional processing, and self-awareness, such as the PFC and insula (Hölzel et al., 2011; Hernández et al., 2020). These structural changes are accompanied by functional alterations in brain networks implicated in emotion regulation and self-referential processing, leading to improvements in mental health outcomes. The insula in particular appears to play a prominent role in emotional regulation that is affected by meditation practices (Gotink et al., 2016; Sezer et al., 2022). In addition, the insula has been postulated to be involved in spiritual experiences, especially in the context of patients with temporal lobe seizures (Gschwind & Picard, 2016). Such patients who report ecstatic experiences during seizures have been found to have localized activation in the anterior insula. In addition, direct stimulation of this area has produced intense feelings of arousal and bliss. Thus, the insula, in addition to its connections with the limbic and cortical areas, may play a prominent role in spiritual experiences.

Moreover, spirituality has been linked to increased levels of positive emotions such as gratitude, compassion, and altruism, which have been associated with enhanced psychological well-being and resilience (Emmons & McCullough, 2003; Sharma et al., 2017). Neuroscientific research has shown that engaging in acts of kindness or altruism activates reward circuits in the brain, leading to feelings of pleasure and satisfaction (Marsh et al., 2014). These positive emotions, in turn, promote resilience to stress and adversity by buffering against the negative effects of psychological distress.

Furthermore, spiritual beliefs and practices have been found to foster social connectedness and social support, which are crucial determinants of mental health and well-being (Pargament et al., 2013). Neuroimaging studies have demonstrated that social interactions and feelings of social belongingness activate brain regions involved in reward processing and emotional regulation, such as the ventral striatum and anterior cingulate cortex (Inagaki & Eisenberger, 2013). By promoting social cohesion and fostering a sense of belongingness, spirituality may enhance individuals' ability to cope with stressors and adversity, thereby promoting mental health and resilience.

As mentioned above, there is also an explosion of research into the potential beneficial effects of psychedelic compounds for disorders such as depression, anxiety, and PTSD (Rhee et al., 2023; Zaretsky et al., 2024). Some early studies have shown that these effects are mediated in part by the spiritual nature of the experiences. Future studies can more specifically explore the acute and long-term effects of psychedelic compounds on brain function, particularly as they relate to changes in mental health.

In general, studying the beneficial aspects of spirituality on mental health with neuroscience provides compelling evidence for the therapeutic effects of spiritual beliefs and practices.

By elucidating the neurobiological mechanisms underlying these effects, researchers can develop targeted interventions to harness the potential of spirituality for promoting psychological well-being and resilience. However, it is essential to approach this research with caution and sensitivity to the diverse cultural and religious contexts in which spirituality operates and to prioritize ethical considerations in studying potentially sensitive topics.

Neuroscience of the Deleterious Effects of Spirituality on Mental Health

Studying the negative aspects of spirituality on mental health through the lens of neuroscience similarly provides valuable insights into the biological connections. While spirituality is often associated with positive outcomes such as improved well-being and resilience, there is growing recognition that it can also have detrimental effects on mental health in certain circumstances (Bentzen et al., 2015). One area of concern is the phenomenon of religious or spiritual struggles, which encompass experiences of doubt, guilt, and conflict related to one's beliefs or practices. These struggles have been linked to increased psychological distress and poorer mental health outcomes (Exline et al., 2016). Neuroscientific research can help elucidate the underlying neural mechanisms through which such struggles contribute to mental health difficulties.

Neuroimaging studies have begun to uncover the neural correlates of religious and spiritual struggles, shedding light on their impact on brain function and structure. For example, research has shown that individuals experiencing religious doubt or uncertainty exhibit patterns of brain activity associated with heightened emotional distress and cognitive conflict (van Elk et al., 2010). Furthermore, chronic exposure to stressors related to religious or spiritual conflicts may lead to alterations in brain circuits implicated in emotion regulation and self-referential processing (Exline et al., 2016). Understanding these neurobiological mechanisms is crucial for developing targeted interventions to alleviate the negative effects of spiritual struggles on mental health.

Another area of interest in studying the negative aspects of spirituality on mental health is the phenomenon of religious or spiritual abuse. Religious or spiritual abuse involves the misuse of power and authority within religious or spiritual contexts, leading to psychological harm and trauma (Linnville et al., 2016). Neuroscientific research can provide insights into how experiences of religious or spiritual abuse affect brain function and contribute to mental health disorders such as PTSD and depression. For example, neuroimaging studies have shown that individuals who have experienced trauma exhibit alterations in brain regions involved in fear processing and emotion regulation (Lanius et al., 2010). Examining the neural correlates of religious or spiritual abuse can help identify biomarkers of vulnerability to such experiences and inform the development of therapeutic interventions.

Finally, prominent negative effects of spirituality can include those individuals who follow cults or commit violent acts in the name of their tradition or God. Following such religious and spiritual paths can be dangerous for the individual and society at large. However, little is known about the brain mechanisms that predispose individuals to pursue negative paths of spirituality. Future neuroimaging studies can assess predisposing factors that might lead an individual to more positive or negative views on spirituality. Factors may include an altered balance between cognitive and emotional processes that leads to poor decision-making regarding spiritual paths.

By elucidating the neurobiological mechanisms underlying spiritual struggles, religious or spiritual abuse, or cult behaviors, researchers can develop more effective interventions to mitigate these adverse effects on mental health.

Limitations of Research on the Neuroscience of Spirituality

Studying spirituality through the lens of neuroscience offers valuable insights into the neural correlates of religious and spiritual experiences. However, this interdisciplinary approach comes with important methodological challenges and limitations. One notable limitation is the inherent complexity and subjectivity of spirituality itself. Spirituality encompasses a wide range of beliefs, practices, and experiences that are deeply personal and culturally influenced. As such, attempting to reduce spirituality to measurable neural activity may oversimplify its multifaceted nature (Schjoedt et al., 2013). In addition, there are many diverse emotional, cognitive, and experiential aspects that contribute to religious and spiritual experiences. Clarifying these elements and also differentiating the psychological from the spiritual can be very difficult. For example, differentiating the fear, awe, and arousal emotions that each can potentially be felt during spiritual experiences may involve overlapping brain regions.

Another limitation arises from the methodological challenges in studying spirituality using neuroscientific techniques. Most neuroimaging studies rely on tasks or stimuli that can be standardized and controlled in laboratory settings. However, spiritual experiences often occur spontaneously and are influenced by various contextual factors, making them difficult to replicate under controlled conditions (Newberg & Waldman, 2017). This discrepancy between the naturalistic context of spiritual experiences and the controlled environment of neuroscientific experiments poses a significant challenge to researchers. For example, studying certain practices while lying in an MRI may not be possible, especially if these practices involve certain postures or movements. There are also many challenges in studying spiritual experiences associated with psychedelic compounds, including issues with regard to mechanism, subjective effects, and potential long-term consequences (Barksdale et al., 2024).

Furthermore, the interpretation of neuroimaging data related to spirituality requires careful consideration of cultural and individual differences. Brain activity associated with spiritual experiences may vary across different religious traditions, cultural backgrounds, and personal beliefs (Kapogiannis et al., 2009). Without accounting for these factors, the generalizability of findings may be limited. Additionally, individual differences in cognitive and emotional processing can influence how spiritual experiences are perceived and encoded in the brain, further complicating the interpretation of neuroimaging results (Beauregard & Paquette, 2006).

Moreover, the reductionist nature of neuroscience poses philosophical challenges to the study of spirituality. Neuroscience seeks to understand complex phenomena by analyzing their underlying neural mechanisms. However, spirituality encompasses aspects of consciousness, meaning, and transcendence that may transcend the physical realm (Beauregard, 2014). Attempting to explain spiritual experiences solely in terms of neural activity may overlook their profound existential and metaphysical significance.

Thus, while neuroscience offers valuable tools for investigating the neural underpinnings of spirituality, it also presents several limitations. Addressing these limitations requires interdisciplinary collaboration, methodological innovation, and a nuanced understanding of spirituality's subjective and cultural dimensions. By acknowledging these challenges, researchers can strive to develop more comprehensive approaches to studying spirituality and spiritual experiences that integrate neuroscientific insights with insights from psychology, anthropology, and philosophy.

Future Directions in Neurotheology

The exploration of the neurobiological correlates of religious and spiritual phenomena, often termed "neurotheology," offers a wide range of avenues for future research. One approach involves delving into the diverse spectrum of spiritual practices, including meditation, prayer, rituals, and specific traditions, both across different traditions and within them. Another aspect ripe for investigation lies in examining the incredible variety of religious and spiritual experiences, varying from mild to profound mystical encounters. Furthermore, there is potential in studying specific conditions associated with intense experiences such as near-death states, pathological disorders, or altered states induced by substances.

Future studies in this field can leverage the advancements in cognitive neuroscience. Utilizing cutting-edge neuroimaging techniques, such as those employed in the Human Connectome Project (Smith, 2013), offers detailed insights into the intricate connectivity patterns of brain structures. Explorations into the resting brain and the default mode network can elucidate how the functional connectivity of different brain regions correlates with religious and spiritual phenomena. Additionally, investigations of various neurotransmitter systems and their associations with different practices and experiences hold promise for further understanding.

Efforts should also focus on refining the assessment of the phenomenological and psychological aspects of religious and spiritual experiences. Developing effective methodologies to evaluate the impact of these experiences on cognitive, emotional, sensory, and behavioral domains is crucial for interpreting neuroscientific findings accurately. Such studies can also evaluate the impact of spirituality on mental health problems, particularly from a neuroscientific perspective.

In summary, the future of research into the neurobiological underpinnings of religious and spiritual phenomena appears promising and filled with vast possibilities.

References

Adair, J. C., Gilmore, R. L., Fennell, E. B., Gold, M., & Heilman, K. M. (1995). Anosognosia during intracarotid barbiturate anesthesia: unawareness or amnesia for weakness. *Neurology*, *45*(2), 241–243. https://doi.org/10.1212/wnl.45.2.241

Aghajanian, G. K., & Marek, G. J. (1999). Serotonin and hallucinogens. *Neuropsychopharmacology*, *21*, 16S–23S. https://doi.org/10.1016/S0893-133X(98)00135-3

Amihai, I., & Kozhevnikov, M. (2015). The influence of Buddhist meditation traditions on the autonomic system and attention. *BioMed Research International*, *2015*, 731579. https://doi.org/10.1155/2015/731579

Barker, S. A., Monti, J. A., & Christian, S. T. (1981). N, N-dimethyltryptamine: an endogenous hallucinogen. *International Review of Neurobiology*, *22*, 83–110.

Barksdale, B. R., Doss, M. K., Fonzo, G. A., & Nemeroff, C. B. (2024). The mechanistic divide in psychedelic neuroscience: An unbridgeable gap?. *Neurotherapeutics: The Journal of the American Society for Experimental NeuroTherapeutics*, *21*(2), e00322. https://doi.org/10.1016/j.neurot.2024.e00322

Beauregard, M. (2014). *Spiritual brain: A neuroscientist's case for the existence of the soul*. HarperCollins.

Beauregard, M., & Paquette, V. (2006). Neural correlates of a mystical experience in Carmelite nuns. *Neuroscience Letters*, *405*(3), 186–190. https://doi.org/10.1016/j.neulet.2006.06.060

Bentzen, M., La Cour, P., & Koenig, H. G. (2015). The association between religiosity and depression in two cohorts of Danish adults. *The International Journal of Psychiatry in Medicine*, 49(2), 109–123.

Brewer, J. A., Garrison, K. A., & Whitfield-Gabrieli, S. (2013). What about the "Self" is processed in the posterior cingulate cortex? *Frontiers in Human Neuroscience*, *7*, 647. https://doi.org/10.3389/fnhum.2013.00647

Bucci, D. J., Conley, M., & Gallagher, M. (1999). Thalamic and basal forebrain cholinergic connections of the rat posterior parietal cortex. *Neuroreport, 10*, 941–945. https://doi.org/10.1097/00001756-199904060-00009

Bulbulia, J. & Schjoedt, U. (2011). Toward an evolutionary social neuroscience of religion. *Religion, Brain & Behavior, 1*(3), 220–222. https://doi.org/10.1080/2153599X.2011.647851

Buttle, H. (2015). Measuring a journey without goal: Meditation, spirituality, and physiology. *Biomedical Research International*, 891671. https://doi.org/10.1155/2015/891671

Cornwall, J., & Phillipson, O. T. (1988). Mediodorsal and reticular thalamic nuclei receive collateral axons from prefrontal cortex and laterodorsal tegmental nucleus in the rat. *Neuroscience letters, 88*(2), 121–126. https://doi.org/10.1016/0304-3940(88)90111-5

d'Aquili, E. G., & Newberg, A. B. (1993). Religious and mystical states: A neuropsychological model. *Zygon, 28*, 177–200.

d'Aquili, E. G., & Newberg, A. B. (1999). *The mystical mind: Probing the biology of religious experience.* Fortress Press.

Davis, M. (1992). The role of the amygdala in fear and anxiety. *Annual Reviews in Neuroscience, 15*, 353–375. https://doi.org/10.1146/annurev.ne.15.030192.002033

Destexhe, A., Contreras, D., & Steriade, M. (1998). Mechanisms underlying the synchronizing action of corticothalamic feedback through inhibition of thalamic relay cells. *Journal of Neurophysiology, 79*(2), 999–1016. https://doi.org/10.1152/jn.1998.79.2.999

Devaney, K. J., Levin, E. J., Tripathi, V., Higgins, J. P., Lazar, S. W., & Somers, D. C. (2021). Attention and default mode network assessments of meditation experience during active cognition and rest. *Brain Sciences, 11*(5), 566. https://doi.org/10.3390/brainsci11050566

Durkheim, E. (1926). *The elementary forms of the religious life* (J. W. Swain, Trans.). George Allen & Unwin, LTD. (1915).

Emmons, R. A., & McCullough, M. E. (2003). Counting blessings versus burdens: An experimental investigation of gratitude and subjective well-being in daily life. *Journal of Personality and Social Psychology, 84*(2), 377–389. https://doi.org/10.1037/0022-3514.84.2.377

Engström, M., Pihlsgård, J., Lundberg, P., & Söderfeldt, B. (2010). Functional magnetic resonance imaging of hippocampal activation during silent mantra meditation. *Journal of Alternative and Complementary Medicine, 16*(12), 1253–1258. https://doi.org/10.1089/acm.2009.0706

Exline, J. J., Grubbs, J. B., Homolka, S. J., & Toner, K. (2016). Religious and spiritual struggles. In R. F. Paloutzian & C. L. Park (Eds.), *Handbook of the psychology of religion and spirituality* (Second ed.) (pp. 380–398). The Guilford Press.

Ferguson, M. A., Nielsen, J. A., King, J. B., Dai, L., Giangrasso, D. M., Holman, R., Korenberg, J. R., & Anderson, J. S. (2018). Reward, salience, and attentional networks are activated by religious experience in devout Mormons. *Social Neuroscience, 13*(1), 104–116. https://doi.org/10.1080/17470919.2016.1257437

Fernandez-Duque, D., & Posner, M. I. (2001). Brain imaging of attentional networks in normal and pathological states. *Journal of Clinical and Experimental Neuropsychology, 23*(1), 74–93. https://doi.org/10.1076/jcen.23.1.74.1217

Fingelkurts, A. A., Fingelkurts, A. A., & Kallio-Tamminen, T. (2016). Long-term meditation training induced changes in the operational synchrony of default mode network modules during a resting state. *Cognitive Processing, 17*(1), 27–37. https://doi.org/10.1007/s10339-015-0743-4

Foote, S. L., & Morrison, J. H. (1987). Extrathalamic modulation of cortical function. *Annual Review of Neuroscience, 10*, 67–95. https://doi.org/10.1146/annurev.ne.10.030187.000435

Fox, K. C., Dixon, M. L., Nijeboer, S., Girn, M., Floman, J. L., Lifshitz, M., Ellamil, M., Sedlmeier, P., & Christoff, K. (2016). Functional neuroanatomy of meditation: A review and meta-analysis of 78 functional neuroimaging investigations. *Neuroscience and Biobehavioral reviews, 65*, 208–228. https://doi.org/10.1016/j.neubiorev.2016.03.021

Frith, C. D., Friston, K., Liddle, P. F., & Frackowiak, R. S. (1991). Willed action and the prefrontal cortex in man: A study with PET. *Proceedings of the Royal Society B: Biological Sciences, 244*(1311), 241–246. https://doi.org/10.1098/rspb.1991.0077

Gay, P. (Ed.). (1995). *The Freud reader*. W. W. Norton.

Gellhorn, E., & Kiely, W. F. (1972). Mystical states of consciousness: Neurophysiological and clinical aspects. *Journal of Nervous and Mental Disease*, 154, 399–405. https://doi.org/10.1097/00005053-197206000-00002

Gotink, R. A., Meijboom, R., Vernooij, M. W., Smits, M., & Hunink, M. G. (2016). 8-week mindfulness based stress reduction induces brain changes similar to traditional long-term meditation practice: A systematic review. *Brain and Cognition, 108*, 32–41. https://doi.org/10.1016/j.bandc.2016.07.001

Gschwind, M., & Picard, F. (2016). Ecstatic epileptic seizures: A Glimpse into the multiple roles of the insula. *Frontiers in Behavioral Neuroscience, 10*, 21. https://doi.org/10.3389/fnbeh.2016.00021

Guglietti, C. L., Daskalakis, Z. J., Radhu, N., Fitzgerald, P. B., & Ritvo, P. (2013). Meditation-related increases in $GABA_B$ modulated cortical inhibition. *Brain Stimulation*, *6*(3), 397–402. https://doi.org/10.1016/j.brs.2012.08.005

Hernández, S. E., Dorta, R., Suero, J., Barros-Loscertales, A., González-Mora, J. L., & Rubia, K. (2020). Larger whole brain grey matter associated with long-term Sahaja Yoga Meditation: A detailed area by area comparison. *PloS one*, 15(12), e0237552. https://doi.org/10.1371/journal.pone.0237552

Herzog, H., Lele, V. R., Kuwert, T., Langen, K. J., Rota Kops, E., & Feinendegen, L. E. (1990). Changed pattern of regional glucose metabolism during yoga meditative relaxation. *Neuropsychobiology*, *23*(4), 182–187. https://doi.org/10.1159/000119450

Hölzel, B. K., Carmody, J., Vangel, M., Congleton, C., Yerramsetti, S. M., Gard, T., & Lazar, S. W. (2011). Mindfulness practice leads to increases in regional brain gray matter density. *Psychiatry Research: Neuroimaging*, *191*(1), 36–43. https://doi.org/10.1016/j.pscychresns.2010.08.006

Inagaki, T. K., & Eisenberger, N. I. (2013). Neural correlates of giving support to a loved one. *Psychosomatic Medicine*, *75*(7), 694–700. https://doi.org/10.1097/PSY.0b013e3182359335

Ingvar, D. H. (1994). The will of the brain: Cerebral correlates of willful acts. *Journal of Theoretical Biology*, *171*, 7–12. https://doi.org/10.1006/jtbi.1994.1206

James, W. (1902). *The varieties of religious experience*. Mentor.

Jevning, R., Wallace, R. K., & Beidebach, M. (1992). The physiology of meditation: a review. A wakeful hypometabolic integrated response. *Neuroscience and Biobehavioral Reviews*, *16*(3), 415–424. https://doi.org/10.1016/s0149-7634(05)80210-6

Jevning, R., Wilson, A. F., & Davidson, J. M. (1978). Adrenocortical activity during meditation. *Hormones and Behavior*, *10*(1), 54–60. https://doi.org/10.1016/0018-506x(78)90024-7

Jevtovic-Todorovic, V., Wozniak, D. F., Benshoff, N. D., & Olney, J. W. (2001). A comparative evaluation of the neurotoxic properties of ketamine and nitrous oxide. *Brain Research*, *895*(1-2), 264–267. https://doi.org/10.1016/s0006-8993(01)02079-0

Juckel, G., Mendlin, A., & Jacobs, B. L. (1999). Electrical stimulation of rat medial prefrontal cortex enhances forebrain serotonin output: implications for electroconvulsive therapy and transcranial magnetic stimulation in depression. *Neuropsychopharmacology*, *21*(3), 391–398. https://doi.org/10.1016/S0893-133X(98)00097-9

Kapogiannis, D., Barbey, A. K., Su, M., Zamboni, G., Krueger, F., & Grafman, J. (2009). Cognitive and neural foundations of religious belief. *Proceedings of the National Academy of Sciences*, *106*(12), 4876–4881. https://doi.org/10.1073/pnas.0811717106

Karnath, H. O., Ferber, S., & Himmelbach, M. (2001). Spatial awareness is a function of the temporal not the posterior parietal lobe. *Nature*, *411*, 950–953. https://doi.org/10.1038/35082075

Kemp, A. H., & Quintana, D. S. (2013). The relationship between mental and physical health: insights from the study of heart rate variability. *International Journal of Psychophysiology*, *89*(3), 288–296. https://doi.org/10.1016/j.ijpsycho.2013.06.018

Kiss, J., Kocsis, K., Csaki, A., Gorcs, T.J., Halasz, B. (1997). Metabotropic glutamate receptor in GHRH and beta-endorphin neurons of the hypothalamic arcuate nucleus. *Neuroreport*, *8*, 3703–3707. https://doi.org/10.1097/00001756-199712010-00009

Kjaer, T. W., Bertelsen, C., Piccini, P., Brooks, D., Alving, J., & Lou, H. C. (2002). Increased dopamine tone during meditation-induced change of consciousness. *Cognitive Brain Research*, *13*(2), 255–259. https://doi.org/10.1016/s0926-6410(01)00106-9

Koenig, H. G. (2012). Religion, spirituality, and health: The research and clinical implications. *ISRN Psychiatry*, *2012*, 1–33. https://doi.org/10.5402/2012/278730

Kreiman, G., Koch, C., & Fried, I. (2000). Imagery neurons in the human brain. *Nature*, *408*(6810), 357–361. https://doi.org/10.1038/35042575

Lanius, R. A., Vermetten, E., & Pain, C. (2010). *The impact of early life trauma on health and disease: The hidden epidemic*. Cambridge University Press.

Larson, D. B., Swyers, J. P., & McCullough, M. E. (Eds.). (1998). *Scientific research on spirituality and health: A consensus report*. National Institute for Healthcare Research.

Lau, W. K., Leung, M. K., Chan, C. C., Wong, S. S., & Lee, T. M. (2015). Can the neural-cortisol association be moderated by experience-induced changes in awareness?. *Scientific Reports*, *5*, 16620. https://doi.org/10.1038/srep16620

Lazar, S. W., Bush, G., Gollub, R. L., Fricchione, G. L., Khalsa, G., & Benson, H. (2000). Functional brain mapping of the relaxation response and meditation. *Neuroreport*, *11*(7), 1581–1585.

Libby, D. J., Worhunsky, P. D., Pilver, C. E., & Brewer, J. A. (2012). Meditation-induced changes in high-frequency heart rate variability predict smoking outcomes. *Frontiers in Human Neuroscience*, *6*, 54. https://doi.org/10.3389/fnhum.2012.00054

Linnville, S. E., Bagwell-Gray, M., & Madigan, L. M. (2016). What do we know about the link between childhood religiousness and abuse? A review of the literature. *Trauma, Violence, & Abuse*, 17(4), 444–458.

Manfridi, A., Brambilla, D., & Mancia, M. (1999). Stimulation of NMDA and AMPA receptors in the rat nucleus basalis of Meynert affects sleep. *The American Journal of Physiology*, *277*(5), R1488–R1492. https://doi.org/10.1152/ajpregu.1999.277.5.R1488

Marsh, A. A., Kanai, R., & Nour, M. M. (2014). Neuroanatomy of giving it up: Dopamine and altruism. *Journal of Neuroscience*, *34*(50), 16835–16837.

Newberg, A., Alavi, A., Baime, M., Pourdehnad, M., Santanna, J., & d'Aquili, E. (2001). The measurement of regional cerebral blood flow during the complex cognitive task of meditation: A preliminary SPECT study. *Psychiatry Research*, *106*(2), 113–122. https://doi.org/10.1016/s0925-4927(01)00074-9

Newberg, A., Wintering, N.A., Morgan, D., & Waldman, M. R. (2006). The measurement of regional cerebral blood flow during glossolalia: A preliminary SPECT study. *Psychiatry Research: Neuroimaging*, *148*(1), 67–71. https://doi.org/10.1016/j.pscychresns.2006.07.001

Newberg, A. B. (2018). *Neurotheology: How science can enlighten us about spirituality*. Columbia University Press.

Newberg, A. B., Amsterdam, J. D., Wintering, N., Ploessl, K., Swanson, R. L., Shults, J., & Alavi, A. (2005). 123I-ADAM binding to serotonin transporters in patients with major depression and healthy controls: a preliminary study. *Journal of nuclear medicine: Official publication, Society of Nuclear Medicine*, *46*(6), 973–977.

Newberg, A. B., Iversen, J. (2003). The neural basis of the complex mental task of meditation: Neurotransmitter and neurochemical considerations. *Medical Hypothesis*, *61*(2), 282–291. https://doi.org/10.1016/s0306-9877(03)00175-0

Newberg, A. B., & Waldman, M. R. (2016). *How enlightenment changes your brain: The new science of transformation*. New York, NY: Penguin Random House.

Newberg, A. B., & Waldman, M. R. (2017). *How enlightenment changes your brain: The new science of transformation*. Penguin.

Newberg, A. B., Wintering, N., Khalsa, D. S., Roggenkamp, H., & Waldman, M. R. (2010). Meditation effects on cognitive function and cerebral blood flow in subjects with memory loss: A preliminary study. *Journal of Alzheimer's Disease*, *20*(2), 517–526. https://doi.org/10.3233/JAD-2010-1391

Newberg, A. B., Wintering, N., Yaden, D. B., Zhong, L., Bowen, B., Averick, N., & Monti, D. A. (2017). Effect of a one-week spiritual retreat on dopamine and serotonin transporter binding: A preliminary study. *Religion, Brain & Behavior*, *8*(3), 265–278. https://doi.org/10.1080/2153599X.2016.1267035

Newman, J., & Grace, A. A. (1999). Binding across time: The selective gating of frontal and hippocampal systems modulating working memory and attentional states. *Consciousness & Cognition*, *8*, 196–212. https://doi.org/10.1006/ccog.1999.0392

O'Halloran, J. P., Jevning, R., Wilson, A. F., Skowsky, R., Walsh, R. N., & Alexander, C. (1985). Hormonal control in a state of decreased activation: potentiation of arginine vasopressin secretion. *Physiology & Behavior*, *35*(4), 591–595. https://doi.org/10.1016/0031-9384(85)90146-5

Olds, M. E., & Forbes, J. L. (1981). The central basis of motivation, intracranial self-stimulation studies. *Annual Reviews in Psychology*, *32*, 523–574. https://doi.org/10.1146/annurev.ps.32.020181.002515

Otto, R. (1923). *The idea of the holy: An inquiry into the non-rational factor in the idea of the divine and its relation to the rational* (J. W. Harvey, Trans.). Oxford University Press. (1917).

Panda, R., Bharath, R. D., Upadhyay, N., Mangalore, S., Chennu, S., & Rao, S. L. (2016). Temporal dynamics of the Default Mode Network characterize meditation-induced alterations in consciousness. *Frontiers in Human Neuroscience*, *10*, 372. https://doi.org/10.3389/fnhum.2016.00372

Pardo, J. V., Fox, P. T., & Raichle, M. E. (1991). Localization of a human system for sustained attention by positron emission tomography. *Nature*, *349*, 61–64. https://doi.org/10.1038/349061a0

Pargament, K. I., Ano, G. G., & Wachholtz, A. B. (2013). The religious and spiritual dimensions of coping with stress. In S. Folkman (Ed.), *The Oxford handbook of stress, health, and coping* (pp. 134–150). Oxford University Press.

Peng, C. K., Mietus, J. E., Liu, Y., Khalsa, G., Douglas, P. S., Benson, H., & Goldberger, A. L. (1999). Exaggerated heart rate oscillations during two meditation techniques. *International Journal of Cardiology*, *70*(2), 101–107. https://doi.org/10.1016/s0167-5273(99)00066-2

Peres, J. F., Moreira-Almeida, A., Caixeta, L., Leao, F., & Newberg, A. (2012). Neuroimaging during trance state: A contribution to the study of dissociation. *PLoS One*, *7*(11):e49360. https://doi.org/10.1371/journal.pone.0049360

Pietrowsky, R., Braun, D., Fehm, H. L., Pauschinger, P., & Born, J. (1991). Vasopressin and oxytocin do not influence early sensory processing but affect mood and activation in man. *Peptides*, *12*, 1385–1391. https://doi.org/10.1016/0196-9781(91)90224-d

Posner, M. I., & Petersen, S. E. (1990). The attention system of the human brain. *Annual Review of Neuroscience*, *13*, 25–42. https://doi.org/10.1146/annurev.ne.13.030190.000325

Rhee, T. G., Davoudian, P. A., Sanacora, G., & Wilkinson, S. T. (2023). Psychedelic renaissance: Revitalized potential therapies for psychiatric disorders. *Drug Discovery Today*, *28*(12), 103818. https://doi.org/10.1016/j.drudis.2023.103818

Saver, J. L., & Rabin, J. (1997). The neural substrates of religious experience. *The Journal of Neuropsychiatry and Clinical Neurosciences*, *9*(3), 498–510. https://doi.org/10.1176/jnp.9.3.498

Schjoedt, U., Sørensen, J., Nielbo, K. L., Xygalatas, D., Mitkidis, P., & Bulbulia, J. (2013). Cognitive resource depletion in religious interactions. *Religion, Brain & Behavior*, *3*(1), 39–55. https://doi.org/10.1080/2153599X.2012.736714

Schleiermacher, F. D. E. (1999). *The Christian Faith*. Edited by H.R. Mackintosh & J.S. Stewart. T & T Clark.

Sezer, I., Pizzagalli, D. A., & Sacchet, M. D. (2022). Resting-state fMRI functional connectivity and mindfulness in clinical and non-clinical contexts: A review and synthesis. *Neuroscience and Biobehavioral Reviews*, *135*, 104583. https://doi.org/10.1016/j.neubiorev.2022.104583

Shaji, A. V., & Kulkarni, S. K. (1998). Central nervous system depressant activities of melatonin in rats and mice. *Indian Journal of Experimental Biology*, *36*, 257–263.

Sharma, V., Marin, D. B., Koenig, H. K., Feder, A., Iacoviello, B. M., Southwick, S. M., & Pietrzak, R. H. (2017). Religion, spirituality, and mental health of U.S. military veterans: Results from the National Health and Resilience in Veterans Study. *Journal of Affective Disorders*, *217*, 197–204. https://doi.org/10.1016/j.jad.2017.03.071

Skinner, B. F. (1953). *Science and human behavior*. Macmillan.

Smith, S. (2013). Introduction to the NeuroImage special issue "Mapping the Connectome". *NeuroImage*, *80*, 1. https://doi.org/10.1016/j.neuroimage.2013.07.012

Strassman, R. J., Clifford, R., Qualls, R., & Berg, L. (1996). Differential tolerance to biological and subjective effects of four closely spaced doses of N,N-Dimethyltrypamine in humans. *Biological Psychiatry*, *39*, 784–795. https://doi.org/10.1016/0006-3223(95)00200-6

Streeter, C. C., Jensen, J. E., Perlmutter, R. M., Cabral, H. J., Tian, H., Terhune, D. B., Ciraulo, D. A., & Renshaw, P. F. (2007). Yoga Asana sessions increase brain GABA levels: A pilot study. *Journal of Alternative and Complementary Medicine*, *13*(4), 419–426. https://doi.org/10.1089/acm.2007.6338

Tao, J., Liu, J., Egorova, N., Chen, X., Sun, S., Xue, X., Huang, J., Zheng, G., Wang, Q., Chen, L., & Kong, J. (2016) Increased hippocampus-medial prefrontal cortex resting-state functional connectivity and memory function after Tai Chi Chuan Practice in elder adults. *Frontiers in Aging Neuroscience*, *8*, 25. https://doi.org/10.3389/fnagi.2016.00025

Thayer, J. F., Åhs, F., Fredrikson, M., Sollers, J. J., III, & Wager, T. D. (2012). A meta-analysis of heart rate variability and neuroimaging studies: implications for heart rate variability as a marker of stress and health. *Neuroscience and Biobehavioral Reviews*, *36*(2), 747–756. https://doi.org/10.1016/j.neubiorev.2011.11.009

Thomas, A. G., Vornov, J. J., Olkowski, J. L., Merion, A. T., & Slusher, B. S. (2000). N-Acetylated alpha-linked acidic dipeptidase converts N-acetylaspartylglutamate from a neuroprotectant to a neurotoxin. *The Journal of Pharmacology and Experimental Therapeutics*, *295*(1), 16–22.

Tooley, G. A., Armstrong, S. M., Norman, T. R., & Sali, A. (2000). Acute increases in night-time plasma melatonin levels following a period of meditation. *Biological Psychology*, *53*(1), 69–78. https://doi.org/10.1016/s0301-0511(00)00035-1

Travis, F. (2001). Autonomic and EEG patterns distinguish transcending from other experiences during Transcendental Meditation practice. *International Journal of Psychophysiology*, *42*(1), 1–9. https://doi.org/10.1016/s0167-8760(01)00143-x

van Elk, M., Rutjens, B. T., van der Pligt, J., & van Harreveld, F. (2010). Priming of supernatural agent concepts and agency detection. *Religion, Brain & Behavior*, *1*(3), 185–200.

Van Praag, H., & De Hann, S. (1980). Depression vulnerability and 5-hydroxytryptophan prophylaxis. *Psychiatry Research*, *3*(1), 75–83. https://doi.org/10.1016/0165-1781(80)90049-9

Vogt, B. A., Finch, D. M., & Olson, C. R. (1992). Functional heterogeneity in cingulate cortex: the anterior executive and posterior evaluative regions. *Cerebral Cortex*, *2*(6), 435–443. https://doi.org/10.1093/cercor/2.6.435-a

Vollenweider, F. X., Leenders, K. L., Scharfetter, C., Antonini, A., Maguire, P., Missimer, J., & Angst, J. (1997). Metabolic hyperfrontality and psychopathology in the ketamine model of psychosis using positron emission tomography (PET) and [18F]fluorodeoxyglucose (FDG). *European Neuropsychopharmacology*, *7*(1), 9–24. https://doi.org/10.1016/s0924-977x(96)00039-9

Vollenweider, F. X., Vontobel, P., Hell, D., & Leenders, K. L. (1999). 5-HT modulation of dopamine release in basal ganglia in psilocybin-induced psychosis in man--a PET study with [11C]raclopride. *Neuropsychopharmacology*, *20*(5), 424–433. https://doi.org/10.1016/S0893-133X(98)00108-0

Walton, K. G., Pugh, N. D., Gelderloos, P., & Macrae, P. (1995). Stress reduction and preventing hypertension: preliminary support for a psychoneuroendocrine mechanism. *Journal of Alternative and Complementary Medicine*, *1*(3), 263–283. https://doi.org/10.1089/acm.1995.1.263

Webb, J. R., Toussaint, L. L., & Dula, C. S. (2014). Ritualistic, theistic, and existential spirituality: Initial psychometric qualities of the RiTE measure of spirituality. *Journal of Religion & Health*, *53*(4), 972–985. https://doi.org/10.1007/s10943-013-9697-y

Yaden, D. B., & Newberg, A. B. (2022). *The varieties of spiritual experience: 21st century research and perspectives*. Oxford University Press.

Yaden, D. B., Nguyen, K. D. L., Kern, M. L., Belser, A. B., Eichstaedt, J. C., Iwry, J., Wintering, N., Hood, R. W., & Newberg, A. B. (2016). Of roots and fruits: A comparison of psychedelic and non-psychedelic mystical experiences. *Journal of Humanistic Psychology*, *57*(4), 338–353.

Zaretsky, T. G., Jagodnik, K. M., Barsic, R., Antonio, J. H., Bonanno, P. A., MacLeod, C., Pierce, C., Carney, H., Morrison, M. T., Saylor, C., Danias, G., Lepow, L., & Yehuda, R. (2024). The psychedelic future of post-traumatic stress disorder treatment. *Current Neuropharmacology*, *22*(4), 636–735. https://doi.org/10.2174/1570159X22666231027111147

Zikopoulos, B., & Barbas, H. (2006). Prefrontal projections to the thalamic reticular nucleus form a unique circuit for attentional mechanisms. *The Journal of neuroscience : the official journal of the Society for Neuroscience*, *26*(28), 7348–7361. https://doi.org/10.1523/JNEUROSCI.5511-05.2006

Chapter 9

Models and Mechanisms of the Association of Spirituality with Health and Well-Being

Sebastian Binyamin Skalski-Bednarz, Loren L. Toussaint, Karol Konaszewski, Janusz Surzykiewicz, and Everett L. Worthington, Jr.*

Spirituality is a complex and multifaceted aspect of human existence. It encompasses a sense of connection to something greater than oneself, whether it is expressed through religion, nature, or personal beliefs. It is increasingly evident that spirituality plays a substantial role in promoting health and well-being, and these associations not only have significant statistical effects in research but are also based on increasingly sophisticated theoretical models. Therefore, this chapter will be a journey through different theoretical perspectives on the relationship between spirituality and health. In the first step, we will discuss the concepts of health at the core of this subject, and subsequently, through a synthesis of research and theoretical insights, we will delve into the impact of spirituality on health and well-being. The papers cited in this chapter were selected based on searches of the PubMed database in the summer of 2023 using various combinations of the keywords spirituality, health, well-being, religion, faith, conceptual model, mechanisms, and theoretical approach.

Definition of Health

Health and well-being are multifaceted concepts influenced by many factors. Their definitions are often subject to evolving perspectives, reflecting our changing understanding of what it means to live a fulfilling and healthy life (see details in Chapter 3). The World Health Organization (WHO; 1946) defined *health* as "a state of complete physical, mental, and social well-being and not merely the absence of disease or infirmity" (p. 100). This comprehensive definition emphasizes that health is not merely the absence of illness but also encompasses mental and social well-being. It underscores the importance of balance and harmony in one's physical, mental, and social dimensions for an overall state of health.

Based on this perspective, one can distinguish two different health paradigms that offer seemingly opposite lenses through which we can examine well-being and illness: pathogenesis and salutogenesis (Strümpfer, 1990). *Pathogenesis* is the traditional approach, concentrating on the causes and mechanisms of disease. In contrast, *salutogenesis*, introduced by Antonovsky (1984), shifts our focus from disease and risk factors to understanding the origins of health and what promotes it. This model posits that health and disease result from the dynamic interplay between stressors, generalized resistance resources, and an individual's sense of coherence. It underscores the intricacy of health at both individual and community levels and highlights the critical role of effective stress management in maintaining health. Furthermore, salutogenesis is linked to *well-being*, which is often characterized by feelings of contentment, happiness, and life satisfaction (Piotrowicz & Cianciara, 2011).

* Corresponding Author: sebastian.skalski@humanitas.edu.pl.

DOI: 10.4324/9781003440048-11

Pathogenic Approach

The pathogenic model emphasizes the identification of disease risk factors and the mitigation of harm. This approach primarily focuses on diagnosing and treating illnesses after they manifest, but it can also focus on disease prevention. In the pathogenic paradigm, spirituality can influence health behaviors, coping mechanisms, and resilience in the face of illness. For example, individuals with strong spiritual beliefs may be more likely to engage in healthy practices, such as regular meditation or prayer, which can positively impact their physical and mental health (Ahles et al., 2016). Furthermore, spirituality can be a source of emotional support and resilience during illness, helping individuals navigate the emotional and psychological challenges that arise (Konaszewski et al., 2022).

The understanding of the impact of spirituality on health and well-being in this paradigm can be achieved through the lens of the *stress-and-coping model* (Lazarus & Folkman, 1984), recognized as the gold standard in the field of stress psychology. This model explains how individuals manage adversity. Thus, spirituality can be perceived as a coping strategy that helps people cope with stress, promoting better health outcomes. Lazarus and Folkman claimed that the effects of a stressful situation and its severity depend on cognitive evaluation, responses to the stressor, and coping methods. A cognitive appraisal consists of three stages: primary appraisal, secondary appraisal, and reappraisal. The first of these determines the meaning of a situation for a person. Primary evaluation is subjective and is not necessarily relevant to the situation. In addition, it is a critical point for the emergence of a stress response because recognizing an event in terms that are irrelevant to well-being or favorable-positive does not disrupt the balance in the individual's relationship with the environment and, consequently, is not a source of stress. When a situation is considered stressful, it is considered either (potentially) harmful, threatening, or challenging. In a stressful situation, besides suffering harm, there is the possibility of receiving some benefit. Thus, stress can be accompanied by negative as well as positive emotions, and each might lead to spiritual growth or spiritual struggles. Secondary evaluation, on the other hand, assesses one's ability to cope with the event. It is a complex process where the individual considers the coping strategies available and their likely effectiveness and consequences. A feedback loop between primary evaluation and secondary evaluation determines the strength of the stress experienced and the accompanying emotional reactions. The individual, based on their feelings or on new information from the environment, can also make a reappraisal. Its task is to correct (i.e., modify) the previous "picture" of the event based on experience subsequent to the initial stressor. According to Lazarus and Folkman, when a stressful situation arises, an individual undertakes activities to deal with the stressor and return to homeostasis. "Religious coping" contains solid and available strategies for some individuals. The use of spirituality for coping can have instrumental and expressive functions. The first concerns human activity based on the problem, and its purpose is to reduce the impact of the stressor (primary function). The second focuses on health-related emotions and has adaptive functions.

Pargament (1997) embedded the stress-and-coping model in the context of faith. His theory is known as religious coping, and it provides a comprehensive exploration of spirituality as an adaptation mechanism, promoting good health. He defines *religion* as the pursuit of meaning associated with the sacred, while spirituality is characterized as a quest for the sacred (Pargament, 2007). Pargament pointed to the profound spiritual dimension of religion, emphasizing that it should not be underestimated because it deals with a higher facet of human potential. *Coping*, as defined by Pargament (1997), involves the search for meaning during times of stress, with religious coping strategies specifically addressing life events intertwined with the sacred (Pargament & Abu Raiya, 2007). Pargament (1997) asserted that spirituality's involvement in coping is grounded in its accessibility as part of the human orientation system. Spirituality's compelling nature is particularly evident in individuals with a strong religious orientation, such as church members, who tend to employ and benefit from religious coping strategies (Pargament et al., 2001). These assumptions are supported by empirical evidence that people frequently turn to facets of their faith when confronted with stress to seek to regain control (Sasaki et al., 2011), restore mental equilibrium after stressful experiences (Pargament et al., 1998; Zinnbauer & Pargament, 2005), seek meaning in life (Pargament, 1997), and cultivate meaningful social relationships (Páez et al., 2018). Previous studies also showed that individuals with firm religious and spiritual commitments often maintain a positive life evaluation, even in adverse circumstances, resulting in higher levels of well-being and lower levels of perceived stress (Ramsay, 2020; Saud et al., 2021; Vishkin et al., 2019). Furthermore, according to Pargament (2011), religion can play an active role in every stage of coping, both in facilitating the discovery, maintenance, and transformation of significance and in adapting to changing temporal, contextual, and situational dynamics. However, spirituality can also be a source of distress and a detriment to health. A pertinent illustration in this context is the concept of *spiritual struggles*, which encompasses various forms of distress and conflict related to religious and spiritual aspects of life (Abu-Raiya et al., 2015). These struggles emerge when specific elements of a person's belief system, practices, or experiences become focal points of negative thoughts, emotions, worry, or conflict (Exline, 2013). Research consistently demonstrates that religious struggles and tensions are inversely related to well-being, life satisfaction, quality of life, self-esteem, coping resources, internal locus of control, optimism, gratitude, prosocial sensitivity, and prosocial behavior (Koenig, 2012; Konaszewski et al., 2022). In later chapters, other authors will present more detailed explanations of spiritual coping (both similarly and more broadly construed) in the face of specific health challenges; in this chapter, we focus more on the salutogenic approach.

Salutogenic Approach

In contrast to pathogenesis, salutogenesis encourages a proactive understanding of health by exploring the origins of well-being. It posits that health is the absence of disease plus a state of complete physical, mental, and social well-being (see WHO, 1946). It directs our attention to the factors that promote health, resilience, and the capacity to cope with life's challenges. Within the salutogenic framework, spirituality is seen as a resource contributing to the overall sense of coherence – a key concept in Antonovsky's (1984) theory. A strong sense of coherence, characterized by comprehensibility, manageability, and meaningfulness, is associated with better health outcomes. Spirituality can give individuals a sense of purpose, inner peace, and a moral compass to guide their health-related decisions.

Salutogenesis emphasizes that the spectrum of health ranges from a complete absence of well-being to an utmost state of health (Antonovsky, 1984). This theory implies that individuals possess the capacity and potential to control progress toward improved health by leveraging their available resources. Salutogenesis comprises two main components: *generalized resistance resources*, which refer to the characteristics of individuals, families, or communities that serve as assets in coping with stressors, and a *sense of coherence*, which pertains to one's ability to utilize available resources for managing stress and promoting health (Koenig, 2012). In recent years, the salutogenic framework has undergone exploration and expansion, leading to the creation of the "salutogenesis umbrella" (Lindström & Eriksson, 2010). This umbrella encompasses concepts such as gratitude, self-efficacy, forgiveness, connectedness, coping, and well-being, embodying a valuable resource for life and actively pursuing behaviors aimed at sustaining and enhancing good health, even in the absence of illness (Bandura, 1997; McCullough et al., 2002). However, can spirituality contribute to a sense of coherence, facilitating the effective coping necessary for salutogenesis?

Spirituality as a Predictor

According to the model of Ellison and Levin (1998), spirituality and religious involvement can directly bolster coping through several mechanisms that might prevent illness and promote well-being: (1) by reducing the likelihood of encountering specific major and chronic stressors, as well as acute stressors; (2) by furnishing cognitive and institutional frameworks that render specific stressors less intimidating to individuals than they would otherwise appear; (3) by cultivating relatively high levels of both objective and subjective social resources; and (4) by enhancing valuable psychological resources, with particular emphasis on fostering positive self-perceptions. Beyond that, these authors have proposed theoretical models, viewed as alternative hypotheses, describing the connections between biobehavioral and psychosocial factors and health outcomes. The *suppressor model* suggests a fully recursive relationship, where poor health prompts increased religious activity and coping responses, subsequently mitigating detrimental effects on mental health. The *distress-deterrent model* posits independent and opposing effects of poor health and religion on mental health without a reciprocal influence. In the *prevention model*, religion exerts both direct and indirect protective effects on mental health by preventing physical morbidity. The *moderator model* posits an interactive relationship where the impact of poor health on mental health varies based on the degree of religious involvement. Last, the *health effects model*, like the suppressor model, suggests that poor health suppresses certain religious activities and may lead to negative psychosocial effects. These approaches provide varied perspectives on the complex interplay between religion, mediating factors, and mental health (Ellison & Levin, 1998; Levin, 1996; Levin & Chatters, 1998).

On the other hand, Koenig (1994) outlined how spirituality and religious faith promote the mental health of older adults suffering physical challenges. Among these, religious faith can provide hope for change and healing and is a paradigm and role model for understanding human suffering; it also includes a focus on interpersonal relationships, seeking forgiveness of oneself and others, provides a sense of control and self-determination, and gives access to a supportive community. Religious faith promises an afterlife and ready accessibility that reflect positive cognitive perspectives and emotional states conducive to individual adjustment.

In contrast, Kaplan (1976) proposed that religious rituals, beliefs, and spiritual values can serve as supportive elements, equipping individuals with competencies to address well-being and prevent illness. It is worth noting that this thesis has found affirmation in many studies. For instance, Diener et al. (1999) demonstrated that certain aspects of religious commitment, such as religious attendance or intrinsic religiousness, positively correlate with well-being. Poloma and Pendleton (1990), through random telephone interviews with residents of Akron, Ohio, in the United States, discovered a notably strong association between religious and spiritual dimensions and well-being. The link between spirituality and well-being appears to be robust across various cultural contexts (Pérez & Rohde, 2022; Piedmont, 2007). Tiliouine and Belgoumidi (2009) demonstrated that religiousness predicts a sense of meaning and life satisfaction among Muslim students in Algeria. Additionally, the role of spirituality and religion in ameliorating or mitigating anxiety has been well-established within the realm of psychological literature. Abdel-Khalek (2007) found that religiousness among Muslim Kuwaiti adolescents was linked to improved physical health, enhanced well-being, and reduced anxiety levels. Antonovsky (1984) himself firmly asserted that religious commitment serves as a tangible expression of the sense of coherence. He believed that empirical findings in the field of health and religion would ultimately coalesce into a comprehensive theoretical approach for the relationship between worldview and health.

Levin (1998) developed a comprehensive socio-epidemiological model that sought to thoroughly account for the potential health benefits of faith and spirituality. His model established connections between various religious or spiritual expression dimensions and health outcomes through mediating psychosocial and behavioral pathways, activating specific, well-established salutogenic mechanisms. He suggested that feeling *transcendence* may contribute to improved health by promoting positive attitudes and cognitive abilities such as optimism, resilience, and hope, which have been demonstrated to have physiological effects (e.g., Arnetz & Ekman, 2006). Second, *religious commitment*, such as affiliation with a specific religious denomination or belief system, can contribute to better health by reducing health-compromising behaviors like smoking, drinking, and unhealthy eating, all of which are recognized to increase the risk of disease and impair overall well-being. Third, *active participation in religious fellowship* (e.g., attending worship services) fosters better health by offering social support, facilitating integration into social networks, and helping in times of need – all known to enhance coping skills and mitigate the adverse effects of stressful life events (e.g., Ahles et al., 2016; Reutter & Bigatti, 2014). Fourth, *engaging in religious worship practices*, including prayer, may influence health through the positive psychodynamic effects of ritual, leading to the generation of positive emotions like contentment, catharsis, and love, which are known to be associated with psychophysiological and psychoneuroimmunological responses (e.g., Alcorta, 2017; Hulett & Armer, 2016). Finally, *religious and theological beliefs* and worldviews could impact health through their alignment with salutary health-related beliefs and personality traits, which are recognized to influence health-related behaviors, patterns of healthcare utilization, and overall health status (e.g., Holt et al., 2014; Krause et al., 2017).

Despite the recognition of multidimensional relationships, one of the most important spiritual paths as a determinant of a sense of coherence is its ability to make meaning. This resource can be a part of the broader intellectual dimension of spirituality. However, due to the empirical validity of this phenomenon (see, e.g., Chapter 19), it requires deeper discussion, especially because the significance of seeking and experiencing meaning has been a recurring theme in philosophical discussions on the good life, tracing its origins back to ancient Greece (if not all the way back to day one, so to speak). The psychological exploration of meaning-making gained momentum in the 1940s, mainly through the pioneering work of Frankl (1963), who posited that the "quest for meaning" constitutes a fundamental human drive. *Meaning in life* can be defined as a personal phenomenon encompassing an awareness of order, coherence, and purpose in one's existence; the pursuit and achievement of valuable objectives; and a concomitant sense of self-realization, order, and coherence within one's life. It entails emotional, motivational, cognitive, relational, and personal aspects linked to realizing purpose, efficacy, value, justification, and self-esteem (Steger, 2012). Engaging with religion or spirituality may enhance one's perception of meaning in life because it allows individuals to recognize a purpose or rationale behind the events they encounter (Frankl, 1963). Spirituality can offer insights into what the future may hold and how to lead a fulfilling present life. It can prompt individuals to reflect on what truly matters, given the limited time available and whether their existing priorities remain relevant, and these contemplations can sometimes lead to a challenging crisis of meaning. However, if one can find a compelling reason to embrace each day, life can take on a precious quality, ultimately contributing to improved health and overall well-being. Interestingly, this aspect of spirituality can also resonate with non-believers. For example, Peteet and Balboni (2013) demonstrated that individuals who do not identify as religious still often value the opportunity to share their deepest concerns with another human being. Spiritual values and rituals assist individuals in persevering and transcending losses and upheavals by nurturing a sense of purpose, unity, connection, and meaning. They provide avenues for reestablishing one's identity, strengthening bonds, and reinforcing fundamental social principles of empathy and benevolence toward others (Park, 2010).

Cognitive-Behavioral Approach

A look at the connection between spirituality and mental health is provided by cognitive-behavioral conceptualizations. James and Wells (2003) distinguished two primary mechanisms involving spirituality: first, these spiritual beliefs (schema) offer generic mental models that act as a foundation for shaping evaluations of life events; second, they establish a groundwork for self-regulating cognitive processes. These mechanisms can have positive or negative effects when dealing with stressful life events, contingent upon their content and form. More precisely, the variable *spiritual-religious orientation* has been linked to forming spiritual mental models, which are generic belief systems influencing appraisals, especially those related to stressful life events. A beneficial spiritual belief system enables individuals to find meaning in challenging events that may otherwise be difficult to explain. The content of these beliefs shapes situational stress appraisals and affects an individual's response, aligning with Crystal Park's stress-and-coping meaning-making model (Park & Folkman, 1997). The certainty with which the belief system is maintained can act as a buffer against mental health problems. For instance, if the content leads individuals to blame themselves or a punishing God for negative events, the mental model may increase vulnerability to mental disturbance. This aligns with Petersen and Roy's (1985) idea that spirituality offers an interpretative framework, contributing to individuals' perceptions of themselves and the purpose of life events. Furthermore, this approach aligns with findings from attribution theory, suggesting that spiritual-religious attributions for life events contribute to maintaining a sense of meaning and control. At the same time, Petersen and Roy (1985) observed that the content of the beliefs comprising the mental model moderates the association between the generic framework and positive mental health. This hypothesis is supported by evidence indicating that positive beliefs, as seen in intrinsic religiousness, are more frequently associated with positive mental health, while negative beliefs, such as feelings of abandonment or punishment by a Higher Power, are connected to poorer mental health (James & Wells, 2003). Furthermore, several studies (e.g., Lavrič & Flere, 2008; Power & McKinney, 2014) support the importance of maintaining a strong generic model consisting of the presence or absence of religious beliefs. Those who strongly believe in their position, irrespective of religious denomination, tend to have lower distress, highlighting the benefits of a salient framework. Uncertainty about religious beliefs is associated with greater distress, emphasizing the importance of having a guiding existential framework.

In contrast, Wells and Matthews (2015/1994) proposed the *self-regulatory executive function model*, offering a comprehensive understanding of the interplay between appraisals, attentional control, and beliefs in emotional disorder maintenance, which can successfully be used to explain the relationship between spirituality and health. *Emotional disorder* is conceptualized within this model as a cognitive-attentional syndrome involving self-focused attention and perseverative thinking, such as worry and rumination. This syndrome hampers the processing of disconfirming information and sustains a preoccupation with threats. Spiritually related beliefs and behaviors can influence cognitive processes, affecting attention to internal events. Some spiritual individuals may intensify their focus on internal cognitive processes due to concerns about "sinful" thinking, while meditative prayer may enhance self-regulation by providing moments of modified awareness, reducing self-focus and worry. According to Wells and Matthews, spiritual expression contributing to self-regulation is positively associated with mental health, while those who increase their self-focus and worry yield negative outcomes. Some beliefs may exacerbate emotional disorders, evident in obsessive-compulsive disorder, where intrusive thoughts are viewed as sinful, necessitating control (Wells & Papageorgiou, 1998). Additionally, religiousness and spirituality might foster concepts of "thought control" and "rituals as penance." Meditative prayer, akin to other meditative procedures, is suggested to diminish self-focused attention and reinforce symptoms of stress. It should be noted that studies on mindfulness meditation from Eastern religions demonstrate benefits, while limited research on meditative prayer has indicated potential positive effects on psychological symptoms, perceived control, and acceptance, especially when incorporating a religious component (James & Wells, 2003; see also Chapter 22).

Integrated Approach

Understanding the intricate relationship between spirituality and well-being is complex, drawing insights from diverse academic disciplines such as cognitive and social psychology, neuroscience, epidemiology, and medicine. Various models of how spiritual practices impact mental health abound, as briefly presented above, ranging from influences on health behaviors and social support to psychological and biological factors. Based on Baetz and Toews (2009), these multileveled mechanisms operate synergistically. Thus, influences at one level do not exclude those at another and indeed might be intertwined with them. Such synergistic, multilevel mechanisms might indicate that the potency of spirituality lies in its complete integration into the fabric of life. The theoretical journey in this field has evolved beyond establishing a connection between spirituality and health to probing into the underlying factors shaping this intricate association. Within the *social domain*, Baetz and Toews (2009) gave attention to potential mediators, such as health behaviors, group connectedness, and social resources, in influencing the nexus between spirituality and health. Moving into the *psychological dimension*, their model incorporates the concepts of extrinsic and intrinsic spiritual-religious orientation, highlighting their role in shaping mental models that guide the appraisal of life events, providing individuals with a sense of meaning and control, especially in times of stress. *Religious coping* emerges as an independent pathway, revealing the nuanced impact of internalized and intrinsically motivated spiritual practices on mental health, while blind faith has been found to exhibit adverse effects. Exploring the *biological perspective* through neurotheology, with their model Baetz and Toews explored the neurophysiological underpinnings of spirituality. Physiological variables, including neurohormonal, neuroimmunologic, and cardiovascular functioning, were posited as potential mediators, with associations between religiousness and lower cortisol reactivity and positive reappraisal coping linked to lower depressive symptoms, underscoring potential benefits of religious and spiritual practices on physical and mental health. Incorporating the *genetic dimension* into the theoretical framework illuminated the interplay between spiritual beliefs, practices, and mental health. In this way, Baetz and Toews underscored the robust environmental influence of familial spiritual beliefs and practices. In contrast, *genetic factors* are thought to contribute to personal devotion, emerging as a protective factor against substance use, dependence, and the depressogenic effects of significant stressors.

Like the conception of Baetz and Toews (2009), Cheadle and Dunkel Schetter (2017) emphasized strong associations between spirituality and enhanced physical and mental health outcomes. These positive outcomes include diminished mortality rates, lowered risks of cancer and cardiovascular disease, and alleviation of depression. In this paradigm, their theoretical framework delineates social, behavioral, psychological, and biological mechanisms through which religiousness and spirituality may exert their potential influence on health. *Social mechanisms*, grounded in the inherent social aspects of spiritual practices, entail pathways connecting these factors to mental and physical health outcomes via social support and interaction. *Behavioral mechanisms* involve the rituals and practices associated with religiousness and spirituality, influencing health through emotional processing and promoting positive health behaviors. *Psychological mechanisms* are used to explain that spiritual dimensions impact health by conceptualizing them as worldviews that give individuals meaning and purpose. Positive psychosocial resources, such as optimism, mastery, self-esteem, and gratitude, were identified as potential mediators in this process. The less-explored realm of *biological mechanisms* was used to suggest links between religiousness, spirituality, and relevant biological markers, including cortisol levels and markers of inflammation. While not as extensively studied, these biological pathways may contribute to the overall impact of spirituality on health. These proposed models depict a synergistic interplay of multiple determinants, forming a complex amalgamation of necessary and sufficient conditions or a network or cascade of determinants creating a blend of direct and indirect connections from cause to effect. Viewing these mediating factors as "links in a chain" may better elucidate their role in connecting spirituality with health and well-being.

Spirituality as an Interventional Resource

Spirituality is acknowledged as a powerful coping strategy and a system potentially well-suited for providing meaning to life. In explaining the mechanisms underlying these effects, spirituality can be viewed not only as a direct input (predictor) but also as a buffering variable that influences the effects of other factors, such as negative appraisal, on health and well-being. For instance, Pargament (2006) postulated that discovering strength, hope, and meaning in spiritual beliefs can also lead to what is referred to as *spiritual transformation*, characterized as a profound and intricate shift in an individual's beliefs, values, and inner comprehension, resulting in a deeper connection with a transcendent or Higher Power. This transformation involves an evolutionary process in which individuals undergo profound personal growth, increased self-awareness, and a heightened sense of purpose, fostering a more meaningful and fulfilling existence (Skalski-Bednarz et al., 2022). While the precise definition of spiritual transformation differs across theoretical frameworks, it typically involves a journey of self-discovery, a quest for inner wisdom, and an exploration of existential questions, ultimately leading to profound self-transformation (Kremer & Ironson, 2009). One prominent theory in this realm is the *faith development model* (Fowler & Dell, 2006), which delineates six progressive stages of faith, spanning from an initial, simplistic belief system to a complex and integrated worldview characterized by a profound sense of interconnectedness and unity with the divine. Another influential framework is the *integral theory of consciousness* (Wilber, 1997), which posits that spiritual transformation entails integrating various aspects of human experience, encompassing cognitive, emotional, social, and moral dimensions, culminating in heightened spiritual awareness and consciousness. Moreover, transpersonal psychology contributes valuable insights into spiritual transformation by emphasizing the transcendent and spiritual dimensions of human experience (Caplan et al., 2003; Schneider et al., 2015). This approach recognizes that the transformational process involves moving "beyond" the egoic self to embracing a broader sense of identity that encompasses interconnectedness with all living beings and the cosmos.

Spiritual transformation is sometimes likened to post-traumatic growth, as both constructs involve a process of personal evolution wherein individuals undergo significant psychological and emotional changes, often leading to a more positive and enriched perspective on life (Calhoun & Tedeschi, 2014). Spiritual transformation frequently occurs when individuals confront existential crises or profound life changes, compelling them to seek a deeper understanding of their place in the world and their spiritual connections (Shaw et al., 2005). Similarly, post-traumatic growth is triggered by experiencing traumatic events that prompt individuals to reevaluate their values, priorities, and beliefs to find meaning and purpose in their lives (Sarıalioğlu et al., 2022). Finally, spiritual transformation and post-traumatic growth are associated with positive individual outcomes. For example, spiritual transformation can enhance emotional well-being, increase resilience, and foster inner peace (Hall & Edwards, 2018). Similarly, post-traumatic growth is linked to improved psychological functioning, greater life satisfaction, and a renewed sense of purpose and appreciation for life (Calhoun & Tedeschi, 2014).

Spirituality as an Outcome

Increasingly, various theoretical concepts feature spirituality as a specific result of positive adaptation. Brady et al. (1999) showed that spiritual well-being was related to the ability to enjoy life despite adversity, suggesting that spirituality may be an important clinical target and should be addressed in health measurement. This observation corresponds with the *biopsychosocial-spiritual model* (Engel, 1977), recognizing spirituality as a critical dimension and providing a holistic understanding of health outcomes (together with biological, psychological, and social factors). Incorporating spirituality into the biopsychosocial model acknowledges its significant role in shaping an individual's well-being, thus contributing to a more comprehensive approach to healthcare. When considering or encouraging spirituality as an outcome or clinical target, it is important to note that a predetermined, specific belief system is not to be imposed (Toussaint et al., 2012). Rather, an autonomous, self-directed, "salient, searching pursuit of the transcendently sacred ritualistic, theistic, and/or existential aspects of the human condition" (Webb et al., 2014, p. 974; for more details, see Chapters 1 and 44 on the ritualistic, theistic, and existential [RiTE] model of spirituality), as otherwise described throughout this chapter, may be an appropriate recommendation.

The contemporary understanding of spiritual well-being has emerged from theoretical and research inquiries focusing on the quality of life in the salutogenic paradigm, the broader concept of human health, and their positive perspective, particularly concerning religion. Fryback and Reinert (1999) articulated spiritual health as a state that assists individuals in discovering meaning and purpose in life, while Ortabag et al. (2011) claimed that spiritual health can promote the adoption of healthy behaviors. Consequently, spiritual well-being is recognized as an indicator of mental health that encompasses the positive experience of one's life (Diener, 2009), potentially contributing to increased longevity (Diener & Chan, 2011).

The National Interfaith Coalition on Aging (1975) defined spiritual well-being as "the affirmation of life in a relationship with God, self, community, and environment that nurtures and celebrates wholeness" (p. 1). This definition suggests that spiritual well-being encompasses two factors: religious aspects and socio-psychological aspects, in alignment with Moberg's (1974) earlier conceptualization that spiritual well-being is two-dimensional, comprising both vertical and horizontal components. The *vertical dimension* pertains to the subjective sense of well-being with God. In contrast, the *horizontal dimension* encompasses existential well-being, representing meaning and life satisfaction without referencing the religious domain. In other words, existential well-being pertains to understanding what to do and why, one's identity, and one's sense of belonging concerning life's ultimate concerns (Blaikie & Kelsen, 1979). Although these two dimensions of spiritual well-being are distinct, they can also interact with each other, as individuals function as integrated systems. Previous reports have indicated that spiritual well-being is linked to crucial well-being indicators, specifically self-esteem and assertiveness (Koenig, 1997). However, the relevance of these traditional measures and outcomes has waned, giving way to more modern and nuanced understandings of spirituality and psychological health.

Kaczorowski (1989) observed negative associations between spiritual well-being and anxiety in cancer patients, while Yates et al. (1981) identified positive associations between spiritual well-being and life satisfaction. Subsequent studies have found that spiritual well-being is associated with reduced depression in individuals with terminal cancer (Bekelman et al., 2007), women living with HIV (Safiya et al., 2009), and the general population (Genia, 2009). Additionally, McClain et al. (2003) noted that spiritual well-being decreases the desire for a hastened death in palliative care patients. In contrast, Phillips et al. (2006) discovered positive associations between spiritual well-being and quality of life, as well as mental and physical health status, in a sample of people living with HIV. Parts III, IV, V, and VI of this volume provide an extensive review of the current state-of-the-science regarding particular associations of spirituality (broadly construed) with physical, mental, and social health and well-being.

Conclusions and Future Approaches

This comprehensive review sheds light on the evolving theoretical landscape at the juncture of spirituality, religion, and health, delineating the nuanced perspectives and significant advancements in understanding their intricate connections. An examination of diverse theoretical approaches reveals an increased emphasis on sophisticated conceptualizations and the dynamic influence of spirituality on health outcomes. It underscores the importance of spiritual dimensions, such as the relationship with a personal deity, in nurturing hope, optimism, and subjective well-being, extending beyond the influence of personality. Furthermore, spirituality acts as a protective buffer against stressors such as negative appraisals, a phenomenon that is notably more pronounced within religious contexts, as elaborated by Levin (1998). Additionally, spiritual practices have been demonstrated to enhance health outcomes by fostering positive behaviors and emotional well-being, although they generally do not surpass secular interventions in effectiveness (Captari et al., 2018).

However, this review also highlights the necessity for a more profound critique and integration of religion and spirituality. While Levin's classification of religion provides insightful observations, an in-depth examination of spirituality's various dimensions – religious, nature-based, humanistic, transcendent, and self-oriented – and their distinct impacts on health is merited. Future research should rigorously assess the strengths and limitations of existing models and theories, exploring their efficacy for specific health outcomes and the possibility of amalgamating these models for a more cohesive understanding of spirituality's role in health. Such analysis might illuminate how different spiritual dimensions, particularly when contextualized within religious traditions, significantly predict well-being, surpassing the realms of personality.

Furthermore, theoretical constructs such as spiritual well-being emphasize the pivotal role of spirituality as an essential facet of human wellness. Yet, as investigations delve into integrated models illustrating spirituality's effects through neurophysiological changes, it becomes evident that the field continues to wrestle with evolving methodologies and theoretical frameworks necessary for fully comprehending such data. The correlations between spiritual practices and positive neurophysiological outcomes, including alterations in cortisol levels and inflammation markers, necessitate further elucidation through enhanced research methodologies, solid theoretical foundations, and cross-disciplinary collaborations.

In summary, this review not only furnishes a detailed overview of current theoretical progress but also advocates for a more refined critique and theoretical amalgamation in future research. By focusing on these areas, we can propel our comprehension of the complex interplay between spirituality, religion, and health forward, underscoring the imperative for ongoing exploration of spirituality's varied roles and its comprehensive influence on personal well-being and health outcomes.

Acknowledgement

SBS-B is grateful to the Polish National Agency for Academic Exchange (NAWA) for a visiting professorship under the NAWA-Bekker BPN/BEK/2022/1/00021 at Luther College in Decorah, IA, where the writing of this chapter took place

References

Abdel-Khalek, A. M. (2007). Religiosity, happiness, health, and psychopathology in a probability sample of Muslim adolescents. *Mental Health, Religion & Culture*, *10*(6), 571–583. https://doi.org/10.1080/13674670601034547

Abu-Raiya, H., Pargament, K. I., & Krause, N. (2015). Religion as problem, religion as solution: religious buffers of the links between religious/spiritual struggles and well-being/mental health. *Quality of Life Research*, *25*(5), 1265–1274. https://doi.org/10.1007/S11136-015-1163-8

Ahles, J. J., Mezulis, A. H., & Hudson, M. R. (2016). Religious coping as a moderator of the relationship between stress and depressive symptoms. *Psychology of Religion and Spirituality*, *8*(3), 228–234. https://doi.org/10.1037/REL0000039

Alcorta, C. (2017). Religion, social signaling, and health: a psychoneuroimmunological approach. *Religion, Brain & Behavior*, *7*(3), 243–246. https://doi.org/10.1080/2153599X.2016.1156559

Antonovsky, A. (1984). The sense of coherence as a determinant of health. In J. D. Matarazzo (Ed.), *Behavioral health: A handbook of health enhancement and disease prevention* (pp. 114–129). John Wiley.

Arnetz, B. B., & Ekman, R. (Eds.). (2006). *Stress in health and disease*. Wiley. https://doi.org/10.1002/3527609156

Baetz, M., & Toews, J. (2009). Clinical implications of research on religion, spirituality, and mental health. *The Canadian Journal of Psychiatry*, *54*(5), 292–301. https://doi.org/10.1177/070674370905400503

Bandura, A. (1997). *Self-efficacy: The exercise of control*. W.H. Freeman.

Bekelman, D. B., Dy, S. M., Becker, D. M., Wittstein, I. S., Hendricks, D. E., Yamashita, T. E., & Gottlieb, S. H. (2007). Spiritual well-being and depression in patients with heart failure. *Journal of General Internal Medicine*, *22*(4), 470–477. https://doi.org/10.1007/S11606-006-0044-9

Blaikie, N. W. H., & Kelsen, G. P. (1979). Locating self and giving meaning to existence: A typology of paths to spiritual well-being based on new religious movements in Australia. In D. O. Moberg (Ed.), *Spiritual well-being: Sociological perspectives* (pp. 133–151) University Press of America.

Brady, M. J., Peterman, A. H., Fitchett, G., Mo, M., & Cella, D. (1999). A case for including spirituality in quality of life measurement in oncology. *Psychooncology*, *8*(5), 417–428.

Calhoun, L. G., & Tedeschi, R. G. (2014). The foundations of posttraumatic growth: An expanded framework. *Handbook of Posttraumatic Growth: Research and Practice*, 3–23. https://doi.org/10.4324/9781315805597-8

Caplan, M., Hartelius, G., & Rardin, M. A. (2003). Contemporary viewpoints on transpersonal psychology. *Journal of Transpersonal Psychology*, *35*(2), 143–162.

Captari, L. E., Hook, J. N., Hoyt, W., Davis, D. E., McElroy-Heltzel, S. E., & Worthington Jr, E. L. (2018). Integrating clients' religion and spirituality within psychotherapy: A comprehensive meta-analysis. *Journal of Clinical Psychology*, *74*(11), 1938–1951. https://doi.org/10.1002/jclp.22681

Cheadle, A. C. D., & Dunkel Schetter, C. (2017). Untangling the mechanisms underlying the links between religiousness, spirituality, and better health. *Social and Personality Psychology Compass*, *11*(2). https://doi.org/10.1111/spc3.12299

Diener, E. (2009). Subjective well-being. 11–58. https://doi.org/10.1007/978-90-481-2350-6_2

Diener, E., & Chan, M. Y. (2011 Happy people live longer: Subjective well-being contributes to health and longevity. *Applied Psychology: Health and Well-Being*, *3*(1), 1–43. https://doi.org/10.1111/J.1758-0854.2010.01045.X

Diener, E., Suh, E. M., Lucas, R. E., & Smith, H. L. (1999). Subjective well-being: Three decades of progress. *Psychological Bulletin*, *125*(2), 276–302. https://doi.org/10.1037/0033-2909.125.2.276

Ellison, C. G., & Levin, J. S. (1998). The religion-health connection: Evidence, theory, and future directions. *Health Education & Behavior*, *25*(6), 700–720. https://doi.org/10.1177/109019819802500603

Engel, G. L. (1977). The need for a new medical model: A challenge for biomedicine. *Science*, *196*(4286), 129–136. https://doi.org/10.1126/science.847460

Exline, J. J. (Ed.). (2013). Religious and spiritual struggles. In *APA handbook of psychology, religion, and spirituality (Vol 1): Context, theory, and research.* (pp. 459–475). American Psychological Association. https://doi.org/10.1037/14045-025

Fowler, J. W., & Dell, M. L. (2006). Stages of faith from infancy through adolescence: Reflections on three decades of faith development theory. In *The handbook of spiritual development in childhood and adolescence* (pp. 34–45). Publisher??

Frank, R. (1963). Polyphase codes with good nonperiodic correlation properties. *IEEE Transactions on Information Theory*, *9*(1), 43–45. https://doi.org/10.1109/TIT.1963.1057798

Fryback, P. B., & Reinert, B. R. (1999). Spirituality and people with poetentially fatal diagnoses. *Nursing Forum*, *34*(1), 13–22. https://doi.org/10.1111/J.1744-6198.1999.TB00231.X

Genia, V. (2009). Evaluation of the spiritual well-being scale in a sample of college students. *The International Journal for the Psychology of Religion*, *21*(1), 25–33. https://doi.org/10.1207/S15327582IJPR1101_03

Hall, T. W., & Edwards, K. J. (2018). The initial development and factor analysis of the Spiritual Assessment Inventory:*JournalofPsychologyandTheology*,*24*(3),233–246.https://doi.org/10.1177/009164719602400305

Holt, C. L., Clark, E. M., & Roth, D. L. (2014). Positive and negative religious beliefs explaining the religion–health connection among African Americans. *The International Journal for the Psychology of Religion*, *24*(4), 311–331. https://doi.org/10.1080/10508619.2013.828993

Hulett, J. M., & Armer, J. M. (2016). A systematic review of spiritually based interventions and psychoneuroimmunological outcomes in breast cancer survivorship. *Integrative Cancer Therapies*, *15*(4), 405–423. https://doi.org/10.1177/1534735416636222

James, A., & Wells, A. (2003). Religion and mental health: Towards a cognitive-behavioural framework. *British Journal of Health Psychology*, *8*(3), 359–376. https://doi.org/10.1348/135910703322370905

Kaczorowski, J. M. (1989). Spiritual well-being and anxiety in adults diagnosed with cancer. *The Hospice Journal*, *5*(3–4), 105–115. https://doi.org/10.1080/0742-969X.1989.11882658

Kaplan, B. H. (1976). A note on religious beliefs and coronary heart disease. *Journal of the South Carolina Medical Association*, *72*(Suppl), 60–64.

Koenig, H. G. (1994). Religion in aging and health: Theoretical foundations and methodological frontiers. In J. S. Levin (Ed.), *Religion in aging and health* (pp. 18–55). Sage.

Koenig, H. G. (1997). Use of religion by patients with severe medical illness. *Mind Body Medicine*, *2*, 31–36.

Koenig, H. G. (2012). Religion, spirituality, and health: The research and clinical implications. *ISRN Psychiatry*, *2012*, 1–33. https://doi.org/10.5402/2012/278730

Konaszewski, K., Skalski, S. B., Niesiobędzka, M., & Surzykiewicz, J. (2022). Religious struggles and mental health in the Polish population during the COVID-19 pandemic. Mediation effects of resilience as an "ability to bounce back". *Journal of Beliefs & Values*, *44*(1), 1–19. https://doi.org/10.1080/13617672.2022.2075645

Krause, N., Hill, P. C., Emmons, R., Pargament, K. I., & Ironson, G. (2017). Assessing the relationship between religious involvement and health behaviors. *Health Education & Behavior*, *44*(2), 278–284.https://doi.org/10.1177/1090198116655314

Kremer, H., & Ironson, G. (2009). Everything changed: Spiritual transformation in people with hiv. *International Journal of Psychiatry in Medicine*, *39*(3), 243–262. https://doi.org/10.2190/PM.39.3.c

Lavrič, M., & Flere, S. (2008). The role of culture in the relationship between religiosity and psychological well-being. *Journal of Religion and Health*, *47*(2), 164–175. https://doi.org/10.1007/s10943-008-9168-z

Lazarus, R. S., & Folkman, S. (1984). *Stress, appraisal, and coping*. Springer Publishing Company.

Levin, J. (1998). From psychosomatic to theosomatic: the role of spirit in the next new paradigm. *Presidential Address*, *9*(1), 1–26.

Levin, J. S. (1996). How religion influences morbidity and health: Reflections on natural history, salutogenesis and host resistance. *Social Science & Medicine*, *43*(5), 849–864. https://doi.org/10.1016/0277-9536(96)00150-5

Levin, J. S., & Chatters, L. M. (1998). Research on religion and mental health. In *Handbook of religion and mental health* (pp. 33–50). Elsevier. https://doi.org/10.1016/B978-012417645-4/50070-5

Lindström, B., & Eriksson, M. (2010). The hitchhiker's guide to salutogenesis: Salutogenic pathways to health promotion. In *Folkhälsan research center*, Health promotion research.

McClain, C. S., Rosenfeld, B., & Breitbart, W. (2003). Effect of spiritual well-being on end-of-life despair in terminally-ill cancer patients. *The Lancet*, *361*(9369), 1603–1607. https://doi.org/10.1016/S0140-6736(03)13310-7

McCullough, M. E., Emmons, R. A., & Tsang, J.-A. (2002). The grateful disposition: A conceptual and empirical topography. *Journal of Personality and Social Psychology*, *82*(1), 112–127. https://doi.org/10.1037/0022-3514.82.1.112

Moberg, D. O. (1974). Spiritual well-being in late life. In J. F. Gubrium (Ed.), *Late life: Communities and environment policy* (pp.). Charles C. Thomas.

National Interfaith Coalition on Aging. (1975). *Spiritual wellbeing: A definition*. NICA.

Ortabag, T., Ozdemir, S., Bakir, B., & Tosun, N. (2011). Health promotion and risk behaviors among adolescents in Turkey. *Journal of School Nursing*, *27*(4), 304–315. https://doi.org/10.1177/1059840511408322

Páez, D., Martínez-Zelaya, G., Bilbao, M., García, F. E., Torres-Vallejos, J., Vargas, S., Sierralta, E., & da Costa, S. (2018). Religiosity, psychosocial factors, and well-being: An examination among a national sample of Chileans. *Psychology of Religion and Spirituality*, *10*(2), 138–145. https://doi.org/10.1037/rel0000156

Pargament, K., Feuille, M., & Burdzy, D. (2011). The Brief RCOPE: Current psychometric status of a short measure of religious coping. *Religions*, *2*(1), 51–76. https://doi.org/10.3390/REL2010051

Pargament, K. I. (1997). *The psychology of religion and coping*. Guilford Press.

Pargament, K. I. (2006). The meaning of spiritual transformation. In J. D. Koss-Chioino & P. Hefner (Eds.), *Spiritual transformation and healing: Anthropological, theological, neuroscientific, and clinical perspectives* (pp. 10–24). AltaMira Press.

Pargament, K. I. (2007). *Spiritually integrated psychotherapy: Understanding and addressing the Sacred.* Guilford Press.

Pargament, K. I., & Abu Raiya, H. (2007). A decade of research on the psychology of religion and coping: Things we assumed and lessons we learned. *Psyke & Logos*, *28*(2), 25. https://doi.org/10.7146/pl.v28i2.8398

Pargament, K. I., Koenig, H. G., Tarakeshwar, N., & Hahn, J. (2001). Religious struggle as a predictor of mortality among medically ill elderly patients. *Archives of Internal Medicine*, *161*(15), 1881. https://doi.org/10.1001/archinte.161.15.1881

Pargament, K. I., Zinnbauer, B. J., Scott, A. B., Butter, E. M., Zerowin, J., & Stanik, P. (1998). Red flags and religious coping: Identifying some religious warning signs among people in crisis. *Journal of Clinical Psychology*, *54*, 77–89.

Park, C. L. (2010). Making sense of the meaning literature: An integrative review of meaning making and its effects on adjustment to stressful life events. *Psychological Bulletin*, *136*(2), 257–301. https://doi.org/10.1037/a0018301

Park, C.L., & Folkman, S. (1997). Meaning in the context of stress and coping. *Review of General Psychology*, *1*, 115–144.

Pérez, S., & Rohde, D. (2022). The relationship between religious/spiritual beliefs and subjective well-being: A case-based comparative cross-national study. *Journal of Religion and Health*, *61*(6), 4585–4607. https://doi.org/10.1007/s10943-022-01550-4

Peteet, J. R., & Balboni, M. J. (2013). Spirituality and religion in oncology. *CA: A Cancer Journal for Clinicians*, *63*(4), 280–289. https://doi.org/10.3322/caac.21187

Petersen, L. R., & Roy, A. (1985). Religiosity, anxiety, and meaning and purpose: Religion's consequences for psychological well-being. *Review of Religious Research*, *27*(1), 49. https://doi.org/10.2307/3511937

Phillips, K. D., Mock, K. S., Bopp, C. M., Dudgeon, W. A., & Hand, G. A. (2006). Spiritual well-being, sleep disturbance, and mental and physical health status in HIV-infected individuals. *Issues in Mental Health Nursing*, *27*(2), 125–139. https://doi.org/10.1080/01612840500436917

Piedmont, R. L. (2007). Spirituality as a robust empirical predictor of psychosocial outcomes: A cross-cultural analysis. In *Advancing quality of life in a turbulent world* (pp. 117–134). Dordrecht: Springer Netherlands.

Piotrowicz, M., & Cianciara, D. (2011). Salutogenesis –new approach to health and disease. *Przeglad Epidemiologiczny*, *65*(3), 521–527.

Poloma, M. M., & Pendleton, B. F. (1990). Religious domains and general well-being. *Social Indicators Research*, *22*(3), 255–276. https://doi.org/10.1007/BF00301101

Power, L., & McKinney, C. (2014). The effects of religiosity on psychopathology in emerging adults: Intrinsic versus extrinsic religiosity. *Journal of Religion and Health*, *53*(5), 1529–1538. https://doi.org/10.1007/s10943-013-9744-8

Ramsay, J. E. (2020). Coping with COVID-19: The role of religion in times of crisis. In *How to Prepare for the Next Pandemic* (pp. 95–111). World Scientific. https://doi.org/10.1142/9789811230059_0007

Reutter, K. K., & Bigatti, S. M. (2014). Religiosity and spirituality as resiliency resources: Moderation, mediation, or moderated mediation?. *Journal for the Scientific Study of Religion*, *53*(1), 56–72. https://doi.org/10.1111/jssr.12081

Safiya, G. D., Marcia, M. H., Colleen, D., & Laderman, G. (2009). Spiritual well-being, depressive symptoms, and immune status among women living with HIV/AIDS. *Women & Health*, *49*(2–3), 119–143. https://doi.org/10.1080/03630240902915036

Sarıalioğlu, A., Çiftçi, B., & Yıldırım, N. (2022). The transformative power of pain and posttraumatic growth in nurses with Covid-19 PCR positive. *Perspectives in Psychiatric Care*, *58*(4), 2622–2630. https://doi.org/10.1111/ppc.13102

Sasaki, J. Y., Kim, H. S., & Xu, J. (2011). Religion and well-being. *Journal of Cross-Cultural Psychology*, *42*(8), 1394–1405. https://doi.org/10.1177/0022022111412526

Saud, M., Ashfaq, A., Abbas, A., Ariadi, S., & Mahmood, Q. K. (2021). Social support through religion and psychological well-being: COVID-19 and coping strategies in Indonesia. *Journal of Religion and Health*, *60*(5), 3309–3325. https://doi.org/10.1007/s10943-021-01327-1

Schneider, K. J., Pierson, J. F., & Bugental, J. F. T. (2015). *The handbook of humanistic psychology: Theory, research, and practice*. Sage Publications, Inc.

Shaw, A., Joseph, S., & Linley, P. A. (2005). Religion, spirituality, and posttraumatic growth: a systematic review. *Mental Health, Religion & Culture*, *8*(1), 1–11. https://doi.org/10.1080/1367467032000157981

Skalski-Bednarz, S. B., Konaszewski, K., Toussaint, L. L., Büssing, A., & Surzykiewicz, J. (2022). Positive religious coping acts through perception of nature and silence in its association with well-being and life satisfaction among Polish Catholics. *Frontiers in Public Health*, *10*, 4170. https://doi.org/10.3389/FPUBH.2022.1020007

Steger, M. F. (2012). Making meaning in life. *Psychological Inquiry*, *23*(4), 381–385. https://doi.org/10.1080/1047840X.2012.720832

Strümpfer, D. J. W. (1990). Salutogenesis: A new paradigm. *South African Journal of Psychology*, *20*(4), 265–276. https://doi.org/10.1177/008124639002000406

Tiliouine, H., & Belgoumidi, A. (2009). An exploratory study of religiosity, meaning in life, and subjective well-being in Muslim students from Algeria. *Applied Research in Quality of Life*, *4*(1), 109–127. https://doi.org/10.1007/s11482-009-9076-8

Toussaint, L. L., Webb, J. R., & Keltner, W. (2012). Religion, spirituality, and mental health. In J. D. Aten, K. A. O'Grady, & E. L. Worthington, Jr. (Eds.), *The psychology of religion and spirituality for clinicians: Using research in your practice* (pp. 331–356). Routledge.

Vishkin, A., Ben-Nun Bloom, P., Schwartz, S. H., Solak, N., & Tamir, M. (2019). Religiosity and emotion regulation. *Journal of Cross-Cultural Psychology*, *50*(9), 1050–1074. https://doi.org/10.1177/0022022119880341

Webb, J. R., Toussaint, L. L., & Dula, C. S. (2014). Ritualistic, theistic, and existential spirituality: Initial psychometric qualities of the RiTE measure of spirituality. *Journal of Religion & Health*, *53*(4), 972–985. https://doi.org/10.1007/s10943-013-9697-y

Wells, A., & Matthews, G. (2015). *Attention and emotion: A clinical perspective* (Classic ed.). Psychology Press. https://doi.org/10.4324/9781315747187 (Routledge, 1994).

Wells, A., & Papageorgiou, C. (1998). Relationships between worry, obsessive–compulsive symptoms and meta-cognitive beliefs. *Behaviour Research and Therapy*, *36*(9), 899–913. https://doi.org/10.1016/S0005-7967(98)00070-9

Wilber, K. (1997). An integral theory of consciousness. *Journal of Consciousness Studies*, *4*(1), 71–92.

World Health Organization (WHO). (1946). *Preamble to the constitution of the World Health Organization as adopted by the International Health Conference*. New York. https://apps.who.int/gb/bd/PDF/bd47/EN/constitution-en.pdf?ua=1

Yates, J. W., Chalmer, B. J., James, P. S., Follansbee, M., & McKegney, F. P. (1981). Religion in patients with advanced cancer. *Medical and Pediatric Oncology*, *9*(2), 121–128. https://doi.org/10.1002/MPO.2950090204

Zinnbauer, B. J., & Pargament, K. I. (2005). Religiousness and spirituality. In B. J. Zinnbauer & K. I. Pargament (Eds.), *Handbook of the psychology of religion and spirituality* (pp. 21–42). Guilford Press.

Part III

Health and Well-Being-Related Outcomes

Chapter 10

Spirituality and Chronic Medical Illness

*Maya Joshi Delity and Amy Wachholtz**

Chronic illness is defined generally as conditions that are not immediately life-threatening, last one year or more, and require ongoing medical attention or limit activities of daily living or both (Centers for Disease Control and Prevention, 2024a). While there is some variation in what conditions are encompassed by the term chronic medical illness, most sources concur that heart disease (see Chapter 12), diabetes, obesity, arthritis, cancer (see Chapter 13), and chronic kidney disease fall under the definition of chronic medical illnesses (Bernell & Howard, 2016). While not a comprehensive list, multiple sclerosis (MS), Parkinson's disease (PD), epilepsy, and irritable bowel disease are also usually included under the chronic illness definition (Roger & Hatala, 2018). More than 47% of the United States population has at least one chronic illness, and almost 30 million people suffer from multiple chronic illnesses (Centers for Disease Control and Prevention, 2024a). These illnesses are responsible for $3.8 trillion in annual healthcare costs and are the leading causes of high care requirements, disability, and death (Centers for Disease Control and Prevention, 2024a).

Chronic medical illness is widely understood and treated within the biopsychosocial model (Hatala, 2013). The biopsychosocial model acknowledges illness as a complex interaction of biological, psychological, and social factors (Engel, 1977). Many researchers believe that the biopsychosocial model should be expanded to include spirituality (McKee & Chappel, 1992; Sulmasy, 2002), arguing that holistic and effective healthcare must consider the totality of a patient's relational existence (Sulmasy, 2002). Evidence supports this argument, as 70% of adults in the United States consider themselves "spiritual in some way" and identify spirituality as an important aspect of their life (Alper, 2023). Furthermore, a growing body of literature in "Spirituality and Health" has revealed a significant influence of spiritual beliefs on both mental (Wachholtz & Sambamthoori, 2013) and physical health outcomes (Damiano et al., 2016; Wachholtz & Sambamoorthi, 2011). While it is important to highlight that the literature exploring religious and spiritual relations with chronic illness demonstrates both negative and positive associations, a substantial amount of literature indicates that spirituality enhances already existing pathways in biopsychosocial domains, such as social support, coping and health behaviors, and psychosomatics (Roger & Hatala, 2018). Thus, it follows that a biopsychosocial-spiritual model of chronic medical illness will offer a nuanced understanding of disease and provide opportunities for unique and augmented treatment approaches.

The following chapter will explore the existing literature in "Spirituality and Health" in the context of a range of chronic medical illnesses. We discuss results from literature searches in

* Corresponding Author: AMY.WACHHOLTZ@UCDENVER.EDU.

DOI: 10.4324/9781003440048-13

PubMed and PsycInfo. Key search terms included "chronic medical illness," "diabetes," "chronic kidney disease," "epilepsy," "neurological conditions," "Parkinson's disease," "gastrointestinal diseases," "spirituality," "religion," and "existentialism"; additional search terms were added as we delved further into the literature.

Spirituality

Finding a unifying definition of spirituality is extremely complex, especially in multicultural contexts. The World Health Organization recognizes that spiritual health is a component of complete health, yet even this august organization, with its international network of scholars and practitioners, struggles to find an adequate definition to encompass the term "spirituality" across cultures (Peng-Keller et al., 2022). Spirituality is often defined as the experience of transcendence, connectedness, meaning, and purpose in life. These definitions reflect a construction of spirituality that is individualistic and broader than religion (Astrow et al., 2001). Instead, religion can be viewed as a platform through which individuals may express their spirituality. It is important to note that both spirituality and religion hold myriad definitions that vary widely according to different cultural, ethnic, and religious backgrounds (Koenig, 2008). Moreover, conceptualization of spirituality, even within one culture, may differ between theologians, scientists, and laypersons (La Cour & Götke, 2012). Thus, it is unsurprising that understandings and measures of these concepts vary widely across research literature.

In this chapter, we will be using the term spirituality as conceptualized with the RiTE Model of Spirituality as defined in this book (see Chapters 1 and 44 and Chapter 11: Health, Well-Being, and Chronic Pain, this volume; see also Webb et al., 2014) This model defines spirituality as a construct that encompasses three categories that can overlap and may look different across cultures. The first concept, otherwise known as "religiousness," is Ritualistic Spirituality or a structured connection with deity. The second, otherwise and formerly known as "spirituality," is Theistic Spirituality, which is defined as a non-structured connection with a deity. Finally, the last concept is Existential Spirituality, which is defined by a non-theistic, yet transcendent search for meaning and purpose, and potentially includes individuals otherwise known as agnostic or atheist. This three-part definition of spirituality allows for significant flexibility to address cultural and religious differences in the internal interpretation and external expression of spirituality, while also allowing space for individuals with non-theistic or agnostic approaches to spirituality.

Diabetes

Diabetes is a chronic illness arising from either insufficient insulin production by the pancreas or ineffective use of insulin within the body (World Health Organization, 2023a). Insulin is a hormone that plays a crucial role in regulating blood sugar, or glucose, levels. Type 1 diabetes (formerly known as insulin-dependent or childhood-onset diabetes) is marked by inadequate insulin production, necessitating daily insulin injections. Currently, there is no known method to prevent Type 1 diabetes (World Health Organization, 2023a). Type 2 diabetes involves insulin resistance coupled with a gradual decline in insulin production, resulting in elevated blood sugar levels if untreated. Long term, Type 2 diabetes can cause significant harm to the body's nerves and blood vessels. Unlike Type 1, Type 2 diabetes is often preventable, with risk factors including obesity, lack of physical activity, and genetics (World Health Organization, 2023a). Individuals who are 45 years or older or are African American, Hispanic, Native American,

South Asian, or Filipino are at a higher risk for diabetes (Centers for Disease Control and Prevention, 2024b). While other types of diabetes exist, such as gestational diabetes, existing literature on spirituality and diabetes focuses on Type 2 diabetes.

Roughly 38.1 million adults in the United States are affected by diabetes, with Type 2 diabetes accounting for 90–95% of all diabetes cases (Centers for Disease Control and Prevention, 2024c). Health care costs for patients with diabetes are 2.3 times higher than for patients without diabetes (American Diabetes Association, 2018). As of 2022, the direct medical costs ($307 billion) and indirect reduced productivity costs ($106 billion) associated with diabetes are $413 billion, demonstrating a 35% increase in economic costs of diabetes since 2012 (American Diabetes Association, 2018; Parker et al., 2024). The prevalence of Type 2 diabetes in adults is highest in American Indian and Alaska Native adults (13.6%), followed by Black adults (12.1%), adults of Hispanic origin (11.7%), Asian adults (9.1%), and White adults (6.9%). Among Asian adults, Asian Indian (10.8%) and Filipino (12.2%) subgroups have the highest prevalence. Among adults of Hispanic origin, Puerto Rican (13.3%) and Mexican (11.1%) adults have the highest prevalence (Centers for Disease Control and Prevention, 2024c).

The documented connection between maintaining a healthy lifestyle and chronic illness prevention is widely recognized (Kushner & Sorensen, 2013). Within this context, psychosocial elements are recognized as significant contributors to the onset, maintenance, and psychological adjustment of various chronic illnesses, including Type 2 diabetes (Bellou et al., 2018; Hackett & Steptoe, 2017; Tuncay et al., 2008). Among these psychosocial factors, religion and spirituality hold a profound influence in American society (Alper, 2023), impacting social dynamics, lifestyle choices, ideologies, and coping styles. However, the impact of religion or spirituality on Type 2 diabetes largely remains limited.

The existing research that has investigated the role of spirituality in Type 2 diabetes has yielded very mixed results. Several studies have explored spirituality as a possible protective or risk factor for Type 2 diabetes. One cross-sectional study in Canada of 5,442 adults found that individuals who attended religious services more than once a week had lower prevalent odds of type 2 diabetes compared to individuals attending less than once a year (Banerjee et al., 2014). Conversely, a cross-sectional study of 4,344 Black Christians from the National Survey of American Life found increased odds of Type 2 diabetes among those attending religious services at least once a week compared to non-attenders. Interestingly, they also highlight notable differences by denomination, with the odds of Type 2 diabetes much lower for Presbyterians and Catholics compared to Baptists. While these studies demonstrate spirituality as having a dual role as both a protective factor and a risk factor in diabetes, other research provides contrasting findings by revealing a lack of any significant impact of spirituality on diabetes. Spence et al. (2022) examined data from a 14-year prospective Nurses' Health Study of 46,713 women with self-reported spiritual beliefs and 42,825 women with self-reported spiritual service attendance to assess Type 2 diabetes risk. They found no significant differences in hazard ratios for Type 2 diabetes between women who used religious or spiritual coping compared to women who did not (Spence et al., 2022). Further, the study demonstrated no significant differences in hazard ratios for Type 2 diabetes between women who attended spiritual meetings or services and women who did not (Spence et al., 2022).

In addition to examining spirituality as a protective factor for diabetes, some research has focused on spirituality as a coping tool for diabetes management and psychological adjustment to diabetes. One study consisting of 109 Black women with diabetes examined the role of both religion and spirituality on glycemic control, the crucial process of maintaining optimal blood glucose levels in diabetic individuals through consistent adherence to diabetes health behaviors, such as medication compliance, diet, exercise, and blood glucose monitoring (Association of Diabetes Care Education Specialists & Kolb, 2021). The study found that when clinically significant factors, including body mass index, age, income, education, and diabetes medication, were held constant, both religion and spirituality had significant relationships with glycemic control (Newlin et al., 2008). Interestingly, these relationships were not the same, with negative associations between religion and glycemic control, and positive associations between spirituality and glycemic control. Newlin et al. (2008) proposed that women experiencing sub-optimal glycemic control, which may be accompanied by symptoms like vision change and neuropathic pain, may demonstrate elevated levels of religiousness due to an increased reliance on a higher power to cope with emotional distress. While religion, as measured in this study, captures a direct, supportive, and personal connection with a higher power, spirituality in this study encompasses life's purpose, meaning, and satisfaction. Women who exhibited greater spirituality tended to demonstrate more optimal glycemic control, suggesting that spirituality fosters successful diabetes self-management practices (Newlin et al., 2008). It is also possible that spirituality is related to better glycemic control through reduced stress levels, given the positive association between cortisol – our body's stress hormone – and blood glucose levels (Hucklebridge et al., 1999). Though this study did not show mediating effects of stress levels as measured by diabetes-specific emotional distress or diabetes-specific social support, the authors suggest these findings could represent model misspecification and indicate that the use of global mental psychosocial measures, rather than diabetes-specific psychosocial measures, may offer meaningful insights (Newlin et al., 2010).

However, other research using diabetes-specific emotional distress to measure mental health in diabetic populations has found significant associations with spirituality. Using the Spiritual Well-Being Scale (Paloutzian & Ellison, 1982), which operationalizes existential well-being and religious well-being in two subscales, one study (N = 45) demonstrated that Black women who exhibited high existential well-being had lower emotional distress (Newlin et al., 2010). The study found that religious well-being was not significantly associated with emotional distress among Black women with diabetes. Further, the same study examined how spirituality related to coping strategies that Black women with diabetes use in stressful events concerning diabetes self-management. They found that both existential and religious well-being were positively associated with cognitive reframing coping strategies, or behaviors aimed at reevaluating the meaning attached to stress and understanding it within a different context. Further, the study found that existential well-being, but not religious well-being, was positively associated with direct assistance coping, or obtaining help from others to manage stress (Newlin et al., 2010). One possible explanation for the findings of this study is that spirituality cultivates a sense of responsibility and obligation, self-efficacy, and meaning-making, thereby enhancing the capacity for effective self-management of diabetes.

In contrast to the quantitative approaches in the previously described studies, more recent literature has utilized qualitative methodology to offer insights into the experiential impact of spirituality among formerly unhoused Black individuals navigating the complexities of diabetes management. Choi and Hastings (2019) conducted semi-structured interviews of 42 formerly unhoused Black individuals with Type 2 diabetes and explored perceptions of spirituality in diabetes self-management. While 19 participants did not identify a specific religious affiliation, 17 participants identified as Christian, 2 participants identified as

Buddhist, and 2 participants identified as atheist. Interviews revealed that spirituality was a source of hope and meaning in the context of diabetes, promoted coping and resilience mechanisms, and fostered diabetes self-management practices (Choi & Hastings, 2019). Moreover, spirituality increased self-reliance and equanimity in the face of diabetes-related stressors (Choi & Hastings, 2019).

While existing studies examining spirituality in diabetic populations focus predominantly on American and Christian samples, a recent pilot randomized controlled trial explored the feasibility of incorporating supernatural beliefs into diabetes self-management interventions (Pan et al., 2024). Supernatural belief explanatory models, which attribute health and illness to non-scientific factors, may be rooted in religion and spirituality. Given that current diabetes management programs in China are not resulting in optimal glycemic control for a significant portion of patients, many healthcare providers have advocated for culturally and spiritually sensitive clinical care. Thus, this study compared self-efficacy outcomes between a control group that watched a standard diabetes self-management video and an intervention group that watched the same video supplemented with information on using supernatural beliefs as a resource in managing diabetes. However, the intervention group had a follow-up loss rate ten times higher than the control group, indicating a potential cultural resistance to integrating religious and spiritual topics into clinical care in China (Pan et al., 2024). It is possible that cultural nuances affected the acceptance of spiritual concepts in healthcare, and it may be beneficial to investigate alternative interventions that would better resonate with this patient population.

Several limitations within the existing research on spirituality and diabetes warrant consideration. Much of the research predominantly focuses on specific religious affiliations or spiritual practices, potentially neglecting the diversity of spiritual beliefs and experiences within populations. Existing studies primarily consist of Christian samples, overlooking how the perspectives of individuals from other spiritual backgrounds use spirituality to cope with diabetes. Furthermore, the underrepresentation of racial and ethnic groups beyond White and Black populations in diabetes and spirituality research is another critical limitation. While diabetes disproportionately affects Black adults in the United States, other racial and ethnic groups, such as Native American, Hispanic, South Asian, and Filipino individuals, also experience high prevalence rates of the disease in the United States (Centers for Disease Control and Prevention, 2024c). These groups possess unique cultural identities and spiritual systems that may influence their experiences with diabetes differently. Future research should prioritize the inclusion of diverse racial, ethnic, and spiritual populations, exploring the nuanced interplay between spirituality, cultural factors, and diabetes outcomes across different communities and spiritual traditions. Additionally, the scarcity of large-scale, high-quality quantitative studies investigating the relationship between spirituality and diabetes poses limitations. The existing literature predominantly comprises smaller-scale and qualitative studies, often limited in scope and generalizability. Future research should aim to utilize rigorous quantitative methodology in larger samples.

The chronic nature of diabetes necessitates a collaborative and multifaceted approach to disease management. Some limited evidence suggests that spirituality may serve as a protective factor for diabetes risk in certain populations; however, further research is needed to elucidate the precise role of spirituality in diabetes risk. Existing literature generally indicates that spirituality may be a valuable coping resource in diabetes management, emphasizing the importance of integrating religious and spiritual considerations into clinical practice to promote holistic and patient-centered care for diabetic populations.

Chronic Kidney Disease

Chronic kidney disease is the gradual loss of kidney function, in which glomeruli in the kidneys lose their ability to clean and filter blood. When kidney function deteriorates past a certain level, toxic waste and extra fluid accumulate in the body, which may contribute to and/or be a consequence of high blood pressure, heart disease, stroke, and early death. In the United States, chronic kidney disease affects an estimated 35.5 million adults overall (Centers for Disease Control and Prevention, 2024d), with prevalence rates of 19.5% among Black adults, 14% among Hispanic adults, 14% among Asian adults, and 11.7% among White adults (Centers for Disease Control and Prevention, 2024d). Chronic kidney disease is most commonly attributable to hypertension and diabetes, explaining the overlap in racial prevalence between diabetes and chronic kidney disease (Centers for Disease Control and Prevention, 2024d). Progressive chronic kidney disease is associated with adverse clinical outcomes, including end-stage kidney disease. End-stage kidney disease, also referred to as end-stage renal disease, is the final stage of chronic kidney disease and occurs when kidney function is no longer adequate for long-term survival without kidney transplantation or dialysis. Though life can be prolonged by hemodialysis (HD), peritoneal dialysis, or kidney transplantation, there is no cure for chronic kidney disease (Smeltzer & Bare, 2003).

While chronic kidney disease can be managed, its progressive nature means it cannot be fully cured. Consequently, prioritizing the enhancement of health-related quality of life rather than solely focusing on reducing mortality and morbidity is widely acknowledged as an important therapeutic goal (Mapes et al., 2003). This emphasis is particularly significant given extant evidence of compromised quality of life among individuals living with chronic kidney disease (Fukuhara et al., 2007; Hedayati et al., 2009). Recognized as critical to quality of life, spirituality has garnered increased attention for its association with enhanced psychosocial adaptation to illness and reduced reliance on healthcare services (Koenig et al., 1999). Several studies have examined spiritual well-being within the context of chronic kidney disease.

Qualitative studies provide evidence that spirituality improves quality of life by prompting individuals to seek meaning and purpose when confronted with the challenges of chronic kidney disease. Al-Ghabeesh and Suleiman (2014) employed a phenomenological approach to better understand the lived experiences of patients with end-stage renal disease who were undergoing HD treatment. Participants (N = 10) emphasized their reliance on faith through the phrase "trust in God." This spiritual grounding was identified by participants as the foundation of resilience amidst the challenges of chronic kidney disease. Additional findings from this study, as well as other qualitative studies, suggest spirituality facilitates better health behaviors, medication adherence, and coping (Al-Ghabeesh & Suleiman, 2014; Molzahn et al., 2012). While these studies present potential limitations in their depth of analysis by modern qualitative standards, they provide nuanced information beyond mere associations on the role of spirituality in chronic kidney disease. In particular, qualitative studies offer unique opportunities to generate insights about underrepresented populations within this field of research, whose spiritual beliefs and lifestyle habits may cultivate distinctive outcomes for chronic kidney disease.

Walton (2007) examined the role of spirituality among Native Americans undergoing HD, utilizing qualitative interviews to develop knowledge and establish theoretical foundations for further research among members of this population, which is underrepresented in research. Within the interviews, participants endorsed prayer as a powerful coping skill for the stress of HD treatment, in that it alleviated suffering, honored their beliefs, addressed past traumas, and fostered community connections (Walton, 2007). Moreover, prayer rituals were often incorporated into their treatment routines. Despite potential cultural hesitancy towards technological interventions like dialysis within Native American communities, this research suggests that embracing a culturally sensitive approach to dialysis, coupled with the integration of spiritual practices, could enhance the acceptance of the treatment (Walton, 2007).

Another study explored the role of religion and spirituality in coping with chronic kidney disease and HD among individuals from Thailand who identified as Buddhist (N = 17) and Muslim (N = 3) in Thailand (Yodchai et al., 2017). Similar to previously discussed studies, findings indicated that religious and spiritual beliefs played a significant role in helping to find meaning in patients' lives despite dealing with chronic kidney disease. However, distinct from Buddhist and Muslim religious frameworks, respectively, patients in this study attributed their chronic kidney disease to either karmic disease or a test from Allah. These perceptions led patients to greater acceptance of illness (Yodchai et al., 2017). To counterbalance their karma, participants engaged in acts of merit-making (performing good deeds to generate positive karma), a practice deeply ingrained in Buddhist tradition. Merit-making, reading Dharma books, meditating, and praying were important coping mechanisms that enhanced purpose and meaning among these patients (Yodchai et al., 2017). In Thai culture, these acts may take place in a specific religious context, but not necessarily. Regardless of the specific religion practiced, Yodchai et al. (2017) highlighted that religion and spirituality were deeply intertwined with daily life and could not be distinctly separated into secular and sacred components. They emphasized that Western conceptualizations of religion and spirituality may not fully encompass the nuances of Eastern conceptualizations and cultures.

The concept of spiritual or religious well-being may sometimes be used in a Western cultural context to examine more expanded concepts of wellness in relation to psychological adjustment to illness. Patients receiving HD treatment for chronic kidney disease must adjust daily to their treatment schedule, dietary limitations, and other potential complications, all of which can cause mental and physical stress. Tanyi and Werner (2003) investigated the relationship between spirituality and psychological adjustment among 65 White and Black women undergoing HD. They found that higher levels of spirituality, including spiritual well-being, religious well-being, and existential well-being, were linked to better adjustment to illness, underscoring the potential influence of spirituality on coping mechanisms and well-being in chronic illness (Tanyi & Werner, 2003). However, the sample was comprised only of Christian individuals, limiting its generalizability.

In another study of 253 Canadian patients diagnosed with stage four or five chronic kidney disease, associations were found between existential well-being and various domains of health-related quality of life, such that higher existential well-being correlated to lower perceived burden of kidney disease, fewer effects of kidney disease, improved symptom management, improved cognitive function, improved sleep patterns, and higher quality of social interactions (Davison & Jhangri, 2010). Notably, individuals who reported higher levels of existential well-being tended to perceive a greater overall quality of life concerning their health (Davison & Jhangri, 2010). Within this study, the existential dimension of spirituality exerted a more substantial influence on the quality of life compared to measures of religious well-being (Davison & Jhangri, 2010), underscoring the unique impact of existential considerations on individuals' well-being in the context of late-stage chronic kidney disease.

Another study used data from the Southern Community Cohort Study to examine end-stage kidney disease risk in 76,443 adults with generally low socioeconomic status who were recruited from 12 states in the southeast United States between 2002 and 2009 (Nair et al.,

2020). High levels of spirituality were associated with a 20% decrease in end-stage kidney disease (ESKD) risk among Black adults, though this association was not observed among their White counterparts (Nair et al., 2020). Notably, this relationship in Black adults persisted even after adjusting for various psychosocial and behavioral factors, including depressive symptoms, social support networks, and tobacco usage frequency (Nair et al., 2020). However, upon introducing clinical covariates into the analysis, such as hypertension, diabetes, BMI, and estimated glomerular filtration rate (eGFR), the statistical significance of the link between spirituality and ESKD risk among Black participants dissipated. It is important to note that the same equation for eGFR estimation was used for both Black and White adults. While this outcome suggests that clinical factors may more accurately predict the risk of end-stage kidney disease than spirituality alone in statistical models, Nair et al. (2020) highlight the clinical significance of spirituality in mitigating psychosocial distress associated with medical illnesses, implying that despite statistical nuances, spirituality remains an essential consideration in the holistic management of chronic kidney disease.

Existing research on spirituality and chronic kidney disease emphasizes spirituality as a contributing factor to adjustment mechanisms and overall well-being in patients suffering from chronic kidney disease. Qualitative studies have laid important foundational understandings, illuminating how religion and spirituality serve as sources of strength in navigating kidney disease, fostering coping mechanisms, and promoting positive health behaviors. However, to attain a more comprehensive understanding, further quantitative studies utilizing constructs that operationalize spirituality or religion measures are warranted. Future research should aim to conduct randomized control trials among diverse populations to investigate interventions that reflect the role of religion and spirituality in effective coping strategies for chronic kidney disease. Moreover, the existing research suggests that healthcare professionals should recognize and support individuals' coping strategies, tailored to their unique spiritual beliefs, values, and cultural contexts.

Further examination of spirituality and chronic kidney disease may also reduce health disparities. Within the United States, individuals who identify as Black, individuals with lower incomes, and individuals with decreased education report a higher degree of spirituality, a higher degree of comfort from religion, and a greater frequency of service attendance in comparison with those who do not belong to these groups (Hackett et al., 2014). Given the disproportionate burden of end-stage kidney disease faced by individuals belonging to these groups in the United States, assessing the effects of religiousness on kidney disease risk may help identify novel mechanisms for culturally tailored strategies to prevent kidney disease in these vulnerable populations (Tarver-Carr et al., 2002).

Epilepsy

According to the World Health Organization, epilepsy is a chronic brain disorder affecting about 50 million people worldwide (World Health Organization, 2024). It involves recurrent seizures, which are brief episodes of involuntary movement that can be partial or generalized, sometimes causing loss of consciousness and control over bowel or bladder function. Seizures result from excessive electrical discharges in brain cells, which can occur in different brain regions. They range from brief lapses of attention or muscle jerks to severe convulsions and can vary in frequency from less than once a year to multiple times a day.

In patients with epilepsy, spirituality has received varying attention. It is important to note that past research has linked epilepsy to mystical states (Dewhurst & Beard, 1970; Hansen &

Brodtkorb, 2003) and found hyperreligiosity and mystic attraction during interictal periods (Hansen & Brodtkorb, 2003). Hyperreligiosity in epilepsy is a feature of Gastaut-Geschwind syndrome, which also includes hypergraphia (compulsive writing), altered sexual behavior, aggression, stickiness or viscosity, preoccupation with details, seriousness, and circumstantiality (Devinsky & Schachter, 2009). However, less research has examined the role spirituality may play in disease management and quality of life in patients with epilepsy, despite evidence that psychosocial variables, including some that are directly correlated to spirituality, are strong predictors of quality of life in neurological conditions (Giovagnoli et al., 2009; Gramstad et al., 2001). Considering that spirituality has been shown to impact conditions that are highly comorbid with epilepsy, including mood disorders and migraine headaches (Seidenberg et al., 2009), spirituality is an important factor to investigate and understand, and may offer insights for new comprehensive care strategies for epilepsy patients.

Aligning with the concept that quality of life encompasses biological, social, psychological, and spiritual factors, one study utilized a factor analysis of spiritual measures (spiritual, religious, and personal beliefs) and psychological measures (State-Trait Anxiety Inventory and Beck Depression Inventory) to examine the position of spirituality in a multidimensional model of quality of life in patients with neurological disorders (Giovagnoli et al., 2019). The study included 199 adult patients with neurological conditions, specifically 88 with epilepsy, 32 with ischemic vascular disorders, 28 with tumors, 22 with MS, and 66 healthy controls (Giovagnoli et al., 2019). While epilepsy patients reported significantly lower spirituality and lower quality of life compared to healthy subjects (Giovagnoli et al., 2019), spiritual factors contributed to the prediction of quality of life in patients to a greater extent than to the quality of life in healthy controls. In addition to spiritual factors, socioeconomic factors and mood-related variables impacted quality of life in patients, supporting a biopsychosocial-spiritual model for epilepsy.

It is important to consider spirituality as a factor in epilepsy care while also understanding how different uses and expressions of spirituality impact epilepsy patients. For example, spiritual coping strategies vary widely and are used differently based on religious frameworks and cultural contexts. Spiritual coping can be classified as positive, involving collaboration with a higher power (e.g., God) or seeking comfort from spiritual activities, or negative, involving beliefs in a punitive higher power or deferring responsibility to a higher power to solve one's problems (Pargament, 2001). Tedrus et al. (2013) found that, among 110 patients with epilepsy in Brazil, positive spiritual coping strategies were used more frequently than negative spiritual coping strategies, though both types of spiritual coping were employed to deal with epilepsy (Tedrus et al., 2013). The patients who relied more on negative spiritual coping rather than positive spiritual coping experienced a poorer quality of life, emotional well-being, and lower energy levels (Tedrus et al., 2013), demonstrating the differential effects of spirituality on epilepsy based on the way spirituality is used. Further, spiritual coping scores were significantly higher in patients practicing some form of religion compared to those who did not. This suggests that religious practices enhance the relevance of these coping mechanisms for individuals in this population and highlights that while spirituality is an important component of holistic health, its role is nuanced and may not be universally applicable.

The relationship between spiritual coping and quality of life, emotional well-being, and energy levels demonstrated by Tedrus et al. (2013) may be explained by health behaviors, such as medication adherence. In patients with epilepsy, non-adherence to antiepileptic medication decreases symptom control, lowers productivity, and reduces quality of life (Hovinga et al., 2008). One study consisting of 760 patients with epilepsy in Iran found that religiousness and both positive and negative spiritual coping were strong predictors of medication adherence (Lin et al., 2018). In this study, medication adherence was measured by both a subjective, self-report questionnaire and objective blood samples of antiepileptic drug serum levels. Patients who utilized more negative spiritual coping strategies demonstrated lower medication adherence (Lin et al., 2018), which could explain previous findings from Tedrus et al. (2013) regarding associations between negative spiritual coping and worse mental health. Lin et al. (2018) also found that negative religious coping and medication adherence, both separately and together, mediated the relationship between religiousness and quality of life. These findings emphasize that the way spirituality/religion is used impacts health behaviors and quality of life outcomes in a clinically meaningful way. Therefore, it may be important for health care providers to ask about patients' views on spirituality and its role in their epilepsy management to enhance medication adherence.

Cultural factors also offer a nuance that may impact how spirituality is used by and impacts patients with epilepsy. Ismail et al. (2005) explore the influence of spiritual and religious beliefs on the explanation of the cause of epilepsy in patients of South Asian origin using semi-structured interviews. In addition to the South Asian patients with epilepsy, 20 who identified as Muslim, six who identified as Sikh, and four who identified as Hindu, nominated caregivers, healthcare professionals, and community members who were also interviewed. The study found that over half of the responders, especially those who identified as Muslim, attributed their illness to fate and the will of God (Ismail et al., 2005). Some individuals from Sikh backgrounds viewed their illness as a punishment for sins of a past life, demonstrating that doctrines of karma influence interpretations of illness (Ismail et al., 2005). Of importance, a strong network of traditional healers was discussed within this community, and many patients, especially those of Islamic faith, utilized religio-spiritual treatments from South Asian cultures. Ismail et al. (2005) emphasized that this network provides a parallel and complementary system of healthcare, rather than an alternative to Western medicine, highlighting the importance of cultural and spiritual sensitivity in epilepsy care in underrepresented racial and spiritual populations. The qualitative findings of this study offer strong implications for future research, including that integrative spiritual and cultural treatments should be explored, developed, and implemented into standard care for epilepsy.

Parkinson's Disease

The World Health Organization defines PD as "a brain condition that causes problems with movement, mental health, sleep, pain and other health issues" (World Health Organization, 2023b). Global estimates in 2019 demonstrated over 8.5 million individuals live with PD, and estimates suggest that, in 2019, PD was the cause of 329,000 deaths (World Health Organization, 2023b). PD is a progressive and debilitating disease due to the degradation of the neurons that respond to dopamine in the basal ganglia, for which the cause is still unknown. The distinct pathology of dopaminergic neurons in PD has been regarded as an opportunity to examine the role that dopaminergic networks play in the practice, experience, and maintenance of religious or spiritual beliefs.

Redfern et al. (2020) conducted a study involving 42 patients with PD and 39 healthy controls matched for age, gender, educational attainment, and disability. Over a one-year period, the study observed expected declines in mobility and cognition within the PD group. Despite these declines, there were no significant changes in religiousness and spirituality scores or in reports of interest in religious faith or spirituality among the PD patients. Anecdotal reports indicated that decreasing mobility, loss of driving ability, increased emotional lability, and tiredness did cause reduced participation in some religious and spiritual practices.

Another study offers quantitative evidence for such anecdotal reports, demonstrating that PD patients (N = 22) reported lower engagement with religious practices and organized religious activities compared to age-matched healthy controls (McNamara et al., 2006). Moreover, PD patients in this study exhibited lower levels of daily spirituality, religious and spiritual coping, religious support, and overall religiousness compared to age-matched controls. Interestingly, the reduced religiousness was primarily associated with performance on the Stroop task, a measure of prefrontal neuropsychological function (Vendrell et al., 1995), rather than age, education, mood, or medication-related factors. The authors posit that prefrontal dysfunction may explain decreased religiousness in PD patients, asserting that stable forms of religiousness require the motivational support typically provided by dopaminergic drive centers in the neostriatal and limbic-prefrontal circuits. Indeed, neuroimaging and neuropsychological studies have established the activation of prefrontal networks in religious practices, indicating that dopaminergic activity may be crucial for religiousness (Azari et al., 2001; McNamara et al., 2003). Considering that PD is associated with the loss of dopaminergic neurons in the central and forebrain, it follows that PD patients may exhibit fewer signs of spirituality and religiousness. If dopaminergic activity is crucial for religiousness, it is unsurprising that PD patients exhibit fewer overt signs of religiousness.

Still, Redfern et al. (2020) was not the only study to show no changes in spirituality in PD patients, indicating that the progressive loss of dopaminergic neurons in PD may not impact religious practice and belief. Among 85 patients with PD, most patients reported no change in their religious or spiritual beliefs following their diagnosis of PD (Ghourchian et al., 2023). However, higher levels of spirituality and religiousness were associated with younger age, female gender, lower educational attainment, Christian religious affiliation, and better mental health status among PD patients (Ghourchian et al., 2023), and greater spirituality and religiousness were linked to lower levels of anxiety. While this evidence suggests that PD may not reduce spirituality through dopaminergic neuron degradation, it is possible that greater spirituality promotes dopaminergic pathways that are also implicated in mental health (Belujon & Grace, 2017). Thus, spirituality may offer a protective effect, through reinforced dopaminergic neuron pathways, on the psychiatric manifestations of PD (Han et al., 2018).

Given the mixed findings regarding spirituality and PD, future research is needed to disentangle how PD may impact spirituality through neurological and psychological pathways. Such investigations will offer insights into how to promote well-being for patients with PD, as well as how neurological systems promote or inhibit spiritual coping and beliefs.

Multiple Sclerosis

Another common chronic neurological condition, or neurological autoimmune disease, is MS, a disease that is estimated to affect almost one million individuals in the United States (Wallin et al., 2019). In MS, the immune system cells that normally protect us from viruses, bacteria, and unhealthy cells mistakenly attack myelin in the central nervous system, including the brain, optic nerves, and spinal cord (National Institute of Neurological Disorders and Stroke, 2023). Myelin is a substance that makes up the protective sheath that coats nerve fibers (axons). Thus, nerves may be abnormally activated or damaged in MS, leading to changes in vision and cognition, weakness, and pain (please see Chapter 11 of this volume for an in-depth review of the influence of spirituality on chronic pain). Given that pain is one of the primary and most debilitating symptoms of MS, spirituality, as a part of the well-established biopsychosocial-spiritual model of pain, may be especially important to examine within patients dealing with MS.

Sparaco et al. (2022) found a complex relationship between religiousness and health outcomes, including pain, in a sample of 92 MS patients. Within their study, patients who endorsed more religious practice and faith demonstrated worse physical functioning, worse physical pain, worse general health, and more consequent limitation. Moreover, there was a positive correlation between religious practice and qualitative aspects of pain, such that patients who reported greater religious practices demonstrated higher sensory, affective, and evaluative aspects of pain related to MS. This finding is contrary to other literature that suggests religious activities have analgesic effects on pain (see Chapter 11, this volume), and the authors posit that structural or functional changes in neural circuits resulting from MS may contribute to unique effects of religious activities on pain in MS patients (Sparaco et al., 2022). In addition, disability scores were significantly higher among practicing believers compared to non-practitioners, indicating a higher level of disability in those engaging in religious practices (Sparaco et al., 2022). These findings suggest that more disabled MS patients, who experience a poorer quality of life and greater physical pain, may be more likely to turn to faith and religious practices for comfort. This interpretation may be more accurate than the notion that religious engagement results in greater disability, given that previous research has demonstrated the positive impact of religiousness on quality of life in patients with MS (Yamout et al., 2013). Specifically, religiousness, in addition to depression, social support, years of education, and living area, was a significant predictor of overall quality of life in 201 patients with MS. Similar to the research reviewed in this chapter on epilepsy, these findings reinforce the inclusion of spirituality within biopsychosocial models and treatments of chronic illness.

Fibromyalgia

Fibromyalgia (FM) is a chronic pain condition that is characterized by widespread musculoskeletal pain. Pain is the main symptom of FM; however, sleep disturbances, cognitive impairment, and fatigue are also common clinical symptoms of this syndrome (Dizner-Golab et al., 2023). Chronic fatigue syndrome, anxiety, rheumatic arthritis, and irritable bowel syndrome (IBS) increase the risk of developing FM (Queiroz, 2013). Given the close associations of FM with several autoimmune disorders (e.g., rheumatoid arthritis and lupus), it is unsurprising that researchers have begun to explore possible autoimmune origins of FM. While available evidence does not provide a clear pathogenesis of FM in general or support autoimmune origins, there continues to be debate regarding the pathophysiology and classification of FM (Clauw et al., 2023). At present, the World Health Organization classifies FM as a chronic pain condition, in accordance with the IASP criteria for ICD-11 (Nicholas et al., 2019). Thus, Chapter 11: Health, Well-Being, and Chronic Pain in this volume may provide more comprehensive and relevant information to the study of spirituality and FM (i.e., in the specific context of pain).

FM is a complex disease that has several overlapping syndromes and frequent comorbidities. Thus, multimodal treatment plans are most effective for FM patients, with interdisciplinary approaches addressing rheumatic, neurological, sleep, psychiatric, gastrointestinal, and psychological concerns (Dizner-Golab et al., 2023). Recent research has advocated for such approaches to consider addressing spiritual concerns as well.

One study examined how spirituality impacts satisfaction with life in 590 FM patients (Biccheri et al., 2016). The results showed significant mediation pathways, such that higher levels of spirituality enabled the use of problem-focused coping and coping through seeking social support, which in turn led to greater satisfaction with life. Further, this study found that emotion-focused coping did not intervene in the spirituality–life satisfaction relationship and was negatively correlated with life satisfaction. The authors assert that patients with a higher level of spirituality utilize practices that reduce the negative impact of their symptoms on quality of life. Indeed, free expression responses included at the end of this study revealed that patients benefited from several practices that may be spiritual, including relaxation therapy, yoga, meditation, and some psychotherapies (Biccheri et al., 2016).

FM patient testimonies documenting the benefits of spiritual practices (Biccheri et al., 2016) are backed by empirical evidence. For example, one randomized controlled trial evaluated the effectiveness of a meditation awareness training for treating FM (Van Gordon et al., 2017). Meditation awareness training draws from Buddhist models of mental health and is a second-generation mindfulness-based intervention, which is intentionally more acknowledging of the spiritual components of mindfulness compared to first-generation mindfulness-based interventions. A total of 74 adults with FM received an 8-week meditation awareness, and 74 adults with FM received an active control intervention known as cognitive behavior therapy for groups. Assessments performed at pre-, post-, and 6-month follow-up phases revealed that the meditation awareness training participants experienced significant and sustained improvements compared to the control group participants in FM symptomatology, pain perception, psychological distress, sleep quality, non-attachment (to self, symptoms, and environment), and civic engagement. Non-attachment to self, a common Buddhist meditative concept, appeared to be an important therapeutic mechanism of change, partially mediating treatment effects for psychological distress and sleep quality, and almost fully mediating treatment effects for FM symptomatology and pain perception (Van Gordon et al., 2017). The principle of non-attachment, presented to participants in certain second-generation mindfulness-based trainings, originates from the Buddhist belief that suffering results from an individual's attachment to themselves and external factors like wealth, relationships, and reputation. This study highlights potential advantages of second-generation mindfulness practices, which consciously incorporate spiritual components, over more traditional, first-generation mindfulness approaches.

The empirical evidence reviewed on FM and spirituality invites further discussion on the integration of spiritual elements in therapeutic interventions for FM. Future research directly comparing first-generation mindfulness interventions (i.e., mindfulness-based stress reduction (MBSR) and mindfulness-based cognitive therapy) to second-generation mindfulness interventions for FM may help identify the specific contributions of spiritual elements to therapeutic outcomes. Ultimately, this line of inquiry may pave the way for more holistic and effective treatment strategies for FM, which is especially important given that treatment for FM is complex. For a deeper discussion of psychotherapy interventions for pain based on spiritual frameworks, please refer to Chapter 11: Health, Well-Being, and Chronic Pain in this volume.

Inflammatory Bowel Disease and Irritable Bowel Syndrome

Inflammatory bowel diseases (IBD), such as Crohn's disease and ulcerative colitis, are chronic and recurring inflammatory conditions of the gastrointestinal tract (Centers for Disease Control and Prevention, 2024e) that affect an estimated 3.1 million adults (1.3%) in the United States (Centers for Disease Control and Prevention, 2024f). IBD may manifest in symptoms such as abdominal pain, bloody diarrhea, and nausea and vomiting. Some of these symptomatic patterns are also seen in IBS, a functional gastrointestinal disorder characterized by chronic diarrhea, constipation, bloating, and/or abdominal pain. IBS is often diagnosed after IBDs are ruled out, and, unlike IBD, IBS cannot be attributed to a specific structural or metabolic abnormality. Both IBD and IBS impose considerable physical and psychological burdens on patients (Gralnek et al., 2000; Kappelman et al., 2008; Weimers & Munkholm, 2018). These burdens lead to isolation, poor quality of life, and stigmatization for patients with IBD and IBS (Frank et al., 2002; Sajadinejad et al., 2012). To manage their gastrointestinal illnesses, patients employ a wide array of psychosocial, alternative, and complementary strategies, which may include spiritual practices and beliefs (Cramer et al., 2017; Rawsthorne et al., 1999; Swarup et al., 2017).

There have been mixed findings regarding the role of spirituality and spiritual coping in IBD. One study investigated the impact of coping strategies on mental health and quality of life in 102 patients with Crohn's disease in Brazil (de Campos et al., 2020). Their findings revealed that negative spiritual coping was significantly associated with depressive and anxiety symptoms, but not with quality of life, after statistical adjustments for gender, smoking, and years with the disease were made. However, this study showed no associations between positive coping strategies and quality of life or mental health (de Campos et al., 2020). Conversely, Freitas et al. (2015) demonstrated that, among 147 patients with IBD in Brazil, positive religious coping was correlated with lower levels of psychological distress and with greater health-related quality of life. Anxiety symptoms fully mediated the effect of positive religious coping on overall health-related quality of life, suggesting that positive religious coping enhances quality of life for patients with IBD by reducing anxiety symptoms (Freitas et al., 2015). These two studies, both conducted in Brazil, reveal mixed findings that may be attributed to variations in the measurement of spirituality or inconsistent definitions of spirituality and religion, highlighting the need for standardized measurement tools and definitions of spirituality.

Another study compared spiritual well-being in 155 adolescents with and without IBD and found that levels of spiritual well-being were similar between adolescents with IBD and their healthy counterparts (Cotton et al., 2009). While spiritual well-being had a significant association with mental health across all adolescents, the presence of IBD moderated the relationship between mental health and spiritual well-being, with higher spiritual well-being more strongly related to better emotional functioning and decreased depressive symptoms in adolescents with IBD compared to healthy peers. Cotton et al. (2009) highlight this finding as an indicator that spiritual well-being could play a particularly significant role in the mental health of chronically ill adolescents, in contrast to their healthy peers. These findings raise the question of how spiritual well-being can be improved among individuals who are struggling with IBD.

While limited research has investigated spiritual interventions for patients with IBD, there has been research on the use of MBSR (Kabat-Zinn, 1993) for management of IBD, which may improve spiritual well-being. MBSR is established in the spiritual traditions of Buddhism, where mindfulness, the practice of developing conscious awareness of the present moment with openness and without judgment, is actively practiced (Kabat-Zinn & Hanh, 2009). In addition to mindfulness meditation, MBSR incorporates *hatha yoga*, a practice of Hinduism and Buddhism (Burley, 2000). Despite MBSR being grounded in spiritual and religious principles and practices, it is often presented in secular contexts and is not necessarily designed for spiritual or religious populations. Zernicke et al. (2013) conducted a treatment-as-usual wait-list control trial to investigate the impact of MBBR on IBS. Both the group randomized to

MBSR (n = 43) and the group randomized to a treatment-as-usual waitlist (n = 47) exhibited a decrease in IBS symptom severity scores over time; however, the improvement was greater for the MBSR group than the controls. Of note, the change in symptom severity for the MBSR group was clinically meaningful, exhibiting a decrease in symptoms from severe to moderate. However, both groups demonstrated improved spiritual well-being over time (Zernicke et al., 2013). While there are several possible explanations for this, the lack of significant improvement in spiritual well-being for the MBSR group compared to controls may indicate that MBSR does not address spiritual well-being in patients with IBS in a unique manner, despite being heavily rooted in spiritual frameworks. Given the evidence that spiritual well-being could improve quality of life in those suffering from gastrointestinal diseases and disorders, future research should aim to develop and test other spiritual interventions. Moreover, the possibility that spiritually based interventions may influence spiritual well-being differentially in individuals depending on their own spiritual backgrounds and traditions should be considered (i.e., MBSR may enhance spiritual well-being in patients who identify as Buddhist or Hindu) and examined in order to provide diverse and patient-centered treatment options to manage IBD or IBS.

Conclusions

The exploration of spirituality in relation to chronic medical conditions reveals a vital, yet underexamined, dimension of patient care and self-management. Existing literature demonstrates that spirituality may improve disease symptoms, quality of life, and psychological adjustment to illness, suggesting that novel biopsychosocial-spiritual interventions for chronic illness could benefit patients. Expanding research on the nuanced relationship between spirituality and chronic medical conditions is crucial for the development of such interventions, especially when considering the limitations in existing research. Future research should prioritize the inclusion of diverse samples and utilize rigorous methodology and study designs to ensure comprehensive and generalizable findings.

The establishment of the National Institutes of Health (NIH) Religion, Spirituality, and Health Scientific Interest Group (RSH-SIG) represents a significant step forward in this endeavor. The NIH RSH-SIG (https://oir.nih.gov/sigs/religion-spirituality-health-scientific-interest-group) aims to enhance communication, encourage collaboration, and facilitate the exchange of information and resources both within the NIH and the wider research community, thus elevating the discourse surrounding the intersection of religion, spirituality, and health. This initiative addresses the historical underrepresentation of spirituality within scientific and medical fields. The NIH RSH-SIG offers opportunities to overcome existing limitations within the field of spirituality and health, such as limited funding opportunities and a lack of standardization, ultimately contributing to a more holistic understanding of health and well-being.

References

Al-Ghabeesh, S., & Suleiman, K. (2014). The lived experience of patients' with end stage renal disease on hemodialysis: A phenomenological study. *International Journal of Medicine and Medical Sciences*, *47*(1), 1423–1429.

Alper, B. A., Rotolo, M., Tevington, P., Justin, N., Kallo, A. (2023). Spirituality among Americans. *Pew Research Center's Religion & Public Life Project*. Retrieved April 3, 2024, from https://www.pewresearch.org/religion/2023/12/07/spirituality-among-americans/

American Diabetes Association. (2018). Economic costs of diabetes in the US in 2017. *Diabetes Care*, *41*(5), 917–928. https://doi.org/10.2337/dci18-0007

Association of Diabetes Care Education Specialists, & Kolb, L. (2021). An effective model of diabetes care and education: The ADCES7 Self-Care Behaviors™. *The Science of Diabetes Self-Management and Care*, *47*(1), 30–53. https://doi.org/10.1177/0145721720978154

Astrow, A. B., Puchalski, C. M., & Sulmasy, D. P. (2001). Religion, spirituality, and health care: Social, ethical, and practical considerations. *The American Journal of Medicine*, *110*(4), 283–287. https://doi.org/10.1016/s0002-9343(00)00708-7

Azari, N. P., Nickel, J., Wunderlich, G., Niedeggen, M., Hefter, H., Tellmann, L., Herzog, H., Stoerig, P., Birnbacher, D., & Seitz, R. J. (2001). Neural correlates of religious experience. *European Journal of Neuroscience*, *13*(8), 1649–1652. https://doi.org/10.1046/j.0953-816x.2001.01527.x

Banerjee, A. T., Boyle, M. H., Anand, S. S., Strachan, P. H., & Oremus, M. (2014). The relationship between religious service attendance and coronary heart disease and related risk factors in Saskatchewan, Canada. *Journal of Religion and Health*, *53*, 141–156. https://doi.org/10.1007/s10943-012-9609-6

Bellou, V., Belbasis, L., Tzoulaki, I., & Evangelou, E. (2018). Risk factors for type 2 diabetes mellitus: An exposure-wide umbrella review of meta-analyses. *PloS one*, *13*(3), e0194127. https://doi.org/10.1371/journal.pone.0194127

Belujon, P., & Grace, A. A. (2017). Dopamine system dysregulation in major depressive disorders. *International Journal of Neuropsychopharmacology*, *20*(12), 1036–1046. https://doi.org/10.1093/ijnp/pyx056

Bernell, S., & Howard, S. W. (2016). Use your words carefully: What is a chronic disease? *Frontiers in Public Health*, *4*, 212747. https://doi.org/10.3389/fpubh.2016.00159

Biccheri, E., Roussiau, N., & Mambet-Doué, C. (2016). Fibromyalgia, spirituality, coping and quality of life. *Journal of Religion and Health*, *55*, 1189–1197. https://doi.org/10.1007/s10943-016-0216-9

Burley, M. (2000). *Haṭha-yoga: Its context, theory, and practice*. Motilal Banarsidass Publ.

Centers for Disease Control and Prevention. (2024a). About chronic diseases. Retrieved April 6, 2024, from https://www.cdc.gov/chronic-disease/about/index.html

Centers for Disease Control and Prevention. (2024b). Diabetes risk factors. Retrieved April 2, 2024, from https://www.cdc.gov/diabetes/risk-factors/index.html

Centers for Disease Control and Prevention. (2024c). National diabetes statistics report. Retrieved March 10, 2024, from https://www.cdc.gov/diabetes/php/data-research/index.html

Centers for Disease Control and Prevention. (2024d). Chronic kidney disease in the United States. Retrieved May 1, 2023, from https://www.cdc.gov/kidney-disease/php/data-research/index.html

Centers for Disease Control and Prevention. (2024e). What is inflammatory bowel disease (IBD)? Retrieved May 25, 2024, from https://www.cdc.gov/inflammatory-bowel- disease/about/index.html

Centers for Disease Control and Prevention. (2024f). Prevalence of IBD. Retrieved May 21, 2024, from https://www.cdc.gov/inflammatory-bowel-disease/php/facts-stats/index.html

Choi, S. A., & Hastings, J. F. (2019). Religion, spirituality, coping, and resilience among African Americans with diabetes. *Journal of Religion & Spirituality in Social Work: Social Thought*, *38*(1), 93–114. https://doi.org/10.1080/15426432.2018.1524735

Clauw, D., Sarzi-Puttini, P., Pellegrino, G., & Shoenfeld, Y. (2023). Is fibromyalgia an autoimmune disorder? *Autoimmunity Reviews*, 103424. https://doi.org/10.1016/j.autrev.2023.103424

Cotton, S., Kudel, I., Roberts, Y. H., Pallerla, H., Tsevat, J., Succop, P., & Yi, M. S. (2009). Spiritual well-being and mental health outcomes in adolescents with or without inflammatory bowel disease. *Journal of Adolescent Health*, *44*(5), 485–492. https://doi.org/10.1016/j.jadohealth.2008.09.013

Cramer, H., Schäfer, M., Schöls, M., Köcke, J., Elsenbruch, S., Lauche, R., Engler, H., Dobos, G., & Langhorst, J. (2017). Randomised clinical trial: Yoga vs written self-care advice for ulcerative colitis. *Alimentary Pharmacology & Therapeutics*, *45*(11), 1379–1389. https://doi.org/10.1111/apt.14062

Damiano, R. F., Costa, L. A., Viana, M. T. S., Moreira-Almeida, A., Lucchetti, A. L., & Lucchetti, G. (2016). Brazilian scientific articles on "Spirituality, Religion and Health". *Archives of Clinical Psychiatry (São Paulo)*, *43*, 11–16. https://doi.org/10.1590/0101-60830000000073

Davison, S. N., & Jhangri, G. S. (2010). Existential and religious dimensions of spirituality and their relationship with health-related quality of life in chronic kidney disease. *Clinical Journal of the American Society of Nephrology*, *5*(11), 1969–1976. https://doi.org/10.2215/CJN.01890310

de Campos, R., Lucchetti, G., Lucchetti, A. L. G., da Rocha Ribeiro, T. C., Chebli, L. A., Malaguti, C., Gaburri, P. D., Pereira, L. M. N., de Almeida, J. G., & Chebli, J. M. F. (2020). The Impact of Spirituality and Religiosity on Mental Health and Quality of Life of Patients with Active Crohn's Disease. *Journal of Religion and Health*, *59*(3), 1273–1286. https://doi.org/10.1007/s10943-019-00801-1

Devinsky, J., & Schachter, S. (2009). Norman Geschwind's contribution to the understanding of behavioral changes in temporal lobe epilepsy: The February 1974 lecture. *Epilepsy & Behavior*, *15*(4), 417–424. https://doi.org/10.1016/j.yebeh.2009.06.006

Dewhurst, K., & Beard, A. W. (1970). Sudden religious conversions in temporal lobe epilepsy. *The British Journal of Psychiatry*, *117*(540), 497–507. https://doi.org/10.1192/bjp.117.540.497

Dizner-Golab, A., Lisowska, B., & Kosson, D. (2023). Fibromyalgia–etiology, diagnosis and treatment including perioperative management in patients with fibromyalgia. *Reumatologia*, *61*(2), 137–148. https://doi.org/10.5114/reum/163094

Engel, G. L. (1977). The need for a new medical model: A challenge for biomedicine. *Science*, *196*(4286), 129–136. https://doi.org/10.1126/science.847460

Frank, L., Kleinman, L., Rentz, A., Ciesla, G., Kim, J. J., & Zacker, C. (2002). Health-related quality of life associated with irritable bowel syndrome: Comparison with other chronic diseases. *Clinical Therapeutics*, *24*(4), 675–689. https://doi.org/10.1016/S0149-2918(02)85143-8

Freitas, T. H., Hyphantis, T. N., Andreoulakis, E., Quevedo, J., Miranda, H. L., Alves, G. S., Souza, M. H., Braga, L. L., Pargament, K. I., Soczynska, J. K., McIntyre, R. S., & Carvalho, A. F. (2015). Religious coping and its influence on psychological distress, medication adherence, and quality of life in inflammatory bowel disease. *Revista Brasileira de Psiquiatria*, *37*(3), 219–227. https://doi.org/10.1590/1516-4446-2014-1507

Fukuhara, S., Yamazaki, S., Hayashino, Y., & Green, J. (2007). Measuring health-related quality of life in patients with end-stage renal disease: Why and how. *Nature Clinical Practice Nephrology*, *3*(7), 352–353. https://doi.org/10.1038/ncpneph0510

Ghourchian, S., Gruber-Baldini, A. L., Shakya, S., Reich, S. G., von Coelln, R., Savitt, J. M., & Shulman, L. M. (2023). Spirituality in Parkinson's Disease within a Sample from the USA. *Journal of Religion and Health*, *62*(6), 4177–4191. https://doi.org/10.1007/s10943-023-01817-4

Giovagnoli, A. R., da Silva, A. M., Federico, A., & Cornelio, F. (2009). On the personal facets of quality of life in chronic neurological disorders. *Behavioural Neurology*, *21*(3–4), 155–163. https://doi.org/10.3233/BEN-2009-0243

Giovagnoli, A. R., Paterlini, C., Meneses, R. F., & da Silva, A. M. (2019). Spirituality and quality of life in epilepsy and other chronic neurological disorders. *Epilepsy & Behavior*, *93*, 94–101. https://doi.org/10.1016/j.yebeh.2019.01.035

Gralnek, I. M., Hays, R. D., Kilbourne, A., Naliboff, B., & Mayer, E. A. (2000). The impact of irritable bowel syndrome on health-related quality of life. *Gastroenterology*, *119*(3), 654–660. https://doi.org/10.1053/gast.2000.16484

Gramstad, A., Iversen, E., & Engelsen, B. A. (2001). The impact of affectivity dispositions, self-efficacy and locus of control on psychosocial adjustment in patients with epilepsy. *Epilepsy Research*, *46*(1), 53–61. https://doi.org/10.1016/S0920-1211(01)00261-3

Hackett, C., Grim, B., Stonawski, M., Skirbekk, V., Kuriakose, N., & Potančoková, M. (2014). Methodology of the pew research global religious landscape study. In *Yearbook of international religious demography 2014* (pp. 167–175). Brill.

Hackett, R. A., & Steptoe, A. (2017). Type 2 diabetes mellitus and psychological stress - a modifiable risk factor. *Nature Reviews. Endocrinology*, *13*(9), 547–560. https://doi.org/10.1038/nrendo.2017.64

Han, J. W., Ahn, Y. D., Kim, W.-S., Shin, C. M., Jeong, S. J., Song, Y. S., Bae, Y. J., & Kim, J.-M. (2018). Psychiatric manifestation in patients with Parkinson's disease. *Journal of Korean Medical Science*, *33*(47), e300. https://doi.org/10.3346/jkms.2018.33.e300

Hansen, B. Å., & Brodtkorb, E. (2003). Partial epilepsy with "ecstatic" seizures. *Epilepsy & Behavior, 4*(6), 667–673. https://doi.org/10.1016/j.yebeh.2003.09.009

Hatala, A. R. (2013). Towards a biopsychosocial–spiritual approach in health psychology: Exploring theoretical orientations and future directions. *Journal of Spirituality in Mental Health, 15*(4), 256–276. https://doi.org/10.1080/19349637.2013.776448

Hedayati, S. S., Bosworth, H. B., Briley, L. P., Sloane, R., Pieper, C., Kimmel, P. L., & Szczech, L. A. (2009). Response to 'Death or hospitalization of patients on chronic hemodialysis is associated with a physician-based diagnosis of depression'. *Kidney International, 75*(8), 861–862. https://doi.org/10.1038/ki.2008.672

Hovinga, C. A., Asato, M. R., Manjunath, R., Wheless, J. W., Phelps, S. J., Sheth, R. D., Pina-Garza, J. E., Zingaro, W. M., & Haskins, L. S. (2008). Association of non-adherence to antiepileptic drugs and seizures, quality of life, and productivity: Survey of patients with epilepsy and physicians. *Epilepsy & Behavior, 13*(2), 316–322. https://doi.org/10.1016/j.yebeh.2008.03.009

Hucklebridge, F., Clow, A., Abeyguneratne, T., Huezo-Diaz, P., & Evans, P. (1999). The awakening cortisol response and blood glucose levels. *Life Sciences, 64*(11), 931–937. https://doi.org/10.1016/S0024-3205(99)00019-3

Ismail, H., Wright, J., Rhodes, P., & Small, N. (2005). Religious beliefs about causes and treatment of epilepsy. *British Journal of General Practice, 55*(510), 26–31.

Kabat-Zinn, J. (1993). Mindfulness meditation: Health benefits of an ancient Buddhist practice In Goleman D & Gurin J (Eds.), *Mind/body medicine* (pp. 259–275). Consumer Reports Books.[Google Scholar].

Kabat-Zinn, J., & Hanh, T. N. (2009). *Full catastrophe living: Using the wisdom of your body and mind to face stress, pain, and illness*. Delta.

Kappelman, M. D., Rifas Shiman, S. L., Porter, C. Q., Ollendorf, D. A., Sandler, R. S., Galanko, J. A., & Finkelstein, J. A. (2008). Direct health care costs of Crohn's disease and ulcerative colitis in US children and adults. *Gastroenterology, 135*(6), 1907–1913. https://doi.org/10.1053/j.gastro.2008.09.012

Koenig, H. G. (2008). Concerns about measuring "spirituality" in research. *The Journal of Nervous and Mental Disease, 196*(5), 349–355. https://doi.org/10.1097/NMD.0b013e31816ff796

Koenig, H. G., Idler, E., Kasl, S., Hays, J. C., George, L. K., Musick, M., Larson, D. B., Collins, T. R., & Benson, H. (1999). Editorial: Religion, spirituality, and medicine: A rebuttal to skeptics. *International Journal of Psychiatry in Medicine, 29*(2), 123–131. https://doi.org/10.2190/C2FB-95VW-FKYD-C8RV

Kushner, R. F., & Sorensen, K. W. (2013). Lifestyle medicine: The future of chronic disease management. *Current Opinion in Endocrinology, Diabetes, and Obesity, 20*(5), 389–395. https://doi.org/10.1097/01.med.0000433056.76699.5d

La Cour, P., & Götke, P. (2012). Understanding of the word "spirituality" by theologians compared to lay people: An empirical study from a secular region. *Journal of Health Care Chaplaincy, 18*(3–4), 97–109. https://doi.org/10.1080/08854726.2012.720543

Lin, C.-Y., Saffari, M., Koenig, H. G., & Pakpour, A. H. (2018). Effects of religiosity and religious coping on medication adherence and quality of life among people with epilepsy. *Epilepsy & Behavior, 78*, 45–51. https://doi.org/10.1016/j.yebeh.2017.10.008

Mapes, D. L., Lopes, A. A., Satayathum, S., McCullough, K. P., Goodkin, D. A., Locatelli, F., Fukuhara, S., Young, E. W., Kurokawa, K., Saito, A., Bommer, J., Wolfe, R. A., Held, P. J., & Port, F. K. (2003). Health-related quality of life as a predictor of mortality and hospitalization: The Dialysis Outcomes and Practice Patterns Study (DOPPS). *Kidney International, 64*(1), 339–349. https://doi.org/10.1046/j.1523-1755.2003.00072.x

McKee, D. D., & Chappel, J. N. (1992). Spirituality and medical practice. *The Journal of Family Practice, 35*(2), 201–205. https://go.exlibris.link/SbZ2Zv2X

McNamara, P., Andresen, J., & Gellard, J. (2003). Relation of religiosity and scores on fluency tests to subjective reports of health in older individuals. *The International Journal for the Psychology of Religion, 13*(4), 259–271. https://doi.org/10.1207/S15327582IJPR1304_3

McNamara, P., Durso, R., & Brown, A. (2006). Religiosity in patients with Parkinson's disease. *Neuropsychiatric Disease and Treatment*, *2*(3), 341–348. https://doi.org/10.2147/nedt.2006.2.3.341

Molzahn, A., Sheilds, L., Bruce, A., Stajduhar, K., Makaroff, K. S., Beuthin, R., & Shermak, S. (2012). People living with serious illness: stories of spirituality. *Journal of Clinical Nursing*, *21*(15–16), 2347–2356. https://doi.org/10.1111/j.1365-2702.2012.04196.x

Nair, D., Cavanaugh, K. L., Wallston, K. A., Mason, O., Stewart, T. G., Blot, W. J., Ikizler, T. A., & Lipworth, L. P. (2020). Religion, spirituality, and risk of end-stage kidney disease among adults of low socioeconomic status in the southeastern United States. *Journal of Health Care for the Poor and Underserved*, *31*(4), 1727–1746. https://doi.org/10.1353/hpu.2020.0129

National Institute of Neurological Disorders and Stroke. (2023). Multiple Sclerosis. Retrieved May 23, 2024, from Www.ninds.nih.gov. https://www.ninds.nih.gov/health-information/disorders/multiple-sclerosis

Newlin, K., Melkus, G. D., Peyrot, M., Koenig, H. G., Allard, E., & Chyun, D. (2010). Coping as a Mediator in the Relationships of Spiritual Well-Being to Mental Health in Black Women with Type 2 Diabetes. *International Journal of Psychiatry in Medicine*, *40*(4), 439–459. https://doi.org/10.2190/PM.40.4.g

Newlin, K., Melkus, G. D., Tappen, R., Chyun, D., & Koenig, H. G. (2008). Relationships of Religion and Spirituality to Glycemic Control in Black Women With Type 2 Diabetes. *Nursing Research*, *57*(5), 331–339. https://doi.org/10.1097/01.NNR.0000313497.10154.66

Nicholas, M., Vlaeyen, J. W., Rief, W., Barke, A., Aziz, Q., Benoliel, R., Cohen, M., Evers, S., Giamberardino, M. A., & Goebel, A. (2019). The IASP classification of chronic pain for ICD-11: Chronic primary pain. *Pain*, *160*(1), 28–37. https://doi.org/10.1097/j.pain.0000000000001390

Paloutzian, R. F., & Ellison, C. W. (1982). Loneliness, spiritual well-being and quality of life. In L. A. Peplau & D. Perlman (Eds.), *Loneliness: A sourcebook of current theory, research, and therapy* (pp. 224–237).

Pan, S. W., Wachholtz, A., Strand, M., Wang, W., Wu, S., Dong, Z., Wang, Q., Liang, Y., Zhou, G., Mao, D., & Tang, Y. (2024). Supernatural beliefs-based intervention to improve type-2 diabetes self-management: A pilot randomized controlled trial from China. *Journal of Religion and Health*. https://doi.org/10.1007/s10943-024-02061-0

Pargament, K. I. (2001). *The psychology of religion and coping: Theory, research, practice*. Guilford press.

Parker, E. D., Lin, J., Mahoney, T., Ume, N., Yang, G., Gabbay, R. A., ElSayed, N. A., & Bannuru, R. R. (2024). Economic Costs of Diabetes in the U.S. in 2022. *Diabetes Care*, *47*(1), 26–43. https://doi.org/10.2337/dci23-0085

Peng-Keller, S., Winiger, F., & Rauch, R. (2022). *The Spirit of Global Health: The World Health Organization and the 'Spiritual Dimension' of Health, 1946-2021*. Oxford University Press. https://doi.org/10.1093/oso/9780192865502.001.0001

Queiroz, L. P. (2013). Worldwide epidemiology of fibromyalgia. *Current Pain and Headache Reports*, *17*, 356. https://doi.org/10.1007/s11916-013-0356-5

Rawsthorne, P., Shanahan, F., Cronin, N. C., Anton, P. A., Löfberg, R., Bohman, L., & Bernstein, C. N. (1999). An international survey of the use and attitudes regarding alternative medicine by patients with inflammatory bowel disease. *The American Journal of Gastroenterology*, *94*(5), 1298–1303. https://doi.org/10.1016/S0002-9270(99)00136-7

Redfern, C., Mason, S. L., Barker, R. A., & Coles, A. (2020). Parkinson's disease and spirituality. *NeuroRehabilitation*, *46*(1), 31–39. https://doi.org/10.3233/nre-192947

Roger, K. S., & Hatala, A. (2018). Religion, spirituality & chronic illness: A scoping review and implications for health care practitioners. *Journal of Religion & Spirituality in Social Work: Social Thought*, *37*(1), 24–44. https://doi.org/10.1080/15426432.2017.1386151

Sajadinejad, M. S., Asgari, K., Molavi, H., Kalantari, M., & Adibi, P. (2012). Psychological issues in inflammatory bowel disease: An overview. *Gastroenterology Research and Practice*, *2012*(1), 106502. https://doi.org/10.1155/2012/106502

Seidenberg, M., Pulsipher, D. T., & Hermann, B. (2009). Association of epilepsy and comorbid conditions. *Future Neurology*, *4*(5), 663–668. https://doi.org/10.2217/fnl.09.32

Smeltzer, S. C., & Bare, B. (2003). *Brunner & Suddarth's textbook of medical-surgical nursing*. 10th ed. Philadelphia: USA: Lippincott Williams & Wilkins.

Sparaco, M., Miele, G., Abbadessa, G., Ippolito, D., Trojsi, F., Lavorgna, L., & Bonavita, S. (2022). Pain, quality of life, and religiosity in people with multiple sclerosis. *Neurological Sciences*, *43*(5), 3247–3254. https://doi.org/10.1007/s10072-021-05759-1

Spence, N. D., Warner, E. T., Farvid, M. S., VanderWeele, T. J., Zhang, Y., Hu, F. B., & Shields, A. E. (2022). Religious or spiritual coping, religious service attendance, and type 2 diabetes: A prospective study of women in the United States. *Annals of Epidemiology*, *67*, 1–12. https://doi.org/10.1016/j.annepidem.2021.09.012

Sulmasy, D. P. (2002). A biopsychosocial-spiritual model for the care of patients at the end of life. *The Gerontologist*, *42 Spec No 3*, 24–33. https://doi.org/10.1093/geront/42.suppl_3.24

Swarup, N., Nayak, S., Lee, J., Pai Raikar, S., Hou, D., Sockalingam, S., & Lee, K. J. (2017). Forming a support group for people affected by inflammatory bowel disease. *Patient Preference and Adherence*, 277–281. https://doi.org/10.2147/PPA.S123073

Tanyi, R. A., & Werner, J. S. (2003). Adjustment, spirituality, and health in women on hemodialysis. *Clinical Nursing Research*, *12*(3), 229–245. https://doi.org/10.1177/1054773803253163

Tarver-Carr, M. E., Powe, N. R., Eberhardt, M. S., LaVeist, T. A., Kington, R. S., Coresh, J., & Brancati, F. L. (2002). Excess risk of chronic kidney disease among African-American versus white subjects in the United States: A population-based study of potential explanatory factors. *Journal of the American Society of Nephrology*, *13*(9), 2363–2370. https://doi.org/10.1097/01.ASN.0000026493.18542.6A

Tedrus, G. M. A. S., Fonseca, L. C., Magri, F. D. P., & Mendes, P. H. M. (2013). Spiritual/religious coping in patients with epilepsy: Relationship with sociodemographic and clinical aspects and quality of life. *Epilepsy & Behavior*, *28*(3), 386–390. https://doi.org/10.1016/j.yebeh.2013.05.011

Tuncay, T., Musabak, I., Gok, D. E., & Kutlu, M. (2008). The relationship between anxiety, coping strategies and characteristics of patients with diabetes. *Health and Quality of Life Outcomes*, *6*, 1–9. https://doi.org/10.1186/1477-7525-6-79

Van Gordon, W., Shonin, E., Dunn, T. J., Garcia-Campayo, J., & Griffiths, M. D. (2017). Meditation awareness training for the treatment of fibromyalgia syndrome: A randomized controlled trial. *British Journal of Health Psychology*, *22*(1), 186–206. https://doi.org/10.1111/bjhp.12224

Vendrell, P., Junqué, C., Pujol, J., Jurado, M. A., Molet, J., & Grafman, J. (1995). The role of prefrontal regions in the Stroop task. *Neuropsychologia*, *33*(3), 341–352. https://doi.org/10.1016/0028-3932(94)00116-7

Wachholtz, A., & Sambamoorthi, U. (2011). National trends in prayer use as a coping mechanism for health concerns: Changes from 2002 to 2007. *Psychology of Religion and Spirituality*, *3*(2), 67–77. https://doi.org/10.1037/a0021598

Wachholtz, A. B., & Sambamthoori, U. (2013). National trends in prayer use as a coping mechanism for depression: Changes from 2002 to 2007. *Journal of Religion and Health*, *52*, 1356–1368. https://doi.org/10.1007/s10943-012-9649-y

Wallin, M. T., Culpepper, W. J., Campbell, J. D., Nelson, L. M., Langer-Gould, A., Marrie, R. A., Cutter, G. R., Kaye, W. E., Wagner, L., & Tremlett, H. (2019). The prevalence of MS in the United States: A population-based estimate using health claims data. *Neurology*, *92*(10), e1029–e1040. https://doi.org/10.1212/WNL.0000000000007035

Walton, J. (2007). Prayer warriors: A grounded theory study of American Indians receiving hemodialysis. *Nephrology Nursing Journal*, *34*(4), 377–386.

Webb, J. R., Toussaint, L., & Dula, C. S. (2014). Ritualistic, theistic, and existential spirituality: Initial psychometric qualities of the RiTE measure of spirituality. *Journal of Religion and Health*, *53*, 972–985. https://doi.org/10.1007/s10943-013-9697-y

Weimers, P., & Munkholm, P. (2018). The natural history of IBD: Lessons learned. *Current Treatment Options in Gastroenterology*, *16*, 101–111. https://doi.org/10.1007/s11938-018-0173-3

World Health Organization. (2023a). Diabetes. Retrieved April 2, 2023, from https://www.who.int/news-room/fact-sheets/detail/diabetes

World Health Organization. (2023b). Parkinson disease. Retrieved May 20, 2024, from https://www.who.int/news-room/fact-sheets/detail/parkinson-disease

World Health Organization. (2024). *Epilepsy*. World Health Organization. Retrieved June 3rd, 2024 from https://www.who.int/news-room/fact-sheets/detail/epilepsy

Yamout, B., Issa, Z., Herlopian, A., El Bejjani, M., Khalifa, A., Ghadieh, A. S., & Habib, R. H. (2013). Predictors of quality of life among multiple sclerosis patients: A comprehensive analysis. *European Journal of Neurology*, *20*(5), 756–764. https://doi.org/10.1111/ene.12046

Yodchai, K., Dunning, T., Savage, S., & Hutchinson, A. M. (2017). The role of religion and spirituality in coping with kidney disease and haemodialysis in Thailand. *Scandinavian Journal of Caring Sciences*, *31*(2), 359–367. https://doi.org/10.1111/scs.12355

Zernicke, K. A., Campbell, T. S., Blustein, P. K., Fung, T. S., Johnson, J. A., Bacon, S. L., & Carlson, L. E. (2013). Mindfulness-based stress reduction for the treatment of irritable bowel syndrome symptoms: A randomized wait-list controlled trial. *International Journal of Behavioral Medicine*, *20*(3), 385–396. https://doi.org/10.1007/s12529-012-9241-6

Chapter 11

Spirituality and Chronic Pain

*Maya Joshi Delity and Amy Wachholtz**

Chronic pain is a debilitating condition that impacts daily functioning and has been linked to higher suicide risk (Interagency Pain Research Coordinating Committee, 2016), depression (Zis et al., 2017), anxiety (Asmundson & Katz, 2009), and substance use (Ditre et al., 2019). In 2021, the United States had an estimated prevalence of 20.9% of adults (51.6 million persons) who had experienced chronic pain and 6.9% (17.1 million persons) who had experienced high-impact chronic pain (Rikard, 2023). This has resulted in tremendous economic burdens; the annual health care costs due to pain range from $560 to $635 billion and are greater than the annual costs of $309 billion for heart disease, $243 billion for cancer, and $188 billion for diabetes (Gaskin & Richard, 2012).

The opioid epidemic remains a significant public health concern in the United States and is especially relevant to chronic pain populations. Prescription opioid misuse and opioid-related deaths continue to rise rapidly each year (National Institute on Drug Abuse, 2023), with 25% of patients prescribed opioids for chronic pain misusing them, and 12% of chronic pain patients developing an opioid use disorder (Carberg, 2023). As such, increased attention is being focused on non-pharmacological interventions for chronic pain. In particular, a growing body of literature has examined the relationship between spirituality/religion and chronic pain. The following chapter summarizes the existing research on chronic pain and spirituality, utilizing results from literature searches in PubMed and PsycINFO. Key search terms included "chronic pain," "pain," "spirituality," "religion," and "existentialism"; additional search terms were added as we delved further into the literature. We will review empirical evidence for both advantageous and disadvantageous relationships between chronic pain and spirituality and discuss future directions for research.

Pain

Pain processing is a vital function of our body and is biologically required for survival. In a healthy functioning body, the perception of pain starts with a signal from peripheral nociceptors on A-delta or C fibers that synapse onto the dorsal horn of the spinal cord (Garland, 2012). From there, a fast reflex response ascends and synapses in the thalamus. This signal is then relayed to higher cortical regions, including the somatosensory cortex, the cingulate, and the insula (Tracey & Mantyh, 2007). Different descending systems exist along this path that have the potential to downregulate ascending signals. Similarly, each of the locations along

* Corresponding Author: AMY.WACHHOLTZ@UCDENVER.EDU.

DOI: 10.4324/9781003440048-14

this path can become dysregulated when overwhelmed, resulting in a breakdown or remodeling of neuronal pathways. This process of dysregulated learning in pain circuits demonstrates the transition from acute to chronic pain. It is important to note that cognitions, behavior, and emotion can influence pain circuits and contribute to their regulation (Melzack & Wall, 1965). Thus, chronic pain is best understood as a biopsychosocial illness.

The biopsychosocial model conceptualizes illness as a complex interaction of biological, psychological, and social factors (Engel, 1977). This model emphasizes the reciprocal interactions between individuals and their environment and facilitates an interdisciplinary approach to the treatment of medical illness and pain. The Gate Control Theory of Pain (Melzack & Wall, 1965) and the Neuromatrix Theory of Pain (Melzack, 1999) further illustrate the relationship between psychological and biological factors of pain. In contrast to historical biomedical theories that defined pain and tissue damage in an isomorphic relationship, these theories posit that pathways involving cognitions, emotions, and behavior can influence the pain signal, thereby influencing the subjective experience of pain. Extensive research has established evidence for both the Gate Control and Neuromatrix models, identifying psychosocial variables such as depression, anxiety, and distress as robust influences on the onset and maintenance of chronic pain (Asmundson & Katz, 2009; Bair et al., 2003; Linton et al., 2011). Likewise, social support, self-efficacy, and pain-related fear have been shown to moderate pain perception and disability from pain (Brown et al., 2003; Eisenberger et al., 2011; Keefe et al., 1997; Lee et al., 2015). A growing body of work has advocated for the biopsychosocial model to include spirituality (McKee & Chappel, 1992; Sulmasy, 2002), suggesting that illness disrupts biological, interpersonal, and spiritual relationships. This proposed addition to the biopsychosocial model of chronic pain is consistent with the Gate Control and Neuromatrix theories, given that spirituality offers a variety of pathways that can modify the subjective experience of pain.

Spirituality

This chapter will use the term spirituality as conceptualized by the RiTE Model of Spirituality defined in this book (see Chapters 1 and 44, this volume; see also Webb et al., 2014) and as discussed in detail in Chapter 10 of this volume. Briefly, the RiTE model incorporates Ritualistic Spirituality or "religiousness," Theistic Spirituality or "spirituality," and Existential Spirituality or "agnostic and atheist," allowing for flexibility across various interpretations and expressions of spirituality.

Evidence for an Advantageous Relationship between Pain and Spirituality

Although research examining spirituality and pain yields some conflicting results, in a review of spirituality and pain literature, spirituality in chronic pain populations was associated with meaning and purpose, self-efficacy, and coping techniques such as prayer, social support, relaxation, and feeling loved (Wachholtz et al., 2007). These spiritual coping techniques are thought to be the core mechanism through which spirituality improves pain experience. It is important to note that each of these techniques fits differently within definitions of spirituality. For example, the literature examining prayer and religious attendance tends to reflect ritualistic forms of spirituality, whereas the studies exploring meditation include ritualistic, theistic, and existential forms of spirituality.

Prayer

Prayer is one coping technique that has been shown to improve pain experience and is often executed in the context of ritualistic frameworks of spirituality. Dezutter et al. (2011) studied 202 Flemish chronic pain patients and found that prayer was related to increased pain tolerance. However, prayer was not related to pain severity. Positive reappraisals mediated the relationship between prayer and pain tolerance. The researchers hypothesize that through praying, individuals were able to reframe their pain conditions into more positive and meaningful terms.

Another study examined the effects of prayer on 92 migraine headache patients in Iran. Patients were randomized to receive either 40 milligrams of propranolol twice a day for two months or 40 milligrams of propranolol twice a day for two months with prayer. Patients' pain was measured at the beginning of the study and three months after intervention, and they found that while pain was significantly reduced in both groups at follow-up, pain was significantly lower in the prayer group compared to the propranolol-only group (Tajadini et al., 2017). The reduced pain suggests that prayer may be an efficacious addition to pharmaceutical interventions for chronic pain, highlighting the need for integrative and holistic treatment approaches to pain.

Investigators have also examined prayer as an intervention, rather than simply a coping strategy (Eilami et al., 2019). Seventy-six cancer patients in Iran were assigned to a control or experimental group involving "prayer psychotherapy," which consisted of four training sessions centered around religious attitudes within the Islamic faith, specific prayers from Islamic sacred scriptures, and emphasis on the importance of a peaceful attitude around illness and a faithful belief in the positive potential of prayer. Compared to a control group, the prayer psychotherapy group had significantly lower pain scores after the intervention.

These studies provide evidence that prayer can be used to cope with chronic pain and may also be an effective intervention for chronic pain, especially when it is used in the context of one's personal beliefs and identity. In other words, prayer is more useful for pain patients who are already religious than non-religious pain patients, suggesting that prayer needs to be meaningful for it to be an effective pain management tool.

Meditation

Meditation has received wide attention as a preventative and rescue intervention for chronic pain, as well as acute pain. The potential benefits of meditation for acute pain are somewhat less studied compared to chronic pain, but are extremely important, especially when considering that opioids are the primary intervention. While opioids can be necessary and useful for managing acute pain, exploring additional rescue interventions may mitigate the associated risks of prescribing opioids to patients, such as opioid use disorder. One study demonstrated that when hospitalized patients with either "intolerable pain" or "inadequate pain control" were treated with a single 15-minute mindfulness meditation, approximately one-third of the patients reported at least a 30% reduction in pain intensity. This reduction in pain is comparable to the effect of five milligrams of oxycodone (Garland, 2012). Moreover, although a weekend mindfulness meditation course did not reduce perceived pain for women going through childbirth, it did lower rates of opioid analgesia use in labor (Duncan et al., 2017). Future research exploring meditation as a treatment for acute pain may elucidate opportunities to manage acute pain in varying clinical contexts, potentially preventing the development of chronic pain and opioid misuse (Roberts et al., 2022).

There are a wide variety of meditation traditions and techniques from all of the "Big 5" world religions (i.e., Judaism, Christianity, Islam, Hinduism, and Buddhism) as well as many other religious and spiritual groups. Many of the meditation techniques that have gained popularity and have been empirically studied in the United States derive from Indian or Chinese spiritual systems such as Hinduism or Buddhism (Kong et al., 2016; Singla, 2011) but have been presented in a more secular context in Western psychotherapy (Kabat-Zinn, 1993; Kabat-Zinn et al., 1985). While secular components of meditation have been widely studied and implemented in the treatment of chronic pain (e.g., Benson & Klipper, 1975; Kabat-Zinn, 1993; la Cour & Petersen, 2015), the effects of meditation in spiritual contexts (or spirituality-based meditation) on chronic pain may not be as well known. Indeed, the secular practice of meditation has recently been questioned, especially given that many Western practices of meditation may not be congruent with the spiritual frameworks and values they originate from (Dimidjian & Linehan, 2003). These considerations are discussed further later in this chapter (see Future Directions).

Carson et al. (2005) were among the first to examine loving-kindness meditation as a therapeutic treatment for chronic pain patients. They examined 43 patients with chronic low back pain, who were randomly assigned to an 8-week loving-kindness program or standard care provided through their medical outpatient programs. Patients in the 8-week loving-kindness program showed significant improvements in pain and psychological distress (Carson et al., 2005). In contrast, there were no changes in the usual care group. Later work built on these findings, showing that only a single exposure to a Buddhist loving-kindness (among non-Buddhist individuals) based guided meditation significantly reduced migraine pain and emotional tension in 27 migraine patients (Tonelli & Wachholtz, 2014), demonstrating the immediate analgesic effects of meditation on migraine pain. Additionally, these studies suggest that, unlike prayer, spiritual meditation's efficacy on chronic pain may not depend on prior spiritual identity.

Wachholtz and Pargament (2008) compared spiritual meditation with three other meditation groups – internally focused secular meditation, externally focused secular meditation, and progressive muscle relaxation – in a group of 83 migraine patients. Findings demonstrated that participants practicing spiritual meditation had greater decreases in the frequency of migraine headaches and negative affect and anxiety and greater increases in pain tolerance, headache-related self-efficacy, daily spiritual experiences, and existential well-being (Wachholtz & Pargament, 2008). Moreover, a study of the effects of meditation practice on migraine medication usage showed that migraine frequency decreased in the spiritual meditation group compared to other types of meditation groups. Further, after adjusting for headache frequency, migraine medication use decreased in the spiritual meditation group compared to other groups (Wachholtz et al., 2017).

Another study found that compared to a relaxation group, participants in a spiritual meditation group showed an increase in pain tolerance on cold pressor tests and a decrease in pain intensity ratings for heat from quantitative sensory testing. The meditation group also showed a higher level of spiritual well-being (Sollgruber et al., 2018). While many studies hypothesize that spiritual meditation acts on secondary factors associated with chronic pain conditions, this study suggests that spiritual meditation may also have a more direct effect on acute nociceptive stimuli processing.

This literature demonstrates that there are multifarious forms of meditation that can improve the chronic pain experience. Spiritual meditation may be especially impactful for addressing pain tolerance, pain frequency, pain medication use, and psychological well-being.

Moreover, spiritual meditation appears to be effective in improving short-term and long-term pain experiences. This spiritual technique has been studied within several realms of spirituality, including ritualistic, theistic, and existential, providing encouraging evidence for its generalizability. Future research should aim to further examine the mechanisms of spiritual meditation as potential therapeutic targets for chronic pain.

Religious Attendance

Religious attendance, an aspect of ritualistic spirituality or religiousness, has also been studied as a form of coping for chronic pain. Attending religious services may facilitate engagement in other forms of coping, such as prayer, or offer foundations for social support, which is linked to less severe pain and less distress (Jensen et al., 2002; Waltz et al., 1998).

In one study of 37,000 participants in Canada, religious individuals were less likely to have chronic pain and fatigue, while spiritual individuals who did not engage in regular religious attendance were more likely to have chronic pain and fatigue (Baetz & Bowen, 2008).

This evidence suggests that frequent religious attendance may be a protective factor for chronic pain and fatigue. The same study also found that chronic pain patients who were religious or spiritual were more likely to use positive coping mechanisms than chronic pain patients who were not religious or spiritual (Baetz & Bowen, 2008).

Harrison et al. (2005) examined 127 African American individuals with sickle cell disease and found that more frequent attendance at church was related to lower sensory and affective experiences of pain, as well as fewer symptoms of somatization, depression, and anxiety. Frequent church attendance was also associated with lower self-reports of pain intensity among these individuals with sickle cell disease (Harrison et al., 2005).

The literature suggests that religious attendance has a salubrious impact on chronic pain. It is likely that religious attendance has an influence on social support, cognitive reframing, and other religious coping tools such as prayer, therefore providing a wide range of benefits for chronic pain sufferers.

Evidence for a Disadvantageous Relationship between Pain and Spirituality

Though there has been substantial literature in support of a positive relationship between pain and spirituality, some studies have also demonstrated a negative impact of spirituality on chronic pain outcomes. It is important to acknowledge that certain spiritual beliefs or coping styles can lead to maladaptive coping. Previous research delineates three forms of spiritual coping (Pargament et al., 1988) that stem from ritualistic practices of spirituality more so than theistic or existential. "Collaborative" coping involves an active personal exchange with a higher power in which there is a shared responsibility for one's own health. "Deferred" coping involves a passive deferral of responsibility for one's own health to a higher power. "Self-Directed" coping does not involve a higher power at all and emphasizes personal agency. Later, a fourth form of coping was identified. "Abandoned" describes an individual feeling fully responsible for their health because they are being abandoned or punished by God (Phillips III et al., 2004). This fourth form was associated with poorer psychological outcomes, including anxiety, depression, and self-esteem. Pargament (1997) also describes positive religious coping and negative religious coping, which also tend to be associated with advantageous and disadvantageous health-related outcomes (see Chapter 38, this volume), respectively, including in the context of pain.

Such findings regarding negative spiritual coping styles have been extended to pain-related outcomes, in addition to psychological outcomes. One study examined the use of positive and negative spiritual coping in a sample of 61 chronic pain patients. Here, positive coping was defined as an individual looking to a higher power for strength, comfort, and support and was associated with adaptive outcomes. Conversely, negative coping was defined as an individual viewing their pain as punishment from a higher power ("Punishing God") or feeling abandoned by God ("Absent God"). The study found that negative coping was associated with worse pain-related outcomes (Bush et al., 1999).

Rippentrop et al. (2005) examined 122 patients with chronic musculoskeletal pain. Although they hypothesized that spirituality would be significantly associated with better physical health, the study interestingly found that private religious activities like prayer and meditation were related to poorer physical health. However, the researchers posit that this effect may be a result of more severely disabled patients feeling the greatest need to rely on their faith for comfort.

Another cross-sectional study examined the impact of prayer and religious attendance on self-reports of pain, psychopathology, and healthcare utilization in 67 Black patients with sickle cell disease (O'Connell-Edwards et al., 2009). The study utilized a comprehensive self-report of psychopathology that included measures for anxiety, depression, hostility, obsessive-compulsivity, interpersonal sensitization, and somatization. Healthcare utilization consisted of reports of the number of hospitalizations, the number of emergency department visits, and the number of days hospitalized. Interestingly, this study found support for a curvilinear model of religious coping, such that moderate frequency of religious coping was associated with salubrious pain and psychopathology outcomes, compared to extremes of religious coping. In particular, those who endorsed moderate levels of religious coping showed significantly decreased anxiety, hostility, and affective reactions to pain. Those who engaged in the highest frequency of religious attendance generally reported the highest levels of psychopathology and affective reactions to pain, suggesting that extreme levels of religious coping are especially maladaptive. However, moderate religious coping was associated with significantly greater emergency department visits than low or high religious coping. This study highlights that extremes of spiritual coping are less effective in pain management and suggests an optimal level of spiritual coping to produce beneficial outcomes.

In line with these findings, Dezutter et al. (2011) found that individuals who were religiously non-affiliated and engaged in high levels of prayer had increases in pain severity and decreases in pain tolerance. Conversely, individuals who were religiously affiliated and engaged in high levels of prayer demonstrated decreases in pain severity and increases in pain tolerance. These striking findings highlight that prayer is only an effective pain management strategy when individuals believe in it. These findings were consistent across a wide range of belief systems. Thus, while spiritual coping techniques may offer favorable outcomes for those who affiliate with a religion, it may in fact be harmful to those who do not associate with a religion, emphasizing the importance of "believing" rather than merely "using" spiritual techniques.

Mechanisms of Spiritual Coping

As discussed, there are many forms of spiritual coping that have been linked to positive outcomes in chronic pain management. Further, some studies have suggested that spirituality acts as a protective factor against chronic pain. To better understand this relationship, the mechanisms through which spirituality influences pain have also been investigated. Wachholtz et al. (2007) outlined several pathways through which spiritual practices and coping strategies may facilitate better pain outcomes (see Figure 11.1). These pathways encompass the biopsychosocial-spiritual model of pain, demonstrating the potential for spiritual practices and unique spiritual factors to influence psychosocial factors, thereby altering physiological processes related to pain. Substantial literature has provided support for these pathways and mechanisms, such as self-efficacy, cognitive reframing, and meaning-making.

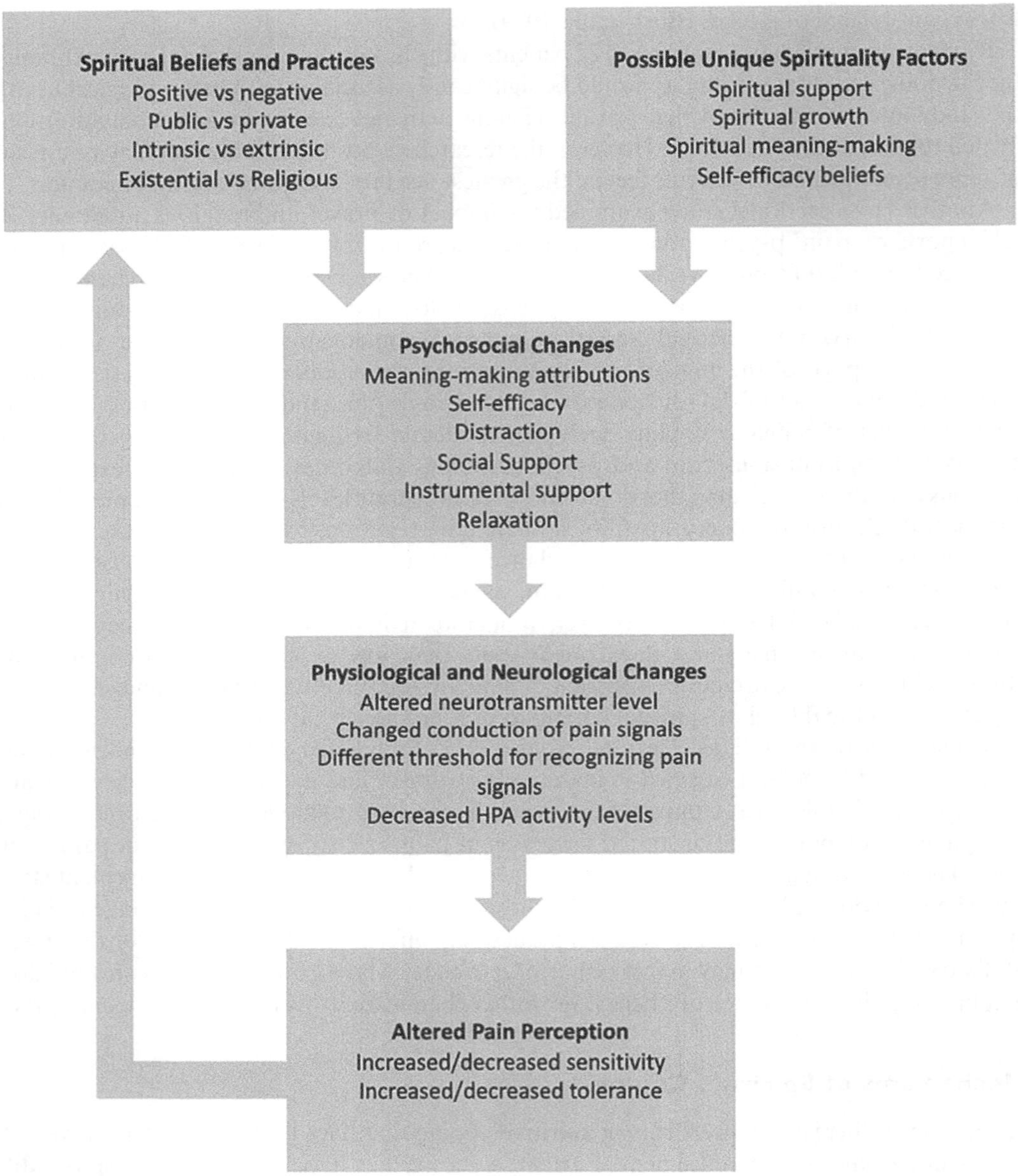

Figure 11.1 Potential Pathways between Spirituality and Pain.

Adapted from Wachholtz et al. (2007).

Pain self-efficacy refers to the belief held by individuals with chronic pain in their ability to carry out certain activities, even when experiencing pain. In a sample of 135 older adults with chronic pain, researchers found a significant positive correlation between pain self-efficacy and spirituality, suggesting pain self-efficacy may be a mechanism through which spirituality affects pain (Asadi-Piri et al., 2021). Another recent study replicated these results, finding that in a cross-sectional study of 150 chronic pain patients, spiritual health was associated with greater pain self-efficacy (Vasigh et al., 2020).

Dezutter, Wachholtz, and Corveleyn (2011) found that cognitive positive reappraisals mediated the relationship between prayer and pain tolerance. They posited that by praying, individuals were able to reframe their pain condition into more positive and meaningful terms (Dezutter et al., 2011). Such positive reappraisals are one technique that can facilitate meaning-making, a process that has been identified as a mediating variable through which spirituality influences chronic pain. A review found that pain tolerance was increased for individuals who were self-efficacious and open to seeking a connection to a meaningful spiritual practice (Lysne & Wachholtz, 2011), and this phenomenon has been further elucidated in neuroimaging studies. For instance, one study utilized functional magnetic resonance imaging (fMRI) in practicing Catholics and atheists, in which all participants were shown religious and non-religious images, received painful stimulation, and were then asked to rate their pain (Wiech et al., 2008). The study found that when the religious group was presented with a religious image, individuals were able to down-regulate pain perception, resulting in decreased pain ratings. However, this group demonstrated no differences in pain perception when presented with a non-religious image. Further, non-religious controls did not exhibit any modulation of pain during presentation of either image. The study reports that activation of the right ventrolateral prefrontal cortex (VLPFC) only occurred in the Catholic sample when individuals were shown a religious image and was accompanied by a decrease in subjective pain intensity. Indeed, research has consistently identified the role of the right VLPFC in cognitive down-modulation of pain (Lieberman et al., 2004; Wager et al., 2004), suggesting that religious belief that is meaningful to the individual may support engagement of pain-regulatory brain processes. This study is especially relevant to the aforementioned Gate Control and Neuromatrix theories of pain, as it demonstrates that spirituality has the potential to influence neural pathways of pain if the spirituality is meaningful to that individual.

In another study, 62 Portuguese adults with chronic musculoskeletal pain completed measures of spirituality, pain intensity, physical and psychological function, and pain coping (Ferreira-Valente et al., 2020). The studies revealed that spirituality – as hope and a positive perspective toward life – is linked with better psychological function and coping responses of ignoring pain sensations and coping self-statements. Further, spirituality – as a search for meaning and a sense of purpose – was associated with the coping response of task persistence. Task persistence was defined as "how often someone continued an activity despite pain," which also may be an indicator of self-efficacy. Thus, the study intimates an association between self-efficacy and spiritual meaning-making.

These studies demonstrate that spirituality may be a salubrious resource in not only positive psychological adjustment, but also in the ability to facilitate down-regulation of pain pathways in the brain. The literature suggests that various spiritual coping skills can promote self-efficacy, meaning-making, and positive pain coping and reframing, which in turn may alter the pain experience.

Future Directions

While the current literature offers evidence for the potential benefit of spirituality for chronic pain patients, there is also support for negative and differential outcomes. Of importance, the existing research is limited in its generalizability and inclusivity. Though more recent work has expanded its definitions of spirituality to be more encompassing of different religious backgrounds and the broad range of spiritual connections experienced by humankind, further research is needed to understand how spirituality impacts chronic pain across cultures. It should be noted that most of the foundational literature that exists regarding spirituality, coping, and chronic pain is based on non-diverse samples. For instance, the religious coping styles outlined by Pargament et al. (1988) and Phillips III et al. (2004) were developed from predominantly white and Christian samples. Furthermore, little research exists on spirituality and chronic pain in the context of non-Abrahamic spiritual frameworks, although many forms of meditation derived from Buddhist and Hindu traditions have been studied in a secular context for pain management (Singla, 2011). However, such Western, secularized meditation practices are actually vastly different from the Eastern spiritual practices and contexts they were developed from (Schmidt, 2011), and it has been suggested that reconnecting these meditation practices with their spiritual roots may enhance clinical practice and outcomes (Dimidjian & Linehan, 2003). Yoga is another spiritual practice that has been shown to be an effective alternative treatment for chronic pain (Schmid et al., 2019); however, it has not been studied within the true spiritual or cultural contexts of Hinduism. In fact, the inception of yoga as a Hindu spiritual practice is widely underrecognized. Acknowledgment of the spiritual frameworks that some alternative and complementary approaches to health and well-being come from is important, and studying these interventions with an in-depth understanding of the religious backgrounds they come from may allow for more nuanced findings. Indeed, Park et al. (2017) emphasizes the importance of considering spirituality variables within the religious culture in which they are embedded, asserting that this will facilitate a more sophisticated interpretation of the connection between spirituality and health (Park et al., 2017). Though many medical and social scientists lack adequate knowledge and openness to religious cultures (Best et al., 2016), engaging in these cultures with an open mind will result in advancement of the field as a whole. Future research should expand its scope of exploration to investigate how spirituality in different contexts around the globe may impact chronic pain outcomes and pain management.

In addition to including more diverse and inclusive samples and definitions of spirituality, improvement in the methodology of studies would allow for more in-depth understandings of the pathways between spirituality and chronic pain. In order to enhance the methodological rigor of research, it has been recommended that studies utilize prospective designs, experimental approaches, psychometrically robust measures of spirituality and health outcomes, appropriate statistical analyses with adequate power for moderator analyses, and control for established protective factors (Park et al., 2017; Rosmarin et al., 2011). There is also a call for consistency in conceptualization of spirituality variables across studies (Park et al., 2017; Rosmarin et al., 2011). Importantly, more randomized controlled trials could strengthen the use of spiritual coping practices as a non-pharmacological intervention for chronic pain.

Conclusions

The research summarized in this chapter highlights that spirituality can have a powerful impact on the pain experience. There is substantial evidence to support that, in some cases, spirituality facilitates better pain management, especially if aligned with the patients' beliefs.

Studies also emphasize the role of self-efficacy, cognitive reframing, meaning-making, and social support in the link between spirituality and improved pain outcomes. Conversely, some research demonstrates an association between spirituality and maladaptive pain coping, suggesting that the way and extent to which one engages in spirituality is important to its influence on chronic pain. Nevertheless, the integration of spiritual interventions with standard care (i.e., prayer, meditation, spiritual social support, and spiritual psychotherapy) may offer unique benefits to chronic pain patients, without the hazardous risks, escalated costs, or side effects of analgesic medications, surgeries, or devices.

References

Asadi-Piri, Z., Harvey, I. S., Imani-Nasab, M.-H., Zare, S., Nouraei Motlagh, S., & Cheraghi, N. (2021). Spirituality and pain self-efficacy in older adults with chronic pain: Evidence from Iran. *Journal of Religion, Spirituality & Aging*, *33*(3), 298–310. https://doi.org/10.1080/15528030.2020.1845277

Asmundson, G. J., & Katz, J. (2009). Understanding the co-occurrence of anxiety disorders and chronic pain: State-of-the-art. *Depression and Anxiety*, *26*(10), 888–901. https://doi.org/10.1002/da.20600

Baetz, M., & Bowen, R. (2008). Chronic pain and fatigue: Associations with religion and spirituality. *Pain Research and Management*, *13*(5), 383–388. https://doi.org/10.1155/2008/263751

Bair, M. J., Robinson, R. L., Katon, W., & Kroenke, K. (2003). Depression and pain comorbidity: a literature review. *Archives of Internal Medicine*, *163*(20), 2433–2445. https://doi.org/10.1001/archinte.163.20.2433

Benson, H., & Klipper, M. Z. (1975). *The relaxation response*. Morrow New York.

Best, M., Butow, P., & Olver, I. (2016). Doctors discussing religion and spirituality: A systematic literature review. *Palliative Medicine*, *30*(4), 327–337. https://doi.org/10.1177/0269216315600912

Brown, J. L., Sheffield, D., Leary, M. R., & Robinson, M. E. (2003). Social support and experimental pain. *Psychosomatic Medicine*, *65*(2), 276–283. https://doi.org/10.1097/01.PSY.0000030388.62434.46

Bush, E. G., Rye, M. S., Brant, C. R., Emery, E., Pargament, K. I., & Riessinger, C. A. (1999). Religious coping with chronic pain. *Applied Psychophysiology and Biofeedback*, *24*, 249–260. https://doi.org/10.1023/A:1022234913899

Carberg, C. (2023). Prescription Opioid Addiction Statistics. Retrieved November 23, 2023, from https://www.addictionhelp.com/prescription-opioids/statistics/#:~:text=25%25%20of%20patients%20prescribed%20opioids,(OxyContin%C2%AE%2C%20Percocet%C2%AE)

Carson, J. W., Keefe, F. J., Lynch, T. R., Carson, K. M., Goli, V., Fras, A. M., & Thorp, S. R. (2005). Loving-kindness meditation for chronic low back pain: results from a pilot trial. *Journal of Holistic Nursing*, *23*(3), 287–304. https://doi.org/10.1177/0898010105277651

Dezutter, J., Wachholtz, A., & Corveleyn, J. (2011). Prayer and pain: the mediating role of positive re-appraisal. *Journal of Behavioral Medicine*, *34*(6), 542–549. https://doi.org/10.1007/s10865-011-9348-2

Dimidjian, S., & Linehan, M. M. (2003). Defining an agenda for future research on the clinical application of mindfulness practice. *Clinical Psychology: Science and Practice*, *10*(2), 166–171. https://doi.org/10.1093/clipsy.bpg019

Ditre, J. W., Zale, E. L., & LaRowe, L. R. (2019). A reciprocal model of pain and substance use: Transdiagnostic considerations, clinical implications, and future directions. *Annual Review of Clinical Psychology*, *15*, 503–528. https://doi.org/10.1146/annurev-clinpsy-050718-095440

Duncan, L. G., Cohn, M. A., Chao, M. T., Cook, J. G., Riccobono, J., & Bardacke, N. (2017). Benefits of preparing for childbirth with mindfulness training: a randomized controlled trial with active comparison. *BMC Pregnancy and Childbirth*, *17*(1), 140. https://doi.org/10.1186/s12884-017-1319-3

Eilami, O., Moslemirad, M., Naimi, E., Babuei, A., & Rezaei, K. (2019). The Effect of Religious Psychotherapy Emphasizing the Importance of Prayers on Mental Health and Pain in Cancer Patients. *Journal of Religion and Health*, *58*(2), 444–451. https://doi.org/10.1007/s10943-018-0696-x

Eisenberger, N. I., Master, S. L., Inagaki, T. K., Taylor, S. E., Shirinyan, D., Lieberman, M. D., & Naliboff, B. D. (2011). Attachment figures activate a safety signal-related neural region and reduce pain experience. *Proceedings of the National Academy of Sciences*, *108*(28), 11721–11726. https://doi.org/10.1073/pnas.1108239108

Engel, G. L. (1977). The need for a new medical model: A challenge for biomedicine. *Science*, *196*(4286), 129–136. https://doi.org/10.1126/science.847460

Ferreira-Valente, A., Damião, C., Pais-Ribeiro, J., & Jensen, M. P. (2020). The role of spirituality in pain, function, and coping in individuals with chronic pain. *Pain Medicine*, *21*(3), 448–457. https://doi.org/10.1093/pm/pnz092

Garland, E. L. (2012). Pain processing in the human nervous system: a selective review of nociceptive and biobehavioral pathways. *Primary Care: Clinics in Office Practice*, *39*(3), 561–571. https://doi.org/10.1016/j.pop.2012.06.013

Gaskin, D. J., & Richard, P. (2012). The economic costs of pain in the United States. *Journal of Pain*, *13*(8), 715–724. https://doi.org/10.1016/j.jpain.2012.03.009

Harrison, M. O., Edwards, C. L., Koenig, H. G., Bosworth, H. B., Decastro, L., & Wood, M. (2005). Religiosity/spirituality and pain in patients with sickle cell disease. *Journal of Nervous and Mental Disease*, *193*(4), 250–257. https://doi.org/10.1097/01.nmd.0000158375.73779.50

Interagency Pain Research Coordinating Committee. (2016). National Pain Strategy: a comprehensive population health-level strategy for pain. Retrieved November 23, 2023, from https://www.iprcc.nih.gov/node/5/national-pain-strategy-report

Jensen, M. P., Ehde, D. M., Hoffman, A. J., Patterson, D. R., Czerniecki, J. M., & Robinson, L. R. (2002). Cognitions, coping and social environment predict adjustment to phantom limb pain. *Pain*, *95*(1-2), 133–142. https://doi.org/10.1016/S0304-3959(01)00390-6

Kabat-Zinn, J. (1993). Mindfulness meditation: health benefits of an ancient Buddhist practice In Goleman D & Gurin J (Eds.), *Mind/body medicine* (pp. 259–275). Consumer Reports Books.[Google Scholar].

Kabat-Zinn, J., Lipworth, L., & Burney, R. (1985). The clinical use of mindfulness meditation for the self-regulation of chronic pain. *Journal of Behavioral Medicine*, *8*(2), 163–190. https://doi.org/10.1007/bf00845519

Keefe, F. J., Lefebvre, J. C., Maixner, W., Salley, A. N., Jr., & Caldwell, D. S. (1997). Self-efficacy for arthritis pain: relationship to perception of thermal laboratory pain stimuli. *Arthritis & Rheumatology*, *10*(3), 177–184. https://doi.org/10.1002/art.1790100305

Kong, L. J., Lauche, R., Klose, P., Bu, J. H., Yang, X. C., Guo, C. Q., Dobos, G., & Cheng, Y. W. (2016). Tai Chi for Chronic Pain Conditions: A Systematic Review and Meta-analysis of Randomized Controlled Trials. *Scientific Reports*, *6*, 25325. https://doi.org/10.1038/srep25325

la Cour, P., & Petersen, M. (2015). Effects of mindfulness meditation on chronic pain: A randomized controlled trial. *Pain Medicine*, *16*(4), 641–652. https://doi.org/10.1111/pme.12605

Lee, H., Hübscher, M., Moseley, G. L., Kamper, S. J., Traeger, A. C., Mansell, G., & McAuley, J. H. (2015). How does pain lead to disability? A systematic review and meta-analysis of mediation studies in people with back and neck pain. *Pain*, *156*(6), 988–997. https://doi.org/10.1097/j.pain.0000000000000146

Lieberman, M. D., Jarcho, J. M., Berman, S., Naliboff, B. D., Suyenobu, B. Y., Mandelkern, M., & Mayer, E. A. (2004). The neural correlates of placebo effects: a disruption account. *NeuroImage*, *22*(1), 447–455. https://doi.org/10.1016/j.neuroimage.2004.01.037

Linton, S. J., Nicholas, M. K., MacDonald, S., Boersma, K., Bergbom, S., Maher, C., & Refshauge, K. (2011). The role of depression and catastrophizing in musculoskeletal pain. *European Journal of Pain*, *15*(4), 416–422. https://doi.org/10.1016/j.ejpain.2010.08.009

Lysne, C. J., & Wachholtz, A. B. (2011). Pain, Spirituality, and Meaning Making: What Can We Learn from the Literature? *Religions*, *2*(1), 1–16. https://doi.org/10.3390/rel2010001

McKee, D. D., & Chappel, J. N. (1992). Spirituality and medical practice. *The Journal of Family Practice*, *35*(2), 201, 205–206, 208.

Melzack, R. (1999). From the gate to the neuromatrix. *Pain, Suppl 6*, S121–S126. https://doi.org/10.1016/s0304-3959(99)00145-1

Melzack, R., & Wall, P. D. (1965). Pain mechanisms: a new theory. *Science, 150*(3699), 971–979. https://doi.org/10.1126/science.150.3699.971

National Institute on Drug Abuse. (2023). Drug overdose death rates. Retrieved November 23, 2023, from https://nida.nih.gov/research-topics/trends-statistics/overdose-death-rates#:~:text=Opioid%2Dinvolved%20overdose%20deaths%20rose,with%2080%2C411%20reported%20overdose%20deaths

O'Connell-Edwards, C. F., Edwards, C. L., Pearce, M., Wachholtz, A. B., Wood, M., Muhammad, M., Leach-Beale, B., Shelby, R., McDougald, C. S., & Harrison, M. O. (2009). Religious coping and pain associated with sickle cell disease: Exploration of a non-linear model. *Journal of African American Studies, 13*, 1–13. https://doi.org/10.1007/s12111-008-9063-4

Pargament, K. I. (1997). *The psychology of religious coping: Theory, research, practice*. Guilford Press.

Pargament, K. I., Kennell, J., Hathaway, W., Grevengoed, N., Newman, J., & Jones, W. (1988). Religion and the problem-solving process: Three styles of coping. *Journal for the Scientific Study of Religion*, 90–104. https://doi.org/10.2307/1387404

Park, C. L., Masters, K. S., Salsman, J. M., Wachholtz, A., Clements, A. D., Salmoirago-Blotcher, E., Trevino, K., & Wischenka, D. M. (2017). Advancing our understanding of religion and spirituality in the context of behavioral medicine. *Journal of Behavioral Medicine, 40*, 39–51. https://doi.org/10.1007/s10865-016-9755-5

Phillips III, R. E., Pargament, K. I., Lynn, Q. K., & Crossley, C. D. (2004). Self-directing religious coping: A deistic god, abandoning god, or no god at all? *Journal for the Scientific Study of Religion, 43*(3), 409–418. https://doi.org/10.1111/j.1468-5906.2004.00243.x

Rikard, M., Strahan, A., Schmit, K., Guy, G. (2023). Chronic Pain Among Adults — United States, 2019–2021. *Morbidity and Mortality Weekly Report, 72*, 379–385. http://doi.org/10.15585/mmwr.mm7215a1

Rippentrop, E. A., Altmaier, E. M., Chen, J. J., Found, E. M., & Keffala, V. J. (2005). The relationship between religion/spirituality and physical health, mental health, and pain in a chronic pain population. *Pain, 116*(3), 311–321. https://doi.org/10.1016/j.pain.2005.05.008

Roberts, R. L., Hanley, A. W., & Garland, E. L. (2022). Mindfulness-based interventions for perioperative pain management and opioid risk reduction following surgery: a stepped care approach. *The American Surgeon, 90*(5). https://doi.org/10.1177/00031348221114019

Rosmarin, D. H., Wachholtz, A., & Ai, A. (2011). Beyond descriptive research: Advancing the study of spirituality and health. *Journal of Behavioral Medicine, 34*, 409–413. https://doi.org/10.1007/s10865-011-9370-4

Schmid, A. A., Fruhauf, C. A., Sharp, J. L., Van Puymbroeck, M., Bair, M. J., & Portz, J. D. (2019). Yoga for people with chronic pain in a community-based setting: A feasibility and pilot RCT. *Journal of Evidence-Based Integrative Medicine, 24*, https://doi.org/10.1177/2515690X19863763

Schmidt, S. (2011). Mindfulness in east and west–is it the same? In H. Walach, S. Schmidt, & W. Jonas (Eds.), *Neuroscience, consciousness and spirituality: Studies in neuroscience, consciousness, and spirituality* (Vol. 1, pp. 23–38). Springer.

Singla, R. (2011). Origins of mindfulness & meditation: Interplay of eastern & western psychology. *Psyke & Logos, 32*(1), 220–239.

Sollgruber, A., Bornemann-Cimenti, H., Szilagyi, I.-S., & Sandner-Kiesling, A. (2018). Spirituality in pain medicine: A randomized experiment of pain perception, heart rate and religious spiritual well-being by using a single session meditation methodology. *PloS one, 13*(9), e0203336. https://doi.org/10.1371/journal.pone.0203336

Sulmasy, D. P. (2002). A biopsychosocial-spiritual model for the care of patients at the end of life. *The Gerontologist, 42*(Spec No 3), 24–33. https://doi.org/10.1093/geront/42.suppl_3.24

Tajadini, H., Zangiabadi, N., Divsalar, K., Safizadeh, H., Esmaili, Z., & Rafiei, H. (2017). Effect of prayer on intensity of migraine headache: A randomized clinical trial. *Journal of Evidenced-Based Complementary and Alternative Medicine, 22*(1), 37–40. https://doi.org/10.1177/2156587215627551

Tonelli, M. E., & Wachholtz, A. B. (2014). Meditation-based treatment yielding immediate relief for Meditation-Naïve Migraineurs. *Pain Management Nursing*, *15*(1), 36–40. https://doi.org/10.1016/j.pmn.2012.04.002

Tracey, I., & Mantyh, P. W. (2007). The cerebral signature for pain perception and its modulation. *Neuron*, *55*(3), 377–391. https://doi.org/10.1016/j.neuron.2007.07.012

Vasigh, A., Tarjoman, A., & Borji, M. (2020). Relationship between spiritual health and pain self-efficacy in patients with chronic pain: A cross-sectional study in West of Iran. *Journal of Religion and Health*, *59*(2), 1115–1125. https://doi.org/10.1007/s10943-019-00833-7

Wachholtz, A. B., Malone, C. D., & Pargament, K. I. (2017). Effect of different meditation types on migraine headache medication use. *Behavioral Medicine*, *43*(1), 1–8. https://doi.org/10.1080/08964289.2015.1024601

Wachholtz, A. B., & Pargament, K. I. (2008). Migraines and meditation: Does spirituality matter? *Journal of Behavioral Medicine*, *31*(4), 351–366. https://doi.org/10.1007/s10865-008-9159-2

Wachholtz, A. B., Pearce, M. J., & Koenig, H. (2007). Exploring the relationship between spirituality, coping, and pain. *Journal of Behavioral Medicine*, *30*(4), 311–318. https://doi.org/10.1007/s10865-007-9114-7

Wager, T. D., Rilling, J. K., Smith, E. E., Sokolik, A., Casey, K. L., Davidson, R. J., Kosslyn, S. M., Rose, R. M., & Cohen, J. D. (2004). Placebo-induced changes in fMRI in the anticipation and experience of pain. *Science*, *303*(5661), 1162–1167. https://doi.org/10.1126/science.1093065

Waltz, M., Kriegel, W., & Bosch, P. V. T. P. (1998). The social environment and health in rheumatoid arthritis: marital quality predicts individual variability in pain severity. *Arthritis & Rheumatology*, *11*(5), 356–374. https://doi.org/10.1002/art.1790110507

Webb, J. R., Toussaint, L., & Dula, C. S. (2014). Ritualistic, theistic, and existential spirituality: Initial psychometric qualities of the RiTE measure of spirituality. *Journal of Religion and Health*, *53*, 972–985. https://doi.org/10.1007/s10943-013-9697-y

Wiech, K., Farias, M., Kahane, G., Shackel, N., Tiede, W., & Tracey, I. (2008). An fMRI study measuring analgesia enhanced by religion as a belief system. *Pain*, *139*(2), 467–476. https://doi.org/10.1016/j.pain.2008.07.030

Zis, P., Daskalaki, A., Bountouni, I., Sykioti, P., Varrassi, G., & Paladini, A. (2017). Depression and chronic pain in the elderly: links and management challenges. *Clinical Interventions in Aging*, *12*, 709–720. https://doi.org/10.2147/cia.S113576

Chapter 12

Spirituality and Cardiovascular-Related Outcomes

Kevin S. Masters, Kristin E. Rabil, and Nicholas D. Kellar*

Cardiovascular disease (CVD) remains the leading cause of death in the United States and worldwide (Murphy et al., 2024; World Health Organization [WHO], 2021). Overall, CVD accounts for about a third of all deaths, and though sometimes thought of as a disease of rich countries, about 75% of CVD deaths take place in low- or middle-income countries (WHO, 2021). CVD constitutes a broad range of disorders of the heart and circulatory (blood vessel) system, including myocardial infarction (MI), heart failure (HF), and cerebrovascular disease, among many others. Several conditions predict the development of CVD and are therefore referred to as risk factors. These are often the focus of study in psychological or behavioral research and include hypertension (HTN), hypercholesterolemia, hyperlipidemia, hyperglycemia (and type 2 diabetes mellitus), abdominal obesity, and a clustering of these conditions forming the metabolic syndrome. Behaviors that predict both risk factors and CVD have garnered significant attention and empirical investigation. These include cigarette smoking, sedentary or insufficiently active lifestyle, and unhealthy diet (e.g., Krause et al., 2019; Mente et al., 2023; Ockene & Miller, 1997). Direct relations between psychological factors and various CVDs have been found for depression, anxiety, Type D personality, chronic daily stressors, post-traumatic stress disorder, and even, in the case of Takotsubo syndrome, significant acute stress (see Waldstein et al., 2022 for an overview and detail). Alternatively, psychological variables such as meaning, purpose, optimism, gratitude, positive affect, vitality, and religiousness and spirituality (R/S) have, in at least some studies, demonstrated protective relationships with cardiovascular (CV) outcomes (e.g., Boehm & Kubzansky, 2022; Levine et al., 2021; Masters et al., 2023).

The processes that connect behavioral factors with CVD are reasonably well understood (e.g., poor quality diets high in calories lead to obesity and hypercholesterolemia). Effects from psychological characteristics are thought to travel through two pathways: (1) psychological effects on behavioral practices; and (2) direct psychological effects on physiological processes (e.g., CV reactivity to psychological stress). Social support is often discussed as a psychosocial factor that can influence both behavioral and psychological functioning (see Masters, 2022). We presume that relationships with, or effects of, R/S on CV outcomes occur via the same processes.

Studying R/S in relation to CV outcomes is challenging. Both R/S and CV outcomes are multidimensional constructs, resulting in many possible targets for investigation. But perhaps

* Corresponding Author: kevin.masters@ucdenver.edu; The second and third authors contributed equally to the preparation of this manuscript.

DOI: 10.4324/9781003440048-15

more basic are considerations of the definition(s) of R/S. Previous investigators have addressed these issues (e.g., Hill et al., 2000; Kapuscinski & Masters, 2010; Paloutzian & Park, 2021). It has been generally concluded that both R/S concern understanding and relationship with what is thought of as sacred (e.g., divine being, higher power, and ultimate reality) or transcendent and that they are related, but not identical, constructs. Though many people experience their spirituality within the context of a religious organization formed around various doctrinal statements and containing a specific clerical structure, religiousness may contain aspects that are not specifically spiritual (e.g., social functions). Further, there is widespread agreement that spiritual understandings and experiences may occur without a religious context. Thus, it is possible to be religious but not spiritual or spiritual but not religious, though the latter is more likely.

Recently, Webb et al. (2014) organized this literature into a three-dimensional model of spirituality, referred to as the RiTE (Ritualistic, Theistic, and Existential) Model of Spirituality (see Chapters 1 and 44 of this volume). The comprehensive nature of their approach has much to recommend for future investigation. Only time will tell how widely it is adopted. Unfortunately, the literature relating R/S with CV function has not been guided by a consistent definition of either religiousness or spirituality. With the task before us of reviewing the literature, we were bound to the definitions and, more so, operationalizations of R/S that previous investigators utilized. Recognizing the multidimensional nature of these constructs, we attempted to broadly survey the literature with a focus on areas that have received the most empirical study from researchers, but also areas that had not been the focus of previous reviews. This resulted in the inclusion of sections emphasizing R/S behaviors, beliefs, communities, and interventions. To locate these studies, we conducted a multimethod, systematic search of literature published in the last 10 years across PubMed and PsycINFO. Using a standardized set of search terms, broadly covering religion, spirituality, and CV outcomes, we initially gathered 348 articles. These articles were reviewed, and a subset of them (k = 32) formed the basis for this chapter. Articles beyond the 10-year limit were included based on previous familiarity, searches of article reference lists, and the articles' ability to add both results and historical context.

Service Attendance

The most studied R/S variable in the CV literature has been religious service attendance (Meng et al., 2019). This is perhaps a function of the variable being included in epidemiological studies not specifically focused on R/S and due to the ease of assessment. Attending may be a proxy for other potentially important processes that will be noted throughout the chapter. Nevertheless, service attendance has been an important variable that has demonstrated significant relationships between R/S and several CV health outcomes.

Healthy Populations

Powell et al.'s (2003) systematic review of the R/S and health literature provides a starting point for discussion of service attendance and health. Through evaluation of 11 high-quality longitudinal studies, all-cause mortality was found to decrease by 25–30% through a dose-effect relationship with service attendance. R/S were also correlated to a decrease in overall CV risk and mortality, which was moderated by health behaviors and lifestyle. Although results were stronger in women than men, the relationship was significant in both. Chida et al. (2008) followed the systematic review with a meta-analysis examining relationships between R/S and all-cause and cause-specific mortality (including CV) in prospective observational cohort studies. Six studies in the meta-analysis examining CV disease were among healthy populations and found a protective relationship for R/S, broadly operationalized as service attendance, regarding CV mortality.

An example of a higher-quality study in the Powell et al. (2003) review was conducted by Hummer et al. (1999). They examined the service attendance relation to mortality and found that even when controlling for race, gender, and socioeconomic status in a nationally representative sample, all-cause mortality was lower, in a dose-response manner, for people who attended at least once a week compared to those who never attended. Cause-specific mortality for circulatory (i.e., CV) disease, which accounted for 42.6% of deaths, was also significantly higher for individuals who never attended compared to those who attended more than once per week. Their work demonstrated that R/S attendance has relationships with all-cause and CV mortality, though these effects were tempered by socioeconomic status, race, gender, and lifestyle (Hummer et al., 1999). Although not specific to CVD, it was notable that African Americans who attended services at least once a week demonstrated an almost 14-year difference in life expectancy at age 20 compared with those who never attended (Hummer et al., 1999).

In a 31-year longitudinal study of 6,545 residents of Alameda County, California, infrequent attendance was associated with a greater risk of mortality from circulatory diseases (Oman et al., 2002). These findings held in a model controlling only age and sex and in a full model that controlled for a range of demographics, social connection, and health behaviors. Though relative hazards were reduced when adjusting for social connections, models controlling for health behavior demonstrated more robust effects.

Social connections, health behaviors, and other potential mechanisms are mediated by physiological processes that include allostatic load (AL; see McEwen, 1998). AL, or specifically allostatic overload, is conceptualized as a physiological marker of repeated or chronic stress in daily life characterized by perturbations of physiological systems. Allostatic overload occurs, for example, if an individual continues to experience a physiological stress response following cessation of the stressor. In short, AL is the wear and tear on the body. Measures of AL include CV variables such as blood pressure and known CV risk factors such as cholesterol and homocysteine, along with measures of other systems. One possible pathway between R/S, including attendance, and CV outcomes lies in the possibility of reduced stress leading to adaptive allostatic responses.

In a longitudinal study utilizing NHANES III (Third National Health and Nutrition Examination Survey) data for individuals between 40 and 65 years of age, followed up to 18 years, Bruce et al. (2017) examined 5,449 Americans to investigate how service attendance related to AL and all-cause mortality. They demonstrated a higher adjusted mortality for non-attenders that was only somewhat attenuated when controlling for AL, suggesting that AL plays a role in the attendance-mortality relationship, but a significant independent relationship remains for attendance. Overall, in fully adjusted models, including demographic, health, socioeconomic, and behavioral covariates, a 55% decrease in all-cause mortality was found for frequent attenders (more than once a week) versus non-attenders. They also observed that non-attenders had significantly higher overall AL than attenders, in part due to greater percentages of the non-attenders being at high risk based on cholesterol and systolic blood pressure values.

Diverse Populations

Studies of Women

Though CVD is the leading cause of death worldwide in males and females, it is important to determine if R/S, particularly service attendance, manifests the same relationships in subgroups as in the general population. Li et al. (2016) conducted a longitudinal study of 74,534 healthy women followed from 1992 to 2012 and found a 33% decrease in all-cause mortality for women attending services at least once per week compared to non-service-attending women. Additionally, for that same comparison, they found a decrease in CVD mortality accounted for, in part, by smoking (22% of variance) and social support (23% of variance).

The Women's Health Initiative (Schnall et al., 2010) studied over 92,000 women across an average of 7.7 years. In models progressively adjusted for demographic, socioeconomic, self-reported health, psychosocial, health behavior, depression, and physical activity variables, religious service attendance demonstrated a protective effect against mortality for those who attended weekly or less than once per week compared with those who never attended. Depending on the model, service attendance had a protective relationship with all-cause mortality of 10–20%. However, service attendance did not predict CVD morbidity or mortality.

Ethnicity and Race

The Multi-Ethnic Study of Atherosclerosis (Feinstein et al., 2010) deliberately selected a multi-ethnic sample and examined the attendance and health relationship as well as possible mediators. During a mean follow-up of 4.1 years, they found that service attendance was not predictive of CVD events in a large and ethnically diverse sample (N = 5,474) that included White, Black, Hispanic, and Chinese participants. Across these groups, greater service attendance was related to decreased smoking but increased rates of obesity. The relationships between R/S and smoking are well established, but findings regarding diet/nutritional intake and weight are less clear. The investigators also provided cross-sectional analyses of subclinical coronary heart disease as indicated by coronary artery calcification, carotid intima-media thickness, left ventricular mass, and ankle brachial index, but none of the results were significant.

C-reactive protein (CRP) is a biomarker of general bodily inflammation as well as CV inflammation and is a risk factor for coronary artery disease and MI. Ferraro and Kim (2014) found that in a sample of US Black and White individuals without CV disease, CRP was inversely correlated with service attendance for Black attenders but not for White attenders.

Meng et al. (2019) conducted a systematic review to investigate the literature related to HTN and R/S, including possible race and gender differences. They found that the relationship between greater attendance and HTN was not consistent across different racial groups. For example, Bell et al. (2012) found in their nationally representative sample (N = 12,488) that the non-Hispanic White and Black service attenders had lower systolic blood pressure than non-attenders, but this was not the case for Hispanic attenders. Differences based on nationality have also been investigated. In two studies (Hill et al., 2014; Hill et al., 2017), investigators found significant relationships between CV markers and service attendance in both the United States (2014) and Mexican (2017) populations. Service attendance was correlated to lower pulse rates and AL compared to non-attendance, regardless of nationality.

Gender Differences

Similarly, Meng et al.'s (2019) review found conflicting results regarding gender and service attendance relative to blood pressure. For example, studies from Fonnebo (1988) in Norway (N = 37,981) and Bland et al. (1991) in New York (N = 1,409) did not find gender differences. The Duke Established Population for Epidemiologic Studies of the Elderly (Koenig, 1998) showed a 2–4/1–4 mmHg blood pressure difference (i.e., lower) for attenders, but gender only played a significant role in private religious practices and not service attendance.

Nevertheless, other studies suggest gender differences may exist. Service attendance is related to lower blood pressure in middle-aged Black women but not Black men and in Mexican American men at higher risk for HTN but not Mexican American women (Meng, 2019). Similarly, Maselko et al. (2007) found weekly attending males, aged 70–80, had higher AL-blood pressure risk than their weekly attending female colleagues. However, age may be a moderator of gender differences. Tartaro et al. (2005) found that weekly service-attending undergraduate men had lower blood pressure compared with undergraduate women. This mixed literature suggests that there may be male-female differences in the relations of religious service attendance with biomarkers of CVD, but understanding these differences is not clear.

Conclusions

Though space prohibited a full presentation of the studies, a relatively strong literature has investigated R/S service attendance and CV outcomes. Overall, the pattern of findings suggests that R/S attendance is related to better CV outcomes, though there are notable exceptions to the overall trend. In some cases (e.g., Schnall et al., 2010), relationships between attendance and CV outcomes were not found, whereas relations with all-cause mortality were. As research in the area has progressed, studies have become increasingly sophisticated, making better use of adequate controls and covariates to reduce the likelihood of rival hypotheses to account for the findings and examining specific populations.

R/S-Based Practices

Research has addressed the relationships between R/S-based practices and CV-related outcomes. Aspects of religious lifestyles, including prayer, exercise, and diet, have been investigated. We will highlight several studies that discuss various types of prayer in healthy populations as well as prayer as a coping mechanism for cardiac patients. Several other R/S practices are associated with CV outcomes, and we will discuss reviews and independent studies that illustrate the role of religious influences on diet and exercise in relation to CV outcomes.

Prayer

Several studies suggest that prayer yields beneficial CV outcomes in healthy populations. May et al. (2020) examined daily partner-focused petitionary prayer, whereby healthy, married couples that were assigned to pray for their spouses had improved CV efficiency as compared to waitlist and meditation groups. Specifically, left ventricular workload decreased, and coronary perfusion and blood flow increased for those in the prayer condition (measured by pulse wave analysis). Improved relationship quality accompanied the improvements in CV efficiency, pointing to the potential roles of interpersonal and social factors in the relationship between partner-focused petitionary prayer and CV outcomes.

Other forms of prayer have been shown to have benefits for CV health. Salat is an Islamic prayer practiced five times a day that involves several different postures and includes both obligatory and voluntary rituals. Chamsi-Pasha and Chamsi-Pasha (2021) reviewed approximately 26 studies on salat with Muslims worldwide and concluded that systolic blood pressure decreased after prayer and that those who regularly pray salat generally have lower blood pressure. We can hypothesize that these benefits are rooted in individual, meditation-like exercise as well as the social support contexts in which they are conducted. Salat activates the parasympathetic nervous system and deactivates the sympathetic nervous system, promoting relaxation and having similar benefits to meditation. Further, heart rate and blood pressure changes documented during salat may also be triggered by various maneuvers and changes in posture, leading the authors to consider it a form of exercise. The researchers also note the importance of the sense of community that accompanies salat in enhancing CV outcomes but acknowledge the need for more research (Chamsi-Pasha & Chamsi-Pasha, 2021).

Prayer, however, is a complex and diverse practice. Anderson and Nunnelley (2016) reviewed the associations of private prayer (i.e., praying by oneself) with mental and physical health outcomes and found mixed results. Similarly, Buck et al. (2009) utilized data from the Chicago Community Adult Health Study to assess the relationships between several R/S variables (attendance, prayer, spirituality, and R/S participation) and measures of blood pressure. They found a complex pattern of results wherein spirituality predicted higher diastolic blood pressure in the full analytic model (including sociodemographic, health, and possible mediating R/S variables) but not systolic blood pressure or HTN (as measured, not diagnosed). Prayer predicted HTN in the base models but not in the full model, and did not predict systolic or diastolic blood pressure. Further, Skipper et al. (2022) found that Black men with diagnosed HTN were significantly more likely to pray than Black men without HTN. It is possible that those with HTN were engaging in prayer as a means of religious coping, rather than prayer being a cause of their HTN. The use of prayer as a coping mechanism has been seen in cardiac patients as well. In coronary artery bypass patients, the majority used prayer to cope, and this was associated with more favorable mental health outcomes after surgery (Ai et al., 2000). In a separate sample of cardiac patients, the use of prayer to cope before surgery was associated with less mental fatigue after cardiac surgery, but it had no effect on physical fatigue (Ai et al., 2012).

In first-time MI or coronary artery revascularization bypass surgery patients, increases in religious coping were associated with improved quality of life outcomes (Trevino & McConnell, 2014), supporting the notion that religious coping brings psychological benefits to cardiac patients who engage in these behaviors. Prayer is often a form of religious coping, but the practices are not identical; for example, religious coping can include activities such as understanding stressful events through a religious lens or reading sacred texts. In a prospective study of R/S coping and incident HTN in Black women, Cozier et al. (2018) found that the extent to which women reported utilizing R/S positive coping in response to stressful events was associated with a 13% risk reduction for incident HTN. This relationship was found only when other R/S measures were controlled. Notably, more frequent prayer predicted higher incident HTN.

Methodologically, it can be difficult to distinguish the direction of the relationship between prayer and health conditions. It is important to study both cross-sectional and longitudinal associations between prayer and health to try and ascertain the temporal nature of the relationships. Though always being wary of presuming causality in any type of observational study, one might be tempted to conclude that a positive relationship between prayer and a negative health outcome is due to prayer leading to poor health when, in fact, it could be that patients are engaging in more prayer because of declining health (Ai et al., 1998).

Religiously Influenced Lifestyle Practices

In addition to prayer, there are other R/S-based practices related to CV outcomes. For instance, in a comparison of Buddhist monks and nuns versus non-religious Tibetans, the Buddhist monks and nuns had lower systolic and diastolic blood pressure, triglycerides, low-density lipoprotein cholesterol, and blood glucose as compared to the non-religious Tibetan residents, which was attributed to Buddhist practices (meditation-like activity) and a vegetarian diet (Meng et al., 2018). Both the meditation and diet were based on religious principles. Similarly, in Japan, those who considered themselves to be religious were less likely to smoke and consume alcohol and were more likely to exercise regularly (Kobayashi et al., 2015).

Fasting is another religious behavior that could have effects on CV outcomes. In a review of 36 studies on Ramadan fasting (refraining from food, drinking, smoking, and sex during the holy month), investigators found that fasting was shown to improve lipid profiles and decrease blood pressure and body mass index in patients with HTN (Salim et al., 2013). More recently, however, Kokkinopoulou et al. (2023) examined rates of metabolic syndrome in members of the Christian Orthodox Church who have consistently fasted since childhood during the 180–200 fasting days throughout the year, including the 40 days before Christmas and 48 days before Easter. During this fast, members avoid meat, dairy, and eggs. No constraints exist regarding the quantity and timing of food, and thus, members may adopt a plant-based diet. There was no statistically significant difference in the prevalence of metabolic syndrome in those who fasted versus those who did not.

Overall, religious lifestyle factors, including diet and exercise, are related to CV health. Considerable evidence supports the notion that, for some people, practices based on religious belief influence their adherence to certain lifestyles, which may then have CV benefits. To be clear, anyone who does not smoke, for example, gains CV benefit regardless of religious status. But in this section, we explore groups who maintain healthy lifestyles *because* of their religious beliefs and community. In a study of 257 Polish immigrants in Germany, those who considered themselves more religious were at lower risk of smoking and drinking alcohol, as compared with those who were less religious (Morawa & Erim, 2018). They were also more likely to be overweight or obese compared to the less religious, but no relationship was found between their religiousness and physical activity. Intrinsic religiousness, or the centrality of religion in one's life, may be a protective factor for health broadly, as well as for specific CV markers. The centrality of religion in the Polish immigrants and its association with lower smoking and drinking presented an example of how their beliefs were related to their lifestyle, which could have benefits for their overall health.

Evidence also suggests that some religious groups practice health-enhancing behaviors more than the general population and experience CV benefits. For example, members of the Church of Jesus Christ of Latter-day Saints (Latter-day Saints; previously referred to as Mormons) are encouraged to prioritize family life and well-balanced diets while avoiding the use of alcohol, tobacco, coffee, or other substances, and they show reduced mortality rates relative to the general population (Enstrom & Breslow, 2008). This group practices these health behaviors at high rates, as demonstrated by a group of Mormon high priests, or long-term devout members. Enstrom (1989) found that 76% of high priests exercise often or sometimes, 82% regularly get seven to eight hours of sleep, and 75% have never smoked in their lives. Additionally, Enstrom compared the Latter-day Saint group to a group of "Mormon-like" individuals in Alameda County, California, who were not Latter-day Saints but attended church weekly and did not smoke. These individuals demonstrated similar benefits as the Latter-day Saints in their standardized mortality ratios, including all-cause mortality and CV disease. Moreover, Loma Linda, California, was identified as one of the "Blue Zones" of the world because its inhabitants outlive the rest of the American population by 10 years (Buettner & Skemp, 2016). Loma Linda is home to Seventh-day Adventists, who maintain a plant-based diet, abstain from tobacco, and rest on the Sabbath (Buettner & Skemp, 2016). Seventh-day Adventists have long been studied because they have a lower risk of coronary heart disease as compared to other Californians, part of which could be explained by their religious lifestyles and community (Fraser, 1999). The increase in health-enhancing behaviors by these religious groups strengthens the idea that religiously based lifestyles have effects on CV health.

Church-Placed and Faith-Based Interventions

We have established that religious practices and health behaviors based on religious principles play a role in CV health. A different, but related, line of research explores *interventions* we refer to as "church-placed" or "faith-based." The primary point of distinction is the extent to which the interventions integrate aspects of the faith belief system into their content versus conducting standard health interventions at a house of worship. We do not intend to be exclusive with the use of "church," we recognize and respect the various types of worship settings across faiths; however, nearly all the research in this area has been conducted in churches.

Maroney et al. (2023) reviewed results of 81 church-placed intervention studies, looking only at articles that examined CV risk factors in adults as primary outcomes. Many of these studies were randomized controlled trials (47%), whereas 14% were non-randomized studies, and another 39% were pre-post studies without comparison groups. Meta-analytic findings indicate that these interventions improved diets, increased physical exercise, reduced weight, and reduced blood pressure in participants. Though the authors referred to their review as consisting of "church-placed" interventions, using our nomenclature, many of these studies were also "faith-based." For example, 43% included scripture and prayer in the intervention components.

Perhaps the most extensive intervention study specifically focusing on a religious population was conducted by Proeschold-Bell et al. (2017). They conducted a 2-year randomized controlled trial of a multicomponent health intervention (Spirited Life) that targeted both metabolic syndrome and stress among United Methodist clergy in North Carolina. They successfully randomized 1,114 participants. The intervention had several aspects, but what was required was an initial 3-day workshop that included cognitive-behavioral skills-based interventions from the Williams LifeSkills stress management program (Williams & Williams, 1993, 2006). Specifically included for this population was significant theological content integrated into the workshops. Though theological study is an important aspect of the job of clergy, the investigators surmised that demands on clergy often limit their ability to take the lessons of scripture and apply them to their own lives (e.g., caring for one's health as an aspect of Christian stewardship). Results demonstrated significant reductions in metabolic syndrome at 12 months that were maintained at 24 months. These improvements centered on central obesity, HDL cholesterol, and blood pressure.

Further, these church-placed and faith-based interventions have been an effective way to bridge gaps in the healthcare system by reaching minority communities, particularly African American and Latin American populations. In the review conducted by Maroney et al. (2023), 74% of the studies were in predominantly African American churches, 11% were in churches with multiracial membership, and 5% were in predominantly Hispanic churches. For minority communities, it may be beneficial to have an intervention that addresses health disparities within an institution that the community trusts and seeks comfort in. The authority and influence that the church has in people's lives is significant, and the sense of belonging that comes with having a community that shares similar beliefs can be powerful in shaping behavior. Fraser (1999) suggests that religious communities embedding healthy lifestyles into their beliefs and practices will elicit positive results through the social support that people receive by being with others who also believe the body to be sacred and worthy of protection.

A few specific studies will be highlighted. Lynch et al. (2019) tested the feasibility and acceptability of an intervention to address Black-White health disparities in CV disease. The primary aim was to increase vegetable consumption, with secondary aims of weight and blood pressure reduction. This study is of particular interest for several reasons. First, it was both church-placed and faith-based. For instance, a Bible study was part of the intervention. The content of the Bible study focused on scripture that explicitly taught eating healthier, and the team encouraged prayer and faith as supports for behavior change. Further, the intervention was delivered by pastors and church members. Two hundred and six people enrolled in this nine-month program, 90% of whom were African American. The intervention was integrated into existing church activities, such as Bible study and small group sessions, and the results were promising. Not only were there dietary improvements indicated by vegetable consumption, but participants also showed significant decreases in weight and blood pressure. Importantly, participants rated Bible study to be the most helpful aspect of the intervention, demonstrating the importance of aligning interventions with community beliefs and values, and it is thought that the success of the intervention was largely related to the collaboration of pastors, church leaders, and researchers. The trust that church members have in their faith and church leaders added credibility to the program.

Derose et al. (2019) conducted a pilot study in African American and Latino churches that involved mobile messaging, pastor sermons, cooking and nutrition classes, and a church garden to target diet and exercise. Preliminary findings suggested that participants had significant weight loss, decreased body mass index, and improved diet, but there were no significant changes in blood pressure or physical activity. Challenges to implementation were noted, particularly with respect to deciding the dosage of certain activities, but the initial findings support the multilevel approach to implementing these programs in churches.

Another intervention program was created specifically to reduce HTN in African Americans, though for this pilot, the researchers were more interested in determining feasibility, acceptability, and retention than reductions in HTN (Skolarus et al., 2018). This program utilized text messaging to reach out to church members and encourage healthy habits, leveraging a low-cost communication strategy. Participants did not have changes in their blood pressure at the end of the intervention, but 100% reported satisfaction with the intervention, and the researchers are confident in its feasibility moving forward.

Many of these interventions are in the pilot testing phase and have demonstrated strong signals of physiological improvements along with widespread acceptability and feasibility of integrating health interventions into communities of faith. We are aware that some investigators have followed their pilots with larger-scale studies that are ongoing. We strongly encourage continued work in this domain. These interventions leverage crucial factors that could help encourage healthy living, namely the social support that comes with a faith community, alignment of the interventions with the group's values and beliefs, and the ability to reach groups characterized by health disparities within institutions they trust. These interventions used a community-based participatory research approach, integrating the trusted social network that the church provides people with the research, and including the community in decision-making.

As noted, many of the studies have been conducted in African American or Latino churches, highlighting the role of the church in reaching groups that are often excluded from health initiatives. It is possible that, with adaptations, these interventions could be applied to other groups who similarly face health disparities and do not trust health authorities. Case and Deaton (2015) observed that while mortality rates have generally declined from 1999 to 2013, they increased for middle-aged White non-Hispanic men and women primarily characterized by lower education and socioeconomic status. The deaths were explained primarily by drug and alcohol poisonings, suicide, and chronic liver diseases, the so-called "deaths of despair." It is possible that similarly developed church-placed/faith-based interventions may provide an entrée into these populations as well.

Conclusion

Though research into the relations between R/S and CV outcomes has significantly increased in both depth and breadth, only the very top of the surface has been scratched. Significant work remains to not only firmly establish and specify recognized relationships but also to seek greater understanding of causal mechanisms and, at the very practical level, develop spiritual interventions that target both psychological and behavioral variables that influence CV outcomes. We are particularly optimistic regarding the latter. Sustained health- and CV-related psychological and behavioral change is difficult, with most studies finding disappointingly high rates of return to baseline over the long run. Church-placed/faith-based interventions, however, may have a significant "secret sauce" because they involve the integration of health-related changes into existing communities of faith. These communities are structured to combine substantial social support within an encompassing, spiritual worldview. This combination may prove to be potent not only in terms of reaching and initiating changes among those who are underserved and lack trust in the healthcare system, but also in maintaining health gains over time due to the personal and spiritual infrastructure in place to uphold the changes. Only time and extensive research will tell if our hunches are correct, but we sincerely hope that both investigators and funders will have an interest in pursuing this line of research because the potential benefits are tremendous. Meanwhile, we are also bullish on the continued investigation of basic R/S and CV relationships and precise delineation of potent processes that are involved therein. Both R/S and, unfortunately, CVD are widespread among millions of people. Further development of understanding of their relations is important for the scientific agenda.

References

Ai, A. L., Bolling, S. F., & Peterson, C. (2000). The use of prayer by coronary artery bypass patients. *International Journal for the Psychology of Religion*, *10*(4), 205–220. https://doi.org/10.1207/S15327582IJPR1004_01

Ai, A. L., Dunkle, R. E., Peterson, C., & Boiling, S. F. (1998). The role of private prayer in psychological recovery among midlife and aged patients following cardiac surgery. *The Gerontologist*, *38*(5), 591–601. https://doi.org/10.1093/geront/38.5.591

Ai, A. L., Wink, P., & Shearer, M. (2012). Fatigue of survivors following cardiac surgery: Positive influences of preoperative prayer coping: Prayer coping and vitality after cardiac surgery. *British Journal of Health Psychology*, *17*(4), 724–742. https://doi.org/10.1111/j.2044-8287.2012.02068.x

Anderson, J. W., & Nunnelley, P. A. (2016). Private prayer associations with depression, anxiety and other health conditions: An analytical review of clinical studies. *Postgraduate Medicine*, *128*(7), 635–641. https://doi.org/10.1080/00325481.2016.1209962

Bell, C.N., Bowie, J. V., & Thorpe, R. J. Jr. (2012). The interrelationship between hypertension and blood pressure, attendance at religious services, and race/ethnicity. *Journal of Religion and Health*, *51*(2), 310–322. https://www.jstor.org/stable/41653771

Bland, S. H., Krogh, V., Winkelstein, W., & Trevisan, M. (1991). Social Network and Blood Pressure: A Population Study. *Psychosomatic Medicine*, 53(6), 598–607. https://doi.org/10.1097/00006842-199111000-00002

Boehm, J. K., & Kubzansky, L. D. (2022). Positive psychological well-being and cardiovascular disease. In S. R. Waldstein et al. (Eds.), *Handbook of cardiovascular behavioral medicine* (pp. 541–569). Springer Nature. https://doi.org/10.1007/978-0-387-85960-6_27

Bruce, M. A., Martins, D., Duru, K., Beech, B. M., Sims, M., Harawa, N., Vargas, R., Kermah, D., Nicholas, S. B., Brown, A., & Norris, K. C. (2017). Church attendance, allostatic load and mortality in middle aged adults. *PLoS One*, *12*(5), e0177618. https://doi.org/10.1371/journal.pone.0177618

Buck, A. C., Williams, D. R., Musick, M. A., & Sternthal, M. J. (2009). An examination of the relationship between multiple dimensions of religiosity, blood pressure, and hypertension. *Social Science & Medicine*, *68*(2), 314–322. https://doi.org/10.1016/j.socscimed.2008.10.010

Buettner, D., & Skemp, S. (2016). Blue zones: Lessons from the world's longest lived. *American Journal of Lifestyle Medicine*, *10*(5), 318–321. https://doi.org/10.1177/1559827616637066

Case, A., & Deaton, A. (2015). Rising morbidity and mortality in midlife among white non-Hispanic Americans in the 21st century. *Proceedings of the National Academy of Sciences*, *112*(49), 15078–15083. https://doi.org/10.1073/pnas.1518393112

Chamsi-Pasha, M., & Chamsi-Pasha, H. (2021). A review of the literature on the health benefits of Salat (Islamic prayer). *The Medical Journal of Malaysia*, *76*(1), 93–97.

Chida, Y., Steptoe, A., & Powell, L. H. (2008). Religiosity/spirituality and mortality. *Psychotherapy and Psychosomatics*, *78*(2), 81–90. https://doi.org/10.1159/000190791

Cozier, Y. C., Yu, J., Wise, L. A., VanderWeele, T. J., Balboni, T. A., Argentieri, M. A., Rosenberg, L., Palmer, J. R., & Shields, A. E. (2018). Religious and spiritual coping and risk of incident hypertension in the black women's health study. *Annals of Behavioral Medicine*, *52*(12), 989–998. https://doi.org/10.1093/abm/kay001

Derose, K. P., Williams, M. V., Flórez, K. R., Ann Griffin, B., Payán, D. D., Seelam, R., Branch, C. A., Hawes-Dawson, J., Mata, M. A., Whitley, M. D., & Wong, E. C. (2019). Eat, pray, move: A pilot cluster randomized controlled trial of a multilevel church-based intervention to address obesity among African Americans and Latinos. *American Journal of Health Promotion: AJHP*, *33*(4), 586–596.https://doi.org/10.1177/0890117118813333

Enstrom, J. E. (1989). Health practices and cancer mortality among active California Mormons. *JNCI Journal of the National Cancer Institute*, *81*(23), 1807–1814. https://doi.org/10.1093/jnci/81.23.1807

Enstrom, J. E., & Breslow, L. (2008). Lifestyle and reduced mortality among active California Mormons, 1980–2004. *Preventive Medicine*, *46*(2), 133–136. https://doi.org/10.1016/j.ypmed.2007.07.030

Feinstein, M., Liu, K., Ning, H., Fitchett, G., & Lloyd-Jones, D. M. (2010). Burden of CV risk factors, subclinical atherosclerosis, and incident CV events across dimensions of religiosity: The multi-ethnic study of atherosclerosis. *Circulation*, *121*(5), 659–666. https://doi.org/10.1161/circulationaha.109.879973

Ferraro, K. F., & Kim, S. (2014). Health benefits of religion among Black and White older adults? Race, religiosity, and C-reactive protein. *Social Science and Medicine*, *120*, 92–99. https://doi.org/10.1016/j.socscimed.2014.08.030

Fonnebo, V. (1988). The Tromso Heart Study: Diet, religion, and risk factors for coronary heart disease. *American Journal of Clinical Nutrition*, 48(3), 826–829. https://doi.org/10.1093/ajcn/48.3.826

Fraser, G. E. (1999). Diet as primordial prevention in Seventh-Day Adventists. *Preventive Medicine*, *29*(6), S18–S23. https://doi.org/10.1006/pmed.1998.0415

Hill, P. C., Pargament, K. I., Hood, R. W., McCullough, J. M. E., Swyers, J. P., Larson, D. B., & Zinnbauer, B. J. (2000). Conceptualizing religion and spirituality: Points of commonality, points of departure. *Journal for the Theory of Social Behaviour*, *30*, 51–77. https://doi.org/10.1111/1468-5914.00119

Hill, T. D., Rote, S. M., & Ellison, C. G. (2017). Religious participation and biological functioning in Mexico. *Journal of Aging and Health*, *29*(6), 951–972. https://doi.org/10.1177/0898264317716244

Hill, T. D., Rote, S. M., Ellison, C. G., & Burdette, A. M. (2014). Religious attendance and biological functioning: A multiple specification approach. *Journal of Aging and Health*, *26*(5), 766–785. https://doi.org/10.1177/0898264314529333

Hummer, R. A., Rogers, R. G., Nam, C. B., & Ellison, C. G. (1999). Religious involvement and U.S. adult mortality. *Demography*, *36*(2), 273–285.

Kapuscinski, A. N., & Masters, K. S. (2010). The current status of measures of spirituality: a critical review of scale development. *Psychology of Religion and Spirituality*, *2*(4), 191–205. https://doi.org/10.1037/a0020498

Kobayashi, D., Shimbo, T., Takahashi, O., Davis, R. B., & Wee, C. C. (2015). The relationship between religiosity and CV risk factors in Japan: A large–scale cohort study. *Journal of the American Society of Hypertension*, *9*(7), 553–562. https://doi.org/10.1016/j.jash.2015.04.003

Koenig, H. G., George, L. K., Hays, J. C., Larson, D. B., Cohen, H. J., & Blazer, D. G. (1998). The relationship between religious activities and blood pressure in older adults. *International Journal of Psychiatry in Medicine*, *28*(2), 189–213. https://doi.org/10.2190/75JM-J234-5JKN-4DQD

Kokkinopoulou, A., Rodopaios, N. E., Koulouri, A.-A., Vasara, E., Papadopoulou, S. K., Skepastianos, P., Dermitzakis, E., Hassapidou, M., & Kafatos, A. G. (2023). Impact of christian orthodox church fasting on metabolic syndrome components in adults aged 18–49 years. *Nutrients*, *15*(7), 1755. https://doi.org/10.3390/nu15071755

Krause, W. E., Powell, K. E., Haskell, W. L., Janz, K. F., Campbell, W. W., Jakicic, J. M., Troiano, R. P., Sprow, K., Torres, A., Piercy, K. L., and 2018 Physical Activity Guidelines Advisory Committee. (2019). Physical activity, all-cause and cardiovascular mortality, and cardiovascular disease. *Medicine & Science in Sports and Exercise*, 51(6), 1270–1281. Doi: 10.1249/MSS.0000000000001939

Levine, G. N., Cohen, B. E., Commodore-Mensah, Y., Fleury, J., Huffman, J. C., Khalid, U., Labarthe, D. R., Lavretsky, H., Michos, E. D., Spatz, E. S., Kubzansky, L. D. on behalf of the American Heart Association Council on Clinical Cardiology; Council on Arteriosclerosis, Thrombosis and Vascular Biology; Council on Cardiovascular and Stroke Nursing; and Council on Lifestyle and Cardiometabolic Health. (2021). Psychological health, well-being, and the mind-heard-body connection: A scientific statement from the American Heart Association. *Circulation*, 143:00–00, doi:10.1161/CIR.0000000000000947

Li, S., Stampfer, M. J., Williams, D. R., & VanderWeele, T. J. (2016). Association of religious service attendance with mortality among women. *JAMA Internal Medicine*, *176*(6), 777–785. https://doi.org/10.1001/jamainternmed.2016.1615

Lynch, E., Emery-Tiburcio, E., Dugan, S., White, F. S., Thomason, C., Jenkins, L., Feit, C., Avery-Mamer, E., Wang, Y., Mack, L., & Ragland, A. (2019). Results of alive: A faith-based pilot intervention to improve diet among African American church members. *Progress in Community Health Partnerships: Research, Education, and Action*, *13*(1), 19–30. https://doi.org/10.1353/cpr.2019.0005

Maroney, K., Laurent, J., Alvarado, F., Gabor, A., Bell, C., Ferdinand, K., He, J., & Mills, K. T. (2023). Systematic review and meta-analysis of church-based interventions to improve CV disease risk factors. *The American Journal of the Medical Sciences*, *366*(3), 199–208. https://doi.org/10.1016/j.amjms.2023.05.010

Maselko, J., Kubzansky, L., Kawachi, I., Seeman, T., & Berkman, L. (2007). Religious service attendance and allostatic load among high-functioning elderly. *Psychosomatic Medicine*, *69*(5), 464–472. https://doi.org/10.1097/PSY.0b013e31806c7c57

Masters, K. S. (2022). Religion, spirituality, and cardiovascular disease. In S. R. Waldstein et al. (Eds.), *Handbook of cardiovascular behavioral medicine* (pp. 655–674). Springer Nature. https://doi.org/10.1007/978-0-387-85960-6_27

Masters, K. S., Boehm, J. K., Boylan, J. M., Vagnini, K. M., & Rush, C. L. (2023). The scientific study of positive psychology, religion/spirituality, and physical health. In E. B. Davis, E. L. Worthington, Jr., & S. A. Schnitker (Eds.), *Handbook of positive psychology, religion, and spirituality* (pp. 329–342). Springer. https://doi.org/10.1007/978-3-031-10274-5

May, R. W., Cooper, A. N., & Fincham, F. D. (2020). Prayer in marriage to improve wellness: Relationship quality and CV functioning. *Journal of Religion and Health*, *59*(6), 2990–3003. https://doi.org/10.1007/s10943-019-00829-3

McEwen, B. S. (1998). Stress, adaptation, and disease: Allostasis and allostatic load. *Annals of the New York Academy of Sciences*, *840*(1), 33–44.

Meng, Q., Xu, Y., Shi, R., Zhang, X., Wang, S., Liu, K., & Chen, X. (2018). Effect of religion on hypertension in adult Buddhists and residents in China: A cross-sectional study. *Scientific Reports*, *8*, 8203. https://doi.org/10.1038/s41598-018-26638-4

Meng, Q., Zhang, X., Shi, R., Liao, H., & Chen, X. (2019). Correlation between religion and hypertension. *Internal Emergency Medicine*, *14*(2), 209–237. https://doi.org/10.1007/s11739-018-1791-4

Mente, A., Dehghan, M., Rangarajan, S., O'Donnell, M., Hu, W., Dagenais, G., Wielgosz, A., Lear, S. A., Wie, L., Diaz, R., Avezum, A., Lopez-Jaramillo, P., Lanas, F., Swaminathan, S., Kaur, M., Vijayakumar, K., Mohan, V., Gupta, R., Szuba, A.,… Yusuf, S. (2023). Diet, cardiovascular disease, and mortality in 80 countries. *European Heart Journal*, 44, 2560–2579. https://doi.org/10.1093/eurheartj/ehad269

Morawa, E., & Erim, Y. (2018). Health-related lifestyle behavior and religiosity among first-generation immigrants of polish origin in germany. *International Journal of Environmental Research and Public Health*, *15*(11), 2545. https://doi.org/10.3390/ijerph15112545

Murphy, S. L., Kochanek, K. D., Xu, J. Q., Arias, E. (2024). *Mortality in the United States, 2023. NCHS Data Brief, no 521*. Hyattsville, MD: National Center for Health Statistics. https://doi.org/10.15620/cdc/170564

Ockene, I. S., & Miller, N. H., for the American Heart Association Task Force on Risk Reduction. (1997). Cigarette smoking, cardiovascular disease, and stroke: A statement for healthcare professionals from the American Heart Association, *Circulation*, 96(9), 3243–3247. https://doi.org/10.1161/01.CIR.96.9.3243

Oman, D., Kurata, J. H., Strawbridge, W. J., & Cohen, R. D. (2002). Religious attendance and cause of death over 31 years. *International Journal of Psychiatry in Medicine*, *32*(1), 69–89. https://doi.org/10.2190/rjy7-crr1-hcw5-xveg

Paloutzian, R. F., & Park, C. L. (2021). The psychology of religion and spirituality: how big the tent? *Psychology of Religion and Spirituality*, *13*(1), 3–13. https://dx.doi.org/10.1037/rel0000218

Powell, L. H., Shahabi, L., & Thoresen, C. E. (2003). Religion and spirituality: Linkages to physical health. *American Psychologist*, *58*(1), 36–52. https://doi.org/10.1037/0003-066X.58.1.36

Proeschold-Bell, R. J., Turner, E. L., Bennett, G. G., Yao, J., Li, X.-F., Eagle, D. E., Meyer, R. A., Williams, R. B., Swift, R. Y., Moore, H. E., Kolkin, M. A., Weisner, C. C., Rugani, K. M., Hough, H. J., Williams, V. P., & Toole, D. C. (2017). A 2-year holistic health and stress intervention: Results of an rct in clergy. *American Journal of Preventive Medicine*, *53*(3), 290–299. https://doi.org/10.1016/j.amepre.2017.04.009

Salim, I., Al Suwaidi, J., Ghadban, W., Alkilani, H., & Salam, A. M. (2013). Impact of religious Ramadan fasting on CV disease: A systematic review of the literature. *Current Medical Research and Opinion*, *29*(4), 343–354. https://doi.org/10.1185/03007995.2013.774270

Schnall, E., Wassertheil-Smoller, S., Swencionis, C., Zemon, V., Tinker, L., O'Sullivan, M. J., Van Horn, L., & Goodwin, M. (2010). The relationship between religion and CV outcomes and all-cause mortality in the Women's Health Initiative Observational Study. *Psychology and Health*, *25*(2), 249–263. https://doi.org/10.1080/08870440802311322

Skipper, A. D., Towns, T., Moye, R. G., & Rose, D. (2022). Examining the frequency of religious practices among hypertensive and non-hypertensive black men. *Journal of Healthcare, Science and the Humanities*, *12*(1), 41–58. https://www.ncbi.nlm.nih.gov/pmc/articles/PMC10351480/

Skolarus, L. E., Cowdery, J., Dome, M., Bailey, S., Baek, J., Byrd, J. B., Hartley, S. E., Valley, S. C., Saberi, S., Wheeler, N. C., McDermott, M., Hughes, R., Shanmugasundaram, K., Morgenstern, L. B., & Brown, D. L. (2018). Reach out churches: A community-based participatory research pilot trial to assess the feasibility of a mobile health technology intervention to reduce blood pressure among African Americans. *Health Promotion Practice*, *19*(4), 495–505. https://doi.org/10.1177/1524839917710893

Tartaro, J., Luecken, L. J., Gunn, H. E. (2005). Exploring heart and soul: effects of religiosity/spirituality and gender on blood pressure and cortisol stress responses. *Journal of Health Psychology*, *10*(6),753–766. https://doi.org/10.1177/1359105305057311

Trevino, K. M., & McConnell, T. R. (2014). Religiosity and religious coping in patients with CV disease: Change over time and associations with illness adjustment. *Journal of Religion and Health*, *53*(6), 1907–1917. https://doi.org/10.1007/s10943-014-9897-0

Waldstein, S. R., Kop, W. J., Suarez, E. C., Lovallo, W. R., & Katzel, L. I. (Eds.). (2022). *Handbook of cardiovascular behavioral medicine*. Springer. https://doi.org/10.1007/978-0-387-85960-6

Webb, J. R., Toussaint, L., & Dula, C. S. (2014). Ritualistic, theistic, and existential spirituality: Initial psychometric qualities of the RiTE measure of spirituality. *Journal of Religion and Health*, *53*(4), 972–985. https://doi.org/10.1007/s10943-013-9697-y

Williams, R. B., & Williams, V. P. (1993). *Anger kills: seventeen strategies for controlling hostility that can harm your health*. New York Times Books: New York.

Williams, R. B., & Williams, V. P. (2006). *In control*. Rodale Press: New York.

World Health Organization. (2021, June 11). Cardiovascular diseases (CVDs). https://www.who.int/news-room/fact-sheets/detail/cardiovascular-diseases-(cvds)

Chapter 13

Spirituality and Cancer-Related Outcomes

*Elizabeth Palmer Kelly, Julia A. McGee, and Timothy M. Pawlik**

Despite numerous advances in diagnosis and treatment, cancer remains the second most common cause of death in the United States. According to the American Cancer Society, there will be nearly 2 million new cancer cases in 2023 (Siegel et al., 2023). Additionally, the incidence of cancer-related mortality has decreased 33% since 1991, resulting in 3.8 million fewer cancer-related deaths (American Cancer Society, 2023). Ultimately, these data suggest that more individuals are living with or are survivors of cancer than ever before, with a current estimated 18 million Americans with a history of a cancer diagnosis living today (Siegel et al., 2023). Despite the decrease in cancer-related mortality, a cancer diagnosis still represents a life-altering and potentially life-threatening event that often requires multiple difficult treatment-related decisions and challenging therapies across the care continuum.

There is a renewed interest in the role of spirituality and how spirituality should be integrated into the care of patients diagnosed with cancer. Historically, individuals providing spiritual and medical care were one and the same. Over the last century, the transition to a disease-centered, cure-oriented model of care has dominated the medical field (Palmer Kelly, Paredes et al., 2022b). In the early 2000s, the Institute of Medicine advocated that care models should be more patient-, relationship-, and family-centered (Institute of Medicine Committee on Quality of Health Care in America, 2001). Consequently, the role of spirituality and religion in healthcare has expanded, serving as a means to address patient needs in a patient-centered manner through a more comprehensive and complementary approach. In this chapter, we explore differing definitions and concepts related to spirituality and religion and subsequently review well-documented influences, both positive and negative, of spirituality and religion on cancer patient care outcomes, such as health, well-being, and quality of life. The potentially intervening effects of social support and health behaviors on patient outcomes are also discussed. We conclude the chapter by discussing the limitations of the current research and potential future directions.

Operational Definition of Spirituality, Including a Brief Contrast with the RiTE Multidimensional Model

Defining the concepts of spirituality and religion within the healthcare context can present many challenges. For many individuals, spirituality is a deeply personal construct. Within the cancer literature, there is considerable variation in the conceptualization of spirituality and

* Corresponding Author: Tim.Pawlik@osumc.edu.

DOI: 10.4324/9781003440048-16

religion, including perspectives that view them as distinct concepts, distinct but overlapping concepts, religion as a specific type of spirituality, or interchangeable concepts (Palmer Kelly, Paredes et al., 2022b). More recently, both the National Institute for Complementary and Integrative Health (NCCIH) and the US Department of Veterans Affairs have incorporated spirituality as a domain of whole-person health (Langevin, 2023; US Department of Veterans Affairs, 2023). Specifically, the NCCIH considers spirituality as a vital component for restoring health, promoting resilience, and preventing disease across the lifespan (National Center for Complementary and Integrative Health, 2023). We define spirituality as "individualistic, informal, and as a means of establishing relationships to the sacred and to search for answers to fundamental life questions" (Taylor & Chatters, 2010, p. 282). Furthermore, we use spirituality as an umbrella term that is often inclusive of, but not limited to, religion.

A broad definition empowers patients to articulate their own understanding of what spirituality encompasses, enabling them to self-identify the practices, beliefs, or experiences they consider spiritual and understand how these contribute to their overall "whole person health" (Koenig et al., 2012). This approach ensures inclusivity in both research and clinical interventions, facilitating a nuanced understanding of the multidimensional nature of spirituality. Moreover, this expansive definition promotes cultural humility, adopting a "not-knowing stance" where we learn from patients about their individual perspectives on spirituality.

Webb and colleagues developed the RiTE Model of Spirituality to operationalize a broadened understanding of spirituality. The model defines spirituality as "the salient, searching pursuit of the transcendently sacred ritualistic, theistic, and/or existential aspects of the human condition" (Webb et al., 2014, p. 974). Within this definition, three constructs are delineated: (1) Ritualistic Spirituality, characterized by a "structured connection with deity"; (2) Theistic Spirituality, involving a "non-structured connection with deity"; and (3) Existential Spirituality, encompassing a "transcendent, yet non-theistic search for meaning and purpose" (Webb et al., 2014; see also Chapters 1 and 44 of this volume). This model acknowledges the inclusivity of both theistic and non-theistic perspectives, striving to accommodate the multidimensional nature of spirituality. While the RiTE model definition aligns with our conceptualization, as cited above, in recognizing the diverse nature of spirituality, it diverges in its perspective on a "balance" between ritualistic, theistic, and existential spirituality as indicative of spiritual "health" or "optimal" spirituality. Instead, our approach is more patient-led, allowing individuals to define what spiritual health means for themselves.

Definition of the Aspects of Spirituality Under Consideration and a Brief Discussion of How the Major Spiritual Belief Systems Understand the Aspects of Spirituality Under Consideration

Various facets of spirituality play significant roles in the healthcare and cancer care context, including spiritual well-being, spiritual care, spiritual needs, religion, and negative or positive religious coping. Aligned with the heightened emphasis on "whole person health" and patient-centered care in cancer, the spiritual domain of well-being has emerged as a frequently employed construct. Spiritual well-being is characterized by a sense of connection to others, the surrounding world, and a transcendent force (Bożek et al., 2020). It is closely associated with the concept of spiritual health, defined as "a purposeful life, transcendence and [the] actualization of different dimensions and capacities of human beings. Spiritual health creates a balance between [the] physical, psychological and social aspects of human life" (Ghaderi et al., 2018, p. 3).

Likewise, within the context of cancer care, there is an increased emphasis on enhancing the patient-centered care experience. To achieve this objective, it is imperative to ensure that patients have access to spiritual care and that their spiritual needs are adequately addressed. Spiritual care is delineated as "providing professional attention to the subjective spiritual and religious worlds of patients, comprised of perceptions, assumptions, feelings, and beliefs concerning the relationship of the sacred to their illness, hospitalization, and recovery or possible death" (VandeCreek, 2010, p. 1). Through the provision of spiritual care, the aim is to meet the spiritual needs of patients, which may encompass communication/fellowship or access to resources necessary for the execution of specific religious rituals. This approach allows for the customization of spiritual care to accommodate the needs of patients who adhere to religious or specific spiritual traditions. When spiritual needs are adequately addressed, it contributes to fostering patient spiritual well-being, health, and potential growth (Yousefi & Abedi, 2011).

The Pew Research Center's Religious Landscape Study estimates that approximately 3 in 4 Americans adhere to a religious belief system (Pew Research Center, n.d.). As noted, religion falls within the broader category of spirituality and may be denoted in the literature as religion, religiousness, religiosity, or faith. Religion is commonly defined as a tradition characterized by mutually agreed-upon beliefs and practices (Hall & Curlin, 2004). In the study of religion in cancer care, it is often portrayed as a coping mechanism – a means of navigating the challenges posed by a diagnosis or treatment. Consequently, patients may employ both positive and negative coping mechanisms associated with religion. Positive religious coping reflects a secure relationship with "God" and encompasses positive behaviors and thought processes. Conversely, negative religious coping, also termed "spiritual struggle," can manifest across interpersonal, intrapersonal, and divine dimensions. This includes conflicts with religious others, questioning, guilt, and perceived distance from or negative views of a higher power (Jenkins & Pargament, 1995; Pargament, 2007).

Theory and Research in Support of a Positive Relationship between Spirituality, Health, and Well-Being

To date, a substantial body of evidence indicates that spirituality exerts a positive influence on the health and well-being of patients diagnosed with cancer. Numerous systematic reviews have consistently established a positive relationship between spirituality and patient quality of life. In a systematic review and meta-analysis conducted by Kruizinga et al. (2016), the authors noted that following spiritual interventions, patients reported a moderately positive effect on their quality of life ($d = 0.50$, 95% CI: 0.20, 0.79). However, this effect diminished over time, and at 3–6 months post-intervention, the impact of spiritual interventions was small and statistically insignificant ($d = 0.14$, 95% CI: 0.08, 0.35). Notably, subgroup analysis at 3–6 months revealed that Western studies retained a small but significant effect ($d = 0.17$, 95% CI: 0.05, 0.29).

Similarly, a review by Visser, Garssen, and Vingerhoets (2010) reported that most of the cross-sectional studies (31 of 36) included in their review noted a positive association between spirituality and patient perception of well-being. However, four studies with a longitudinal design yielded mixed results. Additional reviews by Bauerei et al. (2018), as well as Xing et al. (2018), documented significant positive effects of existential/spiritual interventions on patient quality of life ($g = 0.21$; CI: 0.01, 0.42, $d = 0.19$, $p = 0.005$, respectively). In addition, Bai and Lazenby (2015) reported a positive association (ranging from 0.36 to 0.70) between overall spiritual well-being and quality of life.

In 2014, three meta-analyses examined the relationship between religion, spirituality, and the physical, mental, and social health among patients diagnosed with cancer. The authors categorized spirituality and religion into distinct constructs: affective (emotional), behavioral (actions/behaviors), cognitive (thoughts), and "other." The three meta-analyses included 1,341 effects from over 44,000 patients (Park et al., 2015). Concerning physical health, encompassing physical well-being, functional well-being, and physical symptoms, spirituality and religion were associated with overall better physical health, even after accounting for sociodemographic and clinical variables (e.g., lower levels of stress hormones, lower incidence of hypertension, heart disease, and chronic pain). Affective spirituality and religion exhibited the strongest association with overall physical health, followed by cognitive and other spirituality and religion. In exploring specific subdomains of physical health, affective R/S demonstrated associations with physical well-being ($z = 0.167$, $P < .001$), functional well-being ($z = 0.343$, $P < .001$), and physical symptoms ($z = 0.282$, $P < .001$). Cognitive R/S was linked to physical well-being ($z = 0.079$, $P < .05$) and functional well-being ($z = 0.090$, $P < .01$). "Other" R/S was associated with functional well-being ($z = 0.100$, $P < .05$) (Jim et al., 2015). Moreover, spirituality and religion were related to social health ($z = .20$; $P < .0001$), comprising social well-being, social distress, and social support. Once again, the affective dimension of spirituality and religion exhibited the strongest relationship with social health ($z = 0.031$, $P < .01$) (Sherman et al., 2015).

Regarding patient mental health, which included the subdomains of emotional well-being, general distress, depression, anxiety, and cancer-specific distress, the correlation with spirituality and religion generally exhibited a positive trend. Affective and cognitive spirituality and religion were significantly associated with all 5 categories of mental health outcomes ($z = 0.269$–0.424 and $z = 0.088$–0.124, respectively); "other" spirituality and religion were significantly associated with depression and emotional well-being ($z = 0.134$ and $z = 0.124$, respectively). Behavioral spirituality and religion were not associated with any subdomains of mental health (Salsman et al., 2015).

Overall, the results from the three meta-analyses demonstrated that spirituality and religion were modestly but significantly related to the physical, mental, and social health of patients diagnosed with cancer. Notably, the largest effect size was observed for the affective dimension of spirituality and religion in relation to mental health. Affective spirituality and religion also demonstrated a moderate association with both physical and social health. Cognitive spirituality and religion exhibited very modest associations with all three dimensions of health examined, while behavioral spirituality and religion were only associated with social health (Park et al., 2015). The affective dimension of spirituality and religion may play a particularly crucial role in the well-being of patients diagnosed with cancer, providing feelings of peace and comfort that aid in coping and act as a buffer against mental health challenges throughout the cancer care continuum.

A meta-analysis by Oh and Kim (2014) also noted a positive association between patient spirituality and mental health. Specifically, spiritual interventions, compared with the usual care of psychosocial effects, demonstrated moderate positive effects on patient depression ($d = -0.62$, $p = 0.001$) and large positive effects on patient anxiety ($d = -0.87$, $p = 0.02$). Similarly, Xing et al. (2018) reported that spiritual interventions had a small to moderate positive effect on depression and hopelessness ($d = -0.33$, $p = 0.01$ and $d = -0.38$, $p = 0.008$, respectively) and a moderate effect on patient anxiety ($d = -0.58$, $p = 0.03$). Additionally, a review by Hulett and Armer (2016) focused on objective psychoneuroimmunological outcomes in breast cancer survivors to connect spirituality-based interventions and psychosocial outcomes. The authors noted that cortisol was the most common biomarker, with 8 studies reporting positive changes in cortisol activity, which was associated with positive mental health outcomes, and four studies noted stable or no change in cortisol levels. Better mental health can have important implications for health care in general, including better treatment compliance as well as increased engagement around therapeutic options.

Most recently, Echeverri-Herrera et al. (2022) reported that patient spirituality was inversely associated with self-reported financial toxicity in a population of Hispanic breast cancer survivors. While more research is needed, spirituality may be an important target for interventions to help alleviate the financial stress of cancer for this community, as cancer is one of the most expensive diseases in the United States.

Research in Support of a Negative Relationship Between Spirituality/Health/Well-Being

While much research suggests a positive relationship between spirituality and the overall health and well-being of cancer patients, it is crucial to acknowledge the complexity of this relationship and recognize the existence of negative influences. For instance, spirituality and religion have been linked to the receipt of more aggressive end-of-life care and less frequent advanced care planning. In a recent review by Santos Carmo et al. (2023), high spiritual support from the religious communities of patients diagnosed with cancer was associated with less hospice care and more aggressive end-of-life care. When examining specific denominations, Catholics were the least likely to sign a Do Not Resuscitate (DNR) order, and Buddhists/Taoists received more aggressive interventions at the end of life. Interestingly, the same review noted that spiritual care administered by the medical team was associated with higher referrals to hospice and less aggressive end-of-life care.

While many patients draw support and hope from their religious and spiritual beliefs during cancer care, some patients experience spiritual distress and feelings of anger or abandonment by their God or religious community, concepts often referred to in the literature as "negative religious coping." Patients diagnosed with cancer who experience negative religious coping are more likely to have increased levels of depression and decreased adherence to medication and treatment plans, which could ultimately lead to negative outcomes (Jim et al., 2015). In one review (Thuné-Boyle et al., 2006), 4 of the 17 included studies noted that negative religious coping was harmful, with patients experiencing more psychological distress, poor psychosocial adjustment, increased levels of anxiety, increased cancer-related stress, reduced life satisfaction, diminished emotional well-being, and decreased social well-being. To date, there are limited data on whether spirituality may influence specific biomarkers or other physical/biological parameters.

The Relevance of Health Behaviors and Social Support – Two Common Mechanistic Intervening Variables

Spirituality and religion exert both direct and indirect influences on mechanistic variables such as health behaviors and social support. When considering the direct impact of spirituality and religion on health behaviors, it is important to acknowledge that many religious faiths prescribe explicit rules about healthcare and treatment that can significantly influence cancer outcomes. For instance, some religions, like Judaism, actively encourage the seeking of medical treatment, while others have specific rules that can directly impact a patient's treatment options (e.g., Jehovah's Witnesses, who are prohibited from receiving blood transfusions) (Woolley, 2005). Moreover, certain religions articulate explicit guidelines regarding health behaviors, which can indirectly contribute to reducing the risk for specific types of cancer. For example, several religions discourage or prohibit the use of alcohol and tobacco products, both of which are well-established risk factors for multiple types of cancers (McCaffree, 2002; Zygogianni et al., 2011). Additionally, religions that advocate for more modest dress may inadvertently limit individuals' exposure to the sun, thereby reducing the risk of skin cancer.

A review by Hoff et al. (2008) aimed to explain the association between religion and reduced cancer risk. While the review was limited by its exclusive focus on Christianity, the results indicated a decrease in the risks of lifestyle-associated cancer risk factors such as tobacco smoking, alcohol consumption, diet, physical activity, and reproductive factors. In turn, the association between membership in a religious Christian community and cancer risk may be the adoption of a healthy lifestyle intrinsic to religious practices within these communities. A study by Park, Waddington, and Abraham (2018) examined different dimensions of spirituality and religion with health behaviors among breast cancer survivors. Spiritual identity, religious coping, and private prayer were associated with fruit and vegetable intake. Both service attendance and religious identity (marginally) were related to engaging in less physical activity, while private prayer was positively related. Afterlife beliefs and private prayer were positively associated with BMI.

Social support is a factor associated with improved quality of life and overall well-being among patients with cancer (Ell et al., 1992). Higher levels of spirituality have been consistently linked to increased optimism, promoting hope, resilience, and improved coping mechanisms, all of which contribute to better well-being and quality of life (Ciria-Suarez et al., 2021; Rock et al., 2014; Thuné-Boyle et al., 2006). Faith-based communities also can serve as vital sources of support for individuals diagnosed with cancer. A study by Howsepian and Merluzzi (2009) investigated the relationship between religious beliefs and perceived social support with patient adjustment to cancer. The findings indicated that religious beliefs were more strongly associated with perceived social support than with the psychosocial adjustment to cancer itself. While not directly impacting psychosocial adjustment, religious beliefs may represent a crucial component of social support, which, in turn, directly influences psychosocial adjustment to cancer.

A qualitative study by our own research group sought to characterize the type of social support religious and spiritual beliefs offered patients diagnosed with cancer. Previous research has suggested that social support may be most influential when there is "optimal matching," defined as the "right" type and level of support offered by the "right" person in their social network (Fife et al., 2013; Nausheen et al., 2009). We defined 4 types of social support as described in House (1987): 1) Emotional/nondirective guidance (sharing of life experiences), 2) Informational/directive guidance (advice and suggestions), 3) Appraisal (providing information for self-evaluation), and 4) Instrumental/tangible (physical labor and tasks). Spirituality and religion were often discussed relative to appraisal/feedback support, as participants often looked to their faith for strength and inspiration. Discussions about spirituality and religion were most often classified as appraisal social support. Participants discussed finding inspirational quotes or Bible verses that gave them the motivation and strength during their cancer journey (Palmer Kelly et al., 2019). For example:

> *"But um I remember… I really felt like God was saying, 'you're going to walk through … the valley of the shadow death. You're going to go through this and come out the other side.' So, I think gave me a different perspective of everything knowing that I was going to get through it. And so, it was, we just I think looked at it differently, we're like, 'this too shall pass'.*

The benefits of spirituality/religion have been previously reported, with data suggesting that spirituality and religion may facilitate "meaning-making" or searching for purpose around the experience of cancer (Breitbart et al., 2010). The role of spirituality and religion may be more a means to cope with the cancer diagnosis and treatment rather than as a functional means to support positive psychosocial adjustment (Robb et al., 2007).

Limitations

Much of the literature has discussed the limitations of the study of spirituality in cancer care. Methodologically, the lack of consistency and a clear definition of spirituality (and religion), along with accompanying measurements, continues to be a significant challenge. Scholars have recently attempted to address this issue by developing multidimensional measures of spirituality and religion or by categorizing spirituality into different dimensions (e.g., affective and cognitive). A comprehensive conceptual model, such as the RiTE model/definition of spirituality, could be instrumental in standardizing definitions and measurements across studies. Many studies examining both the patient and provider perspective and cancer care are self-reported in survey-style studies. While these studies undoubtedly contribute valuable insights, there is a potential for bias in the sampling frame. Specifically, individuals with strong opinions on the incorporation of spirituality in cancer care, whether in favor or against, may be more likely to volunteer to participate. In contrast, individuals who fall somewhere in the middle might be less inclined to participate, even though they may be the ones who could benefit from or support the integration of spirituality in their cancer care.

In a comprehensive umbrella review conducted by our research group, we noted a limited focus on diverse populations, particularly African American/Black and adolescent/young adult cancer survivors (Gibson & Hendricks, 2006; McNeil, 2016; Mistretta, 2017; Mollica & Nemeth, 2013; E. J. Taylor et al., 2015). The review demonstrated that less than 20% of the included studies specifically addressed the unique experiences of these populations. This oversight is particularly significant given the persistently high mortality rates and shorter life spans among Black Americans compared with other racial/ethnic groups facing cancer challenges in the United States. Despite an overall decline in death rates from 2007 to 2016 across all racial groups, mortality gaps persist for most types of cancer among Black patients (American Cancer Society, 2023). To address these disparities, it is crucial to create opportunities for open and culturally sensitive discussions that incorporate patient beliefs and values. Integrating spirituality and religion into clinical discussions has shown promise in facilitating meaningful conversations across diverse racial and ethnic backgrounds. However, the evidence indicates a particularly influential role of spirituality and religion for Black patients in the cancer context. Compared with White cancer patients, spirituality among Black patients has been identified as a potential catalyst for improved quality of life and health-related outcomes (Culver et al., 2002). Recognizing the impact of diverse spiritual beliefs in clinical interactions is integral to fostering equitable and patient-centered cancer care for Black individuals.

Future Directions for the Science of Spirituality, Health, and Well-being in the Context of Cancer-Related Outcomes

The methodologies employed to study spirituality and patient health and well-being in the context of cancer care are limited, warranting utilization of more sophisticated research designs. It is crucial to employ longitudinal studies with larger datasets to explore the role of spirituality at various points in the cancer care continuum. Unfortunately, such datasets are currently scarce, preventing nuanced subset analyses to understand how patients' spiritual needs or the general impact of spirituality may vary based on the care continuum. Research done by our group used a retrospective chart review to characterize the utilization of spiritual care services among 14,322 cancer patients. We noted that patients at more advanced stages of disease or with more severe prognoses were more likely to use spiritual care services at the hospital (Hyer et al., 2020). Prospective studies to confirm these findings and allow for more nuanced analysis are needed.

Future research directions should also involve the development of interventions supporting the integration of spirituality into clinical cancer care. While much of the current intervention research focuses on end-of-life care, it is crucial to recognize that spirituality is important to patients across the entire care continuum. A systematic review by our team indicated that patient spirituality and religion can influence treatment decision-making (Palmer Kelly, Myers et al., 2022a). To ensure broader applicability, interventions should be translatable and disseminated across various healthcare settings, considering the wide variability in resources that support patient spirituality and religion across different hospital systems. Additionally, interventions targeting healthcare providers and addressing their specific barriers to spiritual care are essential when integrating spirituality into clinical cancer care. These interventions should go beyond educational and curriculum development, as personal discomfort is identified as a consistent barrier for providers, regardless of formal training (McGee et al., 2023). Therefore, interventions with self-reflective components are needed to address these barriers effectively.

Conclusion

Spirituality and religion have an increasing role in the context of cancer care and cancer-related illnesses. In particular, spirituality can play a significant role in the healthcare and cancer care context, including spiritual well-being, spiritual care, spiritual needs, religion, and negative or positive religious coping. Aligned with the heightened emphasis on "whole person health" and patient-centered care in cancer, the spiritual domain of well-being needs to be addressed by cancer care providers. Social support and health behaviors can mediate the effects of spirituality on patient outcomes. Healthcare providers need to address specific barriers to spiritual care and integrate spirituality into clinical cancer care. Future studies will need to better define the role of spirituality and religion in impacting cancer pathophysiology, biomarkers, and physiologic responses to cancer treatment.

References

American Cancer Society. (2023). Cancer facts & figures 2023. https://www.cancer.org/content/dam/cancer.org/research/cancer-facts-and-statistics/annual-cancer-facts-and-figures/2023/2023-cancer-facts-and-figures.pdf

Bai, M., & Lazenby, M. (2015). A systematic review of associations between spiritual well-being and quality of life at the scale and factor levels in studies among patients with cancer. *Journal of Palliative Medicine*, *18*(3), 286–298. https://doi.org/10.1089/jpm.2014.0189

Bauereiß, N., Obermaier, S., Selçuk Özünal, E., & Baumeister, H. (2018). Effects of existential interventions on spiritual, psychological, and physical well-being in adult patients with cancer: Systematic review and meta-analysis of randomized controlled trials. *Psycho-Oncology*, *27*, 2531–2545. https://doi.org/10.1002/pon.4829

Bożek, A., Nowak, P. F., & Blukacz, M. (2020). The relationship between spirituality, health-related behavior, and psychological well-being. *Frontiers in Psychology, 11*. https://doi.org/10.3389/fpsyg.2020.01997

Breitbart, W., Rosenfeld, B., Gibson, C., Pessin, H., Poppito, S., Nelson, C., Tomarken, A., Timm, A. K., Berg, A., Jacobson, C., Sorger, B., Abbey, J., & Olden, M. (2010). Meaning-centered group psychotherapy for patients with advanced cancer: A pilot randomized controlled trial. *Psycho-Oncology*. https://doi.org/10.1002/pon.1556

Ciria-Suarez, L., Calderon, C., Fernández Montes, A., Antoñanzas, M., Hernández, R., Rogado, J., Pacheo-Barcia, V., Ansensio-Martínez, E., Palacín-Lois, M., & Jimenez-Fonseca, P. (2021). Optimism and social support as contributing factors to spirituality in Cancer patients. *Supportive Care in Cancer, 29*(6). https://doi.org/10.1007/s00520-020-05954-4

Culver, J. L., Arena, P. L., Antoni, M. H., & Carver, C. S. (2002). Coping and distress among women under treatment for early stage breast cancer: Comparing African Americans, Hispanics and non-Hispanic whites. *Psycho-Oncology*. https://doi.org/10.1002/pon.615

Echeverri-Herrera, S., Nowels, M. A., Qin, B., Grafova, I. B., Zeinomar, N., Chanumolu, D., Duberstein, P. R., & Bandera, E. V. (2022). Spirituality and financial toxicity among Hispanic breast cancer survivors in New Jersey. *Supportive Care in Cancer, 30*(12). https://doi.org/10.1007/s00520-022-07387-7

Ell, K., Nishimoto, R., Mediansky, L., Mantell, J., & Hamovitch, M. (1992). Social relations, social support and survival among patients with cancer. *Journal of Psychosomatic Research, 36*(6), 531–541. https://doi.org/10.1016/0022-3999(92)90038-4

Fife, B. L., Weaver, M. T., Cook, W. L., & Stump, T. T. (2013). Partner interdependence and coping with life-threatening illness: The impact on dyadic adjustment. *Journal of Family Psychology, 27*(5), 702–711. https://doi.org/10.1037/a0033871

Ghaderi, A., Tabatabaei, S. M., Nedjat, S., Javadi, M. & Larijani, B. (2018). Explanatory definition of the concept of spiritual health: A qualitative study in Iran. *Journal of Medical Ethics and History of Medicine*, 11, 3. https://www.ncbi.nlm.nih.gov/pubmed/30258553

Gibson, L. M., & Hendricks, C. S. (2006). Integrative review of spirituality in African American breast cancer survivors. *The ABNF Journal : Official Journal of the Association of Black Nursing Faculty in Higher Education, Inc, 17*(2), 67–72.

Hall, D. E., & Curlin, F. (2004). Can physicians' care be neutral regarding religion? *In Academic Medicine*. https://doi.org/10.1097/00001888-200407000-00012

Hoff, A., Johannessen-Henry, C. T., Ross, L., Hvidt, N. C., & Johansen, C. (2008). Religion and reduced cancer risk – What is the explanation? A review. *European Journal of Cancer, 44*(17), 2573–2579. https://doi.org/10.1016/J.EJCA.2008.08.001

House, J. S. (1987). Social support and social structure. *Sociological Forum*. https://doi.org/10.1007/BF01107897

Howsepian, B. A., & Merluzzi, T. V. (2009). Religious beliefs, social support, self-efficacy and adjustment to cancer. *Psycho-Oncology, 18*(10). https://doi.org/10.1002/pon.1442

Hulett, J. M., & Armer, J. M. (2016). A systematic review of spiritually based interventions and psychoneuroimmunological outcomes in breast cancer survivorship. *Integrative Cancer Therapies, 15*(4), 405–423. https://doi.org/10.1177/1534735416636222

Hyer, J. M., Paredes, A. Z., Kelley, E. P., Tsilimigras, D., Meyer, B., Newberry, H., & Pawlik, T. M. (2020). Characterizing pastoral care utilization by cancer patients. *American Journal of Hospice and Palliative Medicine®*, 104990912095108. https://doi.org/10.1177/1049909120951082

Institute of Medicine (US) Committee on Quality of Health Care in America. (2001). Crossing the quality chasm: A new health system for the 21st century. In *Institute of medicine*. National Academies Press. https://doi.org/10.17226/10027

Jenkins, R. A., & Pargament, K. I. (1995). Spirituality and religion as resources for coping with cancer. *Journal of Psychosocial Oncology, 13*(1–2), 51–74. https://doi.org/10.1300/J077V13N01_04

Jim, H. S. L., Pustejovsky, J. E., Park, C. L., Danhauer, S. C., Sherman, A. C., Fitchett, G., Merluzzi, T. V., Munoz, A. R., George, L., Snyder, M. A., & Salsman, J. M. (2015). Religion, spirituality, and physical health in cancer patients: A meta-analysis. *Cancer*, *121*(21), 3760–3768. https://doi.org/10.1002/cncr.29353

Koenig, H. G., King, D. E., & Carson, V. Benner. (2012). *Handbook of religion and health* (2nd ed.). [References]. *(2012)*, 1.

Kruizinga, R., Hartog, I. D., Jacobs, M., Daams, J. G., Scherer-Rath, M., Schilderman, J. B. A. M., Sprangers, M. A. G., & Van Laarhoven, H. W. M. (2016). The effect of spiritual interventions addressing existential themes using a narrative approach on quality of life of cancer patients: A systematic review and meta-analysis. In *Psycho-oncology* (Vol. 25, Issue 3, pp. 253–265). John Wiley and Sons Ltd. https://doi.org/10.1002/pon.3910

Langevin, H. M. (2023). *Including spirituality into a fuller picture of research on whole person health.* National Center for Complementary and Integrative Health.

McCaffree, J. (2002). Dietary restrictions of other religions. *Journal of the American Dietetic Association*, *102*(7). https://doi.org/10.1016/S0002-8223(02)90212-9

McGee, J., Palmer Kelly, E., Kelly-Brown, J., Stevens, E., Waterman, B. L., & Pawlik, T. M. (2023). Assessing the impact of provider training and perceived barriers on the provision of spiritual care: A mixed methods study. *Journal of Cancer Education*, *38*(1). https://doi.org/10.1007/s13187-021-02115-x

McNeil, S. B. (2016). Spirituality in adolescents and young adults with cancer: A review of literature. *Journal of Pediatric Oncology Nursing*, *33*(1), 55–63. https://doi.org/10.1177/1043454214564397

Mistretta, E. G. (2017). Spirituality in young adults with end-stage cancer: A review of the literature and a call for research. *Annals of Palliative Medicine*, *6*(3), 279–283. https://doi.org/10.21037/apm.2017.06.17

Mollica, M., & Nemeth, L. (2013). Spirituality measurement in African American cancer survivors. *Journal of Holistic Nursing*, *31*(3), 214–225. https://doi.org/10.1177/0898010113495713

National Center for Complementary and Integrative Health. (2023, November 22). *NCCIH strategic plan FY 2021–2025: Mappying the pathway to research on whole person health.* National Center for Complementary and Integrative Health.

Nausheen, B., Gidron, Y., Peveler, R., & Moss-Morris, R. (2009). Social support and cancer progression: A systematic review. In *Journal of Psychosomatic Research* (Vol. 67, Issue 5, pp. 403–415). https://doi.org/10.1016/j.jpsychores.2008.12.012

Oh, P.-J., & Kim, S. H. (2014). The effects of spiritual interventions in patients with cancer: A meta-analysis. *Oncology Nursing Forum*, *41*(5), E290–301. https://doi.org/10.1188/14.ONF.E290-E301

Palmer Kelly, E., Meara, A., Hyer, M., Payne, N., & Pawlik, T. M. (2019). Understanding the type of support offered within the caregiver, family, and spiritual/religious contexts of cancer patients. *Journal of Pain and Symptom Management*, *58*(1). https://doi.org/10.1016/j.jpainsymman.2019.03.003

Palmer Kelly, E., Myers, B., Henderson, B., Sprick, P., White, K. B., & Pawlik, T. M. (2022a). The influence of patient and provider religious and spiritual beliefs on treatment decision-making in the cancer care context. *Medical Decision Making*, *42*(1), 125–134. https://doi.org/10.1177/0272989X211022246

Palmer Kelly, E., Paredes, A. Z., Tsilimigras, D. I., Hyer, J. M., & Pawlik, T. M. (2022b). The role of religion and spirituality in cancer care: An umbrella review of the literature. *Surgical Oncology*, *42*, 101389. https://doi.org/10.1016/j.suronc.2020.05.004

Pargament, K. I. (2007). *Spiritually integrated psychotherapy: Understanding and addressing the sacred.* Guildford Press.

Park, C. L., Sherman, A. C., Jim, H. S. L., & Salsman, J. M. (2015). Religion/spirituality and health in the context of cancer: Cross-domain integration, unresolved issues, and future directions. *Cancer*, *121*(21), 3789–3794. https://doi.org/10.1002/cncr.29351

Park, C. L., Waddington, E., & Abraham, R. (2018). Different dimensions of religiousness/spirituality are associated with health behaviors in breast cancer survivors. *Psycho-Oncology*, *27*(10). https://doi.org/10.1002/pon.4852

Pew Research Center. (n.d.). *Religion in America: U.S. religious data, demographics and statistics.* Retrieved November 22, 2018, from http://www.pewforum.org/religious-landscape-study/

Robb, C., Haley, W. E., Balducci, L., Extermann, M., Perkins, E. A., Small, B. J., & Mortimer, J. (2007). Impact of breast cancer survivorship on quality of life in older women. *In Critical Reviews in Oncology/Hematology*. https://doi.org/10.1016/j.critrevonc.2006.11.003

Rock, E. E., Steiner, J. L., Rand, K. L., & Bigatti, S. M. (2014). Dyadic influence of hope and optimism on patient marital satisfaction among couples with advanced breast cancer. *Supportive Care in Cancer, 22*(9). https://doi.org/10.1007/s00520-014-2209-0

Salsman, J. M., Pustejovsky, J. E., Jim, H. S. L., Munoz, A. R., Merluzzi, T. V., George, L., Park, C. L., Danhauer, S. C., Sherman, A. C., Snyder, M. A., & Fitchett, G. (2015). A meta-analytic approach to examining the correlation between religion/spirituality and mental health in cancer. *Cancer, 121*(21), 3769–3778. https://doi.org/10.1002/cncr.29350

Santos Carmo, B. Dos De Camargos, M. G., Santos Neto, M. F. Dos Paiva, B. S. R., Lucchetti, G., & Paiva, C. E. (2023). Relationship between religion/spirituality and the aggressiveness of cancer care: A scoping review. In *Journal of Pain and Symptom Management* (Vol. 65, Issue 5). https://doi.org/10.1016/j.jpainsymman.2023.01.017

Sherman, A. C., Merluzzi, T. V., Pustejovsky, J. E., Park, C. L., George, L., Fitchett, G., Jim, H. S. L., Munoz, A. R., Danhauer, S. C., Snyder, M. A., & Salsman, J. M. (2015). A meta-analytic review of religious or spiritual involvement and social health among cancer patients. *Cancer, 121*(21), 3779–3788. https://doi.org/10.1002/cncr.29352

Siegel, R. L., Miller, K. D., Wagle, N. S., & Jemal, A. (2023). Cancer statistics, 2023. *CA: A Cancer Journal for Clinicians, 73*(1). https://doi.org/10.3322/caac.21763

Taylor, E. J., Petersen, C., Oyedele, O., & Haase, J. (2015). Spirituality and spiritual care of adolescents and young adults with cancer. *Seminars in Oncology Nursing, 31*(3), 227–241. https://doi.org/10.1016/j.soncn.2015.06.002

Taylor, R. J., & Chatters, L. M. (2010). Importance of spirituality and religion in the lives of African Americans, Caribbean Blacks and Non-Hispanic Whites. *Journal of Negro Education, 79*(3), 280–294. https://muse.jhu.edu/article/806982

Thuné-Boyle, I. C., Stygall, J. A., Keshtgar, M. R., & Newman, S. P. (2006). Do religious/spiritual coping strategies affect illness adjustment in patients with cancer? A systematic review of the literature. *Social Science & Medicine, 63*(1), 151–164. https://doi.org/10.1016/j.socscimed.2005.11.055

US Department of Veterans Affairs. (2023, November 22). *Spirit & Soul.* Whole Health.

VandeCreek, L. (2010). Defining and advocating for spiritual care in the hospital. *Journal of Pastoral Care and Counseling, 64*(2). https://doi.org/10.1177/154230501006400205

Visser, A., Garssen, B., & Vingerhoets, A. (2010). Spirituality and well-being in cancer patients: A review. *Psycho-Oncology, 19*(6), 565–572. https://doi.org/10.1002/pon.1626

Webb, J. R., Toussaint, L., & Dula, C. S. (2014). Ritualistic, theistic, and existential spirituality: Initial psychometric qualities of the RiTE measure of spirituality. *Journal of Religion and Health, 53*(4). https://doi.org/10.1007/s10943-013-9697-y

Woolley, S. (2005). Jehovah's Witnesses in the emergency department: What are their rights? *Emergency Medicine Journal, 22*(12). https://doi.org/10.1136/emj.2004.023382

Xing, L., Guo, X., Bai, L., Qian, J., & Chen, J. (2018). Are spiritual interventions beneficial to patients with cancer? A meta-analysis of randomized controlled trials following PRISMA. *Medicine (Baltimore), 97*(35), e11948. https://doi.org/10.1097/md.0000000000011948

Yousefi, H., & Abedi, H. A. (2011). Spiritual care in hospitalized patients. *Iranian Journal of Nursing and Midwifery Research, 16*(1), 125–132.

Zygogianni, A., Kyrgias, G., Mystakidou, K., Antypas, C., Kouvaris, J., Papadimitriou, C., Armonis, V., Alkati, H., & Kouloulias, V. (2011). Potential role of the alcohol and smoking in the squamous cell carcinoma of the head and neck: Review of the current literature and new perspectives. *Asian Pacific Journal of Cancer Prevention 12*(2), 339–344.

Chapter 14

Spirituality and HIV-Related Outcomes

*Vivian S. Vigliotti**

Spirituality is a deeply personal and multifaceted aspect of the human experience. It provides a sense of connection to something greater than oneself and encompasses a wide range of beliefs, practices, and experiences that involve exploring the meaning and purpose of life and the interconnectedness of all things. Spirituality is a multifaceted concept involving a quest for deeper understanding, self-awareness, and connection to the universe, often expressed through religious practices, prayer, meditation, or acts of kindness. It significantly influences values, ethics, and moral perspectives, providing guidance and strength during challenges, fostering hope, resilience, and inner peace. In this regard, religiousness and spirituality have been found to be associated with better outcomes related to HIV and people living with HIV (PLWH), as will be the focus of this chapter.[1] The diversity of spiritual beliefs and experiences underscores the unique and individual nature of each person's spiritual journey, shaped by personal beliefs, cultural backgrounds, and life experiences.

Spirituality and Its Relevance to Health and Well-Being

Spirituality significantly impacts health, offering coping strategies for stress and trauma. It encourages healthy lifestyles, potentially reducing the risk of HIV and enhancing overall well-being. Positive emotions associated with spirituality, such as hope and optimism, can also boost the body's natural healing processes (Baysal, 2022). Spiritual experiences, like feeling connected to nature or a divine presence, are associated with enhanced well-being and reduced stress (Preston et al., 2023). Spirituality significantly contributes to mental, emotional, and physical well-being, influencing coping, emotional regulation, social support, and life satisfaction holistically (Yousefi Afrashteh et al., 2023).

How Spirituality Is Related to Chronic Medical Conditions

Spirituality and its relationship with chronic medical conditions, including HIV, is a topic of significant interest in medical and psychological research (Bożek et al., 2020), including with respect to HIV/PLWH (Grill et al., 2020). It often serves as a coping mechanism for individuals dealing with chronic illnesses and provides a sense of purpose and hope during prolonged health challenges. Chronic health conditions such as HIV often lead to stress, anxiety, and depression, and engaging with spirituality has been linked to improved mental health outcomes. Religiousness/spirituality provides a source of psychological strength and resilience to reduce symptoms of anxiety and depression and enhance overall well-being (Koenig, 2012).

* Corresponding Author: vivvig1523@gmail.com.

DOI: 10.4324/9781003440048-17

Over 39 million people globally were living with HIV in 2022, with about 1.3 million individuals newly infected with HIV in the same year (UNAIDS, 2023). Biomedical, behavioral, and structural factors are needed to halt transmission and reduce HIV incidence. However, attention to cultural context is needed for biomedical modalities to be effective and have maximum population impact (Vigliotti et al., 2020). Spirituality plays a role in primary HIV prevention due to its influence on upstream social and cultural factors such as a person's values, social networks, structures, and norms (Vigliotti et al., 2020). People living with HIV (PLWH) often face stigma, leading to higher depressive symptoms and lower mental health-related quality of life (HRQoL). Research has found that engagement in religious activity has helped address the deleterious relationship between stigma and depression for PLWH (Davis et al., 2023).

Spirituality fosters hope and resilience, essential qualities for individuals dealing with chronic illnesses, including HIV/PLWH. Studies have suggested that spiritual practices can alter the perception of pain to reduce its intensity and improve pain coping mechanisms (Bukhori et al., 2022). Believing in a higher power or a purpose beyond the illness can also inspire endurance through difficult treatments and maintain optimism about the future. In the context of terminal chronic illnesses, spirituality often plays a significant role in end-of-life care (Singh & Ajinkya, 2012). It provides comfort, addresses existential concerns, and helps patients and their families navigate the complex emotions associated with mortality.

Spirituality and Better Health and Well-Being

The significance of religion and spirituality as key social determinants influencing public health practice has prompted the field of epidemiology to play a crucial role in addressing enduring inquiries regarding the causal association between religion and health, including mortality (Ransome, 2020). Several aspects of spirituality have been associated with better health and well-being among individuals struggling with persistent health concerns (as evidenced in the various chapters of this volume). A sense of meaning and purpose in life is an existential aspect of spirituality that can help individuals navigate persistent health concerns through motivation to engage in life, maintain hope, and pursue positive health behaviors, such as primary HIV prevention activities outlined by the United States Department of Health and Human Services: condom use, HIV testing, number of sexual partners, and Pre-Exposure Prophylaxis (PrEP) (Vigliotti et al., 2020).

Religious or spiritual communities can provide crucial social support, reducing feelings of isolation and fostering emotional well-being (Koenig, 2012). Spirituality offers coping mechanisms like prayer and mindfulness, aiding in stress management and resilience (Koenig, 2012). Moreover, engaging in spiritual practices correlates with improved psychological well-being and life satisfaction (Preston et al., 2023). In a study of 177 individuals living with HIV, researchers investigated the impact of spiritual coping on HIV disease progression and health behaviors. Positive spiritual coping was associated with sustained undetectable viral load and CD4-cell preservation over four years, independently of sociodemographic variables and substance use disorder, suggesting its potential as an interventional aid in achieving undetectable viral load and preventing substance use onset/relapse (Kremer et al., 2015).

Spirituality often involves a sense of connection to something greater than oneself, which can provide comfort and perspective, reducing existential distress and fear associated with chronic illnesses. For PLWH, higher levels of spirituality have been associated with improvements in life satisfaction, functional health status, HRQoL, and overall well-being

(Cotton et al., 2006). Further, integrating spiritual beliefs and practices into healthcare approaches in a respectful and culturally sensitive manner can enhance overall support and improve the quality of life for PLWH (Davis et al., 2023). However, it is important to note that the impact of spirituality on health and well-being is highly individual and can vary based on personal beliefs, cultural context, and the specific nature of the health concern.

Operationally Defining Spirituality

Spirituality encompasses personal exploration, purpose, and interconnectedness with the universe, addressing existential questions about life and morality. It shapes beliefs, values, and overall well-being, reflecting the human condition. My approach for examining spirituality, health, and well-being for PLWH emphasizes inclusivity and the belief in something greater than earthly existence. It focuses on personal growth and a holistic understanding of the universe, aligning closely with existential spirituality within the RiTE model (see Chapters 1 and 44, this volume).

Aligning my personal belief with my research approach recognizes that religion exerts a pervasive influence on norms, values, structures, and institutions to shape individuals' behaviors and decisions. Defined broadly as a system encompassing symbols, rites, experiences, and rituals, religion holds profound and lasting effects, generating motivations through concepts of existence and evoking awe and dependence on a power greater than oneself. The study of religion is timely and imperative for HIV prevention activities, acknowledging its impactful role in shaping individual perspectives and behaviors (Vigliotti et al., 2020).

Contrast with the RiTE Multidimensional Model of Spirituality

The RiTE model categorizes spirituality into three dimensions: Ritualistic, Theistic, and Existential, representing different aspects of spiritual beliefs and practices (Webb et al., 2014). Individuals may exhibit varying degrees of inclination toward each dimension, leading to diverse spiritual experiences. This nuanced understanding allows for respectful engagement with spirituality.

My operational definition of spirituality emphasizes personal exploration, interconnectedness, and the pursuit of meaning beyond organized religion. In contrast, the RiTE model provides a structured framework categorizing spirituality based on specific dimensions. While my definition is holistic and individual-focused, the RiTE model offers a systematic analysis of spirituality. Both perspectives stress the importance of respecting diverse spiritual beliefs and practices, emphasizing inclusive engagement with spirituality.

Understanding Spirituality Across Belief Systems

Monotheistic Perspectives on Spirituality

Monotheistic perspectives refer to religious or spiritual beliefs centered around the worship or acknowledgment of a single, all-powerful, and supreme deity. While monotheistic perspectives share common features, there are variations and interpretations within each monotheistic religion (Basinger, 2020). These differences can stem from theological, cultural, and historical factors, leading to diverse practices and beliefs even within the broader category of monotheism.

Monotheistic religions, such as Judaism, Christianity, and Islam, emphasize the oneness of God. Followers believe in a singular, transcendent deity who is omnipotent (all-powerful), omniscient (all-knowing), omnipresent (present everywhere), and benevolent (all-good) (Khimjee, 2018). The focus is on a personal relationship with this divine being, often involving prayer, worship rituals, and adherence to religious teachings and commandments. A study, conducted through face-to-face interviews with 22 mothers diagnosed with HIV, found that 95% of them engaged in prayer, with active prayers being more common than receptive ones. Supplicatory or petitionary prayers for help and health were the most frequent type, while adoration was the least reported, with the majority of mothers perceiving prayer as a positive coping mechanism linked to outcomes such as support, positive attitude/affect, and peace (James Baesler et al., 2003).

Monotheistic religions typically have sacred scriptures or texts that serve as guidelines for belief, morality, and conduct. Monotheistic perspectives often provide followers with moral and ethical principles derived from the teachings of the one God (Alapo, 2022). Monotheistic religions typically include beliefs about an afterlife, where individuals are rewarded or punished based on their actions and faith in the one God. As a relevant example, Zimbabwe is a highly religious country, where 84% of the population aged 15 years and above are Christians (Wüthrich-Grossenbacher et al., 2023). Although religiousness can help improve outcomes with HIV and PLWH, Zimbabwe faces significant HIV challenges, with 1.3 million adults living with HIV and a high prevalence among adolescents, especially females aged 15–29. Risk behaviors, including multiple sexual partnerships, have increased since 2010, highlighting the urgent need for innovative, culture-specific prevention and care strategies to achieve Sustainable Development Goal 3 of ending the AIDS epidemic by 2030 and to better support young people living with HIV in Zimbabwe (Wüthrich-Grossenbacher et al., 2023).

Polytheistic and Non-Theistic Perspectives on Spirituality

Spirituality involves a personal quest for profound answers to existential inquiries, exploring the meaning and connection with the sacred or transcendent, which may or may not involve participation in religious practices or belonging to a specific religious community. Therefore, individuals who are spiritual may not necessarily affiliate themselves with a particular religion (Borges et al., 2021).

Polytheistic spirituality encompasses the worship of multiple deities, each representing distinct powers and domains, in contrast to monotheistic religions. Diverse polytheistic practices, including prayers directed toward specific deities for various concerns, can impact coping mechanisms and crisis responses, highlighting the complexity of religious experiences and suggesting areas for further investigation in resilience studies (Gan et al., 2023). Polytheistic spirituality, seen in ancient cultures such as Greek, Roman, Hindu, and indigenous traditions, regards nature as sacred, emphasizing rituals that honor its spirits, fostering personal connections with deities, and highlighting the diverse and interconnected nature of this belief system.

Non-theistic spirituality emphasizes the sacred or transcendent aspects of life without involving belief in a personal god, focusing on inner experiences, mindfulness, and interconnectedness. For people living with HIV, non-theistic spiritual practices can offer pathways to inner peace, enlightenment, and self-realization, contributing positively to their mental and emotional well-being. Research shows that non-theistic daily spiritual experiences (DSEs) are beneficially correlated with improved self-rated health, better emotional functioning, reduced anxiety, and less anger, aligning with previous studies linking non-theistic DSEs to positive psychological well-being (Kent et al., 2020).

Existential spirituality explores the individual's quest for meaning and purpose in a seemingly indifferent or chaotic universe. Rooted in existential philosophy, this perspective acknowledges the absence of inherent meaning in the universe and places the responsibility on individuals to create their own purpose (Ghaderi et al., 2018). A study involving 52 men living with HIV revealed a positive correlation between overall quality of life, social support, effective coping strategies, and existential well-being (Tuck et al., 2001). Additionally, Tuck et al. identified a negative association between existential well-being and perceived stress, uncertainty, psychological distress, and emotion-focused coping strategies. Through self-reflection, personal responsibility, and embracing life's uncertainties, individuals can find a deep sense of spiritual fulfillment within the framework of existential spirituality.

Salubrious Relationship Between Spirituality and Well-Being

Theoretical Frameworks Supporting Positive Correlations Between Spirituality and Health

The following theoretical frameworks highlight the complex interplay between spirituality and various aspects of health. The biopsychosocial model suggests that health and well-being are influenced not only by biological factors but also by psychological and social factors, including spirituality (Karunamuni et al., 2021). Positive spiritual beliefs and practices are associated with reduced stress, enhanced coping mechanisms, and improved mental well-being. These psychological benefits can positively influence physiological processes, such as immune function. More specifically, elevated cortisol levels, indicative of stress-related neuroendocrine activity, can adversely impact immune system functioning among HIV-infected individuals, stimulating HIV viral replication and influencing various immunologic measures relevant to HIV pathogenesis and disease progression. Research discovered that having a more positive view of God predicts better immune function as measured by CD4 counts in people with HIV (Bormann et al., 2009).

Additionally, social support networks often found within religious or spiritual communities contribute to overall health by providing emotional assistance and encouraging healthy behaviors. Social support is vital for resilience among African-American women living with HIV, as it has been consistently linked to lower HIV-related stigma and reduced loneliness, stress, and depressive symptoms. Specifically, studies show that social support, including emotional and instrumental assistance, can mitigate the adverse effects of HIV-related stigma on depression in this population (Lipira et al., 2019).

Psychoneuroimmunology (PNI) explores the interactions between psychological factors, the nervous system, and the immune system. Studies within this framework suggest that positive spiritual beliefs and practices can modulate the immune response and reduce inflammation (McCain et al., 2005). For example, meditation and prayer have been linked to demonstrable effects on brain and immune function in positive ways (Davidson et al., 2003). A strong immune system is essential for overall health, and spiritual practices are believed to support immune function through these psychoneuroimmunological mechanisms. Psychological interventions like relaxation and meditation training have been linked to enhanced immunity, including increased activity and numbers of NK cells in HIV-infected individuals. Additionally, cognitive coping strategies, relaxation techniques, and social support have shown potential for inducing changes in IgG and CD4+ T lymphocytes among HIV-infected patients (Chacin-Fernández et al., 2019).

Spirituality provides individuals with coping mechanisms to deal with stressors by providing a sense of meaning, purpose, and control. By providing a framework for understanding life events, spirituality reduces the perception of stress and its negative impact on health, especially when diagnosed with a chronic disease like HIV (Arrey et al., 2016). Engaging in prayer, meditation, or religious rituals can activate the relaxation response, leading to reduced stress hormone levels and promoting a sense of calm and well-being.

Empirical Research on the Positive Impact of Spirituality on Mental, Physical, and Social Well-Being

Empirical research involves direct observation and structured data analysis and has consistently demonstrated spirituality's positive impact on mental, physical, and social well-being. However, this impact varies based on individual beliefs and cultural contexts. The complex mechanisms through which spirituality influences well-being intertwine with psychological, social, and biological factors, prompting ongoing research to deepen the understanding of spirituality's contribution to health and wellness.

HIV targets CD4 cells, weakening the immune system and progressing to AIDS if left untreated, which can be fatal. However, highly active antiretroviral therapy (HAART) has significantly extended the lives of HIV-infected individuals, allowing for nearly normal life expectancy with early diagnosis and treatment. Despite advancements, around 1.1 million people live with HIV/AIDS in the United States, with approximately 50,000 new infections annually (Watkins-Hayes, 2014). Individuals with strong spiritual beliefs may experience enhanced immune function, as positive emotions like hope and optimism, associated with spirituality, can bolster the body's natural defense mechanisms. Previous research highlights the crucial role of spirituality and optimism as psychosocial factors influencing the health and well-being of PLWH. Studies indicate that higher levels of spirituality and forgiveness, traits often encouraged by religious communities, are associated with improved immunological markers and slowed disease progression, including greater preservation of CD4+ T cells and improved HIV viral load over time (Ironson et al., 2006). Additionally, optimism has been positively correlated with enhanced immunity and a slower progression of HIV, while both spirituality and optimism are linked to lower levels of distressing HIV-related symptoms, which can significantly impact medication adherence, quality of life, and overall health in PLWH (Gay et al., 2011).

Health Behaviors and Social Support within the Context of Salubrious Spirituality

The salubrious effect of spirituality on health and well-being implies a positive, health-promoting aspect of spirituality, focusing on practices that contribute to a person's overall health and quality of life. Examining health behaviors and social support within the context of spirituality involves understanding how specific spiritual beliefs and practices can influence individuals' health-related choices and their social connections.

The salubrious effect of spirituality may encourage adherence to healthy lifestyle behaviors. Spiritual beliefs emphasizing the importance of the body as a sacred vessel can motivate individuals to care for their physical health. These practices not only enhance mental well-being but also have physiological benefits, such as reducing stress hormones and promoting relaxation. Regular engagement in these practices can lead to improved mental and physical health. Individuals influenced by spirituality in a salubrious fashion may be more inclined to seek preventive HIV healthcare measures, including primary prevention activities such as PrEP, secondary treatment as prevention (TasP), or antiretroviral therapy (ART) as prevention or treatment (Vigliotti et al., 2020). This proactive approach to health can lead to early detection of diseases and better overall health outcomes.

Religion and spirituality have been associated with higher survival and improved biological markers among PLWH. A study found that religious attendance at least monthly among PLWH was associated with higher social support, less unhealthy alcohol and drug use, lower depression, and reduced mortality risk in a larger sample from the Veterans Aging Cohort Study (Doolittle et al., 2021).

In summary, the salubrious effect of spirituality encompasses health-promoting behaviors and strong social support networks within spiritual communities. These factors can have a significant impact on an individual's physical, mental, and social well-being, emphasizing the interconnectedness of spirituality and holistic health.

Deleterious Relationship Between Spirituality and Well-Being

Theoretical perspectives suggesting negative associations between spirituality and health outcomes are limited, as spirituality and religiosity are generally linked to positive health effects such as enhanced well-being, improved coping mechanisms, and social support.

While numerous studies highlight the positive effects of religious engagement, it is crucial to recognize circumstances where it may adversely affect psychological and physical well-being. Instances of religious struggle, such as questioning beliefs, feeling abandoned by God, or exhibiting high extrinsic religiosity, have been associated with compromised mental health (Hill et al., 2017). Studies show that religious involvement can undermine psychological well-being when individuals struggle with their religious beliefs (Hill et al., 2017), feel abandoned by God (Allen et al., 2008), exhibit high levels of extrinsic religiosity (Ardelt & Koenig, 2006), and combine strong religious beliefs with low religious attendance (Mannheimer & Hill, 2015). Additionally, negative social interactions within religious communities have been linked to lower self-esteem and increased depression among older adults (Page et al., 2020).

Religious beliefs among HIV-positive teens have been linked to increased spiritual distress, with reports indicating a higher likelihood of feeling abandoned by God and perceiving HIV as a punishment from a divine entity. These beliefs have further correlated with poor medication adherence, highlighting the complex interplay between religious perceptions and health behaviors among this demographic (Lyon et al., 2014). This is consistent with non-HIV-related research suggesting that indicators of religious struggle, such as doubts about God's love or attributing health issues to negative spirits, have been linked to an elevated risk of mortality in elderly hospital patients (Pargament et al., 2001). The negative aspects of religious involvement among PLWH remain less explored and understood compared to the positive aspects. There is a need for further research to delve into and explain these complex processes, acknowledging that religious involvement can have both salutary and detrimental effects on individuals' mental and physical well-being.

Limitations and Methodological Considerations

Methodological Challenges in Studying Spirituality and Its Impact on Health

Studying the impact of spirituality on HIV and PLWH presents several challenges. Spirituality is a complex and multifaceted concept, making consistency across studies difficult. Establishing causality between spirituality and health is complex; existing research often shows correlations without clarifying direct causation. Epidemiology can apply its methods to religion and health research to establish causality and guide interventions (Ransome, 2020). As religious landscapes evolve, researchers must adapt their approaches to affirm causal claims.

Cultural, religious, and social contexts influence the relationship between spirituality and health. Spiritual beliefs significant in one culture may not apply in another, requiring careful consideration when designing and interpreting studies on spirituality and health (Oji et al., 2017). Moreover, spiritual experiences are deeply personal and subjective, making objective quantification challenging. Researchers must account for individual interpretations of spirituality, ensuring diverse perspectives and experiences are included in their analyses. Randomized field experiments exploring public health outcomes, including spirituality, are scarce (Krause, 2017).

Research Alignment with the Dimensions of the RiTE Model

The empirical research regarding health and well-being among PLWH aligns with the RiTE model by illustrating how different aspects of spirituality interconnect with psychological, social, and biological factors, demonstrating its positive impact on mental well-being through symptom reduction. Additionally, the physiological benefits of spiritual practices, such as enhanced immune function and improved pain management, underscore spirituality's role in promoting holistic health by positively affecting both mental and physical well-being among PLWH.

Furthermore, the emphasis on social support networks within spiritual communities aligns with the relational aspect of the RiTE model. The role of spiritual communities in providing emotional support, fostering compassion, and encouraging positive social behaviors reflects the transformative and experiential dimensions of the model. The salubrious effect of spirituality can similarly facilitate health-promoting behaviors, which is also consistent with the RiTE model's emphasis on the integrative and transformative nature of spirituality.

Future Directions in Spiritual Health Research

Exploration of Understudied Aspects of Spirituality and Their Potential Impact on Health

While the relationship between spirituality and health has been a subject of growing interest, there are still several understudied aspects that warrant further exploration. Most research has focused on the impact of spirituality within mainstream religious traditions. However, there is a need to explore the health implications of a broader range of spiritual beliefs, including those outside organized religions, such as agnosticism, atheism, or unconventional spiritual practices (see Chapter 6, this volume).

In this regard, leading AIDS organizations anticipate the importance of faith and health collaborations in expanding community-based HIV services, yet the effective strategies for such collaborations remain largely unexplored. A 2021 study aimed to establish a comprehensive global research agenda by identifying priority research questions from key stakeholders at the intersection of HIV healthcare and faith, aiming to address urgent needs, enhance coordination, and promote the utilization of research findings. The global research agenda was crafted through interviews, focus groups, and online questionnaires with stakeholders worldwide, highlighting ten research themes such as addressing stigma and engaging faith communities. Participants emphasized the importance of more primary research and collaboration to ensure effective utilization of results. They also stressed the need to align research priorities with diverse religious traditions and local contexts for maximum impact (Ndlovu-Teijema et al., 2021).

Overall, research on spirituality and health predominantly originates from Western, Christian cultures, necessitating exploration of diverse cultural contexts and indigenous belief systems, including with respect to PLWH. Further investigation into negative aspects of spirituality, such as distress and conflicts with medical interventions, can enrich the understanding of spirituality's relationship with health and inform tailored interventions for the diverse population of PLWH (Ironson et al., 2016).

Interdisciplinary Approaches: Integrating Psychology, Sociology, and Theology

Interdisciplinary approaches are crucial for gaining a comprehensive understanding and enrichment of the potential impact of spirituality on health. Integrated research designs that incorporate methodologies from psychology, sociology, and theology that assess mental health outcomes, sociological avenues among community dynamics, and theological insights can help to understand the spiritual aspects of the participants' experiences. Intersectionality guides discussions, mobilization efforts, and research on HIV by recognizing it as an epidemic rooted in intersecting inequalities. Sociologists play a crucial role in providing evidence-based research that acknowledges HIV's intersectional nature and integrates this understanding into conceptual frameworks, methodologies, and practical applications.

The sociology of HIV/AIDS has significantly influenced responses to the epidemic by challenging biomedical and individual behavioral approaches, emphasizing social dimensions like racial inequality, economic conditions, and cultural norms in understanding HIV risk and experiences. Sociologists have also advanced intersectional approaches, highlighting how HIV status intersects with race, class, gender, and sexuality, shaping identity and transmission risk (Watkins-Hayes, 2014). Furthermore, the field demonstrates a model for conducting respectful yet rigorous research on all aspects of human behavior, addressing complexities and power imbalances in examining intimate aspects of people's lives (Watkins-Hayes, 2014). Involving communities, religious institutions, policymakers, healthcare providers, and religious leaders in research efforts fosters culturally sensitive collaboration to integrate findings into healthcare policies and practices while solidifying a holistic and inclusive approach to spirituality and health.

Recommendations for Inclusive and Diverse Research Methodologies

Researching spirituality and health in relation to HIV and PLWH requires attention to cultural and belief contexts. Ethical guidelines, including culturally sensitive informed consent and confidentiality, must be rigorously followed to respect the experiences of PLWH.

Developing or adapting culturally tailored measures helps assess spirituality in a manner that is inclusive of the diverse expressions within different communities. Collaborating with PLWH and community members ensures these measures accurately reflect their spiritual experiences (Coughlin, 2016). Further, using community-based participatory research (CBPR) approaches enables collaboration with PLWH from the study's inception to its interpretation, ensuring the research aligns with their cultural values and beliefs.

Mixed-methods research combines quantitative and qualitative methods, enabling a comprehensive understanding of spirituality and health in PLWH. This approach captures both the scope and depth of the phenomenon (Maragh-Bass et al., 2021). Qualitative methods, in particular, offer insights into the richness and diversity of spiritual experiences among PLWH, shedding light on how spirituality is lived and expressed in different contexts (Wilson et al., 2015).

Applying an intersectionality framework to understand how various social identities (e.g., race, ethnicity, gender, and sexual orientation) intersect with spirituality and health helps to recognize that individuals may have multiple intersecting identities that influence their experiences and health outcomes. For example, strategies to address HIV-related stigma, within the framework of intersectionality, can focus on promoting resilience among Black women living with HIV. Resilience resources encompass modifiable strength-based factors that can be targeted for intervention (Earnshaw et al., 2013). For these individuals, religiosity, social support, and ethnic identity emerge as potential resilience resources, mitigating the adverse impact of HIV-related stigma on psychosocial outcomes such as depression. Further, the consistent association between greater social support and lower HIV-related stigma is evident, with social support linked to reduced loneliness, stress, and depressive symptoms, particularly among women living with HIV (Serovich et al., 2001). Lastly, research indicates that a strong sense of ethnic identity may foster resilience in the face of stigma and discrimination, correlating with lower anxiety, depression, and psychological stress, as well as greater coping, optimism, and self-esteem (Lipira et al., 2019). Additionally, stronger ethnic identity is associated with less HIV-related risk-taking among young, Black women and reduced perceived stress among women living with HIV (Beadnell et al., 2003).

By incorporating these recommendations, researchers can contribute to more inclusive and culturally sensitive studies on spirituality and health, fostering a better understanding of the complex and varied ways in which spirituality impacts well-being across different cultural and belief contexts, all of which is particularly relevant to PLWH.

Ethical Considerations and Guidelines for Conducting Spirituality-Related Research

Ethical considerations in spirituality research are crucial due to the deeply personal nature of spiritual beliefs. Researchers must prioritize informed consent, ensuring participants understand the study's purpose and potential risks. Cultural sensitivity is essential to respect diverse beliefs, while confidentiality and anonymity protect participants' privacy and autonomy. Competence and training are necessary for engaging with diverse spiritual backgrounds, and research design should allow authentic expression of beliefs. Finally, researchers must balance beneficence and nonmaleficence, maximizing benefits while minimizing harm to participants, to conduct ethical and respectful spirituality-related research.

In this regard, research with respect to HIV is complex. A study identified three ethical domains in HIV remission research: recruitment and informed consent, transmission risks and partner protection, and ancillary and continuing care. It discussed challenges in informed consent procedures and suggested staged re-consent or comprehension assessment for those diagnosed with acute HIV infection. The authors emphasized the need for a comprehensive understanding of acute HIV infection's biomedical, psychological, social, and behavioral dimensions to address ethical concerns in study design and approval processes (Gilbertson et al., 2021).

Additional examination of ethical considerations highlighted the need for increased attention to emerging ethical issues in HIV cure research across six categories: social value, scientific validity, fair selection of participants, favorable benefit/risk balance, informed consent, and respect for enrolled participants and community. These issues encompass considerations such as the scalability of research, study design, equity in participant selection, risk perception, informed consent processes, and community perspectives. The focus on addressing evolving ethical challenges can ensure responsible and inclusive HIV cure research practices (Dubé et al., 2021).

Conclusion

The synthesis of theoretical frameworks and empirical research underscores the intricate relationship between spirituality and well-being, revealing its multifaceted impact on mental, physical, and social dimensions. Empirical research consistently demonstrates the positive impact of spirituality on mental, physical, and social well-being, emphasizing its multifaceted nature across individual beliefs and cultural contexts. Spiritual beliefs are associated with enhanced immune function, optimism, and offering psychosocial support crucial for PLWH. The salubrious effect of spirituality fosters health-promoting behaviors and strong social networks, encouraging proactive health measures among PLWH, yet it is important to acknowledge potential deleterious effects such as religious struggle and negative social interactions.

Methodological challenges persist in studying spirituality's influence on health, requiring interdisciplinary approaches, culturally sensitive measures, and mixed-methods research to grasp spirituality's nuanced role, including among PLWH. Ethical considerations are paramount in spirituality-related research, ensuring informed consent, cultural competence, and respect for participants' autonomy while addressing emerging ethical issues in HIV cure research to uphold responsible and inclusive practices.

Note

1 My literature review search process through PsycINFO and PubMed databases included empirical articles that investigated spirituality, chronic diseases, and human immunodeficiency virus (HIV) care and prevention activities. I included articles in the English language published since 2000.

References

Alapo, R. (2022). Religion and Spirituality Across Cultures. In *Diversity and Multi-Cultural Education in the 21st Century*. https://pressbooks.cuny.edu/oalapo/chapter/religion-and-spirituality-across-cultures/

Allen, R. S., Phillips, L. L., Roff, L. L., Cavanaugh, R. & Day, L. (2008). Religiousness/spirituality and mental health among older male inmates. *The Gerontologist*, *48*(5), 692–697. https://doi.org/10.1093/geront/48.5.692

Ardelt, M. & Koenig, C. S. (2006). The Role of Religion for Hospice Patients and Relatively Healthy Older Adults. *Research on Aging*, *28*(2), 184–215. https://doi.org/10.1177/0164027505284165

Arrey, A. E., Bilsen, J., Lacor, P. & Deschepper, R. (2016). Spirituality/Religiosity: A Cultural and Psychological Resource among Sub-Saharan African Migrant Women with HIV/AIDS in Belgium. *PloS One*, *11*(7), e0159488. https://doi.org/10.1371/journal.pone.0159488

Basinger, D. (2020). Religious Diversity (Pluralism). In E. N. Zalta (Ed.), *The Stanford Encyclopedia of Philosophy* (Winter 2020). Metaphysics Research Lab, Stanford University. https://plato.stanford.edu/archives/win2020/entries/religious-pluralism/

Baysal, M. (2022). Positive psychology and spirituality: A review study. *Spiritual Psychology and Counseling*, *7*(3), 359–388. https://doi.org/10.37898/spc.2022.7.3.179

Beadnell, B., Stielstra, S., Baker, S., Morrison, D. M., Knox, K., Gutierrez, L. & Doyle, A. (2003). Ethnic identity and sexual risk-taking among African-American women enrolled in an HIV/STD prevention intervention. *Psychology, Health & Medicine*, *8*(2), 187–198. https://doi.org/10.1080/1354850031000087564

Borges, C. C., Dos Santos, P. R., Alves, P. M., Borges, R. C. M., Lucchetti, G., Barbosa, M. A., Porto, C. C. & Fernandes, M. R. (2021). Association between spirituality/religiousness and quality of life among healthy adults: a systematic review. *Health and Quality of Life Outcomes*, *19*(1), 246. https://doi.org/10.1186/s12955-021-01878-7

Bormann, J. E., Aschbacher, K., Wetherell, J. L., Roesch, S. & Redwine, L. (2009). Effects of faith/assurance on cortisol levels are enhanced by a spiritual mantram intervention in adults with HIV: a randomized trial. *Journal of Psychosomatic Research*, *66*(2), 161–171. https://doi.org/10.1016/j.jpsychores.2008.09.017

Bożek, A., Nowak, P. F. & Blukacz, M. (2020). The Relationship Between Spirituality, Health-Related Behavior, and Psychological Well-Being. *Frontiers in Psychology*, *11*, 1997. https://doi.org/10.3389/fpsyg.2020.01997

Bukhori, B., Hidayanti, E. & Situmorang, D. D. B. (2022). Religious coping strategies for people with HIV/AIDS (PLWHA) Muslims in Indonesia: A qualitative study with a telling-the-stories. *Heliyon*, *8*(12), e12208. https://doi.org/10.1016/j.heliyon.2022.e12208

Chacin-Fernández, J., Chacin Fuenmayor, M., Piñerua-Shuhaibar, L. & Suarez-Roca, H. (2019). Psychological intervention based on psychoneuroimmunology improves clinical evolution, quality of life, and immunity of children with leukemia: A preliminary study. *Health Psychology Open*, *6*(1), 2055102919838902. https://doi.org/10.1177/2055102919838902

Cotton, S., Puchalski, C. M., Sherman, S. N., Mrus, J. M., Peterman, A. H., Feinberg, J., Pargament, K. I., Justice, A. C., Leonard, A. C. & Tsevat, J. (2006). Spirituality and religion in patients with HIV/AIDS. *Journal of General Internal Medicine*, *21*(Suppl 5), S5–S13. https://doi.org/10.1111/j.1525-1497.2006.00642.x

Coughlin, S. S. (2016). Community-based participatory research studies on HIV/AIDS prevention, 2005–2014. *Jacobs Journal of Community Medicine*, *2*(1), 019.

Davidson, R. J., Kabat-Zinn, J., Schumacher, J., Rosenkranz, M., Muller, D., Santorelli, S. F., Urbanowski, F., Harrington, A., Bonus, K. & Sheridan, J. F. (2003). Alterations in brain and immune function produced by mindfulness meditation. *Psychosomatic Medicine*, *65*(4), 564–570. https://doi.org/10.1097/01.psy.0000077505.67574.e3

Davis, C. W., Hook, J. N., Hodge, A. S., DeBlaere, C., Davis, D. E., Van Tongeren, D. R. & Vosvick, M. (2023). Religious relief: Exploring the role of religion and spirituality among a broad range of people living with HIV. *Spirituality in Clinical Practice*, *10*(2), 168–183. https://doi.org/10.1037/scp0000252

Doolittle, B. R., McGinnis, K., Ransome, Y., Fiellin, D. & Justice, A. (2021). Mortality, Health, and Substance Abuse by Religious Attendance Among HIV Infected Patients from the Veterans Aging Cohort Study. *AIDS and Behavior*, *25*(3), 653–660. https://doi.org/10.1007/s10461-020-03028-4

Dubé, K., Kanazawa, J., Taylor, J., Dee, L., Jones, N., Roebuck, C., Sylla, L., Louella, M., Kosmyna, J., Kelly, D., Clanton, O., Palm, D., Campbell, D. M., Onaiwu, M. G., Patel, H., Ndukwe, S., Henley, L., Johnson, M. O., Saberi, P., … Sugarman, J. (2021). Ethics of HIV cure research: an unfinished agenda. *BMC Medical Ethics*, *22*(1), 83. https://doi.org/10.1186/s12910-021-00651-1

Earnshaw, V. A., Bogart, L. M., Dovidio, J. F. & Williams, D. R. (2013). Stigma and racial/ethnic HIV disparities: moving toward resilience. *The American Psychologist*, *68*(4), 225–236. https://doi.org/10.1037/a0032705

Gan, S. K.-E., Wong, S. W.-Y. & Jiao, P.-D. (2023). Religiosity, Theism, Perceived Social Support, Resilience, and Well-Being of University Undergraduate Students in Singapore during the COVID-19 Pandemic. *International Journal of Environmental Research and Public Health*, *20*(4). https://doi.org/10.3390/ijerph20043620

Gay, C., Portillo, C. J., Kelly, R., Coggins, T., Davis, H., Aouizerat, B. E., Pullinger, C. R. & Lee, K. A. (2011). Self-reported medication adherence and symptom experience in adults with HIV. *The Journal of the Association of Nurses in AIDS Care: JANAC*, *22*(4), 257–268. https://doi.org/10.1016/j.jana.2010.11.004

Ghaderi, A., Tabatabaei, S. M., Nedjat, S., Javadi, M. & Larijani, B. (2018). Explanatory definition of the concept of spiritual health: a qualitative study in Iran. *Journal of Medical Ethics and History of Medicine*, *11*, 3. https://www.ncbi.nlm.nih.gov/pubmed/30258553

Gilbertson, A., Tucker, J. D., Dubé, K., Dijkstra, M. & Rennie, S. (2021). Ethical considerations for HIV remission clinical research involving participants diagnosed during acute HIV infection. *BMC Medical Ethics*, *22*(1), 169. https://doi.org/10.1186/s12910-021-00716-1

Grill, K. B., Wang, J., Cheng, Y. I. & Lyon, M. E. (2020). The Role of Religiousness and Spirituality in Health-related Quality of Life of Persons Living with HIV: A Latent Class Analysis. *Psychology of Religion and Spirituality*, *12*(4), 494–504. https://doi.org/10.1037/rel0000301

Hill, T. D., Christie-Mizell, C. A., Vaghela, P., Mossakowski, K. N. & Johnson, R. J. (2017). Do Religious Struggles Mediate the Association between Day-to-Day Discrimination and Depressive Symptoms? *Religions*, *8*(8), 134. https://doi.org/10.3390/rel8080134

Ironson, G., Kremer, H. & Lucette, A. (2016). Relationship Between Spiritual Coping and Survival in Patients with HIV. *Journal of General Internal Medicine*, *31*(9), 1068–1076. https://doi.org/10.1007/s11606-016-3668-4

Ironson, G., Stuetzle, R. & Fletcher, M. A. (2006). An increase in religiousness/spirituality occurs after HIV diagnosis and predicts slower disease progression over 4 years in people with HIV. *Journal of General Internal Medicine*, *21*(Suppl 5), S62–S68. https://doi.org/10.1111/j.1525-1497.2006.00648.x

James Baesler, E., Derlega, V. J., Winstead, B. A. & Barbee, A. (2003). Prayer as Interpersonal Coping in the Lives of Mothers with HIV. https://digitalcommons.odu.edu/communication_fac_pubs/12/?? utm_source=digitalcommons.odu.edu%2Fcommunication_fac_pubs%2F12/?&utm_medium=PDF&utm_campaign=PDFCoverPages

Karunamuni, N., Imayama, I. & Goonetilleke, D. (2021). Pathways to well-being: Untangling the causal relationships among biopsychosocial variables. *Social Science & Medicine*, *272*, 112846. https://doi.org/10.1016/j.socscimed.2020.112846

Kent, B. V., Stroope, S., Kanaya, A. M., Zhang, Y., Kandula, N. R. & Shields, A. E. (2020). Private religion/spirituality, self-rated health, and mental health among US South Asians. *Quality of Life Research: An International Journal of Quality of Life Aspects of Treatment, Care and Rehabilitation*, *29*(2), 495–504. https://doi.org/10.1007/s11136-019-02321-7

Khimjee, H. (2018). *Second Edition: the Attributes of God in the Monotheistic Faiths of Judeo-Christian and Islamic Traditions*. iUniverse. https://play.google.com/store/books/details?id=VIRoDwAAQBAJ

Koenig, H. G. (2012). Religion, spirituality, and health: the research and clinical implications. *ISRN Psychiatry*, *2012*, 278730. https://doi.org/10.5402/2012/278730

Krause, N. (2017). Invited Commentary: Explaining the Relationship Between Attending Worship Services and Mortality-A Brief Excursion Into the Contribution of Social Relationships in Religious Institutions [Review of Invited Commentary: Explaining the Relationship Between Attending Worship Services and Mortality-A Brief Excursion Into the Contribution of Social Relationships in Religious Institutions]. *American Journal of Epidemiology*, *185*(7), 523–525. https://doi.org/10.1093/aje/kww180

Kremer, H., Ironson, G., Kaplan, L., Stuetzele, R., Baker, N. & Fletcher, M. A. (2015). Spiritual coping predicts CD4-cell preservation and undetectable viral load over four years. *AIDS Care*, *27*(1), 71–79. https://doi.org/10.1080/09540121.2014.952220

Lipira, L., Williams, E. C., Nevin, P. E., Kemp, C. G., Cohn, S. E., Turan, J. M., Simoni, J. M., Andrasik, M. P., French, A. L., Unger, J. M., Heagerty, P. & Rao, D. (2019). Religiosity, Social Support, and

Ethnic Identity: Exploring "Resilience Resources" for African-American Women Experiencing HIV-Related Stigma. *Journal of Acquired Immune Deficiency Syndromes*, *81*(2), 175–183. https://doi.org/10.1097/QAI.0000000000002006

Lyon, M. E., Garvie, P., He, J., Malow, R., McCarter, R. & D'Angelo, L. J. (2014). Spiritual well-being among HIV-infected adolescents and their families. *Journal of Religion and Health*, *53*(3), 637–653. https://doi.org/10.1007/s10943-012-9657-y

Mannheimer, A. H. & Hill, T. D. (2015). Deviating from Religious Norms and the Mental Health of Conservative Protestants. *Journal of Religion and Health*, *54*(5), 1826–1838. https://doi.org/10.1007/s10943-014-9951-y

Maragh-Bass, A. C., Gamble, T., El-Sadr, W. M., Springer, S. A., Linas, B. P., Eron, J. J., Felsen, U. R., Myers, J. E., Johnson, W. D., & D'Adamo, C. R. (2021). Examining stigma, social support, and gender differences in unsuppressed HIV viral load among participants in HPTN 065. *Journal of Behavioral Medicine*, *44*(2), 159–171. https://doi.org/10.1007/s10865-020-00186-7

McCain, N. L., Gray, D. P., Walter, J. M. & Robins, J. (2005). Implementing a comprehensive approach to the study of health dynamics using the psychoneuroimmunology paradigm. *ANS. Advances in Nursing Science*, *28*(4), 320–332. https://doi.org/10.1097/00012272-200510000-00004

Ndlovu-Teijema, M. T., Kok, M. O., van Elsland, S. L., Smeets, H., Barstow, D., van Rooyen, L. & van Furth, A. M. (2021). Setting the global research agenda for community-based HIV service delivery through the faith sector. *Health Research Policy and Systems / BioMed Central*, *19*(1), 81. https://doi.org/10.1186/s12961-021-00718-w

Oji, V. U., Hung, L. C., Abbasgholizadeh, R., Terrell Hamilton, F., Essien, E. J. & Nwulia, E. (2017). Spiritual care may impact mental health and medication adherence in HIV+ populations. *HIV/AIDS*, *9*, 101–109. https://doi.org/10.2147/HIV.S126309

Page, R. L., Peltzer, J. N., Burdette, A. M. & Hill, T. D. (2020). Religiosity and Health: A Holistic Biopsychosocial Perspective. *Journal of Holistic Nursing: Official Journal of the American Holistic Nurses' Association*, *38*(1), 89–101. https://doi.org/10.1177/0898010118783502

Pargament, K. I., Koenig, H. G., Tarakeshwar, N. & Hahn, J. (2001). Religious struggle as a predictor of mortality among medically ill elderly patients: a 2-year longitudinal study. *Archives of Internal Medicine*, *161*(15), 1881–1885. https://doi.org/10.1001/archinte.161.15.1881

Preston, J. L., Coleman, T. J., 3rd & Shin, F. (2023). Spirituality of Science: Implications for Meaning, Well-Being, and Learning. *Personality & Social Psychology Bulletin*, 1461672231191356. https://doi.org/10.1177/01461672231191356

Ransome, Y. (2020). Religion, Spirituality, and Health: New Considerations for Epidemiology. *American Journal of Epidemiology*, *189*(8), 755–758. https://doi.org/10.1093/aje/kwaa022

Serovich, J. M., Kimberly, J. A., Mosack, K. E. & Lewis, T. L. (2001). The role of family and friend social support in reducing emotional distress among HIV-positive women. *AIDS Care*, *13*(3), 335–341. https://doi.org/10.1080/09540120120043982

Singh, D. K. M. & Ajinkya, S. (2012). Spirituality and religion in modern medicine. *Indian Journal of Psychological Medicine*, *34*(4), 399–402. https://doi.org/10.4103/0253-7176.108234

Tuck, I., McCain, N. L. & Elswick, R. K., Jr. (2001). Spirituality and psychosocial factors in persons living with HIV. *Journal of Advanced Nursing*, *33*(6), 776–783. https://doi.org/10.1046/j.1365-2648.2001.01711.x

UNAIDS. (2023). *Global HIV & AIDS statistics — Fact sheet*. UNAIDS. https://www.unaids.org/en/resources/fact-sheet

Vigliotti, V., Taggart, T., Walker, M., Kusmastuti, S. & Ransome, Y. (2020). Religion, faith, and spirituality influences on HIV prevention activities: A scoping review. *PloS One*, *15*(6), e0234720. https://doi.org/10.1371/journal.pone.0234720

Watkins-Hayes, C. (2014). Intersectionality and the Sociology of HIV/AIDS: Past, Present, and Future Research Directions. *Annual Review of Sociology*, *40*(1), 431–457. https://doi.org/10.1146/annurev-soc-071312-145621

Webb, J. R., Toussaint, L. & Dula, C. S. (2014). Ritualistic, theistic, and existential spirituality: initial psychometric qualities of the RiTE measure of spirituality. *Journal of Religion and Health*, *53*(4), 972–985. https://doi.org/10.1007/s10943-013-9697-y

Wilson, P. A., Valera, P., Martos, A. J., Wittlin, N. M., Muñoz-Laboy, M. A., & Parker, R. G. (2015). Contributions of qualitative research in informing HIV/AIDS interventions targeting Black MSM in the United States. *The Journal of Sex Research*, *53*(6), 642–654. https://doi.org/10.1080/00224499.2015.1016139

Wüthrich-Grossenbacher, U., Midzi, N., Mutsaka-Makuvaza, M. J. & Mutsinze, A. (2023). Religious and traditional beliefs and practices as predictors of mental and physical health outcomes and the role of religious affiliation in health outcomes and risk taking. *BMC Public Health*, *23*(1), 2170. https://doi.org/10.1186/s12889-023-17030-7

Yousefi Afrashteh, M., Abbasi, M. & Abbasi, M. (2023). The relationship between meaning of life, perceived social support, spiritual well-being and pain catastrophizing with quality of life in migraine patients: the mediating role of pain self-efficacy. *BMC Psychology*, *11*(1), 17. https://doi.org/10.1186/s40359-023-01053-1

Chapter 15

Spirituality and Medical Rehabilitation

George Fitchett and Kate Fiona Jones*

Traumatic injuries such as spinal cord injury (SCI) and traumatic brain injury (TBI) affect the lives of millions of people around the world. A report from the Global Burden of Disease Study 2019 estimates 27.16 million new cases of TBI globally in 2019, 48.99 million prevalent cases, and 7.08 million years lived with disability (YLDs). For SCI, there were 0.91 million new cases in 2019, 20.64 million prevalent cases, and 6.20 million YLDs (Guan et al., 2023).

For the person who is injured, the impact of an SCI or TBI can be devastating and involve major biographical disruption (Bourke et al., 2015). A person with SCI may experience changes to their mobility, continence, and sexual function, and a person with TBI may experience all of these as well as changes in cognitive functioning and behavior. These changes can have far-reaching psychological and social consequences, impacting personal relationships and the ability to return to previous work and leisure activities (Budd et al., 2022). Medical rehabilitation can play a crucial role in assisting a person to adjust to their new life following injury.

In this chapter, we discuss the role of religion/spirituality (R/S) within the context of medical rehabilitation. The first part of the chapter summarizes research about the prevalence of R/S coping and the evidence for the positive and negative associations between R/S and important outcomes, including functional status, psychological well-being, and quality of life (QOL). The second section describes processes that may link R/S and outcomes for medical rehabilitation patients. The third section describes research related to spiritual care. In the fourth section, we focus on rehabilitation professionals, their knowledge and attitudes about R/S, and education to improve their knowledge in this area. In the final section, we offer a critical review of the existing research and highlight areas for future study.

The focus of the chapter is shaped by the existing research. Most of that research focuses on adults with SCI or TBI. It also includes people with stroke as well as medical rehabilitation inpatients with diverse conditions. There are two studies of people with burn injuries (Ajoudani et al., 2019; Jibeen et al., 2018). Research participants include patients and their caregivers, and in some studies, rehabilitation professionals. We found no research about children or adolescents; there is one study about parents of children with TBI (Ayesha et al., 2022).

For this chapter, we have selected research known to us from our own work in the area, described below. We supplemented that with research identified by new searches in PubMed, Medline, and PsycInfo. We have accepted these investigators' conceptualizations of R/S, most frequently operationalized in their choice of measures. In the final section of the chapter, we will offer critical reflections about this. Other reviews of research in this

* Corresponding Author: george_fitchett@rush.edu.

DOI: 10.4324/9781003440048-18

area are available for interested readers (Gibbs et al., 2020; Jones, Pryor et al., 2018c; Jones et al., 2016; Jones, Paal et al., 2021).

Religion/Spirituality and Rehabilitation Outcomes

We begin with an overview of the research that reports the prevalence of R/S coping with traumatic injury and reports of the beneficial associations between R/S and rehabilitation outcomes. Then we review the evidence about the prevalence of R/S distress or struggle (e.g., feeling abandoned or punished by God) and the harmful associations such distress may have with rehabilitation outcomes.

Functional Improvement

Our review identified several studies which explored the relationship between R/S and perceived health during or following rehabilitation. Using the Brief Multidimensional Measure of Religiousness/Spirituality (BMMRS; Fetzer Institute, 1999) and subscales of the SF-36 (Ware et al., 1993), Johnstone and Yoon (2009) conducted a cross-sectional study of R/S coping in a sample of 118 rehabilitation outpatients (52% TBI, 27% cerebral vascular accidents, and 21% SCI). They identified that "positive spiritual experience" and "forgiveness" were associated with General Health Perception. In regression models adjusted for demographic variables, none of the BMMRS subscales, tested simultaneously, were significant predictors of General Health Perception or General Mental Health. When only considering the TBI sample in a separate paper (Johnstone et al., 2009), "meaning" and "values/beliefs" were associated with General Health Perception, and hierarchical regressions indicated that "values/ beliefs" and "forgiveness" significantly predicted General Health Perception beyond that accounted for by demographic variables. In another study, spiritual well-being was identified as a significant predictor of perceived health status (Forchheimer & Tate, 2007).

A few studies explored the relationship between R/S and physiological change. Johnstone and Glass (2008) found that a greater level of spiritual experience (such as transcendence) was significantly associated with reduced right parietal lobe functioning (such as after TBI). In one study, greater spiritual coping was negatively associated with physical functioning (Functional Independence Measure, Craig Handicap Assessment, and Reporting Technique) (Chlan et al., 2011). Three studies, however, found no significant relationship between R/S and functional outcomes for patients with stroke (Morgenstern et al., 2011) and SCI (Matheis et al., 2006; Piderman et al., 2011).

Psychological Well-Being

Among 17 quantitative studies where psychological well-being or mental health of participants was a key area of interest, the majority focused on the experience of the person with the injury or condition. Three involved caregiver participants only, and one involved both the caregivers and the patient.

Administering the Religious Coping Questionnaire to older people in outpatient rehabilitation in Brazil, Luccetti et al. (2011) found that religiousness was related to significantly fewer depressive symptoms. Mixed findings were reported by Giaquinto and colleagues in two studies exploring the impact of religious beliefs upon coping and psychological well-being (Giaquinto et al., 2010; Giaquinto & Spiridigliozzi, 2007). Although the first of their studies suggested that religious beliefs may positively impact coping (Giaquinto & Spiridigliozzi, 2007), the second (Giaquinto et al., 2010) did not find any significant relationships between religious beliefs and a number of variables, including anxiety and depression. Using the Index of Core Spiritual Experiences (INSPIRIT; Kass et al., 1991), which measures the occurrences of experiences that convince a person that God exists and that evoke feelings of closeness with God, Mahalik et al. (2007) found that spirituality was positively associated with positive psychological coping strategies (such as cognitive restructuring, information seeking, and emotional expression), but not with negative psychological coping strategies (such as wish-fulfilling fantasy, self-blame, or threat minimization).

Cultural factors appear to have had some influence in studies investigating religion. Many studies recruited participants within a predominantly Christian cultural context and explored a range of spiritual issues (Baldacchino et al., 2013a, 2013b; Gillespie, 2019; Laures-Gore et al., 2018; Marini & Glover-Graf, 2011; Robinson-Smith, 2002; Rodriguez et al., 2013). In a study where 67% of the sample were Christian, Marini and Glover-Graf (2011) found that 72% of participants believed that God or a Spiritual Power gave them meaning or purpose in life, and 48% believed there was a spiritual reason for their SCI. In a study by Gillespie (2019), almost all participants referenced how their belief in God helped them cope with their acquired brain injury (ABI), facilitating posttraumatic growth. Two studies specifically explored the nature of prayer as a coping strategy within the context of disability (Robinson-Smith, 2002; Rodriguez et al., 2013). Prayer requests to God or a Higher Power were made for physical improvement and functioning, emotional and personal resiliency, improvement in self-efficacy and QOL, and spiritual assistance and growth.

Several studies explored the role of R/S as a coping strategy for participants holding Muslim beliefs, with studies from Turkey (Akturk & Akturk, 2020), Iran (Ajoudani et al., 2019; Alquwez & Alshahrani, 2021; Azar et al., 2022; Babamohamadi et al., 2011; Hatefi et al., 2020; Torabi Chafjiri et al., 2017), and Pakistan (Jibeen et al., 2018). Moderately high levels of spiritual well-being were found among individuals with SCI in Turkey, and it was an important factor in coping (Akturk & Akturk, 2020). Two studies of caregivers of individuals with SCI reported mixed findings on the relationship between religious coping and depression. One study found religious coping to be significantly associated with lower levels of stress, anxiety, and caregiver burden, but not with depression (Hatefi et al., 2020). The other reported an association for both religious and existential coping strategies and lower levels of depression (Alquwez & Alshahrani, 2021), though the use of high religious coping strategies was associated with increased depression. R/S was also found to play a factor in reducing caregiving burden among caregivers of older stroke survivors (Torabi Chafjiri et al., 2017). Among burn survivors, Ajoudani, Jafarizadeh, and Kazamzadeh (2019) found spirituality played a mediating role between social support and post-traumatic growth.

Qualitative studies explored the relationship between the Muslim faith and coping in further depth. Azar, Radfar, and Baghaei (2022) concluded that the spirituality of Iranian stroke survivors increased motivation for self-care and adaptation, reduced stress, and assisted participants to accept the reality of their condition. This was achieved through supplication and religious beliefs. And Babamohamadi et al. (2011) identified three coping strategies for individuals after SCI in Iran: seeking help from religious beliefs, hope, and making efforts toward independence/self-care. Most participants in the study believed that their condition was divine fate/providence and/or a divine test and sought help for this through prayer and belief. Last, a study in Pakistan (Jibeen et al., 2018) found that spiritual transcendence was associated with psychological adjustment in a Muslim community of individuals with burns.

A contrast with those from a Christian or Muslim cultural context was provided by three studies. Spirituality from a Canadian First Nations perspective was explored by Keightley et al. (2011) among elders and traditional healers working among people with brain injury. In this community, spirituality was something which pervaded all other aspects of health and wellness. Participants contrasted their way of bringing healing with Western approaches, but also spoke of how there was a desire to see Western healthcare professionals work together with traditional healers to provide care. A study from China (Wang et al., 2022) among individuals with stroke, where 84.1% of the sample identified as being "without religious beliefs," found that spiritual need was associated with spiritual well-being, self-transcendence, and social support. Finally, in a Sri Lankan study where all the participants identified as religious, and over 85% as Buddhist, Xue (2016) found that if an individual with SCI perceived benefits through spirituality or religion, they were less likely to be depressed.

Other researchers looked beyond religiousness alone and considered different components of spirituality or spiritual well-being. Utilizing the Spiritual Well-being Scale, Sekely et al. (2020) found that existential well-being, not religious well-being, was a predictor of reduced depressive symptomology among individuals with TBI. Both religious and existential well-being were found to uniquely predict psychosocial adjustment among people with multiple sclerosis and mitigate perceived uncertainty associated with adaptation to the condition (McNulty et al., 2004).

Two studies used the BMMRS to explore the relationship between different dimensions of R/S and both physical and mental health subscales of the SF-36. General mental health was shown to have significant associations with the BMMRS "religious support scale" among individuals with SCI (Franklin et al., 2008) and the BMMRS "religious and spiritual coping scale" for individuals with stroke (Johnstone et al., 2008). There were no associations between any of the BMMRS subscales and general health in either of these studies. Cohen, Yoon, and Johnstone (2009) focused on the association between the BMMRS subscales and mental health among a heterogenous group of rehabilitation patients. They found that positive spiritual experiences and positive congregational support were both positively correlated with mental health. Religious practices such as prayer did not have a significant association with mental health, and after regression analyses, congregational support was the only scale to predict mental health.

Other studies conceptualized spiritual well-being using broader measures, such as the Functional Assessment of Chronic Illness Therapy-Spiritual (FACIT-SP; Murphy et al., 2010; Peterman et al., 2002), which encompasses meaning, peace, and faith. Two studies reported negative associations between spiritual well-being and depression among individuals with SCI (Siddall et al., 2017; Wilson et al., 2017). A third study of both individuals with SCI and their caregivers found that greater spiritual well-being was associated with lower levels of depression and anxiety (Jones et al., 2019). Such findings were further confirmed in a study with both TBI and SCI caregivers (Simpson et al., 2020), with greater levels of spirituality associated with lower levels of caregiver burden and positively associated with hope, which contributed toward resilience. Spirituality had an indirect effect on positive affect, which was negatively associated with depression. Another study considering the impact of spirituality on hope (Yıldırım Üşenmez et al., 2022) observed a weak but positive correlation between spiritual well-being and hope for individuals with SCI. And using the WHOQOL-SRPB (WHOQOL SRPB Group, 2006) with stroke survivors and their caregivers, two related studies (one cross-sectional, one longitudinal; Bolgeo et al., 2022; Pucciarelli et al., 2020) observed that spirituality played a protective role, with the survivor's spirituality associated with lower levels of depression among caregivers. It was also noted, however, that higher levels of spirituality for both the survivor and the caregiver were associated with higher levels of anxiety (Bolgeo et al., 2022).

Only a few studies considered the role of other aspects of spirituality, such as hope and gratitude. In one study, both these constructs were identified as outcomes of participants' utilization of sources of spiritual strength and contributors toward family resilience (Jones, Dorsett, and Simpson et al., 2018b).

Quality of Life and Life Satisfaction

Alongside its impact upon functional outcomes and psychological well-being, the relationship between R/S with life satisfaction or QOL was frequently investigated among the studies. Seven of these studies were conducted with individuals with SCI (Brillhart, 2005; Chlan et al., 2011; Forchheimer & Tate, 2007; Hajiaghababaei et al., 2018; Matheis et al., 2006; Siddall et al., 2017; Webb et al., 2010), two with TBI (Philippus et al., 2016; Waldron-Perrine et al., 2011), and three with a mixed group that included rehabilitation patients (Kim et al., 2000; Riley et al., 1998; Tate & Forchheimer, 2002). All studies found some relationship between R/S and life satisfaction; details of many of these studies can be found in two scoping reviews (Jones, Pryor, et al., 2018c; Jones et al., 2016).

Health-related QOL was another frequent outcome of interest. Both religious and existential well-being were identified by Hajiaghababaei et al. (2018) as factors which contributed to health-related QOL after SCI. Among caregivers of individuals with TBI, Hanks et al. (2020) found that existential well-being moderated the relationship between functional impairment of the individual with TBI and health-related QOL for the caregivers.

Prevalence of R/S Struggles and Harmful Associations with Rehabilitation Outcomes

R/S beliefs, practices, and coping come in many forms and have diverse effects. In addition to the R/S beliefs and coping that are associated with better outcomes, as shown in the research we just reviewed, there are other R/S beliefs and coping, such as those associated with R/S struggle (e.g., feeling angry with God or abandoned by God). A substantial body of research in diverse clinical populations finds these beliefs are associated with poorer outcomes for factors such as emotional well-being and QoL (Bockrath et al., 2022). There is a modest body of research about R/S struggle and related types of R/S beliefs and coping among medical rehabilitation patients and those living with SCI and TBI, and the findings are consistent with work in other clinical populations.

Several studies provide information about the prevalence of R/S struggle and related beliefs among medical rehabilitation patients. In an early study of 37 SCI patients, 25% were angry with God and asked why God allowed them to suffer (Salisbury et al., 1989). Another study of 100 former rehabilitation patients reported that 23% believed that God was punishing them (Anderson et al., 1993). Kim et al. (2000) examined changes in spiritual well-being in a sample of 155 medical rehabilitation patients (stroke 30%, SCI 17%, and TBI 7%). They found that nearly similar proportions experienced gains (37%) and declines (32%) in spiritual well-being between admission and 3 months post-discharge. Using chaplains' assessments of spiritual distress in a sample of 203 Swiss geriatric patients in medical rehabilitation, Monod et al. (2012) reported some spiritual distress in 65% of the sample and severe distress in 22%.

Marini and Glover-Graf (2011) conducted an extensive survey of past and current R/S beliefs and disability in a sample of 157 people with SCI; the time since injury was 5 years or greater for 48% of respondents. They found 26% of respondents reported they were at one time angry with God for their disability, and 10% reported currently feeling that way. Those who felt angry with God currently also reported feeling their disability made them a worse person, they felt abandoned by God, and they believed they and/or their family were being punished for having sinned.

In an early study, Fitchett et al. (1999) examined the association between multiple dimensions of R/S (e.g., beliefs, practices, and coping) and adjustment and recovery at admission and 4 months post-discharge among 96 medical rehabilitation inpatients (49% joint replacement, 17% stroke, 17% amputation, and 17% other). In adjusted models, no R/S measure was associated with better follow-up adjustment or recovery. However, in adjusted models, admission R/S struggle was associated with poorer follow-up functional status (activities of daily living). The proportion of patients who expressed "anger with God for letting this happen," one of the R/S items, was 6.3%.

Another study examined the association between three types of R/S appraisals, sacred loss (a sanctified aspect of life has been lost), desecration (a sanctified aspect of life has been violated), and benevolent religious appraisal (e.g., trying to find a lesson from God in what happened) and emotional adjustment among 70 medical rehabilitation inpatients (30% stroke, 10% SCI, and 10% TBI; Magyar-Russell et al., 2013). Data was collected at admission and 6–8 weeks post-discharge. Among these patients, 71.4% and 58.6% endorsed some degree of sacred loss, and 42.9% and 40.0% endorsed some degree of desecration at admission and follow-up, respectively. The investigators found that sacred loss and desecration uniquely predicted anxiety, depression, and posttraumatic growth, and benevolent religious appraisal only posttraumatic growth. Positive and negative religious coping, however, were partial mediators, suggesting that although religious and spiritual appraisals can play an important role, they work in combination with other factors to contribute toward psychological well-being.

Returning to the study mentioned earlier by Johnston and Yoon (2009), conducted with a mixed group of rehabilitation patients, an inverse correlation between negative spiritual experiences ("I feel a higher power is punishing me for my sins or lack of spirituality;" "I wonder whether a higher power has abandoned me") and the General Mental Health subscale of the SF-36 ($r = -.18$, $p < 0.05$) was observed. Among these patients, 27.2% reported "significant loss in faith" (32% and 33% for SCI and TBI patients, respectively, and 12.5% for stroke patients). Another study with this sample reported that 40% of the SCI patients reported some negative spiritual experience; the proportions for TBI and stroke patients were 39.3% and 31.3%, respectively (Jones et al., 2015). A unique study (Ayesha et al. 2022) examined R/S and general psychological distress (GHQ-12) in 302 Pakistani parents of children with TBI; 99% of the sample were Muslim. They found a moderate correlation between R/S struggle coping and GHQ 12 ($r = 0.22$; $p = 0.000$).

How Religion and Spirituality Contribute to Rehabilitation Outcomes

At the beginning of the chapter, we reviewed research about the association between R/S and rehabilitation outcomes. Here, we summarize research that focuses on four specific ways in which R/S may *contribute* to those outcomes (i.e., possible explanatory models): meaning-making, spiritual transformation, R/S and self-perception, and the role of forgiveness. While we recognize that these processes themselves can also be considered outcomes, our point here is that they may play a role in the contribution of R/S to other outcomes such as QoL and emotional adjustment.

Religion/Spirituality and Illness Narratives and Meaning-Making

Traumatic injury or illness often causes severe biographical disruption and precipitates the need for meaning-making. Research has described themes and narrative processes associated with the meaning-making process. An influential framework developed by Arthur Frank (2013) describes three types of illness narratives: chaos, restitution, and quest. A rehabilitation spiritual care provider, Robert Mundle (2015a), used this framework to provide an in-depth description of the role of R/S in the three-month rehabilitation journey of Clare (pseudonym), a 77-year-old woman with hemiparesis after a lytic spinal lesion and stroke. Mundle traces Clare's journey from feeling she is in a "dark night of the soul" (chaos) to being reminded of God's love through a statue (the Sacred Heart of Jesus) in the hospital chapel. Clare's hope that she will walk again (restitution) is challenged when she learns she will need a wheelchair. Mundle describes how Clare discovers a new purpose (narrative) as she finds her religious devotion during her rehabilitation has caused her to be a "testimony," a source of encouragement, to other patients and staff. Mundle (2015b) provides a similar analysis for another patient, Iris (pseudonym), an 82-year-old woman in geriatric medical rehabilitation with a severe and painful ankle injury.

Smith and Sparkes (2005) used Frank's typology in their analysis of three different narratives of hope among 14 men in the United Kingdom who suffered SCI while playing sport. Concrete hope for recovery shaped by a restitution narrative was the most common type of hope, shared by 11 of the 14 men. Two men described narratives of transcendent hope, which embrace uncertainty and are shaped by a quest narrative. One man shared a narrative of despair or loss of any kind of hope, shaped by a chaos narrative. Smith and Sparkes describe the ways in which these various narratives facilitate and limit identity reconstruction for these men.

In another study, DeSanto-Madeya (2006) examined the meaning of living with SCI. She interviewed 20 people, aged 22–55, who had been living with SCI for 5–10 years. At the same time, she also interviewed a member of their family (11 spouses, 9 mothers). She found seven themes in her analysis of the interviews for both the persons with SCI and their family members. They included looking for understanding of a life that is unknown, stumbling along an unlit path, being chained to the injury, and moving forward in a new way of life. The participants described living with SCI as a continuous learning experience. The study findings can help persons living with SCI, their family members, and the health professionals who care for them better understand the experience of living with SCI.

Spiritual Transformation

Several qualitative studies explored how, for some people affected by injury or a condition such as stroke, a spiritual transformation or awakening can take place through suffering (Boswell et al., 2001; Chow & Nelson-Becker, 2010; McColl et al., 2000). These studies depicted R/S and disability to be "inextricably related" (Boswell et al., 2001). This was the case in a qualitative study with eight stroke survivors. The losses after stroke and associated feelings of despair leading to loss of hope were explored by Chow and Nelson-Becker (2010). Personal spiritual resources were discovered over time and included finding renewed purpose in life, hope, and transformation through spiritual connection and transcendence. McColl et al. (2000) explored a number of changes in spiritual beliefs among individuals with TBI and SCI, and these included a greater awareness of self; a change in their view of their own independence; a sense of purpose in life not present before the onset of the disability; greater awareness of their own mortality and vulnerability; a new understanding of trust and dependence on others; loss of some significant relationships; greater appreciation and closeness with others and the world; and greater understanding of other disadvantaged groups.

Religion/Spirituality and a Non-Physical Sense of Self

In an early article, Ellen Idler (1995) examined the role of R/S in self-rated health, specifically the non-physical sense of self of clients randomly selected from an urban rehabilitation clinic in the United States. Semi-structured interviews were conducted with 146 clients. She found that clients who reported greater religiousness also reported a greater non-physical sense of self (e.g., "To what extent do you think of yourself as a religious person?"). Clients with higher levels of disability were also more likely to report having sought help from religion. Summarizing her work, Idler observes that people may use spiritual or religious beliefs to cope with illness or disability. These beliefs, she notes, can help a person refocus on "aspects of the self to which a painful, or nonfunctioning, or unattractive physical body is irrelevant. The inner, spiritual self can be beautiful and whole even when the material, physical body is broken or diseased" (p. 700).

The process described by Idler is supported by a study of self-reported health and disability in a sample of 28 stroke survivors in the United Kingdom (Mavaddat et al., 2021). The study examined transcripts of interviews with 3 groups of survivors: 8 survivors with significant physical disability but high self-rated health, 7 survivors with minimal disability yet low self-rated health, and 13 survivors with minimal disability and high self-rated health. In contrast to the group with minimal disability and low self-rated health, the group with significant disability and high self-rated health "relied on God and drew strength from their faith for their rehabilitation, intentionally practiced gratitude and acceptance of their limitations and exhibited altruistic characteristics, looking beyond themselves and their own situation to consider befriending and helping others" (p. 9).

Forgiveness

As traumatic injuries may be frequently caused by one's own behavior or that of another person, issues of forgiveness, of self and/or of others, often play an important role in rehabilitation. Rehabilitation spiritual care provider John Bauman (2008) suggests that unresolved issues with forgiveness, including guilt or anger, can compromise patients' motivation for rehabilitation (see also Webb, 2007/2003). He clarifies what forgiveness is and is not and describes the use of a four-stage process of forgiveness with an older woman who blamed herself for her injury. Bauman's view about the important role of forgiveness is supported by research by Webb et al. (2010). They surveyed a community-based sample of 140 adults with SCI about forgiveness. They found that greater forgiveness of self was significantly associated with better health behavior as well as greater life satisfaction. In addition, forgiveness of others was significantly associated with better self-reported health status. This study did not examine the role of R/S in forgiveness, though forgiveness is a common spiritual value shared by all mainstream world religions/belief systems (e.g., Webb et al., 2012).

Spiritual Care

In this section, we describe research about patients' interest in receiving spiritual care and descriptions about the care offered by spiritual care providers (chaplains) and others. There is some evidence that medical rehabilitation patients desire spiritual care. One early study of 100 discharged rehabilitation patients, 38% with stroke, found that 54% desired spiritual care visitation and 41% reported they received insufficient spiritual care (Anderson et al., 1993). Another study, among Australian road trauma rehabilitation patients who received spiritual care from a chaplain, reported that 19 of 21 patients described the chaplains' care as somewhat or very important (Calder et al., 2011).

There are two extended case studies by spiritual care providers that describe their spiritual care in the rehabilitation context. In the first case study, Katherine Piderman (2015) describes her care for Angela (pseudonym), a 17-year-old girl who suffered an SCI when her car went off the road. The focus of the case study is a conversation with Angela in which she tearfully asks the chaplain, "They say that there must be a reason. I feel so hurt by God. Betrayed. (sobbing) Why did God do this to me?" The case illustrates how a spiritual care provider responded to this young woman's spiritual distress. In the second case study, Jeffery Murphy (2017) describes his care for Wayne (pseudonym), who suffered an SCI and became quadriplegic at the age of 25. The case describes Murphy's relationship with Wayne, which begins with his post-accident ICU admission and continues over 18 months with Wayne's multiple readmissions for treatment of pressure ulcers, urinary infections, and other conditions. During this time, Wayne is struggling to find meaning and says to Murphy, "Why doesn't God take me home?" Murphy affirms Wayne's R/S struggle and tries to help him find some source of meaning and hope.

Australian chaplains conducted a pilot study with 21 rehabilitation patients who had suffered severe orthopedic injuries after road trauma (Calder et al., 2011). Using surveys and interviews, the investigators found 9 themes in the patients' descriptions of what they appreciated about the chaplains' care, including the chaplain's attentive listening, unconditional care, and assistance with R/S concerns. Some patients valued the chaplains' contributions to their motivation to recover, particularly when they experienced a setback. In another article, a medical rehabilitation chaplain described their clinical role, which included being present, listening to sacred stories, and supporting patients' search for meaning (Sailus, 2017). Sailus also described chaplains' ability to liaise with community religious leaders to address specific religious and/or cultural needs, to offer consultation on ethical issues, and to provide support to other healthcare staff.

The literature on spiritual care interventions is limited. Rehabilitation chaplain Margaret Thompson (2022) developed a group intervention, Grace Notes, designed to support spiritual well-being for patients with ABI. The intervention links themes associated with ABI rehabilitation and adjustment (e.g., problem solving, social skills, attention, and community) with an array of easily accessible spiritual practices from diverse traditions (e.g., visualization, meditation, and gratitude journal). Thompson et al. (2022) found preliminary evidence for the acceptability and benefits of Grace Notes. The article includes a link to a facilitator's manual and participant resources. Thrisna Dewi et al. (2020) conducted a clinical trial that examined the effects of 7 days of daily use of Emotional Freedom Techniques (tapping or rubbing acupressure points while focusing on troubling issues or fears; Church & Feinstein, 2017) and repetition of the Gayatri Mantra on QOL of post-acute stroke Hindu patients in Indonesia. There were 23 patients each in the control and intervention arms of the study; all participants received usual rehabilitation. Compared to the control participants, the intervention participants experienced significant improvements in QOL.

Dekker et al. (2020) describe the importance of learning what gives the client meaning and learning about their fundamental beliefs as the first step in working with them to set meaningful overall as well as specific rehabilitation goals. Their approach builds on research about global meaning for clients in rehabilitation. It also builds on the recognition that motivation for rehabilitation is improved when rehabilitation goals are grounded in fundamental beliefs. They identify the chaplain as the person with the training to interview the client to help them identify fundamental beliefs and articulate them for the rehabilitation team.

Rehabilitation Professionals and Religion/Spirituality

Spiritual care is most often provided by spiritual care specialists such as chaplains. However, there is an increasing argument for all members of the multidisciplinary team to feel comfortable and competent to provide some level of spiritual care when required (Jones et al., 2021). Rehabilitation professionals' perspectives on spirituality and spiritual care have been an area of interest for some time (Kilpatrick & McCullough, 1999). However, only a few studies have considered staff perspectives or training needs. We identified six studies that considered staff perspectives regarding R/S within the context of rehabilitation. Most were conducted in Western contexts (United States and Australia), with one conducted in the Middle East.

The earliest of these papers explored spirituality with 15 rehabilitation professionals. In this qualitative study, a clear distinction between spirituality and religion emerged, with participants viewing *spirituality* as personal and about connection and *religion* as external and "organized and institutional" with "rituals, rites and rules" (Morrison-Orton, 2004). A few years later, Gebhardt (2008) conducted a similar study with rehabilitation nurses, but in this case with the focus on spiritual care. Spiritual care was understood by participants as encompassing respect, support, and building a relationship. It was demonstrated through the "little things" that happened in nurse-patient interactions, a situation through which they as staff might gain or receive something from patients as a "bonus"; or during times when they felt they were being used in some way by a higher power. Comfort was gained in spiritual care provision through more practice and developing a stronger sense of their own spirituality.

Two studies by Jones and colleagues in Australia considered the perspectives of rehabilitation professionals regarding spirituality and spiritual care (Jones, Dorsett, and Briggs et al., 2018a; Jones et al., 2020b). The first of these was a small focus group study with 12 SCI professionals (Jones, Dorsett, and Briggs et al., 2018a). Spirituality was conceptualized by participants as (i) a sense of meaning and purpose; (ii) a belief in, or connection to, something or someone; and (iii) life values or "goodness." Spirituality was viewed as both a help and a hindrance in SCI rehabilitation; a help because of the hope and coping it facilitated, and a hindrance because it led some patients to believe they might be miraculously healed, or spiritual questions resulted in blame or anger that then impacted other aspects of the person's life. Spirituality was seen to be indirectly addressed in practice; however, barriers were identified: the perceptions that spirituality is a private matter, that therapist–patient boundaries needed to be respected, and that an unwelcome sharing of a patient's beliefs might result in discomfort for staff.

The second study by Jones et al. (2020b) explored the perceptions of 125 Australian rehabilitation professionals from a range of clinical contexts. An adapted version of the Royal College of Nursing Spirituality Survey (McSherry & Jamieson, 2011) was administered online. The top-rated identified spiritual need for patients was a "need for a source of hope and strength," followed closely by "a need for meaning and purpose." A key finding from this study was that although participants agreed that spirituality was a fundamental aspect of healthcare, 85% did not believe they received enough education or training. Training in basic knowledge and skills in recognizing spiritual issues was selected by most participants (92%) as an area of need.

A comparison to the studies above is provided by Omu and Reynolds (2014), who interviewed ten rehabilitation professionals working with Muslim stroke survivors in Kuwait. Like Jones, Dorsett, and Briggs et al. (2018a), R/S was viewed as both a potential help and hindrance toward self-efficacy. The influence of R/S was viewed positively in relation to empowerment and support, continuity of the moral self, and patients viewing disability as a test of resilience and something to accept. However, R/S could also have a potential negative effect on self-efficacy when the stroke was viewed as punishment from God or something to be accepted without question or action.

Of all the studies which considered the perspectives of rehabilitation professionals, only one examined their relationship with spiritual care specialists (Poncin et al., 2020). In that study, the authors considered what motivated rehabilitation professionals to refer patients to chaplains. Their findings revealed that although many referrals were driven by difficulties in the patient-professional relationship, staff also valued how the role of spiritual care facilitated access to a sense of identity for patients and assisted them to explore meaning in their lives within the context of rehabilitation. Chaplains were perceived as being able to offer something different to patients "at another level," compared to others on the multidisciplinary team.

Only one spiritual care training program for rehabilitation professionals was identified in our review, with the findings presented in two papers (Jones et al., 2020a; Jones et al., 2022). The training comprised two modules for staff working in the areas of TBI and SCI: the first is a self-study module that participants completed in their own time, and the second is a workshop to increase participants' skills, comfort, and confidence in addressing spiritual care. In an exploratory controlled trial, the training was demonstrated to significantly increase levels of spiritual care competency, confidence, comfort, and understanding of existential spirituality for those who attended the training ($n = 41$) compared to those who did not ($n = 32$) (Jones et al., 2020a). Qualitative data identified one overarching theme of increased awareness with the realization from participants that "spirituality is everybody's business." Six sub-themes pertaining to how this new awareness was experienced included increased awareness of the nature of spirituality, realization of the importance of spirituality to patients, a desire to keep spirituality on the radar, identifying barriers to providing spiritual care, incorporating spirituality into practice, and recognizing spirituality as personally meaningful.

Discussion

As can be seen from the work we have discussed above, the past 30 years have seen growth in research about R/S and medical rehabilitation. The studies have examined R/S for patients with SCI and TBI in acute rehabilitation and those living with these injuries in the community. They have included studies of inpatient rehabilitation samples with diverse conditions, including stroke. There is also a small body of research about the caregivers of these patients. While most of the research comes from Western nations, there is an important body of research from other religious and cultural contexts, including the Middle East and Asia. The consistency of findings about the role of R/S in rehabilitation across these diverse religious/ cultural contexts adds strength to evidence for the observed associations.

In this review, we found several key findings. Among medical rehabilitation patients, R/S coping is common and important. There is some evidence that R/S has beneficial associations with emotional well-being (e.g., depression); however, the evidence for this is not consistent. In contrast, the evidence for positive associations between R/S and QoL and life satisfaction is quite consistent; we describe 12 studies that found beneficial associations. The research also reports positive effects on self-rated health. Consistent with research in other clinical contexts, we also described research that found harmful effects of R/S distress on rehabilitation outcomes. The prevalence of R/S distress in the existing research ranges from 5% to 60%. As noted, most of the research in this field focuses on psychological outcomes; indeed, there is little research on associations between R/S and physical/functional health and none for social health.

While the research about R/S and medical rehabilitation is growing, its quality is limited. A large proportion of the studies use small samples from a single clinic. Almost all of the research is cross-sectional, and a considerable proportion of the work is qualitative (though qualitative research is important). The research we reviewed used diverse measures and conceptualizations of R/S. It included measures that focus mostly on religion, such as the BMMRS, and others, such as the SWB and FACIT-Sp, that include both religion and spirituality. As we saw in the research about R/S distress, R/S are multi-dimensional, and different dimensions of R/S may have different associations with rehabilitation outcomes. A close examination of these differences may strengthen our understanding of the processes through which R/S affects rehabilitation outcomes. Johnstone et al. (2009) used the subscales of the BMMRS to begin to investigate this question. Continuing this line of research will be important to clarifying how to integrate attention to R/S in clinical practice. The contribution of Webb's three-part conceptualization of spirituality (i.e., the RiTE Model of Spirituality; see Chapters 1 and 44 of this volume) is yet to be tested in medical rehabilitation. It should be noted that the items in some measures of R/S, including the meaning and peace subscales of the FACIT-Sp and the existential well-being subscale of the SWB, overlap with items used to measure constructs such as depression and QoL. In light of this, Harold Koenig (2008, p. 349), a leading religion-health investigator, has described associations involving these measures as "meaningless and tautological." In this regard, of note, Webb and colleagues, when developing a measure of their RiTE Model, recognized the conceptual limitations of the existential well-being subscale of the SWB and deliberately sought to avoid similar limitations in their conceptualization of existential spirituality.

Despite its limitations, we believe there is sufficient evidence regarding the importance of R/S, both its beneficial and harmful associations, to recommend routine attention to R/S issues in medical rehabilitation. Specifically, we urge rehabilitation professionals to give attention to patients' global meaning in setting rehabilitation goals as described by Dekker et al. (2020). We also urge clinicians to give attention to R/S distress and to make referrals to professional spiritual care providers as indicated. In this regard, further research to develop targeted measures to screen for R/S distress (Fitchett & Risk, 2009) is important.

There are several other areas that should be priorities for future research about R/S and medical rehabilitation. Currently, there is no research that addresses these issues in children and adolescents, and the research about caregivers is still quite limited. Continued growth of research in non-Western cultural contexts is also important. While qualitative research provides rich insights about the role of R/S in rehabilitation, the research in this field needs more rigorous methods in order to advance. To strengthen our understanding of the protective and harmful associations of R/S, good measures of multiple dimensions of R/S should be included in large, cooperative, longitudinal studies. Longitudinal studies should also be used to describe the prevalence, trajectory, and possible predictors of R/S distress. Collaborative projects that involve multiple clinical contexts are important in order to examine R/S in large and diverse samples.

The research about R/S interventions is very limited and should be a priority for future work. In addition to research about best methods to screen for R/S distress, we urge research that tests the benefits of R/S practices such as mantra repetition (Thrisna Dewi et al., 2020). Research is also needed about individual and group interventions that focus on meaning-making. We need evidence to help us understand who is most likely to benefit from these types of interventions and when is the best time to offer them in the trajectory of rehabilitation and recovery. We hope this review provides a helpful foundation for this important work.

References

Ajoudani, F., Jafarizadeh, H., & Kazamzadeh, J. (2019). Social support and posttraumatic growth in Iranian burn survivors: The mediating role of spirituality. *Burns*, *45*(3), 732–740. https://doi.org/10.1016/j.burns.2018.10.013

Akturk, S., & Akturk, U. (2020). Determining the spiritual well-being of patients with spinal cord injury. *The Journal of Spinal Cord Medicine*, *43*, 69–76. https://doi.org/10.1080/10790268.2018.1490875

Alquwez, N., & Alshahrani, A. A. (2021). Influence of spiritual coping and social support on the mental health and quality of life of the Saudi informal caregivers of patients with stroke. *Journal of Religion and Health*, *60*, 787–803. https://doi.org/10.1007/s10943-020-01081-w

Anderson, J.M., Anderson, L.J., Felsenthal, G. (1993). Pastoral needs and support within an inpatient rehabilitation unit. *Archives of Physical Medicine and Rehabilitation*, *74*(6), 574–578. https://doi.org/10.1016/0003-9993(93)90154-3

Ayesha, A.S., Saba, S., Kashif, M., Khan, D.A., Haque, A., Naseer, M.I., Abuzenadah, A.M., Hashem, A.M., & Rehman, S.U. (2022). The relationship between psychological disability and religious practice and coping strategies in caregivers of children with traumatic brain injury in Pakistani population. *Healthcare (Basel)*. *10*(11), 2158. https://doi.org/10.3390/healthcare10112158

Azar, N. S., Radfar, M., & Baghaei, R. (2022). Spiritual self-care in stroke survivors: A qualitative study. *Journal of Religion and Health*, *61*(1), 493–506. https://doi.org/10.1007/s10943-020-01030-7

Babamohamadi, H., Negarandeh, R., & Dehghan-Nayeri, N. (2011). Coping strategies used by people with spinal cord injury: A qualitative study. *Spinal Cord*, *49*, 832–837. https://doi.org/10.1038/sc.2011.10

Baldacchino, D., Torskenaes, K., Kalfoss, M., Borg, J., Tonna, A., Debattista, C., Decelis, N., & Mifsud, R. (2013a). Spiritual coping in rehabilitation– A comparative study: part 1. *British Journal of Nursing* *22*(4), 228–232. https://doi.org/10.12968/bjon.2013.22.4.228

Baldacchino, D., Torskenaes, K., Kalfoss, M., Borg, J., Tonna, A., Debattista, C., Decelis, N., & Mifsud, R. (2013b). Spiritual coping in rehabilitation–A comparative study: part 2. *British Journal of Nursing* *22*(7), 402–408. https://doi.org/10.12968/bjon.2013.22.7.402

Bauman, J. (2008). The role of forgiveness in rehabilitation. *Journal of Health Care Chaplaincy*. *14*(2),75–82. https://doi.org/10.1080/08854720802129018

Bockrath, M. F., Pargament, K. I., Wong, S., Harriott, V. A., Pomerleau, J. M., Homolka, S. J., Chaudhary, Z. B., & Exline, J. J. (2022). Religious and spiritual struggles and their links to psychological adjustment: A meta-analysis of longitudinal studies. *Psychology of Religion and Spirituality*, 14(3), 283–299. https://doi.org/10.1037/rel0000400

Bolgeo, T., De Maria, M., Vellone, E., Ambrosca, R., Simeone, S., Alvaro, R., & Pucciarelli, G. (2022). The association of spirituality with anxiety and depression in stroke survivor-caregiver dyads: An actor-partner interdependence model. *Journal of Cardiovascular Nursing*, *37*(4), E97–E106. https://doi.org/10.1097/JCN.0000000000000798

Boswell, B. B., Knight, S., Hamer, M., & McChesney, J. (2001). Disability and spirituality: A reciprocal relationship with implications for the rehabilitation process. *The Journal of Rehabilitation*, *67*(4), 20.

Bourke, J.A., Hay-Smith, E. J., Snell, D. L., & DeJong, G. (2015). Attending to biographical disruption: The experience of rehabilitation following tetraplegia due to spinal cord injury. *Disability and Rehabilitation. 37*(4), 296–303. https://doi.org/10.3109/09638288.2014.918188

Brillhart, B. (2005). A study of spirituality and life satisfaction among persons with spinal cord injury. *Rehabilitation Nursing, 30*(1), 31–34. https://doi.org/10.1002/j.2048-7940.2005.tb00353.x

Budd, MA., Gater, DR Jr., & Channell, I. (2022). Psychosocial consequences of spinal cord injury: A narrative review. *Journal of Personalized Medicine. 12*(7), 1178. https://doi.org/10.3390/jpm12071178

Calder, A., Badcoe, A., & Harms, L. (2011). Broken bodies, healing spirits: Road trauma survivor's perceptions of pastoral care during inpatient orthopaedic rehabilitation. *Disability and Rehabilitation. 33*(15-16), 1358–1366. https://doi.org/10.3109/09638288.2010.532280

Chlan, K., Zebracki, K., & Vogel, L. (2011). Spirituality and life satisfaction in adults with pediatric-onset spinal cord injury. *Spinal Cord, 49*, 371–375. https://doi.org/10.1038/sc.2010.80

Chow, E. O. W., & Nelson-Becker, H. (2010). Spiritual distress to spiritual transformation: Stroke survivor narratives from Hong Kong. *Journal of Aging Studies, 24*(4), 313–324. https://doi.org/10.1016/j.jaging.2010.06.001

Church, D., & Feinstein, D. (2017). The manual stimulation of acupuncture points in the treatment of post-traumatic stress disorder: A review of clinical emotional freedom techniques. *Medical Acupuncture*, 29(4), 194–205. https://doi.org/10.1089/acu.2017.1213

Cohen, D., Yoon, D. P., & Johnstone, B. (2009). Differentiating the impact of spiritual experiences, religious practices, and congregational support on the mental health of individuals with heterogeneous medical disorders. *International Journal for the Psychology of Religion, 19*(2), 121–138. https://doi.org/10.1080/10508610802711335

Dekker, J., de Groot, V., Ter Steeg, AM., Vloothuis, J., Holla, J., Collette, E., Satink, T., Post, L., Doodeman, S., & Littooij, E. (2020). Setting meaningful goals in rehabilitation: Rationale and practical tool. *Clinical Rehabilitation. 34*(1), 3–12. https://doi.org/10.1177/0269215519876299

DeSanto-Madeya, S. (2006). The meaning of living with spinal cord injury 5 to 10 years after the injury. *Western Journal of Nursing Research. 28*(3), 265–289. https://doi.org/10.1177/0193945905283178

Fetzer Institute & National Institute on Aging Working Group. (1999). *Multidimensional measurement of religiousness/spirituality for use in health research*. Kalamazoo, MI: Fetzer Institute. Available at https://fetzer.org/resources/multidimensional-measurement-religiousnessspirituality-use-health-research

Fitchett, G., & Risk, J. L. (2009). Screening for spiritual struggle. *Journal of Pastoral Care & Counseling. 63*(1-2), 4-1-12. https://doi.org/10.1177/154230500906300104

Fitchett, G., Rybarczyk, B. D., deMarco, G. A., & Nicholas, J. J. (1999). The role of religion in medical rehabilitation outcomes: A longitudinal study. *Rehabilitation Psychology, 44*(4), 333–353. https://doi.org/10.1037/0090-5550.44.4.333

Forchheimer, M., & Tate, D. G. (2007). The relationship of spirituality and depression to health among people with spinal cord injury. *Topics in Spinal Cord Injury Rehabilitation, 12*(3), 23–34. https://doi.org/10.1310/sci1203-23

Frank, A. (2013) *The wounded storyteller: Body, illness, and ethics* (2nd edn). University of Chicago Press.

Franklin, K. L., Yoon, D. P., Acuff, M., & Johnstone, B. (2008). Relationships among religiousness, spirituality, and health for individuals with spinal cord injury. *Topics in Spinal Cord Injury Rehabilitation, 14*(2), 76–81. https://doi.org/10.1310/sci1402-76

Gebhardt, M. C. (2008). Rehabilitation nurses' experiences providing spiritual care. *Spirituality and Health International, 9*, 230–240. https://doi.org/10.1002/shi.353

Giaquinto, S., Sarno, S., Dall'Armi, V., & Spiridigliozzi, C. (2010). Religious and spiritual beliefs in stroke rehabilitation. *Clinical and Experimental Hypertension, 32*, 6. https://doi.org/10.3109/10641960903443566

Giaquinto, S., & Spiridigliozzi, C. (2007). Possible influence of spiritual and religious beliefs on hypertension. *Clinical and Experimental Hypertension, 29*(7), 457–464. https://doi.org/10.1080/10641960701615683

Gibbs, L.A.L., Anderson, M.I., Simpson, G.K., Jones, K.F. (2020). Spirituality and resilience among family caregivers of survivors of stroke: A scoping review. *NeuroRehabilitation, 46*(1), 41–52. https://doi.org/10.3233/NRE-192946

Gillespie, E. (2019). A qualitative pilot study of spirituality in long-term recovery in acquired brain injury. *The Journal of Pastoral Care & Counseling*, *73*(2), 96–105. https://doi.org/10.1177/1542305019853588

Guan, B., Anderson, D.B., Chen, L., Feng, S., & Zhou, H. (2023). Global, regional and national burden of traumatic brain injury and spinal cord injury, 1990-2019: A systematic analysis for the Global Burden of Disease Study 2019. *BMJ Open*, *13*(10), e075049. https://doi.org/10.1016/S1474-4422(18)30415-0

Hajiaghababaei, M., Saberi, H., Rahnama, P., & Montazeri, A. (2018). Spiritual well-being and quality of life in patients with spinal cord injury: A study from Iran. *Journal of Spinal Cord Medicine*, *41*(6), 653–658. https://doi.org/10.1080/10790268.2018.1466479

Hanks, R. A., Boileau, N. R., Norman, A. L., Nakase-Richardson, R., Mariouw, K. H., & Carlozzi, N. E. (2020). Spirituality and outcomes in caregivers of persons with traumatic brain injury (TBI). *Rehabilitation Psychology*, *65*(4), 347–359. https://doi.org/10.1037/rep0000304

Hatefi, M., Vaisi-Raygani, A., Borji, M., & Tarjoman, A. (2020). Investigating the relationship between religious beliefs with care burden, stress, anxiety, and depression in caregivers of patients with spinal cord injuries. *Journal of Religion and Health*, *59*(4), 1754–1765. https://doi.org/10.1007/s10943-019-00853-3

Idler, E. L. (1995). Religion, health, and nonphysical senses of self. *Social Forces*, *74*(2), 683–704. https://doi.org/10.2307/2580497

Jibeen, T., Mahfooz, M., & Fatima, S. (2018). Spiritual transcendence and psychological adjustment: The moderating role of personality in burn patients. *Journal of Religion and Health*, *57*(5), 1618–1633. https://doi.org/10.1007/s10943-017-0484-z

Johnstone, B., Franklin, K. L., Yoon, D. P., Burris, J., & Shigaki, C. (2008). Relationships among religiousness, spirituality, and health for individuals with stroke. *Journal of Clinical Psychology in Medical Settings*, *15*(4), 308–313. https://doi.org/10.1007/s10880-008-9128-5

Johnstone, B., & Glass, B. A. (2008). Support for a neuropsychological model of spirituality in persons with traumatic brain injury. *Zygon*, *43*(4), 861–874. https://doi.org/10.1111/j.1467-9744.2008.00964.x

Johnstone, B., & Yoon, D. P. (2009). Relationships between the Brief Multidimensional Measure of Religiousness/Spirituality and health outcomes for a heterogeneous rehabilitation population. *Rehabilitation Psychology*, *54*(4), 422–431. https://doi.org/10.1037/a0017758

Johnstone, B., Yoon, D. P., Rupright, J., & Reid-Arndt, S. (2009). Relationships among spiritual beliefs, religious practises, congregational support and health for individuals with traumatic brain injury. *Brain Injury*, *23*(5), 411–419. https://doi.org/10.1080/02699050902788501

Jones, A., Cohen, D., Johnstone, B., Yoon, D. P., Schopp, L. H., McCormack, G., & Campbell, J. (2015). Relationships between negative spiritual beliefs and health outcomes for individuals with heterogeneous medical conditions. *Journal of Spirituality in Mental Health*, *17*(2), 135–152. https://doi.org/10.1080/19349637.2015.1023679

Jones, K., Paal, P., Symons, X., & Best, M. (2021). The content, teaching methods and effectiveness of spiritual care training for healthcare professionals: A mixed-methods systematic review. *Journal of Pain and Symptom Management*, *62*(3), e261–e278. https://doi.org/10.1016/j.jpainsymman.2021.03.013

Jones, K. F., Dorsett, P., Briggs, L., & Simpson, G. (2018a). The role of spirituality in spinal cord injury (SCI) rehabilitation: Exploring health professional perspectives. *Spinal Cord Series and Cases*, *4*(1), 54. https://doi.org/10.1038/s41394-018-0078-3

Jones, K. F., Dorsett, P., Simpson, G., & Briggs, L. (2018b). Moving forward on the journey: spirituality and family resilience after spinal cord injury. *Rehabilitation Psychology*, *63*(4), 521–531. https://doi.org/10.1037/rep0000229

Jones, K. F., Pryor, J., Care-Unger, C., & Simpson, G. (2018c). Spirituality and its relationship with positive adjustment following traumatic brain injury: A scoping review. *Brain Injury*, *32*(13-14), 1612–1622. https://doi.org/10.1080/02699052.2018.1511066

Jones, K. F., Pryor, J., Care-Unger, C., & Simpson, G. (2020a). Effectiveness of spiritual care training for rehabilitation professionals: An exploratory controlled trial. *NeuroRehabilitation*, *47*(4), 393–403. https://doi.org/10.3233/NRE-203221

Jones, K. F., Pryor, J., Care-Unger, C., & Simpson, G. (2020b). Rehabilitation health professionals' perceptions of spirituality and spiritual care: The results of an online survey. *NeuroRehabilitation*, *46*(1), 17–30. https://doi.org/10.3233/NRE-192857

Jones, K. F., Pryor, J., Care-Unger, C., & Simpson, G. (2022). "Spirituality is everybody's business": An exploration of the impact of spiritual care training upon the perceptions and practice of rehabilitation professionals. *Disability and Rehabilitation*, *44*(8), 1409–1418. https://doi.org/10.1080/09638288.2020.1820586

Jones, K. F., Simpson, G., Briggs, L., & Dorsett, P. (2016). Does spirituality facilitate adjustment and resilience among individuals and their families after SCI? *Disability and Rehabilitation*, *38*(10), 921–935. https://doi.org/10.3109/09638288.2015.1066884

Jones, K. F., Simpson, G., Briggs, L., Dorsett, P., & Anderson, M. (2019). A study of whether individual and dyadic relations between spirituality and resilience contribute to psychological adjustment among individuals with spinal cord injuries and their family members. *Clinical Rehabilitation*, *33*(9), 1503–1514. https://doi.org/10.1177/0269215519845034

Kass, J. D., Friedman, R., Lesserman, J., Zuttermeister, P., & Benson, H. (1991). Health outcomes and a new index of spiritual experience. *Journal for the Scientific Study of Religion*, *30*(2), 203–211. https://doi.org/10.2307/1387214

Keightley, M., King, G. E., Shu-Hyun, J., White, R. J., Colantonio, A., Minore, J. B., Katt, M. V., Cameron, A., Bellavance, A. M., & Longboat-White, C. H. (2011). Brain injury from a First Nations' perspective: Teachings from elders and traditional healers. *Canadian Journal of Occupational Therapy*, *78*(4), 237–245. https://doi.org/10.2182/cjot.2011.78.4.5

Kilpatrick, S., & McCullough, M. (1999). Religion and spirituality in rehabilitation psychology. *Rehabilitation Psychology*, *44*(4), 388–402. https://doi.org/10.1037/0090-5550.44.4.388

Kim, J., Heinemann, A. W., Bode, R. K., Sliwa, J., & King, R. B. (2000). Spirituality, quality of life, and functional recovery after medical rehabilitation. *Rehabilitation Psychology*, *45*(4), 365–385. https://doi.org/10.1037/0090-5550.45.4.365

Koenig, H. G. (2008). Concerns about measuring "spirituality" in research. *Journal of Nervous and Mental Disease 196*(5) 349–355. https://doi.org/10.1097/NMD.0b013e31816ff796

Laures-Gore, J. S., Lambert, P. L., Kruger, A. C., Love, J., & Davis, D. E. (2018). Spirituality and post-stroke aphasia recovery. *Journal of Religion and Health*, *57*(5), 1876–1888. https://doi.org/10.1007/s10943-018-0592-4

Lucchetti, G., Granero, A. L., Badan-Neo, A. M., Peres, P. T., Peres, M. F. P., Moreira-Almeida, A., Gomes, C., & Koenig, H. (2011). Religiousness affects mental health, pain, and quality of life in older people in an outpatient rehabilitation setting. *Journal of Rehabilitation Medicine*, *43*, 316–322. https://doi.org/10.2340/16501977-0784

Magyar-Russell, G., Pargament, K. I., Trevino, K. M., & Sherman, J. E. (2013). Religious and spiritual appraisals and coping strategies among patients in medical rehabilitation. *Research in the Social Scientific Study of Religion*, *24*, 93–135. https://doi.org/10.1163/9789004252073_006

Mahalik, J., Johnstone, B., Glass, B. A., & Yoon, D. P. (2007). Spirituality, psychological coping, and community integration for persons with traumatic brain injury. *Journal of Religion, Disability and Health*, *11*(3), 65–77. https://doi.org/10.1300/J095v11n03_06

Marini, I., & Glover-Graf, N. M. (2011). Religiosity and spirituality among persons with spinal cord injury: Attitudes, beliefs, and practices. *Rehabilitation Counseling Bulletin*, *54*(2), 82–92. http://rcb.sagepub.com/content/54/2/82.abstract

Matheis, E. N., Tulsky, D. S., & Matheis, R. J. (2006). The relation between spirituality and quality of life among individuals with spinal cord injury. *Rehabilitation Psychology*, *51*(3), 265–271. https://doi.org/10.1037/0090-5550.51.3.265

Mavaddat, N., Sadler, E., Lim, L., Williams, K., Warburton, E., Kinmonth, A.L., Mckevitt, C., & Mant. J. (2021). What underlies the difference between self-reported health and disability after stroke? A qualitative study in the UK. *BMC Neurology*, *21*(1), 315. https://doi.org/10.1186/s12883-021-02338-x

McColl, M. A., Bickenbach, J., Johnston, J., Nishihama, S., Schumaker, M., Smith, K., Smith, M., & Yealland, B. (2000). Changes in spiritual beliefs after traumatic disability. *Archives of Physical Medicine and Rehabilitation*, *81*(6), 817–823. http://linkinghub.elsevier.com/retrieve/pii/S0003999300901175?showall=true

McNulty, K., Livneh, H., & Wilson, L. M. (2004). Perceived uncertainty, spiritual well-being, and psychosocial adaptation in individuals with multiple sclerosis. *Rehabilitation Psychology*, *49*(2), 91–99. https://doi.org/10.1037/0090-5550.49.2.91

McSherry, W., & Jamieson, S. (2011). An online survey of nurses' perceptions of spirituality and spiritual care. *Journal of Clinical Nursing*, *20*(11-12), 1757–1767. https://doi.org/10.1111/j.1365-2702.2010.03547.x

Monod, S., Martin, E., Spencer, B., Rochat, E., & Büla, C. (2012). Validation of the Spiritual Distress Assessment Tool in older hospitalized patients. *BMC Geriatrics*, *12*, 13. https://doi.org/10.1186/1471-2318-12-13

Morgenstern, L. B., Sánchez, B. N., Skolarus, L. E., Garcia, N., Risser, J. M., Wing, J. J., Smith, M. A., Zahuranec, D. B., & Lisabeth, L. D. (2011). Fatalism, optimism, spirituality, depressive symptoms, and stroke outcome: a population-based analysis. *Stroke*, *42*(12), 3518–3523. https://doi.org/10.1161/strokeaha.111.625491

Morrison-Orton, D. J. (2004). How rehabilitation professionals define the concepts of spirituality and religion when working with individuals with disabilities. *Journal of Social Work in Disability & Rehabilitation*, *3*(2), 37–55. https://doi.org/10.1300/J198v03n02_04

Mundle, R. (2015a). "I should be closer to God because of this"—A case study of embodied narratives and spiritual reconstruction in spinal cord injury and stroke rehabilitation, *Journal of Disability & Religion*, *19*(1), 30–49. https://doi.org/10.1080/23312521.2014.990551

Mundle, R. (2015b). A narrative analysis of spiritual distress in geriatric physical rehabilitation. *Journal of Health Psychology*. *20*(3), 273–285. https://doi.org/10.1177/1359105314566609

Murphy, J.N. (2017). The chaplain as the mediator between the patient and the interdisciplinary team in ethical decision making: A chaplaincy case study involving a quadriplegic patient. *Health & Social Care Chaplaincy*, *5*(2), 241–256. https://doi.org/10.1558/hscc.34301

Murphy, P.E., Canada, A.L., Fitchett, G., Stein, K., Portier, K., Crammer, C., & Peterman, A.H. (2010). An examination of the 3-factor model and structural invariance across racial/ethnic groups for the FACIT-Sp: A report from the American Cancer Society's Study of Cancer Survivors-II (SCS-II). *Psychooncology*, *19*(3), 264–272. https://doi.org/10.1002/pon.1559

Omu, O., & Reynolds, F. (2014). Religious faith and self-efficacy among stroke patients in Kuwait: Health professionals' views. *Disability and Rehabilitation*, *36*(18), 1529–1535. https://doi.org/10.3109/09638288.2014.892641

Peterman, A.H., Fitchett, G., Brady, M.J., Hernandez, L., & Cella, D. (2002). Measuring spiritual well-being in people with cancer: The functional assessment of chronic illness therapy--Spiritual Well-being Scale (FACIT-Sp). *Annals of Behavioral Medicine*, *24*(1), 49–58. https://doi.org/10.1207/S15324796ABM2401_06

Philippus, A., Mellick, D., O'Neil-Pirozzi, T., Bergquist, T., Guller Bodien, Y., Sander, A. M., Dreer, L. E., Giacino, J., & Novack, T. (2016). Impact of religious attendance on psychosocial outcomes for individuals with traumatic brain injury: a NIDILRR funded TBI model systems study. *Brain Injury*, *30*(13-14), 1605–1611. https://doi.org/10.1080/02699052.2016.1199903

Piderman, K.M. (2015). 'Why did God do this to me?': Angela, a 17-year-old girl with spinal injury. In G. Fitchett & S. Nolan (Eds.), *Spiritual care in practice: Case studies in healthcare chaplaincy* (pp 69–89). London: Jessica Kingsley Publishers.

Piderman, K. M., Mueller, P. S., Theneau, T. M., Stevens, S. R., Hanson, A. C., & Reeves, R. K. (2011). A pilot study of spirituality and inpatient rehabilitation outcomes in persons with spinal cord dysfunction and severe neurological illnesses. *Journal of Pastoral Care & Counseling*, *65*(4), 1–13. https://doi.org/10.1177/154230501106500402

Poncin, E., Niquille, B., Jobin, G., Benaim, C., & Rochat, E. (2020). What motivates healthcare professionals' referrals to chaplains, and how to help them formulate referrals that accurately reflect patients' spiritual needs. *Journal of Health Care Chaplaincy*, *26*, 1–15. https://doi.org/10.1080/08854726.2019.1582211

Pucciarelli, G., Vellone, E., Bolgeo, T., Simeone, S., Alvaro, R., Lee, C. S., & Lyons, K. S. (2020). Role of spirituality on the association between depression and quality of life in stroke survivor-care partner dyads. *Circulation: Cardiovascular quality and outcomes*, *13*(6), e006129. https://doi.org/10.1161/CIRCOUTCOMES.119.006129

Riley, B. B., Perna, R., Tate, D. G., Forchheimer, M., Anderson, C., & Luera, G. (1998). Types of spiritual well-being among persons with chronic illness: their relation to various forms of quality of life. *Archives of Physical Medicine and Rehabilitation*, *79*(3), 258–264. http://linkinghub.elsevier.com/retrieve/pii/S0003999398900041?showall=true

Robinson-Smith, G. (2002). Prayer after stroke: Its relationship to quality of life. *Journal of Holistic Nursing*, *20*(4), 352–366. https://doi.org/10.1177/089801002237592

Rodriguez, V. J., Glover-Graf, N. M., & Blanco, E. L. (2013). Conversations with God: Prayer and bargaining in adjustment to disability. *Rehabilitation Counseling Bulletin*, *56*(4), 215–228. https://doi.org/10.1177/0034355213477477

Sailus, M.C. (2017). The role of the chaplain in the interdisciplinary care of the rehabilitation patient. *Rehabilitation Nursing*, *42*(2), 90–96. https://doi.org/10.1002/rnj.222

Salisbury, S.R., Ciulla, M.R., & McSherry, E. (1989). Clinical management reporting and objective diagnostic instruments for spiritual assessment in spinal cord injury patients. *Journal of Health Care Chaplaincy*, *2*(2), 35–64. https://doi.org/10.1300/J080v02n02_05

Sekely, A., Xie, Y., Makani, A., Brown, T., & Zakzanis, K. K. (2020). Spiritual well-being as a predictor of emotional impairement following mild traumatic brain injury. *Journal of Clinical Psychology in Medical Settings*, *27*, 859–866. https://doi.org/10.1007/s10880-019-09687-3

Siddall, P. J., McIndoe, L., Austin, P., & Wrigley, P. J. (2017). The impact of pain on spiritual well-being in people with a spinal cord injury. *Spinal Cord*, *55*(1), 105–111. https://doi.org/10.1038/sc.2016.75

Simpson, G., Anderson, M., Jones, K. F., Genders, M., & Gopinath, B. (2020). Do spirituality, resilience and hope mediate outcomes among family caregivers after traumatic brain injury or spinal cord injury? A structural equation modelling approach. *NeuroRehabilitation* *46*(1), 3–15. https://doi.org/10.3233/NRE-192945

Smith, B., Sparkes, A.C. (2005). Men, sport, spinal cord injury, and narratives of hope. *Social Science in Medicine*, *61*(5), 1095–1105. https://doi.org/10.1016/j.socscimed.2005.01.011

Tate, D. G., & Forchheimer, M. (2002). Quality of life, life satisfaction, and spirituality: comparing outcomes between rehabilitaton and cancer patients. *American Journal of Physical Medicine and Rehabilitation*, *81*, 400–410. https://doi.org/10.1097/00002060-200206000-00002

Thompson, M., Rabusch, S., Radomski, M.V., Marquardt, V., Kath, K., Kreiger, R., & Squires, K. (2022). Grace Notes: Feasibility of a manualized intervention to advance spiritual well-being for clients with acquired brain injury. *Journal of Health Care Chaplaincy*, *28*(4), 497–509. https://doi.org/10.1080/08854726.2021.1929764

Thrisna Dewi, N.L.P., Arifin, M.T., & Ismail, S. (2020). The Influence of Gayatri Mantra and Emotional Freedom Technique on quality of life of post-stroke patients. *Journal of Multidisciplinary Healthcare*, *13*, 909–916. https://doi.org/10.2147/JMDH.S266580

Torabi Chafjiri, R., Navabi, N., Shamsalinia, A., & Ghaffari, F. (2017). The relationship between the spiritual attitude of the family caregivers of older patients with stroke and their burden. *Clinical Interventions in Aging*, *12*, 453–458. https://doi.org/10.2147/CIA.S121285

Üşenmez, T.Y. Budak, F.K., & Yılmaz, R. (2022). The effect of spiritual well-being on hope in immobile patients suffering from paralysis due to spinal cord injuries. *Journal of Religion and Health*, *61*(5), 4051–4061. https://doi.org/10.1007/s10943-021-01376-6

Waldron-Perrine, B., Rapport, L. J., Hanks, R. A., Lumley, M., Meachen, S., & Hubbarth, P. (2011). Religion and spirituality in rehabilitation outcomes among individuals with traumatic brain injury. *Rehabilitation Psychology*, *56*(2), 107–116. https://doi.org/10.1037/a0023552

Wang, Z., Zhao, H., Zhu, Y., Zhang, S., Xiao, L., Bao, H., Wang, Z., Wang, Y., Li, X., Zhang, Y., & Pang, X. (2022). Needs for nurses to provide spiritual care and their associated influencing factors among elderly inpatients with stroke in China: A cross-sectional quantitative study. *Palliative & Supportive Care*, *20*(3), 407–416. https://doi.org/10.1017/S1478951522000426

Ware, J. E., Snow, K. K., Kosinski, M., & Gandek, B. (1993). *SF-36 health survey: Manual and interpretation guide*. Boston, MA: The Health Institute, New England Medical Center.

Webb, J. R. (2007). Spiritual factors and adjustment in medical rehabilitation: Understanding forgiveness as a means of coping. In A. E. DellOrto & P. W. Power (Eds.), *The psychological and social impact of illness and disability* (5th ed., pp. 455–471). Springer. (Reprinted from *Journal of Applied Rehabilitation Counseling*, *34*(3), 16-24: 2003)

Webb, J. R., Toussaint, L., Kalpakjian, C. Z., & Tate, D. G. (2010). Forgiveness and health-related outcomes among people with spinal cord injury. *Disability and Rehabilitation*, *32*(5), 360–366. https://doi.org/10.3109/09638280903166360

Webb, J. R., Toussaint, L. L., & Conway-Williams, E. (2012). Forgiveness and health: Psycho-spiritual integration and the promotion of better healthcare. *Journal of Health Care Chaplaincy*, *18*(1-2), 57–73. https://doi.org/10.1080/08854726.2012.667317

WHOQOL SRPB Group (2006). A cross-cultural study of spirituality, religion, and personal beliefs as components of quality of life. *Social Science & Medicine*, *62*(6),1486–1497. https://doi.org/10.1016/j.socscimed.2005.08.001

Wilson, C. S., Forchheimer, M., Heinemann, A. W., Warren, A. M., & McCullumsmith, C. (2017). Assessment of the relationship of spiritual well-being to depression and quality of life for persons with spinal cord injury. *Disability and Rehabilitation*, *39*(5), 491–496. https://doi.org/10.3109/09638288.2016.1152600

Xue, S., Arya, S., Embuldeniya, A., Narammalage, H., da Silva, T., Williams, S., & Ravindran, A. (2016). Perceived functional impairment and spirituality/religiosity as predictors of depression in a Sri Lankan spinal cord injury patient population. *Spinal Cord*, *54*(1158-1163). https://doi.org/10.1038/sc.2016.56

Chapter 16

Awakened Awareness

A Process of Supported Spiritual Individuation in Emerging Adult College Students

Suza C. Scalora, Amy L. Chapman, Elisabeth J. Mistur, Abigail A. Crete, Micheline R. Anderson, and Lisa Miller*

Awakened Awareness for Adolescents (AA-A) is a science-driven, designed process for nurturing spiritual individuation in adolescents and emerging adults. The impact of this process is demonstrated through this qualitative research study, revealing participants' support for spiritual individuation. Awakened Awareness (AA) for adults as a guided process of spiritual awakening evolved over two decades (1998–2020) of clinical science and teaching into an accretive arc of support for the awakening of human relational transcendent awareness (Miller, 2011). AA-A is an adaptation of this process specifically for adolescents and emerging adults (17–25 years of age) (by Miller, Scalora, and Anderson 2018–2020) that has been quantitatively assessed for feasibility and helpfulness in an open trial format (Scalora et al., 2022). This current study examines the spiritual individuation process supported by the AA-A, using qualitative data analysis, revealing the foundational pillars as experienced by emerging adult college students who participated in the AA-A program.

Often, the impetus for engagement with the AA-A program is a catalytic moment in a college student's life that necessitates a supported process for spiritual individuation. AA-A embraces the range of life events that may prompt emerging adults to reengage with the process of spiritual individuation, such as spiritual injury or spiritual struggles, through examination, reflection, and augmented relational transcendent awareness, all toward reconstructing their own spiritual identity. Over the arc of its eight sessions, AA-A guides students through a developmental and integrative process of an emerging, lived, spiritual identity.

State of Mental Health on College Campuses in the United States

Within the past decade, mental health crises have surged among college students in the United States. Over 60% of college students meet the criteria for at least one mental health problem, an increase of almost 50% from 2013 (Flannery, 2023; Lipson et al., 2022). The COVID-19 pandemic intensified mental health problems further; in the academic year 2021–2022, 44% of college students reported symptoms of depression, 37% anxiety, and 15% reported seriously contemplating suicide (Heinze et al., 2022). And yet, many are treatment-averse: 67% of anxious and depressed emerging adults do not access mental health services (Active Minds, 2022). Reasons for this aversion to mental health care include minimization of relevant symptoms, difficulty in understanding mental health issues, and the expectation that stress is prevalent in college (Barbayannis et al., 2022). The mental health crisis is also compounded for

* Corresponding Author: drsuzascalora@gmail.com.

DOI: 10.4324/9781003440048-19

sexual and gender minorities (SGM) and ethnic and racial minorities, the latter of whom are less likely to seek help for mental health conditions (Borgogna et al., 2019; Colarossi, 2022; Horowitz et al., 2020). A multitude of factors contribute to inequities in mental health access and treatment for minority populations. Barriers such as mental health stigma and inclusivity and eligibility concerns keep students from availing themselves of the existing resources (Anderson, 2018; Dunbar et al., 2017). Thus, more evidence-based, culturally appropriate, accessible interventions are needed on college campuses.

The mental health crisis on college campuses is exacerbated by insufficient mental health resources and persistent barriers to access. In response, higher education institutions are urged to provide more comprehensive and accessible mental health and wellness services. Spiritual-Mind-Body (SMB) interventions, as innovative, inclusive, and targeted prevention strategies, are gaining traction and being explored as potential resources for emerging adults (Abrams, 2022; Bruffaerts et al., 2019; McPhillips, 2023; Museus, 2023; Scalora et al., 2020; Scalora et al., 2022).

Spirituality

Spirituality here is understood as a quest for the Transcendent that dwells both beyond and within the self, based upon scientific evidence of an innate human capacity to engage in relational transcendence (Kendler et al., 1997, 1999). The Transcendent is recognized by many appellations across religious traditions and cultures, signifying a divine or Ultimate Truth: G-d, Hashem, Jesus, Allah, a Higher Power, the Universe, cosmic energy, and Ultimate Reality (Hill et al., 2000; Hodges, 2002; Koenig, 2012). The personal dimension of spirituality is understood as a dynamic, nurturing relationship with a loving and guiding transcendent force, accompanied by an awareness of living within a sanctified cosmos (Barton & Miller, 2015).

Relational spirituality, or "ways of relating to the sacred" (Shults & Sandage, 2006, for an overview), accentuates the mutual influences between spirituality and personal relationships throughout human development. Relationships – particularly with spiritual mentors or within communities – often shape identity and catalyze spiritual maturation and the process of spiritual individuation (Desrosiers et al., 2011; McAdams, 1993). This framework views relational dynamics as foundational in the construction of spiritual identity and meaning-making, with spirituality influencing ways of relating to the Transcendent and, by extension, ways of relating to the self and others (Sandage et al., 2008). Such relationships are pivotal in emerging adulthood, defined by identity exploration and consolidation (Arnett & Tanner, 2006).

Relational spirituality is critical for supported spiritual individuation. Relational spirituality provides the scaffolding for spiritual individuation, emphasizing the formative influence of relational dynamics in this developmental arc (Benson et al., 2019). The "spiritual self" concept, integral to identity formation in emerging adults, underscores the role of community and interpersonal relationships in shaping an individual's inner spiritual identity (Markstrom, 1999). The supported spiritual individuation process – the awakening or deepening of spiritual consciousness – is facilitated by relational spirituality, with genuine community experiences and spiritually oriented relationships fostering growth and providing stability during transformative experiences (Grof & Grof, 1989; Peck, 2010). Overall, the nurturing of relational spirituality, as foundational to spiritual individuation in emerging adulthood, strengthens the core in whole-person development.

Relationship Between Spirituality and Health and Well-Being

Personal spirituality, particularly during adolescence (12–18 years of age), emerges as a potent protective factor against depressive disorders and substance use and misuse, with findings indicating a 40–80% decreased risk for adult depression (Bonelli et al., 2012; Miller, 2013; Miller et al., 2000; Miller et al., 1997). Empirical research has shown a positive association between personal spirituality and mental health, including lower rates of depression, anxiety, and substance misuse (Koenig et al., 2012). Personal spirituality is instrumental to developing a robust and healthy identity formation and may offer a buffer against the recurrence of various psychopathologies (King, 2019; McNamara et al., 2010; Oppong, 2013).

The processes through which spirituality confers these health benefits indicate that it supports adaptive interpersonal interactions, motivates healthy lifestyle choices, and increases emotional well-being as well as positive character strengths (Barton & Miller, 2015; Ford et al., 2023). Moreover, personal spirituality serves as a resource for effective stress-coping strategies, instills a sense of existential purpose, provides ethical orientation, and cultivates a social support system, all of which are associated with reduced psychological distress, improved mental health and quality of life, and overarching life satisfaction and wellness (Ano & Vasconcelles, 2005; Pargament, 1997). A growing evidence base supports the role of spirituality in brain health, stress physiology, and other biomarkers that support overall somatic health (Anderson et al., 2023; McClintock et al., 2019; Miller et al., 2013; Miller, 2021).

Spiritual-Mind-Body Wellness Interventions

To fill a gap in mental health on-campus services, SMB wellness interventions have been shown to function as an adjunct to mental health services (Scalora et al., 2020; Scalora et al., 2022). SMB wellness interventions often include practices such as meditation, Tai chi, yoga, and mindfulness, contributing to reduced levels of stress, anxiety, depression, and negative mood symptoms among college students (Leung & Pong, 2021; Novak et al., 2020). Previous work has shown that AA-A, an SMB wellness intervention developed by three of the authors of this chapter (LM, SS, and MA), can lead to significant reductions in depression and anxiety and significant improvements in numerous spiritual well-being variables (Anderson et al., 2023; Mistur et al., 2022; Mistur et al., 2024; Scalora et al., 2022). AA-A may also induce a recovery process from high rates of post-traumatic stress symptomology by supporting a spiritually oriented perception and awareness of personal and relational spirituality (Scalora et al., 2022). AA-A also provides physiological improvements in stress reactivity and recovery that are directly linked to a process of spiritual recovery (Anderson et al., 2023). Notably, SMB wellness interventions on college campuses, including AA-A, have been found to attract a highly diverse subset of students, with higher representation of ethnic minority and SGM students (Craig & Austin, 2016; Mistur et al., 2024; Scalora et al., 2022). These findings suggest that SMB wellness interventions may impact student wellness via psychological and physiological pathways, provide a culturally inclusive and supportive environment for spiritual individuation, and improve stress, anxiety, and depression.

Developmental Tasks and Risks of Emerging Adulthood

Emerging adulthood represents a distinct stage of development: a lifespan transition encapsulating late adolescence and adulthood (18–25 years of age), characterized by exploration and growth along multiple dimensions, marking a period of change and enhanced possibilities (Arnett, 2000; Arnett, 2023; Denton et al., 2008). During this time, multiple developmental tasks are crucial to successful maturation into adulthood. Notably, emerging adulthood is also the period when approximately three-quarters of lifetime mental health disorders have their first onset, a higher rate than for any other adult age group (Pedrelli et al., 2014; Viner & Tanner, 2023; Wood et al., 2018), potentially impacting an individual's ability to complete developmental tasks and transition smoothly into adult roles (Schulenberg & Zarrett, 2006). Often, this first onset overlaps with higher education experiences and can have deleterious short- and long-term effects, including reduced academic performance, withdrawal from college or university, legal issues, relationship problems, and reduced earnings (Cooper, 2022). Providing effective support and resources on college campuses is critical for supporting at-risk emerging adults. This approach can help them to successfully navigate this vulnerable stage of life and promote successful development into subsequent decades of adulthood.

Identity Exploration and Resolution

Emerging adulthood is characterized by moral, spiritual, religious, and emotional explorations of identity in the search for pathways into work, education, family, and romantic relationships (Arnett & Tanner, 2006). Emerging adult development, often in much of the United States (but differing by region of the world), is directed toward autonomous individuation, a central characteristic of emerging adulthood, accompanied by increased intrinsic motivation for action and increased autonomy (Fraser-Thill, 2023). Emerging adults in the United States often explore, experiment with, and evaluate many identities to develop a coherent sense of self unique to their beliefs and values as part of the transition to full-fledged adulthood (Layland et al., 2018; Marcia, 1980; Nice & Joseph, 2022; Tanner, 2006). Identity resolution during emerging adulthood in an individualistic society plays a crucial role in an integrated sense of self, mental health, and well-being, or, alternatively, mental health struggles, in adulthood (Erikson, 1968; Mitchell et al., 2021; Sokol, 2009).

Spiritual Individuation

Spiritual individuation refers to an exploration and development of the self in the spiritual realm that parallels the other developmental lines occurring during emerging adulthood (Arnett, 2000; Barry & Abo-Zena, 2014; Benson et al., 2012; Desrosiers et al., 2011; Fowler, 1981; Marcia, 1980; Scalora et al., 2022). Spiritual individuation is a process of psychological change and integration, seeking a more authentic and meaningful relationship to the Transcendent, which may lead to the development of a unique set of spiritual beliefs and practices. This development of personal spirituality may or may not be connected to a religious denomination or the organized practice of religion (Mistur et al., 2022) and could include processes of reconstruction, reauthorization, or even alienation of prior religious affiliation, spiritual beliefs, and familial and cultural expectations.

Further, spiritual individuation in emerging adulthood involves an individual's journey to find their own spiritual identity, integral to understanding their place in the larger existential context as they transition from adolescence to adulthood. Crises such as spiritual struggle, spiritual injury, loss of meaning, trauma, depression, stress, and existential and identity questioning are often antecedents to spiritual individuation, particularly in the critical developmental stage of emerging adulthood. This period often overlaps with the procurement of higher education, a time of heightened intellectual and philosophical exploration.

To understand how these crises may catalyze spiritual individuation, it is essential to recognize the interplay between crisis and development. James Marcia's identity status model (1966) provides a framework for understanding identity formation from late adolescence to young adulthood. Marcia describes four identity statuses: identity diffusion, identity foreclosure, identity moratorium, and identity achievement. These statuses are determined by the presence or absence of crisis and commitment in various life domains, including spirituality. Crises prompt individuals to explore different beliefs and values (identity moratorium), and if successful, lead to commitment (identity achievement) (Marcia, 1980). Through this lens, supported spiritual individuation may involve deconstructing previously held beliefs in light of some developmental crisis, challenge, or trauma, or perhaps an inner call, with successful resolution resulting in a reconstructed spiritual identity. Support for spiritual individuation may help to offset or resolve these crises.

"Wired" for Personal Spirituality in Emerging Adulthood

Research exploring the confluence of genetics and spirituality has illuminated a developmental phenomenon: the maturation of personal spirituality during adolescence into emerging adulthood. This process has been conceptualized as a contemporary empirical analogue to the "spiritual awakening" that is rooted in various faith traditions (Miller, 2013). This terminology captures the transformative period wherein, during adolescence and emerging adulthood, a surge of genetic expression underlying the awakening process is biologically influenced and culturally (and for some people religiously) enriched.

A genetic-epidemiologic twin study of female adults (mean age 30) found that approximately 29% of the variability between individuals in a two-way personal relationship with the Transcendent is attributed to broad heritability. This pivotal finding suggests that genetic factors may contribute to the physiological framework – the "wiring" – that facilitates personal spiritual experiences (Kendler et al., 1997; Miller, 2013). During adolescence, this physiological predisposition related to spirituality is more pronounced. In another longitudinal twin study, assessing spirituality in adolescents initially around 14–15 years of age and again at 18–19 years of age, a nearly 50% augmentation in the heritable influence on spirituality throughout adolescence into emerging adulthood was found (Koenig et al., 2008).

These findings suggest a biologically predetermined upsurge – akin to an internal clock and in parallel with other lines of development that are similarly heightened during adolescence – that underpins the unfolding of spiritual awareness. This period is receptive to external influences, indicating the significance of an environment that supports the emergence of this spiritual capacity during the transition from middle adolescence to emerging adulthood for optimal mental health. Thus, this phenotypical surge suggests a critical period that is intrinsically hardwired, developmentally critical, and epigenetic in nature.

Need for Supported Spiritual Individuation

Emerging adulthood can be marked by profound spiritual emergence. Spirituality is not taught: the heritable portion of one's spirituality must be nurtured to be fully expressed. From a developmental perspective, the increased capacity for spiritual emergence, an existential quest to find one's inner meaning, purpose, and identity, can be fraught with frustration and disappointment when answers are not found. A spiritual struggle often termed the "dark night of the soul" may emerge as individuals grapple with existential questions, disorientation, and feelings of meaninglessness and purposelessness (Campbell, 2003). Developmental depression (DD) has been proposed as a subtype of moderate depression, a normative developmental process of spiritual individuation, identity exploration, and existential questioning that can present as mood symptomology during emerging adulthood (Barton et al., 2017; Miller, 2013; Miller & Barton, 2015). Two-thirds of depression in emerging adult college students is positively associated with developmental tasks such as identity development and spiritual individuation, indicating that DD may be normative for emerging adults (Barton et al., 2017; Mariano & Damon, 2008). Identity exploration can lead to feelings of existential confusion, self-doubt, and depressive symptoms, especially for those who struggle to establish a clear sense of self. In clinical literature regarding the post-pubertal onset of depression (i.e., during late adolescence) and its association with spiritual and existential questioning or struggle, a pervasive sense of anguish is often experienced and inherent to the spiritual individuation process (Miller & Barton, 2015). Those who integrate this struggle into their spiritual worldview often emerge not only recovered but also with a personal ownership of spiritual views (Musgrave et al., 2002). Spiritual individuation has been associated with positive mental health outcomes and overall well-being (Bożek et al., 2020; Miller & Barton, 2015). Thus, with support, spiritual individuation can be a process of personal growth and self-actualization, fostering identity development and autonomy in decision-making. Without it, emerging adults are at risk for role confusion, disorientation, and loss of purpose and are left vulnerable to the clinical presentation of DD. However, a clear data-driven process of supported spiritual individuation has not been developed to date, and without it, interventions aiming to support spirituality among emerging adults may be ineffective.

RiTE Multidimensional Model and Awakened Awareness for Adolescents

The pillars of AA-A presented here complement the RiTE model of spirituality (Webb et al., 2014; see also Chapters 1 and 44, this volume). One of the core helpful values of the RiTE model is its clarification of various constructs of religion and spirituality, including reverence for a deity or not, attention to questions of meaning and purpose, the level of structure given to one's practice of spirituality, and the inclusion of contemplative practices (Webb et al., 2014). While AA-A does not attempt to consider *how* these dimensions of spirituality are related to each other, the students' qualitative data demonstrates that the process for many (but not all) people involves questioning, exploration, and resolution in spiritual development; for others, a deepening of faith is less driven by questioning and more by exploration of faith experience. AA-A elucidates the process by which emerging adults engage with their relationship with the Transcendent, address questions of meaning and purpose, and develop a distinct personal spiritual identity.

In contrast, AA-A does not focus on understanding *how* religion and spirituality converge and diverge. Instead, AA-A presents a process through which emerging adults, regardless of beliefs, practices, or religious affiliations, navigate spiritual individuation supported by AA-A as realizing an opportunity within hard-wired human development. As such, AA-A is concerned with the pillars that support spiritual individuation, as well as the ways in which spiritual development proceeds.

Awakened Awareness for Adolescents (AA-A) Intervention

AA-A is a 90-minute, eight-session, group-based SMB wellness intervention. It was designed to cultivate an enhanced spiritual perception among emerging adult college students to support the developmental tasks of spiritual individuation and identity development. Through the integration of novel guided spiritual visualizations, receptive transcendent contemplation, meta-cognitive reflections, and relational spirituality practices, AA-A engenders a perceptual shift into spiritual awareness. Namely, AA-A helps to shift perception from a materialistic perspective, termed "Achievement Awareness," which emphasizes the attainment of accomplishments to bolster self-worth, toward an enhanced capacity to interact with oneself, others, and life from a spiritual perspective, termed AA. This spiritual perspective underscores one's inherent worth and connection to one's higher self and Higher Power/Transcendent, within or outside a faith tradition (Miller, 2005, 2011).

AA-A is founded upon 25 years of basic and clinical science, foremost MRI studies (Miller, 2021, for a review) on the human innate neural capacity for spiritual awareness and some of the pathways through which it is fostered. To foster in vivo the pathway identified as supportive of spiritual awareness, the AA program was developed through a 15-year iterative process on adults (Miller, 2013) and is based upon an accretive arc on strengthening natural spirituality. AA was then adapted into AA-A specifically to support the unique spiritual developmental passage of late adolescents and emerging adults (Scalora et al., 2022). AA emphasizes *in vivo* practices that 1) expand relationality to embrace a relationship with one's Higher Power/ Transcendent, Higher Self, and the sacred essence or deep spiritual core in fellow human beings and nature, 2) build awareness of the interplay between internal experiences (inner life) and external occurrences (outer life), and 3) foster spiritual awareness as a guiding principle in perception and decision-making. The adaptation for adolescents and emerging adults, AA-A, extends the work to support the development of awareness of an inner life, a sense of a deeper self that may or may not be seen socially, and enhances the capacity to engage others at this deeper, more spiritual level (Scalora et al., 2022).

To assess whether spiritual individuation in emerging adulthood could be supported through a brief eight-week intervention, the authors implemented a mixed-methods approach to study AA-A. The intervention study was conducted from Fall 2018 to Spring 2021, and the process of spiritual individuation presented here is derived from the qualitative data from that study. More detailed findings about the study have been previously published, focusing on the feasibility and acceptability of the intervention (Scalora et al., 2022) as well as a case study of participants' experiences during the COVID-19 pandemic (Mistur et al., 2022).

Method

Participants and Procedure

Participants were undergraduates aged 18–25 across two sister university campuses in the Northeast United States. From Fall 2018 through Spring 2021, a total of 15 AA-A groups were delivered, and 131 participants completed AA-A (completed post-test and attended at least 1 session; 2 attended 1 session): $N = 131$, mean age: 19.85, mean attendance sum: 5.89, $SD = 1.74$, median number of sessions attended: 6) All groups were delivered in person until spring 2020, after which AA-A transitioned to virtual delivery due to the COVID-19 outbreak. From Fall 2020 to Spring 2021, AA-A was held online (Mistur et al., 2022). The sample was varied across multiple domains, including gender, sexual orientation, religion, ethnicity, and international student status (see Tables 16.1 and 16.2 for complete demographics).

Participants enrolled in AA-A were invited to participate in the research study, and the data were collected and analyzed under the purview of the Institutional Review Board (IRB) of Columbia University, Teachers College.

Table 16.1 Sociodemographic Characteristics of Participants – Part 1

Baseline characteristic	*n*	%
Gender		
Female	102	77.9%
Male	21	16.0%
Transgender and gender non-conforming	8	6.1%
Sexual orientation		
Heterosexual	74	56.5%
Gay/Lesbian	13	9.9%
Bisexual	30	22.9%
Questioning	7	5.3%
Queer/Pansexual	4	3.1%
Prefer not to answer	3	2.3%
Race/ethnicity		
White/Caucasian	52	39.7%
Asian	24	18.3%
Latino/a	11	8.5%
Black/African American	23	17.6%
American Indian	1	0.8%
Multiracial	16	12.2%
Middle Eastern	1	0.8%
Black Caribbean	1	0.8%
Year in school		
Freshman	30	22.9%
Sophomore	28	21.4%
Junior	33	25.2%
Senior	36	27.5%
International/doesn't apply	3	2.3%
Employment		
Yes	52	39.7%
No	79	60.3%

Note: N=131.

Table 16.2 Sociodemographic Characteristics of Participants – Part 2

Baseline characteristic	*n*	%
Household of origin income		
Above 200,000 USD	22	16.8%
100,000–200,000 USD	26	19.8%
75,000–100,000 USD	24	18.3%
50,000–75,000 USD	16	12.2%
30,000–50,000 USD	18	13.7%
15,000–30,000 USD	14	10.7%
Less than 15,000 USD	5	3.8%
Other/NA	6	4.6%
Marital status		
Married	1	0.8%
Single – Never Married	130	99.2%

(*Continued*)

Table 16.2 (Continued)

Baseline characteristic	*n*	%
International status		
Yes	27	20.6%
No	104	79.4%
Clinical characteristics		
Elevated depression[a]	49	37.4%
Elevated anxiety[b]	50	38.2%
Elevated post-traumatic stress[c]	96	73.3%
Religious affiliation		
Buddhist	1	0.8%
Eastern Orthodox	2	1.5%
Hindu	3	2.3%
Jewish	13	9.9%
Muslim	4	3.1%
Protestant Christian	18	13.7%
Roman Catholic	14	10.7%
Other	15	11.5%
None	61	46.6%
Importance of religion or spirituality		
Highly Important	30	22.9%
Moderately Important	43	32.8%
Slightly Important	37	28.2%
Not Important at All	21	16.0%

Note: N=131.

[a] PHQ-9 (Kroenke et al., 2001) score ≥ 10.
[b] GAD-7 (Spitzer et al., 2006) score ≥ 10.
[c] PCL-C (Weathers et al., 1994) score ≥ 30.

Data Collection and Analysis

This current study utilized two types of qualitative data sources: open-ended written responses and semi-structured interviews. Two different interpretivist methodological approaches were employed, which provided a more comprehensive understanding of the phenomenon. In this instance, the use of Grounded Theory (Charmaz, 2014) and Interpretive Phenomenological Analysis (IPA) (Smith & Osborn, 2015) allowed the researchers to inductively analyze participants' in-process and summative experiences with AA-A while also putting those experiences into dialogue with the rest of their lives, providing a more holistic and nuanced understanding of the spiritual individuation process that may not have been possible with a single approach.

During each AA-A group, participants completed open-ended surveys asking about their experiences in each session. Following the conclusion of the AA-A group, participants completed program evaluations. Data from the weekly open-ended surveys and program evaluations were analyzed using a grounded theory approach (Charmaz, 2014), which allows for a systematic yet flexible method for iteratively conducting data analysis.

Additionally, 62 semi-structured interviews were conducted throughout the intervention. Interview data was analyzed using IPA, which examines how participants understand a personal experience; in particular, IPA uses a double hermeneutic approach, as the researcher is making sense of how a participant has made meaning of a certain experience (Chapman & Greenhow, 2021; Smith & Osborn, 2015).

Rigor

Throughout data analysis, an emphasis was placed on attention to credibility, dependability, confirmability, and transferability (Patton, 2014). An audit trail was kept tracking researcher memos, insights, and decisions. Each piece of data was independently coded and then brought to the research group for discussion and consensus. Researchers looked for counterexamples and alternative explanations to their emerging understanding of the data throughout analysis (Creswell & Miller, 2000). Each researcher, and the team as a whole, engaged in reflexivity, acknowledging their beliefs, values, and prior experience so as to consider whether who they were served as a lens of expertise or a potential influence of bias at any point of analysis.

Results

AA-A Pillars of Support of Spiritual Individuation

During the process of AA-A, students engage in groups that welcome direct personal spiritual experience, practice, struggle, and reflection. Data analysis confirms the student experience of AA-A as garnering support for the spiritual individuation process as intended by the AA-A model. These designed pillars of support in the AA-A model include 1) Group leaders: The vital role of group leaders provides guidance and a structural framework for spiritual development; 2) Spiritual language: The utilization of specific terminologies that convey spiritual concepts, enhancing understanding of self, communication with others, and the Transcendent; 3) Community: The formative influence and synergistic interplay of a spiritual community, together in a shared and sacred space, serve as a support for spiritual growth and accretion; 4) Relational spirituality: Spiritual connections for individuals in a direct, lived relationship with the sacred Transcendent (whether their own term might be Higher Power, G-d, Jesus, Hashem, Allah, Universe, or another sacred word), together with fostering awareness of interpersonal relationships grounded in a sacred spiritual presence (while always embracing pluralism of expression); 5) Spiritual resource provision: The availability of both material and non-material resources that support spiritual practices and pedagogical approaches, facilitating deeper spiritual engagement and learning.

There is a dynamic interplay among these pillars of designed support in AA-A, highlighting their contributory roles in the process of supported spiritual awakening and spiritual individuation.

Pillar 1: Role of Group Leaders

For college students, who are often at a critical juncture of identity formation amid the search for existential meaning, the presence of group leaders can anchor and support the spiritual individuation process, providing the non-judgmental guidance needed to navigate this complex inner terrain. An essential aspect of the leader's role is to create a secure and confidential space where students feel comfortable, valued, and understood to explore their insights, doubts, and deep questions about life and themselves with non-judgmental guidance (Travis & Ryan, 2004). In AA-A, an emphasis is placed on a "non-guru approach" for group leaders, whereby spiritual concepts are presented within a universal, non-judgmental framework which refrains from imposing specific beliefs or doctrines. This approach underscores the importance of autonomy in the spiritual exploration process, allowing students to cultivate their understanding and beliefs, as illustrated by a student who shared, "I always felt safe and comfortable in the sessions. I never felt judged — very healthy, kind environment. The team [group leaders] running the group are all so kind and fantastic."

For many students, the impact of feeling valued by group leaders was an important aspect of AA-A. For instance, one student stated, "Group leaders made me feel like my thoughts were valuable and worth listening to." Some students shared that group leaders acted as guides and role models, exemplifying spiritual notions taught in AA-A (Schure et al., 2008) and guiding students in interpreting their experiences within a spiritual framework (Shapiro & Carlson, 2009). One student described, "The group leaders were really good listeners and offer really sage guidance and are the most valuable aspects of AA-A."

In sum, the AA-A group leader is not merely a facilitator but a shepherd of the individuation process, providing guidance, spiritual resources, and a model for spiritual growth, and is instrumental in nurturing the development of a distinct, participant-congruent spiritual identity among emerging adults in an academic setting.

Pillar 2: Spiritual Language

Spiritual language is one of the pillars of designed support in AA-A for spiritual individuation. Spirituality, while inherently personal and often nebulous, benefits from a shared language that can deliver clarity to internal struggles and spiritual questions. Participants in AA-A articulated that the introduction of spiritual terminology provided them with the linguistic tools necessary to name previously ineffable experiences. This newfound vocabulary not only facilitated communication about their spiritual journeys but also enabled participants to recognize the universality of their experiences and their relevance to personal identity. The acquisition of spiritual language serves as a scaffold for individuals to explore and express their spiritual experiences and beliefs, which is integral to the process of self-discovery and spiritual individuation (Fuertes & Dugan, 2021; Mistur et al., 2022).

The language used in AA-A aims toward a universal nature that is central to this spiritual framework. The core language and related participant observations are outlined below.

AA is a framework that augments spiritual perception, enhancing students' relational transcendent awareness, namely that of their inherent connection to a higher self, the spiritual core in fellow people and living beings, and a living bi-directional relationship with a Higher Power/transcendent entity, which may exist within or outside traditional religious paradigms (Miller, 2005, 2011). AA was developed over 20 years at Columbia University, Teachers College, based upon 1) science on innate human spiritual awareness and developmental processes, and 2) practices aligned in an accretive arc shown to sustain and support natural awakening (Miller, 2011). AA offers a transformative lens through which students perceive, understand, and connect with the self, others, and the environment, an evolved self-awareness that acknowledges the interplay between one's internal experiences and external occurrences to cultivate a sense of inner peace. As seen here, students who participated in the AA-A intervention reported moments of and desire for an AA perspective:

> I wish I didn't feel like everything I have is incredibly fragile and about to be taken away from me. I wish I had the confidence that I will be ok no matter what happens. I wish I could get myself to see success more broadly than it has been taught to me all my life. I wish I could be more at peace in my mind.

The *Higher Self* is the eternal and intrinsic part of oneself in AA-A that perceives life from a spiritual perspective and views life through an AA lens. Conceptualized as a constant loving presence, the higher self represents the spiritual essence of an individual. Many students experienced learning about the higher self as an aspect of self that is imbued with qualities of love and kindness, offering a compassionate viewpoint toward one's experiences and actions and others and increasing their sense of self-reliance. For example,

> I have a hard time showing love and understanding to myself, so it was very interesting to have to visualize my higher self and look for support in her. It helps me realize I have myself as a source of support whenever I want to – and I do not have to resort to other people.

This transformative realization fostered a paradigm shift toward self-reliance, highlighting the critical role of spiritual individuation in developing an autonomous and self-sufficient identity. Additionally, the higher self advocates for a more expansive conception of self-identity that incorporates emotional and spiritual dimensions of love and acceptance. Students described their higher self as a compassionate guide helping navigate disappointments, reminding them of their inherent worth and the natural role of mistakes along life's journey. As one student explained:

> My higher self acknowledges the reality of the situation and clarify that it does not define who I am, as it is only one particular experience of my existence. She would also invite me to be compassionate and understanding with myself and would remind me that it is not a complete loss and I can move forward and learn from myself.

Students further articulated that their higher self loves them, offering a more holistic and balanced perspective in contrast to their Achievement Awareness self.

Life Beyond Achievement Awareness. Achievement Awareness in AA-A is a perceptual lens that is inherently goal-oriented and accomplishment-focused. However, while this orientation toward goals and accomplishments is fundamental, its excessive application can potentially undermine well-being and spiritual growth. Numerous students realized that relying on external validation and tangible achievements for their sense of self-worth offered a limited vantage point on life, ultimately proving unsatisfactory. As one student shared:

> Connecting with my higher self was very emotional for me. It made me realize that grades, income, status, they all don't matter. What's important is that I value myself and those who love me. Connecting with my higher self allowed me to see that I was more than my grades or accomplishments.

This awareness led many students to recognize the often detrimental impact of primarily prioritizing goals and accomplishments. For instance, one student stated, "This week I got very overwhelmed about the amount of commitments I have made this semester and realized that I've taken on an unhealthy amount of responsibilities and my mental health is suffering as a result." Such recognitions were sometimes accompanied by relief or appreciation of having a different lens through which to see themselves and recognize their worth. As this student shared:

> I remembered my acceptance into X University. I can vividly go back to that memory, and feel the shock, delight, and excitedness that I had when I got in. It made me also a bit sad

> that that excitedness dulled after a while when I began to think about what else I wanted to achieve. I think this reflects the materialistic & temporary downsides of the Achievement Awareness.

Many students reported that AA provided them with a respite from the demands of Achievement Awareness and supported them in finding meaning in their life path through contact with their higher self.

Providing a space for students' inquiry into life's big questions in AA-A, including their belief in and conceptualizations of a *higher power*, revealed a continuum of interpretations, ranging from established religious beliefs to discovering novel spiritual constructs. Some students acknowledged an enduring, pre-existing connection with a higher power, reflective of faith traditions: as various students reported, "My higher power is God, and he is perfect and loving," "My higher power is Jesus. Kind, loving, accepting, smiling, wanting what is best for me" and "My higher power is La Virgen de Guadalupe."

In contrast, many students identified as spiritual but not religious (SBNR) and engaged in a transformative process of redefining their spiritual beliefs, and dialogues with a higher power manifested as an aspect of nature. One student described the meaning of and relationship with their higher power in this way:

> My higher power is the sun. I love seeing it every morning when I wake up. It is something that shines brightly not only for me, but for everyone else as well. It makes me feel happy and free. It's not always shining brightly, but I know that it's always there and will never go away or let me down.

Some students identified as humanists, finding spirituality in relationships with other human beings. For example, one student shared, "My higher power is universal love and shows up in moments where humans act to improve their lives and the lives of others."

Conversely, a subset of students expressed uncertainty or inner struggle toward the concept of a higher power; this may signify a stage of spiritual exploration or skepticism within the spiritual individuation process. This uncertainty or "existential questioning" can be a critical aspect of spiritual growth, as it prompts introspection and the potential evaluation or reevaluation of one's spiritual beliefs. One student stated, "I'm not sure about my higher power-nothing came to mind for me. I eventually settled on an approximation of the God from my youth, but then made edits to be less problematic." Another student described uncertainty about the notion of a higher power, "My higher power was really hard for me to reach/imagine. Maybe because I have trouble w/ the religious/the spiritual? I kind of think my higher power is 'Fate/the universe' because I sometimes have trust in forces around me."

Research indicates that such transitions in faith can have profound psychological implications, potentially leading to increased open-mindedness and psychological resilience or emotional distress and disorientation (Ferguson, 2022). The students' evolving faith narrative underscores the importance of examining the psychological and spiritual dimensions of belief systems as they relate to identity development and spiritual individuation in emerging adulthood.

Pillar 3: Community

A sense of belonging to a community in AA-A can support the collective aspect of spiritual growth by allowing students to learn from and support one another while still nurturing individual paths (Astin et al., 2003). Fowler (1981) posits that a community serves as a mirror, reflecting individual aspects of spirituality that may not be evident in isolation. A spiritual community can establish norms that validate spiritual experiences and practices, thereby strengthening personal spiritual beliefs, encouraging spiritual practices, and supporting spiritual individuation (Canda et al., 2019; Mistur et al., 2022). The group setting of AA-A provided a sense of community and accountability, encouraging regular participation in habit-building and, in turn, building a sense of self-efficacy. As one student said, "Having a spiritual community is nourishing. Committing to do something [AA-A] like this every week made me proud of myself. Happier, more self-worth + confidence. Better connections."

Pillar 4: Relational Spirituality

Relational spirituality is a multifaceted concept encompassing the spiritual dimensions of interpersonal relationships (Faver, 2004; Mahoney, 2013) and the individual's dynamic relationship with a Higher Power/Transcendent (Davis et al., 2008). The term describes the positive interconnectedness between individuals and "ways of relating to the sacred" (Shults & Sandage, 2006, p. 161). In AA-A, authentic relationships developed from an AA lens instead of an Achievement Awareness lens, described here by a student:

> When I'm neglecting myself, I also neglect my relationships with others. I think only of how they can make me happy and what they have to offer me, instead of how what each of us brings to the relationship is something to be appreciated.

Relationships in AA-A were grounded in relational spirituality, as evidenced by the connections made between students and the impact of these deep relationships on students' development of an AA lens.

Pillar 5: Spiritual Resources

Integrating diverse spiritual resources was integral in fostering spiritual individuation, supporting spiritual awareness, and enhancing students' identity development. Participants described the importance of spiritual resources (spiritual visualizations and practices) in AA-A: "The guided meditations and the concepts of higher self, Awakened Awareness, Achievement Awareness, and Augmented Awareness were helpful as included in my daily life," and "The meditations were definitely the most help for my spiritual journey for they allowed me to continue important conversations with myself outside the sessions."

AA-A leverages five interconnected pillars to support spiritual individuation, emphasizing a non-linear interplay between these elements. AA-A's SMB approach highlights the components involved in supported spiritual individuation, accentuating the critical importance of a supportive, non-judgmental, and safe environment and community in nurturing individual spiritual growth, facilitating a comprehensive framework for understanding and fostering spiritual development.

Supported Process of Spiritual Individuation

This section describes supported spiritual individuation facilitated by AA-A, a science-driven process. The five phases of this process were seen in this study and summarized into a diagram

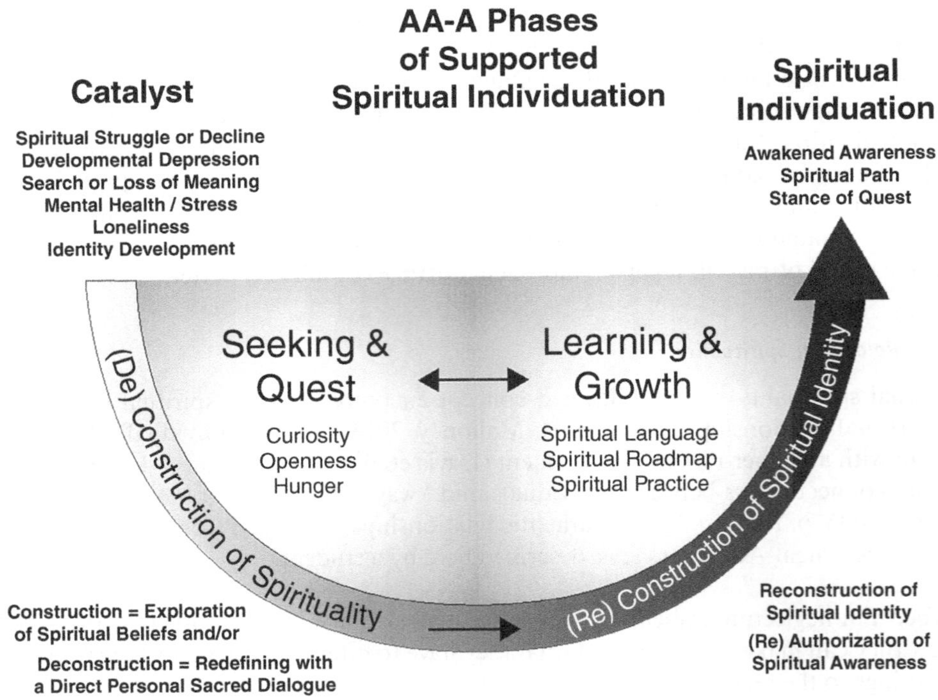

Figure 16.1 Experience of the Phases of AA-A in the Process of Supported Spiritual Individuation in Emerging Adult College Students.

(Figure 16.1) to reflect their relationships. The five phases involved in the process of supported spiritual individuation include 1) catalyst, 2) seeking/quest, 3) (de)construction of spirituality, 4) new learning and growth, and 5) (re)construction of spiritual identity.

Phase 1: Catalyst

Catalysts in AA-A serve as critical junctures in one's developmental trajectory with the capacity to destabilize pre-existing constructs of identity and spiritual orientation and provoke an unexpected reassessment of beliefs and values. Within our study, participants identified a range of catalysts, characterized by psychological distress, existential disorientation, and pervasive uncertainty that precipitated their transformative journey: 1) spiritual struggle, reflecting a conflict within one's spiritual or religious beliefs; 2) spiritual decline, denoting a loss of meaning in pre-established spiritual or religious beliefs; 3) mental health problems, involving conditions such as depression and anxiety that impact one's psychological well-being; 4) loss of or search for meaning, indicating a quest for existential purpose; 5) feelings of loneliness and isolation, highlighting a lack of meaningful social connections; 6) identity questioning, involving a reevaluation of one's sense of self; and 7) stress, arising from academic and social pressures and life transitions. These identified catalysts underline the multidimensional nature of the experiences that can initiate the journey toward spiritual individuation among students.

Spiritual Struggle. Emerging adulthood often entails wrestling with existential questions such as identity, life's purpose, and one's place in the universe, which are intrinsically connected to the quest for sacred meaning and ultimate significance (Pargament & Exline, 2021). Existential explorations can precipitate spiritual struggles and can be associated with psychological distress and diminished psychological functioning (Ellison & Lee, 2010). However, it is crucial that these struggles are not conflated with pathology. Rather, they represent a potential catalyst for spiritual growth and spiritual individuation, even as they may concurrently pose risks for psychological problems (Abu-Raiya et al., 2015). Empirical studies show a link between spiritual struggles and poorer mental health, including higher levels of depression, anxiety, and difficulty regulating emotions (for a review, see Pargament & Exline, 2021; Dworsky et al., 2016).

Some students engaged in AA-A after a loss in familial faith: "I was raised a Roman Catholic, and while I do believe there is a God, somehow I haven't been recognizing him (praying to, thinking of) as of recent (about seven months). I feel like I am, indeed, losing faith." Another student described existential questions: "I'm not sure about my higher power. It was clearer last week. I'm feeling incredibly, incredibly discouraged right now. The world seems like an incredibly large place, and it's hard for me to imagine something connecting it all," while another student expressed a desire to feel a connection to the Transcendent, "I wish I felt some sort of spiritual connection to the universe, and I believed in the afterlife- I wish the people I've lost were still here."

Encounters with spiritual struggle can expand spiritual awareness and connection to a transcendent power and/or higher self. Such struggles, while potentially detrimental to well-being, also present opportunities for spiritual transformation and individuation (Mistur et al., 2022).

Spiritual decline is characterized by a weakening of spiritual associations with a sense of self, perception of others and the world, and spiritual beliefs (Cole et al., 2008; Crete et al., 2020; Greyson & Khanna, 2014). The dissolving of spiritual associations can take the form of a loss of meaning, a sense of isolation, and a disconnection from a higher power or the Transcendent. Emerging adults are particularly susceptible to the effects of spiritual decline, as the critical juncture of personal and spiritual exploration leaves them vulnerable to experiences that challenge their spiritual frameworks (Smith-MacDonald et al., 2018). One student shared a lack of resonance with their familial religion that left them feeling isolated and unloved by their higher power:

> So, I grew up in a very religious household, and as much as I pushed back on that concept of a higher power. I always, (scoffs) I was, kind of manipulated into believing that was the baseline, and that was the way, even if I was rejecting it. So, coming into this [AA-A], I asked my higher power if It loved me? And it said no!

Some students experiencing spiritual decline spoke of a sense of isolation and disconnection, not only from familial or traditional religious contexts but also from a sense of divine love and their higher power.

Loss of or Search for Meaning. An individual's pursuit of meaning and purpose in life (Mitchell et al., 2010) is particularly salient during emerging adulthood. This spiritual quest is frequently catalyzed by a sense of disconnection or disillusionment with previously held values, religious affiliations, and spiritual beliefs. Such experiences precipitate a critical reevaluation and, often, a reconstruction of one's spiritual orientation (Holland et al., 2006). Empirical data from our sample illuminated the complex processes by which students navigate their search for meaning and purpose within the context of a college environment, including the phenomenon of spiritual dislocation – the loss of previously held purpose and meaning – and the subsequent active search for new sources of meaning. These findings underscore the necessity of creating spaces and offering support for spiritual exploration on college campuses, recognizing the unique challenges and opportunities this setting presents for students.

Mental Health Problems. Numerous students reported frustration over struggling with mental health issues, leading them to seek change and support in AA-A. Mental health issues such as depression, trauma, and stress are relevant to the experience of existential questioning and loneliness and can act as catalysts for spiritual individuation. These challenges may prompt individuals to seek more profound meaning and purpose, fostering spiritual growth (McKenna-Plumley et al., 2023).

Moreover, students reported that mental health challenges frequently led to negative self-appraisals. For instance, one student described their struggle with mental health, characterizing their relationship with self as profound self-loathing and a pervasive sense of inadequacy: "I deal with chronic depression, severe anxiety, and daily panic attacks, so my relationship with myself as of now is a deep self-loathing that reminds me of my inadequacy."

In certain instances, students' awareness of their relationship to self was marred by a critical inner voice, exemplified by a student's reflection on the relentless nature of their self-criticism:

> My self-talk is much less compassionate. If it is someone I unequivocally love, I will be very gentle and not get angry at them for making mistakes I'd decimate myself for if I'd made them. It's easier to rationalize why someone else's failure will be ok than my own. My relationship with myself is not good. I truly do not like or approve of myself. When I do something well, all that means is that I've escaped my own wrath for another day. In the instances I do find my inner voice trying to comfort me, even then, it only brings me more pain. A recurring and omnipresent example of this is my OCD, which I have had for many years now. My inner voice tells me to act out compulsions and avoid something bad happening but doing the behavior only ever brings more distress in the end.

These narratives highlight the intricate relationship between mental health issues and self-perception, illustrating the profound influence of psychological well-being on identity formation and self-appraisal.

In some cases, the severity of students' mental health struggles necessitated a medical leave of absence. Upon return, these students sought support through AA-A, indicating the perceived value of this program in addressing mental health concerns.

Our findings elucidate that *loneliness and isolation* are prevalent within our sample and were motivators for AA-A engagement. Loneliness, an emotional state characterized by distress due to the absence of fulfilling interpersonal relationships, has been linked to adverse mental health outcomes, including depression and suicidal tendencies (Chang et al., 2017; Donovan et al., 2017; Heinrich & Gullone, 2006). Notably, emerging adults have been identified as the demographic most susceptible to loneliness (Bruce et al., 2019); 73% of college students reported feeling alone, and 45% experienced chronic, pervasive loneliness (Linder, 2024). A student shared that "Coming to college has been so rough because I'm very unhappy and I had such high expectations for college. I haven't made any friends really and feel very left out of the community." International students are especially at risk due to adjusting to life in a foreign country without social support networks (Trusty & Chun-Kennedy, 2023). This can be seen in the following example of an international student who realized through participation in AA-A that feeling alone was a significant issue:

> Even though I used to practice meditation before I came to college, I couldn't focus to meditate alone in my room. When I first joined AA-A, it's weird, I don't know exactly why, but maybe because of peers in the group, I was making friends, and I knew I was not alone and there were people who were willing to help me. The first AA-A session was a turning point for me. Before the first session, I was under heavy stress, and after that session, I knew that I was not alone. There were friends taking it [AA-A] together and there were some very kind instructors [group leaders], willing to help me. Those kind of things were really helpful. My choice to join AA-A was one of the best decisions I've made during the semester. The lack of community was one of the biggest problems for me.

Establishing interpersonal relationships between the students, their peers, and the group leaders fostered a sense of belongingness. This experience was exemplified through an anecdotal account shared by one of the group leaders, in which the student expressed gratitude for the AA-A program, noting that "AA-A is my family." This statement not only underscores the significance of the social bonds formed within the group but also highlights the role such connections play in engendering a sense of community and familial support among participants.

Negative self-talk, encompassing critical, derogatory, or pessimistic thoughts about oneself, can intensify loneliness and isolation (Sowislo & Orth, 2013). It was observed that students' inner voice frequently served a dual role, both contributing to and reflecting feelings of loneliness, thereby affecting their perceptions of their social interactions and self-concept (Masi et al., 2010), exhibited here:

> I saw my inner "voice" as a scared, sad, hurt, confused being. My relationship with myself seems dependent, but at the same time exhausting. I don't know how to change what I say to myself, and without that "voice" I feel scared and alone.

Our findings indicate that students were grappling with experiences of isolation and loneliness, which can catalyze students to seek deeper meaning in life and forge meaningful connections with others, potentially initiating a journey toward spiritual individuation (Brown et al., 2021).

Identity Development. Emerging adulthood is recognized as a developmental stage distinguished by the experimentation with diverse identities, belief systems, values, and ethical frameworks, alongside the pursuit of distinct trajectories in vocational, educational, and interpersonal domains (Arnett & Tanner, 2006). A supportive environment within a university setting, where spiritual community and guidance from group leaders are available, facilitates a safe space for students to contemplate life's profound questions. This process is exemplified by one student's introspective struggle with identity: "My higher self and I look the same but we're not the same. I don't know who she is or who I am. There's anger involved but I don't know where it comes from. I'm still so abstract." There is a paradoxical nature to this developmental stage, marked by intense desire for self-knowledge and the simultaneous experience of an elusive sense of self as described by this student:

> I wish I knew who I am and who I want to be – I wish I knew what I want to do with my life – I wish I were more assertive and more comfortable in social interactions – I wish I wasn't so stuck in my head and could let go, "be myself."

These experiences highlight the intricate relationship between self-knowledge and spiritual individuation.

Stressful life events or prolonged periods of *stress* have been identified as significant factors that can precipitate feelings of existential loneliness, driving individuals toward a search for spiritual connection and understanding (McKenna-Plumley et al., 2023). This experience is particularly evident among undergraduates in the United States, with evidence suggesting that those who experience higher stress levels have lower academic performance, social withdrawal, and less satisfaction with life (Misra & McKean, 2000).

Furthermore, numerous studies highlight the association between high levels of stress and the development or exacerbation of mental health disorders such as depression and anxiety (Dusselier et al., 2005). The pervasive "stress culture" within universities, characterized by a competitive, evaluative academic environment to excel and the glorification of overwork, contributes significantly to the mental health burden faced by students and perpetuates an Achievement Awareness perspective, often leading to a detrimental cycle of stress, a tenuous relationship with self, and poor mental health outcomes. A student's reflection encapsulates the impact of the evaluative ethos on their stress levels:

> I think an evaluative mindset definitely creates a more stressful mood for myself. I think often this evaluation is a subset of external constant evaluation, like because a grade might be partially determined by participation, I judge if I say 'smart' things in class.

Students identified stress as a catalyst for seeking out AA-A. By fostering a sense of community and providing spiritual practices and a space for self-reflection and spiritual exploration, AA-A offered a valuable resource for students navigating the complexities of college life. One student poignantly articulated the search for a more authentic and supportive community, contrasting it with the prevailing campus culture:

> I was looking for a community because I felt like the people around me at school were so stress culture, staying up all night studying, and it wasn't human. And now to put words to it – it was very much like Achievement Awareness came first. That was even, in terms, of how you present yourself, as a person, so that you present yourself as not being someone who has tons of feelings. That was really hard, and I was really lonely for a long time.

Phase 2: Seeking/Quest

Seeking is the deliberate and introspective journey undertaken as individuals transition from adolescence to full-fledged adulthood. Emerging adults engage in "seeking" to forge a coherent and authentic identity (Arnett, 2023). Openness and curiosity emerged as important factors in seeking through the process of spiritual individuation.

Openness refers to a psychological trait characterized by a willingness to engage in new experiences, consider novel ideas, and exhibit receptivity to diverse and new perspectives. Openness is associated with a heightened capacity for introspection and a broad-minded approach to life's complexities and possibilities inherent in this developmental stage (Benedek et al., 2014). Emerging adults with high levels of openness are more likely to embark on identity exploration, a quest for meaning, and to understand their purpose in life (Bleidorn & Schwaba, 2017; McCrae & Costa, 1997). The significance of openness in fostering genuine interactions and embracing life's opportunities is captured in this student's reflection:

> Openness, in place of judgment, allows me to see things as they are/what they offer as opposed to the limitation/outline of my judgment of them. I believe it is vital to be open with one another and to accept others openly; only that way can we have genuine interaction and connectedness.

A student's account of living life through the lens of AA describes the transformative potential of embracing openness, highlighting its capacity to broaden horizons and uncover paths that align more closely with one's authentic self. "Awakened Awareness would help prevent me from only seeing what my Achievement Awareness wants, by being more open-minded and adaptable, I can open doors to opportunities that are better for me."

In the developmental stage of emerging adulthood, *curiosity* is characterized by the formation of a coherent sense of self, driving individuals to question and seek a deeper understanding of their beliefs, values, and purpose in life (Kashdan & Fincham, 2004). Curiosity facilitates the exploration of and encourages engagement with a wide range of spiritual traditions, philosophies, and practices, enabling them to discern what resonates with their personal experiences and inner truths (Piedmont, 1999). This exploratory process is essential for spiritual individuation to unfold, as it allows individuals to construct an authentic spiritual identity. Curiosity may lead students to seek out programs like AA-A to facilitate self-discovery and enhance their awareness of the world. A student described their reason for engaging in AA-A: "A curiosity to learn more about the world around me and about myself."

AA-A also allowed for an unfolding of curiosity in the wake of the most difficult of experiences for students. Following the death of a parent, one student joined AA-A to seek answers and understanding within the supportive framework of AA-A. Upon completing AA-A, the student articulated a profound shift in their perspective and emotional state and a reawakening of their inner self, characterized by a deepened sense of love and curiosity toward the world:

> I felt a renewed sense of self and love for the world. It was internal love and external love. I literally came back alive because feeling the fascination for books reminded me of what was true in myself, that I have this self that will never die and can never be smothered out because there's this me inside. Being fascinated with these books reminded me of this sense of self that I had. It was renewed love for the world around me and realizing that it's just beautiful, and how much curiosity I have to learn new things.

Phase 3: (De)Construction of Spirituality

The third component of the model for supported spiritual individuation involves the intricate process of constructing or deconstructing one's spiritual beliefs. This critical phase entails an examination and potential reevaluation of pre-existing spiritual or religious beliefs, concepts, and values, or the redefinition of one's sacred dialogue with the Transcendent. A notable trend that emerged within this process was spiritual decline, which is frequently precipitated by spiritual injury or a growing incongruence between familial beliefs and an individual's developing identity. Such disconnection from previously held beliefs, and often from the related faith community, can lead to existential crisis, loss, and confusion.

One student's narrative exemplifies the deconstruction of familial beliefs:

> In my childhood I had been exposed to a higher power, but I don't know if I would have called it "my" higher power, because I was rushed into this from birth. "This is your higher power – this is what you're supposed to believe and how you're supposed to believe." I remember the first time that we did the Hosting Council [an AA-A practice taught to Dr. Lisa Miller by the late Dr. Gary Weaver], and I discussed this in the group, when I called upon the higher power, there was really nothing there. No higher power, no kind of higher energy showed up. I think it was because at that moment I didn't really know what I believed in. I didn't really know if there was a higher power. I hadn't even begun that process of discovery.

The process of constructing or deconstructing one's spirituality at this crucial life stage represents a critical juncture, illuminating a new path that substantially influences the individual's identity formation. Coming out as gay and the subsequent rejection one student experienced in his faith community led him to deconstruct his faith and consider which parts he'd like to leave behind and which parts he would like to continue to live by:

> When I was coming out, I started questioning a lot of the fundamentals of what God is and I don't know what a relationship with God means… And [I was] feeling trapped by a lot of the ritual and very small parts of religion that I often saw within the Orthodox community that didn't come along with the bigger things … [I've been] doing a lot of thinking about what that looks like for me and how I wanna be a part of it…up until then, I had a very positive experience with Judaism…it's something that I do want to figure out how to manage and *deal* with and think about… and still believ[e] in something bigger than myself and feel like there *is* bigger purpose for why we might be here, or there's some sort of moral responsibility I have to…help people or try to make the world a better place.

For these students, deconstructing and analyzing the building blocks of their worldviews resulted in reconstructing them into a personal spirituality congruent with their sense of self, fostering spiritual individuation.

Phase 4: Learning and Growth

Learning and growth in AA-A is part of the supported spiritual individuation process. This journey involves the development of new perspectives and insights about one's relationship with oneself and others, a higher self, a higher power, and one's meaning and purpose in life as supported by resources, including spiritual language, meditations, and practices, which together provide a structured spiritual framework. A poignant illustration of this learning process is provided by a student's reflection on their evolving understanding of spirituality:

> I feel it's important to note I viewed spirituality/religion as a very black and white thing. I wanted all the right answers, and I wanted to know all the rules and how it worked. I would ask specific questions related to [spirituality/religion] and my parents would give me answers. I think what I was completely missing is that spirituality is absolutely not black and white. It's the most abstract f-king thing out there and it's very much about self-exploration and coming to your own conclusions.

Students were not given theological answers from AA-A group leaders, but resources to support their learning and growth, which they used to alleviate stress and improve mental health issues. One student shared their experience:

> I've been experiencing more anxiety than usual, and that anxiety can snowball very easily. However, I reminded myself about the Road to Life [meditation] to ground myself and remember that there are always more doors to open and the important thing for me is to keep moving and not feel like it's the end of the world.

Group leaders observed that many students reported experiences of an AA perspective prior to having the language to describe such an experience. This is exemplified by this student's statement: "It's interesting because I felt Awakened Awareness before this [AA-A], and I didn't know how to articulate it. I think that's another use that I derived from this class."

Numerous students reported the idea of a "relationship with yourself" introduced in AA-A as a novel concept, recognizing how a negative relationship with the self can influence their self-perception and interaction with self. The shift from Achievement Awareness to AA often involves differentiating the higher self from an "ideal self," which is often an internalization of external or even societal standards. This insight is captured in a student's narrative, where she discerns that the critical voice demanding perfection in her academic work, an Achievement Awareness perspective, is not hers, but her mother's, instilled in her from a young age:

> I knew there were two different sides of my thinking. I thought one wasn't really me because I can't be both. You guys [group leaders] helped me realize the one that's criticizing is not really me – it [AA-A] cleared things up for me. When I get a 95 [on an assignment], there's that part of me that says, "It should have been 100. You could have done better," but then the other part says, "You tried your best and that's already enough." I thought that's my higher self, and the one that says "You could have done better" is mostly from what others expect of me. I grew up with my mom always wanting 100. I feel like that was more my mom's voice – it was what I was hearing because of her, so it wasn't really my voice.

These accounts highlight the transformative capacity of a spiritual language, practices, and roadmap in facilitating the process of spiritual individuation.

Phase 5: (Re)Construction of Spiritual Identity

AA-A supported many students who had the building blocks to put the pieces together to construct or re-construct their spiritual identity. Through the supported spiritual individuation process, they discovered awareness of their interiority, awareness of their relationship with self, and/or awareness of the spiritual vernacular.

(Re) Authorization of Spiritual Awareness. Student narratives elucidated a pattern of reauthorizing an innate spiritual awareness via the acquisition of spiritual language, spiritual practices, and a spiritual roadmap provided by AA-A group leaders. For example, this student described a change she experienced as a result of participating in AA-A:

> I've been able to engage in better conversations with both of my parents now about, I'm not Catholic, but I can also be religious. We can engage in those conversations about spirituality. At the end of the day, they really value that I'm very spiritual…through all the conversations

> we've had, we can both see that I don't need to subscribe to Catholicism. If that's what they want, they can do that. But that is not, the only thing that links us to spirituality.

Another student spoke about feeling unauthorized in their sense of spirituality and religion in the past and shared about their recent process of reclaiming their spiritual awareness connected to Judaism through engaging in identity exploration and with spiritual communities:

> Sometimes it felt like [my beliefs] didn't *count* as Judaism because it didn't come with the rituals, and I think a lot of it is about reclaiming it and being like "No! This *is* coming from a place of Judaism, and this *is* from my sense of Judaism." I think that there's a lot in there, in terms of my spiritual journey or connection with Judaism. When I got to college, I joined the Jewish acapella group… I was then able to engage deeply and meaningfully with my Jewish identity and Jewish community without it being ritual in nature…so that's…my process in terms of trying to figure out spirituality.

For some, AA-A provided a frame for their existing but previously unsupported experiences. One student, identifying as neither spiritual nor religious, narrated an experience of a secular upbringing without prior engagement in spiritual matters. She recounts a transformative shift in her relational orientation toward life, moving toward a connection with a "kinder, higher self," and adopting a more mindful approach to daily life beyond "my to-do list." This change also brought about a newfound sense of purpose and a feeling of connectedness with a higher power, which she identifies as the "universe." She reflects, "I never thought about it [higher power, universe] until sitting at home after coming home from college between sophomore and junior year and AA-A."

Reconstruction of spiritual identity often entails relational spirituality. Students shared transformative experiences that led to a personal and reciprocal relationship with the Transcendent, distinct from communal beliefs traditionally imposed upon them. This narrative captures the essence of supported spiritual individuation as a deeply personal journey, facilitated by AA-A's spiritual meditative practices:

> Because of the program [AA-A], I started to ask myself certain things and I would come back to Hosting Council meditation in the hopes that when I called upon the higher power, eventually something would show up. I remember the second or third time that I did it in my room, I called upon the higher power, and somebody actually showed up. It was the Virgin Mary, but in her Latin American manifestation, the Virgin of Guadalupe. That was such a powerful moment because she's a figure that I'd always been exposed to, but it had always been forced. Like, this is who you are supposed to believe in, this is who you are supposed to love. But I realized that through the meditation, my love for her could be something personal, that it could be a personal belief as opposed to a sort of communal belief. As opposed to, we're all supposed to believe in her because that's just the way things are. Now I feel like I'm building my devotion towards the Virgin Mary, specifically the Virgin of Guadalupe. A month later after doing this meditation more continuously, I decided, "You know what? I'm going to go get a candle." Like, one of those religious candles to just be in contact with her, one on one, and see what happens. I lit it in my room, and I did a little prayer, and the candle itself, it became so strong, so powerful. It became bright, and that resonated with me. So, I feel like just the very notion of a higher power as translated through the program, it's really set into motion a whole bunch of beautiful things.

Discussion

This study investigated the experiences of emerging adult college students engaged in an SMB wellness intervention, AA-A, aimed at supporting spiritual individuation and identity development within a collegiate setting. The objective was to delineate the spiritual individuation process among this demographic through supported spiritual individuation facilitated by AA-A.

Overall results indicate that the AA-A design supports spiritual individuation. To illustrate the AA-A Model, we present an exemplar of the supported spiritual individuation process that unfolded during AA-A. Alana (a pseudonym) is a 21-year-old senior who engaged with an AA-A group in spring 2020, initially on campus and then online after the onset of the COVID-19 pandemic. Alana identifies as a Christian, bisexual, Black female and described being active in faith communities at home and college. Alana was in psychotherapy for anxiety when she joined AA-A.

Catalyst

Spiritual struggle and the onset of the pandemic served as catalysts for Alana's engagement in AA-A. As a senior, Alana endured several losses in transitioning from campus to home, including on-campus learning and experiences, community, and in-person graduation, as well as a loss of independence in moving home.

Alana struggled with motivation and negative self-talk whenever she perceived herself as unproductive. She perceived herself through an Achievement Awareness lens, only as good as her last accomplishment. Although the university converted its grading system to pass/fail for that spring semester, Alana was unable to allow this change to relax her because she viewed herself through an Achievement Awareness lens, stating:

> I'm about finishing super strong, and I have put a lot of pressure on this semester, so it's been hard to let go of that. I still have my thesis to finish, and I really want departmental honors with that, and so I'm struggling to be chill even though everything is pass/fail because I still feel like there's a lot on the line.

Seeking/Quest

Alana sought the AA-A program to delve into mindfulness and meditation as a strategy to mitigate her anxiety. As she recounts:

> It's been an anxious and depressed time amidst all of the pandemic chaos...my self-talk has definitely been abrasive, harsh, hurtful, and negative ... my internal landscape has been rocky lately, but I'm trying to cut myself some slack. I want to let go of my attachment to external, quantitative-style validations. I have a lot of anxiety, and I want to let go. The Road of Life [meditation] was opening yourself up to trying to embrace change and embrace a new path and thinking about what if this might be better for you and what if you took this other path that seems like more opening yourself up to receiving what is or following what feels better and is more appropriate for you, even if things don't work out.

Alana utilized the spiritual resources provided in AA-A to support her spiritual quest with the spirit of openness and curiosity, moving her along the path of spiritual individuation.

(De) Construction of Spirituality

Alana was on her path of spiritual individuation when she sought further support in AA-A, revealing a spiritual struggle with her faith and perception of God that was directly affecting her mood and functioning:

> I am in an odd position because I care deeply about my religion and religious community, and I study religion. But I also feel that I am in a personal place of struggle with my religion/spirituality and my relationships with my Higher Power and myself.

She appeared to realize the depth of her spiritual struggle during AA-A, which catalyzed her to move along her path. The SBNR affiliation of AA-A opened the door to spiritual support not only for those who did not identify as religious, but also for those like Alana who were religious. Alana was able to utilize the pluralistic, non-judgmental space of AA-A toward safe spiritual exploration outside the bounds of a specific theology amidst her own process of deconstructing and questioning her previously known sense of spirituality.

Learning and Growth

Through AA-A spiritual practices, language, and peer sharing, Alana began to recognize that her negative self-talk may be contributing to her anxiety and expressed a desire to be kinder to herself. She exhibits an openness to new knowledge and integrates spiritual concepts that open new perspectives: "I learned to be mindful and pay attention to how my 'inner roommate' is treating me." To counteract her critical self-talk and anxiety, she chose to practice the AA-A meditations and lessons outside of the group sessions. Alana began engaging in an active dialogue with her higher self to cope with her anxiety and transform her relationship with herself:

> This week's been rough because I've been super anxious about my thesis and tomorrow's deadline. So, one day before I started working, I did the *higher self* meditation and found that 'talking' with my higher self got me into a better mental state and helped me face my work.

Alana utilized the *relational spirituality* concepts provided in AA-A to cultivate spiritual practices to support her spiritual and mental well-being. Alana highlighted the significance of the community fostered by AA-A in affirming her experiences and cultivating relationships grounded in authentic connection through a spiritual perspective. She reflects on her engagement with AA-A virtual sessions and the shared experience of impostor syndrome, stating:

> For me, it's nice that I'm still with people and have some distance, but still get the conversation, and we're still able to do the small group chats…I like having the group and being able to talk and hear…from my peers about their experiences because it's validating; I think a lot of our experiences overlap. What people were sharing on Tuesday was the most meaningful session, hearing what people were sharing, things like imposter syndrome comes up a lot when you talk to students, but yet even though we know that we are all feeling imposter syndrome, you still have trouble shaking it or feeling you need to overwork because everyone else is and seems to be doing so much better than you – even though we know it, it's still something that persists.

Alana found a connection with herself through AA-A language and resources and a connection with her peers in AA-A when participating in a remote format. The group format of AA-A provides an immediate counter to isolation, and the spiritual concepts and tools to support spiritual individuation offer a long-term counter to isolation through relational spirituality – a focus on building relationships with self, higher self, higher power, and others.

(Re)Construction of Spiritual Identity

Before AA-A, Alana perceived God as judgmental, and her perspective started to shift when she began engaging in an active dialogue with her higher self. Alana was in the process of deconstructing pre-existing beliefs and redefining her personal, sacred dialogue with God:

> I have been having a hard time with my faith and my perception of God. I realized that I'd feel better about God if I thought about God like my higher self, someone there to support me and give me advice and be compassionate and loving.

Alana was cultivating a more secure and loving relationship with God and engaging in spiritual community, both of which appeared to support her along her path out of struggle and into spiritual transformation and individuation. Alana experienced a reconstruction of her spiritual identity through her new spiritual awareness of and relationship with her higher self and re-authorization of her spirituality by discovering a loving and compassionate relationship with God through her AA-A journey:

> I learned to be mindful and pay attention to how my self-talk is treating me, and work on how I can pivot away from hyper-critical and judgmental internal thoughts about myself and others to engaging with my higher self…With Awakened Awareness, we can learn to accept our thoughts and feelings and not let them overcome us, but also open ourselves up to fostering a positive relationship between ourselves and our higher self and Higher Power. With Awakened Awareness, we can also open ourselves up to new pathways and connections in life that may not be what we intended or wanted for ourselves, but that will serve us better.

Overall, Alana was able to increase her self-compassion and begin to resolve her spiritual struggle, which improved her ability to engage and be effective in her religious and secular worlds.

Conclusion

In this chapter, we utilized a qualitative design to identify college student engagement with the pillars of AA-A, a science-driven program to support the endemic developmental tasks of spiritual individuation and identity development. The student's qualitative experience of the pillars of the AA-A process offers a rich and nuanced understanding of one path of supported spiritual individuation.

AA-A was designed to support spiritual awakening and spiritual individuation and provide targeted prevention against the risk of the diseases of despair that are often linked with spiritual struggles. By prioritizing the creation of spiritually supportive spaces and interventions, colleges and universities can play a pivotal role in potentiating spiritual individuation, thereby contributing to students' mental health and overall well-being.

More must be done to address the college mental health crisis. Our series of studies on AA-A and other research has shown the importance of supporting spirituality as part of identity development, holistic wellness, and stable mental health. Institutions of higher education are well suited to support emerging adult spirituality, which includes supporting spiritual individuation. Spiritual individuation in emerging adults is shown by previous research to be an essential process of whole-person development, foundational to lifelong mental health and thriving. The AA-A process presented in this chapter elucidates the pillars of support for spiritual individuation and the factors that drive it. Through AA-A, tools for engagement are provided that are inherently necessary, impactful, and effective in supporting spiritual awakening and individuation among emerging adult college students.

References

Abrams, Z. (2022). Student mental health is in crisis. Campuses are rethinking their approach. *Monitor on Psychology*. *53*(7). Retrieved on January 1, 2024, from https://www.apa.org/monitor/2022/10/mental-health-campus-care

Abu-Raiya, H., Pargament, K. I., Krause, N., & Ironson, G. (2015). Robust links between religious/spiritual struggles, psychological distress, and well-being in a national sample of American adults. *American Journal of Orthopsychiatry*, *85*(6), 565. https://doi.org/10.1037/t04021-000

Active Minds. (2022). Statistics. *Active Minds*. Retrieved on December 23, 2023, from https://www.activeminds.org/about-mental-health/statistics/

Anderson, M. R., Scalora, S. C., Crete, A., Mistur, E. J., & Miller, L. (2023). Physiological Recovery from Stress is Associated with Spiritual Recovery: Findings from Awakened Awareness, a College-Based Spiritual-Mind-Body Intervention. *Integrative Medicine Reports*, *2*(1), 129–137. https://doi.org/10.1089/imr.2023.0026

Anderson, M. S. (2018). Barriers to the utilization of mental health services on college campuses by African-American students. *McNair Scholars Research Journal*, *11*(1), 3. Retrieved on January 5, 2024, from http://commons.emich.edu/mcnair/vol11/iss1/3/

Ano, G. G., & Vasconcelles, E. B. (2005). Religious coping and psychological adjustment to stress: A meta-analysis. *Journal of clinical psychology*, *61*(4), 461–480. https://doi.org/10.1037/e411162005-006

Arnett, J. J. (2000). Emerging adulthood: A theory of development from the late teens through the twenties. *American psychologist*, *55*(5), 469.

Arnett, J. J. (2023). *Emerging adulthood: The winding road from the late teens through the twenties*. Oxford University Press. https://doi.org/10.1093/oso/9780197695937.001.0001

Arnett, J. J., & Tanner, J. L. (Eds.). (2006). *Emerging adults in America: Coming of age in the 21st century*. American Psychological Association. https://doi.org/10.1037/11381-000

Astin, J. A., Shapiro, S. L., Eisenberg, D. M., & Forys, K. L. (2003). Mind-body medicine: state of the science, implications for practice. *The Journal of the American Board of Family Practice*, *16*(2), 131–147. https://doi.org/10.3122/jabfm.16.2.131

Barbayannis, G., Bandari, M., Zheng, X., Baquerizo, H., Pecor, K. W., & Ming, X. (2022). Academic Stress and Mental Well-Being in College Students: Correlations, Affected Groups, and COVID-19. *Frontiers in psychology*, *13*, 886344. https://doi.org/10.3389/fpsyg.2022.886344

Barry, C. M., & Abo-Zena, M. M. (2014). Emerging adults' religious and spiritual development. *Emerging Adults' Religiousness and Spirituality: Meaning-making in an Age of Transition*, 21–38. https://doi.org/10.1093/acprof:oso/9780199959181.003.0002

Barton, Y. A., Barkin, S. H., & Miller, L. (2017). Deconstructing depression: A latent profile analysis of potential depressive subtypes in emerging adults. *Spirituality in Clinical Practice*, *4*(1), 1–21.

Barton, Y. A., & Miller, L. (2015). Spirituality and positive psychology go hand in hand: An investigation of multiple empirically derived profiles and related protective benefits. *Journal of Religion and Health*, *54*, 829–843. https://doi.org/10.1007/s10943-015-0045-2

Benedek, M., Jauk, E., Sommer, M., Arendasy, M., & Neubauer, A. C. (2014). Intelligence, creativity, and cognitive control: The common and differential involvement of executive functions in intelligence and creativity. *Intelligence*, *46*, 73–83. https://doi.org/10.1016/j.intell.2014.05.007

Benson, P. L., Roehlkepartain, E. C., & Rude, S. P. (2019). Spiritual development in childhood and adolescence: Toward a field of inquiry. In *Beyond the Self* (pp. 205–213). Routledge. https://doi.org/10.4324/9780203764688

Benson, P. L., Scales, P. C., Syvertsen, A. K., & Roehlkepartain, E. C. (2012). Is youth spiritual development a universal developmental process? An international exploration. *The Journal of Positive Psychology*, *7*(6), 453–470. https://doi.org/10.1080/17439760.2012.732102

Bleidorn, W., & Schwaba, T. (2017). Personality development in emerging adulthood. In *Personality development across the lifespan* (pp. 39–51). Academic Press. https://doi.org/10.1016/b978-0-12-804674-6.00004-1

Bonelli, R., Dew, R. E., Koenig, H. G., Rosmarin, D. H., & Vasegh, S. (2012). Religious and spiritual factors in depression: review and integration of the research. *Depression research and treatment*, *2012*. (1), 962860. https://doi.org/10.1155/2012/962860

Borgogna, N. C., McDermott, R. C., Aita, S. L., & Kridel, M. M. (2019). Anxiety and depression across gender and sexual minorities: Implications for transgender, gender nonconforming, pansexual, demisexual, asexual, queer, and questioning individuals. *Psychology of Sexual Orientation and Gender Diversity*, *6*(1), 54. https://doi.org/10.1037/sgd0000306

Bożek, A., Nowak, P. F., & Blukacz, M. (2020). The relationship between spirituality, health-related behavior, and psychological well-being. *Frontiers in Psychology*, *11*, 1997. https://doi.org/10.3389/fpsyg.2020.01997

Brown, V., Morgan, T., & Fralick, A. (2021). Isolation and mental health: thinking outside the box. *General Psychiatry*, *34*(3). https://doi.org/10.1136/gpsych-2020-100461

Bruce, L. D., Wu, J. S., Lustig, S. L., Russell, D. W., & Nemecek, D. A. (2019). Loneliness in the United States: A 2018 national panel survey of demographic, structural, cognitive, and behavioral characteristics. *American Journal of Health Promotion*, *33*(8), 1123–1133. https://doi.org/10.1177/0890117119856551

Bruffaerts, R., Mortier, P., Auerbach, R. P., Alonso, J., Hermosillo De la Torre, A. E., Cuijpers, P., Demyttenaere, K., Ebert, D. D., Green, J. G., Hasking, P., Stein, D. J., Ennis, E., Nock, M. K., Pinder-Amaker, S., Sampson, N. A., Vilagut, G., Zaslavsky, A. M., & Kessler, R. C. (2019). Lifetime and 12-month treatment for mental disorders and suicidal thoughts and behaviors among first year college students. *International Journal of Methods in Psychiatric Research*, *28*(2), e1764. https://doi.org/10.1002/mpr.1764

Campbell, J. (2003). *The hero's journey: Joseph Campbell on his life and work* (Vol. 7). New World Library.

Canda, E. R., Furman, L. D., & Canda, H. J. (2019). *Spiritual diversity in social work practice: The heart of helping*. Oxford University Press, USA.

Chang, E. C., Wan, L., Li, P., Guo, Y., He, J., Gu, Y., … & Hirsch, J. K. (2017). Loneliness and suicidal risk in young adults: does believing in a changeable future help minimize suicidal risk among the lonely?. *The Journal of psychology*, *151*(5), 453–463. https://doi.org/10.1080/00223980.2017.1314928

Chapman, A., & Greenhow, C. (2021). Applying a critical lens to teachers' use of social media for civic education. *Contemporary Issues in Technology and Teacher Education*, *21*(2), 526–555. https://doi.org/10.3102/1687245

Charmaz, K. (2014). Grounded theory in global perspective: Reviews by international researchers. *Qualitative inquiry*, *20*(9), 1074–1084. https://doi.org/10.1177/1077800414545235

Colarossi, J. (2022, April 21). *Mental Health of College Students is Getting Worse*. The Brink. Boston University. Retrieved on December 10, 2023, from https://www.bu.edu/articles/2022/mental-health-of-college-students-is-getting-worse/

Cole, B. S., Hopkins, C. M., Tisak, J., Steel, J. L., & Carr, B. I. (2008). Assessing spiritual growth and spiritual decline following a diagnosis of cancer: reliability and validity of the spiritual transformation scale. *Psycho-Oncology: Journal of the Psychological, Social and Behavioral Dimensions of Cancer*, *17*(2), 112–121. https://doi.org/10.1002/pon.1207

Cooper, V.E. (2022, August 12). An Essential Education: Mental Health First Aid for Emerging Adults. *Mental Health First Aid from National Council for Mental Wellbeing*. Retrieved on January 1, 2024, from https://www.mentalhealthfirstaid.org/2022/08/an-essential-education-mental-health-first-aid-for-emerging-adults/

Craig, S. L., & Austin, A. (2016). The AFFIRM open pilot feasibility study: A brief affirmative cognitive behavioral coping skills group intervention for sexual and gender minority youth. *Children and Youth Services Review*, *64*, 136–144. https://doi.org/10.1016/j.childyouth.2016.02.022

Creswell, J. W., & Miller, D. L. (2000). Determining validity in qualitative inquiry. *Theory into practice*, *39*(3), 124–130. https://doi.org/10.1207/s15430421tip3903_2

Crete, A., Anderson, M., Scalora, S., Mistur, E., Fuller, O., & Miller, L. (2020). Spiritual decline as a predictor of posttraumatic stress. *Religions*, *11*(11), 575. https://doi.org/10.3390/rel11110575

Davis, D. E., Hook, J. N., & Worthington Jr, E. L. (2008). Relational spirituality and forgiveness: The roles of attachment to God, religious coping, and viewing the transgression as a desecration. *Journal of Psychology & Christianity*, *27*(4), 293–301.

Denton, M. L., Pearce, L. D., & Smith, C. (2008). Religion and spirituality on the path through adolescence. *National study of Youth and religion*, *22*, 2010.

Desrosiers, A., Kelley, B. S., & Miller, L. (2011). Parent and peer relationships and relational spirituality in adolescents and young adults. *Psychology of Religion and Spirituality*, *3*(1), 39–54. https://doi.org/10.1037/a0020027

Donovan, N. J., Wu, Q., Rentz, D. M., Sperling, R. A., Marshall, G. A., & Glymour, M. M. (2017). Loneliness, depression and cognitive function in older US adults. *International Journal of Geriatric Psychiatry*, *32*(5), 564–573. https://doi.org/10.1002/gps.4495

Dunbar, M. S., Sontag-Padilla, L., Ramchand, R., Seelam, R., & Stein, B. D. (2017). Mental health service utilization among lesbian, gay, bisexual, and questioning or queer college students. *Journal of Adolescent Health*, *61*(3), 294–301. https://doi.org/10.1016/j.jadohealth.2017.03.008

Dusselier, L., Dunn, B., Wang, Y., Shelleyii, M. C., & Whalen, D. F. (2005). Personal, health, academic, and environmental predictors of stress for residence hall students. *Journal of American College Health*, *54*(1), 15–24. https://doi.org/10.3200/jach.54.1.15-24

Dworsky, C. K. O., Pargament, K. I., Wong, S., & Exline, J. J. (2016). Suppressing spiritual struggles: The role of experiential avoidance in mental health. *Journal of Contextual Behavioral Science*, *5*(4), 258–265. https://doi.org/10.1016/j.jcbs.2016.10.002

Ellison, C. G., & Lee, J. (2010). Spiritual struggles and psychological distress: Is there a dark side of religion? *Social Indicators Research*, *98*, 501–517.

Erikson, E.H. (1968). *Identity: Youth and Crisis*. New York: W.W. Norton & Company.

Faver, C. A. (2004). Relational spirituality and social caregiving. *Social Work*, *49*(2), 241–249. https://doi.org/10.1093/sw/49.2.241

Ferguson, S. (2022, October 11). Loss of Faith: What to Do When You Feel Like You're Losing it. *Psych Central*. Retrieved February 26, 2024, from https://psychcentral.com/lib/the-pain-of-losing-your-faith

Flannery, M.E. (2023, March 29). *The Mental Health Crisis on College Campuses*. National Education Association. Retrieved December 10, 2023, from https://www.nea.org/nea-today/all-news-articles/mental-health-crisis-college-campuses

Ford, T., Lipson, J., & Miller, L. (2023). Spiritually grounded character: A latent profile analysis. *Frontiers in Psychology*, *13*. https://doi.org/10.3389/fpsyg.2022.1061416

Fowler, J. W. (1981). *Stages of Faith: The Psychology of Human Development and the Quest for Meaning*. Harper Collins.

Fraser-Thill, R. (2023). What is individuation in psychology? *verywell mind*. Retrieved December 30, 2023, from https://www.verywellmind.com/individuation-3288007

Fuertes, A., & Dugan, K. (2021). Spirituality through the lens of students in Higher Education. *Religions*, *12*(11), 924. https://doi.org/10.3390/rel12110924

Greyson, B., & Khanna, S. (2014). Spiritual transformation after near-death experiences. *Spirituality in Clinical Practice*, *1*(1), 43–55. https://doi.org/10.1037/scp0000010

Grof, S., & Grof, C., (1989). *Spiritual emergency: When personal transformation becomes a crisis*. Tarcher: Distributed by St. Martin's Press.

Heinrich, L. M., & Gullone, E. (2006). The clinical significance of loneliness: A literature review. *Clinical Psychology Review*, *26*(6), 695–718. https://doi.org/10.1016/j.cpr.2006.04.002

Heinze, J., Eisenberg, D., & Zhou, S. (2022). Healthy Minds Study 2021-2022. Healthy Minds Network. Retrieved December 10, 2023, from https://healthymindsnetwork.org/hms/

Hill, P. C., Pargament, K. I., Hood, R. W., McCullough, J. M. E., Swyers, J. P., Larson, D. B., & Zinnbauer, B. J. (2000). Conceptualizing religion and spirituality: Points of commonality, points of departure. *Journal for the Theory of Social Behaviour*, *30*(1), 51–57. https://doi.org/10.1111/1468-5914.00119

Hodges, S. (2002). Mental health, depression, and dimensions of spirituality and religion. *Journal of Adult Development*, *9*(2), 109–115. https://doi.org/10.1023/a:1015733329006

Holland, J. M., Currier, J. M., & Neimeyer, R. A. (2006). Meaning reconstruction in the first two years of bereavement: The role of sense-making and benefit-finding. *OMEGA-Journal of Death and Dying*, *53*(3), 175–191. https://doi.org/10.2190/fkm2-yjty-f9vv-9xwy

Horowitz, A. G., Berona, J., Busby, D. R., Eisenberg, D., Zheng, K., Pistorello, J., Albucher, R., Coryell, W., Favorite, T., Walloch, J. C., & King, C. A. (2020). Variation in suicide risk among subgroups of sexual and gender minority college students. *Suicide and Life-Threatening Behavior*, *50*(5), 1041–1053. https://doi.org/10.1111/sltb.12637

Kashdan, T. B., & Fincham, F. D. (2004). Facilitating curiosity: A social and self-regulatory perspective for scientifically based interventions. *Positive Psychology in Practice*, 482–503. https://doi.org/10.1002/9780470939338.ch30

Kendler, K. S., Gardner, C. O., & Prescott, C. A. (1997). Religion, psychopathology, and substance use and abuse; a multimeasure, genetic-epidemiologic study. *The American Journal of Psychiatry*, *154*(3), 322–329. https://doi.org/10.1176/ajp.154.3.322

Kendler, K. S., Neale, M. C., Sullivan, P., Corey, L. A., Gardner, C. O., & Prescott, C. A. (1999). A population-based twin study in women of smoking initiation and nicotine dependence. *Psychological Medicine*, *29*(2), 299–308. https://doi.org/10.1017/s0033291798008022

King, P. E. (2019). Religion and identity: The role of ideological, social, and spiritual contexts. In *Beyond the self* (pp. 197–204). Routledge.

Koenig, H. G. (2012). Religion, spirituality, and health: the research and clinical implications. *ISRN psychiatry*, *2012*, 1–33. https://doi.org/10.5402/2012/278730

Koenig, H. G., King, D., & Carson, V. B. (2012). *Handbook of Religion and Health*. Oxford University Press.

Koenig, L. B., McGue, M., & Iacono, W. G. (2008). Stability and change in religiousness during emerging adulthood. *Developmental Psychology*, *44*(2), 532–543. https://doi.org/10.1037/0012-1649.44.2.532

Kroenke, K., Spitzer, R. L., & Williams, J. B. (2001). The PHQ-9. *Journal of General Internal Medicine*, *16*(9), 606–613. https://doi.org/10.1046/j.1525-1497.2001.016009606.x

Layland, E. K., Hill, B. J., & Nelson, L. J. (2018). Freedom to explore the self: How emerging adults use leisure to develop identity. *The Journal of Positive Psychology*, *13*(1), 78–91. https://doi.org/10.1080/17439760.2017.1374440

Leung, C. H., & Pong, H. K. (2021). Cross-sectional study of the relationship between the spiritual wellbeing and psychological health among university students. *PLOS ONE*, *16*(4). https://doi.org/10.1371/journal.pone.0249702

Linder, J., (2023). Loneliness in College Students Statistics: Market Report & Data. *Gitnux Market Data Report* 2024. Retrieved March 20, 2024, from https://gitnux.org/loneliness-in-college-students-statistics/

Lipson, S. K., Zhou, S., Abelson, S., Heinze, J., Jirsa, M., Morigney, J., … & Eisenberg, D. (2022). Trends in college student mental health and help-seeking by Race/ethnicity: Findings from the National Healthy Minds Study, 2013–2021. *Journal of Affective Disorders*, *306*, 138–147. https://doi.org/10.1016/j.jad.2022.03.038

Mahoney, A. (2013). The spirituality of us: Relational spirituality in the context of family relationships. In *APA Handbook of Psychology, Religion, and Spirituality (Vol 1): Context, Theory, and Research*, 365–389.

Marcia, J. E. (1966). Development and validation of ego-identity status. *Journal of personality and social psychology*, *3*(5), 551–558. https://doi.org/10.1037/h0023281

Marcia, J. E. (1980). Identity in adolescence. In J. Adelson (Ed.), *Handbook of Adolescent Psychology*, *9*(11), 159–187. New York: Wiley and Sons.

Mariano, J. M., & Damon, W. (2008). The role of spirituality and religious faith in supporting purpose in adolescence. In R. M. Lerner, R. W. Roeser, & E. Phelps (Eds.), *Positive youth development and spirituality: From theory to research* (pp. 210–230). Templeton Foundation Press.

Markstrom, C. A. (1999). Religious involvement and adolescent psychosocial development. *Journal of Adolescence*, *22*(2), 205–221. https://doi.org/10.1006/jado.1999.0211

Masi, C. M., Chen, H. Y., Hawkley, L. C., & Cacioppo, J. T. (2010). A meta-analysis of interventions to reduce loneliness. *Personality and Social Psychology Review*, *15*(3), 219–266. https://doi.org/10.1177/1088868310377394

McAdams, D. P. (1993). *The stories we live by: Personal myths and the making of the self.* William Morrow & Co.

McClintock, C. H., Worhunsky, P. D., Balodis, I. M., Sinha, R., Miller, L., & Potenza, M. N. (2019). How spirituality may mitigate against stress and related mental disorders: A review and preliminary neurobiological evidence. *Current Behavioral Neuroscience Reports*, *6*(4), 253–262. https://doi.org/10.1007/s40473-019-00195-0

McCrae, R. R., & Costa, P. T. (1997). Conceptions and correlates of openness to experience. In R. Hogan, J. Johnson, & S. Briggs (Eds), *Handbook of personality psychology* (pp. 825–847). Academic Press. https://doi.org/10.1016/B978-012134645-4/50032-9

McKenna-Plumley, P. E., Turner, R. N., Yang, K., & Groarke, J. M. (2023). "it's a feeling of complete disconnection": Experiences of existential loneliness from youth to older adulthood. *BMC psychology*, *11*(1), 408. https://doi.org/10.1186/s40359-023-01452-4

McNamara Barry, C., Nelson, L., Davarya, S., & Urry, S. (2010). Religiosity and spirituality during the transition to adulthood. *International Journal of Behavioral Development*, *34*(4), 311–324. https://doi.org/10.1177/0165025409350964

McPhillips, D. (2023). Mental health struggles are driving more college students to consider dropping out, survey finds. *CNN health*. Retrieved on January 1, 2024, from https://www.cnn.com/2023/03/23/health/mental-health-college-dropout-survey-wellness/index.html

Miller, L. (2005). Interpersonal psychotherapy from a spiritual perspective. In L. Sperry & E. P. Shafranske (Eds.), *Spiritually Oriented Psychotherapy*, 153– 175. https://doi.org/10.1037/10886-007

Miller, L. (2011). An experiential approach for exploring spirituality. In Aten, J., McMinn, M., & Worthington, E., *Spiritually Oriented Interventions for Counseling and Psychotherapy*, 325–343. https://doi.org/10.1037/12313-013

Miller, L. (2013). Spiritual awakening and depression in adolescents: A unified pathway or "two sides of the same coin". *Bulletin of the Menninger Clinic*, *77*(4), 332–348. https://doi.org/10.1521/bumc.2013.77.4.332

Miller, L. (2021). *The awakened brain: The new science of spirituality and our quest for an inspired life.* Random House; New York, NY.

Miller, L., & Barton, Y. A. (2015). Developmental depression in adolescents: A potential sub-type based on neural correlates and comorbidity. *Journal of Religion and Health*, *54*, 817–828. https://doi.org/10.1007/s10943-015-0047-0

Miller, L., Davies, M., & Greenwald, S. (2000). Religiosity and substance use and abuse among adolescents in the National Comorbidity Survey. *Journal of the American Academy of Child and Adolescent Psychiatry*, 39, 1190–1197. https://doi.org/10.1097/00004583-200009000-00020

Miller, L., Warner, V., Wickramaratne, P., & Weissman, M. (1997). Religiosity and depression: Ten-year follow-up of depressed mothers and offspring. *Journal of the American Academy of Child & Adolescent Psychiatry*, *36*(10), 1416–1425.

Misra, R., & McKean, M. (2000). College students' academic stress and its relation to their anxiety, time management, and leisure satisfaction. *American Journal of Health Studies*, *16*(1), 41. https://doi.org/10.1037/1072-5245.11.2.132

Mistur, E. J., Scalora, S. C., Crete, A. A., Anderson, M. R., Athan, A. M., Chapman, A. L., & Miller, L. J. (2022). Inner Peace in a Global Crisis: A Case Study of Supported Spiritual Individuation in Acute Onset Phase of COVID-19. *Emerging Adulthood*, *10*(6), 1543–1560. https://doi.org/10.1177/21676968221111965

Mistur, E. J., Scalora, S. C., Crete, A. A., Anderson, M. R., Jain, K., Huang, C., Noumair, D. A., Miller, L. (2024). Supporting sexual and gender minority college student wellness: Differential needs and outcomes in a spiritual-mind-body intervention. *Psychology of Sexual Orientation and Gender Diversity*. Advance online publication. https://doi.org/10.1037/sgd0000775

Mitchell, G., Murray, J., Wilson, P., Hutch, R., & Meredith, P. (2010). "Diagnosing" and "Managing" spiritual distress in palliative care: Creating an intellectual framework for spirituality useable in clinical practice. *Australasian Medical Journal*, *3*(6), 364–369. https://doi.org/10.4066/amj.2010.338

Mitchell, L. L., Lodi-Smith, J., Baranski, E. N., & Whitbourne, S. K. (2021). Implications of identity resolution in emerging adulthood for intimacy, generativity, and integrity across the adult lifespan. *Psychology and Aging*, *36*(5), 545–556. https://doi.org/10.1037/pag0000537

Museus, S. (2023). The Hechinger Report. Retrieved December 23, 2023, from https://hechingerreport.org/opinion-our-students-face-a-mental-health-crisis-and-college-campuses-are-part-of-the-problem/

Musgrave, C. F., Allen, C. E., & Allen, G. J. (2002). Spirituality and health for women of color. *American Journal of Public Health*, *92*(4), 557–560.

Nice, M. L., & Joseph, M. (2022). The features of emerging adulthood and individuation: Relations and differences by college-going status, age, and living situation. *Emerging Adulthood*, *11*(2), 271–287. https://doi.org/10.1177/21676968221116545

Novak, B. K., Gebhardt, A., Pallerla, H., McDonald, S. B., Haramati, A., & Cotton, S. (2020). Impact of a university-wide interdisciplinary mind-body skills program on student mental and emotional well-being. *Global Advances in Health and Medicine*, *9*, 216495612097398. https://doi.org/10.1177/2164956120973983

Oppong, S. H. (2013). Religion and identity. *American International Journal of Contemporary Research*, *3*(6), 10–16.

Pargament, K. I. (1997). *The psychology of religion and coping: Theory, research, and practice*. Guilford.

Pargament, K. I., & Exline, J. J. (2021). *Working with spiritual struggles in psychotherapy: From research to practice*. Guilford Publications.

Patton, M. Q. (2014). *Qualitative research & evaluation methods: Integrating theory and practice*. Sage publications.

Peck, M. S. (2010). *The different drum: Community making and peace*. Simon and Schuster.

Pedrelli, P., Nyer, M., Yeung, A., Zulauf, C., & Wilens, T. (2014). College students: mental health problems and treatment considerations. *Academic psychiatry*, *39*(5), 503–511. https://doi.org/10.1007/s40596-014-0205-9

Piedmont, R. L. (1999). Does spirituality represent the sixth factor of personality? Spiritual transcendence and the five-factor model. *Journal of Personality*, *67*(6), 985–1013. https://doi.org/10.1111/1467-6494.00080

Sandage, S. J., Jensen, M. L., & Jass, D. (2008). Relational spirituality and transformation: Risking intimacy and alterity. *Journal of Spiritual Formation and Soul Care*, *1*(2), 182–206. https://doi.org/10.1177/193979090800100205

Scalora, S., Anderson, M., Crete, A., Drapkin, J., Portnoff, L., Athan, A., & Miller, L. (2020). A spirituality mind-body wellness center in a university setting; A pilot service assessment study. *Religions*, *11*(9), 466. https://doi.org/10.3390/rel11090466

Scalora, S. C., Anderson, M. R., Crete, A., Mistur, E. J., Chapman, A., & Miller, L. (2022). A campus-based spiritual-mind-body prevention intervention against symptoms of depression and trauma; An open trial of awakened awareness. *Mental Health & Prevention*, *25*. https://doi.org/10.1016/j.mhp.2022.200229

Schulenberg, J. E., & Zarrett, N. R. (2006). Mental Health During Emerging Adulthood: Continuity and Discontinuity in Courses, Causes, and Functions. *Emerging Adults on America: Coming of Age in the 21st Century.*, 135–172. https://doi.org/10.1037/11381-006

Schure, M. B., Christopher, J., & Christopher, S. (2008). Mind–body medicine and the art of self-care: teaching mindfulness to counseling students through yoga, meditation, and qigong. *Journal of Counseling & Development*, *86*(1), 47–56. https://doi.org/10.1002/j.1556-6678.2008.tb00625.x

Shapiro, S. L., & Carlson, L. E. (2009). The art and science of mindfulness: Integrating mindfulness into psychology and the helping professions. *American Psychological Association*. https://doi.org/10.1037/11885-000

Shults, F. L., & Sandage, S. J. (2006). *Transforming spirituality: Integrating theology and psychology*. Baker Academic. p. 161.

Smith, J. A., & Osborn, M. (2015). Interpretative phenomenological analysis as a useful methodology for research on the lived experience of pain. *British journal of pain*, *9*(1), 41–42. https://doi.org/10.1177/2049463714541642

Smith-MacDonald, L. A., Morin, J. S., & Brémault-Phillips, S. (2018). Spiritual dimensions of moral injury: Contributions of Mental Health Chaplains in the Canadian Armed Forces. *Frontiers in Psychiatry*, *9*, 592. https://doi.org/10.3389/fpsyt.2018.00592

Sokol, J. T. (2009). Identity development throughout the lifetime: An examination of Eriksonian theory. *Graduate Journal of Counseling Psychology*, *1*(2), 14.

Sowislo, J. F., & Orth, U. (2013). Does low self-esteem predict depression and anxiety? A meta-analysis of longitudinal studies. *Psychological Bulletin*, *139*(1), 213–240. https://doi.org/10.1037/a0028931

Spitzer, R. L., Kroenke, K., Williams, J. B., & Löwe, B. (2006). A brief measure for assessing generalized anxiety disorder: the GAD-7. *Archives of Internal Medicine*, *166*(10), 1092–1097.

Tanner, J. L. (2006). Recentering during emerging adulthood: A critical turning point in life span human development. In *Emerging Adults in America: Coming of Age in the 21st Century*, 21–55. https://doi.org/10.1037/11381-002

Travis, J. W., & Ryan, R. S. (2004). *The wellness workbook: How to achieve enduring health and vitality*. Celestial Arts.

Trusty, T. W., & Chun-Kennedy, C. (2023). *International Students Are More Socially Isolated Than Domestic Students, and the Gap is Growing After COVID-19*. Center for Collegiate Mental Health. Penn State, Student Affairs. Retrieved March 21, 2024, from https://ccmh.psu.edu/index.php?day=07&id=44%3Ainternational-students-are-more-socially-isolated-than-domestic-students-and-the-gap-is-bigger-after-covid-19&month=09&option=com_dailyplanetblog&view=entry&year=2023

Viner, J., & Tanner, J. L. (2023). Psychiatric Disorders in Emerging Adulthood. *Yellowbrick*. Retrieved January 1, 2024, from https://yellowbrickprogram.com/papers/psychiatric-disorders-in-emerging-adulthood/

Weathers, F. W., Litz, B., Herman, D., Juska, J., & Keane, T. (1994). PTSD Checklist—Civilian Version. *Journal of Occupational Health Psychology*.

Webb, J. R., Toussaint, L., & Dula, C. S. (2014). Ritualistic, theistic, and existential spirituality: Initial psychometric qualities of the RiTE measure of spirituality. *Journal of Religion and Health*, *53*(4), 972–985. https://doi.org/10.1007/s10943-013-9697-y

Wood, D., Crapnell, T., Lau, L., Bennett, A., Lotstein, D., Ferris, M., & Kuo, A. (2018). Emerging Adulthood as a Critical Stage in the Life Course. *Handbook of Life Course Health Development*, 123–143.

Chapter 17

Spirituality and Suicidal Behavior

Benjamin B. Hall and Jameson K. Hirsch*

Suicide is a prevalent public health concern and the 17th leading cause of death worldwide (World Health Organization [WHO], 2021); approximately one in every 100 deaths is by suicide (WHO, 2021). The causes of suicide are multifactorial, necessitating a comprehensive and interdisciplinary approach to understanding associated predisposing, precipitating, and protective factors. The scientific literature, characterized by a biopsychosocial perspective, demonstrates the complexity of suicidal behavior, with evidence for an array of contributing factors, including genetics, neurophysiology, social isolation, sociocultural influences, adverse life events, and psychopathology (Liu & Miller, 2014; Mullins et al., 2022; Xu et al., 2023). Historically, suicide research has sought to identify risk factors responsible for suicidal behavior in an attempt to highlight potential areas of focus for suicide prevention and intervention strategies. In recent decades, some researchers have shifted their attention to resiliency factors relevant to suicide risk, and a growing body of empirical evidence supports a positive psychological approach to suicidology (see Hirsch et al., 2018). Indeed, the focus of "positive suicidology" includes factors such as psychological virtues (e.g., forgiveness, humility, gratitude, and honesty), positive life events (e.g., marriage, job promotions, and childbirth), and positive cognitive styles (e.g., future orientation and cognitive flexibility), as well as spirituality and religiousness.

Religion, Spirituality, and Health and Well-Being

The extant literature highlights a largely salubrious association between religiousness/spirituality (R/S) and health and well-being in general (Koenig et al., 2024). This includes the positive effect of spirituality on a range of physical health outcomes, including cardiovascular disease (Masters & Hooker, 2013), health behaviors (Roff et al., 2005), and general mental health (Rosmarin & Koenig, 2020); indeed, several other chapters in this volume have focused on the linkages between spirituality, health, and well-being. Despite support for the benefits of spirituality on health and well-being, there is growing concern related to the challenges of conceptualizing and measuring spirituality (Jastrzębski, 2022). The academic literature demonstrates myriad factors that comprise the various conceptualizations of R/S. For example, cognitive factors (e.g., forgiveness, gratitude, and belief in a higher power), social factors (e.g., social support and belongingness), and behavioral factors (e.g., prayer, meditation, and health behaviors) are all components of the construct of R/S described in the literature

* Corresponding Author: bhall4@harding.edu.

DOI: 10.4324/9781003440048-20

(e.g., Connors et al., 1996; Monod et al., 2011; Underwood & Teresi, 2002). Given the breadth of factors associated with R/S, a parsimonious and consensus definition of religiousness or spirituality has become a challenge for researchers. Indeed, more than 40 conceptualizations of spirituality exist in the psychological literature (Zinnbauer & Pargament, 2005). Nevertheless, several common themes have emerged in the scientific endeavor to define R/S. For example, a common approach to distinguishing spirituality from religiousness is to define religiousness as a subcategory of spirituality, whereby spirituality serves as a broader term that encompasses the aspects traditionally viewed as religious (Jastrzębski, 2022). As such, for the remainder of this chapter, the term spirituality will be used in reference to the factors associated with both spiritual functioning and religiousness.

Defining Spirituality

As discussed in the first chapter of this book (see also Chapter 44), the RiTE Model of Spirituality (Webb et al., 2014; Webb, 2021) is a relatively recent conceptualization founded on three dimensions of spiritual functioning: ritualistic, theistic, and existential. To review, the ritualistic domain of spirituality encompasses the aspects of spirituality traditionally associated with organized religion (e.g., church attendance and religious rituals). The theistic domain of spirituality refers to aspects of spiritual functioning concerned with a personal connection or relationship with a deity, higher power, or sacred concept (e.g., nature). Finally, the existential domain of spirituality is characterized by a "transcendent, yet non-theistic, search for meaning or purpose" (Webb, 2021, p. 61). The RiTE Model of Spirituality provides advantages over other unidimensional conceptualizations of spirituality in that it allows for more discrete categorization of aspects of spirituality. This is particularly useful when describing the association of spirituality with health- and well-being-related outcomes. For example, ritualistic spirituality is more strongly linked to social well-being (e.g., Hastings, 2016), whereas existential spirituality is more closely linked to positive psychological virtues (e.g., Hall et al., 2020). The RiTE Model of Spirituality also allows for a more inclusive view of spirituality that extends to non-theistic expressions of spirituality.

Despite preliminary support for the RiTE Model, most research on spirituality, health, and well-being approaches the topic from a constricted view of spiritual functioning. The aim of our chapter is to review empirical data on the association between spirituality and suicide risk in the context of the ritualistic, theistic, and existential aspects of the RiTE Model, which conceptualizes spirituality as "the salient, searching pursuit of the transcendently sacred ritualistic, theistic, and/or existential aspects of the human condition" (Webb et al., 2014, p. 974). We begin with a review of the existing literature on spirituality and suicide risk, which we categorize into the respective dimensions of spirituality as defined by the RiTE Model of Spirituality (i.e., ritualistic, theistic, and existential). We then shift our focus to the potential limitations facing the study of spirituality and suicide. Finally, we address the potential implications of this conceptualization of spirituality in the context of suicide risk and note future directions for the study of the spirituality-suicide link.

Ritualistic Spirituality and Suicidal Behavior

Much of the research regarding spirituality and suicidal behavior focuses on the ritualistic (i.e., religious) aspects of spirituality, such as the association between structured religious practices, including prayer, church attendance, scripture reading, or other religious prescriptions, and suicide risk. For example, across clinical samples (i.e., 144 adults receiving psychotherapy; 248 older adults with depression), greater religious service attendance is associated with less suicidal ideation (Price & Callahan, 2017; Rushing et al., 2013) and, more broadly (e.g., in health professionals), is associated with a five-fold decrease in suicide risk (VanderWeele et al., 2016). The effect of religious service attendance on reduced suicide risk may also be more robust than other religious behaviors (e.g., prayer and studying scripture), perhaps, as we note below, due to its relation to increased social support (Hastings, 2016). For example, in a study of 272 college students in the southern United States, religious service attendance was more strongly associated with reduced suicide risk than private religious behaviors (e.g., prayer, Bible study; Kim et al., 2021). Moreover, the association between religious service attendance and reduced suicide risk has been demonstrated among cross-cultural samples, including adolescents and young adults from Trinidad and Tobago (Toussaint et al., 2015; Ali & Maharajh, 2005) and adolescents in the United Kingdom (Kay & Francis, 2006), although additional research is needed to clarify this association in non-Western, non-Christian societies. The effect of religious service attendance on suicide is commonly attributed to the social support conferred by religious service attendance (Hastings, 2016). Social support is a known protective factor for suicide (Datta & Nakhaie, 2022), and previous research supports the assertion that religious service attendance is indirectly associated with suicide through the role of increased social support (Hovey et al., 2014; Robins & Fiske, 2009; Rushing et al., 2013).

The associations between other manifestations of ritualistic spirituality (e.g., prayer and studying scriptures) and suicidal behavior have been investigated less frequently. In one study, Toussaint et al. (2015) found that frequency of prayer was inversely associated with suicidal ideation and suicide planning. Jongkind et al. (2019) found a significant bivariate correlation between frequency of prayer and suicidal ideation; however, frequency of prayer was no longer related to suicidal ideation in regression models after accounting for age, gender, marital status, and depressive symptoms. Frequency of prayer has been more commonly linked to prominent risk factors for suicide (e.g., depression, anxiety, substance use, and health behaviors). For example, Boelens et al. (2012) found that a six-week prayer intervention was associated with reduced depression and anxiety at a 1-month and 1-year follow-up. In an analysis of studies prior to 2016, Anderson and Nunnelley (2016) found that prayer was associated with less depression in nine out of eleven studies reviewed. Other studies have evaluated the association between broader religious practices and suicide risk. For example, in a sample of 321 young adults who self-identified as Modern Orthodox Jews, Hamdan and Peterseil-Yaul (2020) found that religious commitment, as measured by frequency of observing the Sabbath, attending synagogue, and keeping kosher, was associated with reduced suicidal ideation. Finally, Kim et al. (2021) found that private religious activities, including meditation, Bible study, and prayer, cumulatively were negatively associated with suicide risk, though to a lesser degree than religious service attendance.

Although much research highlights a salubrious association between ritualistic spirituality and suicide risk, there may be ritualistic aspects of spirituality that increase one's risk for suicide. For example, in prior research, individuals who engage in religious behaviors due to fear, guilt, or societal pressures are at greater risk for adverse psychological outcomes (e.g., depression, anxiety, and poor psychological adjustment; Ryan et al., 1993). Moreover, adverse emotional experiences, such as fear or guilt, are a common motivation for engagement in religious behaviors (e.g., prayer and confession; Hermann et al., 2015) and are both associated with increased risk for suicide (Exline et al., 2000). Further research is needed to directly assess the causal pathways between ritualistic spirituality and suicide risk; however, the extant literature supports the notion that engagement in ritualistic spirituality may, in some cases, be associated with suicidal behavior.

It is important to note that the aspects of spirituality discussed above are operationally defined as ritualistic expressions of spirituality, yet they do not necessarily indicate one's degree of belief in, relationship with, or meaningfulness of a connection with a deity or sacred object (e.g., nature). Those characteristics may be better captured by theistic or existential expressions of spirituality, as we review below. As such, the ritualistic qualities of spirituality may exist in the absence of either theistic or existential spirituality. For example, an individual may self-identify as Jewish and practice the cultural behaviors consistent with Judaism (e.g., observing the Sabbath and keeping kosher) without the belief in God, as traditionally described by the religion of Judaism. It is also important to note that some aspects of ritualistic spirituality may cross over into the domains of theistic or existential spirituality. For example, prayer may be considered a structured and organized practice in religious systems, but may also occur as an informal, non-structured, and relational experience better characterized by theistic spirituality (Büssing et al., 2016).

Theistic Spirituality and Suicidal Behavior

Theistic spirituality, defined as "a non-structured connection with deity" (Webb et al., 2014, p. 973), is represented in the literature by numerous concepts, including perceptions of a deity, experiences of deity, attachment to God, or the degree of importance that one places on their spiritual beliefs. Davis et al. (2021, p. 401) describe this type of spirituality as "theistic relational spirituality" and suggest that this aspect of spirituality is represented by one's beliefs about God ("God's traits and ways of thinking, feeling, and behaving toward humans;" p. 403) and one's experiences of God (i.e., the emotions and behaviors experienced in one's relationship to a deity). Previous research suggests that beliefs about deity and experiences of deity are both positively and negatively associated with suicide risk. That is, positive perceptions and experiences of God are associated with reduced risk for suicide, whereas negative perceptions and experiences of God are associated with increased suicide risk (Exline et al., 2000; Jongkind et al., 2019). Regarding perceptions of God, Jongkind et al. (2019) differentiate between a positive-supportive representation of God and a passive-distressing representation of God. Positive-supportive representations describe a view of a deity as positive, authoritative, and beneficial to one's life, whereas passive-distressing representations describe a negative, distant, and angry view of a deity. In a study of 155 Christian adults with depression, Jongkind et al. found that a positive-supportive God representation was associated with decreased suicidal ideation, while a passive-distressing God representation was associated with increased suicidal ideation. This result is consistent with other research. For example, in a study of US military veterans, the perception of being punished by God was positively associated with a history of suicide attempts (Smigelsky et al., 2020). Similarly, in a sample of men in early recovery from substance use disorders, a perception of God as cruel or distant was associated with an increased risk of suicide (Currier et al., 2020). Conversely, the belief that God is in control of one's life was protective of suicidal ideation in a nationally representative sample of American adults (Upenieks, 2022). Likewise, Teismann et al. (2017) found that trust in a higher power moderated the relation between depressive symptoms and suicide ideation among 427 German adults.

Another manifestation of theistic spirituality found in the literature is the widely studied concept of religious coping (Pargament et al., 2000). Religious coping refers to the use of religious beliefs or practices as a resource for coping with adverse life events, and may be adaptive (i.e., positive religious coping) or maladaptive (i.e., negative religious coping; Pargament et al., 2000). Pargament et al. (2011) characterize positive religious coping as "a sense of connectedness with a transcendent force, a secure relationship with a caring God, and a belief that life has a greater benevolent meaning" (p. 58). In contrast, negative religious coping represents a tension or struggle with the divine, questioning one's spiritual beliefs, or the sense that a demonic force is negatively influencing one's life. As a construct, religious coping aligns most closely with theistic spirituality, given its emphasis on one's unstructured connection with a deity (e.g., "Tried to put my plans into action together with God"), rather than engagement in ritualistic behaviors, such as religious service attendance (Pargament et al., 2011, p. 57). Although religious coping may be expressed through ritualistic practices (e.g., praying for forgiveness), it reflects a personal, intrinsic motivation for responding to life stressors based on one's individual relationship with a deity (Pargament et al., 2011).

Broadly, positive religious coping is beneficially associated with mental health outcomes, including reduced suicide risk. For example, in a study of 94 adult outpatients with major depressive disorder, positive religious coping was negatively associated with suicidal ideation (De Berardis et al., 2020). Likewise, Suresh et al. (2020) found that positive religious coping was related to lower risk for suicide among 310 older adults who were homebound. Sinnott et al. (2023) provide further support for the link between positive religious coping and reduced suicide risk and suggest that meaning in life may play an important role in the effect of positive religious coping on suicide. Positive religious coping is also a protective factor for prominent suicide risk factors, including depression (Mahamid & Bdier, 2021), PTSD (Gerber et al., 2011), and psychological adjustment to stress (Ano & Vasconcelles, 2005). Further, in a study of over 500 Muslim and Christian participants, positive religious coping was associated with a reduced likelihood of having had a mental disorder (Thomas & Barbato, 2020). Yet, research on the beneficial effects of religious coping on mental health and suicide is mixed, with multiple studies showing that negative religious coping may have a more robust effect on mental health outcomes than positive religious coping (Kopacz et al., 2018). Indeed, negative religious coping has been linked to a wide range of adverse mental health outcomes. Trevino et al. (2014) found that negative religious coping was a robust predictor of suicidal ideation among a sample of adult patients with advanced cancer. Further, among 7427 Muslims across 11 countries, negative religious coping was associated with suicide attempts (Eskin et al., 2020). Negative religious coping is also linked to risk factors for suicide, including increased depression and anxiety, decreased subjective well-being (Rosmarin et al., 2017), and posttraumatic stress (Arkin et al., 2024).

Research on negative religious coping has evolved over recent decades, leading to the exploration of additional potentially deleterious aspects of spirituality. For example, spiritual struggle is a more recent conceptual framework that encompasses negative aspects of religious experience, and occurs "when some aspect of religious belief, practice or experience becomes a focus of negative thoughts or emotions, concern or conflict" (Exline et al., 2014, p. 208). Although spiritual struggle reflects aspects of both ritualistic spirituality and existential spirituality, to a limited degree, it is predominantly characterized by contention in one's personal, unstructured relationship with deity, or theistic spirituality. Like negative religious coping, spiritual struggle has been linked to increased suicide risk. For example, in a longitudinal study of US veterans, Currier et al. (2018) found that spiritual struggles were associated with an increased risk for suicide. This finding was confirmed among combat veterans seeking treatment for PTSD (Raines et al., 2017), men in recovery from substance use disorders (Currier et al., 2020), and patients with psychosis (Rosmarin et al., 2014).

In sum, the extant literature indicates that theistic spirituality may have both a negative and positive association with suicidality. Theistic spirituality may manifest in adaptive methods of coping with adverse life events (e.g., positive religious coping) or in maladaptive coping behaviors (e.g., negative religious coping) or distress related to one's connection with deity (e.g., spiritual struggle). It is important to note that the literature related to theistic spirituality uses language and measurement that emphasizes one's relationship with God, a deity, or a higher power; however, there may also be aspects of spirituality that are independent of the theistic focus within theistic spirituality (Hodge, 2003). For example, the construct of spirituality has also been equated to non-theistic qualities of life such as meaning, purpose, and positive psychological virtues (e.g., Schuurmans-Stekhoven, 2011). These aspects of spiritual functioning epitomize the concept of existential spirituality.

Existential Spirituality and Suicidal Behavior

Existential spirituality describes a non-theistic pursuit of purpose and meaning in life (Webb et al., 2014) and has been similarly defined as "an individual's belief in ultimate truth and meaning in life" (Jang, 2016, p. 213). It can be argued that meaning and purpose are inherently transcendent qualities and, thus, are immanent in our conceptualization of spirituality. Existential spirituality can be broadly construed, posing a particular challenge for its conceptualization and measurement. As such, our review of the literature on existential spirituality and suicide risk is not intended to be comprehensive but, rather, is intended to highlight some of the literature that broadly examines factors consistent with the framework of existential spirituality.

To our knowledge, only one study has directly examined the relation between existential spirituality and suicide risk using the RiTE measure of spirituality (Hall et al., 2020). Hall and colleagues found that existential spirituality, as measured by the RiTE measure of spirituality (Webb et al., 2014), was inversely associated with suicide risk, and this linkage was serially mediated by self-forgiveness and psychache (i.e., psychological pain; Shneidman, 1993); that is, greater existential spirituality was related to greater self-forgiveness and, in turn, to less psychache and reduced suicide risk. Of note, Hall et al. (2020) examined the RiTE dimensions (i.e., ritualistic, theistic, and existential) in the context of one another and found that existential was thusly associated, but ritualistic and theistic were not. This study supports previous hypotheses (e.g., Schnitker & Emmons, 2017) and theory (Webb et al., 2015), which indicate that positive psychological variables (e.g., forgiveness, gratitude, and humility) play an important role in spiritual functioning. Further, positive psychological variables have been linked to increased well-being and reduced suicide risk. For example, forgiveness, in various forms (e.g., forgiveness of self, forgiveness of others, and forgiveness of God), has been linked to reduced suicide risk in multiple studies (e.g., Sansone et al., 2013; Kopacz et al., 2016; see also Webb, 2021). Relatedly, in a meta-analysis of 38 studies, Gao et al. (2022) found that forgiveness was consistently associated with fewer negative emotions and greater life satisfaction, positive emotionality, and subjective well-being. Similarly, gratitude and humility, among other positive psychological virtues (e.g., hope and compassion), are associated with reduced suicide risk and other adverse mental health outcomes (e.g., depression and anxiety; Kleiman et al., 2013; Krause et al., 2016; Valikhani et al., 2019).

Positive psychological characteristics, such as gratitude or forgiveness, appear to be important contributors to existential spirituality, as they are associated with meaning in life, the primary telos of existential spirituality. In a study of undergraduate students in Taiwan

(Lin, 2021), meaning in life fully mediated the relation between gratitude and suicidal ideation. Damreihani et al. (2018) conducted a 6-session, group-based positive psychological intervention (e.g., writing a letter of forgiveness; keeping a gratitude log) for mothers of children with cancer, which resulted in increased meaning in life, hope in life, and life satisfaction, factors that are linked to reduced suicide risk. For example, in a study of 375 Black young adults, meaning in life was significantly associated with reduced suicide risk (Goodwill & Hope, 2024) and, similarly, in a study of US military veterans, meaning in life buffered the association between moral injury and suicide risk (Corona et al., 2019). Finally, in a systematic review and meta-analysis of 11 studies by Li et al. (2024), meaning in life was consistently and significantly associated with reduced risk for suicide among adolescents and young adults.

Similar to meaningfulness and consistent with the tenets of existential spirituality, reasons for living (Linehan et al., 1983) are related constructs that reflect a sense of purpose in life. In a study of more than 600 Australian men by McLaren (2020), reasons for living, including family responsibilities, child-related concerns, confidence in coping with life, and moral objections to suicide, were inversely related to suicidal ideation. Similarly, in a study of Chinese adults, reasons for living, in addition to hope, significantly predicted less suicidal ideation (Luo et al., 2016). Of note, there is some evidence that reasons for living are associated with meaning in life, providing a potential explanation for the link between reasons for living and suicide. For example, in a sample of older adults, meaning in life significantly mediated the relation between reasons for living and suicide ideation (Heisel et al., 2016).

The literature reviewed here represents only a portion of the constructs that may warrant consideration for integration into the psychology of existential spirituality. Indeed, factors that relate to a "transcendent, yet non-theistic, search for meaning and purpose" (Webb, 2021, p. 61) are numerous and not fully explored. Moreover, many of these factors (e.g., positive psychological traits and meaning in life) are not traditionally conceptualized as elements of spiritual functioning. Nevertheless, as we have reviewed, there is mounting evidence that these constructs are closely related to spirituality (see also Chapter 7, this volume) and play an important role in the link between spirituality and health and well-being, including suicide risk.

Limitations in the Scientific Study of Spirituality and Suicide

Despite many decades of progress in the psychological study of religion and spirituality, and its application to the understanding and prevention of suicide, significant limitations exist. As previously noted, a primary challenge in the field is the lack of consensus regarding the definition and measurement of spirituality (Jastrzębski, 2022). An overarching goal of our review of the literature is to highlight the utility of the RiTE Model of Spirituality (Webb et al., 2014; Webb, 2021) as a conceptual framework through which the extant literature can be viewed and by which future research on spirituality and suicide can be informed. Moving toward a consensus definition of spirituality will allow for a more standardized interpretation of the scientific literature and reduce the prevalence of conflicting results in research.

A second limitation of the research on spirituality and suicide risk is methodological. There are two particular methodological issues facing the study of spirituality and suicide, including the use of cross-sectional, correlational designs and a lack of spiritual diversity in sampling methods (Abu-Raiya, 2017). A significant percentage of studies on spirituality and suicide risk are limited by their ability to draw causal conclusions due to the use of cross-sectional data. Use of experimental designs and longitudinal data will improve confidence in research conclusions and will better inform our understanding and prevention of suicide. Additionally, most studies evaluating spirituality and suicide risk rely primarily on Western cultures and the Christian religion. Although diverse religious worldviews are increasingly represented in the literature (Rosmarin et al., 2017; Thomas & Barbato, 2020), expanded inclusion of diverse religious and spiritual perspectives is critical for a comprehensive understanding of the relation between spirituality and suicide.

Finally, despite the growing body of research on spirituality and suicide risk, there continues to be a dearth of translational research efforts applied toward the prevention of suicide. That is, the primary contribution of the study of spirituality and suicide, thus far, is descriptive, offering explanations as to what aspects of spirituality are associated with risk for suicide. Yet, little work has applied this knowledge to the prevention of suicide. This is due, perhaps, to the notion that one's religious or spiritual orientation is deeply personal and outside of the scope of clinical intervention (Isaac et al., 2016). In the next section, we discuss potential future directions for the study of spirituality and suicide and highlight several efforts to integrate spirituality into preventative efforts for suicide.

Future Directions for the Study of Spirituality and Suicide

A noble objective for the psychology of spirituality is the development of methods to prevent and treat suicide, particularly given the increasing rates of suicide in recent decades (Martínez-Alés et al., 2022). Attempts to develop spiritually informed clinical interventions for suicide show promising results. For example, spiritual and religious group psychotherapy is a 10-session treatment that has shown efficacy in reducing suicidal ideation among patients with depression (Ebrahimi et al., 2014). Similarly, Ramos et al. (2018) found that religiously integrated cognitive-behavioral therapy was as effective at reducing suicidal ideation as conventional cognitive-behavioral therapy among adult patients with major depressive disorder and chronic medical illness. Regarding spiritually related risk factors for suicide (e.g., negative religious coping and spiritual struggle; Eskin et al., 2020), therapeutic interventions to address spiritually related distress may also be an avenue for ameliorating suicide risk. Several studies have demonstrated therapeutic interventions that reduce spiritual distress or spiritual struggle. For example, religious cognitive-behavioral therapy has been demonstrated to reduce spiritual distress among patients with depression (Pearce et al., 2016; Pearce & Koenig, 2016). Interventions for spiritual struggle, such as Winding Road, a 9-session treatment protocol, also show promise for the reduction of spiritual distress (Reist Gibbel et al., 2019).

Previous research also supports the use of positive psychological interventions for suicide risk. In a randomized controlled trial of hospitalized adults with suicidal ideation (N = 201), keeping a gratitude diary for one week was shown to reduce the severity of suicidal thoughts (Ducasse et al., 2019). Further, cognitively-based compassion training (CBCT), a 6-session group intervention, was shown to improve levels of compassion, and greater levels of improvement in compassion were predictive of less suicidal ideation in a randomized controlled trial of African-American suicide attempters (LoParo et al., 2018). In addition to the beneficial effects on suicide risk, positive psychological interventions (e.g., forgiveness therapy and kindness interventions) are shown to improve adverse mental health outcomes, including depression, anger, stress, and anxiety (Akhtar & Barlow, 2018; Kerr et al., 2015). Future research should continue to build on these efforts to develop effective interventions for suicide and other health-related outcomes.

Conclusion

In sum, spirituality is a complex component of human functioning that, despite a wealth of research, is limited by a lack of conceptual clarity and methodological issues that constrain our understanding of its implications for health and well-being. Likewise, suicide is a growing public health concern that warrants a multidimensional approach to understanding the risk and protective factors involved. The RiTE Model of Spirituality (Webb et al., 2014; Webb, 2021), composed of ritualistic, theistic, and existential dimensions of spirituality, is a valuable conceptual model of spiritual functioning that incorporates elements traditionally described as religious or spiritual (e.g., church attendance, prayer, meditation, and connection to deity) while also broadening the scope of spirituality to include such factors as meaning in life, reasons for living, and positive psychological virtues (i.e., existential spirituality). Given the evidence for a robust association between spirituality and risk for suicide, it is imperative that the psychology of spirituality continue to pursue a deeper understanding of the spiritual and religious factors that contribute to and protect against suicide.

References

Abu-Raiya, H. (2017). A critique from within: Some important research issues that psychologists of religion and spirituality should further work on. *Mental Health, Religion & Culture*, *20*(6), 544–551. https://doi.org/10.1080/13674676.2017.1377945

Akhtar, S., & Barlow, J. (2018). Forgiveness therapy for the promotion of mental well-being: A systematic review and meta-analysis. *Trauma, Violence, & Abuse*, *19*(1), 107–122. https://doi.org/10.1177/1524838016637079

Ali, A., & Maharajh, H. D. (2005). Social predictors of suicidal behaviour in adolescents in Trinidad and Tobago. *Social Psychiatry and Psychiatric Epidemiology: The International Journal for Research in Social and Genetic Epidemiology and Mental Health Services*, 40(3), 186–191. https://doi.org/10.1007/s00127-005-0846-9

Anderson, J. W., & Nunnelley, P. A. (2016). Private prayer associations with depression, anxiety and other health conditions: An analytical review of clinical studies. *Postgraduate Medicine*, 128(7), 635–641. https://doi.org/10.1080/00325481.2016.1209962

Ano, G. G., & Vasconcelles, E. B. (2005). Religious coping and psychological adjustment to stress: A meta-analysis. *Journal of Clinical Psychology*, 61(4), 461–480. https://doi.org/10.1002/jclp.20049

Arkin, M., Lowe, S. R., Poon, C. Y. S., & Rhodes, J. E. (2024). Associations between religious coping and long-term mental health in survivors of Hurricane Katrina. *Psychology of Religion and Spirituality*, *16*(1), 63–71. https://doi.org/10.1037/rel0000483

Boelens, P. A., Reeves, R. R., Replogle, W. H., & Koenig, H. G. (2012). The effect of prayer on depression and anxiety: maintenance of positive influence one year after prayer intervention. *International Journal of Psychiatry in Medicine*, 43(1), 85–98. https://doi.org/10.2190/PM.43.1.f

Büssing, A., Frick, E., Jacobs, C., & Baumann, K. (2016). Health and life satisfaction of Roman Catholic pastoral workers: Private prayer has a greater impact than public prayer. *Pastoral Psychology*, *65*(1), 89–102. https://doi.org/10.1007/s11089-015-0672-2

Connors, G. J., Tonigan, J. S., & Miller, W. R. (1996). A measure of religious background and behavior for use in behavior change research. *Psychology of Addictive Behaviors*, *10*(2), 90–96. https://doi.org/10.1037/0893-164X.10.2.90

Corona, C. D., Van Orden, K. A., Wisco, B. E., & Pietrzak, R. H. (2019). Meaning in life moderates the association between morally injurious experiences and suicide ideation among US combat veterans: Results from the national health and resilience in veterans study. *Psychological Trauma: Theory, Research, Practice, and Policy*, *11*(6), 614–620. https://doi.org/10.1037/tra0000475

Currier, J. M., Fadoir, N., Carroll, T. D., Kuhlman, S., Marie, L., Taylor, S. E., Smith, T., Isaak, S. L., & Sims, B. M. (2020). A cross-sectional investigation of divine struggles and suicide risk among men in early recovery from substance use disorders. *Psychology of Religion and Spirituality*, 12(3), 324–333. https://doi.org/10.1037/rel0000286

Currier, J. M., McDermott, R. C., McCormick, W. H., Churchwell, M. C., & Milkeris, L. (2018). Exploring cross-lagged associations between spiritual struggles and risk for suicidal behavior in a community sample of military veterans. *Journal of Affective Disorders*, 230, 93–100. https://doi.org/10.1016/j.jad.2018.01.009

Damreihani, N., Behzadipour, S., Haghpanh, S., & Bordbar, M. (2018). The effectiveness of positive psychology intervention on the well-being, meaning, and life satisfaction of mothers of children with cancer: A brief report. *Journal of Psychosocial Oncology*, *36*(3), 382–388. https://doi.org/10.1080/07347332.2018.1427173

Datta, R. P., & Nakhaie, R. (2022). Suicidal ideation and social integration in three Canadian provinces: The importance of social support and community belonging. *Canadian Review of Sociology*, 59(Suppl 1), 74–97. https://doi.org/10.1111/cars.12396

Davis, E. B., Granqvist, P., & Sharp, C. (2021). Theistic relational spirituality: Development, dynamics, health, and transformation. *Psychology of Religion and Spirituality*, *13*(4), 401–415. https://doi.org/10.1037/rel0000219

De Berardis, D., Olivieri, L., Rapini, G., Serroni, N., Fornaro, M., Valchera, A., ... & Di Giannantonio, M. (2020). Religious coping, hopelessness, and suicide ideation in subjects with first-episode major depression: An exploratory study in the real world clinical practice. *Brain Sciences*, 10(12), 912. https://doi.org/10.3390/brainsci10120912

Ducasse, D., Dassa, D., Courtet, P., Brand, A. V., Walter, A., Guillaume, S., Jaussent, I., & Olié, E. (2019). Gratitude diary for the management of suicidal inpatients: A randomized controlled trial. *Depression and Anxiety*, *36*(5), 400–411. https://doi.org/10.1002/da.22877

Ebrahimi, H., Kazemi, A. H., Fallahi Khoshknab, M., & Modabber, R. (2014). The effect of spiritual and religious group psychotherapy on suicidal ideation in depressed patients: A randomized clinical trial. *Journal of caring sciences*, *3*(2), 131–140. https://doi.org/10.5681/jcs.2014.014

Eskin, M., Baydar, N., El-Nayal, M., Asad, N., Noor, I. M., Rezaeian, M., Abdel-Khalek, A. M., Al Buhairan, F., Harlak, H., Hamdan, M., Mechri, A., Isayeva, U., Khader, Y., Khan, A., Al Sayyari, A., Khader, A., Behzadi, B., Öztürk, C. Ş., Agha, H., ... Khan, M. M. (2020). Associations of religiosity, attitudes towards suicide and religious coping with suicidal ideation and suicide attempts in 11 Muslim countries. *Social Science & Medicine*, *265*. https://doi.org/10.1016/j.socscimed.2020.113390

Exline, J. J., Pargament, K. I., Grubbs, J. B., & Yali, A. M. (2014). The Religious and Spiritual Struggles Scale: Development and initial validation. *Psychology of Religion and Spirituality*, 6(3), 208–222. https://doi.org/10.1037/a0036465.supp

Exline, J. J., Yali, A. M., & Sanderson, W. C. (2000). Guilt, discord, and alienation: The role of religious strain in depression and suicidality. *Journal of Clinical Psychology*, *56*(12), 1481–1496. https://doi.org/10.1002/1097-4679(200012)56:12<1481::AID-1>3.0.CO;2-A

Gao, F., Li, Y., & Bai, X. (2022). Forgiveness and subjective well-being: A meta-analysis review. *Personality and Individual Differences*, *186*(Part B). https://doi.org/10.1016/j.paid.2021.111350

Gerber, M. M., Boals, A., & Schuettler, D. (2011). The unique contributions of positive and negative religious coping to posttraumatic growth and PTSD. *Psychology of Religion and Spirituality*, 3(4), 298. https://doi.org/10.1037/a0023016

Goodwill, J. R., & Hope, M. O. (2024). Religion and suicide in black emerging adults: Examining pathways through hope and meaning in life. *Journal of Youth and Adolescence*. https://doi.org/10.1007/s10964-023-01930-3

Hall, B. B., Webb, J. R., & Hirsch, J. K. (2020). Spirituality and suicidal behavior: The mediating role of self-forgiveness and psychache. *Psychology of Religion and Spirituality*, *12*(1), 36. https://doi.org/10.1037/rel0000182

Hamdan, S., & Peterseil-Yaul, T. (2020). Exploring the psychiatric and social risk factors contributing to suicidal behaviors in religious young adults. *Psychiatry Research*, 287. https://doi.org/10.1016/j.psychres.2019.06.024

Hastings, O. P. (2016). Not a lonely crowd? Social connectedness, religious service attendance, and the spiritual but not religious. *Social Science Research*, *57*, 63–79. https://doi.org/10.1016/j.ssresearch.2016.01.006

Heisel, M. J., Neufeld, E., & Flett, G. L. (2016). Reasons for living, meaning in life, and suicide ideation: Investigating the roles of key positive psychological factors in reducing suicide risk in community-residing older adults. *Aging & Mental Health*, *20*(2), 195–207. https://doi.org/10.1080/13607863.2015.1078279

Hermann, A. D., Simpson, A. J., Lehtman, M. J., & Fuller, R. C. (2015). Does guilt motivate prayer? *Journal for the Scientific Study of Religion*, *54*(3), 540–554. https://doi.org/10.1111/jssr.12208

Hirsch, J. K., Chang, E. C., & Rabon, J. K. (Eds.). (2018). *A positive psychological approach to suicide: theory research, and prevention*. Springer.

Hodge, D. R. (2003). The intrinsic spirituality scale: A new six-item instrument for assessing the salience of spirituality as a motivational construct. *Journal of Social Service Research*, *30*(1), 41–61. https://doi.org/10.1300/J079v30n01_03

Hovey, J. D., Hurtado, G., Morales, L. R. A., & Seligman, L. D. (2014). Religion-based emotional social support mediates the relationship between intrinsic religiosity and mental health. *Archives of Suicide Research*, 18(4), 376–391. https://doi.org/10.1080/13811118.2013.833149

Isaac, K. S., Hay, J. L., & Lubetkin, E. I. (2016). Incorporating spirituality in primary care. *Journal of Religion and Health*, *55*(3), 1065–1077. https://doi.org/10.1007/s10943-016-0190-2

Jang, S. J. (2016). Existential spirituality, religiosity, and symptoms of anxiety-related disorders: A study of belief in ultimate truth and meaning in life. *Journal of Psychology and Theology*, *44*(3), 213–229. https://doi.org/10.1177/009164711604400304

Jastrzębski, A. K. (2022). The challenging task of defining spirituality. *Journal of Spirituality in Mental Health*, *24*(2), 113–131. https://doi.org/10.1080/19349637.2020.1858734

Jongkind, M., Van Den Brink, B., Schaap, J. H., Van Den Velde, N., & Braam, A. W. (2019). Dimensions of religion associated with suicide attempt and suicide ideation in depressed, religiously affiliated patients. *Suicide and Life-Threatening Behavior*, *49*(2), 505–519. https://doi.org/10.1111/sltb.12456

Kay, W. K., & Francis, L. J. (2006). Suicidal ideation among young people in the UK: Churchgoing as an inhibitory influence? *Mental Health, Religion & Culture*, 9(2), 127–140. https://doi.org/10.1080/13694670500071745

Kerr, S. L., O'Donovan, A., & Pepping, C. A. (2015). Can gratitude and kindness interventions enhance well-being in a clinical sample?. *Journal of Happiness Studies*, *16*, 17–36. https://doi.org/10.1007/s10902-013-9492-1

Kim, Y. J., Crutchfield, J., & Kim, Y. K. (2021). Effects of church attendance vs private religious activities on suicidal ideation: A study of rural US college students. *Journal of Religion and Health*, 60(4), 2560–2572. https://doi.org/10.1007/s10943-021-01224-7

Kleiman, E. M., Adams, L. M., Kashdan, T. B., & Riskind, J. H. (2013). Grateful individuals are not suicidal: Buffering risks associated with hopelessness and depressive symptoms. *Personality and Individual Differences*, 55, 595–599. https://doi.org/10.1016/j.paid.2013.05.002

Koenig, H. G., VanderWeele, T. J., & Peteet, J. R. (2024). *Handbook of religion and health* (3rd ed.). Oxford University Press.

Kopacz, M. S., Crean, H. F., Park, C. L., & Hoff, R. A. (2018). Religious coping and suicide risk in a sample of recently returned veterans. *Archives of Suicide Research*, 22(4), 615–627. https://doi.org/10.1080/13811118.2017.1390513

Kopacz, M. S., Currier, J. M., Drescher, K. D., & Pigeon, W. R. (2016). Suicidal behavior and spiritual functioning in a sample of Veterans diagnosed with PTSD. *Journal of Injury & Violence Research*, 8(1), 6–14.

Krause, N., Pargament, K. I., Hill, P. C., & Ironson, G. (2016). Humility, stressful life events, and psychological well-being: Findings from the Landmark Spirituality and Health Survey. *The Journal of Positive Psychology*, 11(5), 499–510. https://doi.org/10.1080/17439760.2015.1127991

Li, S., Luo, H., Huang, F., Wang, Y., & Siu Fai Yip, P. (2024). Associations between meaning in life and suicidal ideation in young people: A systematic review and meta-analysis. *Children & Youth Services Review*, *158*. https://doi.org/10.1016/j.childyouth.2024.107477

Lin, C.-C. (2021). Gratitude and suicidal ideation in undergraduates in Taiwan: The mediating role of self-esteem and meaning in life. *Omega: Journal of Death and Dying*, 84(1), 177–193. https://doi.org/10.1177/0030222819882845

Linehan, M. M., Goodstein, J. L., Nielsen, S. L., & Chiles, J. A. (1983). Reasons for staying alive when you are thinking of killing yourself: The reasons for living inventory. *Journal of Consulting and Clinical Psychology*, 51(2), 276–286. https://doi.org/10.1037/0022-006X.51.2.276

Liu, R. T., & Miller, I. (2014). Life events and suicidal ideation and behavior: A systematic review. *Clinical Psychology Review*, *34*(3), 181–192. https://doi.org/10.1016/j.cpr.2014.01.006

LoParo, D., Mack, S. A., Patterson, B., Negi, L. T., & Kaslow, N. J. (2018). The efficacy of cognitively-based compassion training for African American suicide attempters. *Mindfulness*, *9*(6), 1941–1954. https://doi.org/10.1007/s12671-018-0940-1

Luo, X., Wang, Q., Wang, X., & Cai, T. (2016). Reasons for living and hope as the protective factors against suicidality in Chinese patients with depression: A cross sectional study. *BMC Psychiatry*, *16*. https://doi.org/10.1186/s12888-016-0960-0

Mahamid, F. A., & Bdier, D. (2021). The association between positive religious coping, perceived stress, and depressive symptoms during the spread of coronavirus (COVID-19) among a sample of adults in Palestine: Across sectional study. *Journal of religion and health*, 60, 34–49. https://doi.org/10.1007/s10943-020-01121-5

Martínez-Alés, G., Jiang, T., Keyes, K. M., & Gradus, J. L. (2022). The recent rise of suicide mortality in the United States. *Annual Review of Public Health*, *43*, 99–116. https://doi.org/10.1146/annurev-publhealth-051920-123206

Masters, K. S., & Hooker, S. A. (2013). Religiousness/spirituality, cardiovascular disease, and cancer: Cultural integration for health research and intervention. *Journal of Consulting and Clinical Psychology*, *81*(2), 206–216. https://doi.org/10.1037/a0030813

McLaren, S. (2020). Rurality, reasons for living, and suicidal ideation among Australian men. *Death Studies*. https://doi.org/10.1080/07481187.2020.1863520

Monod, S., Brennan, M., Rochat, E., Martin, E., Rochat, S., & Büla, C. J. (2011). Instruments measuring spirituality in clinical research: a systematic review. *Journal of General Internal Medicine*, *26*(11), 1345–1357. https://doi.org/10.1007/s11606-011-1769-7

Mullins, N., Kang, J., Campos, A. I., Coleman, J. R. I., Edwards, A. C., Galfalvy, H., Levey, D. F., Lori, A., Shabalin, A., Starnawska, A., Su, M.-H., Watson, H. J., Adams, M., Awasthi, S., Gandal, M., Hafferty, J. D., Hishimoto, A., Kim, M., Okazaki, S., … et al. (2022). Dissecting the shared genetic architecture of suicide attempt, psychiatric disorders, and known risk factors. *Biological Psychiatry*, *91*(3), 313–327. https://doi.org/10.1016/j.biopsych.2021.05.029

Pargament, K. I., Feuille, M., & Burdzy, D. (2011). The brief RCOPE: Current psychometric status of a short measure of religious coping. *Religions*, *2*(1), 51–76. https://doi.org/10.3390/rel2010051

Pargament, K. I., Koenig, H. G., & Perez, L. M. (2000). The many methods of religious coping: Development and initial validation of the RCOPE. *Journal of Clinical Psychology*, 56(4), 519–543. https://doi.org/10.1002/(SICI)1097-4679(200004)56:4<519::AID-JCLP6>3.0.CO;2-1

Pearce, M. J., & Koenig, H. G. (2016). Spiritual struggles and religious cognitive behavioral therapy: a randomized clinical trial in those with depression and chronic medical illness. *Journal of Psychology and Theology*, *44*(1), 3–15. https://doi.org/10.1177/009164711604400101

Pearce, M. J., Koenig, H. G., Robins, C. J., Daher, N., Shaw, S. F., Nelson, B., … & King, M. B. (2016). Effects of religious versus conventional cognitive-behavioral therapy on gratitude in major depression and chronic medical illness: A randomized clinical trial. *Journal of Spirituality in Mental Health*, *18*(2), 124–144. https://doi.org/10.1080/19349637.2015.1100971

Price, S. D., & Callahan, J. L. (2017). Religious attendance serves as a protective variable against suicidal ideation during treatment. *Pastoral Psychology*, 66(1), 103–115. https://doi.org/10.1007/s11089-016-0725-1

Raines, A. M., Currier, J., McManus, E. S., Walton, J. L., Uddo, M., & Franklin, C. L. (2017). Spiritual struggles and suicide in veterans seeking PTSD treatment. *Psychological Trauma: Theory, Research, Practice and Policy*, 9(6), 746–749. https://doi.org/10.1037/tra0000239

Ramos, K., Erkanli, A., & Koenig, H. G. (2018). Effects of religious versus conventional cognitive–behavioral therapy (CBT) on suicidal thoughts in major depression and chronic medical illness. *Psychology of Religion and Spirituality*, 10(1), 79–87. https://doi.org/10.1037/rel0000113

Reist Gibbel, M., Regueiro, V., & Pargament, K. I. (2019). A spiritually integrated intervention for spiritual struggles among adults with mental illness: Results of an initial evaluation. *Spirituality in Clinical Practice*, *6*(4), 240–255. https://doi.org/10.1037/scp0000207

Robins, A., & Fiske, A. (2009). Explaining the relation between religiousness and reduced suicidal behavior: social support rather than specific beliefs. *Suicide & Life-Threatening Behavior*, 39(4), 386–395. https://doi.org/10.1521/suli.2009.39.4.386

Roff, L. L., Klemmack, D. L., Parker, M., Koenig, H. G., Sawyer-Baker, P., & Allman, R. M. (2005). Religiosity, smoking, exercise, and obesity among southern, community-dwelling older adults. *Journal of Applied Gerontology*, *24*(4), 337–354. https://doi.org/10.1177/0733464805278132

Rosmarin, D. H., & Koenig, H. G. (Eds.). (2020). *Handbook of spirituality, religion, and mental health* (Second ed.). Academic Press.

Rosmarin, D. H., Malloy, M. C., & Forester, B. P. (2014). Spiritual struggle and affective symptoms among geriatric mood disordered patients. *International Journal of Geriatric Psychiatry*, 29(6), 653–660. https://doi.org/10.1002/gps.4052

Rosmarin, D. H., Pirutinsky, S., Carp, S., Appel, M., & Kor, A. (2017). Religious coping across a spectrum of religious involvement among Jews. *Psychology of Religion and Spirituality*, 9(Suppl 1), S96–S104. https://doi.org/10.1037/rel0000114

Rushing, N. C., Corsentino, E., Hames, J. L., Sachs-Ericsson, N., & Steffens, D. C. (2013). The relationship of religious involvement indicators and social support to current and past suicidality among depressed older adults. *Aging & Mental Health*, 17(3), 366–374. https://doi.org/10.1080/13607863.2012.738414

Ryan, R. M., Rigby, S., & King, K. (1993). Two types of religious internalization and their relations to religious orientations and mental health. *Journal of Personality and Social Psychology*, *65*(3), 586–596. https://doi.org/10.1037//0022-3514.65.3.586

Sansone, R. A., Kelley, A. R., & Forbis, J. S. (2013). The relationship between forgiveness and history of suicide attempt. *Mental Health, Religion & Culture*, 16(1), 31–37. https://doi.org/10.1080/13674676.2011.643860

Schnitker, S. A., & Emmons, R. A. (2017). The psychology of virtue: Integrating positive psychology and the psychology of religion. *Psychology of Religion and Spirituality*, 9(3), 239–241. https://doi.org/10.1037/rel0000133

Schuurmans-Stekhoven, J. B. (2011). Is it God or just the data that moves in mysterious ways? How well-being research may be mistaking faith for virtue. *Social Indicators Research*, *100*(2), 313–330. https://doi.org/10.1007/s11205-010-9630-7

Shneidman, E. (1993). *Suicide as psychache: A clinical approach to self-destructive behavior*. Lanham, MD: Rowman & Littlefield Publishers, Inc.

Sinnott, S. M., Park, C. L., George, J. R., Gnall, K. E., & David, A. B. (2023). Use of religious and spiritual responses after trauma to prevent posttraumatic stress symptoms and suicidality: The role of meaning in life. *Clinical psychology & psychotherapy*, Advance online publication. https://doi.org/10.1002/cpp.2902

Smigelsky, M. A., Jardin, C., Nieuwsma, J. A., Brancu, M., Meador, K. G., Molloy, K. G., & Elbogen, E. B. (2020). Religion, spirituality, and suicide risk in Iraq and Afghanistan era veterans. *Depression and Anxiety*, 37(8), 728–737. https://doi.org/10.1002/da.23013

Suresh, M. E., McElroy-Heltzel, S. E., & Shannonhouse, L. R. (2020). Predicting suicide risk in older homebound adults during COVID-19: The role of religious coping. *Journal of Psychology and Christianity*, *39*(4), 301–312.

Teismann, T., Willutzki, U., Michalak, J., Siegmann, P., Nyhuis, P., Wolter, M., & Forkmann, T. (2017). Religious beliefs buffer the impact of depression on suicide ideation. *Psychiatry Research*, 257, 276–278. https://doi.org/10.1016/j.psychres.2017.07.060

Thomas, J., & Barbato, M. (2020). Positive religious coping and mental health among Christians and Muslims in response to the COVID-19 pandemic. *Religions*, *11*(10), 498. https://doi.org/10.3390/rel11100498

Toussaint, L., Wilson, C. M., Wilson, L. C., & Williams, D. R. (2015). Religiousness and suicide in a nationally representative sample of Trinidad and Tobago adolescents and young adults. *Social Psychiatry and Psychiatric Epidemiology: The International Journal for Research in Social and Genetic Epidemiology and Mental Health Services*, *50*(9), 1441–1450. https://doi.org/10.1007/s00127-015-1045-y

Trevino, K. M., Balboni, M., Zollfrank, A., Balboni, T., & Prigerson, H. G. (2014). Negative religious coping as a correlate of suicidal ideation in patients with advanced cancer. *Psycho- Oncology*, 23(8), 936–945. https://doi.org/10.1002/pon.3505

Underwood, L. G., & Teresi, J. A. (2002). The Daily Spiritual Experience Scale: Development, theoretical description, reliability, exploratory factor analysis, and preliminary construct validity using health-related data. *Annals of Behavioral Medicine*, *24*(1), 22–33. https://doi.org/10.1207/S15324796ABM2401_04

Upenieks, L. (2022). Religious/spiritual struggles and well-being during the COVID-19 pandemic: Does "talking religion" help or hurt?. *Review of Religious Research*, 64(2), 249–278. https://doi.org/10.1007/s13644-022-00487-0

Valikhani, A., Ahmadnia, F., Karimi, A., & Mills, P. J. (2019). The relationship between dispositional gratitude and quality of life: The mediating role of perceived stress and mental health. *Personality and Individual Differences*, 141, 40–46. https://doi.org/10.1016/j.paid.2018.12.014

VanderWeele, T. J., Li, S., Tsai, A. C., & Kawachi, I. (2016). Association between religious service attendance and lower suicide rates among US women. *JAMA psychiatry*, 73(8), 845–851. https://doi.org/10.1001/jamapsychiatry.2016.1243

Webb, J. R. (2021). *Understanding forgiveness and addiction: Theory, research, and clinical application*. Routledge.

Webb, J. R., Hirsch, J. K., & Toussaint, L. (2015). Forgiveness as a positive psychotherapy for addiction and suicide: Theory, research, and practice. *Spirituality in Clinical Practice*, 2(1), 48–60. https://doi.org/10.1037/scp0000054

Webb, J. R., Toussaint, L., & Dula, C. S. (2014). Ritualistic, theistic, and existential spirituality: Initial psychometric qualities of the RiTE measure of spirituality. *Journal of Religion and Health*, 53(4), 972–985. https://doi.org/10.1007/s10943-013-9697-y

World Health Organization. (2021). Suicide worldwide in 2019: global health estimates. https://www.who.int/publications/i/item/9789240026643

Xu, Y. E., Barron, D. A., Sudol, K., Zisook, S., & Oquendo, M. A. (2023). Suicidal behavior across a broad range of psychiatric disorders. *Molecular Psychiatry*, *28*(7), 2764–2810. https://doi.org/10.1038/s41380-022-01935-7

Zinnbauer, B. J., & Pargament, K. I. (2005). Religiousness and spirituality. In R. F. Paloutzian, & C. L. Park (Eds.), *Handbook of the psychology of religion and spirituality*, *54*, 1–6. New York, NY: Guilford.

Chapter 18

Spirituality and Addictive Behavior

*Trever Dangel**

Religious and spiritual experiences, beliefs, and practices are often vital elements of the recovery process for individuals struggling with addiction (Subhani et al., 2022). Yet, efforts to gain an empirical understanding of the relationship between spirituality and addictive behavior have only begun in earnest over the past few decades. The goal of this chapter is to provide an overview of the key theoretical developments and empirical findings concerning spirituality's associations with addictive behavior. While attempts to define what behaviors can be considered "addictive" are ongoing (e.g., Sussman, 2017), this chapter will primarily focus on addictive behavior in the context of substance use (e.g., alcohol, opioids, and marijuana). Other types of addictive behavior that have gained more intensive empirical attention in recent years, including gambling, sex, and internet use, will also be discussed.

Defining Spirituality

Scholars have attempted to define religion and spirituality from a psychological perspective throughout the field's history (see Pargament et al., 2013, for a more in-depth discussion of the history of these definitions). Although spirituality and religion are commonly viewed as opposing or otherwise mutually exclusive constructs (see Chapter 3, this volume), extant literature has demonstrated a gradual integration of the two over the last few decades (Hill et al., 2000). For example, Pargament et al. (2013) define spirituality as "the search for the sacred" (p. 14). In their discussion of the RiTE model of spirituality, Webb et al. (2014) similarly define spirituality as "The salient, searching pursuit of the transcendently sacred ritualistic, theistic, and/or existential aspects of the human condition" (p. 974; see also Chapters 1 and 44, this volume). Both definitions include religion as an important (and for some individuals, necessary) mechanism for spiritual experiences or practices while acknowledging that religion may also serve additional nonspiritual functions. That is, while the primary function of religion is to facilitate spirituality, religion may serve other nonspiritual goals that may be fulfilled through membership in a traditional faith community (e.g., social support).

In the pursuit of arriving at a consensus-oriented yet inclusive definition of spirituality, this chapter defines spirituality as follows: *the cognitive, affective, social, or behavioral processes by which individuals experience personal connection to, or understanding of, the sacred.* This definition builds upon the search-centered conceptualizations of spirituality described above by honoring the dynamic and evolving nature of spirituality over the life course, while also explicitly grounding the definition of spirituality in its primary functions: connection with, experience of, and understanding of the sacred. These experiences of connection and understanding, in turn, support the individual's well-being and motivation in their lifelong search

* Corresponding Author: tdangelphd@gmail.com.

DOI: 10.4324/9781003440048-21

for the sacred (Pargament, 2013). Simply put, this definition honors spirituality as a search for the sacred while also delineating the purpose and mechanisms of said search. Each definition referenced above may have its own unique utility depending on the context in which it is used, but all of them consider the individual's connection to the sacred to be the core defining element of spirituality.

Addictive Behavior

Much like spirituality, arriving at a consensus definition of addictive behavior is an ongoing endeavor within the field of addiction research. Scholars have, however, generally agreed upon several key features that may distinguish when a given behavior has crossed the threshold of addiction. These include 1) an inability to stop engaging in the target behavior, 2) long-term harm resulting from the behavior, 3) short-term achievement of a desired emotional state such as pleasure or relief, and 4) intense preoccupation with the target behavior (see Maté & Maté, 2022, Chapter 16; Sussman & Sussman, 2011). By extension, this implies that virtually *any* behavior can be potentially addictive if the individual's relationship to it involves the above characteristics. Indeed, this broadened idea of addiction has resulted in a rapid acceleration of research into various behaviors that had previously gone unexamined as candidates for addiction – often referred to as "process addictions" or "behavioral addictions" – such as work, sex, internet use, and shopping (e.g., Sussman, 2017).

Regardless of its ultimate definition, available epidemiological data consistently demonstrate the significant global public health consequences of addiction. While a full review of epidemiological data for the numerous potentially addictive substances and behaviors is beyond the scope of this chapter (see Webb, 2021, Chapter 1), some exemplary data readily demonstrate the magnitude of the problem. In the United States, recent estimates placed the total economic burden of opioid-related deaths and disorders at over $1 trillion in 2017 alone when considering costs related to healthcare, criminal justice, lost productivity, and mortality (Florence et al., 2021). Recent data from the United States also estimated that average annual death rates from drug overdoses have increased from 6.1 per 100,000 in 1999 to 20.7 per 100,000 in 2018, a more than three-fold increase in less than 20 years (Hedegaard et al., 2020).

Although there appears to be a recent downtrend in global alcohol consumption (World Health Organization [WHO], 2023), its societal effects continue to be significant. For example, alcohol use contributed to three million deaths and over 132 million disability-adjusted life years lost (DALYs) in 2016 (WHO, 2018). Considering the significant societal consequences of opioid and alcohol use alone (only two of many addictive substances), the few examples mentioned above highlight the arguably urgent need to address the problem of addictive behavior using all available resources, including spirituality.

Spirituality and Addictive Behavior

Although addiction is not exclusively addressed through spiritual means, nearly every mainstream spiritual belief system in existence today attempts to address the problem of addictive or otherwise compulsive behaviors to some degree. Some religious/spiritual texts prescribe explicit behavioral rules or rituals concerning the use or non-use of various substances (e.g., alcohol use and Islam [Michalak & Karen, 2006]). More broadly, numerous spiritual practices and teachings in both mono- and polytheistic traditions are designed to assist individuals in changing undesired patterns of thinking and/or behavior (e.g., the use of mindfulness practices in Buddhism [Harvey, 2013]). Several spiritual constructs, such as gratitude, forgiveness, and mindfulness (see below), are also believed to serve as key mechanisms of the spirituality–addiction association; several of these constructs do not necessarily require religious or deistic beliefs, broadening their utility to those who identify as spiritual but do not endorse belief in a deity. Multiple theoretical models have been developed that directly or indirectly describe the various ways in which spirituality may influence the development and extinction of addictive behavior. These models are summarized below, followed by a more in-depth discussion of the empirical findings that support the models and the linkages between spirituality and addiction more generally.

Theoretical Associations

Explanatory models of spirituality and addiction have invoked a variety of psychological mechanisms to explain how spirituality may aid or hinder individuals in the recovery process. One of the earliest models, developed by Neff and MacMaster (2005), attempts to describe the various behavioral, social, and spiritual processes that facilitate behavior change during faith-based substance misuse treatment. The model posits that effective faith-based interventions facilitate progression through a spiritual transformation process that leads to a more positive relationship to one's higher power, increased forgiveness of oneself and others, improved self-acceptance, meaning in life, social connectedness, and positive coping strategies. Proposed mechanisms included (but were not limited to) treatment program elements such as an accepting and empathic environment, development of more positive spiritual appraisals, spiritual coping, and social learning principles.

Additional models have emphasized a particular aspect of spirituality and the ways in which it may influence specific forms of addictive behavior or addiction outcomes more broadly. For example, a theoretical model of the forgiveness–addiction association has begun to accumulate empirical support (see Webb, 2021, Chapter 5). This model posits a variety of social (e.g., social support), psychological (e.g., existentially driven distress), and behavioral (e.g., health behaviors) mediators linking forgiveness and addiction- and suicide-related outcomes, in addition to several moderator variables such as shame. Similarly, Lyons et al. (2010) proposed the Spiritual/Forgiveness/Purpose (SFP) model of recovery. The model posits that spirituality facilitates the recovery process through increases in forgiveness and purpose in life, both of which are associated with decreased feelings of resentment. The authors noted that these mechanisms are theorized to be only partial mediators, as many other factors are likely to contribute to the spirituality–addiction association. In the context of problematic pornography use, Grubbs et al. (2019) have proposed a "moral incongruence" model to explain the relationship between religiousness and self-perceptions of problematic pornography use. The model suggests that religiously based moral disapproval of pornography may result in a sense of moral incongruence that subsequently leads to feelings of psychological distress regarding pornography use.

Broader models of the relationship between spirituality and health also suggest numerous other potential mechanisms germane to the context of addiction. For example, Cheadle and Dunkel Schetter (2017) propose a model wherein both spirituality and religiousness influence physical and mental health outcomes through a variety of social, behavioral, psychological, and biological mechanisms. A large number of these mechanisms have been identified as having salutary or deleterious associations with addiction-related outcomes (see below). The following sections provide a thematically organized and integrated summary of these findings.

Empirical Associations

The literature reviewed below attempts to answer the following questions: 1) Does spirituality demonstrate causal or longitudinal associations with addiction? 2) What mechanisms might explain spirituality's relationship to addiction-related outcomes? The search process utilized combinations of the following primary search terms within the PsycINFO and PubMed databases: "spiritu*," "religio*," "review," "meta*," "addict*," "recover*," "substance use," "alcohol*," and "drug*." Terms for specific spirituality-related constructs (e.g., forgiveness, gratitude, and hope) were also included in the search to produce more targeted results for each construct. Previously published literature reviews, meta-analyses, and book chapters were also examined for additional citations not previously identified in the search. In addition to studies concerning longitudinal associations, the following broad themes were also identified as areas of empirical support for the spirituality–addiction association: positive psychological constructs, existential well-being, social factors, spiritual coping practices, and behavioral mechanisms.

Longitudinal and Effectiveness Studies

Before discussing the intervening variables linking spirituality and addiction, it is important to first address the broader empirical question of whether a causal link between the two exists *at all*. Available literature suggests that the short answer to this question is yes.

First, a variety of well-controlled studies have identified that longitudinal increases in spirituality are associated with improved substance use treatment-related outcomes after controlling for other important variables. This finding has been observed primarily within the context of Alcoholics Anonymous (Alcoholics Anonymous [AA], 2001). For example, Kelly et al. (2011) found that in a large inpatient aftercare sample, increases in spirituality/religiousness partially mediated the association between AA attendance and drinking outcomes over a 15-month period. Specifically, increased spirituality/religiousness accounted for 23% and 20% of AA's indirect effects on percentage of days abstinent and drinks per drinking day, respectively. Krentzman et al. (2013) replicated this finding in a more diverse sample with additional spirituality measures and found that AA involvement predicted increases in private religious practices, which then predicted increases in percentage of days abstinent and fewer drinks per drinking day. Two other seminal studies by Robinson et al. (2007, 2011) using outpatient and community samples point to spirituality's beneficial effects independent of AA involvement. In both studies, multiple spirituality-related variables demonstrated salutary changes at six months relative to baseline levels, including daily spiritual experiences, purpose in life, self-forgiveness, and negative religious coping. These changes, in turn, predicted improvements in drinking outcomes at nine months relative to baseline, even after controlling for AA participation.

Second, literature utilizing randomized clinical trial designs suggests that spiritually informed treatments may provide iterative benefits beyond those of more secular treatments. Kelly et al. (2020) conducted an extensive review of literature pertaining to the effectiveness of both AA (a spiritual, mutual-help program [AA, 2001]) and Twelve-Step Facilitation Therapy [TSF; see Nowinski, 2012] relative to other treatments such as Cognitive-Behavioral Therapy. Their review incorporated findings from 27 studies (21 of which were randomized controlled trials) involving a mixture of manualized and non-manualized treatments with over 10,000 participants. In summarizing their findings, they noted, "There is high quality evidence that manualized AA/TSF interventions are more effective than other established treatments, such as CBT, for increasing abstinence." (p. 2) They also reported that these treatments appear to be "at least as effective as other treatments for other alcohol-related outcomes." (p. 2). A meta-analysis by Hai et al. (2019) found similar results for the efficacy of spirituality-informed interventions relative to nonspiritual interventions for general substance use outcomes. A total of 16 randomized controlled trials comparing the two types of interventions were analyzed, with spirituality-informed interventions demonstrating relatively larger effect sizes.

Finally, previously published literature reviews have consistently identified both positive and negative empirical associations between spirituality and/or religiousness and addiction-related outcomes. These findings span a variety of addictive behaviors, including substance use (Connery & Devido, 2020), internet use (Dossi et al., 2022), and sex and pornography use (Grubbs & Hook, 2016; Jennings et al., 2021). Although numerous limitations and caveats to the above literature are warranted and discussed below, there appears to be ample evidence to say that spirituality and religiousness can play a significant and direct role in the recovery process.

Positive Psychological Constructs

In the late 2000s and early 2010s, scholars began to explore the parallels between spirituality and positive psychology in the context of addiction (e.g., Krentzman, 2013). While a number of positive psychological constructs facilitated by spirituality may be conceptually relevant to addiction, this section will focus on forgiveness, gratitude, and mindfulness. Each of these constructs has received significant empirical attention in both the spirituality and positive psychology literature and has been implicated as a potential mechanism of the spirituality–addiction association.

Forgiveness in its various manifestations (e.g., state, trait, of self, and of others) has been identified as a key mediator of the spirituality–addiction association. Theoretical models posit that forgiveness facilitates addiction recovery by allowing individuals to more effectively cope with various negative emotions such as shame, resentment, and condemnation; self-forgiveness has been implicated as an especially important dimension of forgiveness in the addiction recovery process (Lyons et al., 2010; Webb et al., 2017; Webb et al., 2015). Indeed, empirical research has suggested that self-forgiveness may be the most critical dimension of forgiveness to achieving long-term recovery while also being the most difficult to achieve (see Charzyńska et al., 2018; Webb, 2021; Webb et al., 2017).

Forgiveness has also demonstrated other potential routes of influence on addiction-related outcomes identified in the Webb model, including salutary associations with a variety of negative affective states (Dangel & Webb, 2018; Webb et al., 2009), purpose in life (Lyons et al., 2011), and health behaviors (Webb & Brewer, 2010). While some studies have found deleterious associations between various dimensions of forgiveness and addiction-related outcomes, the vast majority of studies investigating the forgiveness–addiction association have found salutary associations (see Webb, 2021, Chapter 6 for the most up-to-date review of this literature).

Research on *gratitude* and addiction is in its early stages but rapidly accelerating. Salutary associations between gratitude and addictive behaviors have been observed in the context of substance use (e.g., Krentzman, 2017) and compulsive sexual behavior (Wnuk et al., 2023). Apart from its associations with specific addiction-related outcomes, gratitude also appears to be associated with improved quality of life during the recovery process. For example, Krentzman et al. (2015) found that a gratitude-based intervention for individuals in treatment for alcohol use disorder was associated with decreases in negative affect and increases in unactivated positive affect (i.e., feeling calm, at ease, or relaxed) at the end of the intervention.

Recent studies suggest that gratitude's role in addiction recovery, while generally beneficial, is nuanced and context-dependent. Specifically, studies using naturalistic and longitudinal designs by Krentzman and colleagues (Krentzman, 2017; Krentzman & Finn, 2019) suggest that gratitude may function differently for those in active recovery versus those who are not. Krentzman (2017) explored the longitudinal relationship between gratitude and abstinence among individuals entering an outpatient alcohol treatment program. For individuals who were still actively drinking six months into treatment, high levels of gratitude were actually associated with lower levels of abstinence another six months later. However, future abstinence was more likely for still-drinking individuals with low gratitude and for already-abstinent individuals with high gratitude. As such, it was posited that gratitude for sobriety (rather than gratitude more generally) may be a motivating factor for working toward abstinence. In explaining possible reasons for these somewhat counterintuitive findings, Krentzman stated, "Endorsement that life is good as is would offer low motivation for change. Conversely, frequent drinkers with low gratitude might have been motivated by their negative view of the status quo" (2017, p. 33). Krentzman also provided the caveat that "efforts to increase gratitude among those with alcohol-use disorders who are abstinent might be beneficial but might be contraindicated among those who are drinking frequently" (p. 34).

Mindfulness is one of the most intensively studied spirituality-related constructs in the context of addiction. Indeed, multiple published meta-analyses and literature reviews support the assertion that mindfulness-based interventions are effective in the treatment of addictive behaviors, including substance use, binge eating, and gambling (Godfrey et al., 2015; Li et al., 2017; Sancho et al., 2018).

Mindfulness has been identified as a mechanism between spirituality and a large number of physical and mental health outcomes (see Chapter 24, this volume), with mindfulness itself influencing health through a number of different cognitive, behavioral, and emotional pathways (Greeson et al., 2011; Gu et al., 2015). This then raises the question of which pathways may be involved in the relationship between mindfulness and addiction recovery specifically. A recent literature review by Rosenthal et al. (2021) suggested that three primary mechanisms may play a role. They first noted that increased mindfulness may allow individuals to recalibrate their habitual responses toward drug-related cues that produce a craving response, such that they are able to re-sensitize themselves toward natural reward cues rather than drug-related cues. Second, mindfulness also appears to enhance a variety of executive functions relevant to addiction, including impulse control, attention, and emotional response inhibition. Finally, the authors suggested that mindfulness may also influence addiction outcomes through an increased ability to regulate negative affective states and the stress response, both of which may contribute to engagement in addictive behavior.

Existential Well-Being

Religion and spirituality are inextricably linked to deep existential questions concerning one's purpose, the meaning of one's existence, and one's relationship to the sacred or the universe at large. The ways in which individuals attempt to cope with and resolve these questions, in turn, have direct implications for their mental well-being (Stauner et al., 2020). This section summarizes extant literature regarding the role of the above existential factors in the relationship between spirituality, addiction, and recovery.

As mentioned above, meaning and purpose in life have been theoretically implicated in the spirituality–addiction association (Neff & MacMaster, 2005; Lyons et al., 2010; Webb et al., 2015). Support for this theoretical assertion comes in two forms. First, longitudinal studies have found positive associations between these two variables and addiction-related outcomes. For example, the Robinson et al. (2007) study mentioned above found that increases in purpose in life during treatment significantly predicted abstinence from alcohol six months later. Similar results were found in a later study related to purpose in life and abstinence from cocaine, even after controlling for depressive symptoms (Martin et al., 2011).

Second, additional research has also suggested an inverse pattern; that is, a sense of meaninglessness and purposelessness is associated with poorer addiction-related outcomes (e.g., Schnetzer et al., 2012). Such feelings have been found to be associated with negative affective states such as depression and intense psychological pain, which are in turn associated with increased engagement in addictive behaviors (Dangel & Webb, 2018; Kleftaras & Katsogianni, 2012). Webb and colleagues have labeled this existentially and philosophically driven psychological distress as "ExistAngst" in their model (Webb et al., 2015). Such findings regarding the importance of meaning and purpose could also be considered analogous to the Existential Spirituality dimension of the RiTE model, which greatly emphasizes the aspects of spirituality relevant to such pursuits (Webb et al., 2014).

In sum, the research described above supports a long-held and intuitive but empirically under-examined assertion regarding the importance of establishing a coherent and stable sense of existential well-being in one's life in the context of addiction. Further investigation is warranted to determine the relative importance of these existential well-being components in relation to other known mechanisms of the spirituality–addiction association.

Spirituality as a Unique Catalyst for Belonging and Coping

A key function of spirituality, and religion in particular, is to facilitate a sense of social connectedness and community with other people and/or some sort of higher, transcendent entity. A sense of social connection and belonging has been shown to have direct ties to addiction-related outcomes when one's social connections are pro-abstinence (Kelly, 2017). Additionally, spiritual and religious beliefs support the utilization of novel coping strategies that may play a role (both salubrious and deleterious) in the recovery process (Connery & Devido, 2020). This section summarizes extant literature on these two novel elements of spirituality and their associations with addictive behavior.

Spirituality and Belongingness. As mentioned above, a sense that one's life involves consistent, supportive, and meaningful bonds with others can be highly beneficial for the recovery process. Indeed, empirical studies suggest that these social bonds play a role in the development of and recovery from addictive behaviors. Religious service attendance and other forms of socially oriented spiritual involvement have been largely observed to show positive correlations with supportive social ties (Bradley et al., 2019) and inverse relationships with a variety of addictive behaviors (Livne et al., 2021). Feelings of isolation and loneliness, conversely, are associated with increased engagement in addictive behaviors (Ingram et al., 2020).

Social support has then, in turn, been identified as a protective factor in the recovery process through its stress-buffering effects as well as selection mechanisms involved in choosing recovery-conducive peer networks. For example, one of the primary drivers of positive outcomes within Twelve-Step approaches to recovery appears to be the adaptive changes that occur in one's peer networks as a result of group membership (see Kelly, 2017). While it is true that secular forms of social support likely play a role in the recovery process, scholars have observed that spiritual/religious forms of support may demonstrate unique associations with substance use outcomes above that of general support (e.g., Debnam et al., 2012). Of note, these findings regarding the mediating role of social support are not unanimous, with some studies finding no association between social support and addictive behavior outcomes (e.g., Webb et al., 2011) and others finding the type of social support to be more or less relevant (e.g., less social undermining, but not constructive social support; Webb et al., 2012).

Spiritual and Religious Coping. Numerous studies have found that utilization of spiritually or religiously based coping strategies (e.g., spiritual/religious cognitive appraisals of events, seeking support from clergy, and experiencing connectedness to a higher power; see Pargament et al., 2000) can impact recovery outcomes. As mentioned, these coping strategies can be both positive and negative, leading to salutary or deleterious associations with addictive behavior depending on the type of coping strategy being used. The significance of spiritual and religious coping has been observed in a variety of samples, including college students (Gallucci et al., 2018) and inpatient treatment samples (Medlock et al., 2017). Negative coping strategies, while used less frequently than positive ones, have shown deleterious associations with addiction-related outcomes (Galluci et al., 2018; Medlock et al., 2017).

It is also worth noting that the strength of the above associations may be moderated by a variety of factors. For example, it is possible that the relative salience of religious coping may differ for men and women (Krause et al., 2018). Other factors, such as depressive symptoms, may also produce differential associations between religious coping and addictive behaviors (Horton & Loukas, 2013). Future studies are needed to further clarify the variables that may moderate the relationship between religious coping and addictive behavior (e.g., demographic characteristics, comorbid symptoms, and specific addictive substances or behaviors).

Behavioral Mechanisms

A final prevalent theme observed in this review concerns the ways in which spirituality may be related to addictive behavior via social learning and behavioral conditioning principles. As mentioned above, some spiritual belief systems may explicitly prohibit the use of various substances; still, more belief systems view compulsive or unmoderated behaviors of all kinds as immoral, harmful, or otherwise against the core teachings of that system. These views are then reinforced within communal systems that consistently enact behavioral consequences for adhering or not adhering to group norms related to addictive behaviors. Indeed, extant literature suggests that a variety of social mechanisms may play a role in the spirituality–addiction association. These include beliefs about the potential harm of the substance, peer group norms, and expectancies about the effects of using the substance (e.g., Cox et al., 2012; Sauer-Zavala et al., 2014).

While the social mechanisms mentioned above may play a preventative role in developing addictive behaviors, other studies also suggest that these social mechanisms may have secondary negative effects for some individuals. Specifically, if individuals do engage in compulsive or addictive behaviors, violation of the social norms or religious tenets described above may produce internal distress and a sense of stigma that further exacerbates the behavior. This premise is reflected in the moral incongruence model of pornography use described above (Grubbs et al., 2019).

At the individual level, spiritual and religious beliefs may also strengthen a variety of mental processes that, in turn, enhance one's ability to avoid or moderate undesired behaviors. In an extensive review of this literature, McCullough and Willoughby (2009) discussed a large volume of evidence (including studies investigating substance use) that religiousness in particular can influence a variety of processes, including goal selection, self-control, self-regulation, and self-monitoring. The authors posit that religious individuals are able to strengthen these processes as a result of frequent subjection to monitoring both by one's faith community and directly by a supernatural entity, as well as through consistent engagement in the ritualistic aspects of various faith traditions (i.e., ritualistic spirituality within the RiTE model).

Conclusions, Limitations, and Future Directions

In conclusion, the literature reviewed in this chapter illustrates the multifaceted and complex relationship between spirituality and addiction. Scholars have not only established that the two constructs are indeed related, but are now firmly in the process of understanding the various mechanisms that may be involved in this relationship. These mechanisms play a variety of roles ranging from preventative to protective to deleterious. Moreover, the relative salience of each mechanism may vary depending on a variety of factors, including demographic factors, belief status, and the specific type of addictive behavior. It should be noted that the literature reviewed in this chapter is neither a definitive nor exhaustive survey of all literature pertaining to the topic of spirituality and addiction. Other mechanisms not discussed here may also be involved in the spirituality–addiction association. Furthermore, as with many scientific observations, none of the trends described above are unanimously supported in all contexts, suggesting that much remains to be learned about the conditions in which certain mechanisms may be more or less relevant.

Despite all of the evidence described above concerning the role of spirituality in addiction (both positive and negative), the literature on this topic is limited by a variety of factors. First, as is evident in this chapter, much of the literature on the spirituality–addiction association has tended to emphasize substance use, and alcohol use in particular. Although other substances and behavioral addictions have begun to receive more empirical attention, more research is needed to determine how spirituality's relative influence may differ across different types and subtypes of addictive behaviors. Similarly, while constructs like forgiveness and mindfulness have been extensively studied in the addiction literature (e.g., entire books, mediation meta-analyses, and manualized interventions), less is known about other spirituality-related constructs. Further study into newer or otherwise lesser-studied constructs will ideally lead to a deeper understanding of the unique ways in which spirituality may influence the addiction and recovery process.

A second and related issue is the substantial variability in methodology and measures used in the studies discussed in this chapter. Studies utilizing more rigorous methods, such as longitudinal and experimental designs, are smaller in number compared to those using cross-sectional designs with fewer methodological or statistical controls in place. Additionally, more formal empirical tests of specific theoretical models of spirituality and addiction are needed. Although informed by theory and prior research, many studies in this chapter were not explicitly designed to test a specific theoretical model of the spirituality–addiction association. Formal tests of these explanatory models are necessary to further refine our understanding of which theorized mechanisms are ultimately empirically supported. Regarding measurement, the significant variability in how the above constructs are defined and measured across studies poses limitations to generalizability and replication across contexts. Taken together, these two limitations highlight the need for continued efforts to study spirituality and addiction using theoretically grounded and methodologically sound research designs that will ultimately enhance their generalizability.

A final limitation of the above literature is that studies are often limited to Western samples using primarily White and male college students. This is particularly relevant for religion and spirituality research in that these studies are also often designed in the context of Judeo-Christian belief systems and/or with religiously homogeneous samples. Given the inextricable links between religious/spiritual traditions and cultural, historical, geographical, and political influences, more research with historically underrepresented groups is needed to provide a more nuanced and unbiased understanding of spirituality's potential linkages to addiction.

As more is learned about the role spirituality may play in mental health, researchers and clinicians will be well-positioned to translate this knowledge into applied treatment contexts to improve the lives of those struggling with addiction. Despite the field's historical reticence to consider spirituality as a subject worthy of investigation, there has been a rapid accumulation of knowledge on this topic over the past two decades. This may signify that the field of psychology has begun to appreciate the arguably central role of spirituality in helping individuals to navigate the often challenging and arduous journey of addiction and recovery.

References

Alcoholics Anonymous (2001). *Alcoholics Anonymous* (4th ed.). Author

Bradley, C. S., Hill, T. D., Burdette, A. M., Mossakowski, K. N., & Johnson, R. N. (2019). Religious attendance and social support: Integration or selection? *Review of Religious Research*, *62*(1), 83–99. https://doi.org/10.1007/s13644-019-00392-z

Charzyńska, E., Gruszczyńska, E., & Heszen, I. (2018). Forgiveness and gratitude trajectories among persons undergoing alcohol addiction therapy. *Addiction Research & Theory*, *26*(4), 282–293. https://doi.org/10.1080/16066359.2018.1429595

Cheadle, A. C. D., & Schetter, C. D. (2017). Untangling the mechanisms underlying the links between religiousness, spirituality, and better health. *Social and Personality Psychology Compass*, *11*(2), Article e12299. https://doi.org/10.1111/spc3.12299

Connery, H. S., & Devido, J. (2020). Spirituality/religion and substance use disorders. In D. H. Rosmarin & H. G. Koenig (Eds.), *Handbook of Spirituality, Religion, and Mental Health* (2nd ed., pp. 119–138). Elsevier. https://doi.org/10.1016/C2017-0-04790-0

Cox, R. B., Danelia, K., Larzelere, R. E., & Blow, A. J. (2012). Do peers and perceived risk mediate the association of religiosity with the likelihood and extent of recent substance use among Venezuelan youth? *International Perspectives in Psychology: Research, Practice, Consultation*, *1*(1), 15–31. https://doi.org/10.1037/a0026832

Dangel, T. & Webb, J. R. (2018). Forgiveness and substance use problems among college students: Psychache, depressive symptoms, and hopelessness as mediators. *Journal of Substance Use*, *23*(6), 618–625, https://doi.org/10.1080/14659891.2018.1489003

Debnam, K., Holt, C., Clark, E. M., Roth, D. L.., & Southward, P. (2012). Relationship between religious social support and general social support with health behaviors in a national sample of African Americans. *Journal of Behavioral Medicine*, *35*(2), 179–189. https://doi.org/10.1007/s10865-011-9338-4

Dossi, F., Buja, A., & Montecchio, L. (2022). Association between religiosity or spirituality and internet addiction: A systematic review. *Frontiers in Public Health*, *10*, Article e 980334. https://doi.org/10.3389/fpubh.2022.980334

Florence, C., Luo, F., & Rice, K. (2021). The economic burden of opioid use disorder and fatal opioid overdose in the United States, 2017. *Drug and Alcohol Dependence*, *218*, Article e108350. https://doi.org/10.1016/j.drugalcdep.2020.108350

Gallucci, A. R., (2018). Examining the relationship between religious coping and the misuse of prescription stimulants among a sample of undergraduate students. *Substance Use and Misuse*, *53*(9), 1571–1579. https://doi.org/10.1080/10826084.2017.1416405

Godfrey, K. M., Gallo, L. C., & Afari, N. (2015). Mindfulness-based interventions for binge eating: A systematic review and meta-analysis. *Journal of Behavioral Medicine*, *38*(2), 348–362. https://doi.org/10.1007/s10865-014-9610-5

Greeson, J. M., Webber, D. M., Smoski, M. J., Brantley, J. G., Ekblad, A. G., Suarez, E. C., & Wolever, R. Q. (2011). Changes in spirituality partly explain health-related quality of life outcomes after mindfulness-based stress reduction. *Journal of Behavioral Medicine*, *34*(6), 508–518. https://doi.org/10.1007/s10865-011-9332-x

Grubbs, J. B., & Hook, J. N. (2016). Religion, spirituality, and sexual addiction: A critical evaluation of converging fields. *Sexual Addiction & Compulsivity*, *23*(2-3), 155–166. https://doi.org/10.1080/10720162.2016.1150925

Grubbs, J. B., Perry, S. L., Wilt, J. A., & Reid, R. C. (2019). Pornography problems due to moral incongruence: An integrative model with a systemic review and meta-analysis. *Archives of Sexual Behavior*, *48*(2), 397–415. https://doi.org/10.1007/s10508-018-1248-x

Gu, J., Strauss, C., Bond, R., & Cavanagh, K. (2015). How do mindfulness-based cognitive therapy and mindfulness-based stress reduction improve mental health and wellbeing? A systematic review and meta-analysis of mediation studies. *Clinical Psychology Review*, *37*, 1–12. https://doi.org/10.1016/j.cpr.2015.01.006

Hai, A. H., Franklin, C., Park, S., DiNitto, D. M., & Aurelio, N. (2019). The efficacy of spiritual/religious interventions for substance use problems: A systematic review and meta-analysis of randomized controlled trials. *Drug and Alcohol Dependence*, *202*, 134–148. https://doi.org/10.1016/j.drugalcdep.2019.04.045

Harvey, P. (2013). *An introduction to Buddhism: Teachings, history, and practices* (2nd Ed). Cambridge University Press.

Hedegaard, H., Miniño, A. M., & Warner, M. (2020). *Drug overdose deaths in the United States, 1999–2018*. Center for Disease Control. https://www.cdc.gov/nchs/data/databriefs/db356-h.pdf

Hill, P. C., Pargament, K. I., Hood, R. W., Jr., McCullough, M. E., Swyers, J. P., Larson, D. B., & Zinnbauer, B. J. (2000). Conceptualizing religion and spirituality: Points of commonality, points of departure. *Journal for the Theory of Social Behaviour*, *30*(1), 51–77. https://doi.org/10.1111/1468-5914.00119

Horton, K. D., & Loukas, A. (2013). Depressive symptoms, religious coping, and cigarette smoking among post-secondary vocational students. *Psychology of Addictive Behaviors*, *27*(3), 705–713. https://doi.org/10.1037/a0031195

Ingram, I., Kelly, P. J., Deane, F. P., Baker, A. L., Goh, M. C. W., Raftery, D. K., & Dingle, G. A. (2020). Loneliness among people with substance use problems: A narrative systematic review. *Drug and Alcohol Review*, *39*(5), 447–483. https://doi.org/10.1111/dar.13064

Jennings, T. L., Lyng, T., Gleason, N., Finotelli, I., & Coleman, E. (2021). Compulsive sexual behavior, religiosity, and spirituality: A systematic review. *Journal of Behavioral Addictions*, *10*(4), 854–878. https://doi.org/10.1556/2006.2021.00084

Kelly, J. F. (2017). Is Alcoholics Anonymous religious, spiritual, or neither? Findings from 25 years of mechanisms of behavior change research. *Addiction*, *112*(6), 929–936. https://doi.org/10.1111/add.13590

Kelly, J. F., Humphreys, K., & Ferri, M. (2020). Alcoholics Anonymous and other 12-step programs for alcohol use disorder. *Cochrane Database of Systematic Reviews*. https://doi.org/10.1002/14651858.CD012880.pub2

Kelly, J. F. Stout, R. B., Magill, M., Tonigan, J. S., & Pagano, M. E. (2011). Spirituality in recovery: A lagged mediational analysis of Alcoholics Anonymous' principal theoretical mechanism of behavior change. *Alcoholism: Clinical and Experimental Research*, *35*(3), 454–463. https://doi.org/10.1111/j.1530-0277.2010.01362.x

Kleftaras, G., & Katsogianni, I. (2012). Spirituality, meaning in life, and depressive symptomatology in individuals with alcohol dependence. *Journal of Spirituality in Mental Health*, *14*(4), 268–288. https://doi.org/10.1080/19349637.2012.730469

Krause, N., Pargament, K. I., Hill, P. C., & Ironson, G. (2018). Assessing gender differences in the relationship between religious coping responses and alcohol consumption. *Mental Health, Religion, & Culture*, *21*(1), 93–104. https://doi.org/10.1080/13674676.2018.1455652

Krentzman, A. R. (2013). Review of the application of positive psychology to substance use, addiction, and recovery research. *Psychology of Addictive Behaviors*, *27*(1), 151–165. https://doi.org/10.1037/a0029897

Krentzman, A. R. (2017). Gratitude, abstinence, and alcohol use disorders: Report of a preliminary finding. *Journal of Substance Abuse Treatment*, *78*, 30–36. https://doi.org/10.1016/j.jsat.2017.04.013

Krentzman, A. R., Cranford, J. A., & Robinson, E. A. R. (2013). Multiple dimensions of spirituality in recovery: A lagged mediational analysis of Alcoholics Anonymous' principle theoretical mechanism of behavior change. *Substance Abuse*, *34*(1), 20–32. https://doi.org/10.1080/08897077.2012.691449

Krentzman, A. R., & Finn, M. T. M. (2019). Gratitude while drinking, gratitude while recovering: A study of alcohol use disorders. *Journal of Recovery Science*, *1*(3). https://doi.org/10.31886/jors.13.2019.39

Krentzman, A. R., Mannella, K. A., Hassett, A. L., Barnett, N. P., Cranford, J. A., Brower, K. J., … Meyer, P. S. (2015). Feasibility, acceptability, and impact of a web-based gratitude exercise among individuals in outpatient treatment for alcohol use disorder. *The Journal of Positive Psychology*, *10*(6), 477–499. https://doi.org/10.1080/17439760.2015.1015158

Li, W., Howard, M. O., Garland, E. L., McGovern, P., & Lazar, M. (2017). Mindfulness treatment for substance misuse: A systematic review and meta-analysis. *Journal of Substance Abuse Treatment*, *75*, 62–96. https://doi.org/10.1016/j.jsat.2017.01.008

Livne, O., Wengrower, T., Feingold, D., Shmulewitz, D., Hasin, D., & Lev-Ran, S. (2021). Religiosity and substance use in U.S. adults: Findings from a large-scale national survey. *Drug and Alcohol Dependence*, *225*, Article e108796. https://doi.org/10.1016/j.drugalcdep.2021.108796

Lyons, G. C. B., Deane, F. P., Caputi, P., & Kelly, P. J. (2011). Spirituality and the treatment of substance use disorders: An exploration of forgiveness, resentment and purpose in life. *Addiction Research & Theory*, *19*(5), 459–469. https://doi.org/10.3109/16066359.2011.555022

Lyons, G. C. B., Deane, F. P., & Kelly, P. J. (2010). Forgiveness and purpose in life as spiritual mechanisms of recovery from substance use disorders. *Addiction Research and Theory*, *18*(5), 528–543. https://doi.org/10.3109/16066351003660619

Martin, R. A., MacKinnon, S., Johnson, J., & Rohsenow, D. J. (2011). Purpose in life predicts treatment outcome among adult cocaine abusers in treatment. *Journal of Substance Abuse Treatment*, *40*(2), 183–188. https://doi.org/10.1016/j.jsat.2010.10.002

Maté, G., & Maté, D. (2022). *The Myth of Normal: Trauma, Illness, & Healing in a Toxic Culture*. Avery.

McCullough, M. E., & Willoughby, B. L. B. (2009). Religion, self-regulation, and self-control: Associations, explanations, and implications. *Psychological Bulletin*, *135*(1), 69–93. https://doi.org/10.1037/a0014213

Medlock, M. M., Rosmarin, D. H., Connery, H. S., Griffin, M. L., Weiss, R. D., Karakula, S. L., & McHugh, R. K. (2017). Religious coping in patients with severe substance use disorders receiving acute inpatient detoxification. The *American Journal on Addictions*, *26*(7), 744–750. https://doi.org/10.1111/ajad.12606

Michalak, L., & Karen, T. (2006). Alcohol and Islam: An overview. *Contemporary Drug Problems: An Interdisciplinary Quarterly*, *33*(4), 523–562. https://doi.org/10.1177/009145090603300401

Neff, J. A., & MacMaster, S. A. (2005). Spiritual mechanisms underlying substance abuse behavior change in faith-based substance abuse treatment. *Journal of Social Work Practice in the Addictions*, *5*(3), 33–54. https://doi.org/10.1300/J160v05n03_04

Nowinski, J. (2012). Facilitating 12-Step recovery from substance abuse. In S. T. Walters & F. Rotgers (Eds.), *Treating substance abuse: Theory and technique* (Third ed., pp. 191–223). Guilford Press.

Pargament, K. I. (2013). Searching for the sacred: Towards a nonreductionistic theory of spirituality. In K. I. Pargament, A. Mahoney, & E. P. Shafranske, (Eds.), *APA handbook of psychology, religion, and spirituality (Vol 1): Context, theory, and research* (pp. 257–273). American Psychological Association.

Pargament, K. I., Koenig, H. G., & Perez, L. M. (2000). The many methods of religious coping: Development and initial validation of the RCOPE. *Journal of Clinical Psychology*, *56*(4), 519–543. https://doi.org/10.1002/(SICI)1097-4679(200004)56:4<519::AID-JCLP6>3.0.CO;2-1

Pargament, K. I., Mahoney, A., Exline, J. J., Jones, J. W., & Shafranske, E. P. (2013). Envisioning an integrative paradigm for the psychology of religion and spirituality. In K. I. Pargament, A. Mahoney, & E. P. Shafranske, (Eds.), *APA handbook of psychology, religion, and spirituality (Vol 1): Context, theory, and research* (pp. 3–19). American Psychological Association.

Robinson, E. A. R., Cranford, J. A., Webb, J. R., & Brower, K. J. (2007). Six-month changes in spirituality, religiousness, and heavy drinking in a treatment-seeking sample. *Journal of Studies on Alcohol and Drugs*, *68*(2), 282–290. https://doi.org/10.15288/jsad.2007.68.282

Robinson, E. A. R., Krentzman, A. R., Webb, J. R., & Brower, K. J. (2011). Six-month changes in spirituality and religiousness in alcoholics predict drinking outcomes at nine months. *Journal of Studies on Alcohol and Drugs*, *72*(4), 660–668. https://doi.org/10.15288/jsad.2011.72.660

Rosenthal, A., Levin, M. E., Garland, E. L., & Romanczuk-Seiferth, N. (2021). Mindfulness in treatment approaches for addiction- underlying mechanisms and future directions. *Current Addiction Reports*, *8*, 282–297. https://doi.org/10.1007/s40429-021-00372-w

Sancho, M., De Gracia, M., Rodriguez, R. C., Mallorqui-Bague, N., Sanchez-Gonzalez, J., Trujols, J., … Menchon, J. M. (2018). Mindfulness-based interventions for the treatment of substance and behavioral addictions: A systematic review. *Frontiers in Psychiatry*, *9*. https://doi.org/10.3389/fpsyt.2018.00095

Sauer-Zavala, S., Burris, J. L., & Carlson, C. R. (2014). Understanding the relationship between religiousness, spirituality, and underage drinking: The role of positive alcohol expectancies. *Journal of Religion & Health*, *53*(1), 68–78. https://doi.org/10.1007/s10943-012-9598-5

Schnetzer, L. W., Schulenberg, S. E., & Buchanan, E. M. (2012). Differential associations among alcohol use, depression, and perceived life meaning in male and female college students. *Journal of Substance Use*, *18*(4), 311–319. https://doi.org/10.3109/14659891.2012.661026

Stauner, N., Exline, J. J., & Wilt, J. A. (2020). Meaning, religious/spiritual struggles, and well-being. In K. E. Vail & C. Routledge (Eds.), *The Science of Religion, Spirituality, and Existentialism* (pp. 287–303). Elsevier. https://doi.org/10.1016/C2018-0-01248-7

Subhani, M., Talat, U., Knight, H., Morling, J. R., Jones, K. A., Aithal, G. P., … Rennick-Egglestone, S. (2022). Characteristics of alcohol recovery narratives: Systematic review and narrative synthesis. *PLoS ONE*, *17*(5). https://doi.org/10.1371/journal.pone.0268034

Sussman, S. (2017). *Substance and behavioral addictions: Concepts, causes, and cures*. Cambridge University Press.

Sussman, S., & Sussman, A. N. (2011). Considering the definition of addiction. International Journal of Environmental Research and Public Health, 8(10), 4025–4038. https://doi.org/10.3390/ijerph8104025

Webb, J. R. (2021). *Understanding forgiveness and addiction: Theory, research, and clinical application*. Routledge.

Webb, J. R., & Brewer, K. (2010). Forgiveness, health, and problematic drinking among college students in Southern Appalachia. *Journal of Health Psychology*, *15*(8), 1257–1266. https://doi.org/10.1177/1359105310365177

Webb, J. R., Hill, S. K., & Brewer, K. G. (2012). Dimensions of social support as mediators of the forgiveness-alcohol outcome relationship. *Addictive Disorders & Their Treatment*, *11*(2), 64–75. https://doi.org/10.1097/ADT.0b013e31822dcd56

Webb, J. R., Hirsch, J. K., & Toussaint, L. (2015). Forgiveness as a positive psychotherapy for addiction and suicide: Theory, research, and practice. *Spirituality in Clinical Practice*, *2*(1), 48–60. https://doi.org/10.1037/scp0000054

Webb, J. R., Robinson, E. A. R., & Brower, K. J. (2009). Forgiveness and mental health among people entering outpatient treatment with alcohol problems. *Alcoholism Treatment Quarterly*, *27*(4), 368–388. https://doi.org/10.1080/07347320903209822

Webb, J. R., Robinson, E. A. R., & Brower, K. J. (2011). Mental health, not social support, mediates the forgiveness-alcohol outcome relationship. *Psychology of Addictive Behaviors*, *25*(3), 462–473. https://doi.org/10.1037/a0022502

Webb, J. R., Toussaint, L., & Dula, C. S. (2014). Ritualistic, theistic, and existential spirituality: Initial psychometric qualities of the RiTE Measure of Spirituality. *Journal of Religion & Health*, *53*(4), 972–985. https://doi.org/10.1007/s10943-013-9697-y

Webb, J. R., Toussaint, L. L., & Hirsch, J. K. (2017). Self-forgiveness, addiction, and recovery. In L. Woodyatt, E. L. Worthington Jr., M. Wenzel, & B. J. Griffin (Eds.), *Handbook of the psychology of self-forgiveness* (pp. 265–277). Springer.

Wnuk, M., Krentzman, A. R., & Charzyńska, E. (2023). The 12-step pathway to spiritual growth and gratitude and its relationship with well-being among the members of Sexaholics Anonymous in Poland. *Journal of Religion & Health*. https://doi.org/10.1007/s10943-023-01892-7

World Health Organization. (2018). Global status report on alcohol and health 2018. https://iris.who.int/bitstream/handle/10665/274603/9789241565639-eng.pdf?sequence=1

World Health Organization. (2023). World health statistics 2023: monitoring health for the SDGs, Sustainable Development Goals. https://cdn.who.int/media/docs/default-source/gho-documents/world-health-statistic-reports/2023/world-health-statistics-2023_20230519_.pdf

Chapter 19

Spirituality, Meaning Making, and Trauma Recovery

Crystal L. Park[*] *and Mariel Emrich*

In this chapter, we elaborate on the roles that spirituality can play in processes of meaning-making in recovering from trauma. Trauma refers to exposure to actual or threatened death, serious injury, or sexual violence (American Psychiatric Association, 2013) and can result in a range of mental health sequelae (e.g., posttraumatic stress disorder, depression, suicidality, and moral injury). Given the pervasive influences of spirituality (Park, 2013) and the high prevalence of trauma (Benjet et al., 2016), this intersection is critical in advancing current approaches to trauma recovery and resilience (Park et al., 2017). We begin with a brief review of the meaning-making model and then describe ways that spirituality can potentially influence this process. We then review the empirical evidence in four key areas within the context of trauma: (a) global meaning, (b) trauma appraisals, (c) engagement in meaning-making, and (d) resultant meanings made. We conclude with directions for future research.

The Meaning-Making Model

The meaning-making model is a conceptual framework that helps explain people's day-to-day functioning in the world and how they may regain functioning after highly stressful or traumatic events. The model focuses on two levels of meaning: global and situational (Park, 2017) (see Figure 19.1). Global meaning comprises people's fundamental beliefs – about the world, other people, and their own identity in that world – as well as their unique hierarchies of goals, and values, and their sense of meaning and purpose. Situational meaning refers to the influences of global meaning, in conjunction with the context of a particular situation, on one's appraisals of and subsequent responses to a particular situation. Situational meaning encompasses the meanings assigned to these experiences, the potential discrepancies between global and appraised meaning, the processes involved in reconciling those discrepancies (i.e., "meaning making"), and the changes resulting from these reconciliation processes (i.e., "meaning made").

When individuals encounter potentially significant stressors, they evaluate and assign meaning to them in an effort to grasp their personal significance (Lazarus & Folkman, 1984). This *appraised meaning* is shaped by a combination of their overarching beliefs and goals (i.e., their global meaning) and the specific details of the situation at hand (i.e., their situational meaning). For example, those with a strong sense that stressful situations are amenable to change may try to understand an event in terms of the specific aspects that can be modified,

* Corresponding Author: crystal.park@uconn.edu.

DOI: 10.4324/9781003440048-22

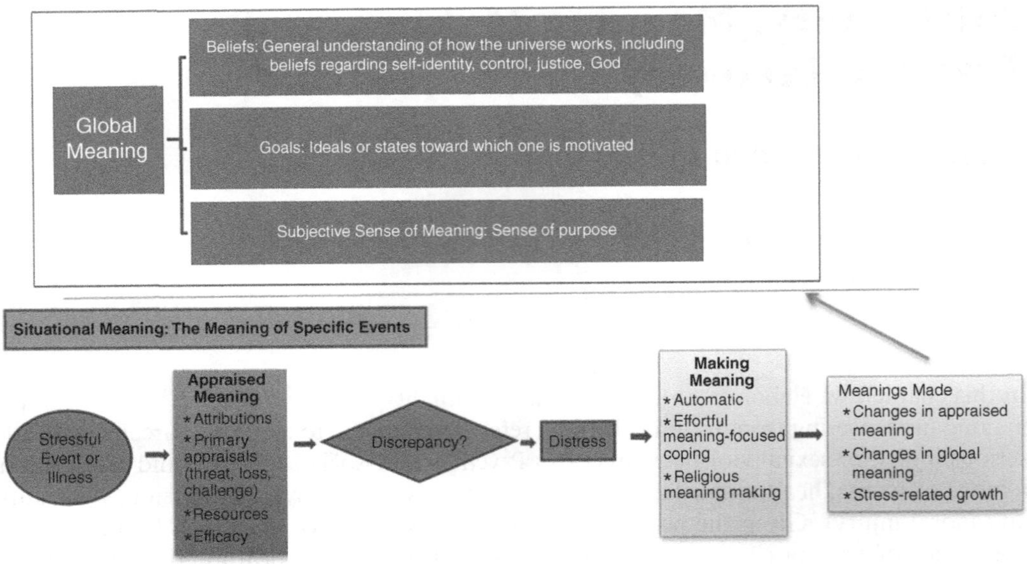

Figure 19.1 The Meaning-Making Model.

while someone who believes in a "just world" (Lerner & Miller, 1978) might focus more on identifying what prior mistake or offense he or she committed to deserve the present adversity.

Following appraisal of the meaning of an event, individuals determine the extent to which that assigned meaning is congruent with their global beliefs and their desires and goals. According to the meaning-making model, individuals experience distress when they perceive the trauma and its aftermath as conflicting with their deeply ingrained core beliefs and life objectives. Traumatic events may violate or even "shatter" global beliefs and goals. For example, a traumatic event might violate a person's global beliefs, such as being in control of their fate or that God would protect them. Global goals such as being healthy and safe and maintaining relationships with loved ones can be threatened or taken away by traumatic events. In particular, individuals who experience interpersonal traumas (e.g., physical or sexual trauma) compared to non-interpersonal traumas (e.g., natural disasters) may be at greater risk for their global beliefs to be violated due to feelings of betrayal and disruptions of trust in others (Lilly et al., 2011).

Perceiving such violations or discrepancies may initiate individuals' engagement in cognitive and emotional processing efforts – "meaning making" – to rebuild their meaning systems in a way that incorporates their understanding of the trauma (Park, 2010). *Making meaning* involves either reevaluating the traumatic event to align it more closely with their pre-trauma beliefs and goals (i.e., altering the situational meaning) or adjusting their core beliefs and goals to incorporate their experiences (i.e., modifying their global meaning). These shifts in meaning, or the meanings constructed, can reduce the perceived disconnect between their core beliefs and goals and the traumatic event. Meaning-making can be adaptive to the extent that it may result in reducing distress and restoring global meaning (Brown et al., 2019). However, failing to reduce discrepancies between situational and global meaning may lead to rumination, intrusive thoughts, and depression (Hayes et al., 2017).

Meaning-making may result in a variety of meanings made, including changes in appraisals of the traumatic event (e.g., coming to see the trauma and its aftermath from a more adaptive perspective, such as reduced self-blame), changes in global meaning (e.g., changing one's global beliefs, identity, values, or life goals), and perceived stress-related or post-traumatic growth (e.g., perceptions of increased appreciation for life, stronger connections with family and friends, or greater awareness of one's strengths; Park, 2017). Individuals' ability to successfully engage in meaning-making following trauma can be influenced by the surrounding sociocultural context (Theisen-Womersley, 2021). Successful meaning-making reduces perceived discrepancies between appraised and global meanings and restores a sense of a meaningful world and a worthwhile life, ultimately aiding psychological adaptation to the trauma and fostering future resilience.

Spirituality and Its Potential Roles in the Meaning-Making Model

Spirituality often plays a key role in individuals' global meaning and thus can exert effects throughout their meaning-making processes. Spirituality is a broad and variously defined term that can refer to a range of different phenomena (see Chapter 3, this volume). In this chapter, we aimed to hew closely to the definition of spirituality proposed by Webb et al. (2014) in their RiTE model: "the salient, searching pursuit of the transcendently sacred ritualistic, theistic, and/or existential aspects of the human condition" (p. 974; see also Chapters 1 and 44, this volume). Operationally, this definition includes both structured (ritualistic) and non-structured (theistic) connections with deity as well as existential spirituality, the transcendent, yet non-theistic search for meaning and purpose. Thus, in the present chapter, we are concerned not only with theistic aspects of spirituality but with existential aspects as well.

Often, individuals' global meaning systems have a religious or spiritual foundation (Park, 2020), including their understanding of God or of the divine (e.g., as loving and benevolent, wrathful, or distant) and their beliefs about the nature of people (e.g., inherent goodness, being made in God's image, and sinful human nature) and this world (e.g., the coming apocalypse and the illusory nature of reality) as well as, perhaps, the next (e.g., Heaven, reincarnation) (Newton & McIntosh, 2013). Religion also forms the core of many individuals' identities in terms of how they understand themselves as a religious or spiritual being (e.g., as unworthy of God or as created in God's image; Hardy et al., 2017) as well as their social identification with a religious group. Religion underlies or is integrated into the overarching goals of many individuals, including not only their ultimate fate but also the values and motives for their earthly pursuits (e.g., family, career, achievements, leisure, and volunteering) (Emmons, 2003). Even those persons not expressly religious often have deep spiritual influences in these aspects of global meaning that provide a sense of meaning in their lives (George & Park, 2016). Collectively, these spiritual elements of global meaning influence how individuals live their day-to-day lives and may be especially salient when individuals are faced with highly stressful or traumatic events (Park, 2013).

Empirical Studies Testing Spiritual Meaning-Making Following Trauma

The growing interest in spirituality in the context of trauma has led to an expanding body of work on spirituality in meaning-making following trauma. For example, several recent systematic reviews on specific aspects of these relations have been published, including on spirituality and disasters (Aten et al., 2019), meaning in life and posttraumatic stress symptoms (PTSS) (Fischer et al., 2020), religiousness and trauma outcomes (Kucharska, 2020), and trauma and religious beliefs (Leo et al., 2021). Because a systematic review of such a large body of literature is neither feasible nor appropriate for a book chapter, our aim here is to highlight some recent studies showcasing both the potentially helpful and harmful aspects of spirituality on trauma recovery using the meaning-making framework. We used PsycINFO, PubMed, CINAHL, and Google Scholar to identify relevant literature and reviewed the reference sections of papers to identify other relevant literature. We focused on studies that examined aspects of spirituality in four key areas of the meaning-making model in the context of trauma: (a) global meaning, (b) appraisals of the trauma, (c) engagement in meaning-making, and (d) meanings made.

Spirituality as Protective or Vulnerable Global Meaning in the Context of Trauma

According to the meaning-making model, global meaning, including one's general or dispositional spirituality (Kucharska, 2020), can influence all aspects of meaning-making after experiencing trauma. Some studies have examined spirituality in this way, as a general predictor of how well people respond to and cope with traumatic experiences. These studies simply test spirituality as a potential protective or exacerbating factor in recovery; although they may hypothesize specific pathways of meaning-making through which spirituality may exert influence, they do not empirically test those pathways. While these studies are potentially hypothesis-generating, they are less informative than studies examining pathways such as meaning-making. A brief review of such studies is provided here with a focus on those that examined spirituality in terms of global meaning (beliefs, goals, and sense of meaning).

Studies focusing explicitly on religious beliefs (e.g., in God, in an afterlife) and trauma symptoms have produced mixed results. For example, assessed two years after the L'Aquila (Italy) Earthquake, survivors who reported being high in religiosity had the lowest levels of PTSS, while those high in spirituality reported higher levels of PTSS (Stratta et al., 2013), suggesting a protective value for organizational and ritual aspects of religiosity but a potential liability for spirituality per se.

One cross-sectional study found that religious commitment was unrelated to suicidality in a sample of combat-exposed US veterans and did not moderate effects of moral injury on suicidality (Ames et al., 2019). In another cross-sectional study of US veterans and active duty military, religious commitment was unrelated to PTSS (Koenig et al., 2019). Similarly, in a study of war-zone US veterans from the post-9/11 era who screened positive for spiritual struggle, current religious commitment was not associated with posttraumatic outcomes, including PTSS and moral injury. In contrast, veterans' recollections of their religious commitment retrospectively recalled from prior to joining the military were uniquely linked with *worse* outcomes even after controlling for covariates (Currier et al., 2023). Still other studies have shown the potential value of high spiritual meaning in life. In a sample of Hurricane Katrina survivors assessed within the first few months after Hurricane Katrina, spiritual meaning buffered against PTSS caused by resource loss (Haynes et al., 2017).

These mixed results suggest that explicitly religious beliefs and commitments may not be protective of distress in the face of traumatic experiences; however, the cited studies are scant, and more research is needed to understand whether and how religious meanings can serve as protective or vulnerability factors, especially if they are firmly in place prior to the traumatic event. For example, as reviewed in the next section, different spiritual meaning systems may render individuals more or less vulnerable to violations of global meaning (Park, 2013).

One aspect of global spirituality, a sense of meaning or purpose in life, appears to be robustly related to better outcomes for survivors of trauma. A systematic review of the literature on a sense of meaning in life found nearly uniform results across many trauma-exposed samples: a higher sense of meaning and purpose in life was consistently related to lower levels of adverse symptoms following trauma (Fischer et al., 2020). For example, in a recent cross-sectional study of US veterans exposed to traumatic events who experienced clinically meaningful guilt, greater meaning in life was associated with lower depression, anxiety, and PTSS even when controlling for avoidant coping (Morse et al., 2024).

However, nearly all of these studies examining spiritual meaning systems (e.g., religious beliefs, commitments, and meaning in life) have assessed these elements of global meaning and PTSS post-trauma. A serious limitation of these study designs is that they cannot rule out the possibility that those who experienced trauma or are more distressed by it may seek out spiritual experiences as a coping response. Thus, prospective longitudinal studies are sorely needed. Yet very few prospective studies are available to truly test the protective effects of spiritual meaning against the deleterious impacts of trauma.

One rare study that addresses this issue prospectively was already in progress prior to Hurricane Katrina, focusing on mostly non-Hispanic Black low-income mothers living in or near New Orleans. Following the hurricane, this study demonstrated that purpose in life assessed one year prior to Hurricane Katrina *did not* predict PTSS at one or two years after the hurricane (Lowe et al., 2013). This prospective study of Katrina survivors suggests that elements of global meaning prior to a trauma may *not* provide strong protection, although post-trauma, the associations may be more consistently salutary.

Appraisals of Trauma Experience/Meaning Violations

Spiritual meaning systems often encompass core values, beliefs, and principles that shape individuals' understanding of the world and their own lives. A traumatic or challenging event can conflict with these deeply held beliefs, goals, or values. For example, if a person strongly believes in the benevolence of a higher power or the fairness of the universe but experiences a significant tragedy, they may experience a rupture in their global beliefs, which is highly distressing (Park, 2017).

Some recent research suggests that global spiritual beliefs influence appraisals of and recovery from trauma. For example, a study of survivors of the 2016 Louisiana Flood found that holding theodicies (i.e., understandings of God's role in suffering) of a suffering God and providence were *positively* related to PTSS. However, these same beliefs in benevolent theodicies buffered the link between perceptions of the flood as violating global beliefs and PTSS (McElroy-Heltzel et al., 2018). This study suggests benevolent theodicies might create vulnerabilities to violation when encountering extreme stressors, but may also help to minimize the impact of damage sustained; perhaps, over time, as individuals make meaning of their traumatic experiences, more salutary effects of benevolent global meaning emerge. More research is needed to understand how theodicies and other global spiritual beliefs influence the course of recovery when experiencing trauma.

Spiritual appraisals of trauma often involve *attributions*, individuals' understanding of why a particular event occurred. Attributions can have a naturalistic or supernatural religious character. For example, some individuals may attribute an airplane crash to inclement weather or pilot error, while others may attribute it to God's intentions to punish the victims or to teach a lesson. These types of religious or spiritual attributions are often assessed in the context of disaster (Aten et al., 2012). Religious attributions take diverse forms and can range from God's punishment to God's efforts to teach a lesson; findings regarding religious attributions and subsequent distress are quite inconsistent and appear to depend on how the questions are asked as well as the type of traumatic event (see Park & Blake, 2020, for a review). Effects of such attributions may also depend on the extent to which those attributions are consistent with one's beliefs. For example, a longitudinal study examined whether attributing Hurricane Michael to God predicted later distress over and above pre-hurricane levels of distress in a sample of college students in Florida. The relationship between attributing the hurricane to God and distress was buffered by beliefs in divine forgiveness: for students who attributed the hurricane to God but had high beliefs in divine forgiveness, those attributions were essentially unrelated to distress, while for those with low beliefs in divine forgiveness, those attributions were related to higher distress (Fincham & May, 2021). Thus, seeing the hurricane as the work of a benign and forgiving God appeared to minimize the impact of casting the hurricane as divinely caused.

One type of religious response to trauma involves perceiving that the event represents God's punishment for their sins or that God is angry at or abandoning them. Although typically reported at low levels, these perceptions are consistently associated with poorer mental health after many life events (see Aten et al., 2019). While often termed *negative religious coping*, these religious responses do not, in fact, constitute coping, which involves efforts made to manage a situation or the distress it causes (Lazarus & Folkman, 1984), but rather describe a set of appraisals in the wake of traumatic events (Grey et al., 2023; Sinnott et al., 2024). Construing these responses of feeling abandoned or punished by God as appraisals is consistent with the meaning-making model, which posits that people often assign specific meanings to their traumatic events that are of a spiritual nature (Park, 2013).

Recent studies of trauma have highlighted how these negative religious appraisals relate to poorer post-trauma adjustment and functioning. For example, in a sample of survivors of Hurricane Katrina assessed two years later, negative religious coping (feeling the event was related to "God punishing me for my sins") was positively associated with major depression and poorer quality of life but not PTSS (Henslee et al., 2015), but in a sample of college student survivors of Katrina assessed two to three months after the hurricane, negative religious coping (i.e., negative religious appraisals) was positively associated with PTSS (Wood et al., 2021). Similarly, for survivors of the L'Aquila (Italy) Earthquake, negative religious coping was related to higher levels of PTSS and suicidality (Stratta et al., 2012). Many cross-sectional studies have consistently reported these associations of negative religious coping and PTSS, including in college students who had experienced childhood interpersonal trauma (Walker et al., 2022), college students in Botswana coping with disastrous drought (Shannonhouse et al., 2019), Columbian survivors of armed conflict and of a landslide (Chen et al., 2021), survivors of the 2005 Pakistani earthquake (Feder et al., 2013), US veterans and active duty military (Koenig et al., 2019), college students who had experienced sexual harassment on campus (Sujadi et al., 2023), and survivors of the 2010 Haiti earthquake (Blanc et al., 2016; Mesidor & Sly, 2019). A study of Muslim trauma survivors suggested that these negative religious appraisals were related to higher levels of PTSS through negative secular appraisals (i.e., more negative self and world views and self-blame) (Berzengi et al., 2017).

A longitudinal study of Operation Enduring Freedom/Operation Iraqi Freedom/Operation New Dawn (OEF/OIF/OND) US veterans shed more light on these associations by examining the potential mediating role of meaning in life in a three-assessment-point study over a year. Baseline spiritual struggle predicted PTSS and suicidality at subsequent 6- and 12-month time points. Further, higher levels of baseline spiritual struggle predicted increases in 12-month PTSS and suicidality, with decreased 6-month sense of meaning in life fully mediating this association (Sinnott et al., 2024).

In the aggregate, studies reviewed here indicate that spiritual beliefs and commitments or goals may not facilitate resilience in the face of trauma. However, these studies were virtually all conducted long after the traumatic event had occurred, and spirituality itself may change following trauma, as discussed below. Thus, it may be that spiritual beliefs and goals held prior to trauma are helpful in resisting distress in ways that subsequent spirituality may not be, but research to adequately address this issue has yet to be conducted.

Engaging in Meaning-Making Processes

Spirituality has been proposed to be helpful in making meaning of highly stressful and traumatic events by providing alternative ways to understand or reframe the event that help to reduce or eliminate the gap between their appraisal of the event and their global meaning. Spiritual meaning-making can also involve reconsidering one's global ways of understanding God and the world or revising one's spiritual commitments or identity. Researchers often measure religious coping using the Brief RCOPE positive religious coping scale, which taps religious meaning-making but only as part of a somewhat broader construct that also includes relying on religion for both support and guidance and trying to become closer to God. The RCOPE contains at least two explicit religious meaning-making items ("Tried to put my plans into action together with God" and "Tried to see how God might be trying to strengthen me in this situation") along with some others that might refer to efforts to make meaning (e.g., "Looked for a stronger connection with God") could represent an effort to change global meaning (Pargament et al., 2011).

Perhaps surprisingly, so-called positive religious coping has not demonstrated strong salutary relations with recovery following trauma. Some studies have indeed reported positive effects. For example, in a cross-sectional sample of college students in Mississippi affected by Hurricane Katrina, which had landed a few months previously, spiritual well-being (including meaning in life as well as peace and faith) helped buffer the impact of resource loss on PTSS (Haynes et al., 2017). Similarly, in cross-sectional studies of survivors of Hurricane Katrina assessed two months afterwards, positive religious coping (looking to God for strength and guidance) was related to less PTSS (Wood et al., 2021) and assessed two years afterwards, with less PTSS, depression, and alcohol use and higher quality of life (Henslee et al., 2015).

Yet other studies have not demonstrated beneficial effects of spiritual meaning-making as assessed by positive religious coping using the Brief RCOPE. In a prospective study of mostly non-Hispanic Black low-income mothers living in or near New Orleans, positive religious coping was not related to PTSS at assessments made one, two (Lowe et al., 2013), and even 13 years after the hurricane (Arkin et al., 2024). Similarly, in cross-sectional studies, positive religious coping was unrelated to PTSS for survivors of the 2005 Pakistani earthquake (Feder et al., 2013), Indonesian college students who had experienced sexual harassment on campus (Sujadi et al., 2023), and college students who had experienced childhood interpersonal trauma (Walker et al., 2022).

In a cross-sectional study of middle-aged and older survivors of the Louisiana flood, religious coping was not related to PTSS or depression, although it was related to lower levels of worry (Cherry et al., 2021) and in the abovementioned study of college students dealing with disastrous drought in Botswana, positive religious coping was associated with greater distress, although it mitigated to some extent the impact of resource loss on PTSS (Shannonhouse et al., 2019). Several studies have even found positive associations: in cross-sectional studies, positive religious coping was *positively* related to PTSS in survivors of the 2010 Haiti earthquake (Mesidor & Sly, 2019), in crime scene investigators (Rosansky et al., 2019), in survivors of a landslide in Columbia (Chen et al., 2021), and in survivors of the 2015 Nepal earthquake (Baral & Bhagawati, 2019).

Longitudinal prospective studies, which examine change over time in distress and thus might be more useful in understanding the meaning-making process, have also yielded minimal evidence of helpful effects of spiritual meaning-making. In the abovementioned study of US OEF/OIF/OND veterans, positive religious coping was associated with subsequent decreases in suicidality but was not related to subsequent PTSS (Sinnott et al., 2024). In a sample of African American adult sexual assault survivors, high endorsement of religious coping at baseline did not predict a reduction in PTSS one year later (Bryant et al., 2015). A one-month longitudinal study of US Army soldiers deployed to Iraq found that greater use of positive religious coping at baseline predicted *greater* distress 1 month later (Cornish et al., 2017). One study used the full RCOPE rather than the abbreviated positive and negative coping scales from the Brief RCOPE in order to examine associations of specific religious strategies in samples of trauma-exposed students and community members. This study found substantial positive relations between making meaning by reappraising the event as God's punishment or due to demonic factors, or God's lack of power, and PTSS. This study also found a slight potentially protective effect of making meaning through actively surrendering to God (Lehmann & Steele, 2020).

In sum, studies assessing meaning-making of trauma through spiritual pathways have largely demonstrated a lack of beneficial effects. This lack of evidence for spiritual meaning-making could be due to the near-universal use of the brief RCOPE positive coping scale, which does not specifically isolate religious meaning-making. The study of trauma-exposed individuals using the full RCOPE found a weak signal for one type of more explicitly spiritual meaning-focused coping. More studies are needed that measure the different types of spiritual meaning-making and further examine whether adequate meaning is made per the meaning-making model (Park, 2017).

Spiritual Meaning Made and Recovery from Trauma

Meaning-making is considered to be adaptive, especially or only to the extent that it results in reducing discrepancies between global beliefs and goals and the appraised meaning of the trauma (Park, 2017). Discrepancies can be reduced by making changes in the global meaning or in appraisals of the trauma. These *meanings made* are outcomes of the meaning-making process and can take many different forms. Changes in global meaning can include shifts in spiritual beliefs, in spiritual goals and commitments, and in a sense of meaning in life. In addition, individuals may shift their appraisals of the traumatic event over time, perhaps to a more benevolent one that helps them to integrate it into their global meaning system (Park, 2010).

Self-reported changes in global spiritual meaning following trauma appear to be common. For example, the abovementioned sample of war-zone US veterans from the post-9/11 era who screened positive for spiritual struggle reported their current religious commitment as substantially lower than their recollected religious commitment (Currier et al., 2023). In a web-based sample of people reporting having experienced a trauma, 24.9% reported experiencing a decrease in religious beliefs, while 19.4% reported a strengthening of their religious beliefs. Reporting a decrease in religious beliefs was associated with higher levels of PTSS, but reporting an increase was unrelated to levels of PTSS (ter Kuile & Ehring, 2014). Similarly, a study conducted two to three years after the 9/11 terrorist attacks in the United States found that bereaved individuals who reported a decrease in the importance of religion were more likely to have experienced complicated grief, posttraumatic stress disorder, or major depression than those who reported no change (Seirmarco et al., 2012). In a sample of people who had suffered traumatic loss, those who committed to spiritual and religious goals following the loss were more likely to report that they had recovered from the trauma and had found meaning in it (Emmons et al., 1998). Together, these findings suggest that perceived changes in spiritual meaning may be important determinants of posttraumatic outcomes. Important to note, however, is that these perceived changes in beliefs and commitments were recollected following the trauma; due to retrospective bias, the validity of people's reported changes in spiritual global meaning must be regarded with extreme caution.

Another outcome of spiritual meaning-making is perceptions of post-traumatic growth or positive changes (e.g., Lehmann & Steele, 2020). These reports of positive changes may include having more appreciation for life, improved coping skills, closer relationships with others, increased compassion, greater life meaning, and deeper spirituality. Such perceptions of positive change are both very common and very strongly linked with positive religious coping (e.g., Gerber et al., 2011; Thrombre et al., 2010). These beliefs are often taken at face value as indicating genuine positive change (Park et al., 2023). Yet while these beliefs in positive change may be regarded by individuals as genuine, favorable outcomes of the trauma, they have been shown to reflect a trait-like positive outlook or efforts to cope rather than accurately reflecting growth (Frazier et al., 2009; Park et al., 2023). Thus, while they do not constitute genuine growth, these perceptions may help people to feel their trauma was less discrepant with their global meaning.

In addition to changing one's global spiritual meaning, meaning-making can result in changes in how one understands or appraises the situation. Aside from the commonly studied meaning made of perceptions that the event led to posttraumatic growth, very little research has examined changes in appraised meanings of a trauma over time. Thus, this aspect of recovery – changes in appraised meaning of the trauma – appears to be an important area for future research. For example, appraisals that a trauma was caused by God or was a sign of God's punishment or abandonment have been shown to be associated with high levels of posttraumatic stress, as reviewed above. Perhaps spiritual meaning-making practices, such as prayer and seeking a closer relationship with God, help individuals, over time, to see the event as less of an intentional punishment. Such a possibility awaits future research.

Limitations to the Research

We mentioned some of the limitations of this research as we reviewed each area of research above. Here, we highlight the most important methodological issues that underlie the lion's share of extant work, setting the scene for our suggestions for future research.

First, as is true of trauma literature more broadly, nearly all of the research in this area has been carried out post-trauma. This lack of pre-trauma baseline data is understandable, given the unpredictable nature of trauma, yet the extent to which this lack of prospective data precludes truly addressing our research questions cannot be overstated. The very nature of trauma is a violent reordering of global meaning (Park et al., 2017), yet most studies, by necessity, assess as "baseline" some point *after* the trauma has occurred.

In addition, although researchers are moving toward longitudinal research to examine the unfolding of recovery processes over time, the bulk of the research remains cross-sectional. This leaves researchers attempting to describe longitudinal processes with data that has all been collected at a single time point, which is simply temporally impossible to model. Further, measurement of different aspects of spirituality and the meaning-making model in the context of trauma has been overly simplistic, especially with the reliance on the Brief RCOPE as the primary assessment tool. Finally, very few studies include critical covariates in their analyses, rendering ruling out competing explanations impossible. Thus, many of the results reviewed here could be due to unexamined covariates (e.g., age, socioeconomic status, and education). Non-significant findings reported could also be due to hidden moderators (e.g., type of trauma, types of spiritual and religious practices, religious denomination, time since trauma, and prior trauma exposure).

Another limitation we must acknowledge is that the dimensions of spirituality included in studies of spiritual meaning-making of trauma have been mostly limited to formal religious variables, especially meaning-making coping, along with existential spirituality, primarily in terms of meaning in life. The studies have seldom included aspects of theistic or existential spiritual global meaning in terms of specific beliefs, theodicies, or goals.

One strength of the corpus of studies reviewed is that it comprises studies conducted from fairly diverse points of view; the studies highlighted in this chapter come from all over the world and represent a wide swath of sociodemographic diversity. Further, these studies include individuals dealing with a wide range of different traumas.

Future Directions for the Science of Spirituality and Making Meaning of Trauma

These findings suggest several avenues for future research. First, prospective longitudinal study designs are ideal for addressing these research questions, aiming to understand the potential protective nature of spirituality in the meaning-making process following trauma. However, because researchers cannot predict trauma exposure, it is logistically challenging to obtain baseline measurements prior to individual traumatic events. The rare prospective studies that exist were typically already collecting data for an existing study before a community trauma occurred (e.g., Hurricane Katrina; Lowe et al., 2013). Another possible methodological approach for future research could be to recruit very large nationally representative samples and follow them over time, knowing that inevitably a significant proportion of the sample will experience a trauma over the course of the study (e.g., Frazier et al., 2009).

Second, measurements of both aspects of spirituality and of the components of the meaning-making model in the context of trauma need to be far more sophisticated and nuanced. Employing more comprehensive measures, such as the Brief Multidimensional Measure of Religion and Spirituality (Fetzer/NIA, 1999) that tap a broader range of dimensions of spirituality, would be informative. Moreover, using measures to empirically assess each aspect of the meaning-making model (Park & George, 2013) could help unpack the role of spirituality in each aspect of the model. For example, violations of meaning can be directly assessed with the Global Meaning Violation Scale (Park et al., 2016). Another advance in this research would be to consider covariates (e.g., income, education, and age) as well as factors that may strengthen or weaken the relationships of spirituality, trauma exposure, and meaning making (e.g., type of trauma, types of spiritual and religious practices, religious denomination, time since trauma, and prior trauma exposure).

Relatedly, although many trauma types were represented throughout this review (e.g., combat, natural disasters, and terrorist attacks), many studies focused on a singular trauma type, which limits the comparisons that can be made across different traumatic experiences. Future studies may choose to include mixed trauma samples in order to make comparisons in meaning-making processes in individuals who experienced different types of trauma. Lastly, it is common for trauma survivors to experience multiple traumatic events over their lifetime (Kilpatrick et al., 2013), and because effects are often cumulative, taking a trauma history into account is critical when assessing meaning-making processes.

Given the limitations of current research, drawing solid conclusions is premature. We are optimistic that future research following these more rigorous practices will better illuminate the potential roles of spirituality in making meaning of trauma.

References

American Psychiatric Association. (2013). *Diagnostic and statistical manual of mental disorders* (5th ed.). American Psychiatric Association.

Ames, D., Erickson, Z., Youssef, N. A., Arnold, I., Adamson, C. S., Sones, A. C., ... & Koenig, H. G. (2019). Moral injury, religiosity, and suicide risk in US veterans and active duty military with PTSD symptoms. *Military Medicine*, *184*(3–4), e271–e278. https://doi.org/10.1093/milmed/usy148

Arkin, M., Lowe, S. R., Poon, C. Y. S., & Rhodes, J. E. (2024). Associations between religious coping and long-term mental health in survivors of Hurricane Katrina. *Psychology of Religion and Spirituality*, *16*(1), 63–71. https://doi.org/10.1037/rel0000483

Aten, J., Bennett, P., Hill, P., Davis, D., & Hook, J. (2012). Predictors of God concept and God control after Hurricane Katrina. *Psychology of Religion and Spirituality*, *4*(3), 182–192. https://doi.org/10.1037/a0027541

Aten, J. D., Smith, W. R., Davis, E. B., Van Tongeren, D. R., Hook, J. N.,... & Hill, P. C. (2019). The psychological study of religion and spirituality in a disaster context: A systematic review. *Psychological Trauma 11*(6), 597–613. https://doi.org/10.1037/tra0000431

Baral, A. I., & Bhagawati, K. C. (2019). Posttraumatic stress disorder and coping strategies among adult survivors of earthquake, Nepal. *BMC Psychiatry*, *19*, 118. https://doi.org/10.1186/s12888-019-2090-y

Benjet, C., Bromet, E., Karam, E. G., Kessler, R. C., McLaughlin, P., ... Koenen, K. C. (2016). The epidemiology of traumatic event exposure worldwide: Results from the World Mental Health Survey Consortium. *Psychological Medicine*, *46*(2), 327–343. https://doi.org/10.1017/S0033291715001981

Berzengi, A., Berzenji, L., Kadim, A., Mustafa, F., & Jobson, L. (2017). Role of Islamic appraisals, trauma-related appraisals, and religious coping in the posttraumatic adjustment of Muslim trauma survivors. *Psychological Trauma*, *9*(2), 189–197. http://doi.org/10.1037/tra0000179

Blanc, J., Rahill, G. J., Laconi, S., & Mouchenik, Y. (2016). Religious beliefs, PTSD, depression and resilience in survivors of the 2010 Haiti earthquake. *Journal of Affective Disorders*, *190*, 697–703. https://doi.org/10.1016/j.jad.2015.10.046

Brown, L. A., Belli, G. M., Asnaani, A., & Foa, E. B. (2019). A review of the role of negative cognitions about oneself, others, and the world in the treatment of PTSD. *Cognitive Therapy and Research*, *43*, 143–173. https://doi.org/10.1007/s10608-018-9938-1

Bryant-Davis, T., Ullman, S., Tsong, Y., Anderson, G., Counts, P., Tillman, S., ... & Gray, A. (2015). Healing pathways: Longitudinal effects of religious coping and social support on PTSD symptoms in African American sexual assault survivors. *Journal of Trauma & Dissociation*, *16*(1), 114–128. https://doi.org/10.1080/15299732.2014.969468

Chen, Z. J., Bechara, A. O., Worthington Jr, E. L., Davis, E. B., & Csikszentmihalyi, M. (2021). Trauma and well-being in Colombian disaster contexts: Effects of religious coping, forgivingness, and hope. *The Journal of Positive Psychology*, *16*(1), 82–93. https://doi.org/10.1080/17439760.2019.1663254

Cherry, K. E., De Vito, A. N., Calamia, M. R., Elliott, E. M., Yu, S., Sampson, L.,...& Nguyen, Q. P. (2021). Disaster stressors and psychological well-being in older adults after a flood. *Psychology and Aging*, *36*(5), 660–666. https://doi.org/10.1037/pag0000602

Cornish, M. A., Lannin, D. G., Wade, N. G., & Martinez, M. (2017). Can use of positive religious coping predict greater distress? An examination of Army soldiers on deployment. *Journal of Counseling Psychology*, *64*(3), 302–310. https://doi.org/10.1037/cou0000200

Currier, J. M., Manalo, M., & McDermott, R. C. (2023). Examining the unique role of premilitary religious commitment in posttraumatic symptomatology among post-9/11 veterans. *Traumatology*, *29*(1), 1–5. https://doi.org/10.1037/trm0000361

Emmons, R. A. (2003). Personal goals, life meaning, and virtue: Wellsprings of a positive life. In C. L. M. Keyes & J. Haidt (Eds.), *Flourishing: Positive psychology and the life well-lived* (pp. 105–128). American Psychological Association.

Emmons, R. A., Cheung, C., & Tehrani, K. (1998). Assessing spirituality through personal goals: Implications for research on religion and subjective well-being. *Social Indicators Research*, *45*, 391–422. https://doi.org/10.1023/A:1006926720976

Feder, A., Ahmad, S., Lee, E. J., Morgan, J. E., Singh, R., Smith, B. W.,... Charney, D. S. (2013). Coping and PTSD symptoms in Pakistani earthquake survivors: Purpose in life, religious coping and social support. *Journal of Affective Disorders*, *147*, 156–163. https://doi.org/10.1016/j.jad.2012.10.027

Fetzer Institute & National Institute on Aging Working Group. (1999). *Multidimensional measurement of religiousness/spirituality for use in health research*. Fetzer Institute.

Fincham, F. D., & May, R. W. (2021). Divine forgiveness protects against psychological distress following a natural disaster attributed to God. *The Journal of Positive Psychology*, *16*(1), 20–26. https://doi.org/10.1080/17439760.2019.1689411

Fischer, I. C., Shanahan, M. L., Hirsh, A. T., Stewart, J. C., & Rand, K. L. (2020). The relationship between meaning in life and post-traumatic stress symptoms in US military personnel: A meta-analysis. *Journal of Affective Disorders*, *277*, 658–670. https://doi.org/10.1016/j.jad.2020.08.063

Frazier, P., Tennen, H., Gavian, M., Park, C., Tomich, P., & Tashiro, T. (2009). Does self-reported posttraumatic growth reflect genuine positive change? *Psychological Science*, *20*(7), 912–919. https://doi.org/10.1111/j.1467-9280.2009.02381.x

George, L. S., & Park, C. L. (2016). Meaning in life as comprehension, purpose, and mattering. *Review of General Psychology*, *20*, 205–220. https://doi.org/10.1037/gpr0000077

Gerber, M. M., Boals, A., & Schuettler, D. (2011). The unique contributions of positive and negative religious coping to posttraumatic growth and PTSD. *Psychology of Religion and Spirituality*, *3*(4), 298. https://doi.org/10.1037/a0023016

Grey, I., Thomas, J., Mansour Jamaleddine, J., Yaktine, T., & Cheung, C. M. (2023 online first). Religious coping and levels of posttraumatic stress disorder symptomatology after the Beirut explosion. *Psychological Trauma: Theory, Research, Practice, and Policy*, *16*(1), 39–48. https://doi.org/10.1037/tra0001529

Hardy, S. A., Nadal, A. R., & Schwartz, S. J. (2017). The integration of personal identity, religious identity, and moral identity in emerging adulthood. *Identity*, *17*(2), 96–107. https://doi.org/10.1080/15283488.2017.1305905

Hayes, A. M., Yasinski, C., Grasso, D., Ready, C. B., Alpert, E., McCauley, T., ... & Deblinger, E. (2017). Constructive and unproductive processing of traumatic experiences in trauma-focused cognitive-behavioral therapy for youth. *Behavior Therapy*, *48*(2), 166–181. https://doi.org/10.1016/j.beth.2016.06.004

Haynes, W. C., Van Tongeren, D. R., Aten, J., Davis, E. B., Davis, D. E., Hook, J. N., Boan, D., & Johnson, T. (2017). The meaning as a buffer hypothesis: Spiritual meaning attenuates the effect of disaster-related resource loss on posttraumatic stress. *Psychology of Religion and Spirituality*, *9*(4), 446–453. http://doi.org/10.1037/rel0000098

Henslee, A. M., Coffey, S. F., Schumacher, J. A., Tracy, M., Norris, F. H., & Galea, S. (2015). Religious coping and psychological and behavioral adjustment after Hurricane Katrina. *The Journal of Psychology*, *149*, 630–642. https://doi.org/10.1080/00223980.2014.953441

Kilpatrick, D. G., Resnick, H. S., Milanak, M. E., Miller, M. W., Keyes, K. M., & Friedman, M. J. (2013). National estimates of exposure to traumatic events and PTSD prevalence using DSM-IV and DSM-5 criteria. *Journal of Traumatic Stress*, *26*(5), 537–547. https://doi.org/10.1002/jts.21848

Koenig, H. G., Youssef, N. A., Ames, D., Oliver, R. J. P., Volk, F., Teng, E. J., & Hill, T. D. (2019). Dimensions of religiosity and PTSD symptom clusters in US veterans and active duty military. *Journal of Religion and Health*, *58*, 805–822. https://doi.org/10.1007/s10943-019-00817-7

Kucharska, J. (2020). Religiosity and the psychological outcomes of trauma: A systematic review of quantitative studies. *Journal of Clinical Psychology*, *76*(1), 40–58. https://doi.org/10.1002/jclp.22867

Lazarus, R. S., & Folkman, S. (1984). *Stress, appraisal, and coping*. Springer.

Lehmann, C., & Steele, E. (2020). Going beyond positive and negative: Clarifying relationships of specific religious coping styles with posttraumatic outcomes. *Psychology of Religion and Spirituality*, *12*(3), 345–355. http://doi.org/10.1037/rel0000310

Leo, D., Izadikhah, Z., Fein, E. C., & Forooshani, S. A. (2021). The effect of trauma on religious beliefs: A structured literature review and meta-analysis. *Trauma, Violence, & Abuse*, *22*(1), 161–175. https://doi.org/10.1177/1524838019834076

Lerner, M. J., & Miller, D. T. (1978). Just world research and the attribution process: Looking back and ahead. *Psychological Bulletin*, *85*(5), 1030–1051. https://doi.org/10.1037/0033-2909.85.5.1030

Lilly, M. M., Valdez, C. E., & Graham-Bermann, S. A. (2011). The mediating effect of world assumptions on the relationship between trauma exposure and depression. *Journal of Interpersonal Violence*, *26*(12), 2499–2516. https://doi.org/10.1177/0886260510383033

Lowe, S. R., Manove, E. E., & Rhodes, J. E. (2013). Posttraumatic stress and posttraumatic growth among low-income mothers who survived Hurricane Katrina. *Journal of Consulting and Clinical Psychology*, *81*(5), 877–889. http://doi.org/10.1037/a0033252

McElroy-Heltzel, S. E., Davis, E. B., Davis, D. E., Aten, J. D., Van Tongeren, D. R., Hook, J. N., & Hwang, J. (2018). Benevolent theodicies protect against PTSD following a natural disaster. *Journal of Psychology & Christianity*, *37*(1), 6–16.

Mesidor, J. K., & Sly, K. F. (2019). Religious coping, general coping strategies, perceived social support, PTSD symptoms, resilience, and posttraumatic growth among survivors of the 2010 earthquake in Haiti. *Mental Health, Religion & Culture*, *22*(2), 130–143. https://doi.org/10.1080/13674676.2019.1580254

Morse, J. L., Wooldridge, J. S., Afari, N., Angkaw, A. C., Schnurr, P. P., Lang, A. J., Capone, C., & Norman, S. B. (2024). Associations among meaning in life, coping, and distress in trauma-exposed U.S. military veterans. *Psychological Services*, *21*(2), 247–253. https://doi.org/10.1037/ser0000755

Newton, T., & McIntosh, D. N. (2013). Unique contributions of religion to meaning. In J. A. Hicks & C. Routledge (Eds.), *The experience of meaning in life: Classical perspectives, emerging themes, and controversies* (pp. 257–269). Dordrecht: Springer Netherlands.

Pargament, K., Feuille, M., & Burdzy, D. (2011). The Brief RCOPE: Current psychometric status of a short measure of religious coping. *Religions*, *2*(1), 51–76. https://doi.org/10.3390/rel2010051

Park, C. L. (2010). Making sense of the meaning literature: An integrative review of meaning making and its effects on adjustment to stressful life events. *Psychological Bulletin*, *136*(2), 257–301. https://doi.org/10.1037/a0018301

Park, C. L. (2013). Religion and meaning. In R. F. Paloutzian & C. L. Park (Eds.), *Handbook of the psychology of religion and spirituality*, 2nd Edition (pp. 357–379). Guilford.

Park, C. L. (2017). Distinctions to promote an integrated perspective on meaning: Global meaning and meaning-making processes. *Journal of Constructivist Psychology*, *30*(1), 14–19. https://doi.org/10.1080/10720537.2015.1119082

Park, C. L. & Blake, E. B. (2020). Resilience and recovery following disasters: The meaning making model (pp. 9–25). In S. E. Schulenberg (Ed.), *Positive psychological approaches to disaster: Meaning, resilience, and posttraumatic growth*. Springer.

Park, C. L., & George, L. S. (2013). Assessing meaning and meaning making in the context of stressful life events: Measurement tools and approaches. *The Journal of Positive Psychology*, *8*(6), 483–504. https://doi.org/10.1080/17439760.2013.830762

Park, C. L., Riley, K. E., George, L., Gutierrez, I., Hale, A., Cho, D., & Braun, T. (2016). Assessing disruptions in meaning: Development of the Global Meaning Violation Scale. *Cognitive Therapy and Research*, *40*, 831–846. https://doi.org/10.1007/s10608-016-9794-9

Park, C. L., Currier, J. M., Harris, J. I., & Slattery, J. M. (2017). *Trauma, meaning, and spirituality: Translating research into clinical practice*. American Psychological Association.

Park, C. L., Wilt, J., Russell, B. S., & Fendrich, M. (2023). Does perceived post-traumatic growth during the Covid-19 pandemic reflect actual positive changes? *Anxiety, Stress, & Coping*, *36*(6), 661–673. https://doi.org/10.1080/10615806.2022.2157821

Rosansky, J. A., Cook, J., Rosenberg, H., & Sprague, J. E. (2019). PTSD symptoms experienced and coping tactics used by crime scene investigators in the United States. *Journal of Forensic Sciences*, *64*(5), 1444–1450. https://doi.org/10.1111/1556-4029.14044

Seirmarco, G., Neria, Y., Insel, B., Kiper, D., Doruk, A., Gross, R., & Litz, B. (2012). Religiosity and mental health: Changes in religious beliefs, complicated grief, posttraumatic stress disorder, and major depression following the September 11, 2001 attacks. *Psychology of Religion and Spirituality*, *4*(1), 10–18. https://doi.org/10.1037/a0023479

Shannonhouse, L. R., Bialo, J. A., Majuta, A. R., Zeligman, M. R.,…& Hook, J. N. (2019). Conserving resources during chronic disaster: Impacts of religious and meaning-focused coping on Botswana drought survivors. *Psychological Trauma: Theory, Research, Practice, and Policy*, *11*(2), 137–146. http://doi.org/10.1037/tra0000420

Sinnott, S., Park, C. L., George, J., Gnall, K., & David, A. B. (2024). Use of religious and spiritual responses after trauma to prevent posttraumatic stress symptoms and suicidality: The role of meaning in life. *Clinical Psychology & Psychotherapy*, *31*(1), e2902. https://doi.org/10.1002/cpp.2902

Stratta, P., Capanna, C., Riccardi, I., Carmassi, C., Piccinni, A., Dell'Osso, L., & Rossi, A. (2012). Suicidal intention and negative spiritual coping one year after the earthquake of L'Aquila (Italy). *Journal of Affective Disorders*, *136*(3), 1227–1231. https://doi.org/10.1016/j.jad.2011.10.006

Stratta, P., Capanna, C., Riccardi, I., Perugi, G., Toni, C., Dell'Osso, L., & Rossi, A. (2013). Spirituality and religiosity in the aftermath of a natural catastrophe in Italy. *Journal of Religion and Health*, *52*, 1029–1037. https://doi.org/10.1007/s10943-012-9591-z

Sujadi, E., Meditamar, M. O., Fadhli, M., Ahmad, J., Bustami, Y., & Indra, S. (2023). Posttraumatic stress disorder among sexual harassment victims: The role of social support, resilience, and religious coping. *International Journal of Public Health Science*, *12*(2), 846–858. https://doi.org/10.11591/ijphs.v12i2.21952

ter Kuile, H., & Ehring, T. (2014). Predictors of changes in religiosity after trauma: Trauma, religiosity, and posttraumatic stress disorder. *Psychological Trauma: Theory, Research, Practice, and Policy*, *6*(4), 353–360. https://doi.org/10.1037/a0034880

Theisen-Womersley, G. (2021). Culturally informed manifestations of trauma. In G. Theisen-Womersley (Ed.), *Trauma and resilience among displaced populations: A sociocultural exploration* (pp. 113–146). Springer.

Thombre, A., Sherman, A. C., & Simonton, S. (2010). Religious coping and posttraumatic growth among family caregivers of cancer patients in India. *Journal of Psychosocial Oncology*, *28*(2), 173–188. https://doi.org/10.1080/07347330903570537

Walker, H. E., Wamser-Nanney, R., & Howell, K. H. (2022). Relationships between childhood interpersonal trauma, religious coping, post-traumatic stress symptoms, and resilience. *Journal of Interpersonal Violence*, *37*(13–14), NP11296–NP11314. https://doi.org/10.1177/0886260521991883

Webb, J. R., Toussaint, L. L., & Dula, C. S. (2014). Ritualistic, theistic, and existential spirituality: Initial psychometric qualities of the RiTE measure of spirituality. *Journal of Religion & Health*, *53*(4), 972–985. https://doi.org/10.1007/s10943-013-9697-y

Wood, Z. B., Wang, D. C., Lee, C., Barnes, H., Abouezzeddine… & Aten, J. (2021). Social support, religious coping, and traumatic stress among Hurricane Katrina survivors of southern Mississippi: A sequential mediational model. *Traumatology*, *27*(4), 336–345. https://doi.org/10.1037/trm0000328

Part IV

Predictors, Interventions, and Clinical Perspectives

Chapter 20

Addressing Spirituality in Treatment-Related Settings

Big Picture Issues

*Edward P. Shafranske**

How should healthcare professionals respond to the psychological suffering of their patients, particularly those for whom spirituality plays a role in their lives? How might clinicians enter their clients' unique systems of meaning, catalyze their personal strengths, and marshal social, institutional, and spiritual supports? What religious or spiritual resources might be available to combat a patient's demoralization, anxiety, or depression? More simply, how can mental health professionals help facilitate processes of healing to promote therapeutic change, mental health, and well-being?

This chapter aims to answer these questions by presenting the *big picture issues* that inform the provision of psychological care that explicitly considers patients' or clients' religious and spiritual (R/S) dimensions.[1] These issues include (1) the medical or healthcare framework in which processes of healing, including psychological treatment, are situated; (2) the unique role of R/S in meaning-making, coping, and psychological health; (3) the associations between R/S and mental health; (4) a framework for incorporating spirituality into psychological treatment; (5) the essentials of practice when integrating R/S in treatment, including best practices in interviewing, assessment, and the use of spiritually informed therapy approaches and interventions; (6) ethics and professionalism; and (7) professional readiness, education, and clinical training in the provision of spiritually responsive care.

The following discussion draws upon a substantial body of literature that comprises the applied psychology of religion and spirituality.[2] This review offers theory and the findings of science-informed research that examines the relationships between R/S and mental health, provides an orientation to clinical practice, and proposes guidelines for integrating R/S in psychological treatment. The aim of this review is to present current clinical approaches to advance best practices for addressing spirituality in psychological treatment.

An expansive framework is proposed, based on evidence-based practice, that includes differing levels of R/S integration based on presenting problems, client preferences, and therapist expertise. The discussion includes the essential issues psychologists, other mental health professionals, and the professions themselves face when integrating R/S in treatment, including developing an understanding of trends in contemporary expressions of R/S, approaches to interviewing and assessment, incorporating spiritually informed clinical approaches (including interventions and resources), enhancing coping, addressing spiritual struggles, and safeguarding the patient through ethical practice. We conclude by considering the present status of clinical competence and offering recommendations for graduate education, training, and approaches to continuous professional development. The chapter is oriented toward examining general principles and professional practices, which should be tailored to the uniqueness of each clinical relationship.

* Corresponding Author: edward.shafranske@pepperdine.edu.

DOI: 10.4324/9781003440048-24

For many clients, religion, broadly conceived (James, 1902/1982), plays a role in their lives, contributes to their health, combats disillusionment, and enhances flourishing (Davis et al., 2023). In some cases, R/S is their centerpiece, in which spiritual beliefs, values, affiliations, and practices directly influence their actions. For others, spirituality plays a lesser role or is seemingly absent or dormant, only coming to the fore when evoked by personal hardships, medical challenges, or traumatic events. Incorporating R/S in healthcare can be delicate, requiring knowledge, skill, tact, a clear sense of ethics and professional boundaries, and, most importantly, deep respect for the client's autonomy and well-being. The questions opening this chapter can only be answered by the clinician's keen attention to their client's unique religiosity, spirituality, or the absence of a transcendent spiritual dimension. Including R/S in psychological treatment is fostered by a commitment to understand, as best they can, the client's subjective experience and worldview, including their conceptions and experiences of what is considered personally sacred or transcendent realities and faith commitments. Through an intentional approach, healthcare providers can offer an integrative, holistic view of health and facilitate processes of healing that routinely incorporate R/S in treatment.

A Comprehensive Framework

Throughout history, the provision of healthcare has been influenced by the cultural, philosophical, and scientific understanding of the time. A through-line of common elements in psychological healing has been identified.[3] Approaches to ameliorate suffering are inevitably culture-bound and orient how suffering is understood and treated (American Psychiatric Association, 2013; American Psychological Association, 2017a), including determining and delimiting the relevance of spirituality (see also Chapter 3 of this volume). During much of the 20th century, medicine operated within the biomedical paradigm, influenced by the Cartesian framework of mind-body. The assumption of a fundamental schism between the mind and body led to a materialistic reductionism in which other factors were excluded or minimized. Further, as Foucault (1994/1963) observed, the "medical gaze" became oriented to physical symptoms and disease mechanisms, abandoning the relational connection between physician and patient and considerations of meaning.[4]

While advances were made, evidence accumulated regarding the impacts of non-physical co-determinants on disease processes, and the prevailing biomedical model was challenged. George L. Engel (1977), a prominent figure in medicine, asserted, "all three levels, biological, psychological, and social, must be taken into account in every health care task" (p. 164). The introduction of the biopsychosocial model (Engel, 1977) marked a dramatic shift – "science itself was evolving from an exclusively analytic, reductionistic, and specialized endeavor to become more contextual and cross-disciplinary" (Borrell-Carrió et al., 2004, p. 1). Although not without its critics (Ghaemi, 2009), this change brought greater attention to the individual patient's subjective experience, for example, a shift of focus from a circumscribed experience of physical or psychological pain to a broadened sensitivity of the experience of suffering. This emphasis acknowledged that, for patients, suffering is complex, and they do not distinguish physical and non-physical sources of suffering in the same way that physicians do (Cassell, 1988). The new model invoked innovations in "patient-centered, relationship-centered care" (Borrell-Carrió, p. 4) and reinforced the need to "expand the domain of medical knowledge to address the needs of each patient" (p. 5). Attention to the conceptual foundations in medicine and health service psychology is required when making efforts to incorporate a patient's subjective, meaning-making experiences of psychological suffering (Verhagen, 2017).

To illustrate, when medication is used for the treatment of depression, it provides not only a biochemical agent, but the physician *prescribes meanings* for the patient's suffering (Pais Silva Guerra, 2021; Suijker, 2023). However, experiences of mental illness extend beyond the manualized diagnostic assessments of depression and a reductionistic understanding of neurotransmitters. And for some patients, their experiences and root causes of their suffering are not found in the narrowly focused medical nomenclature. Patient-centered care acknowledges the patient as the 'meaning-creating'" subject of their experience (Shafranske, 1997) in which spirituality plays a role (Kheriaty & Cihak, 2012; Rosmarin & Koenig, 2020) and supports the relational dimensions in healing (Sandange et al., 2020).

Introducing R/S into psychological therapeutics and healthcare reflects the expanded understanding that was initiated by the adoption of the biopsychosocial model. However, that paradigm has its own self-defined limits, and a full consideration of spirituality in treatment stretches the model's ontological, philosophical, and clinical boundaries. Are we on the cusp of another paradigmatic development, another expansion of the domains of knowledge, and the evolution of clinical practice? And are we ready to adopt a model that explicitly integrates spirituality in healthcare? The answers are complex.

The proposed biopsychosocial-spiritual model acknowledges spirituality to be a dimension of human experience that, for many people, plays a crucial role in their lives and contributes in unique ways to health and healing. It places value on the patient's subjective experience and expands the "disease causative framework to a more comprehensive model" (Saad et al., 2017, pp. 1–2). Such an expansion of the biopsychosocial model is justified by the body of empirical evidence establishing significant, although complex and at times contradictory, associations between R/S and health (see Part III of this volume; Masters et al., 2023) and mental health (Koenig, 2018; Shafranske, 2023).

The adoption of the biopsychosocial-spiritual model would have far-reaching impacts and would be "perhaps the boldest model yet" (Jones, 1994), in which a constructive relationship between science and the profession of psychology would mature. It would highlight how science and our professional practices are infused with metaphysical assumptions (O'Donohue, 1989) and beliefs, and perhaps find a place for transcendence. It would allow for consideration that science and religion are each a valid source of knowledge and human understanding (Jones, 1981). Theory-building and study would continue of the nonmaterial factors influencing human life, including spirituality in its varied forms, expressions, and effects. Consideration of spiritually informed psychology and applied practices would not be in opposition to traditional positivistic modes of scientific study or their application. As Miller (2012) put it, "post-materialist spiritual psychology can live alongside and cross-fertilize work conducted from a materialist perspective; the two are not exclusive, and both are true" (p. 2). An overarching framework can be envisioned in which multiple factors affecting health and psychological treatment may be considered. Theorizing across ontological and interdisciplinary lines provides opportunities to better understand complex interactions rather than positing isolated causalities.

Writing about the biopsychosocial model, Bolton and Gillett (2019) suggest that the evolution of life ends up with human psychological and social phenomena, and these phenomena have lives of their own; although, "they can bump into one another and affect one another, that they, causally interact, as opposed to being in parallel universes" (pp. 34–35). Their approach may usefully be applied in our discussion – spirituality and religion also have lives of their own and similarly interact in meaningful ways with other biopsychosocial factors influencing health and healing. Returning to the discussion of depression, allowing "space" for consideration of the spiritual aspects of depression does not refute biochemical explanations but expands understanding. Addressing spirituality in clinical settings goes beyond a formulaic use of a religious- or spiritual-accommodative intervention or appropriation of an approach. As discussed in this section, the integration of R/S in health involves a major shift in the medical or healthcare paradigm, which informs the ways in which health professionals, including mental health professionals, view health, illness, and psychological healing.

Religion, Spirituality, and Meaning Making in Mental Health

Humans appear "to possess a general need for a well-functioning meaning system" (Park et al., 2013, p. 159), and "the quest for meaning is a key part of what makes us human, and uniquely so" (Baumeister et al., 2013). Finding out what really matters in life and holding onto it, particularly in the face of adversity, contributes to well-being and mental health (Pargament, 2007; Shafranske, 2023). Meaning systems serve several constructive and adaptive functions (Park et al., 2013; see also Chapter 19 of this volume), including:

- Provide a cognitive structure that helps make sense of the world by organizing experience into a cohesive worldview.
- Provide a sense of mastery or control over one's future and life circumstances.
- Provide meaning to eliminate or manage distressing feelings of uncertainty.
- Maintain a sense of identity or self-concept.
- Provide satisfactory answers to questions of identity and existence; and
- Provide goals that are essential for providing an overarching purpose and direction to one's life, including values.

Meaning contributes to managing and ordering the complexity that life presents to us as sentient and social beings (Peterson, 2013). Ascendant among the meanings people construct is their sense of "meaning in life," which is conceptualized as a unique and positive subjective and emotional experience (King & Hicks, 2021). It is associated with important positive life outcomes, and "those who report a high sense of meaning in life appear to be better off than others" (p. 564). Overarching purpose, which is a component of meaning in life, serves as "a central, self-organizing life aim that organizes and stimulates goals, manages behaviors, and provides a sense of meaning" (McKnight & Kashdan, 2009, p. 242). Enough good things cannot be said about having and successfully maintaining meaning in life.

Religion meets the need for a meaning system and, for some people, serves an essential role for "maintaining a coherent, organized view of the world and themselves and a clear sense of where they are going and why" (Park et al., 2013, p. 160; Park, 2005). R/S systems of meaning answer the fundamental questions that science cannot. Science, the penultimate expression of positivism, furnishes knowledge about material things and processes, but, as Smith (2001) observed, "on existential and global meanings it is silent" (p. 198). R/S beliefs and values translate global meaning into goals that shape daily life and sustain meaning throughout. Further, religion provides a reliable meaning system in stressful circumstances and furnishes religious attributions that offer comfort and buttress personal meaning (Park et al., 2013).

Religion, particularly in its institutional forms, furnishes broad-based conceptions and explanations that provide a sense of how the world works (Koltko-Rivera, 2004), furnishes guidance as to how to live, and "tells us what goals to have in the grand scheme" (King & Hicks, 2021, p. 572). In addition to beliefs, values, moral teachings, rituals, etc., religion provides the grand meta-narratives that link the believer to the transcendent and provide depictions of ultimate meaning (Rizzuto, 2005; Rizzuto & Shafranske, 2013). These "culturally accepted leitmotifs and symbols promote personal signification" (Shafranske, 2002, p. 228) within a setting of shared human purpose and virtuous living (Shafranske, 2009, 2023).

Further, R/S has the power to evoke powerful emotional experiences (Geertz, 1966/1973) that have the potential to contribute to well-being (Fredrickson, 2002) and set in motion an upward spiral of positive experience (Van Cappellen et al., 2021; Wormley et al., 2025). Such experiences support mental health and reciprocally reinforce engagement in meaning-making.

Whereas religion may be defined as "a search for significance that occurs within the context of established institutions that are designed to facilitate spirituality," spirituality constitutes the fundamental "search for the sacred" (Pargament, 2013, pp. 257–258; see also Hill et al., 2000). Spirituality is usually highly individualistic, with very limited or no engagement with institutional religion. Although the appearances in expression appear dissimilar, Pargament et al. (2013) proposed that spirituality and religion are interrelated rather than isolated (see also Hill et al., 2000; Zinnbauer et al., 1999).

> People do not follow their religious and spiritual paths in isolation. They undertake their journeys within a larger field of social and cultural forces, including religious group, age, ethnicity, family, community, and culture. These forces shape the nature of the individual's religious and spiritual trek over the life span.
>
> (Pargament et al., 2013, p. 6)

Religion and spirituality are complex, multi-leveled phenomena that involve multiple dimensions (Pargament, 2013; Pargament et al., 2013) and provide pathways to meaning – pathways that may contribute to well-being. Webb (2014) proposed the RiTE model of spirituality, which set aside the conundrum of differentiating between individual religiosity and spirituality and identified three aspects – *ritualistic spirituality*, *theistic spirituality*, and *existential spirituality* (Webb, 2021; see also Chapters 1 and 44 of this volume). *Ritualistic spirituality* includes a structured connection with a deity, *theistic spirituality* involves a non-structured connection to a deity, and *existential spirituality* refers to a transcendent, yet non-theistic search for meaning and purpose. *Existential spirituality* contributes directly to our discussion of meaning. Each form of spirituality contributes to the search for meaning; however, *existential spirituality* is independent of ritualistic and theistic spirituality. This approach connects spirituality to the body of theoretical and empirical work on meaning-making. We turn briefly to consideration of R/S involvement in which the construction of meaning may take root and be nourished.

Meaning-Making and R/S Coping

Meaning-making and coping are intrinsically linked. Park and Folkman (1997) referred to "meaning making as coping" (p. 124), in which the impacts of stressful events are addressed by the search for meaning (or cognitive appraisals of the situation). The meaning-making process "is considered successful when people achieve reconciliation either by changing the appraised meaning of the situation to assimilate it into preexisting global meaning, or by changing their beliefs or goals to accommodate the event" (p. 124). Viewed from the perspective of the transactional model of stress-and-coping (Lazarus & Folkman, 1984),

R/S provides pathways in which beliefs, activities, rituals, and affiliations with others contribute to coping (Gall & Guirguis-Younger, 2013). Nonreligious coping methods indeed work; what then are the unique features of R/S coping? Pargament (1997) addressed the distinctive contributions of religion to the coping process:[5]

> … religion offers a response to the problem of human insufficiency. Try as we might to maximize significance through our own insights and experiences or those of others, we remain human, finite, and limited. At any time we may be pushed beyond our immediate resources, exposing our basic vulnerability to ourselves and the world. To this most basic of existential crises, religion holds out solutions.
>
> (p. 310)

Implications for Treatment

The recognition of the importance of meaning in life to well-being and, second, the finding that religion, broadly considered, is positively related to meaning in life (King & Hicks, 2021) constitute one of the big issues on which the applied psychology of R/S stands. Clinical work can be enhanced by recognizing the role that religion and spirituality play by providing individual- and community-based pathways to establish and sustain meaning and foster the development of a coherent set of purposeful goals that are integral to well-being. Further, R/S offer pathways for coping with stressful events, particularly in those situations in which clients have limited control of the outcomes. Also, clinicians should be attuned to threats to meaning that may underlie presenting problems and contribute to the psychological symptoms patients are experiencing. Problems of meaning are often associated with trauma and the development of PTSD (Janoff-Bulman, 1992); however, other life events can pose threats to a person's sense of meaning. For example, the impacts of loss of a job or a special relationship may be expressed in anxieties about financial security or the challenges of finding another position or relationship. These manifest concerns are, of course, legitimate in themselves, but their presentation may mask threats to personal meaning or erode confidence in or participation in religion or spirituality. Each of which requires clinical attention.

Religion, Spirituality, and Mental Health

The associations between religion, spirituality, and mental health have been extensively studied (e.g., over 11,000 journal articles over the past 20 years), and their findings highlight the importance of addressing spirituality in treatment (Koenig, 2018; Koenig et al., 2012; Rosmarin & Koenig, 2020). The findings of a recent review of systematic reviews and meta-analyses conducted over the past 20 years showed modest but significant associations between R/S and better mental health (Shafranske, 2023). Consistent with past reviews of the empirical literature, "*on the balance*, it appears that religious beliefs and practices rooted within established religious traditions are generally associated with better mental health, higher social functioning, and fewer self-destructive tendencies" (emphasis in original; Koenig & Larson, 2001, p. 72). A comprehensive review of this literature is beyond the scope of this chapter; however, the following summary presents the major findings regarding depression, anxiety, and trauma-related disorders (drawn from Koenig, 2018; Koenig, King, & Carson, 2012, Rosmarin & Koenig, 2020; and Shafranske, 2023). See Parts III and IV of this volume for detailed reviews of various aspects of the association of R/S with health and well-being.

Mood Disorders

Most empirical studies have found positive effects of R/S on mood disorders, including a lower likelihood of developing depression, lower depression, and faster remission among more religious individuals; however, these associations are modest, and a large proportion of the studies showed no association. Therefore, R/S does not universally predict salutary outcomes. "The effects of R/S on depression may depend on what kind of depression, what kind of religion, what kind of individual, and what kind of situation the individual is in" (Koenig, King, & Carson, 2012, p. 173).

Anxiety Disorders

Associations between anxiety and R/S are complex, and findings are mixed; however, recent prospective research finds that "R/S may buffer against anxiety symptoms or increase treatment response" (Koenig, 2018, p. 89). In sum, the mixed associations are based on differences between positive R/S beliefs and personal orientation/relationship with a benevolent God versus negative mindsets and mistrust in God, which accentuate stress and anxiety.

Trauma-Related Disorders

The consequences of trauma exposure are multifaceted and unique to each person, and recovery is complex. For many trauma survivors, religious coping is used to find meaning, gain mastery and control, feel comfort from God, nurture intimacy with God and others, and, for some, experience life transformation (Pargament et al., 2013; Park et al., 2017; see also Chapter 19 of this volume). Religious/spiritual involvement has generally been found to be associated with better mental health outcomes following trauma and adversity. However, this is not always the case. For some people, trauma exposure can negatively impact R/S and weaken the potentially positive benefits of R/S. Also, most people do not change their R/S beliefs after trauma exposure, but significant changes can occur, either in increasing or decreasing religious beliefs and practices.

Acquiring familiarity with the literature regarding the associations between R/S and mental health, including the use of R/S interventions and resources in psychological treatment, prepares clinicians to bring the full complement of resources to address a patient's suffering. Understanding the scientific evidence is important since it addresses and may correct any overly positive, negative, or simplistic assumptions about the impacts of R/S involvement. Close inspection of this literature reveals the complexity within these associations and reveals the significant challenges in conducting research that aims to establish causal relationships between R/S beliefs, practices, and psychological health (see Koenig, 2018, and Koenig et al., 2012, for discussions of the methodological challenges). Much of the research on religion relies on forms of institutional participation as measures of R/S involvement; however, these indicators do not fully capture the extent to which R/S is integrated into daily life. Similarly, difficulties abound in operationalizing and measuring spirituality, which, by its nature, is highly idiosyncratic, and, in Koenig's assessment (2018), has "become a nebulous and poorly defined term that is of little use when conducting research (because of overlapping definitions with mental health)" (p. 311). Research programs examining R/S in terms of depth of commitment and integration both during and absent times of distress would better assess the associations with mental health and well-being.

A Framework for Incorporating Spirituality into Psychological Treatment

A review of the literature finds that formal standards of practice do not exist for incorporating spirituality into psychological treatment.[6] Professional associations, such as the American Psychological Association, commonly address R/S as multicultural features (2017a); however, they do not provide established standards or offer specific guidance about the means of integrating spirituality into treatment.[7] The following components are proposed to establish a framework for practice:

- An evidence-based approach to professional practice establishes the essential features of a clinical approach through which spirituality may be addressed in treatment. It builds upon knowledge from the psychology of religion and spirituality, highlights the importance of clinical expertise, and identifies and situates R/S as salient multicultural features and prioritizes patient preferences (Shafranske, 2013).
- Guidelines and competencies establish the overarching aims of the integration framework and identify the requisite knowledge, skills, and attitudes that prepare clinicians to address spirituality in psychological treatment.
- A comprehensive model that describes a range of approaches that may address R/S in healthcare, including integrative and stand-alone approaches to spirituality-informed psychological treatments.

An Evidence-Based Framework

With the adoption in 2005 of evidence-based professional practice as the standard in professional practice (American Psychological Association, APA Presidential Task Force on Evidence-Based Practice, 2006), psychologists are duty-bound to integrate the "*best available research* with *clinical expertise* in the context of *patient characteristics, culture, and preferences*" [emphasis added] (p. 273). While these *Guidelines* only apply to psychologists, they provide a useful starting point for developing a framework for incorporating spirituality into psychological treatment, no matter one's professional affiliation.

Best Available Research

The research base incorporates contributions from the applied psychology of religion and spirituality. This literature includes the psychology of meaning-making, religious coping, empirical research on the associations of R/S and mental health and treatment, the theory and demographics of contemporary expressions of R/S, and approaches to R/S interventions, including empirically supported, evidence-based approaches to religious accommodative psychotherapies.

Clinical Expertise

Clinical competence is required to ethically provide psychological services that integrate R/S into professional practice. Advances in graduate education and clinical training are necessary to support the development of expertise in the applied psychology of R/S in the curriculum, clinical training, clinical supervision, and consultation. A competency-based model identifies the knowledge, skills, and attitudes that ensure readiness to address R/S in psychological treatment.

Patient Characteristics, Culture, and Preferences

This guideline highlights the necessity for psychologists to consider the client's R/S, together with other intersecting multicultural identities, and a treatment approach that incorporates the client's preferences for integrating R/S. It legitimizes taking account of client preferences in treatment planning. Incorporating R/S into psychological treatment begins with developing an understanding of the patient's spiritual and religious background, beliefs, and practices (SRBBP) (Vieten & Lukoff, 2022). Obtaining such information is aligned with professional standards, multicultural guidelines, and reports.[8] In general, these documents frame consideration of R/S as a feature of multicultural identity (see also Chapter 2 of this volume). An emphasis is placed on respect for R/S diversity and its contributions to the client's worldview; however, few recommendations are provided in these standards about how such awareness is to be used in psychotherapy.

Developing an understanding of the client's R/S involvement and asking their preferences provides information to guide the nature of incorporating R/S in treatment. For some clients, R/S plays a central role in their meaning-making and coping; for others, R/S holds little personal relevance. Although the evidence is limited,[9] survey data show that most clients view the inclusion of R/S in treatment to be relevant, if not desirable. Harris, Randolph, and Gordon (2016) in their systematic review of 64 peer-reviewed journal articles, reported, "The majority of studies found that clients often have spiritual or religious problems, and they frequently want and expect to talk about spiritual or religious topics in mental health counseling" (p. 269; see also Worthington et al., 1996). Yamada et al. (2020) published the findings of a survey of 2050 recipients of California mental health services in which 80% agreed or strongly agreed that spirituality was important to their mental health, and 70% reported they wanted the system "to do more to support clients and families in terms of using their spirituality as a wellness and recovery resource" (p. 284). Oxhandler, Ellor, and Stanford (2018) reported the findings of an online survey that included 245 current or former mental health counseling clients. Although there were mixed views of who should initiate the discussion, a majority responded favorably toward integrating R/S in practice, and over 80% opined that "a good therapist is sensitive to clients' religious/spiritual beliefs" (p. 343). Christiano (2024) discussed the findings of a mixed-methods study of a community-based convenience sample (N=187), which found variability in spiritual sensitivity ratings of therapists by clients with a strong interest in spiritual practice. A total of 44% of respondents reporting "much" strength and resilience from spiritual practices were most likely to report that they "seldom" felt spiritually understood by their therapists.

These studies suggest that many clients view R/S as important and have a preference that a place be made for inclusion in psychological treatment. However, there appears to be variability regarding who initiates the discussion and regarding which psychological issues R/S would be relevant. Studies in medicine have found similar variability regarding the initiation of discussion of R/S and the clinical context, that is, the severity of the medical condition. To conclude, the incorporation of client preferences in psychological treatment advances client-centered care, is aligned with the principles of evidence-based professional practice, fosters an appreciation of the client's R/S beliefs, values, and practices, and encourages the development of the working alliance by collaborating on the means to achieve the therapy goals (Bordin, 1979; see Captari et al., 2022).

Guidelines and Competencies

Clinical practice guidelines provide recommendations regarding professional practices to ensure the quality of patient care. They are based on reviews of the existing evidence, and in the medical context, guide clinician decision-making and can be used in making systematic improvements in patient care. In contrast to standards, professional practice guidelines are aspirational (APA, n.d.) and, for our purposes, inform rather than dictate the discussion of "what is required" to address spirituality in treatment-related settings. Although related to guidelines, competencies define the requisite knowledge, skills, and attitudes that are assembled to perform a specific professional activity (Falender & Shafranske, 2021) and are directed at the individual clinician or trainee. Guidelines are essential for developing evidence-based approaches to R/S integration, whereas competencies can be used by clinicians to assess their readiness for integrating spirituality in treatment. The following draft of the guidelines was developed by the *Task Force to Develop Professional Practice Guidelines for Addressing Religion and Spirituality in the Practice of Psychology*.[10]

Guideline 1: Psychologists seek to appreciate that spirituality and religion are distinct, often overlapping, expressions of human experience that, for many, are core areas of diversity and identity.
Guideline 2: Psychologists strive to become aware of how their own R/S background and beliefs, or their attitudes toward religion and/or spirituality, might influence or bias their reactions to clients.
Guideline 3: Psychologists aspire to recognize and attend to problems related to spirituality and religion that may adversely influence people's psychological well-being.
Guideline 4: Psychologists work to gain awareness of the ways that spirituality and religion may support psychological well-being and support clients in accessing their spiritual and religious strengths and resources.
Guideline 5: Psychologists endeavor to inquire about people's R/S practices, backgrounds, and beliefs as a routine part of psychological practice.
Guideline 6: Psychologists practice within the boundaries of their competence in addressing R/S concerns and are willing to consult, refer, and collaborate with spiritual care professionals, clergy, and other qualified individuals when indicated.

These *Guidelines* provide a starting point, which can be tailored to meet the orientations of other allied mental health professions and settings, to establish aspirational principles for professional practice.

A Comprehensive Framework for Integrating R/S in Treatment

The development of a comprehensive framework must take into consideration the diverse forms of religiosity and spirituality, as well as the variability in the degree to which R/S is integrated in global life meaning, daily appraisals of significance, and as a resource for coping and flourishing. One approach will not fit all; rather, a comprehensive framework must provide guidance for addressing spirituality with those clients for whom R/S has little or no value and for those in whom R/S is core to their identity, relationships, and living. Saunders, Miller, and Bright (2010) provide a model that describes the continuum of spiritual care currently offered in psychotherapy. They identified the following approaches clinicians likely adopt when addressing spirituality in treatment, and range from avoidance to exercising an explicit focus:[11]

- Spiritually avoidant care is characterized by "the explicit or implicit attempt, on the part of a psychologist, to avoid conversations with patients about their religious beliefs and practices (SRBP)" (cf. p. 357).

- Spiritually conscious care is defined "as an approach that assesses SRBP in a respectful and sensitive manner to determine its general importance to a patient, but also to assess the influence, if any, of SRBP on the presenting problem, and the potential of SRBP as a resource to help recovery" (p. 359).
- Spiritually integrated psychotherapy is defined "as an approach that utilizes a patient's SRBP in the treatment of emotional problems … and [focuses] on a patient's SRBP to facilitate the goals of psychotherapy, which are the alleviation of distress and impairment" (cf. p. 358).
- Spiritually directive care is an approach "wherein treatment focuses on a patient's SRBP as the explicit object of attention. The potential outcome of a spiritually directive, psychotherapy might be the conservation, or perhaps the transformation of SRBP (Sperry & Shafranske, 2005). Using this approach, the patient might be aided in evaluating or reconstructing his or her faith perspective" (p. 357).

These categories reflect varying degrees of integration and, in the best of circumstances, are aligned with patient preferences and characteristics, including the degree of R/S salience and involvement and culture, paired with the clinician's experience and expertise. The other forms of integration provide approaches that can be tailored to the needs of the patient, the presenting problems, and the salience of spirituality. Treatments may involve *implicit* or *explicit* forms of integration reflecting the degree to which attention and spiritual resources are incorporated in treatment (Tan, 1996). Implicit integration is a more covert approach that respects and takes into consideration spirituality but does not initiate discussion of R/S issues per se nor systematically incorporate spiritual resources such as prayer, scripture, sacred texts, and rituals in treatment. Implicit integration may be reflected in spiritually conscious care in which spirituality is acknowledged and addressed as one among other factors affecting the patient. Explicit integration refers to a more overt approach that directly and systematically deals with spiritual or religious issues in therapy and uses spiritual resources, referrals to church or other religious groups or lake counselors, or other religious practices. "It emphasizes the spirituality of both a therapist and client as foundational to effective therapy and human growth and healing" (Tan, 1996, p. 368). Explicit integration is used in both spiritually integrated psychotherapy and spiritually directed psychotherapy. Further, in some forms of explicit integration, for example, theistic integrative psychotherapy (Richards, 2005), emphasis is placed on healing as a spiritual process in which therapy may play a role and in which "clients may be encouraged to explore how their faith in God and personal spirituality may assist them in their treatment and recovery" (p. 265).

The discussion on integration has focused primarily on the individual clinician level; however, bringing spirituality more fully into healthcare settings involves changes in the medical culture as reflected in the emerging biopsychosocial-spiritual model and at the institutional level involving policy development and implementation. Long et al. (2024) assembled an expert panel, which concluded the following:

> In a reimagined clinical and public health system, spiritual factors would be routinely considered in creating person- and community- centered policy and practice. Although the intersections between spirituality and well-being have existed through millennia, a compelling body of empirical research currently allows policy makers to learn from and build on numerous contemporary models of integrated health policies and practices … As empirical scholarship increasingly illuminates these connections, public health systems must seek

> additional ways to recognize spiritual determinants of health as a vital dimension, and extension, of whole-person, whole-community well-being.
>
> (p. 788)

Establishing a framework to address spirituality in treatment involves a full commitment at all levels of the healthcare system.

The Essentials of Practice

The overarching principles of respect, humility, commitment to the well-being of patients, and professionalism provide the foundation for ethical and effective clinical practice. Besides knowledge and skills, the clinician's personal and professional values play a crucial role when integrating R/S in treatment. Central to ethics and good practice is respecting the patient's right to form their own spiritual beliefs, worldviews, religious affiliations, and practices. In addition to acknowledging the patient's autonomy, respect involves an appreciation that each person must find their own way in making sense of their existence. Respect, of course, does not require agreement with the client's R/S beliefs or assent to their ontological truth claims.

Conceptions of intellectual and cultural humility anchor ethical practice and safeguard against the dangers of disregarding or minimizing the client's viewpoints and the attributions they make about the events in their daily life. Broadly speaking, intellectual humility speaks to people's willingness to reconsider their views, to avoid defensiveness when challenged, and to moderate their own need to appear "right." It is sensitive to counter-evidence, realistic in outlook, strives for accuracy, shows little concern for self-importance, and is corrective of the natural tendency to prioritize one's own needs and, for our discussion, to prioritize our personal beliefs and faith commitments (John Templeton Foundation, n.d.). In the clinical setting, cultural humility reflects an openness to understand the experiences and worldview of the other and the meanings they create. Assuming a position of cultural humility is not so much a clinical competency as an aspirational orientation (Davis et al., 2018; Hook et al., 2025; Owen et al., 2011). Adopting a multicultural orientation to treatment (Hook, 2018) or, for our application, a spiritually sensitive orientation, offers the clinician a way of "being in session" (p. 90) that heightens awareness of the influence of R/S in the patient's present situation and provides opportunities for understanding. Although healthcare professionals may strive (or assume) to offer healthcare in a *value-neutral* fashion, they are human beings "whose values and morals [and R/S beliefs and commitments] must participate in their human relationship with the client" (Jones, 1994, p. 191) and, therefore, impact their understanding. Although well-intended, in my view, we cannot "ethically bracket" (Kocet & Herlihy, 2014) or set aside our personal beliefs and values; rather, we should cultivate awareness of the personal and professional factors that influence our understanding of and work with patients [see special issue psychologists' reflections on integration in their clinical work (Mangione & Plante, 2022; Shafranske, 2023)].

Assessing Spiritual and Religious Background, Beliefs, and Practices (SRBBP)

The assessment of SRBBP is conducted to obtain a comprehensive and clinically meaningful understanding of the client within the context of the biopsychosocial-spiritual model to address their psychological difficulties and mental health issues. It is not a "fishing expedition" but is *explicitly* and *intentionally* linked to patient care. A thorough understanding of SRBBP contributes to clinical formulation, which includes inquiring about the background, present status, and impacts of R/S and identifies spiritual struggles as well as spiritual resources. It is important for clinicians to have a general understanding of the functions and features of R/S, to recognize SRBBP in terms of intersectionality with other individual and cultural contexts, and to know about the demographic trends in R/S.

Demographics of Religious and Spiritual Involvement

Demographic research points to a broad landscape of R/S beliefs and involvement in the United States. A total of 78% of participants in a Gallup poll conducted in 2023 in the United States reported belief in God (Evans et al., 2025), down from 92% in a 2010 poll (Newport, 2010). The *2023–24 Religious Landscape Study* (RLS) conducted by the Pew Research Center (2025) reported that the percentage of US adults who say that religion is "Very" important in their lives dropped from 56% in 2007, to 53% in 2014, and to 38% in 2023; there was correspondingly a significant increase in "Not too/Not at all" from 16%, 22%, and 26%, respectively (p. 157). Younger adults are leading the long-term shift away from formal religious affiliation; more than 3 in 10 Generation Z and millennials have no religious preference (Jones, 2025), and the "Unaffiliated," are predicted to increase from 16.4% to 25.6% by 2050 (Pew Forum, 2015). Consistent with declines in religious salience, 80% of US adults say, "Religion's influence in American life is declining as high as it's ever been"; interestingly, 49% say this is a bad thing (Pew Research Center, 2024). Finally, "nearly half of Americans (47%) describe themselves as religious, another 33% say they are spiritual but not religious, and 2% volunteer they are both" (Jones, 2023). See Chapter 1 for a related discussion of global and US demographic trends related to religion and spirituality. What do these demographic trends mean? At first glance, the trends reflect declines in formal religious affiliation, but the findings may not be as clear as they initially appear regarding religious involvement. Levin et al. (2022) examined the extent to which religious "nones" were actually not religious in their personal lives, based on data from five recent US population surveys. They reported that many who check "None" on surveys displayed a wide variety of R/S practices and beliefs, for example, attending religious services, praying, meditating, and believing in God. Although not entirely refuting the apparent declines in formal affiliation, the study points to the complexity in assessing R/S involvement.

These findings point to the importance of carefully assessing a client's religiousness and spirituality, including changes in affiliation. Also, leaving a faith tradition may reflect a past spiritual struggle in which doctrinal beliefs were no longer held or spiritual needs were unfulfilled. Particularly for the unaffiliated, a void in faith or religious support may result, initiating a pursuit of other sources of meaning or social support. Some people seek psychotherapy as an adjunctive or primary means to address existential questions, transform personal faith, or engage in a spiritual quest (Shafranske & Sperry, 2005).

Conducting the Assessment

Acquiring an understanding of how R/S functions in a person's life is challenging given that "the specific ways of experiencing religion and the specific psychological processes involved in the realization of the religion-related goals, seem to vary importantly across groups, differing in ethnicity, social, economic status, social, cultural group level-factors, theological traditions, and broad, cultural dimensions involving culture-specific personality, cognitions, emotions, social relations, and morality" (Saroglou & Cohen, 2013, p. 345; Richards & Bergin, 2014; Richards, 2024). Returning to our earlier discussion, conducting the assessment requires respect, cultural humility, and sensitivity to the client's reactions and the salience of R/S; however, it also offers an opportunity for the client to discuss matters of personal meaning and significance, which may contribute to the development of the therapeutic alliance.

The following content areas, drawn from a review of the literature, constitute areas for focus during the early assessment phase and throughout treatment (Shafranske, 2013, p. 600):

1 *Salience*. How important is religion and/or spirituality in the life of the client from the client's perspective?
2 *Integration*. In what ways and to what extent does R/S contribute to the client's global life meaning and impact their daily life, including their values, decision-making, goals, behaviors, and ongoing appraisals of significance?
3 *Spiritual and Religious Background, Beliefs, and Practices*. How does the client experience R/S? What are their core beliefs, values, affiliations, and practices? What role does R/S, including affiliation with a faith community, play in their daily life and as a source of support or conflict?
4 *Coping*. To what extent does the client employ R/S sources of positive coping, and how effective are these resources in enhancing psychological adjustment and well-being (Pargament, 2007)?
5 *Struggles/Conflict*. To what extent are the client's present difficulties related to R/S conflicts or spiritual struggles (Exline & Rose, 2013; Pargament & Exline, 2022)? Does the client use negative religious coping, including "red flags," such as conflict, loss, or anger toward God? Do the client's psychological difficulties and/or psychiatric/medical conditions impair their use of religious resources, that is, clinically significant religious impairment?
6 *Potential Impacts on Treatment*. Does the client believe that religious or spiritual healing plays a role in his or her treatment, and what role does psychological treatment play? If religiously affiliated, does the client's faith community support mental health treatment? Does the R/S background of the clinician affect the client's participation in treatment?

Developing an understanding of the impacts of the client's recent and present R/S involvement is important when considering the degree to which R/S will become a focus within treatment and a potential source of therapeutic resources. The clinician must be attuned to salience as well as the possible use of spirituality as a means to bypass emotional conflicts (see Chapter 41). The clinician should also become familiar with or obtain consultation when evaluating R/S experiences that appear anomalous or are inconsistent with culture-specific expressions of religiousness to differentiate religious delusions from non-pathological beliefs and experiences (American Psychiatric Association, 2022). Although recommending a comprehensive examination of R/S, there are three areas that require particular attention (i.e., spiritual struggles, trauma, and moral injury).

A body of theory and empirical evidence has established that *spiritual struggles* influence not only R/S involvement but also psychological coping and well-being (Exline & Rose, 2013; Pargament & Exline, 2022). See Chapter 38 for a comprehensive discussion of spiritual struggles. The six types of spiritual struggle (Pargament & Exline, 2022) are:

1 *Divine struggles* take the form of anger or disappointment with God and feeling punished, abandoned, or unloved by God.
2 *Demonic struggles* involve worries that problems are caused by the devil or evil spirits and feelings of being attacked or tormented by the devil.

3 *Interpersonal spiritual struggles* reflect conflicts with other people and institutions about secret issues, anger at organized religion, and feeling hurt, mistreated, or offended by others in relation to religious or spiritual issues.
4 *Struggles with doubt* are marked by feeling confused about religious/spiritual beliefs and feeling troubled by doubts or questions about religion/spirituality.
5 *Moral struggles* take the form of tensions and guilt about not living up to one's higher standards and wrestling with attempts to follow moral principles [see Chapter 39 of this volume for a related discussion regarding temptation].
6 *Struggles of ultimate meaning* involve questions about whether one's life has a deeper meaning and whether life really matters (p. 9).

Experiences of *trauma* often pose an existential threat (Sandage et al., 2020, p. 8) and shatter the assumptions held within R/S beliefs and conceptions of the world – even more so when trauma is experienced in the context of one's R/S belief system. Such events can increase both psychological and spiritual vulnerabilities. There is evidence that complex interactions can occur in which psychology and spirituality conjoin in the process of recovery. On the one hand, "spiritual resources can contribute substantially to recovery from trauma," and on the other hand, "spiritual struggles and distress can compound mental health challenges and impede healing" (Captari & Worthington, 2024, p. 195). Clinicians must bring a nuanced approach to assessing the impacts of R/S in the treatment of trauma, including oscillating positions of hope and despair. See Chapter 19 for much more discussion regarding trauma and meaning-making.

Moral injury results when a person perpetrates, fails to prevent, or bears witness to acts that transgress deeply held moral beliefs and expectations (Litz et al., 2009). The consequences include long-lasting psychological, biological, spiritual, behavioral, and social impacts. Treatments integrating a spiritual perspective have been found to have promise in addressing the impacts of moral injury and trauma (Harris et al., 2015; Harris et al., 2018; Park et al., 2017). See Chapter 40 for a comprehensive discussion of moral injury.

Assessment Approaches and Procedures

Assessing SRBBP is started during the opening phase but continues throughout the treatment as the therapeutic process deepens and pathways are opened to a more incisive grasp of the dynamics contributing to their suffering and recovery. A comprehensive discussion of the various assessment procedures and tools is beyond the scope of this chapter; however, the major approaches are delineated in Hodge (2013) and in the previously recommended texts (see Endnote[7]). Clinicians should initiate a discussion by asking open-ended questions about religion and spirituality within the context of learning about the patient's presenting problems, background, context, and history. Such early inquiry often provides a glimpse into the present degree of salience and integration of R/S; however, it is important to consider the role of R/S and challenges and transitions, including experiences of conversion, de-conversion, and transformation (Paloutzian et al., 2013). Besides the use of open-ended questions and structured interviews such as the Structured Clinical Interview for Spiritual Problems and Psychiatric Problems (SSOPP) (Lukoff, 2014) to collaboratively explore the client's R/S involvement, life maps, R/S genograms, and empirically validated assessment tools such as the brief Religion Coping Inventory (RCOPE; Pargament et al., 1998) or research instruments, such as the Screener for Spiritual Struggles (Pargament & Exline,

2022, adapted from Exline et al., 2014) may be used. The nature and attention given to examining spirituality and religious involvement should be carefully aligned with salience ascribed by the client, the presenting difficulties, and the client's interest, and with informed consent.

Integrating Religion and Spirituality in Treatment: Intervention Approaches

The *big picture* suggests there is a recognition within the healthcare *Zeitgeist* of the relevance of R/S in psychological and other psychosocial and behavioral treatments; see, for example, policy statements of the Substance Abuse and Mental Health Services Administration (2016). However, an informal review of the clinical literature and anecdotal evidence suggests wide variability in implementing explicit R/S treatment protocols and interventions. Historically, clinicians have incorporated the exploration of R/S into their existing therapy models and tailored their general treatment interventions to address spirituality (Richards & Bergin, 2005). These religiously accommodative interventions "modify an existing secular treatment to include methods and goals that reflect certain values, beliefs, or practices, promoted by religious institutions or psychological treatments created specifically for use with people who belong to specific religious or spiritual subgroups" (Worthington et al., 2013, pp. 651–652). In other instances, spiritual practices and R/S resources, such as prayer, meditation, and use of scriptures, may be encouraged or incorporated in psychotherapy (Plante, 2009, 2024), virtues-based approaches may be integrated (Captari et al., 2023; Fowers, 2005; Shafranske, 2023), or formal community-based programs addressing forgiveness, for example, may be implemented (Worthington, 2024; Ho et al., 2024). McMinn et al. (2024) propose conceptualizing integration that includes assimilative (introducing R/S interventions into standard treatments), accommodative (adapting a standard psychotherapy regimen to include R/S), collaborative (mental health professionals and religious leaders working in tandem), and emergent (innovative, new developments). As previously discussed, the range of approaches may vary from avoidant to explicit integration. Spiritually avoidant care is *a priori* problematic and inappropriate given its intentional disregard for the patient's personal and cultural features, values, preferences, and existing resources.[12] Careful assessment, aligning the client's preferences and values and the expertise of the clinician, guides the nature of spiritually responsive forms of integration, which may include spiritually directive care. A seamless integration approach should be developed in which assessment leads to case formulation and results in a treatment plan which incorporates forms of spiritually responsive care (i.e., spiritually conscious care, spiritually integrated psychotherapy, or spiritually directed care).

The arc in the development of approaches to address spirituality in treatment settings is focused on religiously accommodative interventions (e.g., Worthington et al., 2011; Worthington et al., 2013) and spiritually integrative psychotherapies (Captari et al., 2022; Captari & Worthington, 2024). Captari et al. (2018) conducted a meta-analysis of 97 studies (N = 7,181) examining the efficacy of tailoring treatment to patients' R/S beliefs and values. They reported that R/S-adapted psychotherapy resulted in greater improvement in clients' psychological and spiritual functioning compared with no treatment and non-R/S psychotherapies. Captari, Sandage, and Vandiver (2022), in their discussion of real-world clinical practice, suggest that integration can take the forms of "(a) recommending stand-alone interventions, (b) tailoring evidence-based treatments, or (c) developing and testing new approaches" (p. 315). The use of these (and future) cutting-edge, empirically supported, spiritually integrated treatments will advance the implementation of therapy approaches to address spirituality within mental health. Likewise, the principles discussed herein are also relevant to and translatable for application in the medical model, including allopathic, osteopathic, and other allied approaches to otherwise traditional physical healthcare, thus fulfilling the ideals of the biopsychosocial-spiritual model of comprehensive healthcare; indeed, they are consistent with the World Health Organization's definition of health[4]. As these intervention protocols are developed, they should be used with careful attention to the fit with the client's preferences and values, applicability to the treatment issues, informed consent, and sensitivity to avoid dropout (Currier, 2024). Efforts to integrate R/S in mental health treatment are not without iatrogenic risks. In a sample of 989 current mental health clients, about 1 in 10 respondents reported harmful experiences, which included a lack of openness to the client's R/S, the therapist imposing their own beliefs, and a perceived negative bias toward the client's R/S (Oxhandler et al., 2018). Further, healthcare professionals should consider the role others may play, such as religious authorities (e.g., clergy, rabbis, and imams), and are encouraged to consider consultation or referral in patient care.

Ethics and Professionalism

Laws and professional ethics govern the conduct of healthcare provision, safeguarding individual patients and the public, and establishing standards of care. The following areas of ethics and professional conduct, drawn from the literature (Currier et al., 2023; Dike et al., 2022; Hathaway & Ripley, 2009; Gonsiorek et al., 2009), should be considered when addressing spirituality in treatment settings.

Respect for the client as a human being is the superordinate principle on which the professional relationship and the therapeutic alliance are established. Respect is infused in every aspect of the treatment process and conveyed by the clinician's interest, genuine concern, and commitment to the client's well-being. It is imperative when incorporating R/S in treatment. The following attitudes and behaviors affirm respect:

- Respect and uphold the rights and dignity of the client.
- Attend to the multicultural intersectional identities that contribute to the client's sense of self and worldview.
- Respect the autonomy and self-determination of the client to form their own R/S beliefs, values, affiliations, practices, and worldview.
- Obtain informed consent to discuss R/S and integrate R/S interventions.

Maintaining appropriate boundaries, including monitoring and stopping the use of personal influence, is closely aligned with respect and includes the following:

- Do not impose personal beliefs, attitudes, or judgments on the client through overt or covert influence or by disregarding, invalidating, disputing, or ignoring the client's R/S beliefs, values, affiliations, practices, and worldview.
- Engage in reflective practice to identify and manage R/S (and other forms of) countertransference.
- Maintain appropriate boundaries, particularly when participating in a faith community in which your client is affiliated.
- Engage in ethical decision-making when considering or entering a multiple relationship with the client.

Establishing competence in implementing spiritually responsive care is required, while recognizing that maintaining competence is a dynamic process that necessitates a commitment to ongoing professional development. Developing competence is particularly challenging, given the general paucity of preparation in graduate school and clinical training, as well as advances in the field. Consider the following:

- Practice within your scope of competence.
- Engage in reflective practice and metacompetence to identify deficiencies or gaps in knowledge or abilities required to provide spiritually responsive care.
- Seek consultation with R/S professionals and mental health professionals with expertise in the applied psychology of religion and spirituality, as appropriate.

Psychological treatment, like other healthcare services, is guided by several contextual influences. Clinicians must be mindful of the following:

- Review and comply with the principles and code of ethics of your respective profession and employment setting.
- Review and comply with all federal, state, local, and employment setting regulations, including those affecting the inclusion of R/S in mental health practices. This review includes statutes and policies about church/state restrictions and conscience clauses, that is, US state statutes that allow health professionals, including psychology graduate students, to refuse to provide care to patients based on the trainee's religious beliefs (Grzanka et al., 2020; see also Erickson Cornish, Riva, & Smith, 2015; Wise et al., 2015), and restrictions on specific treatments, for example, sexual orientation therapy (Appelbaum, 2014; see Davison & Walden, 2024 for a review of the literature). Of note, statutes and policies can vary across legal jurisdictions – whether within the United States (or any other given country) or internationally.

For psychologists, review the following resolutions adopted by the American Psychological Association (APA):

- Within its 2007 resolution (American Psychological Association, 2008, pp. 432, 433), APA condemned "prejudice directed against individuals or groups, derived from or based on religious or spiritual beliefs" and "encourages all psychologists to act to eliminate discrimination based on or derived from religion and spirituality," and
- "Encourages individuals and groups to work against any potential adverse psychological consequences to themselves, others, or society that might arise from religious or spiritual attitudes, practices, or policies," and
- Psychologists are encouraged to recognize that it is outside the role and expertise of psychologists to adjudicate religious or spiritual tenets (e.g., doctrine, sin, or transgression).
- In its 2009 report on appropriate affirmative responses to sexual orientation distress and change efforts (American Psychological Association, 2009), the APA task force draws attention to the vital role of religion and discriminates between the contributions of religion and psychological science.

Although ethical codes appear straightforward, their application is often complex. Healthcare professionals should become familiar with decision-making processes that guide ethical conduct when integrating spirituality in treatment settings (see Barnett & Johnson, 2011, for an overview of stages and processes that inform R/S ethical issues and dilemmas). The establishment of clinical competence serves as the centerpiece of professional ethics, as does relevant continuing education. We turn now to the discussion of readiness and offer recommendations to enhance professional preparation.

Professional Readiness, Education, and Clinical Training

The final *big picture* issue in this chapter is expressed as a question: "Are mental health professionals adequately prepared, i.e., competent, to address spirituality in treatment?" Here's what we know: the research suggests that most mental health professionals receive almost no education and training about how to assess R/S as clinical variables or integrate R/S in treatment (Vieten et al., 2024). And, although 47.1% of the professionals surveyed had not received much R/S training, many (i.e., 57.8%) perceived themselves to be highly competent in R/S clinical integration practices (Vieten et al., 2023).[13]

Shafranske and Cummings (2013), in their review of the extant research, concluded that psychologists' training in the psychology of R/S and in how to incorporate RS into treatment was generally inadequate. Vieten et al. (2016) reported that the majority of psychologists (52.2%–80.7%) replied that "they had received little or no training, and between 29.7% and 58.6% had received no training at all, in these competencies" (p. 92). Several surveys have been conducted within the profession of social work and point to similar trends; for example, only 13% of social workers had taken a course on R/S, and 46% sought continuing education on R/S (Oxhandler et al., 2015; Oxhandler & Parrish, 2018). A study of over 3500 Brazilian medical students found that the majority believed that spirituality has an impact on patients' health (71.2%); over three-quarters of the students considered it relevant (75.3%), although nearly one-half (48.7%) felt unprepared to integrate spirituality into their practice of medicine (Lucchetti et al., 2013). Given the apparent insufficiency in education and training, clinicians may rely on their own personal R/S to guide their efforts to integrate spirituality into treatment. Which may or may not be productive and could be problematic.

Systematic efforts must be taken within the graduate education and training trajectory to enhance professional preparation and the establishment of sufficient competence for clinicians to address spirituality in treatment (Vieten et al., 2024) and to counter barriers to training (Currier et al., 2023; Tanega et al., 2025). A recent survey of mental health educators suggested that there may be support for strengthening the curriculum in this area based on their personal involvement in R/S (Polson et al., 2025). Using a competency-based approach to education and clinical training, including clinical supervision, provides a pedagogical model to develop clinical competence (Falender & Shafranske, 2021; Shafranske, 2016). A first step is the identification of the knowledge, skills, and attitudes that are assembled to form competence to address R/S in psychotherapy and other mental health services (Oxhandler et al., 2019). Vieten and Lukoff (2022; see Table 1, p. 32) and the Association for Spiritual, Ethical, and Religious Values in Counseling (2016) have identified competencies that can be used to develop benchmarks for use in education and training. Recent projects have been initiated to advance education and training opportunities to enhance existing academic curricula and clinical training (Pearce et al., 2019; Pearce et al., 2020; Pearce et al., 2024; see also the Spiritual and Religious Competencies Project[14]).

Closing Remarks

Addressing spirituality in treatment is complex. It requires specialized clinical competence that prepares the clinician to integrate R/S in holistic patient-centered or person-centered care. Advances in the applied psychology of religion and spirituality will be supported by empirical research that further examines the properties and functions of R/S on processes of healing and mental and physical health. Advances in education and clinical training are required to develop and sustain clinical competence. It is through these efforts that we will be prepared to facilitate processes of healing to promote therapeutic change, mental health, and well-being.

Notes

1 The terms *client* and *patient* will be used interchangeably throughout this chapter.

2 To illustrate the size of the literature base, over 11,000 journal articles were published between 2001 – 2020 in which R/S and mental health were the focus (Shafranske, 2024, p. 345) and about 1600 peer-reviewed journal articles were published between 2001 and 2024. The development of this chapter, emphasized the contributions from well-established scholars in the applied psychology of religion and spirituality, major reviews of the literature, authoritative texts, and edited handbooks, and proposed guidelines.

3 Common elements include compassionate understanding, confiding, confessional, and cathartic moments, emotional expression, explanation and persuasion, promotion or self-understanding and change to master difficult illness-related situations (Jackson, 1999).

4 Of note, this approach to health is inconsistent with the World Health Organization's 1946 prioritization of a more comprehensive definition of health as being "a state of complete physical, mental and social well-being and not merely the absence of disease or infirmity" (World Health Organization, 2025, p. 1). Which definition serves as a guiding principle for this edited volume (see Chapters 1 and 44).

5 See Pargament (1997) for an explication of the theory and research on religious coping and Pargament (2007) for further clinical applications.

6 The American Psychological Association and the American Counseling Association have published texts on integrating R/S in psychological treatment and counseling, e.g., Richards & Bergin (2005) and Cashwell & Young (2020), respectively; however, formal standards involving required compliance by members of their respective organizations have not been established.

7 There is a large collection of texts that provide a foundation for understanding the psychology of religion, spirituality, and mental health and applied practice. The following books (arranged by author) provide a starting point and illustrate the available scholarly and clinical resources. Aten & Leach, *Spirituality and the therapeutic process: A comprehensive resource from intake to termination*, 2008; Aten, McMinn, & Worthington, Jr., *Spiritually oriented interventions for counseling and psychotherapy*, 2011; Aten, O'Grady, Worthington, Jr., *The psychology of religion and spirituality for clinicians*, 2012; Currier, Fox, & Vieten, *Handbook of training in spiritual and religious competencies in mental health professions*, in press; Griffith & Griffith, *Encountering the sacred in psychotherapy: How to talk with people about their spiritual lives*, 2002; Koenig, VanderWeele, & Peteet, *Handbook of religion and health* (3rd ed.)., 2023; Miller, *The Oxford handbook of psychology and spirituality* (2nd ed.), 2024; Paloutzian & Park, *Handbook of the psychology of religion and spirituality* (2nd ed.), 2013; Pargament, *Spiritually integrated psychotherapy: Understanding and addressing the sacred*, 2007; Pargament & Exline, *Working with spiritual struggles in psychotherapy: From research to practice*, 2022; Pargament, Exline, & Jones, *APA handbook of psychology, religion, and spirituality, Volume 1, Context, theory, and research*, 2013; Pargament, Mahoney, & Shafranske, *APA handbook of psychology, religion, and spirituality, Volume 2, An applied psychology of religion and spirituality*, 2013; *Plante, Spiritually informed therapy (SIT): Wisdom and evidence based strategies that work*, 2024; Richards & Bergin, *A spiritual strategy for counseling and psychotherapy* (2nd ed.), 2005; Richards & Bergin, *Handbook of psychotherapy and religious diversity* (2nd ed.), 2014; Richards, Allen, & Judd, *Handbook of spiritually integrated psychotherapies*, 2023; Sandage, Rupert, Stavros, & Devor, *Relational spirituality in psychotherapy: Healing suffering and promoting growth*, 2020; Sperry,

Spirituality in clinical practice: Theory and practice of spiritually oriented psychotherapy, 2012; and Sperry & Shafranske, *Spiritually oriented psychotherapy*, 2005.

8 For example, professional standards, e.g., *ACA Code of Ethics* (American Counseling Association, 2014), and the Joint Commission (2022), multicultural guidelines, e.g., *Multicultural guidelines: An ecological approach to context, identity, and intersectionality* (American Psychological Association, 2017a) and *Standards and indicators for cultural competence in social work practice* (National Association of Social Workers, 2015), and reports, e.g., *American Psychiatric Association Resource Document on Ethics at the Interface of Religion, Spirituality, and Psychiatric Practice* (American Psychiatric Association, 2021) and *WPA Position Statement on Spirituality and Religion in Psychiatry* (World Psychiatry, 2016).

9 Of the 64 studies that were examined only 18 studies of spirituality in mental health counseling were conducted obtaining data from actual clients.

10 The *Task Force to Develop Professional Practice Guidelines for Addressing Religion and Spirituality in the Practice of Psychology* is chaired by Cassandra Vieten, Kari O'Grady, Joseph Currier. The members include:

> Christine Agaibi, Kevin Armstrong, George Fitchett, Nicholas Gibson, Bill Hathaway, Tyler Lefevor, David Lukoff, Kevin Masters, Glen Milstein, Elizabeth O'Brien Oden, Innocent Okozi, Kenneth I. Pargament, Michelle Pearce, Ben O'Dell, Holly Oxhandler, Edward Shafranske, Timothy Sisemore, Floyd Thompkins, and Stephanie Winklejohn Black.

11 The model (Saunders, Miller, and Bright (2010) is descriptive in nature and does not intend to be prescriptive. It offers a theoretical depiction rather than empirical description of therapists' approaches.

12 All of which is counter to the ethical guidelines, code of conduct, and professional standards developed and adopted by the American Psychological Association (2008, 2017b).

13 Importantly, Currier, Fox, and Vieten (in press) have a forthcoming, open-access edited book set for release in 2025 entitled: *Handbook of Training in Spiritual and Religious Competencies in Mental Health Professions*.

14 Spiritual and Religious Competencies Project, contact: spiritual.competency@southalabama.edu.

References

American Psychiatric Association. (2013). *Cultural Concepts in DSM-5*. Author. https://www.psychiatry.org/File%20Library/Psychiatrists/Practice/DSM/APA_DSM_Cultural-Concepts-in-DSM-5.pdf

American Psychiatric Association. (2022). *Diagnostic and Statistical Manual of Mental Disorders* (5th ed., text rev.). Arlington, VA: American Psychiatric Publishing.

American Psychological Association. (2008). Resolution on religious, religion-based, and/or religion-derived prejudice. *American Psychologist*, *63*(5), 431–434. https://doi.org/10.1037/0003-066X.63.5.360. See also: https://www.apa.org/about/policy/religious-discrimination.pdf

American Psychological Association. (2009). Resolution on appropriate affirmative responses to sexual orientation distress and change efforts. Accessed July 2, 2025 from: https://www.apa.org/about/policy/sexual-orientation. See also: https://www.apa.org/about/policy/sexual-orientation.pdf

American Psychological Association. (2017a). Multicultural guidelines: An ecological approach to context, identity, and intersectionality. Retrieved from: http://www.apa.org/about/policy/multicultural-guidelines.pdf

American Psychological Association. (2017b). Ethical principles of psychologists and code of conduct. Accessed July 2, 2025 from: https://www.apa.org/ethics/code. See also: https://www.apa.org/ethics/code/ethics-code-2017.pdf

American Psychological Association, Presidential Task Force on Evidence-Based Practice. (2006). Evidence-based practice in psychology. *American Psychologist*, *61*(4), 271–285. https://doi.org/10.1037/0003-066X.61.4.271

Appelbaum, P. S. (2014). Regulating psychotherapy or restricting freedom of speech? California's ban on sexual orientation change efforts. *Psychiatric Services*, *65*(1), 1–3. https://doi.org/10.1176/appi.ps.650101

Association for Spiritual, Ethical, and Religious Values in Counseling. (2016). Competencies for addressing spiritual and religious issues in counseling. Retrieved from https://www.aservic.org/competencies/

Aten, J. D., & Leach, M. M. (Eds.). (2008). *Spirituality and the therapeutic process: A comprehensive resource from intake to termination*. American Psychological Association. https://doi.org/10.1037/11853-000

Aten, J. D., McMinn, M. R., & Worthington, E. L., Jr. (2011). *Spiritually oriented interventions for counseling and psychotherapy*. American Psychological Association. https://doi.org/10.1037/12313-000

Aten, J. D., O'Grady, K. A., & Worthington, E. L., Jr. (Eds.). (2012). *The psychology of religion and spirituality for clinicians: Using research in your practice*. Routledge/Taylor & Francis Group.

Barnett, J. E., & Johnson, W. B. (2011). Integrating spirituality and religion into psychotherapy: Persistent dilemmas, ethical issues, and a proposed decision-making process.*Ethics & Behavior*, *21*(2), 147–164. https://doi.org/10.1080/10508422.2011.551471

Baumeister, R. F., Vohs, K. D., Aaker, J. L., & Garbinsky, E. N. (2013). Some key differences between a happy life and a meaningful life. *The Journal of Positive Psychology*, *8*(6), 505–516. https://doi.org/10.1080/17439760.2013.830764

Bolton, D., & Gillett, G. (2019). The biopsychosocial model 40 years on. In D. Bolton & G. Gillett (Eds.), *The biopsychosocial model of health and disease: New philosophical and scientific developments*. Palgrave Pivot, Cham. https://doi.org/10.1007/978-3-030-11899-0_1

Bordin, E. S. (1979). The generalizability of the psychoanalytic concept of the working alliance. *Psychotherapy: Theory, Research & Practice*, *16*(3), 252–260. https://doi.org/10.1037/h0085885

Borrell-Carrió, F., Suchman, A. L., & Epstein, R. M. (2004). The biopsychosocial model 25 years later: principles, practice, and scientific inquiry. *Annals of family medicine*, *2*(6), 576–582. https://doi.org/10.1370/afm.245

Captari, L. E., Hook, J. N., Hoyt, W., Davis, D. E., McElroy, H. S. E., & Worthington, E. L. (2018). Integrating clients' religion and spirituality within psychotherapy: A comprehensive meta-analysis. *Journal of Clinical Psychology*, *74*(11), 1938–1951. https://doi.org/10.1002/jclp.22681

Captari, L. E., Sandage, S. J., & Vandiver, R. A. (2022). Spiritually integrated psychotherapies in real-world clinical practice: Synthesizing the literature to identify best practices and future research directions. *Psychotherapy*, *59*(3), 307–320. https://doi.org/10.1037/pst0000407

Captari, L. E., Sandage, S. J., Vandiver, R. A., Jankowski, P. J., & Hook, J. N. (2023). Integrating positive psychology, religion/spirituality, and a virtue focus within culturally responsive mental healthcare. In E. B. Davis, E. L. Worthington, Jr., & S. A. Schnitker (Eds.), *Handbook of positive psychology, religion, and spirituality* (pp. 413–428). Springer Nature Switzerland AG. https://doi.org/10.1007/978-3-031-10274-5_26

Captari, L. E., & Worthington, E. L., Jr. (2024). Assessing and treating trauma impacts in religious and spiritual populations: Introduction to the special issue. *Spirituality in Clinical Practice*, *11*(3), 195–202. https://doi.org/10.1037/scp0000380

Cashwell, C. S. & Young, J. S. (Eds.). (2020). *Integrating spirituality and religion into counseling: A guide to competent practice*. American Counseling Association.

Cassell, E. J. (1988). The nature of suffering and the goals of medicine. *The New England Journal of Medicine*, *306*(11), 639–645. https://doi.org/10.1056/NEJM198203183061104

Christiano, A. (2024). Understanding the needs and experiences of spiritual and religious clients seeking mental health counseling. *Berkeley Undergraduate Journal*, 38(1), 1–24, 10.5070/B3.36704

Currier, J. M., Fox, J., Vieten, C. (Eds.). (in press). *Handbook of training in spiritual and religious competencies in mental health professions*. Oxford University Press.

Currier, J. M., Fox, J., Vieten, C., Pearce, M., & Oxhandler, H. K. (2023). Enhancing competencies for the ethical integration of religion and spirituality in psychological services. *Psychological Services*, *20*(1), 40–50. https://doi.org/10.1037/ser0000678

Currier, J. M., Swift, J. K., Sanders, P., & Richards, P. S. (2024). Preventing dropout in spiritually integrated psychotherapies: What are the effective methods of attending to clients' spirituality? *Psychotherapy*, *61*(3), 184–190. https://doi.org/10.1037/pst0000530

Davis, D. E., DeBlaere, C., Owen, J., Hook, J. N., Rivera, D. P., Choe, E., Van Tongeren, D. R., Worthington, E. L., & Placeres, V. (2018). The multicultural orientation framework: A narrative review. *Psychotherapy*, *55*(1), 89–100. https://doi.org/10.1037/pst0000160

Davis, E. B., Worthington, E. L., Jr., & Schnitker, S. A. (Eds.). (2023). *Handbook of positive psychology, religion, and spirituality*. Springer Nature Switzerland AG. https://doi.org/10.1007/978-3-031-10274-5

Davison, G. C., & Walden, K.-R. (2024). History and iatrogenic effects of conversion therapy. *Annual Review of Clinical Psychology*, *20*, 333–354. https://doi.org/10.1146/annurev-clinpsy-080822-052144

Dike, C., Briz, L., Fadus, M., Martinez, R., May, C., Milone, R., Nesbit-Bartsch, A., Powell, T., Witmer, A. & Brendel, R. (2022). Religion, spirituality, and ethics in psychiatric practice. *The Journal of Nervous and Mental Disease*, *210* (8), 557–563. doi: 10.1097/NMD.0000000000001505

Engel, G. L. (1977). The need for a new medical model: a challenge for biomedicine. *Science* (New York, N.Y.), *196*(4286), 129–136. https://doi.org/10.1126/science.847460

Erickson Cornish, J. A., Riva, M. T., & Smith, R. D. (2015). Responding to the conscience clause: A complex and crucial issue in the education and training of health service psychologists. *Training and Education in Professional Psychology*, *9*(4), 271.

Evans, J., Lesage, K., Miner, W., Starr, K. J., & Corichi, M. (2025, May 6). Believing in spirits and life after death in common around the world. https://www.pewresearch.org/religion/2025/05/06/god-spirits-and-the-natural-world/

Exline, J. J., Pargament, K. I., Grubbs, J. B., & Yali, A. M. (2014). The Religious and Spiritual Struggles Scale: Development and initial validation. *Psychology of Religion and Spirituality*, *6*(3), 208–222. https://doi.org/10.1037/a0036465

Exline, J. J., & Rose, E. D. (2013). Religious and spiritual struggles. In R. F. Paloutzian & C. L. Park (Eds.), *Handbook of the psychology of religion and spirituality* (2nd ed., pp. 380–398). The Guilford Press.

Falender, C. A. & Shafranske, E. P. (2021). *Clinical supervision. A competency-based approach* (2nd Ed.). Washington, DC: American Psychological Association. https://doi.org/10.1037/0000243-000

Foucault, M. (1994). *The birth of the clinic: An archaeology of medical perception* (A. M. Sheridan Smith, Trans.). Vintage. (Original work published 1963)

Fowers, B. J. (2005). *Virtue and psychology: Pursuing excellence in ordinary practices*. American Psychological Association. https://doi.org/10.1037/11219-000

Fredrickson, B. L. (2002). How does religion benefit health and well-being? Are positive emotions active ingredients? *Psychological Inquiry*, *13*(3), 209–213.

Gall, T. L., & Guirguis-Younger, M. (2013). Religious and spiritual coping: Current theory and research. In K. I. Pargament, J. J. Exline, & J. W. Jones (Eds.), *APA handbook of psychology, religion, and spirituality (Vol. 1): Context, theory, and research* (pp. 349–364). American Psychological Association. https://doi.org/10.1037/14045-019

Geertz, C. (1973). Religion as a cultural system. In C. Geertz (Ed.), *The interpretation of cultures* (pp. 87–125). Basic Books.

Ghaemi, S. N. (2009). The rise and fall of the biopsychosocial model. *The British journal of psychiatry: The journal of mental science*, *195*(1), 3–4. https://doi.org/10.1192/bjp.bp.109.063859

Gonsiorek, J. C., Richards, P. S., Pargament, K. I., & McMinn, M. R. (2009). Ethical challenges and opportunities at the edge: Incorporating spirituality and religion into psychotherapy. *Professional Psychology: Research and Practice*, *40*(4), 385–395. https://doi.org/10.1037/a0016488

Griffith, J. L., & Griffith, M. E. (2002). *Encountering the sacred in psychotherapy: How to talk with people about their spiritual lives*. Guilford Press.

Grzanka, P. R., DeVore, E. N., Frantell, K. A., Miles, J. R., & Spengler, E. S. (2020). Conscience clauses and sexual and gender minority mental health care: A case study. *Journal of Counseling Psychology*, *67*(5), 551–567. https://doi.org/10.1037/cou0000396

Harris, J. I., Park, C. L., Currier, J. M., Usset, T. J., & Voecks, C. D. (2015).Moral injury and psycho-spiritual development: Considering the developmental context.*Traumatology*, 21(3), 166–174. https://doi.org/10.1037/trm0000038

Harris, J. I., Usset, T. J., Voecks, C. D., Thuras, P. D., Currier, J. M., & Erbes, C. R. (2018).Theodicy and spiritual distress among veterans managing posttraumatic stress.*International Journal for the Psychology of Religion*, 28(2), 105–115.

Harris, K. A., Randolph, B. E., & Gordon, T. D. (2016). What do clients want? Assessing spiritual needs in counseling: A literature review. *Spirituality in Clinical Practice*, *3*(4), 250–275. https://doi.org/10.1037/scp0000108

Hathaway, W. L., & Ripley, J. S. (2009). Ethical concerns around spirituality and religion in clinical practice. In J. D. Aten, M. R. McMinn, & E. L. Worthington Jr. (Eds.), *Spiritually oriented interventions for counseling and psychotherapy* (pp. 25–52). American Psychological Association.

Hill, P. C., Pargament, K. I., Hood, R. W. Jr., McCullough, M. E., Swyers, J. P., Larson, D. B., & Zinnbauer, B. J. (2000). Conceptualizing religion and spirituality: Points of commonality, points of departure. *Journal for the Theory of Social Behaviour*, 30(1), 51–77.

Ho, M. Y., Worthington, E. L., Jr., Cowden, R. G., Bechara, A. O., et al. (2024). International REACH forgiveness intervention: A multisite randomized controlled trial. *BMJ Public Health*, 2, e000072. DOI: 10.1136/bmjph-2023-000072

Hodge, D. R. (2013). Assessing spirituality and religion in the context of counseling and psychotherapy. In K. I. Pargament, A. Mahoney, & E. P. Shafranske (Eds.), *APA handbook of psychology, religion, and spirituality (Vol. 2): An applied psychology of religion and spirituality* (pp. 93–123). American Psychological Association. https://doi.org/10.1037/14046-005

Hook, J. N. (2018). A way of being in session: Cultivating cultural humility in clinical supervision. *American Journal of Psychotherapy*, 72(2), 90–97.

Hook, J. N., Davis, D., Owen, J., & DeBlaere, C. (2025). Developing a multicultural orientation. In J. N. Hook, D. Davis, J. Owen, & C. DeBlaere (Eds.), *Cultural humility: Engaging diverse identities in therapy* (*2nd ed.*, pp. 21–48). American Psychological Association. https://doi.org/10.1037/0000462-002

Jackson, S. W. (1999). *Care of the psyche: History of psychological healing*. Yale University Press.

James, W. (1982). *The varieties of religious experience*. Penguin Books. (Original work published 1902)

Janoff-Bulman, R. (1992). *Shattered assumptions: Towards a new psychology of trauma*. Free Press.

John Templeton Foundation. (n.d.). Intellectual humility. https://www.templeton.org/discoveries/intellectual-humility

Jones, J. (1981). *The texture of knowledge. An essay on religion and science*. Lanham.

Jones, J. M. (2023). In U.S., 47% identify as religious, 33% as spiritual. Retrieved from https://news.gallup.com/poll/511133/identify-religious-spiritual.aspx

Jones, J. M. (2025). Religious preferences largely stable in U. S. since 2020. https://news.gallup.com/poll/659339/religious-preferences-largely-stable-2020.aspx

Jones, M. (2023). *In U.S., 47% Identify as Religious, 33% as Spiritual*. (Gallup). https://news.gallup.com/poll/511133/identify-religious-spiritual.aspx

Jones, S. L. (1994). A constructive relationship for religion with the science and profession of psychology: Perhaps the boldest model yet. *American Psychologist*, *49*(3), 184–199. https://doi.org/10.1037/0003-066X.49.3.184

Kheriaty, A., & Cihak, J. (2012). *The Catholic guide to depression: How the saints, the sacraments, and psychiatry can help you break its grip and find happiness again*. Sophia Institute Press.

King, L. A., & Hicks, J. A. (2021). The science of meaning in life. *Annual Review of Psychology*, *72*, 561–584. https://doi.org/10.1146/annurev-psych-072420-122921

Kocet, M. M., & Herlihy, B. J. (2014). Addressing value-based conflicts within the counseling relationship: A decision-making model. *Journal of Counseling & Development*, *92*(2), 180–186. https://doi.org/10.1002/j.1556-6676.2014.00146.x

Koenig, H. G. (2018). *Religion and mental health: Research and clinical applications*. Academic Press.

Koenig, H. G., King, D. E., & Carson, V. B. (2012). *Handbook of religion and health* (2nd ed.). Oxford University Press.

Koenig, H. G., & Larson, D. B. (2001). Religion and mental health: Evidence for an association. *International Review of Psychiatry*, *13*(2), 67–78. https://doi.org/10.1080/09540260124661

Koenig, H. G., VanderWeele, T. & Peteet, J. R. (2023). *Handbook of religion and health* (3rd ed.). Oxford University Press.

Koltko-Rivera, M. E. (2004). The psychology of worldviews. *Review of General Psychology*, *8*(1), 3–58. https://doi.org/10.1037/1089-2680.8.1.3

Lazarus, R., & Folkman, S. (1984). *Stress, appraisal, and coping*. Springer.

Levin, J., Bradshaw, M., Johnson, B. R., & Stark, R. (2022). Are religious "nones" really not religious?: Revisiting Glenn, three decades later. *Interdisciplinary Journal of Research on Religion*, *18*, Article 7.

Litz, B. T., Stein, N., Delaney, E., Lebowitz, L., Nash, W. P., Silva, C., & Maguen, S. (2009). Moral injury and moral repair in war veterans: A preliminary model and intervention strategy. *Clinical Psychology Review*, 29(8), 695–706. https://doi.org/10.1016/j.cpr.2009.07.003

Long, K. N. G., Symons, X., VanderWeele, T. J., Balboni, T. A., Rosmarin, D. H., Puchalski, C., Cutts, T., Gunderson, G. R., Idler, E., Oman, D., Balboni, M. J., Tuach, L. S., & Koh, H. K. (2024). Spirituality as a determinant of health: Emerging policies, practices, and systems. *Health Affairs*, *43*(6), 783–790. https://doi.org/10.1377/hlthaff.2023.01643

Lucchetti, G., de Oliveira, L. R., Koenig, H. G., Leite, J. R., & Lucchetti, A. L. (2013). Medical students, spirituality and religiosity — results from the multicenter study SBRAME. *BMC Medical Education*, *13*(1), Article 162. https://doi.org/10.1186/1472-6920-13-162

Lukoff, D. (2014). From personal experience to clinical practice to research: A career path leading to public policy changes in integrating spirituality into mental health. *Spirituality in Clinical Practice*, *1*(2), 145–152. https://doi.org/10.1037/scp0000016

Mangione, L., & Plante, T. G. (2022). Psychologists' reflections on the integration of spirituality in clinical practice. *Spirituality in Clinical Practice*, *9*(2), 81–83. https://doi.org/10.1037/scp0000286

Masters, K. S., Boehm, J. K., Boylan, J. M., Vagnini, K. M., & Rush, C. L. (2023). The scientific study of positive psychology, religion/spirituality, and physical health. In E. B. Davis, E. L. Worthington, Jr., & S. A. Schnitker (Eds.), *Handbook of positive psychology, religion, and spirituality* (pp. 329–343). Springer Nature Switzerland AG. https://doi.org/10.1007/978-3-031-10274-5_21

McKnight, P. E., Kashdan, T. B. (2009). Purpose in life as a system that creates and sustains health and well-being: An integrative, testable theory. *Review of General Psychology*, *13*(3), 242–251. https://doi.org/10.1037/a0017152

McMinn, M. R., Neff, M. A., Snow, K. N., & Schollars, N. (2024). Counseling and psychotherapy within and across faith traditions. In L. J. Miller (Ed.), *The Oxford handbook of psychology and spirituality* (2nd ed., pp. 364–387). Oxford University Press. https://doi.org/10.1093/oxfordhb/9780190905538.013.16

Miller, L. J. (Ed.). (2012). *The Oxford handbook of psychology and spirituality*. Oxford University Press. https://doi.org/10.1093/oxfordhb/9780199729920.001.0001

Miller, L. J. (Ed.). (2024). *The Oxford handbook of psychology and spirituality* (2nd ed.). Oxford University Press. https://doi.org/10.1093/oxfordhb/9780190905538.001.0001

Newport, F. (2010). In U.S., increasing number have no religious identity. Retrieved from https://news.gallup.com/poll/128276/Increasing-Number-No-Religious-Identity.aspx

O'Donohue, W. (1989). The (even) bolder model: The clinical psychologist as metaphysician-scientist-practitioner. *American Psychologist*, *44*(12), 1460–1468. https://doi.org/10.1037/0003-066X.44.12.1460

Owen, J., Leach, M. M., Wampold, B., & Rodolfa, E. (2011). Client and therapist variability in clients' perceptions of their therapists' multicultural competencies. *Journal of Counseling Psychology*, *58*(1), 1–9. https://doi.org/10.1037/a0021496

Oxhandler, H. K., Ellor, J. W., & Stanford, M. S. (2018). Client Attitudes toward Integrating Religion and Spirituality in Mental Health Treatment: Scale Development and Client Responses. *Social work*, *63*(4), 337–346. https://doi.org/10.1093/sw/swy041

Oxhandler, H. K., Moffatt, K. M., & Giardina, T. D. (2019). Clinical helping professionals' perceived support, barriers, and training to integrate clients' religion/spirituality in practice. *Spirituality in Clinical Practice*, *6*(4), 279–291. https://doi.org/10.1037/scp0000189

Oxhandler, H. K., & Parrish, D. E. (2018). Integrating clients' religion/spirituality in clinical practice: A comparison among social workers, psychologists, counselors, marriage and family therapists, and nurses. *Journal of Clinical Psychology*, *74*(4), 680–694. https://doi.org/10.1002/jclp.22539

Oxhandler, H. K., Parrish, D. E., Torres, L. R., & Achenbaum, W. A. (2015). The integration of clients' religion and spirituality in social work practice: A national survey. *Social Work*, *60*(3), 228–237. https://doi.org/10.1093/sw/swv018

Pais Silva Guerra, C. S. (2021). A critical approach to subjectivation processes in psychiatry and their correlation with distinct political ideas. *Dialogues in Philosophy, Mental & Neuro Sciences*, *14*(1), 1–8.

Paloutzian, R. F., Murken, S., Streib, H., & Rößler-Namini, S. (2013). Conversion, deconversion, and spiritual transformation: A multilevel interdisciplinary view. In R. F. Paloutzian & C. L. Park (Eds.), *Handbook of the psychology of religion and spirituality* (2nd ed., pp. 399–421). The Guilford Press.

Pargament, K. I. (1997). *The psychology of religion and coping: Theory, research, practice*. Guilford Press.

Pargament, K. I. (2007). *Spiritually integrated psychotherapy: Understanding and addressing the sacred*. The Guilford Press.

Pargament, K. I. (2013). Searching for the sacred: Toward a non-reductionistic theory of spirituality. In K. I. Pargament (Ed.-in-Chief), J. J. Exline & J. Jones (Assoc. Eds.), *APA handbooks in psychology: APA handbook of psychology, religion, and spirituality: Vol 1. Context, theory, and research* (pp. 257–274). American Psychological Association. https://doi.org/10.1037/14045-014

Pargament, K. I., & Exline, J. J. (2022). *Working with spiritual struggles in psychotherapy: From research to practice*. The Guilford Press.

Pargament, K. I., Mahoney, A., Exline, J. J., Jones, J. W., & Shafranske, E. P. (2013). Envisioning an integrative paradigm for the psychology of religion and spirituality. In K. I. Pargament, J. J. Exline, & J. W. Jones (Eds.), *APA handbook of psychology, religion, and spirituality (Vol. 1): Context, theory, and research* (pp. 3–19). American Psychological Association. https://doi.org/10.1037/14045-001

Pargament, K. I., Smith, B. W., Koenig, H. G., & Perez, L. (1998). Patterns of positive and negative religious coping with major life stressors. *Journal for the Scientific Study of Religion*, *37*(4), 710–724. https://doi.org/10.2307/1388152

Park, C. L. (2005). Religion and meaning. In R. F. Paloutzian & C. L. Park (Eds.), *Handbook of the psychology of religion and spirituality* (pp. 295–314). The Guilford Press.

Park, C. L., Currier, J. M., Harris, J. I., & Slattery, J. M. (2017). *Trauma, meaning, and spirituality: Translating research into clinical practice*. American Psychological Association. https://doi.org/10.1037/15961-000

Park, C. L., Edmondson, D., & Hale-Smith, A. (2013). Why religion? Meaning as motivation. In K. I. Pargament, J. J. Exline, & J. W. Jones (Eds.), *APA handbook of psychology, religion, and spirituality (Vol. 1): Context, theory, and research* (pp. 157–171). American Psychological Association. https://doi.org/10.1037/14045-008

Park, C. L., & Folkman, S. (1997). Meaning in the context of stress and coping. *Review of General Psychology*, *1*(2), 115–144. https://doi.org/10.1037/1089-2680.1.2.115

Pearce, M. J., Pargament, K. I., Oxhandler, H. K., Vieten, C., & Wong, S. (2019). A novel training program for mental health providers in religious and spiritual competencies. *Spirituality in Clinical Practice*, *6*(2), 73–82. https://doi.org/10.1037/scp0000195

Pearce, M. J., Pargament, K. I., Oxhandler, H. K., Vieten, C., & Wong, S. (2020). Novel online training program improves spiritual competencies in mental health care. *Spirituality in Clinical Practice*, *7*(3), 145–161. https://doi.org/10.1037/scp0000208

Pearce, M. J., Pargament, K. I., Wong, S., Hinkel, H., Salcone, S., Morgan, G., Kemp, D., Brock, B., Kim, E., Oxhandler, H. K., Vieten, C., Fox, J., Polson, E. C., & Currier, J. M. (2024). Enhancing training in spiritual and religious competencies in mental health graduate education: Evaluation of an integrated curricular approach. *PLoS ONE*, *19*(9), 1–21. https://doi.org/10.1371/journal.pone.0306114

Peterson, J. B. (2013). Three forms of meaning and the management of complexity. In K. D. Markman, T. Proulx, & M. J. Lindberg (Eds.), *The psychology of meaning* (pp. 17–48). American Psychological Association. https://doi.org/10.1037/14040-002

Pew Research Center. (2015). *Religiously unaffiliated.* (Pew Research Center) https://www.pewresearch.org/religion/2015/04/02/religiously-unaffiliated/

Pew Research Center (2024). *8 in 10 Americans say religion is losing influence in public life.* (Pew Research Center) https://www.pewresearch.org/religion/2024/03/15/8-in-10-americans-say-religion-is-losing-influence-in-public-life/

Pew Research Center. (2025). *Religious Landscape Study.* (Pew Research Center) https://www.pewresearch.org/collections/religious-landscape-study/

Plante, T. G. (2009). *Spiritual practices in psychotherapy: Thirteen tools for enhancing psychological health.* American Psychological Association. https://doi.org/10.1037/11872-000

Plante, T. G. (2024). *Spiritually informed therapy (SIT): Wisdom and evidence based strategies that work.* Cognella.

Polson, E. C., Oxhandler, H. K., Ander, G., Morgan, G. B., Fox, J., Pearce, M., Vieten, C., Pargament, K., & Currier, J. (2025). The religious and spiritual beliefs and practices of mental health educators: a national study. *Journal of Spirituality in Mental Health*, 1–16. https://doi.org/10.1080/19349637.2025.2470822

Richards, P. S. (2005). Integrative theistic psychotherapy. In L. Sperry & E. P. Shafranske (Eds.), *Spiritually oriented psychotherapy* (pp. 165–186). Washington, DC: American Psychological Association.

Richards, P. S. (2024). Honoring religious diversity and universal spirituality in psychotherapy. In L. J. Miller (Ed.), *The Oxford handbook of psychology and spirituality* (2nd ed., pp. 338–363). Oxford University Press. https://doi.org/10.1093/oxfordhb/9780190905538.013.15

Richards, P. S., Allen, G. E. K., & Judd, D. K. (Eds.). (2023). *Handbook of spiritually integrated psychotherapies.* American Psychological Association. https://doi.org/10.1037/0000338-000

Richards, P. S., & Bergin, A. E. (2005). *A spiritual strategy for counseling and psychotherapy* (2nd ed.). American Psychological Association. https://doi.org/10.1037/11214-000

Richards, P. S., & Bergin, A. E. (Eds.). (2014). *Handbook of psychotherapy and religious diversity* (2nd ed.). American Psychological Association. https://doi.org/10.1037/14371-000

Rizzuto, A.-M. (2005). Psychoanalytic considerations about spiritually oriented psychotherapy. In L. Sperry & E. P. Shafranske (Eds.), *Spiritually oriented psychotherapy* (pp. 31–50). American Psychological Association. https://doi.org/10.1037/10886-002

Rizzuto, A-M., & Shafranske, E. P. (2013). Addressing religion and spirituality in treatment from a psychodynamic perspective. In K. I. Pargament, A. Mahoney, E. P. Shafranske (Eds.), *APA handbook of psychology, religion, and spirituality (Vol 2): An applied psychology of religion and spirituality* (pp. 125–146). American Psychological Association. https://doi.org/10.1037/14046-006

Rosmarin, D. H., & Koenig, H. G. (Eds.). (2020). *Handbook of spirituality, religion, and mental health* (2nd ed.). Elsevier Academic Press.

Saad, M., de Medeiros, R., & Mosini, A. C. (2017). Are We Ready for a True Biopsychosocial-Spiritual Model? The Many Meanings of "Spiritual". *Medicines (Basel, Switzerland)*, *4*(4), 79. https://doi.org/10.3390/medicines4040079

Sandage, S. J., Rupert, D., Stavros, G., & Devor, N. G. (2020). *Relational spirituality in psychotherapy: Healing suffering and promoting growth.* American Psychological Association. https://doi.org/10.1037/0000174-000

Saroglou, V., & Cohen, A. B. (2013). Cultural and cross-cultural psychology of religion. In R. F. Paloutzian & C. L. Park (Eds.), *Handbook of the psychology of religion and spirituality* (2nd ed., pp. 330–354). The Guilford Press.

Saunders, S. M., Miller, M. L., & Bright, M. M. (2010). Spiritually conscious psychological care. *Professional Psychology: Research and Practice*, *41*(5), 355–362. https://doi.org/10.1037/a0020953

Shafranske, E. (1997). Practices in the search for meaning: A response to Hefner. *International Journal for the Psychology of Religion*, *7*(3), 161–166. https://doi.org/10.1207/s15327582ijpr0703_3

Shafranske, E. P. (2002). The psychoanalytic meaning of religious experience. In M. Arieti & F. De Nardi (Eds.)., *Psychoanalisi e religione* (pp. 227–257). Centro Scientifico Editore. [Il significanto dell'esperienza religiosa.]

Shafranske, E. P. (2009). Spiritually oriented psychodynamic psychotherapy. *Journal of Clinical Psychology: In Session*, *65*(2), 147–157. https://doi.org/10.1002/jclp.20565

Shafranske, E. P. (2013). Addressing religiousness and spirituality in psychotherapy: Advancing evidence-based professional practice. In R. Paloutzian & C. Park (Eds.), *The handbook of the psychology of religion and spirituality* (pp. 595–616). New York: Guilford Press.

Shafranske, E. P. (2016) Finding a place for spirituality in psychology training: The use of competency-based clinical supervision. *Spirituality in Clinical Practice*. *3*(1), 18–21. https://doi.org/10.1037/scp0000098

Shafranske, E. P. (2023). The scientific study of positive psychology, religion/spirituality, and mental health. In E. B. Davis, E. L. Worthington, Jr., & S. A. Schnitker (Eds.), *Handbook of positive psychology, religion, and spirituality* (pp. 345–358). Springer Nature Switzerland AG. https://doi.org/10.1007/978-3-031-10274-5_22

Shafranske, E. P. (2024). Religion and spirituality in psychotherapy: A personal bedrock of faith. *Spirituality in Clinical Practice*, *11*(1), 48–54. https://doi.org/10.1037/scp0000359

Shafranske, E. P., & Sperry, L. (2005). Addressing the spiritual dimension in psychotherapy: Introduction and overview. In L. Sperry & E. P. Shafranske (Eds.), *Spiritually oriented psychotherapy* (pp. 11–29). American Psychological Association. https://doi.org/10.1037/10886-001

Smith, H. (2001). *Why religion matters*. HarperSanFrancisco.

Sperry, L. (2012). *Spirituality in clinical practice: Theory and practice of spiritually oriented psychotherapy* (2nd ed.). Routledge/Taylor & Francis Group.

Sperry, L., & Shafranske, E. P. (Eds.). (2005). *Spiritually oriented psychotherapy*. American Psychological Association. https://doi.org/10.1037/10886-000

Substance Abuse and Mental Health Services Administration. (2016). *Creating a healthier life: A step-by-step guide to wellness* (SMA16-4958). U.S. Department of Health and Human Services.https://store.samhsa.gov/product/creating-healthier-life-step-step-guide-wellness/sma16-4958

Suijker, C. A. (2023). Foucault and medicine: challenging normative claims. *Medicine, Health Care, and Philosophy*, *26*(4), 539–548. https://doi.org/10.1007/s11019-023-10170-y

Tan, S.-Y. (1996). Religion in clinical practice: Implicit and explicit integration. In E. P. Shafranske (Ed.), *Religion and the clinical practice of psychology* (pp. 365–387). Washington, DC: American Psychological Association. https://doi.org/10.1037/10199-013

Tanega, C., Currier, J., Fox, J., Pittman, J., & Vieten, C. (2025). Promoting training in spiritual and religious competencies for mental health care: Understanding barriers and facilitators in graduate education. *Psychology of Religion and Spirituality*. Advance online publication. https://dx.doi.org/10.1037/rel0000549

Van Cappellen, P., Edwards, M. E., & Fredrickson, B. L. (2021). Upward spirals of positive emotions and religious behaviors. *Current Opinion in Psychology*, *40*, 92–98. https://doi.org/10.1016/j.copsyc.2020.09.004

Verhagen, P. J. (2017). Psychiatry and religion: consensus reached! *Mental Health, Religion & Culture*, *20*(6), 516–527. https://doi.org/10.1080/13674676.2017.1334195

Vieten, C., Fox, J., Oxhandler, H. K., Pearce, M., Polson, E. C., Pargament, K., Wong, S., & Currier, J. M. (2024). Spiritual and religious competency training for mental health care professionals: How much is enough? *Counselor Education & Supervision*, *63*(3), 187–202. https://doi.org/10.1002/ceas.12311

Vieten, C., & Lukoff, D. (2022). Spiritual and religious competencies in psychology. *American Psychologist*, *77*(1), 26–38. https://doi.org/10.1037/amp0000821

Vieten, C., Oxhandler, H. K., Pearce, M., Fry, N., Tanega, C., & Pargament, K. (2023). Mental health professionals' perspectives on the relevance of religion and spirituality to mental health care. *BMC Psychology*, *11*(1), 439. https://doi.org/10.1186/s40359-023-01466-y

Vieten, C., Scammell, S., Pierce, A., Pilato, R., Ammondson, I., Pargament, K. I., & Lukoff, D. (2016). Competencies for psychologists in the domains of religion and spirituality. *Spirituality in Clinical Practice*, *3*(2), 92–114. https://doi.org/10.1037/scp0000078

Webb, J. R. (2021). *Understanding forgiveness and addiction: Theory, research, and clinical application*. Routledge.

Webb, J. R., Toussaint, L., & Dula, C. S. (2014). Ritualistic, theistic, and existential spirituality: Initial psychometric qualities of the RiTE measure of spirituality. *Journal of Religion and Health*, *53*(4), 972–985. https://doi.org/10.1007/s10943-013-9697-y

Wise, E. H., Bieschke, K. J., Forrest, L., Cohen-Filipic, J., Hathaway, W. L., & Douce, L. A. (2015). Psychology's proactive approach to conscience clause court cases and legislation. *Training and Education in Professional Psychology*, *9*(4), 259–268. https://doi.org/10.1037/tep0000092

World Health Organization. (2025). *Constitution of the World Health Organization*. Geneva: Author. Retrieved April 29, 2025, from https://www.who.int/about/governance/constitution

Wormley, A. S., Vornlocher, C., Aglozo, E. Y., Jayawickreme, E., Johnson, K. A., Moon, J. W., Van Cappellen, P., Verma, A., & Cohen, A. B. (2025). Religion and human flourishing. *The Journal of Positive Psychology*, *20*(1), 43–58. https://doi.org/10.1080/17439760.2023.2297208

Worthington, E. L., Jr. (2024). Forgiveness psychoeducation with emerging adults: REACH forgiveness and community campaigns for forgiveness. *Education Sciences*, *14*(9), 927. https://doi.org/10.3390/educsci14090927

Worthington, E. L., Jr., Hook, J. N., Davis, D. E., Gartner, A. L., & Jennings, D. J., II. (2013). Conducting empirical research on religiously accommodative interventions. In K. I. Pargament, A. Mahoney, & E. P. Shafranske (Eds.), *APA handbook of psychology, religion, and spirituality (Vol. 2): An applied psychology of religion and spirituality* (pp. 651–669). American Psychological Association. https://doi.org/10.1037/14046-034

Worthington, E. L., Jr., Hook, J. N., Davis, D. E., & McDaniel, M. A. (2011). Religion and spirituality. In J. C. Norcross (Ed.), *Psychotherapy relationships that work: Evidence-based responsiveness* (2nd ed., pp. 402–419). https://doi.org/10.1093/acprof:oso/9780199737208.003.0020

Worthington, E. L., Jr., Kurusu, T. A., McCullough, M. E., & Sandage, S. J. (1996). Empirical research on religion and psychotherapeutic processes and outcomes: A 10-year review and research prospectus. *Psychological Bulletin*, *119*(3), 448–487. https://doi.org/10.1037/0033-2909.119.3.448

Yamada, A.-M., Lukoff, D., Lim, C. S. F., & Mancuso, L. L. (2020). Integrating spirituality and mental health: Perspectives of adults receiving public mental health services in California. *Psychology of Religion and Spirituality*, *12*(3), 276–287. https://doi.org/10.1037/rel0000260

Zinnbauer, B. J., Pargament, K. I., & Scott, A. B. (1999). The emerging meanings of religiousness and spirituality: Problems and prospects. *Journal of Personality*, *67*(6), 889–919. https://doi.org/10.1111/1467-6494.00077

Chapter 21

An Overview of Systematic Reviews and Meta-Analyses on the Association Between Religion/Spirituality and Health/Well-Being

Edward (Ward) B. Davis, Zhuo Job Chen, Richard G. Cowden, Tyler J. VanderWeele, Steve Oberg, Greta Bivins, Cate Newcity, Eden Song, and Harold G. Koenig*

A vast body of research has examined the relationships between religiousness/spirituality (R/S) and health/well-being (HWB; Koenig et al., 2024), and a massive but disjointed corpus of systematic reviews and meta-analyses has tried to synthesize these empirical findings. One prior overview of reviews on R/S and HWB was conducted by Oman and Syme (2018), who synthesized 118 reviews published through 2017. However, an enormous body of empirical research on R/S and HWB has been published since then (Koenig et al., 2024), likely including dozens if not hundreds of new reviews. This chapter offers an updated synthesis of systematic reviews and meta-analyses (all-time through January 1, 2024) that have studied this relationship.

Definitions and Conceptual Frameworks

We begin by clarifying our terms and conceptual frameworks. Religion, spirituality, health, and well-being are complex constructs with varied, debated definitions (Harris et al., 2018; Lee et al., 2021). Davis et al. (2023a) have defined *spirituality* and *religion* as follows:

> *Spirituality* refers to people's search for and response to meaning and connection with whatever they perceive as sacred, typically including supernatural entities (e.g., deity/deities, saints, ancestors, karma, or fate/destiny) or aspects of life either viewed as a manifestation of the divine (e.g., close human relationships) or as having transcendent or divine-like qualities (e.g., nature, the universe, [the true self]). *Religion* refers to people's search for and response to sacred meaning… and connection in the context of culturally sanctioned codifications (e.g., of beliefs, values, and morals), rituals (e.g., prayer, meditation, and collective worship), and institutions (e.g., families, faith communities, schools, and organizations).
>
> (p. 280; see also Harris et al., 2018; Pargament et al., 2013)

In short, R/S refers to people's search for and response to sacred meaning and connection. This search and response process can occur through institutional or noninstitutional pathways.

Building on prior work (Davis et al., 2023a, 2023b; Pargament et al., 2013), we affirm that people's R/S is multidimensional (comprised of cognitive, emotional, social, and behavioral facets), multivalent (able to facilitate or undermine health/well-being), and multilevel (embodied at individual, relational, and community levels). This view is

* Corresponding Author: ward.davis@wheaton.edu.

DOI: 10.4324/9781003440048-25

resonant with Webb's (2021) RiTE model of spirituality (see Chapters 1 and 44, this volume) in that both models are multidimensional and ecumenical (applicable across cultures and across monotheistic, polytheistic, and nontheistic R/S), focus on sacred connection and meaning, and operationalize healthy R/S as a harmonious balance and coherent integration across dimensions of R/S. In addition, Davis et al.'s (2023a) Positive Religious and Spiritual Development theory incorporates an appreciation for *contextual adaptiveness* (i.e., "individual–context relations benefiting both the person and his or her ecology," Lerner et al., 2015, p. 608) into this understanding of R/S, defining *healthy R/S* as contextually adaptive, harmonious balance that is coherently well-integrated across dimensions of R/S and across time, situations, and contexts (see also VanderWeele et al., 2023).

Human flourishing is the "relative attainment of a state in which all aspects of a person's life are good, *including the contexts in which that person lives*" (VanderWeele & Lomas, 2023, p. 38), and *well-being* is "the relative attainment of a state in which all aspects of a person's life are good *as they pertain to that individual*" (VanderWeele & Lomas, 2023, p. 38). The current chapter focuses on individuals (i.e., well-being) because little research on R/S has measured flourishing at a level of analysis that extends beyond the individual (Davis et al., 2023b). Even so, we use the conceptual framework of human flourishing to operationalize the core domains of individual well-being (plus one flourishing-facilitative environmental condition: material and financial stability). These five domains are (a) mental and physical health, (b) happiness and life satisfaction, (c) meaning and purpose, (d) character and virtues, and (e) close social relationships (VanderWeele, 2017; VanderWeele et al., 2023).

When it comes to conceptualizing health, we adopt Lomas et al.'s (2024) WHO+ framework, which defines *health* as "a state of complete physical, mental, ... social [and spiritual] well-being and not merely the absence of disease or infirmity" (World Health Organization, 1946, para. 1). This WHO+ framework is especially relevant for people for whom R/S plays a key role in their identity or culture, including approximately 68% of the global population (Diener et al., 2011; VanderWeele & Lomas, 2023). Even as religion and spirituality are strongly interrelated concepts and hence are often referred to collectively as R/S, health and well-being are also strongly interrelated and commonly referred to collectively as HWB.

Regarding the association between R/S and HWB, most modern theories have focused on the bidirectional causal impact R/S and HWB have on each other. These theories suggest R/S and HWB influence one another along four major bidirectional pathways: physical pathways (e.g., genetic, epigenetic, and other biological and neurobiological influences), psychological pathways (e.g., cognitive and emotional habits and coping strategies), behavioral pathways (e.g., healthy behaviors, decision-making habits, and morally good and wise choices and behaviors), and social–environmental pathways (e.g., caregiver nurturance, family and peer influences, social support, and sociocultural and societal influences; Davis et al., 2023a; Koenig et al., 2024). Importantly, because both R/S and HWB are multivalent (Koenig et al., 2024), elements within each causal pathway can vary in how flourishing-facilitative or flourishing-undermining (contextually adaptive or maladaptive) they are (Davis et al., 2023a, 2023b). Moreover, because both R/S and HWB are multilevel—embodied at individual, relational, and community levels—the systemic interactions of R/S and HWB are extremely complex and context-dependent, varying along an enormous array of multilevel, multidimensional combinations of R/S and HWB variables (Koenig et al., 2021; VanderWeele et al., 2023). The current chapter will partly examine how much multilevel research on R/S and HWB has been conducted to date.

Oman and Syme's (2018) Previous Overview of Reviews

In the one prior publication that synthesized systematic reviews and meta-analyses of the association between R/S and HWB, Oman and Syme (2018) identified 118 publications through 2017, including 77 systematic reviews (65.3%), 33 meta-analyses (28.0%), 7 qualitative meta-syntheses (5.9%), and 1 meta-analysis of case studies (0.8%). Oman and Syme (2018) categorized these reviews topically into 26 domains: health behaviors (k = 6), substance misuse (k = 3), coping/adjustment/stress-related growth (k = 5), dementia prevention or coping (k = 2), psychological well-being in healthy populations (k = 4), prayer (k = 6), mortality/longevity (k = 3), physical health (k = 2), crime/delinquency (k = 3), discrimination (k = 1), environmental health (k = 1), infectious diseases (k = 1), nutrition (k = 2), family/youth and reproductive outcomes (k = 2), training or well-being of health or religious professionals (k = 6), spiritual well-being interventions at the end of life (k = 5), referrals and adherence (k = 1), programs for prevention or treatment (k = 6), organizational factors (k = 1), treatments/interventions for individuals (k = 15), mental health and disorders (k = 15), patient psychosocial well-being (k = 10), patient sources of spiritual well-being (k = 6), doctor–patient conversations (k = 2), perspectives on the end of life (k = 1), and specific religious traditions (k = 9).

In their overview chapter, Oman and Syme (2018) reported on the authorship of a subset of reviews published through 2013, which were collectively authored by 223 distinct individuals, with only 18 people contributing to multiple reviews and one person to three or more reviews. They also reported that the reviews published through 2017 synthesized a median of 26 primary studies and appeared collectively in 83 distinct journals, with only 14 journals publishing more than one review. Further, Oman and Syme (2018) used Hill's (1965) considerations to evaluate the strength of the evidence supporting the claim that R/S has a causal effect on HWB. Specifically, they evaluated four of Hill's (1965) nine considerations for appraising causality: (a) *Strength* (i.e., the size of the prospective association between R/S and subsequent HWB), (b) *Consistency* (i.e., how consistently that approximate effect size is observed), (c) *Temporality* (i.e., how much does the R/S–HWB association differ when testing the causal effect of HWB on subsequent R/S [reverse causation]), and (d) *Coherence* (i.e., how much does an evidenced causal effect of R/S on HWB cohere with generally accepted facts about HWB).[1] Ultimately, through appraising the totality of the evidence as of 2017, Oman and Syme (2018) concluded the evidence for causality was strengthened considerably since a seminal *American Psychologist* article in which Levin (1994) used Hill's considerations to appraise causal evidence (through 1993) of the R/S–HWB link. Levin (1994, p. 1480) concluded the evidence for *Strength* was "insufficient," for *Consistency* was "yes," for *Coherence* was "probably yes" (p. 1480), and for *Temporality* was "insufficient." Oman and Syme (2018) concluded the evidence (through 2017) for *Consistency* was still "yes" and for the other three considerations was "probably yes."

The Current Overview of Reviews

This chapter aims to update Oman and Syme's (2018) previous umbrella review by synthesizing all systematic reviews and meta-analyses published through January 1, 2024. There are several reasons this update is needed. First, research on R/S and HWB has grown exponentially in recent decades. A simple PsycINFO search using the string "(religio* OR spirit*) AND (health OR well* OR flourishing)" yields 6,560 all-time results published from inception through 1990; 11,960 through 2000 (0.82× increase since 1990); 29,974 through 2010 (3.57× increase since 1990); 58,338 through 2020 (7.89× increase since 1990); and 69,855 through January 1, 2024 (9.65× increase since 1990). There likely has been a corresponding exponential increase in the number of systematic reviews and meta-analyses on the R/S–HWB association, but that is an open empirical question. Second, in the past 5 years, there have been accelerating advances in artificial intelligence and machine learning (Chenneville et al., 2024), even as there have been accelerating advances in research, statistical, and computational methodologies (Little, n.d.). These advancements have opened new horizons for synthesizing large bodies of research through rigorous meta-analyses and systematic reviews. Third, the walls dividing science and R/S are steadily coming down, and there is increasing openness to incorporating R/S into HWB-related science, practice, policy, and public health work (Koenig et al., 2024). Because systematic reviews and meta-analyses are often what guide data-driven public health work, it is reasonable to assume that not only are there many new systematic reviews and meta-analyses since 2017, but there also is an even more pressing need to synthesize those reviews to guide public health work, reduce health inequities, and optimize societal impact.

Consequently, we set out to conduct the current overview of reviews. Our two guiding research questions echoed those of Oman and Syme (2018): (1) What do the published systematic reviews and meta-analyses of the relationship between R/S and HWB collectively reveal? (2) Using Hill's (1965) considerations for causality, what does the collective body of evidence suggest about the causal relationship between R/S and HWB? Of note, the current overview is part of a broader umbrella review that builds on this chapter's dataset and findings.

Methods

Literature Search and Screening of Search Results Against Eligibility Criteria

To begin, our research team conducted preliminary searches in mid-December 2023 and preregistered the umbrella review on PROSPERO (ID# 2024 CRD42024495180, https://www.crd.york.ac.uk/prospero/display_record.php?RecordID=495180) on January 1, 2024. We then conducted the literature database search using our prespecified search strategy (https://www.crd.york.ac.uk/PROSPEROFILES/495180_STRATEGY_20231219.pdf), with the date range spanning from inception to January 1, 2024. We searched five databases (PsycINFO, MEDLINE/PubMed, Web of Science, Cochrane Library, and Healthevidence.org) and found 27,969 publications after de-duplication and citation searching (see Figure 21.1 for our PRISMA diagram). Two blinded coders independently screened all titles/abstracts and 1,058 full texts to determine if they met all inclusion criteria: (a) must be published in a peer-reviewed journal, scholarly book, or governmental/nongovernmental report; (b) must be published in the English language and only involve primary studies of human participants; (c) must specify its search strategy and the individual primary studies it included in its analyses; and (d) must synthesize primary studies that all or mostly (≥ 90%) include at least one quantitative measure of R/S (e.g., prayer, service attendance, religious/spiritual beliefs, or religious/spiritual coping), and at least one quantitative measure of HWB (e.g., mental health, physical health, behavioral health, or happiness/life satisfaction). Any coding conflicts were resolved by consensus.

Like Oman and Syme (2018), we included systematic reviews and meta-analyses evaluating the effectiveness of a clearly defined or described intervention on at least one HWB outcome.

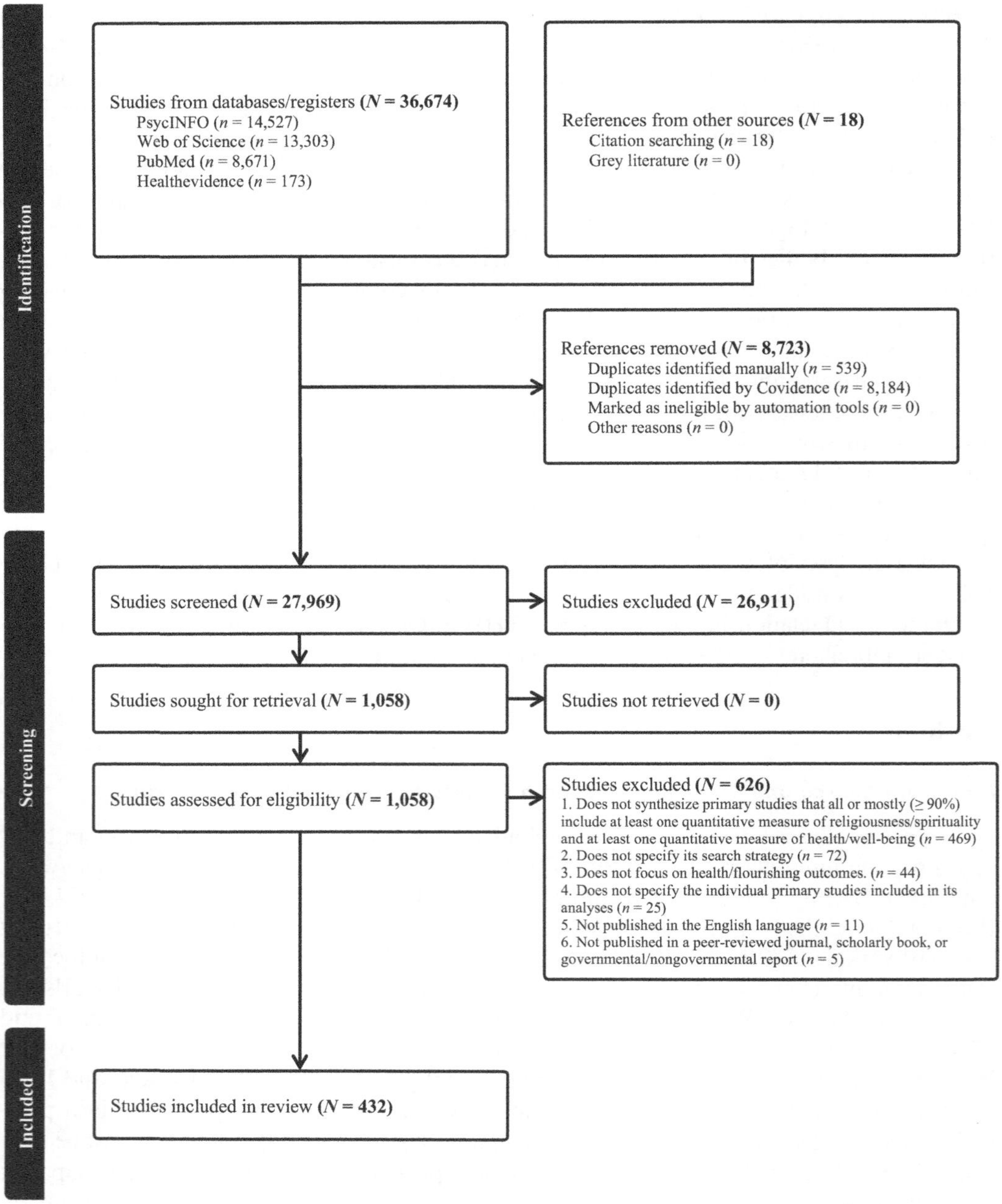

Figure 21.1 PRISMA Diagram.

However, unlike Oman and Syme (2018), we decided to concentrate on systematic reviews and meta-analyses oriented toward (a) understanding and promoting human flourishing/well-being and/or (b) studying the diagnosis, prevention, and treatment of human diseases or disorders. We also restricted our overview to reviews that predominantly included quantitative scientific studies, which excluded some of the types of reviews that Oman and Syme (2018) included in their umbrella review (e.g., qualitative meta-syntheses and case-study meta-analyses). In addition, we excluded commentaries and any reviews that were conducted unsystematically (e.g., did not have a specified search strategy or screening process). Ultimately, 432 reviews met all study criteria.

Data Extraction

All eligible studies were coded by the first author (EBD), who has 19 years of experience scientifically studying the relationship between R/S and HWB and 7 years of experience conducting systematic reviews and bibliometric analyses. Each review was coded along several features, including first author, all authors, number of authors, title, publication year, publication name, publication type (systematic review, meta-analysis, or both), number of studies synthesized, digital object identifier, abstract content, and keywords. Reviews were also coded for the following: (a) whether they were included in the Oman and Syme (2018) umbrella review; (b) whether the review was multilevel (i.e., focused on more than just the individual level of analysis); (c) whether the review synthesized mostly (> 50%) prospective longitudinal studies of the R/S–HWB association; and (d) which of eight HWB dimensions/conditions (mental health, physical health, behavioral health, happiness/life satisfaction, meaning/purpose, character/virtue, social relationships, and material/financial stability) were quantitatively measured by two or more primary studies (one or more if there were ≤ 10 studies in the review). In addition, reviews were coded for whether the review focused predominantly (≥ 90%) on (a) one or more yoga interventions, (b) fasting interventions (e.g., religious fasting during Ramadan), (c) another spiritual intervention (e.g., meditation, tai chi, faith-based interventions, or spiritually integrated psychotherapy), and/or (d) a special population (e.g., youth, older adults, people with mental disorders/difficulties, people with physical diseases/symptoms, or cancer patients).

Results

Next, we conducted bibliometric analyses of the project dataset. The data and data output are openly available at https://osf.io/hty9u/ (Davis et al., 2024), as are all project materials. The main results of data analysis are presented in Table 21.1.

Type of Review

Of the corpus, 270 (62.5%) were systematic reviews, 61 (14.1%) were meta-analyses, and 101 (23.4%) were combined systematic reviews and meta-analyses. Only 60 (13.9%) of the publications were also included in the Oman and Syme (2018) umbrella review, partly because our project's inclusion criteria were more restrictive in some ways (e.g., we excluded reviews that did not have a predominant focus on quantitative studies). At the same time, our umbrella review's criteria were broader than Oman and Syme's (2018) in other ways. Most notably, we included systematic reviews and meta-analyses that focused on yoga interventions and other related spiritual interventions (e.g., tai chi, qi gong, or transcendental meditation). In fact, because such a large proportion of the reviews were yoga reviews, we wanted to look at the corpus from three main vantage points: (a) as a corpus (k = 432), (b) as a subset of all the yoga-focused reviews (k = 154, 35.6% of the corpus), and (c) as a subset of all the reviews that were not yoga-focused (k = 278, 64.4% of the corpus).

Table 21.1 Results From Analyses of Reviews on Religion/Spirituality (R/S) and Health/Well-Being (HWB)

Review characteristic	*All reviews (432 total)*	*Yoga studies (154 total)*	*Nonyoga studies (278 total)*
	k *(%)*	**k** *(%)*	**k** *(%)*
Type of review			
Systematic review	270 (62.5)	87 (56.5)	183 (65.8)
Meta-analysis	61 (14.1)	10 (6.5)	51 (18.3)
Systematic review/meta-analysis	101 (23.4)	57 (37.0)	44 (15.8)
Was included in Oman and Syme's (2018) umbrella review	60 (13.9)	0 (0.0)	60 (100.0)
Decade in which the publication was published			
Before 2000	5 (1.2)	0 (0.0)	5 (1.8)
2000 to 2010	50 (11.6)	5 (3.2)	45 (16.2)
2010 to 2019	203 (47.0)	92 (59.7)	111 (39.9)
2020 to present (through January 1, 2024)	174 (40.3)	57 (37.0)	117 (42.1)
Number of distinct sources (journals or books)	273	102	190
Number of distinct first authors	381	132	249
Number of primary studies synthesized in each review			
2 to 19	226 (52.3)	108 (70.1)	118 (42.4)
20 to 49	124 (28.7)	39 (25.3)	85 (30.6)
50 to 99	53 (12.3)	5 (3.2)	48 (17.3)
100 or more	29 (6.7)	2 (1.3)	27 (9.7)
Overall findings of each review			
Positive R/S–HWB association (≥ 66%)	304 (70.4)	127 (82.5)	177 (63.7)
Negative R/S–HWB association (≥ 66%)	3 (0.7)	1 (0.6)	2 (0.7)
No R/S–HWB association across studies	10 (2.3)	3 (1.9)	7 (2.5)
Mixed R/S–HWB association across studies	95 (22.0)	14 (9.1)	81 (29.1)
Inconclusive	20 (4.6)	9 (5.8)	11 (4.0)
Incorporated R/S and/or HWB at ≥ 1 level of analysis	5 (1.2)	0 (0.0)	5 (1.8)
Examined mostly (> 50%) longitudinal primary studies	281 (65.0)	153 (99.4)	128 (46.0)
Type of HWB dimension(s) measured in each review			
Mental health	296 (68.5)	112 (72.7)	184 (66.2)
Physical health	271 (62.7)	129 (83.8)	142 (51.1)
Behavioral health	125 (28.9)	19 (12.3)	106 (38.1)
Happiness and life satisfaction (including quality of life)	172 (39.8)	85 (55.2)	87 (31.3)
Meaning and purpose (had to be a nontautological measure)	37 (8.6)	2 (1.3)	35 (12.6)
Character and virtues	73 (16.9)	9 (5.8)	64 (23.0)
Social relationships	79 (18.3)	20 (13.0)	59 (21.2)
Material/financial stability (a condition that facilitates HWB)	4 (0.9)	0 (0.0)	4 (1.4)
Number of HWB dimensions measured in each review			
1	147 (34.0)	39 (25.3)	108 (38.8)
2	111 (25.7)	41 (26.6)	70 (25.2)
3 or 4	132 (30.6)	71 (46.1)	61 (21.9)
5 or more	42 (9.7)	3 (1.9)	39 (14.0)
Reviews that focused ≥ 90% on a yoga intervention	154 (35.6)	154 (100.0)	0 (100.0)
Reviews that focused ≥ 90% on a fasting intervention	32 (7.4)	0 (0.00)	32 (11.5)
Reviews that focused ≥ 90% on another spiritual intervention	99 (22.9)	11 (7.1)	88 (31.7)
Reviews that focused ≥ 90% on a special population	304 (70.4)	122 (79.2)	182 (65.5)

Note: Percentages may not sum to 100.0% because of rounding.

Publication Year, Sources, Authors, and Number of Synthesized Primary Studies

For example, the number of nonyoga reviews published began accelerating in the early 2000s, whereas the number of yoga reviews began accelerating in the 2010s. Now both types are growing exponentially in number. In the overall corpus, there were 273 distinct sources overall (263 journals and 10 scholarly books), 1,542 distinct contributing authors, and 381 distinct first authors (132 from yoga reviews and 249 from nonyoga ones). The median number of authors per review was 4 in the overall corpus (M = 4.34, SD = 2.56, range: 1–19), as well as in the yoga (M = 4.40, SD = 2.42, range: 1–19) and nonyoga subgroups (M = 4.31, SD = 2.63, range: 1–16). In contrast, the median and mean number of synthesized primary studies per review varied considerably between the yoga (Mdn = 13, M = 20.16, SD = 26.62, range: 2–258) and nonyoga subgroups (Mdn = 23, M = 84.77, SD = 328.90, range: 2–3,300).

The Oman and Syme (2018) umbrella review found that multiple reviews appeared in 14 of 83 journals (16.9%), most of which had an impact factor (IF) over 2.0. By comparison, in our corpus, we found that multiple reviews appeared in 62 of 263 journals (23.6%). In fact, 51 journals published three (k = 27), four (k = 16), or five or more reviews (k = 8). The eight journals that published five or more reviews were the *Journal of Religion and Health* (k = 31; 2023 2-year IF: 2.2), *Complementary Therapies in Clinical Practice* (k = 14; 2.2 IF), *Cochrane Database of Systematic Reviews* (k = 10; 8.8 IF), *Complementary Therapies in Medicine* (k = 8; 3.3 IF), *Journal of Alternative and Complementary Medicine* (k = 7; 2.4 IF), *Journal of Clinical Psychology* (k = 5; 2.5 IF), *Psychology of Religion and Spirituality* (k = 5; 2.2 IF), and *Supportive Care in Cancer* (k = 5; 2.8 IF; Clarivate Analytics, 2024). These journals are classified in the disciplines of religion, medicine, and psychology, and, like what Oman and Syme (2018) found, all eight journals had 2-year Clarivate (Thomson Reuters) IFs above 2.0.

Regarding authors, Oman and Syme (2018) reviewed the subset of their dataset that was published through 2013, and they found that only 11 of the total 223 individuals (4.9%) had authored more than one review, with just one authoring more than three reviews. In our corpus of 432 reviews, 161 of 1,542 authors (10.4%) had authored more than one review. Fifty-six individuals (3.6%) had contributed to three or more reviews, and 27 (1.8%) had coauthored more than three. The authors who had contributed most often to reviews were Holger Cramer (k = 21), Gustav Dobos (k = 17), Harold G. Koenig (k = 15), Romy Lauche (k = 15), Giancarlo Lucchetti (k = 11), Don E. Davis (k = 10), Joshua N. Hook (k = 10), Petra Klose (k = 7), Jost Langhorst (k = 7), Everett L. Worthington, Jr. (k = 7), and Crystal L. Park (k = 6).

As of 2017, Oman and Syme (2018) found the mean number of primary studies synthesized in reviews was 33.5. Although direct comparisons between umbrella reviews should be done with some caution (e.g., inclusion criteria may differ), in the current corpus, the mean number of primary studies in reviews was substantially higher (M = 61.74, SD = 265.96, range: 2–3,300). With our corpus's enormous range and high standard deviation, it was most appropriate to calculate the median number of studies per review, which was 18. When we segmented our corpus by review-type subgroup, the median for the systematic review subgroup (18) was similar to that of the combined meta-analysis and systematic review/meta-analysis subgroup (19). However, reviews in the systematic review subgroup had a higher mean number of studies (M = 73.91) and more variability in the number of included studies (SD = 324.31) compared to the combined meta-analysis and systematic review/meta-analysis subgroup (M = 41.45, SD = 113.85, respectively).

Outcomes, Methodologies, Interventions, and Populations

We utilized VanderWeele and colleagues' framework for conceptualizing the dimensions of HWB. Based on that framework, we coded each review for whether it had two or more primary studies that quantitatively measured that given dimension. The one exception to that coding rule was that if the review synthesized 10 or fewer studies, we coded if just one primary study measured that dimension. We used these rules to code for the seven dimensions of HWB and the one environmental condition that facilitates HWB—material/financial stability.

Using this coding scheme, we found that most reviews (*k* = 285, 66.0%) measured two or more dimensions of HWB. The remainder (*k* = 147, 34.0%) measured a single HWB dimension in their evaluation of the R/S–HWB associations. Across the reviews, the most commonly measured HWB dimensions were mental health (*k* = 296, 68.5%), physical health (*k* = 271, 62.7%), happiness and life satisfaction (including quality of life; *k* = 172, 39.8%), and behavioral health (including positive behaviors like healthy and prosocial behaviors, as well as negative behaviors like substance misuse, criminal behavior, or disordered eating behavior; *k* = 125, 28.9%). It was somewhat rare for reviews to evaluate the association between R/S and social relationships (e.g., loneliness, social support, or marital satisfaction and stability; *k* = 79, 18.3%) or character and virtues (e.g., hope, optimism, forgiveness, humility, or gratitude; *k* = 73, 16.9%). It was very rare for reviews to examine associations between R/S and the HWB facilitating condition of material/financial stability (*k* = 4, 0.9%) and the HWB dimension of nontautological meaning/purpose (37, 8.6%). However, it is noteworthy that we were quite strict in coding reviews as measuring the meaning/purpose dimension because of valid and strong criticisms of how tautological many R/S measures are (i.e., many R/S measures contain a large percentage of items that assess meaning/purpose, social connections, peacefulness, or well-being, thereby confounding any association with scores on mental health outcome measures; for discussions of this problematic issue, see Koenig, 2008; Koenig et al., 2024; Koenig & Carey, 2024).

Regarding methodologies examined, it was common (*k* = 281, 65.0%) for reviews to evaluate mostly (> 50%) primary studies employing a prospective longitudinal design. However, there was substantial differentiation in how often yoga reviews (*k* = 153/154, 99.4%) and nonyoga reviews (*k* = 128/278, 46.0%) relied on mostly longitudinal studies. Across the corpus, it was rare for reviews to incorporate measures of R/S and/or HWB at more than the individual level of analysis (e.g., at the level of a couple, family, group, congregation, community, or society; *k* = 5, 1.2%).

In terms of interventions and populations, it was common for reviews to focus (≥ 90% of studies in the review) on a particular R/S-incorporative intervention (*k* = 273, 63.2%), including yoga (*k* = 154, 35.6%), fasting (*k* = 32, 7.4%), and/or another spiritual intervention (*k* = 99, 22.9%). It was also common for reviews to focus on a special population (*k* = 304, 70.4%). The most frequently studied special populations were (a) people with physical diseases or symptoms (*k* = 136, 31.5%), (b) a special cultural group (based on nationality, race, ethnicity, gender, sexual orientation, or religious affiliation; *k* = 59, 13.7%), (c) people with psychiatric disorders or difficulties (*k* = 56, 13.0%), (d) Muslim people (*k* = 39, 9.0%), and (e) cancer patients or survivors (*k* = 35, 8.1%). Less commonly, reviews focused on youth (*k* = 31, 7.2%), women (*k* = 25, 5.8%), people coping with a specific stressor or shared experience (*k* = 23, 5.3%), older adults (*k* = 18, 4.2%), trauma-exposed people (*k* = 11, 2.6%), people with neurocognitive disorders (e.g., dementia; *k* = 10, 2.3%), people facing (or caring for someone facing) the end of life (*k* = 7, 1.6%), people with substance use disorders or difficulties (*k* = 4,

0.9%), people involved in the criminal justice system ($k = 4$, 0.9%), or other special population groups ($k = 21$, 4.9%; e.g., athletes, helping health professionals, couples, families, veterans, and religious "nones").

Overall Findings from Reviews

As other large-scale umbrella reviews have done (e.g., Koenig et al.'s [2024] *Handbook of Religion and Health*, 3rd ed.), we coded whether each review's findings generally revealed evidence of a positive R/S–HWB association (i.e., a ≥ 66% threshold of synthesized studies indicated a significant positive relationship between R/S and the measured HWB dimension[s]), a negative relationship (a ≥ 66% threshold of synthesized studies indicated a negative R/S–HWB relationship), a mixed relationship (a substantial mixture of positive and negative associations), no relationship (the review overall indicated no association), or inconclusive evidence. In this corpus, most reviews revealed evidence of a positive association ($k = 304$, 70.4%), but a sizable portion indicated mixed evidence ($k = 95$, 22.0%). A few reviews found inconclusive evidence ($k = 20$, 4.6%) or evidence of either a negative association ($k = 3$, 0.7%) or no association ($k = 10$, 2.3%).

There were noteworthy differences between the overall findings from yoga and nonyoga reviews. Nonyoga reviews were much *less* likely to find evidence of a positive association ($k = 177/278$, 63.7%), relative to yoga reviews ($k = 127/154$, 82.5%). In contrast, nonyoga reviews were much *more* likely to find mixed evidence of an association ($k = 81/278$, 29.1%), relative to yoga reviews ($k = 14/154$, 9.1%).

Discussion

What Do Published Systematic Reviews and Meta-Analyses Collectively Reveal?

There are several conclusions that can be derived from this corpus of 432 systematic reviews and meta-analyses. First, the sheer number of reviews and meta-analyses examining the relationship between R/S and HWB has grown exponentially over the past decade, corresponding to the exponential rise in research interest on R/S and HWB more broadly. Even as research on the relationship between R/S and HWB began accelerating in the early 2000s, our findings suggest that reviews of research on R/S and HWB have begun accelerating in the past several years since Oman and Syme's (2018) review. We anticipate this trend to continue.

Second, the umbrella of what is considered "spiritual" has broadened as well (Koenig et al., 2024), paralleling the broader societal trend toward people becoming more spiritual and less religious (Chen et al., 2023; Kallo, 2024). There has been a particular increase in the number of reviews examining yoga as a spiritual intervention. Authors of those reviews often lament about the low methodological quality of the studies they have synthesized (e.g., Hendriks et al., 2017). Hopefully, the methodological rigor of those and other more spiritually inclusive reviews (e.g., of HWB connections with Eastern, Latin American, African, Oceanic, and other diverse or indigenous spiritualities) will improve, even as the number of people who consider themselves spiritual but not religious rises in several parts of the world.

Third, the collective body of evidence still tends to reveal a positive relationship between R/S and HWB, but the picture is more mixed than the typical review's storyline might suggest. In this overview, only 7.6% of reviews yielded inconclusive evidence, evidence of a negative association, or evidence of no association. The other 92.4% of reviews yielded evidence of a positive

(70.4%) or mixed association between R/S and HWB (22.0%; e.g., some positive, some negative, and/or some null association). The popularized review storyline is often that evidence of a positive association between R/S and HWB is overwhelming, but as we found, nonyoga reviews are increasingly revealing a more complex, nuanced picture (29.1% found mixed evidence). As the quality of research on R/S and HWB keeps improving, we hope there is corresponding growth in the intellectual humility of review authors, the methodological rigor of their reviews, and the overall quality of the evidence they synthesize (Koenig et al., 2024).

Fourth, as one hopeful example, we found that almost two-thirds of published reviews relied mostly on prospective longitudinal studies. That was more common in yoga (99.4%) than nonyoga reviews (46.0%), but even in the latter, it is encouraging that reliance on high-quality prospective longitudinal studies (e.g., with randomization, time-varying exposures, and control for confounding variables and baseline outcomes) is increasing (Koenig et al., 2024). At the same time, below we have discussed some important limitations and caveats to keep in mind when it comes to reviews that synthesize both longitudinal and cross-sectional research.

What Does the Body of Evidence Suggest About the Causal R/S–HWB Relationship?

The reader may recall that Oman and Syme (2018) evaluated four of Hill's (1965) nine considerations for appraising causality: (a) *Strength* (i.e., the size of the prospective R/S–HWB association between R/S and subsequent HWB), (b) *Consistency* (i.e., how consistently this approximate effect was observed), (c) *Temporality* (i.e., how unidirectional or bidirectional this effect is), and (d) *Coherence* (i.e., whether any causal effect coheres with generally accepted facts about HWB). They concluded that, as of 2017, the collective body of evidence indicated "yes" for the *Consistency* consideration and "probably yes" for the other three considerations.

Based on the results of this overview of reviews, we conclude the same four answers. There is generally a small-sized positive association between R/S and HWB; for instance, Lefevor et al. (2021, Table 1) synthesized 20 meta-analyses from 1983 to 2019 and found a median Pearson r of .16 and a mean of .15. In nonyoga reviews, this approximate effect is observed in almost two-thirds of reviews, but around a third of reviews reveal mixed evidence. Many of the reviews that yielded mixed evidence were ones that evaluated the multivalent relationships between R/S and HWB. That is, they examined the association between HWB and both "positive" forms/dimensions of R/S (e.g., positive religious/spiritual coping and religious/spiritual social support) and "negative" forms/dimensions of R/S (e.g., negative religious/spiritual coping [religious/spiritual struggles]). As might be expected, these reviews frequently found evidence of a positive association between HWB and positive R/S but an inverse association between HWB and negative R/S. With the rapid advance of research on religious/spiritual struggles (Pargament & Exline, 2022) and the open science movement's paradigmatic shift toward greater scientific humility, objectivity, integrity, transparency, and reproducibility (Crüwell et al., 2019), we may be seeing a shift in research on R/S and HWB. Perhaps scholars researching the association between R/S and HWB are employing stronger research designs, more complex analytic strategies, increased control for confounding variables, and greater open science practices (e.g., preregistration, registered reports, and open sharing of data/materials). Reviews of these stronger primary studies may not only be improving in the quality of the primary data they are synthesizing but also in their own methodological practices (e.g., use of preregistration, PRISMA guidelines, and standardized tools). We hope such trends continue.

Implications for Theory and Research

For theory and research, perhaps the most important implication of this overview's findings is that theory and research on the associations between R/S and HWB needs to become (a) more multilevel (i.e., examine associations beyond just the individual level of analysis), (b) more multidimensional (i.e., examine associations across several dimensions of R/S and several dimensions of HWB), (c) more multivalent, and (d) less unidirectional. First, theory and research need to examine the complex network of associations beyond the individual level of analysis. For example, how do the effect sizes of the R/S–HWB association differ when examining (a) relational-, community-, and national-level R/S and/or (b) relational-, community-, and national-level HWB? Second, theory and research need to become more multidimensional because doing so will allow for testing Hill's (1965) consideration of *Specificity*. For example, how does evidence for a causal R/S–HWB association differ when examining combinations of specific, validly measured R/S dimensions with specific, validly measured HWB dimensions? Third, theory and research must become more nuanced, recognizing that R/S–HWB associations are complex and multivalent, especially considering how context-sensitive, individually idiosyncratic, and culturally embedded R/S is (Saroglou et al., 2020). For instance, even as there is increasing appreciation of HWB's multivalent nature (Lomas & VanderWeele, 2023) and of the need to study culturally embedded psychological phenomena like personality both from etic (cross-culturally normative) and emic (culturally idiographic) perspectives (Oishi et al., 2021), there must be a corresponding appreciation incorporated into the theory, research, and reviews of R/S–HWB associations (VanderWeele et al., 2023). Fourth, theory and research on R/S and HWB need to become less unidirectionally focused on evaluating the effects of R/S on HWB. Instead, the directional effects of HWB on R/S need to be studied, as do bidirectional effects of R/S and HWB on each other. In fact, in the current corpus, only five reviews evaluated this type of (bi)directionality (Braam & Koenig, 2019; Hardy et al., 2019; Koenig et al., 2012, 2024; Leo et al., 2021).

Implications for Practice

This overview chapter has several implications for practice, but rather than reiterate what we and our colleagues have indicated elsewhere (Balboni et al., 2022; Davis et al., 2023a, 2023b; Koenig et al., 2024), we will merely underscore three major practice implications. First, the collective body of evidence suggests R/S and HWB are usually related positively to each other, so practitioners can confidently ask people to draw on personally congruent R/S practices and resources to cope with their HWB difficulties. At the same time, practitioners need to evaluate and provide appropriate support when a person's R/S has been negatively affected by their HWB difficulties (clinically significant R/S impairment; Hathaway, 2003) and/or when a person is experiencing religious/spiritual struggles of some kind (Pargament & Exline, 2022; Vieten & Lukoff, 2022). Finally, despite their personal beliefs and biases, practitioners need to realize the scientific evidence supporting causal effects of R/S on HWB is steadily increasing in quantity and quality (Koenig et al., 2024). Hence, as part of their practice of cultural humility and culturally responsive clinical practice, practitioners need to become increasingly open to and competent in incorporating patient R/S into their work (Vieten & Lukoff, 2022). This need is especially important given that integrating a patient's R/S into psychotherapy is one of only three demonstrably effective ways to adapt psychotherapy to the patient (the other two ways are patient culture and preferences; Norcross & Wampold, 2019).

Limitations of the Current Overview of Reviews

Like every overview of reviews, this overview has limitations that should be acknowledged. First, although we adhered to the vast majority of the Preferred Reporting Items for Overviews of Reviews (PRIOR guidelines; Gates et al., 2022), we did not adhere to them all.

Most notably, because our preregistered protocol for data extraction and risk of bias assessment was quite rigorous and time-intensive (e.g., independent coding for extracting data and evaluating risk of bias), we chose to shift that phase of data extraction and bias assessment to later in the broader umbrella review project. Hence, in this overview of reviews, only the first author (EBD) conducted data extraction, and there was no formal risk of bias assessment.

Second, we decided a priori to focus on systematic reviews and meta-analyses that were predominantly (≥ 90%) comprised of quantitative studies (not qualitative studies). Several prior overviews and umbrella reviews have made this methodological decision (e.g., Ayano et al., 2023). Nonetheless, it meant a sizable number of reviews were excluded because they contained a substantive portion of qualitative primary studies. We hope other scholars will conduct overviews or umbrella reviews that are more methodologically pluralistic in their inclusion criteria, especially given the rich, nuanced insights that qualitative research on R/S affords.

Third, although many reviews and meta-analyses have relied mostly on prospective longitudinal studies—representing an improvement over the past—more remains to be done. Especially in quantitative meta-analysis, it would be important to exclusively *restrict* attention to such longitudinal studies so as to evaluate causality better. Without such restriction, it is possible that, even if *most* studies are prospective, the cross-sectional studies might be what are driving the more prominent effect sizes. There are some notable examples of such restrictions (Balboni et al., 2022; Chida et al., 2009; Garssen et al., 2021), but future researchers conducting systematic reviews and meta-analyses on R/S and HWB need to do this more frequently, rather than synthesizing both cross-sectional and longitudinal primary studies.

Finally, the current overview did not find many reviews that evaluated certain HWB dimensions (e.g., character/virtues, nontautological meaning/peace, or social relationships), special populations (e.g., youth, older adults, couples, or families), or multilevel interactions (at individual, relational, and community levels). Therefore, more of these types of primary studies, systematic reviews, and meta-analyses are needed.

Conclusions

This overview of reviews sought to explore two related research questions: (1) What do the published systematic reviews and meta-analyses of the relationship between R/S and HWB collectively reveal? and (2) Using Hill's (1965) considerations for causality, what does the collective body of evidence suggest about the causal relationship between R/S and HWB? We found 432 reviews, and they collectively revealed evidence that the relationship between R/S and HWB is generally positive (but sometimes mixed), and this relationship is probably positive in most instances. Even so, as scientific exploration of R/S and HWB continues to evolve at a rapid pace, we eagerly await what future studies, systematic reviews, and meta-analyses might reveal.

There are no potential conflicts of interest with this manuscript.

The data and materials for this study are available on the Open Science Framework at https://osf.io/hty9u/ (Davis, 2024). The PROSPERO preregistration form is available at https://www.crd.york.ac.uk/prospero/display_record.php?RecordID=495180.

Role of Funding

This publication was made possible through the support of grants from the John Templeton Foundation (JTF #61865 and JTF #61665), Templeton Religious Trust (TRT #2022-30967), and Wheaton College Mental Health Collective. The opinions expressed in this publication are those of the authors and do not necessarily reflect the views of the John Templeton Foundation, Templeton Religious Trust, or Wheaton College.

Note

1 Hill's (1965) other five considerations for appraising causality are: (a) *Specificity* (i.e., is the exposure associated with the outcome of interest and no others?), (b) *Biological gradient* (i.e., is there a dose-response curve in the association between exposure and outcome), (c) *Plausibility* (i.e., is the causal evidence concerning the association between the exposure and outcome plausible?), (d) *Experiment* (i.e., how well do interventions targeting the exposure affect the outcome?), and (e) *Analogy* (i.e., the causal relationship between the exposure and outcome may be strengthened if a comparable association is observed either between the same exposure and an analogous outcome or between an analogous exposure and the same outcome).

References

Ayano, G., Demelash, S., Gizachew, Y., Tsegay, L., & Alati, R. (2023). The global prevalence of attention deficit hyperactivity disorder in children and adolescents: An umbrella review of meta-analyses. *Journal of Affective Disorders, 339*, 860–866. https://doi.org/10.1016/j.jad.2023.07.071

Balboni, T. A., VanderWeele, T. J., Doan-Soares, S. D., Long, K. N. G., Ferrell, B. R., ... & Koh, H. K. (2022). Spirituality in serious illness and health. *JAMA, 328*(2), 184–197. https://doi.org/10.1001/jama.2022.11086

Braam, A. W., & Koenig, H. G. (2019). Religion, spirituality and depression in prospective studies: A systematic review. *Journal of Affective Disorders, 257*, 428–438. https://doi.org/10.1016/j.jad.2019.06.063

Chen, Z. J., Cowden, R. G., & Streib, H. (2023). More spiritual than religious: Concurrent longitudinal relations with personality traits, mystical experiences, and other individual characteristics. *Frontiers in Psychology, 13*, e1025938. https://doi.org/10.3389/fpsyg.2022.1025938

Chenneville, T., Duncan, B., & Silva, G. (2024). More questions than answers: Ethical considerations at the intersection of psychology and generative artificial intelligence. *Translational Issues in Psychological Science*. Advance online publication. https://doi.org/10.1037/tps0000400

Chida, Y., Steptoe, A., & Powell, L. H. (2009). Religiosity/spirituality and mortality. A systematic quantitative review. *Psychotherapy and Somatics, 78*(2), 81–90. https://doi.org/10.1159/000190791

Clarivate Analytics. (2024). *2023 journal citation reports*. Author.

Crüwell, S., van Doorn, J., Etz, A., Makel, M. C., Moshontz, H., ... & Schulte-Mecklenbeck, M. (2019). Seven easy steps to open science: An annotated reading list. *Zeitschrift für Psychologie, 227*(4), 237–248. https://doi.org/10.1027/2151-2604/a000387

Davis, E. B. (2024, August 7). Umbrella review of systematic reviews and meta-analyses on religion/spirituality and health/well-being. https://doi.org/10.17605/OSF.IO/HTY9U

Davis, E. B., Day, J. M., Lindia, P., & Lemke, A. (2023a). Religious/spiritual development and positive psychology: Toward an integrative theory. In E. B. Davis, E. L. Worthington, Jr., & S. A. Schnitker (Eds.), *Handbook of positive psychology, religion, and spirituality* (pp. 279–295). Springer Nature. https://doi.org/10.1007/978-3-031-10274-5_18

Davis, E. B., Schnitker, S. A., Worthington, E. L., Jr., & Lacey, E. K. (2023b). Future directions for the positive psychology of religion and spirituality. In E. B. Davis, E. L. Worthington, Jr., & S. A. Schnitker (Eds.), *Handbook of positive psychology, religion, and spirituality* (pp. 493–507). Springer Nature. https://doi.org/10.1007/978-3-031-10274-5_31

Diener, E., Tay, L., & Myers, D. G. (2011). The religion paradox: If religion makes people happy, why are so many dropping out? *Journal of Personality and Social Psychology*, *101*(6), 1278–1290. https://doi.org/10.1037/a0024402

Garssen, B., Visser, A., & Pool, G. (2021). Does spirituality or religion positively affect mental health? Meta-analysis of longitudinal studies. *International Journal for the Psychology of Religion*, *31*(1), 4–20. https://doi.org/10.1080/10508619.2020.1729570

Gates, M., Gates, A., Pieper, D., Fernandes, R. M., Tricco, A. C., … & Hartling, L. (2022). Reporting guideline for overviews of reviews of healthcare interventions: Development of the PRIOR statement. *BMJ 2022*, 378, e070849. http://doi.org/10.1136

Hardy, S. A., Nelson, J. M., Moore, J. P., & King, P. E. (2019). Processes of religious and spiritual influence in adolescence: A systematic review of 30 years of research. *Journal of Research on Adolescence*, *29*(2), 254–275. https://doi.org/10.1111/jora.12486

Harris, K. A., Howell, D. S., & Spurgeon, D. W. (2018). Faith concepts in psychology: Three 30-year definitional content analyses. *Psychology of Religion and Spirituality*, *10*(1), 1–29. https://doi.org/10.1037/rel0000134

Hendriks, T., de Jong, J., & Cramer, H. (2017). The effects of yoga on positive mental health among healthy adults: A systematic review and meta-analysis. *Journal of Alternative and Complementary Medicine*, *23*(7), 505–517. https://doi.org/10.1089/acm.2016.0334

Hill, A. B. (1965). The environment and disease: Association or causation? *Proceedings of the Royal Society of Medicine*, *58*(5), 295–300.

Kallo, A. (2024, January 17). *Around 4 in 10 Americans have become more spiritual over time; fewer have become more religious.* Pew Research Center. https://www.pewresearch.org/short-reads/2024/01/17/around-4-in-10-americans-have-become-more-spiritual-over-time-fewer-have-become-more-religious/

Koenig, H. G. (2008). Concerns about measuring "spirituality" in research. *Journal of Nervous and Mental Disease*, *196*(5), 349–355. https://doi.org/10.1097/NMD.0b013e31816ff796

Koenig, H. G., & Carey, L. B. (2024). Religion, spirituality and health research: Warning of contaminated scales. *Journal of Religion and Health*, *63*, 3729–3743. https://doi.org/10.1007/s10943-024-02112-6

Koenig, H. G., Hill, T. D., Pirutinsky, S., & Rosmarin, D. H. (2021). Commentary on "Does spirituality or religion positively affect mental health?" *International Journal for the Psychology of Religion*, *31*(1), 27–44. https://doi.org/10.1080/10508619.2020.1766868

Koenig, H. G., King, D. E., & Carson, V. B. (2012). *Handbook of religion and health* (2nd ed.). Oxford University Press.

Koenig, H. G., VanderWeele, T. J., & Peteet, J. R. (2024). *Handbook of religion and health* (3rd ed.). Oxford University Press. https://doi.org/10.1093/oso/9780190088859.001.0001

Lee, M. T., Kubzansky, L. D., & VanderWeele, T. J. (Eds.). (2021). *Measuring well-being*. Oxford University Press. https://doi.org/10.1093/oso/9780197512531.001.0001

Lefevor, G. T., Davis, E. B., Paiz, J. Y., & Smack, A. C. P. (2021). The relationship between religiousness and health among sexual minorities: A meta-analysis. *Psychological Bulletin*, *147*(7), 647–666. https://doi.org/10.1037/bul0000321

Leo, D., Izadikhah, Z., Fein, E. C., & Forooshani, S. A. (2021). The effect of trauma on religious beliefs: A structured literature review and meta-analysis. *Trauma, Violence, & Abuse*, *22*(1), 161–175. https://doi.org/10.1177/1524838019834076

Lerner, R. M., Lerner, J. V., Bowers, E. P., & Geldhof, G. J. (2015). Positive youth development and relational–developmental–systems. In R. M. Lerner (Ed.), *Handbook of child psychology and developmental science* (7th ed.; Vol. 1, pp. 607–651).

Levin, J. S. (1994). Religion and health: Is there an association, is it valid, and is it causal? *Social Science & Medicine*, *38*(11), 1475–1482. https://doi.org/10.1016/0277-9536(94)90109-0

Little, T. D. (Ed.). (n.d.). *Methodology in the social sciences literature* [Book series]. Guilford. https://www.guilford.com/browse/research-methods/methodology-social-sciences-series

Lomas, T., Pawelski, J. O., & VanderWeele, T. J. (2024). A flexible map of flourishing: The dynamics and drivers of flourishing, well-being, health, and happiness. *International Journal of Wellbeing, 13*(4), 3665. 1–38. https://doi.org/10.5502/ijw.v13i4.3665

Lomas, T., & VanderWeele, T. J. (2023). The mental illness–health matrix and the mental state space matrix: Complementary meta-conceptual frameworks for evaluating psychological states. *Journal of Clinical Psychology*, *79*, 1902–1920. https://doi.org/10.1002/jclp.23512

Norcross, J. C., & Wampold, B. (2019). Psychotherapy relationships that work (3rd ed.), *Volume 2: Evidence-based therapist responsiveness*. Oxford University Press.

Oishi, S., Kushlev, K., & Benet-Martínez, V. (2021). Culture and personality: Current directions. In O. P. John & R. W. Robins (Eds.), *Handbook of personality: Theory and research* (4th ed., pp. 686–703). Guilford Press.

Oman, D., & Syme, S. L. (2018). Weighing the evidence: What is revealed by 100+ meta-analyses and systematic reviews of religion/spirituality and health? In D. Oman (Ed.), *Why religion and spirituality matter for public health* (pp. 261–281). Springer International Publishing. https://doi.org/10.1007/978-3-319-73966-3_15

Pargament, K. I., & Exline, J. J. (2022). *Working with spiritual struggles in psychotherapy: From research to practice*. Guilford Press.

Pargament, K. I., Mahoney, A., Exline, J. J., Jones, J. W. & Shafranske, E. P. (2013). Envisioning an integrative paradigm for the psychology of religion and spirituality. In K. I. Pargament (Ed.), *APA handbook of psychology, religion, and spirituality* (Vol. 1, pp. 3–19). American Psychological Association. https://doi.org/10.1037/14045-001

Saroglou, V., Clobert, M., & Tapia Valladares, J. (2020). Believing, bonding, behaving, and belonging: The cognitive, emotional, moral, and social dimensions of religiousness across cultures. *Journal of Cross-Cultural Psychology*, *51*(7-8), 551–575. https://doi.org/10.1177/0022022120946488

VanderWeele, T. (2017). On the promotion of human flourishing. *Proceedings of the National Academy of Sciences*, *114*, 8148–8156. https://doi.org/10.1073/pnas.1702996114

VanderWeele, T. J., Case, B. W., Chen, Y., Cowden, R. G., Johnson, B., Lee, M. T., Lomas, T., & Long, K. G. (2023). Flourishing in critical dialogue. *SSM–Mental Health*, *3*, Article 100172. https://doi.org/10.1016/j.ssmmh.2022.100172

VanderWeele, T. J., & Lomas, T. (2023). Terminology and the well-being literature. *Affective Science*, *4*, 36–40. https://doi.org/10.1007/s42761-022-00153-2

Vieten, C., & Lukoff, D. (2022). Spiritual and religious competencies in psychology. *American Psychologist*, *77*(1), 26–38. https://doi.org/10.1037/amp0000821

Webb, J. R. (2021). *Understanding forgiveness and addiction: Theory, research, and clinical application*. Routledge.

World Health Organization. (1946). *Constitution of the World Health Organization*. Author. https://www.who.int/about/accountability/governance/constitution

Chapter 22

Meditation

A Practice for Inner Wisdom and Spiritual Growth

*Jean L. Kristeller**

Overview

Almost all religious traditions have elements of meditative or contemplative practice. Although much of the recent focus on the psychology of meditative practice has been on Buddhist-based mindfulness meditation (see Chapter 24), there has also been substantive interest in Hindu-based mantra meditations and Tibetan practices, with growing recognition of underlying similarities and distinctions among other traditions (Goleman, 1988; Knabb, 2021; Monaghan & Viereck, 2011; Sedlmeier, 2022), including Christian contemplative prayer,[1] a range of Jewish prayer traditions (Hilert & Gutierrez, 2020), and Sufic meditative and mystical traditions (Shafii, 1988; Arasteh & Sheikh, 1989; Ismail et al., 2023). Common elements of practice, such as repetition and detached awareness, appear to facilitate spiritual experience across traditions, but the challenges for systematic research are considerable (Davidson & Kaszniak, 2015). Therefore, further research and clinical application are warranted to more fully explore across the range of meditative practices, their cultural/religious contexts, and effects, including spiritual (Kristeller & Jordan, 2017).

Meditation as a psychotherapeutic approach is arguably unique in drawing so broadly on non-Western traditions, from the earliest influences (Walsh, 1999; Walsh & Shapiro, 2006). Meditation practices may have first entered the West via India, through the development of Catholic Centering prayer by the desert Fathers in the 4th century (Harmless, 2004), and then more recently through Europe, as part of Transcendentalism (Tart, 1992). Carl Jung (1938–1940/2020), in his travels to India, was fascinated by yogic and meditation practices. In Europe, Johannes Schultz (Linden, 2021) drew explicitly on Yogic meditative traditions to develop Autogenic Training, one of the earliest cognitive-behavioral relaxation interventions.

In 1893, at the World Parliament of Religions[2] (WPR) in Chicago, Roshi *Shaku Sōen*, a Japanese Buddhist monk, introduced Zen meditation to a wider audience in a compelling way (Fields, 1992). Zen meditation continued to gain attention in the United States into the mid-20th century through the efforts of D.T. Suzuki, a student of Shaku Soen's and also a monk, who made multiple visits to the United States before and after WWII, teaching at Columbia University, and influencing psychoanalytic theory through the writings of Erich Fromm (Fromm, Suzuki, & De Martino, 1960) and Karen Horney (1987). The upsurge of interest in meditation in the 1960s and 1970s was fueled by three parallel developments: growing intrigue with altered states of consciousness (Tart, 1972); a growing appreciation of Asian spiritual culture (Ram Dass, 1976/2010; Watts, 1957, 1963);[3] and the beginning of mind-body medicine.

* Corresponding Author: Jean.Kristeller@indstate.edu.

DOI: 10.4324/9781003440048-26

Contemporary research is providing evidence for the impact of meditative practice on a wide range of human functions: cognition, physiology, emotion, behavior, sense of self, and the psychology of spirituality, distinct yet intertwined areas. This range of effects is the foundation of the multi-domain model of meditation (Kristeller, 2020), exploration of which will help shape this chapter, which will examine the basic elements of the meditative process and how these are reflected in the major traditions, in contemporary usage, and increasingly supported by substantial research. The therapeutic value of meditation will also be reviewed across these six areas, with special focus on links to spiritual or religious effects and the spiritual domain.

The Meditative Process

As noted, meditation refers to a family of practices grounded in traditional religious contexts, but used therapeutically to an increasing degree over the last 50 years. They have in common intentional focusing of attention, accompanied by an effort to suspend usual analytic thinking (Shapiro & Walsh, 1984; Bishop et al., 2004). One of the earliest and approachable books on meditation written for the general audience, and capturing a sense of wonder and value, was by Patricia Carrington (1977), *Freedom in Meditation*. Numerous models for meditation effects have been proposed; one challenge in understanding the psychology of meditation is separating the *process* of practice from the *effects* of practice, with considerable advances in conceptualizing the core components as neuropsychological processes (Lazar et al., 2005; Goleman & Davidson, 2017), drawing both on current psychological theory and on a growing understanding of the sophisticated but esoteric literatures of Buddhist and Hindu psychology.

At a fundamental level, this review construes meditation as a set of attentional and cognitive processes with predictable and wide-ranging effects (Lutz et al., 2008). While carefully addressed in Chapter 24 in regard to mindfulness meditation, arguably all meditation/contemplative approaches engage the process of momentary attention in related ways. The mind is designed to be constantly scanning the external and internal environment for meaningful information. This is the "monkey mind" of classical Buddhist teaching, jumping quickly to whatever next draws its attention, and in recent theory, to the *wandering mind* (Mrazek et al., 2012). In daily functioning, meaning is based on reward value or potential threat of the experience, and familiarity or novelty. This creates the attachments and aversions of the conditioned mind of contemporary psychology and, in traditional Buddhist psychology, *dependent origination* (Germer et al., 2013).

The mind – and body – are then designed to react as quickly and efficiently as possible, a core aspect of the conditioned mind, which produces automatic, but sometimes unwise, reactions. While we cannot function without such processes, when they become incompatible with higher-level goals, they can be quite troublesome yet difficult to disengage, leading to distress – and perhaps the need for therapeutic intervention, as the mind becomes caught up in deeply embedded self-criticism, anxiety, depression, or "addictive" behaviors.

In the *Abhidhamma*, a classic text laying out core Buddhist psychology (Goleman, 1988; Fulton & Siegel, 2013), meditation is a means for disengaging these unhealthy aspects of self. Kelly (2022) describes Buddhist psychology as addressing the interruption of undesired attachments and reactions, and how transformational experiences, including spiritual or mystical states, can be created. Lee and Tang (2023), drawing on early Buddhist psychology, highlight the easily understood "note, know, choose" distinctions: "noting" a trigger and undesired reaction; "knowing" there are alternatives; and then "choosing" mindfully. After this comes the emergence of higher-level *wisdom*, as the brain/mind is released from conditioned reactions, and can integrate across alternative possibilities.

This process then facilitates the emergence of self-regulatory functions experienced as healthier, more balanced, or in some way "wiser" (Brewer, 2017). As the habitual pull is loosened, that trigger can now link into alternative options. That higher level of brain functioning is also where our spiritual self can be engaged. These responses may be ones we already know how to use – more positive emotions, healthier behaviors, more loving connections with others – or they may be emergent, wiser options from the integrated power of our "wiser," even spiritual, self. Accessing *wisdom* relates to emergent insight in any realm of functioning (Sternberg, 1990; Sternberg & Glück, 2019), perhaps profound or just an ordinary type of decision-making. In a group I was leading, a woman shared that she'd been trying to reconfigure a room in her house, but every idea that arose had some problem. While sitting in meditation practice one day, a totally new solution came into her mind that, as she said, was "perfect" – reflecting a novel option and new neuro-linkages.

Suspension of the conditioned "self," whether for a few moments or longer, may also engage emergence of the spiritual self, with a sense of transcendent merging, of enlightenment, or *satori* in Zen Buddhism, as accounted by James Austin (1998, 2006), an MIT neuroscientist who was introduced to Zen practice during a year-long sabbatical in Kyoto. Particular effects of meditative practice, including spiritual engagement, of course depend on many factors, including the type of meditation, length and context of practice, and the background of the practitioner. Austin (1998), in his substantive 800-page treatise on Zen, shares this experience, including integration of meditative practice into daily activities.

> Meditation practice…helps you pause and examine your mental processes dispassionately. Soon, you identify self-centered behaviors and distractions. After that, a series of small insights then enables you to let go of them. … Slowly, the aspirant who follows the Zen Buddhist path learns to merge the practices of meditative concentration with restraint (*shila*) and insight (*prajna*) … *Reinforcing one another, they gradually bring their coordinated impact into thoughts, attitudes, and behavior. Together, they help one sort things out, observe which options work better, arrive at constructive solutions, keep one's best intentions on-line.* The result can be nothing less than a spiritual renaissance.
>
> (Austin, 1998, p. 126)

Meditation Techniques and Meditative Traditions

Meditative techniques derived from traditional practices can be categorized into three types, though these may overlap or blend with each other: *concentrative techniques*, *mindfulness or insight meditation*, and *guided meditations*. Each can engage the three aspects of Webb's RiTE model of spirituality (Webb et al., 2014; see also Chapters 1 and 44, this volume): (1) ritualistic spirituality, involving intention to connect with the deity, as represented in the religion of a person's tradition or of the tradition being taught; (2) theistic spirituality, involving connection with one or more deities, but which may be independent of any organized religion; and (3) existential spirituality, encompassing a non-theistic yet transcendent search for meaning and purpose, also inclusive of those who identify as agnostic or atheist. See Chapter 24 for an in-depth consideration of this model in relation to mindfulness meditation, which would also extend to other modes of meditation.

As a brief overview, the fundamental distinction between mindfulness and concentrative meditations, behind the vast culturally determined variety of ritualized practice, is in the cognitive process. *Concentrative meditative practices* involve a relatively concrete focus for attention, whether a sound, word (*mantra*), prayer, picture, or image, often framed within a religious context. Transcendental Meditation (TM) and Christian Centering Prayer each engage this approach, in that a mantra or sacred word provides a focus that is spiritual in nature, and also anchors the mind, helping it from straying into discursive or analytic thought (Oman, 2025; Keating, 2002). The use of mantras can be brought into daily activities at any time (Oman, Bormann, & Kane, 2022), much as can be the breath. *Mindfulness meditation* cultivates attentive awareness to whatever may emerge into conscious awareness, often beginning with the breath. *Guided meditations* often introduce a broader focus for attention, such as a personal area for growth or a particular spiritual/religious context. Both traditional and contemporary meditative practices often include "guided" elements: attention is directed to a place in the body, a feeling, a sound, a picture, or a prayer – with intended value related to that focus. These distinctions are further developed and reviewed below.

Most meditation research has been carried out with a limited set of meditation approaches: Zen, Tibetan traditions, TM and its variants, Catholic Centering Prayer, and secular mindfulness meditation, including ones entailing guided practices. Classifying meditation is further complicated by the wide range of techniques, by the religious context, and by issues such as how to consider such related variants as *hatha yoga*, chanting, or certain types of prayer. But all variations contribute to a heightened state of spiritual engagement and inner wisdom.

Concentrative Meditation

The element common to all concentrative techniques is a repetitive object of focus or attention, whether a word or sound (*mantra* or *mantram*) or spiritual phrase, or, less commonly, a picture or physical experience. The Sanskrit term *mantra* derives from the root terms "*man-*," the mind, and "*-tra*," control. The intention is disengagement from usual thought processes and the cultivation of the capacity to sustain attention on a single object, eventually producing the experience of full absorption (*samatha* in Pali, or *samadhi* in Sanskrit).

The best-known mantra-based practice in the United States may still be TM, as introduced by the Maharishi Mahesh Yogi in the 1960s (Yogi, 1963/1995) and still actively promulgated (Rosenthal, 2012; Bhattacharya & Gaur, 2024). It involves the formal transmission of a Sanskrit *mantra* that is repeated silently during two 20-minute sessions a day. Benson's book 'The Relaxation Response' (1975), describes arguably the first intentionally secular meditation, as adapted from TM to examine the effects on cardiac patients at Harvard Medical School (Benson & Wallace, 1972) and then continued to be taught for many years. Other Hindu approaches include those taught through the Himalayan Institute, founded in 1981, with a strong focus on yoga (Ram Dass, 1976/2010), the Vedanta Society, and meditations as part of Easwaran's (1991) integrative approach, drawing on mantra-based and longer spiritual passages. The Vedanta Society in the United States, founded in 1894 by Swami Vivekananda, after he appeared at the 1893 WPR, was inspired by the Indian mystic Sri Ramakrishna (1836–1886), and it remains universalistic, incorporating both Christian and Eastern traditions.

In Tibetan Buddhism, repetition of *Om Mani Padme Hum*[4] and repetitive prostrations are only parts of a complex meditative tradition introduced into the United States by Chogyam Trungpa (1973/2002), who founded Naropa University in Colorado in 1974 after years of teaching outside Tibet. Tibetan Buddhism has gained many adherents in the last 30 years through the teachings of the Dalai Lama (Dalai Lama & Cutler, 1998). The Rinzai sect of Zen Buddhism utilizes the *koan* (a non-logical conceptual "puzzle") as an object of focus to help disengage intellectual functioning more than would repetition of a simple word or phrase (Miura & Sasaki, 1965; Austin, 1998). Other sects of Japanese Buddhism draw heavily on repetitive chanting. Nichiren Buddhism, following the teachings of Nichiren (1222–1282), is one of the largest Buddhist groups outside Japan. Practice includes chanting *Namu myou hou renge kyou* as the mantra, which refers, in Japanese, to dedication to the Lotus Sutra (Teiser & Stone, 2009). In TM and mantra-based Hindu traditions, eyes are typically closed. In Zen, eyes are kept open to guard against sleep and possibly promote other neurological effects (Austin, 1998); other Buddhist traditions have the eyes closed.

Using prayer beads, such as the Catholic rosary, to guide repetitive meditative prayer, is part of many religions (Monaghan & Viereck, 2011). Contemplative Christian traditions also use repetitive prayer; the Jesus Prayer was revived by Father Thomas Merton (1948/1962/2007) and by Father Thomas Keating (1997, 2002) as Catholic Centering Prayer, similar in many ways to other mantra-based meditations. Father Merton went on to connect deeply with Buddhist practices (1968), exploring their interface with Catholic teachings. The central Islamic Sufi practice *(zikr)* is an adsorptive repetition of the name of God, but is also broader than that (Ismail et al., 2023). Sufis are also known for their dancing (the whirling dervishes), entailing repetitive movement, introduced by the mystic and poet Rumi (Breton & Largent, 1998). Jewish prayer may also include repetitive swaying, called "shuckling" (Eisenberg, 2004).

The degree to which the repeated material fully engages multiple sensory faculties varies substantially and may affect the quality of the experience. The simplest variants involve only the breath and a repeated sound, *mantra*, or brief prayer. Traditional mantra meditations or prayers place substantial importance on both the meaning and quality of the repeated sound, with certain sounds, such as *Om*, one of the most deeply established chants/sounds of Hinduism, also evident to some extent in Buddhism (Lipner, 2010), and thought to induce particular neuro-cognitive and emotional benefits (Kumar et al., 2015). Cultivating the ability to remain focused on an object of attention is a key goal of concentrative practice. The primary purpose of this practice has been likened to developing "a laser beam quality of attention" (Urbanowski & Miller, 1996). In the Hindu and Buddhist concentrative meditative traditions, the ability to attain such attentional focus is the beginning of a much longer, intense development of control over various aspects of mind and body, and the path of entry into transcendent or altered states. The neurophysiological processes involved in deep absorption by losing oneself in the repetition of a chant, mantra, or prayer may be one reliable path to deeper spiritual or religious experience (Austin, 1998, 2006).

The immediate effect of concentrative techniques is to disengage the mind from the normal stream of discursive or analytic thinking, including self-judgment, and to cultivate an ability to direct attention. This psychological process may serve to quiet the mind, provide a sense of relaxation, and promote a sense of peace and acceptance. With further practice, this disengagement promotes access to more focused attention in an increasing range of contexts and to other types of mental processing, such as spiritual experience. The rhythmic repetition of a sound or word may also have distinct benefits for what is called "entrainment" or induction of neurological changes dependent on rhythm (Lutz et al., 2009). Synchronization of brain rhythms across the hemispheres is another element in understanding meditation effects and heightened creativity or emergent wisdom, as noted above (Horan, 2009). As the emphasis on a fixed focus decreases, as in TM and in Centering prayer (Keating, 2002; Knabb, 2021), the quality of experience moves toward that of mindfulness meditation. Strikingly, TM and

Centering prayer place similar emphasis on cultivating transcendent experience: in TM, "cosmic consciousness" (Orme-Johnson, 2000), and in Centering prayer, as an experience of God or the divine (Keating, 1997).

Mindfulness/Insight Meditation

Mindfulness meditation primarily uses the breath as the focus of attention, but any object of thought that comes into awareness can serve as a focus as part of "open awareness" practice. One of the best-known definitions of mindfulness is Jon Kabat-Zinn's (2011, p. 291), also noted in Chapter 24 of this volume (p. 4): "the awareness that arises from paying attention, on purpose, in the present moment, and non-judgmentally." There is an emphasis on cultivating a distinct quality of awareness, often referred to as *bare attention*. The goal is to develop a deeper awareness of the nature of one's own mind patterns, without bringing to them emotional reactivity or judgement, either negative (avoidance) or positive (attachment) (Bishop et al., 2004). Mindfulness meditation, therefore, entails the *mindful observation of whatever arises in consciousness*. Within a spiritual context, this clearing away of the daily preoccupations facilitates becoming conscious of the source of God (in Christianity), of cosmic consciousness (in Hinduism), or of the Void (in Buddhism).

Mindfulness/insight or *vipassana* ("to see clearly") meditation developed out of Theravadan Buddhist traditions, and received extensive introduction in the United States by a number of Americans who entered training in Thailand, in the Thai forest monastic tradition, including Kornfield (1993, 2003), Levine (2000), and Thanissaro Bhikkhu (Geoffrey DeGraff) (2006). Among Asian teachers, Thich Naht Hanh, from Vietnam, whose lineage was both Theravadan and Chinese Zen (Ch'an) Buddhism, provided prolific and approachable writings (Nhat Hanh,1975; 1995; 2017) that both universalized and broadened mindfulness approaches, particularly loving-kindness meditation and contemplative walking. Goenka, a highly regarded lay leader in India of spiritually traditional 10-day Vipassana retreats (Hart, 1987), influenced meditation-based interventions in the United States, particularly in prisons and addiction programs (Marlatt, 2002). Mindfulness elements are also present in Zen meditation, particularly in the practice of "shikantaza" or "just sitting," linked to the Japanese Soto Zen school of practice (Masuda & O'Donohue, 2017).

Jon Kabat-Zinn, while coming from a personal background in both Vipassana and Zen traditions, secularized these practices in the Mindfulness-Based Stress Reduction (MBSR) program in the late 1970s, initially designed for and highly effective with chronic pain patients (Kabat-Zinn, 1990; Kabat-Zinn, Lipworth, & Burney, 1985), within a medical setting, and still the most widely used mindfulness-related therapeutic program. Although secularized, our research showed that spiritual engagement deepened over the 8-week program (Carmody et al., 2008). See Chapter 24 for a fuller description of mindfulness practice, MBSR, related programs, and research.

Variations on the MBSR program include Mindfulness-Based Cognitive Therapy (MBCT) (Segal, Williams, & Teasdale, 2002/2013) for treatment of depression, Mindfulness-Based Compassion Therapy (Neff & Germer, 2018) for cultivating feelings of acceptance and compassion toward others and oneself, and Mindfulness-Based Eating Awareness Therapy (MB-EAT) for management of eating-related problems (Kristeller, 2015; Kristeller & Wolever, 2011; Kristeller, Wolever & Lieberstein, in press). These variants well represent the value of bringing a non-reactive quality of mindful awareness and a purposeful disengagement of conditioned reactions to a range of core experiences. Germer, Siegel, and Fulton (2013) provide a deep exploration of ways that mindfulness has become integrated into psychotherapy.

Even if attention is only directed toward the breath, this carries with it an explicit engagement of a psycho-biological system that can have powerful self-regulatory effects (Lehrer, 1983; Lehrer et al., 1999; Shonin & Van Gordon, 2016). For example, Hindu or Buddhist meditative practices that engage the breath as a focus are often noted to produce relaxation effects, whereas in Christian contemplative (meditative) traditions that rarely utilize the breath (though it may be invoked symbolically – "spiritus" is the Latin word for breath), an inherent relaxation effect is not identified as a meditative goal. Another example of an implicit framework is the almost universal spiritual or religious context of traditional meditative practice. Thai Buddhist *metta* (loving-kindness) meditation (Kornfield, 1993; Shapiro & Sahgal, 2012) is explicitly used to cultivate experiences of empathy and compassion, which can be viewed as inherently spiritual – or can be secularized if used in a therapeutic context (Neff & Germer, 2018).

Guided Meditations

Guided meditation is increasingly included in therapeutic uses, bringing focused awareness to chosen *experiences*. The MBSR program includes multiple body awareness practices. John Teasdale and his colleagues (2000, 2002, and 2003) modified MBSR to create MBCT to include cognitive components to prevent relapse in chronic depression. Mindfulness-Based Eating Awareness Training (MB-EAT) includes many guided practices related to taste, hunger, satiety, and eating-related emotions to treat binge eating disorder and broader eating dysregulation (Kristeller, 2004; Kristeller, Wolever & Sheets, 2013; Mason et al., 2016; Kristeller, Wolever & Lieberstein, in press). Mindfully eating specific foods, whether challenging ones like chocolate or healthy alternatives, can be a powerful experience for individuals often eating mindlessly – or compulsively. Compassion-focused meditation (Neff & Germer, 2018), well summarized in Chapter 24, provides a valuable focus, building on MBSR. Being able to deepen and hold a place of compassion for oneself and others is an important aspect of a range of traditional spiritually oriented meditative traditions and has been integrated into other contemporary practices.

Contemplative engagement with more complex material may involve distinct processes. Easwaran combined mantra meditation with the use of longer memorized contemplative texts, drawn from across world religions (Easwaran, 1991), similar to some aspects of Christian contemplative practice (the *lectio divina*) (Knabb, 2021). Long memorized texts may, in a valuable way, link spiritual and intellectual engagement, but they may also be distinctly different from the immediate meditative practice experience associated with simple mantra meditation. Easwaran made the argument for the overlap of meditative approaches, both in regard to broad effects and in relation to spiritual deepening (Oman & Bormann, 2018). Recently, when I inquire if someone has "meditation" experience, and I ask what type, they'll often tell me that they listen to "meditative music" online. While undoubtably relaxing, even spiritual, and distracting from worrisome thoughts, there is likely little value for training qualities of attention or awareness.

Another variation of Easwaran's approach, developed by Bormann and her associates, has people choose a *mantram* that resonates for them from a range of faith traditions. In addition to brief meditative practice in a group, individuals engage in frequent repetition of their mantram "in the back of the mind" throughout the day. Five weeks after the group ended, greater use of the mantram was related to increases in spiritual faith, a sense of meaning and peace on the FACIT-Sp (Peterman et al., 2002) and a deeper quality of life (Bormann et al., 2020).

Concentrative, mindfulness, and guided practices merge within a number of traditions, particularly Tibetan Buddhism, as made clear through the work of researchers over the last 40 years, whose striking findings are shared in the book, *Altered Traits: Science reveals how meditation changes your mind, brain, and body*, by Goleman and Davidson (2017). With personal backgrounds, beginning in the early 1970s in Asia, and professional backgrounds in meditative traditions, they provide an overview of both spiritual and applied areas of meditation practice.

Little research, however, has systematically compared different meditative approaches. A creative study by Dunn et al. (1999) explored brain wave activity in an undergraduate course on meditation; each person was their own control while engaging in concentrative versus mindfulness meditation versus non-meditative relaxation, finding distinct differences among the three in neuro-activity, consistent with concentrative and mindfulness meditation having distinct characteristics, in contrast to a general relaxation state. A neuroimaging review (Beauregard, 2024) of religious, spiritual, and mystical experience, with a focus on meditative approaches, found the temporal lobe to be a common site of spiritual engagement.

Understanding Meditative Effects: Spiritual/Religious Experience within a Multi-Domain Perspective

The processes involved in any meditative practice, of focusing attention and awareness and disengaging analytic thought and self-judgment, are fundamentally cognitive in nature, but are now shown to have a wide range of effects across multiple domains of functioning, including physiological, emotional, and behavioral, or in shifts in relation to self and others (Newberg & Waldman, 2009; Rose et al., 2020). By the mid-1990s, over 1,000 studies had been published across a broad range of outcomes (Murphy, Donovan, & Taylor, 1999). Currently, there are over 10,000, with about 1,000 addressing meditation and spirituality. Models of meditation also incorporate the spiritual goals of practice, but the extent to which these are explicitly acknowledged varies. Shonin, Van Gordon, and Griffith (2013) have strongly voiced the need to acknowledge this inherent spiritual linkage, calling for more substantive research.

The multi-domain model of meditation (Kristeller, 2004) both distinguishes among the range of effects, and acknowledges that interactions occur among them, both because of the integrative nature of the brain and because practice experiences rarely, if ever, focus on only a single domain. Therefore, a multi-domain perspective can help make sense of the broad literature on meditation practice, further addressing complex questions related to the interdependence of effects. Because the focus of this chapter is more on the religious and spiritual aspects of meditation, each domain will only be briefly reviewed, with particular attention to interactions with the spiritual domain. A more extensive review will then be provided of the sixth domain, spiritual and religious effects of practice. The order of the domains is not rigid but draws from both an understanding of the underlying processes and the depth of practice that may be engaged.

Teasdale's model of "Interacting Cognitive Subsystems" (1993), which he and his colleagues have applied to understanding mindfulness meditation effects (Segal, Williams, & Teasdale, 2002/2013; Teasdale, 1999) on depression, focuses primarily on the role of cognitive processing on emotion, and secondarily on physiology, but is consistent with an interactive model of effects across the six domains posited here. Sternberg's model of wisdom (1990; Sternberg & Glück, 2019) might also be considered a highly valuable perspective on the role of meditation on integration across these multiple domains (Kunzman & Baltes, 2005). Lazar's work (Lazar et al., 2005), showing general cortical thickening related to meditation experience, further supports this perspective.

Based on clinical application and on research to date, six domains, as noted above, are posited as heuristically useful: cognitive, physiological, emotional, behavioral, relation to self and others, and spiritual (Kristeller, 2004; see Figure 22.1). Attention/cognition is placed first as the primary process present in all meditation practice, in that the ability to focus and engage awareness is cognitive process. Physiological or health-related effects are next; most people, when first experiencing meditation, note how physically relaxing it feels. Emotional effects represent the next domain, generally as positive experiences but also related to troubling emergent memories. Behavioral change, often involving guided meditation practices, is somewhat more challenging; more time may be needed to shift strong underlying conditioning. Shifts in relation to self and to others may develop naturally with practice, as attachment to self weakens (Kristeller & Johnson, 2005), but can be powerfully heightened by related practices (Neff & Germer, 2018). Health psychology, and more broadly, health care, can gain value from understanding both meditation effects (Ospina et al., 2008) and spiritual engagement (Martin & Carlson, 1988). Cultivation of insight and spiritual well-being are virtually universal goals of meditative practice, now understood to be inherent to practice, independent of religious context, and, as research shows, as reviewed below, occurring with even limited practice, sometimes within a person's first meditation experience. A relatively recent call was released from a group of 18 top investigators suggesting even more attention be given to transpersonal and mystical effects of meditation practice (Vieten et al., 2018).

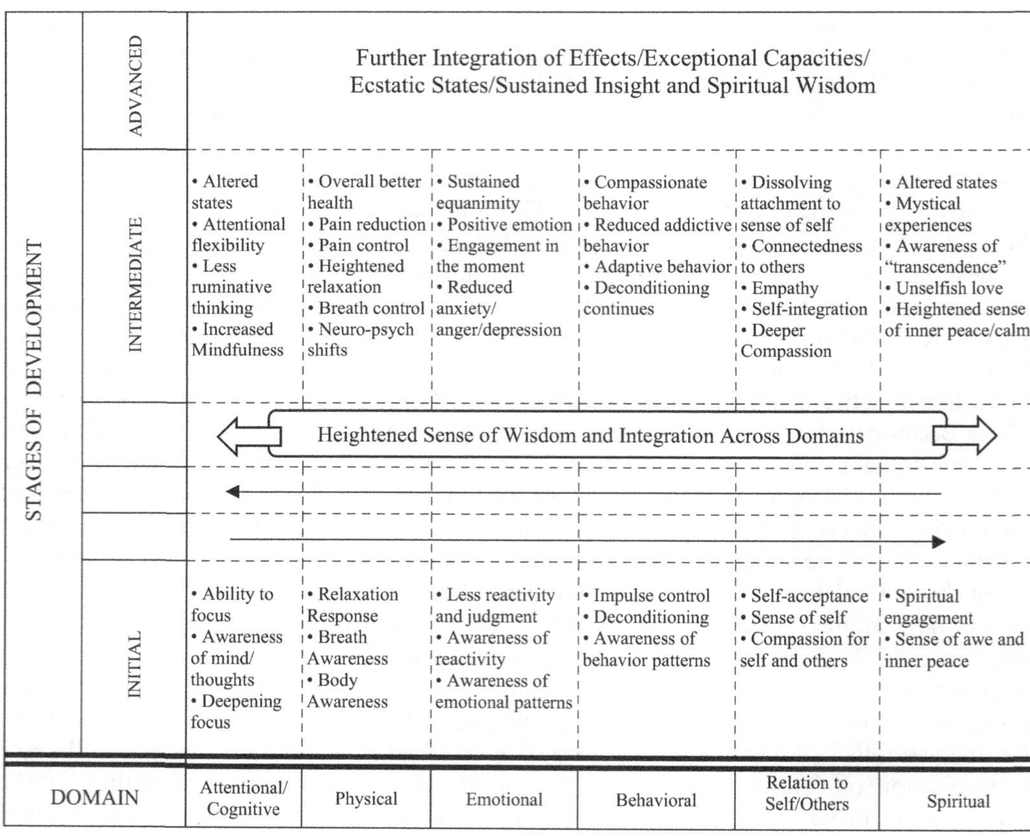

Figure 22.1 Multi-Domain Model of Stages and Interactions of Meditation Effects.[5]

The dashed vertical lines between domains in Figure 22.1 and the larger double-headed arrow line indicate the inherent interdependence and interconnectedness across the domains. If two of the domains can be argued to cross all the others, research and experiential evidence suggest that Attentional/Cognitive impacts each of the others, reflected in the thin arrow going from left to right. And once Spiritual is engaged, it deepens/mediates increases in the others, including an ability to deepen focused attention, as reflected in the horizontal line going left across all other areas of function. The dashed horizontal lines indicate that effects develop with practice, first with those at the bottom, INITIAL, level. The INTERMEDIATE level represents those that appear with more extended practice, but with considerable individual variability in the occurrence of such experiences. Guided meditations and more practice may facilitate growth within each of the domains. The highest ADVANCED level indicates continued growth and integration, with an ongoing sense of spiritual well-being and greater inner wisdom.

Attention/Cognition

All meditative techniques involve disengagement of attention from our usual scanning, analyzing, ignoring, or reacting so that a different type of mental engagement occurs or is cultivated. Mind wandering, engaging the default network of the brain (Mzarek et al., 2012), and reactivity are in contrast to the heightened capacity for attentional focus, a core aspect of all aspects of practice: concentrative, mindfulness, and guided. The earliest related research, in Japan (Kasamatsu & Hirai, 1969), showed that advanced Zen monks, when presented with repetitive sounds, observed the sounds, but neither reacted nor habituated to them. As research has developed, it is more evident that everyone, with practice, becomes able to better draw on their attentional capacities to be aware but less reactive (Lutz et al., 2008, 2009). In a study exploring the neurophysiology of the default mode network (DMN) (where our minds go when we are not focused), brain activity prior to beginning a meditation practice and four months later were compared. Results showed that the primary activity of the DMN had shifted from posterior areas of the brain to integration of activity in the right and left frontal hemispheres (Fingelkurts et al., 2016).

Clinically, an ability to cultivate focused attention showed substantial value for children with Attention Deficit Disorder trained in Samatha meditation (Singh et al., 2018). Shamatha comes from Buddhism and helps cultivate a single point of focus. While this may be on the breath, and therefore a type of mindfulness, it may also add a sound (such as *om*) or another simple *mantra*. In a group of experienced TM practitioners, an fMRI study found higher activity during meditation in attentional and executive functioning areas of the brain, with decreased activity in arousal areas (Mahone et al., 2018). Attention can also be brought in a non-reactive way to thoughts, as it would to feelings, with detached awareness replacing over-identification.

These processes may also promote absorption into religious or symbolic experience. Meditation practices support heightened awareness and alertness – of being fully in the present – often experienced as spiritually powerful. The disengagement cultivated by meditation practice may also allow space for a different type or level of processing, as occurs in trance states, in Buddhist *samadhi* or in the silent space cultivated in contemplative prayer (Keating, 1997). At the same time, mindfulness has also been referred to as the opposite of trance (Brach, 2012). Although unusual, I have had clients who, after their first experience with meditation practice, immediately shared that they had gained a distinct sense of their spiritual self; for others, with only a little practice, they had hallucinatory-type recall of prior memories.

Physical

Most people almost immediately share a sense of relaxation experienced with meditation. This is linked to the physiological shifts meditation produces in the autonomic nervous system through two primary processes: indirectly by disengaging stress-related "fight or flight" reactivity, producing the "relaxation response" (Benson, 1975), and directly by slowing and pacing breathing (Lehrer et al., 1999), representing a shift from sympathetic nervous system dominance to parasympathetic dominance. Such relaxation effects may contribute to a sense of calmness or feelings of inner peace; while distinct, they may not be greater than from other relaxation techniques. A meta-analysis of TM effects on blood pressure found significant reductions, particularly for systolic blood pressure, and more so for individuals over age 65 (Schneider et al., 2022). Newberg and Waldman, in their book, *How God Changes Your Brain* (2009), outline their extensive research, including meditation studies with both religious and non-religious individuals. They've shown that just 12 minutes of daily meditation practice may slow down the aging process. A small study (Robertson, 2022) using Centering Prayer with undergraduates documented improvement in physiology, along with increased general well-being. More active chanting, Sufi dancing, or other related contemplative practices may foster ecstatic states characterized by hyperarousal of a different type (Schimmel, 1975).

Carlson and her colleagues (2007) found substantial health benefits, sustained at one year after the MBSR program, for early-stage cancer patients in regard to immune and endocrine function. Patients with psoriasis receiving usual light treatment were randomized to also receive brief mindfulness guidance, drawn from MBSR, which substantially decreased the number of sessions needed to clear (Kabat-Zinn et al., 1998). Another study of MBSR found heightened activity in frontal areas of the brain related to positive affect, and this mediated degree of improvement in antibody titers to influenza vaccine (Davidson et al., 2003). Van Gordon and his colleagues (2017) found improvement in the treatment of fibromyalgia syndrome using meditation awareness training. Experienced Zen students, in comparison to controls, were exposed to a temperature-related pain stimulus – and asked NOT to meditate as this occurred. Not only did they bear more pain, but their brains also showed little activity in executive, evaluative, or emotional areas during the process (Grant, Courtemanche, & Rainville, 2011).

In a definitive study (Saron, 2013), 30 long-term meditators entered a retreat environment for three months and were compared to a group matched on prior experience. Telomerase response, a marker of stress and long-term cellular viability, was better in the retreat group. Increases in purpose in life, spiritually related, directly mediated this difference (Jacobs et al., 2011), showing the impact of deep practice, even in well-experienced meditators.

Emotional

If meditation is essentially a cognitive process, how does it impact emotional states? One means is by interrupting the escalating cycles of reactivity and arousal that characterize intense emotional experience, whether anxiety (Kabat-Zinn et al., 1992), anger (Bormann & Carrico, 2009; Levine, 2000; Naht Hanh, 2002), or depression (Teasdale et al., 2000; Kuyken et al., 2016; Martin, 1999). With practice, emotional reactivity may be replaced by emotional equanimity, depicted in Figure 22.1, and a more general sense of well-being (Ekman et al., 2005; Goleman, 2003). These effects are, again, applicable to virtually any type of contemplative practice. A 2-month intervention comparing TM to group support for women with a history of domestic violence found TM to be more effective for anxiety and depression at immediate post and 2 months later (Leach & Lorenzon, 2023). In a very early laboratory study (Goleman & Schwartz, 1976), both experienced TM meditators and those introduced to a TM-type meditation showed decreased responses to a highly stressful brief film. Bormann and associates (2006) found broad benefits from spiritual mantram repetition in HIV patients. Multiple studies have shown benefits for PTSD (e.g., Nidich et al., 2018; Bellehsen et al., 2022; Barnes et al., 2016), with a scoping review of spirituality-integrated therapies for PTSD showing TM to be particularly strong (Field et al., 2024). In a meta-analytic review of research on emotion regulation (Naragon-Gainey et al., 2017), high levels of mindfulness and acceptance were most predictive of distress tolerance.

Davidson's now classic work (Lutz et al., 2004), with neuroimaging in highly experienced Tibetan monks, suggests dramatically greater dominance of positive emotions, which are processed in the left prefrontal cortex. This shift may be separate from spiritual development, as Tibetan Buddhism is a practice that encompasses all aspects of adaptive functioning, or it may be related to the attainment of positive states of bliss and euphoria that mark heightened spiritual experience. Austin (1998) and Newberg and Waldman (2009) also draw on neurological models to explain the pervasive emotional well-being associated with most spiritual experiences. Rubik (2011), in a creative study using neurofeedback to enhance positive emotions associated with prefrontal lobe gamma waves, found that TM meditators could do so better than non-meditators.

Conversely, meditation practice may, on occasion, promote the uncovering of traumatic memories or profoundly distressing emotions. While addressed anecdotally in the meditation literature (Miller, 1999), the incidence of such experiences among the general population of novice meditators may be less than 1% (Kabat-Zinn, personal communication, 2004), but higher in psychiatric populations, as has occurred for a small number of my own clients. But such connections may also prove to be very healing (Boorstein, 2000).

Behavioral

"Right action" is a major tenet of Buddhism. As noted, even in the traditional Buddhist literature, meditation is frequently referred to as engaging a deconditioning process, and a means to changing undesirable patterns of attachment or avoidance, readily translating into psychological concepts of conditioning theory. Meditation practice may also improve impulse control, as the mind slows down, allowing space for reflection and the emergence of alternative – and wiser – choices, as people move from "reacting" to "responding," also reducing cravings for addictive-type substances or behaviors, whether alcohol, nicotine, eating, or computer games (Brewer, 2017).

Much of the empirical evidence indeed comes from the addiction literature (Bowen et al., 2009; Marlatt, 2002), which can be difficult to interpret because of the complexities of the presenting problems and possibilities of multiple paths of effect, including change in emotion and cognition. An early meta-analysis of TM with smoking and alcohol intake supported extended benefits for both (Alexander et al., 1994). A randomized study of inpatient treatment for alcohol use disorder found that 3 months post-discharge, those practicing TM twice daily were far less likely to return to any drinking (25% vs. 59%; $p = .02$) or to heavy drinking (0% vs. 47%; $p < .001$). Further, regularity of practice predicted lower psychological distress, craving, and alcohol use at follow-up (Gryczynski et al., 2018). Christian-based Two-Way Prayer Meditation, in AA-based residential programs, led to strong increases in spiritual engagement, along with decreases in psychological distress (Hai et al., 2021). More applicable to everyone is the cultivation of mindful eating, now well documented to decrease compulsive eating, using several variants of MB-EAT (Kristeller et al., 2013; Radin et al., 2020; Kristeller & Epel, 2014).

Relation to Self and Others

A core theme in traditional meditation practice is a shift in the experience of the self. In Buddhism and Hinduism, this may be conceptualized as a fundamental disengagement from a created self (Engler, 1986), followed by a profound experience of the essential self. Further, meta-awareness, perspective-taking, and self-inquiry may be valuable in releasing people from maladaptive self-schemas (Dahl, Lutz, & Davidson, 2015). In Christian prayer, it is a transcending of the self and engagement with God. Such shifts may also relate to disengaging from a single definition of the self: from "I am an addict" to "I am so much more than that, and I'm moving to a more flexible and self-accepting sense of self."

Transformation of the self is the focus of many humanistic approaches to meditation and provides a linkage to spiritual growth. A substantial body of early empirical evidence supports the positive impact of meditation practice on self-growth and self-actualization (Sallis, 1982; Compton & Becker, 1983). While early psychodynamic models of meditation (and religious experience) tended to pathologize religiously oriented meditation (Molino, 1998), contemporary psychodynamic theorists acknowledge its value for helping explore the "deepest" reaches of oneself as a source of peace and wholeness versus a source of infantile conflict and impulses that need to be "tamed and controlled" (Rubin, 1999; Epstein, 2007). Travis (2006), in his work with TM, described an object-referral/self-referral continuum with a progressive dis-embedding of the Self, characterized by higher frontal coherence, higher alpha and lower gamma power during tasks, and heightened response to tasks, with release from the demands of perception, thought, and behavior during meditation practice and daily activity.

Fundamentally, there are also shifts in relation to others. In *metta* meditation within the Buddhist *vipassana* tradition, the focus is on "opening the heart" (Kornfield, 1993) to love and caring for others. A growing ability to experience empathy, compassion, and "loving kindness" is an important aspect of traditional meditation (Davidson & Harrington, 2002; Salzberg, 2002). As noted earlier, Neff and Germer (2018) have developed a widely used therapeutic approach, Mindfulness-Based Compassion Therapy. Semple and Hatt (2012/2024) call for linking spirituality with compassion-related research to explore Buddhist-related mindfulness therapies and positive psychological outcomes, also as reflected in Figure 22.1 in the horizontal bar going from spiritual effects back across all others. Development of compassion can be viewed as a function of dropping away of egoistic concern for one's own needs and shifting to a focus on others, or as a separate path of transformation (Kristeller & Johnson, 2005). Falb and Pargament (2012) call for therapists to engage in meditation for themselves as a way to heighten their own capacity for compassion, which they refer to as relational mindfulness. A study in India (Bubber & Gala, 2022) found that couples who both meditated reported higher levels of spiritual well-being and relationship quality than couples who did not. In the 3-month retreat study mentioned above (Saron, 2013), participants were also evaluated on responses to observed suffering (Rosenberg et al., 2015) and showed consistently heightened responses of sympathetic concern than the comparison group. Monaghan and Viereck (2011) provide an excellent brief summary of loving kindness, also linking it to spiritual engagement. Nurturing compassion and loving-kindness is beautifully addressed in a chapter, "Primed for Love," in Goleman and Davidson's book, *Altered States* (2017).

Meditation: Cultivating Spiritual and Religious Effects

Cultivating Spiritual Experience and Engagement

Not only do all current meditative practices derive from religious traditions, but some argue (e.g., Brach, 2003; Shonin et al., 2013) that all meditation effects can or should be subsumed under spiritual engagement. While a multi-domain model, as posited in Figure 22.1, places spiritual change as the sixth area of effect, more in parallel to, rather than superordinate to, other effects, meditation is virtually synonymous with the cultivation of spiritual growth. Disengaging from worldly concerns, from a preoccupation with self, and toward a cultivation of emotional equanimity are often considered the foundation for spiritual engagement. Rather than seeing spiritual effects as a sixth parallel domain, it could be argued that spirituality be viewed as an integrative domain, crossing all the others. Yet, as noted above, this could be true of other domains, as indicated by the horizontal arrow linking across each of them. The remainder of the chapter will explore the role of meditation in cultivating spiritual development more deeply, and in regard to individual differences and therapeutic context.

What is meant by spiritual effects? A sense of inner peace, of higher levels of meaning, of connectedness with a transcendent (or internal) God, of connectedness with others, increased faith, and a feeling of awe – all these are dimensions that have been linked to the psychology of spirituality (Johnson, Sheets, & Kristeller, 2008). Spirituality is also being integrated into positive psychology; an updated review in relation to mindfulness and other meditation approaches highlights recent research in that area (Shapiro et al., 2024). Datta and Newberg (2020) have creatively summarized the neurotheology literature to explore the potential of contemplative practices for healing in elderly individuals. The question nevertheless remains how a simple cognitive process like meditation can lead an individual to such experiences. More dramatic and esoteric effects include the range of "altered states," "anomalous experience," or enlightenment that have intrigued investigators of meditation for some time (Austin, 1998, 2006; Newberg & Waldman, 2009). At the extreme are effects that might be considered paranormal: out-of-body experiences, levitation, or ESP. Whether such dramatic experiences are functionally contiguous with milder experiences of inner peace and connectedness or whether they involve distinctly different neurophysiology is another question in understanding the psychology of both meditation and religious experience.

An increasing amount of research is being carried out on spiritual change during the initial stages of meditation. One question is whether explicitly engaging spirituality is needed. An earlier study (Wachholtz & Pargament, 2005), drawing on TM, randomized students to one of three 20-minute meditative/relaxation practices to use daily for two weeks: a brief spiritual phrase (e.g., "God is joy."), a secular phrase (e.g., "I am content."), or sitting quietly, trying not to think of stressful things. The spiritual group had the greatest decreases in anxiety and increases in spiritual well-being. This was confirmed in a second study (Wachholtz & Pargament, 2008) with an even stronger focus on spiritual engagement. In Korea, the use of a *mantra*-based Holy Name meditation program for both palliative care patients (Yong & Lee, 2021) and nurse managers (Yong et al., 2020) improved a sense of spiritual well-being and dignity. At the same time, the 8-week MBSR program, designed to be entirely secular, was found to result in substantive changes on the FACIT-Sp. Further, these changes were related to the impact of the program on stress and on medical symptoms (Carmody et al., 2008). In a study of MBSR for depressive symptoms (Greeson et al., 2015), increases in spirituality mediated improvement.

Extending Spiritual Wisdom into Everyday Life

Can eating be a spiritual experience? In a program that might be presumed to be even less likely to engage spiritual effects than MBSR, participants in the 10-week MB-EAT program, focused on overeating but also including general meditation practice, shared with us that they had experienced spiritual growth, also reflected in significant increases on the FACIT-Sp (Kristeller & Jordan, 2018). Similarly to MBSR, increases in spiritual well-being are also related to increases in mindfulness, emotional improvement, and eating regulation and mediated the effects of mindfulness on eating and depression. Thich Naht Hanh, together with Lillian Cheung, a Harvard nutritionist, wrote the book *Savor: Mindful Eating, Mindful Life* (Naht Hanh & Cheung, 2010), beautifully linking one's relationship to food and eating to spiritual engagement, as does Jan Chozen Bays, a physician and Zen practitioner, in her book, *Mindful Eating* (2009). Thich Naht Hanh (2009) included our relationship to eating and food as part of the Five Mindfulness Trainings, the primary teachings of the Buddha. The first is to protect life and to decrease violence in oneself, in the family, and in society. The second is to practice social justice, generosity, and not exploiting other living beings. The third is the practice of responsible sexual behavior. The fourth is the practice of deep listening and loving speech to restore communication and reconciliation. And the fifth is mindful consumption.

A wider range of spiritually-based meditation practices is being explored systematically. A small qualitative study of Brahma Kumaris Raja Yoga meditation reported multiple ways in which cancer patients drew on their spiritual resources, including spiritual connection and self-empowerment, using mind–body-soul healing practices, and post-cancer spiritual growth (Agarwal et al., 2022). A study in an inpatient recovery center reintroduced Christian Two-Way Prayer Meditation, an approach that had once been part of AA in the 1930s, but had been lost in practice. It consists of a daily 10–15 minute practice of sitting quietly, expressing a desire or need to one's God, and then listening silently for a response. Multiple positive effects were found related to spiritual engagement compared to the non-participants, with somewhat weaker effects for overall distress and self-esteem (Hai et al., 2021). Thomas Keating (2002) wrote extensively about the value of Catholic Centering Prayer, expanding out into daily activities, although acknowledging that doing so can be challenging outside of a cloistered environment. Yet Knabb and his associates (Knabb et al., 2020) found that students at two Christian universities, who attended a 4-week spiritually-engaging meditation class, and then used deeply structured Christian contemplative prayer first for 10 minutes daily and then for 2 minutes, showed increases in humility, surrender and non-attachment, although no decreases in anxiety, relative to a wait-list control. In Japan, the traditionally Zen Buddhist practice of "forest walking," called Shinrin-Yoku, or meditating while walking in nature, now has many offerings available for the general public, with a range of studies showing considerable benefit, including spiritual well-being (Hansen & Jones, 2020).

Deepening Spiritual Engagement, Cultivating the Mystical Mind

With more extended practice, the development of what Maslow termed peak experience (1970) may contribute to self-actualization and related personal growth. Considerable attention has been paid by researchers of TM to documenting the state they refer to as "transcendental consciousness," the entry into higher states of consciousness (Alexander et al., 1991). Gifford-May and Thompson (1994), in a qualitative study of 10 meditators across multiple traditions, documented that such transcendent experiences were the most universal of the deep meditative states reported.

As noted, practice may also lead to triggering challenging emotional experience, uncovering traumatic memories, or adaptive regression (Urbanowski & Miller, 1996). While these experiences could be construed as more relevant to the domain of emotional growth rather than spiritual growth, if occurring after more extended practice, they may be part of the journey of the classic "dark night of the soul," leading to a deepening of spiritual engagement, as internal struggles and trauma release their hold on psychic energy. Schmidt and Miller (2004) highlight several ways in which meditation practice may be drawn on when working with trauma patients, including engaging *metta* (loving-kindness). Knabb et al. (2022b) randomized Christian trauma survivors to either a two-week online loving-kindness intervention or to a *lectio divina* meditative intervention, that includes scripture, meditation, prayer and contemplation, finding a greater response to the *lectio divino* program. Another study (Knabb et al., 2022a) compared a 4-week online version of the program to a wait-list control, also post-trauma, with similar findings, including a reduction in trauma-based rumination and other trauma-related symptoms and an increase in attention, present focus, awareness, and acceptance.

Meditation practice is also a path to more intense altered states and mystical experience (Goleman, 1978). Early models, such as Deikman's deautomatization model (1966), focused on how disengagement from usual cognitive processing may open a path to mystical experience, marked by a sense of intense realness, unusual sensations, a sense of unity, ineffability, and trans-sensate experience. Some of these can be quite mild and explained in psychophysiological terms; for example, being so still when sitting that there is virtually no muscle feedback to the brain may lead to feelings of "floating." Other unusual effects, such as Tibetan and Zen Rinzai monks who maintain high body temperatures despite freezing ambient temperatures, although indicators of advanced practice (Benson, 1982), may fall within the realm of physiological effects, such as very slow-paced breathing, rather than spiritual experiences.

Others, such as ecstatic states or peak experiences, engage both emotional and spiritual experience. Of more importance is the possibility that studying such states in advanced meditators may bring a greater understanding of the underlying neurophysiology of intense spiritual and religious experience. Austin's (1998) perspective on the neurophysiology of Zen practice primarily focused on ways to understand *kensho* (the initial experience of enlightenment or "awakening") and *satori* (subsequent and/or more profound experiences of enlightenment). Neuroimaging research on advanced meditators in the Tibetan tradition has investigated the neurological shifts that accompany very specific experiential states (Goleman & Davidson, 2017). The TM-Siddhi program touts the potential of practice in cultivating Hindu *siddhi* ("perfect mastery over mind and body") powers, including processes generally considered within the realm of the paranormal, such as levitation (Goleman, 1988), though without providing scientifically reliable evidence for such. Alan Wallace, known for his work with long-term meditators, proposed a model that explores ways to link basic science/physics with Buddhist philosophy (Wallace, 2007).

Variation in Spiritual Experiences: Stages of Practice and Individual Differences

Individual variation in meditative effects, as in other areas of psychological functioning, is important to consider. Two sources of such variation are apparent. First, given that meditation cultivates skillful means of focusing attention and engaging unique mental abilities, effects would be expected to deepen as the level of practice increases. Further, some individuals may be naturally more endowed with these capacities, independent of practice, as occurs in other areas of human attainment, such as musical or athletic ability.

Level of Practice

One challenge in understanding the literature on meditation is that the preponderance of empirical research has investigated the experiences of novice meditators, whereas most of the traditional literature focuses on highly trained meditators. While more advanced levels of practice have limited bearing on understanding therapeutic applications, they may be more pertinent to spiritual and religious contexts. The early neuroimaging research by Davidson and his team (Lutz et al., 2004) explored changes in highly experienced (e.g., over 10,000 hours of practice) meditators, showing extraordinary capacities to disengage from usual processing. In traditional Eastern meditation literature, stages in shifts of awareness, attention, and cognition are clearly delineated, starting with initial meditative effects, and continuing into advanced levels characterized by altered states of consciousness. Brown and Engler (1980) addressed issues related to progression through stages of practice by novices, in which fascination for the content of the mind that arises may interfere with cultivating adequate concentrative abilities, yet this can be seen as consistent with both traditional training and results found by Dunn et al. (1999), as noted above. Goleman, in *The Meditative Mind* (1988), pointed out that one limit of some traditional classifications of stages of meditative progress is that they start by describing relatively advanced levels (*jhanas*), rarely experienced without substantial practice, while providing an overview of more basic processes relevant for beginners.

Individual Differences in Practice and Experience

Some individuals appear more drawn to some practices than others. At the beginning level, in structured programs such as Kabat-Zinn's MBSR program, individual variation may play less of a role, but understanding who continues to practice may be pertinent to broader issues in the psychology of religion and spirituality. Who is the natural contemplative? Who becomes the mystic or adept? Because meditation practices are so highly structured, exploring this question lends itself to empirical study in ways that other religious practices may not.

Two broader models consider such differences: the concept of spiritual intelligence (Emmons, 2000) and the Jungian model of personality type (1923/1971). Emmons argues that spirituality fits the eight criteria for a unique intelligence under Gardner's multiple intelligences theory (2004), including the existence of exceptional individuals, a set of core operations that promote adaptability, support from psychometric evidence, and encoding in a symbol system. Meditation can be argued to be an effective means to cultivating spiritual intelligence (Kristeller, 2004) in that it promotes core elements of the spiritual experience and related adaptive functioning, there are extraordinary individuals who become meditation masters, and because encoding in a symbol system is evident in a wide range of practices in most religions. The Jungian concept of personality type, operationalized in the Myers-Briggs Type model (Myers, 1962), posits four dimensions: Sensing-Intuitive (i.e., are you more of a "sensor" or more of an "intuitive"?), Thinking-Feeling, Introversion-Extroversion, and Judging-Perceiving, that interface with each other. For example, someone might be an "Introverted/Thinker," or an "Intuitive/Feeler." Richardson (1996) related these categories to variations in religious practices and spiritual orientation, engaging the question of how some individuals may be drawn more strongly to certain practices, both within and across religious traditions. For example, he proposed silent meditation may be more appealing to Intuitive/Thinkers who prefer less adorned settings for spiritual practice, such as a Zen garden or a simple chapel, whereas ritualistic meditation, such as the Jesus Prayer or the Nichiren Lotus Sutra, may appeal to Sensing/Feeling types who resonate more with the rituals of tradition, and also value connection with a teacher or guru more highly.

Meditation, Spirituality, and Psychotherapy

Meditative practice, over the last 50 years, has found its way into the major domains of therapeutic theory and practice: psychodynamic, humanistic/transpersonal, and cognitive-behavioral. The distinctions among these therapeutic approaches have loosened in the face of more integrated perspectives on human functioning. Meditation practice has also been engaged psychotherapeutically in ways that explicitly retain a religious context, whether Buddhist, Christian, or a more integrated perspective.

How should meditation as a path to spiritual growth be considered within the therapeutic context? As spirituality becomes better identified as a universal aspect of psychological capacity and as an appropriate focus for therapy (Miller, 1999), it has become clearer that acknowledging the spiritual power of meditation practice makes it more, rather than less, appropriate as a therapeutic tool (Marlatt & Kristeller, 1999; Rosch, 2002; Rubin, 1996; Welwood, 2000). For example, Tom Plante (2020) reviews a number of ways in which Jesuit-based approaches to meditation can be integrated into psychotherapy.

There are several ways to consider meditation as a therapeutic path within the spiritual and religious context: 1) meditation may be a powerful way to cultivate spiritual resources (i.e., someone's innate "spiritual intelligence"), which then promotes emotional healing within the self and with others, providing the power to let go of addictive behaviors, such as drug or alcohol use – or compulsive eating; 2) meditative prayer can purposefully deeply engage the spiritual self and contribute to well-being; 3) meditative practice may serve as a direct way of healing spiritual distress, feeling abandoned by God, or being separated from the transcendent.

There is also the question of whether meditative practice, while unquestionably healing for many, can stand alone as adequate psychotherapy. Therapists may want to familiarize themselves with the spiritual and religious traditions of different meditation practices, both to understand the perspective of clients already engaged in such practices, and to more knowledgeably encourage a client to seek a deeper personal practice, including within a retreat environment, which is usually identified with a specific spiritual or religious perspective. Some clients may express discomfort with learning meditation even within a therapeutic framework unless they can frame it within an acceptable religious context (such as Christian, in contrast to Buddhist or Hindu).

Psychodynamic Theory

Freud's solution to dealing with the vestiges of pre-Renaissance thinking was to pathologize all of what he perceived as religious or spiritual inclinations. He asserted that such impulses were regressive, neurotic, and counter to healthy development of the self (Freud, 1930/2010; Morvay, 1999), but as Epstein notes (1996), Freud later shifted some of his perspectives on this. Jung took a very different perspective on the value of religious experience, as noted above, but it was Erich Fromm (Fromm et al., 1960) and Karen Horney (Quinn, 1987;

Horney, 1987) who were, within the psychoanalytic tradition, credited with explicitly promoting the value of meditation practice, from the Zen Buddhist tradition and their work with D. T. Suzuki, to foster profound self-development (DeMartino, 1991; Morvay, 1999). Their influences have been more deeply cultivated by writings on meditation of such analytically oriented therapists as Brown and Engler (1980), Rubin (1985, 1996, 1999), and Epstein (2007).

Humanistic/Transpersonal Psychology

During the early phases of interest in meditation as a therapeutic approach, humanistic psychology most directly embraced the spiritual dimensions of human functioning, particularly within the related area of transpersonal psychology, and associations with altered states (Goleman, 1978; Tart, 1972). There was strong interest in the mystical aspects of meditation practice, related to interest in psychedelic drugs, particularly mescaline and LSD. More recent developments are again linking such psychedelic experiences with meditation (Boorstein, 2000).

Cognitive-Behavioral

Behavioral perspectives initially simply side-stepped the issue of the role of religion in human functioning. Yet, paradoxically, we now understand that much of what we call religious beliefs and practices are learned attitudes and conditioned associations to frequently repeated and meaning-embedded rituals. Considering such effects was outside the domain of radical behaviorism, but is much less problematic for contemporary extensions within cognitive behavioral approaches, such as dialectical behaviorism (Linehan, 1993; Linehan & Wilks, 2015), which is explicitly informed by Linehan's personal experiences with Zen and which incorporates limited mindfulness meditative practices, as do a broad range of other approaches, such as Acceptance and Commitment Therapy (ACT) (Hayes, 1984; Hayes et al., 2004). In another example, a clinical trial linked religion-specific *mantras* to cognitive therapy for insomnia, finding substantial results (Behera et al., 2023). Spiritual Self-Schema (3-S+) therapy is another approach that has blended Buddhist teachings, mindfulness and concentrative meditation practice, and cognitive behavioral therapy in a treatment program for persons struggling with drug misuse (Avants & Margolin, 2004; Margolin et al., 2007). A Dutch theorist and clinical psychologist, Maurits Kwee, working with Albert Ellis, integrated Ellis' Rational Emotive Behavior Therapy with Zen perspectives (Kwee & Ellis, 1998), incorporating the value of spiritual growth. Cognitive behavioral perspectives and constructivist approaches (Mahoney, 2003; Rosmarin, 2018) have been reinfused with the value of addressing meaning and spirituality with clients.

Summary and Conclusion

Meditation practices have a history as enduring aspects of virtually all religious traditions. The powerful healing and growth effects of secularized meditative practice are increasingly understood within the context of contemporary psychological theory, but this has generally been at the cost of dismissing or ignoring ways in which meditation has power as a spiritual or religious practice and discipline. Understanding and exploring these aspects of practice is equally important for several reasons: 1) meditative practices were – and still are – shaped by the particular religious traditions from which they developed; 2) personal meditative experience – and religious experience – are affected by culturally defined expectations; 3) the self-transformative processes, both in relation to self and in relation to others, may be best understood within a spiritual context, as is posited by many religious faiths; 4) spirituality is gaining acceptability as a valid psychological construct, and a comprehensive consideration of the psychological impact of meditation therefore inherently engages this dimension. Finally, despite the still limited evidence that spiritual engagement has a mediating effect on change in other aspects of meditation-related growth, the results overall, as summarized, would support the value of assessing spiritual well-being in all outcome research on meditation-based experience.

Related to this, and perhaps of most critical value, is the need at a theoretical level to understand those aspects of meditative practice that may empower spiritual experience via universal psychological processes, as called for by Vieten and her associates (2018). By understanding the religious roots of the major meditative traditions, it may be easier to differentiate the belief structure from the universal aspects of the practice. In understanding meditative processes, we may come to better understand the underlying neurological mechanisms involved in each of the six domains of effects, and their interlinks with spiritual and religious experience.

Notes

1 In Christianity, the term 'contemplation' is the closer usage to the term 'meditation' as it has entered contemporary usage from the Asian traditions, whereas the term 'meditation' in Christianity generally refers to more active, reflective prayer, in which the mind is engaged with sacred content.
2 Also referred to as the Parliament of the World's Religions.
3 Ram Dass changed his name from Richard Alpert in 1967, after leaving Harvard University as faculty member in the Department of Psychology, and travelling to India.
4 *Om* represents a universal sacred sound; *Mani* speaks to love and compassion; *padme* is 'lotus', referring to wisdom; and *hum* refers to enlightenment or release from the negative.
5 Adapted from Kristeller, J.L. (2021). Ch. 14. Mindfulness meditation. In P. Lehrer, R.L. & Woolfolk (Eds.). *Principles and Practice of Stress Management*. 4th Edition. Guilford Press.

References

Agarwal, K., Kelly, L. L., Heintzman, J. C., & Fortune, L. D. (2022). Lived spiritual experiences of cancer survivors with long-term meditation practices: An interpretative phenomenological analysis. *Pastoral Psychology*, *71*(4), 485–501.

Alexander, C. N., Rainforth, M. V., & Gelderloos, P. (1991). Transcendental meditation, self-actualization, and psychological health: A conceptual overview and statistical meta-analysis. *Journal of Social Behavior & Personality* , *6*(5), 189–248.

Alexander, C. N., Robinson, P., & Rainforth, M. (1994). Treating and preventing alcohol, nicotine, and drug abuse through Transcendental Meditation: A review and statistical meta-analysis. *Alcoholism Treatment Quarterly*, *11*(1–2), 13–87.

Arasteh, A. R., & Sheikh, A. A. (1989). Sufism: The way to universal self. In A. A. Sheikh & K. S. Sheikh (Eds.), *Eastern and Western approaches to healing: Ancient wisdom and modern knowledge*. (pp. 146–179): John Wiley & Sons.

Austin, J. H. (1998). *Zen and the brain: Toward an understanding of meditation and consciousness*. MIT Press.

Austin, J. H. (2006). *Zen-brain reflections*. Cambridge, MA: MIT Press.

Avants, S. K., & Margolin, A. (2004). Development of spiritual self-schema therapy for ther treatment of addictive and HIV risk behavior: A convergence of cognitive and Buddhist psychology. *Journal of Psychotherapy Integration*, *14*(3), 253–289.

Barnes, V. A., Monto, A., Williams, J. J., & Rigg, J. L. (2016). Impact of transcendental meditation on psychotropic medication use among active duty military service members with anxiety and PTSD. *Military Medicine*, *181*(1), 56–63.

Bays, J. C. (2009). *Mindful eating: A guide to rediscovering a healthy and joyful relationship with food.* Boulder, Co: Shambala Press.

Beauregard, M. (2024). Neuroimaging and spiritual practice. In L. J. Miller (Ed.), *The Oxford handbook of psychology and spirituality., 2nd ed.* (pp. 632–653). Oxford University Press.

Behera, C. K., Reddy, T. K., Behera, L., Birbaumer, N., & Ika, K. (2023). A meditation based cognitive therapy (HMBCT) for primary insomnia: A treatment feasibility pilot study. *Applied Psychophysiology and Biofeedback*, *48*(3), 369–378.

Bellehsen, M., Stoycheva, V., Cohen, B. H., & Nidich, S. (2022). A pilot randomized controlled trial of Transcendental Meditation as treatment for posttraumatic stress disorder in veterans. *Journal of Traumatic Stress*, *35*(1), 22–31

Benson, H. (1975). *The relaxation response.* William Morrow.

Benson, H. (1982). Body temperature changes during the practice of g Tum-mo yoga. *Nature*, *295*(5846), 234–236.

Benson, H., & Wallace, R. (1972). Decreased blood pressure in hypertensive subjects who practiced meditation. *Circulation*, *46*(1), 130.

Bhattacharya, M. & Gaur, K. (2024). Transcendental meditation, education, health and wellbeing: A spiritual approach. *Journal of Spirituality in Mental Health*, 26 (1), 21–31.

Bishop, S. R., Lau, M., Shapiro, S., Carlson, L., Anderson, N. D., Carmody, J., et al. (2004). Mindfulness: A proposed operational definition., *Clinical Psychology: Science & Practice* (Vol. 11, pp. 230–241): Oxford Univ Press.

Boorstein, Seymour (2000). Transpersonal psychotherapy. *American Journal of Psychotherapy*, *54*(3), 408–423.

Bormann, J. E., & Carrico, A. W. (2009). Increases in positive reappraisal coping during a group-based mantram intervention mediate sustained reductions in anger in HIV-positive persons. *International Journal of Behavioral Medicine*, *16*(1), 74–80.

Bormann, J. E., Gifford, A. L., Shively, M., Smith, T. L., Redwine, L., Kelly, A., et al. (2006). Effects of spiritual mantram repetition on HIV outcomes: A randomized controlled trial. *Journal of Behavioral Medicine*, *29*(4), 359–376.

Bormann, J. E., Kane, J. J., & Oman, D. (2020). Mantram repetition: A portable practice for being mindful. *Mindfulness*, *11*(8), 2031–2033.

Bowen, S., Chawla, N., Collins, S., Witkiewitz, K., Hsu, S., Grow, J., et al. (2009). Mindfulness-based relapse prevention for substance use disorders: A pilot efficacy trial. *Substance Abuse*, *30*(4), 295–305.

Brach, T. (2003). *Radical acceptance: Embracing your life with the heart of a Buddha.* New York: Bantam Books.

Brach, T. (2012). Mindful presence: A foundation for compassion and wisdom. In C. K. Germer & R. D. Siegel (Eds.), *Wisdom and compassion in psychotherapy: Deepening mindfulness in clinical practice.* (pp. 35–47). Guilford Press.

Breton, D., & Largent, C. (1998). *Love, soul, and freedom: Dancing with Rumi on the mystic path.* Hazelden Press.

Brewer, J. (2017). *The craving mind: From cigarettes to smartphones to love—why we get hooked and how we can break bad habits.* New Haven: Yale University Press.

Brown, D. P., & Engler, J. (1980). The stages of mindfulness meditation: A validation study. *Journal of Transpersonal Psychology*, *12*(2), 143–192.

Bubber, S., & Gala, J. (2022). Linking indian yogic practices and modern marriages: Role of meditation in marital wellbeing. *Current Psychology: A Journal for Diverse Perspectives on Diverse Psychological Issues.* doi:10.1007/s12144-022-02826-4

Carlson, L. E., Speca, M., Faris, P., & Patel, K. D. (2007). One year pre-post intervention follow-up of psychological, immune, endocrine and blood pressure outcomes of mindfulness-based stress reduction (MBSR) in breast and prostate cancer outpatients. *Brain, Behavior, and Immunity*, *21*(8), 1038–1049.

Carmody, J., Reed, G., Kristeller, J., & Merriam, P. (2008). Mindfulness, spirituality, and health-related symptoms. *Journal of Psychosomatic Research*, *64*, 393–403.

Carrington, P. (1977). *Freedom in meditation*. Anchor Press/Doubleday.

Compton, W. C., & Becker, G. M. (1983). Self-actualizations and experience with Zen meditation: Is a learning period necessary for meditation?, *Journal of Clinical Psychology* (Vol. 39, pp. 925–929): John Wiley & Sons.

Dahl, C. J., Lutz, A., & Davidson, R. J. (2015). Reconstructing and deconstructing the self: Cognitive mechanisms in meditation practice. *Trends In Cognitive Sciences*, *19*(9), 515–523.

Datta, S., & Newberg, A. (2020). The relationship between the brain and spirituality with respect to aging and neurodegenerative diseases: Clinical and research implications. *Journal of Religion, Spirituality & Aging*, *32*(4), 357–380

Davidson, R. J., & Harrington, A. (Eds.). (2002). *Visions of compassion: Western scientists and Tibetan Buddhists examine human nature*. London: Oxford University Press.

Davidson, R. J., Kabat-Zinn, J., Schumacher, J., Rosenkranz, M., Muller, D., Santorelli, S. F., et al. (2003). Alterations in brain and immune function produced by mindfulness meditation., *Psychosomatic Medicine* (Vol. 65, pp. 564–570): Lippincott Williams & Wilkins.

Davidson, R.J. & Kaszniak, A.W. (2015). Conceptual and methodological issues in research on mindfulness and meditation. *American Psychologist*, 70, 581–592.

Deikman, A. (1966). Deautomatization and the mystic experience. *Psychiatry*, 29, 324–388.

DeMartino, R. J. (1991). Karen Horney, Daisetz T. Suzuki, and Zen Buddhism., *American Journal of Psychoanalysis* (Vol. 51, pp. 267–283): Kluwer Academic Publishers.

Dunn, B. R., Hartigan, J. A., & Mikulas, W. L. (1999). Concentration and mindfulness meditations: Unique forms of consciousness?, *Applied Psychophysiology & Biofeedback*, *24*, 147–165.

Easwaran, E. (1991). *Meditation: A simple 8-point path for translating spiritual ideals into daily life*. Nilgiri Press.

Eisenberg, R. L. (2004). *The JPS guide to Jewish traditions*. The Jewish Publication Society.

Ekman, P., Davidson, R., Ricard, M., & Wallace, B. A. (2005). Buddhist and psychological perspectives on emotions and well-being. *Current Directions in Psychological Science*, *14*, 59–63.

Emmons, R. A. (2000). Is spirituality an intelligence? Motivation, cognition, and the psychology of ultimate concern., *International Journal for the Psychology of Religion* (Vol. 10, pp. 3–26): Lawrence Erlbaum.

Engler, J. (1986). Therapeutic aims in psychotherapy and meditation: Developmental stages in the representation of the self. In Wilber, K., Engler, J., & Brown, D.P. *Transformations of Consciousness*. Boston: Shambala Press.

Epstein, M. (1996). Freud's influence on transpersonal psychology. In B. W. Scotton, A. B. Chinen, & J. R. Battista (Eds.), *Textbook of transpersonal psychiatry and psychology*. (pp. 29–38). New York, NY: Basic Books/Hachette Book Group.

Epstein, M. (2007). *Psychotherapy without the Self: A Buddhist perspective*. New Haven, CT: Yale University Press.

Falb, M. D., & Pargament, K. I. (2012). Relational mindfulness, spirituality, and the therapeutic bond. *Asian Journal of Psychiatry*, *5*(4), 351–354.

Field, T. A., White, D. B., Davis, J., Park, J. S., & Pierson, J. L. (2024). Scoping review of spirituality-integrated psychotherapies for posttraumatic stress disorder. *Spirituality in Clinical Practice*, *11*(3), 203–221.

Fields, R. (1992). *How the Swans Came to the Lake: A Narrative History of Buddhism in America*. Boulder, CO: Shambhala Publications.

Fingelkurts, A. A., Fingelkurts, A. A., & Kallio-Tamminen, T. (2016). Long-term meditation training induced changes in the operational synchrony of default mode network modules during a resting state. *Cognitive Processing*, *17*(1), 27–37.

Freud, S. (1930/2010). *Civilization and its discontents*. W. W. Norton & Company.

Fromm, E., Suzuki, D. T., & De Martino, R. (1960). *Zen Buddhism and psychoanalysis*. New York: Harper Press.

Fulton, P. R., & Siegel, R. D. (2013). Buddhist and western psychology: Seeking common ground. In C. K. Germer, R. D. Siegel, & P. R. Fulton (Eds.), *Mindfulness and psychotherapy., 2nd* ed. (pp. 36–56). The Guilford Press.

Gardner, H. (2004). *Frames of mind: The theory of multiple intelligences.* New York: Basic Books.

Germer, C. K., Siegel, R. D., & Fulton, P. R. (Eds.). (2013). *Mindfulness and psychotherapy, 2nd* ed. New York, NY: Guilford Press.

Gifford-May, D., & Thompson, N. L. (1994). "Deep states" of meditation: Phenomenological reports of experience., *Journal of Transpersonal Psychology* (Vol. 26, pp. 117–138): Journal of Transpersonal Psychology.

Goleman, D. (1978). A taxonomy of meditation-specific altered states. *Journal of Altered States of Consciousness, 4*(2), 203–213.

Goleman, D. (1988). *The meditative mind: The varieties of meditative experience.* Los Angeles: Jeremy P. Tarcher Publishing.

Goleman, D. (2003). *Destructive emotions: How can we overcome them? A scientific dialogue with the Dalai Lama.* New York: Bantam Books.

Goleman, D. & Davidson, R.J. (2017). *Altered traits: Science reveals how meditation changes your mind, brain and body.* Avery/Random House.

Goleman, D. J. & Schwartz, G. E. (1976). Meditation as an intervention in stress reactivity. *Journal of Consulting and Clinical Psychology, 44*(3), 456–466.

Grant, J. A., Courtemanche, J., & Rainville, P. (2011). A non-elaborative mental stance and decoupling of executive and pain-related cortices predicts low pain sensitivity in Zen meditators. *Pain, 152*(1), 150–156.

Greeson, J., Smoski, M., Suarez, E., Brantley, J., Ekblad, A., Lynch, T., & Wolever, R. (2015). Decreased symptoms of depression after mindfulness-based stress reduction: potential moderating effects of religiosity, spirituality, trait mindfulness, sex, and age. *Journal of Alternative and Complementary Medicine, 21,* 166–174. doi:10.1089/acm.2014.0285

Gryczynski, J., Schwartz, R. P., Fishman, M. J., Nordeck, C. D., Grant, J., Nidich, S., … O'Grady, K. E. (2018). Integration of Transcendental Meditation® (TM) into alcohol use disorder (AUD) treatment. *Journal of Substance Abuse Treatment, 87,* 23–30.

Hai, A. H., Wigmore, B., Franklin, C., Shorkey, C., von Sternberg, K., Cole, A. H., Jr., & DiNitto, D. M. (2021). Efficacy of two-way prayer meditation in improving the psychospiritual well-being of people with substance use disorders: A pilot randomized controlled trial. *Substance Abuse, 42*(4), 832–841 doi:10.1080/08897077.2020.1865244

Hansen, M. M., & Jones, R. (2020). The interrelationship of Shinrin-Yoku and spirituality: A scoping review. *Journal of Alternative and Complementary Medicine, 26,* 1093–1104. doi: 10.1089/acm.2020.0193

Harmless, W. (2004). *Desert Christians: An introduction to the literature of early monasticism.* Oxford University Press.

Hart, W. (1987). *The Art of living: Vipassana meditation: As taught by S.* N. Goenka. HarperOne.

Hayes, S. C. (1984). Making sense of spirituality. *Behaviorism, 12*(2), 99–110.

Hayes, S. C., Follette, V. M., & Linehan, M. M. (2004). *Mindfulness and acceptance: Expanding the cognitive-behavioral tradition.* New York, NY: Guilford Press.

Hilert, A. J., & Gutierrez, D. (2020). Jewish meditation in counseling. *Counseling and Values, 65*(2), 126–136. doi:10.1002/cvj.12133

Horan, R. (2009). The neuropsychological connection between creativity and meditation. *Creativity Research Journal, 21*(2–3), 199–222.

Horney, K. (1987). *Our inner conflicts.* New York: Norton.

Ismail, G., Shealy, C., & Nahas, Z. (2023). Psychotherapy through a Sufi Islamic lens: A dialectic of transcendence and acceptance. *Spirituality in Clinical Practice, 10*(3), 200–218. doi:10.1037/scp0000274

Jacobs, T. L., Epel, E. S., Lin, J., Blackburn, E. H., Wolkowitz, O. M., Bridwell, D. A., … Saron, C. D. (2011). Intensive meditation training, immune cell telomerase activity, and psychological mediators. *Psychoneuroendocrinology, 36*(5), 664–681.

Johnson, T. J., Sheets, V. L., & Kristeller, J. (2008). Empirical identification of dimensions of religiousness and spirituality. *Mental Health, Religion, and Culture*, *11*, 745–767.

Jung, C.G. (1923/1971). *Psychological types*. Harcourt, Brace & Co./Princeton University Press.

Jung, C.G. (2020). *Psychology of yoga and meditation (translation of 1938-1940 lectures)*. Princeton University Press.

Kabat-Zinn, J. (1990). *Full catastrophe living*. New York: Delacorte Press.

Kabat-Zinn, J. (2011). Some reflections on the origins of MBSR, skillful means, and the trouble with maps. *Contemporary Buddhism*, *12*(1), 281–306.

Kabat-Zinn, J., Lipworth, L., & Burney, R. (1985). The clinical use of mindfulness meditation for the self-regulation of chronic pain., *Journal of Behavioral Medicine*, *8*, 163–190.

Kabat-Zinn, J., Massion, A. O., Kristeller, J., & Peterson, L. G. (1992). Effectiveness of a meditation-based stress reduction program in the treatment of anxiety disorders. *American Journal of Psychiatry*, *149*(7), 936–943.

Kabat-Zinn, J., Wheeler, E., Light, T., Skillings, A., Scharf, M. J., Cropley, T. G., et al. (1998). Influence of a mindfulness meditation-based stress reduction intervention on rates of skin clearing in patients with moderate to severe psoriasis undergoing phototherapy (UVB) and photochemotherapy (PUVA). *Psychosomatic Medicine*, *60*, 625–632.

Kasamatsu, A. & Hirai, T. (1969). An electroencephalographic study of the Zen meditation (Zazen). *Psychologia*, *12*, 205–225.

Keating, T. (1997). *Active meditations for contemplative prayer*. New York: Continuum.

Keating, T. (2002). *Foundations for centering prayer and the Christian life*. Continuum.

Kelly, B. D. (2022). Beyond mindfulness: Buddhist psychology and the Abhidharma. *Journal of Spirituality in Mental Health*, *25*(1), 71–82. doi:10.1080/19349637.2022.2081952

Knabb, J. (2021). *Christian meditation in clinical practice. A four-step model and workbook for therapists and cliients*. Lisle, IL: IVP Academic.

Knabb, J. J., Vazquez, V. E., Garzon, F. L., Ford, K. M., Wang, K. T., Conner, K. W., … Weston, D. M. (2020). Christian meditation for repetitive negative thinking: A multisite randomized trial examining the effects of a 4-week preventative program. *Spirituality in Clinical Practice*, *7*(1), 34–50. doi:10.1037/scp0000206

Knabb, J. J., Vazquez, V. E., Pate, R. A., Garzon, F. L., Wang, K. T., Edison-Riley, D., … Weber, S. E. (2022a). Christian meditation for trauma-based rumination: A two-part study examining the effects of an internet-based 4-week program. *Spirituality in Clinical Practice*, *9*(4), 253–271. doi:10.1037/scp0000255

Knabb, J. J., Vazquez, V. E., Pate, R. A., Lowell, J. R., Wang, K. T., De Leeuw, T. G., … Park, J. C. (2022b). Lectio divina for trauma symptoms: A two-part study. *Spirituality in Clinical Practice*, *9*(4), 232–252. doi:10.1037/scp0000303

Kornfield, J. (1993). *A path with heart*. Bantam Books.

Kornfield, J. (2003). *After the ecstasy, the laundry*. Bantam Books.

Kristeller, J. (2004). Meditation: Multiple effects, a unitary process? In M. Blows (Ed.), *The relevance of the wisdom traditions in contemporary society: The challenge to psychology*. Eburon Publishing.

Kristeller, J., & Johnson, T. (2005). Cultivating loving kindness: A two-stage model of the effects of meditation on empathy, compassion, and altruism. *Zygon*, *40*, 391–407.

Kristeller, J., & Jordan, K. (2017). Spirituality and meditative practice: Research opportunities and challenges. *Psychological Studies*, *63*(2), 130–139. doi:10.1007/s12646-017-0391-0

Kristeller, J., & Jordan, K. (2018). Mindful eating: Connecting with the wise self, the spiritual self. *Frontiers in Psychology*, *9*, 1–11.

Kristeller, J., Wolever, R.Q., & Sheets, V. (2013). Mindfulness-Based Eating Awareness Treatment (MB-EAT) for binge eating disorder: A randomized clinical trial. *Mindfulness*, *4*, 282–297.

Kristeller, J.L. (2015). *The joy of half a cookie: Using mindfulness to lose weight and end the struggle with food*. Penguin Books.

Kristeller, J.L. (2020). Mindfulness meditation. In P. Lehrer, & R.L. Woolfolk. *Principles and practice of stress management*. 2nd, 3rd, & 4th Editions. Guilford Press.

Kristeller, J. L., & Epel, E. (2014). Mindful eating and mindless eating: The science and the practice. In A. Le, C. T. Ngnoumen, & E. J. Langer (Eds.), *The Wiley Blackwell handbook of mindfulness., Vols. I and II.* (pp. 913–933): Wiley-Blackwell.

Kristeller, J. L., & Wolever, R. Q. (2011). Mindfulness-based eating awareness training for treating binge eating disorder: The conceptual foundation. *Eating Disorders: The Journal of Treatment & Prevention, 19*(1), 49–61.

Kristeller, J.L., Wolever, R.Q., & Lieberstein, A. (in press). *Mindfulness-based eating awareness training (MB-EAT)*. Guilford Press.

Kumar, U., Guleria, A., & Khetrapal, C. (2015). Neuro-cognitive aspects of 'OM' sound/syllable perception: A functional neuroimaging study. *Cognition and Emotion, 29*(3), 432–441. doi:10.1080/02699931.2014.917609

Kunzmann, U., & Baltes, P. B. (2005). The psychology of wisdom: Theoretical and empirical challenges. In R. J. Sternberg & J. Jordan (Eds.), *A handbook of wisdom: Psychological perspectives*. (pp. 110–135). Cambridge University Press.

Kuyken, W., Warren, F. C., Taylor, R. S., Whalley, B., Crane, C., Bondolfi, G., … Dalgleish, T. (2016). Efficacy of mindfulness-based cognitive therapy in prevention of depressive relapse: An individual patient data meta-analysis from randomized trials. *JAMA Psychiatry, 73*(6), 565–574. doi:10.1001/jamapsychiatry.2016.0076

Kwee, M., & Ellis, A. (1998). The interface between rational emotive behavior therapy (REBT) and Zen., *Journal of Rational-Emotive & Cognitive Behavior Therapy, 16*, 5–43.

Dalai Lama, & Cutler, H. C. (1998). *The Art of Happiness*. Riverhead Books.

Lazar, S. W., Kerr, C. E., Wasserman, R. H., Gray, J. R., Greve, D. N., Treadway, M. T., et al. (2005). Meditation experience is associated with increased cortical thickness. *Neuroreport: For Rapid Communication of Neuroscience Research, 16*(17), 1893–1897.

Leach, M. J., & Lorenzon, H. (2023). Transcendental meditation for women affected by domestic violence: A pilot randomized, controlled trial. *Journal of Family Violence*. doi:10.1007/s10896-023-00561-3

Lee, K. C., & Tang, J. L. K. (2023). Note, know, choose: A psychospiritual treatment model based on early Buddhist teachings. *Spirituality in Clinical Practice, 10*(2), 150–167.

Lehrer, P., Sasaki, Y., & Saito, Y. (1999). Zazen and cardiac variability. *Psychosomatic Medicine, 61*(6), 812–821. doi:10.1097/00006842-199911000-00014

Lehrer, P. M. (1983). Progressive relaxation and meditation: A study of psychophysiological and therapeutic differences between two techniques., *Behaviour Research & Therapy, 21*, 651–662.

Levine, M. (2000). *The positive psychology of Buddhism and Yoga: Paths to a mature happiness: With a special application to handling* anger.: Lawrence Erlbaum Associates, Publishers.

Linden, W. (2021). The autogenic training method of J. H. Schultz. In P. M. Lehrer & R. L. Woolfolk (Eds.), *Principles and practice of stress management* (4th ed., pp. 527–552). Guilford Press.

Linehan, M. M. (1993). *Cognitive-behavioral treatment of borderline personality disorder*. New York: Guilford Press.

Linehan, M. M., & Wilks, C. R. (2015). The course and evolution of dialectical behavior therapy. *American Journal of Psychotherapy, 69*(2), 97–110.

Lipner, J. (2010). *Hindus: Their religious beliefs and practices*. Routledge.

Lutz, A., Greischar, L. L., Rawlings, N. B., Ricard, M., & Davidson, R. J. (2004). Long-term meditators self-induce high-amplitude gamma synchrony during mental practice. *Proceedings of The National Academy of Sciences, 101*(46), 16369–16373.

Lutz, A., Slagter, H. A., Dunne, J. D., & Davidson, R. J. (2008). Attention regulation and monitoring in meditation. *Trends In Cognitive Sciences, 12*(4), 163–169.

Lutz, A., Slagter, H. A., Rawlings, N. B., Francis, A. D., Greischar, L. L., & Davidson, R. J. (2009). Mental training enhances attentional stability: Neural and behavioral evidence. *The Journal of Neuroscience, 29*(42), 13418–13427.

Mahone, M. C., Travis, F., Gevirtz, R., & Hubbard, D. (2018). fMRI during Transcendental Meditation practice. *Brain and Cognition, 123*, 30–33.

Mahoney, M. J. (2003). *Constructive psychotherapy: A practical guide*. New York: Guilford Press.
Margolin, A., Schuman-Olivier, Z., Beitel, M., Arnold, R. M., Fulwiler, C. E., & Avants, S. K. (2007). A preliminary study of spiritual self-schema (3-S+) therapy for reducing impulsivity in HIV-positive drug users. *Journal of Clinical Psychology*, *63*(10), 979–999.
Marlatt, G. A. (2002). Buddhist philosophy and the treatment of addictive behavior., *Cognitive & Behavioral Practice*, *9*, 44–49.
Marlatt, G. A., & Kristeller, J. L. (1999). Mindfulness and meditation. In W. R. Miller (Ed.), *Integrating spirituality into treatment: Resources for practitioners*. American Psychological Association. (pp. 67–84).
Martin, J. E., & Carlson, C. R. (1988). Spiritual dimensions of health psychology. In W. R. Miller & J. E. Martin (Eds.), *Behavior therapy and religion: Integrating spiritual and behavioral approaches to change*. (pp. 57–110): Sage Publications, Inc.
Martin, P. (1999). *The Zen path through depression*. New York: Harper.
Maslow, A. H. (1970). *Religions, values, and peak experiences*. The Viking Press, Inc.
Mason, A., Epel, E., Kristeller, J., … Daubenmier, J. (2016). Effects of a mindfulness-based intervention on mindful eating, sweets consumption, and fasting glucose levels in obese adults: Data from the SHINE randomized controlled trial. *Journal of Behavioral Medicine*, *39*(2), 201–213.
Masuda, A., & O'Donohue, W. T. (Eds.). (2017). *Handbook of Zen, mindfulness, and behavioral health*. Springer International Publishing.
Merton, T. (1948/1962/2007). *New seeds of contemplation*. New Directions Publishing.
Merton, T. (1968). *Zen and the birds of appetite*. New Directions Publishing.
Miller, W. R. (1999). *Integrating spirituality into treatment: Resources for practitioners*. American Psychological Association.
Miura, I. & Sasaki, S. F. (1965). *The Zen koan*. Harcourt Press.
Molino, A. (1998). *The couch and the tree: Dialogues in psychoanalysis and* Buddhism.: North Point Press.
Monaghan, P. & Viereck, E. G. (2011). *Meditation: The complete guide. Techniques from East and West to calm the mind, heal the body, and enrich the spirit*. Revised edition. New World Library.
Morvay, Z. (1999). Horney, Zen, and the real self: Theoretical and historical connections., *American Journal of Psychoanalysis*, *59*, 25–35.
Mrazek, M. D., Smallwood, J., & Schooler, J. W. (2012). Mindfulness and mind-wandering: Finding convergence through opposing constructs. *Emotion*, *12*(3), 442–448. doi:10.1037/a0026678
Murphy, M., Donovan, S., & Taylor, E. (1999). *The physical and physiological effects of meditation*. Institute of Noetic Science.
Myers, I. (1962). *The Myers-Briggs Type Indicator*. Consulting Psychologists Press.
Naht Hanh, T. (1975). *The Miracle of Mindfulness*. Beacon Press.
Naht Hanh, T. (1995). *Living Buddha, Living Christ*. Riverhead Books.
Naht Hanh, T. (2002). *Anger: Wisdom for cooling the flames*. Riverhead Trade.
Naht Hanh, T. (2009). *Happiness: Essential mindfulness practices*. Parallax Press.
Naht Hanh, T. (2017). *The Art of Living: Peace and Freedom in the Here and Now*. HarperOne.
Naht Hanh, T., & Cheung, L. (2010). *Savor: Mindful eating, mindful life*. San Francisco, CA: HarperOne/HarperCollins.
Naragon-Gainey, K., McMahon, T. P., & Chacko, T. (2017). The structure of common emotion regulation strategies: A meta-analytic examination. *Psychological Bulletin*, *143*, 384–427.
Neff, K., & Germer, C. (2018). *The mindful self-compassion workbook: A proven way to accept yourself, build inner strength, and thrive*. Guilford Press.
Newberg, A., & Waldman, M. R. (2009). *How God changes your brain: Breakthrough findings from a leading neuroscientist*. New York, NY: Ballantine Books.
Nidich, S., Mills, P. J., Rainforth, M., Heppner, P., Schneider, R. H., Rosenthal, N. E., … Rutledge, T. (2018). Non-trauma-focused meditation versus exposure therapy in veterans with post-traumatic stress disorder: A randomized controlled trial. *The Lancet Psychiatry*, *5*, 975–986. doi:10.1016/S2215-0366(18)30384-5

Oman, D. (2025). What is a mantra? Guidance for practitioners, researchers, and editors. *American Psychologist*, *80*(7), 1032–1044. doi:10.1037/amp0001368

Oman, D., & Bormann, J. E. (2018). Eknath Easwaran's mantram and passage meditation as applied Indian psychology: Psycho-spiritual and health effects. *Psychological Studies*, *63*(2), 94–108. doi:10.1007/s12646-018-0448-8

Oman, D., Bormann, J. E., & Kane, J. J. (2022). Mantram repetition as a portable mindfulness practice: Applications during the COVID-19 pandemic. *Mindfulness*, *13*(6), 1418–1429. doi:10.1007/s12671-020-01545-w

Orme-Johnson, D. W. (2000). An overview of Charles Alexander's contribution to psychology: Developing higher states of consciousness in the individual and the society. *Journal of Adult Development*, *7*, 199–215.

Ospina, M. B., Bond, K., Karkhaneh, M., Buscemi, N., Dryden, D. M., Barnes, V., ... Shannahoff-Khalsa, D. (2008). Clinical trials of meditation practices in health care: Characteristics and quality. *The Journal of Alternative and Complementary Medicine*, *14*(10), 1199–1213. doi:10.1089/acm.2008.0307

Peterman, A. H., Fitchett, G., Brady, M. J., Hernandez, L., & Cella, D. (2002). Measuring spiritual well-being in people with cancer: The Functional Assessment of Chronic Illness Therapy-Spiritual Well-Being Scale (FACIT-Sp). *Annals of Behavioral Medicine*, *24*(1), 49–58.

Plante, T. G. (2020). St Ignatius as psychotherapist? How Jesuit spirituality and wisdom can enhance psychotherapy. *Spirituality in Clinical Practice*, *7*(1), 65–71.

Quinn, S. (1987). *A mind of her own: The life of Karen* Horney.: Summit Books.

Radin, R. M., Epel, E. S., Daubenmier, J., Moran, P., Schleicher, S., Kristeller, J., ... Mason, A. E. (2020). Do stress eating or compulsive eating influence metabolic health in a mindfulness-based weight loss intervention? *Health Psychology*, *39*(2), 147–158.

Ram Dass, B. (1976/2010). *Be Here Now*. Lama Foundation/Three Rivers Press.

Richardson, P. T. (1996). *Four spiritualities: Expressions of self, expressions of spirit: A psychology of contemporary spiritual choice*. Davies-Black Publishing.

Robertson, S. E. (2022). *The psychological and physiological markers of Christian meditation: A quasi-experimental study of centering prayer*. (83). Dissertation. ProQuest Information & Learning.

Rosch, E. (2002). How to catch James's mystic germ: Religious experience, Buddhist meditation and psychology. *Journal of Consciousness Studies*, *9*(9–10), 37–56.

Rose, S., Zell, E., & Strickhouser, J. E. (2020). The effect of meditation on health: A metasynthesis of randomized controlled trials. *Mindfulness*, *11*(2), 507–516.

Rosenberg, E. L., Zanesco, A. P., King, B. G., Aichele, S. R., Jacobs, T. L., ... & Saron, C. D. (2015). Intensive meditation training influences emotional responses to suffering. *Emotion*, *15*, 775–790.

Rosenthal, N. (2012). *Transcendence: Healing and transformation through Transcendental Meditation*. New York: Tarcher.

Rosmarin, D. H. (2018). *Spirituality, religion, and cognitive-behavioral therapy: A guide for clinicians*. The Guilford Press.

Rubik, B. (2011). Neurofeedback-enhanced gamma brainwaves from the prefrontal cortical region of meditators and non-meditators and associated subjective experiences. *Journal of Alternative and Complementary Medicine*, *17*(2), 109–115.

Rubin, J. B. (1985). Meditation and psychoanalytic listening, *Psychoanalytic Review*, *72*, 599–613.

Rubin, J. B. (1996). *Psychotherapy and Buddhism: Toward an integration*. Plenum Press.

Rubin, J. B. (1999). Close encounters of a new kind: Toward an integration of psychoanalysis and Buddhism. *American Journal of Psychoanalysis*, *59*(1), 5–24.

Sallis, J. F. (1982). Meditation and self-actualization: A theoretical comparison. *Psychologia: An International Journal of Psychology in the Orient*. *25*, 59–64.

Salzberg, S. (2002). *Loving kindness: The revolutionary art of happiness* (2nd ed.). Shambala.

Saron, C. (2013). Training the mind—the Shamatha Project. In A. Fraser, Ed., *The Healing power of meditation*. Shambala Publications, 45–65.

Schimmel, A. (1975). *Mystical Dimensions of Islam*. University of North Carolina Press.

Schmidt, A., & Miller, J.J. (2004). Healing trauma with meditation. *Tricycle. Fall issue*, *14*(1), 40–43. https://users.neo.registeredsite.com/3/2/7/12399723/assets/HealingTrauma-Tricycle-Fall_2004.pdf

Schneider, J. K., Reangsing, C., & Willis, D. G. (2022). Effects of transcendental meditation on blood pressure: A meta-analysis. *Journal of Cardiovascular Nursing*, *37*(3), E11–E21.

Sedlmeier, P. (2022). *The psychology of meditation: Varieties, effects, theories, and perspectives*. Göttingen: Hogrefe.

Segal, Z. V., Williams, J. M. G., & Teasdale, J. D. (2002/2013). *Mindfulness-based cognitive therapy for depression*. (2nd ed.). New York: Guilford Press.

Semple, R. J., & Hatt, S. P. (2012/2024). Translation of Eastern meditative disciplines into Western psychotherapy. In L. J. Miller (Ed.), *The Oxford handbook of psychology and spirituality*, 1st/2nd ed. (pp. 484–516). New York, NY: Oxford University Press.

Shafii, M. (1988). *Freedom from the self: Sufism, meditation and psychotherapy*.: Human Sciences Press, Inc.

Shapiro, D. H., & Walsh, R. N. (Eds.). (1984). *Meditation: Classic and contemporary perspectives*. New York: Aldine Publishing Company.

Shapiro, S. L., Carlson, L. E., & Sawyer, B. A. (2024). Mindfulness and positive psychology. In *The art & science of mindfulness: Integrating mindfulness into the helping professions*., *3rd* ed. (pp. 109–121). Washington, DC: American Psychological Association.

Shapiro, S. L., & Sahgal, M. (2012). Loving-kindness. In T. G. Plante (Ed.), *Religion, spirituality, and positive psychology: Understanding the psychological fruits of faith*. (pp. 109–126). Santa Barbara, CA: Praeger/ABC-CLIO.

Shonin, E., & Van Gordon, W. (2016). Experiencing the universal breath: A guided meditation. *Mindfulness*, *7*(5), 1243–1245.

Shonin, E., Van Gordon, W., & Griffiths, M. D. (2013). Mindfulness-based interventions: Towards mindful clinical integration. *Frontiers in Psychology*, *4*, 1–4.

Singh, N., Lancioni, G., Nabors, L., Myers, R., Felver, J., & Manikam, R. (2018). Samatha meditation training for students with attention deficit/hyperactivity disorder: Effects on active academic engagement and math performance. *Mindfulness*, *9*(6), 1867–1876. doi:10.1007/s12671-018-1014-0

Sternberg, R. J. (1990). *Wisdom: Its nature, origins, and development*. Cambridge University Press.

Sternberg, R. J., & Glück, J. (2019). *The Cambridge Handbook of Wisdom*. New York, NY: Cambridge University Press.

Tart, C. T. (Ed.) (1972). *Altered states of consciousness*. Doubleday.

Tart, C. T. (1992). *Transpersonal psychologies: Perspectives on the mind from seven great spiritual traditions*. HarperCollins.

Teasdale, J. D. (1993). Emotion and two kinds of meaning: Cognitive therapy and applied cognitive science. *Behaviour Research & Therapy*, *31*(4), 339–354.

Teasdale, J. D. (1999). Emotional processing, three modes of mind and the prevention of relapse in depression. *Behaviour Research & Therapy*, *37*, S53–S77.

Teasdale, J. D., Moore, R. G., Hayhurst, H., Pope, M., Williams, S., & Segal, Z. V. (2002). Metacognitive awareness and prevention of relapse in depression: Empirical evidence., *Journal of Consulting & Clinical Psychology*, *70*, 275–287.

Teasdale, J. D., Segal, Z. V., & Williams, J. M. G. (2003). Mindfulness training and problem formulation., *Clinical Psychology: Science & Practice*, *10*, 157–160.

Teasdale, J. D., Segal, Z. V., Williams, J. M. G., Ridgeway, V. A., Soulsby, J. M., & Lau, M. A. (2000). Prevention of relapse/recurrence in major depression by mindfulness-based cognitive therapy, *Journal of Consulting & Clinical Psychology*, 68, 615–623.

Teiser, S. F., & Stone, J. I. (2009). *Interpreting the Lotus Sutra: Readings of the Lotus Sūtra*. Columbia University Press.

Thanissaro, B. (2006). *Meditations 3: Dhamma Talks*. Valley Center, CA: Metta Forest Monastery.

Travis, F. (2006). From I to I: Concepts of self on an object-referral/self-referral continuum. In A. P. Prescott (Ed.), *The concept of self in psychology*. (pp. 21–43). Hauppauge, NY: Nova Science Publishers.

Trungpa, C. (1973/2002). *Cutting Through Spiritual Materialism.* Berkeley, CA: Shambala Publications.

Urbanowski, F. B., & Miller, J. J. (1996). Trauma, psychotherapy, and meditation., *Journal of Transpersonal Psychology* (Vol. 28, pp. 31–48): Journal of Transpersonal Psychology.

Van Gordon, W., Shonin, E., Dunn, T., Garcia-Campayo, J., & Griffiths, M. (2017). Meditation awareness training for the treatment of fibromyalgia syndrome: A randomized controlled trial. *British Journal of Health Psychology, 22*(1), 186–206. doi:10.1111/bjhp.12224

Vieten, C., Wahbeh, H., Cahn, B. R., MacLean, K., Estrada, M., Mills, P., ... Delorme, A. (2018). Future directions in meditation research: Recommendations for expanding the field of contemplative science. *PLoS ONE, 13*(11). doi:10.1371/journal.pone.0205740

Wachholtz, A. B., & Pargament, K. I. (2005). Is spirituality a critical ingredient of meditation? Comparing the effects of spiritual meditation, secular meditation, and relaxation on spiritual, psychological, cardiac, and pain outcomes. *Journal of Behavioral Medicine, 28*, 369–384.

Wachholtz, A. B., & Pargament, K. I. (2008). Migraines and meditation: Does spirituality matter? *Journal of Behavioral Medicine, 31*(4), 351–366.

Wallace, B. A. (2007). *Hidden dimensions: The unification of physics and consciousness.* Columbia University Press.

Walsh, R. (1999). Asian contemplative disciplines: Common practices, clinical applications, and research findings. *Journal of Transpersonal Psychology, 31*(2), 83–107.

Walsh, R., & Shapiro, S. (2006). The meeting of meditative disciplines and Western psychology. *American Psychologist, 61*(3), 1–13.

Watts, A. (1957). *The way of Zen.* New York: Pantheon Books.

Watts, A. W. (1963). *Psychotherapy East and West.* New American Library.

Webb, J. R., Toussaint, L., & Dula, C. S. (2014). Ritualistic, theistic, and existential spirituality: Initial psychometric qualities of the RiTE measure of spirituality. *Journal of Religion & Health, 53*(4), 972–985. doi: 10.1007/s10943-013-9697-y

Welwood, J. (2000). *Toward a psychology of awakening. Buddhism, psychotherapy, and the path of personal and spiritual transformation.* Shambala Press.

Yogi, M. M. (1963/1995). *The science of being and the art of living.* Penguin Books.

Yong, J., & Lee, H. (2021). Holy name meditation: A spiritual intervention to conserve the dignity of patients and nurses. In K. Benton & R. Pegoraro (Eds.), *Finding dignity at the end of life: A spiritual reflection on palliative care.* (pp. 112–119). Routledge/Taylor & Francis Group.

Yong, J., Park, J., Park, Y., Lee, H., Lee, G., & Rim, S. (2020). Effects of Holy Name Meditation on the quality of life of hospital middle manager nurses in Korea: A 6-month follow-up. *The Journal of Continuing Education in Nursing, 51*(5), 215–224. doi:10.3928/00220124-20200415-06

Chapter 23

Forgiveness

Everett L. Worthington Jr.[*] and Frederick A. DiBlasio

In this chapter, we seek to provide an update on forgiveness research as it intersects with research on spirituality and health. The literature on the intersection of these three topics is so extensive that a thorough review here is not possible. So, we have made some choices. We summarized associations of forgiveness, health, and well-being by referring to recent reviews and meta-analyses (i.e., Griffin et al., 2020; Toussaint et al., 2020b; Webb, 2021; Webb & Toussaint, 2020). We have provided a non-systematic, review of other aspects: (1) spirituality in relationship to forgiveness (Worthington & Sandage, 2016); (2) highlights of a vast literature on forgiveness and health (Toussaint et al., 2015; Toussaint et al., 2020b; Webb, 2021; Webb & Toussaint, 2020); (3) forgiveness using research of religious and spiritually oriented forgiveness; (4) a review of studies related to Enright's process model (e.g., Enright & Fitzgibbons, 2024; Freedman & Enright, 2020); and (5) brief reviews of literatures on self-forgiveness (Woodyatt et al., 2017; Woodyatt & Wenzel, 2020); divine forgiveness (Fincham & May, 2019, 2023); and intergroup forgiveness (Van Tongeren et al., 2014: Van Tongeren & Lindeman, 2020).

We rely largely on recent reviews when summarizing the research on forgiveness, spirituality, and health to enable most of our discussion herein to be focused on the evidence-based interventions designed to promote forgiveness, health, and well-being. Two interventions have dominated clinical research (Wade et al., 2014). Research on Enright's process model is summarized below (e.g., Freedman & Enright, 2020). Regarding the REACH Forgiveness model, recently, Ho et al. (2024) reported a worldwide randomized controlled trial (RCT) intervention experiment involving 4,598 participants in five non-USA countries. That RCT alone more than doubled the participant base of all previous forgiveness intervention studies (irrespective of which model was used) combined (i.e., through 2020, ~4,100 participants). Because of the imbalance that the new RCT brings to the field and because about one-third of the studies of REACH Forgiveness have targeted religious and spiritual populations, we have focused this chapter on the spiritually accommodated REACH Forgiveness model. Of note, the secular REACH Forgiveness model has been explicitly adapted for use with Christians (see Worthington, 2020, 2024, for more information on the secular version), and the non-adapted secular model has been used within samples of Christians. Thus, we emphasized the REACH Christian-accommodated model, which can provide some illumination regarding spirituality, health, and forgiveness.

* Corresponding Author: eworth@vcu.edu.

DOI: 10.4324/9781003440048-27

Spirituality in Relationship to Forgiveness

Forgiveness-and-Relational-Spirituality Model (Worthington & Sandage, 2016)

Worthington and Sandage (2016) explain how relationships within a spiritual model could predict whether a person forgives and, if so, under what conditions. The model considers the basic aspects of a transgression regarding its relationship to what a person holds to be sacred. Yet, it also understands not just that different sources of spirituality exist and that we are in relationship to each of them, but also that the sources of spirituality are in relationship to each other. That is, there are relationships between aspects of nature. Theological or spiritual constructs are related to each other, and religious or spiritual values, beliefs, and practices are related to each other. And, within nature, for example, constructs have a relationship to each other. So, in the forgiveness-and-relational-spirituality model, we suggested that four classes of agents exist: victim, offender, transgression, and the sacred.

Of course, what is considered to be sacred is what both Davis et al.'s (2015) sources of spirituality and Webb's (2021) RiTE models attempt to identify. It is important to consider how these models relate to each other. Furthermore, whether forgiveness does or does not take place depends on the relationships of victim-offender, victim-transgression, offender-transgression, victim-sacred, similarity or difference of offender-sacred to victim-sacred, and the degree to which the victim feels that a transgression-sacred relationship is a desecration.

Webb's RiTE Multidimensional Model

Because much of this edited book is organized around Webb's RiTE model (Webb et al., 2014; Webb, 2021; see also Chapters 1 and 44, this volume), we will not spend much time summarizing it. *Ritualistic spirituality* involves a structured connection with deity, governed in most cases by theologies – systematic theology (i.e., how the whole theological system fits together), scriptural theology (how the sacred writings reveal truths about the deity), and practical theology (how the theology is handled in daily living). *Theistic spirituality* is defined as a non-structured connection with deity, which can involve a personal relationship with the divinity that is not bound by a formal theological system. *Existential spirituality* is a transcendent yet non-theistic search for meaning and purpose in life. It does not presume a God(s) but is focused on spirituality-based implications for living.

The three types of spirituality are not exclusive of each other. All have belief- and practice-related components that are tied to the beliefs. Each believes in a transcendent aspect separate from the self. For ritual and theistic spiritualities, that is, belief in a deity. For existential spirituality, the transcendent is sacralized knowledge, humanity, nature, or the universe. It is possible to combine all three types of spirituality, or any amounts and combinations of the three. Thus, for example, a Christian with Calvinistic theology (i.e., ritualistic spirituality) could believe in God, Jesus, the Holy Spirit, and the church in ways that were not laid out in Calvinistic theology (i.e., theistic spirituality) and could be pursuing a sense of purpose based on personal experiences rather than religious experiences. In Webb's scheme, spiritual health is presumed to be at the balance point in the center of the three. This assumption has not been empirically tested.

Davis et al.'s (2015) Sources of Spirituality Model

Davis et al. proposed that there are five "sources" of spirituality – religious, nature, humanistic, transcendent, and self-spiritualities. As Webb et al. (2014) did with their RiTE model of spirituality, Davis et al. also created a scale to assess each type of spirituality in their model and provided psychometric evidence of the scale's adequacy. *Religious spirituality* looks to deity and sacred objects (i.e., church, papal edicts, church polity, and sacred rituals, including sacraments). *Nature spirituality* looks to the created order (space-time, natural environment, awe-inspiring nature of the creation, etc.). *Humanistic spirituality* looks to the common wonder of human relations and societal norms that have been created, evolved, or otherwise developed. *Transcendent spirituality* looks to the things beyond the created order, like the presence of a wider spiritual world or unseen beings, or a feeling of something beyond nature or humanism. *Self-spirituality* views the person as a meaning-making, purpose-seeking agent.

How the Sources of Spirituality Map onto the RiTE Model

Religious spirituality can be variously related to the RiTE's ritual and theistic spirituality. The person's view of religion could emphasize ritual within an organized theological system, a mere theistic connection without the emphasis on the theology, or even existential aspects of principle, purpose, and meaning. It is likely that all are involved to some extent. Davis et al.'s nature spirituality is most strongly related to the RiTE's existential spirituality. However, religious spirituality can also venerate nature (i.e., Didn't God create a wonderful creation? Isn't Yosemite National Park awe-inspiring? Aren't human bodies fearfully and wonderfully made?). Davis et al.'s humanistic spirituality is most thoroughly related to the RiTE's existential spirituality. Clearly, a distinct aspect of humans is their existential nature as purposeful, meaning-making, and meaning-seeking unique persons. But again, religious spirituality could venerate the humanity of humans (i.e., people are created in God's image and thus are endowed with characteristics beyond the mere animal). Davis et al.'s transcendent spirituality is generally related to all three types of spirituality in the RiTE model. Yet, it emphasizes the way religious rituals and belief systems point to wonderful things beyond existence. A theistic connection with God or another deity is also more than a psychological connection with a perceived deity. It is a transcendent relationship. Thus, transcendent spirituality is, in most cases, a theology-lite mixture of ritual, theistic, and existential spiritualities. Davis et al.'s self-spirituality is essentially a one-to-one mapping onto the RiTE's existential spirituality. However, self-spirituality could conceive of finding purpose and meaning in religion, nature, humanity, or the transcendent.

In summary, Davis et al.'s sources of spirituality model and the RiTE model seek to get at the same idea – what people hold to be sacred and what its relationships will be to aspects of existence. The aspect of existence that we are most concerned with in this chapter is how people handle interpersonal transgressions. Both models seem to flesh out concepts of the forgiveness-and-relational spirituality model (Worthington & Sandage, 2016).

Religions and Spiritualities and Forgiveness

The following is a brief description of four distinct types of forgiveness.

Divine forgiveness is the perception that one is forgiven by what one holds to be sacred (to the extent the sacred is a moral agent capable of forgiveness). Divine forgiveness (Fincham & May, 2019, 2020, 2023) cannot speak to whether God (or some other deity) actually forgives (or even exists). It can only theorize about how people perceive divine forgiveness of their sins or transgressions against God or humans or nature. Thus, divine forgiveness is typically limited to ritual or theistic spiritualities (in the RiTE model; *religious spirituality* in Davis et al.'s *sources of spirituality*). Fincham and May provided studies outlining the correlations between perceptions of divine forgiveness and mental health and physical health correlates. No interventions to promote a sense of divine forgiveness have yet been developed.

Self-forgiveness is a response to self-condemnation that seeks to restore one's sense of a valued moral self and one's emotional and psychological equanimity. The pursuit of self-forgiveness involves wronging someone or disappointing oneself. There are three preconditions to moving toward self-forgiveness properly. One tries to (a) responsibly make things right with the sacred; (b) make amends for social harms done; and (c) deal with psychological harms to oneself as a result of the wrongdoing or self-disappointment. After those steps have been at least approached, one can pursue emotional self-forgiveness and decisional self-forgiveness (see Griffin et al., 2015, for self-forgiveness intervention steps and the REACH model section below). However, in the intervention, it is usually preferred to help people first experience emotional self-forgiveness and then decide to forgive the self (for more information, see Cornish & Wade, 2015; Cornish et al., 2020; Griffin et al.,2015; Woodyatt & Wenzel, 2020).

Person-to-person forgiveness is forgiving someone who has harmed us. The most-used theory of person-to-person forgiveness is the stress-and-coping theory (Strelan, 2020). A stressor (i.e., an interpersonal transgression) is appraised as a threat to well-being. Also, the amount of injustice experienced is subjectively appraised. The person attempts to cope with stress reactions by seeking to modify stressors, appraisals, stress reactions, or any combination of those. The literature summarizing the basic research on person-to-person forgiveness is huge (for a review of 40 meta-analyses, see Griffin et al., 2020).

There are numerous interventions to promote forgiveness, though two dominate (Wade et al., 2014). The REACH Forgiveness model is mostly investigated as a general psychoeducational model for adults (Worthington, 2024). It has also been most investigated as an explicitly Christian accommodated model and as a secular model with explicitly Christian samples. It has been investigated in psychoeducational groups and in DIY workbook groups. Enright's forgiveness process model has been most investigated as a targeted forgiveness intervention using weekly therapeutic sessions for specific problems (Freedman & Enright, 2020). Enright's forgiveness process model has also been used in studies of children and adolescents, and his story-based model has also been studied for children and adolescents (for a meta-analysis, see Rapp et al., 2022).

Intergroup forgiveness describes how individuals forgive individuals or groups of people of an outgroup with which they might not have had any direct contact. People might be low on intergroup forgiveness for a variety of reasons, such as having had bad experiences with an outgroup, believing members of the outgroup are prejudiced, or being in an ingroup and having prejudice toward other groups. Van Tongeren et al. (2014) and Van Tongeren and Lindemann (2020) found that this process of forgiving is similar to other types of forgiveness. However, group identity factors predict the level of intergroup forgiveness. They identified six factors facilitating forgiveness: empathy, collective guilt, trust, making amends, common superordinate group identification, and contact were positively associated with intergroup forgiveness. Stirred-up negative emotions, perceived victimhood, and strong ingroup identification were negatively associated.

Theory and Research in Support of a Salubrious Relationship Between Forgiveness, Spirituality, Health, and Well-being

The World Health Organization (WHO, 2025) defines health as "a state of complete physical, mental and social well-being and not merely the absence of disease or infirmity" (p. 1). Forgiveness has been shown often to be related to the reduction of physical and mental health symptoms and promotion of well-being, social well-being, and spiritual well-being.

Basic Health- and Well-Being-Related Research

Unforgiveness has been shown to have deleterious physical, mental, and social health effects (see Toussaint et al., 2020b). Forgiveness alleviates those effects and is hypothesized to have positive effects that broaden options and build resources (i.e., Fredrickson, 2001).

One mechanism responsible for negative effects on physical health is chronic activation of the sympathetic nervous system (SNS), which not only produces direct effects on the cardiovascular, immune, gastrointestinal, and sexual-reproductive systems but also has other effects through chronically elevated cortisol and adrenaline (Toussaint et al., 2020b). The parasympathetic nervous system's (PSNS's) vagal tone, which is responsible for calming and inhibiting the SNS, is also dysregulated, which results in flattened heart-rate variability (for a review, see Witvliet, 2020).

Webb and Toussaint (2020) reviewed the research on forgiveness and its effects on mental health symptoms (e.g., depression, anxiety, stress, addiction, and suicide) and well-being. They observed that over 50% of all research studies on the topic since 1947 were published in the six years preceding their review. And that trend has continued with new research attention to resilience, well-being, and flourishing. In the specific context of addictive behavior and suicidal behavior, over 90% of the literature has documented positive associations between forgiveness and psychological outcomes (Webb, 2021).

Social outcomes after forgiving have been reviewed recently. Green et al. (2020) reviewed research on forgiveness and relational repair in non-romantic relationships. They used interdependence theory to understand offering amends, receiving amends, commitment, dependence, asymmetrical power, and relationship alternatives and investments. In romantic relationships, Fincham (2020) reports a causal relation between (a) forgiveness and marital quality and more effective discussions of partners; (b) self-forgiveness and person-to-person forgiveness are intertwined; and (c) forgiveness and religion/spirituality played a larger role than had previously been shown.

Choe et al. (2020) reviewed research on forgiveness in the context of religion and spirituality. Springing from a meta-analysis (Davis et al., 2013), they emphasized methodology more than new findings. Sophisticated designs (i.e., longitudinal, experimental, and interventional) were more often used than in the past. They also observed lingering weaknesses within the field, such as the overreliance on cross-sectional study designs and the lack of programmatic work. Washington-Nortey et al. (2022) reviewed studies on forgiveness and spirituality and focused more on findings, especially hope (26 studies related to hope, forgiveness, and spirituality). When relationships are beset by transgressions, forgiveness is related to hope that the relationship is repairable (see Worthington & Ripley, 2024).

Effects of Forgiveness Interventions on Promoting Forgiveness

Wade et al. (2014) meta-analyzed 54 intervention RCTs on forgiveness interventions. They found four major findings. First, Enright's process model and the REACH Forgiveness model each were represented in one-third of the studies. All other approaches constituted the remaining one-third. Second, they found a strong dose-response relationship between the amount of time spent trying to forgive and the amount of forgiveness. Time was vitally important, more so than the content of the approaches, which were more similar than different. Third, they found that Enright's approach did not differ in effectiveness (once time and severity were controlled) from REACH Forgiveness or all other approaches combined. Fourth, as people forgave, they also experienced a comparable increase in hope and reduction in depression and anxiety.

Wade et al. (2014) meta-analyzed all types of interventions without differentiating their type or target. Recent research shows that this might not be tenable. Rapp et al. (2022) meta-analyzed two interventions for schools by Enright – an intervention based on his process model ($k = 9$; $d = 0.66$) and one based on stories ($k = 9$; $d = 0.27$). They found a substantial difference in the effectiveness of the two approaches. They also analyzed two studies in which investigators used the REACH Forgiveness model ($k = 2$; $d = 0.29$): one effective, the other not as much. As more research accumulates, Wade et al.'s lack of differentiation among school-based treatments for adolescents and children, forgiveness therapy, forgiveness psychoeducational groups, forgiveness self-administered workbooks, and use in couple therapy will likely need refinement.

Method of Our Search

Because Enright's research dealt with mental health, well-being, and physical health, we compiled a list of studies using Wade et al. (2014) and a recent review by Freedman and Enright (2020) in Worthington and Wade (2020). We supplemented that list with other recent reviews and meta-analyses (Rapp et al., 2022), examining the studies for relevance to physical and mental health. The purpose of reviewing Enright's treatments was not to make an exhaustive review, but a targeted review, because some of his studies related directly to health.

On the other hand, we undertook an exhaustive review of REACH Forgiveness studies. We compiled a list of publications involving an experimental or quasi-experimental study of REACH Forgiveness from existing narrative reviews and meta-analyses (Wade et al., 2014; Worthington, 2020, 2024). A total of 30 articles were located. We located 25 studies of REACH Forgiveness psychoeducational groups (19 used the full REACH method; 6 were considered Proto-REACH group studies). We located 5 studies of the REACH Forgiveness DIY workbook (three published 7-hour workbooks, one Christian-accommodated 3-hour workbook, and one Christian-accommodated 7-hour workbook). We then searched PsycINFO and PubMed databases (using REACH, Forgiv*, spiritual*, religio*, health*, depress*, anxi*, well-being*, and flourish*). This resulted in one additional study (Allemand & Flückiger, 2020) involving a Christian Greek Orthodox-accommodated REACH Forgiveness group treatment. However, vital data were missing, which prohibited computing the effect size. Two additional unpublished studies not yet listed in a database, both involving a 3-plus hour DIY REACH Forgiveness workbook, were available by contacting the authors (Ortega Bechara et al., 2024; Ho et al., 2024). Thus, the comprehensive review involved a total of $k = 33$ studies. However, we reported those who used spiritual samples most directly.

Enright's Research on Forgiveness and Physical, Mental, and Social Health

Freedman and Enright (2020) comprehensively reviewed Enright's forgiveness therapy. We have abstracted studies relating to physical, mental, and social health, but refer the reader to the Freedman and Enright review for references. A good portion of research on Enright's model has targeted forgiveness interventions to specific populations and specific problems. Typically, those are first-of-a-kind forgiveness treatment studies on serious mental or physical health conditions. For example, Freedman and Enright (2020) treated 12 female incest survivors and found that after approximately 14.3 months of individual therapy, participants reported increased forgiveness, well-being, and hope and a decrease in depression and anxiety.

Coyle and Enright (1997) reported a study of 10 men receiving a 12-week therapy for expressing hurt from their partner's abortion. Participants experienced increased forgiveness and decreased anxiety, anger, and grief. Lin et al. (2004) treated 7 men and 7 women in a drug rehabilitation facility for 12 hours, randomly assigning them to process (i.e., forgiveness) therapy or a 12-step program alternative treatment control. Those seven receiving the forgiveness therapy forgave more, and they decreased state and trait anger, depression, state and trait anxiety, and vulnerability to drug use when compared to the control group. Reed and Enright (2006) treated 20 women who had experienced spousal emotional abuse for an average of 8 months of individual therapy. The 10 participants who received the process forgiveness treatment had more forgiveness, self-esteem, environmental mastery, and meaning in life and less depression, trait anxiety, and post-traumatic stress symptoms than did the 10 participants in alternative treatment matched controls. People in all four experiments maintained gains in follow-up investigations, demonstrating that the Enright Process model is effective at producing mental health changes.

Enright has also targeted forgiveness with people who have physical disorders. Some examples include the following. Waltman et al. (2009) provided forgiveness therapy to 17 patients who had had myocardial perfusion. Both experimental and control participants were treated in individual therapy for 10 weekly one-hour sessions. Patients who received forgiveness therapy had more forgiveness and fewer anger-recall-induced myocardial perfusion defects. Hansen et al. (2009) used four weeks of individual forgiveness therapy with 20 people terminally ill with cancer in a waiting-list design with 20 others in the wait-list condition. Patients forgave more and reported a higher quality of life, hope, and reduced anger. After the wait-list patients received forgiveness therapy, they too improved on all measures. Lee and Enright (2014) provided 24 weekly one-hour sessions of treatment (over 6 months) to 16 women diagnosed with fibromyalgia who were randomly assigned to either forgiveness therapy or a healthy-lifestyles intervention. The forgiveness intervention participants improved more in forgiveness and fibromyalgia health and reduced state anger (gains maintained at 12-week follow-up) compared to those in the fibromyalgia intervention. Enright found that these intensive forgiveness interventions promoted improvements in physical health conditions.

REACH Forgiveness Psychoeducational Treatments and Forgiveness

REACH Forgiveness is a general psychoeducational protocol that is available as a psychoeducational group or as a do-it-yourself (DIY) workbook. Both modes of delivery use the same content and most of the same activities that individuals can work through to forgive hurts that are at present unforgiven and apply the method broadly to affect dispositional forgivingness.

The core of the REACH Forgiveness method is reaching emotional forgiveness by completing exercises to facilitate emotional forgiveness. The exercises are grouped into five sets with memory prompted by the acronym REACH: R = Recall the hurt. E = Empathy (or other emotions like sympathy, compassion, or even love) to emotionally replace negative, unforgiving resentment and bitterness with more positive emotions. A = giving an Altruistic gift of forgiveness to an offender who does not deserve forgiveness. C = Commit to the forgiveness experienced so that H = you Hold onto the forgiveness when doubts arise. The emotional forgiveness helps people be able to make a decision to forgive, which is a behavioral intention statement to treat the offender as a valued and valuable person henceforth.

The core for reaching emotional forgiveness and decisional forgiveness is the part of a protocol that begins with a self-assessment of the unforgiveness (which, at the end, will be repeated to illustrate to the participant that forgiveness has indeed happened). Then, two types of person-to-person forgiveness are defined – emotional forgiveness and decisional forgiveness. Participants are told of physical health, mental health and well-being, relational health, and spiritual health benefits that have been scientifically shown to accrue when forgiveness occurs. Emotional forgiveness is most powerful in promoting mental health and well-being, and physical health benefits. Decisional forgiveness, which is a behavioral intention to treat the offender better, can aid relationships immediately because the offender sees the changed behavior of the forgiver. Decisional forgiveness is also generally more involved in spiritual well-being. Most religious and spiritual groups advocate decisions to forgive, so decisional forgiveness provides more spiritual congruence. After participants work through the core of the method, people try to generalize its use to other unforgiven hurts or offenses. Finally, the initial self-assessment is repeated to show the participants that they have indeed forgiven their offender. See Chapter 43 of this volume for a more detailed description of the REACH Forgiveness method.

A recent review of all research on groups using REACH Forgiveness was conducted (Worthington, 2024). In each study, an effect size per hour of treatment was calculated. This is the best measure of effectiveness, which was shown by Wade et al.'s (2014) meta-analysis of all interventions on forgiveness. Wade et al. found that there was a linear relationship between time spent trying to forgive and forgiveness effect size (pooling all of a study's state forgiveness scores). In addition, they found that hope changed with a comparable effect size per hour to forgiveness, and depressive and anxious symptoms decreased about half the effect size per hour.

Proto-REACH studies ($k = 6$) investigated parts of the REACH Forgiveness method – usually the definition of forgiveness, benefits, and the R, E, and A steps – prior to its finalization (adding the C and H steps and the portion on generalization) in 1998. In Table 23.1, we summarized the number of studies, mean *N* per study, and effect size per hour for group and DIY workbook studies. From those comparisons, the most important takeaway is that DIY workbooks seem almost twice as effective (range of effect size per hour from 0.16 to 0.17) at promoting forgiveness as are groups (range of effect size per hour from 0.083 to 0.105). Christian group samples were comparable to secular group samples, and Christian workbook samples were comparable to secular workbook samples in effectiveness.

Table 23.1 A Brief Summary of Number of Participants and Effect Size per Hour in Articles on REACH Forgiveness in Groups and DIY Workbooks (person-to-person)

Mean Effect Size per Hour of...	*Number of Studies (k)*	*Mean N per Study*	*Effect size per Hour*
Proto-REACH Group Studies (Pre-2001)	6	82	0.105
All Group Studies (2001 and Later)	19	111	0.083
Groups with Christian Samples	8 of the 19	111	0.091
DIY 7-hour Secular Workbooks	3	67	0.17
DIY 3.34-hour Secular Workbooks	1 (Study of 6 sites in 5 countries	4,598	0.16
Christian DIY Workbooks	3 (1 of 7 hours; 2 of 3.34 hours secular applied to Christians)	210	0.16

In Table 23.2, we tabulated all studies using Christians. For studies involving group psychoeducation ($k = 8$), the effect size per hour ranged from 0.03 (Lampton et al., 2005) to 0.18 (Osei-Tutu et al., 2020) in the extremely Christian-oriented country, Ghana. For DIY workbooks with Christian samples ($k = 3$), the effect size per hour for forgiveness measures ranged from 0.13 (Ortega Bechara et al., 2024) to 0.20 (Greer et al., 2014). Rye and Pargament (2002) and Rye et al. (2005) compared a REACH Forgiveness-like psychoeducational group treatment that was accommodated to Christian belief and practice against a strictly matched REACH Forgiveness secular treatment. They found no differences in forgiveness in both conditions.

REACH Forgiveness Interventions in Light of RiTE Spirituality

Generally, secular REACH Forgiveness groups and DIY workbooks promote forgiveness as a strong search for the purpose and meaning of the offense against them. But more, it is ensconced in a general framework that is aimed at living a virtuous life, with forgiveness

Table 23.2 Summary of Pooled Forgiveness Measures in Research on REACH Forgiveness Groups and DIY Workbooks with Christian Samples (person-to-person)

Author(s) (Date)	*Sample*	*N*	*# Hours*	*Effect Size*	*Effect Size per Hour*
Christian Groups (k = 8)					
Jackson (1999)	Adults from a local church (proto-REACH)	27	12	1.27	0.11
Rye & Pargament (2002)	Christian women students; Christian REACH	58	12	1.53	0.13
Rye et al. (2005)	Divorced adult women in the community (Christian REACH)	149	6	0.28	0.05
Lampton et al. (2005)	Christian students; Christian REACH	65	6	0.15	0.03
Stratton et al. (2008)	Christian students; Christian REACH	114	5.5	0.42	0.07
Worthington et al. (2010)	REACH 5 Churches in the Philippines (secular groups)	33	6	0.92	0.15
Osei-Tutu et al. (2020)	Ghana, Christian adults from local churches	264	6	0.96[a]; 1.05[b]	0.16[a]; 0.18[b]
Toussaint, Griffin et al. (2020a)	Christian students; secular REACH	99	6	0.51	0.08
DIY Workbooks with Christians					
Greer et al. (2014; 7 hours; Christian accommodated REACH)	Christian college students from community churches; Christian REACH	52	7	1.37	0.20
Kurniati et al. ((2020); Brief, Secular DIY Workbook with Christians)	Community adult Indonesia Christians (from Ho et al., 2024; used as control for REACH-Collective)	203	3.34	0.87	0.14
Ortega Bechara et al. (2024; Brief, Secular DIY Workbook with Christians)	Christian Subsample of war survivors from Ho et al. (Colombia)	374	4	0.50	0.13

[a] Christian accommodated
[b] Christian accommodated plus Ghanaian cultural accommodation

being the focal point. However, in addition, spirituality is encouraged in recounting the spiritual benefits of forgiving and through an emphasis on doing morally right actions. Empathy (the second step in REACH) is emphasized. Empathy does not necessarily imply that one is acting spiritually. A con artist is excellent at empathy to be able to swindle people. However, in the context of having committed to attend a group or work through a DIY workbook to become a more forgiving person, we can assume that almost everyone will employ empathy for benevolent purposes. Altruistic giving is emphasized as a key third step in REACH. Gratitude is encouraged for having been forgiven by someone important to the participant. Generosity is also encouraged, as is a humble understanding of one's status as someone who has also done others wrong. Using Webb's RiTE model, the secular version of the REACH Forgiveness protocol is heavily tilted toward promoting existential spirituality.

However, it is important to note that forgiveness has historically, prior to the recent emphasis on the science of forgiveness, been associated with all major religions and thus with religious spirituality (in Davis et al.'s conceptual scheme). Thus, participants will bring to the treatment their own views on religion, spirituality, and the role that forgiveness plays in it. A secular treatment is not necessarily a non-religious or non-spiritual treatment. A secular population is not a non-religious or non-spiritual population. Thus, there are likely people of many religions (including religious "nones" and religious "dones") and various spiritualities within any sample that is "secular." Those people will bring with them their beliefs and practices. For example, Rye and Pargament (2002) discovered that women in a Christian sample who were randomly assigned to a secular REACH-like treatment did as well as those who were randomly assigned to an explicitly Christian-accommodated treatment. One participant in the secular treatment said that they still consulted their religious beliefs and practices about forgiveness, including praying for the offender, searching the Scriptures, and consulting clergy and other wise Christians. The secular REACH Forgiveness appeals to and activates people's existential spirituality. However, the secular REACH Forgiveness model might also appeal to ritualistic and theistic spirituality as well.

What about the Christian-accommodated version of REACH Forgiveness? One of the difficulties in interpreting findings in a meta-analysis of religiously or spiritually accommodated treatments for psychotherapy (i.e., Captari et al., 2018) is that the articles almost never specify how much spiritual accommodation was done. For the REACH studies, over 23 explicit modifications to the secular protocol were made in developing a Christian-accommodated intervention (see Lampton et al., 2005). Given the space allocation of this chapter, only three examples are summarized: (a) engage in a *lectio divina* exercise, listening to Scripture quotes and responding personally; (b) hear decisional forgiveness interpreted as being compatible with Scripture's use of forgiveness; and (c) reflect on Jesus' passion as agape love for the offender.

These modifications consist of about one-third of the secular group activities. We can conclude that the Christian REACH Forgiveness protocol is quite representative of RiTE's ritualistic spirituality. However, numerous times the accommodations appealed to people's experience with God (i.e., discerning God's heart regarding the offender, regarding a time when they needed God's forgiveness, and searching the full Scripture, including the Hebrew and New Testament, for what is said about forgiveness). Thus, although the emphasis is less than for ritualistic spirituality, there is some appeal to theistic spirituality. The remainder of the secular activities, which constitute at least two-thirds of the Christian-accommodated treatment, promote existential spirituality.

REACH Forgiveness Treatments and Outcomes Other Than Forgiveness

As previously mentioned, the World Health Organization (WHO, 2025) defines health as "a state of complete physical, mental and social well-being and not merely the absence of disease or infirmity" (p. 1). Thus, in addition to examining the effects of REACH Forgiveness treatments on forgiveness, we consider the effects, especially on other outcomes that pertain to mental health symptoms and psychological and social well-being.

Psychoeducational group or DIY workbook studies assessed person-to-person forgiveness and other outcomes with many measures. In Tables 23.3 and 23.4, we report non-forgiveness outcome measures for each study. We report effect size per hour (*d*/hr). As a benchmark, 26 hours of secular CBT for depression has an effect size of −1.24, which is *d*/hr = −0.05.

Mental Health and Well-Being

Forgiveness facilitated reductions in depression. Rye et al. (2005) compared secular and Christian REACH Forgiveness groups for depression (*d*/hr = −0.15, secular; *d*/hr = −0.08, Christian). Ortega Bechara et al. (2024) tested a secular workbook with Christians in Colombia (*d*/hr = −0.08). Rye and Pargament (2002) reported a significant pre- to post-treatment change in depression for both secular and Christian models, maintained at follow-up. The results were more modest for other symptoms. For anxiety, Rye and Pargament (2002) reported no change from pre- to post-treatment in either secular or religious models. For trait anger, Rye et al. (2005) reported *d*/hr as −0.01 for secular and −0.02 for Christian. Jackson (1999) reported small changes in shame (*d*/hr = −0.01). Well-being was more robustly affected. Rye and Pargament (2002) found gains for secular and Christian groups for religious well-being, existential well-being, and anticipation of the future (i.e., hope). Ortega Bechara et al. (2024) reported *d*/hr of 0.08 (flourishing), 0.10 (post-traumatic growth), and 0.09 (spiritual growth) for war survivors. Several studies assessed changes in trait forgivingness: Lampton et al. (2005; 0.01), Osei-Tutu et al. (2020; 0.15 for religious, 0.06 for cultural adaptation), Greer et al. (2014; 0.13), and Ortega Bechara et al. (2024; 0.12).

Physical Health and Well-Being

Ortega Bechara et al. (2024) found self-reported sleep quality improved (0.09), and Rye and Pargament (2002) found hostility improved, which has implications for cardiovascular health.

Social Health and Well-Being

Several studies measured indexes of social health and well-being. Lampton et al. (2005) found more positive responses to offenders (0.16), as did Stratton et al. (2008) in two conditions (0.12, 0.14). Osei-Tutu et al. (2020) assessed forbearance (restraint for the good of the relationship or for group harmony; 0.03, 0.01; for Christian and Christian plus culturally accommodated, respectively) and motivation to reconcile (0.09, 0.11).

Whereas several different person-to-person forgiveness interventions have reported mental health effects, Enright's four studies have been most likely to examine physical health effects. Social health and well-being have been assessed occasionally, but there is a deficit in such evidence. Another deficit in intervention studies is that moderators or mediators are understudied in connecting forgiveness interventions to psychological, physical, and social health and well-being outcomes.

Table 23.3 Christian-accommodated REACH Forgiveness (person-to-person) Treatments Non-Forgiveness Measures – Part 1

Author (Date)	*Measures*	*Pre*	*Post*	*Follow*	*d (or if reported Cohen's d)*	*d per hour*
Jackson (1999)						
	Internalized shame	42.00 (17.02)	39.71 (11.51)		−0.16	−0.01
	Perspective taking	18.50 (3.80)	19.64 (3.13)		0.33	0.03
	Empathic concern	20.00 (4.31)	21.36 (3.73)		0.34	0.03
Rye & Pargament (2002)						
Secular (n = 20)	Anxiety	44.00	41.82	36.90*	SD not rep	
Secular	Depression	13.85	5.31***	5.02	SD not rep	
Secular	Anticipation of Future	25.10	26.68**	26.50	SD not rep	
Secular	Hostility	23.65	19.69***	18.30	SD not rep	
Secular	Religious WB	47.50	51.20**	49.78	SD not rep	
Secular	Existential WB	43.08	48.05***	51.62**	SD not rep	
Rel Acccom (n = 19)	Anxiety	40.74	39.74	36.95	SD not rep	
Rel Acccom	Depression	10.00	4.96**	3.84	SD not rep	
Rel Acccom	Anticipation of Future	27.00	28.32**	28.11	SD not rep	
Rel Acccom	Hostility	22.50	20.05*	18.95	SD not rep	
Rel Acccom	Religious WB	48.37	52.41**	51.63	SD not rep	
Rel Acccom	Existential WB	48.41	51.59*	52.63	SD not rep	
Rye et al. (2005)						
Secular (n = 49)	Trait Anger	17.97 (5.28)	17.76 (4.96)	16.69 (4.53)	−0.04	−0.01
Secular	Depression	19.98 (10.62)	11.89 (7.43)	10.97 (8.70)	−0.89	−0.15
Rel Acccom (n = 50)	Trait Anger	17.99 (5.56)	17.30 (5.05)	16.25 (3.98)	−0.13	−0.02
Rel Acccom	Depression	19.08 (10.21)	14.21 (9.62)	12.80 (8.98)	−0.49	−0.08
Lampton et al. (2005)						
	TFS (n = 42)	37.3 (7.45)	37.8 (6.70)		0.07	0.01
	F-PRO (n = 42)	18.4 (5.57)	23.6*** (5.02)		0.99	0.16

TFS = Trait Forgivingness Scale; TRIM-C = Conciliation subscale of the Transgression-Related Inventory of Motivations; F-PRO = Forgiveness-Positive Responses to the Offender; PTG = Post-Traumatic Growth; If *d* is reported, Cohen's *d*, which compares changes to the control condition; if d was computed for the present table, *d* = (Post – Pre) / pooled SD for treatment condition only, *, **, *** = Statistically significant change at the levels of $p < .05$, .01, or .001, respectively.

Table 23.4 Christian-accommodated REACH Forgiveness (person-to-person) Treatments Non-Forgiveness Measures – Part 2

Author (Date)	*Measures*	*Pre*	*Post*	*Follow*	*d (or if reported Cohen's d)*	*d per hour*
Stratton et al. (2008)						
	F-PRO (workshop) n = 22	16.73 (5.36)	20.05 (5.04)	21.82 (5.22)	0.64	0.12
	F-PRO (workshop + essay) n = 17	19.06 (5.10)	23.59 (5.30)	23.47 (5.66)	0.87	0.14
Worthington et al. (2010)	Forgiveness only					
Osei-Tutu et al. (2020)	REACH Christian (RC; n = 135); RC + culture (RCC; n = 129)					
	TRIM-C (RC)	3.34 (1.02)	3.91 (0.97)	4.13 (0.90)	0.57	0.09
	TFS (RC)	3.32 (0.67)	3.91 (0.65)	3.85 (0.63)	0.89	0.15
	Forbearance (RC)	3.42 (0.93)	3.59 (0.79)	3.61 (0.89)	0.20	0.03
	TRIM-C (RCC)	3.44 (0.97)	4.04 (0.88)	4.18 (0.97)	0.65	0.11
	TFS (RCC)	3.42 (0.67)	3.69 (0.72)	3.86 (0.69)	0.38	0.06
	Forbearance (RCC)	3.29 (0.93)	3.35 (1.05)	3.64 (0.90)	0.06	0.01
Toussaint, Griffin et al. (2020a)	Forgiveness only DIY Workbooks					
Greer et al. (2014)	TFS (Christians, n = 25)	30.20 (6.64)	35.40 (5.11)	35.21 (7.33)	0.89	0.13
Kurniati et al. (2020)	Forgiveness only					
Ortega Bechara et al. (2024)	War survivors (n = 176)					
	TFS	3.70 (0.74)	4.02 (0.70)		0.39	0.12
	Flourishing Index	8.69 (1.45)	9.05 (1.18)		0.27	0.08
	PTG	4.03 (0.74)	4.32 (0.73)		0.33	0.10
	Spiritual Growth	3.47 (0.56)	3.65 (0.47)		0.31	0.09
	Sleep Quality	3.89 (0.91)	4.18 (0.84)		0.31	0.09
	Depression Symptoms	0.97 (0.90)	0.70 (0.82)		−0.26	−0.08

TFS = Trait Forgiveness Scale; TRIM-C = Conciliation subscale of the Transgression-Related Inventory of Motivations; F-PRO = Forgiveness-Positive Responses to the Offender; PTG = Post-Traumatic Growth; If *d* is reported, Cohen's *d*, which compares changes to the control condition; if d was computed for the present table, *d* = (Post – Pre)/pooled SD for treatment condition only

Limitations to the Body of Research

Critiques of the Basic Science Research

Research has studied the effects of forgiveness on physical, psychological, and social health outcomes, and some have studied spirituality. As a field, mediation of forgiveness and physical health through SNS and PSNS pathways, and neurohormonal release (e.g., cortisol and oxytocin) is well represented. Less has studied mediation by central nervous system functioning. More brain research is needed. We also know that rumination mediates between forgiveness and mental health symptoms. Little is known about what mediates between forgiveness and well-being measures. The broaden-and-build model has been proposed as a theoretical explanation (Fredrickson, 2001). Yet it does not reveal causal mechanisms. The mediation between forgiveness and social health has been well specified. Wrongdoers who accept responsibility, apologize, express empathy, make amends, and interact positively around the offense promote forgiveness. Little attention has been paid to the contexts in which social apologies might (or might not) occur. Worthington and Sandage's (2016) forgiveness and relational spirituality theory describes ways the forgiveness and spiritual outcome connection is mediated. However, the RiTE model of the ritualistic, theistic, and existential dimensions of spirituality might accelerate that understanding.

Methodologically, the "usual suspects" form a cadre of weaknesses. (1) College students are overrepresented. (2) Low number of diverse samples. (3) Simple research designs have predominated, but increasingly longitudinal designs, prospective designs, and experiments have been used. (4) Most research is unsystematic – almost a catch-as-catch-can approach. Physical difficulties are thought to arise from a stress-and-coping model of forgiveness, and the choice of topics to investigate has seemed to be selected by convenience, personal interest, or grant-driven choices. The general stress-and-coping model has been studied for 75 years. Its findings could be a systematic guide to the study of forgiveness and health. (5) Issues of timing and physical, mental, and social health and well-being reactions are unclear. For example, how long and to what extent must physiological effects be experienced before they manifest as a physical/psychological disorder or before they interrupt social relationships? (6) Are there transgression-related triggers that hasten disorders and forgiveness-related processes that direct people toward health and well-being instead of disorders?

Critiques of the Intervention Research

Not surprisingly, this review showed that the sample sizes in intervention studies were often small, with sample sizes for group studies being between 50 and 100 (less for individual therapies). Another critique is the choice of control condition against which progress can be evaluated. Many studies early in intervention research used either wait-list designs, wait-list cross-over designs, or control conditions that tested people multiple times but provided no or few bona fide no-treatment and alternative-treatment control conditions. Rye and Pargament (2002) and Rye et al. (2005) compared strictly matched secular and Christian-accommodated versions of a REACH-like intervention. Wade et al. (2018) and Goldman and Wade (2012) used process-oriented group therapy (Yalom & Leszcz, 2005). Toussaint, Griffin et al. (2020a) used Luskin's (2002) Forgive for Good as a comparison condition. Osei-Tutu et al. (2020) compared the Christian-accommodated REACH Forgiveness model with one that was also accommodated by considering Ghanaian culture. Kurniati et al. (2020) compared the secular

REACH Forgiveness 3.34-hour DIY workbook with one that was adapted to collectivism, which had previously been shown to be important to Javanese conceptions of forgiveness. Most of these comparisons with strictly matched or competing forgiveness models showed subtle differences in some of the dependent measures, but not generally in the degree of forgiveness experienced.

A brief assessment of dimensions of the RiTE model and definition of spirituality reveals that the REACH Forgiveness model largely appeals to people's existential motives. That is, forgiveness is widely seen as a virtue, even though people are not always keen to practice it in the throes of a severe offense. Virtually all forgiveness interventions alluded to the benefits to the forgiver of forgiving. Wade et al. (2014) found that a linear regression equation showed the dose-response relationship between hours of treatment (T) and forgiveness effect size (*d*). The equation was $d = 0.124 + 0.046 * T$. The intercept (0.124) might be due to two sources: (1) people's initial motivation to forgive and (2) each treatment fostering increased motivation by recounting physical health, mental health, well-being, relationship, and spiritual benefits to the forgiver. Thus, we might infer that by emphasizing the benefits to the forgiver, the person's (RiTE) existential well-being is engaged. Most interventions took little time to recount the benefits. The secular REACH Forgiveness model perhaps took 10 minutes of a group and less than that for the DIY workbooks. Yet that paid off in an inordinate increase in forgiving – likely concentrated in decisional rather than emotional forgiveness.

Future Directions for Research on Forgiveness, Spirituality, and Health and Well-being

Many recommendations regarding future directions of research have been listed within the limitations above. The maturing of forgiveness studies has continued. Worthington and Wade (2020) observed that almost one-third of the authors called for more attention to the offender's behavior as context for forgiveness. In this present review, we are tempted to push the envelope farther. Advances in divine forgiveness and its interplay with self-forgiveness, and more attention to intergroup forgiveness, reconciliation, and culture (including a diversity of religious and spiritual belief systems; that is, much of the extant work is in the context of Christianity) make consideration of a broad context for forgiveness studies needed. In terms of the intersection of forgiveness, spirituality, and health, we must pay more attention to both spiritual and social health. We must move past a laser focus on individual mental and physical health and well-being to consider how forgiveness can inform public health and mental health. These transformations are already underway and must be considered necessary as we move into the second quarter century of the 21st century.

References

Allemand, M., & Flückiger, M. (2020). Different routes, same effects: Managing unresolved interpersonal transgressions in old age. *Geriatric Psychology*, *33*, 223–234. https://doi.org/10.1024/1662-9647/a000237

Captari, L.E., Hook, J.N., Davis, D. E., McElroy-Heltzel, S.E., & Worthington, E. L., Jr (2018). Integrating clients' religion and spirituality within psychotherapy: A comprehensive meta-analysis. *Journal of Clinical Psychology*, *74* (11), 1938–1951 https://doi.org/10.1002/jclp.22681

Choe, E., McLaughlin, A., McElroy-Heltzel, S. E., & Davis, D. E. (2020). Forgiveness and religion/spirituality. In E. L. Worthington, Jr. & N. G. Wade (Eds.), *Handbook of forgiveness* (2nd ed., pp. 107–116). Routledge. https://doi.org/10.4324/9781351123341-11

Cornish, M. A., Griffin, B. J., & Morris, G. W. (2020). Promotion of self-forgiveness. In E. L. Worthington, Jr. & N. G. Wade (Eds.), *Handbook of forgiveness*, 2nd ed. (pp. 288–297). Routledge. https://doi.org/10.4324/9781351123341

Cornish, M. A., & Wade, N. G. (2015). Working through past wrongdoing: Examination of a self-forgiveness counseling intervention. *Journal of Counseling Psychology*, *62*(3), 521–528. https://doi.org/10.1037/cou0000080

Coyle, C. T., & Enright, R. D. (1997). Forgiveness intervention with postabortion men. *Journal of Consulting and Clinical Psychology*, *65*(6), 1042–1046. https://doi.org/10.1037/0022-006X.65.6.1042

Davis, D. E., Rice, K. G., Hook, J. N., Van Tongeren, D. R., DeBlaere, C. Choe, E., & Worthington, E. L., Jr. (2015). Development of the Sources of Spirituality Scale. *Journal of Counseling Psychology*, *62*(3), 503–513. https://doi.org/10.1037/cou0000082

Davis, D. E., Worthington, E. L., Jr., Hook, J. N., & Hill, P. C. (2013). Research on forgiveness and religion/spirituality: A meta-analytic review. *Psychology of Religion and Spirituality*, 5(4), 233–241. https://doi.org/10.1037/a0033637

Enright, R. D., & Fitzgibbons, R. P. (2024). *Forgiveness therapy: An empirical guide for resolving anger and restoring hope*, 2nd ed. American Psychological Association. https://doi.org/10.1037/14526-000

Fincham, F. D. (2020). Forgiveness in marriage. In E. L. Worthington, Jr. & N. G. Wade (Eds.), *Handbook of forgiveness*, 2nd ed. (pp. 142–152). Routledge. https://doi.org/10.4324/9781351123341-14

Fincham, F. D., & May, R. W. (2019). Self-forgiveness and well-being: Does divine forgiveness matter? *The Journal of Positive Psychology*, *14*(6), 854–859. https://doi.org/10.1080/17439760.2019.1579361

Fincham, F. D., & May, R. W. (2020). Divine, interpersonal, and self-forgiveness: Independently related to depressive symptoms? *The Journal of Positive Psychology*, 15(4), 448–454. https://doi.org/10.1080/17439760.2019.1639798

Fincham, F. D., & May, R. W. (2023). Divine forgiveness and interpersonal forgiveness: Which comes first? *Psychology of Religion and Spirituality*, 15(2), 167–173. https://doi.org/10.1037/rel0000418

Fredrickson, B. L. (2001). The role of positive emotions in positive psychology: The broaden-and-build theory of positive emotions. *American Psychologist*, *56*, 218–226. https://doi.org/10.1037/0003-066X.56.3.218

Freedman, S. R., & Enright, R. D. (2020). A review of the empirical research using Enright's process model of interpersonal forgiveness. In E. L. Worthington, Jr., and N. G. Wade (Eds.), *Handbook of forgiveness*, 2nd ed. (pp. 266–276). Routledge. https://doi.org/10.4324/9781351123341-25

Goldman, D. B., & Wade, N. G. (2012). Comparison of forgiveness and anger-reduction group treatments: A randomized controlled trial. *Psychotherapy Research*, *22*(5), 604–620. https://doi.org/10.1080/10503307.2012.692954

Green, J. D., Reid, C. A., Coy, A. E., Hedgebeth, M. B., Kneuer, M. A. (2020). An interdependence analysis of forgiveness, amends, and relational repair in work and family relationships. In E. L. Worthington, Jr. & N. G. Wade (Eds.), *Handbook of forgiveness* (pp. 131–141, 2nd ed.) Routledge. https://doi.org/10.4324/9781351123341-13

Greer, C. L., Worthington, E. L., Jr., Lin, Y., Lavelock, C. R., & Griffin, B. J. (2014). Efficacy of a self-directed forgiveness workbook for Christian victims of within-congregation offenders. *Spirituality in Clinical Practice*, *1*(3), 218–230. https://doi.org/10.1037/scp0000012

Griffin, B. J., Cowden, R. G., & Shawkey, L. (2020). Bibliography of narrative reviews and meta-analyses on forgiveness (2004 - 2018). In E. L. Worthington, Jr., & N. G. Wade (Eds.), *Handbook of forgiveness*, 2nd ed. (pp. 335–344). Routledge. https://doi.org/10.4324/9781351123341-31

Griffin, B. J., Worthington, E. L., Jr., Lavelock, C. R., Greer, C. L., Lin, Y., Davis, D. E., & Hook, J. N. (2015). Efficacy of a self-forgiveness workbook: A randomized controlled trial with interpersonal offenders. *Journal of Counseling Psychology*, *62*(2), 124–136. https://doi.org/10.1037/cou0000060

Hansen, M. J., Enright. R. D., Baskin, T. W., & Klatt, J. (2009). A palliative care intervention in forgiveness therapy for elderly terminally-ill cancer patients. *Journal of Palliative Care*, *25*(1), 51–60. https://doi.org/10.1177/082585970902500106

Ho, M. Y., Worthington, E. L., Jr., Cowden, R. G., Bechara, A. O., Chen, Z. J., Gunatirin, E. Y., Joynt, S., Khalanskyi, V. V., Korzhov, H., Kurniati, N. M. T., Rodriguez, N., Salnykova, A. A., Shtanko, L., Tymchenko, S., Voytenko, V. L., Zulkaida, A., Mathur, M. B., & VanderWeele, T. J. (2024). International REACH Forgiveness intervention: A multisite randomised controlled trial. *BMJ Public Health*, *2*(1), e000072 https://doi.org/10.1136/bmjph-2023-000072

Jackson, R. E. (1999). Reducing shame through forgiveness and empathy: A group therapy approach to promoting prosocial behavior. *Dissertation Abstracts International*, *60*, 1856.

Kurniati, N. M. T., Dwiwardani, C., Worthington, E. L., Jr., Widyarini, N., Citra, A. F., & Widhiarso, W. (2020). Does forgiving in a collectivistic culture affect only decisions to forgive and not emotions? REACH Forgiveness Collectivistic (REACH-FC) in Indonesia. *International Journal of Psychology*, *55*(5), 861–870. https://doi.org/10.1002/ijop.12648

Lampton, C., Oliver, G., Worthington, E. L., Jr., & Berry, J. W. (2005). Helping Christian college students become more forgiving: An intervention study to promote forgiveness as part of a program to shape Christian character. *Journal of Psychology and Theology*, *33*, 278–290. https://doi.org/10.1177/009164710503300404

Lee, Y.-R. & Enright, R. D. (2014) A forgiveness intervention for women with fibromyalgia who were abused in childhood: A pilot study. *Spirituality in Clinical Practice*, *1*(3), 203–217. https://doi.org/10.1037/scp0000025

Lin, W. -F., Mack, D., Enright, R. D., Krahn, D., & Baskin, T. W. (2004). Effects of forgiveness therapy on anger, mood, and vulnerability to substance use among inpatient substance-dependent clients. *Journal of Consulting and Clinical Psychology*, *72*(6), 1114–1121. https://doi.org/10.1037/0022-006X.72.6.1114

Luskin, F. (2002). *Forgive for good: A proven prescription for health and happiness*. HarperCollins.

Ortega Bechara, A., Chen, Z. J., Worthington, E. L., Jr., Cowden, R. G., Toussaint, L. L., Ho, M. Y., Rodriguez, M. A., Mathur, M., & VanderWeele, T. J. (2024). Do forgiveness campaign activities improve forgiveness, mental health, and flourishing? *International Journal of Public Health*, *69*. https://doi.org/10.3389/ijph.2024.1605341

Osei-Tutu, A., Osafo, J., Anum, A., Appiah-Danquah, R., Worthington, E. L., Jr., Chen, Z. J., Cowden, R. G., & Nonterah, C. W. (2020). Is cultural adaptation needed beyond using Christian-accommodated REACH Forgiveness psychoeducational group intervention in Ghana? An efficacy study comparing a Christian-accommodated version against a version accommodated by Christian and cultural adaptations. *Spirituality in Clinical Practice*, *7*(2), 73–88. https://doi.org/10.1037/scp0000215

Rapp, H., Wang Xu, J., & Enright, R. D. (2022). A meta-analysis of forgiveness education interventions' effects on forgiveness and anger in children and adolescents. *Child Development*, *93*(5), 1249–1269. https://doi.org/10.1111/cdev.13771

Reed, G. & Enright, R.D. (2006). The effects of forgiveness therapy on depression, anxiety, and post-traumatic stress for women after spousal emotional abuse. *Journal of Consulting and Clinical Psychology*, *74*(5), 920–929. https://doi.org/10.1037/0022-006X.74.5.920

Rye, M. S., & Pargament, K. I. (2002). Forgiveness and romantic relationships in college: Can it heal the wounded heart? *Journal of Clinical Psychology*, 54, 419–441. https://doi.org/10.1002/jclp.1153

Rye, M. S., Pargament, K. I., Pan, W., Yingling, D. W., Shogren, K. A., & Ito, M. (2005). Can group interventions facilitate forgiveness of an ex-spouse? A randomized clinical trial. *Journal of Consulting and Clinical Psychology*, 73, 880–892. https://doi.org/10.1037/0022-006X.73.5.880

Stratton, S. P., Dean, J. B., Nooneman, A. J., Bode, R. A., & Worthington, E. L., Jr. (2008). Forgiveness interventions as spiritual development strategies: Workshop training, expressive writing about forgiveness, and retested controls. *Journal of Psychology and Christianity*, *27*, 347–357.

Strelan, P. (2020). The stress-and-coping model of forgiveness: Theory, research, and the potential of dyadic coping. In E. L. Worthington, Jr. & N. G. Wade (Eds.), *Handbook of forgiveness* (2nd ed., pp. 63–73). Routledge. https://doi.org/10.4324/9781351123341-7

Toussaint, L. L., Griffin, B. J., Worthington, E. L., Jr., Zoelzer, M., & Luskin, F. (2020a). Promoting forgiveness at a Christian college: A comparison of REACH Forgiveness and Forgive for Good methods. *Journal of Psychology and Theology*, *48*(2), 154–165. https://doi.org/10.1177/0091647120911109

Toussaint, L. L., Worthington, E. L., Jr., & Williams, D. R. (Eds.). (2015). *Forgiveness and health: Scientific evidence and theories relating forgiveness to better health*. Springer Science + Business.

Toussaint, L. L., Worthington, E. L., Jr., Williams, D. R., & Webb, J. R. (2020b). Forgiveness and physical health. In E. L. Worthington, Jr. & N. G. Wade (Eds.), *Handbook of forgiveness*, 2nd ed. (pp. 178–187). Routledge. https://doi.org/10.4324/9781351123341-17

Van Tongeren, D. R., Burnette, J. L., O'Boyle, E., Worthington, E. L., Jr., & Forsyth, D. (2014). A meta-analysis of inter-group forgiveness. *Journal of Positive Psychology*, *9*(1), 81–95. http://doi.org/10.1080/17439760.2013.844268

Van Tongeren, D. R., & Lindemann, R. (2020). Intergroup forgiveness. In E. L. Worthington, Jr. & N. G. Wade (Eds.), *Handbook of forgiveness*, 2nd ed. (pp. 301–311). Routledge. https://doi.org/10.4324/9781351123341-28

Wade, N. G., Cornish, M. A., Tucker, J. R., Worthington, E. L., Jr., Sandage, S. J., & Rye, M. S. (2018). Promoting forgiveness: Characteristics of the treatment, the clients, and their interaction. *Journal of Counseling Psychology*, *65*(3), 358–371. https://doi.org/10.1037/cou0000260

Wade, N. G., Hoyt, W. T., Kidwell, J. E. M., & Worthington, E. L., Jr. (2014). Meta-analysis of psychotherapeutic interventions to promote forgiveness. *Journal of Consulting and Clinical Psychology*, 82(1), 154–170. https://doi.org/10.1037/a0035268

Waltman, M.A., Russell, D.C., Coyle, C.T., Enright, R.D., Holter, A.C., & Swoboda, C. (2009). The effects of a forgiveness intervention on patients with coronary artery disease. *Psychology and Health*, *24*(1), 11–27. https://doi.org/10.1080/08870440801975127

Washington-Nortey, P. M., Worthington, E. L., Jr., & Ahmed, R. (2022). The scientific study of forgiveness, hope, and religion/spirituality. In E. B. Davis, E. L. Worthington, Jr., & S. A. Schnitker (Eds.), *Handbook of positive psychology, religion, and spirituality* (pp. 361–377). Springer. Open access. https://doi.org/10.1007/978-3-031-10274-5

Webb, J. R. (2021). *Understanding forgiveness and addiction: Theory, research, and clinical application*. Routledge. https://doi.org/10.4324/9780429200274

Webb, J. R., Toussaint, L., & Dula, C. (2014). Ritualistic, theistic, and existential spirituality: Initial psychometric qualities of the RiTE measure of spirituality. *Journal of Religion and Health*, *53*(4), 972–985. https://doi.org/10.1007/s10943-013-9697-y

Webb, J. R., & Toussaint, L. L. (2020). Forgiveness, well-being, and mental health. In E. L. Worthington, Jr. & N. G. Wade (Eds.), *Handbook of forgiveness*, 2nd ed. (pp. 188–198). Routledge. https://doi.org/10.4324/9781351123341-18

Witvliet, C. V. O. (2020). Forgiveness, embodiment, and relational accountability: Victim and transgressor psychophysiology research. In E. L. Worthington, Jr. & N. G. Wade (Eds.), *Handbook of forgiveness*, 2nd ed. (pp. 167–177). Routledge. https://doi.org/10.4324/9781351123341-16

Woodyatt, L., & Wenzel, M. (2020). The psychology of self-forgiveness. In E. L. Worthington, Jr. & N. G. Wade (Eds.), *Handbook of forgiveness* (2nd ed., pp. 22–32). Routledge. https://doi.org/10.4324/9781351123341-3

Woodyatt, L., Worthington, E. L., Jr., Wenzel, M., & Griffin, B. J. (Eds.), (2017). *Handbook of the psychology of self-forgiveness*. Springer.

World Health Organization. (2025). *Constitution of the World Health Organization*. Geneva: Author. Retrieved from https://www.who.int/about/governance/constitution

Worthington, E. L. Jr., & Wade, N. G. (Eds.). (2020). *Handbook of forgiveness*, 2nd ed. Routledge. https://doi.org/10.4324/9781351123341

Worthington, E. L., Jr. (2020). An update of the REACH Forgiveness model to promote forgiveness. In E. L. Worthington, Jr. & N. G. Wade (Eds.), *Handbook of forgiveness*, 2nd ed. (pp. 277–287). Routledge. https://doi.org/10.4324/9781351123341-26

Worthington, E. L., Jr. (2024). REACH forgiveness: A narrative analysis of group effectiveness. *International Journal of Group Psychotherapy*, *74*(3), 330–364. https://doi.org/10.1080/00207284.2024.2340593

Worthington, E. L., Hunter, J. L., Sharp, C. B., Hook, J. N., Van Tongeren, D. R., Davis, D. E., Miller, A. J., Gingrich, F. C., Sandage, S. J., Lao, E., Bubod, L., & Monforte-Milton, M. (2010). A psychoeducational intervention to promote forgiveness in Christians in the Philippines. *Journal of Mental Health Counseling*, *32*(1), 75–93. https://doi.org/10.17744/mehc.32.1.t36770728111j864

Worthington, E. L., Jr., & Ripley, J. S. (2024). *Hope, forgiveness and positive psychology in couple therapy*. Routledge, in press.

Worthington, E. L., Jr., & Sandage, S. J. (2016). *Forgiveness and spirituality in psychotherapy: A relational approach*. American Psychological Association. https://doi.org/10.1037/14712-000

Yalom, I., & Leszcz, M. (2005). *The theory and practice of group psychotherapy* (5th ed.) Basic Books.

Chapter 24

Mindfulness

Sabrina G. Zuniga[*], *Jacob Kranendonk, Carla Nikki Cook, Joshua N. Hook, Daryl R. Van Tongeren, and Don E. Davis*

Mindfulness has a rich history. Originating from Buddhist practices thousands of years ago, it has gained popularity in Western culture in recent years. Mindfulness has been conceptualized as a state, trait, intervention, or ethical and moral belief system (Germer, 2004; Harrington & Dunne, 2015). This chapter provides various conceptualizations of mindfulness and how it relates to spirituality, health, and well-being. Specifically, we discuss (1) our definition of spirituality and how it relates to the RiTE model of spirituality (Webb et al., 2014), (2) definitions of mindfulness and how they relate to spiritual and secular traditions, (3) relevant theory and research regarding the impact of mindfulness interventions and dispositional mindfulness on well-being, (4) findings related to mindfulness, health, and social support, and (5) limitations and directions for future research.

Defining Spirituality

Spirituality has many potential meanings, depending on the person or tradition. Hill and Pargament (2008) define spirituality as "a search for the Sacred, a process through which people seek to discover, hold on to, and when necessary, transform whatever they hold sacred in their lives" (Pargament, 1997, p. 65). People may experience closeness or connection with various objects or events (e.g., concepts of God, the Divine, the universe, or any aspect of life representing sacredness) that transform the ordinary into the transcendent – that which is worthy of veneration. Although many practice spirituality within a religious tradition, others may cultivate spiritual experiences outside of organized religion. Thus, spirituality integrates all of life (i.e., self, others, and daily events) through a spiritual lens and "cannot be divorced from daily life" (Hill & Pargament, 2008, p. 65).

Similarly, in the RiTE model, the pursuit of the sacred can be manifested in three, nonexclusive ways: (1) Ritualistic Spirituality, in which individuals and communities engage in structured connections with one or more deities (i.e., formerly known as religiousness); (2) Theistic Spirituality, in which individuals and communities engage in non-structured connection with one or more deities (i.e., formerly known as spirituality), which may be independent of or include minimal or no affiliation with organized religion(s); and (3) Existential Spirituality, which encompasses a non-theistic yet transcendent search for meaning and purpose (i.e., including individuals who identify as agnostic or atheist) (Webb, et al., 2014; (see Chapters 1 and 44 of this volume). The RiTE model suggests that a balance between all three

* Corresponding Author: SabrinaZuniga@my.unt.edu.

DOI: 10.4324/9781003440048-28

dimensions of spirituality promotes healthier relationships with oneself and others (e.g., positive religious coping and respect for others), whereas countereffects lead to imbalance (e.g., negative religious coping, prejudice, and intolerance). Accordingly, we examine mindfulness through the RiTE model of spirituality.

Defining Mindfulness in Spiritual Contexts

There are several definitions of mindfulness. Kabat-Zinn (2011, p. 291) defines mindfulness as "the awareness that arises from paying attention, on purpose, in the present moment, and non-judgmentally." Although this definition may be useful in therapeutic and clinical settings, it does not express the vast religious and multicultural history of mindfulness. Toward that end, we review various conceptualizations of mindfulness across various expressions of spirituality.

One major *non-theistic* religious influence on mindfulness is Buddhism (Hassed, 2021), which encourages mindfulness, both through specific practice and as a way of life, to attain enlightenment (Kang & Whittingham, 2010). Rightful mindfulness (*samma sati*) is featured in the Buddhist eightfold path toward enlightenment, deeming mindfulness as one of the most important and ethical factors in Buddhist practice. Kang and Whittingham (2010) noted that the "right" in right mindfulness emphasizes that practicing mindfulness elicits ethical judgment and discernment in deciding what is wholesome and skillful (*kusala*) and unwholesome/unskillful (*akusala*). This requires both an active, intentional practice and that the practice influence daily life through decision-making.

Attitudinal foundations of mindfulness and mindfulness-based practices have been seen throughout various *polytheistic* religious traditions. Many foundations and empirically based mindfulness interventions mirror Native American religious practices (Proulx & Bergen-Cico, 2022). For example, the Lakota concept of paying attention to *the Sacred Space*, Ute and Lakota prayers, and mindfulness attitudes such as trust, awareness, and non-judgment can be seen in Native American spirituality (Bergen-Cico & Proulx, 2018). Similarly, many Hindu teachings and practices are consonant with mindfulness. For example, Mindfulness-Based Stress Reduction interventions have utilized the Hindu concept of Indra's net to encourage interconnectedness and universality (Kabat-Zinn, 2000).

Monotheistic religions (including Abrahamic faiths) promote forms of prayer that are similar to mindfulness in the psychology literature. For example, in the Islamic tradition, one of the outcomes for engaging in *salat* (i.e., prayer five times a day) is to foster *khushu*, meaning the "equanimity of body, mind, and soul" (Bergen-Cico & Proulx, 2018). Christians are encouraged to adopt a "being" versus "doing" attitude with God (e.g., Luke 10:41–42), which runs parallel to mindfulness "being versus doing" patterns (Hoover, 2018), and Christian accommodative mindfulness (CAM) emphasizes the role of grace and receiving God's love to encourage mindfulness attitudinal foundations of nonjudgment and acceptance (Jones et al., 2023).

Evidence-Based Mindfulness Interventions

Mindfulness and its core attitudinal foundations have been translated into various mindfulness-based interventions (MBIs) that aim to decrease stress and increase psychological well-being. First-generation MBIs, such as Mindfulness-Based Stress Reduction (MBSR) and Mindfulness-Based Cognitive Therapy (MBCT), were created with the intention of reducing stress and enhancing attention (Urrila, 2022) and would likely be categorized as Existential

Spirituality in the RiTE model (Webb et al., 2014). Second-generation MBIs, such as Mindful Self-Compassion (MSC), Mindfulness-Informed Acceptance Commitment Therapy (ACT), and Dialectical Behavioral Therapy (DBT), strive to embrace transcendent, ethical, and value-based conceptualizations of mindfulness and provide opportunities for individuals and groups to incorporate religious practice (e.g., prayer) into mindfulness interventions (Urrila, 2022) and may be applied as practices in all three forms (i.e., Ritualistic, Theistic, and Existential) of spirituality in the RiTE model (Webb et al., 2014). We briefly review different interventions below.

Inspired by Buddhist practices of mindfulness, MBSR was developed to decrease stress and manage medical conditions (e.g., chronic pain) in hospital patients (Kabat-Zinn, 1982), though recent work has applied MBSR to non-clinical samples. The goal of MBSR is to reduce stress by applying mindfulness to challenging situations and increase adaptive responding (Bishop, 2002). According to the MBSR protocol (Woods & Rockman, 2021), participants join a group for 8 weeks and engage in a variety of interventions and practices, including mind-body scans, breathing techniques, mindful movement, sitting and walking meditations, focused meditations, and yoga. They also complete homework outside the sessions. At the end, participants engage in a full-day mindfulness retreat. MBSR has been successfully adapted to various formats (brief, McIndoo et al., 2016; video-conference groups, Moulton-Perkins et al., 2022; self-help, Taylor et al., 2021).

MBCT is an adaptation of MBSR for preventing depression relapse (Segal et al., 2002). Clients learn to use mindfulness practices to disrupt maladaptive thoughts and reactivity that may cause relapse. Whenever clients notice negative thoughts or self-criticism, they learn to engage mindfulness, which promotes awareness, nonjudgment, equanimity, and self-compassion (Feldman & Kuyken, 2011). MBCT entails an eight-week standardized program consisting of weekly, two-hour group sessions. Like MBSR, MBCT involves psycho-education and a variety of structured meditation activities. In addition, participants practice noticing maladaptive thoughts and using mindfulness practices to reduce their reactivity to negative thoughts (Kraines et al., 2022; Segal et al., 2002).

Mindfulness is also a foundational component of *Acceptance and Commitment Therapy* (ACT; Hayes et al., 2006). In ACT, clients learn to "change their relationship" to negative, unwanted thoughts and emotions and to, instead, act based on their cherished values and principles, thoughts, or emotions (Harris, 2019, p. 16). They learn to practice greater cognitive flexibility through six core therapeutic processes, all of which are directly or indirectly related to mindfulness (i.e., acceptance, contact with the present moment, self-as-context, cognitive defusion, committed action, and values; Hayes et al., 2006; Harris, 2019). Common ACT interventions include a range of activities that draw on principles of mindfulness, including meditations, breathing exercises, metaphors (e.g., imagining thoughts as cars passing by or clouds drifting in the sky), or other defusion activities that reduce reactivity to thoughts (Harris, 2019).

Mindfulness skills are also explicitly taught and encouraged in *DBT*, which was originally developed for patients with Borderline Personality Disorder (BPD) (Heard & Linehan, 1994). Linehan (2015) defines mindfulness in the context of DBT as "intentionally living with awareness in the present moment, without judgment or rejecting the moment, and without attachment to the moment" (p. 24). The goals of mindfulness from a DBT framework include (a) reducing suffering and increasing happiness, (b) increasing control within the mind, and (c) experiencing reality for what it is (Linehan, 2015). Clients learn to develop "wise mind," which involves combining the strengths of the "reasonable mind" with those of the "emotional mind" (Linehan, 2015). In addition, clients cultivate "what" skills – what one does while practicing mindfulness, such as observing, describing, and participating. They also develop "how" skills – they learn how to engage a mindful stance, such as being in a state of non-judgment, completing one task at a time, and completing the task effectively.

Finally, additional *self-compassion interventions*, such as Compassion-Focused Therapy (CFT; Gilbert, 2010) and Mindful Self-Compassion (MSC; Germer & Neff, 2019), draw from Buddhist mindfulness philosophy to cultivate compassion toward oneself and others (Neff, 2003). Practitioners encouraging self-compassion acknowledge the necessity of mindfulness. Self-compassion involves three distinct but overlapping components: (a) developing a posture of kindness toward oneself, (b) acknowledging suffering as a part of the common human experience, and (c) acknowledging (without overidentifying with) suffering via mindfulness (Shapiro et al., 2006). Germer and Neff (2019) developed the MSC program, which involves two-and-a-half-hour sessions and one half-day retreat across the course of eight weeks to enhance mindfulness and increase self-compassion. The program provides instruction and space to complete written exercises, meditations, and informal practices that can be implemented in everyday settings.

Mindfulness, Health, and Well-Being

Mindfulness – as an intervention, disposition, state, and religious/cultural practice – has been shown to have various health-related outcomes. Greeson and Chin (2019) proposed that

> the ability to mindfully observe one's present-moment experience with clarity and equanimity enables more effective appraisals of stressors, which in turn, facilitates conscious, healthy decisions, and prevents automatic, unhealthy habitual reactions… mindfulness can promote self-regulation that may ultimately buffer against biological processes and behaviors that contribute to stress-related disease.
>
> (p. 204)

Mindfulness has been shown to influence various factors of physical health related to disease prevention and healthy living. For example, mindfulness practices have been widely tested as an intervention for individuals with cardiovascular and coronary heart disease. Participants of a mindfulness-based blood pressure class reported increased physical activity, improved diet, and decreases in alcohol consumption and systolic blood pressure at a one-year follow-up (Loucks et al., 2019). Black participants with hypertension who completed a mindfulness meditation program had lower blood pressure compared to a relaxation program (Levine et al., 2017; Parswani et al., 2013). MBIs have demonstrated mixed outcomes for participants with coronary heart disease, with some studies demonstrating significant outcomes – decreased systolic blood pressure (Delui et al., 2013; Parswani et al., 2013), heart rate (Delui et al., 2013), heart failure symptoms and clinical scores (Sullivan et al., 2009), and somatic health complaints (Nehra et al., 2013). However, other studies found nonsignificant outcomes, such as no evidence for decreased blood pressure in college students compared to passive controls (Dawson et al., 2020) and no significant improvements in participants with unmedicated hypertension (Blom et al., 2014). Significant outcomes from MBIs in participants for coronary heart disease may be mediated by mindful attention, decreased rumination (Campbell et al., 2012), and autonomic nervous system regulation (Tang et al., 2015). Levine et al. (2017) suggested that mindfulness interventions have some promising outcomes, though MBIs may be more beneficial as an adjunctive intervention.

Mindfulness interventions have also been tested on various other physical conditions, such as chronic pain, diabetes, smoking, cancer, and HIV/AIDS. Mindfulness interventions have demonstrated mixed evidence with diabetes, with a more recent meta-analysis finding decreased body weight, blood pressure, and glycemic control with mindfulness interventions (Priya & Kalra, 2018). According to Loucks et al. (2015, 2016), dispositional mindfulness has been associated with body mass index, physical activity levels, and central adiposity, though it is not related to blood pressure, total cholesterol, or a healthy diet. Regarding chronic pain, Veehof et al. (2011) found a small to medium effect of mindfulness- and acceptance-based interventions on pain intensity and physical well-being. Mindfulness programs may demonstrate moderate improvement for pain reduction compared to nonspecific active controls, though not compared to specific active controls (Goyal et al., 2014). However, Greeson and Chin (2019) suggest that results from MBIs on chronic pain are largely inconclusive due to differences in methodological rigor, chronicity, and co-morbidity.

Although no evidence suggests that mindfulness can prevent or reduce the spread of cancer, many studies have shown that mindfulness interventions can reduce cancer-related stress and increase emotional well-being and health behaviors (De Vibe et al., 2017; Greeson & Chin, 2019). Breast cancer survivors who completed a mindful awareness practice program demonstrated decreased pro-inflammatory gene expression (Bower et al., 2015). In general, with regard to mindfulness, cancer patients tend to report increased quality of life and reduction in anxiety, depression, fatigue, and hostility (Henderson et al., 2012; Schellekens Melanie et al., 2017).

Initial studies also demonstrated that mindfulness interventions may be useful in the treatment of HIV/AIDS and found a reduction in CD4+ helper T lymphocytes (Riley & Kalichman, 2015). However, more recent studies found no significant differences between MBIs and self-management skills groups for patients with HIV/AIDS (Greeson & Chin, 2019; Hecht et al., 2018). Similarly, some research suggests that mindfulness interventions may be associated with smoking cessation (Levine et al., 2017), and dispositional mindfulness may be related to nonsmoking (Loucks et al., 2015).

Johnson et al. (2023) analyzed physical health and mental health outcomes after MBIs in college students and found that mindfulness training typically demonstrated small effect sizes in physical health outcomes, compared to mental health outcomes with small to medium effect sizes. This reflects a major theme in the relationship between mindfulness and physical health reviewed in this chapter: mindfulness may not cure diseases, but it may decrease stressors and maladaptive behaviors related to disease risk (e.g., smoking, mindless eating, and sedentary lifestyle) and increase quality of life and preventative measures (e.g., increased autonomic nervous system functioning, self-care, and physical activity).

The literature on mindfulness and mental health and well-being is vast. For instance, in participants with chronic pain, mindfulness interventions demonstrated a small to medium effect related to decreased depression, anxiety, and quality of life – though not superior to traditional interventions (e.g., CBT) (Veehof et al., 2011). In participants with coronary heart disease or cardiovascular disease, mindfulness interventions reduced anxiety and depression and increased emotional control and coping (Sullivan et al., 2009; Tacón et al., 2004).

Mindfulness interventions tend to outperform active controls with a small effect size and inactive controls with a small to medium effect size on anxiety, depression, and combined mental health outcomes (Goyal et al., 2014; Hoge et al., 2021; Johnson et al., 2023). Similarly, MBIs, compared to passive controls, decreased distress, anxiety, depression, and rumination as well as increased well-being and dispositional mindfulness. However, when compared to active controls, MBIs improved distress and state anxiety, though not depression, well-being, thought suppression, and life satisfaction (Dawson et al., 2020). Longer interventions tended to have larger mental health effects, and intervention type (e.g., MBSR vs. MBCT) was a nonsignificant moderator (Johnson et al., 2023). Larger effects have sometimes been seen in clinical samples versus non-clinical samples (Johnson et al., 2023), though some studies found no significant differences between sample types (Hoge et al., 2021).

Unguided mindfulness-based self-help programs demonstrated small effects for improving depression, anxiety, stress, and well-being, though depression and anxiety outcomes were not sustained with future follow-up (Taylor et al., 2021). Dispositional mindfulness has been positively correlated with higher life satisfaction, negative thought regulation, and emotion regulation (Baer et al., 2006; Kang et al., 2013) and negatively correlated with rumination (Svendsen et al., 2017). Mindfulness has been associated with sustained well-being despite fluctuating life circumstances (Hanley & Garland, 2022; Jo et al., 2022). Additionally, mindfulness and acceptance-based practices have been related to decreased rumination and increased resilience following traumatic events (Thompson et al., 2011).

Recent research has begun to explore the impact of mindfulness on relationships and social support. Dispositional mindfulness was related to relationship satisfaction, mediated by emotion regulation, in a sample of married couples (Wachs & Cordova, 2007). Dispositional mindfulness was positively related to perceived social support in college students with low and moderate trauma-related symptoms, though not for participants with high trauma-related symptoms (Kuhl & Boyraz, 2017). Recent research among Chinese participants has begun examining social support as a mediator in the relationship between mindfulness and burnout. Among Chinese students, perceived social support from teachers mediated the relationship between mindfulness and educational burnout (Wen et al., 2023). Social support partially mediated the relationship between dispositional mindfulness and trauma-related symptoms in Chinese firefighters (Chen et al., 2022), and perceived social support was related to post-traumatic growth for individuals with higher dispositional mindfulness, though not for individuals with lower dispositional mindfulness (Chen et al., 2021). In a sample of Chinese adolescents, mindfulness was inversely related to cyberbullying, mediated by social support and empathy (Liu et al., 2020). Therefore, mindfulness may improve perceived social support through reappraisal, approach-oriented coping, positive emotions, and compassion (Chen et al., 2022). However, more cross-cultural research is needed.

In general, mindfulness is thought to improve well-being through decreased rumination, interruption of racing thoughts, reappraisal, and exposure (Lyall et al., 2021), as well as increased emotion regulation (Fisher et al., 2022; Hölzel et al., 2011; Loucks et al., 2015; Tang et al., 2015). Additionally, mindfulness meditation has been related to increased positive affect related to left-sided anterior brain electrical activity (Davidson et al., 2003). Long-time mindfulness meditation practitioners have higher grey matter density (Lutz et al., 2009) in insula and hippocampal regions, which increases perspective taking (Hölzel et al., 2011) as well as the medial prefrontal cortex, which relates to fear modulation (Luders et al., 2013; Milad et al., 2005). Furthermore, experienced mindfulness meditators have decreased levels of adrenocortical hormones (Vago & Silbersweig, 2012). Mindfulness has additionally been associated with changes in the resting state of the brain (i.e., Default Mode Network), resulting in decreased rumination and increased sensory awareness (Riegner et al., 2023). Taken together, this research supports the salutary effects of mindfulness on a range of outcomes.

Limitations

Despite the strong empirical research base on mindfulness, we note several limitations and directions for future research. First, much of the research focused on the consistent, positive relationship between mindfulness, mental well-being, and reduced psychopathology. Considering this, Johnson et al. (2023) encourage mindfulness researchers to further examine physical health and health behavior outcomes, given that results were largely inconclusive in physical health studies due to differences in methodological rigor as well as an imbalance in the number of studies examining physical health compared to mental health outcomes. Also, some meta-analyses encouraged their audiences to interpret their results with caution due to publication bias. For instance, Levine and colleagues (2017), in their review of acceptance and mindfulness-based interventions, noted difficulty in finding studies that reported nonsignificant results (i.e., file-drawer effect). Similarly, many meta-analyses only included published peer-reviewed articles or unpublished dissertations in English, thus increasing the risk for publication bias toward results that generalize and can be applied only toward English-speaking populations (e.g., Kraines et al., 2022; Querstret et al., 2020). Finally, because MBSR and MBCT treatments reportedly include more standardized protocols, have a stronger evidence base (Querstret et al., 2020), and may reduce heterogeneity in meta-analyses (Gu et al., 2018), MBSR and MBCT were overrepresented in various meta-analyses analyzing MBIs and related health outcomes (e.g., Gu et al., 2018; Querstret et al., 2020). Even within studies analyzing just MBSR and MBCT, MBSR appeared to dominate most studies (Querstret et al., 2020). Gu et al. (2018) noted that by having excluded other MBIs outside of MBSR and MBCT, such as ACT, they may have missed how other factors (e.g., cognitive flexibility) influence the relationship between mindfulness and well-being. However, studies that analyzed ACT, MBSR, and MBCT (e.g., Ma et al., 2022) noted that only post-intervention outcomes could be compared due to the heterogeneity of intervention delivery (e.g., in-person groups for MBSR/MBCT, self-help for ACT), thus decreasing the ability to compare mechanisms of change.

Differences in methodological rigor, study quality, and heterogeneity of studies led many authors to draw inconclusive results and encourage interpretation with caution (Carney et al., 2023; Johannsen et al., 2022; Moulton-Perkins et al., 2022; Pseftogianni et al., 2023; Veehof et al., 2016). Various meta-analyses listed difficulties analyzing studies that did not include a control group (e.g., Carney et al., 2023) or an active comparison group (e.g., Byrne et al., 2019; Carney et al., 2023; Pseftogianni et al., 2023). Other meta-analyses listed high heterogeneity of psychopathology as a limitation even among similar domains (e.g., obsessive-compulsive-related symptoms) (Pseftogianni et al., 2023). On another note, some meta-analyses noted small sample sizes that led to decreased ability to generalize results to other populations as well as being underpowered (Pseftogianni et al., 2023; Strauss et al., 2015). Lastly, some reviews listed sample demographics as a limitation, noting predominantly White samples, lack of race/ethnicity demographic reports, and other studies not examining differences across race/ethnicity or religious groups, which may be important given stigma regarding mindfulness across various racial/ethnic and religious groups (Hoge et al., 2021; Johnson et al., 2023; Sun et al., 2022; Waldron et al., 2018). Waldron et al. (2018) analyzed demographic distributions in MBI studies, and about 79% of participants were White, and only one study specifically examined MBIs in the context of racial/ethnic minorities. Furthermore, Waldron et al. (2018) found that lower SES was rarely represented in MBI studies, as college students tended to be overrepresented.

Several reviews listed mindfulness measurement as a limitation. For example, Kraines et al. (2022) noted how different aspects of mindfulness (e.g., attentional control and selective attention) and cognitive processes (e.g., inhibition and shifting) were labeled differently across studies and may have led to some inconsistencies. Furthermore, Kuyken et al. (2010) listed one-dimensional measurement of mindfulness as a limitation given its various aspects (e.g., decentering, attentional control, and observing). Carney et al. (2023) reported differences in mindfulness measures [e.g., Five Facet Mindfulness Questionnaire (FFMQ; Baer et al., 2006), Mindful Attention Awareness Scale (MAAS; 2003)] as a limitation, suggesting further utilization of the FFMQ due to its multidimensional measurement of mindfulness. Kuyken et al. (2010) note that many studies utilized a self-report measure of mindfulness, thus increasing risk for social desirability responding as compared to behavioral- or neuroscience-related measures. Lastly, Lee et al. (2021) note that only 3% of their studies included qualitative analyses, which is relatively small given the introspective nature of mindfulness.

Directions for Future Research

Recent reviews on mindfulness and mindfulness interventions have provided various directions for future research. Regarding methodological rigor and study quality, researchers suggested applying stronger control and comparison groups (Carney et al., 2023; Greeson & Chin, 2019; Hoge et al., 2021; Veehof et al., 2016), more replication studies, and thorough theoretical backgrounds (Carney et al., 2023; Lee et al., 2021). Regarding mindfulness measurement, researchers suggest utilizing multidimensional measurements of mindfulness, more consistent measures of mindfulness, and including behavioral or neuroscience-related measures (Carney et al., 2023; Kraines et al., 2022; Kuyken et al., 2010). When analyzing the effectiveness of specific MBIs, researchers strongly encouraged including an integrity check to ensure MBIs were properly and thoroughly implemented (Veehof et al., 2016).

To better understand the effectiveness of MBIs, researchers suggested testing for moderators, such as duration of the intervention, amount of training for providers, delivery mode (e.g., in-person, virtual, hybrid, and group), practice effects, or regression to the mean (Kraines et al., 2022; Querstret et al., 2020). To better understand the underlying mechanisms of change for MBIs on health and well-being, researchers suggested analyzing for potential mediators through RCTs and meta-analyses across various interventions (e.g., ACT, DBT, and MSC; Gu et al., 2018). Carney et al. (2023) reminded future researchers to report nonsignificant mediators. In longitudinal studies measuring mediation, researchers suggested applying more intensive and frequent measurements throughout the intervention phase to understand the change process over time (Carney et al., 2023; Veehof et al., 2016). Lastly, Lee et al. (2021) suggested qualitative and mixed-method studies to understand the underlying processes of mindfulness, especially for minority populations.

Regarding multi- and cross-cultural advances in mindfulness research, studies suggested recruiting racially diverse samples (Carney et al., 2023; Waldron et al., 2018), assessing participants' religiosity and spirituality (Abdulkerim & Li, 2022; Jones et al., 2023) with tools such as the Beliefs, Relational, Application, Integration, Diagnostic, Self (BRAIDS; Leighton, 2014) screening tool, and conducting MBIs in diverse racial and religious communities with matching race and/or religion providers (Bergen-Cico & Proulx, 2018). Furthermore, given the new, emerging literature regarding mindfulness and social support, future researchers may examine mindfulness and social support across various cultural groups (Chen et al., 2021, 2022). Hassed (2021) noted the importance of implementing culturally relevant conceptualizations – through metaphors, stories, and humor – when teaching mindfulness to minority racial/ethnic or religious communities. For example, if a participant asks, "why practice mindfulness if prayer is my meditation?" Hassed (2021) suggested prompting a question on "whether they ever find themselves praying on automatic pilot with their attention wandering into daydreams or worldly worries while they pray" (p. 85). Finally, Bergen-Cico and Proulx (2018) strongly encouraged future researchers to consider and acknowledge privilege when conducting research and implementing MBIs in minority communities.

Conclusion

Mindfulness has been utilized across various religious, cultural, and secular traditions. Mindfulness is associated with various health and well-being outcomes due to its emphasis on increasing present-moment contact, emotion regulation, and value-centered living. Though much of the psychological literature focuses on health and well-being outcomes (e.g., decreased mental and physical symptoms, increased quality of life), mindfulness has also been encouraged by various religious traditions to increase connectedness with one's purpose, and even with the Sacred. Although outcomes found in the psychological literature may align more with Existential Spirituality components of the RiTE model of spirituality, mindfulness may be integrated across all three components (i.e., Existential, Theistic, and Ritualistic) of spirituality. Given the outcomes of mindfulness and well-being in an Existential Spirituality context, it may be especially important for researchers to continue examining how mindfulness outcomes manifest in Theistic and Ritualistic contexts, even how mindfulness may influence connection to and seeking the Divine.

References

Abdulkerim, N., & Li, C. (2022). How applicable are mindfulness-based interventions to Muslim clients in the US? *Professional Psychology: Research and Practice*, *53*(3), 253–265. https://doi.org/10.1037/pro0000454

Baer, R. A., Smith, G. T., Hopkins, J., Krietemeyer, J., & Toney, L. (2006). Using Self-Report Assessment Methods to Explore Facets of Mindfulness. *Assessment*, *13*(1), 27–45. https://doi.org/10.1177/1073191105283504

Bergen-Cico, D., & Proulx, J. (2018). Mindfulness and contemplative practices for diverse cultures. In D. Grimes, Q. Wang, & H. Lin (Eds.), *Empirical studies of contemplative practices*. (2018-57991-006; pp. 145–164). Nova Science Publishers.

Bishop, S. R. (2002). What Do We Really Know About Mindfulness-Based Stress Reduction? *Psychosomatic Medicine*, *64*(1), 71.

Blom, K., Baker, B., How, M., Dai, M., Irvine, J., Abbey, S., Abramson, B. L., Myers, M. G., Kiss, A., Perkins, N. J., & Tobe, S. W. (2014). Hypertension Analysis of Stress Reduction Using Mindfulness Meditation and Yoga: Results From the Harmony Randomized Controlled Trial. *American Journal of Hypertension*, *27*(1), 122–129. https://doi.org/10.1093/ajh/hpt134

Bower, J. E., Crosswell, A. D., Stanton, A. L., Crespi, C. M., Winston, D., Arevalo, J., Ma, J., Cole, S. W., & Ganz, P. A. (2015). Mindfulness meditation for younger breast cancer survivors: A randomized controlled trial. *Cancer*, *121*(8), 1231–1240. https://doi.org/10.1002/cncr.29194

Byrne, S. P., Haber, P., Baillie, A., Costa, D. S. J., Fogliati, V., & Morley, K. (2019). Systematic reviews of mindfulness and acceptance and commitment therapy for alcohol use disorder: Should we be using third wave therapies? *Alcohol and Alcoholism*, *54*(2), 159–166. https://doi.org/10.1093/alcalc/agy089

Campbell, T. S., Labelle, L. E., Bacon, S. L., Faris, P., & Carlson, L. E. (2012). Impact of Mindfulness-Based Stress Reduction (MBSR) on attention, rumination and resting blood pressure in women with cancer: A waitlist-controlled study. *Journal of Behavioral Medicine*, *35*(3), 262–271. https://doi.org/10.1007/s10865-011-9357-1

Carney, L. M., Park, C. L., & Hingorany, P. (2023). The mechanisms of mindfulness-based stress reduction and mindfulness-based cognitive therapy for cancer patients and survivors: A systematic review. *Psychology of Consciousness: Theory, Research, and Practice*. https://doi.org/10.1037/cns0000362.supp

Chen, J., Li, J., Zhou, Y., Liu, X., & Xu, W. (2021). Enhancement from being present: Dispositional mindfulness moderates the longitudinal relationship between perceived social support and posttraumatic growth in Chinese firefighters. *Journal of Affective Disorders*, *279*, 111–116. https://doi.org/10.1016/j.jad.2020.09.137

Chen, J., Li, W., An, Y., Zhang, Y., Du, J., & Xu, W. (2022). Perceived social support mediates the relationships of dispositional mindfulness to job burnout and posttraumatic stress disorder among chinese firefighters. *Psychological Trauma: Theory, Research, Practice, and Policy*, *14*(7), 1117–1123. https://doi.org/10.1037/tra0000534

Davidson, R. J., Kabat-Zinn, J., Schumacher, J., Rosenkranz, M., Muller, D., Santorelli, S. F., Urbanowski, F., Harrington, A., Bonus, K., & Sheridan, J. F. (2003). Alterations in brain and immune function produced by mindfulness meditation. *Psychosomatic Medicine*, *65*(4), 564–570.

Dawson, A. F., Brown, W. W., Anderson, J., Datta, B., Donald, J. N., Hong, K., Allan, S., Mole, T. B., Jones, P. B., & Galante, J. (2020). Mindfulness-Based Interventions for University Students: A Systematic Review and Meta-Analysis of Randomised Controlled Trials. *Applied Psychology: Health and Well-Being*, *12*(2), 384–410. https://doi.org/10.1111/aphw.12188

de Vibe, M., Bjørndal, A., Fattah, S., Dyrdal, G. M., Halland, E., & Tanner-Smith, E. E. (2017). Mindfulness-based stress reduction (MBSR) for improving health, quality of life and social functioning in adults: A systematic review and meta-analysis. *Campbell Systematic Reviews*, *13*(1), 1–264. https://doi.org/10.4073/csr.2017.11

Delui, M. H., Yari, M., Khouyinezhad, G., Amini, M., & Bayazi, M. H. (2013). Comparison of Cardiac Rehabilitation Programs Combined with Relaxation and Meditation Techniques on Reduction of Depression and Anxiety of Cardiovascular Patients. *The Open Cardiovascular Medicine Journal*, *7*, 99–103. https://doi.org/10.2174/1874192401307010099

Feldman, C., & Kuyken, W. (2011). Compassion in the landscape of suffering. *Contemporary Buddhism*, *12*(1), 143–155. https://doi.org/10.1080/14639947.2011.564831

Fisher, M. E., Duraney, E., Friess, K., Whitmoyer, P., Andridge, R., & Prakash, R. S. (2022). Trait Mindfulness and Emotion Regulation Responsiveness to Negative Affect in Daily Life. *Mindfulness*, *13*(11), 2796–2811. https://doi.org/10.1007/s12671-022-01996-3

Germer, C. (2004). What is Mindfulness? *Insight Journal*, *22*(3), 24–29.

Germer, C., & Neff, K. (2019). Mindful Self-Compassion (MSC). In I. Ivtzan (Ed.), *Handbook of Mindfulness-Based Programmes* (1st ed., pp. 357–367). Routledge. https://doi.org/10.4324/9781315265438-28

Gilbert, P. (2010). An Introduction to Compassion Focused Therapy in Cognitive Behavior Therapy. *International Journal of Cognitive Therapy*, *3*(2), 97–112. https://doi.org/10.1521/ijct.2010.3.2.97

Goyal, M., Singh, S., Sibinga, E. M. S., Gould, N. F., Rowland-Seymour, A., Sharma, R., Berger, Z., Sleicher, D., Maron, D. D., Shihab, H. M., Ranasinghe, P. D., Linn, S., Saha, S., Bass, E. B., & Haythornthwaite, J. A. (2014). Meditation Programs for Psychological Stress and Well-being: A Systematic Review and Meta-analysis. *JAMA Internal Medicine*, *174*(3), 357–368. https://doi.org/10.1001/jamainternmed.2013.13018

Greeson, J. M., & Chin, G. R. (2019). Mindfulness and physical disease: A concise review. *Current Opinion in Psychology*, *28*, 204–210. https://doi.org/10.1016/j.copsyc.2018.12.014

Hanley, A. W., & Garland, E. L. (2022). Self-transcendence Predicts Better Pre- and Postoperative Outcomes in Two Randomized Clinical Trials of Brief Mindfulness-Based Interventions. *Mindfulness*, *13*(6), 1532–1543. https://doi.org/10.1007/s12671-022-01896-6

Gu, J., Cavanagh, K., & Strauss, C. (2018). Investigating the specific effects of an online mindfulness-based self-help intervention on stress and underlying mechanisms. *Mindfulness*, *9*(4), 1245–1257. https://doi.org/10.1007/s12671-017-0867-y

Harrington, A., & Dunne, J. D. (2015). When mindfulness is therapy: Ethical qualms, historical perspectives. *American Psychologist*, *70*(7), 621–631. https://doi.org/10.1037/a0039460

Harris, R. (2019). *ACT Made Simple: An Easy-To-Read Primer on Acceptance and Commitment Therapy*. New Harbinger Publications.

Hassed, C. (2021). Mindfulness: Is it buddhist or universal? *The Humanistic Psychologist*, *49*(1), 72–88. https://doi.org/10.1037/hum0000169

Hayes, S. C., Luoma, J. B., Bond, F. W., Masuda, A., & Lillis, J. (2006). Acceptance and Commitment Therapy: Model, processes and outcomes. *Behaviour Research and Therapy*, *44*(1), 1–25. https://doi.org/10.1016/j.brat.2005.06.006

Heard, H. L., & Linehan, M. M. (1994). Dialectical behavior therapy: An integrative approach to the treatment of borderline personality disorder. *Journal of Psychotherapy Integration*, *4*(1), 55–82. https://doi.org/10.1037/h0101147

Hecht, F. M., Moskowitz, J. T., Moran, P., Epel, E. S., Bacchetti, P., Acree, M., Kemeny, M. E., Mendes, W. B., Duncan, L. G., Weng, H., Levy, J. A., Deeks, S. G., & Folkman, S. (2018). A randomized, controlled trial of mindfulness-based stress reduction in HIV infection. *Brain, Behavior, and Immunity*, *73*, 331–339. https://doi.org/10.1016/j.bbi.2018.05.017

Henderson, V. P., Clemow, L., Massion, A. O., Hurley, T. G., Druker, S., & Hébert, J. R. (2012). The effects of mindfulness-based stress reduction on psychosocial outcomes and quality of life in early-stage breast cancer patients: A randomized trial. *Breast Cancer Research and Treatment*, *131*(1), 99–109. https://doi.org/10.1007/s10549-011-1738-1

Hill, P. C., & Pargament, K. I. (2008). Advances in the conceptualization and measurement of religion and spirituality: Implications for physical and mental health research. *Psychology of Religion and Spirituality*, *S*(1), 3–17. https://doi.org/10.1037/1941-1022.S.1.3

Hoge, E. A., Acabchuk, R. L., Kimmel, H., Moitra, E., Britton, W. B., Dumais, T., Ferrer, R. A., Lazar, S. W., Vago, D., Lipsky, J., Schuman-Olivier, Z., Cheaito, A., Sager, L., Peters, S., Rahrig, H., Acero, P., Scharf, J., Loucks, E. B., & Fulwiler, C. (2021). Emotion-Related Constructs Engaged by Mindfulness-Based Interventions: A Systematic Review and Meta-analysis. *Mindfulness*, *12*(5), 1041–1062. https://doi.org/10.1007/s12671-020-01561-w

Hölzel, B. K., Lazar, S. W., Gard, T., Schuman-Olivier, Z., Vago, D. R., & Ott, U. (2011). How Does Mindfulness Meditation Work? Proposing Mechanisms of Action From a Conceptual and Neural Perspective. *Perspectives on Psychological Science*, *6*(6), 537–559. https://doi.org/10.1177/1745691611419671

Hoover, J. (2018). Can Christians Practice Mindfulness Without Compromising Their Convictions? *Journal of Psychology and Christianity*, *37*(3), 247–255.

Jo, D., Spencer, S. D., & Masuda, A. (2022). Mindfulness as a Moderator of the Relationship Between Engaged Living and Depression in Emerging Adulthood. *Mindfulness*, *13*(3), 742–750. https://doi.org/10.1007/s12671-022-01831-9

Johannsen, M., Nissen, E. R., Lundorff, M., & O'Toole, M. S. (2022). Mediators of acceptance and mindfulness-based therapies for anxiety and depression: A systematic review and meta-analysis. *Clinical Psychology Review*, *94*, 102156. https://doi.org/10.1016/j.cpr.2022.102156

Johnson, B. T., Acabchuk, R. L., George, E. A., Nardi, W., Sun, S., Salmoirago-Blotcher, E., Scharf, J., & Loucks, E. B. (2023). Mental and Physical Health Impacts of Mindfulness Training for College Undergraduates: A Systematic Review and Meta-Analysis of Randomized Controlled Trials. *Mindfulness*, *14*(9), 2077–2096. https://doi.org/10.1007/s12671-023-02212-6

Jones, T. L., Garzon, F. L., & Ford, K. M. (2023). Christian accommodative mindfulness in the clinical treatment of shame, depression, and anxiety: Results of an N-of-1 time-series study. *Spirituality in Clinical Practice*, *10*(2), 118–130. https://doi.org/10.1037/scp0000221

Kabat-Zinn, J. (1982). An outpatient program in behavioral medicine for chronic pain patients based on the practice of mindfulness meditation: Theoretical considerations and preliminary results. *General Hospital Psychiatry*, *4*(1), 33–47. https://doi.org/10.1016/0163-8343(82)90026-3

Kabat-Zinn, J. (2000). Indra's net at work: The mainstreaming of Dharma practice in society. In *The psychology of awakening: Buddhism, science, and our day-to-day lives* (pp. 225–249). Samuel Weiser.

Kabat-Zinn, J. (2011). Some reflections on the origins of MBSR, skillful means, and the trouble with maps. *Contemporary Buddhism*, *12*(1), 281–306.

Kang, C., & Whittingham, K. (2010). Mindfulness: A Dialogue between Buddhism and Clinical Psychology. *Mindfulness*, *1*(3), 161–173. https://doi.org/10.1007/s12671-010-0018-1

Kang, Y., Gruber, J., & Gray, J. R. (2013). Mindfulness and De-Automatization. *Emotion Review*, *5*(2), 192–201. https://doi.org/10.1177/1754073912451629

Kraines, M. A., Peterson, S. K., Tremont, G. N., Beard, C., Brewer, J. A., & Uebelacker, L. A. (2022). Mindfulness-based stress reduction and mindfulness-based cognitive therapy for depression: A systematic review of cognitive outcomes. *Mindfulness*, *13*(5), 1126–1135. https://doi.org/10.1007/s12671-022-01841-7

Kuhl, M., & Boyraz, G. (2017). Mindfulness, General Trust, and Social Support Among Trauma-Exposed College Students. *Journal of Loss and Trauma*, *22*(2), 150–162. https://doi.org/10.1080/15325024.2016.1212610

Kuyken, W., Watkins, E., Holden, E., White, K., Taylor, R. S., Byford, S., Evans, A., Radford, S., Teasdale, J. D., & Dalgleish, T. (2010). How does mindfulness-based cognitive therapy work? *Behaviour Research and Therapy*, *48*(11), 1105–1112. https://doi.org/10.1016/j.brat.2010.08.003

Lee, J., Kim, K. H., Webster, C. S., & Henning, M. A. (2021). The Evolution of Mindfulness from 1916 to 2019. *Mindfulness*, *12*(8), 1849–1859. https://doi.org/10.1007/s12671-021-01603-x

Leighton, T. J. (2014). The Therapeutics of Counselling Religious Clients: Intake and Assessment. *International Journal of Mental Health and Addiction*, *12*(3), 295–311. https://doi.org/10.1007/s11469-013-9454-1

Lever Taylor, B., Strauss, C., Cavanagh, K., & Jones, F. (2014). The effectiveness of self-help mindfulness-based cognitive therapy in a student sample: A randomised controlled trial. *Behaviour Research and Therapy*, *63*, 63–69. https://doi.org/10.1016/j.brat.2014.09.007

Levine, G. N., Lange, R. A., Bairey-Merz, C. N., Davidson, R. J., Jamerson, K., Mehta, P. K., Michos, E. D., Norris, K., Ray, I. B., Saban, K. L., Shah, T., Stein, R., & Smith, S. C. (2017). Meditation and Cardiovascular Risk Reduction. *Journal of the American Heart Association*, *6*(10), e002218. https://doi.org/10.1161/JAHA.117.002218

Linehan, M. M. (2015). *DBT skills training handouts and worksheets* (Second). Guilford Publications.

Liu, C., Wang, L., Liu, Z., Li, Y., & Yuan, G. (2020). Mindfulness and Cyberbullying Among Chinese Adolescents: The Mediating Roles of Perceived Social Support and Empathy. *Violence and Victims*, *35*(6), 815–827. https://doi.org/10.1891/VV-D-19-00104

Loucks, E. B., Britton, W. B., Howe, C. J., Eaton, C. B., & Buka, S. L. (2015). Positive associations of dispositional mindfulness with cardiovascular health: The New England Family Study. *International Journal of Behavioral Medicine*, *22*(4), 540–550. https://doi.org/10.1007/s12529-014-9448-9

Loucks, E. B., Britton, W. B., Howe, C. J., Gutman, R., Gilman, S. E., Brewer, J., Eaton, C. B., & Buka, S. L. (2016). Associations of Dispositional Mindfulness with Obesity and Central Adiposity: The New England Family Study. *International Journal of Behavioral Medicine*, *23*(2), 224–233. https://doi.org/10.1007/s12529-015-9513-z

Loucks, E. B., Nardi, W. R., Gutman, R., Kronish, I. M., Saadeh, F. B., Li, Y., Wentz, A. E., Webb, J., Vago, D. R., Harrison, A., & Britton, W. B. (2019). Mindfulness-Based Blood Pressure Reduction (MB-BP): Stage 1 single-arm clinical trial. *PLOS ONE*, *14*(11), e0223095. https://doi.org/10.1371/journal.pone.0223095

Luders, E., Kurth, F., Toga, A., Narr, K., & Gaser, C. (2013). Meditation effects within the hippocampal complex revealed by voxel-based morphometry and cytoarchitectonic probabilistic mapping. *Frontiers in Psychology*, *4*. https://doi.org/10.3389/fpsyg.2013.00398

Lutz, A., Greischar, L. L., Perlman, D. M., & Davidson, R. J. (2009). BOLD signal in insula is differentially related to cardiac function during compassion meditation in experts vs. Novices. *NeuroImage*, *47*(3), 1038–1046. https://doi.org/10.1016/j.neuroimage.2009.04.081

Lyall, K., Mikocka-Walus, A., Evans, S., & Cummins, R. A. (2021). Linking Homeostatically Protected Mood, Mindfulness, and Depression: A Conceptual Synthesis and Model of Moodfulness. *Review of General Psychology*, *25*(3), 304–320. https://doi.org/10.1177/10892680211017523

McIndoo, C. C., File, A. A., Preddy, T., Clark, C. G., & Hopko, D. R. (2016). Mindfulness-based therapy and behavioral activation: A randomized controlled trial with depressed college students. *Behaviour Research and Therapy*, *77*, 118–128. https://doi.org/10.1016/j.brat.2015.12.012

Ma, L., Wang, Y., Pan, L., Cui, Z., & Schluter, P. J. (2022). Mindfulness-informed (ACT) and Mindfulness-based Programs (MBSR/MBCT) applied for college students to reduce symptoms of depression and anxiety. *Journal of Behavioral and Cognitive Therapy*, *32*(4), 271–289. https://doi.org/10.1016/j.jbct.2022.05.002

Milad, M. R., Quinn, B. T., Pitman, R. K., Orr, S. P., Fischl, B., & Rauch, S. L. (2005). Thickness of ventromedial prefrontal cortex in humans is correlated with extinction memory. *Proceedings of the National Academy of Sciences*, *102*(30), 10706–10711. https://doi.org/10.1073/pnas.0502441102

Moulton-Perkins, A., Moulton, D., Cavanagh, K., Jozavi, A., & Strauss, C. (2022). Systematic review of mindfulness-based cognitive therapy and mindfulness-based stress reduction via group videoconferencing: Feasibility, acceptability, safety, and efficacy. *Journal of Psychotherapy Integration*, *32*(1), 110–130. https://doi.org/10.1037/int0000216

Neff, K. (2003). Self-Compassion: An Alternative Conceptualization of a Healthy Attitude Toward Oneself. *Self and Identity*, *2*(2), 85–101. https://doi.org/10.1080/15298860309032

Nehra, D. K., Sharma, N., Kumar, P., & Nehra, S. (2013). Efficacy of mindfulness-based stress reduction programme in reducing perceived stress and health complaints in patients with coronary heart disease. *Dysphrenia*, *5*(1), 1–10.

Pargament, K. I. (1997). *The Psychology of Religion and Coping: Theory, Research, Practice*. Guilford Press.

Parswani, M. J., Sharma, M. P., & Iyengar, S. (2013). Mindfulness-based stress reduction program in coronary heart disease: A randomized control trial. *International Journal of Yoga*, *6*(2), 111–117. https://doi.org/10.4103/0973-6131.113405

Priya, G., & Kalra, S. (2018). Mind–Body Interactions and Mindfulness Meditation in Diabetes. *European Endocrinology*, *14*(1), 35.

Proulx, J., & Bergen-Cico, D. (2022). Exploring the Adaptation of Mindfulness Interventions to Address Stress and Health in Native American Communities. In C. M. Fleming, V. Y. Womack, & J. Proulx, *Beyond White Mindfulness* (1st ed., pp. 110–124). Routledge. https://doi.org/10.4324/9781003090922-9

Proulx, J., Croff, R., Oken, B., Aldwin, C. M., Fleming, C., Bergen-Cico, D., Le, T., & Noorani, M. (2018). Considerations for Research and Development of Culturally Relevant Mindfulness Interventions in American Minority Communities. *Mindfulness*, *9*(2), 361–370. https://doi.org/10.1007/s12671-017-0785-z

Pseftogianni, F., Panagioti, M., Birtwell, K., & Angelakis, I. (2023). Mindfulness interventions for obsessive–compulsive and related disorders: A systematic review and meta-analysis of randomized controlled trials. *Clinical Psychology: Science and Practice*, *30*(3), 233–243. https://doi.org/10.1037/cps0000132

Querstret, D., Morison, L., Dickinson, S., Cropley, M., & John, M. (2020). Mindfulness-based stress reduction and mindfulness-based cognitive therapy for psychological health and well-being in non-clinical samples: A systematic review and meta-analysis. *International Journal of Stress Management*, *27*(4), 394–411. https://doi.org/10.1037/str0000165

Riegner, G., Posey, G., Oliva, V., Jung, Y., Mobley, W., & Zeidan, F. (2023). Disentangling self from pain: Mindfulness meditation–induced pain relief is driven by thalamic–default mode network decoupling. *Pain*, *164*(2), 280–291. https://doi.org/10.1097/j.pain.0000000000002731

Riley, K. E., & Kalichman, S. (2015). Mindfulness-based stress reduction for people living with HIV/AIDS: Preliminary review of intervention trial methodologies and findings. *Health Psychology Review*, *9*(2), 224–243. https://doi.org/10.1080/17437199.2014.895928

Schellekens Melanie, P. J., Tamagawa, R., Labelle, L. E., Speca, M., Stephen, J., Drysdale, E., Sample, S., Pickering, B., Dirkse, D., Savage, L. L., & Carlson, L. E. (2017). Mindfulness-Based Cancer Recovery (MBCR) versus Supportive Expressive Group Therapy (SET) for distressed breast cancer survivors: Evaluating mindfulness and social support as mediators. *Journal of Behavioral Medicine*, *40*(3), 414–422. https://doi.org/10.1007/s10865-016-9799-6

Segal, Z. V., Teasdale, J. D., Williams, J. M., & Gemar, M. C. (2002). The mindfulness-based cognitive therapy adherence scale: Inter-rater reliability, adherence to protocol and treatment distinctiveness. *Clinical Psychology & Psychotherapy*, *9*(2), 131–138. https://doi.org/10.1002/cpp.320

Shapiro, S. L., Carlson, L. E., Astin, J. A., & Freedman, B. (2006). Mechanisms of mindfulness. *Journal of Clinical Psychology*, *62*(3), 373–386. https://doi.org/10.1002/jclp.20237

Strauss, C., Thomas, N., & Hayward, M. (2015). Can we respond mindfully to distressing voices? A systematic review of evidence for engagement, acceptability, effectiveness and mechanisms of change for mindfulness-based interventions for people distressed by hearing voices. *Frontiers in Psychology*, *6*. https://doi.org/10.3389/fpsyg.2015.01154

Sullivan, M. J., Wood, L., Terry, J., Brantley, J., Charles, A., McGee, V., Johnson, D., Krucoff, M. W., Rosenberg, B., Bosworth, H. B., Adams, K., & Cuffe, M. S. (2009). The Support, Education, and Research in Chronic Heart Failure Study (SEARCH): A mindfulness-based psychoeducational intervention improves depression and clinical symptoms in patients with chronic heart failure. *American Heart Journal*, *157*(1), 84–90. https://doi.org/10.1016/j.ahj.2008.08.033

Sun, S., Guy, A. A., Zelaya, D. G., & Operario, D. (2022). Mindfulness for Reducing Minority Stress and Promoting Health Among Sexual Minority Men: Uncovering Intervention Principles and Techniques. *Mindfulness*, *13*(10), 2473–2487. https://doi.org/10.1007/s12671-022-01973-w

Svendsen, J. L., Kvernenes, K. V., Wiker, A. S., & Dundas, I. (2017). Mechanisms of mindfulness: Rumination and self-compassion. *Nordic Psychology*, *69*(2), 71–82. https://doi.org/10.1080/19012276.2016.1171730

Tacón, A. M., Caldera, Y. M., & Ronaghan, C. (2004). Mindfulness-Based Stress Reduction in Women With Breast Cancer. *Families, Systems, & Health*, *22*(2), 193–203. APA PsycArticles. https://doi.org/10.1037/1091-7527.22.2.193

Tang, Y.-Y., Hölzel, B. K., & Posner, M. I. (2015). The neuroscience of mindfulness meditation. *Nature Reviews Neuroscience*, *16*(4), 213–225. https://doi.org/10.1038/nrn3916

Taylor, H., Strauss, C., & Cavanagh, K. (2021). Can a little bit of mindfulness do you good? A systematic review and meta-analyses of unguided mindfulness-based self-help interventions. *Clinical Psychology Review*, *89*, 102078. https://doi.org/10.1016/j.cpr.2021.102078

Thompson, R. W., Arnkoff, D. B., & Glass, C. R. (2011). Conceptualizing Mindfulness and Acceptance as Components of Psychological Resilience to Trauma. *Trauma, Violence, & Abuse*, *12*(4), 220–235. https://doi.org/10.1177/1524838011416375

Urrila, L. I. (2022). From personal wellbeing to relationships: A systematic review on the impact of mindfulness interventions and practices on leaders. *Human Resource Management Review*, *32*(3), 100837. https://doi.org/10.1016/j.hrmr.2021.100837

Vago, D., & Silbersweig, D. (2012). Self-awareness, self-regulation, and self-transcendence (S-ART): A framework for understanding the neurobiological mechanisms of mindfulness. *Frontiers in Human Neuroscience*, *6*. https://doi.org/10.3389/fnhum.2012.00296

Veehof, M. M., Oskam, M.-J., Schreurs, K. M. G., & Bohlmeijer, E. T. (2011). Acceptance-based interventions for the treatment of chronic pain: A systematic review and meta-analysis. *Pain*, *152*(3), 533–542. https://doi.org/10.1016/j.pain.2010.11.002

Veehof, M. M., Trompetter, H. R., Bohlmeijer, E. T., & Schreurs, K. M. G. (2016). Acceptance- and mindfulness-based interventions for the treatment of chronic pain: A meta-analytic review. *Cognitive Behaviour Therapy*, *45*(1), 5–31. https://doi.org/10.1080/16506073.2015.1098724

Wachs, K., & Cordova, J. V. (2007). Mindful Relating: Exploring Mindfulness and Emotion Repertoires in Intimate Relationships. *Journal of Marital and Family Therapy*, *33*(4), 464–481. https://doi.org/10.1111/j.1752-0606.2007.00032.x

Waldron, E. M., Hong, S., Moskowitz, J. T., & Burnett-Zeigler, I. (2018). A Systematic Review of the Demographic Characteristics of Participants in US-Based Randomized Controlled Trials of Mindfulness-Based Interventions. *Mindfulness*, *9*(6), 1671–1692. https://doi.org/10.1007/s12671-018-0920-5

Webb, J. R., Toussaint, L., & Dula, C. S. (2014). Ritualistic, Theistic, and Existential Spirituality: Initial Psychometric Qualities of the RiTE Measure of Spirituality. *Journal of Religion and Health*, *53*(4), 972–985. https://doi.org/10.1007/s10943-013-9697-y

Wen, X., Zhang, Q., Wang, S., Liu, X., & Xu, W. (2023). Mindfulness and academic burnout among chinese elementary school students: The mediating role of perceived teacher support. *Teaching and Teacher Education*, *123*, 103991. https://doi.org/10.1016/j.tate.2022.103991

Woods, S. L., & Rockman, P. (2021). *Mindfulness-Based Stress Reduction: Protocol, Practice, and Teaching Skills*. New Harbinger Publications.

Chapter 25

Compassion

Lauren A. Stutts[*]

Spirituality Overview

The landscape of religiousness and spirituality has changed notably in the United States (US) in the last few decades. The Pew Research Center (2022) found that approximately 64% of Americans identify as Christian, 6% identify with other religions, and 30% are not affiliated with a religion. They predict that the percentage of unaffiliated will rise to between 34% and 52% by 2070. Moreover, Smith and Schapiro (2021) found that adults in the US who identified themselves as "more spiritual than religious" rose from 18.5% in 1998 to 33.6% in 2020.

Spirituality is often generally defined as a search for meaning and connection to the universe (Saslow et al., 2013). It is also described as having a strong connection to nature (Naor & Mayseless, 2020). However, Webb et al. (2014) developed a more specific definition by delineating three different types of spirituality: ritualistic, theistic, and existential. Ritualistic spirituality is structured and includes a connection and practices related to a deity or deities. Individuals with ritualistic spirituality are typically involved with an organized religion. Theistic spirituality is non-structured and includes a connection to a deity or deities, though individuals are typically not involved with an organized religion. Lastly, existential spirituality is non-structured and does not include a connection to a deity, deities, or specific religion. Existential spirituality also involves a broader search for meaning. Webb et al. (2014) developed a 30-item survey called the RiTE Measure of Spirituality to assess those three dimensions of spirituality. There are 10 items for each scale: ritualistic (e.g., "I observe or follow the rules of a formal belief system"), theistic (e.g., "I believe in a deity or deities"), and existential (e.g., "I believe that finding meaning and purpose in life is very important"). Participants rate each item on a scale from 1 (*strongly disagree*) to 5 (*strongly agree*). The average score is computed for each dimension, with higher scores indicating stronger spirituality in that dimension. This measure was validated by Webb et al. (2014) and has been effectively used in many studies on spirituality (Dangel & Webb, 2017; Stauber & Stutts, 2021). Please review Chapters 1 and 44 in this book for more detailed information about the RiTE Measure of Spirituality.

This chapter includes studies that utilize a broad definition of spirituality and some that include Webb et al.'s (2014) more specific definition. That said, a lot of research does not define spirituality for the participant but instead allows participants to indicate how spiritual they are based on their own interpretation (Saslow et al., 2013; Smith & Schapiro, 2021). For example, Saslow et al. (2013) asked participants to rate how spiritual they were on a scale from 1 (*not at all*) to 7 (*deeply*). As such, comparing research across studies using different definitions is challenging.

* Corresponding Author: lastutts@davidson.edu.

DOI: 10.4324/9781003440048-29

Compassion Overview

Religion and spirituality inform the concept of compassion, which is divided into two categories in this chapter: compassion for others and self-compassion. Compassion for others is defined as thoughts and feelings of kindness toward others, particularly when others are struggling (Pommier et al., 2020). However, Strauss et al. (2016) consolidated definitions across the literature and found that compassion for others consists of five related components: being able to recognize suffering, acknowledgement of the universality of human suffering, emotion toward the individual who is suffering, being able to tolerate uncomfortable feelings, and having the motivation to reduce suffering.

One way to assess compassion for others is the 16-item Compassion Scale (Pommier et al., 2020). This measure has an overall compassion score and four subscales: kindness (e.g., "If I see someone going through a difficult time, I try to be caring toward that person"), common humanity (e.g., "I realize everyone feels down sometimes, it is part of being human"), mindfulness (e.g., "I pay careful attention when other people talk to me about their troubles"), and indifference (e.g., "I am unconcerned with other people's problems"). Participants indicate how often they behave in the stated manner of those items on a scale from 1 (*almost never*) to 5 (*almost always*). The average score is computed for each subscale, with higher scores indicating higher kindness, common humanity, mindfulness, and indifference. After reverse-scoring the indifference items, the scores are averaged for an overall compassion for others score. This scale was validated by Pommier et al. (2020) and was found to be reliable and valid in an Italian sample (Lucarini et al., 2022).

On the other hand, self-compassion is defined as thoughts and feelings of kindness for oneself, particularly related to one's mistakes and failures (Neff, 2003a). The most common assessment of self-compassion is the validated 26-item Self-Compassion Scale (Neff, 2003b). There is also a short-form version that contains 12 items (Raes et al., 2011) and a state self-compassion scale that assesses current feelings of kindness for oneself (Neff et al., 2021). All three scales have an overall self-compassion score, and the longer version contains six subscales: self-kindness (e.g., "I try to be loving towards myself when I'm feeling emotional pain"), self-judgment (e.g., "I'm disapproving and judgmental about my own flaws and inadequacies"), common humanity (e.g., "When things are going badly for me, I see the difficulties as part of life that everyone goes through"), isolation (e.g., "When I think about my inadequacies, it tends to make me feel more separate and cut off from the rest of the world"), mindfulness (e.g., "When something upsets me I try to keep my emotions in balance"), and over-identification (e.g., "When I'm feeling down I tend to obsess and fixate on everything that's wrong"). Participants rate how often they behave in the stated manner of those items on a scale from 1 (*almost never*) to 5 (*almost always*). The subscales are averaged, and an overall score is averaged after reverse coding, with higher scores indicating higher self-compassion. Self-compassion is indicated by higher levels of self-kindness, common humanity, and mindfulness and lower levels of self-judgment, isolation, and overidentification. This scale has been validated (Neff, 2003b) and has been effectively used in research (Barnard & Curry, 2012; Birnie et al., 2010).

Compassion for others has been found to be positively correlated with self-compassion (Bayır-Toper et al., 2022). Bayır-Toper et al. (2022) further found that authenticity served as a moderator between self-compassion and compassion for others, such that there was a stronger relationship between those two variables for individuals with high authenticity. However, one key distinction between compassion for others and self-compassion is that compassion for others has a central social component – it involves the relationship of oneself toward others, whereas self-compassion does not (Oriol et al., 2022).

The Relationship Between Spirituality and Compassion

Many religions promote compassion for others, and involvement in religion has been associated with more helping behavior toward strangers (Bennett & Einolf, 2017). For example, Krause and Hayward (2015) found a positive correlation between religious commitment and compassion for others. Compassion for others and self-compassion have particular roots in Buddhism (Anālayo, 2022; Neff, 2003a). Compassion for others and for oneself is considered as one compassion concept in Buddhism and is highlighted as having value simultaneously (Quaglia et al., 2021). However, Western approaches typically separate the two or emphasize one over the other in terms of assessments and interventions (Quaglia et al., 2021).

Although religiousness is associated with compassion for others, spirituality also has been shown to be positively related to compassion for others (Saslow et al., 2013). In fact, Saslow et al. (2013) found that spirituality had a stronger relationship to compassion for others than religiosity in a US general population sample. Moreover, they found that individuals who were spiritual were more likely to behave in altruistic ways compared to individuals who were religious. For example, they found that spiritual individuals were more likely to allocate resources to others rather than themselves in a hypothetical scenario.

Minimal research has examined the relationship between religiousness and self-compassion; however, one study found that US clergy who were higher in self-compassion had lower levels of exhaustion (Barnard & Curry, 2012). Moreover, another study found that higher anxiety about one's relationship with God was negatively correlated with self-compassion in a sample of the general population and college students in the US (Homan, 2014). Similar to Saslow et al.'s (2013) finding that spirituality was associated with compassion for others, another study found that spirituality was positively correlated with self-compassion in a Canadian sample (Birnie et al., 2010).

Only a few studies have examined the relationship between spirituality and self-compassion. For example, Stauber and Stutts (2021) found that ritualistic spirituality was correlated with higher self-compassion in a US college student sample. They also found that individuals who spent time in intensive outdoor programs had higher existential spirituality than individuals who did not. Furthermore, Akin and Akin (2017) found that spiritual experiences were correlated with all six self-compassion components (self-kindness, self-judgment, common humanity, isolation, mindfulness, and over-identification) in Turkish university students. However, they found the weakest correlations between spirituality and self-kindness and mindfulness.

Positive Effects of Compassion on Health and Well-Being

Compassion for others confers psychological benefits. For example, Oriol et al. (2022) found that compassion for others predicted higher subjective well-being in a sample of Chileans. They found that this relationship was explained by beneficence, which is the belief of having a positive impact on others. Moreover, Lee et al. (2021) examined the longitudinal effects of compassion for others in a five-year study in the US. They found that compassion for others significantly predicted better physical (e.g., less pain) and psychological well-being (e.g., feeling calm). Similarly, Saarinen et al. (2020) found that higher compassion predicted higher affective well-being (e.g., higher positive affect) in a 15-year longitudinal study in

Finland. Furthermore, they found that higher compassion was significantly related to higher social support and higher cognitive well-being (e.g., higher optimism).

Compassion also has benefits from an evolutionary perspective (Gilbert, 2019). It is theorized to have evolved due to caring responsibilities for offspring. Having caring attitudes, feelings, and behaviors toward others who are suffering allows us to increase survival and promotes human connection. It is also often reciprocal – if an individual helps someone who is suffering, then that person will be more likely to help them when they are suffering.

Similarly, self-compassion has been found to have a relationship with better psychological functioning. For example, a meta-analysis found a strong negative relationship between self-compassion and psychopathology (MacBeth & Gumley, 2012). They found that higher levels of self-compassion were associated with lower levels of depression, anxiety, and stress across a variety of populations. Moreover, Stutts et al. (2018) found that self-compassion moderated the relationship between stress and depression in a US sample of college students. There was a weaker relationship between stress and depression for those with high self-compassion. Similarly, Stutts and Blomquist (2018) found that self-compassion moderated the relationship between weight/shape concerns and disordered eating. There was a weaker relationship between weight/shape concerns and disordered eating for those with high self-compassion. Those two moderation studies suggest that self-compassion serves as a protective factor against negative outcomes.

Self-compassion has also been associated directly with positive outcomes. A meta-analysis found a strong positive relationship between self-compassion and well-being (Zessin et al., 2015). In particular, they found a strong relationship between self-compassion and cognitive well-being (i.e., how one evaluates their life) and psychological well-being (i.e., pursuit of one's optimal functioning). Similar to the results for compassion for others, Lee et al. (2021) found that self-compassion significantly predicted better physical and psychological well-being over a 5-year period in the US.

Negative Effects of Compassion on Health and Well-Being

Although compassion for others has positive relationships with health, it can also have negative effects. One of those effects was coined "compassion fatigue" by Joinson (1992) to describe the negative effects (e.g., anxiety and irritability) of consistent exposure to others' traumas among nurses. However, compassion fatigue is now understood to extend beyond nurses to any individual in a helping profession, such as psychologists, social workers, and other health-care providers (Cavanagh et al., 2020; Newmeyer et al., 2016; Rivera-Kloeppel & Mendenhall, 2023). One way to assess compassion fatigue is the Professional Quality of Life Scale (Stamm, 2009). This scale contains 10 items across three subscales: burnout (e.g., "I think that I might have been affected by the traumatic stress of those I help"), secondary traumatic stress (e.g., "I find it difficult to separate my personal life from my life as a helper"), and compassion satisfaction (e.g., "I get satisfaction from being able to help people"). Individuals rate those items on a scale from 1 (*never*) to 5 (*very often*). The subscale scores are averaged, and higher scores indicate higher levels of burnout, secondary traumatic stress, and compassion satisfaction. Newmeyer et al. (2016) found a strong negative correlation between compassion satisfaction and burnout in trauma therapists in Romania. The researchers also found that religious commitment was positively associated with compassion satisfaction.

In addition to the negative effects of compassion for others, self-compassion has some negative associations. For example, in a qualitative study on self-compassion, Bayır and

Lomas (2016) found that many Turkish individuals view self-compassion as selfish and egocentric, and some viewed self-compassionate people as focusing too much on themselves rather than others. One US study found that the more strongly someone believed self-compassion leads to indulgence and irresponsibility, the less self-compassionately they responded to a stressful event (Chwyl et al., 2021). Moreover, those individuals were less likely to engage in adaptive coping strategies. Another study found that fear of self-compassion was associated with higher depression, anxiety, and stress in a Portuguese sample (Gilbert et al., 2014). Furthermore, individuals in the United Kingdom who had a high level of self-criticism have been found to have a negative physiological response (i.e., greater stress) to compassion-building interventions (Duarte et al., 2015). It was theorized that individuals felt more threatened by those exercises and that thinking positively about themselves was unusual and uncomfortable for them.

Relationships Among Spirituality, Compassion, and Health and Well-Being

Historically, research has focused more on religion's relationship to compassion and health than spirituality. For example, Steffen and Masters (2005) found that having a compassionate attitude served as a significant mediator between intrinsic religiosity and psychological health in a US community and college student sample. This result highlights that it is not necessarily religion that results in better psychological health – having a compassionate attitude is what is important in predicting psychological health, which can happen outside of being religious. Moreover, they found that having a compassionate attitude and reporting compassionate behaviors were negatively associated with depression and stress and were positively associated with social support satisfaction, number of support persons, marital adjustment, and marital commitment.

Homan (2014) examined the relationship among attachment to God, self-compassion, depression, anxiety, and life satisfaction in a US sample. They found that self-compassion was a mediator between the predictors of anxiety about attachment to God and avoidance of God and the outcomes of depression, anxiety, and life satisfaction. This result indicates that not having kindness toward oneself may be a key reason why someone who is anxious about their relationship with God develops depression, for example.

Another study examined religion/spirituality, self-compassion, and health outcomes in Iranian university students and seminary students (Ghorbani et al., 2017). The researchers had individuals select if they were in one of four groups: religious and spiritual, religious but not spiritual, spiritual but not religious, and neither religious nor spiritual. They also included continuous measures of religiosity, spirituality, self-compassion, anxiety, and depression. They found that religiosity and spirituality were negatively correlated with anxiety and depression. Self-compassion was positively correlated with religiosity but not spirituality, and was negatively correlated with anxiety and depression. The majority of seminary students reported being either religious and spiritual or religious only, whereas the majority of university students reported being spiritual only. Participants who identified as religious and spiritual had significantly higher self-compassion, lower anxiety, and lower depression than the other three groups. Therefore, being both religious and spiritual was most beneficial for psychological functioning in Iran among this sample.

Dangel and Webb (2017) examined the relationship among the three dimensions of spirituality from the RiTE Measure of Spirituality (Webb et al., 2014), a variable related to receiving compassion called "affectionate support" (i.e., receiving love and affection from others), and a variable called "psychache" (i.e., psychological distress) in a US college student sample. They found that for each of the three spiritual dimensions, higher affectionate support was associated with lower psychache. Moreover, of the three dimensions, the strongest correlation was between existential spirituality and affectionate support. This research supports the beneficial role of spirituality and affectionate support on psychological functioning.

A subsequent study examined the relationship among the three dimensions of spirituality from the RiTE Measure of Spirituality (Webb et al., 2014), a variable related to self-compassion called "self-forgiveness" (i.e., acceptance of oneself despite a mistake), and suicidal behaviors in a US community sample (Hall et al., 2020). Self-forgiveness was positively correlated with existential spirituality and negatively with suicidal behaviors, and existential spirituality was negatively correlated with suicidal behaviors. In addition, self-forgiveness was found to be a mediator between existential spirituality and suicidal behaviors. In contrast, ritualistic and theistic spirituality were not correlated with self-forgiveness or with suicidal behaviors. These results suggest that existential spirituality may be protective against suicidal behaviors and that increasing self-forgiveness may be a valuable focus for interventions.

Although no previous study to my knowledge has directly examined the three dimensions of spirituality from the RiTE Measure of Spirituality (Webb et al., 2014), compassion for others, self-compassion, and health outcomes, the collective results from Dangel and Webb (2017) and Hall et al. (2020) suggest the particular value of existential spirituality, as it was consistently related to positive outcomes. It appears that the broader focus on meaning and purpose rather than specific rules and rituals from a religion is beneficial for one's health. However, the reasons for these different relationships need to be explored further.

Compassion Interventions

Given the overall benefits of compassion for others and self-compassion, many compassion interventions have been developed. Many of the existing compassion interventions have roots in trainings developed in Buddhism (Makransky, 2012; Quaglia et al., 2021). While Buddhist trainings tend to combine compassion for others and self-compassion, Western interventions tend to emphasize one over the other (Quaglia et al., 2021). Table 25.1 contains a summary of the compassion interventions described in this section.

One popular intervention for compassion for others is called the Compassion Cultivation Training (CCT) program (Goldin & Jazaieri, 2017; Jinpa, 2010). This consists of two-hour weekly group sessions of 20 to 30 individuals for eight to nine weeks. There are six steps to the program divided among those weeks: 1) settling and focusing the mind, 2) practicing loving-kindness and compassion for a loved one, 3) practicing loving-kindness and compassion for oneself, 4) establishing the basis for compassion for others, 5) cultivating compassion for all beings, and 6) practicing active compassion exercises (Goldin & Jazaieri, 2017). After completing the six steps, participants learn how to combine those elements into an integrative compassion practice. The effects of the CCT program have been examined experimentally. For example, a randomized controlled trial assigned adults in the US to either the CCT program or a wait-list control group (Jazaieri et al., 2013). Individuals in the CCT group had increased compassion for others, the ability to receive compassion from others, and self-compassion, whereas the control group did not change on those variables. A similar randomized controlled trial of CCT in the US further examined the effects of CCT on mindfulness, affect, and emotion regulation (Jazaieri et al., 2014). They found that individuals

Table 25.1 Overview of Compassion Interventions

Name of Program	*Main Program Components*	*Current Website about Program*
Compassion Cultivation Training (CCT; Goldin & Jazaieri, 2017; Jinpa, 2010)	1 settling and focusing the mind 2 practicing loving-kindness and compassion for a loved one 3 practicing loving-kindness and compassion for oneself 4 establishing the basis for compassion for others 5 cultivating compassion for all beings 6 practicing active compassion exercises	https://www.compassioninstitute.com/cct/
Compassion Beyond Fatigue (Makransky, 2011)	1 to alleviate burnout and compassion fatigue 2 to become more fully present to others 3 to enhance one's ability to change	Now part of broader SCT program: https://sustainablecompassion.org/
Sustainable Compassion Training (SCT; Condon & Makransky, 2020)	1 field of care 2 becoming more deeply receptive to love and compassion 3 compassionate presence to one's feelings 4 letting be 5 extending love 6 turning our suffering feelings into compassion for others 7 generating a strong will of compassion for action	https://sustainablecompassion.org/
Mindful Self-Compassion (MSC; Neff & Germer, 2013)	1 introduction to self-compassion 2 foundational knowledge about mindfulness 3 application of self-compassion 4 development of a compassionate inner voice 5 importance of living by one's core values 6 coping skills for challenging emotions 7 coping skills for challenging interpersonal relationships 8 how to relate to positive aspects of oneself and life appreciation	https://centerformsc.org/
Loving-Kindness Meditation (LKM; Salzberg, 1995)	1 developing feelings of compassion and love for oneself 2 developing feelings of compassion and love for others 3 developing feelings of compassion and love for the world	An example LKM can be downloaded: https://self-compassion.org/category/exercises/#exercises
Compassion-Focused Therapy (CFT; Gilbert, 2009)	1 psychoeducation about how our brain works and how to reduce shame 2 understanding of how individuals develop coping strategies 3 building compassion strategies cognitively, emotionally, and behaviorally	https://www.mindfulcompassion.com/

in the CCT group had increased mindfulness and happiness and decreased worry and emotional suppression compared to the control group.

In reaction to healthcare providers who experienced compassion fatigue, Makransky (2011) developed a workshop called Compassion Beyond Fatigue, which was built on the foundation of Buddhist practices. This workshop contains three main aims: 1) to alleviate burnout and compassion fatigue, 2) to become more fully present to others, and 3) to enhance one's ability to change. Since the advent of that workshop, it has evolved into a broader program called Sustainable Compassion Training (SCT; Condon & Makransky, 2020). This program adapted practices from Tibetan Buddhism. It includes seven meditations in four categories: receptive mode, deepening mode, inclusive mode, and generating empathy and compassion for action. In the first receptive mode, there are two meditation practices: the field of care, in which individuals reflect on moments of caring connection with others and become more deeply receptive to love and compassion. The deepening mode consists of the next two practices: compassionate presence to one's feelings and letting be, in which individuals focus and accept their current awareness. The inclusive mode occurs next and consists of one practice called extending love, in which individuals learn to relate to others beyond stereotypes and categorization. Lastly, the generating empathy and compassion for action category contains two meditation practices: turning our feelings of suffering into compassion for others and generating a strong will of compassion for action. To my knowledge, there are no published randomized studies that examine the effectiveness of the Compassion Beyond Fatigue program or the SCT program.

In addition to the compassion for other interventions, there are a number of established self-compassion interventions (Stutts, 2022). In fact, a meta-analysis was conducted on 27 randomized controlled trials on self-compassion interventions (Ferrari et al., 2019). They found that self-compassion interventions produced strong effects on reducing disordered eating behaviors and rumination and moderate effects on increasing self-compassion and mindfulness and decreasing depression, anxiety, and self-criticism.

One common self-compassion intervention is called the Mindful Self-Compassion (MSC) program (Neff & Germer, 2013). The MSC program consists of two hours of weekly meetings over eight weeks with a group of 10 to 25 participants (Germer & Neff, 2013). The following topics are covered in the eight sessions: introduction to self-compassion, foundational knowledge about mindfulness, application of self-compassion, development of a compassionate inner voice, importance of living by one's core values, coping skills for challenging emotions, coping skills for challenging interpersonal relationships, and how to relate to positive aspects of oneself and life appreciation. A randomized controlled trial examined the effectiveness of the MSC program in a US sample (Neff & Germer, 2013). Participants were randomized to either the MSC group or a waitlist control group. Participants in the MSC group had increased self-compassion, mindfulness, compassion for others, and life satisfaction and decreased depression, anxiety, stress, and avoidance compared to the control group. Upon follow-up assessments, they found that these benefits lasted for a year in the MSC group.

Another intervention is called a loving-kindness meditation (LKM) (Salzberg, 1995); it is derived from Buddhist traditions (Shonin et al., 2015). LKM focuses on developing loving feelings for oneself, for others, and for the broader world (Salzberg, 1995). LKM vary significantly in terms of length and how they are disseminated (e.g., online and in person, individual and group) (Galante et al., 2014). A meta-analysis of eight LKM studies found that LKM was associated with reductions in negative affect and distress (Shonin et al., 2015). Similarly, another meta-analysis of 24 LKM studies found that LKM had a medium effect on improving positive affect (Zeng et al., 2015).

While many of the interventions discussed previously are mostly group-based, there is an individual or group type of therapy called compassion-focused therapy (CFT) that combines both compassion for others and compassion for oneself (Gilbert, 2009). The therapist receives training on how to interact with patients in a way that is non-judgmental and compassionate, and how to assist their clients in developing compassionate skills toward themselves and others. Gilbert (2014) highlighted the key phases in CFT: psycho-education about how our brain works and how to reduce shame, understanding of how individuals develop coping strategies, and building compassion strategies cognitively, emotionally, and behaviorally. A meta-analysis across 15 studies found that CFT significantly increased self-compassion and self-assurance and decreased self-criticism, fear of self-compassion, anxiety, depression, and disordered eating (Millard et al., 2023). Similarly, another meta-analysis of seven experimental studies and seven observational studies found that CFT significantly decreased participants' level of self-criticism and increased participants' ability to self-soothe (Vidal & Soldevilla, 2023).

Limitations

While the compassion and spirituality literature has valuable findings, there are notable limitations in this field. For example, two review studies highlighted common limitations across the literature: missing theoretical frameworks, inconsistent measurements, designs that were limited or low in quality, high attrition rates, and small sample sizes (Galante et al., 2014; Rivera-Kloeppel & Mendenhall, 2023).

There are a number of participant limitations in studies on compassion. For example, a review article highlighted the lack of studies including children for self-compassion interventions (Ferrari et al., 2019). Another review article found that the majority of participants in self-compassion studies were women (Zessin et al., 2015). Individuals who identified as white were the majority of participants in many studies (Chwyl et al., 2021; Dangel & Webb, 2017; Hall et al., 2020). Due to the homogenous nature of many of the samples, it is difficult to generalize the findings to all people.

Furthermore, many of the surveys implemented in studies are flawed. For example, the existential spirituality subscale is quite general (e.g., items like "I feel that helping others is very important") and lends itself to having a ceiling effect (Stauber & Stutts, 2021). Moreover, many studies don't define "spirituality" and simply ask participants to rate how spiritual they are, which participants could be interpreting differently (Saslow et al., 2013; Smith & Schapiro, 2021). Most studies include self-report measures, which are subject to social desirability bias, particularly for items related to compassion for others. In addition, some individuals may not be aware of their actual level of compassion for others or for themselves.

Another limitation is that it is difficult to assess actual engagement with self-compassion interventions. For example, when listening to a compassion meditation, someone may be fully present while someone else may be distracted, though both complete the meditation. Similarly, it can be difficult to assess the efficacy of interventions across studies because they often have different procedures, lengths of time, and samples (Millard et al., 2023; Vidal & Soldevilla, 2023). Moreover, we do not know the impact of self-compassion interventions years after the interventions or in people's day-to-day lives.

Conclusions

Compassion for others and self-compassion are important factors that are related to spirituality and health. Although there are some negative associations with compassion for others and self-compassion, they are largely qualities that are beneficial to one's health. As such, there are many interventions that have been shown to increase compassion for others and for oneself. However, more research is needed to examine the relationship among spirituality, compassion for others, self-compassion, and health outcomes. The rising number of individuals who are more spiritual than religious suggests that spirituality will continue to become an important variable to examine (Smith & Schapiro, 2021). Future studies should include diverse samples across the lifespan and across cultures. Moreover, research should examine the mechanisms behind the relationship among spirituality, compassion for others, self-compassion, and health outcomes. Creating accessible, simple compassion interventions that are assessed longitudinally would be beneficial. Ultimately, continuing this research is valuable, as it can inform prevention and intervention efforts to improve health and psychological well-being.

References

Akin, A., & Akin, U. (2017). Does self-compassion predict spiritual experiences of Turkish university students? *Journal of Religion and Health*, *56*(1), 109–117. https://doi.org/10.1007/s10943-015-0138-y

Anālayo, B. (2022). Situating mindfulness, part 3: Unmasking Buddhism? *Mindfulness*, *13*(5), 1136–1143. https://doi.org/10.1007/s12671-021-01765-8

Barnard, L. K., & Curry, J. F. (2012). The relationship of clergy burnout to self-compassion and other personality dimensions. *Pastoral Psychology*, *61*(2), 149–163. https://doi.org/10.1007/s11089-011-0377-0

Bayir, A., & Lomas, T. (2016). Difficulties generating self-compassion: An interpretative phenomenological analysis. *The Journal of Happiness & Well-Being*, *4*(1), 15–33.

Bayır-Toper, A., Sellman, E., & Joseph, S. (2022). Being yourself for the 'greater good': An empirical investigation of the moderation effect of authenticity between self-compassion and compassion for others. *Current Psychology: A Journal for Diverse Perspectives on Diverse Psychological Issues*, *41*(7), 4871–4884. https://doi.org/10.1007/s12144-020-00989-6

Bennett, M. R., & Einolf, C. J. (2017). Religion, altruism, and helping strangers: A multilevel analysis of 126 countries. *Journal for the Scientific Study of Religion*, *56*(2), 323–341. https://doi.org/10.1111/jssr.12328

Birnie, K., Speca, M., & Carlson, L. E. (2010). Exploring self-compassion and empathy in the context of mindfulness-based stress reduction (MBSR). *Stress and Health: Journal of the International Society for the Investigation of Stress*, *26*(5), 359–371. https://doi.org/10.1002/smi.1305

Cavanagh, N., Cockett, G., Heinrich, C., Doig, L., Fiest, K., Guichon, J. R., Page, S., Mitchell, I., & Doig, C. J. (2020). Compassion fatigue in healthcare providers: A systematic review and meta-analysis. *Nursing Ethics*, *27*(3), 639–665. https://doi.org/10.1177/0969733019889400

Chwyl, C., Chen, P., & Zaki, J. (2021). Beliefs about self-compassion: Implications for coping and self-improvement. *Personality and Social Psychology Bulletin*, *47*(9), 1327–1342. https://doi.org/10.1177/0146167220965303

Condon, P., & Makransky, J. (2020). Sustainable compassion training: Integrating meditation theory with psychological science. *Frontiers in Psychology*, *11*. https://doi.org/10.3389/fpsyg.2020.02249

Dangel, T., & Webb, J. R. (2017). Spirituality and psychological pain: The mediating role of social support. *Mental Health, Religion & Culture*, *20*(3), 246–259. https://doi.org/10.1080/13674676.2017.1345880

Duarte, J., McEwan, K., Barnes, C., Gilbert, P., & Maratos, F. A. (2015). Do therapeutic imagery practices affect physiological and emotional indicators of threat in high self-critics? *Psychology and Psychotherapy: Theory, Research and Practice*, *88*(3), 270–284. https://doi.org/10.1111/papt.12043

Ferrari, M., Hunt, C., Harrysunker, A., Abbott, M. J., Beath, A. P., & Einstein, D. A. (2019). Self-compassion interventions and psychosocial outcomes: A meta-analysis of RCTs. *Mindfulness*, *10*(8), 1455–1473. https://doi.org/10.1007/s12671-019-01134-6

Galante, J., Galante, I., Bekkers, M.-J., & Gallacher, J. (2014). Effect of kindness-based meditation on health and well-being: A systematic review and meta-analysis. *Journal of Consulting and Clinical Psychology*, *82*(6), 1101–1114. https://doi.org/10.1037/a0037249.supp

Germer, C. K., & Neff, K. D. (2013). Self-compassion in clinical practice. *Journal of Clinical Psychology*, *69*(8), 856–867. https://doi.org/10.1002/jclp.22021

Ghorbani, N., Watson, P. J., Kashanaki, H., & Chen, Z. J. (2017). Diversity and complexity of religion and spirituality in Iran: Relationships with self-compassion and self-forgiveness. *International Journal for the Psychology of Religion*, *27*(4), 157–171. https://doi.org/10.1080/10508619.2017.1340100

Gilbert, P. (2009). Introducing compassion-focused therapy. *Advances in Psychiatric Treatment*, *15*(3), 199–208. https://doi.org/10.1192/apt.bp.107.005264

Gilbert, P. (2014). The origins and nature of compassion focused therapy. *The British Journal of Clinical Psychology*, *53*(1), 6–41. https://doi.org/10.1111/bjc.12043

Gilbert, P. (2019). Explorations into the nature and function of compassion. *Current Opinion in Psychology*, *28*, 108–114. https://doi.org/10.1016/j.copsyc.2018.12.002

Gilbert, P., McEwan, K., Catarino, F., Baião, R., & Palmeira, L. (2014). Fears of happiness and compassion in relationship with depression, alexithymia, and attachment security in a depressed sample. *British Journal of Clinical Psychology*, *53*(2), 228–244. https://doi.org/10.1111/bjc.12037

Goldin, P. R., & Jazaieri, H. (2017). The compassion cultivation training (CCT) program. In E. M. Seppälä, E. Simon-Thomas, S. L. Brown, M. C. Worline, C. D. Cameron, & J. R. Doty (Eds.), *The Oxford handbook of compassion science*. (pp. 237–245). Oxford University Press.

Hall, B. B., Webb, J. R., & Hirsch, J. K. (2020). Spirituality and suicidal behavior: The mediating role of self-forgiveness and psychache. *Psychology of Religion and Spirituality*, *12*(1), 36–44. https://doi.org/10.1037/rel0000182

Homan, K. J. (2014). A mediation model linking attachment to God, self-compassion, and mental health. *Mental Health, Religion & Culture*, *17*(10), 977–989. https://doi.org/10.1080/13674676.2014.984163

Jazaieri, H., Jinpa, G. T., McGonigal, K., Rosenberg, E. L., Finkelstein, J., Simon-Thomas, E., Cullen, M., Doty, J. R., Gross, J. J., & Goldin, P. R. (2013). Enhancing compassion: A randomized controlled trial of a compassion cultivation training program. *Journal of Happiness Studies: An Interdisciplinary Forum on Subjective Well-Being*, *14*(4), 1113–1126. https://doi.org/10.1007/s10902-012-9373-z

Jazaieri, H., McGonigal, K., Jinpa, T., Doty, J. R., Gross, J. J., & Goldin, P. R. (2014). A randomized controlled trial of compassion cultivation training: Effects on mindfulness, affect, and emotion regulation. *Motivation and Emotion*, *38*(1), 23–35. https://doi.org/10.1007/s11031-013-9368-z

Jinpa, T. L. (2010). *Compassion Cultivation Training (CCT): Instruction's manual*. Unpublished.

Joinson, C. (1992). Coping with compassion fatigue. *Nursing*, *22*(4), 116, 118–119, 120.

Krause, N., & Hayward, R. D. (2015). Humility, compassion, and gratitude to God: Assessing the relationships among key religious virtues. *Psychology of Religion and Spirituality*, *7*(3), 192–204. https://doi.org/10.1037/rel0000028

Lee, E. E., Govind, T., Ramsey, M., Wu, T. C., Daly, R., Liu, J., Tu, X. M., Paulus, M. P., Thomas, M. L., & Jeste, D. V. (2021). Compassion toward others and self-compassion predict mental and physical well-being: A 5-year longitudinal study of 1090 community-dwelling adults across the lifespan. *Translational Psychiatry*, *11*(1), 1–9. https://doi.org/10.1038/s41398-021-01491-8

Lucarini, A., Fuochi, G., & Voci, A. (2022). A deep dive into compassion: Italian validation, network analysis, and correlates of recent compassion scales. *European Journal of Psychological Assessment*. https://doi.org/10.1027/1015-5759/a000717

MacBeth, A., & Gumley, A. (2012). Exploring compassion: A meta-analysis of the association between self-compassion and psychopathology. *Clinical Psychology Review*, *32*(6), 545–552. https://doi.org/10.1016/j.cpr.2012.06.003

Makransky, J. (2011). Compassion beyond fatigue: Contemplative training for people who serve others. In J. Simmer-Brown & F. Grace (Eds.), *Meditation and the Classroom: Contemplative Pedagogy for Religious Studies* (pp. 85–94). SUNY Press.

Makransky, J. (2012). Compassion in Buddhist psychology. In C. K. Germer & R. D. Siegel (Eds.), *Wisdom and compassion in psychotherapy: Deepening mindfulness in clinical practice*. (pp. 61–74). The Guilford Press.

Millard, L. A., Wan, M. W., Smith, D. M., & Wittkowski, A. (2023). The effectiveness of compassion focused therapy with clinical populations: A systematic review and meta-analysis. *Journal of Affective Disorders*, *326*, 168–192. https://doi.org/10.1016/j.jad.2023.01.010

Naor, L., & Mayseless, O. (2020). The therapeutic value of experiencing spirituality in nature. *Spirituality in Clinical Practice*, *7*(2), 114–133. https://doi.org/10.1037/scp0000204

Neff, K. D. (2003a). Self-compassion: An alternative conceptualization of a healthy attitude toward oneself. *Self and Identity*, *2*(2), 85–101. https://doi.org/10.1080/15298860309032

Neff, K. D. (2003b). The development and validation of a scale to measure self-compassion. *Self and Identity*, *2*(3), 223–250. https://doi.org/10.1080/15298860309027

Neff, K. D., & Germer, C. K. (2013). A pilot study and randomized controlled trial of the mindful self-compassion program. *Journal of Clinical Psychology*, *69*(1), 28–44. https://doi.org/10.1002/jclp.21923

Neff, K. D., Tóth-Király, I., Knox, M. C., Kuchar, A., & Davidson, O. (2021). The development and validation of the State Self-Compassion Scale (long- and short form). *Mindfulness*, *12*(1), 121–140. https://doi.org/10.1007/s12671-020-01505-4

Newmeyer, M., Keyes, B., Palmer, K., Kent, V., Spong, S., Stephen, F., & Troy, M. (2016). Spirituality and religion as mitigating factors in compassion fatigue among trauma therapists in Romania. *Journal of Psychology and Theology*, *44*(2), 142–151.

Oriol, X., Unanue, J., & Unanue, W. (2022). The longitudinal link between compassion toward others and subjective well-being: The role of beneficence as an underlying psychological process to explain this relationship. *Current Psychology: A Journal for Diverse Perspectives on Diverse Psychological Issues*. https://doi.org/10.1007/s12144-022-03490-4

Pew Research Center. (2022). Modeling the future of religion in America. https://www.pewresearch.org/religion/2022/09/13/modeling-the-future-of-religion-in-america/

Pommier, E., Neff, K. D., & Tóth-Király, I. (2020). The development and validation of the Compassion Scale. *Assessment*, *27*(1), 21–39. https://doi.org/10.1177/1073191119874108

Quaglia, J. T., Soisson, A., & Simmer-Brown, J. (2021). Compassion for self versus other: A critical review of compassion training research. *The Journal of Positive Psychology*, *16*(5), 675–690. https://doi.org/10.1080/17439760.2020.1805502

Raes, F., Pommier, E., Neff, K. D., & Van Gucht, D. (2011). Construction and factorial validation of a short form of the Self-Compassion Scale. *Clinical Psychology & Psychotherapy*, *18*(3), 250–255. https://doi.org/10.1002/cpp.702

Rivera-Kloeppel, B., & Mendenhall, T. (2023). Examining the relationship between self-care and compassion fatigue in mental health professionals: A critical review. *Traumatology*, *29*(2), 163–173. https://doi.org/10.1037/trm0000362.supp

Saarinen, A. I. L., Keltikangas-Järvinen, L., Pulkki-Råback, L., Cloninger, C. R., Elovainio, M., Lehtimäki, T., Raitakari, O., & Hintsanen, M. (2020). The relationship of dispositional compassion with well-being: A study with a 15-year prospective follow-up. *The Journal of Positive Psychology*, *15*(6), 806–820. https://doi.org/10.1080/17439760.2019.1663251

Salzberg, S. (1995). *Loving kindness: The revolutionary art of happiness*. Shambala.

Saslow, L. R., John, O. P., Piff, P. K., Willer, R., Wong, E., Impett, E. A., Kogan, A., Antonenko, O., Clark, K., Feinberg, M., Keltner, D., & Saturn, S. R. (2013). The social significance of spirituality: New perspectives on the compassion–altruism relationship. *Psychology of Religion and Spirituality*, *5*(3), 201–218. https://doi.org/10.1037/a0031870

Shonin, E., Van Gordon, W., Compare, A., Zangeneh, M., & Griffiths, M. D. (2015). Buddhist-derived loving-kindness and compassion meditation for the treatment of psychopathology: A systematic review. *Mindfulness*, *6*(5), 1161–1180. https://doi.org/10.1007/s12671-014-0368-1

Smith, T. W., & Schapiro, B. (2021). Spirituality and religion in the United States, 1998-2020. https://www.norc.org/content/dam/norc-org/pdfs/Spirituality%20and%20Religion%20in%20the%20United%20States,%201998-2020.pdf

Stamm, B. H. (2009). Professional Quality of Life: Compassion Satisfaction and Fatigue Version 5 (ProQOL). https://proqol.org/proqol-measure

Stauber, L. G., & Stutts, L. A. (2021). The relationship among spirituality, self-compassion, and body satisfaction in college students. *Spirituality in Clinical Practice*. https://doi.org/10.1037/scp0000284

Steffen, P. R., & Masters, K. S. (2005). Does compassion mediate the intrinsic religion-health relationship? *Annals of Behavioral Medicine*, *30*(3), 217–224. https://doi.org/10.1207/s15324796abm3003_6

Strauss, C., Lever Taylor, B., Gu, J., Kuyken, W., Baer, R., Jones, F., & Cavanagh, K. (2016). What is compassion and how can we measure it? A review of definitions and measures. *Clinical Psychology Review*, *47*, 15–27. https://doi.org/10.1016/j.cpr.2016.05.004

Stutts, L. A. (2022). Increasing self-compassion: Review of the literature and recommendations. *The Journal of Undergraduate Neuroscience Education*, *20*(2), A115–A119.

Stutts, L. A., & Blomquist, K. K. (2018). The moderating role of self-compassion on weight and shape concerns and eating pathology: A longitudinal study. *International Journal of Eating Disorders*, *51*(8), 879–889. https://doi.org/10.1002/eat.22880

Stutts, L. A., Leary, M. R., Zeveney, A. S., & Hufnagle, A. S. (2018). A longitudinal analysis of the relationship between self-compassion and the psychological effects of perceived stress. *Self and Identity*, *17*(6), 609–626. https://doi.org/10.1080/15298868.2017.1422537

Vidal, J., & Soldevilla, J. M. (2023). Effect of compassion-focused therapy on self-criticism and self-soothing: A meta-analysis. *British Journal of Clinical Psychology*, *62*(1), 70–81. https://doi.org/10.1111/bjc.12394

Webb, J. R., Toussaint, L., & Dula, C. S. (2014). Ritualistic, theistic, and existential spirituality: Initial psychometric qualities of the RiTE measure of spirituality. *Journal of Religion and Health*, *53*(4), 972–985. https://doi.org/10.1007/s10943-013-9697-y

Zeng, X., Chiu, C. P. K., Wang, R., Oei, T. P. S., & Leung, F. Y. K. (2015). The effect of loving-kindness meditation on positive emotions: A meta-analytic review. *Frontiers in Psychology*, *6*. https://doi.org/10.3389/fpsyg.2015.01693

Zessin, U., Dickhäuser, O., & Garbade, S. (2015). The relationship between self-compassion and well-being: A meta-analysis. *Applied Psychology. Health and Well-Being*, *7*(3), 340–364. https://doi.org/10.1111/aphw.12051

Chapter 26

Gratitude and Spirituality

Pathways to Individual and Relational Well-Being

Jenae M. Nelson, Sarah A. Schnitker†, and Jo-Ann C. Tsang*

This handbook covers topics connected to health, well-being, and spirituality. Gratitude sits prominently at this nexus, buoyed by a large catalog of empirical research (Wood et al., 2010). Moreover, gratitude is widely valued across religious and cultural contexts (Emmons & Crumpler, 2000). As such, gratitude is hailed as good medicine for many aspects of life (romantic relationships, Algoe et al., 2010; physical health, Boggiss et al., 2020; spirituality, Krause & Hayward, 2015; workplace, Locklear et al., 2022; subjective well-being, Watkins, 2004). However, chronologically mature psychological phenomena, such as gratitude, are ripe for advancement, criticism, discovery, and innovation (Yadav, 2018). Therefore, in this chapter, we will chronicle the well-known benefits of gratitude pertaining to the themes of this handbook while also endeavoring to uncover the complexities and challenges. In fact, addressing the hidden contours of gratitude may provide the greatest opportunities for innovation.

What Is Gratitude and What Are Its Functions?

Gratitude can be studied and defined on several different levels. On a state level, gratitude is conceptualized as a positive emotional reaction to a valued and intentional positive outcome originating from outside of the self (Emmons & Crumpler, 2000; McCullough et al., 2001; Smith et al., 2017; Tsang, 2006). Gratitude is often other-oriented (Algoe, 2012) and hence can be a social emotion (Ellsworth & Smith, 1988), providing the potential for relationship-related positive effects on well-being. On a trait level, a grateful disposition is a propensity to experience gratitude frequently; individuals with a grateful disposition should have a lower threshold for experiencing gratitude (McCullough et al., 2002). Seminal gratitude theories posit that gratitude evolved to promote reciprocity (Gouldner, 1960) and reinforce relationships (Algoe, 2012). Recent research suggests that gratitude must be relational and accompanied by a desire to repay (i.e., transcendent indebtedness) to produce such outcomes (Nelson, Hardy, & Watkins, 2023). Indeed, gratitude practices that elicit a desire to repay are associated with more empathy and reciprocity than individual gratitude practices (e.g., gratitude lists vs. letters; Nelson, Hardy, et al., 2025; Regan et al., 2023). For these reasons, in this chapter, we include a discussion on indebtedness as an important part of the association between gratitude and well-being.

* Corresponding Author: schnitker.sarah@gmail.com.

† The preparation of this article was supported by grants from the John Templeton Foundation (#61513, 62208) and Templeton World Charity Foundation (#30432). The opinions expressed in this publication are those of the authors and do not necessarily reflect the views of the John Templeton Foundation.

DOI: 10.4324/9781003440048-30

Many theorists have emphasized the social nature of gratitude. Trivers (1971) suggested that gratitude was integral to the process of reciprocal altruism. Later, McCullough and colleagues (McCullough et al., 2001; McCullough et al., 2008) theorized further about the moral and prosocial functions of gratitude. They theorized that gratitude notifies individuals that others have expended costly efforts in order to benefit them (e.g., Heider, 1958), thereby motivating grateful individuals to behave prosocially toward others (DeSteno et al., 2010; Ma et al., 2017; Tsang & Martin, 2019). The expression of gratitude also serves a prosocial function in reinforcing gratitude-eliciting behavior (Simpson et al., 2018). Moreover, the sense of indebtedness that accompanies relational gratitude is a key motivational feature of social exchange (Nelson, Hardy et al., 2023; Nelson, Hardy, & Watkins, 2023).

Algoe's (2012) *find-remind-bind* theory of gratitude focuses more extensively on the social and relational functions of gratitude. Algoe's theory proposed that gratitude enables people to find suitable relationships (including both romantic and friendship relationships), reminds people of the value of existing relationships, and strengthens relational bonds. Evolutionarily, these relational functions of gratitude increase fitness through the accrual of future resources via the cultivation of strong, mutually benefiting relationships (Algoe et al., 2020; Forster et al., 2017; Smith et al., 2017). The relationship-enhancing function of gratitude, along with its associations with spirituality and self-transcendence, provides powerful links between gratitude and psychological as well as physical well-being.

Gratitude as an Aspect of Spirituality and Religion

Gratitude is closely linked to concepts of spirituality and religiousness. In the context of the RiTE model of spirituality (Webb, 2021), researchers often use the term *spirituality* to refer to non-structured searches for meaning, such as theistic spirituality or existential spirituality, whereas they use the term *religiousness* to refer to the search for meaning within the context of a community or institution, such as ritualistic spirituality (Hill et al., 2000). We utilize the terms *spirituality* and *religiousness* in this way in order to provide continuity with previous literature on gratitude and spirituality.

Gratitude and Spirituality

Gratitude is a viable pathway to increased meaning (O'Dea et al., 2024), hope (Witvliet et al., 2019), and self-transcendent aspirations (Oriol et al., 2020). Therefore, gratitude itself can be a form of existential spirituality. Moreover, gratitude can help individuals reappraise situations, transforming cognition and emotion related to adverse life events by cultivating and channeling sacred meaning and purpose (Marple et al., 2024). Helping individuals attend to beneficial outcomes during difficult events may be one way that gratitude buffers against stress and increases well-being (Deichert et al., 2019; Fekete & Deichert, 2022).

Gratitude within Religious Traditions

Religions are conduits and reinforcers of cultural and moral norms such as gratitude (Belzen, 2010). In fact, gratitude is nearly universally valued across world religions (Carlisle & Tsang, 2013; Emmons & Kneezel, 2005). Despite doctrinal conflict, religions seem unified in promoting interpersonal and transcendent gratitude. This may be because gratitude, like religion, is a deeply human endeavor (Nelson, Mangan, et al., 2023). Religions specify what to be grateful for, and rituals are often elaborate expressions of gratitude.

Direct and indirect mentions of gratitude appear in several world religions (Emmons & Crumpler, 2000; Tsang & Martin, 2016). Gratitude is heavily emphasized in Judeo-Christian ritual and doctrine (Emmons & Kneezel, 2005), appearing as a major theme in the Psalms (Emmons & Crumpler, 2000) as well as in Jewish prayers (Schimmel, 2004). Gratitude is a nuanced concept in Islam, which includes concepts related to being grateful for positive outcomes (*shukr*), grateful indebtedness (*imtinaan*), and gratitude in response to hardship (*hamid*; Chalmiers et al., 2023). Gratitude toward other people is strongly linked to gratitude toward Allah (Chalmiers et al., 2023), with many religious rituals being viewed as expressions of gratitude (e.g., fasting during Ramadan; Newman, Balkaya-Ince et al., 2023; Emmons & Crumpler, 2000). In addition, non-Abrahamic faiths also place importance on gratitude. For instance, Hinduism emphasizes the importance of having gratitude for all material and spiritual possessions, includes doctrine related to gratitude toward the self, and expands the notion of gratitude beyond people and toward non-human forms of life (Garg, 2023). Buddhists likewise express gratitude in their practices such as the practice of providing food to the monks as an expression of thanks (Winzer & Gray, 2019).

In short, religious texts across various faiths cultivate and inspire feelings of interpersonal gratitude and gratitude toward transcendent benefactors. Indeed, religious individuals have been found to be higher on trait and state gratitude (Nelson, Mangan, et al., 2023). Research suggests that theists also have the highest levels of transcendent gratitude (Nelson, Mangan, et al., 2023). Other studies link trait gratitude to general religiousness (Emmons & Kneezel, 2005; McCullough et al., 2002), intrinsic religious orientation (Watkins et al., 2003), prayer frequency (Lambert et al., 2009), involvement in religious social groups (Krause & Ellison, 2009) and spirituality (Adler & Fagley, 2005; Emmons & Kneezel, 2005). These links between religiousness/spirituality and gratitude suggest that gratitude has the potential to be a key concept in the association between spirituality and well-being.

Gratitude toward God

Researchers are beginning to investigate how feeling and expressing gratitude to God relates to well-being. Studies reveal that religious/spiritual individuals feel and express gratitude to God for spiritual and religious benefits on a regular basis, along with benefits associated with belongingness needs (Tsang et al., 2023). Interestingly, even non-religious individuals report feeling gratitude toward transcendent entities (Nelson, Mangan, et al., 2023), suggesting that it is a deeply human proclivity to attend to transcendent sources of benefits and feel gratitude toward such entities, whether God, nature, or some other cosmic source. Research demonstrates that having transcendent targets of gratitude may increase well-being beyond the effects of general gratitude (e.g., Rosmarin, Pirutinsky et al., 2011, cf., Aghababaei et al., 2018; Aghababaei & Tabik, 2013) and is associated with self-transcendent emotions (Nelson et al., 2022) and prosocial intentions (Tsang et al., 2023).

Although gratitude to God has a long historical record, research exploring the effects of gratitude to God is a relatively novel area. For example, it is still unclear how gratitude toward God and other transcendent benefactors, such as nature (Tam, 2022) or the universe, affect outcomes such as well-being, self-transcendence, and prosociality. Some have theorized that gratitude toward intangible benefactors may be associated with higher construal levels (Trope & Liberman, 2010; Tsang et al., 2021). Indeed, experiments manipulating construal level (i.e., abstract thinking) found that individuals induced to think with a higher construal level were more likely to mention intangible non-deity benefactors in a gratitude task compared to a control group (Nelson et al., 2022). The intangible non-deity benefactors included agents such as *the universe* and *nature*. However, the manipulation of construal level did not have an effect on whether individuals listed God as a benefactor, suggesting that God may be more tangible to individuals. Interestingly, Tam (2022) found that gratitude toward nature was associated with the anthropomorphism of nature rather than abstract construals.

Pertaining to well-being, transcendent gratitude may simultaneously recruit two mechanisms related to well-being, namely spirituality and gratitude (Nelson, Mangan, et al., 2023). Rosmarin, Pirutinsky et al. (2011) found that gratitude to God accounted for unique variance in predicting well-being beyond general gratitude and religiosity. However, on a daily basis, researchers have found that general gratitude – expressed on a daily basis – predicts most of the variance associated with well-being (Newman, Nezlek et al., 2023). It may be that trait-level gratitude to God is a stronger predictor of well-being in general, but daily fluctuations in gratitude to God are a poor predictor of state-level well-being. Further research is needed to investigate how gratitude to God uniquely leads to long-term associations with well-being.

Contemporary research questions in the psychology of religion pertain to the adaptive qualities of religious belief. The connection between religious belief and physical health is established (e.g., Rosmarin, Wachholtz, et al., 2011), but religious belief such as gratitude to God may also be a cultural adaptation (e.g., Henrich, 2004; Henrich, 2023) that addresses social concerns. For example, the supernatural monitoring hypothesis posits that the belief in an omnipresent deity increases self-monitoring (Gervais & Norenzayan, 2012). Rituals form group cohesion, reduce freeloaders, increase group solidarity, and transmit social morals and norms (e.g., Alcorta & Sosis, 2006; Graham & Haidt, 2010; Norenzayan et al., 2016; Rossano, 2020). More specifically, gratitude and indebtedness to God increase fidelity to God and religious groups, with indebtedness uniquely predicting religious commitment (Nelson, Hardy, & Watkins, 2023), thereby forging enhanced group adherence. Thus, one way that gratitude to God may lead to increases in well-being may be through cultural adaptations that enhance social cooperation and cohesion.

Promoting gratitude to God in addition to interpersonal gratitude may, therefore, be beneficial for individual and group well-being. Religious systems are uniquely positioned to teach grateful reappraisals and promote grateful dispositions, which enhance individual well-being. In turn, religious systems benefit when subscribers feel gratitude and indebtedness to God because it enhances group commitment (Nelson, Hardy, & Watkins, 2023). Religious norms and beliefs produce adaptive responses (e.g., enhanced coordination and prosociality across the religious group), so transcendent gratitude may further promote adaptive responses. From an evolutionary perspective, religious groups that historically engage gratitude may have formed more cooperative, cohesive groups (Smith et al., 2017), enhancing their survival. Whereas interpersonal gratitude promotes social bonds, gratitude toward God may improve adherence to adaptive religious norms and beliefs. In light of the current shifting religious landscape (Pew Research Center, 2019), with many people departing from religious institutions uniquely positioned to transmit adaptive religious beliefs, these themes should be explored.

The Positive Impact of Gratitude on Psychological Well-Being

Perhaps one of the most researched areas in gratitude is the positive association between gratitude and psychological well-being (Wood et al., 2010). Much evidence has accrued linking gratitude on both the trait and state level to various indices of well-being. Correlational studies reveal positive associations between gratitude and such well-being metrics as life satisfaction, subjective well-being, meaning in life, and positive affect, and negative with depressive symptoms (Jans-Beken et al., 2020; Locklear et al., 2022; Wood et al. 2010). For example, in a daily diary study, Newman, Nezlek et al. (2023) found that prayers of thanksgiving, which might be considered a form of state religious gratitude, were more frequent on days when individuals reported higher than average well-being for that day. However, it is difficult to know with correlational studies whether grateful dispositions enhance well-being or whether individuals with higher well-being find it easier to be grateful. Prospective studies provide the opportunity to test whether earlier values of gratitude are related to later values of well-being.

Results of several longitudinal studies support the positive associations between gratitude and well-being (Jans-Beken et al., 2020). Initial levels of gratitude are related to higher later levels of social support and lower later levels of stress and depression (Wood, Maltby, Gillett al., 2008). Zhou and Wu (2016) found that early levels of state gratitude after a natural disaster were associated with later levels of posttraumatic growth. Early levels of trait gratitude have also been associated with later levels of well-being, including higher humility (Kruse et al., 2014) and lower depression (Jans-Beken et al., 2020).

Even though longitudinal studies can provide more evidence in support of a causal association between gratitude and well-being, they still have limitations that prevent making strong causal conclusions. For instance, third variables (e.g., agreeableness, social support) could potentially cause both earlier levels of gratitude and later levels of well-being without there necessarily being a direct causal association between gratitude and well-being. In contrast, well-controlled intervention studies with random assignment and appropriate control groups provide the opportunity to experimentally test the causal association between gratitude and well-being (Wood et al., 2010).

In fact, intervention studies do support a causal association between gratitude and well-being, with some important caveats. Gratitude interventions such as daily gratitude journals, gratitude letters, texting, apps, and thanking people on social media are related to reductions in depression symptoms (Dickens, 2017; Hartanto et al., 2023; Jans-Beken et al., 2020), anxiety symptoms (Cregg & Cheavens, 2021; Hartanto et al., 2023), perceived stress (Hartanto et al., 2023; Locklear et al., 2022) and body dissatisfaction (Geraghty et al., 2010; Wolfe, 2022) as well as increases in happiness, subjective well-being, life satisfaction, optimism, meaning in life, and positive affect (Dickens, 2017; Locklear et al., 2022), especially when compared to a neutral or negative control group (see Nelson, Hardy, et al., 2025, and Wood et al., 2010, for brief descriptions of key gratitude interventions).

Despite these numerous positive outcomes, the effects of gratitude interventions tend to be modest (Cregg & Cheavens, 2021; Davis et al., 2016; Hartanto et al., 2023), and gratitude interventions are not necessarily any more effective than other positive interventions (Dickens, 2017). However, gratitude interventions might elicit greater retention than other effective interventions, such as cognitive restructuring (Geraghty et al., 2010). Although gratitude interventions may not be uniquely related to psychological well-being (Jans-Beken et al., 2020), the low-cost nature of gratitude interventions suggests they can be an important tool alongside other techniques to increase and maintain psychological well-being.

One way that gratitude may affect well-being is by buffering against negative life events or experiences. For example, Datu and Fincham (2022) conducted a longitudinal study assessing the protective effects of gratitude in college students during the COVID-19 pandemic. Gratitude predicted satisfaction of relatedness needs one month later and was inversely associated with later levels of anxiety, stress, and depression. Research shows that gratitude's buffering effects extend to highly vulnerable populations. For example, gratitude attenuated the effects of struggles with meaning on suicide risk in hospitalized patients, demonstrating the protective effects (Schnitker et al., 2021).

Facilitation of adaptive emotion regulation is another reason the emotion of gratitude might be associated with well-being (evinced by increases in positive affect, happiness, joy, and elevation and decreases in negative affect and anger; Jans-Beken et al., 2020; Locklear et al., 2022; Wood et al., 2010). For instance, Boggio et al. (2020) found that four weeks of gratitude writing improved emotion regulation compared to an active control group.

Likewise, the effects of trait gratitude – an individual's average gratefulness response across situations (Fleeson, 2001) – in predicting well-being (see Wood et al., 2010 for a review) are robust or not reducible to other personality factors. Gratitude is associated with Big Five personality traits (e.g., extraversion, neuroticism, and agreeableness), but its associations with well-being outcomes are robust even when controlling for these traits (Wood, 2009). Multiple studies replicate this finding; even after accounting for personality traits in general, a grateful disposition positively predicts hope, positive affect, and happiness (Witvliet, 2019) and is inversely associated with stress responses, depression, and anxiety (Hartanto et al., 2023).

The Positive Impact of Gratitude on Physical Health

In addition to psychological benefits, there is a burgeoning collection of research demonstrating that gratitude can positively impact physical health. The most common areas of research include cardiovascular benefits, inflammation markers, pain perception, and sleep. As of this writing, a search with the terms "gratitude" and "health" in PsycInfo and MEDLINE produced over 350 articles. Early investigations into the association of gratitude and health found that those who wrote gratitude journals self-reported fewer physical symptoms, spent more time exercising, and felt better about their health compared to control groups (Emmons & McCullough, 2003). Emmons and McCullough's findings initiated the large body of literature that now exists demonstrating gratitude's health benefits and the association between gratitude and health.

A recent review found that trait and state gratitude were associated with myriad health benefits ranging from lower levels of endothelial dysfunction, lower inflammation, lower cardiac readmission rates, cardiovascular health, lower levels of HbA1c, lowered heart rate, reduced fatigue, decreased coronary heart disease symptoms, and better mood, sleep, and self-efficacy (Cousin et al., 2021). Out of the studies reviewed, gratitude was most often examined as an intervention for patients with various cardiovascular diseases, and the benefits were varied and impressive. Moreover, evidence from an ecological momentary assessment study suggests that state levels of gratitude are associated with decreased heart rate, blood pressure, and stress, as well as increased sleep quality and exercise over 21 days (Newman et al., 2021). Both trait and state gratitude thus have the potential to affect physiology through enhanced resilience to stress, leading to other potential downstream effects.

A systematic review using the Revised Cochrane risk-of-bias tool, however, found some risk of bias in the literature, suggesting that the link between gratitude and health may not be as robust as initially thought (Boggiss et al., 2020). For example, results across the review were mixed for sleep quality, inflammation markers, and self-reported physical symptoms. The majority of studies examined showed some risk of bias (e.g., lack of randomization, intervention deviations, missing outcome data, measurement bias, selective reporting of results).

These mixed result findings are corroborated by other reviews that have shed some doubt on the persistence and reliability of gratitude interventions on health outcomes (Cregg & Cheavens, 2021; Jans-Beken et al., 2020).

Making Sense of Varying Results of Gratitude on Well-Being

What can explain the mixed results? Many suggest that it is unclear which intervention aspects can be attributed to benefits because there is no standardization of gratitude interventions (Cregg & Cheavens, 2021; Jans-Beken et al., 2020; Wood et al., 2010). For example, few have distinguished between interpersonal gratitude interventions (inclusive of indebtedness, e.g., gratitude letters or gratitude memories) versus interventions that induce more intrapersonal gratitude (e.g., gratitude lists and counting benefits) (Nelson, Hardy, et al., 2025). Intrapersonal gratitude lists may be less connected to gratitude's social and spiritual content, which may reduce the efficacy of the interventions (Nelson, Hardy, et al., 2025). There are many theoretical and practical reasons why social and spiritual content may increase the efficacy of gratitude interventions, not the least being that gratitude evolved to promote cooperation (DeSteno et al., 2010; Smith et al., 2017), transcendence (King et al., 2022; Nelson, Mangan, et al., 2023) and relationships (Algoe, 2012). Moreover, humans are socially motivated and neurologically wired and rewarded for spirituality and attachment (Ferguson et al., 2018, 2022). Spirituality is associated with stress resilience (e.g., Brewer-Smyth et al., 2014)). Additionally, social support has a profound impact on biological markers of stress (e.g., Graff et al., 2019). Thus, we suggest that gratitude practices that predictably and routinely activate spiritual and social content are more likely to tap into motivational circuits and attenuate stress, producing more lasting effects (Nelson, Hardy et al., 2023; Nelson, Hardy, & Watkins, 2023; Nelson, Hardy, et al., 2025).

Nevertheless, gratitude's link with mental and physical health – whether driven by intrapersonal or interpersonal gratitude – is consistent with Fredrickson's (2004) broaden and build theory of positive emotions, which posits that positive emotions broaden people's focus and build resources associated with resilience. Here, we see that gratitude can aid in building resources by strengthening resilience to stress and improving physical health. Yet, gratitude is distinct from other positive emotions inasmuch as it reflects positive social interactions (McCullough et al., 2008) and attends to the needs of attachment and belonging. Thus, we posit that the full benefits of gratitude beyond other positive emotions are only accessed to the extent that gratitude practices build social and spiritual resources. Indeed, others have also argued that gratitude is best understood as inherently relational (Algoe, 2012). Thus, gratitude practices are likely to be most effective when they prompt people to reflect on the social and spiritual nature of gratitude. We will discuss these opportunities for innovation in more detail in the limitations and opportunity section of this chapter.

Mediators of the Relationship between Gratitude and Well-Being

The association between gratitude and physical as well as psychological health and well-being is consistent, if small. What, then, might be the potential mechanisms underlying gratitude's effects on well-being that could be leveraged to improve outcomes? We suggest at least three possible mechanisms, including (1) the individual mechanism of changes in attributions, (2) the social mechanism of enhanced relationships and social connectedness, and (3) indebtedness.

Changing Attributions

Attributions play an important role in eliciting emotions, including gratitude (Weiner, 2014). Wood, Maltby, Stewart, et al. (2008) put forth a social-cognitive model of gratitude, proposing that individuals who are higher in dispositional gratitude tend to appraise outcomes in ways that facilitate higher state gratitude; namely, they appraise benefits as more costly, helpful, and valuable compared to individuals who are lower in dispositional gratitude. Wood, Maltby, Stewart, et al. (2008) found that grateful people were more likely to make these benefit appraisals both after reading vignettes as well as when reporting real-life outcomes and that manipulating these benefit appraisals increased state gratitude. Applying this to well-being, it is possible that individuals with higher grateful disposition, as well as individuals engaging in long-term gratitude interventions, might experience more positive benefit appraisals, and the process of attributing valuable outcomes to benevolent others increases physical and psychological well-being via positive affect and fulfillment of belongingness needs (Wood et al., 2010).

Social Connectedness

In addition to intra-individual mechanisms, gratitude is a social emotion with the potential to affect individuals' relationships and interactions with others. Consistent with Fredrickson's (2004) broaden and build hypothesis of positive emotions and Algoe's (2012) find-remind-bind theory of gratitude, another important way that gratitude might affect well-being is through increased social connectedness, social support, and relationship quality. Gratitude's significant, moderate correlation with prosociality (Locklear et al., 2022; Ma et al., 2017) supports a social mechanism linking gratitude with well-being. Gratitude is associated with prosociality when looking at self-reports (e.g., Yu et al., 2023), peer-reports (e.g., Chang et al., 2012), using scenario methodology (e.g., Tsang, 2021), recall of events (e.g., Mooney et al., 2016), as well as in-lab gratitude inductions with behavioral measures of gratitude (e.g., Tsang & Martin, 2019).

Gratitude facilitates prosociality toward benefactors (Tsang & Martin, 2019), as well as toward third parties ("upstream reciprocity"; DeSteno et al., 2010), and expressions of gratitude can lead witnesses to behave prosocially toward the grateful expressor as well as toward the expressor's benefactor (Algoe et al., 2020). In turn, prosocial behaviors are related to increased well-being, although effect sizes are small (Regan et al., 2022). Some cross-sectional research has found self-reported prosociality mediates the relationship between trait gratitude and well-being (Tian et al., 2015); further research using more rigorous methodology, such as manipulated mediators (Pirlott & MacKinnon, 2016) is needed to more firmly establish the role of prosociality in the relationship between gratitude and well-being.

Likewise, research has linked gratitude with various markers of enhanced relationship quality, such as relationship self-efficacy (Buenconsejo et al., 2023), positive partner perceptions, relationship satisfaction, and relationship investment (McNulty & Dugas, 2019). Gratitude may be particularly strongly associated with well-being in strong relationships. For instance, Algoe and Zhaoyang (2016) randomly assigned couples to a gratitude intervention or a relationship-active control and found that couples in the gratitude condition experienced higher positive affect and ability to adapt to change. Moreover, couples in the gratitude intervention condition who perceived their partners as behaving more responsively reported higher positive affect, relationship satisfaction, ability to adapt to change, and life satisfaction, as well as decreased negative affect, compared to those who perceived their partners as less responsive.

Some research has supported the mediating role of positive interpersonal relationships in the association between gratitude and well-being (Chen et al., 2015; Sun et al., 2014). However, as with prosociality, more rigorous tests of mediation, including manipulating mediators, are needed to more firmly establish relationship quality and social support as mechanisms underlying the link between gratitude and well-being.

Recent research suggests that gratitude-relevant attributions and prosociality may be associated. Ruttan et al. (2024) found that relational attributions for overcoming adversity (e.g., quitting smoking because of support from family members) led individuals to feel more compassionate toward others struggling with similar problems, and this compassion was an important mediator of this effect. Thus, gratitude may be related both to benefit-relevant attributions as well as to prosociality and other relationship-enhancing behaviors, both of which may enhance people's well-being.

Indebtedness: A Hidden Mechanism

In addition to attributions and social connectedness, gratitude may also be linked to well-being through indebtedness. The cognitive attribution of owing a benefactor elicits a feeling of indebtedness, which motivates either an obligation or a desire to repay or pay it forward (Nelson, Hardy, & Watkins, 2023). Notably, indebtedness is considered psychologically distinct from gratitude as construed in the literature (McCullough et al., 2001; Watkins et al., 2006) and is associated with different behavioral, relational, and affective outcomes (Nelson, Hardy et al., 2023; Peng et al., 2018). Indebtedness and gratitude are considered sibling constructs, or constructs that are highly correlated but predict unique variance in outcomes (for a description of sibling constructs, see Lawson & Robins, 2021). Although the majority of researchers acknowledge the two constructs are distinct but related, the nature of their association is an ongoing discussion.

In the past, psychological definitions of indebtedness were confined to "a state of obligation to repay another" (Greenberg, 1980, p. 4 as cited in Watkins et al., 2006, p. 218). This narrow and transactional definition of indebtedness neglects to acknowledge relationships where indebtedness is gladly accepted and one desires to repay (vs. being obligated to), such as with parents and children, and indebtedness to God (Nelson, Hardy, & Watkins, 2023). Extreme versions of this early operationalization of indebtedness positioned gratitude and indebtedness as dichotomous or mutually exclusive constructs (Greenberg & Shapiro, 1971). Studies that operationalize indebtedness in this way typically find that individuals feel an aversion to indebtedness (Greenberg & Shapiro, 1971; Watkins et al., 2006). However, the aversive experience of indebtedness is only one flavor of indebtedness. When indebtedness is construed in agentic terms (i.e., want to repay) versus constrained terms (i.e., have to repay), indebtedness is associated with positive emotions and prosocial behavior (Nelson, Hardy et al., 2023).

Researchers acknowledge that there are social and relational benefits of indebtedness, especially when indebtedness is measured in positive, agentic terms instead of obligated terms (Nelson, Hardy et al., 2023). Individuals frequently choose to remain indebted to others as a means of fostering goodwill and strengthening relationships rather than quickly settling debts and ending the associated dependency. For example, religious exemplars report gladly accepting their indebtedness and dependence on God (Nelson, Hendricks, et al., 2023). In that case, indebtedness, also known as transcendent indebtedness, was positively experienced and associated with several positive relationship outcomes, such as reciprocity and feelings of closeness (Nelson, Hardy et al., 2023; Nelson, Hardy, et al., 2025).

However, some question whether transcendent indebtedness is distinct from gratitude. To address this question, Nelson et al. designed a study with three experimental conditions where individuals were induced to feel (1) gratitude alone, (2) indebtedness alone, and (3) gratitude and indebtedness (Nelson, Hardy et al., 2023). Participants reported significantly different state experiences across the conditions and demonstrated different behaviors. Importantly, in the gratitude and indebtedness condition, participants reported feeling the most transcendent indebtedness, relationship closeness, desire to reciprocate, and exhibited the most prosocial behaviors. Further, indebtedness without gratitude was most likely to be obligatory and was associated with decreases in positive relational outcomes. These findings suggest that gratitude, indebtedness, and the two experienced in tandem all lead to distinct appraisals, affect, and subsequent behaviors (Nelson, Hardy, et al., 2025). Therefore, when it comes to relationship building, the type of indebtedness that an individual cultivates matters (Nelson, Hardy et al., 2023).

Indeed, obligated or transactional indebtedness seems to be associated with negative outcomes, especially in cultures that endorse individualistic values and attitudes (Nelson, Hardy, & Watkins, 2023). These findings coalesce with earlier research suggesting that indebtedness can be aversive (Watkins et al., 2006). However, it is important to remember the synergy that can exist between gratitude and transcendent indebtedness in promoting the maintenance and building of close relationships (Oishi et al., 2019). Many scholars argue that gratitude is not a virtue without a sense of indebtedness (Emmons, 2016; Nelson et al., 2024). Algoe's seminal *find-bind-remind* theory posits that the motivation to repay favors in an appropriate manner is the evolved mechanism of gratitude (2012). Yet, desires to repay a benefactor are motivated more by indebtedness than gratitude (Nelson, Hardy, & Watkins, 2023). This suggests that indebtedness is an important mechanism by which gratitude promotes appropriate reciprocal behavior.

Moreover, research has found that the presence or absence of indebtedness leads to different varieties of gratitude (relational, shallow, transcendent; (Nelson, Hardy et al., 2023). In this way, gratitude may be similar to guilt or love, where the presence or absence of other virtues (e.g., penance, loyalty, patience, fidelity) changes the phenomenological flavor of the virtue.

Further, empirical evidence has found that relational gratitude interventions (e.g., gratitude letters) are more likely to elicit indebtedness than interventions without benefactors (e.g., gratitude lists; Curlee et al., 2023; Nelson, Hardy, et al., 2025; Regan et al., 2023). Moreover, gratitude lists may even suppress indebtedness and empathic responses (compassion, sympathy, and tenderness), whereas gratitude letters are associated with increased indebtedness (Regan et al., 2023) and empathy (Nelson, Hardy, et al., 2025) as well as resourcefulness, generosity, and celebratory emotions (Curlee et al., 2023). These studies provide evidence that relational gratitude interventions may amplify the social and personal benefits of gratitude by activating this positive type of indebtedness.

Transcendent Indebtedness to God

Pioneering research investigating the positive functions of indebtedness involved qualitative interviews exploring the motivations of religious exemplars. Indebtedness to God was found to be highly associated with gratitude to God and motivations to reciprocate via fidelity to God (Nelson, Hendricks, et al., 2023). Moreover, all of the exemplars manifested transcendent indebtedness (i.e., positive affect and desire to repay) rather than transactional indebtedness. This finding has since been replicated (Hodge et al., 2024; Nelson, Hardy et al., 2023; Nelson, Hardy, & Watkins, 2023). Many exemplars in the qualitative study reported that acquiring a sense of indebtedness was part of their spiritual maturation – once they discovered that they could never repay God for all that they had, they came to conclude that God's willingness to remain in an asymmetrical relationship with them was a manifestation of God's love (Nelson, Hendricks, et al., 2023). Subsequent quantitative investigations have demonstrated that transcendent indebtedness to God is positively associated with well-being and spirituality (Nelson, Hardy, & Watkins, 2023), attenuates deconversion (Krok et al., 2024), is associated with breadth and depth of benefit recall (Hodge et al., 2024), and is negatively associated with perfectionism, entitlement, and narcissism (Nelson, Hardy, & Watkins, 2023).

Limitations and Future Directions

Methodological Constraints and Opportunities

Although the research on gratitude is bountiful, there are limitations to the existing literature that need to be considered. First, as with many areas in psychology, nearly all participants are Western and Christian. Although there is reason to believe that gratitude is an innate human emotion, the norms and phenomenology of gratitude vary across cultures and nationalities (Tudge et al., 2018). Therefore, in order to truly understand gratitude across religious contexts and cultures, researchers must expand their population beyond Western, educated, industrialized, rich, and democratic (WEIRD) populations (Henrich et al., 2010). Otherwise, we will not understand the variations of gratitude that exist outside of the norms of convenience samples. Considering the wide variety of religions and cultures, it is imperative to learn from them to complete the human mosaic of gratitude (Nelson et al., 2024).

With much of the foundational work done in this phase of gratitude research, the field is ready for more sophisticated methodologies (Yadav, 2018). Although correlational and cross-sectional research provides a solid base, in order to address more complicated questions, there needs to be more research that allows for inferences about the directionality and causality of effects, such as experimental and longitudinal studies. For example, to assess whether state-level gratitude interventions change trait-level gratitude, longitudinal data and/or ESM burst design must be collected to infer a causal association and observe it over time. Moreover, experimental research can counterbalance the over-reliance on self-report measures, which tend to be problematic due to social desirability bias (Tsang, 2006).

Theoretical and Metaphysical Constraints: Toward a More Relational Well-Being

In recent years, meta-analyses of gratitude interventions have revealed that intervention effects are not long-lasting (Cregg & Cheavens, 2021; Davis et al., 2016; Wood et al., 2010). Addressing the ephemeral nature of gratitude interventions is a pressing concern for those interested in promoting well-being. As previously described, the self-focused structure of many gratitude interventions (e.g., focusing on the benefit to the self rather than the benefactor) may partially explain why many gratitude interventions fail to promote lasting change. Research has found that appreciation of others buffers against the negative psychological and physical responses to stress, but appreciation alone does not have this effect (Deichert et al., 2019).

In addition to continuing research examining ways to make gratitude interventions more relational (e.g., letters vs. lists), we also suggest that focusing on individual well-being may be counterproductive. Therefore, in order to better activate the evolved psychological functions of gratitude (Algoe, 2012), researchers and practitioners should study how to best facilitate transcending self-focus and individual needs (McCullough & Tsang, 2004; Nelson, Mangan, et al., 2023; Smith et al., 2017) moving toward relational well-being focused more on social harmony and relationships (Ng et al., 2017; Tong et al., 2021). Therefore, one relevant area of study might be to examine the motivations underlying gratitude expression and whether these motivations influence the association between gratitude and well-being. For example, would starting a gratitude journal in order to increase one's well-being (presumably an egoistic, individually focused motivation) have similar salubrious effects on well-being compared to experiences of gratitude that are less self-focused (e.g., writing gratitude letters or keeping a gratitude journal to improve relationships)?

Despite gratitude's association with relational well-being in the form of prosociality (Ma et al., 2017) and relationship maintenance behaviors (McNulty & Dugas, 2019), the link between gratitude and relational well-being is not always straightforward. For example, Cazzell et al. (2023) found that having "excessive gratitude" (having a larger discrepancy between levels of gratitude compared to levels of support received from one's relationship partner) was related to negative outcomes such as decreased psychological well-being, decreased sexual satisfaction, and increased aggression. Thus, inappropriate gratitude levels for a given situation or relationship can lead to decreased individual and relational well-being.

Additionally, gratitude's facilitative effect on relationships could lead to negative outcomes in certain circumstances. Zhu et al. (2021) found that gratitude toward a benefactor led to unfair favoritism toward that benefactor after the benefactor acted unfairly toward someone else. Thus, gratitude can lead to violating moral principles in the service of relational goals. Gratitude may also lead to certain negative societal outcomes. Eibach et al. (2015) theorized that norms encouraging gratitude toward sociopolitical systems could lead to justifying unjust systems and cause people to censor oppressed individuals who are dependent on the system.

Similarly, Dixon and Langdridge (2021) suggested that members of disadvantaged groups are expected to respond to help from advantaged group members with gratitude, which preserves the status quo and fosters dependency in disadvantaged groups. Ksenofontov and Becker (2020) demonstrated empirically that individuals induced to express gratitude toward an advantaged group member were less likely to protest that group member's unfair behavior. This suggests that in situations where individuals are disadvantaged, norms and expressions of gratitude can foster the continuation of unjust systems, decreasing well-being at the group and societal level. The relational function of gratitude is, therefore, not uniformly virtuous. More research is needed to delineate the boundary conditions of when gratitude is a virtue (Nelson et al., 2024).

All of these theoretical constraints point to an over-reliance on individualistic approaches in gratitude research and assuming universality of benefits (Nelson, Jeffrey, et al., 2025). Thus, we argue that current definitions, measurements, outcomes, and interventions pertaining to gratitude are too often influenced by an individualistic paradigm (van Zyl et al., 2024). Shifting the focus to the social and communal benefits of gratitude (McCullough et al., 2002) might paradoxically and positively affect individual well-being. Self-transcendence is effective at promoting well-being (Oriol et al., 2020; Schnitker et al., 2019), whereas a self-enhancement focus may detract from this pursuit (Nikitin & Freund, 2021). Indeed, philosophers encourage psychologists to engage in such a shift toward self-transcendent motivations when implementing strategies to increase well-being and character (Marple et al., 2024).

Cultural Constraints: Variations of Gratitude and Indebtedness

As previously mentioned, gratitude research utilizes predominantly WEIRD populations. We will briefly discuss in greater detail some of the reasons why cross-cultural work is needed to better understand gratitude. First, we need to understand how gratitude manifests in majority world populations. Phenomenology and behaviors associated with gratitude are wed to socio-cultural norms; therefore, cultural variation matters (Freitas et al., 2022). However, a fundamental assumption of psychology is that psychological universals exist across cultures (Norenzayan & Heine, 2005). Therefore, many psychologists make the assumption that their findings are generalizable across cultures, a phenomenon called the universality assumption (Kline et al., 2018; Norenzayan & Heine, 2005). Nevertheless, cultural psychologists question this assumption, positing instead that variation is the only universal and that culture shapes psychological constructs (Kline et al., 2018). There is mounting evidence that culture influences and shapes norms surrounding reciprocity, indebtedness, and expressions of gratitude (Tudge et al., 2018), which may change cognitive and behavioral pathways to well-being. Inattention to cultural variation is not isolated to gratitude research but is common across psychology – contributing to the replication crisis (Milfront & Klein, 2018).

Discomfort with indebtedness is an obstacle to developing gratitude (Emmons, 2016; Tudge et al., 2022) and is associated with higher rates of shallow gratitude in the US (Nelson, Hardy et al., 2023). Shallow gratitude is gratitude focused on self-promotion rather than building relationships (Baumeister & Ilko, 1995) and may be inversely related to well-being. The acceptance of indebtedness seems to vary across cultures. For instance, in a global study, Vishkin et al. (2022) found that individuals from South Korea and Turkey reported significantly higher obligated (transactional) indebtedness than the US, India, Israel, and Poland.

Moreover, some cultures intentionally cultivate indebtedness. This can be seen in Naikan therapy, where individuals are prompted to reflect on their indebtedness to others (Fujisaki, 2020). However, the feelings of obligation that can accompany indebtedness seem driven by cultural factors (Naito & Sakata, 2010), so cultural variations surrounding obligatory responses to benefits may have important implications for whether individuals experience positive or negative affect when receiving or recounting favors from others.

Cultural variations associated with autonomy and relatedness help elucidate when obligations relating to gratitude and indebtedness may lead to positive well-being or negative emotionality (Kagitcibasi, 2005). Cultural psychologist Kagitcibasi (2017) explains that though cultures are traditionally categorized by the binary of individualism and collectivism, they would be more accurately classified in terms of autonomy/heteronomy and separateness/relatedness. With this additional dimension, cultures can be categorized as both high on autonomy and relatedness. In other words, separateness and autonomy are distinct categories. This distinction helps explain why researchers found that participants in India, despite belonging to a collectivist culture, reported feeling low levels of obligatory, transactional indebtedness – likely because they place a high value on autonomy (Vishkin et al., 2022). Therefore, Kağıtçıbaşı's cultural model helps researchers understand what variables will likely influence affective responses to gratitude and indebtedness.

For example, research has found that individuals from cultures that value autonomy are more likely to experience an aversion to gratitude and indebtedness (Parker et al., 2017), but researchers are likely conflating heteronomy with relatedness (Kagitcibasi, 2005). Evidence for this conflation is demonstrated by the finding that when obligations are framed as agentically accepted, people view them more positively, especially in individualistic cultures

(Janoff-Bulman & Leggatt, 2002; Nelson, Hardy, et al., 2023). Although the obligation to repay benefactors is associated with negative affect in cultures that value autonomy, such as India and the US, the desire to repay is associated with positive affect (Nelson, Hardy & Watkins, 2023).

Thus, researchers studying the effects of gratitude and indebtedness on well-being should be aware that measurement should reflect these different cross-cultural values. For example, there is evidence that the conceptual distinction between gratitude and indebtedness may be less clear in cultures that value heteronomy and relatedness (e.g., Oishi et al., 2019). In short, gratitude and indebtedness may have different affective responses and associations with well-being depending on the degree to which autonomy and relatedness are valued and captured in measurement.

The few extant cultural comparative studies of gratitude do support the claim that cultural variations exist, but some of that variation can also be attributed to different factors. For example, Oishi et al. (2019) reported that Koreans felt more indebtedness after writing a gratitude letter than Americans. However, Americans felt levels of indebtedness similar to Koreans when expressing gratitude to someone close to them. In this case, relationship closeness was a better predictor of indebtedness than culture alone. Interestingly, gratitude and indebtedness to God are highly correlated, whereas gratitude and indebtedness to humans have a weaker association (Nelson, Hardy & Watkins, 2023; Oishi et al., under review), suggesting that the target of gratitude also changes how much individuals feel indebtedness. Other factors have been found to influence affective responses to gratitude and indebtedness, such as personality level characteristics. For example, low humility (Exline, 2012) and high self-focus (Mathews & Green, 2010) both predict transactional indebtedness. In short, researchers should attend not only to cultural differences but also to individual differences that may lead to within-culture variability.

Other important cultural considerations include the extent to which cultures have an aversion to negative affect and conceptions of well-being. Researchers have found that cultural aversion to negative emotions predicts decreases in self-reports of indebtedness and increases in gratitude (Vishkin et al., 2022). It is likely that this association is partly attributable to how the researchers operationalized obligations (agentic or controlled). Nevertheless, comfort with negative emotions varies across cultures and likely has associations with reports of well-being (Joshanloo & Weijers, 2014). Moreover, even the concept of well-being (e.g., the extent to which individual happiness matters) (Krys et al., 2024) and whether goals are more relational or personal (Jiang & Gore, 2016) are influenced by culture. For these reasons, researchers should attend to cultural and personal variations in norms surrounding negative affect that influence reports of gratitude and indebtedness. In summary, the empirical study of gratitude and well-being needs to include majority world populations (Henrich et al., 2010) and attend to the cultural diversity surrounding norms of reciprocity and affective responses to obligations associated with grateful actions.

Future Research Directions

Although a plethora of studies exist studying the effects of gratitude on well-being (Davis et al., 2016; Jans-Beken et al., 2020; Wood et al., 2010), fewer studies examine the mechanisms that make gratitude interventions more or less successful (Lyubomirsky & Layous, 2013). All the areas of limitations and failings of current gratitude research reveal opportunities ripe for innovation and advancement. For example, we have suggested that including social and spiritual content may be two effective ways of enhancing gratitude interventions. Additionally, we suggest attending to individual and group differences and creating more nuanced and culturally sensitive interventions. Positive psychology generally needs to be more inclusive of majority world populations and be aware of metaphysical assumptions that bias research (Nelson et al., 2024; van Zyl et al., 2024).

Incorporating more diverse perspectives will likely uncover additional moderators of the association between gratitude and well-being. Importantly, gratitude does not increase the well-being of all people in every circumstance. For example, the relationship between dispositional gratitude and positive aspects of well-being is higher in countries with higher levels of individualism and higher in clinical compared to non-clinical samples (Portocarrero et al., 2020). Further research is needed to investigate when and for whom gratitude might increase well-being and health and when other emotions might be better suited to increase well-being, such as moral outrage (Johnston et al., 2013) or indebtedness (Fujisaki, 2020).

Moreover, it is possible that gratitude may need to be counterbalanced with other virtues (Ratchford et al., 2024), such as ambition, in order to be enacted in morally virtuous ways. Gratitude is not a virtue in all circumstances. Particularly in unjust life circumstances such as abuse, gratitude may increase harm and prolong exposure to traumatic events (Wood et al., 2016). Additionally, gratitude's relationship-enhancing function can lead to increased conformity (Ng et al., 2017) and obedience (Tong et al., 2021), which in some cultures are considered virtues, but in other cultures, less so. Gratitude can also lead to bias in favor of a benefactor (Zhu et al., 2021) and the endorsement of unethical pro-organizational behavior (Lu et al., 2021), which upholds the virtue of loyalty but could violate the virtue of fairness (Graham et al., 2009).

Another area of research for the potential "dark side" of gratitude may be related to its socially desirable nature. Because gratitude is valued in many societies, gratitude may become a prescriptive response. This would not be problematic in the case of gratitude in healthy relationships, but societies can often prescribe gratitude as a reaction to difficult life events and injustices. To the extent that individuals may derive meaning from experiencing gratitude in response to negative life events (Chalmiers et al., 2023), this has the potential to increase well-being. However, if individuals instead interpret their ill-being as "not feeling grateful enough" during difficult life circumstances, this might lead to a relationship between gratitude and toxic positivity that might decrease well-being in certain individuals. Future research is needed to define the boundaries of the virtue of gratitude and investigate when gratitude may be more harmful than good.

There are also areas for methodological advancement in the research of gratitude and well-being. Innovative use of ecological momentary assessment (EMA) to examine gratitude in daily life (e.g., Dewall et al., 2012; Jans-Beken et al., 2019; Newman et al., 2021) is a great starting point. This approach can better examine within-person consistency and variability of gratitude across situations. Another innovation that could be applied to gratitude research is an action-based approach to assessment, which has been developed for other virtues (e.g., patience and courage). With patience, researchers have used a goals-based assessment where participants list their goals and then rate their enactment of virtue in relation to their pursuit of each goal (Ratchford et al., 2024; Ratchford & Schnitker, 2024). This methodology takes a unique approach whereby virtues are operationalized as values in action rather than just emotional states or self-schemas. This approach also allows researchers to examine within-person variability across specific actions and domains of life. A modified version of this for gratitude might be the extent to which individuals are motivated by gratitude to act prosocially. For instance, a person may be highly generous but may be motivated by receiving recognition rather than a desire to pay it forward. Grateful motivations may be differentially associated with well-being compared to self-enhancement motivations (Huang & Yang, 2023).

Other understudied moderators that might contribute to variations in gratitude are moral ideals and identity. Although Likert-scale measures can be used to assess identity, we suggest that narrative and textual analysis are often better suited to investigate the associations between gratitude and identity within the self-system. Adding textual analysis to quantitative studies would not be difficult as many gratitude studies already collect text responses from participants in the form of gratitude letters and lists. Especially with the rise of machine learning language analysis with artificial intelligence in recent years, there is much room for innovation that could provide new insights into the connection between gratitude and identity. Moreover, research incorporating machine learning into textual analysis can make discoveries that human coders may neglect (Nelson, Hendricks, et al., 2023).

In summary, much work has been done connecting gratitude to psychological well-being and health, but this work has been done from a relatively limited lens. For this reason, there is still much to learn about gratitude, particularly pertaining to its potential, boundaries, counterparts, and cultural variations. Moreover, as positive psychology more generally expands its metaphysical acumen to include more cultural, relational, and spiritual aspects of gratitude and well-being, interventions and effects will likely become more meaningful for more individuals.

Conclusion

A large body of research demonstrates that practicing gratitude can improve individual well-being. Therefore, gratitude is a highly valued construct in psychology. However, gratitude also has the potential to address social and spiritual needs. Gratitude and indebtedness support and maintain relationships, addressing primal social needs. When it comes to well-being, individual and social needs are not mutually exclusive. Relationships are crucial to individual health and happiness, and relational gratitude has the potential to increase well-being across both contexts. Yet, many gratitude interventions are not designed to address relational health and well-being and may inadvertently be less effective at improving individual well-being.

Additionally, gratitude exercises have the potential to be profound sources of spiritual strength. In view of the RiTE model of spirituality (see Chapters 1 and 44, this volume), gratitude can be a pathway to existential spirituality as it provides an inlet to reappraise difficult circumstances and imbue them with sacred meaning and purpose (Marple et al., 2024). More specifically, gratitude toward a transcendent entity (e.g., nature, God, universe) may combine individual, social, and spiritual mechanisms, leading to increases in existential spirituality and well-being. Although there is some research that questions the contributions of transcendent gratitude above and beyond general gratitude, transcendent gratitude remains highly prevalent, even among the non-religious (Nelson, Mangan, et al., 2023), and therefore a relevant construct that needs to be explored.

Although gratitude has been consistently associated with improved mental, physical, and social well-being, there are circumstances where well-being is not the most adaptive goal. For example, feelings of "ill-being" can motivate individuals and societies toward change when there has been an injustice. Cultural differences, too, will affect whether individuals feel gratitude, indebtedness, or both. Additionally, culture influences whether individual well-being or collective well-being is considered a higher priority and whether other values related to autonomy, heteronomy, relatedness, or separateness are emphasized. These values profoundly shape whether gratitude, indebtedness, or both are appropriate responses. For example, transactional indebtedness seems maladaptive in cultures that value high autonomy, whereas transcendent indebtedness is adaptive and more prevalent. Opposite patterns might exist in other cultures. These remain open research questions, especially as they pertain to well-being.

To this end, we suggest investigating multiple levels of health and well-being (individual, social, cultural, and spiritual) and adopting more nuanced models of gratitude and indebtedness. These nuanced models should acknowledge that not only is well-being complex and culturally construed, but so too is gratitude. We urge researchers to consider ecological contexts that influence appropriate gratitude, spirituality, and social connection – leading to greater health and well-being on individual and communal scales. In essence, we encourage interdisciplinary, culturally sensitive investigations of gratitude that value diverse perspectives – leading to even greater individual and societal health and well-being.

References

Adler, M.G., & Fagley, N.S. (2005). Appreciation: Individual differences in finding value and meaning as a unique predictor of subjective well-being. *Journal of Personality*, *73*, 79–114. https://doi.org/10.1111/j.1467-6494.2004.00305.x

Aghababaei, N., Błachnio, A., & Aminikhoo, M. (2018). The relations of gratitude to religiosity, well-being, and personality. *Mental Health, Religion & Culture*, *21*(4), 408–417. https://doi.org/10.1080/13674676.2018.1504904

Aghababaei, N., & Taghi Tabik, M. (2013). Gratitude and mental health: Differences between religious and general gratitude in a Muslim context: Mental Health, *Religion & Culture: Vol 16*, No 8. https://doi.org/10.1080/13674676.2012.718754

Alcorta, C. S., & Sosis, R. (2006). Why ritual works: A rejection of the by-product hypothesis. *Behavioral and Brain Sciences*, *29*(6), 613–614. https://doi.org/10.1017/S0140525X06009344

Algoe, S. B. (2012). Find, remind, and bind: The functions of gratitude in everyday relationships. *Social and Personality Psychology Compass*, *6*(6), 455–469. https://doi.org/10.1111/j.1751-9004.2012.00439.x

Algoe, S. B., Dwyer, P. C., Younge, A., & Oveis, C. (2020). A new perspective on the social functions of emotions: Gratitude and the witnessing effect. *Journal of Personality and Social Psychology*, *119*(1), 40–74. https://doi.org/10.1037/pspi0000202

Algoe, S. B., Gable, S. L., & Maisel, N. C. (2010). It's the little things: Everyday gratitude as a booster shot for romantic relationships. *Personal Relationships*, *17*(2), 217–233. https://doi.org/10.1111/j.1475-6811.2010.01273.x

Algoe, S. B. & Zhaoyang, R. (2016). Positive psychology in context: Effects of expressing gratitude in ongoing relationships depend on perceptions of enactor responsiveness. *The Journal of Positive Psychology*, *11*(4), 399–415. https://doi.org/10.1080/17439760.2015.1117131

Baumeister, R. F., & Ilko, S. A. (1995). Shallow gratitude: Public and private acknowledgement of external help in accounts of success. *Basic and Applied Social Psychology*, *16*(1–2), 191–209. https://doi.org/10.1080/01973533.1995.9646109

Belzen, J. A. (2010). Psychology of religion: Perspectives from cultural psychology. *Mental Health, Religion & Culture*, *13*(4), 329–347. https://doi.org/10.1080/13674670903415212

Boggio, P. S., Giglio, A. C. A., Nakao, C. K., Wingenbach, T. S. H., Marques, L. M., Koller, S., & Gruber, J. (2020). Writing about gratitude increases emotion-regulation efficacy. *The Journal of Positive Psychology*, *15*(6), 783–794. https://doi.org/10.1080/17439760.2019.1651893

Boggiss, A. L., Consedine, N. S., Brenton-Peters, J. M., Hofman, P. L., & Serlachius, A. S. (2020). A systematic review of gratitude interventions: Effects on physical health and health behaviors. *Journal of Psychosomatic Research*, *135*, 110165. https://doi.org/10.1016/j.jpsychores.2020.110165

Brewer-Smyth, K., & Koenig, H. G. (2014). Could spirituality and religion promote stress resilience in survivors of childhood trauma? *Issues in Mental Health Nursing*, *35*(4), 251–256. https://doi.org/10.3109/01612840.2013.873101

Buenconsejo, J. U., Fincham, F. D., & Datu, J. A. D. (2023). The perks of being grateful to partners: Expressing gratitude in relationships predicts relational self-efficacy and life satisfaction during the COVID-19 pandemic. *Applied Psychology: Health and Well- Being*, *15*(4), 1472–1489. https://doi.org/10.1111/aphw.12447

Carlisle, R. D., & Tsang, J. (2013). The virtues: Gratitude and forgiveness. In K. Pargament, J. J. Exline, & J. W. Jones (Eds.), *APA Handbook of Psychology, Religion, and Spirituality* (pp. 423–437). American Psychological Association.

Cazzell, A., Tsang, J. A., Rivers, A. S., Ratchford, J. L., & Schnitker, S. A. (2023). Find, remind, blind? Support as a context for the adaptive nature of gratitude. *The Journal of Positive Psychology*, *18*(4), 636–648. https://doi.org/10.1080/17439760.2022.2053875

Chalmiers, M. A., Istemi, F., & Simsek, S. (2023). Gratitude to God and its psychological benefits in Islamic contexts: A systematic review of the literature. *Mental Health, Religion & Culture*, *26*(5), 405–417. https://doi.org/10.1080/13674676.2022.2046714

Chang, Y. P., Lin, Y. C., & Chen, L. H. (2012). Pay it forward: Gratitude in social networks. *Journal of Happiness Studies*, *13*, 761–781. https://doi.org/10.1007/s10902-011-9289-z

Chen, L. H., Kee, Y. H., & Chen, M.-Y. (2015). Why grateful adolescent athletes are more satisfied with their life: The mediating role of perceived team cohesion. *Social Indicators Research*, *124*, 463–476.

Cousin, L., Redwine, L., Bricker, C., Kip, K., & Buck, H. (2021). Effect of gratitude on cardiovascular health outcomes: A state-of-the-science review. *The Journal of Positive Psychology*, *16*(3), 348–355. https://doi.org/10.1080/17439760.2020.1716054

Cregg, D. R., & Cheavens, J. S. (2021). Gratitude interventions: Effective self-help? A meta-analysis of the impact on symptoms of depression and anxiety. *Journal of Happiness Studies*, *22*(1), 413–445. https://doi.org/10.1007/s10902-020-00236-6

Curlee, M. S., McIntosh, E., & Ahrens, A. H. (2023). What is gratitude without a benefactor? A daily diary approach. *Cognition and Emotion*, *37*(3), 384–396. https://doi.org/10.1080/02699931.2022.2162005

Datu, J. A. D., & Fincham, F. D. (2022). Gratitude, relatedness needs satisfaction, and negative psychological outcomes during the COVID-19 pandemic: A short-term longitudinal study. *Journal of Clinical Psychology*, *78*(12), 2525–2537. https://doi.org/10.1002/jclp.23364

Davis, D. E., Choe, E., Meyers, J., Wade, N., Varjas, K., Gifford, A., Quinn, A., Hook, J. N., Van Tongeren, D. R., Griffin, B. J., & Worthington, E. L., Jr. (2016). Thankful for the little things: A meta-analysis of gratitude interventions. *Journal of Counseling Psychology*, *63*(1), 20–31. https://doi.org/10.1037/cou0000107

Deichert, N. T., Prairie Chicken, M., & Hodgman, L. (2019). Appreciation of Others Buffers the Associations of Stressful Life Events with Depressive and Physical Symptoms. *Journal of Happiness Studies*, *20*(4), 1071–1088. https://doi.org/10.1007/s10902-018-9988-9

DeSteno, D., Bartlett, M. Y., Baumann, J., Williams, L. A., Wickens, L. (2010). Gratitude as moral sentiment: Emotion-guided cooperation in economic exchange. *Emotion*, *10*(2), 289–293. https://doi.org/10.1037/a0017883

Dewall, C. N., Lambert, N. M., Pond Jr, R. S., Kashdan, T. B., & Fincham, F. D. (2012). A grateful heart is a nonviolent heart: Cross-sectional, experience sampling, longitudinal, and experimental evidence. *Social Psychological and Personality Science*, *3*(2), 232–240. https://doi.org/10.1177/1948550611416675

Dickens, L. R. (2017). Using gratitude to promote positive change: A series of meta-analyses investigating the effectiveness of gratitude interventions. *Basic and Applied Social Psychology*, *39*(4), 193–208. https://doi.org/10.1080/01973533.2017.1323638

Dixon, J., & Langdridge, D. (2021). Beyond prejudice as antipathy. In C. Tileagă, M. Augoustinos, & K. Durrheim (Eds.), *The Routledge International Handbook of Discrimination, Prejudice and Stereotyping* (pp. 213–230). Taylor and Francis.

Eibach, R. P., Wilmot, M. O., & Libby, L. K. (2015). The system-justifying function of gratitude norms. *Social and Personality Psychology Compass*, *9*(7), 348–358. https://doi.org/10.1111/spc3.12184

Ellsworth, P.C., & Smith, C.A. (1988). Shades of joy: Patterns of appraisal differentiating pleasant emotions. *Cognition & Emotion*, 2, 301–331. https://doi.org/10.1080/02699938808412702

Emmons, B., & McCullough, M. E. (2003). Counting blessings versus burdens: An experimental investigation of gratitude and subjective well-being in daily life. *Journal of Personality and Social Psychology*, *84*(2), 377–389. http://doi.org/10.1037/0022-3514.84.2.377

Emmons, R. A. (2016). Is gratitude the queen of virtues and ingratitude king of the vices? In D. Carr (Ed.), *Perspectives on Gratitude: An interdisciplinary approach*. Routledge.

Emmons, R.A., & Crumpler, C.A. (2000). Gratitude as a human strength: Appraising the evidence. *Journal of Social and Clinical Psychology*, *19*, 56–69. https://doi.org/10.1521/jscp.2000.19.1.56

Emmons, R.A., & Kneezel, T.T. (2005). Giving thanks: Spiritual and religious correlates of gratitude. *Journal of Psychology and Christianity*, *24*, 140–148

Exline, J. J. (2012). Humility and the Ability to Receive from Others. *Journal of Psychology & Christianity*, *31*(1), 40–50.

Fekete, E. M., & Deichert, N. T. (2022). A Brief Gratitude Writing Intervention Decreased Stress and Negative Affect During the COVID-19 Pandemic. *Journal of Happiness Studies*. https://doi.org/10.1007/s10902-022-00505-6

Ferguson, M. A., Nielsen, J. A., King, J. B., Dai, L., Giangrasso, D. M., Holman, R., … Anderson, J. S. (2018). Reward, salience, and attentional networks are activated by religious experience in devout Mormons. *Social Neuroscience*, *13*(1), 104–116. https://doi.org/10.1080/17470919.2016.1257437

Ferguson, M. A., Schaper, F. L., Cohen, A., Siddiqi, S., Merrill, S. M., Nielsen, J. A., … Fox, M. D. (2022). A neural circuit for spirituality and religiosity derived from patients with brain lesions. *Biological Psychiatry*, *91*(4), 380–388. https://doi.org/10.1016/j.biopsych.2021.06.016

Fleeson, W. (2001). Toward a structure- and process-integrated view of personality: Traits as density distributions of states. *Journal of Personality and Social Psychology*, *80*, 1011–1027. https://doi.org/10.1037/0022-3514.80.6.1011

Forster, D. E., Pedersen, E. J., Smith, A., McCullough, M. E., & Lieberman, D. (2017). Benefit valuation predicts gratitude. *Evolution and Human Behavior*, *38*(1), 18–26. https://doi.org/10.1016/j.evolhumbehav.2016.06.003

Fredrickson, B. L. (2004). Gratitude, Like Other Positive Emotions, Broadens and Builds. In R. A. Emmons & M. E. McCullough (Eds.), *The psychology of gratitude*. (2004-00298-008; pp. 145–166). Oxford University Press. https://doi.org/10.1093/acprof:oso/9780195150100.003.0008

Freitas, L. B. L., Palhares, F., Cao, H., Liang, Y., Zhou, N., Mokrova, I. L., Lee, S., Payir, A., Kiang, L., Mendonça, S. E., Merçon-Vargas, E. A., O'Brien, L., & Tudge, J. R. H. (2022). How weird is the development of children's gratitude in the United States? Cross-cultural comparisons. *Developmental Psychology*, *58*(9), 1767–1782. https://doi.org/10.1037/dev0001383

Fujisaki, C. (2020). A study evaluating mindfulness and naikan-based therapy: AEON-HO for attachment style, self-actualization, and depression. *Psychological Reports*, 123(2), 239–251. https://doi.org/10.1177/0033294118811106

Garg, N. (2023). Development and validation of Hindu Gratitude Scale (HGS-15): A *rnas* perspective. *Journal of Religion and Health 62*, 3622–3639.

Geraghty, A. W. A., Wood, A. M., & Hyland, M. E. (2010). Attrition from self-directed interventions: Investigating the relationship between psychological predictors, intervention content and dropout from a body dissatisfaction intervention. *Social Science and Medicine*, *71* (1), 30–37.

Gervais, W. M., & Norenzayan, A. (2012). Like a camera in the sky? Thinking about God increases public self-awareness and socially desirable responding. *Journal of Experimental Social Psychology*, *48*(1), 298–302.

Gouldner, A. W. (1960). The Norm of Reciprocity: A Preliminary Statement. *American Sociological Review*, *25*(2), 161–178. https://doi.org/10.2307/2092623

Graff, T. C., Luke, S. G., & Birmingham, W. C. (2019). Supportive hand-holding attenuates pupillary responses to stress in adult couples. *PLoS One*, *14*(2), e0212703. https://doi.org/10.1371/journal.pone.0212703

Graham, J., & Haidt, J. (2010). Beyond Beliefs: Religions Bind Individuals Into Moral Communities. *Personality and Social Psychology Review (PSPR)*, *14*(1), 140–150.

Graham, J., Haidt, J., & Nosek, B. A. (2009). Liberals and conservatives rely on different sets of moral foundations. *Journal of Personality and Social Psychology*, *96*(5), 1029–1046.

Greenberg, M. S. (1980). A theory of indebtedness. In K. J. Gergen, M. S. Greenberg, & R. H. Willis. (Eds.), *Social exchange: Advances in theory and research* (pp. 3–26). Springer US.

Greenberg, M. S., & Shapiro, S. P. (1971). Indebtedness: An adverse aspect of asking for and receiving help. *Sociometry*, *34*(2), 290–301. https://doi.org/10.2307/2786418

Hartanto, A., Kaur, M., Kasturiratna, K. T. A. S., Quek, F. Y. X., & Majeed, N. M. (2023) A critical examination of the effectiveness of gratitude intervention on well-being outcomes: a within-person experimental daily diary approach, *The Journal of Positive Psychology*, *18*(6), 942–957. https://doi.org/10.1080/17439760.2022.2154704

Heider, F. (1958/1982). *The Psychology of Interpersonal Relations*. Psychology Press. https://doi.org/10.4324/9780203781159

Henrich, J. (2004). Cultural group selection, coevolutionary processes and large-scale cooperation. *Journal of Economic Behavior & Organization*, *53*(1), 3–35. https://doi.org/10.1016/S0167-2681(03)00094-5

Henrich, J. (2023). How Culture Made Us Uniquely Human. *Zygon*, *58*(2), 405–424. https://doi.org/10.1111/zygo.12894

Henrich, J., Heine, S. J., & Norenzayan, A. (2010). The weirdest people in the world. *Behavioral and Brain Sciences*, *33*, 61–83. https://doi.org/10.1017/S0140525X0999152X

Hill, P. C., Pargament, K. I., Hood, Jr., R. W., McCullough, M. E., Swyers, J. P., et al. (2000). Conceptualizing religion and spirituality: Points of commonality, points of departure. *Journal for the Theory of Social Behavior*, *30*, 51–77.

Hodge, A. S., Ellis, H. M., Zuniga, S., Zhang, H., Davis, C. W., McLaughlin, A. T., ... & Van Tongeren, D. R. (2024). Linguistic and thematic differences in written letters of gratitude to God and gratitude toward others. *The Journal of Positive Psychology*, *19*(1), 83–94. https://doi.org/10.1080/17439760.2023.2265330

Huang, M., & Yang, F. (2023). Self-transcendence or self-enhancement: People's perceptions of meaning and happiness in relation to the self. *Journal of Experimental Psychology: General*, *152*(2), 590–610. https://doi.org/10.1037/xge0001297

Janoff-Bulman, R., & Leggatt, H. K. (2002). Culture and social obligation: When "shoulds" are perceived as "wants". *Journal of Research in Personality*, 36(3), 260–270. https://doi.org/10.1006/jrpe.2001.2345

Jans-Beken, L., Jacobs, N., Janssens, M., Peeters, S., Reijnders, J., Lechner, L., & Lataster, J. (2019). Reciprocal relationships between state gratitude and high-and low-arousal positive affects in daily life: A time-lagged ecological assessment study. *The Journal of Positive Psychology*, *14*(4), 512–527. https://doi.org/10.1080/17439760.2018.1497684

Jans-Beken, L., Jacobs, N., Janssens, M., Peeters, S., Reijnders, J., Lechner, L., & Lataster, J. (2020). Gratitude and health: An updated review. *The Journal of Positive Psychology*, *15*(6), 743–782. https://doi.org/10.1080/17439760.2019.1651888

Jiang, T., & Gore, J. S. (2016). The relationship between autonomous motivation and goal pursuit: A cross-cultural perspective. *Asian Journal of Social Psychology*, *19*(2), 101–111. https://doi.org/10.1111/ajsp.12115

Johnston, M. E., Sherman, A., & Grusec, J. E. (2013). Predicting moral outrage and religiosity with an implicit measure of moral identity. *Journal of Research in Personality*, *47*(3), 209–217. https://doi.org/10.1016/j.jrp.2013.01.006

Joshanloo, M., & Weijers, D. (2014). Does thinking about the meaning of life make you happy in a religious and globalised world? A 75-nation study. *Journal of Psychology in Africa*, *24*(1), 73–81. https://doi.org/10.1080/14330237.2014.904093

Kagitcibasi, C. (2005). Autonomy and Relatedness in Cultural Context: Implications for Self and Familykag. https://doi.org/10.1177/0022022105275959

Kagitcibasi, C. (2017). *Family, Self, and Human Development Across Cultures: Theory and Applications*. Routledge. https://doi.org/10.4324/9781315205281

King, P. E., Baer, R. A., Noe, S. A., Trudeau, S., Mangan, S. A., & Constable, S. R. (2022). Shades of gratitude: Exploring varieties of transcendent beliefs and experience. *Religions*, *13*(11), 1091. https://doi.org/10.3390/rel13111091

Kline, M. A., Shamsudheen, R., & Broesch, T. (2018). Variation is the universal: Making cultural evolution work in developmental psychology. *Philosophical Transactions of the Royal Society B: Biological Sciences*, *373*(1743), 20170059. https://doi.org/10.1098/rstb.2017.0059

Krause, N., & Ellison, C.G. (2009). Social environment of the church and feelings of gratitude toward God. *Psychology of Religion and Spirituality*, *1*, 191–205. https://doi.org/10.1037/a0016729

Krause, N., & Hayward, R. D. (2015). Humility, compassion, and gratitude to God: Assessing the relationships among key religious virtues. *Psychology of Religion and Spirituality*, *7*(3), 192–204. psyh. https://doi.org/10.1037/rel0000028

Krok, D., Falewicz, A., & Szcześniak, M. (2024). Do Catholic religious practices attenuate the deconversion of emerging adults in Poland? The mediating role of transcendent indebtedness. *Religions*, *15*(1), 85. https://doi.org/10.3390/rel15010085

Kruse, E., Chancellor, J., Ruberton, P. M., & Lyubomirsky, S. (2014). An upward spiral between gratitude and humility. *Social Psychological and Personality Science*, *5*(7), 805–814. https://doi.org/10.1177/1948550614534700

Krys, K., Kostoula, O., van Tilburg, W. A. P., Mosca, O., Lee, J. H., Maricchiolo, F., Kosiarczyk, A., Kocimska-Bortnowska, A., Torres, C., Hitokoto, H., Liew, K., Bond, M. H., Lun, V. M.-C., Vignoles, V. L., Zelenski, J. M., Haas, B. W., Park, J., Vauclair, C.-M., Kwiatkowska, A., … Uchida, Y. (2024). Happiness Maximization Is a WEIRD Way of Living. *Perspectives on Psychological Science*, 17456916231208367. https://doi.org/10.1177/17456916231208367

Ksenofontov, I., & Becker, J. C. (2020). The harmful side of thanks: Thankful responses to high-power group help undermine low-power groups' protest. *Personality and Social Psychology Bulletin*, *46*(5), 794–807. https://doi.org/10.1177/0146167219879125

Lambert, N.M., Fincham, F.D., Braithwaite, S.R., Graham, S.M., & Beach, S.R.H. (2009). Can prayer increase gratitude? *Psychology of Religion and Spirituality*, *1*, 139–149. https://doi.org/10.1037/a0016731

Lawson, K. M., & Robins, R. W. (2021). Sibling constructs: What are they, why do they matter, and how should you handle them? *Personality and Social Psychology Review*, *25*(4), 344–366. https://doi.org/10.1177/10888683211047101

Locklear, L. R., Sharon Sheridan, & Kong, D. T. (2022). Appreciating social science research on gratitude: An integrative review for organizational scholarship on gratitude in the workplace. *Journal of Organizational Behavior*. https://doi.org/10.1002/job.2624

Lu, L., Yuchu, H., & Jia, L. (2021). Leader forgiveness and employee's unethical pro-organizational behavior: The roles of gratitude and moral identity. *Frontiers in Psychology*, *12*, ArtID: 698802. https://doi.org/10.3389/fpsyg.2021.698802

Lyubomirsky, S. & Layous, K. (2013). How do simple positive activities increase well-being? *Current Directions in Psychological Science*, *22*(1), 57–62.

Ma, L. K., Tunney, R. J., & Ferguson, E. (2017). Does gratitude enhance prosociality?: A meta-analytic review. *Psychological Bulletin*, *143*(6), 601–635. https://doi.org/10.1037/bul0000103

Marple, C. A., Jeffrey, A., & Schnitker, S. A. (2024). Reappraisal as a means to self-transcendence: Aquinas's model of emotion regulation informs the extended process model. *Philosophical Psychology*. https://doi.org/10.1080/09515089.2024.2307991

Mathews, M. A., & Green, J. D. (2010). Looking at me, appreciating you: Self-focused attention distinguishes between gratitude and indebtedness. *Cognition & Emotion*, *24*(4), 710–718. https://doi.org/10.1080/02699930802650796

McCullough, M.E., Emmons, R.A., & Tsang, J.-A. (2002). The grateful disposition: A conceptual and empirical topography. *Journal of Personality and Social Psychology*, *82*, 112–127. https://doi.org/10.1037/0022-3514.82.1.112

McCullough, M. E., Kilpatrick, S. D., Emmons, R. A., & Larson, D. B. (2001). Is gratitude a moral affect? *Psychological Bulletin*, *127*(2), 249–266. https://doi.org/10.1037/0033-2909.127.2.249

McCullough, M. E., Kimeldorf, M. B., & Cohen, A. D. (2008). An Adaptation for Altruism: The Social Causes, Social Effects, and Social Evolution of Gratitude. *Current Directions in Psychological Science*, *17*(4), 281–285. https://doi.org/10.1111/j.1467-8721.2008.00590.x

McCullough, M. E., & Tsang, J.-A. (2004). Parent of the Virtues? The Prosocial Contours of Gratitude. In R. A. Emmons & M. E. McCullough (Eds.), *The psychology of gratitude*. (2004-00298-007; pp. 123–141). Oxford University Press. https://doi.org/10.1093/acprof:oso/9780195150100.003.0007

McNulty, J. K., & Dugas, A. (2019). Attributions, forgiveness, and gratitude as relationship maintenance processes. In B. G. Ogolsky & J. K. Monk, (Eds.). *Relationship maintenance: Theory, process, and context*. Cambridge University Press.

Milfront, T., & Klein, R. (2018). Replication and Reproducibility in Cross-Cultural Psychology. https://journals.sagepub.com/doi/full/10.1177/0022022117744892?casa_token=vkS-wWqYrRoAAAAA%3AtLYiEsxoOrTPwN1T170D1-R8MsqXVmJ5NsFAnGi2AeqEwsFOnztJkjVn9k9xOfMdGipmwmQGzxkG

Mooney, L., Strelan, P., & McKee, I. (2016). How forgiveness promotes offender pro-relational intentions: The mediating role of offender gratitude. *British Journal of Social Psychology*, *55*(1), 44–64.

Naito, T., & Sakata, Y. (2010). Gratitude, indebtedness, and regret on receiving a friend's favor in Japan. *Psychologia: An International Journal of Psychological Sciences*, 53(3), 179–194. https://doi.org/10.2117/psysoc.2010.179

Nelson, J., Hardy, S., Amelang, R., Ratchford, J., Tice, D., & Schnitker, S. (2025). More than grateful: Interpersonal gratitude cultivates empathy and transcendent indebtedness, leading to prosocial behavior. *OSF*. https://doi.org/10.31234/osf.io/8brpk_v1

Nelson, J. M., Hardy, S. A., Tice, D., & Schnitker, S. A. (2023). Returning thanks to God and others: Prosocial consequences of transcendent indebtedness. *The Journal of Positive Psychology*, *19*(1), 121–135. https://doi.org/10.1080/17439760.2023.2190926

Nelson, J. M., Hardy, S. A., & Watkins, P. (2023). Transcendent indebtedness to God: A new construct in the psychology of religion and spirituality. *Psychology of Religion and Spirituality*, *15*(1), 105–117. https://doi.org/10.1037/rel0000458

Nelson, J. M., Hendricks, J. J., Cazier, J. C., Hardy, S. A., & Wingate, D. (2023). Religious exemplars' experience of indebtedness to God: Employing innovative machine learning to explore a novel construct. *The Journal of Positive Psychology*, *19*(1), 136–148. https://doi.org/10.1080/17439760.2023.2190925

Nelson, J. M., Jeffrey, A., Ferguson, M. A., & Schnitker, S. A. (2025). Learning from Anishinaabe principles of relationality, process, and reciprocity to expand the reach of positive psychology and address loneliness. *International Journal of Applied Positive Psychology*, *10*(1), 26. https://doi.org/10.1007/s41042-024-00212-y

Nelson, J. M., Mangan, S. A., Baer, R. A., Ramdass, J., & King, P. E. (2023). How diverse beliefs shape the experience of transcendent gratitude. *The Journal of Positive Psychology*, *19*(1), 11–24. https://doi.org/10.1080/17439760.2023.2239785

Nelson, J. M., Schnitker, S. A., Williams, E., & Tsang, J.-A. (2022). Intangible benefactors and the contribution of construal level and attitude accessibility in predicting gratitude and expansive emotions. *Religions*, *13*(9), 9. https://doi.org/10.3390/rel13090866

Nelson, J. M., Tsang, J.-A., & Schnitker, S. A. (2024). Gratitude: From relational emotion to contextualized virtue inclusive of indebtedness. In R. M. Lerner (Ed.), *Oxford handbook of character*. Oxford University Press.

Newman, D.B., Balkaya-Ince, M., Nelson, J. M., Tsang, J., & Schnitker, S. A. (2023). *Feelings of Gratitude to Allah and People and their Associations with Affect in Daily Life* [Manuscript submitted for publication]. Department of Psychology and Neuroscience, Baylor University.]

Newman, D. B., Gordon, A. M., & Mendes, W. B. (2021). Comparing daily physiological and psychological benefits of gratitude and optimism using a digital platform. *Emotion*, *21*(7), 1357–1365. https://doi.org/10.1037/emo0001025

Newman, D. B., Nezlek, J. B., & Thrash, T. M. (2023). The dynamics of prayer in daily life and implications for well-being. *Journal of Personality and Social Psychology*, *124*(6), 1299–1313.

Ng, J. W. X., Tong, E. M. W., Sim, D. L. Y., Teo, S. W. Y., Loy, X., & Giesbrecht, T. (2017). Gratitude facilitates private conformity: A test of the social alignment hypothesis. *Emotion*, *17*(2), 379–387. https://doi.org/10.1037/emo0000249

Nikitin, J., & Freund, A. M. (2021). Does focusing on others enhance subjective well-being? The role of age, motivation, and relationship closeness. *Psychology and aging*, *36*(1), 69. https://doi.org/10.1037/pag0000489

Norenzayan, A., & Heine, S. J. (2005). Psychological universals: What are they and how can we know?. *Psychological bulletin*, *131*(5), 763. https://doi.org/10.1037/0033-2909.131.5.763

Norenzayan, A., Shariff, A. F., Gervais, W. M., Willard, A. K., McNamara, R. A., Slingerland, E., & Henrich, J. (2016). The cultural evolution of prosocial religions. *Behavioral & Brain Sciences*, *39*, N.PAG-0. https://doi.org/10.1017/S0140525X14001356

O'Dea, M. K., Igou, E. R., & van Tilburg, W. A. P. (2024). Preventing boredom with gratitude: The role of meaning in life. *Motivation and Emotion*, *48*(1), 111–125. https://doi.org/10.1007/s11031-023-10048-9

Oishi, S., Koo, M., Lim, N., & Suh, E. M. (2019). When gratitude evokes indebtedness. *Applied Psychology Health and Well-Being*, 11(2), 286–303. https://doi.org/10.1111/aphw.12155

Oriol, X., Unanue, J., Miranda, R., Amutio, A., & Bazán, C. (2020). Self-transcendent aspirations and life satisfaction: The moderated mediation role of gratitude considering conditional effects of affective and cognitive empathy. *Frontiers in Psychology*, *11*. https://doi.org/10.3389/fpsyg.2020.02105

Parker, S. C., Majid, H., Stewart, K. L., & Ahrens, A. H. (2017). No thanks! Autonomous interpersonal style is associated with less experience and valuing of gratitude. *Cognition & Emotion*, 31(8), 1627–1637. https://doi.org/10.1080/02699931.2016.1256274

Peng, C., Nelissen, R. M., & Zeelenberg, M. (2018). Reconsidering the roles of gratitude and indebtedness in social exchange. *Cognition and Emotion*, *32*(4), 760–772. https://doi.org/10.1080/02699931.2017.1353484

Pew Research Center. (2019, October 17). In U.S., Decline of Christianity Continues at Rapid Pace. *Pew Research Center's Religion & Public Life Project*. https://www.pewforum.org/2019/10/17/in-u-s-decline-of-christianity-continues-at-rapid-pace/

Pirlott, A. G., & MacKinnon, D. P. (2016). Design approaches to experimental mediation. *Journal of Experimental Social Psychology*, *66*, 29–38.

Portocarrero, F. F., Gonzales, K., & Ekema-Agbaw, M. (2020). A meta-analytic review of the relationship between dispositional gratitude and well-being, *Personality and Individual Differences*, *164*(1), 110101.

Ratchford, J. L., Cazzell, A. R., Wood, E., Owens, B., Quinn, R., & Schnitker, S. A. (2024). The virtue counterbalancing model: An illustration with patience & courage. *The Journal of Positive Psychology*, *19*(3), 406–418. https://doi.org/10.1080/17439760.2023.2178960

Ratchford, J. L., & Schnitker, S. A. (2024). Virtue in pursuit of goals: A goals-based approach to patience measurement. *Journal of Personality Assessment*, *106*(2), 181–195. https://doi.org/10.1080/00223891.2023.2219846

Regan, A., Radošić, N., & Lyubomirsky, S. (2022). Experimental effects of social behavior on well-being. *Trends in Cognitive Sciences*, 26(11), 987–998.

Regan, A., Walsh, L. C., & Lyubomirsky, S. (2023). Are some ways of expressing gratitude more beneficial than others? Results from a randomized controlled experiment. *Affective Science*, *4*(1), 72–81.. https://doi.org/10.1007/s42761-022-00160-3

Rosmarin, D., Wachholtz, A., & Ai, A. (2011). Beyond descriptive research: Advancing the study of spirituality and health. *Journal of Behavioral Medicine*, *34*(6), 409–413. https://doi.org/10.1007/s10865-011-9370-4

Rosmarin, D. H., Pirutinsky, S., Cohen, A. B., Galler, Y., & Krumrei, E. J. (2011). Grateful to God or just plain grateful? A comparison of religious and general gratitude. *The Journal of Positive Psychology*, *6*(5), 389–396. https://doi.org/10.1080/17439760.2011.596557

Rossano, M. J. (2020). Ritual as resource management. *Philosophical Transactions of the Royal Society of London. Series B, Biological Sciences*, *375*(1805), 20190429. https://doi.org/10.1098/rstb.2019.0429

Ruttan, R. L., Zhang, T., Barli, S. B., & DeCelles, K. A. (2024). Relational attributions for one's own resilience predict compassion for others. *Journal of Personality and Social Psychology*. Advance online publication. https://doi.org/10.1037/pspi0000438

Schimmel, S. (2004). Gratitude in Judaism. In R.A. Emmons & M.E. McCullough (Eds.), *The psychology of gratitude* (pp. 37–57). Oxford University Press.

Schnitker, S. A., Currier, J. M., Abernethy, A. D., Witvliet, C. Vanoyen, Foster J. D., Root Luna, L. M., Vanharn, K., & Carter, J. (2021). Gratitude and patience moderate meaning struggles and suicidal risk in a cross-sectional study of inpatients at a Christian psychiatric hospital. *Journal of Personality, 89*(6), 1191–1205. https://doi.org/10.1111/jopy.12644

Schnitker, S. A., King, P. E., & Houltberg, B. (2019). Religion, spirituality, and thriving: Transcendent narrative, virtue, and telos. *Journal of Research on Adolescence, 29*(2), 276–290.

Simpson, B., Harrell, A., Melamed, D., Heiserman, N., & Negraia, D. V. (2018). The Roots of Reciprocity: Gratitude and Reputation in Generalized Exchange Systems. *American Sociological Review, 83*(1), 88–110. https://doi.org/10.1177/0003122417747290

Smith, A., Pedersen, E. J., Forster, D. E., McCullough, M. E., & Lieberman, D. (2017). Cooperation: The roles of interpersonal value and gratitude. *Evolution and Human Behavior*, 38(6), 695–703. https://doi.org/10.1016/j.evolhumbehav.2017.08.003

Sun, P., Jian, H., Chu, M., & Qian, F. (2014). Gratitude and school well-being among Chinese university students: Interpersonal relationships and social support as mediators. *Social Behavior and Personality, 42*(10), 1689–1698.

Tam, K.-P. (2022). Gratitude to nature: Presenting a theory of its conceptualization, measurement, and effects on pro-environmental behavior. *Journal of Environmental Psychology, 79*. https://doi.org/10.1016/j.jenvp.2021.101754

Tian, L., Du, M. & Huebner, E.S. (2015). The effect of gratitude on elementary school students' subjective well-being in schools: The mediating role of prosocial behavior. *Social Indicators Research, 122*, 887–904. https://doi.org/10.1007/s11205-014-0712-9

Tong, E. M. W., Ng, C.-X., Ho, J. B. H., Yap, I. J. L., Chua, E. X. Y., Ng, J. W. X., Ho, D. Z. Y., & Diener, E. (2021). Gratitude facilitates obedience: New evidence for the social alignment perspective. *Emotion, 21*(6), 1302–1316. https://doi.org/10.1037/emo0000928

Trivers, R. L. (1971). The Evolution of Reciprocal Altruism. *The Quarterly Review of Biology, 46*(1), 35–57.

Trope, Y, & Liberman, N. (2010). Construal-level theory of psychological distance. *Psychological Review, 117*(2), 440–463. https://doi.org/10.1037/a0018963

Tsang, J. (2021). (Un)special favors: Gratitude for group-based benefits. *The Journal of Positive Psychology, 16*(1), 27–37.

Tsang, J., & Martin, S. R. (2016). A psychological perspective on gratitude and religion. In D. Carr (Ed.), *Perspectives on gratitude: An interdisciplinary approach*. (2016-22140-011; pp. 154–168). Routledge/Taylor & Francis Group; https://www.lib.byu.edu/cgi-bin/remoteauth.pl?url=http://search.ebscohost.com/login.aspx?direct=true&db=psyh&AN=2016-22140-011&site=ehost-live&scope=site

Tsang, J., Medenwaldt, J. M., Alwood, H. N., Nelson, J. M., & Schnitker, S. A. (2023). Writing about gratitude toward God produces differential content and outcomes compared to gratitude toward other benefactors among U.S. adults. *The International Journal for the Psychology of Religion, 33*(3), 169–197. https://doi.org/10.1080/10508619.2023.2192106

Tsang, J.-A. (2006). Gratitude and prosocial behaviour: An experimental test of gratitude. *Cognition and Emotion, 20*(1), 138–148. https://doi.org/10.1080/02699930500172341

Tsang, J.-A., & Martin, S. R. (2019). Four experiments on the relational dynamics and prosocial consequences of gratitude. *The Journal of Positive Psychology, 14*(2), 188–205. https://doi.org/10.1080/17439760.2017.1388435

Tudge, J., & Freitas, L. B., De, L. (2018). *Developing Gratitude in Children and Adolescents*. Cambridge University Press; nlebk. https://www.lib.byu.edu/cgi-bin/remoteauth.pl?url=http://search.ebscohost.com/login.aspx?direct=true&db=nlebk&AN=1578719&site=ehost-live&scope=site

Tudge, J. R. H., Navarro, J. L., Payir, A., Merçon-Vargas, E. A., Cao, H., Zhou, N., Liang, Y., & Mendonça, S. (2022). Using cultural-ecological theory to construct a mid-range theory for the development of gratitude as a virtue. *Journal of Family Theory & Review, 14*(2), 157–174. https://doi.org/10.1111/jftr.12432

van Zyl, L. E., Gaffaney, J., van der Vaart, L., Dik, B. J., & Donaldson, S. I. (2024). The critiques and criticisms of positive psychology: A systematic review. *The Journal of Positive Psychology*, *19*(2), 206–235. https://doi.org/10.1080/17439760.2023.2178956

Vishkin, A., Szymaniak, K., Solak, N., Kim, M. Y., Kitayama, S., (2022). *Cultural Variation in the Correlates of Gratitude [Conference presentation]*. Gratitude to God Convening, Palm Springs, CA, United States.

Watkins, P., Scheer, J., Ovnicek, M., & Kolts, R. (2006). The debt of gratitude: Dissociating gratitude and indebtedness. *Cognition & Emotion*, *20*(2), 217–241. https://doi.org/10.1080/02699930500172291

Watkins, P. C. (2004). Gratitude and Subjective Well-Being. In R. A. Emmons & M. E. McCullough (Eds.), *The psychology of gratitude*. (2004-00298-009; pp. 167–192). Oxford University Press. https://doi.org/10.1093/acprof:oso/9780195150100.003.0009

Watkins, P.C., Woodward, K., Stone, T., & Kolts, R.L. (2003). Gratitude and happiness: Development of a measure of gratitude, and relationships with subjective well being. *Social Behavior and Personality: An International Journal*, *31*, 431–451. https://doi.org/10.2224/sbp.2003.31.5.431

Webb, J. R. (2021). *Understanding forgiveness and addiction: Theory, research, and clinical application*. Routledge.

Weiner, B., (2014). The emotional consequences of causal attributions. In M. S. Clark & S. T. Fiske (Eds.), *Affect and cognition* (pp. 185–209). Psychology Press.

Winzer, L., & Gray, R. S. (2019). The role of Buddhist practices in happiness and health in Thailand: A structural equation model: Journal of Happiness Studies: An Interdisciplinary Forum on Subjective Well-Being. *Journal of Happiness Studies: An Interdisciplinary Forum on Subjective Well-Being*, *20*(2), 411–425. https://doi.org/10.1007/s10902-017-9953-z

Witvliet, C. V.O., Richie, F. J., Root Luna, L. M., & Van Tongeren, D. R. (2019). Gratitude predicts hope and happiness: A two-study assessment of traits and states. *The Journal of Positive Psychology*, *14*(3), 271–282. https://doi.org/10.1080/17439760.2018.1424924

Wolfe, W. L. (2022). Does gratitude induction buffer the adverse effect of thin ideal media exposure on women's body image? *North American Journal of Psychology*, *24*(1), 7–26.

Wood, A. M., Emmons, R. A., Algoe, S. B., Froh, J. J., Lambert, N. M., & Watkins, P. (2016). A dark side of gratitude? Distinguishing between beneficial gratitude and its harmful impostors for the positive clinical psychology of gratitude and well-being. In A. Wood & J. Johnson (Eds.), *The Wiley handbook of positive clinical psychology* (pp. 137–151). John Wiley & Sons. https://doi.org/10.1002/9781118468197.ch10

Wood, A. M., Froh, J. J., & Geraghty, A. W. A. (2010). Gratitude and well-being: A review and theoretical integration. *Clinical Psychology Review*, *30*(7), 890–905. https://doi.org/10.1016/j.cpr.2010.03.005

Wood, A. M., Joseph, S., & Maltby, J. (2009). Gratitude predicts psychological well-being above the Big Five facets. *Personality and Individual Differences*, 46(4), 443–447. https://doi.org/10.1016/j.paid.2008.11.012

Wood, A. M., Maltby, J., Gillett, R., Linley, P. A., & Joseph, S. (2008). The role of gratitude in the development of social support, stress, and depression: Two longitudinal studies. *Journal of Research in Personality*, *42*, 854–871.

Wood, A. M., Maltby, J., Stewart, N., Linley, P. A., & Joseph, S. (2008). A social–cognitive model of trait and state levels of gratitude. *Emotion*, 8, 281–290.

Yadav, M. S. (2018). Making emerging phenomena a research priority. *Journal of the Academy of Marketing Science*, *46*(3), 361–365. https://doi.org/10.1007/s11747-017-0575-0

Yu, Q., Wang, P., Xia, X., Zhao, L., Zhu, S., & Wang, W. (2023). The mediating roles of social support and basic psychological needs in the relationship between gratitude and adolescent prosocial behavior. *Current Psychology: A Journal for Diverse Perspectives on Diverse Psychological Issues*, *43*, 15342–15351.

Zhou, X., & Wu, X. (2016). Understanding the roles of gratitude and social support in posttraumatic growth among adolescents after Ya'an earthquake: A longitudinal study. *Personality and Individual Differences*, *101*, 4–8. https://doi.org/10.1016/j.paid.2016.05.033

Zhu, R., Xu, Z., Su, S., Feng, C., Luo, Y., Tang, H., … Liu, C. (2021). From gratitude to injustice: Neurocomputational mechanisms of gratitude-induced injustice. *NeuroImage*, *245*, 118730. https://doi.org/10.1016/j.neuroimage.2021.118730

Chapter 27

Hope

Research on Well-Being and Psychological Interventions

*Jennifer S. Ripley** and *Jessica McCleese*

Few psychological factors have had a more significant social science and medical research footprint than hope. The term "hope" will return over 50,000 references in the PsycINFO database and approximately 10,000 references in PubMed with as wide-ranging topics as hope in Sudanese refugee children, palliative care, couple therapy, mental illness, suicide, and trauma from disaster. The idea of hope in medicine and mental health sparked with Karl Menninger (1959) and C.R. Snyder (1989) and then became a forest fire of research activity. Snyder defined hope as "a cognitive set that is based on a reciprocally derived sense of successful (a) agency (goal-directed determinism) and (b) pathways (planning of ways to meet goals)" (Snyder, 1989, p. 571). Today, the medical and psychological community considers hope one of the most well-researched and top virtues for human flourishing and well-being. It's been called the most important virtue (Scioli & Biller, 2009), and Martin Seligman's lab research listed hope as one of the top five virtues to predict life satisfaction (Park et al., 2005).

Hope wasn't always a super-star virtue. Historically, philosophers and poets have shaken their fists at hope. Ancient Greek writers thought of hope as a vice, not a virtue. Euripides called hope "man's curse" (Aeschylus, 424 BCE, 1961) with fatalistic assumptions about a world where humans have little influence or agency. In the myth of Pandora, she released pain and suffering from the box (really a casket) but imprisoned hope in the box and withheld it from humanity (Hesiodus, 700 BCE, 1980). Most interpretations of the myth indicate that Pandora was withholding blind or false hope from humanity, while others consider the remaining hope a future salvific device for humankind. The ambiguity of the meaning of hope is part of the ancient puzzle: Is hope a salvation or a curse? Sophocles' Antigone considers hope a curse when she declares,

> We are of the tribe that asks questions, and we ask them to the bitter end until no tiniest chance of hope remains to be strangled by our hands. We are of the tribe that hates your filthy hope, your docile, female hope; hope, your whore.
>
> (Sophocles, 441 BCE, 1947, p. 24)

The modern psychological and health communities have rejected Antigone's declaration and decided that Hope is a virtue, or at the least that it has a robust correlation with life satisfaction (Park, 2013). It is no accident that the changes in hope emerged as hierarchical power structures began to diminish, and the Abrahamic faiths emerged with their emphasis on

* Corresponding Author: jennrip@mail.regent.edu.

DOI: 10.4324/9781003440048-31

individual freedom and hope (Davis et al., 2021). Even among the so-called ragpickers in Mumbai, India, tainted as the lowest caste of India with no chance of improving their state, there is still hope for their children to escape the lowest caste and poverty through education (Shepherd et al., 2022). The modern invention of mass education becomes the vehicle for hope, showing the robust tenacity of hope to survive in all environments.

Religion and spirituality are a seedbed for the concept of hope, particularly for religions with a benevolent deity or deities, as an attachment to a benevolent deity is foundational to hope for most people (Allen, 2013; Pruyser, 1987). Indeed, attachment and trust in a benevolent deity or spiritual realm appear frequently in the hope literature as a robust human perception (Allen, 2013).

Definition of Religion/Spirituality

There is a developing body of research on attachment to the divine as a basis for hope (Allen, 2013). Therefore, we will use relational spirituality as the primary model of religion/spirituality (R/S). Relational spirituality is "ways of relating to the sacred" (Sandage et al., 2020, p. 24). The sacred can include both the traditional and non-traditional versions of R/S and include anything that is imbued with sacred qualities that set it apart from the rest of life. The Relational Spirituality Model includes dwelling and seeking. Dwelling consists of commitments, community, and connection, while seeking involves questing or exploring religious aspects of self and the world. This model is especially appealing since relational spirituality has interdisciplinary roots in theology, psychology, social cognition, attachment, and interpersonal neurobiology. It can be theistic (Davis et al., 2021), as seen in the World's monotheistic religions, or non-theistic and existential. Relational spirituality can also be adaptive or maladaptive, allowing for flourishing or diminishing life satisfaction, making it a robust research model.

Hope and Religion/Spirituality

Pruyser (1987) defined hope as embedded within a secure attachment to a divine figure or object, and the research on R/S and hope has supported that perception in research. Research reflects human ideas, society, and functioning, so the tangling of hope and R/S is unsurprising. Even those who self-define as agnostic or atheistic often still have experiences of the sacred or divine, making R/S an almost universal experience of humanity.

In their study of hope in religion, Scioli and Biller (2009) reviewed references to hope in ten religions (Australian Aboriginal, Buddhist, Hindu, Judaism, Ifa in West Africa, native American, Islam, Catholic, Orthodox, and Protestant Christianity). They noted that attachment-based hope existed in all religions except Buddhism (which is salvation-based hope). This attachment to the divine provided hope through sacred texts such as Dreamtime stories of Aborigines or the Rig Veda in Hinduism. Some references to hope are related to survival, while others hope in divine justice, such as the Qur'an, "He shows you the lightning causing fear and hope" (Surah 13:12). Jewish hope is particularly focused on survival, as major themes of the Torah include hope in preserving and sustaining the survival of the Jewish people (Scioli & Biller, 2009). Philosophers such as Ernst Bloch have emphasized the theme across major religions to be delivered by a divine actor toward something good in the future. For atheistic hope, leaders like Bertrand Russell have proposed science as mastery of the world and love for others (attachment) as the sources of hope. As Russell (2013) said in his memoir, "The good life is one inspired by love and guided by knowledge. Neither love without knowledge nor knowledge without love can produce a good life." The theme of hope in world religion is central, with attachment to the Divine as the primary means for most people to find hope.

Extant Research on Hope and Aspects of Life Satisfaction

The scientific research on hope skews toward a positive influence on human flourishing. Meta-analytic research has established the value of hope to predict positive affect, optimism, self-esteem, and social support in adolescents (Yarcheski & Mahon, 2016) and adults (Corrigan et al., 2023). Hope is a key ingredient in recovery from mental illness (van Weeghel et al., 2019) using the CHIME conceptual framework for recovery, which contains hope as a central element. The basic research in psychological health has advanced to a level where many meta-analytic studies have supported hope as an important positive factor in well-being and life satisfaction (Alarcon et al., 2013; Reichard et al., 2013; Yarcheski & Mahon, 2016).

Strong lines of research in the medical literature indicate that hope predicts healthy behaviors, compliance with medical advice, prevention activities, and adjustment to living with illness (Duncan et al., 2021). In a review of 73 studies of hope in the healthcare literature, Olsman (2020) demonstrated that attachment to peers increased hope in patients, while loss of health negatively impacted hope. Hope was able to motivate change in addressing health problems and improve decision-making.

Snyder's (1989) two-component theory of agency and pathways has received extensive research. Most researchers propose that *agency thinking* and *pathways thinking* are independent factors (Tong et al., 2010). They appear to affect life satisfaction and flourishing differently, with agency thinking as the more potent factor in most research. In particular, the agency aspect of hope predicts accomplishment (Day et al., 2010) and provides resiliency against depression and anxiety (Corrigan et al., 2023). Pediatric cancer patients' agency thinking was predictive of lowering anxiety, whereas pathways thinking was not (Germann et al., 2018). Parents of disabled children with greater agency thinking had better life satisfaction and coping (Lloyd & Hasting, 2009), with similar findings in stroke survivors (Gum et al., 2006).

When All Hope Is Gone: Deleterious Effects of Hope

Futile hope was the concern of the ancient writers and the burden of medical and mental health providers everywhere. The balance of truth and hope in the face of terminal illness or unrecoverable loss is essential. Buddhist teachings particularly emphasize that hope can have a dark side, encouraging striving toward goals that cannot be attained, which can damage one's health, resources, and relationships (Dunlap, 2020).

Medical ethicist Marleen Eijkolt (2020) coined the phrase "False Hope Harms" as an ethical dilemma in communicating information to patients about the lack of medicine's ability to assist them with suffering or illness. False hope is characteristic of patients who persist in seeking unproven or even harmful medical treatments. Not all medical providers agree that false hope is necessarily harmful, stating that it can buoy a patient and their family's agency to engage in activities that have a low chance of helping but still could help. Snyder and Rand (2003) made a strong case in the *American Psychologist*, the flagship scientific journal of the American Psychological Association, against false hope concepts, stating that high-hope people are *more* likely to adjust their goals in the face of obstacles, are no more likely to have positive biases than low-hope people, tend to achieve goals more often, and tend to produce more effective pathways.

To address the issue of false hope, ethicists Pergert and Lutzen (2012) proposed relational ethics as a means to balance truth and hope. They present the case of a terminally ill teen and differences of opinion between the family and medical providers on what to tell the teen regarding the fact that medicine had no further treatment options for her. The upcoming loss of her young life was certain and needed to be accepted. They propose that relational ethics would engage all parties to focus on pain management as a different type of hope for the girl and her family. They also proposed that discussing her brief timeline would allow the family to address existential issues together and with any spiritual leaders. Using the relationships of the oncology care team as an attachment provided a sense of peace to the family and pointed them to existential hope. Meaning-making in the face of loss and suffering is an especially important aspect of R/S (Park, 2013) and a pathway for hope.

Mental healthcare has unique situations where permanent loss has to be addressed, and futile hope could harm patients. Persistence of hope in domestic violence situations would be one case where a victim of domestic violence puts themselves in harm's way out of a false hope that their family member will not violate them again (Ybarra & Lohr, 2002). This dark side of hope has some research from McNulty (2011), who has indicated that forgiveness of domestic violence perpetrators can lead to increased violence if the abuser has antisocial, narcissistic, or other traits low in empathy. Even within this paradigm of the dark side of forgiveness, McNulty doesn't preclude forgiveness as a means of addressing violence but instead recommends against communicating forgiveness in ways that indicate to the abuser that they will not be held responsible for the harm they have inflicted.

Other false-hope circumstances in mental healthcare might include diagnosis of severe persistent mental illness, palliative care, grief, long-term disability, loss of a job or possessions, and divorce. In these circumstances, the loss is permanent, and sometimes patients cannot accept the loss. The research on these circumstances has not yet investigated the agency and pathways of high versus low-hope individuals who face permanent loss. Even if activities cannot obtain the original goal, will they allow the individual to let go of the lost thing with a sense that they tried everything? For others, it can take time to accept that a longed-for door has been closed to them. The goals of therapy in these circumstances would be to help clients determine if the goal is lost, understand the meaning of the goal in their lives, weigh the benefits and costs of continued pursuit of lost pathways, avoid harming themselves or others in their pursuit or grief, and encourage the client's agency to find meaning and hope in other aspects of their life.

Religion, Hope, and Scientific Research

Most of the social science research in R/S and hope has focused on hope in the face of loss, trauma, illness, and death through R/S attachment or ideas. Research on R/S resiliency and natural disasters has found hope to be an important direct predictive factor (Aten et al., 2019). A study of parents with a child with terminal cancer also found that R/S strengthened general and existential hope (Broadhurst & Harrington, 2016).

In 2022, researchers set out to provide a working definition of hope by examining previous literature and combining that with five studies they completed among laypeople. They defined hope as "a *belief that a positive future outcome is possible* combined with *a desire for that outcome*" (Luo et al., 2022, p.762). In religious clients, hope and faith could be intimately connected with one another. The actual words faith and hope are sometimes used interchangeably with one another to provide religious clients with therapeutic approaches that encourage them and provide them with the motivation to engage in more satisfying outcomes.

Hope may also be an important moderator between R/S and resilient functioning. Raney et al. (2022) conducted a study of 491 hurricane victims, finding that hope was a strong moderator between prayer and coping with depressive symptoms. Participants with high trait-hope and high prayer engagement were resilient to depressive symptoms, while those with low trait-hope and high prayer were significantly more depressed (Raney et al., 2022). This is not unusual in R/S research, where hopeless R/S strivings are deleterious to people while hopeful R/S strivings strengthen (Eche et al., 2022). Agli et al. (2015) proposed in a study with dementia patients that hope might be the mechanism for R/S resiliency, as they find meaning in aspects of their lives where they are able to be effective. Even in the most painful and difficult circumstances, hope continues to find a way out of Pandora's box into the lives of humans who are suffering.

Measuring Hope

There are several scales to measure hope, the first developed by Snyder (Snyder et al., 1991). The items show good internal consistency, with Cronbach's alpha ranging from .74 to .84 (Snyder et al. 1991). A dispositional scale for children was developed (Snyder et al., 1997) with a similar strong two-factor structure along agency thinking and pathways thinking. A state hope scale (Snyder et al. 1996) is a six-item scale to measure current hope, with an expectation of fluctuation over time. It also has good internal consistency and discriminant validity (Snyder et al., 1996).

Beyond Snyder's measures, there are dozens of empirically supported measures of Hope ranging from specific conditions such as Schizophrenia (Choe, 2014) to multidimensional measures of hope applied to psychotherapy (Larson et al., 2020). Herth Hope Index (Herth, 1992) was developed in a medical setting with good consistency and convergent validity. The Herth measure proposed a three-factor structure of time, expectancy, and attachment. Ward and Wampler (2010) developed a hope scale to reflect their alternative theory, where hope focuses on a relationship (attachment) and doesn't assume emotions result from cognitive appraisal. The Multidimensional Hope in Psychotherapy and Counseling scale (Larson et al., 2020) found six factors with 34 items: future, spirituality, cognitive, therapeutic relationship, other relationships, and emotion. Hope is studied in medical and therapeutic settings and in ecclesiastical work. Within theistic Hope, a new measure of Eschatological Hope (van Oyen Witvliet et al., 2022) supports the construct of hope in a positive, just, and loving eternal future with the Divine. The common theme of hope in attachment persists across many of the measures of hope developed after Snyder.

Social Support and Hope

With the common theme of attachment throughout the literature, it's not surprising that the construct of social support would be an important predictor of hope. Meta-analytic research on social support and hope has focused primarily on children or mental health conditions. A meta-analysis of the nursing literature studying social support and hope among adolescents found that both parent social support and hope were significant (Mahon & Yarcheski, 2017). Leamy et al.'s (2018) review of 97 studies found hope to be one of the five major recovery processes for mental illness. Research has extended to the family members of those with mental health problems and found hope to be a key factor in predicting the support of family (McCarthy et al., 2023). Longitudinal studies of disaster victims find social support and hope to contribute to mental health (Cherry et al., 2023). A strong trend supports that social support and hope are "in the mix" as predictors of various types of well-being.

A model is still needed to understand how hope and social support constructs might relate to each other, the mechanisms for how they influence well-being, and in what context. One study of rural Chinese adolescents (Lu, 2023) found that parental emotional warmth indirectly affected hope, mediated through perceived social support, with boys having a stronger correlation than girls. A similar study of Chinese elderly adults (Zhang et al., 2022) found a mediation model fit with hope mediating between social support and loneliness. A study of 275 Israeli citizens under social distancing restrictions during the COVID-19 outbreak found that social participation predicted post-traumatic growth mediated both directly and indirectly through hope and social support (Laslo et al., 2022). These, and many other similar studies, are finding support for hope as a mediator between social attachment factors and well-being or functioning.

Hope as Intervention

The vast majority of research has studied Hope as a common factor in mental health and medical research (Duncan et al., 2021). Still, there are some interventions that have been developed and built on hope as a conceptual framework. Within medical settings, three types of Hope interventions include curative hope work when patients are getting better, palliative hope work for patients to feel better, and dismantling hope when patients are past recovery (Peraklya et al., 1991). Medical professionals using support and attachment through sharing more personally is a key component of hope with patients and is an important intervention to assist patients in all three types of hope (Pergert & Lutzen, 2012).

More traditional clinical research has demonstrated hope as helpful in addressing medical and mental health problems. A clinical study of diabetes patients in a peer support group in Iran that focused on hope showed increased hope after completing 16 hours of group intervention (Ghazavi et al., 2015). Of note, peer support is a type of attachment that is an important factor in medical compliance, which is a key concern in the treatment of diabetes. These diabetic patients were in the "getting better" modality of treatment. While intervention research in medicine is not extensive, it does consider the prognosis of the medical condition and attachment to peers or medical professionals when utilizing hope as an intervention.

The field of positive psychology has developed interventions and strategies to increase hopefulness in a community or clinic (Lopez et al., 2015). These interventions encourage hopeful cognitions to reduce stress and often focus on enrichment or non-clinical community participants. A meta-analysis of 27 studies showed significant, although small, effect sizes for hope interventions to enhance psychotherapy (Weis & Speridakos, 2011). Despite the importance of hope as a common factor, the researchers concluded that hope enhancement treatments, as they have currently been studied, did not have evidence of contributing to improving outcomes beyond regular psychotherapy. However, the interventions described used common psychotherapy techniques, so the findings that treatment did not produce above and beyond psychotherapy does not mean that hope interventions were ineffective. These studies often targeted enrichment or enhancement interventions with a ceiling effect. The authors also did not differentiate between the three scenarios as described by Peraklya et al., which may be an important factor to consider when engaging in Hope-focused interventions.

Spiritually Integrated Psychotherapy and Hope

Spiritually integrated psychotherapy is an interdisciplinary approach to treatment that uses healthy practices, cognitions, and relationships from a client's spirituality together with psychotherapy to create interventions. There are spiritually integrated psychotherapies developed, to varying degrees, for all of the major religions, addressing a variety of clinical problems. Islamic hope therapy focuses on instilling hope in the mercy of God, meaning, and purpose in life as a pathway for change and to speed healing (Rassool & Khan, 2023). This approach has yet to be tested in clinical research environments. Still, it demonstrates how spirituality and hope may combine to provide an approach to treating clients that is congruent with their traditions and beliefs.

Hope-focused couple therapy (Worthington et al., 1997; Ripley & Worthington, 2014) is an empirically supported treatment designed as a spiritually integrated therapy in the Christian tradition that uses agency and pathways thinking to promote change. The strategy uses various couple therapy techniques, such as communication or forgiveness interventions, with a simple strategy to increase faith, work, and love within the couple. The interventions and strategy combine to increase hope for couples. Hope is necessary for the couple to have the courage to change the relational dynamic. However, hope is engaged indirectly through a strategy with good techniques rather than directly promoting hope. Hope is fostered by encouraging agency, which partners gain from success in early strategic techniques. Couples also increase pathways thinking, which engages each couple's overall strategy for change. After hope is engaged, the emotional bond can be repaired or improved. Couple therapists agree that repairing and maintaining the relationship's emotional bond is the most important active ingredient for couple therapy (Ripley, Worthington, et al., 2023b). Finally, the outcomes of this treatment would include increased satisfaction, stability, and maturity in the relationship.

Christian therapists widely use the Hope approach (Hook et al., 2011; Ripley, Solfelt, et al., 2023a). Hope-focused couple therapy is spiritually integrated with an ecumenical Christian tradition that is often altered for other religions or non-religious people by focusing on positive virtues instead of specific Christian virtues. Research on the approach demonstrated efficacy in over a dozen published studies of enrichment and psychotherapy (Ripley, Solfelt et al., 2023a). Two clinical studies have demonstrated that both the spiritually integrated version of Hope-focused couple therapy and the standard secular version are equally effective in promoting change in couple satisfaction (Ripley, Solfelt, et al., 2023a). The authors propose that spiritual integration addresses religious diversity in improving relationships despite no outcome differences in relationship functioning. However, spiritually integrated therapy may be superior in addressing spiritual needs and strivings (Sandage et al., 2022).

Hope-Focused and Couple Therapy: Case-Related Examples

Most couples enter the therapy process with at least a few hopes, and many also express these hopes, although not always in ways that are beneficial for the actual goal-setting and achieving therapy outcomes. Married individuals *hope* that therapy will have some long-term benefit or that the current therapist will be "more skilled" than the last therapist. Others hope that "my husband will quit his job" that demands so much of his time or that "my wife will start enjoying sex more." All of these are examples of the hopes that one of the individuals might have for the therapy process. When couples are able to use positive religious coping (which comes from a secure attachment with God) and spiritual practices (attending worship services, reading sacred texts, or praying), they find that they are more satisfied with their marriages and experience a higher level of personal well-being (Jerome et al., 2023; Lai et al., 2023).

We have found this to be practically relevant in our work with religious couples. Dr. McCleese once worked with a couple, Chris and Nikki, who had been married for 13 years before beginning services. They were both committed to their Christian faith, attended church services together, and even served in ministry together as part of the prayer team. But this couple felt disconnected emotionally and noted that they felt more like "good friends" than a couple in a "good marriage." They both noted that divorce due to dissatisfaction was not an option because this was not something congruent with their Christian faith. Even so, they felt like they did not have the marriage that God designed for them. They believed that they should feel more emotionally connected because the Bible promised they would "become one" (Gen. 2:24). As they described what this meant for them, both noted a desire to be vulnerable with one another, a desire to know that each would be fully accepted and loved by the other, and a hope that they would "fall in love again" so that they actually wanted to spend time together.

The Hope approach starts with techniques, as that is what clients experience in the room. Several techniques from Hope-Focused Marriage Counseling (Ripley & Worthington, 2014) were implemented for Chris and Nikki. We started by assessing their core vision for their marriage and their thoughts and beliefs about where their difficulties were and why these difficulties came to be. Specifically, they both felt like they had lost the emotional intimacy in the marriage due to raising two sons, busy work schedules, and full weekends with child and ministry responsibilities. They placed a high value on parenting and church involvement, which both saw as a strength in their relationship. Both agreed that these two activities left them with little time to spend alone. One of their biggest concerns was that backing away from these responsibilities to make time for one another would mean that they were not fully engaged in these activities, making them feel like they were not adhering well to their Christian beliefs and faith practices.

Since Chris and Nikki firmly believed that their religious practices were important for them and their marriage, it was helpful to have them connect their hope in God with their relationship needs. For religious couples, hope can grow when they see their marriage as a sacred partnership. Mahoney et al. (1999) developed a definition of sanctification in this regard as "the degree to which partners believe their marriage is a manifestation of their beliefs or experiences of God and their religious faith" (p. 323). They further assert that sanctification refers to God being active in and reflected in the marriage relationship. Through this research, Mahoney et al. found that couples high in sanctification described their marriages as having transcendent qualities, such as being blessed or holy, and held strong convictions that their marriage reflected their beliefs and experiences about God. Other researchers have similarly found a positive association between sanctification and marital satisfaction (Ellison et al., 2011; Pargament & Mahoney, 2005; Rusu et al., 2015; Stafford, 2016), specifically in the areas of increasing one's efforts to view their marriage positively, protect their marriage, increase support for their partner, and be satisfied with their marriage.

Dr. McCleese encouraged Nikki and Chris in their service to the community through their church, shared prayers, and religious holidays. Couples involved in more joint religious activities and have greater perceptions of having spiritual significance associated with their marriage also have better marriage functioning (Dew et al., 2020). The marriages were characterized by higher marital satisfaction, more perceived benefit for both husband and wife, less conflict within the marriage, and greater collaboration between the husband and wife. Furthermore, research (Mahoney et al., 2022) has shown that people put greater effort and derive greater benefit from areas of their life to which they attribute greater sanctity, further proving that emphasizing the sanctity of marriage for religious couples can lead to better therapy outcomes. As Chris and Nikki began reflecting on this concept of the sanctity of their marriage, they could extend their spiritual practices of prayer for others in the church to prayer specifically for one another and the marriage.

Prayer research indicates that those with high hope and high prayer activity tend to have better outcomes, which applied to this couple (Raney et al., 2022). For this couple, their hope in their relationship, their Higher Power, and therapy were high, so mutual prayer was helpful to them. This also extended to specific prayer times for one another before one left for work in the morning and to prayer as a family through short devotion time with their children once a week. During their prayer time as a couple, Chris and Nikki would practice vulnerability by sharing their current needs, concerns, or anxieties. After they prayed together, they would end the prayer with a quick blessing over one another and their marriage. This helped them feel a greater commitment to growing their emotional connection. One of the primary emphases of the Hope approach is to build the emotional connection or bond of the couple through their hope, strategy, and therapy techniques. This couple was ready to repair their bond, and prayer was a technique that fit the treatment strategy and brought hope to the couple.

Rather than commit to the value of "not divorcing," Chris and Nikki became committed to growing their emotional connection by intentionally spending time together and speaking about the high value they put on each other and their commitment to the marriage. At termination, Chris and Nikki both noted that they were proud of themselves for committing to weekly date nights and felt that their alone time together had strengthened their bond. They also attributed much of their growth to their religious hope that God was involved in their relationship and helped them relate better. Chris and Nikki brought in a photo frame with digital pictures of their last several date nights together for a final exercise we labeled a "Joshua Memorial." This is a final session activity where a couple creates something that symbolizes their work in couple therapy together. They noted that the pictures could be updated and planned to update them each quarter with their favorite dates. Truly, Chris and Nikki left therapy with a much greater hope for their long-term emotional connection than what they had when they began sessions.

Not only did sanctification produce a more positive marital experience for Chris and Nikki, but sanctification predicts improved sexual connection. Couples who believe in the sanctity of their marital sexuality have been found to experience higher levels of sexual satisfaction and smaller declines in sexual satisfaction, which also leads to a closer relationship and greater relational well-being (Dew et al., 2020; Hernandez-Kane & Mahoney, 2018). Specifically, couples that have higher levels of perceived sanctification of their marital sexual relationship, defined as a "specific belief consistent with diverse religious teachings about the meaning and reverence of sexual intimacy…in other words, viewing sexual intimacy with a partner as a sacred experience…" (Hernandez-Kane, 2018, p. 423). Couples also reported greater frequency of sex, sexual satisfaction, and marital satisfaction one year later. Dr. McCleese recently found this to be the case with a couple who were actually struggling to complete the act of intercourse. Jonas and Sierra had been married for just three weeks when they entered therapy. They reported that they had been "unable to have sex all the way" on their wedding night due to the pain that Sierra experienced when penetration was attempted. They both noted waiting to have sex until marriage and believed that this would be one way to honor

God in their marriage. They also noted their surprise and disappointment that they falsely believed that remaining virgins until marriage would guarantee a satisfying sexual relationship. Despite their false hope that virginity before marriage would guarantee their sexual success, they continued to believe that sex was a divine gift from God and that they worked on their sexual relationship with one another with a focus on kindness and grace. They believed their faith would help them to have success with intercourse as well as a closer, more fulfilling relationship overall.

Jonas and Sierra spent just over a year working on improving their sexual communication with one another as they simultaneously worked on successfully completing the act of intercourse. This included talking about sexual disappointments and fears within their relationship, as well as their belief that God would heal their bodies and gift them with a positive experience in their marital intimacy. They engaged in sensate focus exercises with one another as well as pelvic floor therapy and dilator use for her and anxiety-reduction techniques for both of them. Specifically, they would spend a few minutes focusing on their faith that God would heal their bodies and their emotions surrounding sex each evening, and she would also say a short "faith-prayer" prior to practicing with her dilators. After fourteen months and successful, pain-free penetration, Jonas and Sierra attributed God as the primary source of their healing and their determination and willingness to continue with treatment as other contributing factors to their success.

Conclusions on Hope

Research on hope in human functioning and flourishing is advanced and extensive, with thousands of studies where hope is a key construct of research in health and well-being, including physical, mental, and social (Duncan et al., 2021; Park & Chen, 2016). The research has been inclusive of various cultures, groups, and conditions. The research in healthcare is robust, including demonstrating the importance of hope in treating those with various medical and mental health conditions. What is currently lacking is an understanding of the models, mechanisms, and contexts where hope plays a key role in human functioning. Mediating models are promising, but more theoretically based advanced models would advance the body of research.

The role of eschatological or divine hope in research remains relatively small (van Oyen Witvliet et al., 2022). The research on prayer (Raney et al. 2022) is especially intriguing as hope played the moderator role in research. There may be situations where low hope paired with high spiritual activities and strivings can increase distress and create vulnerabilities.

It is possible that other factors are involved in low hope, focusing on hope in a particular outcome, such as speedy healing from disease. Low hope may be a temporary pathway of lament through a "dark night of the soul" toward spiritual maturity. Low hope may be a means of resolution after wrestling with the Divine or existential limitations. Other R/S factors may be worth exploring, such as negative attachment to God, anger with God, or isolation from spiritual support systems. This research could help enlighten the relationship between other R/S constructs and hope.

The "dark side" of hope is also poorly researched. While Snyder and Rand (2003) argued that those with high trait hope are less likely to engage in harmful behaviors, there are still settings and situations where hope can lead to harm, such as returning to domestic violence relationships out of unlikely or futile hope of change (McNulty, 2011). Researchers who are willing to study futile hope would contribute significantly to the literature.

Finally, interventions that utilize hope explicitly are understudied. Given the extensive research base for the importance of hope, it is surprising how little medical or therapeutic interventions are designed to address hope. Future research can examine direct versus indirect interventions to improve hope. It's possible that directly intervening to improve hope could create reactance, and indirectly fostering hope through good interventions and strategies may be as effective. Researchers could benefit from research on the role of interventions to increase attachment to the Divine, family, friends, or others in maintaining hope. Distinguishing the role of agency thinking versus pathways thinking as specific interventions has not been directly studied. Finally, techniques to help clients as they face losses to redirect hope away from goals that can no longer be accomplished to focus on deeper underlying meaningful life goals may be promising as an intervention.

References

Aeschylus, (424 BCE/ 1961). *Prometheus bound; The suppliants; Seven against Thebes; The Persians.* (P. Vellacott, Ed.) Penguin.

Agli, O., Bailly, N., & Ferrand, C. (2015). Spirituality and religion in older adults with dementia: A systematic review. *International Psychogeriatrics, 27*, 715–725. http://doi.org/10.1017/S1041610214001665

Alarcon, G. M., Bowling, N. A., & Khazon, S. (2013). Great expectations: A meta-analytic examination of optimism and hope. *Personality and Individual Differences, 54*(7), 821–827. https://doi.org/10.1016/j.paid.2012.12.004

Allen, J. G. (2013). Hope in human attachment and spiritual connection. *Bulletin of the Menninger Clinic, 77*, 302–331. http://doi.org/10.1521/bumc.2013.77.4.302

Aten, J. D., Smith, W. R., Davis, E. B., Hook, J. N., Ranter, J., Van Tongeren, D. R., Davis, D. E., Shannonhouse, L., DeBlaere, C., O'Grady, K., & Hill, P. C. (2019). A psychological study of religion and spirituality in a disaster context: A systematic review. *Psychological Trauma: Theory, Research, Practice, and Policy, 11*, 597–613. http://doi.org/10.1037/tra0000431

Broadhurst, K., & Harrington, A. (2016). A mixed method thematic review: The importance of hope to the dying patient. *Journal of Advanced Nursing, 72*, 18–32. http://doi.org/10.1111/jan.12765

Cherry, K. E., Miller, L. R., Bordes, P. J., Calamia, M. R., Elliott, E. M., Sampson, L., & Galea, S. (2023). Longitudinal assessment of mental health after a flood: Roles of social support, hope, recovery stressors, and prior lifetime trauma. *Aging & Mental Health, 27*(12), 2446–2456. https://doi.org/10.1080/13607863.2023.2191927

Choe, K. (2014). Development and preliminary testing of the Schizophrenia Hope Scale, a brief scale to measure hope in people with schizophrenia. *International Journal of Nursing Studies, 51*, 927–933. http://doi.org/10.1016/j.ijnurstu.2013.10.018

Corrigan, J. A., & Schutte, N. S. (2023). The relationship between the hope dimensions of agency thinking and pathways thinking with depression and anxiety: A meta-analysis. *International Journal of Applied Positive Psychology, 8*, 211–255. http://doi.org/10.1007/s41042-023-00099-1

Davis, E. B., Granqvist, P., & Sharp, C. (2021). Theistic relational spirituality: Development, dynamics, health, and transformation. *Psychology of Religion and Spirituality, 13*(4), 401–415. https://doi.org/10.1037/rel0000219

Day, L., Hanson, K., Maltby, J., Proctor, C., & Wood, A., (2010). Hope uniquely predicts objective academic achievement above intelligence, personality, and previous academic achievement. *Journal of Research in Personality, 44*, 550–553. http://doi.org/10.1016/j.jrp.2010.05.009

Dew, J. P., Eucker, J. E., & Willoughby, B. J. (2020). Joint religiosity and married couples' sexual satisfaction. *Psychology of Religion and Spirituality, 12*, 201–212. http://doi.org/10.1037/rel0000243

Duncan, A. R., Jaini, P. A., & Hellman, C. M. (2021). Positive psychology and hope as lifestyle medicine modalities in the therapeutic encounter: A narrative review. *American Journal of Lifestyle Medicine, 15*, 6–13. . http://doi.org/10.1177/1559827620908255

Dunlap, R. (2020). A Zen Buddhist conception of hope in enlightenment. In C. Blöser & T. Stahl (Eds.), *The moral psychology of hope*. (pp. 209–226). Rowman & Littlefield International.

Eche, I. J., Eche, I. M., Pires, C., Achibiri, A. (2022). A systematic mixed-studies review of hope experiences in parents of children with cancer. *Cancer Nursing*, *45*, E43–E58. . http://doi.org/10.1097/NCC.0000000000000841

Eijkolt, M. (2020). Medicine's collision with false hope: The false hope harms (FHH) argument. *Bioethics*, *34*, 803–811. https://doi.org/10.1111/bioe.12731

Ellison, C. G., Henderson, A. K., Glenn, N. D., & Harkrider, K. E. (2011). Sanctification, stress, and marital quality. *Family Relations: An Interdisciplinary Journal of Family Studies*, *60*, 404 – 420. http://doi.org/10.1111/j.1741-3729.2011.00658.x

Germann, J. N., Leonard, D., Heath, C. L., Stewart, S. M. Leavey, P. J., & Alarcon, A. (2018). Hope as a predictor of anxiety and depressive symptoms following pediatric cancer diagnosis. *Journal of Pediatric Psychology*, *43*, 152–161. http://doi.org/10.1093/jpepsy/jsx097

Ghazavi, Z., Khaledi-Sardashti, F., Kajbaf, M. B., & Esmaielzadeh, M. (2015). Effect of hope therapy on the hope of diabetic patients. *Iran Journal of Nursing and Midwifery Research*, *20*, 75–80. PMCID: PMC4325418

Gum, A., Snyder, C. R., Duncan, P. W. A. G., & Aben, A. (2006). Hopeful thinking, participation, and depressive symptoms three months after a stroke. *Psychology and Health*, *21*, 319–334. http://doi.org/10.1080/14768320500422907

Hernandez-Kane, K. M., & Mahoney, A. (2018). Sex through a sacred lens: Longitudinal effects of sanctification of marital sexuality. *Journal of Family Psychology*, *32*(4), 425–434. https://doi.org/10.1037/fam0000392

Herth, K. (1992). Abbreviated instrument to measure hope: Development and psychometric evaluation. *Journal of Advanced Nursing*, *17*, 1251–1259. https://doi.org/10.1111/j.1365-2648.1992.tb01843.x

Hesiodus (1980). *Works and Days*. Penguin Classics.

Hook, J.N., Worthington, E.L., Jr., Ripley, J.S., & Davis, D.E. (2011). Christian approaches for helping couple: Review of empirical research and recommendations for clinicians. *Journal of Psychology and Christianity*, *30*, 213–222.

Jerome, A., Allen Heath, M., Williams, M., Winters, R., & Cutrer-Párraga, E. A. (2023). Traversing trauma: Resilient women's religious and spiritual stories of hope and strength. *Professional Psychology: Research and Practice*, *54*(2), 177–187. https://doi.org/10.1037/pro0000491

Lai, G. J., Tan, K., Tan, M., Cheong, G., Cheng, C., & Mathew, M. (2023). Dyadic positive and negative religious coping among older Singaporean couples and marital satisfaction. *Journal of Family Psychology*, *37*(2), 268–274. https://doi.org/10.1037/fam0001025

Larson, D.J., Whelton, W.J., Rogers, T., McElheran, J., Tremblay, H., Dushinski, K., Chaodraka, M., Herth, K., Green, J., Schalk, K., & Domene, J. (2020). Multidimensional Hope in Counseling and Psychotherapy Scale. *Journal of Psychotherapy Integration*, *30*, 407–422. http://doi.org/10.1037/int0000198

Laslo, R. R., George, L. S., & Margalit, M. (2022). Social participation and posttraumatic growth: The serial mediation of hope, social support, and reappraisal. *Journal of Community Psychology*, *50*(1), 47–63. https://doi.org/10.1002/jcop.22490

Leamy, M., Bird, V., Le Boutillier, C., Williams, J., & Slade, M. (2018). Conceptual framework for personal recovery in mental health: Systematic review and narrative synthesis. *The British Journal of Psychiatry*, *199*, 445–452. http://doi.org/10.1192/bjp.bp.110.083733

Lloyd, T.J., & Hastings, R. (2009). Hope as a psychological resilience factor in mothers and fathers of children with intellectual disabilities. *Journal of Intellectual Disability Research*, *53*, 957–968. http://doi.org/10.1111/j.1365-2788.2009.01206.x

Lopez, S. J., Pedrotti, J. T., & Snyder, C. R. (2015). *Positive psychology: The scientific and practical explorations of human strengths*, *3rd* ed. Sage Publications, Inc.

Lu, C. (2023). The relationship between parental emotional warmth and rural adolescents' hope: The sequential mediating role of perceived social support and prosocial behavior. *The Journal of Genetic Psychology*, *184*, 260–273. http://doi.org/10.1080/00221325.2022.2161343

Luo, S. X., van Horen, F., Millet, K., & Zeelenberg, M. (2022). What we talk about when we talk about hope: A prototype analysis. *Emotion*, *22*(4), 751–768. https://doi.org/10.1037/emo0000821

Mahon, N.E., & Yarcheski, A. (2017). Parent and friend social support and adolescent hope. *Clinical Nursing Research*, *26*, 224–240. https://doi.org/10.1177/1054773815619881

Mahoney, A., Pargament, K. I., Jewell, T., Swank, A. B., Scott, E., Emery, E., & Rye, M. (1999). Marriage and the spiritual realm: The role of proximal and distal religious constructs in marital functioning. Journal of Family Psychology, 13, 321–338. https://doi.org/10.1037/0893-3200.13.3.321

Mahoney, A., Wong, S., Pomerleau, J. M., & Pargament, K. I. (2022). Sanctification of diverse aspects of life and psychosocial functioning: A meta-analysis of studies from 1999 to 2019. *Psychology of Religion and Spirituality*, *14*(4), 585–598. https://doi.org/10.1037/rel0000354

McCarthy, J., Higgins, A., McCarthy, B., Flynn, A.B., & Gijbels, H. (2023). Family members perspectives on hope when supporting a relative experiencing mental health problems. *International Journal of Mental Health Nursing*, *32*, 1405–1415. http://doi.org/10.1111/inm.13185

McNulty, J. K. (2011). The dark side of forgiveness: The tendency to forgive predicts continued psychological and physical aggression in marriage. *Personality and Social Psychology Bulletin*, *37*(6), 770–783. https://doi.org/10.1177/0146167211407077

Menninger, K. (1959). The academic lecture: Hope. *The American Journal of Psychiatry*, *116*, 481–491. https://doi.org/10.1176/ajp.116.6.481

Olsman, E. (2020). Hope in health care: A synthesis of review studies. In: van den Heuvel, S.C. (eds) *Historical and Multidisciplinary Perspectives on Hope*. Springer, Cham. https://doi.org/10.1007/978-3-030-46489-9_11

Pargament, K. I., & Mahoney, A. (2005). Sacred matters: Sanctification as a vital topic for the psychology of religion. *International Journal for the Psychology of Religion*, *15*, 179 –198. http://doi.org/10.1207/s15327582ijpr1503_1

Park, C. L. (2013). Religion and meaning. In R. F. Paloutzian & C. L. Park (Eds.), *Handbook of the Psychology of Religion and Spirituality* (pp. 357–379). The Guilford Press.

Park, J., & Chen, R.K. (2016). Positive psychology and hope as means to recovery from mental illness. *Journal of Applied Rehabilitation Counseling*, *47*, 34–42.

Park, N., Peterson, C., & Seligman, M.E.P. (2005). Strengths of character and well-being. *Journal of Social and Clinical Psychology*, *23*. https://doi.org/10.1521/jscp.23.5.603.50748

Perakyla, A. (1991). Hope work in the care of seriously ill patients. *Qualitative Health Research*, *1*(4), 407–433. https://doi.org/10.1177/104973239100100402

Pergert, P., & Lutzen, K. (2012). Balancing truth-telling in the preservation of hope: A relational ethics approach. *Nursing Ethics*, *19*, 21–29. https://doi.org/10.1177/0969733011418551

Pruyser, P.W. (1987). Maintaining hope in adversity. *Bulletin of the Menninger Clinic*, *51*, 463–474. PMID: 3676542

Raney, A.A., Ai, A.L., & Paloutzian, R.F. (2022). Faith factors, character strengths, and depression following Hurricane Michael. *The International Journal for the Psychology of Religion*, *32*, 330–346. http://doi.org/10.1080/10508619.2022.2029045

Rassool, G.H., & Khan, W.N.A. (2023). Hope in Islamic psychotherapy. *Journal of Spirituality in Mental Health*. https://doi.org/10.1080/19349637.2023.2207751

Reichard, R. J., Avey, J. B., Lopez, S., & Dollwet, M. (2013). Having the will and finding the way: A review and meta-analysis of hope at work. *The Journal of Positive Psychology*, *8*(4), 292–304. https://doi.org/10.1080/17439760.2013.800903

Ripley, J., Solfelt, L., Ord, A., Garthe, R. C., Worthington, E. L., Jr., & Channing, T. (2023a). Short- and long-term outcomes of hope-focused couple therapy. *Spirituality in Clinical Practice*, *10*, 271–288. https://doi.org/10.1037/scp0000286

Ripley, J. S., & Worthington, E. L., Jr. (2014). *Couple therapy: A new Hope-focused Approach*. InterVarsity Press.

Ripley, J.S., Worthington, E.L., Jr., Kent, V., Loewer, E., & Chen, J. (2023b). Spiritually incorporating couple therapy in practice: Christian-accommodated couple therapy as an illustration. *Psychotherapy, 59*(3), 382–391. https://doi.org/10.1037/pst0000411

Russell, B. (2013). *What I Believe* 2nd edition. Routledge.

Rusu, P. P., Hilpert, P., Beach, S. R. H., Turliuc, M. N., & Bodenmann, G. (2015). Dyadic coping mediates the association of sanctification with marital satisfaction and well-being. *Journal of Family Psychology, 29*(6), 843–849. https://doi.org/10.1037/fam0000108

Sandage, S.J., Jankowski, P.J., Paine, D.R., Exline, J.J., Ruffing, E.G., Rupert, D., Stavros, G.S., & Bronstein, M. (2022). Testing a relational spirituality model of psychotherapy clients' preferences and functioning, *Journal of Spirituality in Mental Health, 24*, 1–21. https://doi.org/10.1080/19349637.2020.1791781

Sandage, S.J., Rupert, D., Stavros, G., & Devor, N.G. (2020). *Relational spirituality in psychotherapy: Healing suffering and promoting growth.* American Psychological Association.

Scioli, A., & Biller, H. B. (2009). *Hope in the age of anxiety: A guide to understanding and strengthening our most important virtue.* Oxford University Press.

Shepherd, D.A., Maitlis, S., Parida, V., Wincent, J., & Lawrence, T.B. (2022). Intersectionality in intractable dirty work: How Mumbai ragpickers make meaning of their work and lives. *Academy of Management Journal, 65*, 1680–1708. http://doi.org/10.5465/amj.2019.0125

Snyder, C.R. (1989). Reality negotiation: From excuses to hope and beyond. *Journal of Social and Clinical Psychology, 8*, 130–157. http://doi.org/10.1521/jscp.1989.8.2.130

Snyder, C.R., Harris, C., Anderson, J.R., Holleran, S.A., Irving, L.M., Sigmon, S.T., et al., (1991). The will and the ways: Development and validation of an individual differences measure of hope. *Journal of Personality and Social Psychology, 60*, 570–585. http://doi.org/10.1037/0022-3514.60.4.570

Snyder, C.R., Hoza, B., Pelham, W.E., Rapoff, M., Ware, L., Danovsky, M., et al., (1997). The development and validation of the Children's Hope Scale. *Journal of Pediatric Psychology, 22*, 399–421. http://doi.org/10.1093/jpepsy/22.3.399

Snyder, C.R., & Rand, K.L. (2003). The case against false hope. *American Psychologist, 58*(10), 820–822. https://doi.org/10.1037/0003-066X.58.10.820

Snyder, C. R., Sympson, S. C., Ybasco, F. C., Borders, T. F., Babyak, M. A., & Higgins, R. L. (1996). Development and validation of the State Hope Scale. *Journal of Personality and Social Psychology, 70*, 321–335. http://doi.org/10.1037/0022-3514.70.2.321

Sophocles (443 BCE/ 1947). *Antigone* (L. Galantiere, Translator). Samuel French Publishers.

Stafford, L. (2016). Marital sanctity, relationship maintenance, and marital quality. *Journal of Family Issues, 37*(1), 119–131. https://doi.org/10.1177/0192513X13515884

Tong, E.M.W., Frederickson, B.L., Chang, W., & Lim, Z.X. (2010). Re-examining hope: The roles of agency thinking and pathways thinking. *Cognition and Emotion, 24*, 1207–1215. http://doi.org/10.1080/02699930903138865

Van Weeghel, J., Boetien, D., van Zelst, C., & Hasson-Ohayon, I. (2019). Conceptualizations, assessments, and implications of personal recovery in mental illness: A scoping review of systematic reviews and meta-analyses. *Psychiatric Rehabilitation Journal, 42*, 160–181. http://doi.org/10.1037/prj0000356

Ward, D.B., & Wampler, K.S. (2010). Moving up the continuum of hope: Developing a theory of hope and understanding its influence in couples therapy. *Journal of Marital and Family Therapy, 36*, 212–228. http://doi.org/10.1111/j.1752-0606.2009.00173.x

Weis, R., & Speridakos, E.C. (2011). A meta-analysis of hope enhancement strategies in clinical and community settings. *Psychology of Well-Being, 1*, 5. https://doi.org/10.1186/2211-1522-1-5

Witvliet, C. V. O., Hall, M. E. L., Exline, J., Wang, D. C., Root Luna, L. M., Van Tongeren, D. R., Myers, D. G., Abernethy, A. D., & Witvliet, J. D. (2022). The Eschatological Hope Scale: Construct development and measurement of theistic eschatological hope. *Journal of Psychology and Christianity, 41*(1), 16–35.

Worthington, E. L., Jr., Hight, T. L., Ripley, J. S., Perrone, K. M., Kurusu, T. A., & Jones, D. R. (1997). Strategic hope-focused relationship-enrichment counseling with individual couples. *Journal of Counseling Psychology*, *44*(4), 381–389. https://doi.org/10.1037/0022-0167.44.4.381

Yarcheski, A., & Mahon, N.E. (2016). Meta-analyses of predictors of hope in adolescents. *Western Journal of Nursing Research*, *38*, 345–368. https://doi.org/10.1177/0193945914559545

Ybarra, L. and Lohr, S. (2002), Estimates of repeat victimization using the national crime victimization survey. *Journal of Quantitative Criminology*, *18*, 1–21. https://www.jstor.org/stable/23366729

Zhang, R., Gao, Y., & Xie, P. (2022). The role of perceived social support for loneliness in the Chinese elderly: Hope and core self-evaluations as mediators. *Current Psychology*, *42*, 29172–29178. http://doi.org/10.1007/s12144-022-03967-2

Chapter 28

Humility

Yejin Lee, Aaron T. McLaughlin, Jamian Coleman, Hee Chan Woo, Anna L. Scott, Joshua N. Hook, Daryl R. Van Tongeren and Don E. Davis[*†]

Humility is a popular topic of discourse within several world religions and influential philosophies (Lundberg, 2010). Indeed, several religious teachings and traditions identify humility as a desirable character strength. For example, the Islamic sacred text of *The Qur'an* (M.A.S. Abdel Haleem, Trans., 2004) houses verses such as, "successful indeed are the believers who humble themselves in their prayers" (Al-Mu'minun 23:1–2). Similarly, in the *Holy Bible* (i.e., Christian sacred text), you can find verses such as "God opposes the proud but gives grace to the humble" (New International Version, 2011, Proverbs 3:34). The Bhagavadgītā (Hinduism) and the Qur'an (Islam) commend humility as a virtue juxtaposed with arrogance. In Buddhism, humility is conceptualized as an absence of conceit. Revered figures in Judaism (e.g., Moses), Christianity (e.g., Jesus), and Confucianism (e.g., Confucius) are characterized as being humble. Accordingly, many reviews have surveyed the literature and pointed to beneficial associations of humility with health and well-being (Van Tongeren, Davis et al., 2019a). Benefits include meaning in life, strong relationships, lower blood pressure, and less stress (Van Tongeren, Hook et al., 2019b). At first glance, the case seems closed: Reviews on humility, health, and well-being typically report that humility is beneficial, and more humility is needed. However, humility is not equally extolled and valued across worldviews. The ancient Greeks viewed humility as a vice resembling a form of self-debasement (Chappell, 2020), and the "dark" side of humility is receiving increased attention among philosophers, theologians, and psychologists (e.g., Floyd-Thomas, 2020; Priebe & Van Tongeren, 2021; Van Tongeren et al., 2023). In recognition of this tension and acknowledgement of the influence of spiritual contexts on how humility is perceived or valued (Hill et al., 2023; Porter et al., 2017), in this chapter, we review the "light" (i.e., salubrious) and "dark" (i.e., deleterious) sides of humility, health, and well-being.

This review builds on the work of prior reviews assessing associations of humility and well-being (e.g., Toussaint & Webb, 2017; Worthington & Allison, 2018) by examining the potential benefits and drawbacks of humility on outcomes of physical health, depression, anxiety, life satisfaction, and meaning in life. We also consider the relationships of humility with health and well-being within the context of spirituality. Thus, we define humility within the context of spirituality and then review the literature to explore the benefits and drawbacks of

* Corresponding Author: ddavis88@gsu.edu.

† Supplemental Tables will be placed in an OSF page upon completion of the project https://docs.google.com/spreadsheets/d/1P7nZkHmOA_Z32Bh1ZQnR-kbNSmPx19IDbie12iQr4bM/edit?usp=sharing.

DOI: 10.4324/9781003440048-32

humility on health and well-being. Next, we provide a brief overview of humility interventions and conclude with a discussion of limitations and future directions for the scientific study of humility, health, and well-being.

Fundamental Concepts

Humility

Although there is a lack of full consensus among researchers with regards to the definition of humility, most agree that humility involves intrapersonal (e.g., holding an accurate view of oneself, owning one's limitations) and interpersonal aspects (e.g., being oriented to the needs of others; Davis et al., 2011; Van Tongeren, Davis et al., 2019a). In this chapter, we include studies whose conceptual or operational definitions of humility might differ, but also fall under this larger umbrella of intrapersonal and interpersonal definitions of humility. We also consider studies in which subdomains of humility are expressed in different contexts (e.g., intellectual humility, theistic humility, and cultural humility). Our approach aligns with theory that treats humility as a relationship-specific personality judgement (Davis et al., 2011).

Spirituality

We define spirituality broadly as a sense of closeness, connection, or oneness with the sacred (Hill et al., 2001; Davis et al., 2015). The "sacred" refers to any object or being that individuals sanctify (Hill et al., 2001). Examples include a theistic being, the transcendent, nature, humanity, marriage, and even oneself (Pargament, 2002). This definition of spirituality includes theistic (e.g., monotheistic, polytheistic) and non-theistic searches for meaning and purpose in the face of existential concerns (e.g., death, isolation, meaninglessness, and freedom). Further, this conceptualization of spirituality is compatible with the RiTE model of spirituality that distinguishes various types of spirituality (e.g., ritualistic [religious], theistic, existential). This facilitates inclusion of a wide range of spiritual expressions (Webb et al., 2014; see also, Chapters 1 and 44 of this volume).

Health and Well-Being

Health and well-being are conceptualized in a variety of ways within the empirical literature. For the purposes of this chapter, we focused on humility's relationships with physical health, mental health (i.e., depression, anxiety), and well-being (i.e., life satisfaction, meaning in life). Physical health was operationalized as subjective or objective indicators of somatic symptoms and general health (e.g., blood pressure). We chose depression and anxiety as operationalizations of mental health as they represent the two most common diagnoses according to the World Health Organization ("Mental Disorders", n.d.). In terms of well-being, we included studies that measured life satisfaction and meaning in life, two constructs distinguished in the literature as representative of hedonic and eudaimonic well-being, respectively (Ryan & Deci, 2001). *Hedonic well-being* refers to subjective pleasure and happiness, which is most often captured through self-report of one's perceived life satisfaction. *Eudaimonic well-being* refers to self-actualization and flourishing, which is often measured by assessing levels of perceived meaning in life (Ryan & Deci, 2001; Ryff, 1989).

Theory of Humility, Health, and Well-Being

The Light Side: Salubrious Effects

In a prior review, Toussaint and Webb (2017) presented a theoretical model that outlines several mechanisms through which humility generates positive effects on health. In this model, humility eases one's mental and physical burdens, which in turn allows for better health. Thus, in the context of spirituality, one way in which a person's humility affects their own health may be through effects on a person's cognitive appraisals of experiences with religious/spiritual stress, struggle, and trauma, or threats to their worldview (Toussaint & Webb, 2017). In such situations, individuals who are higher in humility might experience less rumination, have a greater ability to cope with negative emotions, possess a greater openness to experience, and maintain a secure sense of identity (Chancellor & Lyubomirsky, 2013).

Another causal mechanism for effects of humility on health might be the quality of one's social relationships or social support (Van Tongeren, Hook et al., 2019b). Humility serves prosocial functions, in that people who are perceived to be high in humility benefit from the formation of new social bonds and the maintenance of strong relationships. Moreover, humility can buffer the potential costs of conflict or competition in relationships (i.e., *social oil hypothesis*, see Van Tongeren, Davis et al., 2019a for a review). On the other hand, less humility predicts less social support, which in turn can lead to fewer resources that contribute to one's health and well-being (Davis et al., 2013). Together, the *humility-health hypothesis* suggests that people higher in humility will engage in a range of intrapersonal and interpersonal behaviors that contribute to better health.

Surely, humility may show stronger associations with some indicators of well-being over others. For example, in what we might call the *humility-well-being hypothesis*, Aghababaei and colleagues argue that humility, as measured by the HEXACO, is more strongly and consistently related to indicators of eudaimonic well-being rather than hedonic well-being (Aghababaei & Arji, 2013; Aghababaei et al., 2016). If this hypothesis is correct, then humility might be a long-term investment in relationships that can result in short-term decreases in pleasure, but over longer periods of time, embed people within a relationship network that provides a basis for meaning in life. Such relationships may provide meaning even amidst the adversity that individuals will inevitably face within a broader community.

The Dark Side: Deleterious Effects

It is also likely that the benefits of humility may have important boundary conditions. Such a theory suggests that, in certain contexts, humility can be detrimental to one's health and well-being. For example, humility norms can be applied unequally. If women are expected to express greater humility than men in workplace negotiations, they may get less social credit or reward for expressing humility; see Priebe & Van Tongeren, 2021). In such cases, virtue language may create a structure for maintaining social advantages (e.g., the ability for some to act more selfishly or assertively without being labeled arrogant). In other cases, we imagine that if leaders are under pressure to appear decisive and strong, expressions of humility may undermine trust of subordinates.

Humility may cause disadvantages in times of uncertainty. When engaging existential doubts, humility toward one's beliefs, values, and worldview (i.e., intellectual humility) might undermine existential security (called the *trade-off hypothesis of humility*; Van Tongeren et al.,

2016). In a set of two studies, Van Tongeren et al. (2023) observed that existential humility predicted greater death anxiety and lower levels of religious well-being. Furthermore, McLaughlin et al. (2023) observed through latent profile analyses that groups of individuals with higher levels of intellectual humility reported higher levels of anxiety and negative affect in the United States and Hong Kong, but not the Netherlands.

Given that the literature is beginning to identify important boundary conditions for associations of humility, health, and well-being (such as inequality and uncertainty), it is important to clarify contextual factors that explain when humility is beneficial or costly to health and well-being. As such, the primary aim of this chapter is to summarize observations in the literature regarding salubrious and deleterious associations of humility with physical health, depression, anxiety, life satisfaction, and meaning in life.

Method

We set several inclusion criteria. First, we only included empirical articles (written in English); theoretical articles and case studies were excluded. Second, we only included articles containing (a) a measure of humility and (b) one or more measures of general health, depression, anxiety, life satisfaction, and meaning. Type of measurement, sample, and design were allowed to vary. The search for articles on humility and health/well-being occurred in two phases. First, a search on PsycINFO and Google Scholar was conducted as part of a larger study for all empirical studies that included the term "humility" prior to 2019. We identified 182 studies from this prior search to screen for inclusion. Then, we conducted another search on PsycINFO on August 31, 2023. We searched for all articles that included the term "humility" between 2019 and 2023 ($N = 953$). In total, this search strategy yielded a total of 1,135 articles to screen for inclusion in this chapter.

The coding process occurred in three rounds (see Supplemental Table 1). Coders met multiple times to receive training for the screening and extraction process led by the first author. In the first round of coding, three members of the research team screened abstracts based on inclusion criteria. These team members included one faculty member in the field of Counselor Education, one doctoral student studying Counseling Psychology, and one master's level student in a CACREP program for rehabilitation counseling. This process yielded 552 articles that were in English, empirical, and included a measure of humility for full-text review. In the second round, two members of the research team screened texts for measures of health, depression, anxiety, life satisfaction, and meaning (a postdoctoral research associate with training in Counseling Psychology and the first author's advisor who is a full professor in a Counseling Psychology program). This resulted in 127 articles. In the third round of coding, the first author reviewed all articles for inclusion in the review. Articles without specific target DVs and duplicates were excluded. This process yielded a total of 89 studies. Supplemental Table 2 presents data from each included study and a summary of key findings related to humility and health.

Results

Associations of humility, health, and well-being were the primary topic of interest in about 25% of the studies (22 out of 89). Nevertheless, an additional 60% ($N = 47$) of studies reported correlations of humility with outcomes of health and well-being, and about 15% ($N = 11$) included variables of humility and health for which the authors did not report correlations.

As we examined humility, physical health, depression, anxiety, life satisfaction, and meaning in life in broad terms, we allowed for various measures to be represented in the review. Measures used in each study are detailed in Supplemental Table 2.

Humility and Physical Health

The *humility-health hypothesis* suggests that people higher in humility will engage in a range of intrapersonal and interpersonal behaviors that contribute to better physical health. In our review, twelve studies examined the relationship between humility and health (see Supplemental Table 3); 11 of which reported null or weak positive associations (*r*s = |.00–.33|). Notably, no studies reported a negative association between humility and health. Van Tongeren, Hook and colleagues' set of studies (2019) provides clues to understand when humility may have health benefits, if at all. Across two studies, the researchers found a general pattern in which the benefits of humility on physical and mental health were greatest in dyads where both partners were humble rather than when only one partner was humble. In their second study, they specifically found this pattern assessing blood pressure. Overall, these findings may align with a more nuanced perspective on humility's health benefits. At the individual level, the benefits of humility for physical health may heavily depend on contextual factors, such as the quality of one's surrounding relationships. People may tend to have better health in relationships or larger systems that are characterized by a culture of humility. That said, most of the empirical research in this area has not found much of a meaningful relationship between humility and physical health. More work is needed to test the effects of relational factors on the relationship of humility and one's physical health.

Humility and Mental Health

Next, we explored the association between humility and mental health to test the conflicting theories on the link between humility and mental health. One theory suggests that individuals who are higher in humility experience less rumination and have a greater ability to cope with negative emotions, leading to better mental health (Chancellor & Lyubomirsky, 2013). On the other hand, another theory suggests that humility may come at a cost to one's mental health, especially when it comes to existential matters (i.e., *trade-off hypothesis*; Van Tongeren et al., 2016). Of the 39 studies assessing the relationship of humility with mental health, results from studies converged to support a weak positive association between humility and mental health (see Supplemental Table 4). There were 59 total correlations reported concerning the association of humility with mental health. Of these, 52 correlations were either non-significant, $p > .05$ ($n = 25$), weak positive ($rs = |.13–.29|$, $n = 24$), or weak negative ($rs = |.16–.23|$; $n = 3$). Of the remaining seven correlations, there were four moderate positive ($r \geq |.30|$), one moderate negative, and two strong negative associations ($r \geq |.50|$; see Supplemental Table 4). Once again, these findings align with the idea that the benefits (or risks) of humility for an individual's mental health may depend on a variety of contextual factors that are currently not well understood.

Salubrious Associations

Many studies found a small positive association between humility and mental health symptoms. Noting that three studies reported a moderate positive association between humility and mental health, we examined these studies to identify potential moderators that could be examined in future work (Brown et al., 2013; Van Tongeren, Hook et al., 2019b; Winkeljohn Black, 2019). In each of these studies, an interpersonal aspect of humility was included. For example, Brown et al. (2013) found a moderate association ($r = -.37, p < .01$) between a social-comparison measure of humility (Humility Inventory; Brown et al., 2013) and anxiety (State-Trait Anxiety Inventory; Spielberger et al., 1983) in a sample of 620 undergraduates in the United States (57.1% female, 65.5% White). This measure involves a subscale that measures esteem for others, or the extent to which individuals have an orientation toward others' needs.

Two studies found a moderate association between humility and mental health in the context of the relationship with one's partner. Winkeljohn Black et al. (2019) and Van Tongeren, Hook et al. (2019b) studied humility and mental health in the same sample of 69 heterosexual married couples (71.7% White, *M*age = 30.80). The benefits of humility for mental health (e.g., less depressive symptoms) were greatest in couples in which both partners were humble, and when perceptions of others' humility were not too discrepant from their expectations of others' humility. These results suggest that the context of an interpersonal relationship may be crucial to determining when humility provides benefits to an individual's mental health.

Deleterious Associations

Six studies showed negative associations between humility and mental health (Charbonneau et al., 2021; Lee, 2022; Tilka, 2017; Van Tongeren et al., 2023, McLaughlin et al., 2023). Three studies align with the trade-off hypothesis of humility. Namely, within contexts of uncertainty, humility may be associated with more distress (Van Tongeren et al., 2016). For example, McLaughlin et al. (2023) observed in a sample of 1,030 adults from the United States, the Netherlands, and Hong Kong, that humility regarding one's beliefs about existential matters was typically associated with certain relational benefits (i.e., more empathy, greater perspective-taking, lower defensiveness), but also certain intrapersonal costs (i.e., higher reports of anxiety and negative affect). Further, considering intrapersonal costs of existential humility, Van Tongeren et al. (2023) observed humility to come at the cost of one's spiritual well-being in two studies (including one longitudinal study). They found a small association ($r = .16, p = .024$) between existential humility and death anxiety among a sample of 203 undergraduate students at a religious university (74.4% female, 85% White, 85% currently religious) and a moderate association ($r = .31, p < .001$) in a sample of 1,151 U.S. community members (61.7% female, 73.5% White, 57% currently religious, 75.8% faith in God). These results suggest that humility toward one's spiritual, religious, or existential beliefs may come at a cost to mental health.

Likewise, several other studies showed initial support for deleterious associations between humility and mental health. For example, in a sample of 328 East Asian undergraduate students (62.1% female, 57.9% Chinese American, 47.6% Christian, *M*age = 20.27), Lee (2022) found that humility had a small deleterious association with anxiety ($r = .23, p < .01$). These associations were mediated by an individual's tendency to engage in avoidant coping strategies. This study suggests that there is nuance in the association between humility and mental health when examined in the context of humility being endorsed as an Asian value. Another study found a large deleterious association between humility and mental health. In a dissertation study, Tilka (2017) studied the associations between humility, religious/spiritual struggle, and posttraumatic growth in a sample of 97 breast cancer patients (100% female, 80.4% White, 62.9% Christian, *M*age = 42.26). Within this context, Tilka (2017) found a large deleterious association ($r = .51, p < .01$) between humility and mental health (e.g., more symptoms of depression, anxiety, and stress).

Taken together, we see continued support for the idea that the relationship between humility and mental health benefits might depend on a variety of contextual factors related to the culture of the individual and the relationships within which they are embedded. In some ways, this makes sense, given that humility involves orienting to the interests of others while also appropriately attending to one's own needs. Some situations and contexts may make this balance particularly difficult to accomplish.

Humility and Well-Being

We then explored the literature examining associations between humility and two indicators of well-being: life satisfaction (hedonic well-being) and meaning in life (eudaimonic well-being). Specifically, we sought to clarify whether humility is more strongly associated with certain aspects of eudaimonic well-being rather than hedonic well-being as suggested in prior research (Aghababaei & Arji, 2013; Aghababaei et al., 2016). A summary of the included studies is presented in Supplemental Tables 5 and 6. Of the 41 studies examining life satisfaction and 22 studies examining meaning in life, results converged to suggest a weak or null relationship between humility and life satisfaction and meaning in life. There were 46 total correlations reported testing the association between humility and life satisfaction. Of these, 43 correlations were either non-significant, $p > .05$ ($n = 23$) or weak positive ($rs = |.09–.25|$; $n = 20$). Two correlations were moderate positive, one correlation was strong positive, and no associations were negative. Similarly, there were 24 total correlations reported testing the association between humility and meaning in life. Of these, 18 correlations were either non-significant, $p > .05$ ($n = 5$) or weak positive ($rs = |.15–.29|$, $n = 13$). Six correlations were moderate and positive, which are reviewed below. Overall, these results suggest that humility has a significant but weak positive relationship with life satisfaction and meaning in life. Of note, in our review, we did not find evidence supporting the idea that humility is more strongly related to eudaimonic well-being than it is to hedonic well-being.

Salubrious Associations

As demonstrated above, many studies provided support for positive associations between humility and well-being. Although most studies presented small positive correlations, five studies reported medium and large relationships between humility and well-being (Chen et al., 2023; Cuthbert et al., 2018; Hill et al., 2021; Tong et al., 2019; Yukhymenko-Lescroart & Sharma, 2020).

Two of these studies assessed humility in the spiritual domain, observing medium to large associations with life satisfaction. In a sample of 353 Protestant, Catholic, and Orthodox Christians from the United States (51.1% male, 62.6% White, 60.4% Protestant, *M*age = 34.94), Hill et al. (2021) found that theistic humility showed a salubrious association with life satisfaction ($r = .40$, $p < .01$). In another sample of 71 Christian pastors and lay leaders (60% female, 60.7% White, 100% Protestant, *M*age = 42.50), spiritual humility was associated with life satisfaction ($r = .47$, $p < .01$). One explanation is that measures of spiritual humility or theistic humility may assess a different construct than other measures of humility. Prior work on religiousness shows consistent links between religious involvement and life satisfaction (Yaden et al., 2022) and meaning in life (Park, 2013). Thus, in accordance with the hypothesis of humility being associated with well-being through the development of a strong network of social support, perhaps humility in religious and spiritual domains promotes well-being by engaging spiritual and social relationships.

Two other studies found a moderate correlation between humility and meaning in life. One study by Tong et al. (2019) specifically found these associations in a sample of 122 undergraduates in Singapore (79.5% female, *M*age = 20.71). Results suggested that humility was associated with a total score of psychological well-being (includes a measure of purpose) at two timepoints (T1: $r = .31$, $p < .001$; T2: $r = .40$, $p < .001$). In another sample of 511 university students (66.0% female; 39.1% White, *M*age = 32.75), Yukhymenko-Lescroart and Sharma (2020) found several medium associations among subscales of the Sense of Purpose scale and humility, *r*s = .35–.45, $p < .001$.

Altogether, some early work on humility and well-being led some scholars to speculate that humility might lead to greater eudaimonic well-being. For example, in samples of Iranian (Study 1, $N = 422$; Study 4, $N = 251$), Polish (Study 2, $N = 221$; Study 5, $N = 226$), and Malay (Study 3, $N = 255$) students, Aghababaei et al. (2016) concluded that humility had stronger associations with purpose in life than life satisfaction. In these studies, however, correlations for both life satisfaction (*r*s = .13–.16) and purpose in life (*r*s = .23–.26) were all small. As studies accumulated, these associations were not consistently replicated. Thus, there appears to be more nuance in the relationship of humility with well-being. For example, Tong et al. (2019) found medium associations between humility and purpose in life at two timepoints. However, humility did not predict changes in purpose over time. Thus, they concluded that humility may have limited influence over promoting meaning in life and overall psychological well-being.

Deleterious Associations

Three studies observed humility to have deleterious associations with meaning in life (McLaughlin et al., 2023; Zhang et al., 2019). In the studies on existential humility by McLaughlin et al. (2023), associations of humility and meaning in life were quite nuanced. For example, in a sample of 340 adults in the United States (50.3% female, *M*age = 46.67), those with moderate belief commitment and humility (Moderates), and those with low commitment but high humility (Intellectually Diffident) reported lower meaning in life than those with high commitment and low humility (Intellectually Arrogant) and those with high commitment and high humility (Committed and Humble). However, people with high commitment and high humility were quite rare (appearing only in U.S. samples and not at all in the Hong Kong and the Netherlands samples). Thus, it was most common to see individuals report higher levels of humility with slightly lower levels of commitment, which predicted lower levels of meaning.

Zhang et al. (2019) studied how the makeup of religious groups, as either ideologically homogeneous or diverse, influences meaning in a sample of 229 undergraduate students at public universities (74.2% female, 39.7% White, 66.4% Christian, *M*age = 20.70). Participants were randomized into either an ideologically homogeneous or ideologically diverse condition. Results suggested that intellectual humility was negatively associated with meaning in the ideologically homogenous condition but was not associated with meaning in the ideologically diverse condition. This suggests that, in the context of being with others who share ideological worldviews, humility is associated with less meaning. However, moderation results suggested the benefits of humility for the ideologically diverse condition. Specifically, they found that the ideologically diverse condition reported a lower sense of meaning than participants in the ideologically homogenous condition. Still, this association was moderated by humility such that individuals with high levels of intellectual humility did not report a difference in meaning compared to the ideologically homogenous condition.

Once again, the pattern of results fits a more nuanced storyline: the relationship between humility and life satisfaction or meaning in life likely depends on important contextual factors, especially cultural or relationship factors that determine whether people are likely to reciprocate humble behavior. If people tend to cooperate in response to humility, then humility ought to lead to benefits. In contrast, in situations involving lower trust, we might expect that humility could backfire, and humble people may begin to question themselves and their willingness to focus on the interests of others, sometimes at personal cost.

Potential for Humility Interventions

Given the research and theory that humility may be associated with positive outcomes to health and well-being, researchers have begun to develop interventions to foster greater humility. This literature is still in its infancy however, as very few studies have studied the efficacy of humility interventions on health and well-being outcomes. In a recent review, Davis et al. (2023) provided a content analysis on humility interventions that exist within the literature. They reviewed seven studies that involve interventions that target humility. Two studies sought to increase humility through distanced perspective (Grossmann et al., 2021; Kross & Grossmann, 2012) and another through growth mindset (Porter & Schumann, 2018). Other studies had individuals read an article about humility (Porter et al., 2020), complete a workbook on humility (Lavelock et al., 2017), or prime participants with perception of their relational partner's responsiveness (Reis et al., 2018). Each of these studies demonstrated support for increasing humility pre-to-post intervention. However, other studies showed null results. For example, neither attending a class on humility (Meagher et al., 2019) nor using a workbook to increase humility in a sample of religious leaders (Cuthbert et al., 2018) demonstrated increases in humility after the intervention. Research has yet to establish a robust, feasible intervention that initiates a change in trait-measures of humility. Furthermore, effectiveness of existing interventions has not been tested over time. This research suggests that stronger conceptual work must first be completed in order to develop interventions that can specifically target humility.

Discussion

Humility is a virtue that is a part of major world religious and spiritual traditions. Therefore, it is important to explore how humility is associated with health and well-being. Scholars have long argued that humility, as a virtue, generates positive effects on health. Various mechanisms have been presented for this association, including less rumination (Chancellor & Lyubomirsky, 2013) and increased quality of one's social support (Van Tongeren, Hook et al., 2019b). These mechanisms are especially pertinent within spiritual contexts as humility may influence an individual's cognitive appraisals of their experiences with religious/spiritual stress or threats to their worldview. Despite such theories, however, the majority of studies reviewed in this chapter suggest nonexistent or weak salubrious associations between humility, health, and well-being. Furthermore, some studies even show deleterious associations between humility and health in spiritual contexts (Van Tongeren et al., 2023). Thus, evidence supporting robust links between humility, health, and well-being across conditions seems to be lacking.

A few studies demonstrate medium or strong associations between humility, health, and well-being, suggesting the existence of contextual factors that outline when humility may actually be associated with health and well-being (e.g., Hill et al., 2021; Van Tongeren, Hook et al., 2019b; Winkeljohn Black et al., 2019). Notably, this included benefits of humility with well-being in religious and spiritual domains. Specifically, studies that included an interpersonal aspect examining humility and health (i.e., among romantic partners) demonstrate larger associations between humility and health. These results support theory and work establishing the benefits of humility on interpersonal relationships through protecting against relational wear due to conflict (i.e., social oil hypothesis; Worthington et al., 2017) and through positive perceptions of their partner's lack of arrogance (i.e., social bond hypothesis; Davis et al., 2013). Thus, given weak direct associations among humility, health, and well-being, it is possible that humility is linked to greater health and well-being depending on contextual factors (such as low levels of uncertainty or social pressures), and through mechanisms such as strengthening of a network of social support (Krause, 2010; Krause et al., 2016).

We also sought to clarify the degree to which humility shows stronger associations with some indicators of well-being over others. In several studies, Aghababaei and colleagues argue that humility is more strongly associated with indicators of eudaimonic well-being than hedonic well-being (Aghababaei & Arji, 2013; Aghababaei et al., 2016). We specifically reviewed the literature on meaning in life and life satisfaction and did not find evidence to support this claim, as both indicators of well-being were either unrelated or weakly associated with humility. Given overall weak associations in research thus far, it may be too early to conclude that humility has implications for well-being at all, let alone stronger associations with eudaimonic well-being over hedonic well-being. However, our review is limited in that we only reviewed two indicators of well-being: life satisfaction and meaning in life. Further, we did not formally synthesize and analyze effect sizes. To further test these associations, future research may benefit from conducting a formal meta-analysis that also includes other indicators of hedonic and eudaimonic well-being.

Implications for Conceptualizations of Spirituality

Results of this study should be considered within the context of the specific expressions of spirituality that are represented in this review. The RiTE model of spirituality (Webb et al., 2014) was used to examine conceptualizations of spirituality. This model of spirituality expands the understanding of sacred human experiences to include (a) Ritualistic Spirituality (i.e., ritualistic or structured connection with deity), (b) Theistic Spirituality (i.e., non-structured, non-religious connection with deity), and (c) Existential Spirituality (i.e., a transcendent, yet non-theistic search for meaning and purpose). The studies included in this review primarily explored spirituality within the context of Ritualistic Spirituality as most studies examined spirituality within organized religious contexts. Specifically, the majority of studies were conducted among White Protestant Christian populations. Theistic Spirituality and Existential Spirituality were not represented in studies included in this review; that is, our search of the literature did not extract any studies reflective of non-Ritualistic Spirituality. Ritualistic expressions of spirituality are the most common form of spirituality in the United States, and as such, the review is thereby limited to spirituality that espouses the existence of a monotheistic deity. In this regard, the extant research does not consider polytheistic, atheistic, or non-ritualistic monotheistic understandings of spirituality.

Limitations in the Research on Humility and Health

Several methodological, conceptual, and diversity-related limitations exist within the current literature on humility, health, and well-being. One limitation that significantly impairs humility research is a lack of consensus around conceptualizations of humility (but for an example of initial efforts to consolidate, see Van Tongeren, Davis et al., 2019a). Specifically, there is a lack of synthesis of theory that explains how and why humility works. Not only does this make it difficult to establish a gold standard of measurement of humility, but it also leads researchers to conduct research that lacks a strong conceptual and theoretical base. Second, much of the studies examining humility, health, and well-being are correlational rather than experimental in nature. Thus, directionality of associations among variables cannot be determined. Moreover, although most researchers have conceptualized humility to be a predictor of well-being, it may be that the directionality of associations is the other way around such that well-being predicts greater humility (Tong et al., 2019). Third, the majority of studies used convenience samples of undergraduate students. The most commonly represented demographic across studies in this review were White, Protestant Christian, American individuals. Lack of diversity in the research on religion/spirituality and humility makes it difficult to generalize these results to individuals who identify with different cultural and spiritual identities. As such, the current literature demonstrates only a narrow understanding of how humility-based spirituality impacts health and well-being. Given these limitations, we offer several areas to be considered for future research on the intersections of humility and religion/spirituality.

Directions for Future Research

Conceptual and Theoretical Development of Humility

Research on humility, health, and well-being in a spiritual context is ripe for several research directions. For humility research to flourish, the field must first move toward a conceptual synthesis of humility. In its current state, the lack of consensus on definitions of humility has deterred specific research directions testing humility and health. To further understand the associations between humility, health, and well-being, it is important to develop and test stronger theories that can clarify how people can grow in humility through applied work. Indeed, research on humility interventions is still in its infancy. Initial work has provided evidence for the benefits of certain practices such as taking a distanced perspective in increasing humility (Grossmann et al., 2021; Kross & Grossmann, 2012). However, the feasibility of interventions that can be integrated in daily practices are lacking. Moreover, much of these interventions rely on individual effort. Interdisciplinary work that explores how certain religious/spiritual groups promote the development of character traits like humility within a network of relationships may be important for the development of humility interventions that result in beneficial outcomes for one's well-being. As such, future research may specifically benefit from synthesizing and testing theories of humility and health.

Testing Causal Models

Most research on humility and health has been correlational and cross-sectional. This type of research design is limited in that directionality of associations among variables cannot be determined. Specifically, although many researchers conceptualize humility to predict increases in well-being, this hypothesis cannot be tested using correlational methods. In fact, Tong et al. (2019) observed well-being to predict humility, but not vice versa, in a cross-lagged analysis. Thus, it is possible that the associations between humility, health, and well-being can be better parsed out using experimental methods. Causal models can also be used to test mediators through which humility is associated with health and well-being. One mediator that may be tested is social support, as research has demonstrated preliminary associations among humility and health through the benefits of interpersonal relationships (Krause, 2010; Krause et al., 2016). Another area for research that may be tested using causal models is the association between humility and eudaimonic versus hedonic well-being. Studies in this review suggested that correlations between humility and well-being (i.e., purpose in life and life satisfaction) have been weak. However, these claims should be tested causally to further explore whether humility is more strongly associated with eudaimonic well-being than hedonic well-being (Aghababaei et al., 2016). Greater applied work through experimental methods would do well for testing the efficacy of humility interventions.

Diversity Considerations

Future research may be more inclusive of expressions of spirituality that are not conducted in Western philosophies and worldviews, most of which include monotheistic conceptualizations of spirituality. Specifically, future research may explore Theistic and Existential Spirituality across various religious and nonreligious spiritual traditions around the world. We recommend researchers to be inclusive of polytheistic and atheistic expressions of spirituality. Testing these associations may show differential associations between humility, health, and well-being across race/ethnicity, spiritual affiliations, and cultural contexts. For example, examining humility from a social justice perspective, research has suggested that cultural humility may not be as beneficial for individuals of color compared to their White counterparts in the United States (Moon & Sandage, 2019). Furthermore, other research demonstrated that students of color may be more susceptible to intellectual servility, a construct that captures intellectual humility in unhealthy excess (McElroy-Hetzel et al., 2023). These studies provide preliminary evidence for the claim that humility may not be equally beneficial for all individuals. Future research may specifically examine differential associations that may exist across various expressions of spirituality across the world.

Conclusion

Results from the current review suggest that the associations between humility, health, and well-being are not as clear-cut as was previously concluded. Despite generating much nuance in our understanding of humility and its benefits, this chapter has highlighted numerous areas that are ripe for advancing research on humility and health. We need strong research methodology to clarify how humility is related to health and well-being. Such methods may include meta-analytic synthesis, moderation tests that engage leading theories on health and humility (e.g., humility–well-being hypothesis, trade-off hypothesis, and cultural contexts), causal designs that test humility interventions, and longitudinal studies that employ potential mechanisms (e.g., rumination, social support). Moreover, such advancements in the study of humility, health, and well-being may be facilitated by interdisciplinary conversations that examine humility in the context of spirituality.

References

"Mental Disorders."(n.d.), World Health Organization, https://www.who.int/news-room/fact-sheets/detail/mental-disorders. Retrieved 6 November 2023.

Aghababaei, N., & Arji, A. (2013). Well-being and the HEXACO model of personality. *Personality and Individual Differences*, *56*, 139–142. https://doi.org/10.1016/j.paid.2013.08.037

Aghababaei, N., Błachnio, A., Arji, A., Chiniforoushan, M., Tekke, M., & Fazeli Mehrabadi, A. (2016). Honesty–humility and the HEXACO structure of religiosity and well-being. *Current Psychology*, *35*, 421–426. https://doi.org/10.1007/s12144-015-9310-5

Brown, S. L., Chopra, P. K., & Schiraldi, G. R. (2013). Validation of the Humility Inventory (HI), a five-factor, self-report measure of humility. *The International Journal of Educational and Psychological Assessment*, *12*(2), 57–77.

Chancellor, J., & Lyubomirsky, S. (2013). Humble beginnings: Current trends, state perspectives, and hallmarks of humility. *Social and Personality Psychology Compass*, *7*(11), 819–833. https://doi.org/10.1111/spc3.12069

Chappell, S. G. (2020). Humility among the ancient Greeks. In M. Lafano, M. P. Lynch, & A. Tanesini (Eds.), *The Routledge handbook of philosophy of humility* (pp. 187–201).

Charbonneau, B. D., Reed, M., & Powell, D. M. (2021). Self-verification behavior as an employment interview tactic. *International Journal of Selection and Assessment*, *29*(3-4), 393–411. https://doi.org/10.1111/ijsa.12349

Chen, J. M., Joel, S., & Castro Lingl, D. (2023). Antecedents and consequences of LGBT individuals' perceptions of straight allyship. *Journal of Personality and Social Psychology*, *125*(4), 827–851. https://doi.org/10.1037/pspi0000422

Cuthbert, A. D., Davis, E. B., Aten, J. D., Short, A., Yarborough, C. A., Lavelock, C. R., Worthington, E. L., Jr., Davis, D. E., Hook, J. N., & Van Tongeren, D. R. (2018). Cultivating humility in religious leaders: The effectiveness of a spiritually integrated positive psychology intervention. *Spirituality in Clinical Practice*, *5*(4), 227–239. https://doi.org/10.1037/scp0000185

Davis, D. E., Bowes, S., McLaughlin, A., Hsu, W., Gazaway, S., McElroy-Hetzel, S., Van Tongeren, D. R., & Hook, J. N. (2023). In search of convergent creativity: content analysis of research on intellectual humility, *The Journal of Positive Psychology*, *18*(2), 304–315, https://doi.org/10.1080/17439760.2022.2154706

Davis, D. E., Hook, J. N., Worthington, E. L., Jr., Van Tongeren, D. R., Gartner, A. L., Jennings, D. J., & Emmons, R. A. (2011). Relational humility: Conceptualizing and measuring humility as a personality judgement. *Journal of Personality Assessment*, *93*(3), 225–234. https://doi.org/10.1080/00223891.2011.558871

Davis, D. E., Rice, K., Hook, J. N., Van Tongeren, D. R., DeBlaere, C., Choe, E., & Worthington, E. L., Jr. (2015). Development of the Sources of Spirituality Scale. *Journal of Counseling Psychology*, *62*(3), 503–513. https://doi.org/10.1037/cou0000082

Davis, D. E., Worthington Jr., E. L., Hook, J. N., Emmons, R. A., Hill, P. C., Bollinger, R. A., & Van Tongeren, D. R. (2013). Humility and the development and repair of social bonds: Two longitudinal studies. *Self and Identity*, *12*(1), 58–77. https://doi.org/10.1080/15298868.2011.636509

Floyd-Thomas, S. (2020). Oppressive humility: A womanist view of humility, flourishing, and the secret of joy. In D. Collins, R. McAnnally-Linz, E. C. Rosa (Eds.), *The joy of humility: The beginning and end of the virtues*. (1st ed., pp 13–42). Baylor University Press.

Grossmann, I., Dorfman, A., Oakes, H., Santos, H. C., Vohs, K. D., & Scholer, A. A. (2021). Training for wisdom: The distanced-self-reflection diary method. *Psychological Science*, *32*(3), 381–394. https://doi.org/10.1177/0956797620969170

Hill, P. C., DiFonzo, N., Jones, C. E., & Bell, J. S. (2023). Measurement at the intersection of positive psychology and the psychology of religion/spirituality. In E. B. Davis, E. L. Worthington Jr., & S. A. Schnitker (Eds.), *Handbook of Positive Psychology, Religion, and Spirituality* (pp. 37–52). Springer.

Hill, P. C., Lewis Hall, M. E., Wang, D., & Decker, L. A. (2021). Theistic intellectual humility and well-being: does ideological context matter? *The Journal of Positive Psychology*, *16*(2), 155–167. https://doi.org/10.1080/17439760.2019.1689424

Hill, P. C., Pargament, K. I., Hood, R. W., Jr., McCullough, M. E., Swyers, J. P., Larson, D. B., Zinnbauer, B. J. (2001). Conceptualizing religion and spirituality: Points of commonality, points of departure. *Journal for the Theory of Social Behaviour*, *30*(1), 51–77. https://doi.org/10.1111/1468-5914.00119

Holy Bible: New International Version (2011). Biblica. https://www.biblegateway.com/versions/New-International-Version-NIV-Bible/ (Original Work published 1978).

Krause, N. (2010). Religious involvement, humility, and self-rated health. *Social indicators research*, *98*, 23–39. https://doi.org/10.1007/s11205-009-9514-x

Krause, N., Pargament, K. I., Hill, P. C., & Ironson, G. (2016). Humility, stressful life events, and psychological well-being: Findings from the landmark spirituality and health survey. *The Journal of Positive Psychology*, *11*(5), 499–510. https://doi.org/10.1080/17439760.2015.1127991

Kross, E., & Grossmann, I. (2012). Boosting wisdom: Distance from the self-enhances wise reasoning, attitudes, and behavior. *Journal of Experimental Psychology: General*, *141*(1), 43–48. https://doi.org/10.1037/a0024158

Lavelock, C. R., Worthington, E. L., Griffin, B. J., Garthe, R. C., Elnasseh, A., Davis, D. E., & Hook, J. N. (2017). Still Waters Run Deep: Humility as a Master Virtue. *Journal of Psychology and Theology*, *45*(4), 286–303. https://doi.org/10.1177/009164711704500404

Lee, J. (2022). The Mediating Effect of Avoidant Coping on the Relationship between Asian Values and Psychological Distress among East Asian Americans. *Journal of Asia Pacific Counseling*, *12*(1), 117–132. https://doi.org/10.18401/2022.12.1.7

Lundberg, C. D. (2010). *Unifying truths of the world's religions*. New Fairfield, CT: Heavenlight Press.

McElroy-Hetzel, S. E., Davis, D. E., Hook, J. N., & Battaly, H. D. (2023). Too much of a good thing: Differentiating intellectual humility from servility in higher education, *Journal of Moral Education*, *52*(1), 21–33. https://doi.org/10.1080/03057240.2022.2126829

McLaughlin, A. T., Van Tongeren, D. R., McElroy-Heltzel, S. E., Bowes, S. M., Rice, K. G., Hook, J. N., Dewall, N. C., & Davis, D. E. (2023). Intellectual humility in the context of existential commitment. *The Journal of Positive Psychology*, *18*(2), 289–303. https://doi.org/10.1080/17439760.2022.2154705

Meagher, B. R., Gunn, H., Sheff, N., & Van Tongeren, D. R. (2019). An intellectually humbling experience: Changes in interpersonal perception and cultural reasoning across a five-week course. *Journal of Psychology and Theology*, *47*(3), 217–229. https://doi.org/10.1177/0091647119837010

Moon, S. H., & Sandage, S. J. (2019). Cultural humility for people of color: Critique of current theory and practice. *Journal of Psychology & Theology*, *47*(2), 76–86. https://doi.org/10.1177/0091647119842407

Pargament, K. I., & Mahoney, A. (2002). Spirituality: Discovering and conserving the sacred. In C. R. Snyder & S. J. Lopez (Eds.), *Handbook of positive psychology* (pp. 646–659). Oxford University Press.

Park, C. L. (2013). Religion and meaning. In R. F. Paloutzian & C. L. Park (Eds.), *Handbook of the psychology of religion and spirituality* (pp.357–378). New York: The Guilford Press.

Porter, S. L., Rambachan, A., & de Cea, A. V., Rabinowitz, D., Pardue, S., & Jackson, S. (2017). Religious perspectives on humility. In E. L. Worthington, Jr., D. E. Davis, & J. N. Hook (Eds.), *Handbook of humility: Theory, research, and applications* (pp. 47–61). Routledge/Taylor & Francis Group.

Porter, T., & Schumann, K. (2018). Intellectual humility and openness to the opposing view. *Self and Identity*, *17*(2), 139–162. https://doi.org/10.1080/15298868.2017.1361861

Porter, T., Schumann, K., Selmeczy, D., & Trzesniewski, K. (2020). Intellectual humility predicts mastery behaviors when learning. *Learning and Individual Differences*, *80*, 101888. https://doi.org/10.1016/j.lindif.2020.101888

Priebe, C. & Van Tongeren, D. R. (2021). Women pay a steeper price for arrogance: Examining presentation style, gender, and humility. *The Journal of Positive Psychology, 18*(1), 121–129. https://doi.org/10.1080/17439760.2021.1991451

Reis, H. T., Lee, K. Y., O'Keefe, S. D., & Clark, M. S. (2018). Perceived partner responsiveness promotes intellectual humility. *Journal of Experimental Social Psychology*, 79, 21–33. https://doi.org/10.1016/j.jesp.2018.05.006

Ryan, R. M., & Deci, E. L. (2001). On happiness and human potentials: A review of research on hedonic and eudaimonic well-being. *Annual Review of Psychology, 52*, 141–166. https://doi.org/10.1146/annurev.psych.52.1.141

Ryff, C. D. (1989). Happiness is everything, or is it? Explorations on the meaning of psychological well-being. *Journal of Personality and Social Psychology, 57*(6), 1069–1081. https://doi.org/10.1037/0022-3514.57.6.1069

Spielberger, C. D. (1983). State-Trait Anxiety Inventory for Adults (STAI-AD) *[Database record]. APA PsycTests*. https://doi.org/10.1037/t06496-000

The Qur'an (M.A.S. Abdel Haleem, Trans.). (2004). Oxford University Press. https://quran.com/ (Original Work published 2004).

Tilka, N. A. (2017). *Humility, religious/spiritual struggle, and posttraumatic growth in breast cancer patients: Integrating quantitative and qualitative methods* (Doctoral dissertation, Biola University).

Tong, E. M., Lum, D. J., Sasaki, E., & Yu, Z. (2019). Concurrent and temporal relationships between humility and emotional and psychological well-being. *Journal of Happiness Studies, 20*, 1343–1358. https://doi.org/10.1007/s10902-018-0002-3

Toussaint, L. L., & Webb, J. R. (2017). The humble mind and body: A theoretical model and review of evidence linking humility to health and well-being. In E. L. Worthington, Jr., D. E. Davis, & J. N. Hook (Eds.), *Handbook of humility: Theory, research, and applications* (pp. 178–191). Routledge/Taylor & Francis Group.

Van Tongeren, D. R., Davis, D. E., Hook, J. N., & Johnson, K. A. (2016). Security versus growth: Existential tradeoffs of various religious perspectives. *Psychology of Religion and Spirituality, 8*(1), 77–88. https://doi.org/10.1037/rel0000050

Van Tongeren, D. R., Davis, D. E., Hook, J. N., & Witvliet, C. V. O. (2019a). Humility. *Current Directions in Psychological Science, 18*, 463–468. https://doi.org/10.1177/0963721419850153

Van Tongeren, D. R., Hook, J. N., Ramos, M. J., Edwards, M., Worthington Jr, E. L., Davis, D. E., Ruiz, J. M., Reid, C. A., Garthe, R. C., Nonterah, C. W., Cowden, R. G., Opare-Henaku, A., Connelly, R., Omoruyi, O., Nkomo, T. S., & Osae-Larbi, J. A. (2019b). The complementarity of humility hypothesis: Individual, relational, and physiological effects of mutually humble partners. *The Journal of Positive Psychology, 14*(2), 178–187. https://doi.org/10.1080/17439760.2017.1388433

Van Tongeren, D. R., Severino, M., Kojima, Y., Miskowski, K., & Blank, S. (2023). Is There a Dark Side to Humility? Cross-Sectional and Longitudinal Evidence for Existential Costs of Humility. *The International Journal for the Psychology of Religion, 33*(2), 136–150. https://doi.org/10.1080/10508619.2022.2143662

Webb, J. R., Toussaint, L., & Dula, C. S. (2014). Ritualistic, theistic, and existential spirituality: Initial psychometric qualities of the RiTE measure of spirituality. *Journal of Religion and Health, 53*(4), 972–985. https://doi.org/10.1007/s10943-013-9697-y

Winkeljohn Black, S., Brelsford, G. M., Worthington, E. L., Davis, D. E., Hook, J. N., Van Tongeren, D. R., Reid, C.A., Garthe, R.C., Griffin, B.J., Nonterah, C.W., & Cairo, A. H. (2019). How do humility prototypes affect the association between perceptions of spouse's humility and depressive symptoms and couple conflict?. *The Journal of Positive Psychology, 14*(6), 836–844.

Worthington, Jr., E. L., & Allison, S. T. (2018). Humility, mental health, and physical health. In E. L. Worthington, Jr. & S. T. Allison, *Heroic humility: What the science of humility can say to people raised on self-focus* (pp. 91–103). American Psychological Association. https://doi.org/10.1037/0000079-006

Worthington Jr., E. L., Davis, D. E., & Hook, J. N. (Eds.). (2017). *Handbook of humility: Theory, research, and applications*. New York, NY: Routledge.

Yaden, D. B., Batz-Barbarich, C. L., Ng, V., Vaziri, H., Gladstone, J. N., Pawelski, J. O., Tay, L. (2022). A meta-analysis of religion/spirituality and life satisfaction. *Journal of Happiness Studies*, *23*, 4147–4163. https://doi.org/10.1007/s10902-022-00558-7

Yukhymenko-Lescroart, M. A., & Sharma, G. (2020). Examining the factor structure of the revised sense of purpose scale (SOPS-2) with adults. *Applied Research in Quality of Life*, *15*, 1203–1222. https://doi.org/10.1007/s11482-019-09729-w

Zhang, H., Hook, J. N., Farrell, J. E., Mosher, D. K., Captari, L. E., Coomes, S. P., Van Tongeren, D. R., & Davis, D. E. (2019). Exploring Social Belonging and Meaning in Religious Groups. *Journal of Psychology and Theology*, *47*(1), 3–19. https://doi.org/10.1177/0091647118806345

Chapter 29

Over 50 Years in Clinical Practice

A Tribute to Philip H. Friedman, Ph.D.

Jon R. Webb, Loren L. Toussaint, Everett L. Worthington, Jr., Peta Stapleton, and Anthony Scioli*

Dr. Phil Friedman had originally agreed to contribute a chapter to this edited book project, *Handbook of Spirituality, Health, and Well-Being: A Psychological Perspective*. He was unable to complete his chapter due to some health-related problems that he was experiencing. From time to time, I had thought about replacing what would have been his chapter, with a chapter written in tribute to him. That is, a chapter with contributions from a handful of people that knew him professionally. As one of my talents is procrastinating, I wound up deciding at the last minute to do this, and of course several people agreed. What follows is our heart-felt tribute to Philip H. Friedman, Ph.D. (1941–2024). May his memory be a blessing.

From Jon R. Webb

As I was finalizing the proposal for this book project, including making final decisions regarding all of the topics I wanted to include, I was thinking of all of the people I was planning on inviting and hoping would agree to be contributors. During this process, I started wondering who I might know who had been engaged in the provision of mental healthcare for a long time, and if any of these people had surpassed 50 years. I thought a person with this kind of longevity would have a very valuable perspective regarding addressing religious/spiritual issues in counseling and psychotherapy, drawn from over a *half-century* of experience. Needless to say, my friend Phil Friedman came to mind. Phil was the first person I asked to contribute to this book. And, I was so excited to get his 50-year perspective that Phil was the only person I asked to contribute before even submitting the proposal to Routledge!

I first met Phil nearly 20 years ago – in the spring of 2006 – when attending a mid-year research conference of the Society for the Psychology of Religion and Spirituality (Division 36 of the American Psychological Association) at Loyola University Maryland. We would visit at this conference in Columbia, Maryland many times over the subsequent years. In an endearing way, I found Phil to be a little quirky. Also, I remember attending and being fascinated by his presentations on different topics related to pressure points, energy healing, and tapping techniques (see Friedman, 2009). For the first couple of times that I was exposed to these things by Phil, I found myself a little taken aback, as these methods are not necessarily commonly encountered in current, mainstream approaches to counseling and psychotherapy (and there seemed to be a palpably awkward feeling in the room, as he would invite us to participate in his demonstrations). Ultimately, I thought about how – being born, raised, and still a believing member of the Church of Jesus Christ of Latter-day Saints – I know a little about

* Corresponding Author: jon.r.webb@ttu.edu.

DOI: 10.4324/9781003440048-33

what it is like to be alone in a crowd while holding a minority worldview, and decided to pay closer attention to what he had to offer. And, what he had to offer was his lifetime of professional experience and wisdom in the service of my professional development, to include research collaboration. But, more importantly, kindness, compassion, support, and heart-warming interaction; indeed, genuine friendship. On both fronts, professional and personal, this Sage had time for me. After all, what did a green assistant professor and newly licensed psychologist in the mid-2000s have to offer a seasoned scientist-practitioner who had been actively engaged in the clinical practice of psychology since said newbie was all of about 2 years old (i.e., since 1968)?

After moving from East Tennessee to West Texas in 2017, on more than one occasion I found myself having long phone conversations with Phil – catching up on a personal level, and discussing research projects. In these last several years, I was fortunate to be able to work with him in the context of examining the psychometric qualities of assessment tools he developed and used in his private practice to track the progress of his clients. Never resting on his laurels, he was determined to ensure the scientific rigor of his clinical work. With colleagues, we published a paper in the scientific journal *Nurse Education in Practice* regarding the validation of the Friedman Life Balance scale among nursing students in China (Zhao et al., 2023).

As I began to mention at the outset of this chapter, I emailed Phil on November 12, 2022 to verify my assumption about his years of experience and to ask him if he would write a chapter for this book, to be entitled something to the effect of, "Life Balance, Spiritual Awakening, and Psychotherapy: Observations after Over 50 years in Clinical Practice." Phil enthusiastically agreed to my inquiry, again, before I even submitted my actual proposal to the publisher for review. Upon finalizing the contract with Routledge in March 2023, I emailed Phil again, to formalize his contribution. After some back and forth about what the nature of the content would be, he agreed. This back and forth was not so much about hesitancy, but transparency. In the end, knowing our shared interest in forgiveness, he told me that his perspective on and approach to forgiveness, including self-forgiveness, would be a focus of his chapter, and that it would be different, including as influenced by Energy Healing, Positive Pressure Point Techniques, and *A Course in Miracles* (see Foundation for Inner Peace, 2007). He wanted to be sure that this would be acceptable to me, knowing that there would be other forgiveness content deliberately included in this book. During this email conversation, I emphasized to Phil my view that he, after having over 50 years of clinical experience, had a uniquely credible perspective to share on the association between spiritual transformation and psychotherapeutic outcome. I was eager for him to share his wisdom in this book. Also, during this time, Phil was experiencing some long-term problems with his health, which impacted his day-to-day life. I received another email from him in July 2023 graciously informing me of his need to step away from the project, wanting me to know sooner, rather than at the last minute, and apologizing for letting me down. Of course, he was not letting me down, and there was no need for an apology; but, that was my friend, Phil! Nearly a year later, sadly, I learned that he had recently passed away. An obituary was shared with me, and I share it here: Dr. Philip H. Friedman.[1] Also, for an accounting of Phil's scholarly endeavors, see here: Google Scholar.[2]

Phil Friedman left an indelible impression on me as a professional and as a friend; for which, I am eternally grateful. I have many fond memories of Phil. One of which is that he ended each email with: Many Blessings for Peace, Love, and Happiness. I miss Phil, and his influence. I look forward to seeing and visiting with him again someday.

From Loren L. Toussaint

A Phone Message

In the summer of 2005, I had completed my first year of teaching at Luther College. I had a wife and two young daughters. I had just returned home from my mother's funeral, having lost her to cancer. Shortly after my return, I decided to check in at my office. At that time, the only way to getting any work done was to be in your office where your corded phone and desktop computer were located. I checked my email and my phone messages, and much to my surprise, I had a message from Dr. Phil Friedman, whom I had never met before. He had read some research that I had done on forgiveness and was writing to ask if I might be interested in some collaboration.

I returned the call. Phil explained that he had some interesting data from clinical patients and that we might be able to work productively together. I thought this sounded interesting. And frankly, I needed a spark after losing my mom, and I needed to get going again in the right direction. Little did I know that this was that spark. Anyone who knew Phil, I think, would agree that he brought plenty of spark to any collaboration. He and I spoke for what was probably two hours in our first conversation. We agreed that we had lots of common interests and could probably work well together and so we launched a collaboration, examining forgiveness and gratitude as correlates of happiness.

A Scientist-Practitioner

I will admit that as a full-time clinical psychologist, I expected that the vast majority of Phil's time and energy would be put into working with patients and that any scientific objectives would come as a distant second. There is only so much time a person has after all. I was conservatively anticipating that perhaps this was an interest of his and that eventually his clinical focus would overshadow any interests in research. I could not have been in for a bigger surprise. As a full-time therapist, I was astonished at just how much energy and enthusiasm Phil had for research. He made it a significant part of his practice. He embodied the scientist-practitioner model. He saw patients all week long and then did data entry and analyses all weekend long!

Scholarship

The work that Phil and I began as a result of our earliest conversations led to some early insights and contributions regarding the connections between forgiveness, gratitude, and happiness. In short, we found that forgiveness and gratitude were linked to multiple forms of happiness, and positive beliefs and feelings served as important mechanisms (Toussaint & Friedman, 2009). At that time in our early work, there was not much research on this topic. Nonetheless, Phil had the foresight to collect data using multiple measures of forgiveness, gratitude, and happiness. In fact, Phil had collected data from 72 clinical outpatients using the Heartland Forgiveness Scale (Thompson et al., 2005), the Transgression Related Interpersonal Motivations Inventory (McCullough et al., 1998), the Gratitude Questionnaire-Six (McCullough et al., 2002), the Gratitude, Resentment, and Appreciation Test (Watkins et al., 2003), the Bradburn Affect Balance Scale (Bradburn, 1969), the Fordyce Well-Being scale (Fordyce, 1988), the Satisfaction with Life Scale (Diener et al., 1985), and the Friedman affect and belief scales (Friedman, 1993, 1998). I thought this was incredible! The sample was unique and the measures were state-of-the-art, so we had the components of a strong paper. We presented this paper at the Midyear Conference on Religion and Spirituality (APA Division 36) in Baltimore, Maryland. This was the first time that Phil and I met face-to-face. I quickly learned that Phil was a great guy with an easy laugh and a quick smile. But what I also learned from him was that attending a conference was more than simply showing up, giving your paper, and engaging in simple polite conversation. Phil was hungry for understanding. In some of the earliest sessions that I attended with him, I felt a little uncomfortable with just how assertive he was in asking questions. I was still relatively new to the whole conference scene, but Phil really made it seem natural to get right into the mix with leaders in the field, ask questions, insist on answers, and gain insights for your continuing work. I still try to follow his example at every conference I attend.

Contributions

In addition to the work that Phil and I originally did on forgiveness, gratitude, and well-being, Phil continued to do research throughout the next 20 years that I knew him. He was a pioneering clinician and scientist. He did not hesitate to investigate some of the most interesting and innovative areas of psychology, including much work in energy psychology (Friedman, 2000). Phil always brought his expertise in science to all of his projects. He continued to collect data, write presentations and papers, and he even wrote a few books along the way (e.g., Friedman, 2009).

Measurement

If you look at Phil's website, one of the things that you will notice quickly is that he has a section reserved for all of his measurement tools (https://friedmanscales.com/). Phil not only enjoyed developing measures, but he continued to do it throughout his career, even in his much later years. Most recently, he developed a measure of life balance that Dr. Jon Webb and I assisted him with. He published the measure and used it consistently in his work. Just a few years ago, a colleague from China, Dr. Fangfang Zhou, led a translation and validation project for the tool in China (Zhao et al., 2023).

Later Years

Over the last few years, I continued to keep in touch with Phil. He was always very supportive and encouraging of my work. He watched things closely and every time he saw a new contribution of mine (a talk, paper, etc.), he was one of the first to email and provide his congratulations. As I learned that he was struggling with health issues, I checked in every so often to see how he was doing. Regrettably it was usual only to find that he was continuing to struggle. This did not dampen his mood or his enthusiasm for the science and practice of psychology. If I am not mistaken, I believe he saw patients right up until the day before he passed. Now that is a psychologist at heart! Phil was a wonderful man, offered many contributions to the science and practice of psychology, and provided some gentle advice and an opportunity to me as a young scholar. He always remained one of my biggest fans. I am grateful to Phil Friedman for the time and energy he spent with me and for all of the wonderful collaborations. I am honored to be asked to contribute to this tribute, and I hope these cherished memories add to honoring the practitioner, scholar, and man that he was.

From Everett L. Worthington, Jr.

I was very involved in Division 36 of the American Psychological Association (Society for the Psychology of Religion and Spirituality) throughout the period of about 2000 through 2017, when my salary retired from Virginia Commonwealth University. I often ran into Phil during those years, and it was always a pleasure. He was very interested in talking about forgiveness during that period. He had an active practice, and he had found that many of his clients' lives turned on whether they could forgive.

He came at forgiveness uniquely. He was highly influenced by *A Course in Miracles*, and sought to integrate that with his clinical practice. Inevitably, that led to creative interventions. His thoughts were not in the mainstream of the developing field of forgiveness studies, but that did not deter him. He was an original mind with a fervent commitment to *A Course in Miracles*. Doing things that helped his clients was far more important to Phil than toeing some orthodox line. We had many conversations that almost inevitably extended past conferences into email exchanges. Those exchanges lasted from 2012 to 2019.

Although we collaborated on his research, we never actually published anything together. I was always happy to contribute what little I could to his practice-oriented research. He consulted me on two scales he was developing when he was 78 and only in partial practice. He was trying to get someone in full-time vigorous practice to administer the scales and run the psychometrics for him.

In November 2016, Phil reached out to me through email requesting feedback on the scales that he sent me. After acknowledging his exemplary work as a practitioner-scientist, always seeking to better his practice through clinical research, I offered my critique of the items – based on having taught a graduate level course on psychometrics for several years and having created and published about 40 instruments of my own (with many other failed, unpublished instruments).

Phil wrote and published not only about forgiveness but also about gratitude. He was very open to feedback. Indeed, in December 2016, he emailed again to say that he had revised a scale based on my feedback, and that there were now two scales, The Friedman Life Balance Scale and the Friedman Benefits Scale. Hoping to find someone in full-time practice to help with psychometric development, he emphasized that these scales were based almost entirely on client feedback and likely consistent with current neuroscience, including the neuroplasticity of the brain.

In 2019, characteristically for Phil, who was 78 at that time, he got excited about self-forgiveness. Loren Toussaint – always generous with his time and resources, and a collaborator on forgiveness and health articles with Phil – had sent him some research articles on self-forgiveness. Browsing through those, he came across Davis et al. (2015). And, I had just been a co-editor for the *Handbook of the Psychology of Self-Forgiveness* (Woodyatt et al., 2017). So, Phil emailed me about self-forgiveness, and I sent along a copy of the book and numerous other articles (including Griffin et al., 2018; Griffin et al., 2015), published and (at that time) in press. As always, Phil was appreciative and intellectually engaged with the material.

As you see, Phil was "semi-retired" and 78 years old, and yet he was still plugging away at scientifically bettering what could be done to help his (and others') clients. He was a gentleman and a practitioner-scholar. He never stopped trying to help people. He was a model for all of us. It was my privilege to know and interact with him over the years.

From Peta Stapleton

I first met Dr. Philip Friedman in 2019 – not in person, but over email, as is often the way in academic circles these days. I was the guest editor for a special edition of a journal titled *Mind-Body Approaches that are Revolutionizing the Health Field*, and Dr. Phil submitted a paper for consideration. Ironically, and somewhat humorously in hindsight, we did not accept his paper. It went on to be published elsewhere, but what began as a simple academic exchange blossomed into a lasting collegial relationship grounded in mutual curiosity, respect, and a shared passion for helping others heal.

Over the years, Phil and I stayed in touch. He would often send updates on his latest research and insights from his client work, particularly in the area of forgiveness – an area he devoted so much of his life's work to. He was extraordinarily generous with his time and resources. I teach into a Master of Psychology program, and Phil never hesitated to share the psychological measures and questionnaires he had developed over decades, freely offering them for use in my teaching. His Friedman Assessment Scales on Well-Being, Affect, Life Balance, Spiritual Awakening, and others, provided real, meaningful tools for students beginning their journey into the healing professions.

Our conversations often explored the evolving landscape of therapy. We bonded over our shared enthusiasm for the emerging "fourth wave" approaches – energy-based and somatic modalities like Emotional Freedom Techniques, EMDR, and, more recently, Accelerated Resolution Therapy (ART). I remember when I first brought ART trainers to Australia. Phil, already trained in the U.S., was thrilled. We would swap stories over email about using ART with our clients, sharing insights and breakthroughs, always with that spark of excitement that comes when something really works. Phil had this remarkable openness to new ideas – he was never stuck in one framework, always seeking out the most effective tools for the people he served.

In 2024, I finally launched a podcast called *The 4th Wave in Therapy*. When it came time to invite guests, Phil was at the top of my list. I am so grateful he said yes. What followed was one of the most extraordinary conversations I have had in my career. We talked about his early days in the field, training under some of the original giants of Cognitive Behavioral Therapy (CBT) – at a time when CBT itself was considered fringe or even "quackery." Phil laughed as he recalled those days and pointed out the irony of having seen so many therapies once dismissed later embraced by the mainstream.

Phil was truly ahead of his time. While many clinicians only recently started exploring the transformative potential of 4th wave therapies, Phil had already been using them for years. His relentless drive was always about one thing: helping his clients. And if that meant learning something new, challenging the status quo, or integrating the spiritual with the scientific, he was all in. That is what made him so special – his deep compassion, intellectual courage, and unwavering commitment to healing.

Just a few months after that interview was recorded, I received the heartbreaking news that Phil had passed away. I was quietly devastated. And yet, I felt so profoundly grateful that we had captured his voice, his wisdom, and his journey through the decades. Even at the end, he was still seeing clients from his nursing home – still showing up, still making a difference.

Phil's legacy is vast. He was the author of the books: *The Forgiveness Solution: The Whole-Body Rx for Finding True Happiness, Abundant Love, and Inner Peace* (Friedman, 2009), and *Creating Well-Being: The Healing Path to Love, Peace, Self-Esteem and Happiness* (Friedman, 1989). He developed powerful models such as the ICBEST psychotherapy model, Integrative

Forgiveness Psychotherapy (IFP), the Positive Pressure Point Techniques (PPPT), and the Digital Assessment and Tracking Approach (DATA). His work was deeply influenced by *A Course in Miracles* and the teachings of Siddha Yoga – spiritual paths that clearly infused his work with grace and compassion.

Phil was not just a psychologist – he was a visionary, a pioneer, a true giant in the field of psychology. And yet, he was also humble, curious, and kind. His presence in my professional life was a gift. I miss our emails. I miss his insights. But I know his work lives on – not only in the many clients and students he touched, but in all of us who carry forward the tools, teachings, and spirit he so generously shared.

You can access our conversation online at Evidence Based EFT,[3] or by going directly to YouTube.[4] It is a beautiful reminder of who Phil was – a man with a deep heart, a brilliant mind, and an unshakable belief in our ability to heal.

Rest well, Phil. Your work continues.

From Anthony Scioli

I met Phil Friedman approximately 20 years ago. I was presenting at a conference in Philadelphia. Phil approached me after a talk on the psychology of hope and asked if I would like to contribute to a paper session he was organizing for the *International Society for Quality-of-Life Studies (ISQOLS)*. I explained to Phil that I had never been to a meeting of ISQOLS. In fact, I had never heard of the organization! I would have to do additional research to link hope with quality of life, etc. I was unsure. Phil, always cheerful and encouraging, assured me that I would be fine, everything would be great. It was a fabulous association! I submitted to his bursts of positiveness, attended the conference, and thus began a 20-year friendship.

Several years later, at another conference, Phil turned to me,

> Would you like to know how I ended up at that conference in Philadelphia? Well, a few months earlier, I attended another conference. I stopped at an unattended poster. I noticed some business cards strewn on a chair. For some reason, I picked up one of the cards, turned it over, and someone had handwritten the title and date of the conference in Philadelphia.

Phil then chuckled, convinced that his longtime interests in energy psychology, synchronicity, and spirituality was a player in this quirky drama.

Like other colleagues who are paying tribute to Phil in this volume, I have wonderful memories of gathering year after year, in early March, for the annual midwinter meetings of APA Division 36 (Psychology of Religion and Spirituality). Phil was a regular presenter, sharing data collected in the course of his clinical practice. We had a close group of a dozen or so colleagues who had become friends. Some of the best times were spent in the late afternoon happy hours and dinners, continuing to discuss theory and research. Beyond the midwinter meetings, I recall when Phil spent a week at my home in the Boston area, attending the 2008 APA convention. A humorous situation occurred a few blocks from the convention site, inside a copy center. Phil entered to make a few copies. I waited in my car, by the curb, looking through the glass wall. As Phil walked toward the exit, he spotted a man hunched over a desk. Concerned, Phil shook the man's shoulder. The man awoke from a deep sleep and castigated Phil for ruining his nap! Fortunately, Phil was able to maintain his wry sense of humor and muttered a few words best left out from this tribute!

A few years ago, my wife and I took the train to Philadelphia for a party in honor of Phil's 75th birthday. Although it was not a surprise party, Phil was overcome by the presence of family and close friends and was moved to tears of gratitude. I was struck by the diversity of friends and colleagues that came to honor Phil that day, young and old, from near and far, academics and non-academics, spiritual dwellers and perpetual seekers.

I found Phil remarkable in several respects. First, I admired his efforts to bridge traditional psychological theories and methods with the farthest edges of positive psychology in the potential application of energy models for the purpose of assessment and emotional healing. Phil had a very strong academic background, a B.A. from Columbia and a Ph.D. in clinical psychology from the University of Wisconsin. For scholars and scientists, it is exceedingly difficult to shed dogma in the form of quasi-religious paradigms. In recognition of these challenges, Lee Cronbach (1957) wrote about the "two disciplines" of experimental and correlational psychology. C. P. Snow (1959) followed with the two cultures of science and humanism. Phil was equally comfortable providing a workshop on energy dynamics, discussing the nuances of forgiveness, or sharing endless rows of survey data that he had collected.

Phil was trained as a clinician. He directed training for many years and maintained a private practice. Clinical psychology has long upheld a "scientist-practitioner" ideal, the so-called "Boulder model". In reality, very few clinical psychologists conduct research. Very few researchers, even those with a clinical degree, are actively involved in the delivery of therapy or assessment services. Phil was among that small group at the tiny intersection of the science-practice Venn diagram. Phil developed questionnaires, integrated his tools with those of his colleagues, and distributed them within and beyond his clinical practice. More than once, I witnessed Phil rebut criticisms of his empirical findings at an academic conference by drawing on his vast experience in the clinic.

Thirdly, during conference presentations as well as impromptu small group discussions, Phil was a model of composure, nearly phlegmatic at times but more often humorous than aloof. Phil had a knack for turning an aggressive challenge into a comedy play or a "misunderstanding" that left all sides with plenty of dignity for another day. Indeed, Phil seemed to have embodied Kipling's (1910/2017) classic dictate to "keep your head when all about you are losing theirs." We academics can get a little too serious, a bit too ego-involved, for matters that ultimately will not decide the future fate of humankind! Phil seemed to understand that the relationships mattered more than the abstractions and the ego, the energy and the spirit were the key!

I miss Phil's warmth, his humor, and the stimulating exchanges that preceded each Spring at the midwinter meetings and followed in the closing months of Summer at APA. I hope to continue attending these and other conferences in the coming years, but they may or may not carry the same energy or spirit. I equivocate here, not knowing if Phil and his energy will intersect once more with his friends and colleagues who hold out hope for another happy hour!

Notes

1 https://www.huffandlakjer.com/obituary/dr-philip-friedman.
2 https://scholar.google.com/citations?hl=en&user=bFTWGiwAAAAJ.
3 https://www.evidencebasedeft.com/Dr-Phil-Friedman.
4 https://youtu.be/mt1-GXoFYP0.

References

Bradburn, N. M. (1969). *The structure of psychological well-being*. Aldine.

Cronbach, L. J. (1957). The two disciplines of scientific psychology. *American Psychologist, 12*(11), 671–684. https://doi.org/10.1037/h0043943

Davis, D. E., Ho, M. Y., Griffin, B. J., Bell, C., Hook, J. N., Van Tongeren, D. R., DeBlaere, C., Worthington, E. L., Jr., & Westbrook, C. J. (2015). Forgiving the self and physical and mental health correlates: A meta-analytic review. *Journal of Counseling Psychology, 62*(2), 329–335. https://doi.org/10.1037/cou0000063

Diener, E., Emmons, R. A., Larsen, R. J., & Griffin, S. (1985). The satisfaction with life scale. *Journal of Personality Assessment, 49*, 71–75. https://doi.org/10.1207/s15327752jpa4901_13

Fordyce, M. W. (1988). A review of research on the happiness measures: A sixty second index of happiness and mental health. *Social Indicators Research, 20*(4), 355–381. https://doi.org/10.1007/BF00302333

Foundation for Inner Peace. (2007). *A course in miracles: Combined volume* (Third ed.). Foundation for Inner Peace.

Friedman, P. H. (1989). *Creating well-being: The healing path to love, peace, self-esteem and happiness*. R&E Publishers, Inc.

Friedman, P. H. (1993). *Friedman Belief Scale and Research Manual*. Foundation for Well-Being. Plymouth Meeting, PA.

Friedman, P. H. (1998). *Friedman Affect Scale*. Foundation for Well-Being. Plymouth Meeting, PA.

Friedman, P. H. (2000). *Integrative healing manual*. Foundation for Well-Being. Plymouth Meeting, PA.

Friedman, P. H. (2009). *The forgiveness solution: The whole-body Rx for finding true happiness, abundant love, and inner peace*. Conari Press.

Griffin, B. J., Worthington, E. L., Jr., Davis, D. E., Hook, J. N., & Maguen, S. (2018). Development of the Self-Forgiveness Dual-Process Scale. *Journal of Counseling Psychology, 65*(6), 715–726. https://doi.org/10.1037/cou0000293

Griffin, B. J., Worthington, E. L., Jr., Lavelock, C. R., Greer, C. L., Lin, Y., Davis, D. E., & Hook, J. N. (2015). Efficacy of a self-forgiveness workbook: A randomized controlled trial with interpersonal offenders. *Journal of Counseling Psychology, 62*(2), 124–136. https://doi.org/10.1037/cou0000060

Kipling, R. (1910/2017). If--. *Objective Standard: A Journal of Culture & Politics, 12*(4), 77–78.

McCullough, M. E., Emmons, R. A., & Tsang, J.-A. (2002). The grateful disposition: A conceptual and empirical topography. *Journal of Personality and Social Psychology, 82*(1), 112–127. https://doi.org/10.1037/0022-3514.82.1.112

McCullough, M. E., Rachal, K. C., Sandage, S. J., Worthington, E. L., Jr., Brown, S. W., & Hight, T. L. (1998). Interpersonal forgiving in close relationships: II. Theoretical elaboration and measurement. *Journal of Personality and Social Psychology, 75*(6), 1586–1603. https://doi.org/10.1037/0022-3514.75.6.1586

Snow, C. P. (1959). Two cultures. *Science, 130*(3373), 419. https://doi.org/10.1126/science.130.3373.419

Thompson, L. Y., Snyder, C. R., Hoffman, L., Michael, S. T., Rasmussen, H. N., Billings, L. S., Heinze, L., Neufeld, J. E., Shorey, H. S., Roberts, J. C., & Roberts, D. J. (2005). Dispositional forgiveness of self, others, and situations. *Journal of Personality, 73*(2), 313–359. https://doi.org/10.1111/j.1467-6494.2005.00311.x

Toussaint, L. L., & Friedman, P. (2009). Forgiveness, gratitude, and well-being: The mediating role of affect and beliefs. *Journal of Happiness Studies, 10*(6), 635–654. https://doi.org/10.1007/s10902-008-9111-8

Watkins, P. C., Woodward, K., Stone, T., & Kolts, R. L. (2003). Gratitude and happiness: Development of a measure of gratitude and relationships with subjective well-being. *Social Behavior and Personality: An International Journal, 31*(5), 431–452. https://doi.org/10.2224/sbp.2003.31.5.431

Woodyatt, L., Worthington, E. L., Jr., Wenzel, M., & Griffin, B. J. (Eds.). (2017). *Handbook of the psychology of self-forgiveness*. Springer Nature.

Zhao, F., Friedman, P. H., Toussaint, L., Webb, J. R., & Freedom, J. (2023). Translation and validation of the Chinese version of the Friedman life balance scale among nursing students: A psychometric analysis. *Nurse Education in Practice, 66*, 1–9, Article 103505. https://doi.org/10.1016/j.nepr.2022.103505

Chapter 30

Spirituality, Health, and Well-Being in Collegiate Recovery Programs

Declan P. Murphy, William F. Gerber, and George E. Comiskey*

The aim of this chapter is to explore the role and prevalence of spirituality among collegiate recovery program (CRP) students and determine its impact on their health and well-being. CRPs are university- and college-based programs that recognize and support students, who are in recovery from addiction, to achieve academically and grow in recovery. Although not implicitly prescribed, many CRPs have a spiritual component within their programming. The chapter will include a brief history and evolution of CRPs. Additionally, an analysis of multiple CRPs that have a spiritual component will be explored, culminating in an in-depth analysis of the most prolific CRP, located at Texas Tech University.

The Historical Development of Collegiate Recovery Programs

CRPs were instituted to support college students in recovery from an alcohol or other drug use disorder to acquire a college education while protecting and enhancing their recovery (Harris et al., 2014). The founders of the collegiate recovery movement recognized the challenge and risks of pursuing education while in recovery from substance use in "abstinence hostile environments" due to the prevalence of alcohol and drug use and it being synonymous with college life (Cleveland et al., 2007; Laudet et al., 2015). The overall goal of CRPs is to provide services and support to higher education students who are in recovery so they can complete their education and maintain their sobriety (Bugbee et al., 2016). The roots of the Collegiate Recovery movement can be sourced to Brown University, when in 1977 Bruce Eliot Donovan founded the first CRP after recovering from his own alcohol use disorder. Donovan began supporting the growing number of students on campus with alcohol and drug-related problems. In 1986, Dr. Carl Anderson, (a professor in recovery) founded the Center for the Study of Addiction and Recovery (CSAR), at Texas Tech University. CSAR offered academic support to students and provided a space for recovery meetings. In the 1990s, Dr. Kitty Harris succeeded Dr. Carl Anderson and made significant contributions to the collegiate recovery movement at a national level when securing a SAMHSA grant to design a CRP replication model based on the Texas Tech CRP. This led to several colleges and universities establishing CRPs nationwide (Association of Recovery in Higher Education [ARHE], 2022). Since the first CRP opened over fifty years ago there has been a steady increase in the number of colleges opening CRPs to support students in recovery from addiction. There are currently 151 CRPs in thirty-eight states throughout the United States, and a growing number in other countries (Jason et al., 2021; ARHE 2022).

* Corresponding Author: decmurph@ttu.edu.

DOI: 10.4324/9781003440048-34

However, there are many other colleges and universities that provide support to students in addiction recovery but are not ARHE registered.

As more collegiate recovery centers opened in the decades following their inception in 1977 research began to emerge examining this population in terms of the educational and recovery experiences and outcomes of the students they serve. As CRPs are still a relatively young and emergent movement, much of the research has been descriptive in nature, by tracking their growth and development, more so than scientific evaluative research (Brown et al., 2018). Furthermore, a standardized CRP model has yet to be established meaning each CRP operates in institutions of higher education from various levels of support and funding (Hennessy et al., 2022). Therefore, each CRP model is unique and reflective of their own needs, resources, and cultural context. CRPs may have different services and activities for their students, although there will be some common features too.

The Place of Spirituality in Collegiate Recovery Communities

Regarding the incorporation of a spiritual component in CRPs, some may not require or practice spirituality, nor might spirituality be defined or mentioned in CRP handbooks and curriculums. However, we do know that most CRP models were founded and incorporate 12-Step recovery services (Harris et al., 2007). Due to the spiritual nature of 12-Step recovery, many students in CRPs acquire and express a sense of spirituality in their lives. Indeed, one study found that 92% of CRP students considered themselves spiritual people (Cleveland et al., 2007).

Addiction recovery definitions continue to evolve, and debate continues on an agreed upon universal definition. This has led to researchers collaborating to reach a consensus on what recovery entails (Ashford et al., 2019). Recent definitions of addiction recovery indicate that it is something much more than abstinence (Cano et al., 2017). Indeed, some definitions of recovery imply and emphasize a spiritual component, that supports and improves overall well-being (Ashford et al., 2019). While not all recovering persons embrace spirituality many report that a spiritual connection to the transcendent is part of their recovery (Laudet & White, 2008). Spirituality is considered a founding and vital component of Twelve-Step recovery (Dermatis & Galanter, 2016; Galanter et al., 2007). Spirituality was also found to be a factor that enhances the likelihood of positive recovery outcomes and of global functioning (Laudet & White, 2008). Webb's framework for spirituality in addiction and recovery incorporates ritualism, theism, and existentialism (Webb, 2021; see Chapters 1 and 44 of this volume). More recently, the International Society of Addiction Medicine (ISAM) recommended the incorporation of Spirituality into the clinical care of addiction treatment (Galanter et al., 2021). Spirituality in recovery is a multifaceted concept that is often difficult to define. However, it is generally understood to refer to a person's sense of connection to something larger than themselves, whether it be a higher power, nature, their support group, or humanity-at-large.

It is clear that both traditional and contemporary approaches to addiction recovery advocate and incorporate a spiritual component to the recovery process. Although it is neither prescribed nor compulsory, CRPs also recognize and support the incorporation of spirituality in the recovery process. According to the programming section of the ARHE website, (the administrative body that represents CRPs in the United States), CRPs provide programming for academic, social, and spiritual life and invites students from all identities across all spectrums of race, ethnicity, gender, gender identity, sexual orientation, ability status, justice-involvement, veteran status, and religious status (ARHE, 2022). From a spirituality perspective, not all CRPs will implicitly indicate a prescribed spiritual component. However, there is often an inherent spiritual component to recovery (Dosset & Metcalf-White, 2019) and in that context, spirituality is a feature in the lives of CRP students (Cleveland et al., 2007). In this regard, CRPs generally don't prescribe or prioritize any one particular faith or denomination over another, rather they welcome all spiritual pathways. CRPs strive to create inclusive environments where students from diverse recovery backgrounds feel welcome and supported in their journey of personal growth and development (ARHE, 2022). What CRPs do is provide space and context in a higher education environment for the multiple ways spirituality is addressed, explored, and fully realized in the context of addiction recovery. The next section of the paper will review literature on CRPs with spirituality featured in their curriculum definitions.

Collegiate Recovery Programs with a Spiritual Dimension

As previously stated, CRPs have yet to be standardized, consequently various models exist that are unique to each university. The following section of the chapter reviews three CRPs with a spiritual component in their programming. The final model to be reviewed, The Texas Tech CRP, is more detailed as all three authors are current staff and researchers at Texas Tech University.

The Healing Pillars of Collegiate Recovery

The CRP located at the Community College of Philadelphia (2024) includes a spiritual component in their CRP definition and is called "The Healing Pillars" model of collegiate recovery (DiRosa & Scoles, 2020). All the pillars are of a spiritual nature, the first pillar is Hope. Hope is fostered among the CRP students due to being in community with peers and staff who believe in them and support them in meeting their goals. This is consistent with research on hoping and coping in CRPs (Kimball et al., 2017). The second pillar of the model is secure supportive relationships; this pillar recognizes the need for social networks that understand and support a lifestyle of recovery. Additionally, relationships are promoted beyond the college environment in wider community to develop awareness of addiction and recovery and build partnerships with community. Pillar three of the model is Self-Reflection, this pillar fosters a sense of spirituality through activities such as transformational yoga and recovery meditation, both of which include a spiritual dimension. The fourth pillar of the model is competence and mastery; this model involves students in addiction recovery taking supplementary courses in recovery-based living. It is felt that students in recovery require dedicated coaching in managing their recovery in college environments where drinking is prevalent. The additional class is to help students in recovery be best prepared to master the skills necessary to maintain their recovery. The fifth pillar of the model encourages the building and strengthening of community relationships where CRP students can provide service and support. Service to others is at the heart of the fifth pillar, it promotes a sense of altruism among the students in giving back to the community (DiRosa & Scoles, 2020).

The Strength-based Collegiate Recovery Model

A proposed collegiate recovery model, titled "The strength-based collegiate recovery model," also includes spirituality and religious activities (Scoles, 2021). The genesis of this model was formed on the premise that students in recovery should be viewed from a strength-based perspective. This CRP highlights the strength and wisdom that students in addiction recovery bring to a college campus as a result of their suffering and adversity. The ability to overcome addiction is seen as a valuable strength, and that all stakeholders in college campuses can learn from CRP students. The authors argue that CRP students demonstrate incredible resilience in overcoming obstacles and adversity, and as a result have developed personal virtues and traits that include compassion in caring for others, having a sense of faith, spirituality and humility (Scoles, 2021). The model posits that by the nature of their experience with adversity and their strength in overcoming it, CRP students have a sense of spirituality and altruism about them which is seen as one of their strengths. The model is designed to support and empower the students to see and utilize the strength they have within themselves. The students also engage with local communities to offer their support and service, again highlighting the altruistic and spiritual philosophy of the model.

The Center for Students in Addiction Recovery - Texas Tech University

All of the authors of this chapter are current staff and researchers working out of the Center for Students in Addiction Recovery (CSAR) at Texas Tech University. The following section of the chapter will provide a detailed account of the Spiritual dimension of the Texas Tech CSAR. The Texas Tech CSAR recognizes and supports the important spiritual component of recovery in their programming. The roots of Texas Tech CSAR are steeped in the spiritual 12-Step programming instituted by the founder Dr. Carl Anderson. The recovery model at this CSAR integrates and indeed celebrates the spiritual component that is so often an inherent part of addiction recovery, in general. Since its establishment in 1986, research has shown the prevalence of spirituality in this community (Cleveland et al., 2007). Loyal to the founding vision, the Texas Tech model encourages and harnesses the spiritual dimension at the core of CSAR life. What aids in the process and harnessing of the spiritual component of this model is the established length of recovery time that is required to gain admission into Texas Tech CSAR. Students entering the Texas Tech CSAR must have a minimum of 1 year of abstinent-based recovery within their first semester. Therefore, our students arrive with existing levels of recovery capital. To understand the formula of the Texas Tech CSAR, it is important to understand recovery capital.

Recovery capital was developed to help explain the complex process of individual recovery from addiction (Cloud & Granfield, 2008). A simplified definition of recovery capital is provided by Best and Laudet (2010), "the sum of resources necessary to initiate and sustain recovery from substance misuse" (p. 2). It is in this recovery capital context and nature that the Texas Tech model considers and approaches the spiritual dimension of the CRP Model. The recovery capital framework was introduced by (Granfield & Cloud, 1999) as a means to understand how "natural recovery" from addiction was achieved without formal drug treatment or self-help groups such as 12-Step programs (Morton et al., 2016). Since its inception, recovery capital has gained authority as a way to understand and assess the addiction recovery process, and the necessary components that make it possible (Dekkers et al., 2021). Recovery capital is defined as the sum of internal and external resources necessary to initiate and sustain recovery from substance use (Cloud & Granfield, 2008). More recently, recovery capital has been defined as the resources and capacities that enable growth and human flourishing (Best & Ivers, 2022). Recovery researchers (White & Cloud, 2008) created a three-domain recovery capital framework, the three domains being personal, social and community capital. Hewitt (2007) introduced another recovery capital domain, described as "growth capital." Growth capital is based on an individual's desire for positive growth and is developed throughout the recovery process with a continued focus on building momentum gained in recovery (Hewitt, 2007).

At the heart of the Texas Tech CSAR model is a vision and commitment to develop recovery capital, through the personal, social and community domains. However, this CRP model also incorporates an additional and dedicated spiritual component, i.e., *spiritual* recovery capital. Texas Tech CSAR students are afforded the opportunity to build all three recovery capital domains; that is, personal, social and community recovery capital while also growing what we describe and define as spiritual recovery capital. The students accrue a spiritual capacity through their recovery informed lifestyle. Figure 30.1 illustrates the four interconnected components that result in the acquirement of *Spiritual Capital*. The following section will describe how each component is expressed in daily CRP life at Texas Tech.

Recovery

As previously mentioned, Texas Tech CSAR students have an established level of recovery earned before entry, which affords them the capacity to access and engage in all four components of the Spiritual Capital model. While our students enter CRP life with adequate initial recovery, it is imperative that the students continue to grow in their overall recovery capital. The National Institute of Drug Abuse (NIDA) indicates that established abstinent-based recovery facilitates the ability to voluntarily adopt a lifestyle characterized by continuous and positive growth (NIDA, 2024). The Texas Tech CSAR students demonstrate positive change and growth via a multitude of personally determined and community-based practices that are reflective of a maturing recovery. These practices and rituals unfold and occur in their daily lives in CRP and educational life. Examples of such rituals that take place at Texas Tech CSAR, include morning prayer and reflection, action-based compassion, meditation, reading of spiritual texts and the carrying of an attitude of gratitude throughout their day. Furthermore, the students adopt a recovery informed approach to the inevitable challenges they encounter in university life. These practices and examples of action-based recovery are indicative of the tools acquired and available upon entering, and during their time spent in the Texas Tech

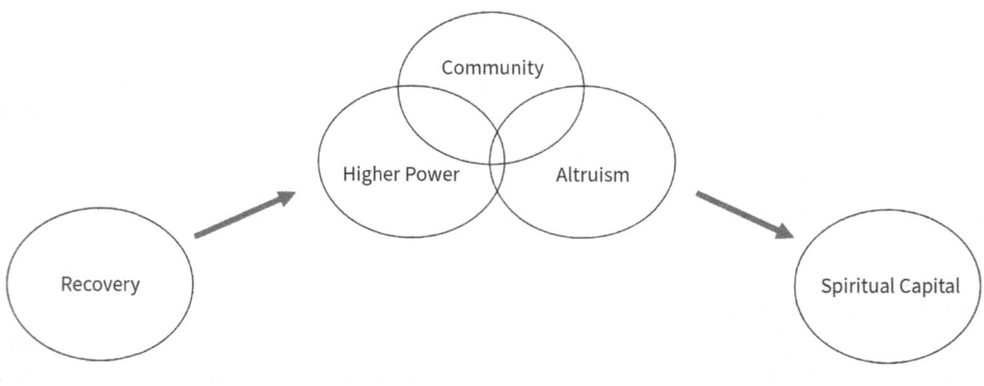

Figure 30.1 Texas Tech CSAR Spirituality Model.

Note: Recovery allows for the growth in Community, Altruism, and a Higher Power which produces Spiritual Capital.

CSAR. To assist the students in gaining further recovery capital, Texas Tech CSAR incorporates and assigns additional recovery activities, such as weekly seminars and celebration of recovery. Recovery support meetings are also held daily which provide opportunities for recovery maintenance and growth. These specific components are described in depth as related to the component they apply to; that is, Higher Power, Community and Altruism.

Higher Power

The concept of a Higher Power has long been associated with 12-Step fellowship and addiction recovery (Ruisard, 2020) and the collegiate recovery movement is itself rooted in 12-Step fellowships (Kimball et al., 2022). The Texas Tech model recognizes that spirituality is a process that most often begins with the discovery and the development of a relationship with a higher power of the students own understanding and choosing. Due to the established recovery gained by students upon entry to the Texas CSAR, they will have already embarked upon this journey. However, Texas Tech CSAR acknowledges the complex and nuanced nature of this relationship and therefore facilitates the diverse conceptualization of a Higher Power among its students. In that sense, there is no prescribed Higher Power at the TTU CSAR, as it is respected as a very intimate and individual journey. In recognition of the many spiritual persuasions among the CRP students, the Texas Tech model facilitates multiple recovery meetings such as Refugee Recovery (Levine, 2014) and traditional 12-Step recovery meetings. The students also have access to an onsite meditation room which is frequently used for times of reflection and mindfulness practices. Weekly seminars are also held with theme-centered discussions and reflections which include discussions on the relationship with a Higher Power. These activities and facilities are carefully designed to ensure students have a dedicated space to participate in rituals which sustain and grow the very important relationship they have with their Higher Power. The prevalence of, and commitment to a Higher Power among Texas Tech CRP students was captured in a study which found that 87% of students reported a relationship with a Higher Power. Furthermore, the study found that 76% of students indicated that they had continuous and direct experiences with God, reflecting an active and ongoing relationship with their Higher Power (Cleveland et al., 2007). The research conducted at the Texas Tech CSAR along with observational data suggest that the program is successful in ensuring the deepening and strengthening of student relationships with their Higher Power (Bell et al., 2009; Cleveland et al., 2007; Kimball et al., 2022).

Altruism

Texas Tech CSAR encourages a sense of altruism among its students. Evidence suggests that Altruism is a component of recovery (Rettie et al., 2021). One of the key features central to 12-Step recovery is the importance of "giving back" (Alcoholics Anonymous [AA], 1981). Altruism occurs in daily life at the Texas Tech CSAR in both formal and informal ways. It is a close-knit community of approximately 100 students who commune and support each other both academically and in respect of their recovery. Indeed, one study at Texas Tech showed that CRP students attribute much of their recovery growth to the support of their peers in recovery (Cleveland & Groenendyk, 2010). Furthermore, studies have shown that CRP students support each other when encountering stigma associated with addiction and recovery on college campuses (Scott et al., 2016). In addition to supporting each other, students at Texas Tech are dedicated to extending their support and altruism to the wider community. Indeed, this CRP has two student organizations dedicated to altruistic pursuits, (1) ASAS, Association of Students Acting in Service and (2) POWER, Providing the Outside World with Empowerment and Resources. These student organizations engage in both formal and informal acts of service on the university campus and also the wider surrounding community. Some service activities include fundraising for the local unhoused community and providing them with hot meals. The students regularly host panels and presentations in local high schools and in the university on addiction and recovery. Such events allow students to share their experience, strength, and hope. POWER specifically supports incarcerated individuals and does so by regularly visiting prisons and jails. On these occasions, the students provide hope and resources for incarcerated individuals to access recovery and education. A sense and spirit of altruism permeates through connections, outreach, and service of Texas Tech CSAR students.

Community

Although spirituality is a deeply personal and intimate experience, it is also a community experience. The Substance Abuse and Mental Health Services Administration (SAMHSA, 2020) includes Community as one of the four dimensions of their working definition of Recovery. Community is not only important to overall recovery, but also essential in creating a sense of hope and belonging among students in recovery. At the Texas Tech CSAR, community life creates a sanctuary of safety and refuge in university campuses that have been described as abstinent hostile environments (Cleveland et al., 2007). In recognition of the important role of community, CRP programming at Texas Tech is designed to facilitate meaningful community congregations. These congregations are exhibited in a number of different ways. Community lunches are a monthly opportunity for all of the members of the Texas Tech CSAR to commune and break bread together. Weekly celebration of recovery (Texas Tech University, 2024) meetings provide the space for students to applaud and celebrate their peers in recovery. Each celebration of recovery meeting begins and ends with a prayer and moment of reflection. Each week at celebration of recovery, the entire CRP community congregates to hear the experience of strength and hope of a selected student's testimony. These meetings also provide a space to recognize and celebrate sobriety milestones which are acknowledged through presentations of coins and chips. In addition to weekly and monthly community gatherings, the pinnacle of Texas Tech CSAR community life occurs at the annual graduation and gratitude meal each December. At this event, students who are on the cusp of graduating are celebrated and afforded the opportunity to share words of gratitude to their peers, staff and the donors who provide important financial scholarships. These donors are all invited guests of the evening along with alumni and university dignitaries. The reverence of this event is reflected in the reciting of the Serenity Prayer (Shapiro, 2008) and a reflection at both the beginning and ending of the event. Aside from the larger community gatherings celebrated, smaller and more intimate student led gatherings occur in the basement of the CRP. The basement is a dedicated space for students to study, commune and to utilize the meditation and seminar rooms. The spirit of community that is fostered at the CRP ensures that students are connected to each other through friendship and faith and provides an ongoing opportunity for spiritual connection.

Spiritual Recovery Capital

The philosophy of the Texas Tech CSAR, which is steeped in 12-Step traditions, recognizes that spirituality is a vital component of recovery. As previously mentioned, the mission of the

Texas Tech CSAR is to create the conditions for students to grow their recovery. Consistent with an overarching principle of Recovery Capital wherein one acquires and accumulates further recovery capital (i.e., Recovery Capital builds upon itself), the Texas Tech CSAR facilitates the acquisition of what we define as "Spiritual Recovery Capital." Although Spiritual Capital is referenced in literature in the context of spirituality more broadly (Guest, 2016) it is not, until now, defined in the context of addiction recovery. We argue that our definition of Spiritual Recovery capital as it applies to addiction recovery provides an effective framework to describe the important component of spirituality in addiction recovery. Additionally, it adds another important dimension to the recovery capital framework. We define Spiritual Recovery Capital as a process of acquiring and embodying a new sense of self and the divine which manifests and is expressed through attitudes and actions of an altruistic nature supportive of the addiction recovery experience. Since the inception of the Texas Tech CSAR in 1986, a multitude of evidence (some empirical, some anecdotal) including published papers, Texas Tech archives, observations, and written and verbal testimonies demonstrates that the students in recovery have acquired and have at their disposal a sense of spirituality (Cleveland et al., 2007; Harris et al., 2007, Kimball et al., 2022). As is demonstrated in the Texas Tech CSAR model, the students have at their disposal the component of spirituality which can be nourished and expressed in CRP and educational student life. In summary, spirituality is expressed in various ways, such as prayer, meditation and coming together in community, which are all underpinned by a relationship with a higher power of their understanding and choice. Having acquired and embodied a sense of spirituality, the students are then capable and committed to altruistically giving back what they have acquired in recovery.

Collegiate Recovery Program Students and Spirituality

Having reviewed the spiritual component of CRP models, the following section of the chapter explores the literature that describes the prevalence and the various expressions of spirituality among CRP students. While CRPs orient in a fashion that allows for the holding and expression of a spiritual component of recovery it is important to note that spirituality is a deeply personal and individualized aspect of recovery. While some students may find solace and strength in traditional religious practices, the majority of CRP students explore and practice spirituality in a more secular or non-traditional context (Cleveland et al., 2007).

A study exploring the daily lives of CRP students captured the role spirituality plays in their day-to-day life (Cleveland et al., 2007). Among the findings, CRP students didn't identify as religious, with two-thirds reporting no current religious affiliation, however the vast majority (92%) described themselves as being spiritual. Notably, not one participant stated they were atheistic or agnostic, which indicates strong faith among this population. These findings align very much with the founder of the Texas Tech CRP who states in his recently published book that "the path to recovery is a spiritual path that should not be confused with a religious path" (Anderson, 2022, p. 135). Furthermore, close to 75% reported reading spiritual literature and / or other holy writings at the present time (Cleveland et al., 2007). The high proportion of CRP members reading scriptures might seem inconsistent with their low affiliation with religion, however, when these spiritual practices are considered in the context of this community's 12-Step orientation, it is consistent with other research outlining the spiritual nature of 12-Step recovery (Dermatis & Galanter, 2016). It appears from this study that the CRP students drew much of their spiritual experiences outside of organized religion. Consistent with this 12-Step experience and orientation, 87% of the CRP students in this study reported having direct experiences with God and 76% reported continuous experiences with God. Findings from this study indicate a relationship with a Higher Power, which is central to 12-Step recovery. The same study found further evidence of the important role spirituality plays in the lives of CRP students as demonstrated in their commitment and attendance to 12-Step meetings, which are of a spiritual nature. Students reported attendance at least one 12-Step meeting on 42% (550) of the 1,319 study days. The students also indicated that they applied at least one of the 12-Steps on 77% of the study days. These findings suggest that CRP students are spiritual not only in theory, but also in practice; they live spiritual lives in word and deed (Cleveland et al., 2007). More recently a national study of CRP students found that three-quarters (72%) of participants identified 12-Step based groups as their primary pathways to recovery, which they continued to engage with. Considering the spiritual nature of 12-Step recovery, this study again highlights the significant role and part spirituality plays for the CRP students (Smith et al., 2023).

In another study, Cleveland and Groenendyk (2010) describe further evidence of the pivotal role of spirituality among CRP students. The participants demonstrated high levels of engagement in spiritual practices which they considered to be crucial self-improvement strategies. When CRP students were asked what self-improvement behaviors and strategies they engaged in, they reported reading 12-Step literature, the Bible, and going to church. Indeed, the most common self-improvement behaviors they participated in out of a 365-day period were, reading Alcoholics Anonymous literature (107 days), reading the Bible (or other holy book; 96 days), and reading Narcotics Anonymous literature (64 days). Such evidence reflects a population that is committed and engaged in spiritual practices in support of their recovery programs. Considering the high number of days students engaged in spiritual practices, it appears that spirituality is embedded in their daily habits and behaviors. While the community is generally organized around 12-Step principles that may seem religious, their low church attendance does not suggest they are conventionally religious, but rather spiritual in nature (Cleveland & Groenendyk, 2010).

Still more evidence of a spiritual component among CRP students was found in a national survey of CRP students (Laudet et al., 2015). The survey reported a significant percentage of CRP students were actively engaging in 12-Step recovery principles and practices. Furthermore, the study highlighted that those students were committed to service, seeing it as an important component of the student lifestyle. Service and acts of altruism are again indicative of a spiritual persuasion. A study of the experiences of college students in recovery from substance use (Iarussi, 2018) revealed that spirituality was a feature of the students' lives, and they utilized it as an effective and healthy coping mechanism. The students in the study also indicated they acquired and expressed a spiritual life through 12-Step recovery. The participants reported that prayer, meditation and contact with a higher power were all important practices that reduced stress. Mel Ash (1993), in his book, *The Zen of Recovery*, wrote "Our spiritual awakenings are meaningless if not expressed in real actions within the context of our real lives" (p. 63). This quote summarizes the experience of spirituality in the lives of CRP students, as spirituality is a prominent feature of their recovery in both word and action (Cleveland et al., 2007).

Experiences of Suffering and Adversity among CRP Students

Any conversation about spirituality and addiction recovery would not be complete without also considering the role of suffering in the addiction and recovery process. Very often, suffering is a precursor or antecedent to addiction (Tarter & Reynolds, 2022). In terms of CRP students, it would appear that suffering, struggle, and adversity are prevalent, particularly during and before their period of addiction. Indeed, the founder of the Texas Tech Collegiate Recovery Program, Dr. Carl Anderson, describes this in his book titled *Addiction Recovery at Texas Tech University* (Anderson, 2022). Anderson explains that "the CRP from its inception was composed of broken lives, wholly transformed when coming to believe and surrender their lives to a Higher Power" (p. 44). The Jesuit Priest and contemplative Fr. Richard Rohr (2023) also argues that suffering is a gateway and portal to transformation. And, the poet and songwriter, Leonard Cohen (1992) speaks of the brokenness being the place where the light gets in. Similarly, the mystic Rumi (Arloo, 2024) also alluded to the value of suffering when stating "the wound is where the light enters and touches you" (p. 1).

The literature on CRP students indicates that suffering is prevalent among this population. Collectively speaking, the CRP student population has been characterized in the literature as vulnerable, marginalized, and stigmatized (Watts et al., 2019). Research has highlighted the widespread prevalence of psychiatric conditions among CRP students, in addition to their substance use disorder. A multi-site study of emerging adults in CRPs conducted by Hennessy et al. (2021) found that of 861 students surveyed, 77% reported they also had a mental health condition. Most CRP students reported mental health and substance use treatment histories. Approximately nearly one-half reported a history of eating disorders or other compulsive behaviors (46%) and over two-thirds (69%) reported histories of mental health concerns more generally. Results indicated a complex history of mental health and substance use recovery needs among students (Hennessy et al., 2021). The same study found that 56% of students had criminal justice involvement and experienced periods of being unhoused. Notably, many reported being in recovery from multiple behavioral addictions—for example, eating disorders, and sex and love addiction. A national survey of CRP students of 2015 also found high rates of co-occurring addictions in this under-examined population and underlined the need for recovery support programs and college health services that provide integrated support for mental health and behavioral addictions to SUD-affected young people (Laudet et al., 2015). Similar evidence was reported among students attending CRPs, who reported a wide range of mental and behavioral health concerns in addition to substance use disorders, highlighting the need for continued support for recovery and well-being at higher education institutions (Nichols et al., 2023).

A study exploring the experiences of stigma among CRP participants (n = 17) in addiction recovery reported on the difficult experiences of stigma among students in addiction recovery in college settings (Scott et al., 2016). The participants found themselves in the unique and difficult situation of wanting to establish a new life that is disconnected from alcohol and drug use, only to be situated in a college culture that is immersed in alcohol and drug use. The participants reported feeling awkward and self-conscious because they could not partake in what was considered a social norm. They also felt anxious about disclosing their status of being in recovery as they felt that too would lead to judgment and stigma. Negotiating a social life as a people who do not drink was found to be both challenging and stressful. The students in the study had access to a CRP which supports students in addiction recovery. Through and in the CRP they found sanctuary and reprieve from the pressures of trying to fit into a culture incompatible with addiction recovery. The CRP provided the participants with a recovery culture that supported a lifestyle focused on recovery. In managing this identity dilemma, the participants also demonstrated problem solving skills, also an element of personal capital (see above), by seeking out people and groups who do not engage in drinking. This study highlights the crucial role and importance of collegiate recovery support in educational settings, while also demonstrating the challenges and risks students in recovery experience, especially those without access to on campus recovery support (Scott et al., 2016).

Another study also shed light on self-stigma among students in addiction recovery in college settings. The study recruited participants (n = 80) from 33 universities, which all had CRPs. This is the only study that explored levels of self-stigma and its association with educational goals and outcomes. The findings revealed that students in recovery experience high levels of self-stigma which contribute to self-defeating beliefs which impact educational outcomes and ambition. Essentially, the participants felt that because of their association with addiction, educational and career goals were relatively pointless. Societal stigma associated with addiction was internalized becoming self-stigma, which acted as a demotivator to succeed academically. In respect of the findings, the authors recommended specific psychological supports to help students in recovery to identify and reduce self-stigmatizing tendencies (Watts et al., 2019). More recently, a doctoral dissertation explored levels of self-stigma and self-compassion among students in addiction recovery (Humberger, 2022). Similar results found that students in recovery internalized societal stigma leading to higher levels of self-stigma. Interestingly, students with less than one year of abstinence had higher levels of self-stigma than students with longer time in recovery. Furthermore, and demonstrative of a spiritual factor, the longer students had in addiction recovery, the more self-compassion they had toward themselves around recovery identity. In addition, the study reported that male students were more comfortable than female and non-binary students in disclosing their recovery status.

In summary, students in CRPs have experienced significant suffering in terms of mental health problems, homelessness, and incarceration. In addition to their experience with addiction, which is also traumatic, this can make the transition to higher education more difficult. Despite the adversity and unique challenges students in addiction recovery encounter, evidence informs that these students tend to thrive in higher education (Murphy, 2023).

CRP Students Transcending Suffering and Adversity

The literature on CRP students indicates that suffering is prevalent among this population. However, there is also compelling evidence demonstrating that these students transcend suffering with the aid of spirituality (Iarussi, 2018). In contrast to characteristics that highlighted significant levels of adversity, CRP students are also characterized in a resilient light (Scoles, 2021). Indeed, they were found to be motivated by past failures and can function as effective on-campus leaders. Further, students in recovery are more altruistic and have a sense of responsibility to self and others (Bratter & Parker, 1994). Bratter and Parker (1994) further advocate for the recovering student by appealing to college admission teams "not to dismiss recovering college students based on their records only, because they may have matured to become stronger because of their struggle to transcend self-destructive behavior" (p. 24). These descriptions of students in recovery alluded to maturing strength found in and from their struggle. Students in recovery from addiction are described as altruistic, selfless, and determined to restore and recover their life. For many, the opportunity to go to higher education represents a further and important step in their recovery process. Despite the many challenges and risks associated with college life for this population, these students bring a sense of service and altruism to the campus community (Iarussi, 2018). Furthermore, they bring a level of maturity beyond their years due to their experiences with addiction and adversity. This was articulated in a study which found students in recovery felt that they arrive on college campuses "all partied out" and consequently could apply themselves more appropriately to their academics and recovery (Bell et al., 2009). Consistent with spiritual practices of service and charity, students in a CRP considered themselves as "helpers" and that helping others through adversity was one of their main priorities (Iarussi, 2018). The countercultural experience of strength and hope that these students bring to the college campus has led to calls for more support and recognition from college administration (Murphy, 2023). CRP students bring a unique strength and experience to higher education settings which is reflected in their impressive recovery and academic outcomes.

CRP Student Outcomes

Despite the suffering and adversity associated with CRP students, evidence suggests that this population is succeeding on many fronts. So, what happens in the lives of CRP students, when spirituality, education, and recovery combine? Research shows impressive outcomes related to health and academics. Indeed, research spanning three decades demonstrates evidence of academic excellence among this population (Hennessy et al., 2021; Laudet, et al., 2014; Smith et al., 2023). Academic outcomes in the United States are often measured by Grade Point Average (GPA) scores and graduation numbers. In both categories, students in recovery excel. Indeed, students in CRPs were found to have higher GPA scores and graduation numbers than those in the general student population (Laudet et al., 2014). Furthermore, research on students who graduated from CRPs showed their success continues after college as evidenced by their successful career trajectories (Brown et al., 2019). Past students attributed much of their academic and career success to the support they experienced in CRPs. Strong evidence shows that when students in recovery are supported in college, they tend to flourish academically. In addition, membership of CRPs does not only support academic performance but also fosters personal growth and development (Murphy, 2023). As the science of collegiate recovery is a young and emergent field, studies have yet to be conducted as to what factors promote academic success among this group. However, we do know a relationship exists between academic excellence and spirituality (Wood & Hilton, 2012). Moreover, a study of the experiences of college students in recovery from substance use (Iarussi, 2018) demonstrated that students utilized spirituality as an effective coping mechanism when faced with academic stress. The students in the study also indicated that they acquired their spiritual life through 12-Step recovery as facilitated by their CRP. The participants reported that prayer, meditation and contact with a higher power were all important practices that reduced stress.

A doctoral dissertation exploring college reentry experiences after a leave of absence due to substance use provided further evidence of academic success among students in addiction recovery (Pesetski, 2015). The participants ($n = 4$) all successfully completed their degree after reentry. The participants attributed much of their academic success to the principles and practices, including those of a spiritual nature, gained in treatment. The participants stated that these skills were acquired in treatment and subsequently applied and utilized in college resulting in academic success. These findings indicate that spiritual practices can help students in recovery in their academic pursuits. Indeed, this was also found in another study (Kimball et al., 2022) which also indicated that having a strong spiritual connection was of crucial importance in the participants' ability to set and accomplish other healthy goals. Essentially, the participants were able to reach out for help when they needed it, and most often the help they sought was through their Higher Power. (Kimball et al., 2022). It is possible that the spiritual principles that CRP students implement could have a positive effect on their academic performance.

A standout health-related outcome associated with students in a CRP shows that once individuals enter CRPs, return-to-use figures drop to as low as 4.4% (Laudet et al., 2014). Currently, there is no research to explain what factors contribute to this low return-to-use figure, however considering their committed and disciplined approach to their spiritual practices, it may indeed be a side effect or result of spiritual commitment. For example, participants in a study of CRP students found that they developed a sense of agency and an ability to consistently make healthy choices which they attributed to the spiritual connection that they discovered in recovery. The same study showed that having a strong spiritual connection was of crucial importance in the participants' ability to set and accomplish other healthy goals. Essentially, the participants were able to reach out for help in times of struggle, and most often the help they sought was from their Higher Power. The ability to be vulnerable and ask for help when required had the effect of bringing success in other areas of their lives (Kimball et al., 2022). Further research on CRP students found that building hopeful relationships with a God of their understanding helped mitigate craving and increase contemplation toward change for individuals in recovery. The participants in the study defined hope in a variety of different ways including having "faith," and knowing that "my Higher Power will take care of me." Ultimately, as the students found hope in a Higher Power, they had a greater ability to cope and perform in healthy ways (Kimball et al., 2017). It is evident that CRP students succeed in higher education, and their educational and recovery pursuits are aided by their spiritual experience and resources i.e., "spiritual recovery capital."

Spirituality Influencing Positive Identity Change in Addiction Recovery

Research has shown that addiction recovery is a multifaceted process that encompasses more than a reduction in addiction symptomology. Being in recovery from drugs and alcohol misuse also requires a pivotal shift in identity from one that is aligned with active use, to one that values recovery and well-being, which has been reported using varying frameworks (Best et al., 2016; Biernacki, 1986; Leamy et al., 2011). To date, there are many models of recovery identity transformation in the literature. The Social Identity Model of Recovery (SIMOR; Best et al., 2016) and the Social Identity Model of Cessation Maintenance (SIMCM; Frings & Albery, 2015) both argue that the mechanism of recovery is a process of social identity transformation in which a person's most salient identity shifts from being defined by membership of a group whose norms and values revolve around substance use, to being defined by membership of a group whose norms and values encourage recovery. The individual's new social identity is strengthened as their sense of belonging grows within the recovery-oriented group and they become more aware of differences to the substance using group. Their identity in-turn enhances their recovery efforts by reinforcing the norms and behaviors of recovery. Biernacki (1986, p. 141) also wrote about this social identity shift stating "addicts [sic] must fashion new identities, perspectives, and social world involvements wherein the addict identity is excluded or dramatically depreciated." In addition to being a social process, identity development has been cited as an important element of an individuals' journey to recovery. Students enrolled in CRPs also undergo a change in self-perception or identity, which further strengthens their recovery. This occurs in a CRP setting in a number of ways. Firstly, by spending time with people in recovery and engaging in spiritual activities mentioned here, such as service work, meditation and recovery meetings, the students begin to see themselves as a person in recovery, doing recovery activities as opposed to their former addict way of living (Kimball et al., 2022). Through acquiring new social networks, who engage in spiritual practices in support of overall well-being, a new identity emerges. Kimball et al. (2022) found that students in CRPs undergo a shift in their identity, and crucially note that spirituality plays a role in the development of a new identity.

Conclusion

CRPs were instituted in the 1970s to recognize and support students in addiction recovery on college campuses. The founders recognized the precarious nature of being a person in recovery in college environments that are synonymous with alcohol and drug-fueled activities (as well as co-morbid or separate behavioral addictions). Furthermore, CRPs were founded on the traditions of 12-Step recovery, which at its heart is a spiritual program. As such, CRP students acquire a sense of spirituality (whether based in theism or otherwise), which is often born by virtue of suffering. Indeed, suffering and adversity is prevalent among CRP students and is often a conduit to a new life aided by a sense of spirituality. What transpires among CRP students having experienced a spiritual awakening is quite profound. A transformation of mind and spirit occurs as students transition from a life of addiction to a life of recovery. They live spiritual lives in word and deed; such that, it is embedded into their daily behaviors and rituals. These students incorporate prayer, acts of compassion, gratitude, and an overall commitment to living good and ethical lives. Both education and recovery are processes that inspire growth and development in and of themselves, however when the two occur simultaneously self-change is prevalent. The personal and academic outcomes of this population are more than impressive. Research has shown that they academically outperform their peers in the general population, and that they have extremely low levels of relapse. Cloud and Granfield (2008) introduced Recovery Capital to demonstrate factors that make recovery possible; that is, human, social and community capital. The literature on the intersection of CRP and Spirituality and health could be summarized or conceptualized as "Spiritual Recovery Capital." Through a process of suffering, surrender, healing, and service this population has accrued a wealth of "spiritual capital" which appears to be present in various aspects of their lives, including education, health, and relationships, to name a few.

Future Research and Recommendations

CRPs and the students they serve are a relatively understudied field of science. To date, there are no studies dedicated to the intersection of spirituality, health, and collegiate recovery. The available literature would suggest that education, recovery, and spirituality combinedly create impressive outcomes. It is important that future research addresses this population and their spiritual characteristics. Specific studies that explore the role spirituality plays in the academic pursuits of CRP students would be particularly interesting. Addressing this gap in the literature would extend our understanding of students in CRPs, particularly in a spiritual context.

Exploration of the spiritual capital construct and how to quantify spiritual capital will be needed to include its importance in the recovery capital framework. Additional research on the implications of spiritual capital in all recovery settings, aside from collegiate recovery, will be beneficial in assessing the implications spiritual capital has on the recovery of all those struggling with addiction.

References

Alcoholics Anonymous. (1981). *Alcoholics anonymous* (3rd ed.). Alcoholics Anonymous World Services.

Anderson, C. M. (2022). *Addiction recovery at Texas Tech University: Where it all began*. Texas Tech University Press.

Arloo, J. (2024, March 27). The epiphany of pain. *Behavioral and Substance Abuse Counseling*. https://www.bsacounseling.com/2024/03/27/the-epiphany-of-pain/

Ash, M. (1993). *The Zen of Recovery*. Open Road Media.

Ashford, R. D., Brown, A., Brown, T., Callis, J., Cleveland, H. H., Eisenhart, E., Groover, H., Hayes, N., Johnston, T., Kimball, T., Manteuffel, B., McDaniel, J., Montgomery, L., Phillips, S., Polacek, M., Statman, M., & Whitney, J. (2019). Defining and operationalizing the phenomena of recovery: a working definition from the recovery science research collaborative. *Addiction Research and Theory*, *27*(3), 179–188. https://doi.org/10.1080/16066359.2018.1515352

Association of Recovery in Higher Education. (2022). History of collegiate recovery. https://collegiaterecovery.org/collegiate-recovery-history/

Bell, N. J., Kanitkar, K., Kerksiek, K. A., Watson, W., Das, A., Kostina-Ritchey, E., Russell, M. H., & Harris, K. (2009). "It has made College Possible for Me": Feedback on the impact of a university-based center for students in recovery. *Journal of American College Health*, *57*(6), 650–658. https://doi.org/10.3200/jach.57.6.650-658

Best, D., Beckwith, M., Haslam, C., Alexander Haslam, S., Jetten, J., Mawson, E., & Lubman, D. I. (2016). Overcoming alcohol and other drug addiction as a process of social identity transition: the social identity model of recovery (SIMOR). *Addiction Research & Theory*, *24*(2), 111–123. https://doi.org/10.3109/16066359.2015.1075980

Best, D., & Ivers, J. H. (2022). Inkspots and ice cream cones: a model of recovery contagion and growth. *Addiction Research & Theory*, *30*(3), 155–161. https://doi.org/10.1080/16066359.2021.1986699

Best, D., & Laudet, A. (2010). The potential of recovery capital. *The RSA*. https://www.thersa.org/reports/the-potential-of-recovery-capital

Biernacki, P. (1986). *Pathways from heroin addiction: Recovery without treatment*. Temple University Press.

Bratter, T. E., & Parker, T. H. (1994). Bright, angry, recovering students: Their value to colleges. *The Journal of College Admission*, *142*, 23–28.

Brown, A., Ashford, R., Heller, A. T., Whitney, J., & Kimball, T. (2018). Collegiate recovery students and programs: Literature review from 1988-2017. *Journal of Recovery Science*, *1*(1), 1–11.

Brown, A. M., Ashford, R. D., Figley, N., Courson, K., Curtis, B., & Kimball, T. (2019). Alumni characteristics of collegiate recovery programs: A national survey. *Alcoholism Treatment Quarterly*, *37*(2), 149–162. https://doi.org/10.1080/07347324.2018.1437374

Bugbee, B. A., Kimberly Caldeira, M. M., Andrea Soong, M. M., Kathryn Vincent, M. B., & Amelia Arria, M. M. (2016). *Collegiate recovery programs: A win-win proposition for students and colleges*. College Park, MD: Center on Young Adult Health and Development. http://www.cls.umd.edu/docs/CRP.pdf

Cano, I., Best, D., Edwards, M., & Lehman, J. (2017). Recovery capital pathways: Modelling the components of recovery wellbeing. *Drug and Alcohol Dependence*, *181*, 11–19. https://doi.org/10.1016/j.drugalcdep.2017.09.002

Cleveland, H. H. & Groenendyk, A. (2010). Daily lives of young adult members of a collegiate recovery community. In H.H. Cleveland, K.S. Harris & R.P. Wiebe (Eds.), *Substance abuse recovery in college: Community supported abstinence* (pp. 77–95). Springer. https://doi.org/10.1007/978-1-4419-1767-6

Cleveland, H. H., Harris, K. S., Baker, A. K., Herbert, R., & Dean, L. R. (2007). Characteristics of a collegiate recovery community: Maintaining recovery in an abstinence-hostile environment. *Journal of Substance Abuse Treatment*, *33*(1), 13–23. https://doi.org/10.1016/j.jsat.2006.11.005

Cloud, W., & Granfield, R. (2008). Conceptualizing recovery capital: Expansion of a theoretical construct. *Substance Use and Misuse*, *43*(12–13), 1971–1986. https://doi.org/10.1080/10826080802289762

Cohen, L. (1992). Leonard Cohen – anthem. *Genius*. https://genius.com/Leonard-cohen-anthem-lyrics

Community College of Philadelphia. (2024). Office of Collegiate Recovery. https://www.ccp.edu/student-services/student-assistance-centers/office-collegiate-recovery

Dekkers, A., Bellaert, L., Meulewaeter, F., De Ruysscher, C., & Vanderplasschen, W. (2021). Exploring essential components of addiction recovery: a qualitative study across assisted and unassisted recovery pathways. *Drugs: Education, Prevention and Policy*, *28*(5), 486–495. https://doi.org/10.1080/09687637.2021.1943315

Dermatis, H., & Galanter, M. (2016). The role of twelve-step-related spirituality in addiction recovery. *Journal of Religion and Health*, *55*(2), 510–521. https://doi.org/10.1007/s10943-015-0019-4

DiRosa, F., & Scoles, P. (2020). The healing pillars of collegiate recovery: A community college model of recovery and education. *Journal of Student Affairs Research and Practice*, *57*(1), 69–76. https://doi.org/10.1080/19496591.2019.1644116

Dossett, W., & Metcalf-White, L. (2019). Religion, spirituality and addiction recovery: Introduction. *Implicit Religion*, *22*(2).95–100.

Frings, D., & Albery, I. P. (2015). The social identity model of cessation maintenance: Formulation and initial evidence. *Addictive Behaviors*, *44*, 35–42. https://doi.org/10.1016/j.addbeh.2014.10.023

Galanter, M., Dermatis, H., Bunt, G., Williams, C., Trujillo, M., & Steinke, P. (2007). Assessment of spirituality and its relevance to addiction treatment. *Journal of Substance Abuse Treatment*, *33*(3), 257–264. https://doi.org/10.1016/j.jsat.2006.06.014

Galanter, M., Hansen, H., & Potenza, M. N. (2021). The role of spirituality in addiction medicine: a position statement from the spirituality interest group of the international society of addiction medicine. *Substance Abuse*, *42*(3), 269–271. https://doi.org/10.1080/08897077.2021.1941514

Granfield, R., & Cloud, W. (1999). *Coming clean: Overcoming addiction without treatment*. New York University Press.

Guest, M. (2016). In search of spiritual capital: The spiritual as a cultural resource. In K. Flanagan, & P. Jupp (Eds.), *The sociology of spirituality* (pp. 181–200). Ashgate Publishing.

Harris, K. S., Baker, A. K., Kimball, T. G., & Shumway, S. T. (2007). Achieving systems-based sustained recovery: A comprehensive model for collegiate recovery communities. *Journal of Groups in Addiction and Recovery*, *2*(2–4), 220–237. https://doi.org/10.1080/15560350802080951

Harris, K. S., Kimball, T. G., Casiraghi, A. M., & Maison, S. J. (2014). Collegiate recovery programs. *Peabody Journal of Education*, *89*(2), 229–243. https://doi.org/10.1080/0161956X.2014.897095

Hennessy, E. A., Nichols, L. M., Brown, T. B., & Tanner-Smith, E. E. (2022). Advancing the science of evaluating collegiate recovery program processes and outcomes: A recovery capital perspective. *Evaluation and Program Planning*, *91*, 102057. https://doi.org/10.1016/j.evalprogplan.2022.102057

Hennessy, E. A., Tanner-Smith, E. E., Nichols, L. M., Brown, T. B., & Mcculloch, B. J. (2021). A multisite study of emerging adults in collegiate recovery programs at public institutions. *Social Science and Medicine*, *278*, 113955. https://doi.org/10.1016/j.socscimed.2021.113955

Hewitt, A. J. (2007). *After the fire: Post traumatic growth in recovery from addictions [thesis]*. University of Bath, UK.

Humberger, M. (2022). *How word choice influences collegiate recovery: A quantitative analysis on the impact of identifying terms on self-compassion, stigma, and recovery capital [thesis]*. University of Texas at Arlington.

Iarussi, M. M. (2018). The experiences of college students in recovery from substance use disorders. *Journal of Addictions and Offender Counseling*, *39*(1), 46–62. https://doi.org/10.1002/jaoc.12040

Jason, L. A., Salomon-Amend, M., Guerrero, M., Bobak, T., O'Brien, J., & Soto-Nevarez, A. (2021). The emergence, role, and impact of recovery support services. *Alcohol Research: Current Reviews*, *41*(1), 04. https://doi.org/10.35946/arcr.v41.1.04

Kimball, T. G., Hune, N. D., Shumway, S. T., & Bradshaw, S. D. (2022). Exploring the long-term 12-step collegiate recovery experiences of emerging adults: An interpretive phenomenological analysis. *Alcoholism Treatment Quarterly*, *40*(3), 338–357. https://doi.org/10.1080/07347324.2022.2068990

Kimball, T. G., Shumway, S. T., Austin-Robillard, H., & Harris-Wilkes, K. S. (2017). Hoping and coping in recovery: A phenomenology of emerging adults in a collegiate recovery program. *Alcoholism Treatment Quarterly*, *35*(1), 46–62. https://doi.org/10.1080/07347324.2016.1256714

Laudet, A., Harris, K., Kimball, T., Winters, K. C., & Moberg, D. P. (2014). Collegiate recovery communities programs: What do we know and what do we need to know? *Journal of Social Work Practice in the Addictions*, *14*(1), 84–100. https://doi.org/10.1080/1533256X.2014.872015

Laudet, A. B., Harris, K., Kimball, T., Winters, K. C., & Moberg, D. P. (2015). Characteristics of students participating in collegiate recovery programs: A national survey. *Journal of Substance Abuse Treatment*, *51*, 38–46. https://doi.org/10.1016/j.jsat.2014.11.004

Laudet, A. B., & White, W. L. (2008). Recovery capital as prospective predictor of sustained recovery, life satisfaction, and stress among former poly-substance users. *Substance Use and Misuse*, *43*(1), 27–54. https://doi.org/10.1080/10826080701681473

Leamy, M., Bird, V., Le Boutillier, C., Williams, J., & Slade, M. (2011). Conceptual framework for personal recovery in mental health: systematic review and narrative synthesis. *The British Journal of Psychiatry*, *199*(6), 445–452. https://doi.org/10.1192/bjp.bp.110.083733

Levine, N. (2014). *Refuge recovery: A Buddhist path to recovering from addiction*. HarperOne.

Morton, S., O'Reilly, L., & O'Brien, K. (2016). Boxing clever: utilizing education and fitness to build recovery capital in a substance use rehabilitation program. *Journal of Substance Use*, *21*(5), 521–526. https://doi.org/10.3109/14659891.2015.1077281

Murphy, D. (2023). Recommending collegiate recovery programs to institutes of higher education in Ireland. *Alcoholism Treatment Quarterly*. *42*, 1–9. https://doi.org/10.1080/07347324.2023.2278532

Nichols, L. M., Hennessy, E. A., Brown, T. B., & Tanner-Smith, E. E. (2023). Co-occurring mental and behavioral health conditions among collegiate recovery program members. *Journal of American College Health*, *71*(7), 2085–2092. https://doi.org/10.1080/07448481.2021.1955687

NIDA. (2024). *Criminal justice drugfacts*. National Institutes of Health. https://nida.nih.gov/publications/drugfacts/criminal-justice

Pesetski, C. A. (2015). *An exploratory case study of undergraduate students in recovery: An application of recovery capital during reentry* [dissertation]. North Carolina State University.

Rettie, H. C., Hogan, L. M., & Cox, W. M. (2021). Identifying the main components of substance-related addiction recovery groups. *Substance Use and Misuse*, *56*(6), 840–847. https://doi.org/10.1080/10826084.2021.1899228

Rohr, R. (2023). *Falling upward: A spirituality for the two halves of life*,2nd ed. Jossey-Bass.

Ruisard, D. (2020). A power greater: Exploring spirituality in addiction recovery. In M. Jaffe, W. Nicola, J. Floersch, & J. Longhofer (Eds.), *Spirituality in mental health practice: A narrative casebook* (pp. 100–119). Routledge.

SAMHSA. (2020). Recovery and recovery Supports. https://www.samhsa.gov/find-help/recovery

Scoles, P. (2021). Public health, population health and the self-help movement in recovery. *Journal of Behavioral Health and Psychology*, *10*(4). https://doi.org/10.33425/2832-4579/21034

Scott, A., Anderson, A., Harper, K., & Alfonso, M. L. (2016). Experiences of students in recovery on a rural college campus: Social identity and stigma. *SAGE Open*, *6*(4). https://doi.org/10.1177/2158244016674762

Shapiro, F. (2008). *Who wrote the serenity prayer?*. Features | Yale Alumni Magazine. https://yalealumnimagazine.org/articles/2143-who-wrote-the-serenity-prayer

Smith, R. L., Bannard, T., McDaniel, J., Aliev, F., Brown, A., Holliday, E., Vest, N., DeFrantz-Dufor, W., & Dick, D. M. (2023). Characteristics of students participating in collegiate recovery programs and the impact of COVID-19: An updated national longitudinal study *Addiction Research & Theory*, 32(1), 58–67. https://doi.org/10.1080/16066359.2023.2216459

Tarter, R. E., & Reynolds, M. D. (2022). Psychological antecedents and correlates of substance use and addiction. In M. M. Vanyukov (Ed.), *Genetics of Substance Use: Research and Clinical Aspects* (pp. 69–95). Springer International Publishing.

Texas Tech University. (2024). *Recovery Meeting Schedule*. Center for Students in Addiction Recovery. https://www.depts.ttu.edu/hs/csa/meetingschedule.php

Watts, J. R., Chowdhury, D., & Holloway, L. (2019). Success in collegiate recovery programs: results from a phenomenological investigation. *Alcoholism Treatment Quarterly*, *37*(2), 163–180. https://doi.org/10.1080/07347324.2018.1532776

Webb, J. R. (2021). *Understanding forgiveness and addiction: Theory, research, and clinical application* (1st ed.). Routledge. https://doi.org/10.4324/9780429200274

White, W., & Cloud, W. (2008). Recovery capital: A primer for addictions professionals. *Counselor*, *9*(5), 22–27.

Wood, L. J., & Hilton, A. A. (2012). Spirituality and academic success: Perceptions of African American males in the community college. *Religion and Education*, *39*(1), 28–47. https://doi.org/10.1080/15507394.2012.648576

Chapter 31

Spirituality and Sex Offense Treatment Related Outcomes

Jill D. Stinson and Abigail G. Wiser*

Persons who have engaged in sexually abusive behaviors and faced legal sanction for sexual crimes are often required to complete sex offense related treatment, either in a custodial setting like a prison or hospital, or while residing in their communities. Though interventions differ with regard to intensity, modality, and therapeutic orientation, empirical findings suggest that such treatments effectively reduce both general and sex offense specific recidivism (Lösel & Schmucker, 2005; Schmucker & Lösel, 2015, 2017), and that treatment noncompletion is associated with higher risk of sexual reoffending (Olver et al., 2011). Many of these effective treatments share common features, including adherence to principles associated with the Risk-Needs-Responsivity model (Hanson et al., 2009) and use of cognitive behavioral approaches and individualized treatment (Schmucker & Lösel, 2017).

Within the realm of sex offense treatment, however, emphasis on specific content areas can substantially vary. One such content area is the role of religion, faith, and spirituality in the rehabilitative process. In this chapter, we will examine the relationship between spirituality and health and recovery for those who have committed sexual offenses, how considerations of spirituality are incorporated into sex offense treatment, and the role of faith communities in rehabilitation and community reintegration following a sexual offense. We will additionally discuss cautions, criticisms, and limitations within the literature describing religion and spirituality in the context of sex offense treatment, as well as future directions for research and clinical practice.

Defining Spirituality in the Context of Sex Offense Treatment

The RiTE Model of Spirituality (Webb et al., 2014; see also, Chapters 1 and 44 of this volume) includes ritualistic, theistic, and existential aspects of the spiritual experience. In our review of the literature related to the role of spirituality in sex offense treatment, operational definitions of spirituality appear to largely focus on ritualistic aspects of spirituality, or those that seem most closely related to structured or organized religious practice and belief, and theistic features of spirituality, or those that are less centered around religious structure and relate more to conceptualizations of deity and the spirit. Considerations relevant to existential spirituality do appear, mostly in the form of finding meaning or purpose in life post-offense, or in understanding the dichotomy of one's "old self" and a reformed, "new self." Throughout this chapter, we will differentiate these where appropriate in order to best

* Corresponding Author: stinson@etsu.edu.

DOI: 10.4324/9781003440048-35

understand our current state of knowledge in this area. Also of note, much of this literature describes beliefs and practices associated with Christianity, with far more limited inclusion of other faith traditions or religious orientations.

In our efforts to most broadly reflect the differing facets of the RiTE Model of Spirituality in relation to sex offense treatment, we have utilized a combination of search strategies. Searches were conducted using the American Psychological Association's PsycInfo and ProQuest's Religion Database, using terms reflecting both general and specific forms of sex offense treatment (e.g., Good Lives Model, Circles of Support and Accountability) and broad terms for spirituality and specific religious affiliations (e.g., Christianity, Islam, Judaism, Buddhism). Further, once relevant articles were identified, searches based on those authors' other works and references contained within were conducted. Some individual authors were contacted to obtain program materials and media releases describing their programs. From these sources, we extracted the information about incorporation of spirituality into health, recovery, and rehabilitation of persons who have committed sexual offenses.

Spirituality as Related to Health and Recovery in Persons Who Have Sexually Abused

Early research in this area focused on the perpetration of sexual abuse by members of the clergy, spanning multiple faith traditions and denominations. Discussion of treatment needs and spirituality were then precipitated by large-scale investigations into institutional responses to allegations of sexual abuse. Since, more attention has been devoted to understanding experiences of spirituality and religious affiliation among non-cleric samples of persons involved in sex offense treatment. Such effort has been concentrated in three broad areas of spirituality in relation to health and recovery: (1) existential spirituality in the way of understanding meaning in one's experience and defining one's "self," (2) communal spirituality as a source of support, connection, or belongingness, and (3) spirituality and religion as an important source of coping, which appears to align with both ritualistic and theistic aspects of spirituality.

Existential Spirituality: Finding Meaning in One's Experience

A crucial component of health and recovery during the sex offense treatment process is to develop an understanding of what led to sexually abusive behavior and the implications for one's identity and purpose in an offense-free future. In a series of qualitative studies involving men incarcerated for sexual offenses in the UK who represented a variety of faith traditions (e.g., Methodist, Catholic, Quaker, Buddhist), religion and spirituality facilitated self-reflection and provided a sense of purpose. For example, Bell et al.'s (2018) Buddhist participants noted that their ritualistic spirituality practices had fostered growth of existential spirituality. Practicing mindfulness, enhancing self-reflection, awareness of the present moment, and behaving more deliberately and purposefully led to a more defined sense of self, a sense of purpose in their lives, and the ability to change their self-narrative or view of who they are as a person. In a study of Jewish, Christian, Muslim, and non-religious men incarcerated for sexual offenses in Israel, themes of transcendence and recovery were intertwined. Some noted that religious conversion from previously non-religious affiliation had aided them in their treatment and growth (Elisha et al., 2012).

Similar themes of spirituality promoting changes in one's view of the "self" were endorsed by a range of Christian participants in Winder et al. (2018). Participants saw their religious practices and spiritual beliefs as a source of becoming a better person and one who is committed to living in accordance with Christian values like honesty, compassion, and service to God and others. This also contributed to increased personal self-satisfaction in their growth and recovery, as they felt such changes in their lives brought them closer to God (theistic spirituality) (Winder et al., 2018). The role of existential spirituality in promoting health and recovery was further associated with views of redemption and forgiveness common to Christianity and other religious traditions, in that men in sex offense related treatment while in prison spoke to themes of forgiveness, redemption, and resurrection in building new lives and fostering more positive views of themselves as people (Blagden et al., 2020).

Harper et al. (2019) further discuss the potential applicability of an Islamic perspective to existential spirituality and the sense of self within sex offense related treatment. The Islamic Guidance Program (Awan, 2014), for example, was developed to assist Muslim treatment participants in challenging their extremist beliefs and behaviors (i.e., if present; e.g., spreading messages intended to incite hatred and violence directed toward non-Muslim groups, unwillingness to associate with non-Muslim others) in the context of Islamic views of the self and relationship with others. Though not directly applied in the context of sex offending, Harper et al. (2019) describe how views of the self, the faith, religious identity, and Islamic moral standards can aid a person in sex offense related treatment to develop a new, more spiritually healthy view of themselves and their relationship with God and others.

Communal Spirituality: Support, Connection, and Belongingness through Spiritual and Religious Practice

Belongingness and relationships with others represent an important aspect of affiliative health. Beyond the contribution spirituality may make to intrinsic self-view and recovery, communing with others through ritualistic spirituality and shared belief may additionally enable post-offense recovery. Sexual offending is a highly stigmatized behavior, and individual feelings of isolation, ostracism, and loneliness are common once sexually abusive behaviors have been detected and sanctioned (Harper et al., 2024, Tewksbury, 2012). Thus, religious involvement and a sense of spiritual connection may offset the experiences of stigma and isolation felt by those who have committed sexual offenses. In one examination of men incarcerated in prison, it was noted that not only was involvement in spiritual and religious programming beneficial in reducing sexual and non-sexual recidivism, but engaging in religious and spiritual community enhanced perceptions of support, collaboration, and working together in recovery (Stansfield et al., 2020).

Others have similarly described the role of religious community in reducing judgment and shame, while enhancing perceptions of connection. In particular, shared communal religious space (e.g., the prison chapel) and religious personnel or prison chaplains have fostered a feeling of connection to something beyond their shared offense stories or the prison culture, and provided a place of acceptance and non-judgment at the human existential level (Winder et al., 2018). This may appear different across different faith traditions, however. While more Judeo-Christian faith traditions emphasize the role of spiritual community and support in health and recovery, the Buddhist tradition of non-attachment can encourage a more balanced view of relationships and outcomes for men in sex offense related treatment. Here, acceptance of the impermanence of life and the need to challenge unhealthy attachments to sex, possessions, and dysfunctional relationships has been beneficial in refocusing what belongingness means in the larger world (Bell et al., 2018). Specific case studies of four men in sex offense related treatment in the UK of Catholic, Jewish, Bahá'í, and Quaker faiths are provided in Winder et al., (2019) that highlight common themes of acceptance, connection, and attachment to others in the faith community across these traditions that differ in belief and practice. These findings again highlight the importance of spiritual community in addition to existential and other aspects of individual spiritual belief.

Ritualistic and Theistic Spirituality: Finding Ways to Cope

Finally, with regard to aspects of spirituality related to health and recovery, religious and spiritual practices (e.g., prayer or religious meditation, involvement in communal worship activities) offer strategies for coping and changing important emotional, interpersonal, and behavioral patterns. For some, the relationship with God or a deity itself is a source of potential coping – knowing that they can commune with God, that they are accepted and loved by God, and that they can rely on God in times of need serves as resource and source of emotional support and comfort (Winder et al., 2018). For others, participation in religious activities builds new habits and routines, which in turn fosters mechanisms for dealing with everyday problems that incorporate religious practices (Stansfield et al., 2020). However, for some, struggle with religious identity and relationship with a higher power can lead to poorer health and recovery, including increased experiences of hopelessness, shame, depression, and anxiety (Robertson et al., 2020). So, while some may find ritualistic and theistic spirituality as important sources of improved coping, experiencing struggle with religious identity and involvement may have a negative impact.

Spirituality as an Integrated Component of Sex Offense Treatment

Religious observance and spirituality, primarily conceptualized within the bounds of Christianity, have long been a foundational component of rehabilitation across the broader correctional systems in the US and UK (Beedon, 2019; Schaefer et al., 2016). An important assumption underlying this relationship has been that illegal behaviors are similarly immoral, and thus represent a problem or failure to adhere to religious principles (ritualistic spirituality) or a lack of faith (theistic spirituality). Along such lines, correctional institutions were termed "penitentiaries" to highlight the role of penitence and absolution in the rehabilitative process (Beedon, 2019). Early forms of treatment for persons convicted of sexual offenses drew from substance misuse treatment models, some of which incorporated principles of theistic spirituality and religious observance. Given this, it is perhaps surprising that so little literature exists today describing the role of spirituality in the sex offense treatment and rehabilitation process. Here, we summarize several approaches that directly incorporate spiritual principles into treatment, as well as limited data related to their relationship to recidivism and desistence from sexual offending.

12-Step/Sexual Addiction Models

Our earliest models of sex offense treatment utilizing a spiritual framework were drawn from 12-step and addiction models intended for substance misuse treatment. Within such models, an important goal is to develop a genuine relationship with a higher power or the Divine (theistic spirituality) and a sense of "wholeness" as a person within the context of that relationship (existential spirituality) (Earle et al., 1998). An important contrast in such conceptualizations is that a person is working toward authenticity in relation to a higher power versus the individual's previous sexual offending behavior, which is characterized by secrecy and a lack of connection to spiritual principles (Earle et al., 1998). Thus, during the course of treatment, growth or progress is viewed through a lens of theistic and existential spiritual development, with the person finding new connections with spirituality in order to move away from a sense of shame and disconnectedness that characterized their life at the time of an offense. Unfortunately, these views of spirituality within sex offense treatment are also linked with components of treatment that are relatively outdated and ineffectual, including confrontational methods and victim empathy training (Earle et al., 1998). Still, these represent efforts to translate an approach once commonly used to incorporate spirituality into substance misuse treatment into a differing realm of need.

Programs for Clergy Who Have Engaged in Acts of Sexual Abuse

Some efforts to develop treatment incorporating spirituality in sex offense related treatment centers on persons who committed acts of sexual abuse while serving as clergy or other religious leaders. Recognizing the key role of spirituality in the lives of these individuals, treatment can incorporate religious traditions in the recovery process. Songy (2003), for example, draws upon elements of vocational and spiritual discernment in Roman Catholicism and recommends a series of questions for assessing spiritual growth, as well as strategies for calling upon commitments made to God and the Church (ritualistic and theistic spirituality) in a process of psychological recovery and spiritual healing (existential spirituality). Though specific recommendations for treatment modality are not made, Songy (2003) urges collaboration between the Church and treating mental health professionals to promote healing for both the person and their spirit.

Lacambre and colleagues (Lacambre & Bodkin, 2021; Lacambre et al., 2021) have highlighted the complexities of engaging in sex offense specific treatment for clergy (again, Roman Catholic) who have engaged in sexual abuse, and the need to incorporate aspects of religious belief and practice (ritualistic spirituality) into understanding how sexual abuse occurred. For example, identifying important relational dynamics that a religious institution may promote (e.g., religious leaders are privileged and their behaviors sacrosanct; secrecy and confession are normalized) can assist in recognizing aspects of the sexual grooming process that can be addressed in treatment (Lacambre et al., 2021). Further, challenging Church doctrine regarding sexuality and celibacy in treatment (e.g., taking a vow of celibacy erases sexual desires and diminishes the need to take seriously sexual urges) can aid in the development of strategies for appropriately and safely addressing sexual needs and relationships in the future to prevent reoffense (Lacambre et al., 2021). However, also within this model is adherence to the Risk–Needs–Responsivity framework,[1] group and individual psychotherapy using evidence-based approaches, administration of psychotropic and other necessary medications, and assistive therapies to address other important life needs (e.g., recreation, creativity).

Circles of Support and Accountability (CoSA)

CoSA is a reintegration framework designed to facilitate successful and safe community reentry for persons at high risk of sexual recidivism. First implemented in Canada in 1994, a circle of supportive volunteers was formed by a Mennonite pastor to address the reintegration of an individual who had committed serious sexual offenses and was institutionalized for much of his life (Wilson et al., 2007). This first circle led to others, with an official recognition of CoSA by the Ontario Mennonite community in 1996 and a contract with Correctional Services Canada (Wilson et al., 2007). Though not specifically a religious or spiritual treatment approach, CoSA is premised on principles of transformation, responsibility, accountability, and leading a productive life (Azoulay et al., 2019). These principles are characteristic of Mennonite views and reflect elements of existential spirituality and constructive spirituality, or healthy relationships between the individual and others in their community (Webb, 2021).

Since initial implementation, CoSA has spread internationally, though primarily within English-speaking nations (Azoulay et al., 2019). With regard to CoSA's effectiveness, empirical findings from small-scale studies do indicate reductions in sexual recidivism, though these evaluations are not specific to spiritual or religious elements of CoSA programming (Azoulay et al., 2019). A meta-analysis of studies evaluating participation in CoSA during the community reintegration process showed improvements across a range of relevant outcomes. These included emotional and social well-being, involvement in prosocial activities, age-appropriate relationships with others, and improved self-esteem (Clarke et al., 2017), highlighting aspects of existential spirituality that may be fostered through CoSA engagement.

Good Lives Model (GLM)

The GLM is a strengths-based treatment framework for people who have engaged in sexually abusive behaviors that is premised on the idea that people in treatment are striving for achievement and well-being (Ward & Gannon, 2006; Ward & Stewart, 2003), rather than trying to merely address deficits and problems in their lives. To accomplish this, they work toward 11 identified "primary human goods" (Purvis et al., 2011), which include happiness, creativity, knowledge, and community, as well as relevant spiritual constructs like existential spirituality and inner peace.

However, little research has examined the specific spiritual components of the GLM and their effect on sexual recidivism or other measures of treatment success. Harper and colleagues (Harper et al., 2021) developed a questionnaire for use with the GLM, and when subjected to factor analysis, four items directly assessing existential and theistic spirituality loaded onto the same factor. In their research, they determined that endorsing aspects of spirituality on this scale were positively associated with psychological well-being and social connectedness, as well as a somewhat protective effect against general delinquency (Harper et al., 2021). However, this was not a sample of people who were engaged in treatment using the GLM for sexual offending, but a community sample of adults. Additional research is needed to better understand the role of spirituality as a primary human good within the GLM, and its contribution toward sex offense related treatment effectiveness and reduction of sexual recidivism.

Role of Faith Communities in Rehabilitation and Reintegration Following a Sexual Offense

As noted previously, involvement as a part of a larger faith community can offer a source of support during the recovery process, and religious and spiritual traditions have often been incorporated into the fundamental practices of correctional rehabilitation and treatment. A common view is that for some, spirituality and religious communion with others can serve as a crucial catalyst for change (Giordano et al., 2008). This has been shown specifically with regard to those who have committed sexual offenses. In their examination of CoSA, a program premised on fostering community transformation and restoration of relationships, Azoulay et al. (2019) noted that the majority of persons who were returning to communities after convictions for sexual offending believed they would have likely returned to criminal activity if not for the support of CoSA volunteers. Similarly, Elisha et al. (2012) indicated that support and acceptance from religious figures and faith community members were critical in fostering self-acceptance during the recovery process. The emphasis on acceptance and compassion common to Judeo-Christian, Buddhist, and other faith traditions lends itself to including religious leaders and peers in the recovery process (Bell et al., 2018; Robertson et al., 2020), and such views parallel the emphasis given to compassion and self-improvement seen in a range of sex offense treatment modalities.

However, how do members of these faith communities view their role in the recovery process, and how do they view persons who have committed sexual offenses? Does spirituality play a role in determining their level of involvement? One systematic review of recent literature identified several key roles of faith communities in promoting recovery, including: (1) supporting re-entry, (2) fostering connection and building new networks, (3) transformation, and (4) giving back or reparation (Kewley et al., 2015). Such roles underscore the multifaceted nature of the faith community and members' contribution to the recovery process, ranging from logistical tasks (e.g., aiding with finding housing and employment), to social connectedness (e.g., building new social ties), to transforming the self through spiritual growth, to finding ways to improve the community as a way of "righting" previous "wrongs."

Views from within a variety of faith communities underscore the complexities of these roles and relationships. In one broad survey of people in the US from a variety of religious backgrounds, people who identified as Christian Protestant or non-religious were least supportive of proposed measures to limit participation in worship for persons on the sex offender registry, while those of Catholic or other non-Christian religious faiths were the most supportive of such measures (Dum et al., 2020). Further, those with self-assessed strongest religious beliefs and those most likely to ascribe morality to individual choice were the least accepting of persons on the sex offender registry in their faith communities (Dum et al., 2020). Others have found that religious fundamentalism (i.e., belief that there is one religion or set of teachings that is fundamental truth, that evil is an opposing force to be conquered, that religious truth is fundamental and unchanged over time, and that those who follow this religion or teachings have a special relationship with the Divine, as defined by Altemeyer & Hunsberger, 2004) is associated with greater discomfort at the thought of interacting with someone convicted of a sexual offense, more so than was true of someone paroled or found not guilty by reason of insanity for non-sexual offenses (Yelderman et al., 2018). This was true to some extent regardless of social context, in that persons with more religiously fundamentalist views who were primed to imagine this encounter at their church or place of worship versus in another non-religious social context felt equally uncomfortable with interacting with a person convicted of a sexual offense (Yelderman et al., 2018).

Beyond strength or nature of spiritual or religious beliefs, however, the relationship between faith communities and persons in recovery following a sexual offense may vary based on other characteristics of the community or the individual. For example, in a study of attitudes in a large Midwestern US Black Seventh Day Adventist church, members strongly felt that the church should have a role in the recovery and reintegration of youth who had engaged in sexually abusive behaviors (Venable, 2015). Here, the history of Black churches in promoting social growth and help-seeking among church members was cited as a prominent theme, and study participants used more positive and recovery-based terms to describe the youth in question. Additionally, participants centered on the role of the church family in providing support and resources and the need for education within the church to promote successful recovery (Venable, 2015). However, this appeared in contrast to views of the youths' families as responsible for their sexually abusive behavior, either through negligence or failure to impart religious morals, traditions, or beliefs, as well as some who viewed these youths as a potential threat to others within the church itself (Venable, 2015). While many see faith communities involved in recovery in multiple ways, there is inconsistency in perceptions across a range of faith traditions, and even within the same church, regarding how they can or should assist persons in recovery following acts of sexual offending.

Cautions Associated with Spirituality and Sex Offense Related Treatment

Despite a broad view of spirituality as a potentially beneficial component of recovery and reintegration efforts for people who have committed sexual offenses, a number of cautions have been identified by providers, faith communities, and treatment consumers themselves. First, some have described how specific ritualistic and theistic aspects of spirituality and spiritual belief can facilitate and entrench offense-supportive beliefs and attitudes, particularly related to the inevitability of their offending behavior and rationalization of its occurrence. Specifically, this may occur through belief that God or a deity allows things to happen or puts an individual in a given scenario in accordance with a grander plan, thus minimizing the individual's personal responsibility for their behavior (Saradjian & Nobus, 2003; Winder et al., 2018). This was also evident in a discussion of views of Karma among a group of Buddhist men who had sexually offended, as some espoused beliefs that "'Karma decides' what happens" (Bell et al., 2018, p. 108), again suggesting that an individual's sexual offending behavior is beyond their immediate control and accountability. Others have indicated that the themes of penitence, forgiveness, and reparation common to many faith traditions and religious practices can promote an attitude dismissive of continued responsibility. This includes persons who believe that confession absolves them of responsibility (Saradjian & Nobus, 2003), or that subsequent "good" acts can cancel the "bad" they've done as part of their offending (Bell et al., 2018). Relatedly, views that religious participation and spiritual belief (primarily ritualistic spirituality) make one somehow better than others involved in similar treatment, or make one immune to potential temptation, were noted to put those in recovery at risk of inflated self-importance and narcissism that might compromise their ability to address challenges and appropriately manage potential risk to others (Winder et al., 2018).

Another caution noted within the literature is that of strong religious beliefs fostering a sense of hopelessness or exclusion. This may take the form of ritualistic spirituality, where specific tenets of a given faith tradition may inspire feelings of condemnation (Eshuys & Smallbone, 2006; Robertson et al., 2020; Winder et al., 2018), leading to isolation, hopelessness, and a sense of having been abandoned. These could reasonably place an individual at risk of reoffending. This may also be evidenced through theistic spirituality, wherein the person may feel that their deity no longer loves or accepts them because of their behavior (Robertson et al., 2020) and has thus abandoned them during their time of recovery and need for strength.

Finally, it is possible that some persons involved in sex offense related treatment may use overt and observable religious observance as a "mask," purportedly to hide their true struggles with recovery and to appear more functional and stable than they really are, or to use the trust and sense of community common to many religious groups as a source of potential victims to exploit and abuse (Kewley et al., 2015). Here, it is assumed that ritualistic spiritual practices are performative but may not be widely recognized as such by others within the same faith community, who are then left vulnerable to potential manipulation and abuse. This has been discussed more broadly within the context of clergy who have used outward penitence and calls for forgiveness to disguise continued efforts to sexually abuse parishioners within their care (Kewley et al., 2015; Smallbone et al., 2013). Occurrences of this have likely contributed to the inconsistent acceptance of persons who have committed sexual offense within faith communities, as was discussed earlier within this chapter.

Limitations and Future Directions

Our current review of the theoretical and empirical literature related to the incorporation of spirituality into sex offense treatment revealed a number of important limitations. Most notably was a lack of standardization or systematic evaluation of the nature and effectiveness of integrating spirituality into recovery programs for persons who have committed acts of sexual abuse. Though there is a history of incorporating religious traditions and practices into a broad range of recovery programs, including those for substance-related struggles or in correctional settings, a more limited understanding of this emerges for those involved with sex offense treatment. Importantly, many religious traditions include specific moral mandates related to sexuality and sexual behavior, and some authors directly address concerns related to recovery and wellness for members of clergy who have engaged in acts of sexual abuse (e.g., dealing with guilt following acts of sexual violation, coping with feelings of loss of purpose or vocation, and managing sexual urges appropriately in those expected to maintain celibacy). Thus, more clearly defined and systematic empirical efforts to examine the role of spirituality at the levels of the individual, the treatment program, the community reintegration context, and the faith community are needed. This is also true of rigorous evaluation of the effectiveness of such efforts.

A related limitation is that even if such examinations of the effectiveness of spirituality and spiritual practices were to become more common, the field is hindered by unclear and inconsistent integration of spirituality into sex offense treatment at the outset. In our efforts to identify how spirituality was incorporated, it was often difficult to determine the degree to which spirituality was included in treatment programming, as well as what it might look like in actual practice for any given client. While not all clients, clinicians, or agencies may desire the incorporation of spirituality into sex offense treatment programming, for some it may be an element critical to recovery. Notably, clinical researchers have described the lack of training in religious and spiritual competencies across most mental health related disciplines and called for increased and more nuanced attention to the spiritual needs of mental and behavioral health consumers (Currier et al., 2023; Vieten & Lukoff, 2022). This may be a particularly salient need for those who work with individuals who have committed sexual offenses, as the current literature evidences intersecting struggles related to existential, theistic, ritualistic, and community spirituality in this population (Winder et al., 2019).

Limitations in the diversity of facets of spirituality and in the representation of differing faith traditions were also evident. The majority of considerations of spirituality in treatment and recovery involved more ritualistic aspects of spirituality. While these may be more objective in some respects and thus more easily operationally defined and measured for empirical study, it is also likely that these are the most salient aspects of spirituality for those providing sex offense treatment and designing programs to promote rehabilitation and community reintegration for persons who have sexually abused. However, it is also quite likely that some of the more personal and subjective elements of spirituality, such as those incorporated into existential and theistic aspects of spirituality, are highly impactful to the individual and may hold significant promise toward promoting holistic and meaningful recovery. Thus, additional consideration of the comprehensive nature of individual spirituality is needed, along with strategies for assessing these constructs, incorporating them into what are often rather standardized treatment approaches, and training clinicians in broader spiritual competencies. Further, while some of the literature we reviewed involved multiple faith traditions, including Judaism, Buddhism, and Islam, Christianity and Christian viewpoints dominated discussions of spirituality in the context of sex offense treatment. This is potentially reflective of the countries from which literature was drawn, where Christianity may be the predominant faith tradition, or from the fact that we reviewed primarily research disseminated in English. Research findings from languages and cultures less accessible to the authors may have provided greater nuance and depth with regard to the role of other faith traditions and their consideration of spirituality in sex offense treatment.

Finally, despite the commonly noted occurrence of the involvement of faith communities in reintegration for persons who have committed sexual offenses and who are returning to the community, there was little guidance for helping members of those faith communities work most effectively to promote and maintain successful reintegration for these individuals. Interestingly, the conversation related to how to include persons convicted of sexual offenses within a church community has been dominated by insurance companies, as a range of church insurers provide guidance for church leaders and parishioners regarding strategies for keeping congregants safe. These include statements and decision-making tools by US-based insurers like AG Financial (Missouri), Brotherhood Mutual Insurance (Indiana), and GuideOne Insurance (Iowa), or non-profit organizations devoted to enhancing safety and community in faith-based organizations (e.g., Adventist Risk Management Inc., MinistrySafe). Across such guidelines are a number of common recommendations, including considerations of legal liability, safety of children within the congregation, personal accountability and compliance concerns for the person with a history of sexual offending, education regarding sexual abuse, and transparency to members of the congregation. Another common element is some discussion of whether or not to even allow a person with a history of sexual offending to participate in worship activities, often referencing concerns about continued predatory behavior and risks to children. We were unable to locate any empirical evaluation of such practices recommended by insurance companies, or of programs that faith communities may have implemented to foster involvement of persons in recovery in their local congregations. This is clearly then a need for future research, as some of the literature we have presented here suggests ambivalent feelings among church members with regard to involving these individuals in their faith communities, while the individuals themselves may find meaning, purpose, and community in spiritual and religious activities. We need additional information related to the effectiveness and limitations of these programs, as well as strategies for enhancing their success among persons and faith communities who wish to use them.

Conclusions

Perspectives regarding the role of existential, ritualistic, and theistic spirituality, as well as the role of spiritual community, vary broadly across faith traditions and treatment and recovery models for those who have engaged in sexually abusive behavior. Shared elements across existing broad-based sex offense treatment modalities emphasize elements of existential spirituality in the context of developing a new self and understanding one's identity in the context of a larger world, while others more specifically incorporate ritualistic and theistic spirituality as strategies for coping, acceptance, and building a network of support. Few programs directly implement tenets of varying faith traditions, and those that do have seldom been rigorously empirically evaluated. Still, participants in those programs provide qualitative reflections on the meaning of their faith and how it has aided in their recovery from a life of sexual violence perpetration. Though faith communities are said to play a pivotal role, their responses and inclusion of persons in recovery following sexual offending is mixed, with some prioritizing personal and congregational safety, and others seeing themselves as key in facilitating recovery for another individual. Finally, our search revealed a number of cautionary statements describing risks of spiritual involvement in the sex offense related treatment process, as some may become less able to see potential risks in their behaviors behind a mask of spiritual transformation, and others may use the trust of faith communities as a source of potential victims. However, to best understand this complex issue, we need additional research related to spiritual components of health and recovery for those convicted of sexual offenses, representation from a range of faith traditions, and more empirical evaluation of treatment and religious communal programming designed to foster effective and safe rehabilitation for those who have engaged in harmful sexual behaviors.

Note

1 The Risk-Needs-Responsivity model (Bonta & Andrews, 2007) is a rehabilitation approach that emphasizes assessing risk and matching services to level of risk, developing treatment goals that incorporate criminogenic needs, and delivering treatment in a way that considers the client's motivation, strengths, abilities, and preferred method of learning.

References

Adventist Risk Management, Inc.(n.d.) https://adventistyouthministries.org/files/images/Safety-Guidelines-microsite/PDF/GUIDE_SexOffendersInChurch_NADENG.pdf

AG Financial.(n.d.) https://www.agfinancial.org/resources/article/church-liability-and-registered-sex-offenders

Altemeyer, B., & Hunsberger, B. (2004). A revised religious fundamentalism scale: The short and sweet of it. *The International Journal for the Psychology of Religion*, *14*(1), 47–54. https://doi.org/10.1207/s15327582ijpr1401_4

Awan, T. M. (2014). *An Islamic approach to rehabilitation of Muslim prisoners: An empirical case study*. Sang-e-Meel Publications.

Azoulay, N., Winder, B., Murphy, L., & Fedoroff, J. P. (2019). Circles of support and accountability (CoSA): A review of the development of CoSA and its international implementation. *International Review of Psychiatry*, *31*(2), 195–205. https://doi.org/10.1080/09540261.2018.1552406

Beedon, D.K. (2019). Religion and the criminal justice system (CJS): A socio-historical overview. In: *Sexual crime, religion and spirituality*, 1–24. (Winder, B., Blagden, N., Hocken, K., Elliott, H., Lievesley, R., & Banyard, P., Eds.). Palgrave MacMillan.

Bell, K., Winder, B., & Blagden, N. (2018). "Better as a Buddhist": An interpretive phenomenological analysis of the reflections on the religious beliefs of Buddhist men serving a prison sentence for a sexual offence. *Religions*, *9*(4), 101–117. https://doi.org/10.3390/rel9040101

Blagden, N., Winder, B., & Lievesley, R. (2020). "The resurrection after the old has gone and the new has come": Understanding narratives of forgiveness, redemption and resurrection in Christian individuals serving time in custody for a sexual offense. *Psychology, Crime, & Law*, *26*(1), 34–52. https://doi.org/10.1080/1068316X.2019.1634194

Bonta, J., & Andrews, D. A. (2007). Risk-need-responsivity model for offender assessment and rehabilitation. *Rehabilitation*, *6*(1), 1–22.

Brotherhood Mutual Insurance.(n.d.) https://www.brotherhoodmutual.com/resources/safety-library/risk-management-articles/administrative-staff-and-finance/sexual-misconduct/sex-offenders-allowed-to-attend-church/

Clarke, M., Brown, S., & Völlm, B. (2017). Circles of Support and Accountability for Sex Offenders: A Systematic Review of Outcomes. *Sexual Abuse*, *29*(5), 446–478. https://doi.org/10.1177/1079063215603691

Currier, J. M., Fox, J., Vieten, C., Pearce, M., & Oxhandler, H. K. (2023). Enhancing competencies for the ethical integration of religion and spirituality in psychological services. *Psychological Services*, *20*(1), 40. https://doi.org/10.1037/ser0000678

Dum, C. P., Socia, K. M., Long, B. L., & Yarrison, F. (2020). Would God forgive? Public attitudes toward sex offenders in places of worship. *Sexual Abuse*, *32*(5), 567–590. https://doi.org/10.1177/1079063219839498

Earle, R.H., Dillon, D., & Jecmen, D. (1998). Systematic approach to the treatment of sex offenders. *Sexual Addiction & Compulsivity*, *5*, 49–61. https://doi.org/10.1080/10720169808400147

Elisha, E., Idisis, Y., & Ronel, N. (2012). Window of opportunity: Social acceptance and life transformation in the rehabilitation of imprisoned sex offenders. *Aggression and Violent Behavior*, *17*(4), 323–332. https://doi.org/10.1016/j.avb.2012.03.004

Eshuys, D., & Smallbone, S. (2006). Religious affiliations among adult sexual offenders. *Sexual Abuse*, *18*(3), 279–288. https://doi.org/10.1177/107906320601800306

Giordano, P. C., Longmore, M. A., Schroeder, R. D., & Seffrin, P. M. (2008). A life-course perspective on spirituality and desistance from crime. *Criminology*, *46*(1), 99–132. https://doi.org/10.1111/j.1745-9125.2008.00104.x

GuideOne Insurance.(n.d.) https://www.guideone.com/resources/safety-resource-library/dos-and-donts-dealing-sex-offenders-church

Hanson, R. K., Bourgon, G., Helmus, L., & Hodgson, S. (2009). The principles of effective correctional treatment also apply to sexual offenders: A meta-analysis. *Criminal Justice and Behavior*, *36*(9), 865–891. https://doi.org/10.1177/0093854809338545

Harper, C. A., Lievesley, R., Blagden, N., Akerman, G., Winder, B., & Baumgartner, E. (2021). Development and validation of the Good Lives Questionnaire. *Psychology, Crime & Law*, *27*(7), 678–703. https://doi.org/10.1080/1068316X.2020.1849695

Harper, C. A., Rumney, P. N., & Sackey, D. A. (2024). Are sex offending allegations viewed differently? Exploring the effect of offense type and conviction status on criminal stigmatization. *Sexual Abuse*, *36*(1), 33–58. https://doi.org/10.1177/10790632231154168

Harper, C. A., Wilson, C., Hocken, K., Awan, T. M., & Lievesley, R. (2019). Religiously responsive treatment for people convicted of sexual offences. In B. Winder, N. Blagden, K. Hocken, H. Elliot, R. Lievesley, & P. Banyard (Eds.), *Sexual crime, religion and spirituality* (pp. 115–138). Palgrave Macmillan Cham.

Kewley, S., Beech, A. R., & Harkins, L. (2015). Examining the role of faith community groups with sexual offenders: A systematic review. *Aggression and Violent Behavior*, *25*, 142–149. https://doi.org/10.1016/j.avb.2015.07.016

Lacambre, M., & Bodkin, W. (2021). New psychiatric/psychological unit working with the Roman Catholic Church, France in cases of pedophilia. *Association for the Treatment of Sexual Abusers, virtual conference*.

Lacambre, M., Teillard-Dirat, M., & Bodkin, W. (2021). *Stratégies de prise en soins des auteurs de violences Sexuelles - chapitre de l'ouvrage « L'Eglise déchirée » sous la direction de Stéphane Joulain, Karjlin Demasure* et Jean-Guy Nadeau, Ed. Bayard.

Lösel, F., & Schmucker, M. (2005). The effectiveness of treatment for sexual offenders: A comprehensive meta-analysis. *Journal of Experimental Criminology*, *1*, 117–146.

MinistrySafe. Registered sex offenders: Should your church accommodate known offenders?, (n.d.) https://ministrysafe.com/wp-content/uploads/2021/11/ChurchExecutiveRegisteredSexOffenders.pdf

Olver, M. E., Stockdale, K. C., & Wormith, J. S. (2011). A meta-analysis of predictors of offender treatment attrition and its relationship to recidivism. *Journal of consulting and clinical psychology*, *79*(1), 6–21. https://doi.org/10.1037/a0022200

Purvis, M., Ward, T., & Willis, G. (2011). The Good Lives Model in practice: Offence pathways and case management. *European journal of probation*, *3*(2), 4–28. https://doi.org/10.1177/206622031100300202

Robertson, T.M., Magyar-Russell, G.M., & Piedmont, R.L. (2020). Let him who is without sin cast the first stone: Religious struggle among persons convicted of sexually offending. *Religions*, *11*(11), 546–568. https://doi.org/10.3390/rel11110546

Saradjian, A., & Nobus, D. (2003). Cognitive distortions of religious professionals who sexually abuse children. *Journal of interpersonal violence*, *18*(8), 905–923. https://doi.org/10.1177/0886260503253881

Schaefer, L., Sams, T., & Lux, J. (2016). Saved, salvaged, or sunk: A meta-analysis of the effects of faith-based interventions on inmate adjustment. *The Prison Journal*, *96*(4), 600–622. https://doi.org/10.1177/0032885516650883

Schmucker, M., & Lösel, F. (2015). The effects of sexual offender treatment on recidivism: An international meta-analysis of sound quality evaluations. *Journal of Experimental Criminology*, *11*, 597–630. https://doi.org/10.1007/s11292-015-9241-z

Schmucker, M., & Lösel, F. (2017). Sexual offender treatment for reducing recidivism among convicted sex offenders: a systematic review and meta-analysis. *Campbell Systematic Reviews*, *13*(1), 1–75. https://doi.org/10.4073/csr.2017.8

Smallbone, S., Marshall, W. L., & Wortley, R. (2013). *Preventing child sexual abuse: Evidence, policy and practice*. Routledge. https://doi.org/10.4324/9781843925606

Songy, D.G. (2003). Psychological and spiritual treatment of Roman Catholic clerical sex offenders. *Sexual Addiction & Compulsivity*, *10*, 123–137. https://doi.org/10.1080/10720160390230655

Stansfield, R., O'Connor, T., Duncan, J., & Hall, S. (2020). Comparing recidivism of sexual and non-sexual offenders: The role of humanist, spiritual, and religious involvement. *Sexual Abuse*, *32*(6), 634–656. https://doi.org/10.1177/1079063219843903

Tewksbury, R. (2012). Stigmatization of sex offenders. *Deviant Behavior*, *33*(8), 606–623. https://doi.org/10.1080/01639625.2011.636690

Venable, V. M. (2015). Black church members' perspectives on the role of the Black church in the rehabilitative process of juvenile sex offenders. *Social Work and Christianity*, *42*(3), 350–368.

Vieten, C., & Lukoff, D. (2022). Spiritual and religious competencies in psychology. *American Psychologist*, *77*(1), 26. https://doi.org/10.1037/amp0000821

Ward, T., & Gannon, T. A. (2006). Rehabilitation, etiology, and self-regulation: The comprehensive good lives model of treatment for sexual offenders. *Aggression and Violent Behavior*, *11*(1), 77–94. https://doi.org/10.1016/j.avb.2005.06.001

Ward, T., & Stewart, C. A. (2003). The treatment of sex offenders: Risk management and good lives. *Professional Psychology: Research and Practice*, *34*(4), 353. https://doi.org/10.1037/0735-7028.34.4.353

Webb, J. R. (2021). *Understanding forgiveness and addiction: Theory, research, and clinical application*. Routledge. https://doi.org/10.4324/9780429200274

Webb, J. R., Toussaint, L., & Dula, C. S. (2014). Ritualistic, theistic, and existential spirituality: Initial psychometric qualities of the RiTE measure of spirituality. *Journal of Religion and Health*, *53*, 972–985. https://doi.org/10.1007/s10943-013-9697-y

Wilson, R. J., McWhinnie, A., Picheca, J. E., Prinzo, M., & Cortoni, F. (2007). Circles of support and accountability: engaging community volunteers in the management of high-risk sexual offenders. *The Howard Journal of Criminal Justice*, *46*(1), 1–15. https://doi.org/10.1111/j.1468-2311.2007.00450.x

Winder, B., Blagden, N., Hocken, K., Elliott, H., Lievesley, R., & Banyard, P. (Eds.). (2019). *Sexual crime, religion and spirituality*. Springer Nature. https://doi.org/10.1007/978-3-030-26040-8

Winder, B., Blagden, N., & Lievesley, R. (2018). "Because you've got faith it doesn't mean that you've got wings on your back": A qualitative analysis of the accounts of Christian prisoners serving time for a sexual offence. *Journal of Sexual Aggression*, *24*(2), 239–255. https://doi.org/10.1080/13552600.2018.1504553

Yelderman, L. A., West, M. P., & Miller, M. K. (2018). Religious beliefs, religious contexts, and perceived interactions with ex-offenders. *Review of Religious Research*, *60*(3), 305–329. https://doi.org/10.1007/s13644-018-0331-z

Part V

Spirituality, Health, and Well-Being in Context

Chapter 32

Religious and Spiritual Flourishing in Children and Adolescents

William L. Hathaway[*]

The relationship between religion, spirituality and various aspects of human flourishing in children and adolescents has been an increasing focus in psychology and related fields. Work in this area faces multiple definitional challenges. It is also impacted by the evolving models and operationalizations of scientific studies of well-being. Still, progress has been made. Yet, in this chapter it will be argued that a basic reframing of the relationship between religion, spirituality and flourishing is needed to complement the dominant conceptualization of their interrelationship to date.

Religion and Spirituality: Definitional Issues

A longstanding challenge for research on the relationship between religion, spirituality and psychological variables is to generate defensible definitions of religion and spirituality that conceptualize both phenomena well despite their pluriform expressions in human experience (Zinnbauer & Pargament, 2005). Following the conventional usage put forward by Pargament and his associates, the influential two-volume *APA Handbook of Psychology, Religion, and Spirituality* distinguishes the two domains as follows: ".... spirituality is considered a personal or group search for the sacred, and religiousness involves a personal or group search for the sacred and other significant goals that unfolds within a traditional sacred context" (Zinnbauer, 2013, p. 72). Pargament (2007) indicates that people may view a wide range of things in life as sacred. Still for "many people, the sacred is equivalent to higher powers or divine beings" (p. 32). He provides examples of the varied objects of devotion that people view as constituting this "transcendent core" with some having no clear connection to any conventional religion. Furthermore, almost anything in life can be imbued with a sacredness by being related in some meaningful way to what a person holds to be at the sacred core.

Paloutzian (2017) notes that during the first half of the 20th century "...the terms *religion* and *spirituality* were pretty much interchangeable" (p. 12). However, the terms began to be increasingly used in distinctive ways in the later 20th century. Similar challenges arise in other cultural contexts. For instance, Zhang et al. (2021) observe that, in China, diffused folk religion is the normative experience for much of the culture: "While scholars have noted that folk religion played a vital role in Chinese religious life, it is not an institutional religion equipped with independent theologies, organizations, and theists" (p. 578). Some have emphasized the growing differentiation between spirituality and religion for some individuals or groups, particularly in Western contexts. Yet others have tended to deemphasize the importance of such distinctions focusing instead on delineating the different domains or dimensions of both religion and spirituality (Webb et al., 2014).

* Corresponding Author: wh@regent.edu.

DOI: 10.4324/9781003440048-37

Webb et al.'s (2014) RiTE model positions the concept of spirituality as the meta-category subsuming partially overlapping spiritual and religious "sub-constructs" (see Chapters 1 and 44 of this volume). They view spirituality as "…the salient, searching pursuit of the transcendently sacred ritualistic, theistic, and/or existential aspects of the human condition" (p. 974). They label these three subconstructs *ritualistic spirituality, theistic spirituality*, and *existential spirituality*. The RiTE measure of spirituality was developed based on this conception. Webb and his colleagues found supportive data in their initial validation process, both for their construct and the measure.

It may be the case that such a construal of religion and spirituality is particularly pertinent to psychology of religion research where the focus is on psychological functioning as opposed to sociological, philosophical, or comparative religion analyses that focus more broadly on the shared contours of religion. Yet even within scholarly fields that focus on normative beliefs or other more "crystalized" features of religious traditions, scholars frequently acknowledge that *lived religion* can take on idiosyncratic forms that differ from religious conventions in substantial ways (McGuire, 2008). Contemporary psychological scientists and clinicians, operating as they do in a field whose roots are in the study of individual and cultural differences, are particularly predisposed to focus on the way religion and spirituality overlap with the cognitive, emotional, behavioral and social aspects of people's concrete lives. Thus, it is not surprising that the focus in the psychology of religion is not so much on the formal trappings and conventions of religion as on the functional correlates and consequences of an individual's religion or spirituality (Allport, 1950).

Accordingly, in this chapter, the phrase "religious or spiritual functioning" (hereafter RSF) will be used as a single placeholder for the varied psychological forms that religion and spirituality exhibit in human life. By using this single RSF placeholder, there is no assumption being made that religion and spirituality are synonymous semantic categories. The terms "religious" or "spiritual" in RSF will be used consistently with the Pargament tradition.

Well-Being and Flourishing: Definitional Issues

The positive psychology movement has brought increasing attention to what psychological researchers and professionals mean by notions such as happiness, well-being, mental health, or flourishing. The influential positive psychology line of research on subjective well-being has been perhaps most extensively investigated by Deiner and his colleagues (Deiner et al., 1985; Deiner et al., 2003). Frederickson's assertion that human flourishing is heavily connected to a preponderance of positive over negative affect reflects a similar *hedonic* notion that a positive emotional state is, on the balance, core to flourishing (Fredrickson & Losada, 2005; Fredrickson, 2013).

In contrast to such hedonic-focused understandings of well-being, other researchers have emphasized the importance of a broader concept of flourishing associated with the Aristotelian notion of *eudaimonia*. Eudaimonic models typically assert that well-being involves the substantial realization or fulfillment of human potential or aspirations. For instance, Ryan and Deci (2001) argue that well-being is better thought of as a matter of meaning and self-realization than mere experience of pleasure and pain avoidance. The positive psychology champion, Seligman (2011, 2018), has similarly advanced his PERMA model of well-being, arguing that while well-being includes positive emotional states, it also includes much more, such as engagement, relationships, a sense of meaning and purpose, and achievement.

The Global Flourishing Study's (hereafter GFS) large-scale panel investigation of human flourishing also conceptualizes flourishing in multicomponent terms. Drawing from the understanding by VanderWeele (2017), the study conceptualizes human flourishing as broader than psychological well-being while subsuming this domain. It succinctly defines flourishing "as a state in which all aspects of a person's life are good" (p. 8149). That those aspects extend beyond a person's subjective functioning is evident by the domains measured in the GFS's human flourishing measure: happiness and life satisfaction, mental and physical health, meaning and purpose, character and virtue, close social relationships, and financial and material stability.

Such eudaimonic conceptions of well-being extend the focus of well-being studies from the intrapsychic to the social and beyond. They thus make for a hospitable paradigm in which to explore the broad ways spirituality manifests in the lives of people. Prior research, albeit often of a cross-sectional and correlational nature, has found significant relationships between religion/spirituality and these sorts of flourishing domains (Hardy et al., 2019; Koenig et al., 2024). In addition, Koenig et al. (2024) note that

> ...religious belief and practices may also indirectly affect human flourishing and public health through their impact on the four major pathways that lead to human flourishing: marital and family stability, completion of education, obtaining high-quality work and employment, and increasing religious community activity.
>
> (p. 641)

In this chapter, well-being is understood in a eudaimonic manner consistent with the VanderWeele GFS definition.

RSF and Well-Being in Children and Adolescents

The study of RSF in children and adolescents stems back to the early decades of contemporary psychology (e.g., Starbuck, 1901). While Freud (1927/1961) famously claimed that religion was a universal and infantile neurosis, subsequent researchers have often countered that religious involvement, spiritual practices, or beliefs are frequently protective factors for a range of adverse developmental outcomes such as substance misuse (Hardy et al., 2019; Hood et al., 2018). The pace of psychological explorations of religious/spiritual development in childhood and adolescents has accelerated in recent decades (Boyatzis, 2005). The more recent developmental approaches have been dominated by investigations drawn from attachment theory, socialization theory, and the cognitive science of religion. Increasingly nuanced investigations of the relationships between RSF and psychological outcomes have found that different aspects of religion and spirituality may relate in divergent ways to such outcomes, some positive, some negative, and others mixed (Boyatzis, 2013). These findings have led Boyatzis (2013) to state that "rather than asking, "Is religion good for children?" we might ask a more differentiated question.... such as "Under what conditions and on what indexes and in what samples is religion good (and bad) for children?" (p. 508).

Sociologists Pearce et al. (2019) attempted to address just such differentiated questions in their annual review article by examining the "state of theory and research on how and under what conditions religion shapes various adolescent outcomes such as health, education, sexual behavior, and substance use" (p. 201). Like the rapid growth in the developmental psychology of religion noted earlier by Boyatzis, they report a growth in the sociology of religion in adolescence, observing:

> A large share of the research in this area comprises hypothesis-driven studies of whether religious characteristics of youth or their parent/s (e.g., affiliation, frequency of religious service attendance or prayer, or self-reported importance) influence a wide range of well-studied indicators of adolescent well-being. Psychologists have contributed much to this field as well. Using survey data, these types of studies consistently find that various forms of family and/or youth religiousness are positively associated with prosocial youth outcomes and negatively associated with detrimental outcomes. More frequent religious service participation, regular prayer, and high importance attached to one's religious identity have all been linked to, on average, lower delinquency; less drinking, smoking, and drug abuse; later initiation of sexual activity; better mental and physical health; higher grades and educational attainment; and greater civic involvement.
>
> (p. 202)

Yet the authors also note that:

> Although most studies on religion and adolescents present positive or protective associations, there is also evidence that religion can have deleterious effects in the lives of adolescents.
>
> (p. 202)

Some of the observed deleterious findings they report include conservative religious affiliation correlating positively with lower educational attainment, religion serving as a focus of parent–adolescent conflicts, and heightened risks of unintended pregnancies and sexually transmitted diseases when conservatively affiliated youth become sexually active. Drawing on minority stress theory, Hall (2018) similarly offers evidence that negative religious experiences can be a depression risk factor for LGBTQ youth.

Despite this expanding knowledge base, Pearce et al. (2019) note that "this larger body of research focused on positive or negative implications of religion in adolescence has several inherent limitations" (p. 202). The methodology of the research precludes confident conclusions about causal relationships. For instance, the field's heavy reliance on cross-sectional surveys at best shows correlational patterns without any ability to identify temporal patterns of change needed to make a case for a particular hypothesized causal order. Even when a clear theoretical basis for predicted relationships is present, the study designs are insufficient to evaluate precise alternative causal processes that could be at work. In addition, most of the research looks at average effects of religion on the outcomes obscuring individual and group differences that may yield different results in some cases. Yet the reviewers report that research has begun to more systematically focus on causal pathways for religion's influence on youth outcomes. They cite as examples Smith's (2003) theory of religion as a source of three potential causal factors: moral order that proscribes and prescribes patterns of behavior resulting in psychological outcomes, learned competencies that can promote coping and well-being, and social and organizational ties. Despite their hopeful assessment of the emerging causal theorizing, the authors mention Wilde's (2018) assertion that religion's effects depend on its intersection with other variables such as race or gender thus potentially rendering studies that look only at RSF as a direct or main effect unproductive.

Yet Wilde's assertion that religion's effects are always modulated by its intersectionality with other variables remains speculative even if it can be clearly shown to sometimes be so modulated. It is an empirical and perhaps even metaphysical question whether religion can be validly and fruitfully studied as a main, *independent*, or direct effect. Nevertheless, the idea that much more attention needs to be given to the nuanced evaluation of RSF's interactions with context and other variables is gaining traction. For instance, Boyatzis (2024) has recently reaffirmed his case for a *social-ecology* approach to the study of religious and spiritual development in children and adolescents. Building on Bronfenbrenner's social ecology, Boyatzis asserts that "we need to examine how multiple contexts influence children's spirituality" (p. 106).

Whether it is through an examination of the main or independent effects of religion and spirituality on psychological outcomes, its indirect or interactional effects, the focus of all such research is primarily framed with religion playing the role of a contributory variable. The language of protective and risk factors from epidemiology construes RSF as influences which respectively decrease or increase the likelihood of an illness outcome. Regardless of whether one hypothesizes that RSF variables may yield positive, negative, or mixed influences on well-being outcomes, the framing of such a perspective is still one in which religion is a causal factor influencing well-being but in a manner that is to some degree *exogenous* or independent of it. While such a line of research is important and justified, the balance of this chapter will suggest that this preoccupation with RSF as a potential causal influence on well-being, for good or ill or both, may lead the field to overlook an important alternative possibility.

An Endogenous Reframing

In causal modeling and economics, *endogenous variables* are those whose values are determined by other variables. An endogenous variable is thus like a *dependent variable* in experimental design. If RSF is considered something fully distinct from flourishing or well-being but potentially able to impact it, then the existing, nearly exclusive focus on whether RSF is *good* or *bad* for people may make sense. *But what if RSF is itself an aspect of well-being, at least for a subset of humanity?* Then the issue becomes not merely whether religion or spirituality promotes or hinders well-being but what factors contribute to the kind of religion or spirituality that is part of a flourishing life. I will assert that there is already a conceptual grounding in our influential diagnostic systems conducive to such a reframing. While I do not intend to deny the value of studying RSF as a potential influence on well-being, I am suggesting that *only* conceptualizing the relationship in this way is myopic, blinding us to another possibility. I am claiming that it is important for us to consider RSF from an endogenous perspective, as part of what constitutes a flourishing life when present in an optimal way.

Clinically Significant Impairment and Human Functional Domains

As a clinical child psychologist who specialized in Attention-Deficit/Hyperactivity Disorder (ADHD), I encountered other professionals who tended to conclude that either they or their clients had ADHD based on the mere presence of inattentive, overactive or impulsive symptoms even when there was no clear history of clinically significant impairment (Hathaway et al., 2006). The *Diagnostic and Statistical Manual* of the American Psychiatric Association (hereafter DSM 5-TR) requires that clinicians verify that, even when a sufficient number of ADHD symptoms are present to meet a threshold, that the symptoms must also interfere with "social, academic, or occupational functioning" (APA, 2022, p. 69). This criterion is referred to in DSM parlance as the *clinical significance criterion*.

DSM often requires a demonstration that clinically significant impairment be demonstrated for disorder symptoms for a diagnosis to be warranted (Üstün & Kennedy, 2009). As the manual explains: "…a generic diagnostic criterion requiring distress or disability has been used to establish disorder thresholds, usually worded "the disturbance causes clinically significant distress or impairment in social, occupational, or other important areas of functioning" (APA, 2022, p. 23). As critics of this diagnostic criterion have pointed out, the DSM never defines what it means by "other important areas of functioning" (Üstün & Kennedy, 2009). Since the third edition of the DSM, this *functional impairment* requirement has been a feature of the manual's diagnostic system. Üstün and Kennedy (2009) explain that the "…DSM term 'functional impairment' is not specifically defined. It is used to mean limitations in the *social* and *occupational* spheres of life. The DSM-IV-TR also refers to "*other important areas of functioning*," but does not identify them" (p. 83). In contrast, the World Health Organization has created two nosologies: one for diseases and one for areas of health and impairment. The World Health Organization's (2022) *International Classification of Diseases* (hereafter ICD-11) has developed a separate classification system for impaired functioning in various life areas or domains known as the *International Classification of Functioning, Disability and Health* (hereafter ICF; WHO, 2007). *Here is a key point for the present discussion: Despite these taxonomic differences, both systems assume that psychological disorders can adversely impact areas of life that are part of healthy functioning.*

In the DSM nomenclature, this system does not specify what the "other important areas of life" might be that could be impaired by the feature cluster of a disorder; indeed, there is inconsistent mention of the academic, social, or occupational areas. In 1999, a group of psychologists joined me in presenting a symposium at the annual convention of the American Psychological Association arguing that religious functioning should be considered a significant life domain that might be adversely impacted by psychological disorders. The symposium papers were later published as a special issue of the *Religion, Mental Health, and Culture* journal (Hathaway, 2003). The position we took was that, rather than just thinking of religion as an influence on health or religiosity or as just a possible symptom of mental illness, there was already sufficient evidence from psychological studies of religious and spiritual functioning to assert that a flourishing life included healthy religious functioning for many people. Yet psychological disorders could impair such functioning. We considered a range of objections to this endogenous reframing. What about harmful religious beliefs or practices? How could those be considered part of human flourishing? Our counterargument was that there are harmful variations of every significant adaptive life domain. Some social relationships are destructive. Some work settings are toxic. But this does not mean humans should not seek optimal and healthy social or work lives. Likewise, for those who value religiousness and spirituality, seeking an optimal religious/spiritual life is an adaptive goal and, when focused on in this way, it functions as an endogenous variable.

The World Health Organization released its ICF classification in 2001 and its Child and Youth version in 2007. It does provide a much more extensive enumeration of functional domains for human life than the brief discussion of functional impairment areas in the DSM. The ICF system does not imply that every domain must be equally present and actualized in a person's life for the life to be healthy. Not everyone may be engaged in academics or an occupation but if one is impaired in academics or one's work because of an illness (psychological or medical) then these recognizable areas of otherwise healthy human life can be coded through the ICF system.

Both the standard ICF and the Child and Youth version (ICF-CY) of the *International Classification of Functioning, Disability, and Health* (World Health Organization, 2001, 2007) identify religion and spirituality as functional domains grouped together with other community, social and civic "actions and tasks required to engage in organized social life outside the family" (p. 186). The ICF-CY offers the following definition of the religion and spirituality domain:

> Engaging in religious or spiritual activities, organizations and practices for self fulfilment, finding meaning, religious or spiritual value and establishing connection with a divine power, such as is involved in attending a church, temple, mosque or synagogue, praying or chanting for a religious purpose, and spiritual contemplation.
>
> (World Health Organization, 2007, p. 187)

It further distinguishes organized religion and spirituality in this manner: *organized religion* as "engaging in organized religious ceremonies, activities and events" and *spirituality* as "engaging in spiritual activities or events, outside an organized religion" (p. 188).

Whether one agrees with this way of locating RSF in human life, the key idea is that religion and spirituality are aspects of normal, healthy functioning that can be impaired by illness. This framing, while not fully developed, puts religion and spirituality in an endogenous perspective. Rather than focusing on religion or spirituality for purely secondary reasons relevant only to the extent they may be protective or risk increasing for health, this alternative notion is of RSF as an area that might itself be adversely affected by pathology. It makes RSF an area of intrinsic interest. Whatever healthy RSF might be, it is presented as a part of the forms that healthy, flourishing human functioning can take.

Building on this understanding, impaired RSF due to a psychological disorder can be conceptualized as a *clinically significant religious impairment*:

> CSRI can be construed as a reduced ability to perform religious activities, achieve religious goals, or to experience religious states, due to a psychological disorder. This definition does not assert that everyone who is irreligious is psychologically disordered. Nor does it assume that religious or spiritual functioning only relates in a positive manner to mental health. Rather, it assumes that religious/spiritual functioning is a normal and significant domain of adaptive functioning, salient for a substantial subset of the human population. When psychological features interfere with the spiritual/religious life of religious individuals, the possibility of CSRI arises.
>
> (Hathaway, 2003, p. 114)

As noted earlier, Seligman (2011) offered his PERMA model of human flourishing as part of his positive psychology project. Whereas clinical psychology had been focused on alleviating suffering, his proposal was that positive psychology should focus on the promotion of optimal functioning (i.e., *flourishing*). Seligman has observed that, even in cases where negative affective states persist, one may still be able to increase positive emotional states and other areas that contribute to a flourishing life such as elevating a person's sense of meaning or purpose. Research on positive and negative affect has demonstrated that the two affective states are not necessarily orthogonal. They do not necessarily vary in inverse proportion to each other. One can change without the other changing in the same direction or to the same degree. Thus, the relationship appears far more complex than viewing positive and negative affect as opposite poles on a single continuum (LaRowe et al., 2024). But if this is the case, one may not need to reduce negative affect to increase positive affect. That reframing the relationship between positive and negative affect creates a hopeful possibility for individuals with treatment resistant and persistent dysphoric states. They might be able to experience better well-being in life even if the dysphoric state does not substantially reduce.

In an analogous way, I suggest reframing the relationship between RSF and flourishing from one where RSF is merely a contributor to pathology or health to one where it is a dimension of human flourishing may offer similar productive options. On this reframing, the challenge becomes how to advance a model of flourishing RSF that does not arbitrarily privilege specific varieties of religious or spiritual life or that may be tradition specific (VanderWeele et al., 2021). For instance, would a flourishing RSF be more characterized by introverted contemplative or enthusiastic sociality expressions as some religious traditions may assert? Would optimal RSF be more pluriform, for example, by depending on a fit between the way the way spirituality is expressed or instantiated and personality or other idiosyncratic features of a person?

Child and Adolescent RSF Flourishing and ADHD

ADHD is one of the more prevalent child and adolescent disorders that present to child clinicians. While there have been a range of theories for the etiology of ADHD, an influential set of theories view a substantial deficit of self-regulation as central to the disorder (Barkley, 2015; Nigg & Casey, 2005). The *APA Dictionary of Psychology* defines self-regulation as "the control of one's behavior through the use of self-monitoring (keeping a record of behavior), self-evaluation (assessing the information obtained during self-monitoring), and self-reinforcement (rewarding oneself for appropriate behavior or for attaining a goal)" (APA, 2024). Neuroscientific models of self-regulation are often conceptualized as an aspect of an *executive functioning* process (hereafter EF). There is disagreement over the precise definition of EF. Goldstein and Naglieri (2014) identified over 30 definitions used by researchers of the concept. Common to many models are incorporation of processes such as those involved in working memory, attention, response inhibition or action initiation.

Self-regulation and EF are both frequently thought to be instrumental to human flourishing. Bella (2023) asserts such a view after engaging in an interdisciplinary analysis of how problems in self-regulation processes provide insights into the long-recognized human failing known as *akrasia*. Akrasia is a Greek term used by Aristotle and others to denote when a person engages in "intentional behavior against one's judgment" (p. 1). Kryza-Lacombe et al. (2021) conducted an exploratory investigation of the relationship between seven EF process measures and a measure of hedonic and eudaimonic motives for action. They reported that their findings "demonstrate that individual differences in the pursuit of pleasure and meaning are associated with unique executive functioning patterns" but also that "the relation between happiness and executive functioning is complex" (p. 13).

Barkley (2012) has asserted that such modest and sometimes inconsistent findings from neuropsychology related EF measures arise in part because they represent at best some of the multiple low-level cognitive processes that people may harness in pursuit of strategic self-regulation over the course of the life span. When executive functioning tasks that are of substantial importance to a person must be accomplished during the life course, they may find alternative ways to achieve them. If the more discrete weaknesses suggested by laboratory or clinic EF tasks are an issue, individuals may find a way to compensate for them in everyday life or to use alternative processes to achieve their goals. In contrast to neuropsychological or laboratory measures of EF skills, Barkley has found that rating scales assessing self or other reported regulation capacities in everyday life better predict significant life outcomes associated with flourishing or impairment (Barkley, 2011).

Based on his understanding of ADHD as a self-regulation deficit, Barkley and I speculated that ADHD would create predictable problems for conventional RSF (Hathaway & Barkley, 2003). Specifically, we hypothesized that people with ADHD would be more likely, in common conventional religious settings, to experience a variety of RSF problems such as having difficulty with religious socialization or internalizing religious norms (e.g., a kind of akrasia). Hathaway et al. (2003) explored this possibility by developing a problem inventory for religious situations called the *Faith Situations Questionnaire*. The questionnaire collects information from key informants of children and adolescents on 18 of the most common potential problem situations related to conventional religious settings or other religious situations reported for children and teens. The instrument was normed on a U.S. Census approximated sample. The study found that youth who met the criteria for ADHD were substantially more likely to have a greater number of problem situations and a greater severity of problem situations when the problems arose. Using the same 93rd percentile cutoff score for a clinically significant impairment level that Barkley had previously used for the *Home* and *School Situations Questionnaire*, clinical cutoffs were established for the number of problems and problem severity ratings reported by the informants.

A clinical case study using the Faith Situations Questionnaire was conducted by Childers (Hathaway & Childers, 2013). Parents who presented at a training clinic for help with an ADHD diagnosed child's behavior in home, church and other situations were taken through a parent training program incorporating psychoeducation and behavioral interventions. At intake, a clinically significant number and severity of problem situations were reported for the child in faith settings. By treatment termination, both ratings had become subclinical.

This clinical discussion of ADHD, impaired self-regulation and problems in RSF reflects a plausible instance of the clinically significant religious impairment notion suggested by Hathaway (2003). While insufficient to indicate that a child was experiencing religious or spiritual flourishing post-treatment, the RSF-focused outcome assessment did provide evidence that objective indicators of impaired RSF had abated. Rather than viewing religion or spirituality as of secondary concern to the clinical presentation, the religious impairment-endogenous conceptualization prompted Childers to aim at helping the parents effectively manage faith context impairing behaviors, thereby helping the child move to healthier RSF (Hathaway & Childers, 2013).

Such an endogenous perspective also comports well with the social model of disability that construes disabling impairments as arising from barriers society puts in place that interfere with optimal functioning for individuals so diagnosed (Oberholzer, 2019). By promoting awareness and relevant training, religious contexts can often be adjusted in various faith-congruent ways to reduce the barriers present in these settings for healthy RSF in these persons (Grcevich, 2018). Oberholzer (2019) relates a poignant example of flourishing in the context of disability:

> When I first walked into the unit for people with profound intellectual disabilities as a nursing student, I was overwhelmed by the severe disabilities of these people. However, as I got to know them better, I discovered precious human beings, each with their own unique personality. I saw people who were happy, who enjoyed each other's company and who flourished, each in their own way. One of them regarded himself as wealthy because he owned a watch that he treasured with his whole life. He experienced a sense of accomplishment through his ability to read the time, as no-one else had a watch or could tell the time. And he found meaning in the task delegated to him to say grace before mealtimes. I also realized that these

> people have the luxury of expressing both positive and negative emotions without the boundaries of what is supposed to be "socially acceptable." ...This is precisely the characteristics used by Seligman (2011) when he describes what it means to flourish.
>
> (p. 135)

Concluding Comments

Attempts to explore the relationship between spirituality in children and adolescents and flourishing are accelerating. Greater theoretical and methodological sophistication offer promise for an increasingly nuanced understanding of how religion and spiritualty may contribute to well-being. Yet despite this increased sophistication, the prevalent paradigms still share a common preoccupation with viewing spiritual functioning as an influence *on* well-being. This nearly exclusive framing has interfered with the field considering the ways in which religious and spiritual functioning may itself be a *dependent flourishing variable*. There is already conceptual, theoretical, and clinical reason to view an endogenous reframing of religion and spirituality as a well-being domain. But very little research has directly explored things from this perspective, so the current paper represents a call for action.

Beyond the mere empirical work ahead for such a project, examinations of religious and spiritual flourishing in children will have to address value laden visions of just what separate healthy and unhealthy spiritual and religious functioning and how norms about matters such as self-determination or parental rights may impact their transmission and promotion (Hathaway, 2013). Under Wakefield's (1992) influential, albeit contested, analysis of what constitutes a mental disorder, psychopathology involves the presence of harmful dysfunctions where harm is understood based on social norms and values about healthy functioning. In a similar way, visions of flourishing have inherent normativity. Rather than minimize this with quixotic aspiration for a value-neutral model, VanderWeele (2024) has asserted that "because understandings of spiritual well-being will vary across religious and cultural traditions, any reasonable assessment or study of spiritual well-being will require tradition-specific understandings and measures of spiritual well-being" (p. 297).

References

Allport, G. W. (1950). *The individual and his religion: a psychological interpretation*. Macmillan.

American Psychiatric Association. (2022). *Diagnostic and statistical manual of mental disorders: DSM-5-TR* (5th ed., text revision.). American Psychiatric Association Publishing.

American Psychological Association (October 14, 2024). Self-regulation. *APA Dictionary of psychology*. Retrieved from https://dictionary.apa.org/self-regulation

Barkley, R. A. (2011). *Barkley Deficits in Executive Functioning Scale (BDEFS)*. The Guilford Press.

Barkley, R. A. (2012). *Executive functions: What they are, how they work, and why they evolved*. The Guilford Press.

Barkley, R. A. (Ed.). (2015). *Attention-deficit hyperactivity disorder: A handbook for diagnosis and treatment* (4th ed.). The Guilford Press.

Bella, A. F. (2023). Psychological underpinnings of akrasia: A new integrative framework based on self-regulation vulnerabilities and failures. *New Ideas in Psychology*, *70*, 1–11. https://doi.org/10.1016/j.newideapsych.2023.101027

Boyatzis, C. J. (2005). Religious and Spiritual Development in Childhood. In R. F. Paloutzian & C. L. Park (Eds.), *Handbook of the psychology of religion and spirituality* (pp. 123–143). The Guilford Press.

Boyatzis, C. J. (2013). The nature and functions of religion and spirituality in children. In K. I. Pargament, J. J. Exline, & J. W. Jones (Eds.), *APA handbook of psychology, religion, and spirituality (Vol 1): Context, theory, and research*. (pp. 497–512). American Psychological Association. https://doi.org/10.1037/14045-027

Boyatzis, C. J. (2024). Spiritual development during childhood and adolescence. In L. J. Miller (Ed.), *The Oxford handbook of psychology and spirituality., 2nd* ed. (pp. 100–124). Oxford University Press.

Diener, E., Emmons, R. A., Larsen, R. J., & Griffin, S. (1985). The Satisfaction with Life Scale. *Journal of Personality Assessment*, *49*, 71–75. https://doi.org/10.1207/s15327752jpa4901_13

Diener, E., Oishi, S., & Lucas, R. E. (2003). Personality, culture, and subjective well-being: Emotional and cognitive evaluations of life. *Annual Review of Psychology*, *54*, 403–425. https://doi.org/10.1146/annurev.psych.54.101601.145056

Fredrickson, B. L. (2013). Updated thinking on positivity ratios. *American Psychologist*, *68*(9), 814–822. https://doi.org/10.1037/a0033584

Fredrickson, B. L., & Losada, M. F. (2005). Positive Affect and the Complex Dynamics of Human Flourishing. *American Psychologist*, *60*(7), 678–686. https://doi.org/10.1037/0003-066X.60.7.678

Freud, S. (1961). *The future of an illusion*. (J. Strachey, Ed.). Norton. (Original work published 1927).

Goldstein, S., & Naglieri, J. A. (Eds.). (2014). *Handbook of executive functioning*. Springer Science + Business Media. https://doi.org/10.1007/978-1-4614-8106-5

Grcevich, S. (2018). *Mental health and the Church: A Ministry handbook for including children and adults with ADHD, Anxiety, Mood Disorders, and other common mental health conditions*. Zondervan.

Hall, W. J. (2018). Psychosocial Risk and Protective Factors for Depression Among Lesbian, Gay, Bisexual, and Queer Youth: A Systematic Review. *Journal of Homosexuality*, *65*(3), 263–316. https://doi.org/10.1080/00918369.2017.1317467

Hardy, S. A., Nelson, J. M., Moore, J. P., & King, P. E. (2019). Processes of Religious and Spiritual Influence in Adolescence: A Systematic Review of 30 Years of Research. *Journal of Research on Adolescence*, *29*(2), 254–275. https://doi.org/10.1111/jora.12486

Hathaway & Barkley, R. A. (2003). Self-regulation, ADHD, & child religiousness. *Journal of Christianity & Psychology*, *22*, 101–114.

Hathaway, W. L. (2003). Clinically significant religious impairment. *Mental Health, Religion & Culture*, *6*(2), 113–129. https://doi.org/10.1080/1367467021000038174

Hathaway, W. L. (2013). Ethics, religious issues, and clinical child psychology. In D. F. Walker & W. L. Hathaway (Eds.), *Spiritual interventions in child and adolescent psychotherapy* (pp. 17–39). American Psychological Association. https://doi.org/10.1037/13947-002

Hathaway, W. L., & Childers, J. (2013). Assessment of religious and spiritual issues in clinical child psychology. In D.F. Walker & W.L. Hathaway (Eds.), *Spiritual interventions in child and adolescent psychotherapy* (pp. 41–64). American Psychological Association.

Hathaway, W. L., Dooley-Litfin, J., & Edwards, G. (2006). Integrating the results of the evaluation: Ten clinical cases. In R. Barkley (Ed.), *Attention-Deficit Hyperactivity Disorder: A handbook for diagnosis and treatment*, (3rd Ed.). Guilford Press.

Hathaway, W. L., Douglas, D., & Grabowski, K. (2003). Faith Situations Questionnaire: Childhood normative data. *Journal of Psychology and Christianity*, *22*, 141–154

Hood, R. W., Hill, P. C., & Spilka, B. (2018). *The Psychology of Religion: An Empirical Approach* (Fifth Ed.). Guilford Publications.

Koenig, H.G., Vanderweele, T.J., & Peteet, J.R. (2024). *Handbook of religion and health*. (3rd. Ed.). Oxford University Press.

Kryza-Lacombe, M., Tanzini, E., Yali, A. M., & O'Neill, S. (2021). Executive Functioning and the Pursuit of Happiness. *Learning and motivation*, *76*, 101758. https://doi.org/10.1016/j.lmot.2021.101758

LaRowe, L.R., Connell Bohlen, L, & Williams, D.M. (2024). There is no happiness in positive affect: the pervasive misunderstanding of the rotated circumplex model. *Frontiers in Psychology*, *15*. N.P. https://doi.org/10.1017/s0954579405050376

McGuire, M.B. (2008). *Lived religion: Faith and practice in everyday life*. Oxford University Press.

Nigg, J. T., & Casey, B. J. (2005). An integrative theory of attention-deficit/hyperactivity disorder based on the cognitive and affective neurosciences. *Development and Psychopathology*, *17*(3), 785–806. http://doi/10.1017/s0954579405050376

Oberholzer, A. E. (2019). Human flourishing in the lives of children living with disability. *Journal of Disability & Religion*, *23*(2), 127–148. https://doi.org/10.1080/23312521.2019.1571468

Paloutzian, R. F. (2017). *Invitation to the psychology of religion.* (3rd ed.). Guilford Press.

Pargament, K.I. (2007). *Spiritually integrated psychotherapy: Understanding and addressing the sacred.* Guilford Press.

Pearce, L. D., Uecker, J. E., & Denton, M. L. (2019). Religion and Adolescent Outcomes: How and Under What Conditions Religion Matters. *Annual Review of Sociology*, *45*(1), 201–222. https://doi.org/10.1146/annurev-soc-073117-041317

Ryan, R. M., & Deci, E. L. (2001). On happiness and human potentials: A review of research on hedonic and eudaimonic well-being. *Annual Review of Psychology*, *52*, 141–166. https://doi.org/10.1146/annurev.psych.52.1.141

Seligman, M. E. P. (2011). *Flourish: A visionary new understanding of happiness and well-being.* Free Press.

Seligman, M.E.P. (2018). PERMA and the building blocks of well-being. *The Journal of Positive Psychology*, *13*(4), 333–335. https://doi.org/10.1080/17439760.2018.1437466

Smith, C. (2003). Theorizing religious effects among American adolescents. *Journal for the Scientific Study of Religion*, *42*(1), 17–30. https://doi.org/10.1111/1468-5906.t01-1-00158

Starbuck, E. D. (1901). *Psychology of Religion: An Empirical Study of the Growth of Religious Consciousness.* Walter Scott Pub. Co. https://doi.org/10.1037/13725-000

Üstün, B., & Kennedy, C. (2009). What is "functional impairment"? Disentangling disability from clinical significance. *World Psychiatry*, *8*, 82–85. https://doi.org/10.1002/j.2051-5545.2009.tb00219.x

VanderWeele, T. J. (2017). On the promotion of human flourishing. *Proceedings of the National Academy of Sciences*, *114*(31), 8148–8156. https://doi.org/10.1073/pnas.1702996114

VanderWeele, T.J. (2024). *A Theology of health: Wholeness and human flourishing.* University of Notre Dame Press.

VanderWeele, T. J., Long, K. N. G., & Balboni, M. J. (2021). Tradition-specific measures of spiritual well-being. In M. T. Lee, L. D. Kubzansky, & T. J. VanderWeele (Eds.), *Measuring well-being: Interdisciplinary perspectives from the social sciences and the humanities* (pp. 482–498). Oxford University Press. https://doi.org/10.1093/oso/9780197512531.003.0017

Wakefield, J. C. (1992). The Concept of Mental Disorder: On the Boundary Between Biological Facts and Social Values. *American Psychologist*, *47*(3), 373–388. https://doi.org/10.1037/0003-066X.47.3.373

Webb, J. R., Toussaint, L., & Dula, C. S. (2014). Ritualistic, theistic, and existential spirituality: Initial psychometric qualities of the RiTE measure of spirituality. *Journal of Religion and Health*, *53*(4), 972–985. https://doi.org/10.1007/s10943-013-9697-y

Wilde, M.J. (2018). Complex religion: interrogating assumptions of independence in the study of religion. *Sociology of Religion*, *79*(3), pp. 287–298. https://doi.org/10.1093/socrel/srx047

World Health Organization. (2001). *International classification of functioning, disability and health.* (1st ed.). World Health Organization.

World Health Organization. (2007). *International classification of functioning, disability and health: children and youth version: ICF-CY.* (1st ed.). World Health Organization.

World Health Organization. (2022). ICD-11: International classification of diseases (11th revision). https://icd.who.int/

Zhang, C., Lu, Y., & Sheng, H. (2021). Exploring Chinese folk religion: Popularity, diffuseness, and diversities. *Chinese Journal of Sociology*, *7*(4), 575–592. https://doi.org/10.1177/2057150X211042687

Zinnbauer, B. J. (2013). Models of healthy and unhealthy religion and spirituality. In *APA handbook of psychology, religion, and spirituality (Vol 2): An applied psychology of religion and spirituality* (pp. 71–89). American Psychological Association. https://doi.org/10.1037/14046-004

Zinnbauer, B. J., & Pargament, K. I. (2005). Spirituality and religiousness. In R. F. Paloutzian & C. L. Park (Eds.), *Handbook of the psychology of religion* (pp. 21–42). Guilford Press.

Chapter 33

The SPIRIT Model of Well-Being

Sacred Processes Inviting Relational and Individual Transcendence among Couples

Tehya A. Vassar, David C. Dollahite, and Loren D. Marks*

In this chapter, we explore the intersection between two of the most complex, central, and powerful aspects of life: human spirituality and intimate relationships. We draw from our own research with couples from diverse racial, ethnic, and religious backgrounds (Dollahite et al., 2023) as well as from other scholars. As family researchers, we use a definition of spirituality that is relational in nature. Rather than split the sacred between religion and spirituality, we use a four-part framework of spirituality involving sacred *meanings, processes*, and *communities* leading to personal and relational *transcendence*. We abbreviate this as MPC→T.

Spirituality, in the way we are using it here, encompasses institutionalized religion, personal spirituality, and how these interact with close relationships to encourage personal and relational transformation. Many marriages and families of faith strive to operate from their deepest values and understandings (meanings), with a rhythm of life permeated with spiritual practices (processes), and with the support of a local congregation (communities) (Dollahite & Marks, 2009). These three facets of spirituality encourage individuals and couples to move beyond merely self-oriented concerns (transcendence).

The MPC→T Framework

Meanings—including sacred, core beliefs—are the first and most fundamental level of the MPC→T model (Marks & Dollahite, 2011). Individuals interpret religious teachings, texts, and experiences to distill knowledge into personal meanings. In a couple relationship, each partner holds their own meanings. Together, they may develop shared meanings that guide their choices and life as a couple (Marks & Dollahite, 2017).

Processes flow from meanings, religious teachings, and family routines and rituals. This level is action- and interaction-based in that every process involves the behavior of individuals and their interactions with one another. An expansion of in-depth, qualitative research over the past decade has explored and captured several processes in couples and families, including sacrifice (Pippert et al., 2019); forgiveness and reconciliation (Dollahite et al., 2019a; Hendricks et al., 2023b); couple and family prayer (Chelladurai et al., 2018); sacred rituals (e.g., Shabbat in Judaism, see Marks et al., 2018; Ramadan in Islam, see Alghafli et al., 2019); transformation (Goodman et al., 2012, 2013); hope (Kelley et al., 2023); and repentance (Hendricks et al., 2023a). In these studies, meanings and beliefs are enacted through processes.

* Corresponding Author: tehya.vassar@gmail.com.

DOI: 10.4324/9781003440048-38

The third portion of the model, *communities*, refers to people of shared faith who may form a system of support. For a portion of couples and families who are highly religious, their faith community is not merely a support group, it is "family" (Wurm et al., 2018). Meanings and processes share a bidirectional relationship with communities. Communities inform meanings, which shape processes. Meanings and processes direct participation with communities. Therefore, couples, families, and communities shape each other (Marks & Dollahite, 2017).

The final element of the MPC→T model is *transcendence*. When deeply held sacred meanings combine with meaningful sacred processes and with involvement with a faith community, there is the potential for personal and relational transcendence. By personal transcendence, we mean individuals transcending self-oriented concerns. By relational transcendence, we mean a couple transcending their own couple-centric concerns. Research has found that transcendence can help couples deal with adversity (Dollahite et al., 2020). Understanding the deepest held meanings, processes, communities, and transcendence of couples helps frame the intersection between faith and committed partners.

Comparing the MPC→T Model with the RiTE Model

Important insights can be gained by utilizing and integrating the MPC→T model and the RiTE model of Webb, Toussaint, and Dula (2014) together (see Chapters 1 and 44 of this volume). The RiTE model provides a definition of spirituality that is similarly composed of three parts: Ritualistic Spirituality, Theistic Spirituality, and Existential Spirituality. Like the MPC→T model, the RiTE model resists separating spirituality and religion (Webb et al., 2014). Where the RiTE model and the MPC→T model diverge is where the first divides its components to show diverse yet converging expressions of spirituality, and the latter divides its components to highlight processes and relationships in family life. The RiTE model and the MPC→T model complement each other in that the MPC→T model provides a framework for understanding relational aspects of spirituality while the RiTE model helps to explain the psychological underpinnings at play. At each level of the MPC→T model, the RiTE model could be used to understand psychological interactions below the surface. Inspired by the RiTE model, we present a conceptual model on Couple Sacred Processes Inviting Relational and Individual Transcendence (C-SPIRIT) in Chapter Appendix A.

We next review recent research on spirituality and religiousness among couples, marriages, and families and the influences of this intersection on couple well-being and fidelity. We will highlight research with diverse and understudied populations. Finally, we will provide possible implications for well-being.

Literature Review

Generally, the impact of religion on marriages is positive (Lakatos & Martos, 2019; Sabey et al., 2014; Spilman et al., 2013; Wilcox & Wolfinger, 2008). Indeed, Marks et al. (2019) noted that more than 1,000 empirical studies have reported positive associations between religious involvement and psychological, relational, and physical well-being. Religion, however, is complicated by powerful dualities that can act for good or for ill—and sometimes for both simultaneously (Dollahite et al., 2018). We have stated in previous work that "Understanding how to harness the positive power of dualities while more carefully navigating negative and damaging approaches to dualities can be a vitally important asset for families and professionals striving to help them" (Dollahite et al., 2018, p. 238).

After qualitatively studying interview data from 198 highly religious couples with an oversampling of racial and ethnic minorities, Dollahite et al. (2019c) concluded that it could be safely assumed that most highly religious couples experience struggles related to their religion. They summarized that families may choose to remain religious despite the struggles that religion produces because religion also addresses these struggles and helps navigate myriad other struggles as well (Dollahite et al., 2019c).

In this review, we will organize the research according to the MPC→T model of religion in relationships. We will be discussing the ways meanings, processes, and communities encourage individuals and couples to overcome barriers to couple well-being. We will then take a deeper dive into current research on religion's influence on fidelity.

Meanings

Of all the constructs of the MPC→T model, religious meanings may be the most discrete to individuals. Even spouses who share the same commitment to the same faith may have very different interpretations of their religion. Having a shared religion and commitment to religion is predictive of higher martial quality (Dollahite et al., 2019c; Sabey et al., 2014). However, research on the impact of individual and/or contrasting religiousness on marriage tends to be ambiguous about whether these lead to positive or negative relational outcomes (Upenieks et al., 2021). It may be that having a shared faith gives couples something to bond over and thus employ for the benefit of the marriage, while unshared religiousness may be a point of contention or simply be less impactful when only one partner is religiously involved. Notably, in a recent study of 913 older adult couples, wives in homogamous religious marriages reported the best psychological and physical well-being (Upenieks et al., 2021).

Even when couples share the same faith, each partner holds religious meanings of his or her own. It is therefore important to understand the diversity of beliefs and meanings not only within faith groups, but also within families. Expectations that come from individual interpretations of religion can pose challenges to marriages in some cases. In a longitudinal study of 331 married couples, wives' religiousness predicted decreases in her perception of how adequately her husband forgave. This further predicted decreases in both spouses' marital satisfaction (Rose et al., 2018). The researchers explained that religious wives' high expectations for their husbands to practice forgiveness may lead to disappointment (Rose et al., 2018).

Another nuance of religious meaning-making in couples is the divide between intrinsic and extrinsic religiosity. Intrinsic religiosity is internalized as a paradigm for life, while extrinsic religiosity is used as a tool to achieve goals (Lakatos & Martos, 2019). Religiosity seems to improve the stability and quality of relationships only when intrinsic religiosity is reported (Lakatos & Martos, 2019). While religious meanings tend to increase marital commitment, commitment to the preservation of an abusive marriage can be harmful (Lakatos & Martos, 2019). If an individual in an abusive relationship interprets religious teachings about divorce to mean that divorce is always sinful, they may stay in a situation that puts them and/or their children in danger (Lakatos & Martos, 2019). On the other hand, research also indicates that having support from a religious group contributes to successfully leaving an abusive relationship and reconciling healthfully (Mahoney et al., 2019).

Some research has explored the couple-deity triad for meanings that may influence the relationship of the couple. Gardner et al.'s (2008) research suggests that when couples retain a clear focus on their bond and take personal responsibility, then the couple-deity triad can improve the couple's relational and psychological health. In these cases, the couple-deity triad serves to foster empathy, self-validation, mindfulness, reconciliation, and learning, while decreasing hostility and emotional reactivity (Gardner et al., 2008).

One meaning in the couple-deity triad that seems to be detrimental to relationships is theistic triangulation, meaning that one partner perceives an alliance with God against the other. Theistic triangulation is harmful because it creates power imbalances and erodes the relationship (Gardner et al., 2008; Lakatos & Martos, 2019). In cases of theistic triangulation where one partner defers responsibility in the relationship to deity, this partner may feel a sense of "faithfulness" while also reducing their involvement in the reconciliation process and reinforcing the negative triangulation process (Gardner et al., 2008).

Researchers have also observed differences in couple outcomes in connection to the meaning of "God as a transcendent moral authority"—a divine figure to personally guide the couple in matters of right and wrong (Shichida et al., 2015). Shichida et al. (2015) qualitatively evaluated interview data from 48 diverse Christian couples and compared data from the 36 couples that had expressed their view of God as a transcendent moral authority to the 12 who did not. The transcendent moral authority group was distinctive in that they displayed three religious-marital dynamics that engaged God in promoting marital unity: (1) spouses modified their own behavior in marriage to better align with their God model, (2) strived to obey God together, and (3) perceived strength from God in their marital bond. The researchers concluded that having accountability to God motivated spouses to critically reflect on themselves and their behavior in marriage as they attempted to become more aligned with His moral authority. This process reportedly facilitated maintenance of the martial relationship (Shichida et al., 2015).

One religious-spiritual meaning that has yielded fruitful research is relationship sanctification. Relationship sanctification is the perception that a relationship is imbued with a spiritual character or meaning (Mahoney et al., 2003). Marital sanctification is linked to increased commitment, better communication, and higher marital quality (Mahoney et al., 2019). In one study, Mahoney et al. (2003) found that 42% of variance in marital satisfaction for middle-aged couples could be explained by marital sanctification. Evaluating nuances in this finding for an older population, Sabey et al. (2014) found that marital sanctification explained 11.3% of variation in husbands' marital satisfaction and 21.2% of wives' satisfaction in marriages among older adults. Similarly, a recent review of literature on religiosity and marriage summarized,

> The experience of God's true presence in marriage not only sanctifies and strengthens the relationship, but also maintains the desire for the couple to *find meaning and purpose* in their life together. … It deepens the belief that shared religious experience, *shared religious practices*, and presence in a *religious community* will help resolve conflicts and challenges in the relationship.
>
> (p. 268, emphasis added)

We note that this summary integrates all four constructs of the MPC→T model.

Couple Sacred Processes

Long-lasting, quality marriages are not satisfying because they are relatively free of problems but because spouses have learned how to successfully navigate problems as a couple (Timothy-Springer & Johnson, 2018). From their qualitative study of healthy, enduring marriages in

Trinidad, Timothy-Springer and Johnson (2018) found that for a variety of problems and across diverse religious backgrounds, religion was the first tool that couples reported using to deal with adversity together. The sacred processes couples use to strengthen their resiliency will be the focus of this section. We will also note where research has identified religious processes with negative outcomes for couples.

In general, prayer for the well-being of a partner improves relational quality (Mahoney et al., 2019; May et al., 2020). Couples in a qualitative study by Lambert and Dollahite (2006) reported that prayer encouraged better communication and reduced tension during conflict. Prayer for a romantic partner during conflict can act as a self-soothing mechanism that mitigates hostile emotion and emotional reactivity (Fincham et al., 2008). This could be beneficial not only for the relational well-being but also for the psychological well-being of each partner.

Research has connected one specific type of prayer to numerous relational and physical measures of well-being. This prayer is termed partner-focused petitionary prayer (PFPP), meaning prayer for the well-being of a significant other. May et al. (2020) performed a controlled, randomized experimentation to assess the effects of PFPP on relational and cardiovascular outcomes. Compared to the control group and the comparison group, the PFPP group (which engaged in PFPP for three minutes daily) showed significant improvements in cardiovascular efficiency and relationship quality (May et al., 2020). May et al. (2020) explained that PFPP may improve relationship quality and cardiovascular health by providing a break from conflict, a time to reframe negative perspectives, and cognitive and emotional benefits that reduce stress on the heart.

While prayer is generally a beneficial religious process, there are instances where prayer may be detrimental to relationships. If prayer is used to manipulate, guilt, or vilify the other, then such prayer could work against the relationship (Fincham et al., 2008). Further, if prayer serves to reinforce negative relational dynamics (e.g., excessive passivity, dominance, externalization, or internalization), then these issues could be exacerbated by prayer (Mahoney et al., 2019). While prayer is one of the most often studied religious processes, other processes such as spiritual disclosure, reconciliatory religious practices, and grace have begun to emerge in recent studies.

Spiritual disclosure (i.e., when couples share personal perspectives of a spiritual/religious nature with each other) is positively linked to marital quality (Mahoney et al., 2019). Spiritual disclosure increases a special type of intimacy, spiritual intimacy, that reportedly helps couples bring more meaning and closeness into their relationship (Mahoney et al., 2019). Couples may find it easier to engage in spiritual disclosure when they are already feeling close; reconciliation helps couples bridge the gap between hurt and intimacy.

In a large qualitative study, with an oversampling of racial and ethnic minorities, Dollahite et al. (2019a) found that relational reconciliation processes that are tied to religious belief and practice can help transform couple relationships with nonclinical issues. Examples of reconciliation processes in couple relationships include confessing wrongdoing, apologizing, and demonstrating humility. These processes are often related to offering and receiving forgiveness and grace.

Hodge et al. (2022) performed an extensive systematic literature review about grace, defined as "the gift of acceptance given unconditionally and voluntarily to an underserving person by an unobligated giver" (Emmons et al., 2017, p. 277). From their review, the researchers concluded that beliefs and experiences of grace are generally positively associated with better mental health outcomes and increased marital satisfaction.

Clinicians and family researchers may increase the quality of services to families by investigating religious couples' processes surrounding prayer, spiritual disclosure, reconciliation, and grace-giving and -receiving. Future research could investigate dualities, including sensitized attention to the "helps and harms" in these processes (Dollahite et al., 2018).

Religious Communities

Religious communities can sometimes reach couples in need of assistance who may not be reachable by clinicians because of distrust, location, or financial barriers (Mitchell et al., 2023). On the other hand, some couples may distance themselves from religious communities if they feel stigmatized or that they cannot live up to the ideals prescribed by their faith (Dilmaghani, 2018; Smith, 2023; Uecker et al., 2016). Even so, Wilcox and Wolfinger (2008) found in their study of urban, racial minority families that couples in non-nuclear families still show better relational well-being when they are involved with a religious community.

Involvement in a religious community seems to have a more exaggerated effect for men than for women (Wilcox & Wolfinger, 2008). In their study, Wilcox and Wolfinger (2008) found that religion affected not only men's behaviors but also men's perceptions of the quality of their relationships. Religion is one of the few institutions that encourages men to turn toward family and fosters an other-oriented kind of masculinity, in contrast to stereotypical masculinity (Upenieks et al., 2021; Wilcox & Wolfinger, 2008). The influence of religious communities on men's behaviors and perceptions could provide needed fortification to many marriages and families, including those in challenging circumstances, in ethnic minorities, and/or who have immigrated.

For Christian Chinese Americans, having a religious community may help preserve cultural and spiritual values of collectivism and kinship, bridging their Chinese and American identities (Lu et al., 2012; Quek et al., 2021). Similarly, cross-cultural and interracial marriages require "bridging" work. Vazquez et al. (2019) used the Vulnerability-Stress-Adaptation model to explain that religion and spiritual well-being may counteract stress introduced by relationship stigma for couples in Black-White interracial relationships. In such contexts, open discourse regarding clients' faith community resources may help professionals serve clients more effectively and sensitively (Mahoney et al., 2019).

For example, Mitchell et al. (2023) implemented an evidence-based relationship education program in partnership with local churches. The researchers used multilevel modeling analyses to compare pre- to post-workshop changes (in 97 participating couples) and concluded that the intervention was successful in improving communication skills, relationship satisfaction, and commitment. Based on previous data and the researchers' own analyses, Mitchell et al. (2023) suggested that clinicians consider partnering with local churches to disseminate evidence-based relationship interventions. Religious communities are a useful vehicle for helping couples because churches usually have large networks, the ability to offer services at a lower cost, and the benefit of established rapport (Mitchell et al., 2023).

Religion and Fidelity

Perhaps the most salient moral issues tied to religion involve marriage and sexuality. A series of related studies by Leavitt and colleagues indicate that religious teachings are most often in support of fidelity within marriage, but varying religious interpretations and applications can have both positive and negative influences on sexuality within marriage (Allsop et al., 2021; Clarke et al., 2021; Leavitt et al., 2021, in press). Leavitt et al. (in press) qualitatively interviewed 261 highly religious couples, with an oversampling of racial and ethnic minorities, and reported that although the interviewers did not ask questions about intimacy or fidelity, the participants spontaneously and frequently addressed these issues in depth. Three core themes emerged from the researchers' analysis of the interview data: (a) integrity and fidelity strengthened marital quality and stability; (b) integrity and fidelity were core marital values; and (c) religion taught, developed, and motivated marital integrity and fidelity.

The final theme in Leavitt et al.'s (in press) qualitative data, namely, "religion taught, developed, and motivated marital integrity and fidelity," developed into three additional subthemes. These themes were: religion supported marital integrity and fidelity through (1) religious lifestyles, (2) religious beliefs, and (3) a commitment to God. We note that these relate closely to the three aspects of spirituality in the RiTE model: Ritualistic Spirituality, Theistic Spirituality, and Existential Spirituality (Webb et al., 2014). That is, "religious lifestyles" coincide with Ritualistic Spirituality, "a commitment to God" relates to Theistic Spirituality, and "religious beliefs" overlap with Existential Spirituality.

Another qualitative study on religion and martial intimacy was conducted by Kamali et al. (2020), who studied 14 Iranian couples using semi-structured interviews and two weeks' worth of written diaries. Three of the eight main themes that emerged from the data were gratitude, reciprocity in self-sacrifice, and religion. The participants reported that religion facilitated communication and intimacy in their marriages. All reported that religious commitment strengthened their marriage against infidelity. All the wives in the study reported that religion helped men support their families and sustain marital intimacy. An additional theme was that religious commitment could help couples avoid conflict and make amends (Kamali et al., 2020), consistent with other research that has suggested that religiousness may help couples reconcile after infidelity by increasing marital quality and stability (Tuttle & Davis, 2015).

Another study of Iranian married couples was conducted by Rayesh and Kalantar (2018) and found that both marital sanctification and partner-focused petitionary prayer (PFPP) were negatively correlated with marital infidelity. They concluded that these two factors should be considered in future research because marital sanctification and PFPP together explained 21% of the variance in infidelity scores (Rayesh & Kalantar, 2018). PFPP has also been longitudinally linked to fidelity in other research (Mahoney et al., 2019).

Relationship sanctification seems to not only protect against infidelity in marriage but also in committed dating relationships (McAllister et al., 2020). McAllister et al. (2020) used quantitative survey analyses of 716 college-aged students in exclusive relationships to assess the effect of relationship sanctification on cheating. Even after controlling for general religiousness, problematic alcohol use, and trait self-control, the significant negative association between relationship sanctification and cheating remained such that the highest possible sanctification score predicted a 19.8% possibility of cheating, while the lowest possible sanctification score had a 38.1% probability of cheating—a nearly two-fold increase (McAllister et al., 2020). This relationship was partially mediated by permissive sexual attitudes, which were also reduced by relationship sanctification (McAllister et al., 2020).

Esselmont and Bierman (2014) used national survey data from the United States of America (with an oversampling of African Americans, Hispanics, and Asians) to explore associations between religiousness and marital formation and infidelity. Based on their research, Esselmont and Bierman (2014) suggested that when religion influences decisions about the martial formation, this can mean that the marriage commences within a sacred framework. However, beginning a marriage with a religious influence was only associated with lower odds of infidelity when the sacredness of the relationship is maintained by personal religiousness (Esselmont &

Bierman, 2014). Another important finding of Esselmont and Bierman's (2014) research is that religious attendance was not an aspect of personal religiousness that predicted lower odds of infidelity, but placing a high value on religion was. Given that many studies use religious attendance as their main (or only) measure of religiousness (Marks & Dollahite, 2017), this could serve as a warning against using single-item measures to identify religiousness.

While the findings cited thus far have indicated generally positive influences of religious meanings on marital intimacy, research also indicates that some religious meanings (e.g., abuse of male headship and the belief that marital sex is sinful) have a high potential to harm marital intimacy (Dollahite et al., 2019c). Because of this, clinicians should be prepared to harness the strengths of religion *and* to mitigate negative intersections of religion and sexuality for couples (Clarke et al., 2021). Based on their research with an oversampling of racial and ethnic minorities, Clarke et al. (2021) made recommendations for clinicians to accomplish this task. First, clinicians should ask about and understand clients' desires to engage with religiousness in marital counseling; if the client wishes to have religiousness addressed in their treatment, then clinicians should seek to understand how religion and sexuality intersect in the client's marriage (Leavitt et al., in press). Second, Clarke et al. (2021) suggested that clinicians recognize that there are religious dualities, meaning that religion can both address and create problems for marital sexuality. With this knowledge, clinicians may work to employ religious strengths for the benefit of couples (Clarke et al., 2021). Relational sanctification may be a fruitful religious strength for some (Leavitt et al., in press).

Future Directions for Research

The research of spirituality, health, and well-being for couples is growing at a steady pace. In this section, we identify gaps in the research that we deem likely areas of fruitful exploration.

First, more research is needed to understand how religion and spirituality interact with clinical services. Most participants in most studies of spirituality, health, and well-being among couples are non-clinical. However, understanding the experiences of couples who present with clinical issues will be helpful as family researchers and clinicians work to create evidence-based interventions with spirituality in consideration. This is especially important given the historical tensions and divisions between religion and psychology that have dominated the field until the efforts of recent decades have fostered systematic empirical dialogue—instead of pro- or anti-religious dogma (Mahoney et al., 2019; Marks & Dollahite, 2017). Further, some research has begun to identify benefits for couples when religious clergy, clinicians, and researchers partner together (Mahoney et al., 2019; Mitchell et al., 2023; Quek et al., 2021). Researchers may approach these topics by asking questions such as: How often do couples presenting for therapy wish to have their spirituality and/or religion integrated into their treatment? For those who wish to have faith-integrated treatment, what would they want such an approach to look like? When is faith-integrated treatment helpful, and when is it harmful?

A second consideration for future research includes broadening research to clinical samples with focal attention given to how religion can help *and* harm (Dollahite et al., 2018).

Third, our intentional focus on racial and ethnic minority samples in this chapter (consistent with the volume's aim) may create an illusion that most religion and marital research is diversity-rich, but this is *not* the case. Additional effort is needed to capture and represent the array of religious and family experience (Dollahite & Marks, 2020).

Fourth, a similar but even more conspicuous gap in the research involves non-traditional family formations including same-sex couples, couples in second or later-life marriages, couples who have adopted, and couples in multi-generational households. Religion and spirituality may have unique interactions for such couples, but the research is nascent. For example, two recent studies of African American cohabiting couples seem to indicate lower positive associations with religion than their married counterparts (Russell et al., 2021; Skipper et al., 2023). Future research should address the meanings, processes, and community influences involved.

Discussion

The quarterly, peer-reviewed *Journal for the Scientific Study of Religion* (*JSSR*) has been in circulation for more than 60 years and has published thousands of articles addressing sociological, political, anthropological, and psychological aspects of religion. The more recent quarterly journal *Psychology of Religion and Spirituality* (*PRS*) was established by the American Psychological Association (APA) in 2009 and has published hundreds of articles focused primarily on intrapersonal and psychological aspects of religion. Rarely, however, has *JSSR* with its more sociological lens probed deeply into the processes and meanings tied to religion and spirituality for married couples. Conversely, *PRS* has increasingly done so in recent years. While the sociological, political, and psychological impacts of religion and spirituality are vital to examine and understand, we have spent 25 years studying the nexus of faith and family and have found great value there as well.

One key finding and conceptual contribution from our in-depth, qualitative interviews with 300 racially and religiously diverse couples in exemplary marriages has been the discovery that there are at least four different categories of processes of spiritual and/or religious devotion (Dollahite et al., 2019b). These four processes or types include: (a) destructive devotion, (b) selfish devotion (potentially destructive), (c) personal devotion (potentially generative) and (d) generative devotion. "Like nuclear power, water behind a dam, or fire, strong religious or spiritual devotion can have both generative and destructive outcomes depending on its application, approach, and use" (Dollahite et al., 2019b). For our purposes here, we will briefly juxtapose the most harmful process or type with the most relationally helpful type of devotion.

Destructive devotion (sometimes called "toxic faith") is characterized by rigidity, self-righteousness, extremism, a focus on personal goals over relationships, coercion, and divisiveness. As we have summarized,

> Destructive devotion can result from psychopathologies such as obsessive–compulsive disorder, neuroticism, narcissism, and other more serious psychological dysfunctions, such as schizophrenia or bipolar disorder. It also can arise from … misguided efforts to interpret or apply sound religious teachings in obsessive or perfectionistic ways. … Destructive devotion can also result from dysfunctional marital or familial relationships, such as when a spouse tries to leverage religion or God as a way to gain power in the relationship ….
>
> (Dollahite et al., 2019b)

Generative devotion, in sharp contrast, involves religious and spiritual processes, meanings, and approaches that include humility, granting and seeking forgiveness (both divine and in family relations), an other-oriented approach to religious practice (e.g., prayer, studying sacred texts, worship, and serving), a fostering of conflict resolution, and a willingness to sacrifice for and nurture others, especially those in the rising generations. In summary,

> Ultimately, generative devotion is about a process, about continually becoming a better family member—particularly in one's relationships with and actions toward those of the rising generation. This is realized by how one devotes oneself in relation to others in one's

> biological family, one's faith community "family," and the broader human family, as well as how one practices and engages a particular faith system on a personal level.
>
> (Dollahite et al., 2019b)

We have also noted ten "pathways to generative devotion" that are each grounded in multiple research studies. These pathways or processes include:

> marital commitment and fidelity, shared devotion to God, offering relational prayer, relational rituals and practices, relational changes and transformation, enduring struggles through faith, sanctified parent–child connections, relational forgiveness and reconciliation, sacred resource management, and strong faith community.
>
> (Dollahite et al., 2019b)

A careful examination will indicate that most, if not all, of these pathways to generative devotion mesh well with the Ritualistic Spirituality, Theistic Spirituality, and Existential Spirituality elements of the RiTE model (Webb et al., 2014).

We further note that in the RiTE model, all three components of spirituality receive capital "S" treatment. On this point, a leading family theorist, Wes Burr, observed that spirituality is defined so broadly by different persons that it "can include walking in the woods, [watching a game of] football, listening to music, going to an art gallery, enjoying a sunset, or watching a butterfly emerge from a cocoon" (Burr et al., 2012, pp. 8–9). As relational scholars, we are not deeply interested in the countless "spiritual experiences" we have as individuals that effectually end within us with no observable transcending of self. We *do* devote focused interest to spiritual processes and experiences that positively transform individuals in ways that: (a) that transcend time and (b) transcend the self—in other words, have lasting beneficial effect on not just an individual but on their relationships with others, particularly their families. When spiritual processes, meanings, and communities impact us positively, profoundly, relationally, and lastingly, *this* is generative devotion. We also see this as Spirituality with a capital S.

Conclusion

Spirituality that attends to and promotes the long-term well-being of marriage and family life, while fostering an other-oriented, responsive, and respectful approach to relationships in ways that unite rather than divide—and in ways that heal instead of harm—should be explored and encouraged by scholars, practitioners, and spiritual and religious leaders.

Appendix A:

The SPIRIT Model of Well-Being

Sacred Processes Inviting Relational and Individual Transcendence

The SPIRIT model of well-being is a conceptual framework that seeks to identify, understand, and encourage sacred practices that invite relational and personal transcendence in relationships. Various processes have been empirically demonstrated to help individuals and couples transcend barriers that limit personal and couple well-being.

Sacred. The sacred involves what is most meaningful, important, and valued to the couple and family as well as to individuals in a couple or family. What is experienced and valued as sacred can be grounded in religious and spiritual traditions as well as in family and ethnic traditions and values.

Processes. Processes that might invite spiritual transcendence include routines, rituals, traditions, ceremonies, rites, practices, habits, and other patterned behaviors or interactions. Some processes (i.e., spiritual practices in the contemplative traditions) are more likely to lead to so-called spiritual experiences (aka mystical experiences). Other processes (i.e., regular religious routines or rituals) may invite moves toward transcending the self that do not necessarily involve a spiritual or mystical experience. Examples of sacred processes that have been explored in empirical research include couple prayer, rituals, forgiveness, reconciliation, repentance, sacrifice, self-care, gratitude, fidelity, integrity, and hope.

Inviting. Transcendence-inviting practices are those that encourage, facilitate, promote, prompt, and/or support transcendence in individuals and relationships. Practices that invite transcendence are those that place persons and groups of persons (e.g., couples and families) in a setting in which transcendence is more likely to occur. The term inviting is used as opposed to, for example, involving or inspiring, because transcendence cannot necessarily be experienced or achieved in any formulaic way or by merely desiring it. Rather, more likely, transcendent experience ensues when a combination of factors exists.

Relational. Relational transcendence involves a couple or family having experiences that move them beyond concern for only their own couple or family to broader concerns such as neighborhood, community, faith community, culture, nation, humanity, and planet.

Individual. Individual transcendence involves a person moving beyond concern merely for their own self, their own interests, their own needs, wants, and desires. It may involve a person transcending their own time, place, body, marriage, family, faith community, and humanity.

Transcendence. Transcendence involves moving beyond one's own current ways of being, perceiving, experiencing, and acting. It may involve a person/couple/family transcending their own time, place, interests, reality, expectations, and needs. Transcendence can also involve sacred connections with divine beings or realities. It may involve transcending one's own loneliness, anxieties, fears, meaninglessness, and other challenges. It can involve virtues that transcend the self, such as love, kindness, sacrifice, and volunteerism. It can involve deeply held commitments to build and strengthen institutions (such as faith communities or charities) or persons (such as children, grandchildren, or orphans). It may involve sacred experiences that have a profound spiritual or mystical quality, but it may rather involve more mundane experiences such as feeling a connection with a new idea or person or place. Persons, couples, and families may choose to move beyond selfish or self-oriented goals and actions grounded in deeply held convictions whether (or not) they have had a "transcendent experience" that motivated such a move.

References

Alghafli, Z., Hatch, T. G., Rose, A. H., Abo-Zena, M. M., Marks, L. D., & Dollahite, D. C. (2019). A qualitative study of Ramadan: A month of fasting, family, and faith. *Religions*, *10*(2), 123. https://doi.org/10.3390/rel10020123 [Simultaneously published In R. J. Petts (Ed.), *Religion and family life* (pp. 221–235). Basel, Switzerland: MDPI.]

Allsop, D. B., Leavitt, C. E., Clarke, R. W., Driggs, S., Gurr, J. B., Marks, L. D., & Dollahite, D. C. (2021). Perspectives from highly religious families on boundaries and rules about sex. *Journal of Religion and Health*, *60*, 1576–1599. https://doi.org/10.1007/s10943-020-01171-9

Burr, W. R., Marks, L. D., & Day, R. (2012). *Sacred matters*. Routledge. https://doi.org/10.4324/9780203641323

Chelladurai, J., Dollahite, D., & Marks, L. (2018). "The family that prays together": Relational processes associated with family prayer. *Journal of Family Psychology*, *32*, 849–859. https://doi.org/10.1037/fam0000432

Clarke, R. W., Leavitt, C. E., Allsop, D. B., Marks, L. D., & Dollahite, D. C. (2021). How sexuality and religion intersect in highly religious families. *Sexual and Relationship Therapy*. https://doi.org/10.1080/14681994.2021.2014052

Dilmaghani, M. (2018). Exploring the relationship between secularity and marital behavior. *Marriage & Family Review*, *54*(5), 438–458. https://doi.org/10.1080/01494929.2017.1403989

Dollahite, D. C., Hendricks, J. J., & Marks, L. D. (2023). A diversity, equity, and inclusion audit of the American Families of Faith project: Exploring lifespan spiritual development in religiously and racially diverse families. *Religions*, *14*(3), 388. https://doi.org/10.3390/rel14030388

Dollahite, D., & Marks, L. (2009). A conceptual model of processes in a diverse, national sample of highly religious families. *Review of Religious Research*, *50*, 373–391. http://www.jstor.org/stable/25593754

Dollahite, D. C., & Marks, L. D. (Eds.). (2020). *Strengths in diverse families of faith*. Routledge.

Dollahite, D. C., Marks, L. D., Banford Witting, A., LeBaron, A. B., Young, K. P., & Chelladurai, J. M. (2020). How relationship-enhancing transcendent religious experiences during adversity can encourage relational meaning, depth, healing, and action. *Religions*, 11, 519, https://doi.org/10.3390/rel11100519

Dollahite, D. C., Marks, L. D., & Dalton, H. (2018). Why religion helps and harms families. *Journal of Family Theory & Review*, *10*(1), 219–241. https://doi.org/10.1111/jftr.12242

Dollahite, D. C., Marks, L. D., & Barrow, B. H. (2019a). Exploring relational reconciliation processes in Christian, Jewish, and Muslim families. *Family Relations*, *68*(5), 517–533. https://doi.org/10.1111/fare.12371

Dollahite, D. C., Marks, L. D., & Wurm, G. J. (2019b). Generative devotion: A theory of sacred relational care in families of faith. *Journal of Family Theory and Review*, *11*, 429–448. https://doi.org/10.1111/jftr.12339

Dollahite, D. C., Marks, L. D., & Young, K. P. (2019c). Relational struggles and experiential immediacy in religious American families. *Psychology of Religion and Spirituality*, *11*, 9–21. http://dx.doi.org/10.1037/rel0000135

Emmons, R. A., Hill, P. C., Barrett, J. L., & Kapic, K. M. (2017). Psychological and theological reflections on grace and its relevance for science and practice. *Psychology of Religion and Spirituality*, *9*(3), 276–284. https://doi.org/10.1037/rel0000136

Esselmont, C., & Bierman, A. (2014). Marital formation and infidelity: An examination of the multiple roles of religious factors. *Sociology of Religion*, *75*(3), 463–487. https://doi.org/10.1093/socrel/sru036

Fincham, F., Beach, S., Lambert, N., Stillman, T., & Braithwaite, S. (2008). Spiritual behaviors and relationship satisfaction. *Journal of Social and Clinical Psychology*, *27*, 362–388. https://doi.org/10.1521/jscp.2008.27.4.362

Gardner, B. C., Butler, M. H., & Seedall, R. B. (2008). En-gendering the couple-deity relationship. *Contemporary Family Therapy*, *30*, 152–166. https://doi.org/10.1007/s10591-008-9063-5

Goodman, M., Dollahite, D., Marks, L., & Layton, E. (2013). Religious faith and transformational processes in marriage. *Family Relations*, *62*, 808–823. https://doi.org/10.1111/fare.12038

Goodman, M.A., Marks, L.D., & Dollahite, D.C. (2012). Transformational processes and meaning in Latter-day Saint marriage. *Marriage & Family Review*, *48*, 555–582. No DOI

Hendricks, J. J., Marks, L. D., & Dollahite, D. C. (2023a). Personal and relational processes of repentance in religious Jewish, Christian, and Muslim Families. *Review of Religious Research*. https://doi.org/10.1177/0034673X231214274

Hendricks, J. J., Chelladurai, J. M., Marks, L. D., Dollahite, D. C., Kelley, H. H., & Rose, A. (2023b). Exploring personal and relational motivations and processes of forgiveness in religious families. *Family Relations*, *72*, 1014–1031. https://doi.org/10.1111/fare.12733

Hodge, A. S., Hook, J. N., Davis, D. E., Van Tongeren, D. R., Bufford, R. K., Bassett, R. L., & McMinn, M. R. (2022). Experiencing grace: A review of the empirical literature. *The Journal of Positive Psychology*, *17*(3), 375–388. https://doi.org/10.1080/17439760.2020.1858943

Kamali, Z., Allahyar, N., Ostovar, S., Alhabshi, S., & Griffiths, M. D. (2020). Factors that influence marital intimacy. *Cogent Psychology*, *7*(1), 1771118. https://doi.org/10.1080/23311908.2020.1771118

Kelley, H. H., Hendricks, J. J., Chelladurai, J. M., Dollahite, D. C., & Marks, L. D. (2023). "We have hope": Exploring hope in highly religious families. *Family Relations*. https://doi.org/10.1111/fare.12937

Lakatos, C., & Martos, T. (2019). The role of religiosity in intimate relationships. *European Journal of Mental Health*, *14*(2), 260–279. No DOI

Lambert, N. M., & Dollahite, D. C. (2006). How religiosity helps couples prevent, resolve, and overcome marital conflict. *Family Relations*, *55*, 439–449. https://doi.org/10.1111/j.1741-3729.2006.00413.x

Leavitt, C. E., Allsop, D. B., Price, A. A., Marks, L. D., & Dollahite, D. C. (2021). Exploring gender roles in highly religious families. *Religious Research Review*, *63*, 511–533. https://doi.org/10.1007/s13644-021-00476-9

Leavitt, C. E., Clarke, R., Hendricks, J., Marks, L. D., Dollahite, D. C., & Rose, A. H. (in press). *Integrity and fidelity in highly religious marriages*. Family Relations.

Lu, Y., Marks, L. D., & Apavaloiae, L. (2012). Chinese immigrant families and Christian faith community. *Family and Consumer Science Research Journal*, *41*, 118–130. https://doi.org/10.1111/fcsr.12002

Mahoney, A., Pargament, K. I., Murray-Swank, A., & Murray-Swank, N. (2003). Religion and the sanctification of family relationships. *Review of religious research*, 220–236. https://doi.org/10.2307/3512384

Mahoney, A., Pomerleau, J., & Riley, A. (2019). Transcending barriers to build bridges between family psychology and religious organizations. In *APA handbook of contemporary family psychology: Applications and broad impact of family psychology* (pp. 315–335). APA. https://doi.org/10.1037/0000100-020

Marks, L., & Dollahite, D. C. (2011). Mining the meanings from psychology of religion's correlation mountain. *Psychology of Religion and Spirituality*, *3*, 181–193. https://doi.org/10.1037/a0022206

Marks, L. D., & Dollahite, D. C. (2017). *Religion and families*. Routledge.

Marks, L. D., Dollahite, D. C., & Young, K. P. (2019). Struggles experienced by religious minority families in the United States. *Psychology of Religion and Spirituality*, *11*, 247. https://doi.org/10.1037/rel0000214

Marks, L., Hatch, T. & Dollahite, D. (2018). Sacred practices and family processes in a Jewish context: Shabbat as the weekly family ritual par excellence. *Family Process*, *57*, 448–461. https://doi.org/10.1111/famp.12286

May, R. W., Cooper, A. N., & Fincham, F. D. (2020). Prayer in marriage to improve wellness. *Journal of Religion and Health*, *59*, 2990–3003. https://doi.org/10.1007/s10943-019-00829-3

McAllister, P., Henderson, E., Maddock, M., Dowdle, K., Fincham, F. D., & Braithwaite, S. R. (2020). Sanctification and cheating among emerging adults. *Archives of Sexual Behavior*, *49*, 1177–1188. https://doi.org/10.1007/s10508-020-01657-3

Mitchell, E. A., Gordon, K. C., Amer, Z., DiPillo, M., McCall, M., & Wieser, S. (2023). University–church partnerships: A mechanism to enhance relationship health. *Journal of Prevention & Intervention in the Community*, *51*(1), 7–22. https://doi.org/10.1080/10852352.2021.1924595

Pippert, H. D., Dollahite, D. C., & Marks, L. D. (2019). Sacrifice and self-care as relational processes in religious families. *Family Relations*, *68*, 534–548. https://doi.org/10.1111/fare.12388

Quek, K. M. T., Hsieh, N. W. M., & Eppler, C. (2021). Collectivist discourses in relational intersectionality. *Journal of Family Issues*, *42*(11), 2487–2508. https://doi.org/10.1177/0192513X20983387

Rayesh, N., & Kalantar, S. M. (2018). The role of praying for the spouse and sanctification of marriage in reducing infidelity. *Mental Health, Religion & Culture*, *21*(1), 65–76. https://doi.org/10.1080/13674676.2018.1447555

Rose, A., Anderson, S., Miller, R., Marks, L., Hatch, T., & Card, N. (2018). Longitudinal test of forgiveness and perceived forgiveness as mediators between religiosity and marital satisfaction in long-term marital relationships. *The American Journal of Family Therapy*, *46*(4), 356–374. https://doi.org/10.1080/01926187.2018.1547667

Russell, J. A., Skipper, A. D., Rose, A. H., & Kennedy, J. (2021). Sanctification of couple relationships and communal coping in married and cohabiting African American couples. *Journal of Family Psychology*, *35*(8), 1128. https://doi.org/10.1037/fam0000882

Sabey, A. K., Rauer, A. J., & Jensen, J. F. (2014). Compassionate love as a mechanism linking sacred qualities of marriage to older couples' marital satisfaction. *Journal of Family Psychology*, *28*(5), 594. https://doi.org/10.1037/a0036991

Shichida, T., Dollahite, D. C., & Carroll, J. S. (2015). How the perception of God as a transcendent moral authority influences marital connection among American Christians. *Journal of Psychology and Christianity*, *34*, 40–52. http://hdl.lib.byu.edu/1877/7771

Skipper. A. D., Rose, A. H., Card, N. A., Moore, T. J., Lavender-Bratcher, D., & Chaney, C. (2023). Relational sanctification, communal coping, and depression among African American couples. *Journal of Marital and Family Therapy*. https://doi.org/10.1111/jmft.12665

Smith, J. (2023). Family and religion in flux: Relationship complexity, type of religiosity, and race/ethnicity. *Journal of Marriage and Family*, 1–20. https://doi.org/10.1111/jomf.12943

Spilman, S. K., Neppl, T. K., Donnellan, M. B., Schofield, T. J., & Conger, R. D. (2013). Incorporating religiosity into a developmental model of positive family functioning across generations. *Developmental Psychology*, *49*(4), 762. https://doi.org/10.1037%2Fa0028418

Timothy-Springer, R., & Johnson, E. J. (2018). Qualitative study on the experiences of married couples. *Journal of Human Behavior in the Social Environment*, *28*(7), 889–902. https://doi.org/10.1080/10911359.2018.1467291

Tuttle, J. D., & Davis, S. N. (2015). Religion, infidelity, and divorce. *Journal of Divorce & Remarriage*, *56*(6), 475–489. https://doi.org/10.1080/10502556.2015.1058660

Uecker, J. E., Mayrl, D., & Stroope, S. (2016). Family formation and returning to institutional religion in young adulthood. *Journal for the Scientific Study of Religion*, *55*(2), 384–406. https://doi.org/10.1111/jssr.12271

Upenieks, L., Uecker, J. E., & Schafer, M. H. (2021). Couple religiosity and well-being among older adults in the United States. *Journal of Aging and Health*, *34*(2), 266–282. https://doi.org/10.1177/08982643211042159

Vazquez, V., Otero, I., & Goodlow, J. (2019). Relationship stigma and Black-White interracial marital satisfaction: The mediating role of religious/spiritual well-being. *Mental Health, Religion & Culture*, *22*(3), 305–318. https://doi.org/10.1080/13674676.2019.1620189

Webb, J. R., Toussaint, L., & Dula, C. S. (2014). Ritualistic, theistic, and existential spirituality: Initial psychometric qualities of the RiTE measure of spirituality. *Journal of Religion and Health*, *53*, 972–985. https://doi.org/10.1007/s10943-013-9697-y

Wilcox, W. B., & Wolfinger, N. H. (2008). Living and loving "decent": Religion and relationship quality among urban parents. *Social Science Research*, *37*(3), 828–843. https://doi.org/10.1016%2Fj.ssresearch.2007.11.001

Wurm, G. J., Dollahite, D. C., & Marks, L. D. (2018). The inner logic of religion(s): Theoretical implications regarding eight American religious-ethnic communities. *Marriage & Family Review*, *54*, 635–647. https://doi.org/10.1080/01494929.2018.1469570

Chapter 34

Women's Experience with Spirituality in Addiction Recovery

*Heather Austin-Robillard**

Women may have unique experiences with spirituality (e.g., Magaldi et al., 2017) and recovery from addiction (e.g., Kruk & Sandberg, 2013), and thus with the interface between spirituality and addiction recovery. This chapter will focus on the relationship between spirituality and addiction recovery for women.

Author's Definition of Spirituality and the RiTE Model of Spirituality

Before delving into the current literature, it is crucial to understand the author's personal definition of spirituality and how it aligns with the RiTE model, as discussed in Chapters 1 and 44 of this volume. One's own perspective on spirituality can influence how one interacts with the topic. Due to the personal nature this section, I will switch to first person to clarify my perspective.

My view of spirituality is fluid and evolving, aligning more with an agnostic stance rather than organized religion. I resonate with Buddhism's non-theistic principles, though I am not a strict Buddhist. I continue to explore Buddhism to refine my understanding of spirituality.

I see spirituality as a lifelong dialogue with the self, acknowledging that my spiritual views will change over time. Raised Christian, I left the religion at nineteen due to conflicts with its teachings. Although I have attempted to rejoin the Christian faith, I am more drawn to non-theistic spirituality, finding Buddhism particularly appealing.

Key tenets of Buddhism, such as the impermanence of life and the notion that material possessions do not bring happiness, shape my spirituality (McMahen, 2012). Mindfulness and meditation help me connect with my spirituality in the present moment, aligning with Buddhism's Four Noble Truths regarding suffering (Kabat Zinn, 2003; see also *Dhammapada*: 190–192; Easwaran, 2007, p. 171).

Comparing my definition to the RiTE model from Chapters 1 and 44, my spirituality is lowest in Ritualistic Spirituality (RS) and highest in Existential Spirituality (ES). I seek meaning in life and do not adhere to a structured belief system or deity. Instead, I find peace in connecting with the universe through nature and mindfulness. As was mentioned in the dimension of Theistic Spirituality (TS) from the RiTE model, I participate in a more non-structured connection with a higher power. While I do not believe in a specific deity, I connect in general to the larger universe. Knowing I put my faith in the larger universe gives me a sense of peace. It allows me to show gratitude toward how the world and I show up for each other. While my definition of spirituality is one of constant learning and changing, this chapter will take into consideration what the spirituality literature focuses on when it comes to women in recovery from addiction. My experience in the field over the past 14 years, both professionally

* Corresponding Author: heather.austin@ttu.edu.

DOI: 10.4324/9781003440048-39

and personally, connects me deeply to the topic of women's spirituality in addiction recovery. This chapter will explore how the scientific spirituality literature intersects with this field.

Different Belief Systems for Women in Addiction Recovery

This section will include a discussion of the current literature on spirituality within women in recovery from addiction. The literature will be split between monotheistic (Christianity, Catholicism, Judaism, etc.), polytheistic (Taoism, Hinduism, Wiccan, etc.) and non-theistic belief systems (Buddhism, Confucianism, Agnostic, etc.). Because of the popularity of certain belief systems, the potential gaps in the literature will become clear, especially around polytheistic, and non-theistic belief systems.

Monotheistic Belief Systems

Much of the literature reflects on samples of women within a monotheistic belief system, primarily through a Christian lens. This is not surprising as Christianity is the largest religion in the world, followed by 2.4 billion people (Pew Research Center, 2017). Much of this literature highlights how Christian beliefs can reduce the risk for alcoholism (Cochran et al., 1992; Kendler, et al., 2003; Sim et al., 2013). One example of this was an all-female twin study, which found lifetime risk for alcoholism was inversely related with personal devotion behaviors/attitudes, like frequency of prayers, fundamentalist Christian beliefs and conservative religious affiliation (Kendler, et al. 2003). More personal devotion, frequency of prayers and a fundamentalist Christian belief tended to have a lower risk for alcoholism in female-to-female twins. This may be due to the importance of forgiveness that Christianity can promise once individuals access recovery (Lund, 2017).

Throughout the literature there are certain ways these monotheistic organizations aid women in attaining and maintaining treatment and recovery from addiction. Turner et al. (1999) wrote about a study that consisted of 51 African American Christian women and 51 Anglo American Christian women in recovery for 1–5 years. While the authors did not discuss the differences between these two groups, they did find that one third of these women reported religious organizations played a part in the beginning of their recovery. The ways these religious organizations aided these women were mainly through spiritual counseling and prayer. Another important factor for these women were the changes in their spiritual needs from the beginning of their recovery to years after. At the beginning of these women's recovery, they reported spiritual needs of forgiveness of self and forgiveness by others, whereas at the time of interview (1–5 years into recovery), the spiritual needs most desired included unconditional love, self-forgiveness and understanding by others (Turner et al., 1999). This change highlights the impact recovery can have on growth of a woman's spirituality. Other researchers identified positive religious coping scores for Christian women did not predict completion of treatment nor did high negative religious coping predict withdrawal from treatment (Bever, 2019). However, they did highlight that many women in the sample drew on their faith and spirituality as they learned to cope with stress when not using drugs and alcohol. In still another study, of a Christian SUD program, it was found women who completed versus those who withdrew from treatment had more mental health symptoms at entrance (Kerlin, 2017). Together, these studies suggest religious coping may feel beneficial for women but alone it is not enough for successful substance treatment completion, especially among those who have a history of trauma and mental health concerns (Bever, 2019; Kerlin, 2017).

A considerable amount of the literature does not directly indicate monotheistic samples; however, they would denote a 12-Step value system (like Alcoholics Anonymous, AA) (Dobbs Butts, 2001). Though the 12-Step Model is often described as a "spiritual program, not a religious one" (AA, 2001, p. 346; see also AA, 2023) and 12-Step programs are welcoming to adherents of many diverse religious belief systems, as local groups are found worldwide (aa.org/find-aa), arguably the 12-Step Model is derived from the Judeo-Christian beliefs of its founders. Therefore, many related studies on women's recovery can fit into a monotheistic belief system as they tend to use the terms "God" or "Higher Power", which likely denotes one deity or transcendent entity.

Polytheistic Belief Systems

There is little literature on specific polytheistic belief systems. Much of the literature revolves around cultures with a mixture of monotheistic and polytheistic belief systems. For example, a qualitative study conducted in Vancouver, Canada had five women (of 24 total) who identified as from the First Nations heritage. One interesting theme presented was that both First Nation's women, as well as the Caucasian women, expressed benefits from the spiritual cultural teachings of First Nations ceremonies, like sweat lodges and burning ceremonies (Kruk & Sandberg, 2013). Many First Nations tribes espouse both monotheistic and polytheistic belief systems, however there was no clarification of the specific First Nation tribes of these women to determine if their beliefs were of a monotheistic or polytheistic system.

Other polytheistic religions like Hinduism had little research specific to women in recovery from addiction. In one study, there was less drinking among Hindu women (27.9%) compared to Hindu men (49.3%), but this same study did find higher rates of drinking in indigenous (65%) and Hindu (55.1%) populations compared to Buddhist (24.7%) and Christian (10%) populations within India (Chaturvedi & Mahanta, 2004). More research on different polytheistic religions is needed to determine the true impacts for women in recovery.

Non-Theistic Belief Systems

Research on non-theistic religions was sparse as well. One of the studies which focused on a non-theistic belief system was a case study of a woman with severe Alcohol Use Disorder. In this case study, the therapist combined psychotherapy and shamanic methodology (Rich, 2012). Shamanism is a cultural practice for guidance and healing (Connor & Keeney, 2008) and considers all illnesses to have a spiritual component (Harner & Harner, 2000). In this case study, the woman was able to surrender to powerlessness and commit to recovery from her addiction (Rich, 2012).

The Buddhist religion is often included as a non-theistic religion. One of the studies reported on an organization called Recovery Dharma, which incorporates Buddhist principles, like mindfulness and meditation in the treatment of addictions (Recovery Dharma, 2019). In a study conducted by LaBelle et al. (2022), 34% identified as Buddhist, 23% as not committed to any faith, 12.5% as atheist and 7.2% as agnostic. In this study, the female participants experienced less severe consequences for their drug use and engaged in shorter meditation lengths compared to the male participants.

It is imperative to discuss the inclusion of feminist spirituality in addiction recovery for women. Because many religions are based in patriarchal views and traditional treatment centers are framed to be more androcentric, Finfgeld (2002) writes this could be detrimental to women in recovery. Feminist spirituality arose from inspirations from ancient Jungian archetypes, goddesses, Eastern religions, pre-Christian European paganism and Native American and African religions. Mainly, feminist spirituality is "grounded in the context of women's experiences" (Ballou, 1995). In a study written by Finfgeld (2002), it was suggested including feminist spirituality in women's health care is imperative. There are four feminist spirituality themes that could be included in alcohol treatment for women. *Nonhierarchical relationships* by allowing women to be collaborative in the development of their treatment plan. *Lived experiences of ordinary life* which may have led to alcohol use should be explored, especially focusing on oppression. *Nature pantheism* by using intrapersonal and environmental factors for women into their treatment plan to develop a holistic plan. *Personal empowerment* by using bibliotherapy, narrative therapy and other storytelling and rituals to reinforce innate goodness and self-nurturing.

A few studies had samples from all three categories of belief systems (monotheistic, polytheistic, and non-theistic). For example, in a qualitative study, regardless of the type of belief system, women expressed learning to separate religion from spirituality was vital to their recovery (Bradley, 2011). This study had 23 monotheistic, 1 polytheistic and 5 non-theistic participants. The author of this study highlighted the changes in women's spirituality. For example, many women expressed "GOD was no longer a distant, uninvolved being or a being only accessed through a male in a hierarchical position or someone who could only be spoken to through rote prayers" (p. 100). This shows some empowerment in the women's change of personal relationship with their deity once going through recovery.

Gender Differences in Addiction Recovery Spirituality

Another important aspect of this literature was the identification of gender differences in spirituality. The current literature has been inconclusive on whether women utilize spirituality/religiousness more or less than men when it comes to addiction recovery. Women may have a more spiritual frame of mind before entering treatment or recovery, but they do not differ much in the actions of their spirituality compared to men. Again, this is illustrated in Bliss and Ekmark (2013) where women have higher scores on spiritual attitudes but equivalent spiritual behaviors when compared to men. In contradiction, Kelly and Hoeppner (2013) reported that women have significantly higher scores on religious background and behaviors than men at intake, but AA attendance, which is rooted in Judeo-Christian beliefs, appears to work for both genders in increasing confidence and the ability to abstain from drugs and alcohol in high-risk situations. However, men's AA attendance led to a significant reduction in heavy drinking compared to women. Kelly and Hoeppner (2013) also mentioned that this could be because women are *more* likely to drink outside of a social context, therefore, the ability for AA to lead to an increase in one's pro-abstinent network may not be needed as much for women as it could be for men.

In contrast, some literature has displayed a lower level of spirituality at intake for women than men, but an increase in the shift of spirituality through recovery as compared to men. In a Polish sample, Charzyńska (2015) discovered of the individuals entering Alcohol Use Disorder (AUD) treatment, women were *less* spiritually inclined than men. Specifically, women had lower scores on forgiveness for others and higher scores for negative spiritual coping than men when entering treatment. Although, there were no gender differences on positive spiritual coping, at the end of the 8 weeks of treatment though, women experienced higher positive spiritual coping compared to men, while there were no longer differences in negative spiritual coping. What this appears to present is that women may enter with more negative uses of spiritual coping than men, but they have a more intense and rapid shift in their positive spiritual coping through treatment. This was also consistent with Krentzman (2017), where between six months and 30 months, women's spirituality domain of forgiveness of self, increased more rapidly than men's, when controlling for covariates (age, education, AA involvement, baseline drinks per day).

Another aspect of women showing more spiritual growth after recovery is shown in the reference of the common recovery concept of spiritual awakening. In Sweden, Bodin (2006) found that 50% of women and only 31% of men attending AA after inpatient treatment reported having a spiritual awakening.

While women may have a more intense shift in spirituality during recovery, they may attribute less of their recovery to a specific deity. Baker et al. (2007) found women's levels of spirituality and religiousness were equivalent to men's for "belief in GOD", religious beliefs/behaviors, and daily spiritual experiences, but women attributed recovery efforts to God's influence less than male peers. In contrast, spirituality was endorsed as being more important for overcoming their Alcohol Use Disorder compared to men (Kelly & Eddie, 2020).

This literature demonstrates a gender difference in several variables of spirituality and religiousness for individuals entering treatment, as well as during recovery. Women attend less of their recovery efforts to God's influence but have more spiritual awakening during recovery efforts. It also appears more women are already spiritual/religious before entering recovery, whereas men may increase more of their religious behaviors after entering recovery, however, women may have a more rapid and intense growth in their spirituality after recovery than men.

Evidence for Salubrious Associations with Health and Well-Being

Spirituality and addiction recovery are both important to health and well-being (Koeing, 2008; Tabei et al., 2016). This section is focused on the current literature that supports a salubrious relationship between spirituality and health and well-being, in the context of addiction and recovery. There has been literature to show that spirituality plays a positive role in other health-related variables for an individual in recovery (Lovett & Weisz, 2021; Puffer et al., 2012; Tonigan et al., 1996); however, much of this research has not looked at the differences among men and women.

Nevertheless, spirituality can decrease perceived stress in women. For example, it was discovered that a woman's perceived stress was negatively associated with spirituality (Arevalo et al., 2008). That is, the more perceived stress, the less spiritual involvement a woman has. Inversely, the more spiritual involvement a woman has, the less perceived stress they have during substance use treatment. This is consistent with other studies – not necessarily in the context of addiction and recovery – that have found spirituality to have a salubrious association with other types of stressors for women (Dolatian et al., 2017; Lucero et al., 2013).

There is some indication that spirituality can help empower women in their recovery efforts. One example is a qualitative study which illustrated a woman's newfound level of spirituality, brought on by AA, allowed them to have a sense of empowerment by embracing powerlessness over their addiction (Bradley, 2011). While there is a lack of research showing that spirituality can mediate the impact of perceived stress on substance addiction (Arevalo et al., 2008), spirituality may impact addiction *severity* through other individual and contextual factors, like social support and other forms of coping (Prado et al., 2004).

It is also apparent the behaviors women engage in during recovery can be beneficial to them. Longitudinally, women tend to experience less negative religious coping and higher levels of forgiveness for others from baseline to 6 months of recovery compared to men. In the long-term range (between 6 and 30 months), women experience increased self-forgiveness more rapidly than men (Krentzman, 2017). This conveys the unique ability women may have in the rapid and positive impact of spirituality and its relationship to their well-being.

Evidence for Deleterious Associations with Health and Well-Being

Alternatively, there is also literature proclaiming ways spirituality can have a deleterious relationship with health and well-being, in the context of addiction and recovery. Much literature has shown that religion can have a negative relationship with substance use disorders (Lovett & Weisz, 2021; Dermatis & Galanter, 2016; Park et al. 2017.) For example, women can desire to avoid judgment and stigma from religious organizations when struggling with addiction. In a study conducted among Christian women, the participants reported not reaching out for help to religious organizations because they believed the church could not help them or out of fear of being stigmatized (Turner et al., 1999). Similarly, women did not reach out to religious organizations for assistance to maintain recovery because fears of religious leaders misunderstanding addiction. It is important for these women to feel the religious leaders understand addiction and recovery in order to reach out to them for continued maintenance of their recovery.

There is some indication of specific qualities of women that may reduce religious organizations offering help to women. Turner et al. (1999) found that (1) women who had never been married received less help from church, (2) women who never attended treatment or attended treatment only once were less likely to receive help, and (3) women who attributed recovery to treatment, illness or religious conversion were less likely to receive help from the church than those who attributed their recovery to the 12-Step model of addiction recovery. It is possible that those who do not abide by the religious foundations of a Christian church for recovery may not receive help from said religious organizations. This could make it difficult for women, who may have trouble with religion and spirituality before or during the recovery process, to access support.

Health Behaviors and Social Support in Relation to a Salubrious or Deleterious Interface with Spirituality

Since spirituality can be salubrious and deleterious to women's health and well-being, it is important to understand how specific health behaviors and social support may play a role therein. It is also important to note that religious involvement may not be as important a factor to recovery as other social support avenues. In a study of women who struggled with both addiction and HIV, women noted social support being important to their recovery, but there was a lack of support found from religious affiliations (Tangenberg, 2001).

Charzyńska (2015) reported at the beginning of addiction-related treatment, women had more negative religious coping and by the end of treatment they had higher positive religious coping than men. Women also had less forgiveness for others at the beginning of treatment compared to men but by the end of treatment women had a higher forgiveness of God compared to men. Charzyńska (2015) also noted that, given the significant role of religion and spirituality in women's lives, their spiritual beliefs may have a substantial influence on both negative outcomes, such as pathological drinking, and positive outcomes, such as improvements in treatment and rapid spiritual transformation.

Some literature has shown that, for women, age may be a factor that determines positive religious coping. Older women use more positive religious coping compared to younger women. And childhood trauma could also be a variable as the more frequently women experienced symptoms of trauma the more likely they use negative religious coping (Fallot & Heckman, 2005).

The Women for Sobriety (WFS) program is a cognitive-behaviorally based recovery program. Its fundamental approach is to increase women's self-esteem through positive affirmations and thinking. In this program, many women reported choosing not to attend AA because of its religious and God-related underpinnings. However, it was also discovered that most women in WFS were religious (Christian). The founders of this program hypothesize the WFS program illustrates that women can be spiritual and religious but that does not equate to sobriety (Fenner & Gifford, 2012). This again highlights that for women spirituality is a variable that may be related to recovery but is not the sole variable needed to achieve recovery.

Spirituality is important to recovery, but it may not be the main component of recovery. Some literature determines that wisdom could predict the ability to abstain from substances. For example, Digangi et al. (2013) conducted a study looking at wisdom, with a sample of women in recovery. They found the measure of wisdom used in their study included three factors – spirituality, intelligence, and nature/relational. The authors concluded those with higher levels of wisdom felt more confident in their abilities to abstain from substances. Ultimately, it was indicated spirituality is often a core component of recovery programs, which is also a factor of wisdom, because it cultivates complicit recognition that individuals cannot control events in their lives.

Another factor that could relate to whether spirituality is positive or negative in women's recovery is how specific gender dynamics are attended to. For example, a qualitative study identified some unique gender themes that may not be present for male counterparts in the recovery arena. These specific female themes included feelings of sabotaging efforts from family members and struggles with safety and intimacy during the recovery process (Flaherty et al., 2014). Without taking into consideration these unique experiences women have, aspects of spirituality may become a barrier to their health and well-being when participating in recovery.

Dimensions of the RiTE Model Found in the Literature

Many of the studies already presented throughout this chapter discuss elements of the RiTE model which are consistent with RS, given the seeming default approach to spirituality being a more structured connection to deity – especially those studies focused on or derived from the 12-Step Model of addiction and recovery (see AA, 1981, 2001, 2019). Some of the other studies did highlight consistencies with TS, a non-structured connection with deity, and ES, a transcendent, yet non-theistic search for meaning and purpose (see Chapters 1 and 44 of this volume). For example, a qualitative study of 28 women in substance misuse treatment presented the theme of spirituality more broadly construed, as opposed to a dogmatic religiosity, as important to the recovery process. Indeed, many of these women identified spirituality as having an association with nature (Kruk & Sandberg, 2013). This aligns well with ES in the RiTE model as these individuals were searching for meaning and purpose outside of a deity.

Current Diversity-Related Research within the Spirituality of Women in Recovery

Understanding spirituality among diverse women in recovery is vital to explore. The importance of spirituality could be different and vary for racial and ethnic minorities. Without understanding the unique experiences of diverse women in this topic we cannot get a clear understanding of spirituality in women in recovery. However, there is a deficit in the diversity of the samples in the current literature on spirituality in women's recovery.

As with white women versus white men (Krentzman, 2017, Newport, 2006), African American women perceive spirituality as more helpful in their recovery than do African American men (Arnold et al., 2002). Additional studies have also found spirituality to be a protective factor in substance use recovery among African American women (Chu & Sung, 2009; DiClemente, 2013). In other qualitative research, spirituality plays an extensive part in African American women's recovery process, including themes like reclaiming their spirituality (primarily with "God"), trusting the process (especially with their higher power), and by having active faith (Blakey, 2016).

An interesting phenomenological study by Blount, LaGuardia, and Fitzpatrick (2021), interviewed African American women regarding their experiences of getting into and maintaining recovery. Through these interviews, themes of recovery capital (see Best & Hennessy, 2022; Granfield & Cloud, 1999; Hennessy, 2017) emerged and included family, spirituality, religion, and the Black Church. Specifically relating to the Black Church, Jordan et al. (2021) found that the Black Church allowed for the feasibility of treatment for SUD for black men and women. Many of the participants reported feeling the Black Church created a strong sense of Black pride, ethnic identity, spiritualty and relation, and that all of these qualities were important to their recovery. Fallot and Heckman (2005), in a diverse sample, observed that African American women reported significantly more positive religious coping than did white women while negative religious coping did not differ among races.

Brome, Owens, Allen and Vevaina (2002) found spirituality as a key component in positive mental health outcomes among African American women in SUD recovery. African American mothers with high spirituality levels have more positive self-concept, more active coping styles, more positive attitudes toward parenting, more positive perceptions of the family climate and more satisfaction with their social support than those mothers with low spirituality levels. It was established that there was no difference between the levels in the experience of tension, frustration, or anxiety in parenting their children, or difference with social appraisals of their relationship with their children compared to their white counterparts.

A study of Puerto Rican women was conducted using the Spiritual Self-Schema (3-S) framework, which is an 8-week intervention treatment incorporating the client's spiritual beliefs. It is based on a Buddhist framework of helping individuals cognitively shift from the "addicted self" to the "spiritual self". In this study, Latina women had statistically significant changes from baseline to 20 weeks post entry in spirituality, motivation to change drug use and HIV prevention (Amaro et al., 2010).

Native American women have a unique experience as research alludes to their desire to quit using often comes from a spiritual experience, like a vision or a dream (Hawkins et al., 1993; Lowery, 1998). Literature among Native American women has also expressed a need for more culturally based activities to help in their recovery journey, due to a lack of treatment programs attending to this need (Lowery, 1998).

Korean American women may have the highest alcohol consumption of all the Asian American Pacific Islander (AAPI) groups (McCracken et al., 2007). This could potentially be impacted by the Korean American woman's religious denomination. Catholic Korean American women and Independent Christian Women were found to have a heavier alcohol consumption when compared to Korean American women that were more Conservative Christians (Sim et al., 2013). In this study, the authors noted the type of denomination impacted the acceptability of drinking which predicted the alcohol consumption of Korean American women.

Limitations to the Research

The author of this chapter attempted to conduct an exhaustive sweep of the literature surrounding spirituality in women in recovery from addiction. While it is possible some literature was not included in this chapter, based on what was included there are a few limitations to the research. The following section will highlight the methodological issues present in the literature and the limitations regarding diversity-related issues within the research.

One methodological issue seen in the literature occurs with uneven sample sizes – which can make it difficult to know if a fair comparison is possible – with regard to gender differences within spirituality and recovery. While some literature has fairly equitable sample sizes when comparing men and women (Bliss & Ekmark, 2013), many more studies include a larger sample size of males compared to females (Lund, 2017). Some studies attempted to make these sample sizes more equitable. For example, Charzyńska (2015) looked at sex differences in spiritual coping with 245 men and only 98 women over a 6–8-week treatment program. The attempts to make the sample size equitable occurred by using 56 men and 56 women with similar age and education criteria before conducting the related analysis, however, gender differences were not discussed.

Nevertheless, overall, when comparing spirituality in recovery between men and women, many studies have a large grouping of men compared to a small sample of women. Additional examples are briefly described to understand the nature of the problem. Piedmont (2004) had 47 men and only 9 women who completed treatment. Both men and women reported higher pretreatment scores on spirituality and well-being and fewer psychiatric symptoms after completion. In a study looking at the effect of AA attendance on self-efficacy and spirituality among 1726 adults seeking treatment for AUD, only 24% of the sample were female (Kelly & Hoeppner, 2012). Bodin (2006) included 112 men and only 40 women from a Swedish treatment center participating in weekly mixed gender groups for 12 months post treatment to determine gender differences in AA attendance and spiritual awakening. And, while the discrepancy of male versus female inclusion was not as large as some studies, Krentzman (2017) examined men and women's differences in spirituality over 30 months, with the sample being made up of 58% men compared to 41% women.

Even some of the qualitative studies had limited female sample sizes. Flaherty et al. (2014) only had one female compared to five males when considering the differences of secular, spiritual and religious pathways for long-term recovery. The one female in this study was from the AA recovery approach, which only focused on a spiritual modality, rather than exploring the differences among women in the other pathways to recovery. When looking specifically at Christianity, Lund (2017) only had 3 females out of 21 participants. While another qualitative study had a more even quantity with 9 men and 5 women when exploring religion and recovery among a homeless population (Lovett & Weisz, 2021).

Another factor to consider in the methodology of the current literature is the comparison of qualitative (Blount et al., 2021; Bradley, 2011; Charzyńska, 2015; Flaherty et al., 2014; Kruk & Sandberg, 2013; Lovett & Weisz, 2021; Rich, 2012) versus quantitative research (Amaro et al., 2010; Arevalo et al., 2008; Bliss & Ekmark, 2013; Bodin, 2006; Brome et al., 2002; DiGangi et al., 2013; Fallot & Heckman, 2005; Kelly & Hoeppner, 2012; Kendler et al., 2003; Krentzman, 2017; Piedmont, 2004; Turner et al., 1999) on women in recovery from Substance Use Disorders (SUD) and their relationship to spirituality/religion. Qualitative studies are popular. And while qualitative studies offer a deeper insight into personal experiences and meaning, it may lack the applicability and objective measurement provided by quantitative methodologies. This imbalance creates a gap in understating how statistically significant the impact of spirituality truly is on women's recovery.

Also, there was more literature exploring active SUD addiction or treatment in women and their spirituality (Amaro et al., 2010; Arevalo et al., 2008; Bliss & Ekmark, 2013; Charzyńska, 2015; Fallot & Heckman, 2005; Kendler et al., 2003; Piedmont, 2004) as compared to those studies exploring recovery or longitudinal data post treatment and women's spirituality (Blount et al., 2021; Bodin, 2006; Bradley, 2011; Brome et al., 2002; DiGangi et al., 2013; Kelly & Hoeppner, 2012; Krentzman, 2017; Turner et al., 1999). Some of this literature did attempt to observe the difference between those active in their addiction and those who were maintaining sobriety. Kruk and Sandberg (2013) conducted a grounded theory analysis on low-income women's experiences with spirituality and components of harm reduction-based recovery. This study looked at both former and active users, with 10 participants currently clean and 13 actively using drugs.

Future Directions for Women's Spirituality, Health, and Well-Being in Recovery

Based on the current literature thus far, there are a few directions researchers and clinicians should take when considering women's spirituality and its relation to addiction recovery. Because of the overabundance of recovery programs and literature focused on monotheistic and/or ritualistic spirituality, we should explore the impact of how polytheistic and non-theistic belief systems impact a woman's relationship with her spirituality and recovery. Within this, exploring how women participate in spirituality in an existential or theistic way may allow for a better understanding of how those in a polytheistic or non-theistic belief system utilize their spiritual self in their recovery.

Also, some of the limitations imply the need for a clear definition of recovery to truly explore the differences of spirituality in women. Many of the studies identified spirituality as either belonging to a religious affiliation or the authors illustrated for their participants what spiritualty was defined as. For example, a program evaluation for a group therapy called Family Focus with a sample of 43 African American women, identified spirituality as "conscious efforts to live a moral life of sobriety" (Dobbs Butts, 2001). However, this study also used the 12-Step Model as foundational in their program, which is aligned with many Judeo-Christian beliefs. Another study of women expressed the importance of interventions that address the spiritual needs of those with addiction, but emphasized the need to be flexible in its interpretations to include a spirituality that does not include a "higher power" (Arnold et al., 2002). If recovery continues to be identified solely as a connection to a higher power, it will continue to exclude women who find hope and joy outside of a higher power. Without this clear definition researchers are also limited to the methodology conducted thus far.

For example, typical measures of spirituality tend to be in the context of "God" and can exclude sample participants from other belief systems. Being able to utilize more appropriate measures of spirituality will allow for increased inclusivity and a more accurate understanding of the relationship between spirituality and recovery among women.

Conclusion

This chapter explored the complex relationship between spirituality and addiction recovery among women, emphasizing the influence of various belief systems, like monotheistic, polytheistic and non-theistic, on their paths to sobriety. While monotheistic frameworks, particularly those rooted in Judeo-Christina traditions, are prevalent in addiction recovery research, this focus limits the scope of understanding of women's spiritual experiences in a broader spectrum. There is a need for more inclusive approaches to research including polytheistic and non-theistic traditions.

While the predominant monotheistic practices offer significant support to some women, it also introduces challenges related to stigma, judgment and institutional support. The gender specific nuances observed suggest that women may experience a more profound spiritual transformation during recovery due to their pre-existing spiritual inclinations and life experiences. Future research should address these challenges by adopting a more inclusive framework that examines the role of diverse spiritual practices in addiction recovery. Additionally, methodological improvements, such as addressing sample size imbalances and the incorporation of more longitudinal studies are essential for a comprehensive understanding of how spirituality influences long-term recovery outcomes.

References

Alcoholics Anonymous. (1981). *Twelve steps and twelve traditions*. Alcoholics Anonymous World Services. See https://www.aa.org/pages/en_US/twelve-steps-and-twelve-traditions

Alcoholics Anonymous. (2001). *Alcoholics Anonymous: The story of how many thousands of men and women have recovered from alcoholism* (Fourth ed.). Alcoholics Anonymous World Services. See https://www.aa.org/pages/en_US/alcoholics-anonymous

Alcoholics Anonymous. (2019). *Living sober*. Alcoholics Anonymous World Services. See https://www.aa.org/living-sober-book

Alcoholics Anonymous. (2023). Understanding Alcoholics Anonymous and Spirituality. Retrieved August 29, 2024, from https://www.aa.org/sites/default/files/literature/AA%20and%20Spirituality%20Press%20Release%20-%20EN_0.pdf

Amaro, H., Magno-Gatmaytan, C., Meléndez, M., Coréts, D., Arevalo, S., & Margolin, A. (2010). Addiction Treatment Intervention: An Uncontrolled Prospective Pilot Study of Spiritual Self-Schema Therapy with Latina Women. *Substance Abuse, 31*, 117–125. https://doi.org/10.1080/08897071003641602

Arevalo, S., Prado, G., & Amaro, H. (2008). Spirituality, Sense of Coherence and Coping Responses in Women Receiving Treatment for Alcohol and Drug Addiction. *Evaluation and Program Planning, 31*, 113–123. https://doi.org/10.1016/j.evalprogplan.2007.05.009

Arnold, R.M., Avants, S.K., Margolin, A., & Marcotte, D. (2002). Patient Attitudes Concerning the Inclusion of Spirituality into Addiction Treatment. *Journal of Substance Abuse Treatment, 23*, 319–326. https://doi.org/10.1016/S0740-5472(02)00282-9

Baker, M.P., Sellman, J.D., & Horn, J. (2007). The Spiritual Characteristics of New Zealanders Entering Treatment for Alcohol/Other Drug Dependence. *Alcoholism Treatment Quarterly, 24* (4), 137–155. https://doi.org/10.1300/J020v24n04_09

Ballou, M. (1995). Women and Spirit: Two Nonfits in Psychology. *Women & Therapy*, *16*(2–3), 9–20. https://doi.org/10.1300/J015v16n02_04

Best, D., & Hennessy, E. A. (2022). The Science of Recovery Capital: Where Do We Go from Here? *Addiction*, *117*(4), 1139–1145. https://doi.org/10.1111/add.15732

Bever, M. B. (2019). Religious Coping and Christ-Centered Recovery for Women with Substance Use Disorders. *DNP Scholarly Projects*. *16*. https://repository.belmont.edu/dnpscholarlyprojects/16?utm_source=repository.belmont.edu%2Fdnpscholarlyprojects%2F16&utm_medium=PDF&utm_campaign=PDFCoverPages

Blakey, J. M. (2016). The Role of Spirituality in Helping African American Women with Histories of Trauma and Substance Abuse Heal and Recover. *Social Work & Christianity*, *43*(1), 40–59.

Bliss, D.L. & Ekmark, S.S. (2013). Gender Differences in Spirituality in Persons in Alcohol and Drug Dependence Treatment. *Alcoholism Treatment Quarterly*, *31*(1), 25–37. https://doi.org/10.1080/07347324.2013.746625

Blount, T.N., LaGuardia, A.C., & Fitzpatrick, D.C. (2021). African American Women's Substance Use Recovery Experiences: A Phenomenological Inquiry. *Counseling and Values*, *66*(1), 92–110. https://doi.org/10.1002/cvj.12146

Bodin, M. (2006). Gender Aspects of Affiliation with Alcoholics Anonymous After Treatment. *Contemporary Drug Problems*, *33*(1), 123–141. https://doi.org/10.1177/009145090603300106

Bradley, C. (2011). Women in AA: "Sharing Experience, Strength and Hope" The Relational Nature of Spirituality. *Journal of Religion & Spirituality in Social Work: Social Thought*, *30*(2), 89–112. https://doi.org/10.1080/15426432.2011.567111

Brome, D. R. Owens, M.D., Allen, K., & Vevaina, T. (2002). An Examination of Spirituality Among African American Women in Recovery From Substance Abuse. *Journal of Black Psychology*, *26*(4), 470–486. https://doi.org/10.1207/S15327965PLI1303_02

Charzyńska, E. (2015). Sex Differences in Spiritual Coping, Forgiveness, and Gratitude Before and After a Basic Alcohol Addiction Treatment Program. *Journal of Religion and Health*, *54*(1), 1931–1949. https://doi.org/10.1007/s10943-015-0002-0

Chaturvedi, H. K., & Mahanta, J. (2004). Sociocultural Diversity and Substance Use Pattern in Arunachal Pradesh, India. *Drug & Alcohol Dependence*, *74*(1), 97. https://doi.org/10.1016/j.drugalcdep.2003.12.003

Chu, D.C. & Sung, H.E. (2009). Racial Difference in Desistance from Substance Abuse: The Impact of Religious Involvement on Recovery. *International Journal of Offender Therapy and Comparative Criminology*, *53*(6), 697–716. https://doi.org/10.1177/0306624X08320207

Cochran, J. K., Beeghley, L., & Bock, W. E. (1992). The Influence of Religious Stability and Homogamy on the Relationship Between Religiosity and Alcohol Use among Protestants. *Journal for the Scientific Study of Religion*, *31*(4), 441. https://doi.org/10.2307/1386855

Connor, N. & Keeney, B. (2008). *Shamans of the World: Extraordinary First Person Accounts of Healings, Mysteries and Miracles*. Boulders, Sounds True.

Dermatis, H., & Galanter, M. (2016). The Role of Twelve-step-related Spirituality in Addiction Recovery. *Journal of Religion and Health*, *55*, 510–521. https://doi.org/10.1007/s10943-015-0019-4

DiClemente, C.C. (2013). Paths through Addiction and Recovery: The Impact of Spirituality and Religion. *Substance Use and Misuse*, *48*(12), 1260–1261. https://doi.org/10.3109/10826084.2013.808475

DiGangi, J.A., Jason, L.A., Mendoza, L., Miller, S.A., & Contreras, R. (2013). The Relationship Between Wisdom and Abstinence Behaviors in Women in Recovery from Substance Abuse. *The American Journal of Drug and Alcohol Abuse*, *39*(1), 33–37. https://doi.org/10.3109/00952990.2012.702172

Dobbs Butts, J. (2001). Spirituality & Sexuality: A Program for Women in Recovery. *American Journal of Health Studies, Special issue: "The Health of Women of Color"*, *17*(2), 102–106. Retrieved from http://lib-e2.lib.ttu.edu/login?url=https://www.proquest.com/scholarly-journals/spirituality-sexuality-program-women-recovery/docview/210482269/se-2

Dolatian, M., Mahmoodi, Z., Dilgony, T., Shams, J., & Zaeri, F. (2017). The Structural Model of Spirituality and Psychological Well-Being for Pregnancy-Specific Stress. *Journal of Religion and Health*, *56*, 2267–2275. https://doi.org/10.1007/s10943-017-0395-z

Easwaran, E. (2007). *The Dhammapada: Introduced & translated by Eknath Easwaran* (Second ed.). Nilgiri Press.

Fallot, R.D. & Heckman, J.P. (2005). Religious/Spiritual Coping Among Women Trauma Survivors with Mental Health and Substance Use Disorders. *Journal of Behavioral Health Services & Research, 32*(2), 215–226. https://doi.org/10.1007/BF02287268

Fenner, R.M. & Gifford, M.H. (2012). Women for Sobriety: 35 Years of Challenges, Changes and Continuity. *Journal of Groups in Addiction & Recovery, 7*, 142–170. https://doi.org/10.1080/1556035X.2012.705662

Finfgeld, D. L. (2002). Feminist Spirituality and Alcohol Treatment. *Journal of Holistic Nursing : Official Journal of the American Holistic Nurses' Association, 20*(2), 113–127. https://doi.org/10.1177/08910102020002002

Flaherty, M.T., Kurtz, E., White, W.L., & Larson, A. (2014). An Interpretive Phenomenological ANlysis of Secular, Spiritual, and Religious Pathways of Long-term Addiction Recovery. *Alcoholism Treatment Quarterly, 32*, 337–356. https://doi.org/10.1080/07347324.2014.949098

Granfield, R., & Cloud, W. (1999). *Coming clean: Overcoming addiction without treatment*. New York University Press.

Harner, M. & Harner, S. (2000). Core Practices of Shamanic Treatment of Illnesses. *Shamanism, 13*, 19–30. Retrieved from: https://www.imaginatie.nl/wp-content/uploads/2021/11/CorePracticesintheShamanicTreatmentIllness.Harner.pdf

Hawkins, N., Day, S., & Suagee, M. (1993, June). American Indian Women's Chemical Health Project. *A research project conducted by the American Indian Section, Chemical Dependency Division, Department of Human Services, State of Minnesota. Minneapolis: Minnesota Department of Human Services, Chemical Dependency Division.*

Hennessy, E. A. (2017). Recovery Capital: A Systematic Review of the Literature. *Addiction Research & Theory, 25*(5), 349–360. https://doi.org/10.1080/16066359.2017.1297990

Jordan, A., Babuscio, T., Nich, C., & Carroll, K. M. (2021). A Feasibility Study Providing Substance use Treatment in the Black Church. *Journal of Substance Abuse Treatment, 124*, 108218. https://doi.org/10.1016/j.jsat.2020.108218

Kabat-Zinn, J. (2003). Mindfulness-based Interventions in Context: Past, Present and Future. *Clinical Psychology, Science & Practice, 10*(2), 144–156. https://doi.org/10.1093/clipsy.bpg016

Kelly, J. F., & Eddie, D. (2020). The Role of Spirituality and Religiousness in Aiding Recovery from Alcohol and Other Drug Problems: An Investigation in a National US Sample. *Psychology of Religion and Spirituality, 12*(1), 116–123. https://doi.org/10.1037/rel0000295

Kelly, J.F. & Hoeppner, B.B. (2012). Does Alcoholics Anonymous Work Differently for Men and Women? A Moderated Multiple-Mediation Analysis in a Large Clinical Sample. *Drug and Alcohol Dependence, 130*, 186–193. https://doi.org/10.1016/j.drugalcdep.2012.11.005

Kelly, J. F., & Hoeppner, B. B. (2013). Does Alcoholics Anonymous Work Differently for Men and Women? A Moderated Multiple-mediation Analysis in a Large Clinical sample. *Drug and Alcohol Dependence, 130*(1–3), 186–193. https://doi.org/10.1016/j.drugalcdep.2012.11.005

Kendler, K.S., Liu, X.O., Gardner, C.O., McCullough, M.E., Larson, D., & Prescott, C.A. (2003). Dimensions of Religiosity and Their Relationship to Lifetime Psychiatric and Substance Use Disorders. *American Journal of Psychiatry, 160*(3), 496–503. https://doi.org/10.1176/appi.ajp.160.3.496

Kerlin, A. M. (2017). Therapeutic Change in a Christian SUD Program: Mental Health, Attachment, and Attachment to God. *Alcoholism Treatment Quarterly, 35*(4), 395–411. https://doi.org/10.1080/07347324.2017.1355218

Koeing, H.G., (2008). *Medicine, Religion and Health: Where Science and Spirituality Meet*. Templeton Foundation Press.

Krentzman, A.R. (2017). Longitudinal Differences in Spirituality and Religiousness Between Men and Women in Treatment for Alcohol Use Disorders. *Psychology of Religion and Spirituality, 9*(1), S11–S21. https://doi.org/10.1037/rel0000096

Kruk, E. & Sandberg, K. (2013). A Home for Body and Soul: Substance Using Women in Recovery. *Harm Reduction Journal*, *10*, 1–16. https://doi.org/10.1186/1477-7517-10-39

LaBelle, O., Meeks, M., Vest, N., Hastings, M., & Harding, T. (2022). Recovery Dharma: Exploration of a Buddhist-based mutual help organization for the treatment of addiction. *Journal of Social Work Practice in the Addictions*, *22*(3), 175–187. https://doi.org/10.1080/1533256X.2021.1946331

Lovett, K. L. & Weisz, C. (2021). Religion and Recovery among Individuals Experiencing Homelessness. *Journal of Religion and Health*, *60*, 3949–3966. https://doi.org/10.1007/s10943-020-01060-1

Lowery, C.T. (1998). American Indian Perspectives on Addiction and Recovery. *Health and Social Work*, *23*(2), 127–135. https://doi.org/10.1093/hsw/23.2.127

Lucero, S.M., Pargament, K.I., Mahoney, A., & DeMaris, A. (2013). Links Between Religious and Spiritual Coping and Adjustment Among Fathers and Mothers During First Pregnancy. *Journal of Reproductive and Infant Psychology*, *31*(3), 309–322. https://doi.org/10.1080/02646838.2013.798864

Lund, P. (2017). Christian Faith and Recovery from Substance Abuse, Guilt, and Shame. *Journal of Religion & Spirituality in Social Work: Social Thought*, *36*(3), 346–366. https://doi.org/10.1080/15426432.2017.1302865

Magaldi, D., Park-Taylor, J., & Latella, L. E. (2017). Women's Religion and Spirituality. In M. Kopala & M. Keitel (Eds.), *Handbook of counseling women*, 2nd ed. (pp. 418–432). Sage Publications, Inc. https://doi.org/10.4135/9781506300290.n35

McCracken, M., Olsen, M., Chen Jr, M. S., Jemal, A., Thun, M., Cokkinides, V., ... & Ward, E. (2007). Cancer incidence, mortality, and associated risk factors among Asian Americans of Chinese, Filipino, Vietnamese, Korean, and Japanese Ethnicities. *CA: A Cancer Journal for Clinicians*, *57*(4), 190–205. https://doi.org/10.3322/canjclin.57.4.190

McMahan, D. L. (2012). The Enchanted Secular: Buddhism and the Emergence of Transtraditional "Spirituality". *The Eastern Buddhist*, *43*(1/2), 205–223. Retrieved from: http://web.otani.ac.jp/EBS/index.html

Newport, F. (2006). *Religion most important to Blacks, women and older Americans*. Washington, DC: Gallup News Service. https://news.gallup.com/poll/25585/religion-most-important-blacks-women-older-americans.aspx

Park, C. L., Masters, K. S., Salsman, J. M., Wachholtz, A., Clements, A. D., Salmoirago-Blotcher, E., et al. (2017). Advancing our Understanding of Religion and Spirituality in the Context of Behavioral Medicine. *Journal of Behavioral Medicine*, *40*, 39–51. https://doi.org/10.1007/s10865-016-9755-5

Pew Research Center (2017). Christians are the Largest Religious Groups in 2015. *Pewforum.org, USA*, March 31, 2017. https://www.pewresearch.org/religion/2017/04/05/the-changing-global-religious-landscape/pf_17-04-05_projectionsupdate_grl310px/

Piedmont, R.L. (2004). Spiritual Transcendence as a Predictor of Psychosocial Outcome from an Outpatient Substance Abuse Program. *Psychology of Addictive Behaviors*, *18* (3), 213–232. https://doi.org/10.1037/0893-164X.18.3.213

Prado, G., Feaster, D.J., Schwartz, I.A., Pratt, L., Smith, J., & Szapocznik (2004). Religious Involvement, Coping, Social Support and Psychological Distress in HIV-seropositive African American Mothers. *AIDS and Behavior*, *9*(1), 221–235. https://doi.org/10.1023/b:aibe.0000044071.27130.46

Puffer, E. S., Skalski, L. M., & Meade, C. S. (2012). Changes in Religious Coping and Relapse to Drug Use Among Opioid-dependent Patients Following Inpatient Detoxification. *Journal of Religion and Health*, *51*, 1226–1238.

Recovery Dharma. (2019). *Recovery Dharma: How to use Buddhist practices and principles to heal the suffering of addiction* (1st ed.). https://recoverydharma.org/wp-content/uploads/misc-content/Recovery_Dharma-v1.0.pdf

Rich, M.L. (2012). Integrating Shamanic Methodology into the Spirituality of Addiction Recovery Work. *International Journal of Mental Health Addiction*, *10*, 330–353. https://doi.org/10.1007/s11469-011-9341-6

Sim, D. E. K., Hofstetter, C. R., Irvin, V. L., Ayers, J. W., Macera, C. A., Ji, M., & Hovell, M. F. (2013). Do Christian Denominations Exhibit Higher Rates of Alcohol Consumption? A Study of Korean American women in California. *Journal of Religion and Health*, *52*(1), 285–298. https://doi.org/10.1007/s10943-011-9471-y

Tabei, S.Z., Zarei, N, & Joulaei, H. (2016). The Impact of Spirituality on Health. *Shiraz E-Medical Journal*, *17*(6), 1–6. https://doi.org/10.17795/semj39053

Tangenberg, K.M. (2001). Surviving two diseases: Addiction, Recovery, and Spirituality Among Mothers Living with HIV Disease. *Families in Society: The Journal of Contemporary Human Services*, *82*(5), 517–524. https://doi.org/10.1606/1044-3894.174

Tonigan, J. S., Toscova, R., & Miller, W. R. (1996). Meta-analysis of the Literature on Alcoholics Anonymous: Sample and Study Characteristics Moderate Findings. *Journal of Studies on Alcohol*, *57*, 65–72. https://doi.org/10.15288/jsa.1996.57.65

Turner, N. H., O'Dell, K. J., & Weaver, G. D. (1999). Religion and the Recovery of Addicted Women. *Journal of Religion and Health*, *38*, 137148. https://doi.org/10.1023/A:1022978109376

Chapter 35

Spirituality, Health, and Well-Being among Ethnic and Racial Minority Populations

Comfort M. Boye, Ernestina Aidoo, Matilda K. Boye, Declan P. Murphy, Ashnita S. Maxton, Sharon E. Prager, and Jon R. Webb*†

Spirituality plays a crucial role in the health and well-being of ethnic and racial minorities, serving as a foundational element in their coping mechanisms, cultural identity, and community support systems (Douglas et al., 2008; Krause et al., 2018; Kwak, 2022).[1] For many ethnic and racial minority groups, spirituality is deeply intertwined with their cultural heritage, offering a sense of belonging and continuity amidst external pressures of assimilation and marginalization. It provides a framework for understanding life's challenges and adversities, fostering resilience and hope in the face of discrimination and social inequities (Nguyen, 2020). Even during times of psychological distress and other health-related concerns, spirituality is linked to better outcomes (Domanico & Crawford, 2000; Levine et al., 2007). This cultural embeddedness of spirituality not only enhances psychological well-being but also strengthens community bonds, creating networks of support that are vital for navigating the complexities of minority experiences in broader society (Chatters, Mattis, et al., 2011a; Chatters et al., 1989; Hamilton et al., 2016; Nguyen et al., 2016). Although most people consider themselves as spiritual or believe in the divine/deity in one form or another (see Webb, 2021), this is particularly vital for the majority of ethnic and racial minority groups compared to their White counterparts; that is, higher levels of religious participation and higher levels of religious mindedness (i.e., monitoring religious broadcasts, perceiving religious beliefs as important, and seeking spiritual comfort through religion) (Kent et al., 2021; Taylor et al., 1996).

Aim and Structure of This Chapter

This chapter delves into the intricate relationship of spirituality with health and well-being within ethnic and racial minority communities, largely centering on the experiences of Hispanic/Latine American, Black American, and Asian American persons. However, we will reference other ethnic/racial minorities on occasion.[2] This chapter provides a comprehensive examination of spirituality's benefits while addressing potential challenges – among ethnic and racial minorities in the United States.[3] It navigates the nuanced terrain of how spirituality influences the health and wellness of individuals from ethnic and racial minority backgrounds, shedding light on its multifaceted impact on their lives.

* Corresponding Author: cmboye@iu.edu.
† The authors would like to acknowledge Mark E. Mills, MEd for contributions toward the development of this chapter.

DOI: 10.4324/9781003440048-40

Definitions

We define *spirituality* as "the salient, searching pursuit of the transcendently sacred ritualistic, theistic, and/or existential aspects of the human condition" (Webb et al., 2014, p. 974). This definition taps into the fundamental basis of the RiTE model's three-dimensional structure: (1) Ritualistic Spirituality – a structured connection with deity; (2) Theistic Spirituality – a non-structured connection with deity; and (3) Existential Spirituality – a transcendent, yet non-theistic search for meaning and purpose. See Chapters 1 and 44 of this volume for a more detailed discussion of the RiTE model of spirituality.

Well-being is defined as "a state of happiness and contentment, with low levels of distress, overall good physical and mental health and outlook, or good quality of life" (APA, 2015, p. 1154). And, *health* is defined as "a state of complete physical, mental, and social well-being and not merely the absence of disease or infirmity" (World Health Organization, 2025, p. 1).

Method of Review

To evaluate the existing scientific literature concerning the association between spirituality and the health and well-being of ethnic/racial minority populations, we conducted comprehensive searches on PsycINFO and PubMed databases employing the following terms: "'spirit*' AND: (1) 'well-being OR wellbeing OR well being', (2) 'life satisfaction OR satisfaction with life OR quality of life OR Happiness' and (3) 'health' ". The inclusion of "among ethnic/racial minority populations" in all searches aimed to focus the search results. All aspects of health and well-being, such as physical, mental, social, etc., were included. Additionally, we largely limited our resource literature to peer-reviewed articles and edited book chapters as well as looking in the reference sections of articles found. Articles and books of well-known experts in the field of spirituality among ethnic and racial minorities were also reviewed (e.g., Chatters). Finally, other positive psychological virtues (e.g., forgiveness, gratitude, hope) were included in the search.

Understanding Spirituality in Ethnic and Racial Minority Populations

In exploring spirituality within ethnic and racial minority populations, it is imperative to understand the unique dynamics which are shaped by cultural diversity, historical traumas, and communal bonds. Across the globe, nations encompass diverse minority groups (United Nations, 2023), each with its distinct identity and experiences. In the United States, for example, minority communities constitute a significant portion of the population, comprising 41.1% of the total population, with Hispanic/Latine, Black American, and Asian persons constituting 39% (19.1%, 13.6%, and 6.3%, respectively) of the total minority population percentage (i.e., 39% of the aforementioned 41.1%) (United States Census Bureau, 2020).

One defining characteristic of ethnic minority groups in the United States is their inclination toward collectivism, in stark contrast to the predominant individualistic ethos of the White population. This collectivist orientation fosters strong communal ties and a sense of interconnectedness within minority communities. Additionally, these groups often share a collective history of trauma, such as the legacy of slavery and discrimination faced by Black American persons and cultural assimilation confronted by Hispanic/Latine and Asian American persons.

Throughout these shared struggles, religion and spirituality have emerged as foundational pillars of resilience and cultural preservation. The church, in particular, has historically served as a sanctuary for many racial and ethnic minority groups, providing not only a place of worship but also a hub for community organizing, social support, and collective action (Billingsley & Morrison-Rodriguez, 1998; Frazier, 1964). Religion and spirituality offer vital sources of strength and solace, especially in times of adversity. Studies have shown that practices such as prayer, meditation, and communal worship can help alleviate stress, foster a sense of inner peace, and provide a framework for coping with life's challenges (Ahmad et al., 2022; Allen & Smith, 2015; Ochoa et al., 2018). For many individuals within minority communities, faith serves as a guiding light, empowering them to navigate systemic inequalities, confront discrimination, and strive for social justice (Nguyen, 2020).

These historical milestones highlight the profound impact of spirituality on the health and well-being of ethnic and racial minorities, who consistently exhibit higher levels of spiritual engagement (daily spiritual experiences and private religious practices) compared to their White counterparts (Marquine et al., 2015; McCauley et al., 2008). Across various studies, spirituality has been consistently linked to enhanced subjective well-being, increased happiness, improved physical and mental health, and stronger coping mechanisms (Johnstone et al., 2012; Marquine et al., 2015).

Among ethnic and racial minorities living with HIV, for instance, familial influences often outweigh individual considerations, highlighting the communal nature of decision-making within these communities (Delgadillo et al., 2022). This communal approach is also crucial in end-of-life care decisions (Kataoka-Yahiro et al., 2010; Van Dorn et al., 2009). In essence, there is a growing interest in integrating spirituality and religion into treatment options for holistic care (AbdAleati et al., 2016; Fang et al., 2016; Isaac et al., 2016).

At both individual and collective levels, religion and spirituality play multifaceted roles. Individuals may engage in religious practices to affirm their identity within specific ethnic communities (Knott, 2022). Within Black communities, the church serves as not only a spiritual sanctuary but also as a social, cultural, civic, educational, and political institution (Nguyen, 2020). This dynamic institution, when coupled with the steadfast support of family, fosters a profound sense of belonging and fortifies resilience, creating a robust network that empowers individuals to navigate life's challenges with greater confidence and solidarity (Chatters et al., 2018; Nguyen et al., 2019).

Furthermore, church support has been associated with reduced rates of depressive symptoms, serious psychological distress, and anxiety (Chatters et al., 2018). Similarly, religion holds significant sway within Hispanic/Latine communities in the United States, aiding stress-coping during migration, facilitating ethnic community reestablishment, and preserving cultural values and identity (Nabhan-Warren, 2016; Pew Research Center, 2014). In essence, spirituality plays a crucial role in the lives of ethnic and racial minority populations, serving as a source of resilience, cultural identity, and communal solidarity.

Cultural Variations in Spiritual Practices and Health Beliefs

Understanding the diverse cultural variations in spiritual practices and health beliefs is essential for appreciating how Hispanic/Latine American, Black American, and Asian American persons approach health and well-being. Research has consistently demonstrated that Blacks (compared to other racial minorities) are more likely to identify as religious (measured by religious denomination, identification, and service attendance) pointing to the essence of faith in their communities (see Brown et al., 2015). For instance, a systematic review of ethnic minority groups in the United States found that although both patients of African and Hispanic descent facing cancer tend to prefer more aggressive end-of-life treatments and hold fatalistic beliefs (e.g., everything that happens is part of God's plan), African Americans' decisions are linked to their faith-based convictions, specifically, in miracles and God's timing of death (LoPresti et al., 2016).

Moreover, a review by Hong et al. (2018) observed that Blacks who have strong faith in God often exhibit hesitation toward Advanced Care Planning (ACP), fearing that such directives might hasten death. In contrast, increased acculturation among Asian Americans and Latine Americans predicted higher engagement in ACP compared to Blacks, whose primary influence remained their spirituality (Hong et al., 2018). Notably, Black Americans show higher levels of religious participation compared to non-Hispanic whites, irrespective of religious affiliation or socioeconomic status (Chatters et al., 2009). That is, on organizational (e.g., religious service attendance, church activities engagement), non-organizational (e.g., reading religious materials, watching/listening to religious programs, praying), and subjective (e.g., the importance of religion to daily life, taking children to services, self-rated religiosity) levels.

Additionally, the tendency to engage more frequently in private religious practices is particularly more pronounced among African Americans/Blacks, who report higher levels of private religious activities compared to other racial minority groups, as detailed by Delgadillo et al. (2022). The emphasis on private religious engagement among African Americans/Blacks highlights the significant role that personal faith and spirituality play in their lives, potentially reflecting a historical reliance on religion as a source of strength and a coping mechanism in the face of systemic inequalities and social adversities.

Krause et al. (2018) further examined how race/ethnicity influences the relationship between spiritual struggles and health outcomes, introducing the concepts of differential exposure and differential impact hypothesis. Their findings showed that Black American persons experience higher levels of spiritual struggles compared to White and Hispanic counterparts. Despite this, these struggles do not significantly affect general religious practices such as private prayer or church attendance. Interestingly, Black Americans reported fewer symptoms of physical illness, less anxiety, and greater happiness compared to their counterparts. The study also revealed that Black Americans scored significantly higher on the Demonic struggle subscale of the Religious and Spiritual Struggles (RSS) inventory (see Exline et al., 2014), suggesting a stronger belief in the presence of demonic forces, which is often aligned with their affiliation to conservative Christian denominations.

The Intersection of Spirituality and Well-Being among Racial/Ethnic Minorities

In recent years, a growing body of research has honed in on the interplay between spirituality and its profound impact on the health and well-being of ethnic and racial minority populations. To most ethnic and racial minorities, spirituality embodies values, beliefs, and behaviors that align with culture. Scholars have increasingly recognized the significance of spirituality within these communities, delving into how it shapes individuals' lives and exploring ways to integrate spiritual practices into healthcare treatments and interventions (Szaflarski, 2013).

Spirituality and Physical Illness Management

Spirituality and religion often serve as vital coping mechanisms for individuals facing the stress and challenges brought on by physical illnesses (Ahmad et al., 2022). In a qualitative study focusing on Mexican migrant women conducted by Velez et al. (2017), spirituality emerged as a significant factor influencing their decision to seek dental care. Their spirituality and faith fostered a positive outlook on health and encouraged them to replace negative attitudes toward providers and staff with the trust in a higher power to meet their dental care needs. This study highlighted how spirituality acted as a predisposing factor, reinforcing the importance of oral health and motivating these women to prioritize dental care.

Moreover, Kwak (2022) delved into the relationship between spirituality and attitudes toward death among Asian Americans and Pacific Islanders, revealing that heightened levels of spirituality were associated with reduced fear of death within these communities. This underscores the potential of spirituality as a resource for coping with existential concerns and enhancing overall well-being among minority groups. Also, Hong et al. (2018) conducted a systematic review shedding light on the pivotal role of spirituality in shaping engagement in Advanced Care Planning (ACP) among ethnic and racial minorities.

Delgadillo et al. (2022) explored the intersection of spirituality, ethnicity, and health outcomes among racial/ethnic minorities living with HIV. Their study revealed a significant correlation between daily spirituality and various psychosocial factors, including ethnic/minority identity, social support, life satisfaction, and resilience. Notably, Delgadillo et al. (2022) also observed higher engagement in private religious practices among African Americans/Blacks compared to other racial minority groups, indicating the diverse expressions of spirituality within different ethnic communities. This is consistent with studies that have highlighted how spirituality improves emotional health and thereby slowing the progression of HIV (Kremer et al., 2015; Oji et al., 2017).

Spirituality and Mental Health

Racial minorities experience significant psychological distress due to the combined effects of socioeconomic disadvantages and pervasive discrimination, impacting their mental health and overall quality of life (Blankenship et al., 2018; Pitcan et al., 2018; Williams et al., 2008). Research has, however, stressed the importance of spirituality and religious coping strategies during such trying times (Lee et al., 2010). For example, a study by Ochoa and colleagues utilized the Functional Assessment of Chronic Illness Therapy-Spiritual Well-Being (FACIT-Sp) Scale (see Brady et al., 1999), which measures meaning, peace, and faith, to explore the impact of social support and spirituality on the general health perceptions of Hispanic cancer survivors. The findings revealed that overall spirituality was positively correlated with improved mental health outcomes (Ochoa et al., 2018).

Additionally, church-based social support has been associated with a reduced risk of suicidal thoughts and depression (Chatters, Taylor, et al., 2011b; Taylor et al., 2012), providing a crucial protective factor for individuals experiencing mental health challenges. This form of support could encompass a range of activities and interactions within the church community, such as participation in worship services, prayer groups, and community outreach programs, which foster a sense of belonging and connectedness. Engaging in these religious and communal activities can offer emotional comfort, practical assistance, and spiritual guidance, helping individuals to cope with stress and feelings of hopelessness. Furthermore, the moral and ethical teachings of many religious communities often emphasize the value of life and encourage seeking help in times of crisis, thereby contributing to a lower incidence of suicidal ideation among those who are actively involved in church-based social networks.

Contrary to this, African American Catholic women who are religiously affiliated seem to have higher odds of reporting elevated depression symptoms (Scott et al., 2022). Stroope et al. (2022) examined the role of religious group involvement on mental health and self-rated health. While their study revealed lower levels of anxiety and anger for individuals who engaged in group prayers at least once a day, they found religious service attendance to be associated with higher levels of anxiety. Additionally, individuals who received congregational criticism reported higher levels of anxiety and anger. Overall, giving or receiving congregational emotional support was positively associated with self-rated health and mental health functioning.

Spirituality as a Coping Mechanism for Stress and Trauma

Post-traumatic stress disorder and depression are common among migrants and refugees (Lusk & Terrazas, 2015; Lusk et al., 2021). Even those who make it to the United States from Central America and Mexico continue to experience great adversity for several years (Lusk et al., 2021). Migrants experience serial trauma, which occurs on all stages of a migrant journey, including the trauma that occurs in their country of origin that compels them to leave, traumatic experiences endured on the journey, and the adverse experiences migrants face upon arrival at the border (Lusk et al., 2021).

However, studies have identified specific protective factors that are found in the networks and cultures of migrants that serve to maintain the integrity and functioning of individuals who have been in peril (Kirchner & Patiño, 2010). Participant migrants in the Lusk and colleagues' study (2021) reported a constancy of faith in the face of multiple traumas. They prayed together and individually along the journey and reported feelings of solace from engaging in prayer. Furthermore, some migrant participants felt that what was happening to them was in relation to the divine and that their suffering had meaning. They reported that they felt God was accompanying them on their journey. It appears that migrants and refugees enduring traumatic experiences take great strength and comfort in group and community prayer. The ability to mobilize in prayer appears to be a factor in maintaining resilience in the face of adversity, with faith serving as a coping mechanism and a source of meaning amidst the hardship and suffering.

Spirituality also serves as a crucial coping mechanism in countering the impact of stigma by serving as a profound source of solace and resilience for those facing societal stigmatization. For instance, Butler-Barnes et al. (2018) in a sample of 117 African American adolescents in predominantly African American churches observed that their relationship with God was a protective factor against the negative effects of racial stigma beliefs on psychological well-being. Also, for older African American men (50 years and above) living with HIV, stigmatization reinforces the use of spirituality, and the decision to use medication is rooted in spirituality (Miller, 2020). Spirituality also offers a sanctuary where individuals navigate and mitigate the effects of stigma, providing a foundation for emotional strength and a sense of meaning amid challenging circumstances (Himelhoch & Njie-Carr, 2016).

Specifically among racial/ethnic minority elderly individuals, spirituality has been found to play a crucial role in mitigating the effects of disadvantaged economic, social, and health circumstances, which often include high rates of poverty, low levels of education, and poorer health (Chatters et al., 2014). For these elderly populations, spirituality and religious involvement often provide a vital source of hope, meaning, and resilience. Engagement in spiritual practices and participation in religious communities offer emotional and psychological support, helping to counter feelings of isolation and despair from their challenging circumstances. Moreover, spirituality can foster a sense of purpose and belonging, which is particularly important for those who may feel marginalized or disconnected from mainstream society (Lewis et al., 2015). Religious congregations often serve as extended families, providing practical assistance such as meals, transportation, financial aid, and emotional and social support through companionship and a sense of community. The structured support systems within worship communities can also enhance access to healthcare and social services, guiding elderly individuals to resources they might otherwise be unaware of or unable to access. Additionally, the coping strategies derived from spiritual beliefs and practices – such as prayer, meditation, and faith in a higher power – can significantly reduce stress, anxiety, and depression, contributing to better mental health and overall well-being.

Spirituality as a Source of Resilience, Empowerment, and Support

Spirituality serves as a profound source of resilience, empowerment, and support within diverse ethnic communities, including Black, Asian, and Hispanic populations. Among Blacks, the church fosters a strong sense of community and belonging, offering spiritual guidance, emotional sustenance, and practical aid to individuals and families alike (Chatters, Mattis, et al., 2011a; Chatters et al., 2018; Chatters, Taylor, et al., 2011b; Chatters et al., 2002; Chatters et al., 1989). Moreover, the Black Church stands as a beacon of hope and resilience, mobilizing resources and advocating for social justice, equality, and the overall well-being of African American communities (Karl, 2022; Ross-Burnett, 2024). For instance, elderly African Americans, particularly during times of illness, receive assistance, ranging from visitations and help with chores to small financial gifts and transportation services (Morrison, 1991). Additionally, for physically healthy elderly individuals, social support often emanates from smaller, more intimate groups within the church, such as choirs and fellowship gatherings, rather than from the entire congregation (Morrison, 1991). Chatters, Mattis, et al. (2011a), in a study on the use of ministers for serious personal problems, observed that older adults (30 and above) were more likely to contact their clergy for counsel than persons between 18 and 29 years. The study, however, did not report the place of birth nor its role in the results.

Similarly, among Asian Americans, the church plays a vital role in providing support and guidance to immigrants as they navigate the challenges of adapting to a new environment and culture by providing essential information, emotional support, and practical aid crucial for navigating unfamiliar terrain (Ai et al., 2013; Hagan & Ebaugh, 2003).

In Hispanic communities, churches also serve as indispensable sources of support and solidarity, particularly in the form of ethnic congregations. For instance, Derose and Rodriguez (2020) reported that among Latinos, congregations play key roles such as fostering community connections in addition to addressing various social and health-related needs, as well as offering emotional support. Among Hispanic populations, spirituality was significant in promoting resilience and empowerment (López-Cevallos et al., 2021). Additionally, Krause and Hayward (2014), in their work on church-based emotional support, reported that Mexican Americans experience social support within their network in the church, thus a signal of egalitarian communal dynamics. This further indicates that spirituality promotes a collective sense of belonging and mutual aid. They reported that spirituality strengthens personal resilience and coping mechanisms among congregants. Thus, across diverse ethnic groups, spirituality and religious institutions emerge as cornerstones of resilience, empowerment, and support, enriching the lives of individuals and communities alike.

Spirituality, Positive Psychology, Health, and Well-Being

Spirituality and positive psychology are deeply interconnected, as both emphasize the pursuit of meaning, fulfillment, and well-being. Spirituality, which often involves a sense of connection to something greater than oneself, fosters qualities such as compassion, gratitude, and a sense of purpose. These qualities align closely with the goals of positive psychology, which focuses on the strengths and virtues that enable individuals and communities to thrive. For instance, a study by Hong et al. (2024) assessed the roles of purpose in life and ethnic identity as protective factors against suicidal ideation among Asian, Hispanic, and Black American emerging adults who perceived racial discrimination. Their findings revealed that ethnic identity was negatively associated with suicidal ideation, indicating that a strong sense of ethnic identity can lessen suicidal thoughts. Additionally, there was a positive correlation between ethnic identity and intrinsic religiousness. However, for individuals with a weak sense of purpose, racial discrimination was more associated with suicidal ideation.

Ochoa et al. (2018) examined the role of social support and spirituality in the general health perception of Hispanic American cancer survivors. Their findings revealed that while Hispanic Americans reported higher levels of faith, they also indicated lower levels of perceived social support from friends. This was coupled with poorer general health perceptions and mental health as well as higher levels of emotional distress compared to their non-Hispanic White counterparts. This result was, however, nuanced by demographic and medical characteristics in that older survivors, being employed and married, were associated with better outcomes.

There is also a report on the association between ethnic/racial identity and life satisfaction. Specifically, Ajibade et al. (2016), in a study of African Americans, observed a positive association between satisfaction with life and meaning. These associations were partially mediated by high religious commitment (i.e., participation in religious activities). Their findings also showed that spiritual beliefs provide a framework that seeks to empower individuals within minority communities, and also buffers against psychological distress. Captari et al. (2023), in their work on integrating spiritual dimensions in positive psychology for ethnic minorities, reported that spirituality enhances the experience of positive emotions and virtues. They reported spirituality as essential for improving general well-being, thus, greater optimal functioning, reflecting its significance in the context of minority stress and cultural identity. de Rezende-Pinto et al. (2019) described the complexities associated with integrating spirituality and positive psychology and mental health. They argue that while spirituality can promote well-being, it can exacerbate distress, particularly for those who experience spiritual struggle or negative religious coping. Hence, there should be a proper application of spirituality to integrate positive psychological outcomes. Thus, there should be the exploration of culturally sensitive practices within the spirituality-positive psychology association.

Integration of Spirituality into Healthcare

Recent research acknowledges spirituality's profound impact on the health and well-being of ethnic and racial populations (as briefly outlined above), prompting a critical examination of how spirituality can be integrated into healthcare practices. While there have been debates regarding the necessity of this integration (e.g., see Dillard et al., 2021; Isaac et al., 2016;

Kliewer & Saultz, 2006), substantial evidence suggests a positive relationship between spirituality and enhanced mental health resilience and coping abilities among individuals from culturally and linguistically diverse (CALD) backgrounds (Malviya, 2023). Fang et al. (2016), in their synthesis of cultural and spiritual aspects of end-of-life care, underscored the necessity for culturally and spiritually sensitive palliative care. They highlighted the significant impact of spiritual support on the quality of life of terminally ill individuals. In the medical literature, three key arguments have been identified to justify the integration of spirituality into healthcare: (a) the significant role of spirituality in improving overall health, (b) the recognition that patients often grapple with spiritual distress, and (c) spirituality serves as a valuable resource for dealing with sickness (Pujol et al., 2016).

For instance, Szaflarski (2013) highlights a growing interest in understanding the role of spirituality in health outcomes and the development of interventions tailored to ethnic and racial minorities. Building on this, Fang et al. (2016) conducted a comprehensive synthesis of cultural and spiritual aspects of end-of-life care, underscoring the crucial need for culturally sensitive palliative care. Their findings emphasized the significant influence of spiritual support on the quality of life for terminally ill individuals, stressing the importance of incorporating spiritual dimensions into healthcare approaches.

To investigate the suitability of meaning-centered psychotherapy for Chinese immigrants, Leng et al. (2018) observed that the unique needs of this underserved group highlight the importance of culturally tailored interventions. The study emphasized that these needs influence the development of linguistically appropriate services.

Cultural Competence

Cultural competence has been defined to include the awareness and attention to patients' religious and spiritual needs and orientation (Whitley, 2012). In the context of ethnic and racial minorities, cultural competence refers to a set of skills and practices that lead to culturally appropriate services that respect patients' ethnocultural beliefs, values, attitudes, and conventions (Bhui et al., 2007). It enables healthcare providers to deliver services that are considerate and adaptable to the health-related beliefs, practices, and cultural and linguistic needs of a diverse range of patients (Isaac et al., 2016). Cultural competence involves the application of one's awareness to provide equitable and ethical healthcare, recognizing one's cultural perspectives and those of others in a diverse cultural encounter (Garneau & Pepin, 2015). Integrating cultural competency and spirituality in healthcare underscores the recognition that cultural competency encompasses religious and spirituality-based competency. This acknowledgement stems from the understanding that individuals' religious or spiritual orientations permeate their beliefs, values, attitudes, and conventions, influencing their healthcare needs and experiences (Whitley, 2012). Importantly, cultural competence does not necessitate that healthcare providers be affiliated with a particular religion or spiritual belief (Dillard et al., 2021), but to recognize, respect, and honor diverse religious and spiritual belief systems and their role in the provision of compentent healthcare services. And, likewise, that religious and spiritual diversity exists among and within ethnically and racially diverse populations.

Community and Religious Institutions as Health Resources

Many individuals from ethnic and racial minority groups are deeply entrenched in their connections with religious communities, finding that their spiritual needs must be intricately attended to in ways that resonate with their cultural backgrounds (Alcorn et al., 2010; Balboni et al., 2017; Balboni et al., 2013). Within these religious institutions, they often discover not only solace but also invaluable support and guidance (Balboni et al., 2007). These community and religious institutions serve as invaluable health resources, offering not only spiritual guidance but also practical support and a sense of belonging during times of illness and adversity (Balboni et al., 2007).

Despite the reliance on religious institutions for guidance and support, research indicates that a majority of clergy members are inadequately equipped to provide comprehensive spiritual care, particularly in the realm of end-of-life care where medical knowledge is crucial (LeBaron et al., 2015; LeBaron et al., 2016; Sanders et al., 2017). This is nuanced by the scarcity of a comprehensive educational resource for training clergy, specifically on medically related end-of-life care (Abrams et al., 2005; LeBaron et al., 2016; Rodriguez et al., 2011).

Challenges and Barriers to Addressing Spirituality in Minority Health

Understanding spirituality proves challenging due to its multifaceted nature, as highlighted in different definitions and measurement approaches (de Jager Meezenbroek et al., 2012; Garssen et al., 2021; Lun & Bond, 2013). This complexity poses a significant hurdle in effectively gauging the essence of spirituality itself or even particular aspects of it (as the case may be). Many studies tend to narrow their focus, primarily examining church affiliation or attendance as proxies for spirituality. As such, this limited scope predominantly addresses Ritualistic Spirituality, overlooking the broader dimensions of Theistic Spirituality (a non-structured connection with deity) and Existential Spirituality (seeking transcendence and purpose, aside from theism). As a result, a comprehensive understanding of spirituality remains elusive, often constrained by the parameters of measurement tools and definitions of spirituality adopted in any given research endeavor.

The challenge of addressing health within ethnic and racial minority groups is significantly influenced by their deeply rooted spiritual beliefs, shaping their perceptions of illness and treatment. Understanding that the perceived origin of an illness dictates the approach taken to address it becomes increasingly apparent in this context. A notable obstacle arises from the lack of an integrated approach to spirituality within the healthcare system, potentially rendering mental health and well-being services [as well as services related to physical and social health and well-being] less effective or pertinent to the distinct needs of these groups (see Malviya, 2023).

Future Directions and Recommendations

One of the critical challenges in researching the connection between spirituality and health outcomes among racial and ethnic minorities is the absence of standardized measurement instruments that can adequately capture the multidimensional character of spirituality. This is reinforced by the fact that many previous studies use proxy measures, e.g., church attendance or religious affiliation, which mostly capture the ritual aspect of spirituality and ignore its conceptual and existential dimensions. To address this challenge effectively, there is a pressing need for the development and validation of multifaceted, culturally sensitive assessment tools capable of capturing the diverse dimensions of spirituality across various racial and ethnic groups. In this chapter, spirituality is defined expansively to encompass not only religious practices but also unstructured connections with deity, and the transcendent, not necessarily theistic, quest for meaning and purpose in life. It is crucial to employ measures that comprehensively reflect these diverse facets of spirituality to gain a nuanced understanding of its role in shaping health and well-being – whether focused in physical, mental, and/or social contexts. Furthermore, these measures must undergo validation within ethnic and racial minority populations to ensure their applicability, validity, and reliability across different cultural contexts. This process is essential to ascertain that the assessment tools gauge spirituality in a manner consistent with that observed among ethnic and racial minorities, as it does within the White population.

Additionally, the two main tools for exploring cultures – culture-based tools and standardized tools – are both essential for studying the health and spirituality of ethnic and racial minority populations. These techniques will thus be equipped to examine the relationship between spirituality and various health outcomes through diverse channels, thoroughly integrating spirituality into the analysis (Dillard et al., 2021). They also have the advantage of formulating a unique blend of culturally sensitive programs based on groups' needs that include culturally specific medical practices. Similarly, this wide-ranging approach should encompass the impact of spirituality on health in the context of both spiritual and religious minorities.

Currently, studies conducted on this subject have largely focused on the spirituality of large ethnic groups in the United States – Black Americans, Hispanic Americans, and Asian Americans – and the Christian faith. Even when focusing on these minority groups, a significant challenge lies in the broad categorization of Asian, Black, and Hispanic populations within the United States. This approach often overlooks crucial details about the country of origin that may significantly impact spirituality. For example, individuals from diverse Asian countries may have experiences that are unique to them. The inclusion of other faith groups deserves attention too. For example, a Muslim or Sikh might have a community and/or personal practice of spirituality that may interact with their health and well-being in a manner that is specific to their culture irrespective of the country of origin.

Furthermore, and most importantly, we should investigate spirituality as a factor affecting not only the physical, mental, and social health and well-being, but *wholesomeness* of these groups (i.e., how spirituality defines and influences intricately, their being and decision making in both positive and negative ways). These areas could be investigated regarding spiritual beliefs and practices as both protective and resilience factors against concerns related to poor health and well-being, such as depression, anxiety, trauma, post-traumatic depreciation, post-traumatic development, and growth. Also, the research could investigate the downsides of spiritual struggles or conflicts on health and well-being related progress. Moreover, spirituality, cultural identity, and health among religious minority groups can also be assessed. An illustration of this could be the reflection of how spirituality is shaping and being shaped by the acculturation process of immigrants and refugees, which, in turn, influences their health and wellness (Nguyen, 2020).

Carrying out thorough research will require the cooperation of community members, religious leaders, and native practitioners to allow the studies to be culturally aware, respectful, and responsive to these groups' distinctive needs and views. Additionally, the interdisciplinary cooperation between researchers from perspectives such as psychology, public health, anthropology, and religious studies can produce valuable insights and methodologies that may explain the intricate interplay between culture, spirituality, and health/wellness. By widening the scope of research to encompass many different religious minority groups, researchers will be able to see a wider, more comprehensive picture of the different ways in which spirituality can improve health and well-being across numerous cultural settings. This knowledge can be the basis for creating culturally appropriate healthcare practices and interventions that address the specific spiritual and cultural needs of these groups, consequently promoting health equity and improved health outcomes.

Conclusion

Spirituality often serves as a vital resource for coping and resilience, offering psychological and emotional support that can positively influence health outcomes related to physical, mental, and social health and well-being, specifically, among racial/ethnic minorities. However, the measurement of spirituality remains a substantial challenge in this context. The diverse expressions and cultural understandings of spirituality among different racial groups complicate the development of standardized assessment tools. This variability necessitates culturally sensitive and inclusive measurement approaches that can accurately capture the nuances of spirituality in these populations. Addressing this challenge is crucial for advancing our understanding and fostering more effective, holistic healthcare practices that honor the spiritual dimensions of health in ethnic and racial minority communities.

Notes

1 As I (CMB, the first author) reflected on spirituality and its impact on health and well-being, I realized that this was not just a journey of the mind but a pilgrimage of the soul. Each step I took led me deeper into the recesses of my being and the lives of those around me. It began with the simplest of questions, innocuous inquiries about how we are faring in this journey called life. Yet, beneath the surface, these questions held a weighty spiritual significance, tapping into the very essence of our existence. Through moments of trial and tribulation, I came to understand the profound role that my spirituality and faith played as guiding beacons, illuminating the path forward in even the darkest of times. In moments where the compass of my beliefs clashed with the directions offered by others, I struggled to heed their guidance due to the mismatch in our spiritual inclinations. As I navigated these complexities in my role as a counselor, it became abundantly clear that for many of my clients, faith was not just a concept; it was a lifeline, a source of solace and strength in times of turmoil. In seeking counsel, they sought not just advice but a connection, a shared resonance in beliefs that fostered a sense of rapport and understanding beyond words.

2 This chapter focuses on Black, Hispanic, and Asian persons as minorities in the United States due to the larger population sizes, significant socio-political presence, and distinct historical and social contexts that have shaped their unique experiences and challenges. These groups are frequently prioritized in research, policy, and advocacy due to well-documented systemic inequalities and the availability of comprehensive data. However, this focus does not diminish the importance of other ethnic groups, such as Native Americans, Pacific Islanders, and Middle Easterners, among others, who also face significant challenges and require attention for a more inclusive and equitable approach to social justice.

3 There are nuanced differences for ethnic and racial minorities in the United States as compared to other parts of the world. Whilst numerous racial/ethnic minorities in the United States are shaped by centuries of immigration, slavery, and/or colonization, this is not necessarily the case for other parts of the world. For instance, minorities in Europe mostly consist of migrants and refugees whilst minorities in the context of Africa are mostly defined by differences in language, culture, and religion. One theme that cuts across all racial/ethnic minorities, however, is the oppression faced. It is worth noting that as this chapter focuses on minorities in the United States, it may not be generalizable to minorities in other parts of the world.

References

AbdAleati, N. S., Zaharim, N. M., & Mydin, Y. O. (2016). Religiousness and Mental Health: Systematic Review Study. *Journal of Religion and Health*, *55*(6), 1929–1937. https://doi.org/10.1007/s10943-014-9896-1

Abrams, D., Albury, S., Crandall, L., Doka, K. J., & Harris, R. (2005). The Florida Clergy End-of-Life Education Enhancement Project: A description and evaluation. *American Journal of Hospice and Palliative Care*, *22*(3), 181–187. https://doi.org/10.1177/104990910502200306

Ahmad, A., Khan, M. U., & Aslani, P. (2022). The role of religion, spirituality and fasting in coping with diabetes among Indian migrants in Australia: A qualitative exploratory study. *Journal of Religion and Health*, *61*(3), 1994–2017. https://doi.org/10.1007/s10943-021-01438-9

Ai, A. L., Huang, B., Bjorck, J., & Appel, H. B. (2013). Religious attendance and major depression among Asian Americans from a national database: The mediation of social support. *Psychology of Religion and Spirituality*, *5*(2), 78–89. https://doi.org/10.1037/a0030625

Ajibade, A., Hook, J. N., Utsey, S. O., Davis, D. E., & Van Tongeren, D. R. (2016). Racial/ethnic identity, religious commitment, and well-being in African Americans. *Journal of Black Psychology*, *42*(3), 244–258. https://doi.org/10.1177/0095798414568115

Alcorn, S. R., Balboni, M. J., Prigerson, H. G., Reynolds, A., Phelps, A. C., Wright, A. A., Block, S. D., Peteet, J. R., Kachnic, L. A., & Balboni, T. A. (2010). "If God wanted me yesterday, I wouldn't be here today": religious and spiritual themes in patients' experiences of advanced cancer. *Journal of Palliative Medicine*, *13*(5), 581–588. https://doi.org/10.1089/jpm.2009.0343

Allen, G. E. K., & Smith, T. B. (2015). Collectivistic coping strategies for distress among Polynesian Americans. *Psychological Services*, *12*(3), 322–329. https://doi.org/10.1037/ser0000039

APA (American Psychological Association) (2015). *APA dictionary of psychology* (Second ed.). Washington, DC: Author.

Balboni, M. J., Sullivan, A., Enzinger, A. C., Smith, P. T., Mitchell, C., Peteet, J. R., Tulsky, J. A., VanderWeele, T., & Balboni, T. A. (2017). U.S. Clergy Religious Values and Relationships to End-of-Life Discussions and Care. *Journal of Pain Symptom Management*, *53*(6), 999–1009. https://doi.org/10.1016/j.jpainsymman.2016.12.346

Balboni, T. A., Balboni, M., Enzinger, A. C., Gallivan, K., Paulk, M. E., Wright, A., Steinhauser, K., VanderWeele, T. J., & Prigerson, H. G. (2013). Provision of spiritual support to patients with advanced cancer by religious communities and associations with medical care at the end of life. *JAMA Internal Medicine*, *173*(12), 1109–1117. https://doi.org/10.1001/jamainternmed.2013.903

Balboni, T. A., Vanderwerker, L. C., Block, S. D., Paulk, M. E., Lathan, C. S., Peteet, J. R., & Prigerson, H. G. (2007). Religiousness and Spiritual Support Among Advanced Cancer Patients and Associations With End-of-Life Treatment Preferences and Quality of Life. *Journal of Clinical Oncology*, *25*(5), 555–560. https://doi.org/10.1200/jco.2006.07.9046

Bhui, K., Warfa, N., Edonya, P., McKenzie, K., & Bhugra, D. (2007). Cultural competence in mental health care: A review of model evaluations. *BMC Health Services Research*, *7*(1), 15–15. https://doi.org/10.1186/1472-6963-7-15

Billingsley, A., & Morrison-Rodriguez, B. (1998). The Black family in the 21st century and the church as an action system: A macro perspective. *Journal of Human Behavior in the Social Environment*, *1*(2–3), 31–47.

Blankenship, K. M., del Rio Gonzalez, A. M., Keene, D. E., Groves, A. K., & Rosenberg, A. P. (2018). Mass incarceration, race inequality, and health: Expanding concepts and assessing impacts on well-being. *Social Science & Medicine*, *215*, 45–52. https://doi.org/10.1016/j.socscimed.2018.08.042

Brady, M. J., Peterman, A. H., Fitchett, G., Mo, M., & Cella, D. (1999). A case for including spirituality in quality of life measurement in oncology. *Psycho-Oncology*, *8*(5), 417–428. https://doi.org/10.1002/(SICI)1099-1611(199909/10)8:5<417::AID-PON398>3.0.CO;2-4

Brown, R. K., Taylor, R. J., & Chatters, L. M. (2015). Race/ethnic and social-demographic correlates of religious non-involvement in America: Findings from three national surveys. *Journal of Black Studies*, *46*(4), 335–362. https://doi.org/10.1177/0021934715573168

Butler-Barnes, S. T., Martin, P. P., Hope, E. C., Copeland-Linder, N., & Scott, M. L. (2018). Religiosity and Coping: Racial Stigma and Psychological Well-Being among African American Girls. *Journal of Religion and Health*, *57*(5), 1980–1995. https://doi.org/10.1007/s10943-018-0644-9

Captari, L. E., Sandage, S. J., Vandiver, R. A., Jankowski, P. J., & Hook, J. N. (2023). Integrating positive psychology, religion/spirituality, and a virtue focus within culturally responsive mental healthcare. In *Handbook of positive psychology, religion, and spirituality*. (pp. 413–428). Springer Nature Switzerland AG. https://doi.org/10.1007/978-3-031-10274-5_26

Chatters, L. M., Mattis, J. S., Woodward, A. T., Taylor, R. J., Neighbors, H. W., & Grayman, N. A. (2011a). Use of ministers for a serious personal problem among African Americans: Findings from the National Survey of American Life. *American Journal of Orthopsychiatry*, *81*(1), 118–127. https://doi.org/10.1111/j.1939-0025.2010.01079.x

Chatters, L. M., Nguyen, A. W., & Taylor, R. J. (2014). Religion and spirituality among older African Americans, Asians, and Hispanics. In K. E. Whitfield, T. A. Baker, C. M. Abdou, J. L. Angel, L. A. Chadiha, K. Gerst-Emerson, J. S. Jackson, K. S. Markides, P. A. Rozario, & R. J. Thorpe, Jr. (Eds.), *Handbook of minority aging*. (pp. 47–64). Springer Publishing Company.

Chatters, L. M., Nguyen, A. W., Taylor, R. J., & Hope, M. O. (2018). Church and family support networks and depressive symptoms among African Americans: Findings from The National Survey of American Life. *Journal of Community Psychology*, *46*(4), 403–417. https://doi.org/10.1002/jcop.21947

Chatters, L. M., Taylor, R. J., Bullard, K. M., & Jackson, J. S. (2009). Race and ethnic differences in religious involvement: African Americans, Caribbean blacks and non-Hispanic whites. *Ethnic and Racial Studies*, *32*(7), 1143–1163. https://doi.org/10.1080/01419870802334531

Chatters, L. M., Taylor, R. J., Lincoln, K. D., Nguyen, A., & Joe, S. (2011b). Church-based social support and suicidality among African Americans and Black Caribbeans. *Archives of Suicide Research*, *15*(4), 337–353. https://doi.org/10.1080/13811118.2011.615703

Chatters, L. M., Taylor, R. J., Lincoln, K. D., & Schroepfer, T. (2002). Patterns of informal support from family and church members among African Americans. *Journal of Black Studies*, *33*(1), 66–85. https://doi.org/10.1177/002193470203300104

Chatters, L. M., Taylor, R. J., & Neighbors, H. W. (1989). Size of informal helper network mobilized during a serious personal problem among Black Americans. *Journal of Marriage and the Family*, *51*(3), 667–676. https://doi.org/10.2307/352166

de Jager Meezenbroek, E., Garssen, B., van den Berg, M., Tuytel, G., van Dierendonck, D., Visser, A., & Schaufeli, W. B. (2012). Measuring Spirituality as a Universal Human Experience: Development of the Spiritual Attitude and Involvement List (SAIL). *Journal of Psychosocial Oncology*, *30*(2), 141–167. https://doi.org/10.1080/07347332.2011.651258

de Rezende-Pinto, A., Schumann, C.S.C., & Moreira-Almeida, A. (2019). Spirituality, Religiousness and Mental Health: Scientific Evidence. In Lucchetti, G., Prieto Peres, M.F., Damiano, R.F. (Eds.) *Spirituality, Religiousness and Health: From Research to Clinical Practice*. (pp. 69–86). Springer. https://doi.org/10.1007/978-3-030-21221-6_5

Delgadillo, J. D., Campbell, L. M., Marquine, M. J., Heaton, A., Rooney, A. S., Umlauf, A., Jeste, D. V., Moore, D. J., & Moore, R. C. (2022). Higher religiosity and spirituality are associated with ethnic group membership among middle-aged and older adults living with HIV. *HIV Research & Clinical Practice*, *23*(1), 91–98. https://doi.org/10.1080/25787489.2022.2113962

Derose, K. P., & Rodriguez, C. (2020). A Systematic Review of Church-Based Health Interventions Among Latinos. *Journal of Immigrant and Minority Health*, *22*(4), 795–815. https://doi.org/10.1007/s10903-019-00941-2

Dillard, V., Moss, J., Padgett, N., Tan, X., & Kennedy, A. B. (2021). Attitudes, beliefs and behaviors of religiosity, spirituality, and cultural competence in the medical profession: A cross-sectional survey study. *PLoS One*, *16*(6), e0252750. https://doi.org/10.1371/journal.pone.0252750

Domanico, R., & Crawford, I. (2000). Psychological distress among HIV-impacted African-American and Latino males. *Journal of Prevention & Intervention in the Community*, *19*(1), 55–78. https://doi.org/10.1300/J005v19n01_04

Douglas, A. N., Jimenez, S., Lin, H.-J., & Frisman, L. K. (2008). Ethnic differences in the effects of spiritual well-being on long-term psychological and behavioral outcomes within a sample of homeless women. *Cultural Diversity and Ethnic Minority Psychology*, *14*(4), 344–352. https://doi.org/10.1037/1099-9809.14.4.344

Exline, J. J., Pargament, K. I., Grubbs, J. B., & Yali, A. M. (2014). The Religious and Spiritual Struggles Scale: Development and initial validation. *Psychology of Religion and Spirituality*, *6*(3), 208–222. https://doi.org/10.1037/a0036465

Fang, M. L., Sixsmith, J., Sinclair, S., & Horst, G. (2016). A knowledge synthesis of culturally- and spiritually-sensitive end-of-life care: findings from a scoping review. *BMC Geriatric*, *16*, 107. https://doi.org/10.1186/s12877-016-0282-6

Frazier, E. F. (1964). *The Negro Church in America* (New York: Schocken).

Garneau, A. B., & Pepin, J. (2015). Cultural Competence: A Constructivist Definition. *Journal of Transcultural Nursing*, *26*(1), 9–15. https://doi.org/10.1177/1043659614541294

Garssen, B., Visser, A., & Pool, G. (2021). Does Spirituality or Religion Positively Affect Mental Health? Meta-analysis of Longitudinal Studies. *The International Journal for the Psychology of Religion*, *31*(1), 4–20. https://doi.org/10.1080/10508619.2020.1729570

Hagan, J. M., & Ebaugh, H. R. F. (2003). Calling upon the Sacred: Migrants' Use of Religion in the Migration Process. *International Migration Review*, *37*, 1145–1162.

Hamilton, J. B., Worthy, V. C., Kurtz, M. J., Cudjoe, J., & Johnstone, P. A. (2016). Using religious songs as an integrative and complementary therapy for the management of psychological symptoms among African American cancer survivors. *Cancer Nursing*, *39*(6), 488–494. https://doi.org/10.1097/NCC.0000000000000335

Himelhoch, S., & Njie-Carr, V. (2016). "God loves me no matter how I am": a phenomenological analysis of the religious and spiritual experiences of HIV-infected African-American women with depression. *Mental health, religion & culture*, *19*(2), 178–191. https://doi.org/10.1080/13674676.2016.1138934

Hong, J. H., Talavera, D. C., Odafe, M. O., Barr, C. D., & Walker, R. L. (2024). Does purpose in life or ethnic identity moderate the association for racial discrimination and suicide ideation in racial/ethnic minority emerging adults? *Cultural Diversity and Ethnic Minority Psychology*, *30*(1), 1–10. https://doi.org/10.1037/cdp0000245

Hong, M., Yi, E.-H., Johnson, K. J., & Adamek, M. E. (2018). Facilitators and barriers for advance care planning among ethnic and racial minorities in the US: A systematic review of the current literature. *Journal of Immigrant and Minority Health*, *20*(5), 1277–1287. https://doi.org/10.1007/s10903-017-0670-9

Isaac, K. S., Hay, J. L., & Lubetkin, E. I. (2016). Incorporating Spirituality in Primary Care. *Journal of Religion and Health*, *55*(3), 1065–1077. https://doi.org/10.1007/s10943-016-0190-2

Johnstone, B., Yoon, D. P., Cohen, D., Schopp, L. H., McCormack, G., Campbell, J., & Smith, M. (2012). Relationships among spirituality, religious practices, personality factors, and health for five different faith traditions. *Journal of Religion and Health*, *51*, 1017–1041. https://doi.org/10.1007/s10943-012-9615-8

Karl, T. (2022). *Black youths' lived experience with social justice activism within faith based organizations*. Unpublished doctoral dissertation, Capella University.

Kataoka-Yahiro, M. R., Conde, F. A., Wong, R. S., Page, V., & Peller, B. (2010). Advance care planning among Asian Americans and Native Hawaiians receiving haemodialysis. *International Journal of Palliative Nursing*, *16*(1), 32–40. https://doi.org/10.12968/ijpn.2010.16.1.46181

Kent, B. V., Davidson, J. C., Zhang, Y., Pargament, K. I., VanderWeele, T. J., Koenig, H. G., Underwood, L. G., Krause, N., Kanaya, A. M., Tworoger, S. S., Schachter, A. B., Cole, S. A., O'Leary, M., Cozier, Y. C., Daviglus, M. L., Giachello, A. L., Zacher, T., Palmer, J. R., & Shields, A. E. (2021). Religion and spirituality among American Indian, South Asian, Black, Hispanic/Latina, and white women in the study on stress, spirituality, and health. *Journal for the Scientific Study of Religion*, *60*(1), 198–215. https://doi.org/10.1111/jssr.12695

Kirchner, T., & Patiño, C. (2010). Stress and depression in Latin American immigrants: The mediating role of religiosity. *European Psychiatry*, *25*(8), 479–484. https://doi.org/10.1016/j.eurpsy.2010.04.003

Kliewer, S. P., & Saultz, J. (2006). *Healthcare and Spirituality* (1st ed.). CRC Press. https://doi.org/10.1201/9781315379692

Knott, K. (2022). Religion and identity, and the study of ethnic minority religions in Britain. In V. C. Hayes (Ed.), *Identity issues and world religions: Selected proceedings of the fifteenth congress of the International Association for the History of Religions* (Australian Association for the Study of Religions Book Series, Vol. 9-9, pp. 167–175). Australian Association for the Study of Religions. (1986). https://openjournals.library.sydney.edu.au/AASR/issue/view/1149

Krause, N., & Hayward, R. D. (2014). Work at Church and Church-Based Emotional Support Among Older Whites, Blacks, and Mexican Americans. *Journal of Religion, Spirituality & Aging*, *26*(1), 22–40. https://doi.org/10.1080/15528030.2013.854727

Krause, N., Pargament, K. I., Hill, P. C., & Ironson, G. (2018). Assessing the role of race/ethnicity in the relationships among spiritual struggles, health, and well-being. *American Journal of Orthopsychiatry*, *88*(2), 132–141. https://doi.org/10.1037/ort0000255

Kremer, H., Ironson, G., Kaplan, L., Stuetzele, R., Baker, N., & Fletcher, M. A. (2015). Spiritual coping predicts CD4-cell preservation and undetectable viral load over four years. *AIDS Care*, *27*(1), 71–79. https://doi.org/10.1080/09540121.2014.952220

Kwak, J. J. (2022). Death attitudes among older Asian and Pacific Islander Americans: The role of religiosity, spirituality, and psychosocial health factors. *Death Studies*, *46*(3), 648–657. https://doi.org/10.1080/07481187.2020.1752853

LeBaron, V. T., Cooke, A., Resmini, J., Garinther, A., Chow, V., Quiñones, R., Noveroske, S., Baccari, A., Smith, P. T., Peteet, J., Balboni, T. A., & Balboni, M. J. (2015). Clergy Views on a Good Versus a Poor Death: Ministry to the Terminally Ill. *Journal of Palliative Medicine*, *18*(12), 1000–1007. https://doi.org/10.1089/jpm.2015.0176

LeBaron, V. T., Smith, P. T., Quiñones, R., Nibecker, C., Sanders, J. J., Timms, R., Shields, A. E., Balboni, T. A., & Balboni, M. J. (2016). How Community Clergy Provide Spiritual Care: Toward a Conceptual Framework for Clergy End-of-Life Education. *Journal of Pain Symptom Management*, *51*(4), 673–681. https://doi.org/10.1016/j.jpainsymman.2015.11.016

Lee, C. C., Czaja, S. J., & Schulz, R. (2010). The moderating influence of demographic characteristics, social support, and religious coping on the effectiveness of a multicomponent psychosocial caregiver intervention, in three racial ethnic groups. *The Journals of Gerontology: Series B: Psychological Sciences and Social Sciences*, *65B*(2), 185–194. https://doi.org/10.1093/geronb/gbp131

Leng, J., Lui, F., Chen, A., Huang, X., Breitbart, W., & Gany, F. (2018). Adapting meaning-centered psychotherapy in advanced cancer for the Chinese immigrant population. *Journal of Immigrant and Minority Health*, *20*(3), 680–686. https://doi.org/10.1007/s10903-017-0591-7

Levine, E. G., Yoo, G., Aviv, C., Ewing, C., & Au, A. (2007). Ethnicity and spirituality in breast cancer survivors. *Journal of Cancer Survivorship*, *1*(3), 212–225. https://doi.org/10.1007/s11764-007-0024-z

Lewis, T. T., Cogburn, C. D., & Williams, D. R. (2015). Self-reported experiences of discrimination and health: Scientific advances, ongoing controversies, and emerging issues. *Annual Review of Clinical Psychology*, *11*, 407–440. https://doi.org/10.1146/annurev-clinpsy-032814-112728

López-Cevallos, D. F., Flórez, K. R., & Derose, K. P. (2021). Examining the association between religiosity and medical mistrust among churchgoing Latinos in Long Beach, CA. *Translational Behavioral Medicine*, *11*(1), 114–121. https://doi.org/10.1093/tbm/ibz151

LoPresti, M. A., Dement, F., & Gold, H. T. (2016). End-of-life care for people with cancer from ethnic minority groups: A systematic review. *American Journal of Hospice and Palliative Medicine*, *33*(3), 291–305. https://doi.org/10.1177/1049909114565658

Lun, V. M.-C., & Bond, M. H. (2013). Examining the relation of religion and spirituality to subjective well-being across national cultures. *Psychology of Religion and Spirituality*, *5*(4), 304–315. https://doi.org/10.1037/a0033641

Lusk, M., & Terrazas, S. (2015). Secondary Trauma Among Caregivers Who Work With Mexican and Central American Refugees. *Hispanic Journal of Behavioral Sciences*, *37*(2), 257–273. https://doi.org/10.1177/0739986315578842

Lusk, M., Terrazas, S., Caro, J., Chaparro, P., & Puga Antúnez, D. (2021). Resilience, faith, and social supports among migrants and refugees from Central America and Mexico. *Journal of Spirituality in Mental Health*, *23*(1), 1–22. https://doi.org/10.1080/19349637.2019.1620668

Malviya, S. (2023). The Need for Integration of Religion and Spirituality into the Mental Health Care of Culturally and Linguistically Diverse Populations in Australia: A Rapid Review. *Journal of Religion and Health*, *62*(4), 2272–2296. https://doi.org/10.1007/s10943-023-01761-3

Marquine, M. J., Maldonado, Y., Zlatar, Z., Moore, R. C., Martin, A. S., Palmer, B. W., & Jeste, D. V. (2015). Differences in life satisfaction among older community-dwelling Hispanics and non-Hispanic Whites. *Aging & Mental Health*, *19*(11), 978–988. https://doi.org/10.1080/13607863.2014.971706

McCauley, J., Tarpley, M. J., Haaz, S., & Bartlett, S. J. (2008). Daily spiritual experiences of older adults with and without arthritis and the relationship to health outcomes. *Arthritis Care & Research: Official Journal of the American College of Rheumatology*, *59*(1), 122–128. https://doi.org/10.1002/art.23246

Miller, W. L., Jr. (2020). Experiences of stigma and spirituality of older black men living with HIV. *Journal of Social Service Research*, *46*(3), 427–438. https://doi.org/10.1080/01488376.2019.1582451

Morrison, J. D. (1991). The Black Church as a Support System for Black Elderly. *Journal of Gerontological Social Work*, *17*(1-2), 105–120. https://doi.org/10.1300/J083v17n01_09

Nabhan-Warren, K. (2016). Hispanics and religion in America. *In Oxford Research Encyclopedia of Religion*. https://doi.org/10.1093/acrefore/9780199340378.013.79

Nguyen, A. W. (2020). Religion and Mental Health in Racial and Ethnic Minority Populations: A Review of the Literature. *Innovation in Aging*, *4*(5), igaa035. https://doi.org/10.1093/geroni/igaa035

Nguyen, A. W., Chatters, L. M., & Taylor, R. J. (2016). African American extended family and church-based social network typologies. *Family Relations: An Interdisciplinary Journal of Applied Family Studies*, *65*(5), 701–715. https://doi.org/10.1111/fare.12218

Nguyen, A. W., Taylor, R. J., Chatters, L. M., & Hope, M. O. (2019). Church support networks of African Americans: The impact of gender and religious involvement. *Journal of Community Psychology*, *47*(5), 1043–1063. https://doi.org/10.1002/jcop.22171

Ochoa, C. Y., Haardörfer, R., Escoffery, C., Stein, K., & Alcaraz, K. I. (2018). Examining the role of social support and spirituality on the general health perceptions of Hispanic cancer survivors. *Psycho-Oncology*, *27*(9), 2189–2197. https://doi.org/10.1002/pon.4795

Oji, V. U., Hung, L. C., Abbasgholizadeh, R., Terrell Hamilton, F., Essien, E. J., & Nwulia, E. (2017). Spiritual care may impact mental health and medication adherence in HIV+ populations. *HIV AIDS (Auckl)*, *9*, 101–109. https://doi.org/10.2147/hiv.S126309

Pew Research Center. (2014). The shifting religious identity of Latinos in the United States. Retrieved November 20, 2023 from https://www.pewresearch.org/religion/2014/05/07/the-shifting-religious-identity-of-latinos-in-the-united-states/

Pitcan, M., Park-Taylor, J., & Hayslett, J. (2018). Black men and racial microaggressions at work. *The Career Development Quarterly*, *66*(4), 300–314. https://doi.org/10.1002/cdq.12152

Pujol, N., Jobin, G., & Beloucif, S. (2016). 'Spiritual care is not the hospital's business': a qualitative study on the perspectives of patients about the integration of spirituality in healthcare settings. *Journal of Medical Ethics*, *42*(11), 733–737. https://doi.org/10.1136/medethics-2016-103565

Rodriguez, E. G. A. J., Culbertson, T., & Grant, W. (2011). An educational program for spiritual care providers on end of life care in the critical care setting. *Journal of Interprofessional Care*, *25*(5), 375–377. https://doi.org/10.3109/13561820.2011.573104

Ross-Burnett, C. (2024). *Somebody ought to say something: The role of the church in facilitating discussion about race, racism, and diversity, equity, and inclusion efforts*. Unpublished doctoral dissertation, University of Southern California.

Sanders, J. J., Chow, V., Enzinger, A. C., Lam, T. C., Smith, P. T., Quiñones, R., Baccari, A., Philbrick, S., White-Hammond, G., Peteet, J., Balboni, T. A., & Balboni, M. J. (2017). Seeking and Accepting: U.S. Clergy Theological and Moral Perspectives Informing Decision Making at the End of Life. *Journal of Palliative Medicine*, *20*(10), 1059–1067. https://doi.org/10.1089/jpm.2016.0545

Scott, M. J., Robbins, P. A., Conde, E., & Bentley-Edwards, K. L. (2022). Depression in the african american christian community: Examining denominational and gender differences. *Journal of Religion and Health*. https://doi.org/10.1007/s10943-022-01528-2

Stroope, S., Kent, B. V., Zhang, Y., Spiegelman, D., Kandula, N. R., Schachter, A. B., Kanaya, A., & Shields, A. E. (2022). Mental health and self-rated health among U.S. South Asians: the role of religious group involvement. *Ethnicity & health*, *27*(2), 388–406. https://doi.org/10.1080/13557858.2019.1661358

Szaflarski, M. (2013). Spirituality and religion among HIV-infected individuals. *Current HIV/AIDS Reports*, *10*(4), 324–332. https://doi.org/10.1007/s11904-013-0175-7

Taylor, R. J., Chatters, L. M., & Abelson, J. M. (2012). Religious involvement and DSM-IV 12-month and lifetime major depressive disorder among African Americans. *Journal of Nervous and Mental Disease*, *200*(10), 856–862. https://doi.org/10.1097/NMD.0b013e31826b6d65

Taylor, R. J., Chatters, L. M., Jayakody, R., & Levin, J. S. (1996). Black and White differences in religious participation: A multisample comparison. *Journal for the Scientific Study of Religion*, *35*(4), 403–410. https://doi.org/10.2307/1386415

United Nations. (2023). Fight Racism. Retrieved 11/13/2023 from https://www.un.org/en/fight-racism/vulnerable-groups/minorities

United States Census Bureau. (2020). QuickFacts United States. Retrieved 5/20/2024 from https://www.census.gov/quickfacts/fact/table/US/POP010220#POP010220

Van Dorn, R. A., Swanson, J. W., & Swartz, M. S. (2009). Preferences for psychiatric advance directives among Latinos: Views on advance care planning for mental health. *Psychiatric Services*, *60*(10), 1383–1385. https://doi.org/10.1176/appi.ps.60.10.1383

Velez, D., Palomo-Zerfas, A., Nunez-Alvarez, A., Ayala, G. X., & Finlayson, T. L. (2017). Facilitators and Barriers to Dental Care Among Mexican Migrant Women and Their Families in North San Diego County. *Journal of Immigrant and Minority Health*, *19*(5), 1216–1226. https://doi.org/10.1007/s10903-016-0467-2

Webb, J. R. (2021). *Understanding forgiveness and addiction: Theory, research, and clinical application*. Routledge. https://doi.org/10.4324/9780429200274

Webb, J. R., Toussaint, L., & Dula, C. S. (2014). Ritualistic, theistic, and existential spirituality: Initial psychometric qualities of the RiTE measure of spirituality. *Journal of Religion and Health*, *53*, 972–985. https://doi.org/10.1007/s10943-013-9697-y

Whitley, R. (2012). Religious competence as cultural competence. *Transcultural Psychiatry*, *49*(2), 245–260. https://doi.org/10.1177/1363461512439088

Williams, D. R., Neighbors, H. W., & Jackson, J. S. (2008). Racial/ethnic discrimination and health: Findings from community studies. *American Journal of Public Health*, *98*(Suppl 1), S29–S37. https://doi.org/10.2105/AJPH.98.Supplement_1.S29

World Health Organization. (2025). *Constitution of the World Health Organization*. Author. Retrieved April 29, 2025, from https://www.who.int/about/governance/constitution

Chapter 36

Spirituality, Health, and Well-Being among Sexual and Gender Minority Populations

Mark A. Yarhouse, Janet B. Dean, Stephen P. Stratton, and David A. O'Connor*

Introduction and Definitions

A sexual minority is a person who experiences same-sex attraction independent of whether they engage in sexual behavior or elect to use a public sexual identity label (e.g., gay, lesbian, bisexual) (Diamond, 2008, p. 14). A gender minority or gender diverse person is someone who experiences a gender identity that does not align with their biological markers, such as chromosomes, gonads, and genitalia.

Sexual minorities report experiences with various milestone events in the formation of their sexual identity (e.g., gay, lesbian, bisexual). These milestone events include first awareness of one's same-sex sexuality, first disclosure of one's identity, first sexual behavior, the use of a private or public sexual identity label, and so on (Yarhouse, Dean, Stratton & Lastoria, 2018). It has been suggested that sexual minorities who identify with a religious faith tradition may also experience additional milestone events having to do with negotiating what they believe about sexuality, sexual behavior, and/or gender identity and expression in light of the religious faith community in which they were raised or are now a part of (Yarhouse & Zaporozhets, 2019).

Gender minorities do not report the same kinds of milestone events, although they may experience a discordant gender identity at an early age or at a later age. In the U.S. Transgender Survey of over 28,000 transgender adults (James et al., 2016), 60% of adults recalled first experiencing their gender identity prior to puberty, while 40% reported experiencing their gender identity as they currently do sometime after puberty. Gender minorities, like sexual minorities, also often navigate religious doctrinal positions that may reflect norms for sexuality and gender. This brings us to our understanding of religion and spirituality (R/S).

In our previous work in which we studied the experiences of Christian sexual minorities (Yarhouse et al., 2018), we defined spirituality as "personal, private faith" in recognition that some people "may not always care to affiliate with an institution or a structure" (p. 18). We also indicated that spirituality "tends to include our thoughts about our relationship with God, our sense of purpose, and the ways in which we make sense of our existence" (p. 31).

This definition is broader and more generic than the RiTE multidimensional model/definition of spirituality with its emphasis on (1) Ritualistic Spirituality, (2) Theistic Spirituality, and (3) Existential Spirituality (see Chapters 1 and 44 of this volume). It is broader than something more structured or ritualistic, which we tend to associate with religiousness (Ritualistic Spirituality) and may not encompass relation to a deity (Theistic Spirituality) (Webb, 2021, pp. 61–62). In some regards, our approach to spirituality probably best reflects

* Corresponding Author: mark.yarhouse@wheaton.edu.

DOI: 10.4324/9781003440048-41

what the RiTE model defines as Existential Spirituality with the focus on non-theistic search for meaning and purpose.

The aspects of spirituality on which we tend to focus are in contrast to religiousness, which tends to be more focused upon attendance at religious services (e.g., corporate worship or prayer services) and personal practices (e.g., prayer, fasting). The first two subscales of the Duke University Religion Index (DUREL; Koenig & Bussing, 2010) capture this kind of religiousness. However, the third subscale, called intrinsic religiosity, gets at the personal significance of spirituality (i.e., affecting all aspects of one's life), referring to an individual's pursuit of their faith as an end in itself.[1] While the DUREL was designed to assess Western religions (e.g., Christianity, Judaism, and Islam), its authors suggest it could be used in Eastern religious traditions (e.g., Hinduism or Buddhism) with some changes in wording (Koenig & Bussing, 2010). While we consistently use the DUREL (Koenig & Bussing, 2010) in our surveys, we also have asked and measured spirituality with the definition, "spirituality is believing that the reason for existence or the purpose of life at its core is a response to or a relationship with a transcendent being, higher power, or God."

Even so, for many sexual and gender minorities (SGMs) who identify as Christians, forcing a distinction between spirituality and religiousness may be problematic. In our large national studies, these two are always moderately related, with correlation coefficients ranging from .31 to .70 ($p < .001$; Dean, Stratton, Yarhouse, & Lastoria, 2011; Yarhouse et al., 2018; authors' files[2]). While spirituality is typically understood as "an internal mystical process and a source of connectedness to self and others" (Bauer & Johnson, 2019, p. 32) and religiousness as the external component of organized, communal beliefs and practices, many forms of spirituality have practices tethered to corresponding religious concepts shared by those with that particular set of religious beliefs (Westerink, 2012). In other words, as those individuals practice their faith together, they are likely to endorse some degree of religiousness in addition to their spirituality, particularly within Christianity.

Theory and Research

Numerous reviews and meta-analyses have provided evidence for the benefits of R/S for people in general (Lefevor et al., 2023). Religious faith can provide rituals or ceremonies for navigating difficult life circumstances, such as loss and grief. It can provide social connections and belongings. It can provide a meaning-making structure. It can encourage practices that are positive for well-being (e.g., forgiveness) and discourage practices that may be detrimental to well-being (e.g., substance abuse). However, there are times in which people experience religious and spiritual struggles that can lead to reduced psychological health and well-being (LeFevor et al., 2023; Paulez et al., 2023; Exline et al., 2021), and there are groups that may be at greater risk for a mixed experience (both mental health promoting and mental health deteriorating), such as those who are highly religious or spiritual (LeFevor et al., 2023; see also Wilt, Pargament, Exline, Barrera, & Teng, 2019). SGMs, as a group, appear more likely to have mixed experiences with R/S.

The mixed experiences reported by SGMs appear to be related to norms for sexuality, sexual behavior, gender identity, and gender expressions within major world religions. Major world religions reflect various understandings of sexuality and gender. However, some of the largest and most influential world religions, such as Christianity, Islam, and Judaism, have historically anchored their teachings in stories of creation. In these accounts, God created male and female, and it is the complimentary male/female relationship (i.e., the covenant of marriage) that lays the foundation for morally permissible sexual intimacy (Yarhouse, 2015). The adoption of cross-gender or other gender identities apart from those that correspond with one's biological markers can raise concerns within conventionally religious communities.

This theological foundation informs doctrinal positions that have often been at odds with the emergence of the mainstream lesbian, gay, bisexual, transgender, queer, and other (LGBTQ+) community. Some of the most conservative religious voices that argued against legalizing gay marriage, for instance, did so from doctrinal positions informing the definition of marriage as between a man and a woman. Although we see more religious diversity in thought on marriage today, this remains an area of contention that can be difficult for SGMs who wish for a more expansive definition of marriage or otherwise wish for affirmational statements from the faith communities in which they may have grown up.

Spirituality, then, is at times an appealing alternative for SGMs who might leave organized religion but want to retain a sense and experience of the transcendent (Beagan & Hattie, 2015). However, spirituality is only at times studied apart from religiousness, and there are discussions about conceptual overlap and the potential value in distinguishing these concepts and associated practices. In addition, as we noted above, most of the research is on religiousness, including aspects of religiousness that might be closer in conceptualization to spirituality. This is the approach we have taken when we have used elements of the DUREL to measure both religiousness and spirituality.

One final point on developments in theory that affect our understanding of research. It is often noted that religious doctrine may lead to increased homophobia that a person subsequently internalizes, and it is this relationship between religion and homophobia that we see in negative health or mental health associations. However, the construct of homophobia has itself been criticized as problematic on several grounds. For example, in their review of the psychometric properties of measures of homophobia, O'Donohue and Caselles (1993) argued that some measures "make an illegitimately pejorative evaluation of certain open and debatable value positions" (p. 177).[3] For example, a measure of internalized homonegativity developed by Mayfield (2001) after the critique by O'Donohue and Caselles, had similarly problematic items, such as "... it's not ok for men to have sex with each other" and "I believe it is morally wrong for women to have sex with other women." In other words, some measures may make it difficult to hold a conventionally religious perspective on sexuality and gender without scoring higher on homophobia or related constructs. This remains conceptually problematic and points to the concerns about the psychometric properties of some of the measures themselves. It is also a problem in our research experience for those persons who are LGBTQ+ and conventionally religious and have trouble filling out those measures because the measures do not seem to reflect a more diverse worldview.

Theory and Research in Support of a Salubrious Relationship between Spirituality and Health and Well-Being

As we have noted, R/S are generally considered to have a salubrious relationship between health and well-being for the general population. We do see lines of research that suggest a positive relationship between religion/spirituality and SGMs, or at least call into question the view that there is a unilateral negative relationship. For instance, in a study by Kappler, Hancock, and Plante (2013), no differences were found in psychological distress or depression. Kappler et al. also reported no differences in psychological well-being. In contrast, a recent study by Anderson-Carpenter (2021), for example, showed that higher levels of spirituality were associated with increased quality of life among over 2000 gay and bisexual men, a finding consistent with other research in which spirituality was associated with increased well-being. Others have found that religion is a means for SGMs to find meaning and purpose in life (Michaels et al., 2019; Rosenkrantz et al., 2016) as well as improved self-esteem, reduced stress, better mental health, and even better physical outcomes for those with HIV (Dowshen et al., 2011; Gattis et al., 2014; Lease et al., 2005; Porter et al., 2013).

Some research has shown that R/S may even be a protective factor insofar as it is associated with decreased alcohol and substance use among religious sexual minorities (e.g., Drabble et al., 2016). In a national study of sexual minorities at Christian colleges, these students, on average, reported fewer alcohol-related problems than the general college population (Yarhouse et al., 2018, p. 42). In contrast, at a public university, lesbian and bisexual women were found to use more alcohol, tobacco, and other drugs than did heterosexual women (Kerr et al., 2015).

A recent meta-analysis (Lefevor et al., 2023) examined the relationship between R/S and health among sexual minorities. They found that the relationship was positive, albeit small (r = .05). This positive relationship was moderated by a number of variables that suggest more research is needed to gain a more accurate understanding of the relationship itself (Lefevor et al., 2023).

The Trevor Project report (2022), *Religion and Spirituality Among LGBTQ Youth*, indicated the importance of R/S for many LGBTQ youth in the United States. It was reported that one in five participants indicated that their religion or spirituality was important to them, with higher rates among those over 18, from lower socioeconomic backgrounds, residing in the South, or of Native/Indigenous or Middle Eastern/Northern African descent. Nearly a quarter reported engaging in prayer, meditation, or private reflection at least weekly. In terms of mental health, the study found that LGBTQ youth who consider religion or spirituality important reported slightly lower rates of recent depressive symptoms.

In a recently proposed model of stress and resilience among sexual minorities (Lefevor et al., 2023), it was suggested that R/S may affect "general resilience processes" among SGMs, and that this effect "occurs along psychological, social, and behavioral pathways" (p. 7). In terms of the social pathway (which includes social support), the meta-analysis (Lefevor et al., 2021) cited above had mixed support, with about half of the studies indicating positive effects (and half indicating negative effects) (Lefevor et al., 2023). In a study of highly religious Christian sexual minorities, participants identified micro-affirmations as positive experiences in social relationships (Yarhouse et al., 2018, see pp. 205–207, 288–293). Similar micro-affirmations were reported, too, among highly religious gender minorities who identified as Christian (Yarhouse et al., 2021).

It appears that sexual minorities who are able to integrate religious identity and sexual or gender identity report positive physical health and positive mental health (Lefevor et al., 2023). It has been speculated by Lefevor et al. that SGMs of faith

> …may engage more often with [religion/spirituality] and see their faith as a larger part of who they are, which may ultimately be beneficial…. Some have even reported that their [religion/spirituality] involvement helps them cope with the unique minority stressors experienced as a [SGM], such as stigma or discrimination.
>
> (2023, p. 11)

We have been discussing R/S together, but it should be noted that some SGMs choose to no longer identify with an organized religion. They retain spirituality as noted above and appear to experience similar health and mental health benefits (Lefevor et al., 2023; see Levefor et al., 2021). The separation of spirituality from religion was a common theme in a qualitative study of LGBTQ+ persons (Beagan & Hattie, 2015). An interviewed participant, Clare, shared,

> I have a far more articulated and self-aware construct of spirituality than I did when I was going through the motions…. My own spirituality, while deeply framed by that ritual and by that practice, only surfaced once I was able to look at it from the outside.
>
> (p. 106)

Recent structural equation modeling (Shakarian et al., 2021) found that "higher levels of spirituality were associated with psychological well-being" (p. 123). Indeed, the authors observed that spiritual health

> is associated with positive psychological components, such as self-efficacy, resilience, hope, optimism, and hard work; these structures play an essential role in strengthening the psychological strength of individuals in various aspects of life and lead to becoming stronger and increasing competence; consequently, promoting individuals' psychological well-being.
>
> (p. 130)

Coping resources are also an important element to spirituality among SGMs. For example, in a study of young gay and bisexual men (Meanley et al., 2016), spiritual coping was positively associated with psychological well-being. Indeed, for sexual and gender diverse persons of faith, "spirituality may have a more uncomplicated and positive relationship with health because it does not increase stressors while increasing resilience" (Lefevor et al., 2023, p. 12).

In their study comparing sexual and gender minority students at religious and non-religious institutions, Dyer and Erickson (2023) found few differences among SGMs at religious and nonreligious institutions. However, in terms of potential protective factors, the authors noted: "For students at religious and nonreligious universities, religion being important appeared to play a protective role against suicide ideation and anxiety" (p. 188).

Mindfulness and related clinical practices, many of which can be spiritually accommodative in working with persons of faith, have been recommended for helping SGMs navigate conflicts they may experience between their religious identity and their sexual or gender identity (see Tan & Yarhouse, 2010).

Self-acceptance seems to play a major role in the psychological health of sexual minorities. For example, Woodford et al. (2014) found SGM students' self-acceptance, which they measured as self-esteem and LGBTQ+ pride, both mitigated the effects of discrimination and decreased psychological distress. However, in our research with Christian sexual minority college students, we found that self-acceptance does not necessarily mean both accepting one's sexuality and becoming gay-affirming. In fact, gay-affirming ethical and moral beliefs were not even correlated with self-acceptance or psychological distress (Dean et al., 2021). Similarly, in a study by Szymanski (2009), self-esteem moderated the relationship between heterosexist events and psychological distress, with those sexual minorities who reported greater self-esteem showing less psychological distress.

In our nationwide study of sexual minority students at Christian colleges (Dean et al., 2021), we found that cisgender identity (β = .32), social support from heterosexual friends (β = −.29), intrinsic religiosity (β = −.22), and organizational religiosity (i.e., attendance at religious services; $\beta = -.17$) positively predicted psychological health, accounting for about 30% of its variance. Moreover, personal acceptance of same-sex sexual behavior, private religious and spiritual practices, degree of same-sex sexual attraction, private sexual identity, campus view of same-sex sexual behavior, and social support from family, church, college faculty, and sexual minority friends did not predict psychological health among Christian sexual minorities.

Among both Christian and non-Christian, sexual and gender minority youth, Ceatha et al. (2021) also found that positive interpersonal relationships (particularly gay-straight alliances) and faith affiliations were among a variety of protective factors, including some that were not significant predictors in the Dean et al. study, such as cultural affiliations, access to LGBTI+ community networks, and online communities. Likewise, family support, peer support, and spirituality, together with healthy help-seeking beliefs, access to medical and counseling services, engagement in healthy activities, and having trusted adults, emerged as protective factors for suicidal thought and behaviors and depression among sexual and gender minority youth in a study by Rivas-Koehl et al. (2021).

Additional mediational analyses in the Dean et al. (2021) study showed that self-acceptance mediated the relationship between intrinsic religiosity and psychological health as well as the relationship between social support and psychological health. The mediator of self-acceptance itself accounted for 46% and 41% of the variance in the models, respectively. Self-acceptance was positively correlated to both faith and social support. Psychological health for these Christian sexual minorities seemed to depend upon their self-acceptance, which is fostered through supportive relationships with straight, cisgender friends, together with a strong relationship with God.

The research generally supports a positive relationship between R/S and health and well-being among SGMs. However, there is also research in support of the claim of a deleterious relationship between spirituality and health and well-being. It is important to note this separation of the positive and negative outcomes of R/S for SGMs tends to be an artificial bifurcation. There is great intersectionality between R/S and sexual/gender identity, with each person experiencing different consequences related to their experiences, environment, social support, personal faith, self-acceptance, and how they choose to hold these identities together. With that as our frame of reference, we turn to this next section.

Theory and Research in Support of a Deleterious Relationship between Spirituality and Health and Well-Being

Several studies have suggested a deleterious relationship between R/S and health and well-being among the LGBTQ+ community. While we have already shown the relationship is quite complex and nuanced, let us now look at the studies that suggest negative associations. For example, some studies report an increased risk for depression (e.g., D'Augelli, 2002, Foster et al., 2015, Marshal et al., 2011, Ream & Savin-Williams, 2005; Silenzio et al., 2007), anxiety and guilt (Levy & Reeves, 2011; Subhi & Geelan, 2012), low self-esteem (Foster et al., 2015; Ream & Savin-Williams, 2005), and psychological distress (e.g., Lefevor, Janis, & Park, 2017; Wilkinson & Pearson, 2009).

It has also been reported in the literature that there is an increased risk for suicidality among religious LGBTQ+ persons. For example, in a study conducted by Lytle et al. (2018) increased religiousness among gay and questioning participants was associated with greater risk of suicidal ideation (see also, McDermott et al., 2008; Marshal et al., 2011; Ryan et al.,

2009; Silenzio et al., 2007; O'Donnell et al., 2004; D'Augelli et al., 2001). Highly religious lesbian and gay students were also at greater risk for suicidal ideation and lifetime suicide attempts. Similarly, Bettis et al. (2020) reported on a sample of sexual and gender minority youth and reported higher rates of suicidal ideation, past suicidal behavior, and (non-suicidal) self-harm among sexual minority youth. Similarly, gender diverse youth reported higher rates of suicidal ideation in a study by deGraaf et al. (2022).

The explanations for the apparent negative associations between religion/spirituality and the health and well-being of SGMs include homonegativity and associated discrimination and/or condemnation of same-sex behavior (Altman et al., 2012; Foster et al., 2015; Meyer, 2003; Quinn, Dickson-Gomez, & Kelly, 2016). The argument is, in part, that rejection and disapproval lead to internalized homonegativity (e.g., Barnes & Meyer, 2012; Bourn, Frantell, & Miles, 2018; Page, Lindahl, & Malik, 2013; Ream & Savin-Williams, 2005) which puts people at greater risk for mental health concerns, such as depression and low self-esteem. Bourn et al. found that, while religious SGMs used both positive and negative religious coping in responding to internalized homonegativity, the negative religious coping was particularly problematic, resulting in increased emotional suffering (i.e., psychache) and psychological distress (see also Paulez et al., 2023).

However, in our nationwide study of sexual minority students at Christian colleges (Dean et al., 2021), one's personal acceptance of same-sex sexuality was not a significant predictor of psychological distress. Instead, a non-cisgender identity, limited social support (particularly from heterosexual friends), little internalization of one's faith, and limited attendance at religious services were predictors of greater psychological distress, with these variables accounting for thirty percent of the variance. Likewise, in a study of gay men, Lassiter et al. (2019) found that "engaging in religious behaviors without the meaning, connectedness, and intrinsic morality that was associated with spirituality seemed to be a detriment to mental well-being" (p. 414). Moreover, Harris et al. (2008) surveyed sexual minorities experiencing conflict between their religious beliefs and sexual orientation, finding that literal interpretation of Scripture and degree of religious commitment were not associated with greater internalized homonegativity or psychological health, whereas having higher levels of independent, post-conventional religious reasoning was related to lower internalized homonegativity and higher levels of sexual identity development.

Further, in terms of social support, which is often protective factor associated with R/S, some studies have pointed to a potential loss of community and corresponding social support if one were to disclose one's sexuality (Haldeman, 2004; Pitt; 2010; Quinn et al., 2016; Smith et al., 2005; Valera & Taylor, 2011; Woodyard et al., 2000). For example, Meanly et al. (2016) reported on threats to the sense of "purpose, value, and self-worth" when LGBTQ+ youth are excluded or stigmatized in religious communities (p. 9). So, while religious communities can provide a sense of connectedness and belonging, they can likewise be settings in which exclusion can contribute to decreased well-being.

We have also seen related research on the need for acceptance among LGBTQ+ persons (Greene, Brennan, & Britton, 2017) and the preference to remain in one's religious community rather than move to a more affirming religious community setting (e.g., Douglas, 1999; Haldeman, 2004; Quinn, Dickson-Gomez, & Kelly, 2016; Woodyard et al., 2000; Pitt, 2010). Sherkat (2002) found that these more affirming churches may not be adequate to meet the spiritual needs of some religious SGMs. That is, that the theological changes that come with congregations becoming more gay-affirming may not fit with the personal religious beliefs of these individuals, causing them to prefer their less gay-affirming religious community despite any homonegativity that might be present (Brennan-Ing et al., 2013; Barton, 2010; Pitt, 2010; Walton, 2006; Sherkat, 2002). These SGMs may also stay in their less gay-affirming religious communities to avoid the losses (e.g., loss of a community that shares other traditional beliefs about the inspiration of Scripture, for instance) that would come from leaving (Gandy, Natale, & Levy, 2021).

Indeed, the acceptance element may be part of what has been referred to as a social pathway for religious and spiritual resilience among SGMs. In a recent meta-analysis (Lefevor et al., 2023), about half of the studies conducted indicated a negative effect on resilience, as some relationships are characterized by "ostracization, alienation, and loneliness" (Lefevor et al., 2023, p. 7). In addition, in a study of religious and spiritual coping, Meanley et al. (2016) reported that religious participation (but not spirituality) was "negatively associated with [sexual minorities] purpose in life and greater feelings of homonegativity" (p. 45). Religious commitment was also "associated with lower self-esteem and higher internalized homophobia" (p. 45).

It seems particularly detrimental to health if individuals are unable to find a way to hold together their sexual/gender and faith identities (Subhi & Geelan, 2012; Yarhouse et al., 2018). Some cope by rejecting either their sexual identity or their faith identity, both of which seem to lead to poorer mental health outcomes (Yarhouse et al., 2018; Barton, 2010; Walton, 2006; Pitt, 2010; Goodwill, 2000; Heerman et al., 2007; Rodriguez & Ouellette, 2000). More psychological distress seems to arise if individuals try to hold onto both their faith identity and their sexual identity despite the seemingly ever-present conflict (Yarhouse et al., 2018); some lessen this distress by holding both separately through compartmentalization (Yarhouse et al., 2018; Pitt, 2010; Rodriguez & Ouellette, 2000).

The integration of these two identities into one, a religious sexual minority, is possible and may require self-acceptance (Yarhouse et al., 2018; Rodriguez, 2010). The research of Dean et al. (2021) showed that the inability to develop self-acceptance led to a negative relationship between faith and psychological health for these individuals. Self-acceptance seems to serve as a self-regulation strategy in which individuals are able to acknowledge their negative emotions and thoughts without feeling a need to control them (see Wojnarowska et al., 2020; Kivity et al., 2016; MacInnes, 2006). As such, Kapatias et al. (2023) found that SGMs who struggled with emotional regulation were almost seven times more likely to self-harm than their straight, cisgender peers, suggesting higher levels of psychological distress.

There is a complex relationship between religion/spirituality and sexual/gender identity when it comes to mental health and well-being. Some find the tension between the religion/spirituality and sexual or gender identity to be untenable, thus they drop one or the other identity to relieve the psychological distress (Yarhouse et al., 2018). Others find a way to hold both, even if they are in tension. That is, with support, sexual and gender minority students who hold their faith as core to their identity grow toward an even more complex integration that affirms a high value of self, while acknowledging aspects of self that are undeveloped or are not acceptable to their faith, and when they do so, they seem to have positive mental health outcomes.

Clinical Applications

There is a modest but growing literature on the clinical applications of R/S in working with the SGM population (Sun et al., 2021). The most common spiritually based approaches are mindfulness-based practices, such as acceptance, present-moment awareness, emotional regulation, and so on, all of which are loosely grounded in Eastern practices/Buddhist forms, although other religious systems have similar meditative processes. Mindfulness-based interventions are often adjunctive practices for the purpose of attentional training, reducing self-harm, behavioral self-management, and resilience, along with empathy enhancement and spiritual well-being for SGMs (e.g., Kapatais, Williams, & Townsend, 2023).

The Substance Abuse and Mental Health Services Administration (SAMHSA, 2023) published resources on care for sexual and gender minority youth and includes information on navigating different values that may inform those conversations. Positive steps include identifying sources of conflict, supporting adaptive coping, and helping SGM youth "within the context of their intersecting identities" (p. 51), which includes religious identities. Specific to mindfulness-based interventions, it was recommended that mindfulness-based coping be taught to SGMs who have experienced victimization in the school setting (Toomey & Anhalt, 2016).

An area of particular interest may be how clinicians aid SGMs in achieving personally determined and satisfactory congruence between their sexual or gender identities and religious identities. The APA Task Force on Appropriate Therapeutic Responses to Sexual Orientation (2009) cited a few case studies as examples of work with conventionally religious SGMs who wished to achieve personal congruence between their religious and sexual identities. It was noted at that time that there was a need to develop client-centered, identity-focused models for working with conventionally religious SGMs. Such approaches would provide active coping strategies to help SGMs reduce distress, encourage and build multiple sources of support, and facilitate identity exploration and development.

Sexual Identity Therapy (SIT) is one approach that since the publication of the 2009 report has been available to conventionally religious sexual minorities (Yarhouse, 2019). SIT is open-ended, client-centered, and focused on exploration of both religious and sexual identities. The goal of therapy is personal congruence in which a person lives and adopts a sexual identity in keeping with their beliefs and values.

Mindfulness and acceptance have been recommended in helping sexual minority youth accept the reality of their same-sex sexuality rather than attempt to change orientation or internalize negative messages about their sexuality that may lead to negative mental health outcomes, such as depression or anxiety (Tan & Yarhouse, 2010). In this approach,

> mindfulness is applied in SIT to assist individuals with same-sex attraction to become non-judgmentally aware of their thoughts and feelings related to same-sex attraction such that they are able to experience their attractions in an open and honest manner without feeling compelled to either dismiss or augment these attractions.
>
> (p. 500)

As noted above, the goal of such an approach is congruence:

> Mindful awareness of same-sex attraction facilitates congruence because there is less emphasis on changing behaviors, thoughts or feelings, but rather, changing the relationship the individual has to their experiences of same-sex attraction so that they are experienced as neutral, as opposed to aversive.
>
> (p. 500)

A similar posture to what is seen in SIT has been developed for helping clients who experience gender discordance and hold conventionally religious beliefs and values about cross- or other-gender identity and expression. This posture is referred to as Gender and Religious Identity

Therapy (GRIT; Yarhouse & Sadusky, 2022). To date, there are fewer mindfulness-based interventions published for transgender and non-binary clients (Sun et al., 2021). However, in the GRIT approach, many tools for navigating gender identity and religious identity are discussed throughout this approach, and the modules on unpacking feelings and coping and management strategies, in particular, emphasize radical acceptance of one's experience of gender to acknowledge one's feelings and experience as part of one's life at this moment and to prevent a defensive posture of denial.

Limitations

Limitations to the research on sexual and gender identity and religiousness include frequent use of convenience samples, the use of brief religiousness assessments which typically miss important nuances in how people experience their faith, the lack of diversity among participants (i.e., most are Christian and Caucasian), and the limited (but growing) number of studies focused upon gender identity. In addition, the variety of understandings represented across the literature of terminology can make comparisons of measures and results complicated and confusing. For example, the word affirming is commonly used to express valuing of certain aspects of human experience, but a closer inspection of the literature demonstrates less uniformity than is often assumed.

A significant inherent limitation in existing research is the often rigid binary categorization of the impacts of spirituality and religion as either positive or negative for sexual and gender diverse individuals. This dichotomous framing overlooks the multifaceted nature of these relationships, which can simultaneously encompass aspects of support and challenge, acceptance and conflict. This tendency to categorize the impacts of spirituality and religion on SGMs into distinct positive or negative outcomes simplifies a highly complex and nuanced reality. SGMs often experience a spectrum of interactions with spirituality and religion, where positive and negative aspects coexist and are influenced by various mediating factors such as cultural context, personal history, self-acceptance, community support, individual interpretations of spiritual teachings, personal experiences within religious communities, and the varying degrees of acceptance or rejection encountered. The interplay of these factors can result in a spectrum of experiences that defy simple classification as either wholly positive or negative.

Furthermore, this binary view needs to account for intersectional identities and how they pivotally shape experiences with R/S. Factors such as race, ethnicity, socioeconomic status, and geographic location intersect with sexual and gender identities, influencing how individuals engage with and are impacted by spiritual and religious practices and beliefs, creating diverse and unique spiritual and sacred journeys. The research also often overlooks the fluidity within these journeys. As individuals navigate their spiritual paths, their perceptions and interactions with spirituality and religion may evolve, further challenging the notion of fixed positive or negative categorizations. Therefore, a more intersectional approach in research is crucial to understanding the full spectrum of experiences among SGMs concerning spirituality and religion.

Moreover, there is a need for a more critical examination of the constructs and measures used in studying the relationship between spirituality, religion, and the experiences of SGMs. For instance, the conceptualization of homophobia in the context of religious beliefs necessitates a nuanced understanding. It is important to differentiate between doctrinal beliefs and internalized negative attitudes, as they have distinct impacts on the well-being of SGMs.

Future Directions

We see the conversations around health and mental health among sexual and gender diverse persons as benefitting from a more careful, nuanced analysis of the relationship between R/S and SGMs. The mediating variables we noted above seem especially salient. In our own research, the consideration of one's relationship to oneself, whether we think of that as self-acceptance or even grace to self, seems especially important. The relationship to others or what we refer to as social support is also important, and we see in the literature mixed evidence of social support in terms of what is potentially gained and what is potentially lost in supportive relationships. We also see a person's relationship with God or the divine as important for health and well-being.

As far as distinguishing religious communities that are affirming versus non-affirming, it may be more helpful to consider "goodness-of-fit" for sexual and gender diverse persons of faith in their religious communities. When we consider the diversity of beliefs and values held by SGMs themselves, it will be important to support them as they seek out religious communities that share their own beliefs and values. It will also be important in these religious communities to create emotionally and spiritually secure environments in which SGMs can take their sexuality/gender seriously, their religious faith seriously, and the relationship between their sexuality/gender and religious identity seriously.

Notes

1 Intrinsic religiosity was defined by Allport and Ross (1967) in this way: "Persons with this orientation find their master motive in religion. Other needs, strong as they may be, are regarded as of less ultimate significance, and they are, so far as possible, brought into harmony with the religious beliefs and prescriptions. Having embraced a creed, the individual endeavors to internalize it and follow it fully. It is in this sense that he lives his religion" (cited in Koenig & Bussing, 2010, pp. 79).

2 We are currently completing a national study (The Sexual & Gender Identity Project) of sexual/gender minority students at public and private Christian universities.

3 One argument for why such evaluations might be deemed "illegitimately pejorative" by conventionally religious persons is that the evaluations move beyond mental health conceptualizations and into moral conclusions or doctrinal statements, which is beyond the scope of psychology as a behavioral science.

References

Allport, G. W., & Ross, J. M. (1967). Personal religious orientation and prejudice. *Journal of Personality & Social Psychology*, *5*(4), 432–443. https://doi.org/10.1037/h0021212

Altman, D., Aggleton, P., Williams, M., Kong, T., Reddy, V., Harrad, D., Reis, T., & Parker, R. (2012). Men who have sex with men: stigma and discrimination. *Lancet (London, England)*, *380*(9839), 439–445. https://doi.org/10.1016/S0140-6736(12)60920-9

American Psychological Association, Task Force on Appropriate Therapeutic Responses to Sexual Orientation (2009). Report of the American Psychological Association Task Force on Appropriate Therapeutic Responses to Sexual Orientation. Retrieved from http://www.apa.org/pi/lgbc/publications/therapeutic-resp.html

Anderson-Carpenter, K. D. (2021). Do spirituality, rurality, and LGBTQ support increase outness and quality of health in gay and bisexual men? *Journal of Homosexuality*, *69*(6), 1081–1096. https://doi.org/10.1080/00918369.2021.1905382

Barnes, D. M., & Meyer, I. H. (2012). Religious affiliation, internalized homophobia, and mental health in lesbians, gay men, and bisexuals. *American Journal of Orthopsychiatry*, *82*(4), 505–515. https://doi.org/10.1111/j.1939-0025.2012.01185.x

Barton, B. (2010). "Abomination"—Life as a Bible Belt gay. *Journal of Homosexuality, 57*, 465–484. https://doi.org/10.1080/00918361003608558

Bauer, A. S., & Johnson, T. J. (2019). Conceptual overlap of spirituality and religion: An item content analysis of several common measures. *Journal of Spirituality in Mental Health, 21*(1), 14–36. https://doi.org/10.1080/19349637.2018.1437004

Beagan, B. L., & Hattie, B. (2015). Religion, spirituality, and LGBTQ identity integration. *Journal of LGBT Issues in Counseling, 9*(2), 92–117. https://doi.org/10.1080/15538605.2015.1029204

Bettis, A. H., Thompson, E. C., Burke, T. A., Nesi, J., Kudinova, A. Y., Hunt, J. L., Liu, R. T., & Wolff, J. C. (2020). Prevalence and clinical indices of risk for sexual and gender minority youth in an adolescent inpatient sample. *Journal of Psychiatric Research*, 130, pp. 327–332. https://doi.org/10.1016/j.jpsychires.2020.08.022

Bourn, J. R., Frantell, K. A., & Miles, J. R. (2018). Internalized heterosexism, religious coping, and psychache in LGB young adults who identify as religious. *Psychology of Sexual Orientation and Gender Diversity, 5*(3), 303–312. https://doi.org/10.1037/sgd0000274

Brennan-Ing, M., Seidel, L., Larson, B., & Karpiak, S. E. (2013). "I'm created in God's image, and God don't create junk": Religious participation and support among older GLBT adults. *Journal of Religion, Spirituality & Aging, 25*(2), 70–92. https://doi.org/10.1080/15528030.2013.746629

Ceatha, N., Koay, A., Buggy, C. J., James, O., Tully, L., Bustillo, M., & Crowley, D. (2021). Protective factors for LGBTI+ youth wellbeing: A scoping review underpinned by recognition theory. *International Journal of Environmental Research and Public Health, 18*(21), 11682. https://doi.org/10.3390/ijerph182111682

D'Augelli, A. R., Hershberger, S. L., & Pilkington, N. W. (2001). Suicidality patterns and sexual orientation-related factors among lesbian, gay, and bisexual youths. *Suicide and Life-Threatening Behavior, 31*(3), 250–264. https://doi.org/10.1521/suli.31.3.250.24246

D'Augelli, A. R. (2002). Mental health problems among lesbian, gay, and bisexual youths ages 14 to 21. *Clinical Child Psychology and Psychiatry, 7*(3), 433–456. https://doi.org/10.1177/1359104502007003039

Dean, J. B., Stratton, S. P., & Yarhouse, M. A. (2021). The mediating role of self-acceptance in the psychological distress of sexual minority students on Christian college campuses. *Spirituality in Clinical Practice, 8*(2), 132–148. https://doi.org/10.1037/scp0000253

Dean, J. B., Stratton, S. P., Yarhouse, M. A., & Lastoria, M. D. (2011). Same-sex attraction. In M. Lastoria (Ed.), *Sexuality, religiosity, behaviors, attitudes: A look at religiosity, sexual attitudes and sexual behaviors of christian college students (ACSD research series)*, 56–70.

deGraaf, N. M., Steensma, T. D., Carmichael, P., VanderLaan, D. P., Aitken, M., Cohen-Kettenis, P. T., deVries, A. L. C., Kreukels, B. P. C., Wasserman, L., Wood, H., & Zucker, K. J. (2022). Suicidality in clinic-referred transgender adolescents. *European Child & Adolescent Psychiatry, 31*, 67–83. https://doi.org/10.1007/s00787-020-01663-9

Diamond, L. M. (2008). *Sexual fluidity: Understanding women's love and desire*. Cambridge, MA: Harvard University Press.

Douglas, K. B. (1999). *Sexuality and the black church: A womanist perspective*. Orbis

Dowshen, N., Forke, C. M., Johnson, A. K., Kuhns, L. M., Rubin, D., & Garafalo, R. (2011). Religiosity as a protective factor against HIV risk among young transgender women. *Journal of Adolescent Health, 48*(4), 410–414. doi: 10.1016/j.jadohealth.2010.07.021

Drabble, L., Trocki, K. F., & Klinger, J. L. (2016). Religiosity as a protective factor for hazardous drinking and drug use among sexual minority and heterosexual women: Findings from the National Alcohol Survey. *Drug and alcohol dependence, 161*, 127–134. https://doi.org/10.1016/j.drugalcdep.2016.01.022

Dyer, W. J., & Erickson, J. J. (2023). Mental health at religious and non-religious institutions: Examining the role of student religiousness and sexual/gender identity. *Journal of Affective Disorders*, 342, 182–191. https://doi.org/10.1016/j.jad.2023.09.011

Exline, J. J., Przeworski, A., Peterson, E. K., Turnamian, M. R., Stauner, N., & Uzdavines, A. (2021). Religious and spiritual struggles among transgender and gender-nonconforming adults. *Psychology of Religion and Spirituality, 13*(3), 276–286. https://doi.org/10.1037/rel0000404

Foster, K. A., Bowland, S. E., & Vosler, A. N. (2015). All the pain along with all the joy: Spiritual resilience in lesbian and gay Christians. *American Journal of Community Psychology*, *55*, 191–201. https://doi.org/10.1007/s10464-015-9704-4

Gandy, M. E., Natale, A. P., & Levy, D. L. (2021). "We shared a heartbeat": Protective functions of faith communities in the lives of LGBTQ+ people. *Spirituality in Clinical Practice*, *8*(2), 98–111. https://doi.org/10.1037/scp0000225

Gattis, M. N., Woodford, M. R., & Han, Y. (2014). Discrimination and depressive symptoms among sexual minority youth: Is gay-affirming religious affiliation a protective factor? *Archives of Sexual Behavior*, *43*(8), 1589–1599. https://doi.org/10.1007/s10508-014-0342-y

Goodwill, K. A. (2000). Religion and the spiritual needs of Mormon gay men. *Journal of Gay & Lesbian Social Services*, *11*(4), 23–37.

Greene, D. C., Brennan, C., & Britton, P. J. (2017). Exploration of psychological distress in gay, bisexual, and heterosexual Roman Catholic priests. *Psychology of Religion and Spirituality*, *9*(4), 401–411. https://doi.org/10.1037/rel0000047

Haldeman, D. C. (2004). When sexual and religious orientation collide: Considerations in working with conflicted same-sex attracted male clients. *The Counseling Psychologist*, *32*(5), 691–715. https://doi.org/10.1177/0011000004267560

Harris, J. I., Cook, S. W., & Kashubeck-West, S. (2008). Religious attitudes, internalized homophobia, and identity in gay and lesbian adults. *Journal of Gay & Lesbian Mental Health*, *12*(3), 205–225. https://doi.org/10.1080/19359700802111452

Heerman, M., Wiggins, M. I., & Rutter, P. A. (2007). Creating a space for spiritual practice: Pastoral possibilities with sexual minorities. *Pastoral Psychology*, *55*, 711–721. https://doi.org/10.1007/s11089-007-0085-y

James, S. E., Herman, J. L., Rankin, S., Keisling, M. Mottet, L., & Anafi, M. (2016). The report of the 2015 U.S. transgender survey. National Center for Transgender Equality. www.ustranssurvey.org

Kapatais, A., Williams, A. J., & Townsend, E. (2023). The mediating role of emotion regulation on self-harm among gender identity and sexual orientation minority (LGBTQ+) individuals. *Archives of Suicide Research: Official Journal of the International Academy for Suicide Research*, *27*(2), 165–178. https://doi.org/10.1080/13811118.2022.2064254

Kappler, S., Hancock, K. A., & Plante, T. G. (2013). Roman catholic gay priests: Internalized homophobia, sexual identity, and psychological well-being. *Pastoral Psychology*, *62*(6), 805–826. https://doi.org/10.1007/s11089-012-0505-5

Kerr, D., Ding, K., Burke, A., & Ott-Walter, K. (2015). An alcohol, tobacco, and other drug use comparison of lesbian, bisexual, and heterosexual undergraduate women. *Substance Use & Misuse*, *50*, 340–349.

Kivity, Y., Tamir, M., & Huppert, J. D. (2016). Self-acceptance of negative emotions: The positive relationship with effective cognitive reappraisal. *International Journal of Cognitive Therapy*, *9*(4), 279–294. https://doi.org/10.1521/ijct_2016_09_10

Koenig, H., & Bussing, A. (2010). The Duke University Religion Index (DUREL): A five-item measure for use in epidemiological studies. *Religions*, *1*(1), 78–85. https://doi.org/10.3390/rel1010078

Lassiter, J. M., Saleh, L., Grov, C., Starks, T., Ventuneac, A., & Parsons, J. T. (2019). Spirituality and multiple dimensions of religion are associated with mental health in gay and bisexual men: Results From the one thousand strong cohort. *Psychology of Religion and Spirituality*, *11*(4), 408–416. https://doi.org/10.1037/rel0000146

Lease, S. H., Horne, S. G., & Noffsinger-Frazier, N. (2005). Affirming faith experiences and psychological health for caucasian lesbian, gay, and bisexual individuals. *Journal of Counseling Psychology*, *52*(3), 378–388. https://doi.org/10.1037/0022-0167.52.3.378

Lefevor, G. T., Davis, E. B., Paiz, J. Y., & Smack, A. C. P. (2021). The relationship between religiousness and health among sexual minorities: A meta-analysis. *Psychological Bulletin*, *147*(7), 647–666. https://doi.org/10.1037/bul0000321

Lefevor, G. T., Etengoff, C., Davis, E. B., Skidmore, S. J., Rodríguez, E. M., McGraw, J. S., & Rostosky, S. S. (2023). Religion/spirituality, stress, and resilience among sexual and gender minorities: The Religious/Spiritual Stress and Resilience Model. *Perspectives on Psychological Science*, *18*(6), 1537–1561. https://doi.org/10.1177/17456916231179137

Lefevor, G. T., Janis, R. A., & Park, S. Y. (2017). Religious and sexual identities: An intersectional, longitudinal examination of change in therapy. *The Counseling Psychologist*, *45*(3), 387–413. https://doi.org/10.1177/0011000017702721

Levy, D. L., & Reeves, P. (2011).Resolving identity conflicts: Gay, lesbian, and queer individuals with a Christian upbringing. *Journal of Gay and Lesbian Social Services*, *23*(1), 53–68. https://doi.org/10.1080/10538720.2010.530193

Lytle, J. R., Blosnich, S. M., & De Luca, C. B. (2018). Association of religiosity with sexual minority suicide ideation and attempt. *American Journal of Preventive Medicine*, *54*(5), 644–651. https://doi.org/10.1016/j.amepre.2018.01.019

MacInnes, D. L. (2006). Self-esteem and self-acceptance: An examination into their relationship and their effect on psychological health. *Journal of Psychiatric and Mental Health Nursing*, *13*(5), 483–489. https://doi.org/10.1111/j.1365-2850.2006.00959.x

Marshal, M. P., Dietz, L. J., Friedman, M. S., Stall, R., Smith, H. A., McGinley, J., Thoma, B. C., Murray, P. J., D'Augelli, A. R., & Brent, D. A. (2011). Suicidality and depression disparities between sexual minority and heterosexual youth: A meta-analytic review. *Journal of Adolescent Health*, *49*(2), 115–123. https://doi.org/10.1016/j.jadohealth.2011.02.005

Mayfield, W. (2001). The development of an Internalized Homonegativity Inventory for gay men. *Journal of Homosexuality*, *41*, 53–76.https://doi.org/10.1300/J082v41n03_05

McDermott, E., Roen, K., & Scourfield, J. (2008). Avoiding shame: Young LGBT people, homophobia and self-destructive behaviours. *Culture, Health & Sexuality*, *10*(8), 815–829. https://doi.org/10.1080/13691050802380974

Meanly, S., Pingel, E. S., & Bauermeister, J. A. (2016). Psychological well-being among religious and spiritual-identified young gay and bisexual men. *Sex Research & Social Policy*, *13*, 35–45. https://doi.org/10.1007/s13178-015-0199-4

Meyer, I. H. (2003). Prejudice, social stress, and mental health in lesbian, gay, and bisexual populations: Conceptual issues and research evidence. *Psychological Bulletin*, *129*(5), 674–697. https://doi.org/10.1037/0033-2909.129.5.674

Michaels, C., Choi, N.-Y., Adams, E. M., & Hitter, T. L. (2019). Testing a new model of sexual minority stress to assess the roles of meaning in life and internalized heterosexism on stress-related growth and life satisfaction. *Psychology of Sexual Orientation and Gender Diversity*, *6*(2), 204–216. https://doi.org/10.1037/sgd0000320

O'Donnell, L., O'Donnell, C., Wardlaw, D. M., & Stueve, A. (2004). Risk and resiliency factors influencing suicidality among urban African American and Latino youth. *American Journal of Community Psychology*, *33*, 37–49. https://doi.org/10.1023/B:AJCP.0000014317.20704.0b

O'Donohue, W., & Caselles, C. E. (1993). Homophobia: Conceptual, definitional, and value issues. *Journal of Psychopathology and Behavioral Assessment*, *15*(3), 177–195. https://doi.org/10.1007/BF01371377

Page, M. J. L., Lindahl, K. M., & Malik, N. M. (2013). The role of religion and stress in sexual identity and mental health among lesbian, gay, and bisexual youth. *Journal of Research on Adolescence*, *23*(4), 665–677. https://doi.org/10.1111/jora.12025

Paulez, J., Johnson, B. D., Davis, E. B., Lacey, E. K., Sullivan, J., Brandys, T. R. (2023).Religious/ spiritual struggles and life satisfaction among sexual minorities. *Psychology of Religion and Spirituality*, *15*(3), 367–378.

Pitt, R. N. (2010). "Still looking for my Jonathan": Gay black men's management of religious and sexual identity conflicts. *Journal of Homosexuality*, *57*, 39–53. https://doi.org/10.1080/00918360903285566

Porter, K. E., Ronneberg, C. R., & Witten, T. M. (2013). Religious affiliation and successful aging among transgender older adults: Findings from the Trans MetLife Survey. *Journal of Religion, Spirituality & Aging*, *25*(2), 112–138. https://doi.org/10.1080/15528030.2012.739988

Quinn, K., Dickson-Gomez, J., & Kelly, J. A. (2016). The role of the Black Church in the lives of young Black men who have sex with men. *Culture, Health & Sexuality*, *18*(5), 524–537. https://doi.org/10.1080/13691058.2015.1091509

Ream, G. L., & Savin-Williams, R. C. (2005). Reciprocal associations between adolescent sexual activity and quality of youth-parent interactions. *Journal of Family Psychology*, *19*(2), 171–179. https://doi.org/10.1037/0893-3200.19.2.171

Rivas-Koehl, M., Valido, A., Espelage, D. L., Robinson, L. E., Hong, J. S., Kuehl, T., Mintz, S., & Wyman, P. A. (2021). Understanding protective factors for suicidality and depression among U.S. sexual and gender minority adolescents: Implications for school psychologists. *School Psychology Review*, *51*(3), 290–303. https://doi.org/10.1080/2372966x.2021.1881411

Rodriguez, E. M. (2010). At the intersection of church and gay: A review of the psychological research on gay and lesbian Christians. *Journal of Homosexuality*, *57*, 5–38. https://doi.org/10.1080/00918360903445806

Rodriguez, E. M., & Ouellette, S. C. (2000). Gay and lesbian Christians: Homosexual and religious identity integration in the members and participants of a gay positive church. *Journal for the Scientific Study of Religion*, *39*, 333–347. https://doi.org/10.1111/0021-8294.00028

Rosenkrantz, D. E., Rostosky, S. S., Riggle, E. D. B., & Cook, J. R. (2016). The positive aspects of intersecting religious/spiritual and LGBTQ identities. *Spirituality in Clinical Practice*, *3*(2), 127–138. https://doi.org/10.1037/scp0000095

Ryan, C., Huebner, D., Diaz, R. M., & Sanchez, J. (2009). Family rejection as a predictor of negative health outcomes in white and Latino lesbian, gay, and bisexual young adults. *Pediatrics*, *123*(1), 346–352. https://doi.org/10.1542/peds.2007-3524

Shakarian, A., Maroufi, Y., & Nateghi, F. (2021). The structural equation modeling of the relationship between spirituality and psychological well-being mediated by spiritual health. *Health, Spirituality and Medical Ethics Journal*, *8*(2), pp. 123–132.

Sherkat, D. E. (2002). Sexuality and religious commitment in the United States: An empirical examination. *Journal for the Scientific Study of Religion*, *41*(2), 313–323. https://doi.org/10.1111/1468-5906.00119

Silenzio, V. M., Pena, J. B., Duberstein, P. R., Cerel, J., & Knox, K. L. (2007). Sexual orientation and risk factors for suicidal ideation and suicide attempts among adolescents and young adults. *American Journal of Public Health*, *97*(11), 2017–2019. https://doi.org/10.2105/AJPH.2006.095943

Smith, J., Simmons, E., & Mayer, K. H. (2005). HIV/AIDS and the Black Church: what are the barriers to prevention services?. *Journal of the National Medical Association*, *97*(12), 1682–1685.

Subhi, N., & Geelan, D. (2012). When Christianity and homosexuality collide: Understanding the potential intrapersonal conflict. *Journal of Homosexuality*, *59*(10), 1382–1402. https://doi.org/10.1080/00918369.2012.724638

Substance Abuse and Mental Health Services Administration (SAMHSA) (2023). *Moving beyond change efforts: Evidence and action to support and affirm LGBTQI+ Youth*. SAMHSA Publication No. PEP2203-12-001. Rockville, MD: Center for Substance Abuse Prevention. Substance Abuse and Mental Health Services Administration.

Sun, S., Nardi, W., Loucks, E. B., & Operario, D. (2021). Mindfulness-based interventions for sexual and gender minorities: A systematic review and evidence evaluation. *Mindfulness*, *12*(10), 2439–2459. https://doi.org/10.1007/s12671-021-01710-9

Szymanski, D. M. (2009). Examining potential moderators of the link between heterosexist events and gay and bisexual men's psychological distress. *Journal of Counseling Psychology*, *56*, 142–151. https://doi.org/10.1037/0022-0167.56.1.142

Tan, E. S. N., & Yarhouse, M. A. (2010). Facilitating congruence between religious beliefs and sexual identity with mindfulness. *Psychotherapy: Theory, Research, Practice, Training*, *47*(4), 500–511. https://doi.org/10.1037/a0022081

The Trevor Project (2022). Religion and spirituality among LGBTQ youth. https://www.thetrevorproject.org/research-briefs/religion-and-spirituality-among-lgbtq-youth-dec-2022/

Toomey, R. B., & Anhalt, K. (2016). Mindfulness as a coping strategy for bias-based school victimization among Latina/o sexual minority youth. *Psychology of Sexual Orientation and Gender Diversity*, *3*(4), 432–441. https://doi.org/10.1037/sgd0000192

Valera, P., & Taylor, T. (2011). "Hating the sin but not the sinner": A study about heterosexism and religious experiences among Black men. *Journal of Black Studies*, *42*(1), 106–122. https://doi.org/10.1177/0021934709356385

Walton, G. (2006). "Fag church": Men who integrate gay and Christian identities. *Journal of Homosexuality*, *51*(2), 1–17.

Webb, J. R. (2021). *Understanding forgiveness and addiction: Theory, research, and clinical application*. Routledge.

Westerink, H. (2012). Spirituality in psychology of religion: A concept in search of its meaning. *Archive for the Psychology of Religion*, *34*, 3–15.

Wilkinson, L., & Pearson, J. (2009). School culture and the well-being of same-sex-attracted youth. *Gender & Society*, *23*(4), 542–568. https://doi.org/10.1177/0891243209339913

Wilt, J. A., Pargament, K. I., Exline, J. J., Barrera, T. L., Teng, E. J. (2019). Spiritual transformation among veterans in response to a religious/spiritual struggle. *Psychology of Religion and Spirituality*, *11*(3), 266–277. https://doi.org/10.1037/rel0000208

Wojnarowska, A., Kobylinska, D., & Lewczuk, K. (2020). Acceptance as an emotion regulation strategy in experimental psychological research: What we know and how we can improve that knowledge. *Frontiers in Psychology*, *11*, 242. https://doi.org/10.3389/fpsyg.2020.00242

Woodford, M. R., Kulick, A., Sinco, B. R., & Hong, J. S. (2014). Contemporary heterosexism on campus and psychological distress among LGBQ students: The mediating role of self-acceptance. *American Journal of Orthopsychiatry*, *84*(5), 519–529. https://doi.org/10.1037/ort0000015

Woodyard, J. L., Peterson, J. L., & Stokes, J. P. (2000). "Let us go into the house of the Lord": participation in African American churches among young African American men who have sex with men. *Journal of Pastoral Care*, *54*(4), 451–460. https://doi.org/10.1177/002234090005400408

Yarhouse, M. A. (2015). *Understanding gender dysphoria: Navigating Transgender issues in a changing culture*. IVP Academic.

Yarhouse, M. A. (2019). *Sexual identity & faith: Helping clients find congruence*. West Conshohocken, PA: Templeton Press.

Yarhouse, M. A., Dean, J., Stratton, S. P., & Lastoria, M. (2018). *Listening to sexual minorities: A study of faith and sexuality on Christian college campuses*. IVP Academic.

Yarhouse, M. A., Dean, J. B., Stratton, S. P., Keefe, H., & Lastoria, M. (2021). Listening to transgender and gender diverse students on Christian college campuses. *Journal of Religion and Health*, *60*, 4480–4499. https://doi.org/10.1007/s10943-021-01425-0

Yarhouse, M. A., & Sadusky, J. A. (2022). *Gender identity & faith: Clinical posture, tools, and case studies for client-centered care*. Downers Grove, IL: InterVarsity Press Academic.

Yarhouse, M. A., & Zaporozhets, O. (2019). *Costly obedience: What we can learn from the celibate gay Christian community*. Zondervan.

Chapter 37

Clergy Health

Religious and Spiritual Considerations

Anthony Isacco and Thomas G. Plante**

Clergy are recognized leaders within an organized religion. There are a variety of clergy across religions. For example, there is the Catholic priesthood, Christian religious leaders such as pastors, deacons, elders, and bishops, and Jewish rabbis. There are approximately 456,000 clergy in the United States, with 80% male, 20% female, with a mean age of 51 years-old (DataUSA, 2024). This chapter uses the terms 'clergy' and 'religious leader' interchangeably and primarily focuses on those from within Judeo-Christian world religions. Clergy fulfill various roles within their religious community such as leading liturgical services (and thus, are often viewed as representatives of deity on earth), administrative oversight, and leading outreach ministries. The non-clergy members of religious communities (i.e., laity, congregants) often look to their religious leaders for support and guidance and as such, religious leaders are typically held in high regard and maintain a prominent status within the religious community. As a result, it is understandable that clergy health is a popular topic. The high interest in clergy health reflects their community standing, leadership role, and how much people of faith care about their religious leaders. Similarly, scholars have been researching clergy health for decades, with different points of focus such as burn-out, weight management, and stress just to name a few. Indeed, the term 'clergy health' has come to encompass a broad array of concerns, points of focus, and interventions. The purpose of this chapter is to highlight some of the unique health concerns of clergy and to describe evidence-based interventions that address their spirituality, health, and well-being.

Spirituality, Religion, and Clergy

Definition precision and conceptual clarity between 'religion' (i.e., religiousness) and 'spirituality' has been a long-term effort in the extant literature. This chapter aims to provide an operational definition of spirituality in relation to clergy. In addition, we briefly discuss our operational definition in relation to the Ritualistic, Theistic, and Existential (RiTE) multidimensional model of spirituality (Webb et al., 2014; see also Chapters 1 and 44 of this volume). A primary theme of this edited book is to explore the RiTE model across diverse populations, constructs, and applications. Thus, our chapter focuses on the RiTE model in relation to clergy health.

Clergy serve a leading ministerial role within an organized religious community, with the role steeped in theological teaching, faith tradition, and individual spiritualities. Thus,

* Corresponding Authors: aisacco@smumn.edu; tplante@scu.edu.

DOI: 10.4324/9781003440048-42

separating religion and spirituality for clergy would be inauthentic. For clergy, their religion is part of their identity, community affiliation, spiritual beliefs, practices, and service to others. Overall, our conceptualization of spirituality in relation to clergy is that religion (i.e., religiousness) and spirituality are integrative constructs, which may be examined distinctively and with nuance depending on the specific question and constructs (Garfield, Isacco, & Sahker, 2013). Therefore, within this integrative conceptualization, we do not agree with attempts to categorize religion as 'bad' and spirituality as 'good' or vice versa. We support precise empirical studies involving clergy that include clearly defined constructs based on a strong theoretical foundation.

The RiTE Model and Clergy Health

The RiTE model of spirituality is an emergent model within the psychological study of religion and spirituality. Webb et al. (2014) developed the RiTE model of spirituality "to bring clarity and parsimony" to definitions of spirituality and religion. The model posits that there is one overarching spirituality that includes both conventional constructs of religion and spirituality as well as three interrelated dimensions: ritualistic, theistic, and existential (Webb et al., 2014). To our knowledge, the RiTE model has not been applied to research and scholarship with clergy. As a result, we are unable to provide a literature review of the RiTE model explicitly applied to clergy health. The RiTE model offers potential for future research about clergy health and well-being. This chapter contextualizes some key research findings about clergy health within the RiTE model.

The RiTE model offers promise to better understand clergy health as the three dimensions are all applicable to clergy. For example, the major organized religions of clergy in the United States (e.g., Catholicism, Protestant-Christianity, Judaism) are all monotheistic and the clergy role is often considered a calling from God and a bridge between God and the people. Thus, the theistic dimension, with the connection to the Divine, is relevant to clergy health. For example, in a qualitative study of Catholic priests in the United States (Isacco et al., 2016), the primary finding was that participants considered their relationship with God to be central to their health and contributed to unique positive outcomes such as perceived support, enabled authenticity, decreased negative emotions, created balance, and empowered them in their vocation and shared positive outcomes such as decreased stress, increased positive emotions, and enhanced interpersonal relationships. Relatedly, in a German sample of Catholic priests, spiritual dryness marked by a disconnection from God was associated with depressive symptoms, perceived stress, and emotional exhaustion (Bussing et al., 2013). A relationship with God is important to clergy from other Christian denominations and Judaism. The relationship with God is often considered the primary mechanism in which clergy hear their calling to religious leadership. Clergy's daily and dynamic connection with God through prayer is a sustaining spiritual force to their ministry activities. As a result, there is a colloquialism among clergy, which is supported by some empirical evidence (Isacco et al., 2016), that a lack of prayer time with God is predictive of clergy misbehavior, burnout, and other unhealthy behaviors. Such data underscores the importance of the theistic dimension of spirituality for clergy.

The spiritual call from God to clergy is directed at helping and serving other people. Psychological scholarship reinforces that an indicator of an authentic spiritual calling is that the transcendent summons is 'other-oriented' (Dik & Duffy, 2009). For clergy, the helping and serving of people is experienced and practiced within a spiritual framework. They are not social workers, mental health counselors, or other secular helping professions. Clergy serve others primarily through leading the organized practice of religion such as presiding over liturgical services, administering sacraments, teaching the faith, and pastoral care. Those ministerial activities, as conducted as an expression of their spirituality, is consistent with the ritualistic dimension of the RiTE model. The ritualistic dimension of spirituality is the structured connection with God through the organized practice and disciplined observance of the faith (Webb et al., 2014). Moreover, clergy understand their participation in rituals as part of their vocational identity as a spiritual leader, father, shepherd, pastor, teacher (Isacco & Songy, 2022). Taken together, it is important to understand that clergy's ritualistic behaviors are within the context of an organized religion and reflective of an interior spirituality and identity. Such a dynamic is a good example of the inter-relatedness among the theistic and ritualistic dimensions of the RiTE model.

Clergy ritualistic behaviors are also studied within social science research because of observed concerns such as dissatisfaction with ministry and leaving the vocation. Among the concerns, clergy burnout is a prominent area of emphasis. According to Maslach and Leiter (2016, p. 103), burnout is "a psychological syndrome emerging as a prolonged response to chronic interpersonal stressors on the job" and may include a sense of exhaustion, cynicism, detachment from the job, and/or a sense of ineffectiveness. Some researchers have labeled clergy as a "high risk" population because they are exposed to several kinds of vocational stressors and diminishing or limited resources and support (Terry & Cunningham, 2020). Specific to the ritualistic dimension of the RiTE model, clergy are often called upon to "do more with less," which can contribute to burnout and other negative health outcomes. For example, in a cross-sectional study with a sample of primarily Christian clergy from various denominations, Shaw et al. (2021) reported a significant correlation between occupational distress and depression. Furthermore, the researchers found that their clergy sample reported higher levels of occupational demand, criticism, loneliness, and stress than a general population mean (Shaw et al., 2021). Conversely, work-related social support such as support from their denomination and congregation has been found to be positively associated with mental health or lessens the effect of stress on mental health among clergy populations (Terry & Cunningham, 2020).

The spiritual mechanisms that may explain clergy burnout and related health outcomes are varied and complex. Clergy may extend themselves beyond their capacity by becoming involved in too many ritualistic activities. Other clergy may perceive insufficient support from the organized religion that they devoted themselves to, thus becoming angry, hurt, or feeling let down by the very religion that they feel spiritually called to serve. For other clergy, they may experience a shift away from the ritualistic behaviors that nurture their spirituality and are drawn into non-spiritual administrative matters. Clergy that become consumed by administrative matters such as financial decision-making and human resource management often lack the training, skills, desire, and self-efficacy for such work. As a result, it is understandable why clergy question their vocation or leave their clerical roles. Both circumstances (questioning and leaving) illustrate an exemplar connection between the ritualistic and existential dimensions of the RiTE model. The existential dimension focuses on the search for meaning and purpose. Clergy that are experiencing occupation distress, burnout, and are engaged in vocational activities outside of the spiritual dimensions are likely to feel a lack of meaning. Congregational support in the form of providing expertise to administrative matters allow clergy to re-focus on the ritualistic activities of their spiritual calling, which contribute to enhanced meaning associated with their vocation. Newer models of church management are emphasizing co-responsibility among clergy and laity, in part, for these reasons i.e., to capitalize on laity strengths and allow clergy to operate from their strengths as religious-spiritual leaders. Such models are based on data that has documented the negative effects of clergy doing non-clergy activities and thus, the belief that clergy engaging in spiritual-ministerial activities will be happier and find greater meaning in their vocation and stay with it longer.

Taken together, the RiTE model has obvious applicability to clergy and clergy health. For researchers, the RiTE model provides an emergent theoretical conceptualization to generate new hypotheses about clergy health. Researchers need to "break the ice" by applying the RiTE model to clergy samples. We recommend starting with qualitative studies to understand the lived spiritual experience of clergy spirituality in their own words, to capture the voices of diverse and underrepresented groups of clergy, and to use as a springboard for quantitative studies to test emergent hypotheses with larger samples. In the United States, the vast majority of clergy are male but there are female clergy in organized religions (e.g., Anglican). There is scarce research on the experience and health of female clergy. Investigating the health of female clergy within the RiTE model is an intriguing line of inquiry. Moreover, African-American and Black clergy may have unique health needs at the intersection of religious, spiritual, and racial factors. Exploratory research with African-American and Black clergy may provide insight into the applicability of the RiTE model within a multicultural framework. Certainly, as the extant literature matures with the RiTE model, researchers can utilize more sophisticated research designs such as longitudinal studies that track clergy health outcomes, moderation and mediation analyses to understand nuanced relationships between variables, and randomized controlled studies to examine the efficacy of theory-based interventions aimed at improving clergy health.

Religious Context to Clergy Health

As mentioned in our initial conceptualization, religion and spirituality are interwoven with clergy and separating the two constructs would be inauthentic. Similarly, there is a distinct religious/spiritual context to clergy health. This section describes how the clergy role itself impacts health outcomes and behaviors.

Clerics are human but often are treated as if they were demigods. People pursue a clergy vocation typically through a spiritual calling from God. Clergy then assume a role of religious leader within their organized religion. Many clerics in various religious communities usually wear special clothes and live in rectories or religious communities away from laypeople. Their lives, observed from a distance, seem very different from the lives of laypersons; the lifestyle differences may prompt inaccurate perceptions and expectations of clergy health and well-being (McGlone & Sperry, 2012; Ruiz-Prada et al., 2021; Seitz, 2016). Despite the Divine inspiration and spiritual context to their leadership, clerics are human too. This statement might seem obvious but it is critically important to be aware of in work with clergy. Too often, people put clerics on a pedestal expecting them to be perfect, "holier thou art," and not to have any problems or to make any mistakes (Plante, 2020a). People's expectations and way they interact with clergy may reinforce a demigod-like aura or status for clergy. As a result, clergy can feel increased social pressure, pastoral demands, and work-related stress from such expectations (Isacco et al., 2014). Clinically, we have worked with clergy members that "buckle" under such pressure and stress. They feel isolated, alone, and misunderstood. Some struggle with anxiety and perfectionism. All of which is directly tied to the religious/spiritual context of their clergy role.

To highlight the humanity of clerics, we provide a few case examples from our clinical work with clergy in Chapter Appendix A. The case examples illustrate some common issues that clerics experience that call for mental health services and consultation. With clergy clients, cultural competency is needed to adequately assist the cleric or congregation in question to best manage behavioral, psychological, or relational problems. Indeed, religious leaders have been found to struggle with depression, anxiety, personality disorders, addictions of various types (e.g., alcohol, gambling, pornography), and other psychiatric concerns (de Santana et al., 2021; Edwards et al., 2020; Isacco et al., 2022).

The other side to social perceptions of clergy is clergy's self-perceptions. Clericalism is the tendency for a small group of leaders to place special importance on their role above others and to exert power and privilege in decision-making (Doyle 2003; Plante, 2020a; Wilson 2008). Clericalism has been observed among various religious leaders and is a common trap for people in high status and prestigious positions of authority where expectations for perfection and virtuous living are expected (Plante, 2020a). Clerics may feel in a privileged position trying to maintain appearances and avoid admitting to human foibles and difficulties. Clericalism may also engender a narcissistic tendency among religious leaders, which maladaptively enhances their sense of self-importance and prevents self-awareness of their challenges, mistakes, and areas of improvement (Burnham, 2023; Doyle, 2003, Plante, 2020a). Narcissistic personality disorder and/or narcissistic tendencies exacerbate mis-guided, elevated social perceptions of clergy by pulling for admiration from others (Montoro et al., 2022). Narcissism is further correlated with trauma, emotional dysfunction, perceived stress, aggressive behavior, and criminality (Montoro et al., 2022). In short, narcissistic clergy often are at-risk for mental health challenges to themselves and others.

In a qualitative study of Catholic priests (Isacco et al., 2014), participants described how priests developed a "Messiah complex," which is a sense that they need to, and are exclusively capable of, solving problems. A consequence of the Messiah complex is that priests often sacrifice their own health by overfunctioning, disenfranchising parish staff, and do not seek their own help. Indeed, clerics of all religious traditions are human and experience various challenges. Too often, clerics who have significant problems may not get the help that they need for a variety of reasons. We identified narcissism and clericalism as two barriers to help-seeking among clergy. In addition, clergy may encounter help-seeking barriers such as mental health stigma and concerns about the practitioner's cultural competency (Isacco et al., 2014). Concern about confidentiality is often on the minds of clerics especially when they are mandated to attend mental health counseling to do so by a religious superior (e.g., pastors, bishops, seminarian presidents, vocation directors) (Plante, 2013). In such cases, clarifying who the client is and who has access to records is important to do in the informed consent process. Churches have always been concerned about scandals and embarrassment. Church personnel may feel more comfortable referring to professionals who share their faith tradition, beliefs, and practices for example. They may feel that they can trust professionals who share their faith and religious community. Clerics may seek out psychological services on their own or their religious superiors may encourage the cleric to seek professional services (Plante, 2018).

Clergy have been found to rely on spiritual and religious strategies to cope with common psychological or behavioral problems (Manuel, 2012; Wilson, 2008). Some overreliance on spiritual/religious strategies may trend into spiritual bypassing (see Chapter 41, in this volume), which is typically maladaptive avoidance of the mental health concern through spiritualizing and religiousness (Fox, Cashwell, Picciotto, 2017). Clerics may also avoid seeking mental health services through healthy, adaptive religious and spiritual coping (e.g., prayer; Zondag, 2006). Given their religious identity and role, it makes sense that clergy use religious and spiritual means to cope with stress and mental health challenges. Indeed, positive religious coping behaviors are culturally congruent with clergy and should be reinforced by mental health practitioners. Clergy support groups are a nuanced area of empirical inquiry. The intention of such groups is to provide a space for clergy to gain support from each other (i.e., clergy to clergy) to better cope with the pastoral demands and pressures of being a religious leader. Miles and Proeschold-Bell (2013) reported mixed effects of their empirical investigation of support groups with United Methodist Church clergy and cautioned against a uniform endorsement of such an intervention. Gubi (2017) identified some limitations to clergy support groups that may contribute to negative effects such as difficulty with vulnerability, lack of structure, being mandated to attend by a religious superior, and group member sabotaging. It appears that some of the limitations reported by Gubi (2017) could be addressed by having a properly trained professional guide clergy support groups. Future research could investigate a professionally guided group versus a peer guided group. Future research can also continue to investigate the nuances of clergy support groups by identifying what are the positive mechanisms of change for specific healthy outcomes. Overall, clergy that look exclusively to religious-based coping strategies may benefit from 'both/and' thinking as opposed to either/or in selecting help-seeking strategies; a mental health component (e.g., individual counseling) and a religious practice such as prayer may have a more powerful collective effect with clergy rather than one over the other.

Over the past twenty plus years, clergy health has taken on enhanced importance because of increased awareness of clergy sexual abuse of minors. Clerical sexual abuse, especially within the Roman Catholic Church, has received a remarkable amount of media attention during the past several decades and most especially after the *Boston Globe*'s Investigative Spotlight Team published their reports starting in January of 2002. In fact, a 2015 Academy Award best picture feature film entitled, *Spotlight*, highlights the kind of publicity and impact the story of clerical sexual abuse has had in the United States and across the globe (Bishop, 2020; Drohan, 2016; Larson, 2015). The shock and hurt that people have felt from clergy sexual abuse is profound, in part, because of the break in trust from their religious leaders and the religious organizations. Religious organizations have contributed to clergy abuse through unhealthy cultural norms that promoted clericalism and poor leadership (Boston Globe Investigative Staff, 2002).

Certainly, clerical sexual abuse is appalling and reflects not only psychopathology but also legal crimes. The *Diagnostic and Statistical Manual of Mental Disorders* from the American Psychiatric Association (2022) suggests that between 3-5% of men are pedophiles who thus target prepubescent children for sexual gratification (Beech et al., 2016; Beier, 2021; Scherner et al., 2021). This estimate does not take into consideration inappropriate sexual contact between vulnerable adults (Kappler et al., 2020) and sexual predators that target minors who are post pubescent such as teenagers. The latter group are referred to as hebephiles but hebephilia is not considered a psychiatric disorder but is considered illegal in most jurisdictions. Since over a third of women report that they were sexually victimized by an adult male while they were a minor, clearly sexual victimization of minors is common among the general population (Finkelhor, 1984; Finkelhor et al., 1990; Williams, 1994). Sadly, no profession or way of life is immune to sexual abuse of minors. While being careful never to be complaisant, it is not surprising that a small number of clerics from various religions have had histories of sexual victimization of minors. The best available research from multiple independent sources suggests that the clergy abuse crisis in the Catholic Church never exceeded expected incidents from the general population of men and if anything was lower (John Jay College of Criminal Justice, 2004; Plante, 2020b). Of course, one would expect that clerics would be much better behaved than men would be in general, but it is important to note that clerics were never at higher risk than non-clerics regarding the sexual victimization of minors. Furthermore, only 10% of clerical offenders victimized prepubescent children while 90% victimized post pubescent teens (John Jay College of Criminal Justice, 2004). This is important since sexual engagements with post pubescent teens are not considered a psychiatric diagnosis but is still a crime in most jurisdictions (American Psychiatric Association, 2022). Thus, the phrase, "pedophile priest" is a misnomer since even among clerics who have victimized minors only a small percentage have victimized prepubescent children (Plante, 2020b).

The other misnomer is to consider clergy sexual abuse the result of isolated, independent actions of a few clergy members. Investigative journalism, government agencies, victim advocacy groups, and other scholars in the social sciences have largely reached a consensus that religious organizations historically lacked proper environmental safeguards, engaged in poor leadership decisions, and have systematically covered up clergy sexual abuse. Such behaviors on the part of religious leadership reflects organizational clericalism, "institutional failure" (Office of Attorney General, Commonwealth of Pennsylvania, 2023), and an abuse of power. Thus, the cultural norms and practices of religious organizations can exacerbate unhealthy and criminal behavior among the clergy. Much progress has been made to prevent clergy sexual abuse. Religious norms, attitudes, and cultures have changed to embrace more rigorous screening of clergy candidates (Isacco et al., 2022), environmental safeguards, transparent decision-making, and not sheltering clergy from civil and/or canonical justice.

Since 2002 and the advent of what has become known and referred to as "the Dallas Charter," the Catholic Church has policies and procedures in place to all but eliminate sexual victimization by clerics or anyone associated with the Church (United States Conference of Catholic Bishops, 2002a, 2002b). Research conducted by a secular and independent auditing firm has demonstrated that the incidence of clerical sexual victimization has been reduced to five or less credible accusations per year of alleged incidents occurring in the 21st century (United States Conference of Catholic Bishops, 2023). While not zero, these figures are very encouraging and are likely well below those of other professions and certainly below those among the public (Assini-Meytin et al., 2020; Borumandnia et al., 2020). These trends and descriptions certainly do not excuse any cleric of sexual victimization. Moreover, religious institutions and leadership still make bad situations worse by not taking victims' experiences seriously, keeping misbehaving clergy in active ministry, and other poor decision-making. However, it would be hard to find other institutions that have taken the prevention of child sexual abuse more seriously and to greater statistical effect than organized religions over the past twenty years.

The clergy abuse crisis speaks to the expectation that clerics are always perfectly behaved and virtuous. Perhaps no other vocation experiences the same level of media attention and outrage as clergy and some argue, Catholic clergy, in particular (McGlone & Sperry, 2012; Plante & Boccaccini, 1997; Ruiz-Prada et al., 2021; Seitz, 2016). All other high-status professions where virtuous behavior is expected such as physicians, schoolteachers, coaches, and counselors, have incidents of sexual victimization of minors (and typically much higher than clerics) but they receive much less attention than clerics (e.g., Fisher & Anders, 2020; Kocturk, 2020). Certainly, one would appropriately expect clerics to behave better than men and women from secular vocations. However, returning to our two original points in this section, clerics have similar types of psychiatric, behavioral, and relationship challenges that non-clerics do, and clerics are human too (Manuel, 2012; McGlone & Sperry, 2012; Ruiz-Prada et al., 2021; Seitz, 2016).

Interventions to Improve Clergy Health

The theoretical and empirical considerations presented in this chapter provide guidance for mental health practitioners (e.g., psychologists, counselors, social workers) to enhance their effectiveness with clergy. We hypothesize that this guidance will assist practitioners in their work with clergy given that there is a lack of specialized training in this area in most graduate programs and post-graduate continuing education offerings. First and foremost, mental health interventions with clergy need to account for the centrality of religion and spirituality to the identity, health, and well-being of clergy. Mental health practitioners can benefit from conceptualizing clergy concerns from the three interrelated dimensions (theistic, ritualistic, and existential) of the RiTE model to form hypotheses about the saliency of each dimension and how the dimensions are associated with presenting concerns, coping, resilience, and health behaviors.

Understanding the role of religion and spirituality in clerics identity and health is consistent with multicultural competence in the helping professions. Thus, mental health practitioners would benefit by applying guidelines for multicultural competency by conceptualizing the cleric's unique religious and spiritual context to offer culturally congruent interventions (American Psychological Association, 2017b). In addition, practitioner self-awareness is a primary component to multicultural competence. Regardless of one's own personal religious traditions, beliefs, and practices, mental health practitioners working with clergy need to be self-aware and exhibit cultural humility to avoid bias, discrimination, overgeneralizations, projection, transference, and other challenges working with these special clients (Plante, 2013, 2018). For example, mental health practitioners may be unfamiliar with married clergy or female clergy and thus make assumptions and statements that are insensitive and offensive. This may be true for any mental health professional with little if any experience with the religious traditions that the cleric represents. Exhibiting cultural humility is an effective therapeutic approach to learning more about a cleric's background, religiousness, and spirituality. As a result of learning more about the specifics of the cleric, mental health practitioners can adjust their diagnostic and intervention efforts from a more informed perspective (Davis et al., 2021).

One way to increase the probability of clergy receiving culturally congruent care is to refer them to mental health facilities and practices that specifically focus on working with clerics. For example, several inpatient and outpatient hospitals, clinics, and institutes focus on providing services for Catholic clerics and those in religious life. These include, for example, Southdown Institute (https://southdown.on.ca/) in Toronto, Canada, St. Luke's Institute (https://sli.org/) in Maryland, St. John Vianney (https://www.sjvcenter.org/) in Philadelphia, and Guest House (https://guesthouse.org/) in St. Louis. Additionally, there are several solo and group practices that specialize in providing mental health services from an integrative perspective with religious populations. We cannot "vouch" for each practice and practitioner, but we encourage searching for referrals with an explicit identification of religious/spiritual competency in their clinical approach. Organizations such as the Catholic Psychotherapy Association (CPA) maintain a national referral directory (https://cpa.ce21.com/directory), as do other religious groups and traditions. Furthermore, religious organizations (e.g., parishes, dioceses, administrative offices) over the years have maintained their own list of professionals that they have worked successfully with in the past that can work with new referrals. That said, we acknowledge that a common pitfall is countertransference among mental health practitioners that share the same religious/spiritual tradition as the cleric. For example, a mental health practitioner of the same religious tradition as the cleric may experience the same type of reverence and elevated expectations that others within their religious communities have about clerics. Mental health practitioners need to be mindful of their own biases and expectations even if the therapeutic relationship is based on a perceived religious match (Plante, 2013, 2018). Therefore, finding appropriate mental health professionals to work with clerics from a culturally congruent perspective is challenging but doable.

Attending to Confidentiality, Living in a Fishbowl, and the Dynamics of Help Seeking

In addition, when working with clergy, mental health practitioners need to be aware of important factors such as confidentiality (American Psychological Association, 2017a), living in a fishbowl, and the dynamics of help seeking. While all health care clients deserve and expect confidentiality, this is often especially complicated while working with clerics (Plante, 2013, 2018). For example, if they go to a mental health practitioner's office wearing clerical clothes, their confidentiality may be compromised. If they are well known in their local community, confidentiality may be harder to maintain when congregants or others see them going in and out of a mental health practice, clinic, or hospital. Additionally, Catholic clerics as well as some non-Catholic clerics are under a vow of obedience to their bishop or local religious superior who may insist on knowing about the contents or details of mental health evaluations or treatment services thereby compromising confidentiality. The religious superior may be paying for the clinical services, which can increase their expectation of receiving information in return. The payment arrangement complicates the basic question of 'who is the client?' (Isacco et al., 2022). Thus, clear informed consent policies and appropriate boundaries are warranted.

Clerics often live in a fishbowl, not only within their particular religious institution but within their local community. Whatever they do is likely amplified by their role as clerics. If a cleric has too much to drink at a restaurant, bar, or social event, people will take notice and likely talk about it. If a cleric has an angry outburst in public, it will likely be focused on and discussed within the community. Any behavior seen as less than virtuous or less than exemplary is likely to be scrutinized and discussed by community members and even the media. We suggest that mental health practitioners conceptualize clergy health within their broader community, including how the cleric is coping with social perceptions and what are the available social supports. The latter focus on social support is particularly important as some clergy may feel like they cannot seek psychological support from people within their congregation/parish and find clergy support groups unfulfilling.

Therefore, it makes sense that clerics are typically unfamiliar with being the person on the receiving line of help. Their primary role, steeped in the religious and spiritual nature of their vocation, is to help, serve, and support others. Thus, it may be very difficult for a cleric to receive mental health help as it often puts them in an unfamiliar and awkward position. They may resist being considered a patient of mental health services and may be highly embarrassed or uncomfortable. This creates a potentially awkward dynamic between the mental health practitioner and their cleric clients. We suggest that mental health practitioners exhibit empathetic regard and broach this topic with clergy as a gesture toward conveying understanding and nurturing the therapeutic alliance.

The Importance of Consultation

Various consultative strategies could be employed to minimize potential bias and stereotyping as well as ensuring that quality evidence-based and culturally competent services are offered. First, mental health practitioners should seek appropriate consultation or supervision when working with clerics from unfamiliar religious traditions and/or if countertransference is a risk. Second, mental health practitioners can attend workshops and continuing education training when offered by relevant parties. Third, mental health practitioners are encouraged to be good consumers of professional research and scholarship about working with clergy. Mental health professionals may wish to join or consider consulting with colleagues from the Catholic Psychotherapy Association (CPA), the Society for the Psychology of Religion and Spirituality (Division 36 of the American Psychological Association), the Christian Association for Psychological Studies (CAPS) or other similar professional organizations and groups that offer referrals, consultation, and trainings. For those new and inexperienced working with clergy, ongoing consultation and supervision is necessary.

Supporting Healthy Clerics

Mental health interventions with clerics often focus on remediating psychological, psychiatric, behavioral, or relationship concerns. Thus, the interventions can be reactionary rather than intentional. However, there are several important principles that can assist all religious institutions, organizations, and clerics in maintaining good mental health and maximizing the chances of clergy flourishing. First, those interested in pursuing seminary or full-time employment as a cleric or in religious life should be adequately screened to determine if they are psychologically fit for the vocation. Most of the major religious traditions and communities partner with psychologists and other mental health professionals to complete psychological evaluations including psychological testing in order to adequately screen applicants ensuring that they do not already suffer from serious psychological or behavioral dysfunction. Typically, background checks for criminal behaviors, financial problems (e.g., student loan debt) and social media screenings are conducted. Much research has been conducted on how to best complete psychological evaluations for clerics and thus spotting potential problems before they arise is critically important (Isacco et al., 2022; Plante, 2013, 2018, 2022).

Second, offering regular mental health check-ups and opportunities to nip potential problems in the bud is a good strategy to maintain good mental health among clerics. Normalizing mental health services is helpful to destigmatize help-seeking among this population of helpers. Typically, psychological and behavioral problems do not emerge overnight but rather unfold over time. Having access to regular mental health consultation and offering check-ups to ensure that clerics are psychologically healthy can be preventative and responsive to addressing needs as they arise. Along these lines, recent research has highlighted the need to focus on building resilience with clergy through intentional practice of establishing healthy boundaries in various life domains (ministry, interpersonally, emotionally), increasing self-awareness so clergy are attuned to their strengths and vulnerabilities, engaging in uplifting spiritual practices, and tapping into healthy peer support (Sielaff, Davis, & McNeil, 2021). An intentional mental health check-up can assess those areas with clergy and emphasize resilience rather than remediation. We believe that would be a welcomed strength-based approach with many clergy.

Summary and Conclusions

This chapter provided an overview of clergy health. Clergy are a unique cultural group. Religion and spirituality are inherent to their identity and vocation. Clergy experience vocational demands and stressors as well as psychological concerns that are often understood only from within a religious and spiritual perspective. Thus, religion and spirituality are central to clergy health. Although we are not aware of any research that has applied the RiTE model to clergy, we identified how the RiTE model can be used to conceptualize empirical findings and can be used for future research with diverse clergy samples. Mental health interventions need to be offered to clergy from an integrative and culturally competent approach. Practitioners are encouraged to maintain reasonable expectations of clergy. As stated earlier in this chapter, clerics are human too and are not immune to problems in life. We have found that just as one unhealthy cleric can create a ripple effect of unhealthiness in their community, one healthy cleric can have an immensely positive and healthy impact in their community. Therefore, expecting that they will need help and being ready to provide that help when needed can have a profound impact across clergy, religious individuals, and communities.

Appendix A

Case Examples of Clergy

Fr. Art, Roman Catholic priest

Fr. Art is a Roman Catholic priest who was referred for therapy by his bishop after he was caught with pornography on his office computer. Additionally, he was accused of initiating an affair with a married parishioner. Fr. Art admitted to his indiscretions and stated that he feels lonely being in the United States since he was born, raised, trained, and ordained overseas. Parishioners generally like Fr. Art very much and they report that his work as a priest has been exemplary. However, Fr. Art's sexual indiscretions are worrisome and the bishop hoped to find out how Fr. Art can turn this around and get whatever help he needs to address his inappropriate behavior.

Pastor Bob, Baptist minister

Pastor Bob is a Baptist minister that was referred for psychotherapy after he was drunk at a Church dinner function. He slurred his words, made some inappropriate comments, and Church members were concerned about him driving home. One of the Church members insisted that he drive Pastor Bob home and the pastor got angry with him for accusing him of being drunk. The Church elders insisted that Pastor Bob see a therapist who specializes in substance misuse.

Rabbi David, Jewish leader

Rabbi David is a religious leader within an orthodox Jewish community. He has not been getting along very well with both staff and congregants at his synagogue. He is new as the head rabbi and people describe him as being arrogant and quick to put people down. They acknowledge that the previous rabbi served the congregation for 20 years and was beloved. They acknowledge that Rabbi David has big shoes to fill and that perhaps their conflicts with him are a byproduct of the transition from one rabbi to another with very different personalities and management styles. The conflicts have escalated recently and the chair of the board of the synagogue has announced her abrupt resignation. The new board chair asked a mental health professional and member of the congregation to help them figure out what can be done to deal with these conflicts including potential ongoing psychological consultation with Rabbi David.

Sarah, Anglican priest

Sarah is an Anglican priest. She has been ordained five years and serves in an assistant role to the pastor at a large suburban parish outside of a major city. Sarah has felt frustrated with the pastor and congregants over her role and how people greet her. She feels minimized in the parish and reports that congregants often refer to her as the administrative assistant to the pastor. She also reports that she is not given as much responsibility, which the pastor has attributed to her inexperience with parish ministry. Sarah also described confusion over her title, "It feels weird to be called 'Father' by people but I am a priest!" Sarah is contemplating leaving the parish and seeking to minister in a different diocese.

References

American Psychiatric Association. (2022). *Diagnostic and statistical manual of mental disorders* (Fifth edition, Text Revision). Author.

American Psychological Association. (2017a). *Code of Ethics: General Principles*. Washington DC: Author. Retrieved December 4, 2023, from http://www.apa.org/ethics/code/

American Psychological Association (2017b). Multicultural Guidelines: An Ecological Approach to Context, Identity, and Intersectionality. Retrieved from: http://www.apa.org/about/policy/multicultural-guidelines.pdf

Assini-Meytin, L. C., Fix, R. L., & Letourneau, E. J. (2020). Child sexual abuse: The need for a perpetration prevention focus. *Journal of Child Sexual Abuse*, *29*(1), 22–40. https://doi.org/10.1080/10538712.2019.1703232

Beech, A. R., Miner, M. H., & Thornton, D. (2016). Paraphilias in the DSM-5. *Annual Review of Clinical Psychology*, *12*, 383–406. https://doi.org/10.1146/annurev-clinpsy-021815-093330

Beier, K. M. (Ed.). (2021). *Pedophilia, hebephilia and sexual offending against children*: *The Berlin Dissexuality Therapy* (BEDIT) (pp. 73–236). Springer.

Bishop, R. (2020). "Not an Ounce of Hollywood Bullshit": A Narrative Analysis of News Media Coverage of Spotlight's Oscar Win. *Journal of Communication Inquiry*, *44*(2), 157–177. https://doi.org/10.1177/0196859919829482

Borumandnia, N., Khadembashi, N., Tabatabaei, M., & Alavi Majd, H. (2020). The prevalence rate of sexual violence worldwide: a trend analysis. *BMC Public Health*, *20*, 1–7. https://doi.org/10.1186/s12889-020-09926-5

Boston Globe Investigative Staff (2002). *Betrayal: The Crisis in the Catholic Church*. New York: Little Brown.

Burnham, M. J. (2023). Clericalism: What is it and how can we treat it?. *Integratus*, *1*(2), 148–158. https://doi.org/10.1521/intg.2023.1.2.148

Büssing, A., Günther, A., Baumann, K., Frick, E., & Jacobs, C. (2013). Spiritual dryness as a measure of a specific spiritual crisis in catholic priests: associations with symptoms of burnout and distress. *Evidence-Based Complementary and Alternative Medicine : eCAM*, *2013*, 246797. https://doi.org/10.1155/2013/246797

Data USA (2024, February). Clergy. https://datausa.io/profile/soc/clergy?redirect=true

Davis, E. B., Plante, T. G., Grey, M. J., Kim, C. L., Freeman-Coppadge, D., Lefevor, T., Paulez, J. A., Giwa, S., Lasser, J., Stratton, S. P., Deneke, E., & Glowiak, K. (2021). The role of civility and cultural humility in navigating controversial areas in psychology. *Spirituality in Clinical Practice*, *8*(2), 79–87. https://doi.org/10.1037/scp0000236

de Santana, C. M. L., Domingos, L. F., Zanatta, C., & Campos, L. A. M. (2021). Catholic Priests mental health facing contemporary challenges. *International Journal of Development Research*, *11*(07), 48976–48982. https://doi.org/10.37118/ijdr.22518.07.2021

Dik, B. J., & Duffy, R. D. (2009). Calling and vocation at work: Definitions and prospects for research and practice. *The Counseling Psychologist*, *37*(3), 424–450. https://doi.org/10.1177/0011000008316430

Doyle, T. P. (2003). Roman Catholic clericalism, religious duress, and clergy sexual abuse. *Pastoral Psychology*, *51*, 189–231. https://doi.org/10.1023/A:1021301407104

Drohan, M. (2016). Spotlight and investigative journalism: How the film reinforces the essential role of a free, professional press in a democracy. *The Serials Librarian*, *71*(3-4), 212–220. https://doi.org/10.1080/0361526X.2016.1237403

Edwards, L., Bretherton, R., Gresswell, M., & Sabin-Farrell, R. (2020). The relationship between social support, spiritual well-being, and depression in Christian clergy: A systematic literature review. *Mental Health, Religion & Culture*, *23*(10), 857–873. https://doi.org/10.1080/13674676.2020.1838459

Finkelhor, D. (1984). *Child sexual abuse*. New York, 186f.

Finkelhor, D., Hotaling, G., Lewis, I. A., & Smith, C. (1990). Sexual abuse in a national survey of adult men and women: Prevalence, characteristics, and risk factors. *Child abuse & Neglect*, *14*(1), 19–28. https://doi.org/10.1016/0145-2134(90)90077-7

Fisher, L. A., & Anders, A. D. (2020). Engaging with cultural sport psychology to explore systemic sexual exploitation in USA gymnastics: A call to commitments. *Journal of Applied Sport Psychology*, *32*(2), 129–145.https://doi.org/10.1080/10413200.2018.1564944

Fox, J., Cashwell, C. S., & Picciotto, G. (2017). The opiate of the masses: Measuring spiritual bypass and its relationship to spirituality, religion, mindfulness, psychological distress, and personality. *Spirituality in Clinical Practice*, *4*(4), 274–287. https://doi.org/10.1037/scp0000141

Garfield, C.F., & Isacco, A., & Sahker, E. (2013). Religion and spirituality as important components of men's health and wellness: An analytic review. *American Journal of Lifestyle Medicine*, *7*, 27–37. https://doi.org/10.1177/1559827612444530

Gubi, P.M. (2017). Assessing the perceived limitations of reflexive groups for supporting clergy in the Church of England. *Mental Health, Religion & Culture*, *19*:7, 769–780, https://doi.org/10.1080/13674676.2017.1279130

Isacco, A., Sahker, E., Hamilton, D., Mannarino, M. B., Sim, W., & St Jean, M. (2014). A qualitative study of mental health help-seeking among Catholic priests. *Mental Health, Religion & Culture*, *17*(7), 741–757. https://doi.org/10.1080/13674676.2014.910759

Isacco, A., Sahker, E., Krinock, E., Sim, W., & Hamilton, D. (2016). How religious beliefs and practices influence the psychological health of Catholic priests. *American Journal of Men's Health*, *10*(4), 325–337. https://doi.org/10.1177/1557988314567325

Isacco, A., & Songy, D. (2022). Spiritual fatherhood of Catholic priests: Conceptualization and practical applications. *Spirituality in Clinical Practice*, *9*(2), 114–126. https://doi.org/10.1037/scp0000293

Isacco, A., Songy, D. G., & Plante, T. G. (2022). Psychological evaluations of clergy applicants in the Catholic Church: Answering frequently asked questions. *Spirituality in Clinical Practice*, *9*(2), 127. https://doi.org/10.1037/scp0000294

John Jay College of Criminal Justice (2004). *The nature and scope of the problem of sexual abuse of minors by Catholic priests and deacons in the United States*. New York: Author.

Kappler, S., Talitman, E., Cavaliere, C., DeLonghi, G., Sy, M., Simpson, M., & Roncadin, S. (2020). Underdeveloped affective maturity and unintegrated psychosexual identity as contributors to clergy abuse and boundary violations: Clinical observations from residential treatment of Roman Catholic clergy at the Southdown Institute. *Spirituality in Clinical Practice*, *7*(4), 302–309. https://doi.org/10.1037/scp0000234

Kocturk, N. (2020). A retrospective study: According to online news, the victims, perpetrators and characteristics of sexual abuse at schools. *Eurasian Journal of Educational Research*, *20*(86), 115–134. https://doi.org/10.14689/ejer.2020.86.6

Larson, S. (2015, December 8). "Spotlight" and Its Revelations. *The New Yorker*. Retrieved from: https://www.newyorker.com/culture/sarah-larson/spotlight-and-its-revelations

Manuel, G. S. (2012). *Living Celibacy: Healthy Pathways for Priests*. Mahwah: Paulist Press.

Maslach, C., & Leiter, M. P. (2016). Understanding the burnout experience: recent research and its implications for psychiatry. *World psychiatry : Official Journal of the World Psychiatric Association (WPA)*, *15*(2), 103–111. https://doi.org/10.1002/wps.20311

McGlone, G. J., & Sperry, L. (2012). *The inner life of priests*. Liturgical Press.

Miles, A. & Proeschold-Bell, R. J. (2013). Overcoming the challenges of pastoral work? Peer support groups and psychological distress among United Methodist Church Clergy. *Sociology of Religion*, *74*, https://doi.org/10.1093/socrel/srs055

Montoro, C. I., de la Coba, P., Moreno-Padilla, M., & Galvez-Sánchez, C. M. (2022). Narcissistic personality and its relationship with post-traumatic symptoms and emotional factors: Results of a mediational analysis aimed at personalizing mental health treatment. *Behavioral Sciences*, *12*(4), 91. https://doi.org/10.3390/bs12040091

Office of Attorney General, Commonwealth of Pennsylvania (February, 2023). Pennsylvania Diocese Victims Report. https://www.attorneygeneral.gov/report/

Plante, T. G. (2013). Consultation with religious institutions. In K. Pargament (Editor-in-Chief), Exline, J., Jones, J., Mahoney, A, & Shafranske, E. (Assoc. Eds.). *APA handbooks in psychology: APA handbook of psychology, religion, and spirituality*, pp. 511–526. Washington, DC: American Psychological Association.

Plante, T. G. (2018). Ethical issues and challenges working with religious individuals and organizations: Providing culturally competent professional mental health services. In M.M. Leach & E. R. Welfel (Eds.), *The Cambridge handbook of applied psychological ethics*, pp. 366–383. New York: Cambridge University Press.

Plante, T. G. (2020a). Clericalism contributes to religious, spiritual, and behavioral struggles among Catholic priests, *Religions*, *11*(5), 217. https://doi.org/10.3390/rel11050217

Plante, T. G. (2020b). Clergy sexual abuse in the Roman Catholic Church: Dispelling eleven myths and separating facts from fiction. *Spirituality in Clinical Practice*, *7*(4), 220–229.https://doi.org/10.1037/scp0000209

Plante, T. G. (2022). Four lessons learned from 1,000 psychological evaluations of clerics and clerical applicants in the Roman Catholic and Episcopalian Churches. *Spirituality in Clinical Practice*, *9*(2), 140–143.https://doi.org/10.1037/scp0000257

Plante, T. G., & Boccaccini, M. T. (1997). Personality expectations and perceptions of Roman Catholic clergy members. *Pastoral Psychology*, *45*(4), 301–315. https://doi.org/10.1007/BF02282658

Ruiz-Prada, M., Fernández-Salinero, S., García-Ael, C., & Topa, G. (2021). Occupational stress and Catholic priests: A scoping review of the literature. *Journal of Religion and Health*, *60*, 3807–3870. https://doi.org/10.1007/s10943-021-01352-0

Scherner, G., Amelung, T., Schuler, M., Grundmann, D., & Beier, K. M. (2021). Pedophilia and hebephilia. In K.M. Beier (Ed.), *Pedophilia, hebephilia and sexual offending against children: The Berlin dissexuality therapy (BEDIT)* (pp. 1–13). Springer. https://doi.org/10.1007/978-3-030-61262-7

Seitz, J. C. (2016). The Lives of Priests. *American Catholic Studies*, *127*(2), 18–23. http://www.jstor.org/stable/44195832

Shaw, M., Lukman, R., Simmons, L. W., & Reynolds, R. (2021). Clergy wholeness study: How occupational distress, depression, and social support inform the health of clergy. *Journal of Pastoral Care & Counseling*, *75*(1), 23–32. https://doi.org/10.1177/1542305020968046

Sielaff, A. M., Davis, K. R., & McNeil, J. D. (2021). Literature review of clergy resilience and recommendations for future research. *Journal of Psychology and Theology*, *49*(4), 308–323. https://doi.org/10.1177/0091647120968136

Terry, J. D., & Cunningham, C. J. L. (2020). The Sacred and stressed: Testing a model of clergy health. *Journal of Religion and Health*, *59*(3), 1541–1566. https://doi.org/10.1007/s10943-019-00920-9

United States Conference of Catholic Bishops (2002a). *Charter for the Protection of Children and Young People*. Washington, DC: USCCB.

United States Conference of Catholic Bishops (2002b). *Essential norms for diocesan/eparchial policies dealing with allegations of sexual abuse of minors by priests or deacons*. Washington, DC: USCCB.

United States Conference of Catholic Bishops (2023). *2022 annual report on the implementation of the charter for the protection of children and young people*. Washington, DC: Author.

Webb, J. R., Toussaint, L., & Dula, C. S. (2014). Ritualistic, theistic, and existential spirituality: initial psychometric qualities of the RiTE measure of spirituality. *Journal of Religion and Health*, *53*(4), 972–985. https://doi.org/10.1007/s10943-013-9697-y

Williams, L. M. (1994). Recall of childhood trauma: A prospective study of women's memories of child sexual abuse. *Journal of Consulting and Clinical Psychology*, *62*(6), 1167.https://doi.org/10.1037/0022-006X.62.6.1167

Wilson, G. B. (2008). *Clericalism: The Death of Priesthood*. Collegeville: Liturgical Press.

Zondag, H. J. (2006). Narcissism and motivation for the pastorate. *Journal of Empirical Theology* 19: 227–243. https://doi.org/10.1163/157092506778884481

Part VI

Emerging Areas in the Science of Spirituality, Health, and Well-Being

Chapter 38

Religious and Spiritual Struggles and Their Implications for Health and Well-Being

A Concise Review of an Emerging and Promising Line of Inquiry

*Hisham Abu-Raiya**

Religion and spirituality, being a distinctively human phenomenon, have garnered significant attention from prominent figures in the field of psychology, such as William James, Sigmund Freud, and Carl Jung (Wulff, 1997). Strikingly, the exploration of the relationship between religion and spirituality and health and well-being was widely disregarded in scholarly research until the 1990s (Miller & Thoresen, 2003). In recent years, however, this picture has changed significantly as psychologists have displayed an increasing interest in investigating the influence of religion and spirituality on individuals' physical health, mental health, and overall well-being.

By and large, the findings of this body of scholarly research have established positive connections between religious and spiritual beliefs and practices and various indicators of health and well-being (for reviews, see Garssen et al., 2021; Hood et al., 2018; Pargament et al., 2013; Park et al., 2013). For instance, religion and spirituality have been linked to higher levels of meaning in life (Park et al., 2013), attachment security (see Granqvist & Kirkpatrick, 2013, for review), self-control (e.g., McCullough & Willoughby, 2009), comfort (e.g., Exline et al., 2000), life satisfaction (Yaden et al., 2022), and reduced levels of depression and anxiety (see Hood et al., 2018, for review). Furthermore, this line of inquiry has uncovered that religion and spirituality can serve as a valuable coping mechanism for individuals faced with life stressors (for reviews, see Abu-Raiya & Pargament, 2015; Ano & Vasconcelles, 2005; Aten et al., 2019; Gall & Guirguis-Younger, 2013; Pargament, 2011a).

This body of research, however, has largely neglected the more somber aspects of religion and spirituality (Abu-Raiya et al., 2015; Hood et al., 2018). Among these potentially troublesome manifestations, religious and spiritual struggles (r/s struggles) have recently received significant attention within the literature. This chapter constitutes a concise review of this emerging and promising line of inquiry. In the subsequent sections, I make reference to the conceptual framework that provides the most comprehensive understanding of r/s struggles, namely religious/spiritual coping theory (Pargament, 1997), elucidate the nature of the phenomenon, and highlight its various manifestations. Additionally, I discuss the prevalence of r/s struggles and some of the factors that predict their occurrence. Subsequently, I examine the empirical evidence pertaining to the connections between r/s struggles and health and well-being. I conclude by deliberating on promising avenues for future research in this domain.

* Corresponding Author: aburaiya@gmail.com.

DOI: 10.4324/9781003440048-44

Conceptual Framework

Religion and Spirituality

Numerous definitions of religion have been put forth by social scientists and theologians; however, a consensus remains elusive in this matter. This lack of consensus is nicely captured by the words of sociologist J. Milton Yinger (1967): "any definition of religion is likely to be satisfactory only to its author" (p. 108). This assertion is also applicable to spirituality (e.g., Zinnbauer et al., 2015). Pargament (1997) argues that due to the complex and subjective nature of religious and spiritual phenomena, singular definitions are inadequate in capturing their true essence. Pargament adopts a pragmatic approach to this matter and stresses that definitions of religion and spirituality should meet three criteria: (1) they should be tailored to the specific area of research we are interested in; (2) they should exclude any considerations regarding the nature of the transcend reality that are of little relevance to important human issues; and (3) they should be applicable to followers of various religious and spiritual groups (Abu-Raiya & Pargament, 2015). Pargament et al. (2013) provide definitions of religion and spirituality that meet these criteria, and which are specifically designed for psychological research. His operational definitions of these two constructs constitute the foundational framework for this chapter.

Pargament et al. (2013) define spirituality as the "search for the sacred." The *search* pertains to the process of discovering a sacred element in existence, the conservation of the sacred once it has been discovered, and the transformation of the sacred when internal or external pressures necessitate a modification (Pargament, 1997; Pargament & Mahoney, 2005). Pargament and Mahoney (2005) define the *sacred* as divine beings, higher powers, or God and other aspects of life that take on a divine character by virtue of their association with the divine. Pargament et al. (2013) define religion "the search for significance that occurs within the context of established institutions that are designed to facilitate spirituality" (p. 15). In this case, the destination of the search are diverse goals that grant *significance* to people's lives. They include personal ends, such as meaning in life and self-development; social ends, such as intimacy with others and justice in the world; and spiritual ends, such as living a moral and ethical life (Pargament & Mahoney, 2005). The search pertains to the multiple pathways people take to reach their goals. Religious pathways encompass multiple dimensions: ideology, ethical conduct, emotional experience, and social intercourse. Another key element in Pargament et al.' (2013) definition of religion is that religion occurs within the larger contexts of *recognized institutions and traditions* whose principal objective is facilitating *spirituality*. In contrast to the modern tendency among scholars to detach spirituality from religion, Pargament and colleagues' view is that spirituality is the purpose most essential to institutional religious life.

At this juncture, it could prove beneficial to engage in a comparative analysis of Pargament's conceptualizations of spirituality and religion with promising alternative definitions of the terms proposed by the RiTE Model of Spirituality. According to this model, spirituality is defined as "the salient, searching pursuit of the transcendently sacred ritualistic, theistic, and/or existential aspects of the human condition" (Webb et al., 2014, p. 974; see also, Chapters 1 and 44 of this volume). This model was created with the aim of being inclusive of various religious traditions, including monotheistic, polytheistic, Eastern, and Western beliefs, while also addressing the growing dichotomy between religion and spirituality. As a result, the previous concepts of religiousness and spirituality were merged into a comprehensive term, Spirituality, which was further divided into three interconnected dimensions: Ritualistic Spirituality (a structured connection with a higher power, previously known as religiousness),

Theistic Spirituality (a non-structured connection with a higher power, previously known as spirituality), and Existential Spirituality (a non-theistic, yet transcendent search for meaning and purpose; to potentially include individuals otherwise known as agnostic or atheist).

Pargament's and the RiTE models display remarkable similarities. Both portray the act of seeking or pursuing the sacred as being at the core of spirituality. They also disregard any contemplations regarding the essence of the transcendental reality that hold little significance to crucial human matters. Moreover, they encompass various religious traditions. Additionally, they are receptive to the presence of non-theistic manifestations of spirituality, such as the existential form. Furthermore, Pargament's definitions effectively capture the differentiation established by the RiTE Model between Ritualistic Spirituality and Theistic Spirituality, which is based on the structure of the connection with a higher power. The former pertains to what Pargament calls religion, while the latter pertains to what Pargament calls simply spirituality. However, it appears that the designation Ritualistic Spirituality of the RiTE model fails to encapsulate the "search for significance" component that resides at the essence of Pargament's delineation of religion. Of course, the spiritual aspect is fundamental to religion as postulated by Pargament et al. (2013), but the objectives that adherents of a religion strive for are not invariably of a religious nature.

Religious/Spiritual Coping Theory

Building on his definitions of religion and spirituality, Pargament (1997) has developed his spiritual/religious coping theory, which is, arguably, the most comprehensible theory via which we can examine r/s struggles. Abu-Raiya et al. (2015) provided a concise summary of this theory, outlining seven key points: (1) People are goal-directed beings motivated to seek some form of significance in life, be it psychological (e.g., emotional comfort, self-control), social (intimacy with others, social identity), material (e.g., wealth), or physical (e.g., attractiveness, health). (2) In the pursuit of their goals, people draw on a general orienting system consisting of stable beliefs (e.g., assumptive worlds), practices, personality characteristics, and social connections. (3) Spirituality and religion can be intimately interwoven into both the individuals' significant goals and orienting system; that is, people can pursue sacred or ultimate goals (see Emmons, 1999), and they can be oriented by their sacred beliefs, practices, experiences, and relationships. (4) People are generally successful in realizing and sustaining their significant goals. (5) At times, however, people experience major stressors and transitions which threaten and challenge their significant goals and orienting system. (6) Religious and spiritual resources are generally helpful to people confronting major life stressors (see Abu-Raiya & Pargament, 2015 for a recent review). (7) However, some life stressors affect spirituality itself triggering key questions and tensions with respect to one's most fundamental assumptions about the world, values, practices, and relationships that provide orientation and guidance in living. At times, people find themselves spiritually shaken by trauma and transition. The latter two points allude to the two fundamental manners in which religion and spirituality intertwine in the process of coping.

Religious/Spiritual Coping-Definition and Types

Religious/spiritual coping is a coping mechanism which is inherently derived from religious/spiritual beliefs, practices, experiences, emotions, or relationships (Abu-Raiya & Pargament, 2015). As with other methods of coping, religious/spiritual coping methods can be either constructive or destructive. On conceptual and empirical grounds, Pargament et al. (1998) distinguished between two categories of religious/spiritual coping: *Positive religious/spiritual coping* and *negative religious/spiritual coping*. Positive religious/spiritual coping activities reflect a secure relationship with God, a belief that there is a greater meaning to be found, and a sense of spiritual connectedness with others, while negative religious/spiritual coping activities reflect an ominous view of the world and a religious/spiritual struggle to find and conserve significance in life. Factor analysis techniques indicate that positive and negative religious/spiritual coping are higher-order constructs that describe a variety of more specific religious/spiritual coping methods (Pargament et al., 2000). Given that religious/spiritual struggles are at the heart of negative religious/spiritual coping, these two concepts have been employed interchangeably. In recent years, the utilization of religious/spiritual struggles has gained more prevalence, and thus it will be used throughout this chapter. In what follows, I briefly discuss positive religious coping, and then move to r/s struggles, which are the focus of this chapter.

Positive Religious/Spiritual Coping

In difficult times, many people find themselves drawing on their religious and spiritual beliefs, practices, and teachings. Empirical evidence strongly supports this assertion. For example, a national survey of Americans shortly after the September 11, 2001, attacks revealed that 90% of Americans turned to God for solace and support (Schuster et al., 2001). In a sample of Egyptian patients with cancer, 92% voiced their belief that God will help them in their illness (Kesseling et al., 1986). Between 39% and 51% of HIV/AIDS and cancer patients reported drawing on their religion to cope with their illnesses (Simoni et al., 2002; Tarakeshwar et al., 2006; Trevino et al., 2010). Of 189 cancer patients in England, 35%, 31%, and 18% described opportunities for personal prayer, support from people of their faith, and support from a spiritual adviser as important needs, respectively (Sothill et al., 2002).

In the past 20 years, a number of empirical studies have tested the links between religious coping and the health and the well-being of the individual. These studies have established significant associations between both positive religious/spiritual coping and indices of physical and mental health (for reviews, see Abu-Raiya & Pargament, 2015; Cummings & Pargament, 2010; Gall & Guirguis-Younger, 2013. For a relevant meta-analysis, see Ano & Vasconcelles, 2005). To summarize, positive religious coping methods have been associated with lower mortality (Fizpatrick et al., 2007), better self-rated physical health (Boswell et al., 2006), slower disease progression for HIV-1 (Ironson & Hayward, 2008), fewer complications following coronary artery bypass surgery (Ai et al., 2009). Positive religious coping has also been linked to lower levels of distress (Tix & Frazier, 1998), less depression and anxiety (Braxton et al., 2007; Lee, 2007), less helplessness (Arnette et al., 2007), less severe post-trauma symptoms (Meisenhelder & Marcum, 2004), and less suicidality (Rosmarin et al., 2013). Additionally, positive religious coping has been associated with indicators of subjective well-being, including greater happiness, quality of life, post-traumatic growth, and satisfaction with life (Ayele et al., 1999; Gillum et al., 2006; Krumrei et al., 2011; Lee, 2007). These findings were obtained from Christian populations primarily. However, similar findings have been obtained from non-Christian populations as well, such as Jews (e.g., Pirutinsky et al., 2011; Rosmarin et al., 2009b; Rosmarin et al., 2009c) and Muslims (Abu-Raiya et al., 2011; Abu-Raiya et al., 2008; Ai et al., 2003).

Religious and Spiritual Struggles

R/s struggles occur when some aspect of religious and spiritual belief, practice, or experience becomes a focus or a source of tension or internal conflict (Exline et al., 2014; Pargament & Exline, 2021). Research has identified three main forms of r/s struggles: *supernatural* struggles, *interpersonal* struggles, and *intrapersonal* struggles (e.g., Exline, 2013; Exline et al., 2014). Supernatural struggles focus on beliefs about supernatural agents: *Divine* struggles involve tensions or conflict centered on beliefs about God or a perceived relationship with God, and *demonic* struggles involve concern that the devil or evil spirits are attacking an individual or causing negative events. Interpersonal struggles involve negative experiences with religious people or institutions or conflict with others around religious issues. Other such struggles are intrapersonal: they have an inward focus on one's own thoughts or actions. Three types of intrapersonal struggles have emerged as significant: *moral* struggles (in which a person wrestles with attempts to follow moral principles or feels excessive guilt in response to perceived transgressions), *doubt-related* struggles (in which people are troubled by doubts or questions about their beliefs), and *ultimate meaning-related* struggles (in which people feel a lack of deeper meaning in life).

Prevalence

Individuals may exhibit a reluctance to disclose certain types of r/s struggles. For instance, research has indicated that numerous individuals perceive anger directed toward God, which represents a form of divine struggle, as morally objectionable (Exline et al., 2012). Consequently, those who choose to reveal such emotions to others may encounter stigmatizing reactions (Exline & Grubbs, 2011). Another plausible explanation for this unwillingness has been proposed by Abu-Raiya (2017), who posited that individuals who adhere to a religious faith may be consciously or unconsciously motivated to present their *religion* in a positive and desirable manner. Therefore, by acknowledging their experiences of r/s struggles, they run the risk of portraying their religion in a negative light. Abu-Raiya referred to this inclination as "theological desirability."

However, in spite of the potential obstacles to reporting r/s struggles, it has become evident that they are not infrequent; numerous individuals encounter r/s struggles and are willing to report them (e.g., Abu-Raiya et al., 2016a, 2016b; Bryan & Astin, 2008; Exline & Grubbs, 2011; Johnson & Hayes, 2003; McConnell et al., 2006). To illustrate, Johnson and Hayes (2003) found that 25% of more than 5000 university students experienced significant distress related to their religious and spiritual concerns. In a study encompassing a large national sample of university students, 18% indicated that they had frequently questioned their religious/spiritual convictions and 40% occasionally experienced anger toward God (Bryan & Astin, 2008). In their work with a group of adults who reported on an occurrence involving some form of suffering, Exline and Grubbs (2011) ascertained that 54% reported some degree of anger directed toward God. In a study conducted by Abu-Raiya et al. (2016a), it was observed that among 139 Israeli-Palestinian Muslims, the prevalence of various r/s struggles ranged from 1.4% to 40.2%, with struggles related to ultimate meaning and demonic influences being the most commonly reported. Among some sub-groups, r/s struggles can be more prevalent. For example, in a sample of Jamaican patients being treated at a sickle-cell unit, 73.6% strongly agreed that "I feel that stressful situations are God's way of punishing me for sins or lack of spirituality" and 74.1% strongly agreed that "I wonder whether God has abandoned me" (Morgan et al., 2014).

Predictors

Pargament (1997) posited the idea that r/s struggles are more likely to be encountered by individuals who possess a limited "general orienting system": a set of overarching beliefs, practices, relationship patterns, coping resources, and personality characteristics that guide individuals in their quest for significance in life. A limited general orienting system is typically characterized by a lack of breadth and depth, inflexibility, and a lack of benevolence. Consequently, individuals with a limited general orienting system may find themselves ill-equipped to navigate the full spectrum of life experiences, including instances of pain and suffering. Conversely, a strong general orienting system, which is marked by flexibility, breadth, depth, and benevolence, could potentially enhance an individual's ability to effectively cope with life's challenges and stressors. Pargament postulated that markers of a restricted general orienting system would correlate with increased levels of r/s struggles, whereas markers of a more fully developed general orienting system would be associated with reduced levels of r/s struggles.

In line with Pargament's postulations, empirical studies have identified a number of personality traits and situational factors that can serve as risk factors in the development of r/s struggles. These factors encompass neuroticism and pessimism (Ano & Pargament, 2013; Wilt et al., 2017), narcissistic qualities and a sense of entitlement (Grubbs et al., 2013), loneliness (Abu-Raiya et al., 2015), negative appraisals of stressful events (Ano & Pargament, 2013), poor social support (McConnell et al., 2006; Ramirez et al., 2012), not being in committed relationship (Exline et al., 2014), greater dignity-related problems and poorer quality of life (Damen et al., 2021), and perceived addiction to Internet pornography (Grubbs et al., 2017). On the other hand, some other personality and situational factors such as meaningful life goals, worthwhileness of life and viewing life as a gift (King et al., 2017), humility (Grubbs & Exline, 2014), conscientiousness and self-discipline (e.g., Wilt et al., 2016), higher self-esteem (Adom-Fynn et al., 2019/2020), and engagement in healthy practices (e.g., exercise; Pargament et al., 2016) have been identified as protective factors against the occurrence of r/s struggles.

Religious and spiritual variables represent one important subset of the orienting system; Pargament has referred to this subset as the religious orienting system (ROS; Pargament, 1997). ROS consists of both resources and burdens which can facilitate or impede efforts to deal with life challenges and demands. In this vein, Pargament (1997) notes that the ROSs of people vary in their strength. Indicators of a stronger ROS include greater embeddedness of the individual in a religious system, greater commitment to religious beliefs and practices, and religious beliefs that are more positive or benevolent in nature. Conversely, some religious factors might be indicators of a more limited ROS and hence could put the individual at risk of developing r/s struggles (e.g., extrinsic motivation to religion, malevolent religious/spiritual beliefs).

In accordance with Pargament's conceptual framework, empirical investigations have identified numerous religious/spiritual factors that serve as potential precursors for the emergence of r/s struggles. Among these factors are insecure ambivalent attachment to God (Ano & Pargament, 2013; Cooper et al., 2009; Sandage & Crabtree, 2012), negative God image (Abu-Raiya et al., 2016a, 2016b), being part of a religious minority, quest orientation toward religion and seeing God as elusive (Bryant & Astin, 2008), and extrinsic religious orientation (Ake & Horen, 2004). On the other hand, engaging in daily spiritual experiences (Park et al., 2014), positive God image (Abu-Raiya et al., 2016a; Bryant & Astin, 2008), secure attachment to God (Granqvist & Kirkpatrick, 2013), sanctification and religious hope (Abu-Raiya et al., 2016c) have been identified as protective factors against the occurrence of r/s struggles.

Health and Well-Being

A number of cross-sectional studies have linked r/s struggles to emotional distress and poorer well-being (for reviews, see Ano & Vasconcelles, 2005; Exline, 2013; Pargament, 2007; Pargament et al., 2013). Many studies have documented ties between r/s struggles and emotional distress (e.g., Ellison & Lee, 2010), including greater anxiety (e.g., Harris et al., 2014; McConnell et al., 2006), depression (e.g., Ano & Vasconcelles, 2005), and suicidal ideation (e.g., Exline et al., 2000). Other studies have shown strong links between r/s struggles and poorer subjective well-being, including lower life satisfaction (Abu-Raiya et al., 2016a, 2016b; Exline et al., 2014; Park, Wortmann, & Edmondson, 2011). Many of these studies have shown that the associations between increased levels of r/s struggles and poorer levels of health and well-being are robust, thus evident after accounting for potential confounding variables (e.g., Abu-Raiya et al., 2015; Currier et al., 2017; Ellison & Lee, 2010; McConnell et al., 2006).

Yet, because the previously mentioned studies have employed cross-sectional designs, it is not possible, based on these studies, to ascertain the causal relationship between r/s struggles and negative psychological processes. These correlational findings can be explicated by three potential explanations, which Pargament (2009) referred to as primary r/s struggles (i.e., r/s struggles stimulate negative psychological outcomes), secondary r/s struggles (i.e., r/s struggles are the results of negative psychological processes), and complex r/s struggles (both r/s struggles and negative psychological processes occur simultaneously). In order to investigate the direction of causality, longitudinal studies are necessary, and indeed, several such studies have been conducted. A small number of these studies (e.g., Neimeyer & Burke, 2011; Rynolds et al., 2014) have provided support for the secondary r/s struggles model. For example, working with a sample of African Americans who lost a loved one due to homicide, Neimeyer and Burke (2011) found that those who reported more severe grief reactions experienced higher levels of r/s struggles over time.

However, the majority of longitudinal studies conducted within this particular field have indicated that r/s struggles are indicative of future psychological distress and maladjustment, thus providing support for the primary model of r/s struggles (for a recent meta-analysis, refer to Bockrath et al., 2022). These studies utilized varying measures of psychological distress and maladjustment, such as depressive symptoms (e.g., Park et al., 2011; Pirutinsky et al., 2011; Rosmarin et al., 2013), anxiety (Exline et al., 2016; Wilt et al., 2017), symptoms of post-traumatic stress disorder (Currier et al., 2015; Harris et al., 2012), addictive behaviors (Faigin et al., 2014), and suicidal ideation (Currier et al., 2018). A single study even discovered that r/s struggles predicted higher rates of mortality (Pargament et al., 2001). These findings strongly suggest that r/s struggles might lead to distress, agony, and maladjustment.

But what are the mechanisms through which r/s struggles achieve their detrimental consequences? Stated differently, how can these causal links between r/s struggles and poorer health and well-being be explicated? There are two sets of possible explanations: The reductionstic and the non-reductionstic (Abu-Raiya & Pargament, 2015). The basic idea behind the reductionstic explanation is that the links between r/s struggles and well-being are not direct, but rather mediated by non-spiritual variables. According to this line of thinking, r/s struggles lead to some non-spiritual consequences (e.g., emotional negativity, disconnection from one's religious community) and those non-spiritual elements of life eventually lead to negative outcomes. In contrast, according to the non-reductionstic explanation, r/s struggles lead to negative outcomes because they reflect a shaken system of ultimate beliefs and practices and a threat to one's deepest values, commitments, and worldview. From this latter perspective, it is the spiritual character of the struggle that is most directly responsible for its effects on health and well-being.

Limitations and Future Directions

The field of study focused on r/s struggles and their implications for health and well-being has clearly made significant advancements. Currently, we possess well-established conceptual frameworks that allow us to comprehend this phenomenon. Additionally, we have gained a good understanding of the prevalence of these struggles, and certain factors that contribute to their occurrence have been identified. Furthermore, it is now evident that there are strong and consistent associations between r/s struggles and psychological distress and maladjustment, with sufficient evidence of the former predicting the latter over time. However, despite these advancements, there are still limitations and deficiencies in this area of research that need to be addressed in future studies in order to expand and deepen our understanding in this field. In what follows, I discuss some of these limitations.

First, a number of investigations have been conducted on r/s struggles within non-Christian populations, particularly among Muslims (Abu-Raiya et al., 2016a, 2016b; Abu-Raiya et al., 2018); as well as Jews (Pirutinsky et al., 2011; Rosmarin et al., 2009a, 2009b, 2009c). However, the majority of research in this field has been carried out among Christian populations. Consequently, there is a need for studies among individuals who adhere to different religious faiths such as Islam, Judaism, Buddhism, and Hinduism, and spiritual individuals who do not align themselves with acknowledged religious tradition, or individuals who hold the belief of agnosticism or atheism. These studies would enable us to determine whether the theoretical frameworks proposed to explain this phenomenon among Christians are also applicable to individuals from other faiths. Additionally, these investigations would allow us to compare and contrast the findings obtained from Christian populations with those obtained from individuals who follow other religious traditions or align with other spiritual groups. Of particular importance are longitudinal studies that can establish the causal relationship between r/s struggles and health and well-being. To the best of my understanding, with the exception of a handful of studies carried out among Jews (e.g., Pirutinsky et al., 2011), no longitudinal studies exploring this area have been undertaken within non-Christian populations.

Second, a few cross-sectional investigations have indicated that the associations between r/s struggles and health and well-being persist even when factors such as neuroticism, religious commitment, loneliness (Abu-Raiya et al., 2015), and the Big Five personality traits (Wilt et al., 2017) were controlled for. However, the absence of reporting on longitudinal studies that explore potential mediators between r/s struggles and health and well-being leaves unanswered the question of whether the impact of r/s struggles on health and well-being is direct or indirect through other psychological mechanisms. Consequently, there is a need for longitudinal studies that specifically investigate potential mediators between r/s struggles and psychological distress and maladjustment. Studies of this kind will contribute to the resolution of the ongoing discourse between advocates of reductionistic and non-reductionistic explanations mentioned earlier (Abu-Raiya & Pargament, 2015).

Third, the inquiry as to whether the associations between r/s struggles and poorer adjustment are moderated by other factors has not yet been adequately addressed. A few studies have already identified factors that either mitigate or intensify these connections, such as acceptance of struggles (Dworsky et al., 2016), religious commitment, support, hope, and life sanctification (Abu-Raiya et al., 2016c). However, upon reviewing the existing literature, it becomes evident that the examination of moderating variables in the relationship between r/s struggles and health and well-being has not been undertaken in longitudinal studies, thus necessitating the filling of this void in the scholarly discourse. Two prospective domains to extract plausible moderators from are health-related actions and social support, two domains that have consistently been linked to improved mental health and wellness (Nenova et al., 2013; Kawachi & Berkman, 2001; Pargament et al., 2016), and thus can serve as a resource that can alleviate the adverse impact of r/s struggles.

Fourth, until recent years, and more specifically prior to the development of the Religious and Spiritual Struggles Scale (RSSS; Exline et al., 2014), the existing body of research on religious and spiritual struggles, with a few notable exceptions (e.g., Ellison & Lee, 2010; Pargament, et al., 2000), has predominantly concentrated on divine struggles, primarily assessed through the Brief RCOPE (Pargament et al., 1998) or the Religious Comfort and Strain Scale (Exline et al., 2000), while overlooking alternative forms of struggle. Although divine struggles hold significant importance and occupy a central position, they merely represent one type of r/s struggles, and the findings pertaining to them alone fail to provide a comprehensive understanding of this intricate and multifaceted construct. Consequently, it is imperative to conduct studies that encompass the complete spectrum of r/s struggles. As observed, progress has been made in this direction (Abu-Raiya & Pargament, 2015; Abu-Raiya et al., 2016a, 2016b, 2016c; Exline et al., 2014).

Finally, the larger perspective becomes somewhat evident: there are enduring positive connections between religious and spiritual struggles and undesirable indicators of health and well-being. However, the "smaller perspective," the more intricate and detailed perspective, remains ambiguous. The inquiries that demand responses are *which* types of r/s struggles forecast *which* indicators of health and well-being, and which of these struggles exhibit a stronger influence. Investigations that concentrate specifically on these inquiries will contribute substantially to the breadth, depth, and complexity of our comprehension of the role of r/s struggles in our psychological existence, and may possess more pragmatic usefulness for healthcare professionals who possess an interest in aiding clients in navigating their struggles.

References

Abu-Raiya, H. (2017). A critique from within: Some important research issues that psychologists of religion and spirituality should further work on. *Mental Health, Religion & Culture*, *20*(6), 544–551. https://doi.org/10.1080/13674676.2017.1377945

Abu-Raiya, H., Ayten, A., Agbaria, Q., & Tekke, M. (2018). Relationships between religious struggles and well-being among a multinational Muslim sample: A comparative analysis. *Social Work*, *63*(4), 347–356. https://doi.org/10.1093/sw/swy031

Abu-Raiya, H., & Pargament, K. I. (2015). Religious coping among diverse religions: Commonalities and divergences. *Psychology of Religion and Spirituality*, *7*(1), 24–33. https://doi.org/10.1037/a0037652

Abu-Raiya, H., Pargament, K. I., Exline, J., & Agbaria, Q. (2016a). Prevalence, predictors, and implications of religious/spiritual struggles among Muslims. *Journal for the Scientific Study of Religion*, *54*(4), 631–648. https://doi.org/10.1111/jssr.12230

Abu-Raiya, H., Pargament, K. I., & Krause, N. (2016b). Religion as problem, religion as solution: Religious buffers of the links between religious/spiritual struggles and well-being/mental health. *Quality of Life Research*, *25*, 1265–1274.

Abu-Raiya, H., Pargament, K. I., & Mahoney, A. (2011). Examining coping methods with stressful interpersonal events experienced by Muslims living in the United States following the 9/11 attacks. *Psychology of Religion and Spirituality*, *3*, 1–14. http://dx.doi.org/10.1037/a0020034

Abu-Raiya, H., Pargament, K. I., Mahoney, A., & Stein, C. (2008). A psychological measure of Islamic religiousness: Development and evidence for reliability and validity. *The International Journal for the Psychology of Religion*, *18*(4), 291–315. https://doi.org/10.1080/10508610802229270

Abu-Raiya, H., Pargament, K. I., Weissberger, A., & Exline, J. (2016c). An empirical examination of religious/spiritual struggle among Israeli Jews. *The International Journal for the Psychology of Religion*, *26*(1), 61–79.https://doi.org/10.1080/10508619.2014.1003519

Adom-Fynn, D., Asamoah, D., Quainoo, E. A., Tetteh, S. Q., & Acquah, D. (2019/2020). Religious coping and self-esteem of women living with cervical cancer in Ghana. *International Journal of Healthcare Sciences*, *7*(2), 162–179.

Ai, A. L., Peterson, C., & Huang, B. (2003). The effect of religious-spiritual coping on positive attitudes of adult Muslim refugees from Kosovo and Bosnia. *The International Journal for the Psychology of Religion*, *13*(1), 29–47. https://doi.org/10.1207/S15327582IJPR1301_04

Ai, A. L., Wink, P., Tice, N. T., Bolling, S. F., & Shearer, M. (2009). Prayer and reverence in naturalistic, aesthetic, and socio-moral context predicted fewer complications following coronary artery bypass. *Journal of Behavioral Medicine*, *32*, 570–581. https://doi.org/10.1007/s10865-009-9228-1

Ake III, G. S., & Horen, S. G. (2004). The influence of religious orientation and coping on the psychological distress of Christian domestic violence victims. *Journal of Religion & Abuse*, *5*(2), 5–28. https://doi.org/10.1300/J154v05n02_02

Ano, G. G., & Pargament, K. I. (2013). Predictors of spiritual struggles: An exploratory study. *Mental Health, Religion & Culture*, *16*, 419–434. https://doi.org/10.1080/13674676.2012.680434

Ano, G. G., & Vasconcelles, E. B. (2005). Religious coping and psychological adjustment to stress: A meta-analysis. *Journal of Clinical Psychology*, *61*, 461–480.https://doi.org/10.1002/jclp.20049

Arnette, N. C., Mascaro, N., Santana, M. C., Davis, S., & Kaslow, N. J. (2007). Enhancing spiritual well-being among suicidal African American female survivors of intimate partner violence. *Journal of Clinical Psychology*, *63*, 909–924. https://doi.org/10.1002/jclp.20403

Aten, J. D., Smith, W. R., Davis, E. B., Van Tongeren, D. R., Hook, J. N., Davis, D. E., … & Hill, P. C. (2019). The psychological study of religion and spirituality in a disaster context: A systematic review. *Psychological Trauma: Theory, Research, Practice, and Policy*, *11*(6), 597–613. https://doi.org/10.1037/tra0000431

Ayele, H., Mulligan, T., Gheorghiu, S., & Reyes-Ortiz, C. (1999). Religious activity improves life satisfaction for some physicians and older patients. *Journal for the American Geriatrics Society*, *47*, 453–455. https://doi.org/10.1111/j.1532-5415.1999.tb07238.x

Bockrath, M. F., Pargament, K. I., Wong, S., Harriott, V. A., Pomerleau, J. M., Homolka, S. J., Chaudhary, Z. B., & Exline, J. J. (2022). Religious and spiritual struggles and their links to psychological adjustment: A meta-analysis of longitudinal studies. *Psychology of Religion and Spirituality*, *14*(3), 283–299.https://doi.org/10.1037/rel0000400

Boswell, G. H., Kahana, E., & Dilworth-Anderson, P. (2006). Spirituality and healthy lifestyle behaviors: Stress counter-balancing effects on the well-being of older adults. *Journal of Religion and Health*, *45*, 587–602.https://doi.org/10.1007/s10943-006-9060-7

Braxton, N. D., Lang, D. L., Sales, J. M., Wingood, G. M., & DiClemente, R. J. (2007). The role of spirituality in sustaining the psychological well-being of HIV-positive black women. *Women and Health*, 46, 113–129. https://doi.org/10.1300/J013v46n02_08

Bryant, A. N., & Astin, H. S. (2008). The correlates of spiritual struggle during the college years. *Journal of Higher Education 79*(1), 1–27. https://doi.org/10.1080/00221546.2008.11772084

Cooper, L. B., Bruce, A. J., Harman, M. J., & Boccaccini, M. T. (2009). Differentiated styles of attachment to God and varying religious coping efforts. *Journal of Psychology and Theology*, *37*(2), 134–141. https://doi.org/10.1177/009164710903700205

Cummings, J. P., & Pargament, K. I. (2010). Medicine for the spirit: Religious coping inindividuals with medical conditions. *Religions*, *1*(1), 28–53. https://doi.org/10.3390/rel1010028

Currier, J. M., Holland, J. M., & Drescher, K. D. (2015). Spirituality factors in the prediction of outcomes of PTSD treatment for U.S. military veterans. *Journal of Traumatic Stress*, *28*(1), 57–64. https://doi.org/10.1002/jts.21978

Currier, J. M., McDermott, R. C., McCormick, W. H., Churchwell, M. C., & Milkeris, L. (2018). Exploring cross-lagged associations between spiritual struggles and risk for suicidal behavior in a community sample of military veterans. *Journal of Affective Disorders*, *230*, 93–100. https://doi.org/10.1016/j.jad.2018.01.009

Currier, J. M., Smith, P. N., & Kuhlman, S. (2017). Assessing the unique role of religious coping in suicidal behavior among US Iraq and Afghanistan veterans. *Psychology of Religion and Spirituality*, *9*(1), 118–123. https://doi.org/10.1037/rel0000055

Damen, A., Exline, J., Pargament, K., Yao, Y., Chochinov, H., Emanuel, L., … & Fitchett, G. (2021). Prevalence, predictors and correlates of religious and spiritual struggles in palliative cancer patients. *Journal of Pain and Symptom Management*, *62*(3), e139–e147. https://doi.org/10.1016/j.jpainsymman.2021.04.024

Dworsky, C. K. O., Pargament, K. I., Wong, S., & Exline, J. J. (2016). Suppressing spiritual struggles: The role of experiential avoidance in mental health. *Journal of Contextual Behavioral Science*, *5*(4), 258–265. https://doi.org/10.1016/j.jcbs.2016.10.002

Ellison, C. G., & Lee, J. (2010). Spiritual struggles and psychological distress: Is there a dark side of religion? *Social Indicators Research*, *98*, 501–517.doi 10.1007/s11205-009-9553-3

Emmons, R. A. (1999). Religion in the psychology of personality: An introduction. *Journal of Personality*, *67*(6), 874–888. https://doi.org/10.1111/1467-6494.00076

Exline, J. J. (2013). Religious and spiritual struggles. In K. I. Pargament (Editor in Chief), J. J. Exline, & J. W. Jones (Associate Eds.), *APA handbook of psychology, religion, and spirituality (Volume 1): Context, theory, and research*, pp. 459–475). Washington, DC: American Psychological Association. https://doi.org/10.1037/14045-025

Exline, J. J., & Grubbs, J. B. (2011). "If I tell others about my anger toward God, how will they respond?" Predictors, associated behaviors, and outcomes in an adult sample. *Journal of Psychology and Theology*, *39*(4), 304–315.https://doi.org/10.1177/009164711103900402

Exline, J. J., Kaplan, K. J., & Grubbs, J. B. (2012). Anger, exit, and assertion: Do people see protest toward God as morally acceptable? *Psychology of Religion and Spirituality*, *4*(4), 264–277. https://doi.org/10.1037/a0027667

Exline, J. J., Krause, S. J., & Broer, K. A. (2016). Spiritual struggle among patients seeking treatment for chronic headaches: Anger and protest behaviors toward God. *Journal of Religion and Health*, *55*(5), 1729–1747. doi 10.1007/s10943-016-0259-y

Exline, J. J., Pargament, K. I., Grubbs, J. B., & Yali, A. M. (2014). The Religious and Spiritual Struggles Scale: Development and initial validation. *Psychology of Religion and Spirituality*, *6*, 208–222. https://doi.org/10.1037/a0036465

Exline, J. J., Yali, A. M., & Sanderson, W. C. (2000). Guilt, discord, and alienation: The role of religious strain in depression and suicidality. *Journal of Clinical Psychology*, *56*(12), 1481–1496. https://doi.org/10.1002/1097-4679(200012)56:12%3C1481::AID-1%3E3.0.CO;2-A

Faigin, C. A., Pargament, K. I., & Abu-Raiya, H. (2014). Spiritual struggles as a possible risk factor for addictive behaviors: An initial empirical investigation. *The International Journal for the Psychology of Religion*, *24*(3), 201–214.https://doi.org/10.1080/10508619.2013.837661

Fizpatrick, A. L., Standish, L. J., Berger, J., Kim, J., Calabrese, C., & Polissar, N. (2007). Survival in HIV-1 positive adults practicing psychological or spiritual activities for one year. *Alternative Therapeutic Health Medicine*, *13*, 18–24.

Gall, T. L., & Guirguis-Younger, M. (2013). Religious and spiritual coping: Current theory and research. In K. I. Pargament (Editor in Chief), J. J. Exline, & J.W. Jones (Associate Eds.), *APA handbook of psychology, religion, and spirituality (Volume 1): Context, theory, and research* (pp. 459–475). American Psychological Association. https://doi.org/10.1037/14045-019

Garssen, B., Visser, A., & Pool, G. (2021). Does spirituality or religion positively affect mental health? Meta-analysis of longitudinal studies. *International Journal for the Psychology of Religion*, *31*(1), 4–20. https://doi.org/10.1080/10508619.2020.1729570

Gillum, T. L., Sullivan, C. M., & Bybee, D. I. (2006). The importance of spirituality in the lives of domestic violence survivors. *Violence against Women*, *12*(3), 240–250. https://doi.org/10.1177/1077801206286224

Granqvist, P., & Kirkpatrick, L. A. (2013). Religion, spirituality, and attachment. In K. I. Pargament, J. J. Exline, & J. W. Jones (Eds.), *APA handbook of psychology, religion, and spirituality (Vol. 1): Context, theory, and research* (pp. 139–155). American Psychological Association. https://doi.org/10.1037/14045-007

Grubbs, J. B., & Exline, J. J. (2014). Humbling yourself before God: Humility as a reliable predictor of lower divine struggle. *Journal of Psychology and Theology*, *42*(1), 41–49. https://doi.org/10.1177/009164711404200105

Grubbs, J. B., Exline, J. J., & Campbell, W. K. (2013). I deserve better and god knows it! Psychological entitlement as a robust predictor of anger at God. *Psychology of Religion and Spirituality*, *5*(3), 192.

Grubbs, J. B., Exline, J. J., Pargament, K. I., Volk, F., & Lindberg, M. J. (2017). Internet pornography use, perceived addiction, and religious/spiritual struggles. *Archives of Sexual Behavior*, *46*, 1733–1745. doi 10.1007/s10508-016-0772-9

Harris, J. I., Erbes, C. R., Engdahl, B. E., Ogden, H., Olson, R. H., Winskowski, A. M. M., … & Mataas, S. (2012). Religious distress and coping with stressful life events: A longitudinal study. *Journal of Clinical Psychology*, *68*(12), 1276–1286. https://doi.org/10.1002/jclp.21900

Harris, J. I., Erbes, C. R., Winskowski, A. M., Engdahl, B. E., & Nguyen, X. V. (2014). Social support as a mediator in the relationship between religious comforts and strains and trauma symptoms. *Psychology of Religion and Spirituality*, *6*(3), 223–229. https://doi.org/10.1037/a0036421

Hood Jr, R. W., Hill, P. C., & Spilka, B. (2018). *The psychology of religion: An empirical approach* (*5th* edition). New York, NY: Guilford Publications.

Ironson, G., & Hayward, H. (2008). Do positive psychosocial factors predict disease progression in HIV-1? A review of the evidence. *Psychosomatic Medicine*, *70*, 546–554. https://doi.org/10.1097/PSY.0b013e318177216c

Johnson, C. V., & Hayes, J. A. (2003). Troubled spirits: Prevalence and predictors of religious and spiritual concerns among university students and counseling center clients. *Journal of Counseling Psychology*, *50*, 409–419. https://doi.org/10.1037/0022-0167.50.4.409

Kawachi, I., & Berkman, L. F. (2001). Social ties and mental health. *Journal of Urban Health*, *78*, 458–467.

Kesseling, A., Dodd, M. J., Lindsey, A. M., Strauss, A. I. (1986). Attitudes of patients living in Switzerland about cancer and its treatment. *Cancer Nursing*, *9*(2), 77–85.

King, S. D., Fitchett, G., Murphy, P. E., Pargament, K. I., Martin, P. J., Johnson, R. H., … & Loggers, E. T. (2017). Spiritual or religious struggle in hematopoietic cell transplant survivors. *Psycho-Oncology*, *26*(2), 270–277. https://doi.org/10.1002/pon.4029

Krumrei, E. J., Mahoney, A., & Pargament, K. I. (2011). Spiritual stress and coping model of divorce: A longitudinal study. *Journal of Family Psychology*, *25*(6), 383–996. https://doi.org/10.1080/17439760.2011.596557

Lee, E.-K. O. (2007). Religion and spirituality as predictors of well-being among Chinese American and Korean American older adults. *Journal of Religion, Spirituality and Aging*, *19*, 77–100. https://doi.org/10.1300/J496v19n03_06

McConnell, K. M., Pargament, K. I., Ellison, C. G., & Flannelly, K. J. (2006). Examining the links between spiritual struggles and symptoms of psychopathology in a national sample. *Journal of Clinical Psychology*, *62*, 1469–1484. https://doi.org/10.1002/jclp.20325

McCullough, M. E., & Willoughby, B. L. (2009). Religion, self-regulation, and self-control: Associations, explanations, and implications. *Psychological Bulletin*, *135*(1), 69–93. https://doi.org/10.1037/a0014213

Meisenhelder, J. B., & Marcum, J. P. (2004). Responses of clergy to 9/11: Posttraumatic stress, coping, and religious outcomes. *Journal for the Scientific Study of Religion*, *43*, 547–554. https://doi.org/10.1111/j.1468-5906.2004.00255.x

Miller, W. R., & Thoresen, C. E. (2003). Spirituality, religion, and health: An emerging field of study. *American Psychologist*, *58*, 24–35. https://doi.org/10.1037/0003-066X.58.1.24

Morgan, K. A. D., Scott, J. K., Parshad-Asnani, M., Gibson, R. C., O'Garo, K. N., Edwards, C. L. (2014). Associations amongst disease severity, religious coping, and depression in a cohort of Jamaicans with sickle-cell disease. *Mental Health, Religion, and Culture*, *17*, (9), 937–945 https://doi.org/10.1080/13674676.2014.961910

Neimeyer, R. A., & Burke, L. A. (2011). Complicated grief in the aftermath of homicide: Spiritual crisis and distress in an African American sample. *Religions*, *2*(2), 145–164.https://doi.org/10.3390/rel2020145

Nenova, M., DuHamel, K., Zemon, V., Rini, C., & Redd, W. H. (2013). Posttraumatic growth, social support, and social constraint in hematopoietic stem cell transplant survivors. *Psycho-oncology*, *22*(1), 195–202. https://doi.org/10.1002/pon.2073

Pargament, K. I. (1997). *The psychology of religion and coping: Theory, research, practice*. New York, NY: The Guilford Press.

Pargament, K. I. (2007). *Spiritually integrated psychotherapy: Understanding and addressing the sacred*. Guilford Press.

Pargament, K. I. (2009). *Wrestling with the angels: Religious struggles in the context of mental illness*. New York City, New York. October: American Psychiatric Association Institute for Psychiatric Services.

Pargament, K. I. (2011a). Religion and coping: The current state of knowledge. In S. Folkman (Ed.), *Oxford Handbook of stress, health, and coping* (pp. 269–288). New York, NY: Oxford University Press.

Pargament, K. I. (2011b). *Spiritually integrated psychotherapy: Understanding and addressing the sacred*. New York, NY: Guilford Press.

Pargament, K. I., & Exline, J. J. (2021). *Working with spiritual struggles in psychotherapy: From research to practice*. New York, NY: Guilford Publications.

Pargament, K. I., Koenig, H. G., & Perez, L. M. (2000). The many methods of religious coping: Development and initial validation of the RCOPE. *Journal of Clinical Psychology*, *56*(4), 519–543. https://doi.org/10.1002/(SICI)1097-4679(200004)56:4<519::AID-JCLP6>3.0.CO;2-1

Pargament, K. I., Koenig, H. G., Tarakeshwar, N., & Hahn, J. (2001). Religious struggle as a predictor of mortality among medically ill elderly patients: A 2-year longitudinal study. *Archives of* internal *Medicine*, *161*(15), 1881–1885. doi:10.1001/archinte.161.15.1881

Pargament, K. I., & Mahoney, A. (2005). Sacred matters: Sanctification as a vital topic for the psychology of religion. *International Journal for the Psychology of Religion*, *15*(3), 179–198. https://doi.org/10.1207/s15327582ijpr1503_1

Pargament, K. I., Mahoney, A., Exline, J. J., Jones, J. W., & Shafranske, E. P. (2013). Envisioning an integrative paradigm for the psychology of religion and spirituality. In K. I. Pargament, J. J. Exline & J. W. Jones (Eds). *APA handbook of psychology, religion, and spirituality (Vol. 1): Context, theory, and research. APA handbooks in psychology* (pp. 3–19). Washington, DC: American Psychological Association. https://doi.org/10.1037/14045-001

Pargament, K. I., Smith, B. W., Koenig, H. G., & Perez, L. (1998). Patterns of positive and negative religious coping with major life stressors. *Journal for the Scientific Study of Religion*, *37*(4), 710–724. https://doi.org/10.2307/1388152

Pargament, K. I., Wong, S., & Exline, J. J. (2016). Wholeness and holiness: The spiritual dimension of eudaimonics. In Vittersø, J. (Ed.) *Handbook of eudaimonic well-being* (pp. 379–394). Cham: Springer International Publishing.

Pargament, K. I., Wong, S., Pomerleau, J., & Kraus, N. [Landmark Spirituality and Health Study: Spirituality Findings]. Unpublished raw data, personal communication. Park, C. L., Edmondson, D., & Hale-Smith, A. (2013). Why religion? Meaning as motivation. In K. I. Pargament, J. J. Exline, & J. W. Jones (Eds.), *APA handbook of psychology, religion, and spirituality (Vol. 1): Context, theory, and research* (pp. 157–171). American Psychological Association. https://doi.org/10.1037/14045-008

Park, C. L., Edmondson, D., & Hale-Smith, A. (2013). Why religion? Meaning as motivation. In K. I. Pargament, J. J. Exline, & J. W. Jones (Eds.), *APA handbook of psychology, religion, and spirituality (Vol. 1): Context, theory, and research*; pp. 157–171). Washington, DC: American Psychological Association. https://doi.org/10.1037/14045-008

Park, C. L., Lim, H., Newlon, M., Suresh, D. P., & Bliss, D. E. (2014). Dimensions of religiousness and spirituality as predictors of well-being in advanced chronic heart failure patients. *Journal of Religion and Health, 53*, 579–590.https://doi.org/10.1007/s10943-013-9714-1

Park, C. L., Wortmann, J. H., & Edmondson, D. (2011). Religious struggle as a predictor of subsequent mental and physical well-being in advanced heart failure patients. *Journal of Behavioral Medicine, 34*, 426–436. https://doi.org/10.1007/s10865-011-9315-y

Pirutinsky, S., Rosmarin, D. H., Pargament, K. I., & Midlarsky, E. (2011). Does negative religious coping accompany, precede, or follow depression among Orthodox Jews? *Journal of Affective Disorders, 132*(3), 401–405.https://doi.org/10.1016/j.jad.2011.03.015

Ramirez, S. P., Macêdo, D. S., Sales, P. M. G., Figueiredo, S. M., Daher, E. F., Araújo, S. M., ... & Carvalho, A. F. (2012). The relationship between religious coping, psychological distress and quality of life in hemodialysis patients. *Journal of Psychosomatic Research, 72*(2), 129–135.https://doi.org/10.1016/j.jpsychores.2011.11.012

Reynolds, N., Mrug, S., Hensler, M., Guion, K., & Madan-Swain, A. (2014). Spiritual coping and adjustment in adolescents with chronic illness: A 2-year prospective study. *Journal of Pediatric Psychology, 39*(5), 542–551.https://doi.org/10.1093/jpepsy/jsu011

Rosmarin, D. H., Bigda-Peyton, J. S., Öngur, D., Pargament, K. I., & Björgvinsson, T. (2013). Religious coping among psychotic patients: Relevance to suicidality and treatment outcomes. *Psychiatry Research, 210*(1), 182–187.https://doi.org/10.1016/j.psychres.2013.03.023

Rosmarin, D. H., Krumrei, E. J., & Andersson, G. (2009a). Religion as a predictor of psychological distress in two religious communities. *Cognitive Behavior Therapy, 38*(1), 54–64. https://doi.org/10.1080/16506070802477222

Rosmarin, D. H., Pargament, K. I., & Flannelly, K. J. (2009b). Do spiritual struggles predict poorer physical/mental health among Jews?. *International Journal for the Psychology of Religion, 19*(4), 244–258. https://doi.org/10.1080/10508610903143503

Rosmarin, D. H., Pargament, K. I., Krumrei, E. J., & Flannelly, K. J. (2009c). Religious coping among Jews: Development and initial validation of the JCOPE. *Journal of Clinical Psychology, 65*(7), 670–683. https://doi.org/10.1002/jclp.20574

Sandage, S. J., & Crabtree, S. (2012). Spiritual pathology and religious coping as predictors of forgiveness. *Mental Health, Religion & Culture, 15*(7), 689–707.https://doi.org/10.1080/13674676.2011.613806

Schuster, M.A., Stein, B.D., Jaycox, L., Collins, R.L., Marshall, G.N., Elliott, M.N., et al. (2001). A national survey of stress reactions after the September 11, 2001, terrorist attacks. *New England Journal of Medicine, 345*, 1507–1512. https://doi.org/10.1056/NEJM200111153452024

Simoni, J. M., Martone, M.G., & Kerwin, J.F. (2002). Spirituality and psychological adaptation among women with HIV/AIDS: Implications for counseling. *Journal of Counseling Psychology, 49*, 139–147. https://doi.org/10.1037/0022-0167.49.2.139

Soothill, K., Morris, S. M., Harman, J. C., Thomas, C., Francis, B., & McIllmurray, M. B. (2002). Cancer and faith. Having faith–does it make a difference among patients and their informal carers?. *Scandinavian Journal of Caring Sciences, 16*(3), 256–263. https://doi.org/10.1046/j.1471-6712.2002.00097.x

Tarakeshwar, N., Vanderwerker, L.C., Paulk, E., Pearce, M. J., Kasl, S.V., & Prigerson, H. G. (2006). Religious coping is associated with the quality of life of patients with advanced cancer. *Journal of Palliative Medicine, 9*, 646–657.https://doi.org/10.1089/jpm.2006.9.646

Tix, A. P., & Frazier, P. A. (1998). The use of religious coping during stressful life events: Main effects, moderation and mediation. *Journal of Consulting and Clinical Psychology, 66*, 411–422. https://doi.org/10.1037/0022-006X.66.2.411

Trevino, K. M., Pargament, K. I., Cotton, S., Leonard, A. C., Hahn, J., Caprini-Faigin, C. A., et al. (2010). Religious coping and physiological, psychological, social, and spiritual outcomes with patients with HIV/AIDS: Cross-sectional and longitudinal findings. *Aids and Behavior, 14*, 379–389. https://doi.org/10.1007/s10461-007-9332-6

Webb, J. R., Toussaint, L., & Dula, C. S. (2014). Ritualistic, theistic, and existential spirituality: Initial psychometric qualities of the RiTE measure of spirituality. *Journal of Religion and Health*, *53*, 972–985. https://doi.org/10.1007/s10943-013-9697-y

Wilt, J. A., Grubbs, J. B., Exline, J. J., & Pargament, K. I. (2016). Personality, religious and spiritual struggles, and well-being. *Psychology of Religion and Spirituality*, *8*(4), 341. https://doi.org/10.1037/rel0000054

Wilt, J. A., Grubbs, J. B., Pargament, K. I., & Exline, J. J. (2017). Religious and spiritual struggles, past and present: Relations to the Big Five and well-being. *International Journal for the Psychology of Religion 27*, 51–64. https://doi.org/10.1080/10508619.2016.1183251

Wulff, D. M. (1997). *Psychology of religion: Classic and contemporary* (2nd ed.). New York, NY: Wiley.

Yaden, D. B., Batz-Barbarich, C. L., Ng, V., Vaziri, H., Gladstone, J. N., Pawelski, J. O., & Tay, L. (2022). A meta-analysis of religion/spirituality and life satisfaction. *Journal of Happiness Studies*, *23*(8), 4147–4163. https://doi.org/10.1007/s10902-022-00558-7

Yinger, J. M. (1967). Pluralism, religion and secularism. *Journal for the Scientific Study of Religion*, *7*, 104–118. https://doi.org/10.2307/1384190

Zinnbauer, B. J., Pargament, K. I., Cole, B., Rye, M. S., Butfer, E. M., Belavich, T. G., … & Kadar, J. L. (2015). Religion and spirituality: Unfuzzying the fuzzy. *Sociology of Religion*, 36(4), 549–564.

Chapter 39

Understanding the Psychology of Temptation and the Role It Plays in Spirituality, Health, and Well-Being

Ashnita S. Maxton, Comfort M. Boye, Declan P. Murphy, Ernestina Aidoo, Alyssa Hill, Sharon E. Prager, and Jon R. Webb†*

The psychology of temptation has received a considerable amount of attention; however, most of this work is in the context of social psychology, with some work in the context of addiction psychology, and fairly little from the point of view of the psychology of religion and spirituality. Moreover, most scientific research regarding the psychology of temptation has been conducted from a secular perspective with little consideration of its significance within the context of human spirituality. Temptation is typically conceptualized along the lines of having a strong desire to do something, often seen as gratifying in the short term, but harmful in the long term. It can be overpowering and is frequently accompanied by craving-related experiences. As an example, persons recovering from addiction often feel tempted to engage in drug or alcohol use. However, temptation also occurs in everyday situations. For instance, one might feel tempted to eat chocolate while dieting, avoid work to watch television, or buy an expensive item that they cannot afford. Temptation typically carries negative connotations due to its potential to undermine long-term goals and well-being but can also be viewed positively as an opportunity for growth. Webb (2014) proposed a more inclusive definition of temptation (see below) in response to the scientific psychological literature's neglect of the spiritual/transcendent components and implications of temptation. Yet, the construct of temptation still needs much scientific attention in the context of spirituality, including as related to health and well-being.

This chapter will provide an overview of the psychology of temptation and discuss the need to incorporate its spiritual/transcendent-level qualities. In addition to presenting the naturalistic, otherwise secular psychological understanding of temptation as a proxy for struggling with self-control, we provide general descriptions of how the major religious belief systems of the world understand temptation. Also, we discuss implications of the effect of temptation on health and well-being, and briefly discuss the contributions of social psychology, addiction psychology, and the psychology of religion and spirituality to the scientific understanding of temptation, both generally and in the context of health and well-being.

Temptation

The scientific study of temptation in psychology is still a relatively new area of research; however, the concept of temptation has been around for a long time [likely since day one, so to speak (see Carus, 2009)]. Temptation has been described as humans being faced with an internal competition to pursue a short-term desire over a long-term interest or goal (Fishbach &

* Corresponding Author: ashnita.maxton@gmail.com.
† The authors would like to acknowledge Mark E. Mills, MEd for contributions toward the development of this chapter.

DOI: 10.4324/9781003440048-45

Converse, 2011). In universal terms, temptation has been defined as "something that makes you want to do or have something that you know you should not" or, as "the wish to do or have something that you know you should not do or have" (Cambridge Dictionary, 2023). Of note, definitions of temptation in the scientific literature largely do not take into account religious or spiritual notions or implications. To address this, Webb (2014) defined temptation as "the dispositional or situational incidence of being drawn cognitively, affectively, and/or behaviorally to engage in undesirable, illicit, and/or transcendent short-term activities that are inconsistent with personal, societal, and/or transcendent long-term standards" (p. 236).

In the field of psychology, the concept and construct of temptation has often been discussed in the context of being enticed into engaging in undesirable behaviors, typically in a secular setting. Although "undesirable" is a useful notion and can encompass various and many situations and experiences, a more thorough understanding of temptation can be achieved by explicitly broadening the scope of temptation to incorporate not only undesirable concerns, circumstances, and activities, but those with illicit and transcendent implications, as well; for example, violence, theft, and marital infidelity (Webb, 2014). Temptation usually arises when a fundamental human need contends with the power of self-control, leading to a conflict where one's moral values and principles are challenged, ultimately prompting action due to an irresistible allure (Robinson & Berridge, 2000; Vonasch, 2017). Related to this, in the philosophy of religion literature, temptation has been defined "as enticement to act in a way that would be contrary to virtue" (Pelser, 2019, p. 84). Further, Pelser (2019) held that temptation revolves around actions that give rise to desires within a person, instigating an inner struggle as they tackle their conscience in choosing between right and wrong. In this regard, the enticement to stay away from responsibility is a facet of the realm of temptation (Pelser, 2019).

To understand the psychology of temptation, we need to understand its underlying mechanisms and qualities. Many studies aim to uncover why some people are more prone to temptation (Hoffman et al., 2012), what occurs in the brain during temptation and what aids in resisting it (Saunders & Robinson, 2013). Environmental factors significantly influence susceptibility (Saunders & Robinson, 2013), as may visceral urges (Nordgren & Chou, 2011), and the interaction between mood and arousal (Fedorikhin & Patrick, 2010). Understanding these dynamics can help in developing strategies to manage temptation effectively. However, unless we also include the aspects of temptation that reach beyond a naturalistic and secular point of view – that is, its spiritual or transcendent-level qualities – our understanding of temptation and its influence on the human condition will be needlessly limited (Webb, 2014).

Spirituality and the RiTE Model

Spirituality has been conceptualized and enjoys empirical support with respect to being a fundamental aspect of human nature or part of what it means to be human (de Jager Meezenbroek et al., 2012b; Piedmont & Wilkins, 2013). It is also crucial to note that having a healthy spirituality is not contingent upon having faith, or even belief, in deity (Pargament, 2013; Piedmont & Wilkins, 2013; Webb et al., 2014). Spirituality encompasses a transcendent aspect that is characterized by external qualities, which provide a guiding, empowering, and unifying effect in the human experience. These qualities extend beyond ordinary understanding and explanation but are often accessible and encountered by much of the world's population (see Webb, 2021). In simpler terms, spirituality has been defined as the pursuit of the sacred (Pargament, 2013). Spirituality has been understood through various perspectives. When viewed through a subjective lens, spirituality is defined as "one's striving for and experience of a connection with the essence of life" (Garssen et al., 2021, p. 4). This involves central elements such as experiences of meaning in life and a sense of connectedness (de Jager Meezenbroek et al., 2012a). Spirituality has also been defined as "the dimension of human existence involving how individuals pursue and articulate meaning and purpose, as well as how they perceive connections to the present moment, themselves, others, nature, and the significant or sacred" (Puchalski et al., 2009, p. 643; see also Pargament et al., 2017). In this definition, 'sacred' appears somewhat secondary, mentioned after listing various potential functions. Its inclusion, however, brings clarity to spirituality. This definition stands out for its distinctive focus on the sacred as life's ultimate purpose, implying that spiritual significance is conferred only when infused with sacredness (Pargament et al., 2017). The sacred is also described as a core surrounded by a ring, encompassing notions of God (deity), the divine, and transcendent reality, expressed diversely across monotheistic, polytheistic, and non-theistic beliefs, such as Buddhism (Pargament et al., 2017; Pargament & Mahoney, 2005). This viewpoint suggests a shared understanding of a sacred core among individuals of various religious backgrounds *and* those without affiliation, revealing commonalities even amid differing interpretations (Gries et al., 2012).

Though often used interchangeably, religion and spirituality delineate distinct yet interconnected concepts (Garssen et al., 2021). Spirituality denotes a personal, profound bond with God or Ultimate Transcendence, while religion encompasses organized systems with rites, doctrines, and communal practices (Hodge et al., 2001). One can partake in religious rituals without a personal connection to God, and conversely, be spiritual without adhering to organized religion (Hodge et al., 2001). In an effort to bring parsimony and consensus, Webb et al. (2014) introduced the RiTE model of spirituality to merge religiousness and spirituality, and define the unified, overarching construct of *spirituality* as the pursuit of three transcendently sacred dimensions. The RiTE model is multidirectional and proportional, acknowledging varying levels of its dimensions (Webb, 2021). Ritualistic Spirituality involves a structured connection with deity, Theistic Spirituality a non-structured connection with deity, and Existential Spirituality a non-theistic, yet transcendent quest for meaning and purpose. Each dimension encompasses beliefs in the sacred or transcendent, often associated with deity, but also other extrinsic sources such as nature, the universe, and knowledge – emphasizing related or overlapping components among the three dimensions (Webb, 2021). Together, these dimensions form the RiTE Model of Spirituality, underscoring and inclusive of diverse expressions of spirituality and, ideally, a relatively balanced engagement across dimensions (Webb, 2021). See Chapters 1 and 44 of this volume for a more detailed discussion of the RiTE Model.

Temptation and Religions of the World

The concept of temptation exists in many – if not all – religious and spiritual traditions in different forms, but very little scientific research has been done to explore temptation in the explicit context of religion and spirituality (Burris & Rempel, 2012). Perhaps this is due to its assumed primary origin being religion, and the common rift and reluctance of science to examine the metaphysical nature of religiously and/or spiritually oriented constructs. Within religious and spiritual traditions, temptation is often seen as a test of faith, morality, and self-discipline. Different religious traditions have their unique perspectives on temptation, its sources, and ways to overcome it.

Judaic Belief Systems

In Judaism, temptation is regarded as a test of moral character, with numerous stories in the *Torah* highlighting how individuals confront and overcome temptation through faith and adherence to God's commandments. The concept is prominently featured in the *First Book of Moses* through the narrative of Adam and Eve (Genesis 3:4-7). Indeed, temptation is arguably among the first theological principles presented in the Abrahamic faith traditions; that is, Judaism, Christianity, and Islam (see below). This account of the forbidden fruit in the Garden of Eden illustrates how temptation can lead to disobedience and separation from God. The serpent (Satan) entices Eve by appealing to her desires for knowledge, resulting in the Fall. Other stories in the Hebrew Bible (*Tanakh* or Old Testament), such as Joseph's encounter with Potiphar's wife (Genesis 39:6-12), further explore this theme. Joseph resists her advances by recognizing the moral implications and potential betrayal of his master, showcasing the importance of integrity. Additionally, King David's temptation by Bathsheba (2 Samuel 11) serves as a cautionary tale about the dire consequences of succumbing to desire. During Yom Kippur, the holiest day of the year, the focus on repentance underscores the significance of self-reflection and moral accountability, urging individuals to seek forgiveness for their transgressions.

Christian Belief Systems

In Christianity, temptation is frequently depicted as a challenge to one's faith and virtue. In Christianity, one of Satan's many names is the Tempter. In the *Old Testament*, there is the Serpent's temptation of Eve in the Garden of Eden and, in the *New Testament*, there are Satan's temptations of Jesus in the wilderness (Day, 1993). In Christian theology, temptation is often viewed as part of a larger spiritual battle. The Apostle Paul in his letter to Ephesus, reminds believers that their struggle is not merely against "flesh and blood" (Ephesians 6:12) but against spiritual forces. Temptation is not just a personal moral issue but part of the broader conflict between good and evil. People are encouraged to use spiritual resources like prayer, scriptures, and the Holy Spirit to combat temptation. The *Bible* speaks of the "armor of God," (Ephesians 6:11) including faith, truth, and righteousness, to stand against the schemes of the devil, who is often portrayed as the tempter. The *Bible* recounts the temptation of Jesus of Nazareth by Satan in the wilderness (Matthew 4:1-11; Mark 1:12-13; Luke 4:1-13), symbolizing the struggle against sin and highlighting the importance of spiritual strength and reliance on God. This narrative illustrates Jesus' deep connection with God, demonstrated through fasting and prayer, reminding believers that a solid spiritual foundation fosters resilience in the face of temptation. The scripture notes that the devil left Jesus "for a time" (Luke 4:13), suggesting that temptation is not a singular event but an ongoing spiritual battle that requires steadfastness in one's spiritual practices. The Lord's Prayer emphasizes this struggle by including a request to "lead us not into temptation but deliver us from evil" (Matthew 6:9-13; Luke 11:2-4), underscoring the necessity for divine assistance in resisting sin. This prayer acknowledges human vulnerability to temptation, framing it as part of a larger spiritual conflict involving greater forces, such as evil and sin (1 Corinthians 10:13).

Islamic Belief Systems

In Islam, temptation (fitna) is regarded as a test from Allah to assess an individual's faith and commitment to Islamic principles. The *Qur'an* underscores the significance of patience, prayer, and fasting in resisting these challenges, as highlighted in Surah Al-Baqarah

(2:153; 2:183; 2:286). Muslims are encouraged to seek refuge in Allah and to practice self-control and discipline. In Islam, Eblis is the tempter of man (Day, 1993). Temptation is viewed as part of the greater test of life that every individual must face. The *Qur'an* repeatedly emphasizes that human life is a test through which God evaluates a person's faith and righteousness. Surah Al-Baqarah (2:286) states, "Allah does not burden a soul beyond that it can bear." This verse implies that temptations and trials are within the capacity of each individual to overcome. Therefore, while temptations may be difficult, they are not insurmountable, and God does not place undue burden on any individual. The *Qur'an* explains that Satan's primary method of leading people astray is through temptation. Temptation is a subtle invitation to wrongdoing, often presented in a persuasive, quiet manner. While Satan may sometimes appear to offer well-meaning advice, he primarily influences through hidden whispers (Shokr, 2016). However, Islam teaches that Satan cannot compel individuals to sin; it is ultimately up to each person to accept or reject these temptations. People can recite a prayer for refuge from Satan's whispers, as mentioned in Surah An-Nas (114:1-6). Of note, as in the Judeo-Christian scriptural account (see above), the Islamic scriptures recount the temptation and Fall of Adam and his wife in the garden – because of Satan (see *Qur'an*, Surah II: 35-36 & Surah VII: 19-34).

Hindu Belief Systems

In Hinduism, temptation is often associated with the concepts of desire, attachment, and the struggles between the higher self (Atman) and lower instincts (prakriti). The tradition recognizes that human beings experience various temptations that can lead them away from their spiritual path and toward material pursuits. These temptations can manifest as desires for pleasure, power, wealth, or fame, which are seen as distractions from the ultimate goal of life: realizing one's true nature and achieving moksha (liberation) (Sivananda, 1993). In *The Bhagavad Gita* (Chapter 3:36), Arjuna asks Krishna about the nature of action and temptation. Krishna explains that it is desire and anger that lead to sin and suffering, emphasizing the need for self-control and mastery over one's desires. Self-discipline is a significant aspect of Hindu practice, particularly in the context of yoga. The *Yoga Sutras of Patanjali* outline methods for controlling the mind and senses to overcome temptation and achieve inner peace. The practice of asanas (postures), pranayama (breathing exercises), and meditation helps cultivate self-awareness and detachment from desires (Sivananda, 1993).

Buddhist Belief Systems

In Buddhism, human desires and attachments are seen as the root causes of suffering. The Buddha's teachings emphasize the significance of mindfulness, meditation, and ethical conduct as essential tools for overcoming temptation and attaining enlightenment. According to these teachings, even pleasant experiences are entangled in the cycle of samsara, the endless cycle of birth, death, and rebirth driven by karma. For instance, pleasurable experiences can trigger craving or an insatiable longing for more, leading to anxious efforts to maintain or protect the source of that pleasure (MacKenzie, 2018). Buddhism encourages practitioners to overcome the three poisons: greed, hatred, and delusion, while cultivating qualities that lead to genuine happiness and freedom for oneself and others (MacKenzie, 2018). Mara, a symbolic figure in Buddhist texts, represents temptation and desire, embodying the forces that hinder spiritual progress. Mara attempts to distract the Buddha during meditation with offers of sensual pleasures, power, and fear. This story illustrates that enlightenment can only be achieved by confronting these inner obstacles through mindfulness, wisdom, and concentration (Goff, 2014). The Buddha faced these temptations in solitude, relying on his own merit and insight, as outlined in the Four Noble Truths and practiced through the Noble Eightfold Path, which guides individuals toward a life free from material distractions and temptations (Goff, 2014). Mindfulness is a key practice within the Noble Eightfold Path, helping practitioners deepen their understanding of the Four Noble Truths and move closer to enlightenment (Trammel, 2017).

Across these religious/spiritual belief systems, the common themes in dealing with temptation include reliance on a higher power, adherence to ethical and moral codes, and the cultivation of self-discipline and mindfulness. Each tradition offers its followers guidance and practices to help navigate and overcome the challenges posed by temptation.

Differentiating Temptation from Self-Control/Impulsivity

From a Christian perspective, the *Bible* defines temptation to mean

> solicitation to that which is evil, and hence Satan is called 'the tempter' (Matthew 4:3). [Jesus of Nazareth] was in this way tempted in the wilderness. That temptation was not internal, but by a real, active, subtle being. It was not self-sought. It was submitted to as an act of obedience on his part. 'Christ was led, driven. [The notion of] an unseen personal force [which] bore him a certain violence is implied in the words' (Matthew 4:1-11) Easton's Bible Dictionary; see kingjamesbibledictionary.com/Dictionary/tempt

Merriam-Webster (2024) broadly defines self-control as "restraint exercised over one's own impulses, emotions, or desires." Considering the clinical, community, and Biblical terms for self-control, impulsiveness, and temptation, how do we differentiate temptation from self-control and impulsiveness? Dholakia et al. (2006) discuss temptation as a hedonistic principle, which is the motivation behind a psychological approach to avoid pain and indulge in pleasurable activities. Is temptation an emotional response to avoid pain rather than a focus of indulgence? If this is the case, then the temptation would be more in line with the process of impulsivity. The decision-making process in the desire to eat candy has a different association when comparing a partygoer to a diet-conscious individual. The partygoer may view the candy as a treat, whereas the dieting individual views this as a sin or transgression and a reflection of their inability to avoid the temptation (e.g., Griffin & Ross, 1991).

Fujita and Han (2009) conducted three experiments in which they noted that an individual's subjective interpretation of a stimulus was not specific to what the participant thought about, but rather by *how* it was thought about: "Impulsive reactions reflected not only the objective features of temptations but also people's subjective interpretations of those features" (p. 803). It appears that if the individual thinks of the item as off limits or something more desirable than they would normally be permitted, the view of the item changes the longing to obtain it. It can then be described as a temptation, and indulgence in it becomes an impulsive act.

Impulsive construal's reflect both dispositional individual differences (Vallacher & Wegner, 1989) and situational factors (Fujita et al., 2006; Liberman et al., 2007). Temptation can be differentiated from self-control by looking at the psychological roles of "regulatory focus" (Dholakia et al., 2006). Individuals can be promotion-focused (orientation toward positive outcomes) or prevention-focused (orientation away from negative outcomes). Faced with similar desires, the prevention-focused individuals reported lower desire for and had higher self-regulation than their counterparts. The prevention-focused individual can maintain self-control in the face of desire, whereas the "promotional-focused individuals have a higher intensity of desire" (p. 172) and thus, risk for temptation.

Spirituality, Health, and Well-Being

Understanding the interplay between spirituality (including temptation), health, and well-being demands historical insight, theoretical conceptualization, and meticulously conducted empirical examination. In this regard, spirituality has been found to offer several protective benefits. Consistent research findings highlight the positive impact of spirituality on diverse aspects of health, encompassing physical, mental, and social well-being. As examples, spirituality correlates with favorable health results, including subjective well-being, health-related quality of life, improved coping abilities, recovery from mental disorders, and a reduced likelihood of involvement in addictive or suicidal behaviors (Braam & Koenig, 2019; Bożek et al., 2020). Studies show that individuals who engage in regular spiritual or religious practices tend to report lower levels of anxiety and depression (Koenig, 2012), positive self-image (Regnerus, 2003), and reduced engagement in risky behaviors, higher levels of mood and overall well-being (Yonker et al., 2012). Also, the impact of childhood adversity on adult mental health has been observed to be mitigated for individuals engaged in religious practices. Specifically, religious salience and spirituality have served as protective factors, attenuating the adverse effects of child abuse on changes in positive affect over time (Jung, 2018).

Additional studies have delved into the psychological dimensions of religiousness, with implications for health and well-being. For instance, Greenfield et al. (2009) identified a positive correlation between higher levels of spirituality and enhanced well-being, encompassing positive affect, purpose in life, positive relations with others, personal growth, self-acceptance, environmental mastery, and autonomy. Of note, certain associations in the context of spirituality, health, and well-being have been found to be more pronounced among women than men (Ryff, 2021).

Temptation in the Context of Spirituality, Health, and Well-Being

Spiritual frameworks often view temptations not just as obstacles but as opportunities for personal and spiritual growth (Pargament, 2007). Religious traditions such as Christianity, Buddhism, and Islam (and others) provide practices such as prayer, fasting, and mindfulness, which foster self-control and emotional regulation (Fishbach et al., 2003; McNamara, 2002; McCullough & Willoughby, 2009).

The relationship between temptation, religiousness/spirituality, health, and well-being is multifaceted. Temptation often poses challenges to individuals' religious/spiritual beliefs and practices, impacting their overall health and well-being. Spirituality can serve as a guiding force in resisting temptation, promoting healthier behaviors, and enhancing psychological resilience. A strong spiritual foundation may provide individuals with the strength and motivation to overcome temptations that could jeopardize their health and well-being. Conversely, succumbing to temptation may lead to psychological, emotional, and/or spiritual distress and adversely affect one's physical, mental, and social health and well-being. Therefore, understanding the interplay between temptation and religiousness/spirituality is essential for fostering holistic and comprehensive health and well-being. However, very few studies have explicitly examined the effect of temptation on health and well-being while also explicitly incorporating into the research design and analyses the spiritual/transcendent components and implications of temptation. Rather, when the influence of temptation on health and well-being is examined, it is largely from a naturalistic and secular point of view. Related to this, when psychological science examines temptation – whether in general, or with respect to health and well-being – much of the work is from the point of view of social psychology, some from addiction psychology, and, ironically, much less than might otherwise be expected from the psychology of religion and spirituality.

Temptation and Social Psychology

A considerable portion of contemporary research in the psychology of temptation – being enticed to do wrong or being put to test (Tang & Sutarso, 2013) – centers on topics rooted in social psychology. In this context, temptation is perceived as a significant challenge to goal-oriented behavior, and resolving this conflict is considered a matter of exercising self-control (Fedorikhin & Patrick, 2010; Muraven & Shmueli, 2006). With humans facing the constant need to choose between destructive short-term desires (temptations) and constructive long-term interests (goals), self-control becomes the successful resolution of this dilemma (Fishbach & Converse, 2011). Indeed, people with high trait self-control can resist temptation which would otherwise result in negative consequences (Christodoulou et al., 2010; Shi et al., 2023). Those who are typically more self-controlled than others have more self-control resources at their disposal and thus more successful techniques for lowering their risk for engaging in temptation. As a result, they will generally exhibit less impulsive conduct than their less-controlled colleagues (Tsukayama et al., 2012). Studies have added to this understanding, such that gratitude, pre-commitment strategies, and experience avoiding temptation can lessen the effect of continuous exposure to the temptation (Baumeister et al., 2018; Ent et al., 2015; Shi et al., 2023).

Despite individuals' best intentions, they may face many struggles to resist temptation, control their urges, and change their behaviors. One reason for these challenges is the notion of ego depletion. That is, exercising self-control is essential for successful self-regulation and yet, it can become depleted as it is thought to be a limited resource (Muraven, 2012). When individuals experience decision fatigue or stress, their ability to resist temptation may diminish (Baumeister, 2002). Social situations can either deplete or bolster this self-control, depending on the presence of supportive or unsupportive peers (Fishbach & Converse, 2011; Muraven, 2012). When self-control is depleted, subsequent efforts to exercise it become more challenging. However, self-control can be replenished, and the immediate effects of depleted self-control can be managed or overcome (Muraven, 2012).

Temptation and Addiction Psychology

From a secular perspective, temptation is often discussed from a negative viewpoint. However, as with spiritual struggle (see below), temptation can have both positively and negatively valenced expressions and effects (Webb, 2014). In the specific context of addiction and recovery, a person can overcome the temptation for relapse if self-control or the desire to stop using alcohol or other substances is otherwise strong enough. If a person has a support system, additional resources, and a clear understanding of the consequences of relapse, they can view avoiding temptation as honorable. Related to this, successfully resisting temptation can build resilience and thus a view of the process of temptation as an opportunity for growth.

Much of the literature regarding the temptation to use alcohol has been in the context of self-control, desire to drink, and drinking restraint. Self-control has been defined as a set of processes by which urges, desires, emotions, or behaviors that conflict with long-term goals or prevailing rules are overridden or inhibited (Muraven et al., 2002). Without self-control, the person would act in a manner that is either automatic, typical, or otherwise normal for them. For instance, people seeking to limit their drinking but lack the self-control to resist the impulse or temptation to drink may give in and drink (Muraven & Shmueli, 2006). Among hazardous drinkers, temptation was associated with stronger urges to drink alcohol, greater difficulty in controlling urges, and increased alcohol consumption, even when alcohol consumption in the past month was controlled for (Palfai, 2001). Related to this, Good et al. (2020) identified a favorable correlation between trait self-control and achieving general daily goals (i.e., not necessarily goals in the context of addiction recovery). However, daily resistance to temptation did not serve as a mediator between self-control and the habit index, with average daily desire acting as the mediator instead.

A study conducted by Luehring-Jones et al. (2018) investigated the question that drinkers with more self-control may consume less alcohol because they can refrain from acting impulsively more often, as well as because they are less likely to feel enticed to consume alcohol after being exposed to the sight, smell, or notion of alcohol. The results of the study indicated that the relationship between trait self-control and both per-occasion alcohol intake and the frequency of heavy drinking episodes was found to be mediated by automatic alcohol-related associations. Results of another study have indicated that when concealing their thoughts, people with higher trait temptation to drink ingested more alcohol than people with lower trait temptation. Alcohol consumption may be influenced by drinking temptation and degree of self-control (Muraven et al., 2002).

Temptation and the Psychology of Religion and Spirituality

Ironically, very few studies in the psychology of religion and spirituality have explored temptation as a construct immersed in and imbued with religion and spirituality. Consistent with social psychology and addiction psychology, the psychology of religion and spirituality largely approaches temptation by implication through self-control, without necessarily considering its transcendent implications. However, a temptation-related construct known as spiritual struggle (to include religious struggle) has fairly recently emerged in the psychology of religion and spirituality. For an initial perspective regarding the aforementioned seeming natural, yet lack of a home for temptation in the psychology of religion and spirituality, see Webb (2014). Since 2014, while research in the psychology of religion and spirituality has continued to understand temptation ostensibly as an otherwise naturalistic, self-regulatory issue (e.g., Ent et al., 2015; Good et al., 2020; Toh et al., 2021), research regarding spiritual struggle flourishes and continues to evolve (see Chapter 38, this volume).

Although there is fundamental similarity between spiritual and religious struggles, there are important differences. *Spiritual* struggles are driven by "relationships with God or with a transcendent or sacred realm," whereas *religious* struggles "center on teachings, practices, or group dynamics of an organized religious group" (Exline, 2013, p. 460). Six categories of spiritual/religious struggle have been empirically identified, including divine, demonic, interpersonal, moral, doubt, and ultimate meaning (Exline et al., 2014). Pargament (2007) has also categorized religious and spiritual struggles across various domains such as divine struggles (e.g., experiencing anger toward God), intrapersonal struggles (e.g., difficulty forgiving oneself for a wrongdoing), and interpersonal struggles (e.g., feeling betrayed by a religious leader). Many spiritual struggles involve perceiving God (deity) in a negative way, such as viewing God as indifferent, punitive, or untrustworthy (Exline, 2013). According to many religious/spiritual traditions, the spiritual path is challenging, marked by obstacles, wrong turns, and struggle. Even revered religious figures, such as Moses, Gautam Buddha, and Jesus of Nazareth, faced profound conflicts, temptations, and struggles in their respective spiritual journeys. These struggles arise when circumstances threaten one's ultimate spiritual goal, such as enlightenment or union with God (Pargament et al., 2005).

Many studies have documented the association of spiritual/religious struggle with various outcomes related to health and well-being (see Chapter 38, this volume). Although said struggles are often associated with poor outcomes, they can also be beneficial and enhance people's lives (Exline & Rose, 2005). When faith is tested, it may become stronger, particularly if individuals choose faith-building responses during spiritual crossroads (Pargament, 2007). Such moments can either lead to feelings of despair, hopelessness, and meaninglessness, or foster renewal, growth, and transformation (Pargament et al., 2005).

The scientific understanding of temptation developed in the context of social psychology, addiction psychology, and the psychology of religion and spirituality is sophisticated, critically important, and noteworthy. However, the spiritual/transcendent components of the construct of temptation and the implications thereof – including in the context of health and well-being – are largely overlooked. As such, much work remains before we can be confident that our scientific understanding of temptation can be considered sufficiently comprehensive.

Conclusion and Future Directions

In conclusion, temptation is a multifaceted psychological and spiritual construct that plays a significant role in everyday experiences, as well as in more severe contexts, such as addiction and recovery. Although traditionally studied from a naturalistic and secular perspective, there is a critical need to (1) recognize the importance of the transcendent-level qualities of temptation and (2) implement the integration of spirituality and religion into the empirical examination of temptation. However, psychological research has largely overlooked the transcendent, religious, and spiritual dimensions of temptation. Integrating these aspects into a broader definition and assessment of temptation will provide a more nuanced and thorough understanding of how it influences human behavior. Expanding the understanding of temptation to include its transcendent dimensions – whether ritualistic, theistic, or existential, as outlined in Webb's RiTE model of spirituality – will provide a more comprehensive framework for examining how individuals navigate the tension between short-term desires and long-term goals. This broader perspective is especially relevant to health and well-being, both in general and in clinical settings, where spiritual well-being and self-control strategies may be essential for effective treatment and healing (e.g., recovery from addiction). Future research must further explore the intersection of temptation, spirituality, health, and well-being to develop more holistic, evidence-based prevention, intervention, and aftercare strategies. Doing so will not only enhance healthy behavior and clinical practices but also offer individuals more effective tools to resist temptation and foster long-term personal growth.

References

Baumeister, R. F. (2002). Ego depletion and self-control failure: An energy model of the self's executive function. *Self and Identity*, *1*(2), 129–136. https://doi.org/10.1080/152988602317319302

Baumeister, R. F., Tice, D. M., & Vohs, K. D. (2018). The strength model of self-regulation: Conclusions from the second decade of willpower research. *Perspectives on Psychological Science*, *13*(2), 141–145. https://doi.org/10.1177/1745691617716946

Bożek, A., Nowak, P. F., & Blukacz, M. (2020). The Relationship between spirituality, health-related behavior, and psychological well-being. *Frontiers in Psychology*, *11*, 1997. https://doi.org/10.3389/fpsyg.2020.01997

Braam, A. W., & Koenig, H. G. (2019). Religion, spirituality and depression in prospective studies: A systematic review. *Journal of Affective Disorders*, 257, 428–438 https://doi.org/10.1016/j.jad.2019.06.063

Burris, C. T., & Rempel, J. K. (2012). Good and evil in religion: The interpersonal context. In L. J. Miller (Ed.), *The Oxford handbook of Psychology and Spirituality* (pp. 123–137). Oxford University Press. https://doi.org/10.1093/oxfordhb/9780199729920.013.0008

Cambridge University Press. (2023). temptation. *In Cambridge Dictionary*. Retrieved August 8, 2023, from https://dictionary.cambridge.org/us/dictionary/english/temptation

Carus, P. (2009). *The history of the Devil and the idea of evil: From the earliest times to the present day*. NuVision Publications. (1900)

Christodoulou, C., Banfield, G., & Cleanthous, A. (2010). Self-control with spiking and non-spiking neural networks playing games. *Journal of Physiology-Paris*, *104*(3-4), 108–117. https://doi.org/10.1016/j.jphysparis.2009.11.013

Day, J. P. (1993). Temptation. *American Philosophical Quarterly*, *30*(2), 175–181. https://www.jstor.org/stable/20014454

de Jager Meezenbroek, E., Garssen, B., van den Berg, M., Van Dierendonck, D., Visser, A., & Schaufeli, W. B. (2012b). Measuring spirituality as a universal human experience: A review of spirituality questionnaires. *Journal of Religion and Health*, *51*, 336–354. https://doi.org/10.1007/s10943-010-9376-1

de Jager Meezenbroek, E. C., Garssen, B., van den Berg, M., Tuytel, G., van Dierendonck, D., Visser, A., & Schaufeli, W. B. (2012a). Measuring spirituality as a universal human experience: Development of the spiritual attitude and involvement list (SAIL). *Journal of Psychosocial Oncology*, *30*, 141–167. https://doi.org/10.1080/07347332.2011.651258

Dholakia, U. M., Gopinath, M., Bagozzi, R. P., & Nataraajan, R. (2006). The role of regulatory focus in the experience and self-control of desire for temptations. *Journal of Consumer Psychology*, *16*(2), 163–175. https://doi.org/10.1207/s15327663jcp1602_7

Ent, M. R., Baumeister, R. F., & Tice, D. M. (2015). Trait-self-control and the avoidance of temptation. *Personality and Individual Differences 74*, 12–15. https://doi.org/10.1016/j.paid.2014.09.031

Exline, J. J. (2013). Religious and spiritual struggles. In K. I. Pargament, J. J. Exline, & J. W. Jones (Eds.), *APA handbook of psychology, religion, and spirituality* (Vol. 1, pp. 459 – 475). Washington, DC: American Psychological Association. https://doi.org/10.1037/14045-025

Exline, J. J., Pargament, K. I., Grubbs, J. B., & Yali, A. M. (2014). The Religious and Spiritual Struggles Scale: Development and initial validation. *Psychology of Religion and Spirituality*, *6*(3), 208–222. https://doi.org/10.1037/a0036465

Exline, J. J., & Rose, E. (2005). Religious and Spiritual Struggles. In R. F. Paloutzian & C. L. Park (Eds.), *Handbook of the psychology of religion and spirituality* (pp. 315–330). The Guilford Press.

Fedorikhin, A., & Patrick, V. M. (2010). Positive mood and resistance to temptation: The interfering influence of elevated arousal. *Journal of Consumer Research*, *37*, 698–711. https://doi.org/10.1086/655665

Fishbach, A., & Converse, B. A. (2011). Identifying and battling temptation. In K. D. Vohs & R. F. Baumeister (Eds.), *Handbook of self-regulation: Research, theory, and applications* (2nd ed., pp. 244–260). New York, NY: Guilford Press.

Fishbach, A., Friedman, R. S., & Kruglanski, A. W. (2003). Leading us not into temptation: Momentary allurements elicit overriding goal activation. *Journal of Personality and Social Psychology*, *84*(2), 296–309. https://doi.org/10.1037/0022-3514.84.2.296

Fujita, K., & Han, H. A. (2009). Moving beyond deliberative control of impulses: The effect of construal levels on evaluative associations in self-control conflicts. *Psychological Science*, *20*(7), 799–804. https://doi.org/10.1111/j.1467-9280.2009.02372.x

Fujita, K., Trope, Y., Liberman, N., & Levin-Sagi, M. (2006). Construal levels and self-control. *Journal of Personality and Social Psychology*, *90*(3), 351–367. https://doi.org/10.1037/0022-3514.90.3.351

Garssen, B., Visser, A., & Pool, G. (2021). Does Spirituality or Religion Positively Affect Mental Health? Meta-analysis of Longitudinal Studies. *The International Journal for the Psychology of Religion*, *31*(1), 4–20. https://doi.org/10.1080/10508619.2020.1729570

Goff, K. (2014). An Analysis of the Temptation Narratives of Siddhartha Gautama Buddha and Jesus Christ. https://www.rodoni.ch/A13/temptation-buddha-jesus.pdf

Good, M., Linzel, M., & Kosits, R. D. (2020). The role of desire, habit, and temptation resistance in the relation between trait self-control and goal success: A study of religious goals in a highly religious sample. *The International Journal for the Psychology of Religion*, *30*(2), 89–100. https://doi.org/10.1080/10508619.2019.1651192

Greenfield, E. A., Vaillant, G. E., & Marks, N. F. (2009). Do formal religious participation and spiritual perceptions have independent linkages with diverse dimensions of psychological well-being?. *Journal of health and social behavior*, *50*(2), 196–212. https://doi.org/10.1177/002214650905000206

Gries, P., J. Su, and D. Schak. (2012). Toward the scientific study of polytheism: Beyond forced choice measures of religious belief. *Journal for the Scientific Study of Religion 51*(4), 623–637. https://doi.org/10.1111/j.1468-5906.2012.01683.x

Griffin, D.W., & Ross, L. (1991). Subjective construal, social inference, and human misunderstanding. In M.P. Zanna (Ed.), Advances in experimental social psychology (Vol. 24, pp. 319–359). New York: Academic Press.

Hodge, D. R., Cardenas, P., & Montoya, H. (2001). Substance use: Spirituality and religious participation as protective factors among rural youths. *Social Work Research*, *25*(3), 153–161. https://doi.org/10.1093/swr/25.3.153

Hofmann, W., Baumeister, R. F., Förster, G., & Vohs, K. D. (2012). Everyday temptations: An experience sampling study of desire, conflict, and self-control. *Journal of Personality and Social Psychology*, *102*(6), 1318–1335. https://doi.org/10.1037/a0026545

Jung, J. H. (2018). Childhood adversity, religion, and change in adult mental health. *Research on Aging*, *40*(2), 155–179. https://doi.org/10.1177/0164027516686662

Koenig, H. G. (2012). Religion, spirituality, and health: The research and clinical implications. *International Scholarly Research Notices*, *2012*(1), 278730. https://doi.org/10.5402/2012/278730

Liberman, N., Trope, Y., McCrea, S. M., & Sherman, S. J. (2007). The effect of level of construal on the temporal distance of activity enactment. *Journal of Experimental Social Psychology*, *43*(1), 143–149. https://doi.org/10.1016/j.jesp.2005.12.009

Luehring-Jones, P., Tahaney, K. D., & Palfai, T. P. (2018). The effect of self-control on drinking outcomes is mediated by automatic appetitive responses to alcohol. *Personality and Individual Differences*, *125*, 116–119. https://doi.org/10.1016/j.paid.2018.01.011

MacKenzie, M. (2018). Buddhism and the Virtues. *The Oxford handbook of virtue*, 153–170. https://doi.org/10.1093/oxfordhb/9780199385195.013.18

McCullough, M. E., & Willoughby, B. L. B. (2009). Religion, self-regulation, and self-control: Associations, explanations, and implications. *Psychological Bulletin*, *135*(1), 69–93. https://doi.org/10.1037/a0014213

McNamara, P. (2002). The motivational origins of religious practices. *Zygon.*, *37*(1). https://doi.org/10.1111/1467-9744.00418

Merriam-Webster. (2024). self-control. Retrieved November 25, 2024 from https://www.merriam-webster.com/dictionary/self-control

Muraven, M. (2012). Ego depletion: Theory and evidence. In R. M. Ryan (Ed.), *The Oxford handbook of human motivation* (pp. 111–126). New York, NY: Oxford University Press.

Muraven, M., Collins, R. L., & Neinhaus, K. (2002). Self-control and alcohol restraint: an initial application of the self-control strength model. *Psychology of addictive behaviors*, *16*(2), 113. https://doi.org/10.1037/0893-164X.16.2.113

Muraven, M., & Shmueli, D. (2006). The self-control costs of fighting the temptation to drink. *Psychology of Addictive Behaviors*, *20*, 154–160. https://doi.org/10.1037/0893-164X.20.2.154

Nordgren, L. F., & Chou, E. Y. (2011). The push and pull of temptation: The bidirectional influence of temptation on self-control. *Psychological Science*, *22*(11), 1386–1390. https://doi.org/10.1177/0956797611418349

Palfai, T. P. (2001). Individual differences in temptation and responses to alcohol cues. *Journal of studies on alcohol*, *62*(5), 657–666. https://doi.org/10.15288/jsa.2001.62.657

Pargament, K. I. (2007). *Spiritually integrated psychotherapy: Understanding and addressing the sacred.* New York: Guilford Press.

Pargament, K. I. (2013). Searching for the sacred: Toward a non-reductionistic theory of spirituality. In K. I. Pargament, J. J. Exline, & J. W. Jones (Eds.), *APA handbook of psychology, religion, and spirituality (Vol 1): Context, theory, and research.* (pp. 257–273). American Psychological Association. https://doi.org/10.1037/14045-014

Pargament, K. I., & Mahoney, A. (2005). THEORY: "Sacred matters: Sanctification as a vital topic for the psychology of religion". *The International Journal for the Psychology of Religion*, *15*(3), 179–198. https://doi.org/10.1207/s15327582ijpr1503_1

Pargament, K. I., Murray-Swank, N. A., Magyar, G. M., & Ano, G. G. (2005). Spiritual struggle: A phenomenon of interest to psychology and religion. In W. R. Miller & H. D. Delaney (Eds.), *Judeo-Christian perspectives on psychology: Human nature, motivation, and change* (pp. 245–268). https://doi.org/10.1037/10859-013

Pargament, K. I., Oman, D., Pomerleau, J., & Mahoney, A. (2017). Some contributions of a psychological approach to the study of the sacred. *Religion*, *47*(4), 718–744. https://doi.org/10.1080/0048721X.2017.1333205

Pelser, A. C. (2019). Temptation, virtue, and the character of Christ. *Faith and Philosophy*, *36*(1), 81–101. https://doi.org/10.5840/faithphil2019117119

Piedmont, R. L., & Wilkins, T. A. (2013). Spirituality, religiousness, and personality: Theoretical foundations and empirical applications. In K. I. Pargament, J. J. Exline, & J. W. Jones (Eds.), *APA handbook of psychology, religion, and spirituality (Vol 1): Context, theory, and research.* (pp. 173–186). American Psychological Association. https://doi.org/10.1037/14045-009

Puchalski, C., Ferrell, B., Virani, R., Otis-Green, S., Baird, P., Bull, J., Chochinov, H., Handzo, G., Nelson-Becker, H., Prince-Paul, M., Pugliese, K., & Sulmasy, D. (2009). Improving the quality of spiritual care as a dimension of palliative care: The report of the consensus conference. *Journal of Palliative Medicine*, *12*(10), 885–904. https://doi.org/10.1089/jpm.2009.0142

Regnerus, M. D. (2003). Religion and positive adolescent outcomes: A review of research and theory. *Review of religious research*, *44*(4), 394–413. https://www.jstor.org/stable/3512217

Robinson, T. E., & Berridge, K. C. (2000). The psychology and neurobiology of addiction: An incentive–sensitization view. *Addiction*, *95*(8s2), 91–117. https://doi.org/10.1046/j.1360-0443.95.8s2.19.x

Ryff, C. D. (2021). Spirituality and Well-Being: Theory, Science, and the Nature Connection. *Religions*, *12*(11), 914. https://doi.org/10.3390/rel12110914

Saunders, B. T., & Robinson, T. E. (2013). Individual variation in resisting temptation: implications for addiction. *Neuroscience & Biobehavioral Reviews*, *37*(9), 1955–1975. https://doi.org/10.1016/j.neubiorev.2013.02.008

Shi, R., Xu, C., Wei, X., & Zhang, S. (2023). The mediating role of avoiding temptation on the relationship between gratitude and academic engagement. *Current Psychology*, *42*(23), 19775–19785. https://doi.org/10.1007/s12144-022-03137-4

Shokr, A. (2016). Satan's Temptation and Ways of its Prevention from the Perspective of Quran. *Quranic Knowledge Research*, *5*(18), 63–89. https://doi.org/10.22054/rjqk.2016.1856

Sivananda, S. (1993). *All about Hinduism.* The Divine Life Society. ISBN 81-7052-047-9

Tang, T., & Sutarso, T. (2013). Falling or not falling into temptation? Multiple faces of temptation, monetary intelligence, and unethical intentions across gender. *Journal of Business Ethics*, *116*(3), 529–552. https://doi.org/10.1007/s10551-012-1475-3

Toh, W. X., Tan, T. S.-M., & Keh, J. S. (2021). Lead us not into temptation: Differential associations of religious identification with self-regulatory traits and abilities. *Journal of Research in Personality*, *94*, 104143. https://doi.org/10.1016/j.jrp.2021.104143

Trammel, R. C. (2017). Tracing the roots of mindfulness: Transcendence in Buddhism and Christianity. *Journal of Religion & Spirituality in Social Work: Social Thought*, *36*(3), 367–383. https://doi.org/10.1080/15426432.2017.1295822

Tsukayama, E., Duckworth, A. L., & Kim, B. (2012). Resisting everything except temptation: Evidence and an explanation for domain–specific impulsivity. *European Journal of Personality*, *26*(3), 318–334. https://doi.org/10.1002/per.841

Vallacher, R. R., & Wegner, D. M. (1989). Levels of personal agency: Individual variation in action identification. *Journal of Personality and Social Psychology*, *57*(4), 660–671. https://doi.org/10.1037/0022-3514.57.4.660

Vonasch, A. J., Clark, C. J., Lau, S., Vohs, K. D., & Baumeister, R. F. (2017). Ordinary people associate addiction with loss of free will. *Addictive Behaviors Reports*, *5*, 56–66. https://doi.org/10.1016/j.abrep.2017.01.002

Webb, J. R. (2014). Incorporating spirituality into the psychology of temptation: Conceptualization, measurement, and clinical implications. *Spirituality in Clinical Practice*, *1*(3), 231–241. https://doi.org/10.1037/scp0000028

Webb, J. R. (2021). *Understanding forgiveness and addiction: Theory, research, and clinical application*. Routledge.

Webb, J. R., Toussaint, L. L., & Dula, C. S. (2014). Ritualistic, theistic, and existential spirituality: Initial psychometric qualities of the RiTE measure of spirituality. *Journal of Religion & Health*, 53(4), 972–985. https://doi.org/10.1007/s10943-013-9697-y

Yonker, J. E., Schnabelrauch, C. A., & DeHaan, L. G. (2012). The relationship between spirituality and religiosity on psychological outcomes in adolescents and emerging adults: A meta-analytic review. *Journal of Adolescence*, *35*(2), 299–314. https://doi.org/10.1016/j.adolescence.2011.08.010

Chapter 40

Spirituality and Moral Injury

A Review of Findings, Models, and Interventions

Joseph M. Currier, Brandon J. Griffin, Timothy J. Usset, J. Irene Harris, Andrew J. Smith, and Jeffrey M. Pyne*

There is increasing recognition in healthcare professions that spirituality can influence resilience and the etiology, phenomenology, and amelioration of physical and mental health conditions following traumatic events. When considering the array of traumas that people might encounter over the life span, clinical researchers and practitioners are also increasingly focusing on features and sequelae of events that violate peoples' deeply held moral beliefs (Bremault-Phillips et al., 2019; Griffin et al., 2019, 2023; Xue et al., 2022). Rather than only challenging conventions of "right" and "wrong," morally injurious events can undermine peoples' basic sense of humanity and pursuit of belonging, transcendence, and meaning over the life span. In keeping with the RiTE model of spirituality that generally organizes this book (see Chapters 1 and 44, this volume), we define spirituality as a multidimensional construct that captures peoples'

> search for and response to meaning and connection with whatever they perceive as sacred, typically including supernatural entities (e.g., deity/deities, saints, ancestors, karma, or fate/destiny) or aspects of life either viewed as a manifestation of the divine (e.g., close human relationships) or as having transcendent or divine-like qualities (e.g., nature or the universe).
>
> (Davis et al., 2023, p. 280)

Emerging evidence affirms a reciprocal association between Ritualistic, Theistic, and Existential aspects of spirituality and peoples' reactions to morally injurious events and possible trajectories of suffering and recovery post-trauma. This chapter offers an overview of the current scientific and clinical literature on the multifaceted role of spirituality in moral injury. Given proliferating interest in moral injury since the COVID-19 pandemic, the brevity of this chapter precludes us from offering a comprehensive discussion of all models, findings, and assertions in healthcare professions at this time. Instead, drawing on a case from Drs. Usset and Harris' team with a morally injured veteran, the goals of this chapter are to summarize: (1) core features of the moral injury construct, (2) scientific evidence for associations between aspects of spirituality and moral injury, (3) promising models that account for links between spirituality and moral injury, and (4) intervention approaches for addressing spiritual determinants of recovery and healing.

* Corresponding Author: jcurrier@southalabama.edu.

DOI: 10.4324/9781003440048-46

Case Example

Jonathan (identifying details altered or omitted), a 72-year-old White man, pursued care from a Veterans Health Administration (VHA) Chaplain Service for chronic spiritual distress from serving as a combat officer in the Vietnam era. As the chaplain completed a spiritual assessment, Jonathan reported being raised Roman Catholic, serving as an altar boy, and feeling pressured by his family and parish priest to enter the priesthood. He then pursued a theology degree from a Catholic university following high school, but felt strongly that he was not called to the priesthood. Feeling lost and seeking a new direction in life, a friend introduced him to Reserve Officers Training Corps (ROTC) at their university. Given Jonathan's achievement orientation and strong desire for purpose and social connection, he excelled in the ROTC and was affirmed for his high performance and giftedness for military leadership. After earning a bachelor's degree in theology, Jonathan then defied his family's wishes by commissioning as an officer in the U.S. Army and deploying to Vietnam.

Jonathan was not deployed for very long before he began to encounter morally troubling events. His ROTC leaders emphasized using his leadership skills to save lives, but he was more rewarded for taking enemy lives. Although Jonathan did his best to minimize losses, he needed to assign soldiers to positions that held a high likelihood of death in designing battle plans. In turn, Jonathan reported becoming depressed in the assessment but kept a brave and hopeful countenance for his troops because they needed to operate as safely as possible in the combat zone. Despite having planned a long-term military career, Jonathan felt so mired in doubts about his faith after his deployment that he never returned to attending mass or engaging in other lifelong spiritual practices, and sought a law degree. He went on to have a successful law practice after leaving the military, but battled chronic depression symptoms and deep levels of self-doubt, shame, and betrayal about his war-related experiences over ensuing decades.

Conceptualizing Moral Injury

Litz et al. (2009) defined moral injury as disruption in an individual's confidence and expectations about one's own or others' motivation to behave in a just and ethical manner brought about by "perpetrating, failing to prevent, bearing witness to, or learning about acts that transgress deeply held moral beliefs and expectations" (p. 700). Per Litz et al., people internalize beliefs about what is morally acceptable from cultural, social, and ethical rules and norms. They may learn to distinguish right and wrong from their families, school or work, and/or social settings including religious congregations and other faith-based communities. Some people may encounter potentially morally injurious events (PMIEs) in which they (1) witness others act in ways they perceive to be morally wrong or (2) transgress their own moral beliefs either by what they did or believe they failed to do (Currier et al., 2015a). For example, Jonathan both witnessed comrades mistreating civilians as well as directly killed enemy combatants and felt responsible for the deaths of his own soldiers. Either by participating in a PMIE or identifying with a group/institution that is collectively responsible for a PMIE (e.g., military, healthcare), people might go on to experience lasting biological/physical, psychological/emotional, social/relational, and spiritual/existential issues known as moral injury (Griffin et al., 2019; Litz et al., 2009).

Rates and consequences of PMIEs have been studied in a growing number of groups. Like Jonathan's experiences in Vietnam, combat-related PMIEs include participating in a firefight where civilian women or children were harmed, failing to prevent a fellow service member from being injured or killed, and witnessing a fellow service member use excessive violence toward an enemy combatant. Recently, studies of PMIE exposure have also proliferated among civilian healthcare workers on the frontlines of the COVID-19 pandemic due to concerns that exposure may lead to professional burnout and turnover intentions (Griffin et al., 2023; Usset et al., 2024). Examples of healthcare-related PMIEs include restricting testing or treatment from patients due to supply shortages, transmitting an infection to a vulnerable person, and witnessing racial or economic disparities in care or survival rates in persons infected with the SAR-CoV-2 virus (Xue et al., 2022). PMIE exposure has also been studied in first responders (Tappenden et al., 2023), educators working in under-resourced and violent locales (Currier et al., 2015b), and humanitarian aid workers and refugees (Hoffman & Nickerson, 2022).

A growing base of studies affirm the prevalence of PMIEs in these groups. Focusing on military-connected groups, 25–40% of nationally representative samples of military veterans report PMIE exposure by witnessing and 10–25% report participating in a PMIE by what they did or failed to do during their military service (Maguen et al., 2023a; Wisco et al., 2017). Similar rates of exposure have been observed among healthcare workers responding to the COVID-19 pandemic, with approximately 50% reporting exposure via witnessing and 20% endorsing exposure by participating in a PMIE (Amsalem et al., 2021). In such cases, PMIE exposure has been associated with a range of adverse health-related outcomes, such as greater mental health symptom severity (Norman et al., 2021), substance misuse (Maguen et al., 2023b), interpersonal difficulties (Weber et al., 2023), and suicidal thoughts and behaviors (Maguen et al., 2023a). Taken together, this research suggests a sizable group of individuals endorse PMIE exposure as a prerequisite for moral injury. The question then becomes: who among those exposed to a PMIE are likely to experience clinically meaningful and functionally impairing levels of distress and impairment that characterizes moral injury?

Unlike other stressor-related syndromes such as PTSD, moral injury is not codified into diagnostic classification systems and there are not any formalized diagnostic criteria. Discussions of the hallmark symptoms that comprise moral injury also lack consensus. Instead, a range of problems are considered putative signs of moral injury after PMIEs including: intractable feelings of guilt, shame, and disgust; believing that one does not deserve to be happy or have healthy relationships or good jobs; and losing a sense of meaning or purpose in life (Liberati et al., 2021). Like Jonathan, morally injured persons may also experience spiritual struggles, such as feeling abandoned or punished by God or a Higher Power, doubting sacred beliefs they once cherished, and difficulties with self-forgiveness or receiving forgiveness from others (Currier et al., 2019; Evans et al., 2018). Critically, a number of questionnaires have become available that purport to assess moral injury outcomes, beyond mere PMIE exposure (e.g., Currier et al., 2018b; Litz et al., 2022; Norman et al., 2023). Initial findings suggest 10–20% of individuals exposed to a PMIE likely go on to develop the moral injury syndrome (e.g., Mantri et al., 2021).

Spirituality and Moral Injury

Ritualistic, Theistic, and Existential approaches to spirituality [(i.e., conceptually consistent with, yet not necessarily using the RiTE measure of spirituality (see Webb et al., 2014)] are commonly highlighted in theoretical, clinical, and scientific work on moral injury (Harris et al., 2015; Pyne et al., 2023; Wortmann et al., 2017). In many ways, the emergence of moral injury challenges traditional biomedical notions of trauma and invites clinicians and researchers alike to expand their frame of reference to consider peoples' spiritual and/or religious identities (Kinghorn, 2012). However, consistent with historic trends in the moral injury literature as a whole, theoretical and clinical discussions about the spirituality–moral injury link have outpaced rigorous scientific inquiry. Drawing upon a lengthy list of search terms (e.g., "moral injur,*", "moral emotions") and databases (e.g., PsycINFO, MEDLINE), Bremault-Phillips et al. (2019) identified 25 studies that were conducted between 2000 and 2018. Of this group, all but three strictly relied on qualitative methods and case studies. In addition, all of the available studies at the time of their review focused on military-connected individuals or clinicians who address moral injury in their practice. Nonetheless, using the available evidence at the time, Bremault-Phillips et al. identified how spirituality and moral injury recursively influence one another and salient ways that spiritual beliefs, practices, and relationships both help and hinder well-being after exposures to PMIEs.

Since then, other researchers have continued to investigate the role of spirituality in moral injury. In keeping with increasing applications to civilian groups, some of these studies have focused on healthcare-related moral injury (e.g., Xue et al., 2022). Further, as we will discuss below, a growing number of studies examined the effectiveness, feasibility, and acceptability of clinician-chaplain collaborations, chaplain-led interventions, and clinical strategies that target spiritual determinants of moral injury (e.g., Chamberlin et al., 2023; Harris et al., 2011, 2018; Pyne et al., 2018, 2021; Smigelski et al., 2022). However, when considering basic research studies examining spiritual determinants of resilience, suffering, and recovery after PMIE exposures, this literature remains in a nascent phase. At present, the vast majority of studies are still qualitative in nature and quantitative ones almost exclusively relied on cross-sectional designs. However, in combination with theoretical and clinical sources, emerging evidence suggests that spirituality intersects with moral injury in three ways: (1) PMIE exposures and sequelae can influence core dimensions of spirituality, (2) spirituality might influence risk for PMIEs leading to moral injury in varying ways, and (3) spirituality can influence recovery from moral injury for better or worse. We will now summarize key findings for these assertions.

Moral Injury Influences Spirituality

Research has not prospectively examined the role of moral injury in influencing peoples' spirituality or directly focused on spiritual growth in the context of moral injury. However, qualitative studies suggest the PMIE exposures and/or the sequelae can challenge peoples' identities and violate aspects of their spirituality (Bremault-Phillips et al., 2019). Further, in keeping with dynamics of spiritual/religious change in the trauma literature, cross-sectional surveys with warzone veterans who report symptoms of military-related moral injury commonly experience a weakening of Ritualistic Spirituality and decreased importance of spirituality in general (Currier et al., 2019, 2023; Usset et al., 2020). When compared to demographically matched peers from the community, Currier et al. (2014) found Vietnam and Iraq/Afghanistan Veterans presenting for PTSD treatment were less engaged in adaptive aspects of spirituality and had more forgiveness problems and spiritual struggles. Focusing on a large treatment-seeking group of veterans, Fontana and Rosenheck (2004) similarly found weakening of Ritualistic Spirituality was linked with higher utilization of mental health services in the VHA. In such cases, other findings suggest that loss of faith or weakening of spirituality are usually linked with worse suffering from moral injury and/or PTSD. For example, Fontana and Rosenheck concluded:

> [Veterans] appear to be looking to their therapists … to provide the answers and a sense of belonging to a larger whole that is no longer being fulfilled sufficiently by their religious

faith. The possibility that Veterans' continued pursuit of mental health services is driven in part by their search for meaning raises the broader issue of whether spirituality should be more central to the treatment of PTSD.

(p. 582)

Spirituality Influences Development of Moral Injury

From a theoretical view, spirituality might influence the development of moral injury following PMIE exposures in a couple of ways. As we will discuss below, a well-functioning spiritual meaning system could presumably facilitate appraisal processes, relational connections, and other supports that mitigate risk for moral injury (Park et al., 2016). Surveys with trauma-exposed groups also suggest Ritualistic, Theistic, and Existential aspects of spirituality are often concurrently associated with well-being (e.g., MacDonald-Smith et al., 2017). Conversely, whether positive or negative in nature, scholars have suggested naïve or rigid beliefs about God or other sacred matters can increase risk for chronic suffering after PMIEs (Harris et al., 2015; Koenig et al., 2017). For example, internalization of standards of moral perfection or having a simplistic, transactional conception of God or Higher Power might cause self-condemnation, betrayal, and other painful cognitions/emotions. Further, when confronted with PMIEs, people might suffer more severe health-related effects when sacred aspects of life are undermined. In such cases, PMIEs might be equated with more than emotional distress, behavioral dysfunction, or other biomedical outcomes – people might experience PMIEs as a violation of their sacred core or spiritual center (Bremault-Phillips et al., 2019). Also, Evans et al. (2018) found PMIE exposures were concurrently associated with spiritual struggles. However, in keeping with the lack of evidence for dynamics of spiritual/religious change, this line of research has similarly not prospectively examined how pre-trauma spirituality affects the development of moral injury.

Spirituality Influences Recovery from Moral Injury

Notwithstanding the viability of these previous lines of research, stronger evidence affirms ways that spirituality can influence recovery from moral injury. Of studies that directly examined the salubrious roles of spirituality in moral injury, findings revealed inverse links for Ritualistic Spirituality with veterans (e.g., Youssef et al., 2020) and healthcare workers (Mantri et al., 2021). To our knowledge, quantitative research has not studied other aspects of spirituality in the context of moral injury per se. However, persons with possible exposures to PMIEs who are also engaged in adaptive aspects of spirituality (e.g., engaging in prayer or meditation, positive religious coping, service attendance) often report greater well-being (MacDonald-Smith et al., 2017). Although findings are not unequivocal, such spiritual factors have also been concurrently linked with less PTSD symptoms (e.g., Koenig et al., 2018) and reduction of PTSD symptoms over time (e.g., Currier et al., 2015c). Conversely, with advances in measuring moral injury as an outcome, a growing number of studies indicate persons who develop symptoms of moral injury often struggle with their spirituality (e.g., Currier et al., 2019, 2023; Norman et al., 2023). In such cases, longitudinal findings also suggest that spiritual struggles add a distinct burden that can complicate the process of recovery from PTSD, suicidal behavior, and other problems that might occur following PMIEs (e.g., Currier et al., 2015c, 2018b). In fact, when compared to studies on the salubrious role of spirituality, evidence is clearer for the deleterious role of spiritual struggles in perpetuating and/or exacerbating moral injury symptoms over time.

Theoretical Models for Spirituality–Moral Injury Link

Notwithstanding a need for rigorous research, scholars have developed a number of psychological models to explain the apparent complex interplay between spirituality and moral injury. When considering the multifaceted role of spirituality, these models can guide researchers and clinicians to explain phenomena they might observe with participants or patients, inform their conceptual knowledge, make informed predictions or hypotheses, and facilitate a shared language with their colleagues and communities that might lead to advances in clinical research and practice for moral injury. Three of these emerging models for the spirituality–moral injury link include the reciprocal meaning-making model (Park et al., 2016), stress and coping model (Griffin et al., 2021), and psychospiritual developmental model (Harris et al., 2015).

Reciprocal Meaning-Making Model

Park et al.'s (2016) reciprocal meaning-making model asserts that spirituality can highly shape peoples' beliefs, goals, and other dimensions of global meaning that promote a sense of comprehensibility and purpose in life. As highlighted above, this model assumes spirituality and traumas do not occur in a vacuum but can rather recursively influence one another in ways that promote and/or diminish well-being. When faced with the situational meanings of PMIEs or other possible traumas that do not readily fit into one's global meaning system, people often feel compelled to engage in a meaning-making process to reconcile the reality and consequences of these events with their existing spiritual beliefs, values, and goals. In some cases, people with a well-integrated spiritual meaning system may appraise the situational meanings of the traumas in ways that align with existing beliefs, values, and goals and only trigger a moderate and transitory disruption in functioning. However, when people have developed critical or unhealthy beliefs – or have not worked through spiritual aspects of prior traumas in adaptive ways – this model asserts that the occurrence of new PMIEs might exacerbate unhealthy aspects of a pre-existing spiritual meaning system. In other cases, PMIEs might also challenge aspects of one's meaning system in ways that lead to distressing emotions/cognitions related to spirituality while also limiting access to previously adaptive spiritual coping resources. For example, Jonathan not only experienced distressing religious doubts and anger toward God, he also disconnected from his Catholic faith after returning from Vietnam. In turn, he could not harness beliefs, practices, and relationships for comfort and support at a time when he needed them the most.

Stress and Coping Model

Griffin et al. (2021) adapted a stress and coping model to conceptualize the complex role of forgiveness in moral injury, including seeking and receiving forgiveness as well as forgiving oneself and others. Specifically, exposure to PMIEs may constitute a stressor to the extent that someone perceives an event to violate their sacred beliefs about acceptable conduct. Like Jonathan feeling deeply responsible for deaths of his soldiers, individuals usually appraise the event in terms of harm severity (How much suffering resulted from the event?), personal agency (Was the event intended or unanticipated?), extenuating circumstances (What mitigating factors were present during the event?), and the possibility of repair (Is the harm done amenable to reparation?). In so doing, PMIEs appraised as sources of greater harm that are less amenable to repair and within their ability to control typically elicit more distress and evoke a stronger stress-related response. In such cases, forgiveness might facilitate meaningful interpretation and resolution of painful moral emotions/cognitions rooted in perceived violation of moral standards while enhancing perceptions of control, esteem, and belonging. Furthermore, forgiveness can be contrasted with maladaptive coping strategies, such as suppression or self-punishment, which may perpetuate distress and impairment. In such cases, an adapted stress-and-coping model can describe the protective effects of forgiveness in terms of reducing shame/guilt, anger/betrayal, and also core features of moral injury (Griffin et al., 2021, 2024).

Psychospiritual Development

The psychospiritual developmental model originated from clinical observations of a psychologist-chaplain team providing specialty care for moral injury (Harris et al., 2015). Clinicians from both disciplines observed that many PMIEs described by patients were not necessarily "wrong" actions, but moral dilemmas. Consider Jonathan's case again; he opted to place some persons in his command in mortal danger in order to protect others. By making these decisions, Jonathan was deeply affected by mutually exclusive rules he had learned in civilian law, his religious moral codes, and Rules of Engagement for the U.S. Army. In such cases, the team noticed that patients like Jonathan could only conceptualize their actions from one set of rules at a time in ways that led to viewing their actions as categorically "right" or "wrong" rather than on a continuum from "better" to "worse" based on context. Drawing upon James Fowler's work on faith development (Fowler & Dell, 2006), the team observed that resolution of moral injury was often closely related to a transition from Stage 3 (Synthetic-Conventional) to Stage 4 (Individuative-Reflective); as patients like Jonathan increase the capacity to hold multiple moral contexts in awareness simultaneously, they no longer need to judge self or others as "right" or "wrong" and can begin to resolve painful cognitions/emotions about these concerns.

In keeping with research on the spirituality–moral injury link, the study of psychospiritual development is just beginning. Measurement of this construct has been complicated; as individuals in Stage 3 confront PMIEs, they may become frustrated that rules, codes, and expectations they were first taught have failed them, and as categorical thinkers, decry religion and/or their Higher Power as altogether wrong. Usset et al. (2020) addressed measurement issues by developing the Multiscale Measure for Postconventional Spiritual Functioning; by classifying individuals as either affiliated or disaffiliated with faith and as functioning at the conventional (Stage 3) or postconventional (Stage 4) level, this scale can differentiate between conventional affiliates, conventional disaffiliates, postconventional affiliates, and postconventional disaffiliates. Like Jonathan's disaffiliation with Roman Catholicism before he shifted into a postconventional level in his psychospiritual development, Usset et al. indeed found that war-zone veterans in the conventional disaffiliate group generally had worse moral injury symptoms than conventional affiliates and other groups when controlling for exposure to PMIEs and PTSD symptoms. Although more research is needed, this finding suggests postconventional functioning could mitigate risk for PMIEs leading to moral injury or support recovery for persons like Jonathan.

Building a Continuum of Care for Moral Injury

Developing a continuum of clinical and community-based interventions for addressing spiritual determinants of moral injury is a public health priority. The rise of multiculturalism, intersectionality, and emphases on patient-centered and holistic care have led to greater openness to considering patients' spirituality in healthcare systems. However, persons who experience a moral injury might lack access to such care or not be amenable to engaging in these treatments. Studies with veterans also suggest that a subset do not respond to gold standard treatments for PTSD (Steenkamp et al., 2015). As such, we need a range of clinicians and community members with skills and resources to support recovery from moral injury. Three promising strategies for addressing spirituality in moral injury include spiritually integrated modes of psychotherapy delivery, collaborations between clinicians, chaplains, and community resources (Pyne et al., 2018, 2021), and Building Spiritual Strength (Chamberlin et al., 2023; Harris et al., 2011, 2018).

Spirituality Integration in Evidence-Based Psychotherapies

Addressing clients' spirituality in psychotherapy (see also Chapter 20, this volume) is a cornerstone for establishing a continuum of moral injury care. Given the lack of a consensus definition of moral injury and clear evidence to differentiate features of the syndrome from PTSD and other clinical diagnoses, experts have recommended adapting empirically supported treatments (e.g., Prolonged Exposure, Cognitive Processing Therapy). In other cases, researchers developed novel psychotherapies that address features of moral injury (e.g., Building Spiritual Strength, Impact of Killing, Trauma-Informed Guilt Reduction). With the exception of Building Spiritual Strength (Harris et al., 2011, 2018) and a spiritually integrated version of CPT (Koenig et al., 2017), treatments do not address spirituality as a standard part of recovery. Rather, integration of clients' spirituality depends on clinicians' discernment and clinical decision-making. In such cases, research with military veterans suggests that many persons who seek psychotherapy for moral injury might wish to consider spiritual aspects of their suffering and recovery (Currier et al., 2018a). When compared to directive strategies (e.g., discussing sacred scriptures, use of meditation exercises), veterans also appear to be more interested in their clinicians assuming an exploratory and affirming approach (e.g., highlighting spiritual strengths, exploring changes in spirituality). Research suggests that adapting psychotherapy in such ways can support psychological and spiritual outcomes (Captari et al., 2018). As such, clinicians who are treating moral injury will ideally be prepared to attend to spiritual strengths and struggles throughout the treatment process.

Mental Health Clinician/Chaplain Collaboration

Whether as an adjunct to psychotherapy or a stand-alone intervention, chaplains are increasingly addressing moral injury in the VHA and other healthcare settings (e.g., Harris et al., 2018; Smigelsky et al., 2022). Clinicians and chaplains might also partner with clergy in their communities to attend to spiritual concerns in moral injury (Milstein et al., 2010). The Mental Health Clinician/Chaplain Collaboration (MC3) intervention emerged from the VA Clergy Partnership (VCP) project (Sullivan et al., 2014). VCP team members trained community clergy and lay leaders to recognize mental health problems, moral injury symptoms, and how to access VHA resources. The VCP team learned from community action board meetings that community clergy, lay leaders, and VA mental health providers were not only interested in connecting veterans with VHA services but also wanted to connect veterans with community resources. Recognizing this gap in the context of moral injury – underutilization of community resources – we sought a better understanding of this problem from the perspectives of veterans, community clergy, VHA and Department of Defense chaplains, and VHA mental health clinicians (Pyne et al., 2018). Drawing upon qualitative interviews with veterans who were receiving specialty care in a VHA Medical Center or community-based outpatient clinic and focus groups with VA and DoD chaplains, and community clergy, the Mental Health Clinician/Community Clergy Collaboration (MC4) intervention was developed. A training manual was constructed to outline the flow of the clergy-led intervention: description of moral injury, forgiveness, and community reintegration utilizing local congregation, community resources, and service projects.

Community clergy were chosen to deliver the MC4 intervention because of closer proximity to community groups, resources, and projects that may support pathways to community reintegration and facilitate long-term recovery. Focusing on veterans from a PTSD outpatient clinic who were matched with community clergy or lay people based on the veterans' preferences, a pilot study revealed MC4 was feasible, acceptable, and effective in most cases (Pyne et al., 2021). However, using community clergy to deliver the intervention was not wholly feasible because of time constraints. Most community clergy reported they could see one veteran at a time, therefore, increasing the number of veterans receiving the intervention would require similar increases in the number of community clergy needed to deliver the intervention. As such, the next iteration of this intervention is MC3 or Mental Health Clinician/Chaplain Collaboration in which VHA chaplains will deliver intervention. Because VHA chaplains fulfill a pluralistic spiritual support role and are uniquely equipped to utilize spiritual/religious narrative to explore connections between shame/guilt, forgiveness, and reintegration, and collaborate with VA mental health clinicians, we believe the chaplain-led MC3 intervention could represent another viable option for developing a continuum of moral injury care in the coming years.

Building Spiritual Strength

BSS is an 8-session, group-based intervention for moral injury with demonstrated evidence in facilitating reduction in PTSD symptoms and spiritual struggles (Chamberlin et al., 2023; Harris et al., 2011, 2018). Facilitated by chaplains and/or mental health professionals, BSS can accommodate a full spectrum of spiritual diversity (including atheistic) and does not aim to change religious commitments or affiliations. Drawing upon clients' own conceptions of the sacred, the goals of BSS are to develop or improve a supportive relationship with a Higher Power/Ultimate Value to enhance coping and replace maladaptive coping strategies, address moral/spiritual concerns by exploring them through the perspectives of the group members, and changing judgments about themselves and others from categorical to contextual/continuous in ways that decrease condemning judgments toward themselves and others. BSS utilizes silence, journaling, and narrative components to facilitate these goals. For example, clients keep a weekly prayer/reflection log to increase awareness and communication skills with God or Higher Power in a manner that is consistent with their core beliefs/values, and take turns engaging in imaginal dialogues with God or Higher Power in which they can work through painful thoughts/emotions. Clients also share their faith histories, explore explanations of theodicy or philosophical perspectives on evil and suffering, learn skills for spiritual coping and forgiveness processes, and develop community resources for spiritual support following completion of the group.

Returning to Jonathan's case, he benefitted greatly from engaging in a BSS group that was co-led by a chaplain and social worker. Although Jonathan viewed mental health services as stigmatizing, he was amenable to seeing a chaplain who was assisted by a social worker. In turn, his fellow group members invited Jonathan to share his difficult combat-related decisions; over time, the group helped Jonathan to see that his decisions could not be classified as "right" or "wrong," but were the best he could do while managing mutually exclusive codes such as Rules of Engagement and his Catholic faith. In addition, the chaplain helped Jonathan to reconsider God as someone who was there with him when he made difficult decisions, knew that Jonathan attempted to seek the greatest good for the most people, and knew the emotional agony he had experienced since Vietnam. These shifts in Jonathan's thinking led to substantial relief from hopelessness, sadness, shame, and depressive symptoms. The social worker talked with Jonathan about other psychospiritual developmental aspects of his decision-making; for example, she discussed that Jonathan was judging decisions in his 20s harshly with the assumption that the younger version of himself had access to all of the accrued experience and knowledge as a 72-year-old man. In turn, Jonathan softened judgments about his younger self and cultivated acceptance and compassion for himself. After the group, Jonathan worked out a plan to shift his law practice to pro bono work to assist other veterans in ways that were spiritually satisfying; in a follow-up conversation with the chaplain, he was grateful to have the energy to serve God and others unfettered by the doubts and other spiritual struggles that had haunted him for so long.

Conclusion

In conclusion, proliferating interest in moral injury over the past decade is one of the significant developments in healthcare research and practice. In keeping with Jonathan's case, moral injury often creates a "thin space" for clinicians and researchers in which Ritualistic, Theistic, and Existential aspects of many peoples' spirituality cannot be avoided. With advances in measurement (e.g., Currier et al., 2018b; Litz et al., 2022; Norman et al., 2023), there is a need for basic and translational research on the spirituality–moral injury link. Namely, basic research needs to clarify how moral injury affects aspects of spirituality, how spirituality influences risk for PMIEs leading to moral injury, and how spirituality influences recovery from moral injury. In addition, translational research will ideally build upon the work shared earlier in this chapter to establish a viable continuum of care for moral injury to facilitate healing and transformation for persons like Jonathan.

References

Amsalem, D., Lazarov, A., Markowitz, J. C., Naiman, A., Smith, T. E., Dixon, L. B., & Neria, Y. (2021). Psychiatric symptoms and moral injury among US healthcare workers in the COVID-19 era. *BMC Psychiatry*, *21*(1), 546. https://doi.org/10.1186/s12888-021-03565-9

Bremault-Phillips, S., Pike, A., Scarcella, F., & Cherwick, T. (2019). Spirituality and moral injury among military personnel: A mini-review. *Frontiers in Psychiatry*, *10*. https://doi.org/10.3389/fpsyt.2019.00276

Captari, L. E., Hook, J. N., Hoyt, W. T., Davis, D. E., McElroy-Heltzel, S. E., & Worthington, E. L. (2018). Integrating clients' religion and spirituality within psychotherapy. A comprehensive meta-analysis. *Journal of Clinical Psychology*, *74*, 1938–1951. https://doi.org/10.1002/jclp.22681

Chamberlin, E. S., Usset, T. J., Fantus, S., Kondrath, S. R., Butler, M., Weber, M. C., & Wilson, M. A. (2023). Moral injury in healthcare: Adapting the Building Spiritual Strength (BSS) intervention to Health and Strength (HAS) for civilian and military healthcare workers. *Current Treatment Options in Psychiatry*, *10*(3), 234–247. https://doi.org/10.1007/s40501-023-00294-6

Currier, J. M., Drescher, K., & Harris, J. I. (2014). Spiritual functioning among Veterans seeking residential treatment for PTSD: A matched control group study. *Spirituality in Clinical Practice*, *1*, 3–15. https://doi.org/10.1037/scp0000004

Currier, J. M., Farnsworth, J. K., Drescher, K. D., Sims, B. M., & Albright, D. L. (2018b). Development and Evaluation of the Outcomes of Moral Injury Scale – Military Version. *Clinical Psychology & Psychotherapy*, *25*, 474–488. https://doi.org/10.1002/cpp.2170

Currier, J. M., Foster, J. D., & Isaak, S. L. (2019). Moral injury and spiritual struggles in military veterans: A latent profile analysis. *Journal of Traumatic Stress*, *32*(3), 393–404. https://doi.org/10.1002/jts.22378

Currier, J. M., Holland, J. M., & Drescher, K. D. (2015c). Spirituality factors in the prediction of outcomes of PTSD treatment for military veterans. *Journal of Traumatic Stress*, *28*, 57–64. https://doi.org/10.1002/jts.21978

Currier, J. M., Holland, J. M., Rojas-Flores, L., Herrera, S., & Foy, D. (2015b). Morally injurious experiences and meaning in Salvadorian teachers exposed to violence. *Psychological Trauma: Theory, Research, Practice, and Policy*, *7*(1), 24–33. https://doi.org/10.1037/a0034092

Currier, J. M., Manalo, M., & McDermott, R. C. (2023). Examining the unique role of pre-military religious commitment in posttraumatic symptomatology among Post 9/11 veterans. *Traumatology*, *29*, 1–5. https://doi.org/10.1037/trm0000361

Currier, J. M., McCormick, W., & Drescher, K. D. (2015a). How do morally injurious events occur? A qualitative analysis of perspectives of veterans with PTSD. *Traumatology*, *21*(2), 106–116. https://doi.org/10.1037/trm0000027

Currier, J. M., Pearce, M., Carroll, T. D., & Koenig, H. G. (2018a). Military veterans' preferences for incorporating spirituality in psychotherapy or counseling. *Professional Psychology: Research and Practice*, *49*, 39–47. https://doi.org/10.1037/pro0000178

Davis, E. B., Day, J. M., Lindia, P. A., & Lemke, A. W. (2023). Religious/spiritual development and positive psychology: Toward an integrative theory. In E. B. Davis, E. L. Worthington, Jr., & S. A. Schnitker (Eds.), *Handbook of positive psychology, religion, and spirituality* (pp. 279–295). Springer.

Evans, W. R., Stanley, M. A., Barrera, T. L., Exline, J. J., Pargament, K. I., & Teng, E. J. (2018). Morally injurious events and psychological distress among veterans: Examining the mediating role of religious and spiritual struggles. *Psychological Trauma: Theory, Research, Practice, and Policy*, *10*(3), 360–367. https://doi.org/10.1037/tra0000347

Fontana, A., & Rosenheck, R. (2004). Trauma, change in strength of religious faith, and mental health service use among veterans treated for PTSD. *Journal of Nervous and Mental Disease*, *192*, 579–584. https://doi.org/10.1097/01.nmd.0000138224.17375.55

Fowler, J. W., & Dell, M. L. (2006). Stages of Faith From Infancy Through Adolescence: Reflections on Three Decades of Faith Development Theory. In E. C. Roehlkepartain, P. E. King, L. Wagener, & P. L. Benson (Eds.), *The handbook of spiritual development in childhood and adolescence* (pp. 34–45).

Griffin, B. J., Cornish, M., Worthington, E. L., Jr., & Maguen, S. (2021). Forgiveness as a mechanism of repair following military-related moral injury. In J. M. Currier, K. D. Drescher, & J. A. Nieuwsma (Eds.), *Addressing Moral Injury in Clinical Practice*. Washington DC: American Psychological Association. https://doi.org/10.1037/0000204-005

Griffin, B. J., Norman, S. B., Weber, M. C., Hinkson Jr, K. D., Jendro, A. M., Pyne, J. M., … & Maguen, S. (2024). Properties of the modified self-forgiveness dual-process scale in populations at risk for moral injury. *Stress and Health*, e3413. https://doi.org/10.1002/smi.3413

Griffin, B. J., Purcell, N., Burkman, K., Litz, B. T., Bryan, C. J., Schmitz, M., Villierme, C., Walsh, J., & Maguen, S. (2019). Moral injury: An integrative review. *Journal of Traumatic Stress*, *32*(3), 350–362. https://doi.org/10.1002/jts.22362

Griffin, B. J., Weber, M. C., Hinkson, K. D., Jendro, A. M., Pyne, J. M., Smith, A. J., Usset, T., Cucciare, M. A., Norman, S. B., Khan, A., Purcell, N., & Maguen, S. (2023). Toward a dimensional contextual model of moral injury: A scoping review on healthcare workers. *Current Treatment Options in Psychiatry*. https://doi.org/10.1007/s40501-023-00296-4

Harris, J. I., Erbes, C. R., Engdahl, B. E., Thuras, P., Murray-Swank, N., Grace, D., … & Le, T. (2011). The effectiveness of a trauma focused spiritually integrated intervention for veterans exposed to trauma. *Journal of Clinical Psychology*, *67*(4), 425–438. https://doi.org/10.1002/jclp.20777

Harris, J. I., Park, C. L., Currier, J. M., Usset, T. J., & Voecks, C. D. (2015). Moral injury and psycho-spiritual development: Considering the developmental context. *Spirituality in Clinical Practice 2*, 256–266. https://doi.org/10.1037/scp0000045

Harris, J. I., Usset, T., Voecks, C., Thuras, P., Currier, J., & Erbes, C. (2018). Spiritually integrated care for PTSD: A randomized controlled trial of "Building Spiritual Strength". *Psychiatry Research, 267*, 420–428. https://doi.org/10.1016/j.psychres.2018.06.045

Hoffman, J., & Nickerson, A. (2022). The impact of moral-injury cognitions on psychological outcomes in refugees: An experimental investigation. *Clinical Psychological Science, 10*(4), 603–621. https://doi.org/10.1177/21677026211039516

Kinghorn, W. (2012). Combat trauma and moral fragmentation: A theological account of moral injury. *Journal of the Society of Christian Ethics, 32*, 57–74. https://doi.org/10.1353/sce.2012.0041

Koenig, H. G., Boucher, N. A., Oliver, J. P., Youssef, N., Mooney, S. R., Currier, J. M., & Pearce, M. (2017). Rationale for spiritually-oriented cognitive processing therapy in Active Duty Military and Veterans with post-traumatic stress disorder. *Journal of Nervous & Mental Disease, 205*, 147–153. https://doi.org/10.1097/nmd.0000000000000554

Koenig, H. G., Youssef, N. A., Ames, D., Oliver, J. P., Teng, E. J., …, & Pearce, M. J. (2018). Moral injury and religiosity in U.S. veterans with PTSDsymptoms. *Journal of Nervous and Mental Disease, 206*, 325–331. https://doi.org/10.1097/nmd.0000000000000798

Liberati, E., Richards, N., Willars, J., Scott, D., Boydell, N., Parker, J., Pinfold, V., Martin, G., Dixon-Woods, M., & Jones, P. B. (2021). A qualitative study of experiences of NHS mental healthcare workers during the Covid-19 pandemic. *BMC Psychiatry, 21*(1), 250. https://doi.org/10.1186/s12888-021-03261-8

Litz, B. T., Plouffe, R. A., Nazarov, A., Murphy, D., Phelps, A., Coady, A., Houle, S. A., Dell, L., Frankfurt, S., Zerach, G., & Levi-Belz, Y. (2022). Defining and assessing the syndrome of moral injury: Initial findings of the Moral Injury Outcome Scale Consortium. *Frontiers in Psychiatry, 13*, 923928. https://doi.org/10.3389/fpsyt.2022.923928

Litz, B. T., Stein, N., Delaney, E., Lebowitz, L., Nash, W. P., Silva, C., & Maguen, S. (2009). Moral injury and moral repair in war veterans: A preliminary model and intervention strategy. *Clinical Psychology Review, 29*(8), 695–706. https://doi.org/10.1016/j.cpr.2009.07.003

MacDonald-Smith, L., Norris, J. M., Raffin-Bouchal, S., & Sinclair, S. (2017). Spirituality and mental well-being in combat veterans: A systematic review. *Military Medicine, 182*, e1920–e1940. https://doi.org/10.7205/MILMED-D-17-00099

Maguen, S., Griffin, B. J., Vogt, D., Hoffmire, C. A., Blosnich, J. R., Bernhard, P. A., Akhtar, F. Z., Cypel, Y. S., & Schneiderman, A. I. (2023a). Moral injury and peri- and post-military suicide attempts among post-9/11 veterans. *Psychological Medicine, 53*(7), 3200–3209. https://doi.org/10.1017/S0033291721005274

Maguen, S., Nichter, B., Norman, S. B., & Pietrzak, R. H. (2023b). Moral injury and substance use disorders among US combat veterans: Results from the 2019–2020 National Health and Resilience in Veterans Study. *Psychological Medicine, 53*(4), 1364–1370. https://doi.org/10.1017/S0033291721002919

Mantri, S., Lawson, J. M., Wang, Z., & Koenig, H. G. (2021). Prevalence and predictors of moral injury symptoms in health care professionals. *The Journal of Nervous and Mental Disease, 209*(3), 174–180. https://doi.org/10.1097/nmd.0000000000001277

Milstein, G., Manierre, A., & Yali, A. M. (2010). Psychological care for persons of diverse religions: A collaborative continuum. *Professional Psychology: Research and Practice, 41*, 371–381. https://doi.org/10.1037/a0021074

Norman, S. B., Feingold, J. H., Kaye-Kauderer, H., Kaplan, C. A., Hurtado, A., Kachadourian, L., …, & Pietrzak, R. H. (2021). Moral distress in frontline healthcare workers in the initial epicenter of the COVID-19 pandemic in the United States: Relationship to PTSD symptoms, burnout, and psychosocial functioning. *Depression and Anxiety*. https://doi.org/10.1002/da.23205

Norman, S. B., Griffin, B. J., Pietrzak, R. H., McLean, C., Hamblen, J. L., & Maguen, S. (2023). The Moral Injury and Distress Scale: Psychometric evaluation and initial validation in three high-risk populations. *Psychological Trauma: Theory, Research, Practice, and Policy*. https://doi.org/10.1037/tra0001533

Park, C. L., Currier, J. M., Harris, J. I., & Slattery, J. (2016). *Trauma, Meaning, and Spirituality: Translating Research into Clinical Practice*. Washington, DC: APA. https://doi.org/10.1037/15961-000

Pyne, J. M., Currier, J. M., Hinkson, K. D., Usset, T. J., …, & Griffin, B. J. (2023). Addressing religious and spiritual diversity in moral injury care: Five perspectives. *Current Treatment Options in Psychiatry, 10*, 446–462. https://doi.org/10.1007/s40501-023-00308-3

Pyne, J. M., Rabalais, A., Sullivan, S. (2018) Mental health clinician and community clergy collaboration to address moral injury in veterans and role of VA chaplain. *Journal of Health Care Chaplaincy, 15*, 1–19. [Epub ahead of print] PMID:30111274. https://doi.org/10.1080/08854726.2018.1474997

Pyne, J. M., Sullivan, S., Rabalais, A., Jacques, M., Griffin, B. J. (2021) Mental Health Clinician Community Clergy Collaboration to Address Moral Injury Symptoms: A feasibility study. *Journal of Religion and Health, 60*, 3034–3051. PMID: 33864575. https://doi.org/10.1007/s10943-021-01257-y

Smigelsky, M. A., Trimm, V., Meador, K. G., Jackson, G. L., Wortmann, J. H., & Nieuwsma, J. A. (2022). Core components of moral injury groups co-facilitated by mental health providers and chaplains. *Spirituality in Clinical Practice*. https://doi.org/10.1037/scp0000297

Steenkamp, M. M., Litz, B. T., Hoge, C. W., & Marmar, C. R. (2015). Psychotherapy for military-related PTSD: a review of randomized clinical trials. *Journal of the American Medical Association, 314*, 489–500. https://doi.org/10.1001/jama.2015.8370

Sullivan, G., Hunt, J., Haynes, T. F., Bryant, K., Cheney, A., …, & Richison, R. (2014). Partnering with rural faith communities to promote mental health: A multi-site program for veterans. *Progress in Community Health Partnerships: Research, Education, and Action, 8*, 11–19. doi: 10.1353/cpr.2014.0004

Tappenden, P. C., Cole, T. A., Valentine, J. N., & Lilly, M. M. (2023). Examining the psychometric properties of the Expressions of Moral Injury Scale in a sample of first responder. *Psychological Trauma: Theory, Research, Practice, and Policy*. https://doi.org/10.1037/tra0001569

Usset, T. J., Baker, L. D., Griffin, B. J., Harris, J. I., Shearer, R. D., Munson, J., Godzik, C., Torrey, W. C., Bardach, S. H., Mulley, A. G., Jr., Locke, A., Wright, H. M., Call, M., Sexton, B., Shanafelt, T., Smith, A.J. (2024). Burnout and turnover risks for healthcare workers in the United States: Downstream effects from moral injury exposure. *Scientific Reports, 14*, 24915. https://doi.org/10.1038/s41598-024-74086-0

Usset, T. J., Gray, E., Griffin, B. J., Currier, J. M., Kopacz, M. S., Wilhelm, J. H., & Harris, J. I. (2020). Psychospiritual developmental risk factors for moral injury. *Religions*. https://doi.org/10.3390/rel11100484

Webb, J. R., Toussaint, L., & Dula, C. S. (2014). Ritualistic, theistic, and existential spirituality: Initial psychometric qualities of the RiTE measure of spirituality. *Journal of Religion and Health, 53*(4), 972–985. https://doi.org/10.1007/s10943-013-9697-y

Weber, M. C., Smith, A. J., Jones, R. T., Holmes, G. A., Johnson, A. L., Patrick, R. N., … & Griffin, B. J. (2023). Moral injury and psychosocial functioning in health care workers during the COVID-19 pandemic. *Psychological Services*, 20(1), 19. https://doi.org/10.1037/ser0000718

Wisco, B. E., Marx, B. P., May, C. L., Martini, B., Krystal, J. H., Southwick, S. M., & Pietrzak, R. H. (2017). Moral injury in U.S. combat veterans: Results from the national health and resilience in veterans study. *Depression and Anxiety, 34*(4), 340–347. https://doi.org/10.1002/da.22614

Wortmann, J. H., Eisen, E., Hundert, C., Jordan, A. H., Smith, M. W., Nash, W. P., & Litz, B. T. (2017). Spiritual features of war-related moral injury: A primer for clinicians. *Spirituality in Clinical Practice, 4*, 249–261. https://doi.org/10.1037/scp0000140

Xue, Y., Lopes, J., Ritchie, K., D'Alessandro, A. M., Banfield, L., McCabe, R. E., Heber, A., Lanius, R. A., & McKinnon, M. C. (2022). Potential circumstances associated with moral injury and moral distress in healthcare workers and public safety personnel across the globe during COVID-19: A Scoping Review. *Frontiers in Psychiatry, 13*, 863232. https://doi.org/10.3389/fpsyt.2022.863232

Youssef, N. A., Boswell, E., Fiedler, S., Jump. R., Lee, E., …, & Koenig, H. G. (2020). Moral injury, post-traumatic stress disorder, and religious involvement in U.S. Veterans. *Annals of Clinical Psychiatry, 30*, 113–121. PMID: 29697712.

Chapter 41

Spiritual Bypass

Jesse Fox and Craig S. Cashwell**

On March 23rd, 2008, Madeline Neumann died at the age of 11 years old from complications due to an undiagnosed case of diabetes (Fitzsimmons, 2009). During court proceedings that followed the investigation into her death, it would become known that her disease had progressed undiagnosed and untreated to the point that she was no longer able to walk or talk. Instead of taking her to a doctor, her parents, Dale and Leilani, held prayer gatherings for the miraculous healing of her symptoms. The case would eventually go down as the first conviction of reckless homicide in the state of Wisconsin, thus drawing a causal connection between the death of a victim and the practice of faith healing. Prior to her death, her father, Dale, had been working toward ordination as a Pentecostal minister before splitting with his denomination to establish his own religious community, leading up to the time of his daughter's death. During his legal testimony, he stated that "If I go to the doctor, I am putting the doctor before God," and "I am not believing what He said He would do" (The Guardian, 2009). He also testified that he sincerely believed his daughter had the flu, but also that even if she died, God would raise her from the dead (British Broadcasting Company, 2013). The case would cause a chain reaction of legislative efforts to limit the parameters of qualifying exemptions for religious treatments for medical illness to prevent future deaths from occurring when parents do not seek out existing and efficacious medical treatments for religious reasons (Fitzsimmons, 2009). The ruling was later upheld at higher courts of appeal, and the Neumanns served 1 month in prison each year for 10 years (British Broadcasting Company, 2013).

What kind of religious belief or spirituality did Dale and Leilani have that led them to forego medical treatment for their daughter? Although it is not clear how much formal mentorship, education, or training Dale had as a Pentecostal minister or why he wanted to leave that community to begin a new community, it is clear from his own testimony that Dale believed that faith healing was his best effort to practice what he believed (and likely preached): that God was capable of intervening and healing medical conditions like (as he claimed) the flu. Further, it was also clear from his own words that diverting from this path would be a betrayal of the God he served, that if he sought medical attention for his daughter's condition, he would be guilty of lacking faith in the power of God to heal her. Sadly, his appraisal of his daughter's condition as a spiritual ailment in need of healing prayer, combined with his view that taking her to a medical doctor was tantamount to betraying his faith in God, created an insurmountable barrier to care for a treatable medical condition, a decision that would cost 11-year-old Madeline her life.

* Corresponding Authors: jfox2@stetson.edu; ccashwe@clemson.edu.

DOI: 10.4324/9781003440048-47

Is Dale's belief in the healing power of prayer unhealthy or abnormal? Statistically speaking, Dale's belief in the power of prayer to heal was common. The 2010 Baylor Religion Survey (N = 1,714), conducted around the same time as the trial, found that healing prayer was affirmed widely in the United States, with estimated lifetime rates including 78.8% of the United States population praying for healing for oneself, 87.4% for others, and 54.1% asking for healing prayer, while 26.1% participated in laying-on-of-hands and 53.0% in a prayer group (Levin, 2016). Though the efficacy of healing prayer for physical ailments was and remains controversial (see Roberts, Ahmed, and Hall [2007] for a seminal review of intercessory prayer studies), the Neumanns' conviction was relatively rare, as there had been only 50 convictions related to healing prayer in the United States from 1984 to that point (Fitzsimmons, 2009). So, what makes this case different from all the other instances of healing prayer that were not answered?

Operationalizing Spiritual Bypass

In our view, Dale Neumann's pattern of behavior and approach to healing prayer fits many dynamics of spiritual bypass. Since the 1980s, when the term *spiritual bypassing* or *spiritual bypass* was first coined, various definitions of the term have surfaced. Originally, Welwood (1984) described spiritual bypass as a way to "use spiritual practice to rise above the difficulties of unresolved personal problems and emotions" and as a "tendency to try to avoid or prematurely transcend basic human needs, feelings, and developmental tasks" (p. 64). Masters (2010), in the first book devoted exclusively to spiritual bypass, called it a shadow of spirituality, pithily "avoidance in holy drag," and suggested it includes many manifestations such as

> exaggerated detachments, emotional numbing and repression, overemphasis on the positive, anger-phobia, blind or overly tolerant compassion, weak or too porous boundaries, lopsided development (cognitive intelligence often being ahead of emotional and moral intelligence), debilitating judgement about one's negativity or shadow side, devaluation of the personal relative to the spiritual, and delusions of having arrived at a higher level of being.
>
> (p. 2)

Harris (2019) defined spiritual bypass as "a way of avoiding or repressing problems in the rest of life by pretending (to self and others) to be enlightened enough not to ever be bothered by anything" (p. 3). These definitions commonly highlight that core to spiritual bypass is *avoidance*, along with *rationalization* or *spiritualizing* for *how* spirituality is practiced. Others expanded on this to involve a social dimension in which spiritual bypass involves a refusal to acknowledge and address injustices in society, racially and economically, instead overemphasizing promises or hopes of later, spiritual (often heavenly) reward (Avent Harris, 2019; Haas et al., 2022).

In our first set of studies that reported on the development of the *Spiritual Bypass Scale-13* (SBS-13), we relied heavily on these earlier definitions that psychotherapists (primarily) developed while also expanding upon them (Fox et al., 2017). We defined spiritual bypass as "a defensive psychological posture cultivated by a tendency to privilege or exaggerate spiritual beliefs, emotions, or experiences over and against psychological needs creating a means of avoiding or bypassing difficult emotions or experiences" (p. 275). In this definition, we included that, in addition to spiritual bypass being a trait or general tendency, it also involves a way of viewing spirituality as superior to other aspects of mental and physical life. Similar to previous definitions, we considered spiritual bypass to have a defensive quality where a person uses spiritual bypass to guard against pain or discomfort. Accordingly, we consider spiritual bypass most common in circumstances that pose threats to one's personhood, whether those be psychological, physical, or spiritual. Over time, however, we have begun to consider spiritual bypass as *protective*, a term we consider more compassionate toward the struggle of those in bypass.

Upon review of the factor analysis (of our scale), we discovered there were two related facets that emphasized different tendencies of spiritual bypass. The first, *psychological avoidance*, involves those definitional aspects that are perhaps most emphasized by theorists; that is, spiritual bypass as a "process of sidestepping or avoiding difficult emotions, experiences, or circumstances through spiritual beliefs or assumptions" (Fox et al., 2017, p. 283). What we were somewhat surprised to find was a second facet that involved *spiritualizing*, which can be defined as "ways of appraising ordinary scenarios and exaggerating their spiritual significance" (Fox et al., 2017, p. 283). Both facets are important to consider. As we have found in our research, they can relate to other psychosocial variables multivalently (Fox et al., 2017; Fox & Picciotto, 2019).

There are other manifestations of spiritual bypass that are also important to mention, though more empirical research is needed. For example, spiritual bypass can involve a degree of spiritualized narcissism, as appeared to be the case for Dale Neumann, where one's personal perspective becomes unduly influential to the exclusion of wise tradition and other salient perspectives. In their theoretical model of spiritual bypass, for example, Cashwell et al. (2010) tested a mediation model where spirituality was indirectly related via narcissism and alexithymia to anxiety and depression, suggesting that narcissism and the struggle to experience and express emotions in the context of a spiritual worldview may partially define spiritual bypass. In our interviews with people who have gone through spiritual bypass, they echoed these findings and noted that spiritualized narcissism can be particularly powerful when people are put into positions of spiritual authority, therefore creating social and religious environments which demand a blind and unquestioning allegiance to a spiritual leader. Additionally, it may be that spiritual bypass has a close association with perfectionism, or an extremely idealized or obsessive spirituality, where anything that is imperfect is also by definition less holy or sacred and, in essence, profane. An example of this occurs when religious or spiritual people deny being angry about a past offense based on a belief that spiritual people must forgive all grievances, often engaging in pseudo (or false) forgiveness while the unprocessed anger remains. As with spiritual narcissism, this perfectionism may include an underlying personality disorder, such as obsessive-compulsive personality disorder, or it could better be explained by subclinical personality impairments (e.g., narcissism) that uniquely originate from one's spiritual motivations.

Spirituality and Spiritual Bypass

To date, spirituality has no consensus definition in social science. Despite this, there are noteworthy advances in operationalizing spirituality empirically, which can inform the study of spiritual bypass. When we developed the SBS-13 (Fox et al., 2017), it was important that we utilized a measure of spirituality that we could contrast with it. In our thinking, spiritual bypass was not simply another form of spirituality, but rather a particular way that people practiced or appropriated their spirituality. As such, spiritual bypass involves a complicated interplay between spiritual awareness, theological understanding, life experience, and psychological processes like coping styles. Thus, spiritual bypass is not simply a matter of describing a particular religion or spiritual practice and calling it *spiritual bypass*; for one, scholars and spiritual masters from different world religions have observed how it manifests using their various theological and philosophical perspectives, and would agree that spiritual bypass can detract or distract from psycho-social-spiritual development. Because it is a way spirituality is practiced, however, we expected that bypass would be closely related to spirituality and religious commitments (i.e., convergent validity). That is, spiritual bypass will only occur when an individual has a salient identity around religion or spirituality. Put more directly, it would not make much sense to think that an atheist is more prone to spiritual bypass; there is no God to come to the rescue. This made logical sense, as we believed that people who did not have a salient identity as a religious or spiritual person would use a protective factor or defense mechanism other than spiritual bypass, or this may also mean they resign themselves to fate and lose hope if they must solve everything, so we made that part of our inquiry.

In our earliest investigations, we drew upon two operational definitions of spirituality, one that considered spirituality as a trait (or way of being) and another that considered spirituality as a state (or temporary condition in a specific situation). We used Piedmont's (2020) *Assessment of Spirituality and Religious Sentiments* (ASPIRES), which defines spirituality as "the capacity of individuals to stand outside of their immediate sense of time and place to view life from a larger, more objective perspective. This transcendent perspective is one in which a person sees a fundamental unity underlying the diverse strivings of nature and finds a bonding with others that cannot be severed, not even by death" (Piedmont, 1999, p. 988). Piedmont hypothesized that spirituality is a personality dimension, one that is not explained by the Big Five personality traits and is cross-culturally generalizable. Like Piedmont, we controlled for the explanatory power of the Big Five in developing the SBS-13. Spirituality, according to Piedmont, is related to, yet distinct from, religiousness, which Piedmont defines as a *sentiment* that can and does vary depending upon theological and philosophical teachings, practices, and identity. We have found that spiritual bypass is strongly related, as hypothesized, to both spirituality and religiousness. Later, we tested these relationships with two other types of spirituality and religiousness measures. This time, we utilized Davis et al.'s (2015) state spirituality measure, known as the *Sources of Spirituality Scale*. This measure operationalizes spirituality as a "closeness" or "connection" to what one considers sacred. There are five dimensions: theistic, transcendent, self, nature, and humanistic. Each dimension reflects a targeted episode of spiritual experience, where participants are instructed to first select and describe their strongest spiritual experience and rate each item in terms of how relevant it is to the experience they recalled. Again, as expected, spiritual bypass was related most strongly to theistic and transcendent spiritualities. Also of note, spiritual bypass was not related to nature spirituality, suggesting that finding sacredness in the physicality of the natural world is most resistant to spiritual bypass. We also included Worthington and colleagues' (2003) *Religious Commitment Inventory-10*, which defines religiousness in terms of cognitive (belief) and behavioral (actions) factors of commitment to one's tradition. The relationships between spiritual bypass and religious commitment were also strong, with effect sizes that replicated our previous work with Piedmont's measures.

What is perhaps the greatest difference between how spirituality and spiritual bypass are operationalized is not in how they relate to each other, but how they relate to other psychological factors. Previously, researchers have shown that spirituality is most strongly related to positive affect (positively related), while religiousness is most strongly related to negative affect (negatively related) (Piedmont, 2020). We also believe that spiritual bypass has a significant relationship to affective experience. However, spiritual bypass has a multivalent relationship to negative affect, dependent upon what dimension is considered. We have found that psychological avoidance, for instance, is negatively related to depression, whereas spiritualizing is positively related to anxiety. Similarly, consider attitudes one may hold about what may be the best avenue to find help when needed. Similar to the tragic death of Madeline Neumann, we also believed that one of the strongest relationships spiritual bypass manifests toward is in help-seeking attitudes, both psychological and medical. Because spiritual bypass involves a dualistic cosmology, where spirituality is superior to the psychological or material, "if problems arise, the solution is thought to be spiritual and thus to require some spiritual intervention or interventionist" (Fox et al., 2020, p. 182). Our understanding of these mechanisms behind spiritual bypass was consistent with the data we collected on psychological and help-seeking attitudes. We found that while religious commitment had a modest relationship to help-seeking attitudes, this relationship became non-significant when we included spiritual bypass in the model. In every instance, spiritual bypass was predictive of less favorable views of both psychological and medical help. Researchers have found that these relationships can remain stable over time, where spiritual bypass (specifically spiritualizing) has predicted help-seeking stigma at least 1 year later (Ahmad et al., 2023b).

Understanding Spiritual Bypass Through the RiTE Model

Webb's RiTE model of spirituality involves three interrelated constructs, which together can be understood as balancing dimensions of diverse sources of spirituality: ritual (or religious), theological, and existential (Webb et al., 2014; see also Chapters 1 and 44 of this volume). To the best of our knowledge, spiritual bypass has never been investigated or conceptualized utilizing the RiTE model, but there are certain pathways in which this theory would help to illuminate the psychospiritual quality of spiritual bypass. In Webb's model, each of the three dimensions combines toward optimal spirituality, and "while an individual may prefer or incline toward a particular dimension of spirituality, optimal spirituality is thought to include modest to moderate levels of each of the three dimensions, rather than an overbearing focus on one of the dimensions" (p. 975). This assumption in the RiTE model is helpful to conceptualize spiritual bypass as an exaggerated focus on the theological and ritualistic dimensions of spirituality, to the neglect of the existential dimension that emphasizes self-knowledge, pro-sociality, and humanism. Moreover, the RiTE model can also help elucidate the possibilities for non-religious bypass, something which has not been articulated as a type of spiritual bypass, where existential spirituality is myopically accentuated to the exclusion of interpersonal well-being. The source of this hyperfocus on personal existential flourishing could be due to a fatalistic appraisal of the value that human effort has to make any difference to the suffering of the world. For example, despite the efforts of many capable change agents and well-meaning social movements, poverty still destroys human lives in every society on earth. In light of such intractable problems, exclusive focus on personal existential spirituality avoids actively engaging with the broader scope of human suffering.

Healthy or Unhealthy?

Spiritual bypass is commonly understood as an unhealthy and deleterious process that can arrest psycho-social-spiritual development. However, rather than what could be construed as an all-or-nothing perspective (spiritual bypass is just always bad news), we have found that spiritual bypass is more nuanced than being either all healthy or unhealthy. In interviewing people who have helped others through spiritual bypass, in addition to correlational analyses, spiritual bypass can be a coping strategy for trauma or feelings of overwhelm. Additionally, researchers have found intercorrelations between spiritual bypass and depression, suggesting a pattern of negative association. This is only true, however, of psychological avoidance. Spiritualizing, on the other hand, has shown a positive association (also replicated across studies) with anxiety as well as alexithymia. One could argue that these patterns are a unique manifestation of how spiritual bypass is operationalized. In the SBS-13, psychological avoidance is loaded with several items that point toward tendencies to bypass problems through experiential avoidance; these items also assume a very positive God concept. That is, in this scale, God is a rescuer who will take care of problems, so there is no need to feel weighed down by circumstances one cannot control. This positive God image could, in part, be why spiritual bypass can be positively related to self-rated posttraumatic growth. In contrast, spiritualizing includes several items that assume negative spiritual forces or entities are out to get you, and therefore are cause for great fear and need for vigilance to prevent calamities from occurring. In clinical work, then, it seems important to not only consider spiritual bypass, but also assess the extent to which the God image is generally positive or negative, and ways in which the doctrinal (i.e., outer) concept of God differs from the experiential (i.e., inner) image of God.

One observation that deserves more attention about the relative healthiness or unhealthiness of spiritual bypass is how time may play a mediating role in the ultimate causal significance of psychological avoidance and spiritualizing. We have found that spiritual bypass is strongly related to Pargament's coping model using the religious problem-solving framework. For example, we found that spiritual bypass, positively related (as expected) to a *deferring* problem-solving approach that involves abdicating personal responsibility for solving problems one may encounter, and expecting the God of one's understanding to address them instead. Spiritual bypass is also negatively related (as expected) to *self-directed* problem solving, wherein one takes ownership for proactively developing solutions rather than expecting God to handle it. In such scenarios, however, where someone experiences a trauma or episodes of cosmological collapse (where they feel like their whole universe is crumbling), spiritual bypass may help one cope initially to at least maintain some sense of coherence. As time wears on and as the reality of the effects of such catastrophic events continues to linger on or perhaps worsen, it becomes harder to justify such evasion. At the very least, the radical honesty that is required of spiritual growth is missing, and so too is the transformative power which suffering can catalyze. Said another way, we have hypothesized that short-term spiritual bypass is not harmful and may even be helpful and related to post-traumatic growth, whereas a chronic pattern of spiritual bypass that becomes trait-like is psychologically problematic. This chronic response of spiritual bypass occurs unconsciously and becomes a patterned response to the challenges of life.

Further, we have found time and again, in both our qualitative interviews and anecdotal cases in clinical and supervisory settings, that people who are actively spiritually bypassing create frustration and disjointed relationships with the people around them. It is hard for people to feel a genuine connection to the person who is bypassing – whether through psychological avoidance or spiritualizing, or both. This seems logical since spiritual bypass typically involves a lack of comfort with distressing feelings arising in the here and now. Authentic relationships require vulnerability and honesty, that one may feel unsafe or helpless, and that things really may not be well, and while spiritual bypass may restore a sense of personal control over these unmanageable emotional states, it must do so at the expense of disavowing the transparency and honesty of the present moment experience. Thus, it appears that one of the most affected areas of a person's life who is in spiritual bypass is the warmth of genuine relationships and the vulnerability they often require. Also, as we noted above, the more people endorse spiritual bypass items, the less likely it is they are to also view psychological and medical help as viable pathways for addressing problems. Collectively, these findings suggest that the unhealthiest consequences, at least to date, are that chronic spiritual bypass stunts problem solving and the power of authentic relationships and creates narrow solutions to high-stakes decision-making in complex situations that could involve heavy life-or-death consequences and, in some cases, could be associated with greater emotional distress (especially anxiety).

Spiritual Bypass Across Religions and Cultural Locations

When we developed our measure of spiritual bypass, we were very conscious at the time of the prevailing religious groups in the United States. At that time, around 70% of the population was Christian, and an even larger percentage believed in God. We thought it important, at least in our first efforts to study the construct, to include theistic items in the measure, which culturally skews the assessment toward the Abrahamic religions. We had not yet become sophisticated enough to address questions of the universal nature of spiritual bypass in different religious philosophies in one measure. What seems obvious, however, is that spiritual bypass is not limited to just Christianity, or even theistic religions; the term, after all, was coined by Welwood (1984) to describe meditators in a Buddhist context. With these limits in mind, we were surprised to observe, since then, just how religiously and linguistically generalizable the concept can be. The first norming sample included a diverse array of religious identities that approximated the US population, with the majority of the participants representing Christian, while being inclusive of religious minorities (e.g., Muslims) and religiously unaffiliated (e.g., spiritual but not religious). Since then, researchers have found structural stability of the construct in the majority of Hindu, Muslim, and spiritual but not religious samples (Ahmad et al., 2023a; Ahmad et al., 2023b, Toussaint et al., 2021). Further, researchers have translated the original English version into Brazilian Portuguese, Korean, Spanish, and Turkish (Picciotto et al., 2018; Taylor et al., 2021; Motiño et al., 2021; Kasapoğlu, 2023). These scholars have also found evidence of the structural validity of psychological avoidance and spiritualizing as concepts that are not bound by language. Given that it shares no etymological roots with English, the Korean translation of the measure is probably the strongest evidence to date that spiritual bypass is not limited to Western lexicons and is more likely attributed to common religious philosophies.

The work of Ahmad et al. (2023a, 2023b) has been particularly important in extending the research on spiritual bypass beyond Christian populations. In a series of studies, their research team has tested the validity and reliability of spiritual bypass with Muslims living in the United States. They have found that the SBS-13 performs comparably to Christian samples, and have added important model testing analyses to address underlying causal precedent in relation to religious concepts that are germane to Islamic theology and practice, and to psychological functioning. They have found that spiritual bypass is not only structurally distinct from Islamic religiousness, but it also moderates the relationship between religiousness and psychological distress, such that those in greater spiritual bypass report higher rates of negative religious coping. Similarly to Fox et al. (2020), they found that spiritual bypass was not conflated with religious commitments, but instead is an influential variable in the way authentic religious practices are obfuscated. They also conducted the first longitudinal analyses of spiritual bypass, and found that scores remained stable over at least 1 year, with intercorrelations between time points ranging from .69 to .76 (Ahmad et al., 2023b).

Controversies Surrounding Spiritual Bypass

There is little doubt that spiritual bypass is an advanced topic in the psychology of religion and spirituality. To understand it, one must first grasp the dynamic ground from which both religion and spirituality emerge and how they can manifest in various dimensions, all before really being able to fit spiritual bypass into a theory or empirical model of its relationships, first to religion and spirituality, and then to various health constructs, including mental health. Moreover, there is a subtlety to spiritual bypass that can be frustrating to observe, penetrate, and distinguish from the myriad of religious philosophies and practices which it can channel and redirect. Therefore, simple correlations between spiritual bypass and the "x" factor of either religious or psychological significance are not sophisticated enough to pick up on how spiritual bypass can be either a mediator or moderator of spiritual practice. Historically speaking, it may in fact be the case that many of the traditional critiques of religion as inauthentic, rigid, power hungry, exclusive, and abusive probably involve moments in that tradition in which spiritual bypass was particularly acute and prevalent, thus bending what can be authentic spirituality toward a quite different arc. At times, it may be difficult for people to articulate why their experience may be so negative, and they may simply conclude that religion is toxic. What exactly is meant by spiritual bypass may likewise be misinterpreted because it can sound like spiritual bypass is simply falling in line with these same critiques. An example may prove useful.

In a recent study to develop a measure of Christian spiritual surrender, researchers (Shannonhouse et al., 2024) hypothesized that spiritual bypass would not be related to how Christians practice their religion through a process of surrendering to God what they perceive to be outside of their control; indeed, one's very life and existence is regularly surrendered to God in Christian teaching. This practice of surrender is core to authentic Christian living, and therefore can be considered a manifestation of intrinsic religiousness. Simultaneously, Christian teaching equally emphasizes the need for personal and collective responsibility to be participants in the ongoing work of God in the world, and to meet the needs of others, especially for those who are considered excluded from society (i.e., justice or righteousness) (Piedmont et al. 2020). The measure they created is heavily loaded with items that defer to God's control over all situations, and includes only two out of ten items that include any acknowledgement of the Christian's ongoing responsibilities as an active participant in resolving problems they encounter.

How spiritual bypass may relate here is complicated. On the one hand, Christian spiritual surrender theologically involves a grounding trust in the benevolence of a loving God. Unsurprisingly, then, and as an authentic practice in Christianity, surrender positively correlated to spiritual bypass (just as it has with other spiritual and religious measures in every published study to date). One would be surprised if it did not, because spiritual bypass will always be related to one's spirituality, especially if it puts change-making agency onto an external spiritual reality. After all, people authentically embrace aspects of their tradition, like petitionary prayer, while also engaging in spiritual bypass. How healthy this is psychologically depends on *how* they do so. If Christians also embrace their roles as participants in the divine plan for justice, they may draw from a fuller understanding of Christian surrender and be less prone to bypass or prematurely transcend and exclude their potential to be agents of change. For people who are religious, spiritual bypass items such as "When I face a life challenge, I always consult with a spiritual or religious teacher" may be consistent practice of seeking counsel that is intrinsic to many religions, but the subtle elements of spiritual bypass in such an item may be the extremity in which it is phrased and subsequently endorsed (i.e., *always*), especially if no action is taken to directly address the challenge. Of course, spiritual bypass is not limited to single items, but rather a combination of items that are correlated to a latent construct. Thus, simple correlations to items on a measure like the Christian Spiritual Surrender Scale will not say much about the construct, but factor analytic methods could (e.g., structural equation modeling). That is, if spiritual bypass loads significantly onto spiritual or religious constructs and, if distinct, moderation or mediation of relationships occurs (see Ahmad et al., 2023a).

Future Directions

Spiritual bypass opens new avenues for both basic and applied research in the science of spirituality and health. Though important developments in construct validity and reliability of spiritual bypass have gained significant traction, there are certain aspects of this burgeoning field of inquiry that need further attention. The research on spiritual bypass has over-relied on self-reports, and while self-reports are vital to access important features of spiritual bypass, they certainly are limited and can succumb to single-source bias and correlated error in later analysis of findings, particularly for those who are highly avoidant and might minimize their struggles. The SBS-13, in part, reflects our efforts to mitigate the potential bias in self-reports by electing to use less direct items like "I avoid responsibilities by distracting myself with spirituality" and relying on more indirect items that stress nuances without creating expectancy effects in respondents. Be that as it may, it seems clear from anecdotal descriptions of spiritual bypass that it is an observable phenomenon, especially to people who are intimately acquainted with the person in bypass and can distinguish the differences between their authentic spiritual motivations and how these are being appropriated for avoidance or spiritualizing.

Further, it is likely that spiritual bypass includes more facets than just psychological avoidance and spiritualizing. As we noted earlier, interviews and previous clinical observations from a variety of writers have noted that a narcissistic preoccupation with one's own perspective, decision-making capacities, and authority are relevant to spiritual bypass. Some form of extreme idealism or perfectionism is also an important feature that needs focused inquiry. Future work needs to disentangle how much either a spiritualized narcissism or an exaggerated idealism is due to underlying personality pathology, or a distinct feature of spiritual bypass.

These directions remain at the descriptive level. For some time now, researchers have been calling for practice-based evidence or randomized controlled trials testing ways of working through spiritual bypass (e.g., Fox et al., 2020). Until such work materializes, the guidelines for clinical practice remain at the level of clinical expertise and anecdote, and while well-trained clinical experience is an essential component of evidence-based practices, they are still limited and need to be triangulated with the greater diversity of experience across larger samples.

Conclusion

Now, approximately 40 years after Welwood (1984) first coined the term, discussions and empirical examination of spiritual bypass are greater than ever. Blog posts, discussions in religious communities, grant-funded projects, and scholarly debates abound on the topic of spiritual bypass. We have seen others and, at times, been guilty ourselves of being overly critical of those in spiritual bypass. As both mental health and religion scholars continue to explore the phenomenon of spiritual bypass, we hope that it will be done with an understanding of the protective nature of spiritual bypass and deep compassion for the underlying suffering that leads to this protective stance. We also hope that we and other scholars will attend to the nuances of healthy spiritual surrender and not move too quickly to pathologize such a surrendered stance. Ultimately, it will be empirical research, both quantitative and qualitative, that furthers a clinical understanding of how to support authentic spirituality and compassionately address problematic spiritual bypass in those we serve.

References

Ahmad, S. S., McLaughlin, M. M., & Weisman de Mamani, A. (2023a). Spiritual bypass as a moderator of the relationships between religious coping and psychological distress in Muslims living in the United States. *Psychology of Religion and Spirituality*, *15*(1), 32–42. https://doi.org/10.1037/rel0000469

Ahmad, S. S., McLaughlin, M. M., & Weisman de Mamani, A. (2023b). Validation and test–retest reliability of the Spiritual Bypass Scale in Muslims and implications for psychological help-seeking attitudes and self-stigma. *Spirituality in Clinical Practice*, *10*(1), 62–73. https://doi.org/10.1037/scp0000300

Avent Harris, J. R. (2019). The Black Superwoman in spiritual bypass: Black women's use of religious coping and implications for mental health professionals. *Journal of Spirituality in Mental Health*, *23*(2), 180–196. https://doi.org/10.1080/19349637.2019.1685925

British Broadcasting Company. (2013, July 3). US 'prayer cure' couple lose appeal over child's death. https://www.bbc.com/news/world-us-canada-23167489

Cashwell, C. S., Glosoff, H. L., & Hammond, C. (2010). Spiritual bypass: A preliminary investigation. *Counseling and Values*, *54*(2), 162–174. https://doi.org/10.1002/j.2161-007X.2010.tb00014.x

Davis, D. E., Rice, K. I., Hook, J. N., Van Tongeren, D. R., DeBlaere, C., Choe, E., & Worthington, E. L., Jr. (2015). Development of the Sources of Spirituality Scale. *Journal of Counseling Psychology*, *62*, 503–513. https://doi.org/10.1037/cou0000082

Fitzsimmons, E. G. (2009, October 8). Wisconsin Couple Sentenced in Death of Their Sick Child. *The New York Times*. A16. https://www.nytimes.com/2009/10/08/us/08sentence.html

Fox, J., Cashwell, C. S., & Picciotto, G. (2017). The opiate of the masses: Measuring spiritual bypass and its relationship to spirituality, religion, mindfulness, psychological distress, and personality. *Spirituality in Clinical Practice*, *4*(4), 274–287. https://doi.org/10.1037/scp0000141

Fox, J., & Picciotto, G. (2019). The mediating effects of spiritual bypass on depression, anxiety, and stress. *Counseling and Values: Spirituality, Ethics, and Religion in Counseling*, *64*, 227–245. https://doi.org/10.1002/cvj.12116

Fox, J., Picciotto, G., Cashwell, C. S., Worthington, E. L., Jr., Basso, M. J., Brow Corrigan, S., Toussaint, L., & Zeligman, M. (2020). Religious commitment, spirituality, and attitudes toward God as related to psychological and medical help-seeking: The role of spiritual bypass. *Spirituality in Clinical Practice*, *7*(3), 178–196. https://doi.org/10.1037/scp0000216

Haas, J., O'Grady, K. A., Fox, J., Schuermann, H., Toscano, M. E., Taylor, C. (2022). Responses to the 2014 Police Shooting of Michael Brown: Cosmology Episodes and Enacted Environments. *Religions*, *13*, 133. https://doi.org/10.3390/rel13020133

Kasapoğlu, F. (2023). Manevi Baypas Ölçeği'nin Türkçe formunun psikometrik özellikleri. *Turkish Studies*, *18*(3), 1185–1195. https://doi.org/10.7827/TurkishStudies.69317

Levin, J. (2016). Prayer and health: Review, meta-analysis, and research agenda. *Journal of Religion and Health*, *55*(6), 1809–1826.

Masters, R. A. (2010). *Spiritual bypassing: When spirituality disconnects us from what really matters*. North Atlantic Books.

Motiño, A., Saiz, J., Sánchez-Iglesias, I., Salazar, M., Barsotti, T. J., Goldsby, T. L., Chopra, D., & Mills, P. J. (2021). Cross-cultural analysis of spiritual bypass: A comparison between Spain and Honduras. *Frontiers in Psychology*, *12*, 658739. https://doi.org/10.3389/fpsyg.2021.658739

Picciotto, G., Fox, J., Cashwell, C. S., & Neto, F. (2018). The spiritual bypass scale-Brazilian translation and the effects of religious affiliation, age, and gender on levels of psychological avoidance and spiritualizing. *Spiritual Psychology and Counseling*, *3*(1), 23–46. https://doi.org/10.12738/spc.2018.1.0034

Piedmont, R. L. (1999). Does spirituality represent the sixth factor of personality? Spiritual transcendence and the five-factor model. *Journal of Personality*, *67*(6), 985–1013. https://doi.org/10.1111/1467-6494.00080

Piedmont, R. L. (2020). *Assessment of Spirituality and Religious Sentiments, Technical Manual*, 3rd ed. Author (Piedmont).

Roberts, L., Ahmed, I., & Hall, S. (2007). Intercessory prayer for the alleviation of ill health. *The Cochrane Database of Systematic Reviews*, 2009(2), CD000368. https://doi.org/10.1002/14651858.CD000368.pub2

Shannonhouse, L., McMartin, J., Sacco, S. J., Hall, M. E. L., Park, C. L., Kim, D., Silverman, E., Kapic, K., & Aten, J. (2024). Spiritual surrender: Measurement of an emic Christian religious coping strategy. *Spirituality in Clinical Practice*, *11*(2), 173–185. https://doi.org/10.1037/scp0000314

Taylor, C., Fox, J., Worthington, E.L., & Cashwell, C. S. (2021). Adaptation and confirmatory factor analysis of the Spiritual Bypass Scale-13 into Korean. *Mental Health, Religion, and Culture*. Advanced Online Publication: https://doi.org/10.1080/13674676.2021.1977920

The Guardian. (2009). Couple sentenced over daughter's death after prayer instead of medical care. https://www.theguardian.com/world/2009/oct/07/couple-sentenced-daughter-prayer-death

Toussaint, L., Fox, J., Kamble, S., Worthington, E. L., Jr., Cashwell, C. S., & Picciotto, G. (2021). Initial psychometric properties of the Spiritual Bypass Scale in an Indian college student sample. *Psychology of Religion and Spirituality*, *13*(1), 63–66. https://doi.org/10.1037/rel0000302

Webb, J. R., Toussaint, L., & Dula, C. S. (2014). Ritualistic, theistic, and existential spirituality: Initial psychometric qualities of the RiTE measure of spirituality. *Journal of Religion & Health*, *53*(4), 972–985. https://doi.org/10.1007/s10943-013-9697-y

Welwood, J. (1984). Principles of inner work: Psychological and spiritual. *Journal of Transpersonal Psychology*, *16*, 63–73.

Worthington, E. L., Jr., Wade, N. G., Hight, T. L., Ripley, J. S., McCullough, M. E., Berry, J. W., Schmitt, M. M., Berry, J. T., Bursley, K. H., & O'Connor, L. (2003). The Religious Commitment Inventory–10: Development, refinement, and validation of a brief scale for research and counseling. *Journal of Counseling Psychology*, *50*(1), 84–96. https://doi.org/10.1037/0022-0167.50.1.84

Chapter 42

Spirituality, Health, and Well-Being among Families and Persons Living with Intellectual and Developmental Disabilities

Nicole Piland[*]

> The human spirit is one of ability, perseverance, and courage that no disability can steal away.
>
> – Anonymous (n.d.)

Historically, the aims of many disability researchers have involved the exploration of how a child with an Intellectual and Developmental Disability (IDD) impacts parental functioning (Chang & McConkey, 2008; Hastings, 2016; Nelson Goff & Piland Springer, 2018; Ramisch & Piland Springer, 2020). Although there is evidence that parental stress can be heightened in these families, and parents often describe an emotional adjustment process when a diagnosis is received (Bentley et al., 2023; Nelson-Goff et al., 2016; Nelson-Goff et al., 2013), not all families respond poorly to a life with disability. Moreover, some research findings actually shed light on the more positive, transformative ways these individuals influence members of their families (Hastings, 2016; Kausar et al., 2003; Nelson Goff & Piland Springer, 2018) and even depict ways in which these families demonstrate resilience (Knestrict & Kuchey, 2009; Knestrict, 2018).

Thus, the research has shifted away from a deficit-oriented framework and more toward a systemic exploration of disability-related stress and coping in families, where coping has been measured in terms of social support, hope, life satisfaction, and marital satisfaction. This chapter will be used to highlight the spiritual lives of families and persons with an IDD as members of communities, and summarize key findings associated with spirituality, health, and well-being in participants affiliated with various socio-cultural, geographic, and ethnic and religious sub-groups. In addition, commonly applied systemic, theoretical frameworks, assessments, and interventions will be presented. Finally, a discussion and critique of the potential benefits and challenges of the role of spirituality, health, and well-being for this population will be offered in order to more effectively inform future research directions and interventions for these families, specifically through the lens of the RiTE model of spirituality (Webb et al., 2014; see also Chapters 1 and 44 of this volume).

Definitions: Intellectual and Developmental Disability and Spirituality

Disability

Before discussing the role of various belief systems associated with spirituality within this diverse population, the following will serve as a working definition of disability, as disability-related terms are often used interchangeably. A *disability* is 'any condition of the body or

* Corresponding Author: nicole.piland@ttu.edu.

DOI: 10.4324/9781003440048-48

mind (*impairment*) that makes it more difficult for the person with the condition to do certain activities (*activity limitation*) and interact with the world around them (*participation restrictions*)' (Centers for Disease Control (CDC), 2025a; World Health Organization (WHO), 2001). Terms utilized throughout the chapter will be based on disability-related sample inclusion criteria or will be consistent with the terms presented within each study's description.

Roughly, 1–3% of the general population is identified as having an *Intellectual Disability* (ID) (Patel et al., 2020; Zablotsky et al., 2023) and experiences impairment within intellectual functioning and adaptive behavior (AAIDD, 2024). Zablotsky et al. (2023) reported that, 'during 2019–2021, the prevalence of any diagnosed developmental disability in children aged 3–17 years increased from 7.40% in 2019 to 8.56% in 2021' (p. 1). Additionally, boys were more than three times as likely as girls to be diagnosed with autism spectrum disorder (Zablotsky et al., 2023). Ultimately, disability can involve a congenital condition (e.g., spina bifida, Down syndrome (DS)) or conditions that develop after birth (e.g., autism spectrum disorders, juvenile diabetes, and childhood cancer) or conditions due to injury (e.g., traumatic brain injury) or other heritable risk factors (e.g., sickle cell disease) (WHO, 2001). Some disabilities not only include cognitive impairment(s) but may also impact other realms of development, requiring medical and therapeutic intervention (Turns et al., 2018).

The current term used to describe someone with a cognitive or intellectual difference who may also experience delays in development is *Intellectual and Developmental Disability* (IDD), defined as 'differences that are usually present at birth and that uniquely affect the trajectory of the individual's physical, intellectual, and/or emotional development' (NICHD, 2021). Another progressive term used to describe those who experience neuro-cognitive differences is *neurodivergent* (Manalili, 2021); often associated with those who may be diagnosed with autism spectrum disorder (ASD) and/or Attention-Deficit Hyperactivity Disorder (ADHD). Levels of impairment, activity limitations, and participation restrictions can vary significantly from person to person (CDC, 2025a; WHO, 2001), but ideally, are attended to at an individual, familial, and community level.

Spirituality

Spirituality, often expressed within the context of a community setting, is one facet of identity. A multitude of factors can influence a person's development and expression of identity. According to the 2017 Pew Research Center survey data of 5000 adults, about half of the participants surveyed identified as religious and spiritual, and 27% of Americans identified as spiritual, but not religious (Lipka & Gecewicz, 2017). Comparatively, data from the 2020 US Census of American Religion indicates that the majority of Americans identified as religious, specifically 70% as Christian (PRRI, 2020), but approximately one in four identified as religiously *un*affiliated, and about 5% of Americans identified with non-Christian religions.

Thus, the relationship between religion and spirituality is often interrelated and yet can manifest as uniquely as the person who identifies with either or both realms of expression. Moreover, those who identify as spiritual often do not define spirituality in the same way, and some people do not identify with either realm of expression. For the purpose of this chapter, *spirituality* is defined as,

> The dynamic dimension of human life that relates to the way persons (individual and community) experience, express and/or seek meaning, purpose and transcendence, and the way they connect to the moment, to self, to others, to nature, to the significant and/or the sacred.
>
> (Kleiven et al., 2021, as cited in Timmons et al., 2023, p. 2)

In this chapter, the role of spirituality will be discussed in terms of how it can influence parents and caregivers, as well as persons living with a disability. Watts (2011) asserts that 'every person is not without a spiritual nature' and 'possesses an inner spiritual state that some choose to call a soul' (p. 236). He also proposes that spiritual awareness can be 'stimulated and developed' within the ID population (p. 236). Ultimately, the role of spirituality and how disability is viewed can fundamentally serve to inform how individuals and families cope or find meaning and purpose when disability presents in their lives.

Models of Disability

Disability has most often been conceptualized using three specific models of disability: (1) Moral – where the disability is viewed as the result of moral choices or failings of the individual or family affected, (2) Medical – a biological, pathology-based model which subscribes to the identification of a physical problem to be treated or managed, and (3) Social – models emphasize the person's level of impairment as not problematic in and of itself but rather is informed by the social barriers and oppression experienced within their social context (Dan, 2020; Olkin, 2002/2022; Riddle, 2013). Although impairment is defined largely in the context of medical criteria of health, Riddle (2013) emphasizes that disability is a 'socially derived phenomenon, resulting in the oppression of people' (p. 381).

Riddle (2013) also proposes that an *interaction model* is more appropriate for conceptualizing disability, highlighting that the experience of the individual with the disability is influenced by individual factors combined with the context in which they are embedded. Interactional theorists are particularly concerned with 'all of the various forms of disadvantage (both social and individual)' (p. 384). Another disability model proposed in the literature is a *life course model* (Krahn & Fox, 2014). Essentially, this model is used to consider how spirituality and expressions thereof are supported during life transitions, particularly in terms of maintaining social relationships and engaging in meaningful life activities. Ultimately, persons and families within this population are influenced by how disability is viewed and related to within the lived experience, which also includes how disability is spoken about.

Person-First Language and Whole-Person Care

The social context of disability is largely influenced by beliefs, attitudes, and inclusive practices, including the use of language. The terms 'mentally retarded' or 'handicapped,' historically used to describe those who are born with or acquire cognitive impairments and/or live with a physical disability, are now considered derogatory, offensive, and othering (Gallus & Jones, 2018; Rahman, 2019). Another term, 'special needs,' has served as an umbrella term for many decades; however, this term can be experienced as infantilizing and removes important context of the disability, collapsing all persons into a single group. The use of the term *functional needs* is more appropriate when addressing supports or accommodations individuals may benefit from in a particular context (Rahman, 2019).

Currently, the language used and perspectives held about IDD populations have improved and exemplify more sensitive, *person-first language* (NIH, 2024; Rahman, 2019). The shift in language is due to many advocacy efforts, including but not limited to the 2019 'Spread the Word' campaign (Special Olympics, 2024) and the work of the Eunice Kennedy Shriver Foundation (NICHD, 2021) to advance the rights and acceptance of those living with an ID. Although the use of labels or diagnoses can serve to facilitate the acquisition and reimbursement of necessary healthcare services and important interventions, efforts should be made to honor all humans by providing *whole-person care* (NCCIH, 2021) and avoiding language which focuses solely on impairments or participation limitations. People are not their diagnoses nor their disability, and how we talk about and attend to this population needs continued advocacy and advancements in inclusive care practices, which impart value for the whole person, beyond their disability type.

The RiTE Model and Intellectual and Developmental Disability in Families

Over the past two decades, not only have efforts been made to advance the rights of those living with disabilities, but research has progressed to a more strengths-based inquiry about how families successfully navigate life, specifically with regard to the role of spirituality. When considering these families, some aspects of spirituality may be particularly relevant for supporting and enhancing 'optimal' or 'balanced' spirituality as discussed by Webb et al. (2014, p. 975) and Webb (2021, p. 62; see also Chapters 1 and 44 of this volume). The RiTE model (i.e., *ritualistic*, *theistic*, and *existential* spirituality) provides a framework for an assessment of the multidirectional and interconnected dimensions of spirituality that may inform spiritual identity, expression, and well-being (Webb et al., 2014).

Ritualistic Spirituality

First, *ritualistic spirituality*, although not exclusively, involves practices performed or participation within the context of groups, and might serve as a secondary, rather than a primary, spiritual function for this population. For caregivers, considerations may be needed for identifying ways in which their loved one's needs must be supported, adapted, and prioritized. In addition, some may need to determine whether regular participation within a religious or spiritual community is feasible, or whether supportive others are available within that setting to allow caregivers respite for participating in routine, ritualistic practices for their own benefit.

For the loved one with IDD, there may be a range in their understanding of the ritual itself, yet participating in the ritual still affords them an opportunity for and a place where belonging and shared experiences can occur (Boehm & Carter, 2019). In addition, there may be greater value in the aspects of ritualistic practices that can be experienced through the five senses (i.e., sight – statues or candles, smell – incense, sound – music, taste – sacraments, touch – the laying of hands) (Underwood, 1999; Watts, 2011). For some individuals, certain senses may be limited (e.g., vision), yet although one sense may be impaired, other senses may be more attuned (e.g., hearing) (Harris, 2016).

Theistic Spirituality

From a *theistic spirituality* perspective, considerations for persons with an IDD, who may not as easily connect to the abstract nature of deity-based spirituality, may be required. More specifically, IDDs that more greatly affect one's level of intelligence, speech and language, or other features of comprehension may affect a person's ability to fully understand or embrace the concept of connecting to something unseen (e.g., God and Allah). However, attending to and identifying other sensory-based information, like a felt sense of connection, or having a physiological experience (e.g., getting the chills or being moved to tears) may serve as a mechanism to bring such an abstract concept to a more concrete level (Lui et al., 2014). For caregivers, it may be important to ask, does the presence of theistic spirituality serve as a resource or a potential source of anger or blame held toward a higher power(s) or even fuel feelings of guilt, shame, and remorse for past misdeeds thought to be the cause of the disability?

Existential Spirituality

In terms of *existential spirituality*, living with purpose may also be achievable, to varying degrees, but it is important to consider the nuance of how one may achieve a sense of purpose or meaning, both for caregivers and their loved ones. What is meaningful for some may vary significantly, but ultimately, it is important to consider what supports or opportunities for discovering or identifying a meaningful outlet in life are available. Essentially, are these families embedded in a social context which attends to, possesses the resources for, and values the existential dimension of spirituality? Other considerations include (1) the role of caregiver burden and the level of demands required, (2) how those demands may serve as a barrier for following one's dreams or pursuing one's life purpose beyond caregiving, or (3) whether caring for the loved one is viewed as a source of meaning and purpose in and of itself.

Perceptions of Persons with Intellectual and Developmental Disability in Context

This section highlights disability-related perceptions of persons affiliated with monotheistic, polytheistic, and non-theistic religions (see Table 42.1) within several important qualitative studies which illustrate the role of faith, spirituality, and coping associated with disability-related experiences of parents and caregivers. Researchers have utilized structured and semi-structured interviews with a majority of Buddhist, Hindu, Muslim, and non-religious identifying participants raising children with a range of disability types (Chang & McConkey, 2008; Croot et al., 2008; John & Montgomery, 2016; Karaca & Sener, 2021; Shahdadi & Mahmoudirad, 2022).

Essentially, an array of cultural perceptions exists regarding persons born with congenital conditions or those who acquire a disability in their developmental years. For instance, some members of certain religious and cultural groups may consider a person with an IDD as a 'blessing,' a 'gift,' or 'sent by God' (Croot et al., 2008; John & Montgomery, 2016; Karaca & Sener, 2021; Nelson-Goff et al., 2013; Sloper, 2007, 2009), while others might believe the disability is due to bad 'karma' (Chang & McConkey, 2008; Harris, 2016; Wilson, 2019), or serves as a punishment for misdeeds (Croot et al., 2008; Karaca & Sener, 2021).

Monotheistic, Polytheistic, and Non-Theistic Perspectives

In certain cultures, the views and perceptions of disability can be both positive and negative, or simply neutral. For example, Croot et al. (2008) identified a range of beliefs held by a sample of Pakistani, Sunni-Muslim (a monotheistic religion) parents living in the United Kingdom. Parent narratives included descriptions about their child's disability that were both positive and negative, but parents also described misconceptions held by those around them. Descriptions ranged from 'gifts from God,' 'chosen parents,' 'punishment,' 'a curse,' and myths that their loved one was 'contagious.'

Alternatively, within Native American (NA) spirituality, which can be considered polytheistic, animistic, shamanistic, pantheistic, or any combination thereof, the relative functioning

Table 42.1 Qualitative Research on Parent/Caregiver Perspectives

Sample description	*Disability type*	*Themes*	*Religious affiliation*	*Citation*
Home-based Interviews - Parents (N = 117): Taiwan - Mothers (86%) - Fathers (14%)	(20%) Autism, (14%) CP (11%) DS (10%) Epilepsy (4%) ADHD	- The role of **karma**, importance of **family harmony**, responsibility and **duty to care for** the loved one, and **collectivist priority** were of significance in understanding the participant's culture of origin. - Family functioning included both **positive and negative influences** of the child on the family system. - Parental stress included the theme of **pessimism about the future**. - Parents reported **emotional difficulties** and **challenges with physical health**. - Parental coping included: proactive behaviors, acceptance, and distractions.	**49% Buddhists**, 20% other religions, 30% no religion identified	Chang & McConkey, (2008)
Semi-structured Interviews - Mothers (N = 28); Turkey	Down syndrome, Mental disability, Cerebral Palsy, and Hydrocephalus	- value in their **spirituality** when finding acceptance and meaning of their child's diagnosis (existential spirituality) - the role of **unconditional love**. - use of **prayer** and reading the Quran (ritualistic spirituality) as a form of coping, and - **concerns about the future** of their child after they die	**Muslim**	Karaca & Sener (2021)
In-depth interviews - Pakistani, Sunni-Muslims (N = 16), in the United Kingdom - Parents (N = 15) - Grandparents (N = 1)	Severe learning disability (with or without additional physical or sensory disabilities)	- 'gifts from God,' 'chosen parents,' 'punishment,' 'a curse,' and myths that their loved one was 'contagious.'	**Sunni-Muslims**; all parents made reference to ***theologically*** based explanations as to why they had a child with a disability	Croot et al. (2008)

(*Continued*)

Table 42.1 (Continued)

Sample description	*Disability type*	*Themes*	*Religious affiliation*	*Citation*
In-depth, unstructured interviews - Muslim-identifying parents (N = 17); Iran - Mothers (N = 11) - Fathers (N = 6)	Mental Disability Physical Disability, or combined	- **emotional turmoil** - **manifestation of spiritual** (i.e., turning to spirituality), - appeal to **spiritual behavior** [*ritualistic* practices], and - **emotional growth** and excellence (i.e., finding acceptance and gratitude for God) [*theistic* and *existential* spirituality]	**Muslim**	Shahdadi & Mahmoudirad (2022)
Q Methodology & Interviews - Hindu-identifying (N = 20); Western India - (N = 17) Mothers - (N = 3) Fathers	Autism (n = 4), DS (n = 3), Epilepsy (n = 2), CP (n = 1), Unknown ID (n = 10)	3 Explanatory Models of Disability: -Religious Resilience -Search for Treatment & Social Change -Burden to Bear	**Hindu**	John & Montgomery (2016)

of persons with IDD is generally not viewed as problematic, given that the concept of othering or the equivalent word for 'disability' does not exist (Leib-Neri, M., 2015). Key disability-related beliefs within NA spirituality include (1) spoken language is not the measure of competency, (2) lack of eye contact is a sign of respect toward elders, (3) conformity is not expected, (4) a problem is more conceived due to the cause of the disability (imbalance of the spirit), not the disability itself, and (5) IDD can be viewed as 'a gift' or opportunity for learning. Since the NA community does not orient around the concept of 'othering,' difference is not the defining element (Leib-Neri, M., 2015). Thus, the spiritual and cultural beliefs of specific groups may serve to inform stress, coping, and well-being in these families.

Family Functioning, Parental Health, and Stress

In a large, religiously diverse sample, Chang and McConkey (2008) conducted home-based interviews with 117 Taiwanese parents randomly recruited from 21 schools in Taiwan to gain an understanding of the perceptions and experiences of parenting a child diagnosed with autism (20%), cerebral palsy (CP) (14%), DS (11%), epilepsy (10%), and ADHD (4%). The sample included mothers (86%) and fathers (14%); 49% identified as Buddhists, 20% as other religions, and for 30% no religion was identified. Nevertheless, half of the sample identified with a non-theistic philosophy (Galtung, 2003; Segall, 2011).

Five themes were identified from interview data, three of which encapsulated the impact of the child on family functioning, parental health, and stress, whereas two themes were reflective of coping strategies and sources of support. The role of karma, the importance of family harmony, responsibility and duty to care for the loved one, and collectivist priority were of significance in understanding the participant's culture of origin. Family functioning included both positive and negative influences of the child on the family system. Parental stress included the theme of pessimism about the future. In addition, parents reported emotional difficulties and challenges with physical health. Parental coping included three themes: proactive behaviors, acceptance, and distractions.

In terms of social support, parents described social isolation, limited or inadequate formal supports, and a range of informal support experiences, but generally reported more positive informal supports when compared to reports of insensitive professional providers described by some parents. Results were indicative of 'parental dilemmas,' which included positive and negative descriptions of their experiences (Chang & McConkey, 2008, p. 38). Ultimately, their experiences seem to be more similar than different to parents in other countries. The study did not explore the role of Buddhism, religious community, or faith directly. However, the role of acceptance served to help parents either reframe the focus of their child's disability on abilities or accept fate as having a greater purpose for the child's condition – characteristic of existential spirituality.

Spirituality and Coping

To better understand the role of spirituality and coping, Karaca and Sener (2021) conducted interviews with 28 Turkish, Muslim-identifying mothers, whose children (ages 8–17) were receiving intervention services. These mothers reported value in their spirituality when finding acceptance and meaning in their child's diagnosis (*existential* spirituality), as well as the role of unconditional love. Participants also described the use of prayer and reading the Quran (*ritualistic* spirituality) as a form of coping. In addition, these mothers shared concerns about the future of their child after they (i.e., the mothers) died, seemingly due to the limited resources available to children with lifelong care needs in developing countries, like Turkey. Concerns of this nature are representative of the practical reality of having access, or lack thereof, to sufficient resources across the lifespan.

In an attempt to elicit descriptions of spiritual self-care, Shahdadi and Mahmoudirad (2022) conducted qualitative interviews with 17 Muslim-identifying parents (N = 11 mothers, N = 6 fathers) living in Iran. Four themes were identified from the data: emotional turmoil (i.e., frustration, anxiety, confusion, and hopelessness), manifestation of spiritual (i.e., turning to spirituality as a result of the disability), appeal to spiritual behavior [*ritualistic* practices], and emotional growth and excellence (i.e., finding acceptance, gratitude for 'God,' kindness toward others, and psychosocial stability) (*theistic* and *existential* spirituality). Thus, all three realms of RiTE spirituality were reflected within identified themes.

American Culture, Ableism, and Pre-Natal Diagnoses

Although parents may experience their child's diagnosis as an emotional adjustment process (Nelson-Goff et al., 2013), some parents may ultimately choose not to continue the pregnancy when a poor pre-natal diagnosis is detected. In the United States, where the dominant culture is oriented toward an ableist mindset (Manalili, 2021), couples and families have the opportunity to determine the relative health of their baby through pre-natal screening and testing for chromosomal aberrations, like DS (Global, 2018a). Although some parents choose testing to prepare for life ahead, others pursue testing to make decisions related to viability or to terminate a pregnancy based on pre-natal diagnostic information.

In their systematic review, de Graff et al. (2022) report ~74% of prenatally diagnosed DS pregnancies are terminated in the United States. This estimate is down from previous reports of a 92% termination rate of prenatally diagnosed DS pregnancies (Natoli, 2012). Based on their meta-analysis of qualitative literature, Blakeley et al. (2019) identified three themes: (1) all life is precious, (2) hope for a positive outcome, and (3) a life worth living. Across 22 studies involving parental decision-making for termination, the literature review also revealed 10 sub-themes. Although all of the studies reviewed may not have directly asked about the influence of faith, religion, or spiritual beliefs and practices, the role of moral and religious beliefs, hope, and quality of life was prominent within resulting themes. However, the role of religion and spirituality is not fully understood in regard to termination decision-making, and particularly by parents: (1) who choose *not* to pursue pre-natal testing in the first place, (2) those who do and receive positive results, but continue the pregnancy, and (3) those who choose to terminate. Thus, further study is needed in order to delineate the relationship between various dimensions of spirituality, American ableist culture, pre-natal testing, and medical termination.

Ultimately, the role of genetic ethics (Hancock et al., 2021) or the role of religion, faith, or spirituality in terms of decision-making for terminations (de Graaf et al., 2022) is beyond the scope of this chapter. However, the topic does invite the opportunity to consider the influence of various socio-cultural factors on how disability, more broadly, is (1) viewed politically and societally, (2) coped with by parents, caregivers, and other close family members, and (3) how these families are supported within systems of care when faced with pre-natal diagnostic news.

From an existential spirituality, or transcendent, meaning-making perspective, which places value on opportunities for growth as a result of hardship or suffering, one might question: Are we ultimately removing opportunities for personal or soul development when we can utilize medical technology to reduce or potentially remove certain communities from human existence? And who ultimately defines human value, purpose, or one's worth in the world? Up until Roe versus Wade was over-turned (NPR, 2022), the majority of prenatally diagnosed babies were terminated (de Graaf et al., 2022; Hancock et al., 2021; Natoli, 2012), and until or if legislation changes, termination rates for chromosomal-based pre-natal diagnoses would be expected to decline in the coming years.

At last, perceptions of persons with disability and spirituality and coping can be informed by numerous, interdependent sources, including a range of theistic, non-theistic, and cultural influences. Harris (2016) proposes that 'disability studies can benefit from the careful analysis of impermanence, fragility, and suffering developed in Buddhist texts, which suggests all humans lie somewhere in a spectrum of dependence and vulnerability that is often erroneously attributed to disabled persons alone' (p. 45). And perhaps, those living with IDD early on in life are more capable of accepting their vulnerabilities and adapting to relevant impairments when compared to those who acquire a disability in later adulthood.

Spirituality and Religiousness as Resources for Parents and Caregivers

This section includes a summary of findings across select studies that provide a glimpse into the experiences of national and international samples, representing unique disability types and diverse religious or spiritual beliefs and practices. In some of the literature, the global terms ID or IDD were used, and in others, diagnosis-based sample criteria were described (e.g., DS and CP). More specifically, various quantitative studies (see Tables 42.2 and 42.3) have been conducted with parents or caregivers in exploring the role of spirituality (Gallagher et al., 2015; McWhirter & McIntyre, 2021) and religiosity (Boehm & Carter, 2019; Carter, 2021; O'Hanlon, 2013), or aspects of both realms of expression (Xavier & Esperandio, 2023).

Spiritual Involvement

For example, O'Hanlon (2013) conducted a web-based survey using the Spiritual Community Experiences Inventory (SCEI; O'Hanlon, 2009) with 57 parents (i.e., mothers who were mostly affiliated with Protestant religions), the majority of whom were raising a child with autism. Parents, mostly mothers, reported on the frequency of attendance and satisfaction with activities they participated in within their spiritual community. Participation in and support from spiritual clergy were found to be important to participants. Frequency of attendance, amount of support, and satisfaction with support received were found to be significantly related. Essentially, those who reported greater satisfaction with support also reported higher levels of participation. However, more than 66% of participants reported their child had a negative experience. And for those who reported negative experiences, they also reported lower levels of participation in various activities.

The role of spiritual involvement, generally speaking, was also explored by McWhirter and McIntyre (2021), longitudinally, which included 180 parent-caregivers, primarily mothers of 3-year-old children presenting with speech delays. They examined the role of religious and spiritual involvement (RSI), family characteristics, and parent mental health. Parents who reported no involvement did indicate higher levels of stress. Plus, parents with less education and lower income reported higher levels of depression, and parent depression and stress were positively associated with child behavior problems. In this study, RSI could be loosely characterized as *ritualistic* or *theistic* spirituality. However, considerations for identifying different forms of religious or spiritual coping should be further explored to more fully inform when and how religious coping may mediate parental mental health, beyond general involvement.

Table 42.2 Measures of Spirituality and Religiosity in Families Living with Disability – Part 1

Construct	*Measure & developer*	*Items, scales & sub-scales*	*Demographics*		*Disability type*	*Citation*
			Participant role	*Religious affiliation*		
Religiosity	Santa Clara Strength of Religious Faith Questionnaire (SCSRFQ) (Cummings et al., 2015)	2 Scales (short form; 5 Items): Beliefs and Practices, Social Support - For example, I look to my faith to provide meaning and purpose.	(N = 530; IL and TN) Role: 86% Mothers 8.5% Fathers 2.6% Siblings 1.5% Grandparents Ethnicity: 86% Caucasian 7.7% African Am. 3.2% Latino/a 1.9% Asian Am.	18.0% Catholic 14.7% Baptist 13.5% Non-denominational Christian 8.4% Methodist 4.7% Lutheran 4.7% Presbyterian 3.6% Church of Christ 2.4% Bible Church 1.7% Episcopal 1.7% Jewish, and 1.7% Pentecostal	51.7% One ID diagnosis 40.7% ASD 31% DS 15% CP	Boehm & Carter (2019)
Religiosity	Systems of Belief Inventory-15 Rev. (SBI) (Holland et al., 1998)	2 Scales (15 items): - Beliefs and Practices (10), Social Support (5) - For example, I have experienced a sense of hope as a result of my beliefs.	Same as above		Same as above	Boehm & Carter (2019)
Religiosity	Centrality of Religiosity Scale (CRS-R) (Huber & Huber, 2012)	5 Domains (10 or 15 items): Practice, Private Practice, Ideological, Intellectual, and Religious Experience	(N = 129; Brazil) Gender: 91.5% Female 7.8% Male 0.8% Agender Caregiver role: 77.5% Mothers 3.9% Fathers 2.3% Grandparents *Ethnicity unknown*	26.36% Catholic, 17.05% Spiritualist, 17.05% Evangelical (including Pentecostal, Neo-Pentecostal, and Protestant), 2.33% Afro-Brazilian religions, 22.48% believe in God, but no religious affiliation, 8.53% reported different religious affiliations	42.6% DS 14.7% West syndrome 14% Rhett syndrome 9.3% Fragile X syndrome 7.8% Angelman syndrome 3.9% multiple IDD	Xavier & Esperandio (2023)
Religious/ Spiritual	Religious and Spiritual Struggles (RSS) (Esperandio et al., 2022)	6 Domains (24 items): Divine, Demonic, Interpersonal, Moral, Doubt, and Ultimate Meaning	Same as above		Same as above	Xavier & Esperandio (2023)

Table 42.3 Measures of Spirituality and Religiosity in Families Living with Disability – Part 2

Construct	*Measure & developer*	*Items, scales & sub-scales*	*Demographics*		*Disability TYPE*	*Citation*
			Participant role	*Religious affiliation*		
Religious/ Spiritual	Spiritual/ Religious Coping Scale (SRCOPE-14) (Esperandio et al., 2018)	2 Domains (14 items): Positive Religious Coping, Negative Religious Coping	Same as above		Same as above	Xavier & Esperandio (2023)
Religious/ Spiritual	Religious and Spiritual Involvement (RSI)	(1 Item): *Are you involved in church, religious, or spiritual practice?*	(N = 180; parents/caregivers; NW United States) Gender: 92% Female 8% Male Role: 80% Mothers 10% Fathers 7% Foster, adoptive Mother 2% Grandmothers Ethnicity: 77% Caucasian	*Affiliation not provided* 48.3% Religious or spiritual involvement	- 53.3% Speech/ language delay - 15% Global delay - 13.3% ASD - 16.7%Unknown etiology - 1.7% other	McWhirter & McIntyre (2021)
Spiritual	Spiritual Community Experiences Inventory (SCEI) (O'Hanlon, 2009)	2 Domains (36 Items): Participation and Support: [Rel. Education, Youth Activities, Formal Ceremonies, Worship Services, Leader Support, Member Support]	(N = 57; MD county) Gender: 89% Females 10% Males Role: 90% Mothers 10% Fathers *Ethnicity unknown*	62.1% Protestant 17.2% Catholic 5.2% Jewish 1.7% Muslim 13.8% Other	- 41.4% Autism - 29.3% Learning disabilities - 29.3% Mental retardation - 27.6% Speech or language impairment - 36.2% Other disabilities	O'Hanlon (2013)
Spiritual	Beliefs and Values Scale (King et al., 2006)	1 Domain (20 Items): - For example, 'I believe in life after death' and 'I believe there is a heaven'	(N = 32) Gender: 84% Females 16% Males Role: 100% Parents Ethnicity: 84% Caucasian	*Affiliation not provided*	- 66% Autism - 22% Down syndrome - 12% Other syndromes	Gallagher et al. (2015)

Spiritual Practices, Participation, and Priorities

Boehm and Carter (2019) explored spirituality and religiosity, and parent reports of expression included practices, participation, and priorities. This study included 530 parents (86% mothers, 8% fathers) and caregivers (4% grandparents or siblings). The majority (51%) of participants' loved ones were diagnosed with an ID, (40%) ASD, (31%) DS, or (15%) CP. Approximately 90% of the sample identified with a particular religion, out of 36 religious affiliations represented. Catholic, Baptist, and non-denominational Christians accounted for almost half of the sample. Most participants identified the value of faith and congregational involvement (i.e., attendance from never to several times per week, and participation in various activities, with the majority reporting that they participated in at least one activity once or twice a month).

Other key findings included: (1) 90% agreed or strongly agreed that 'God in some form exists' (*theistic* spirituality), (2) 84% experienced 'peace of mind through prayer and meditation' (*ritualistic* spirituality) and experienced hope due to religious beliefs, and (3) 81% reported 'one's life and death follow a plan of God' [*existential* spirituality] (p. 520). Of note, none of these findings were correlated with the child's age, severity of disability, or behavior problems, which is counter to other recent findings (McWhirter & McIntyre, 2021).

Strength of Faith

In addition to spiritual involvement and practices, one study utilized the Santa Clara Strength of Religious Faith Questionnaire (SCSRFQ) for exploring the strength of faith (Cummings et al., 2015). Approximately 73% reported they somewhat agreed or strongly agreed that they enjoyed attending religious functions. However, only 35% somewhat or strongly agreed that they seek out people within their spiritual community when in need. Of note, lower reports of social support were correlated with higher levels of disability severity and reported behavioral problems. Alternatively, Gallagher et al. (2015) reported that parents who held 'strong spiritual beliefs' indicated higher depressive symptoms (p. 362). Thus, beliefs and practices can serve to provide meaning or social support for some families, but the 'experiences and priorities of parents with ID are not homogenous' (Boehm & Carter, 2019, p. 521), and at times, spirituality is a form of coping that is characteristic of a 'last resort' (Gallagher et al., 2015, p. 365).

By highlighting the spiritual practices and participation described in select studies, Carter (2021) presents a valuable review and analysis of the beliefs and practices utilized by families as a form of coping. This information can serve as a guide for assessing needs and implementing service structures that best meet the needs of those living with an IDD and their families. Six key areas from the literature are presented, which highlight that spirituality is (1) relevant, (2) a priority, (3) diverse in its expression, (4) dynamic rather than static, (5) highly influential and valuable, and (6) requires planning and support (Carter, 2021).

Thus, assessment for accommodations (provided within congregations) informed by trained professionals is needed to better meet the spiritual needs of those with IDD and their families. Attention should be given to challenges associated with cognitive and speech impairment, as well as mobility and behavioral support needs. In addition, whether the level of severity or other disability-related factors affects the occurrence of negative experiences should be determined, and if uncovered, clarify why this occurs.

Persons with Intellectual and Developmental Disabilities as Spiritual Beings

The majority of the literature, to date, has examined spirituality in families with parents as primary informants. Thus, few religiously and ethnically diverse quantitative studies have been conducted that directly explore the spiritual perspectives, practices, and experiences of those living with a disability (see Table 42.4; Hodge & Reynolds, 2019; Timmins et al., 2023).

Spiritual Practices and Disability Type

Hodge and Reynolds (2019) recruited a national sample of mostly non-institutionalized persons with a disability (*M* = 45 years old; *SD* = 16.55) and utilized face-to-face interviews combined with the use of computer-assisted technology. Participants responded to items representing eight dimensions of spirituality and religion; the majority identified as European American. The sample included persons with hearing (N = 151), vision (N = 144), physical mobility (N = 451), and emotional or mental disabilities (N = 127). Those with hearing, physical, or emotional disabilities were more likely to indicate the use of prayer more than once daily (*ritualistic* spirituality), but those with all four disability types were more likely to reach a turning point of becoming less involved with religious activities. And, those with physical and emotional disabilities were less likely to attend religious services. Thus, the ways in which those living with a disability engage in spiritual practices may be influenced by the type(s) of disability they possess.

Spiritual Well-Being

Timmins et al. (2023) examined well-being in a national sample of persons with ID aged 40 and older who resided in Ireland. Items from multiple measures were used to create a Personal Wellbeing Index (PWI), which included quality and satisfaction of life, and personal and religious practices. Of the 609 participants who were involved in wave 3 of the longitudinal study, 323 randomly selected participants completed the self-report measures of interest, and in some cases, with proxy assistance. Approximately 75% of the participants indicated that religion was important, and 80% indicated it brought them strength and comfort. The majority (~60%) reported that talking to staff brought them hope, peace, or comfort. However, only 6% reported they were active members in church participation.

In addition, participants reported that they found comfort from talking to friends and family (~50%), listening to music (45%), going for a walk (37%), and praying (35%) (*ritualistic* spirituality). Plus, participants who reported difficulty making friends, having a major illness, being in poorer health, or being less happy were more likely to attend faith-based services. And more specifically, the factors associated with those who reported feeling at peace and at ease after praying were female gender, living in a community group home, experiencing the death of a relative, feeling lonely, and reporting fair or poor physical health. Thus, these findings highlight the importance of connection to others, being involved in religious practices (*ritualistic* spirituality), and having positive outlets for well-being, particularly during difficult times. However, determining potential barriers to participation would help to increase access to and meaningful involvement in such spiritual practices.

Table 42.4 Spirituality Research and Perspectives of those Living with Disability

Methodology	*Disability type*	*Characteristics & themes*	*Religious affiliation*	*Citation*
QUANTITATIVE: - Cross-Sectional, US Survey - Persons with a disability (M = 45 years old); European Americans (N = 2454; 54%) Females	- Hearing (N = 151), - Vision (N = 144), - Physical mobility (N = 451), and Emotional or mental disabilities (N = 127).	- Pray several times a day (N = 891, 29.9%) - God definitely exists (N = 1,874, 63.1%) - Bible is the word of God (N = 995, 33.7%) - Religious experience that changed life (N = 1,196, 40.4%) - Turning point toward religion (N = 1,282, 43.0%) - Turning point away from religion (N = 550, 37.6%) - Religious service attendance (M = 3.57, SD = 2.79) - Confidence in organized religion (M = 2.03, SD = 0.68)	*Affiliation not provided*	Hodge & Reynolds (2019)
- Longitudinal, Wave 3, National Survey and Interviews - Adults with ID (N = 323) aged 40 and older; Ireland - (N = 181, 56%) Females - (N = 142, 44%) Males	Ds (N = 49, 15.2%) Unknown/Other/Don't know/ Missing (N = 274, 84.8%) Level of ID: Mild (N = 117, 40.3%) Moderate (N = 157, 54.1%) Severe/Profound (N = 16, 5.5%)	- 80% indicated religion brought them **strength and comfort**. - Only 6% reported they were active members in **church participation**. - ~60% reported that talking to **staff brought them hope, peace, or comfort**. - 35% participants found comfort from **praying** [*ritualistic* spirituality]	*Affiliation not provided* (n = 215, 74.7%) indicated that **religion was important** in their life	Timmons et al. (2023)
QUALITATIVE: - In-Person Interviews - 20 transition-aged youth and young adults (ages 13-21); US	Diagnosed with Autism or ID (70% male, 30% female), as primary informants (*as opposed to parent perspectives of their loved one's spiritual identity or practices*).	- Types of **involvement with their faith community**, including: prayer, beliefs and behaviors, activities, rites of passage, social connections, and ministry to others [*ritualistic* and *theistic*]. - The **importance of faith and spirituality** in their lives, especially how they benefited from their involvement. - **Feelings of acceptance, being used to help others**, and **being healed**. Elements of **belonging** and **purpose** that brought meaning to their lives [*existential* spirituality].	**Christian**	Lui et al. (2014)

- Semi-Structured Interviews, Photovoice - Native American adults (N = 8, males) - Explored individual, family, and community levels of health and wellness in a small reservation sample	Intellectual and Developmental Disabilities	- Health and wellness activities included: **church** and **spirituality** (family level) [*ritualistic, theistic*], - **Connection to the reservation** was reflected within (community level) themes [*existential*].	**Native American Spirituality**	Williamson et al., (2020)
MIXED METHODS: Quantitative - Spiritual Wellbeing Scale (Paloutzian & Ellison, 1982, 1991). - 47 adults, Alaska; (N = 26) Female; (N = 21) Male; Interview data (N = 15/47)	Intellectual and Developmental Disabilities: **59% Mental Retardation** 19% CP 20% Other	5 Spiritual themes: A **framework** for life [*theistic*], **identity**, **opportunity to contribute** [*existential*], **inner wellbeing**, and **connectedness**. Ethnicity: **74% Caucasian** 19% Alaska Native 4% Asian-Pacific Islander 2% African American	Religious Affiliation: **68% Christian/ Protestant** 17% No preference 9% Catholic 4% Atheist 2% Bahai	Rambow (2016)

Spiritual Involvement and Self-Perceptions of Disability

In their qualitative study, Lui et al. (2014) sought to elicit stories of 20 transition-aged youth and young adult individuals (ages 13–21) diagnosed with autism or ID (70% male and 30% female) as primary informants; half were interviewed without their parents. Lui et al. (2014) sought to identify the role of faith and explore participant views of their disability in the context of their faith; all of them were identified as Christian, per parent report. Interview questions elicited elements of RiTE spirituality.

Participants described their faith-based involvement, including prayer, beliefs and behaviors, activities, rites of passage, social connections, ministry to others, and other expressions. In addition, participants described the importance of faith and spirituality in their lives, especially how they benefited from their involvement. Moreover, participants described feelings of acceptance, being used to help others, and being healed. Their descriptions also included elements of belonging and purpose that brought meaning to their lives, representative of existential spirituality.

Quality of Life

Similar to Lui et al.'s (2014) study, Rambow (2016) explored spiritual well-being and quality of life of 47 adults with IDD from a religiously diverse sample utilizing mixed methods, which included a quantitative assessment using the Spiritual Well-being Scale (SWBS; Paloutzian & Ellison, 1982, 1991). The SWBS included statements of Religious and Existential Wellbeing. Interview data with 15 of the original sample (i.e., the qualitative component of the mixed methods study), the majority of whom identified as Christian, revealed 5 spiritual themes: a framework for life, identity, opportunity to contribute, inner well-being, and connectedness. Having a framework for life could be representative of *ritualistic* and *theistic* spirituality, while identity and having an opportunity to contribute may be reflective of *existential* spirituality.

Thus, caution should be taken in assuming that those living with an IDD are not spiritual or that their unique capacity to express themselves spiritually is of less importance to them. Moreover, what may be of greater importance is identifying what is meaningful, to whom and why, and how opportunities for spiritual expression are secured, which may occur more broadly for some groups. For example, Williamson et al. (2020) explored individual, family, and community levels of health and wellness in a small sample (N = 8, males) of Native American adults with IDD, and wellness activities (family level) included church and spirituality (*ritualistic* and *theistic* spirituality), and connection to the reservation (*existential* spirituality) was reflected within (community level) themes.

In summary, Watts (2011) addresses the role of intellectual competence and spiritual awareness of those with IDDs. Disability studies help to inform caregivers as to the aspects of spirituality that are important, but also ways their loved one may be supported within their respective spiritual communities. Other considerations include the role of symbols as a mechanism for understanding, the value of openness consistent with a 'child-like' mindset, and the influences of close personal relationships for this population (Lui et al., 2014; Rambow, 2016; Timmons et al., 2023; Watts, 2011). Hence, a Bio-Psycho-Social-Spiritual (BPSS) assessment of individuals initiated by healthcare providers and other professionals or community leaders could help inform their desires and the supports needed to honor those desires (Hodge, 2015; Hunt, 2014).

Bio-Psycho-Social-Spiritual Framework

One framework often valued by medical and mental health professionals who work with populations affected by chronic medical and developmental conditions is the BPSS framework (Engel, 1977, 1980; Wright et al., 1996). This framework can be valuable in understanding the unique factors that influence the health and well-being of those raising a loved one, caring for, or living with a disability and/or chronic illness (Dellbridge et al., 2014; Hunt, 2014; McDaniel et al., 2014; Rolland, 2018).

Biological. Many disabilities are congenital in nature, and families are faced with a nuanced parenting journey from birth or shortly thereafter (Turns et al., 2018). In addition, the physical health of caregivers is important in terms of managing the needs of the loved one with IDD and other dependent family members. Assessing for disability is encouraged, as those with multiple forms of disability may become less involved in religious attendance (Hodge & Reynolds, 2019).

Psychological. Researchers have identified the role of caregiver functioning in terms of child behavior problems and parent mental health, which should be considered, as it can be associated with reduced religious or spiritual involvement (McWhirter & McIntyre, 2021). Additionally, Hodge and Reynolds (2019) found that those with physical and emotional disabilities were less likely to attend services, leaving them less connected to a potential support network.

Social. Congregational support (Boehm & Carter, 2021), spouses (Bentley et al., 2023; Brown et al., 2020; Ramisch et al., 2014), friends, extended family members, community organizations, and respite providers have been identified as valuable social support resources for families (Bentley et al., 2015). In addition, the important role of connectedness and belonging has been identified in studies, particularly involving the voices of those living with IDD (Lui et al., 2014; Timmons et al., 2023). However, how mental health clinicians effectively explore the spiritual needs of those with IDD remains under-studied (Loynes & O'Hara, 2015) and warrants the development of professional guidelines (see the Assessment of Spirituality and Religiousness in Families section below). And perhaps, adapting recommendations developed in the context of able-bodied persons could be valuable to this population (e.g., Hodge, 2013).

Spiritual. Families report the role of prayer, faith, and other spiritual practices in describing ways they have coped with the challenges of illness (Pargament, 1997). Research has also demonstrated the value of spirituality for individuals with IDD. Moreover, the role of spirituality can also be of particular importance when individuals and families are faced with anticipatory grief and specific needs related to end-of-life care (Rolland, 2018b; Sulmasy, 2002; Timmins et al., 2023). However, some findings have indicated that spirituality can serve as a source of 'both comfort and frustration' (Gallagher et al., 2015, p. 366). Thus, spiritual assessment may serve as a valuable tool for discerning positive and negative spiritual coping.

Spirituality Life-maps, Genograms, and Eco-Maps

There are various forms of assessment available for gathering one's spiritual history and mapping a desired spiritual future (Hodge, 2001, 2013, 2015). Specifically, spirituality life maps, genograms, and eco-maps can serve as tools for eliciting a deeper understanding of the strengths and resources rooted in family beliefs and practices. Particularly, asking, '*How does your spirituality assist you in dealing with difficulties?*' (Hodge, 2001, p. 43) may evoke a fuller picture of the family's coping process specific to living with disability. Loynes and O'Hara (2015) provide guidance for potential ways mental health clinicians can explore, assess, and support spiritual expression in those living with disability. Ultimately, spirituality, religious affiliation, and epistemology (i.e., orthodox vs. progressive) may vary across family members and become a potential source of conflict. Additionally, exploring the influence of disability and related crises could serve to inform whether spirituality is a source of refuge or a source of disconnection from RiTE spirituality.

Theoretical Frameworks for Understanding Families within the IDD Population

Much of the disability literature has explored stress and coping in families informed by models of family stress and adaptation (McCubbin & Patterson, 1983) and family resilience, including ambiguous loss (Boss, 2006; Walsh, 2003). The Double ABC-X Model of Stress and Adaptation, most frequently represented in the disability literature, proposes that resources and social support, which can include religion, faith, and spirituality (i.e., element 'B'), serve as potential mediators of the impact of a crisis, 'X' (e.g., the diagnosis), and other stressors, as families adapt over time (Brown et al., 2020; Ramisch, 2012; Ramisch et al., 2014).

For instance, Ramisch et al. (2014) explored the role of communication for married couples raising a child with ASD, and the couples reported, 'we communicate' and 'we have foundational expectations.' Although couples did not reveal statements exclusively about religion and faith, they did make statements about having faith or believing in God, and they reported involvement in church. Thus, communication and spiritual beliefs and practices served as resources characteristic of ritualistic and theistic spirituality. However, communication quality or style, along with the role of spirituality (specifically with consideration of the meaning-making process), is indicative of family resilience and needs further exploration.

Family Resilience

Walsh's (2003) Family Resilience Framework helps to inform family resiliency with attention on family belief systems (often associated with religious beliefs and spirituality), organizational patterns, and communication/problem-solving. It is the way families rebound when they are faced with challenges, like disability-related stress, that informs resiliency. For example, Knestrict and Kuchey's (2009) mixed-methods study of parents raising children with severe emotional or behavioral disturbances, rare genetic disorders, and other IDDs found that the majority of participant families were considered 'resilient.' However, socioeconomic status (SES) was a significant factor in accessing the resources and supports necessary for meeting their child's needs.

Specifically, reconstruction was a process that was valuable for identifying the meaning of 'the family' outside of the challenges associated with the role of disability. Essentially, these families reportedly had the time to be reflective, which was seemingly less available to families of a lower SES, who instead were required to attend primarily to the immediate caregiving needs of their loved one. Family belief systems, spiritual rituals, or spirituality more broadly were not directly explored; however, the reconstruction meaning-making process described is most parallel to *existential* spirituality, as discussed previously.

Ambiguous Loss

Boss's (2006) model of *Ambiguous Loss* provides an understanding of the role of boundary ambiguity within family systems in regard to psychological and physical presence or absence; originally, it was used to understand how families navigated traumatic events or faced a loved one's chronic illness. Many IDDs (i.e., ASD, CP, and DS) affect both the psychological and physical presence (or functioning) of the diagnosed person, potentially exacerbating the level of boundary ambiguity within the family (Bentle et al., 2015; Bentley et al., 2023; O'Brien, 2007).

Many researchers have substantiated parent concerns related to the unknown future for their loved one (Chang & McConkey, 2008; Karaca & Sener, 2021), and lower coping strategy scores of mothers are associated with early childhood and adult-aged loved ones (Nelson-Goff et al., 2016). Hence, an exploration of how families successfully reduce boundary ambiguity with regard to early childhood, but especially the adult phase of caregiving and end-of-life planning, warrants further study.

Deleterious Relationship Between Spirituality, Health, and Well-Being

Although there is significant literature to support the beneficial role of spirituality and well-being in families, some families within the IDD community report less than ideal experiences that include negative attitudes, inadequate support, or injurious beliefs (Carte et al., 2016; Gaventa, 2018). O'Hanlon (2013) reported that the majority of participants indicated having negative religious experiences. More specifically, low satisfaction levels with religious experiences were associated with lower participation levels.

Negative Views, Misconceptions, and Stigma of Disability

Some attitudes about disability are largely associated with negative views based on the cause of disability (and perpetuated by common misconceptions), which can also be closely tied to cultural or religious beliefs (i.e., the role of shame and blame for disability, perceived to be due to misdeeds within the family, demonic possession, and suspicion of witchcraft or witches) (Croot et al., 2008; Karaca & Sener, 2021; Rohwerder, 2018; Wilson, 2019). For instance, Wilson (2019) highlights the prominent negative perceptions of disability in India based on Hindu beliefs and practices associated largely with the concept of Karma, but also emphasizes the diversity and fluidity of Hindu beliefs. Thus, additional examination of various religions rooted in Indian culture is warranted.

Moreover, misconceptions are still prominent in developing countries about those living with IDD and include assumptions that they: (1) have nothing to offer or contribute, (2) are unable to have meaningful or sexual relationships, (3) are unable to report sexual abuse, (4) are contagious or bring bad luck, (5) have magical properties, and (6) are witches (Rohwerder, 2018). Shifting these types of negative views and misconceptions comes with education and advocacy efforts, and those efforts are making an impact, but there is still room for change. McConkey et al. (2016) address the role of stigma, perpetuated by families, but highlight that families can also serve as a mechanism for change by nurturing optimal development, addressing inclusive practices, challenging myths and misconceptions, and serving as advocates for the IDD population. Over the past few decades, efforts to improve health care through research (Global, 2018b; Kanne, 2018), create opportunities for meaningful experiences (Carter, 2021), and advance educational policies (NHS, 2018) have been expanded to help change the negative disability narrative (Hastings, 2016) with the goal of improving quality of life for this population.

Health Behaviors and Social-Relational Factors in Families

Numerous studies help inform intervention services for the most vulnerable of families. Although the studies presented below did not directly explore spirituality, they have assessed other realms of health behaviors and social-relational factors, including communication, relational coping, hope, mental health and stress levels, life satisfaction, and marital satisfaction, or a combination thereof. Additionally, many of these studies have utilized measures containing sub-scales that align closely with RiTE spirituality.

Communication

One key variable explored in autism research has been relational communication (Brown et al., 2020; Romney et al. 2025). Communication processes have been found to be valuable in families raising a child with autism, but one study in particular examined the sibling perspective (Romney et al. 2025). Guided by Olsen's Circumplex model (Olsen et al., 1989), established for understanding family functioning associated with the elements of cohesion, flexibility, and communication, Romney et al. (2025) explored the role of family communication through an interpretive phenomenological inquiry. Four key interview data themes with seven families were identified: targeted sibling time, targeted sibling communication, sibling expectations, and an understanding of autism.

Although aspects of autism can create stress for families, these families described ways in which they were intentional about meeting the unique needs of their family together. They organized their efforts to meet the needs of each family member, and they were intentional in their communication and expectations for addressing those needs. Although this study did not directly assess spirituality, the importance of communication was revealed as an important social-relational factor.

Coping and Hope

Several studies have examined coping, hope, and relationship quality both in mothers (Cles et al., 2017; Cless & Stephenson, 2018; Nelson-Goff et al., 2016) and fathers (Bentley et al., 2015) with a child with DS. These studies utilized the Herth Hope Index (Herth, 1992) and Family Crisis Oriented Personal Evaluation Scales (F-COPES; McCubbin et al., 1987/1991) to assess coping strategies, which include sub-scales related to seeking social support and acquiring spiritual support (Bentley et al., 2015, Cless et al., 2017; Nelson Goff et al., 2016). Social and spiritual support are coping strategies employed by parents that are characteristic of *ritualistic* spirituality. In addition, parent descriptions of the role of faith and spirituality were identified within qualitative findings, largely consistent with *existential* spirituality, or meaning-making.

Specific to the role of hope, Kausar et al.'s (2003) study involved face-to-face and online qualitative interviews with 19 parents of children with 'significant developmental disabilities' (i.e., ASD, DS, and Joubert's, Muscular Dystrophy-age 3–18). Results included 8 themes, rooted in the core construct of hope. Two themes in particular could be considered spiritual in nature: (1) the transformative process of raising a child with ID, and (2) the positive influence of their child on them as parents. Participants also described the sense of purpose their child offered them and the value of their child's existence, representative of *existential* spirituality.

Life and Relational Satisfaction

Satisfaction with life and relational satisfaction have also been explored in parents and caregivers (Bentley et al., 2015; Brown et al., 2020; Cless et al., 2017; Turns et al., 2019; Xavier & Esperandio, 2023). Specifically, Bentley et al. (2015) explored the role of hope, life satisfaction, and relational satisfaction utilizing a cluster analysis with a sample of 50 fathers. Three father clusters were identified, based on coping styles: (1) mastering, (2) connecting, and (3) thriving. The connecting cluster described social engagement with significant others as well as those in the community in order to give and receive support. The thriving cluster described the opportunity for personal and spiritual growth associated with their child's DS diagnosis, characteristic of *existential* spirituality.

Similarly, Xavier and Esperandio (2023) explored spiritual coping in parents, a majority of whom had a child with DS, and found that those who identified as highly spiritual and religious used positive spiritual coping, reported lower burden, and had greater satisfaction with life. Over half of the participants were identified as 'highly religious' and spiritual coping was measured using the Religious and Spiritual Struggles (RSS; Esperandio et al., 2022) scale and the Spiritual and Religious Coping Scale (SRCOPE-14; Esperandio et al., 2018), which included RiTE spirituality-oriented items.

Additionally, Brown et al. (2020) examined coping in 69 married couples in terms of marital satisfaction and parenting stress in families with a child diagnosed with autism. Findings indicated that parental coping, as measured using the Dyadic Coping Inventory (DCI; Bodenmann, 2004), was positively associated with marital satisfaction and negatively associated with parental stress. Plus, dyadic coping and stress were mediated by marital satisfaction. Thus, the marital relationship can serve as an important source of support in these families, which can ultimately help inform ways behavioral health professionals can address risk and highlight strengths for enhancing resilience. However, further study is warranted to better understand the combined effect of dyadic coping, spirituality, and marital satisfaction.

Mental Health and Stress

One of the more prevalent areas of study has included the exploration of the impact of the child's functional level on parental functioning, particularly with regard to behavioral problems (Ramisch & Piland Springer, 2020). Essentially, higher levels of behavioral problems have been associated with greater levels of parent stress and less religious or spiritual involvement (Boehm & Carter, 2021). Additionally, parent depression and stress have been found to be positively associated with child behavior problems (McWhirter & McIntyre, 2021). However, the level or severity of behavior problems is not always an indicator of parent mental health and can manifest differently for mothers and fathers (Hastings, 2016).

Representative Analysis of the RiTE Model of Spirituality

In summary, when families possess (a) fewer forms of effective communication, coping strategies, and sources of hope; (b) increased levels of parental stress and diminished mental health; (c) higher levels of child behavior problems; and (d) lower levels of life and marital satisfaction, they may face barriers for engaging in realms of RiTE spirituality. Of the studies highlighted in this chapter, there was evidence of findings that were characteristic of Ritualistic, Theistic, and Existential Spirituality. The most prevalent forms of spirituality, health, and well-being included the ritualistic and existential realms of spirituality. In many cases, it was difficult to disentangle ritualistic and theistic realms because many ritualistic practices are inherently embedded within the theistic beliefs of the identified group.

Nevertheless, Ritualistic spirituality has served as a place of worship and a social support mechanism for connection and belonging. Existential spirituality has largely served as a mechanism for meaning-making and finding purpose within the lived experience of disability. The complex intersectionality of these variables has yet to be fully borne out in the literature. Therefore, researchers should seek a deeper understanding of the systemic dynamics of optimal health across the lifespan and the social-relational implications of spiritual involvement and expression by those affected by disability.

Sample Representation and Research Limitations: Where to Next?

Although research conducted to date has included samples that have become more representative over time (regarding various dimensions of identity), there remain significant gaps in the exploration and understanding of the experiences of certain sub-groups within the IDD population. These studies, both qualitative and quantitative in nature, often include voluntary or convenience samples, and a few studies involve the individual living with IDD as the primary informants.

Gender

The past decade of disability studies literature continues to illuminate participant experiences that primarily of comprise women, as mothers (Boehm & Carter, 2019; Cless et al., 2017; Cless & Stephenson, 2018; John & Montgomery, 2016; Karaca & Sener, 2021; McWhirter & McIntyre, 2021; Nelson-Goff et al., 2016; O'Hanlon, 2013; Shahdadi & Mahmoudirad, 2022), where less than 15% of total samples are represented by fathers, although a focus on fathers, individually, and in the context of marriage or families (Bentley et al., 2015, Brown et al., 2020; Ramisch et al., 2014; Romney et al. 2025; Turns et al., 2019) has gained increased attention.

Race and Ethnicity

The role of race and ethnicity should be more thoughtfully considered, as certain ethnicities are at higher risk for comorbid health conditions (CDC, 2025b, 2025c; Krahn et al., 2015) and poor health outcomes due to the layered burden of being associated with two (or more) underprivileged identities (Blic et al., 2015). Participation in disability studies has often been by Caucasians (Boehm & Carter, 2019; Gallagher et al., 2015; Hodge & Reynolds, 2019; Rambow, 2016); thus, intentional efforts should be made to explore the experiences of families within African American, Asian Pacific Islander, Indian, and Latino communities, who are also more negatively affected by health disparities (Krahn & Fox, 2014; Krahn et al., 2015).

Education and Socioeconomic Status

Education and household income are highly correlated, and the reality is, the working poor or poverty-stricken families remain understudied. Researchers should consider creative ways to elicit involvement of less economically privileged populations, as studies have captured parent concerns related to the future (generally speaking), providing lifelong care, limited available resources (Knestrict & Kuchey, 2009), and barriers for accessing support services

(Chang & McConkey, 2008; Karaca & Sener, 2021). Parental depression has also been found to be associated with lower education levels and lower household income (McWhirter & McIntyre, 2021).

Severity and Types of Disability

Disability severity has been explored in terms of chronic sorrow (O'Brien, 2007), and yet it remains unclear as to what factors may mediate the impact of more severe levels of disability within families (Piland Springer et al., 2018; Ramisch & Piland Springer, 2020). Disability types have often been defined by single indicators (i.e., a chromosomal condition or birth defect, e.g., DS or CP), rather than assessing for various components of physical impairment and participation limitations, which could help inform supports needed in enhancing spiritual experiences. ID is often broadly defined, sometimes unclear, or based on subjective parent severity ratings rather than other sources (i.e., genetic testing, IQ testing, or physician or teacher reports). In addition, inclusion criteria have largely entailed more common neurodevelopmentally affected populations (i.e., ADHD, ASD, CP, and DS), and there are limited studies inclusive of those affected by rarer disorders or complex co-occurring disorders. And although samples exclusive to a single IDD type may help inform the unique characteristics within that disability type, the spectrum and types of impairment within and across groups are often lost.

Religious Affiliation and Spirituality

The majority of IDD samples include Judeo-Christian-affiliated participants (Boehm & Carter, 2019; Rambow, 2016), although some studies have solicited a majority of Buddhist (Chang & McConkey, 2008), Hindu (Wilson, 2019), Muslim (Croot et al., 2008; Karaca & Sener, 2021; Shahdadi & Mahmoudirad, 2022), and/or non-religiously affiliated participants (Amioloa et al., 2023). In certain studies, it is not always clear as to what is meant when 'non-affiliated' or 'no religion' is reported (Chang & McConkey, 2008). Moreover, no studies to date have explicitly explored or identified the perspectives of parents who may yet be spiritual, but align with a non-theistic, atheistic, agnostic, or secular philosophy.

Geographic Region

Research included in this chapter has highlighted experiences of participants residing in countries, including India (John & Montgomery, 2016), Iran (Shahdadi & Mahmoudirad, 2022), Pakistan (Croot et al., 2008), South America (Xavier & Esperandio, 2023), Taiwan (Chang & McConkey, 2008), Turkey (Karaca & Sener, 2021), the United Kingdom (Timmins et al., 2023), and the United States (Hodge & Reynolds, 2019; McWhirter & McIntyre, 2021; O'Hanlon, 2013). However, studies that include participants living in Africa, China, and European countries remain underrepresented. For a comprehensive overview of the literature from a global perspective, Amioloa et al. (2023) offer insights into global differences by region.

Methodology

Self-report survey data and individual interviews are most often utilized in the disability literature. However, John and Montgomery (2016) used Q Methodology, along with parent interviews, to explore models of disability subscribed to by parents for capturing their disability perspectives. Ultimately, some studies include data from more than one family member (Brown et al., 2020; Knestrict & Kuchey, 2009; Ramisch et al., 2014), but few explore the perspectives of siblings (Romney et al. 2025) or families across the lifespan. Additionally, even fewer studies have explored the use of therapeutic interventions for couples or families (Turn et al., 2019). These more unique methodological and systemic approaches have provided notable findings.

For the study of IDD participants, Carter (2021) illuminates the importance of developing and utilizing measures that are normed to accommodate reading and comprehension levels, as well as procedures that elicit the lived experiences of this population. For example, Williamson et al. (2020) implemented a photovoice project in conjunction with participant interviews, with parent or guardian support. Replication of these types of studies would help inform parents' and loved ones' perspectives with various disability types and family structures, combined with attention to therapeutic intervention and the role of spirituality as a strength and resource for enhancing well-being.

Ultimately, there remains a lack of clarity as to who thrives under what conditions, and what we know about those who do not (Hastings, 2016), as well as which interventions are beneficial for those who are struggling. Given the frequency of utilizing convenience samples, single data sources, and lack of adaptive measures, researchers need to consider whose experiences we are not capturing and identify more effective ways to secure involvement with those identified groups. And, if parents or caregivers are involved in data collection, efforts should be taken to reduce demand-related dynamics that may influence responses given by participants with an IDD.

Future Directions: Spirituality, Health, and Well-Being

When accounting for the multi-dimensional nature of family functioning and the unique socio-cultural dimensions of spirituality, there are still 'layers of the onion to peel' for understanding and advancing spirituality, health, and well-being in this population. Within religious settings, there is the need (1) to obtain a clearer picture of 'whether and how families access support,' (2) to assess desired versus actual spiritual expressions and practices, (3) to seek national and international samples, (4) to elicit multi-member perspectives, systemically – parents, siblings, and grandparents, and (5) to explore the role of parent spirituality on child spirituality (Boehm & Carter, 2021, p. 513).

Health and well-being for persons with an IDD continue to be impacted by the perceptions and biases, specifically within larger systems of care (i.e., educational, healthcare, and religious settings). Unfortunately, these families face continued social stigma and non-inclusive educational experiences (NHS, 2018), health disparities (Krahn & Fox, 2014), and increased mortality rates (Kanne, 2018). This population is more likely to (1) develop health conditions over the lifespan that are nuanced by pre-existing health impairments associated with their particular disability (e.g., Alzheimer's in DS) (NIH, 2005; NIA-NIH, 2020), and (2) are often victims of provider 'tunnel vision' or diagnostic overshadowing – where there is a hyper-focus on the primary diagnosis, with other conditions remaining unaddressed or minimized, even though those conditions would warrant treatment in someone of able-bodied status (Kanne, 2018).

Policies

Additionally, there is a need for healthcare policy changes that prohibit insurance plan coverage denials for procedures viewed as 'not medically necessary,' or exclusionary practices that inherently discriminate against the care available to those with an IDD. Families who need these benefits are most often denied coverage for certain procedures and medical interventions, while simultaneously having a greater financial cost associated with raising and supporting their loved one across the lifespan. Krahn and Fox (2014) highlight the importance of 'effectively targeting public health interventions around the needs of disability populations in general and intellectual disability subpopulations in particular' (p. 440).

Mortality

Not only is the mortality rate higher for those with an IDD than in the general population, but Hosking et al. (2016) found that causes of death were most often associated with health care interventions for avoidable deaths (e.g., urinary tract infections and aspirations), at 36% compared to 22.5% of their counterparts without a disability. Thus, with a combined approach of science-informed action, attention to multiple determinants of health, a life course perspective, and the use of both cross-disability *and* disability-specific strategies (Krahn & Fox, 2014), more optimal spirituality, health, and well-being in this population can be achieved, and certain vulnerabilities can be reduced.

Initiatives that include targeted funding and research to determine ways to enhance the quality of life (e.g., Global Down Syndrome Foundation; www.globaldownsyndrome.org) and expand educational and vocational experiences for individuals with DS are improving. However, there is a continued need for (1) respecting and protecting rights, (2) providing inclusion and engagement, (3) enhancing workforce opportunities, and (4) expanding specialist learning disability services (NHS, 2018). Enhancing health and well-being through the expansion of spiritual, educational, and workforce opportunities is the vehicle for persons with IDD to find a meaningful purpose, a key component of existential spirituality.

Therapeutic Interventions for Families

When families encounter emotional and relational challenges, professional intervention may be necessary. Ramisch and Piland Springer (2020) present considerations for identifying and addressing challenges associated with various neurodevelopmental populations. Systemic, therapeutic approaches and practice recommendations for family therapists who work with these families include Structural Family Therapy, as well as transgenerational approaches, which can be utilized to address the inter-relatedness of family members for enhancing affect regulation and family functioning in the context of systemic dynamics (Ramisch, 2012; Ramisch & Piland Springer, 2020).

Postmodern models, particularly Narrative Therapy (White & Epston, 1990), could be used to address the family's identity, as identity may become consumed by the disability (McDaniel et al., 2014). Meaning-making is a key element of Narrative Therapy, and supporting families in the meaning-making process associated with the role of disability would more clearly flesh out the influence of *existential* spirituality in these families. Other therapeutic interventions may be warranted for addressing ongoing grief and loss. Jeter and Turns (2022) specifically address the role of ambiguous loss for parents by identifying grief associated with the unmet expectations of having a healthy baby, specific to children with DS.

When parents present as 'stuck' in the emotions of grief after diagnosis, Jeter and Turns (2022) propose the use of empty chair techniques for acknowledging the milestones potentially not achievable or other anticipated experiences (i.e., not securing a driver's license, going to college, or getting married) that may not become a reality. Exploring ways in which ritualistic or theistic spirituality potentially serves as a mechanism for (1) reaching acceptance of the permanent nature of the disability, (2) finding greater meaning, (3) shifting the disability identity, or (4) managing grief involving disability-related experiences could be valuable for certain families.

Assessment of Spirituality and Religiousness in Families

A variety of measures have been used to identify the role of spirituality in families. The more commonly utilized measures have assessed spiritual and religious coping (SRCOPE; Esperandio et al., 2018), RSSs (Esperandio et al., 2022), the centrality or strength of faith (Huber & Huber, 2012; SCSRFQ; Cummings et al., 2015), and beliefs, practices, and values (SBI-15; Holland et al., 1998; King et al., 2006; SCEI; O'Hanlon, 2009), primarily to assess parent-caregiver perspectives (see Tables 42.2 and 42.3). However, to date, the RiTE measure of spirituality (Webb et al., 2014) has not been administered by disability researchers. This measure is unique in that it incorporates a more comprehensive picture of spirituality with the intention of capturing the intersectionality of ritualistic, theistic, and existential realms that may be unique to specific populations.

One consideration is to modify existing items within the RiTE measure for use with those affected by an ID. By incorporating simple, concrete descriptions, visual representations or symbols, and the use of clarifying questions and pretests, researchers can more reliably elicit the experiences of this population (Hartley & MacLean, 2006). For example, the existential spirituality item, '*There is a right way to treat other people*' (p. 978), could be modified to, *we should be loving or kind to people*, and include an image that represents the item symbolically (e.g., two people in an embrace). Incorporating visuals with descriptions of the activities, beliefs, and practices participants may enjoy could serve to capture relevant, lived spiritual experiences. Moreover, exploring the potentially heightened role of existential spirituality within this population is encouraged for delineating its unique value for those living with disability.

Another consideration for this population is to secure measures translated into various languages or assess spirituality more broadly in order to gain insights into the role of spirituality across cultures and particularly with understudied groups from various regions of the world. To date, the most widely used spirituality measure, available in 20 languages, is the Daily Spiritual Experiences Scale (DSES, Underwood & Teresi, 2002; Underwood, 2011). This measure utilizes less theistic language in an effort to be more inclusive of various belief systems, making it a versatile measure. Another broad measure of spirituality, designed to capture more global beliefs across religious and non-religious perspectives, is the Beliefs and Values Scale (Kin et al., 2006).

Furthermore, spirituality research, which directly elicits the perspectives of those living with disability, is largely qualitative (Table 42.4) and is limited in religious diversity, partly because few assessments or qualitative interview guides have been developed that are appropriate for participants with varying reading and comprehension levels. Thus, in order to further advance the disability-related field, researchers need to incorporate more inclusive assessments and computer-assisted technology for inviting the experiences of those living with disability to participate, as they are a diverse group who not only can benefit from spiritual involvement but who can also serve others in meaningful ways.

Conclusion and Recommendations

In closing, the disability literature has expanded over the past two decades, informing the significance of faith, religiousness, and spirituality as an important resource for these families. Generally, many families thrive or, at a minimum, cope sufficiently with the ambiguity of their lived experiences, despite the reality of the ableist mentality of Western culture and negative beliefs held by some cultural and religious communities. Future research designed to explore the relationship between negative beliefs and reaching acceptance of disability should consider (a) exploring which model(s) of disability participants align with most (i.e., moral, medical, social, interaction, and lifespan), (b) identifying which model(s) are most and least useful for supporting optimal spirituality, and (c) determining interventions for those who are at greater risk for diminished well-being.

Innovative methodological approaches are necessary to account for the range of impairments experienced by participants, as well as to create measures that are appropriate for various disability groups. Perhaps a focus on exploring the *spiritual essence* (i.e., open-mindedness, surrendering to the help of others, unconditional love) of IDD participants, and thinking in terms of a *spectrum of expression* (i.e., identifying what is meaningful and desired and how it is uniquely manifested) could be fruitful for how the next decade of research is conducted. Relational and systemic data for eliciting the interactional components of spirituality in families of under-represented family structures (i.e., LGBTQIA-identifying families, single-parent and blended families, and households with grandparents, siblings, or others as primary caregivers) is also necessary.

Moreover, scientist-practitioners are encouraged to consider the intersectionality of identity, spirituality, and health through BPSS assessment, the combined effect of perceptions, resources, and co-occurring stressors, as well as the role of ambiguous loss. Additional research is needed to discern whether and to what extent higher levels of psychological or intellectual absence, along with greater physical impairment of loved ones, affect health and well-being in families, and what aspects of spirituality mediate greater boundary ambiguity across disability types (Bentley et al., 2023).

Although spirituality and religious practices can serve as a valuable resource, to date, the IDD research indicates mixed reports regarding the spiritual experiences of those living with disability. There is still much to be explored for targeting evidence-based interventions for those most at risk in terms of health and well-being. In essence, significant strides have been made in prioritizing needs and recognizing the desires of those within this community, but there is much work that remains with regards to intentionally enhancing spirituality, health, and well-being.

References

American Association on Intellectual and Developmental Disabilities (AAIDD). (2024). Definition of Intellectual Disability. Retrieved April 6, 2024, from https://www.aaidd.org/intellectual-disability/definition

Amioloa, A., Khodabux, N., Peerally, M.F., Temple, P., Bunn, R., Kuruppaurachchi, K.A.L.A., Roy, M., Hollins, S., & Alexander, R.T. (2023). Intellectual disability, spirituality, religion, and social inclusion across cultures. In S. Tromans, R. Alexander, S. Gangadharan, C. Kapugama, & S. Baumik (Eds.), *Psychiatry of intellectual disability across cultures* (pp. 216–239). Oxford University Press. https://doi.org/10.1093/med/9780198857600.003.0013

Anonymous (n.d.). "The human spirit is one of ability, perseverance, and courage that no disability can steal away." Retrieved from https://www.goodreads.com/quotes/tag/disability

Bentley, G., McCarty, M., Zvonkovic, A., & Springer, N. (2015). Down syndrome and fathering: An exploration of ambiguous loss. *Fathering*, *13*(1), 1–17.

Bentley, G., Thomas-Jackson, S., Nelson Goff, B, & Piland, N. (2023). Ambiguous loss and coping strategies in couples raising a child with Down syndrome: A qualitative directed content analysis study. *Medical Research Archives*, *10*(11). https://doi.org/10.18103/mra.v10i11.3267

Blakeley, C., Smith, D.M., Johnstone, E.D., & Wittkowski, A. (2019). Parental decision-making following a prenatal diagnosis that is lethal, life-limiting, or has long term implications for the future child and family: A meta-synthesis of qualitative literature. *BMC Medical Ethics*, *20*(56), 1–19. https://doi.org/10.1186/s12910-019-0393-7

Blick, M.A., Franklin, M., Ellsworth, D., Havercamp, S.M., & Kornblau, B. (2015). The double burden: Health disparities among people of color living with disabilities. Retrieved from http://nisonger.osu.edu/sites/default/files/u4/the_double_burden_health_disparities_among_people_of_color_living_with_disabilities.pdf

Bodenmann, G. (2004). Dyadic Coping Inventory (DCI) [Database record]. *APA PsycTests*. https://doi.org/10.1037/t01977-000

Boehm, T.L., & Carter, E.W. (2019). Facets of faith: Spirituality, religiosity, and parents of children with intellectual disability, *Intellectual and Developmental Disabilities*, *56*(6), 512–526. https://doi.org/10.1352/1934-9556-57.6.512

Boss, P. (2006). *Loss, trauma and resilience: Therapeutic work with ambiguous loss*. W.W. Norton.

Brown, M., Whiting, J., Kahumoku-Fessler, E., Banford Witting, A., & Jensen, J. (2020). A dyadic model of stress, coping, and marital satisfaction among parents of children with autism. *Family Relations*, *69*, 138–150. https://doi.org/10.1111/fare.12375

Carter, E.W. (2021). Spirituality and supports for individuals with intellectual and developmental disabilities and their families. In L.M. Glidden, L. Abbeduto, L. L. McIntyre, & M. J. Tassé (Eds.), *APA handbook of intellectual and developmental disabilities* (Vol 2): *Clinical and educational implications: Prevention, intervention, and treatment* (pp. 419–442). American Psychological Association. https://doi.org/10.1037/0000195-016

Carter, E.W., Biggs, E. E., & Boehm, T. L. (2016). Being present versus having a presence: Dimensions of belonging for young people with disabilities and their families. *Christian Education Journal: Research on Educational Ministry*, *13*(1), 127–146. https://doi.org/10.1177/073989131601300109

Centers for Disease Control and Prevention. (2025a). Developmental Disability Basics. Retrieved on October 30, 2025 from https://www.cdc.gov/child-development/about/developmental-disability-basics.html

Centers for Disease Control and Prevention. (2025b). Disability and Health Data Now Chart. Retrieved on October 30, 2025 from https://www.cdc.gov/disability-and-health/articles-documents/health-data-now-chart.html

Centers for Disease Control and Prevention. (2025c). Socioeconomic Factors at the Intersection of Race and Ethnicity Influencing Health Risks for People with Disabilities. Retrieved on October 30, 2025 from https://www.cdc.gov/disability-and-health/articles-documents/socioeconomic-factors-race-and-ethnicity.html

Chang, M. & McConkey, R. (2008). The perceptions and experiences of Taiwanese parents who have children with an Intellectual Disability, *International Journal of Disability, Development, and Education*, *55*(1), 27–41. https://doi.org/10.1080/10349120701827961

Cless, J., Nelson Goff, B., & Durtschi, J. (2017). Hope, coping, and relationship quality in mothers of children with down syndrome. *Journal of Marital and Family Therapy*, *44*(2), 307–322. https://doi.org/10.1111/jmft.12249

Cless, J.D., & Stephenson, C. (2018). Perspectives from mothers: Recognizing their strengths and contributions beyond caregiving. In B.S. Nelson Goff & N. Piland Springer (Eds.), *Intellectual and developmental disabilities: A roadmap for families and professionals* (pp. 76–89). Routledge/Taylor & Francis.

Croot, E.J., Grant, G., Cooper, C.L., & Mathers, N. (2008). Perceptions of the causes of childhood disability among Pakistani families living in the UK. *Health and Social Care in the Community*, *16*(6). 606–613. https://doi.org/10.1111/j.1365-2524.2008.00784.x

Cummings, J., Carson, C.S., Shrestha, S. Kunik, M.E., Armento, M.E., Stanley, M.A., & Amspoker, A.B. (2015). Santa clara strength of religious faith questionnaire: Psychometric analysis in older adults. *Aging & Mental Health*, *19*(1), 86–97. https://doi.org/10.1080/13607863.2014.917606

Dan, B. (2020). The metaphysical model of disability: Is this a just world? *Developmental Medicine & Child Neurology*, *63*(3), 240. https://doi.org/10.1111/dmcn.14775

de Graaf, G., Buckley, F., & Skotko, B. (2022). People living with Down syndrome in the USA: Births And Population. https://go.downsyndromepopulation.org/usa-factsheet

Dellbridge, E., Taylor, J., & Hanson, C. (2014). Honoring the "Spiritual" in biopsychosocial-spiritual health care: Medical family therapists on the frontlines of graduate education, clinical practice, and research. In J. Hodgson, A. Lamson, T. Mendenhall, & D.R. Crane (Eds.), *Medical family therapy: Advanced applications* (pp. 197–216). Springer International Publishing. https://doi.org/10.1007/978-3-319-03482-9

Engel, G. L. (1977). The need for a new medical model: A challenge for biomedicine. *Science*, *196*, 129–136. https://doi.org/10.1126/science.847460

Engel, G. L. (1980). The clinical application of the biopsychosocial model. *American Journal of Psychiatry*, 137, 535–544. https://doi.org/10.1176/ajp.137.5.535

Esperandio, M.R.G., Escudero, F.T., Fernandes, M.L., & Pargament, K.I. (2018). Brazilian validation of the brief scale for spiritual/religious coping—SRCOPE-14. *Religions*, *9*(1), 31. https://doi.org/10.3390/rel9010031

Esperandio, M.R.G., Viacava, J.J.C., Franco, R.S., Pargament, K.I., & Exline, J.J. (2022). Brazilian adaptation and validation of the religious and spiritual struggles (RSS) scale—Extended and short version. *Religions*. *13*(4), 282. https://doi.org/10.3390/rel13040282

Gallagher, S., Phillips, A.C., Lee, H., & Carroll, D. (2015). The association between spirituality and depression in parents caring for children with developmental disabilities: Social support and/or last resort. *Journal of Religion and Health*, *54*, 358–370. https://doi.org/10.1007/s10943-014-9839-x

Gallus, K. & Jones (2018). Understanding and supporting identity formation and meaning making. In B.S. Nelson Goff & N. Piland Springer (Eds.), *Intellectual and developmental disabilities: A roadmap for families and professionals* (pp. 61–75). Routledge/Taylor & Francis.

Galtung, J. (2003). Dialogue of faiths: Monotheism, polytheism, pantheism, atheism. *World Affairs*, *7*(2). Retrieved from https://ciaotest.cc.columbia.edu/olj/wa/wa_apr03_c.html

Gaventa, W. C. (2018). *Disability and spirituality: Recovering wholeness*. Waco, TX: Baylor University Press. https://www.baylorpress.com/9781481302791/disability-and-spirituality/

Global Down Syndrome Foundation. (2018a). Prenatal and Newborn Pamphlet. Retrieved on April 6, 2024 from https://www.globaldownsyndrome.org/prenatal-testing-pamphlet/

Global Down Syndrome Foundation. (2018b). Research and Medical Care. Retrieved on April 6, 2024 from https://www.globaldownsyndrome.org/research-medical-care/

Hancock, S., Johansen Taber, K. & Goldberg, J.D. (2021). Fetal screening and whole genome sequencing: Where are the limits? *Expert Review of Molecular Diagnostics*, *21*(5), 433–435. https://doi.org/10.1080/14737159.2021.1919087

Harris, S. (2016). Buddhism and disability. In S. Melcher & A Yong (Eds.), *Studies in religion, theology and disability* (pp. 25–45), Waco, TX, Baylor University Press. https://scholarlypublications.universiteitleiden.nl/handle/1887/3458713

Hartley, S.L. & MacLean, W.E. (2006). A review of the reliability and validity of Likert-typescales for people with intellectual disability. *Journal of Intellectual Disability Research*, *50*(II), 813–827. https://doi.org/10.1111/j.1365-2788.2006.00844.x

Hastings, R. P. (2016). Chapter six - Do children with intellectual and developmental disabilities have a negative impact on other family members? The case for rejecting a negative narrative. *International Review of Research in Developmental Disabilities*, *50*, 165–194. https://doi.org/10.1016/bs.irrdd.2016.05.002

Herth, K. (1992). Herth Hope Index (HHI). *APA PsycTests*. https://doi.org/10.1037/t21563-000

Hodge, D. & Reynolds, C. (2019). Spirituality among people with disabilities: A nationally representative study of spiritual and religious profiles. *Health and Social Work*, *44*(2), 75–85. https://doi.org/10.1093/hsw/hly035

Hodge, D. R. (2001). Spiritual genograms: A generational approach to assessing spirituality. *Families in Societies*, *82*(1), 35–48. https://doi.org/10.1606/1044-3894.220

Hodge, D. R. (2013). Assessing spirituality and religion in the context of counseling and psychotherapy. In K. I. Pargament, A. Mahoney, & E. P. Shafranske (Eds.), *APA handbook of psychology, religion, and spirituality (Vol 2): An applied psychology of religion and spirituality* (pp. 93–123). American Psychological Association. https://doi.org/10.1037/14046-005

Hodge, D. R. (2015). *Spiritual assessment in social work and mental health practice*. New York: Columbia University Press. https://doi.org/10.1080/01609513.2015.1036201

Holland, J. C., Kash, K. M., Passik, S., Gronert, M.K., Sison, A., Lederberg, M., …Fox, B. (1998). A brief spiritual beliefs inventory for use in quality of life research in life-threatening illness. *Psycho-Oncology, 7*, 460–469. https://doi.org/10.1002/(SICI)1099-1611(199811/12)7:6<460::AID-PON328>3.0.CO;2-R

Hosking, F.J., Carey, I.M., Shah, S.M., Harris, T., DeWilde, S., Beighton, C., & Cook, D.G. (2016). Mortality among adults with intellectual disability in England: Comparisons with the general population. *American Journal of Public Health, 106*(8), 1483–1490 https://doi.org/10.2105/AJPH.2016.303240

Huber, S. & Huber, O.W. (2012). The Centrality of Religiosity Scale (CRS). *Religions, 3*(3), 710–724. https://doi.org/10.3390/rel3030710

Hunt, J. (2014). Bio-Psycho-Social-Spiritual assessment? Teaching the skill of spiritual assessment. *Social Work and Christianity, 41*(4), 373–384.

Jeter, K., & Turns, B. (2022). Grieving the child that never was: Treatment of ambiguous loss in parents of children with Down syndrome. *Australian and New Zealand Journal of Family Therapy. 43*(2), 243–256. https://doi.org/10.1002/anzf.1488

John, A., & Montgomery, D. (2016). Parental explanatory models of child's intellectual disability: a Q methodology study. *International Journal of Disability, Development, and Education, 63*(3):293–308. https://doi.org/10.1080/1034912x.2015.1085001

Kanne, S. (2018). "Diagnostic overshadowing." In F. Volkmar (Ed.). *Encyclopedia of autism spectrum disorders* (1–3). NY, Springer. https://doi.org/10.1007%2F978-1-4614-6435-8_398-5

Karaca, A., & Sener, D.K. (2021). Spirituality as a coping method for Mothers of children with developmental disabilities. *International Journal of Developmental Disabilities, 67*(2), 112–120. https://doi.org/10.1080/20473869.2019.1603730

Kausar, S. Jevne, R.F., & Sobsey, D. (2003). Hope in families of children with developmental disabilities. *Journal of Developmental Disabilities*, 10(1), 35–46. https://www.academia.edu/33607481/Hope_in_Families_of_Children_with_Developmental_Disabilities

King, M., Jones, L., Barnes, K., Low, J., Walker, C., Wilkinson, S., et al. (2006). Measuring spiritual belief: Development and standardization of a Beliefs and Values Scale. *Psychological Medicine, 36*, 417–425. https://doi.org/10.1017/S003329170500629X

Kleiven, T., Cusveller, B., Nygaard, M.R., Miksi, C. S., Boughey, A., & McSherry, W. (2021).What do we mean by 'spirituality' and 'spiritual care'? In W. McSherry, A. Boughey, and J. Attard (Eds.) *Enhancing nurses' and midwives' competence in providing spiritual care: Through innovative education and compassionate care* (pp. 21–38). Springer. https://doi.org/10.1007/978-3-030-65888-5_2

Knestrict, T. (2018). Discovering resilience: Moving forward on the journey. In B. Nelson Goff & N. Piland Springer (Eds.), *Intellectual and developmental disabilities: A roadmap for families and professionals* (pp. 17–31). Routledge/Taylor & Francis.

Knestrict, T. & Kuchey, D. (2009). Welcome to Holland: Characteristics of resilient families raising children with severe disabilities. *Journal of Family Studies, 15*(3). 227–244. https://doi.org/10.5172/jfs.15.3.227

Krahn, G. & Fox, M. (2014). Health disparities of adults with Intellectual Disability: What do we know? What do we do? *Journal of Applied Research in Intellectual Disabilities, 27*(5), 431–446. https://doi.org/10.1111/jar.12067

Krahn, G, Walker, D, & Correa-De-Araujo, R. (2015). Persons with disabilities as an unrecognized health disparity population. *American Journal of Public Health, 105*(S2), S198–S206. https://doi.org/10.2105/AJPH.2014.302182

Leib-Neri, M. (2015). "Everything in Nature goes in curves and circles": Concepts of Disability– Health and Medicine in American History. Retrieved from https://lewiscar.sites.grinnell.edu/HistoryofMedicine/uncategorized/everything-in-nature-goes-in-curves-and-circles-native-american-concepts-of-disability/

Lipka, M. & Gecewicz, C. (2017). More Americans now say they're spiritual but not religious. *Pew Research Center*. Retrieved from www.pewresearch.org

Loynes, B. & O'Hara, J. (2015). How can mental health clinicians, working in intellectual disability services, meet the spiritual needs of their service users? *Advances in Mental Health and Intellectual Disabilities*, *9*(1), 9–18. https://doi.org/10.1108/AMHID-10-2014-0035

Lui, E.X., Carter, E.W., Boehm, T.L., Annandale, N.H., & Taylor, C.E. (2014). In their own words: The place of faith in the lives of young people with autism and intellectual disability. *Intellectual and Developmental Disabilities*, *52*(5), 388–404. https://doi.org/10.1352/1934-9556-52.5.388

Manalili, M.A.R. (2021). Ableist ideologies stifle neurodiversity and hinder inclusive education. *Ought: The Journal of Autistic Culture*, *3*(1), Article 6. https://doi.org/10.9707/2833-1508.1072

McConkey, R., Kahonde, C., & McKenzie, J. (2016). Tackling stigma in developing countries: The key role of families. In K. Scior & S. Werner (Eds.). *Intellectual disability and stigma: Stepping out from the margins*. Palgrave Macmillan. https://doi.org/10.1057/978-1-137-52499-7_12

McCubbin, H.I., Olsen, D.H., Larsen, A.S., (1987/1991). Family crisis oriented personal evaluation scales. In Corcoran, K. & Fisher, J. (Eds.), *Measures of clinical practice: A sourcebook* (pp. 294–297), 3rd Ed. (Vol 2). Free Press. https://doi.org/10.1037/t02213-000

McCubbin, H.I., & Patterson, J. (1983). The family stress process: The double ABCX model of adjustment and adaptation. In H. I. McCubbin, M. B. Sussman, & J. M. Patterson (Eds.), *Social stress and the family: Advances and developments in family's stress theory and research*. Haworth. https://doi.org/10.1300/J002v06n01_02

McDaniel, S., Doherty, W., & Hepworth. J. (2014). *Medical family therapy and integrated care* (2nd Ed.). American Psychological Association. https://www.apa.org/pubs/books/4317314

McWhirter, A. C. & McIntyre, L. L. (2021). Associations between religion/spirituality, family characteristics, and mental health among parents with children with developmental delay. *Journal of Mental Health Research in Intellectual Disability*, *14*(3), 301–317. https://doi.org/10.1080/19315864.2021.1909680

National Center for Complementary and Integrative Health (NCCIH), (2021). Whole Person Care: What you Need to Know. Retrieved from https://www.nccih.nih.gov/health/whole-person-health-what-you-need-to-know

National Institute of Aging (NIA-NIH). (2020). Alzheimer's disease in people with down syndrome. Retrieved from https://www.nia.nih.gov/health/alzheimers-causes-and-risk-factors/alzheimers-disease-people-down-syndrome

National Institute of Child Health and Development (NICHD). (2021, November 9). About Intellectual and Developmental Disabilities (IDDs). Retrieved April 6, 2024, from https://www.nichd.nih.gov/health/topics/idds/conditioninfo

National Institute of Health (NIH). (2005). *The surgeon general's call to action to improve the health and wellness of person with disabilities*. Washington, DC: US Department of Health and Human Services, Office of the Surgeon General. Retrieved from https://www.ncbi.nlm.nih.gov/books/NBK44667/

National Institutes of Health (2024). Person-first and Destigmatizing Language. Retrieved April 6, 2024 from https://www.nih.gov/nih-style-guide/person-first-destigmatizing-language

National Public Radio (NPR). (2022, June 24). *Live updates: The Supreme Court overturn Roe v.* Wade. Retrieved from https://www.npr.org/live-updates/supreme-court-roe-v-wade-decision-overturn

Natoli, J., Ackerman, D., Dermott, S. & Edwards, J. (2012). Prenatal diagnosis of Down syndrome: A systematic review of termination rates (1995-2011). *Prenatal Diagnosis*, *32*(2), 142–153. https://doi.org/10.1002/pd.2910

Nelson Goff, B. & Piland Springer, N. (2018). *Intellectual and developmental disabilities: A roadmap for families and professionals (Eds)*. Routledge/Taylor & Francis. https://doi.org/10.4324/9781315562490

Nelson Goff, B., Piland Springer, N., Foote, L., Frantz, C., Peak, M., Tracey, C., Veh, T., Bentley, G. E., & Cross, K. (2013). Receiving the initial Down syndrome diagnosis: A comparison of prenatal and postnatal parent group experiences. *Intellectual and Developmental Disabilities*, *51*(6), 446–457. https://doi.org/10.1352/1934-9556-51.6.446

Nelson Goff, B. S., Monk, J. K., Malone, J. Staats, N. Tanner, A., & Springer, N. P. (2016). Comparing parents of children with Down syndrome at different life span stages. *Journal of Marriage and Family Therapy*, *78*(4), 1131–1148. https://doi.org/10.1111/jomf.12312

NHS. (2018). "The learning disability improvement standards for NHS trusts" (PDF). Archived from the original (PDF) on 2023-07-03. Retrieved 2023-07-03. https://www.england.nhs.uk/wp-content/uploads/2020/08/v1.17_Improvement_Standards_added_note.pdf

O'Brien, M. (2007). Ambiguous loss of families with children with autism spectrum disorders. *Family Relations*, *56*, 135–146. https://doi.org/10.1111/j.1741-3729.2007.00447.x

O'Hanlon, E. (2013). Religion and Disability: The experience of families of children with special needs. *Journal of Religion, Disability, and Health*, *17*, 42–61. https://doi.org/10.1080/15228967.2012.731874

O'Hanlon, E. (2009). *Spiritual community experiences of families of children with disabilities. (Unpublished Doctoral Dissertation)*, University of Maryland, College Park, MD.

Olkin, R. (2002). Could you hold the door for me? Including disability in diversity. *Cultural Diversity and Ethnic Minority Psychology*, *8*, 130–137. https://doi.org/10.1037/1099-9809.8.2.130

Olkin, R. (2022). Conceptualizing disability: Three models of disability. Retrieved from https://www.apa.org/ed/precollege/psychology-teacher-network/introductory-psychology/disability-models

Olson, D. H., Russell, C. S., & Sprenkle, D. H. (1989). *Circumplex model: Systemic assessment and treatment of families*. Psychology Press.

Special Olympics (2024). *About spread the word*. Retrieved from www.Spreadtheword.global

Paloutzian, R. F., & Ellison, C. W. (1982). Spiritual Well-Being Scale (SWBS) [Database record]. *APA PsycTests*. https://doi.org/10.1037/t00534-000

Paloutzian, R. F. & Ellison, C.W. (1991). *Manual for the spiritual wellbeing scale*. NY, New York. Life Advance Inc. https://doi.org/10.1037/t00534-000

Pargament, K. I. (1997). *The psychology of religion and coping: Theory, research, practice*. Guilford Publications.

Patel, D.R., Cabral, M.D., Ho, A, & Merrick, J. (2020). A clinical primer on intellectual disability. *Translational Pediatrics*. (Suppl 1): S23–S35. https://doi.org/10.21037/tp.2020.02.02

Piland Springer, N., Turns, B., & Masterson, M. (2018). A systemic and contextual lens of disability: Family Stress, Ambiguous Loss, and Meaning Making. In B. Nelson Goff & N. Piland Springer (Eds.), *Intellectual and developmental disabilities: A roadmap for families and professionals* (pp. 17–31). Routledge/Taylor & Francis.

PRRI (2020). The 2020 Census of American Religion. Retrieved from https://www.prri.org/wp-content/uploads/2021/07/PRRI-Jul-2021-Religion.pdf

Rahman, L. (2019). *Disability language guide*. Stanford Disability Institute Board. https://disability.stanford.edu/sites/g/files/sbiybj26391/files/media/file/disability-language-guide-stanford_1.pdf

Rambow, T. (2016). *The relationship of spiritual well-being to quality of life in adults with intellectual and developmental disabilities [Unpublished master's thesis]*. Waterford Institute of Technology, Waterford, Ireland.

Ramisch, J. (2012). Marriage and family therapists working with couples who have children with autism. *Journal of Marital and Family Therapy*, *38*, 305–316. https://doi.org/10.1111/j.1752-0606.2010.00210.x

Ramisch, J., & Piland Springer, N. (2020). Systemic approaches for children, adolescents, families living with neurodevelopmental disorders (Ch 48). In K. Wampler, S. Miller, R. Seadall, L. McWey, A. Blow, M. Rastogi, & B.J. Singh (Eds.), *Handbook of systemic family therapy*, Vol (2), Wiley. https://doi.org/10.1002/9781119788393.ch15

Ramisch, J. L., Onaga, E., & Oh, S. M. (2014). Keeping a sound marriage: How couples with children with autism spectrum disorders maintain their marriages. *Journal of Child and Family Studies*, *23*, 975–988. https://doi.org/10.1007/s10826-013-9753-y

Riddle, C. (2013). Defining disability: Metaphysical not political. *Medical Healthcare and Philosophy*, *16*, 377–384. https://doi.org/10.1007/s11019-012-9405-9

Rohwerder, B. (2018). *Disability stigma in developing countries*. K4D Helpdesk Report. Brighton, UK: Institute of Development Studies.

Rolland, J. (2018). Tapping the power of family belief systems. In *Helping couples and families navigate illness and disability: An integrated approach* (Chapter 8, pp. 128–156). Guilford Press.

Rolland, J. (2018b). Helping families with anticipatory loss and suffering. In *Helping couples and families navigate illness and disability: An integrated approach* (Chapter 9, pp. 159–176). Guilford Press.

Romney, J., Fife, S., Reitz, R., Piland, N., Soloski, K., Montgomery, A., Wagner, K. (2025). Relational Patterns of Support and Communication in Families with a Child Diagnosed with Autism: An Interpretive Phenomenological Study. *Journal of Autism and Developmental Disorders*, *55*, 3395–3409. https://doi.org/10.1007/s10803-025-06847-3

Segall, S.Z. (2011). Is Buddhism Non-Theistic? Retrieved from https://www.existentialbuddhist.com/2011/05/is-buddhism-non-theistic/

Shahdadi, H. & Mahmoudirad, G. (2022). The emergence of self-care in parents with disabled children. *International Journal of Children's Spirituality*, *27*(3–4), 176–194. https://doi.org/10.1080/1364436X.2022.2093169

Sloper, K. L. (2007). *Gifts: Mothers reflect on how children with down syndrome enrich their lives*. Woodbine House.

Sloper, K.L. (2009). *Gifts 2: How people with down syndrome enrich the world*. Woodbine House.

Sulmasy, D. (2002). A biopsychosocial-spiritual model for the care of patients at the end of life. *The Gerontologist*, *42*(3), 24–33. https://doi.org/10.1093/geront/42.suppl_3.24

Timmons, F., McCausland, D., Brennan, D. Sheerin, F., Luus, R., McCallion, P., & McCarron, M. (2023). A national cohort study of spiritual and religious practices of older people with intellectual disability. *Journal of Intellectual Disabilities*, *28*(2), 533–548. https://doi.org/10.1177/17446295231163977

Turns, B., Nelson Goff, B.N., Masterson, M., Cless, J., & Cless, A. (2018). Intellectual and developmental disabilities: An overview and introduction. In B Nelson-Goff & N. Piland Springer (Eds.), *Intellectual and developmental disabilities: A roadmap for parents and professionals* (pp. 3–16). Routledge/Taylor & Francis.

Turns, B., Smock Jordan, S., Callahan, K., Whiting, J., & Piland Springer, N. (2019). Assessing the effectiveness of solution-focused brief therapy for couples raising a child with autism: A pilot clinical outcome study. *Journal of Couple and Relationship Therapy*, *18*(3), 257–279. https://doi.org/10.1080/15332691.2019.1571975

Underwood, L. (1999). A working model of health: Spirituality and religiousness as resources: Applications to persons with disability, *Journal of Religion, Disability, and Health*, *3*(3), 55–71. J095v03n03_05.PDF (https://researchintegration.org/documents/disability.pdf)

Underwood, L. & Teresi, J. (2002). The daily spiritual experiences scale: Development, theoretical description, reliability, exploratory factor analysis, and preliminary construct validity using health related data. *Annals of Behavioral Medicine*, *24*(1), 22–33. https://doi.org/10.1207/S15324796ABM2401_04

Underwood, L.G. (2011). The daily spiritual experience scale: Overview and results. *Religions*. *2*(1), 29–50. https://doi.org/10.3390/rel2010029

Walsh, F. (2003). Family resilience: A framework for clinical practice. *Family Process*, *42*(1), 1–18. https://doi.org/10.1111/j.1545-5300.2003.00001.x

Watts, G. (2011). Intellectual Disability and Spiritual Development. *Journal of Intellectual & Developmental Disability*, *36*(4), 234–241. https://doi.org/10.3109/13668250.2011.617731

Webb, J.R. (2021). *Understanding forgiveness and addiction: Theory, research, and clinical application*. Routledge. https://doi.org/10.4324/9780429200274

Webb, J.R., Toussaint, L., & Dula, C.S. (2014). Ritualistic, theistic, and existential spirituality: Initial psychometric qualities of the RiTE measure of spirituality. *Journal of Religious Health*. *53*(4), 972–985. https://doi.org/10.1007/s10943-013-9697-y

White, M. & Epston, D. (1990). *Narrative means to therapeutic ends*. WW Norton & Company, New York.

Williamson, H.J., Brennan, A.C., Tress, S.F., Joseph, D.H., & Baldwin, J.A. (2020). Exploring health and wellness among Native American adults with intellectual and/or developmental disabilities and their family caregivers. *Journal of Applied Research in Intellectual Disabilities*, *33*(3), 327–333. https://doi.org/10.1111/jar.12664

Wilson, A. (2019). Barriers and enablers provided by Hindu beliefs and practices for people with disabilities in India. *Christian Journal for Global Health. 6*(2), 12–23. https://doi.org/10.15566/cjgh.v6i2.250

World Health Organization (WHO). (2001). *International classification of functioning, disability and health (ICF)external icon*. Geneva: WHO.

Wright, L. M., Watson, W. L., & Bell, J. M. (1996). *Belief: The heart of healing in families and illness*. New York: Basic Books.

Xavier, F.T. & Esperandio, M.R.G. (2023). Spirituality and caregiver burden of people with intellectual disabilities: An empirical study. *International Journal of Latin American Religions*, *7*, 17–35. https://doi.org/10.1007/s41603-023-00196-8

Zablotsky, B., Ng, A., Black, L., & Blumberg, S. (2023). Diagnosed Developmental Disabilities in children 3-17 years: United States, 2019-2021. Retrieved April 6, 2024 from NCHS Data Brief, Number 473, July 2023 (cdc.gov), https://www.cdc.gov/nchs/data/databriefs/db473.pdf

Chapter 43

Forgiveness Education and Promotion

A Narrative Review of Methods and Effectiveness

Loren L. Toussaint, Everett L. Worthington, Jr, Richard G. Cowden, Jon R. Webb, and Sebastian Binyamin Skalski-Bednarz*

Forgiveness is a skill that can be taught using various methods, and learning to forgive has relational, social, health, and well-being benefits (Toussaint et al., 2015; Worthington & Wade, 2020; see also Chapter 23 of this volume). Aside from those conversant with its clinical utility, regrettably, familiarity with the most common methods of teaching forgiveness and the evidence supporting the effectiveness of these methods remains limited for many. In this chapter, we seek to increase exposure to forgiveness education approaches and the growing evidence on the effectiveness of forgiveness education by offering a narrative review of exemplary methods and evidence for behavioral scientists, practitioners, and educators of various sorts. To accomplish this, we focus on two key areas. First, we examine education in the formal sense of training, either in a psychoeducational setting or a classroom. Second, we consider attempts to promote forgiveness education and awareness at the community level. We begin by defining forgiveness, which identifies the target endpoint of attempts at forgiveness education and promotion. We then consider the three commonly used psychoeducational approaches and community interventions, summarizing examples of their implementation and evaluation. Finally, we summarize our existing understanding of forgiveness education, noting current limitations, and we suggest possibilities for the future in this area.

Forgiveness Conceptualizations and Definitions

There are several ways to conceptualize forgiveness (for a review, see Worthington, 2020a). Some consider forgiveness from an evolutionary perspective, citing the persistence of this characteristic over time in animal and human species, suggesting that it must have adaptation and survival advantages (McCullough, 2008). Others view forgiveness as a coping response after a stressful interpersonal transgression is appraised to be threatening (Strelan, 2020). Still others view forgiveness within the context of relationships involving the victim, offender, transgression, and the sacred (Worthington & Sandage, 2016). For example, victims tend to forgive relationally close offenders a bit more easily, but sacred desecrations are much more difficult to forgive. Another common way of thinking about forgiveness is as a virtue (Worthington, 2022). According to virtue theory, people identify forgiveness as a valued character goal and practice forgiveness to make it a habitual part of who they are. When challenges to forgiveness arise, those people meet this challenge by showing that forgiveness has become a virtue. There are other approaches to thinking about forgiveness. However,

* Corresponding Author: touslo01@luther.edu.

DOI: 10.4324/9781003440048-49

evolutionary, relational, stress-and-coping, and virtue theories have generated considerable research and are especially relevant to forgiveness education and promotion.

Although there are several ways to think of forgiveness, one commonly agreed-upon definition suggests that it involves replacing negative thoughts, feelings, and motivations directed at an offender with positive ones (McCullough et al., 1998). That is, a victim who originally thinks that the offender is a terrible person, feels angry, and seeks revenge shifts to make a prosocial and unwarranted act of altruism to think better of, feel lovingly toward, and wish well for the offender. Forgiveness is also commonly defined in terms of its decisional versus emotional qualities (Cavalcanti et al., 2019; Worthington, 2020a). *Decisional forgiveness* is the intention to treat an offender as a valued person, move past anger, and give up any desire for revenge. *Emotional forgiveness* involves moving to a place of less unforgiving emotions (e.g., hatred, anger, hostility, resentment, bitterness, and fear; Worthington et al., 2001), perhaps achieving emotional neutrality, and eventually achieving a sense of positive emotional valence regarding an offender.

A key distinction in understanding forgiveness is whether it is considered a malleable state or a stable trait (Toussaint & Webb, 2005). This distinction is important and has implications for what education and promotion of forgiveness can achieve. States are more susceptible to change. They may be direct targets of intervention or education, at least in the short term. Traits (or dispositions) are more consistent and stable across time, place, and occasion. They are less likely to change. Nonetheless, building more forgiving states can be a legitimate target for forgiveness education. They can be useful in specific situations (e.g., contexts of bullying or romantic rejection). They can also be stepping-stones to dispositional forgiveness. Consequently, forgiveness interventions often focus foremost on forgiveness states and changes that result from experiencing education or promotion. Interventions might include attempts to generalize learning across multiple states, with some studies reporting changes in forgiving traits (Nation et al., 2018; Osei-Tutu et al., 2020). Although the experience of a forgiving state is a laudable goal for many, it is the lasting change in one's skills – or, in this case, the development of a forgiving disposition – that might make up one's character that might be considered most relevant to daily life and long-term outcomes.

The term forgiveness is often used when referring to a situation in which a victim is hurt and wronged by an offender, and the victim subsequently attempts to forgive the offender. *This is the focus in this review*. However, forgiveness can also be applied to oneself (Woodyatt et al., 2017). Self-forgiveness applies when people have hurt or offended others or themselves. When this happens, feelings of self-blame, guilt, regret, shame, and low self-esteem (generally, *self-condemnation*) might be experienced frequently (Griffin et al., 2018). Self-forgiveness involves recognizing the wrong that has been done, taking responsibility, apologizing as appropriate, attempting to make amends, and rebuilding self-esteem and acceptance (Worthington, 2013). Self-forgivers would also strive to reorient their values and commit to improving their way of living to prevent future problems from occurring (Cowden, Worthington, et al., 2020b). A key difference from forgiving others is that with self-forgiveness there is a risk that one may simply let oneself off the hook too easily by dodging responsibility for wrongdoing, failing to apologize, never making amends, minimizing the offense, or denying the existence of wrongdoing (Murphy, 2003; Webb et al., 2017; Wenzel et al., 2012). Of note, although forgiveness of others and forgiveness of self are the most frequently studied, there are additional dimensions beginning to receive empirical attention (e.g., forgiveness of God, feeling forgiven by God or others, and seeking forgiveness; see Webb, 2021).

Whether applied to forgiving others or oneself (or to any other dimension of forgiveness), several concepts are frequently mistaken as forgiveness (Enright & North, 1998). Forgiveness is not excusing, condoning, minimizing, or denying hurtful behavior. Neither is it repairing a relationship nor seeking justice. Both reconciliation and justice-seeking are independent of forgiveness. That is, forgiveness of others and self-forgiveness are thought of as intrapersonal experiences, whereas reconciliation is an interpersonal, social experience, and justice-seeking also invokes the legal realm of society (or social realm in organizations).

A final consideration in defining forgiveness is the notion of collectivistic forgiveness (Hook et al., 2012). In most Western societies, people often separate intrapersonal and interpersonal worlds. There is the self, and there are others. In many non-Western societies, this distinction is not made as clearly. The self is more often seen as embedded in the greater familial and social context (Cowden et al., 2019; Kurniati et al., 2020). Forgiveness is simply a more natively social act in collectivistic countries and cultures. More social ramifications are typically considered prior to forgiving. This has implications for the understanding of forgiveness and the approaches taken to forgiveness education and promotion (Cook et al., 2022).

Psychoeducational Approaches to Teaching and Promoting Forgiveness

Three psychoeducational approaches to teaching and promoting forgiveness of others have been used and researched most often. Each has been carefully developed and incorporates the wisdom of science, philosophy, and in some cases religion. All are informed by personal accounts of forgiveness that give resonance to these scholarly and professional models for everyday consumers. These models have been widely used across different populations. We briefly review these approaches and highlight key work supporting their effectiveness using a narrative approach.

Narrative reviews have a long and widely accepted history in the social sciences, providing researchers the opportunity to generally explore a topic of interest while summarizing and critiquing key studies in the literature and offering a view of limitations and suggested future directions (Demiris et al., 2019; Sukhera, 2022). Narrative reviews are intended to be more globally focused on a research question and the broad literature in an area. Narrative reviews offer a bird's-eye view, allowing for integration and synthesis of multiple types of work, including research of various types and designs (Sukhera, 2022). Our narrative review follows guidelines developed in the Scale for the Assessment of Narrative Review Articles (SANRA) to ensure high quality of the present review (Baethge et al., 2019). SANRA guidelines emphasize clear justification for and statement of aims, descriptions and referencing in the literature search, and clear reasoning and presentation of findings. We constructed our review to meet each of these requirements.

Process Model of Interpersonal Forgiveness

Enright's Process Model of interpersonal forgiveness has 20 units combined into four major components. This approach has been widely applied in clinical, educational, and international work (Enright, 2001). The Process Model begins with the Uncovering Phase, which consists of eight units. In Unit 1, people explore the offense, break down any defense mechanisms that might distance them from the injury and inhibit progress, and experience the pain of being hurt. The main goals of Unit 2 include healthy recognition and expression of anger.

In Unit 3, feelings of shame and guilt are confronted and dealt with, if present. Units 4 and 5 require people to find a balance between experiencing the pain of being hurt and living a healthy life. Victims seek suitable ways of effectively managing rumination and emotional expressivity. Units 6 and 7 involve a measured comparison of the victim and offender and a recognition that the offender may not be better off. A hope is to find some form of good from the experience. Unit 8 brings one's worldview into consideration and offers the possibility of developing a positive worldview.

The second major phase (i.e., Units 9 through 11) of the Process Model is the Decision Phase. Unit 9 emphasizes the realizations that change is necessary and that holding unforgiveness does not produce the desired results. Considering forgiveness as a potential option is the focus of Unit 10. This requires that people understand what they are being asked to do. This unit addresses misconceptions about forgiveness – forgiveness is not condoning, excusing, or denying bad behavior. Unit 11 involves making a commitment to forgive.

The third phase of the Process Model (i.e., Units 12 through 15) is the Work Phase. The focus is on the development of key emotional states and virtuous perspectives that support the experience of forgiveness. Cognitive reframing is emphasized in Unit 12, the development of empathy in Unit 13, compassion in Unit 14, and acceptance in Unit 15.

The final phase of the Process Model (i.e., Units 16 through 20) is the Deepening Phase. Unit 16 helps participants find meaning in the offense and the hurt they have experienced. The central theme of Unit 17 is to develop humility and recognize that the need to be forgiven is as important as the need to forgive. In Unit 18, people seek to find some common humanity in suffering and forgiveness. Finally, in Units 19 and 20, the forgiver is encouraged to find a new purpose in life as a result of the injury and experience the emotional release that comes with letting go of unforgiveness.

Key Studies of the Effectiveness of the Process Model of Interpersonal Forgiveness

Searching PsycINFO, PubMed, and Google Scholar (search terms = "forgiveness education," "forgiveness promotion," and "teaching forgiveness") revealed over 30 studies, as of December 23, 2024, that have examined the extent to which the Process Model of interpersonal forgiveness satisfactorily brings about improvements in forgiveness. These trials have involved numerous different samples, such as elderly women (Hebl & Enright, 1993), incest survivors (Freedman & Enright, 1996), individuals with substance use problems (Lin et al., 2004), emotionally abused women (Reed & Enright, 2006), and individuals with chronic illnesses like coronary artery disease (Waltman et al., 2009) and cancer (Hansen et al., 2009). Enright and colleagues have repeatedly studied the application of the Process Model in samples who struggle with specific concerns with physical or mental health. Three separate meta-analytic studies reveal that the Process Model has large effects (ds = 1.26 to 1.66) on forgiveness (Akhtar & Barlow, 2018; Baskin & Enright, 2004; Freedman & Enright, 2020) and emotional well-being ($d = 1.42$) (Baskin & Enright, 2004).

The Process Model has also been used with children and adolescents in schools and child services settings. Investigations have included Northern Ireland (Enright et al., 2007), Turkey (Taysi & Vural, 2016), South Korea (Park et al., 2013), and Pakistan (Rahman et al., 2018), as well as the United States (Freedman, 2018) – often in formal school settings. Meta-analytic findings from 20 studies on the effectiveness of forgiveness education in children revealed that children with an average age of about 12 years who work through an age-appropriate version of the Process Model or another story-based forgiveness approach based on the Process Model show significant gains in forgiveness ($g = .54$) and reductions in anger ($g = .29$). Gains in forgiveness were strongest for children who were taught using the Process Model ($g = .66$) versus those who used the story-based approach ($g = .27$).

In both children and adults, studies investigating the effectiveness of the Process Model show that this approach is useful in helping individuals who have been harmed, often quite deeply, to experience less anger, more forgiveness, and better overall mental health and well-being. Importantly, in most of these studies, intensive one-on-one time between the teacher/counselor and the forgiving individual is needed. Several hours are usually required to work through the model. Often, this model is completed over several days, weeks, or months.

REACH Forgiveness

The REACH Forgiveness model includes a decision to forgive plus five key steps to emotional forgiveness (Worthington, 2008). REACH is an acronym that helps interventionists and clients easily recall the most important aspects of forgiveness. Whereas Enright has used the Process Model generally targeted to specific types of patients or to school settings, the REACH Forgiveness model has almost exclusively been applied in untargeted situations. People with all sorts of offenses are typically engaged in either psychoeducational groups or do-it-yourself (DIY) workbooks to deal with their individual offenses (cf. people with borderline personality disorder diagnoses, see Sandage et al., 2015; or couple enrichment or therapy, see Worthington et al., 2015).

Before engaging with the main elements of the REACH Forgiveness approach, some preparatory work is necessary. The beginning work focuses on readying the individual for the experience of forgiveness. Participants identify an unforgiven offense they will work to forgive and complete some self-assessment instruments prior to convening in the group (or starting the DIY workbook proper). They are first asked to identify the "hardest thing you have ever successfully forgiven." Reflecting on this accomplishment builds optimism and hope that the present offense can be forgiven. Participants then contemplate inspiring quotes about forgiveness. Decisional and emotional forgiveness are defined, followed by a discussion of the benefits of forgiveness to relationships, mental and physical health and well-being, spiritual well-being, and general quality of life. The initial phase of work concludes by inviting participants to decide to forgive. Typically, few participants are ready at that point to forgive, but the offer will be re-extended after working through the REACH Forgiveness steps. After the initial preparatory work, the five steps to REACH Forgiveness are engaged through numerous "exercises" aimed at each step.

The first step is to Recall the hurt as objectively as possible and without exaggerating their own actions, reactions, and emotional responses. The second step is to Empathize with the offender. To foster empathy, several exercises are done. For instance, role-playing the offender, writing a letter from the offender's perspective, and using the empty-chair technique in which victims speak to an empty chair as if their offender were present, then roles are reversed until a dialogue has occurred, revealing the offender's viewpoint fully. Empathizing with the offender is perhaps the most important step in promoting forgiveness. However, if empathy for the offender cannot be developed, then it can be helpful to attempt to develop sympathy or compassion, as these emotions can often help replace or reduce unforgiving emotions.

The third step is offering an Altruistic gift of forgiveness. Participants describe times when they have received undeserved forgiveness from someone in their past. Humility and gratitude are also emphasized as participants' attention is directed to times when they have needed to be forgiven. They are asked to reflect on the necessity of forgiveness for their own wrongdoing and the gratitude they felt when they experienced someone else's forgiveness. They estimate the amount of the unforgiveness they held at the outset of the group (or DIY workbook) that they have forgiven, and they are told they will be asked to express it as a percentage.

In the fourth step, participants Commit to forgiveness. In groups, each person verbalizes the percentage of forgiveness they have experienced so far; individuals who complete a DIY workbook record this percentage in writing. Other objective signs of commitment might include things like completing a certificate of emotional forgiveness or participating in a hand-washing ritual in which a "short-hand" description of the hurt is written in permanent ink on the back of one hand, and participants then attempt to wash it off. The pedagogical focus here is to emphasize that forgiveness might require commitment to repeated "washing" (e.g., forgiving).

The final step is Holding on to forgiveness when doubts occur. In the last step, participants are cautioned that negative responses to future encounters with the offender, either real or imagined, that elicit stress and worry, are not evidence of unforgiveness. Rather, these responses are the body's natural self-protective reaction to threatening situations, whether perceived or real. Participants are encouraged to be aware of these possibly threatening thoughts or environments and either remove themselves from situations that cause them to question their commitment to forgiveness or distract themselves from these unwanted thoughts.

At the conclusion of the five steps to REACH Forgiveness, participants are once again invited to decide to forgive explicitly. A penultimate (and crucial) exercise invites participants to think about ways to not only forgive a single offense but to identify up to ten unforgiven events and apply the REACH steps, in addition to deciding to forgive each one. This promotes generalization and further progress toward practicing forgiveness more habitually. Finally, the same self-assessments that were completed at the outset are repeated, demonstrating how far the person has come.

Key Studies of the Effectiveness of the REACH Forgiveness Model

The REACH Forgiveness model has been extensively tested (Worthington, 2020b). Much like the other forgiveness models, most of these studies have focused on the use of randomized-controlled trials, where the design of the study offers evidence supporting the efficacy of the psychoeducational intervention for forgiveness enhancement and other potential benefits to different facets of well-being. Searching PsycINFO, PubMed, and Google Scholar (using the same search terms and date as above) revealed over 30 randomized-controlled trials of the REACH Forgiveness method. REACH Forgiveness has been shown to be effective in treating clients in psychotherapy (Worthington & Sandage, 2016), including individuals with serious psychiatric disorders such as borderline personality disorder (Sandage et al., 2015) and those in couple enrichment (Worthington et al., 2015) and couple therapy (Ripley et al., 2014).

Outside of the clinic, REACH Forgiveness has been tested and shown to be effective with college students in the United States (Toussaint, Griffin, et al., 2020a) and abroad in Indonesia (Kurniati et al., 2020), the Philippines (Worthington et al., 2010), Australia (Nation et al., 2018), and India (Toussaint, Worthington, et al., 2020b), to name a few. An important feature of many of these studies is that the REACH Forgiveness method has been culturally adapted, offered using DIY workbooks in both hardcopy and online formats, and tailored to Christian or secular beliefs. For example, Ho et al. (2024) recently reported the findings of the largest preregistered randomized-controlled trial to examine the effects of a psychoeducational model of forgiveness. They tested the efficacy of a (nominally) two-hour DIY REACH Forgiveness workbook (https://www.discoverforgiveness.org/tools/the-reach-forgiveness-workbook) among almost 4600 participants across six sites within five countries affected by conflict (or war) in the past or present (i.e., Hong Kong, two sites in Ukraine, Colombia, South Africa, and Indonesia). To date, it is the largest multisite study to examine the effects of a psychoeducational model of forgiveness, and its findings could greatly enrich existing knowledge about the effectiveness of the REACH Forgiveness method in promoting forgiveness among people living in non-Western contexts. This study showed that the brief DIY workbook was effective at reducing unforgiveness (SMD = -0.53), depression symptoms (SMD = -0.22), and anxiety symptoms (SMD = -0.21), as well as increasing individual flourishing (SMD = 0.27). These findings align with a prior meta-analysis of studies examining the effectiveness of REACH Forgiveness (Wade et al., 2014), the results of which showed that REACH Forgiveness was effective in increasing forgiveness (g = .33 to .56), reducing depression (g = .34) and anxiety symptoms (g = .63), and increasing hope (g = 1.00). Wade et al. (2014) also found that REACH Forgiveness and the Process Model were comparable in their effectiveness.

One of the contexts in which forgiveness is likely to have important implications for individual and societal flourishing is Africa. Many countries on the continent have been challenged by exploitation, colonialism, oppression, and numerous violent conflicts, especially in recent history. Although the research on forgiveness in Africa consists of a large number of studies examining multiple features of social, political, and community factors (for a review of almost 100 studies, see Worthington et al., 2020), our focus here is on education and promotion of forgiveness using the REACH Forgiveness method. A recent study tested the efficacy of a group-based, culturally adapted Christian REACH Forgiveness method in Ghana (Osei-Tutu et al., 2020). In this first-of-its-kind study, a large sample (N = 260) of Christian Ghanaians were randomly assigned to a Christian version of REACH Forgiveness, a Christian version of REACH Forgiveness that was also culturally adapted, or a waitlist control group that later received either the standard Christian version or the culturally adapted Christian version. Compared to the control group, participants in both of the REACH Forgiveness groups showed improved forgiveness and conciliatory motivations, decisional and emotional forgiveness, forbearance, and dispositional forgivingness. The standard Christian REACH Forgiveness method and the culturally adapted version performed equally well.

Forgive for Good

The Forgive for Good model of teaching and promoting forgiveness is the outgrowth of the research conducted at the Stanford Forgiveness Project (Luskin, 2002, 2007), which originally was aimed at improving heart health. The Forgive for Good model includes nine steps to forgiveness. The first step is knowing clearly how one feels about an offense and articulating what is unacceptable. Understanding one's feelings and articulating the wrong helps in sharing the offense with and gaining the support of a trusted confidant. In the second step, participants are encouraged to make a commitment to feeling better and to recognize that the benefits of forgiveness are for themselves, not the offender. In the third step, the method aims to develop an understanding of what forgiveness is and is not. Forgiveness is delineated from passivity, condoning, excusing, and denying hurt. Forgiveness is also sharply contrasted with reconciliation. This step also engages participants in positive and peaceful emotional experiences and attempts to reduce blaming and over-personalizing the offense. Participants are encouraged to move away from their exclusive focus on telling a grievance story.

Step four entails a change in perspective. The point of emphasis here is to bring to the victims' attention that things from the past, sometimes the distant past, are negatively impacting their life in the present and potentially even their future. The body's natural tendency when thinking about an offense is to become aroused and show signs of stress responding. The focus of step five is to calm the stress response and decondition the thoughts of the offense from the anxiety and physiological symptoms associated with it. Step six introduces the concept of unenforceable rules, which are expectations about control in one's life. The main point of step six is to bring into resolution that expectations for control can be very stressful, often result in disappointment, and can hold an individual in a place of powerlessness. Participants are reminded that they cannot enforce rules or expectations about how a person should be treated or how life should go. The best that can happen is that one can develop hopes about these things. The difference between unenforceable rules and hopes is clearly contrasted, and the immobilizing nature of rules is supplanted with a motivating orientation toward hopes.

Step seven of the model encourages participants to refocus energy not on replaying thoughts and emotions of the hurtful event, but on finding new ways to meet one's goals in life. Step eight invites participants to look for gratitude-building experiences through one's environment, family, friends, or even everyday experiences. Gratitude is useful because it promotes positive emotion, which can help to replace the negativity of unforgiveness. Finally, step nine encourages participants to reconsider how they think about an offense. Instead of viewing the offense from the perspective of the victim, participants are asked to consider the offense from the perspective of an enduring hero who has survived a terrible experience and become stronger and wiser as a result.

Key Studies of the Effectiveness of the Forgive for Good Model

Searching PsycINFO, PubMed, and Google Scholar (using the same search terms and date as above) revealed that the Forgive for Good model has been evaluated in six trials. In the original randomized trial conducted as part of the Stanford Forgiveness Project, the Forgive for Good training was tested and shown to be effective in improving forgiveness, reducing negative emotions such as hurt and anger, and improving physical vitality in Stanford University undergraduates ($N = 259$) (Luskin, 1999). A similar study in hypertensive patients showed effectiveness in reducing anger expression (a key psychosocial variable relevant to patients with heart conditions). This was another large randomized-controlled trial of the Forgive for Good method ($N = 259$) and showed that the method was effective in bringing about improvements in forgiveness and self-efficacy, with an impact that was maintained for up to four months (Tibbits et al., 2006). Uncontrolled trials have shown the usefulness of Forgive for Good with employees of a financial services corporation in terms of increases in positive emotional states, physical vitality, and health-related quality of life and decreases in stress and anger. In addition, this study also found that sales productivity increased by 24% (Toussaint et al., 2019).

Two interesting cultural adaptations of the Forgive for Good model are important to note. First, similar to Enright's Process Model, the Forgive for Good model has been used with survivors of the Northern Ireland conflict (Luskin & Bland, 2000, 2001). In two small uncontrolled studies (Ns < 20), results showed that the Forgive for Good model of teaching forgiveness was effective in improving forgiveness and optimism levels and decreasing stress and depression symptoms.

The second cultural adaptation of the Forgive for Good model is the Sierra Leone Forgiveness Project (Toussaint et al., 2009). The inception of this project was in 2007. Originally, this project involved a scientist and two assistants traveling to Sierra Leone to conduct forgiveness education work at a preparatory school in the capital city of Freetown, Sierra Leone. Sierra Leone is one of the most underdeveloped and economically challenged countries in the world, and suffered one of the bloodiest civil wars on the continent of Africa from 1991 to 2002. It ranked seventh from the bottom on the Human Development Index in 2020 and has held a consistently low ranking since 1990 (https://hdr.undp.org/en/countries/profiles/SLE). This created challenges around logistics and safety. Nonetheless, training was conducted for one week with 24 Sierra Leonean primary school teachers. Forgiveness lessons were also delivered to pre-K through middle school. Although it was not possible to evaluate the training delivered to the school children (except to gather anecdotal feedback), it was possible to evaluate the Forgive for Good method that was delivered to the school teachers. In a randomized-controlled trial with 24 teachers, Toussaint et al. (2009) found that teachers who received the forgiveness training showed improvements in forgiveness, gratitude, and happiness and decreases in negative affect, stress, and depression symptoms. Overall, the school and its approximately 150 students and teachers received the forgiveness training with much enthusiasm and support.

Given the encouraging results of the initial 2007 Sierra Leone Forgiveness Project, the same research team organized a second training held at Stanford University in 2011 to offer additional didactic work, expand resources and support, and invite more teachers and trainers. During a week-long summit, the second cohort of teachers and trainers from Sierra Leone received additional instruction on the Forgive for Good method, practiced methods of forgiveness education and stress relaxation, and built support networks for continued work in Sierra Leone. Since that time, the Sierra Leone Forgiveness Project has continued to develop in size and scope and has continued to train a growing number of individuals, communities, and ethnic groups in Sierra Leone to embrace forgiveness.

Community Forgiveness Interventions

Community interventions could be construed as a means of reaching a larger audience with balanced attention to internal as well as ecological validity (Trickett, 2009). Community interventions may give up some potency and replicability of their effect, but because they may also reach individuals who may not otherwise have the time, resources, or geographic location to access traditional interventions, they remain an important part of intervention delivery. In many instances, community interventions use an action-research model where community leaders are engaged and offer an important voice in developing the intervention and research design (Trickett, 2009).

Searching PsycINFO, PubMed, and Google Scholar (using the same search terms and dates as above), we identified four studies that have examined community-based forgiveness interventions. The first two studies (Lampton et al., 2005; Stratton et al., 2008) could be considered smaller pilot studies ($N = 100$). They included a limited assessment. A campus-wide awareness-raising campaign was conducted at each university, so all students were exposed to the campaign. Awareness-raising activities included things such as campus religious services focused on forgiveness, essay writing, school newspaper stories on forgiveness, book reviews on forgiveness, and forgiveness debates about how and when to forgive. In each study, students who also participated in traditional psychoeducational interventions (namely REACH Forgiveness psychoeducational groups) were compared to those who did not participate in these groups. In both studies, it is impossible to surmise the independent effect of the community-based intervention either against those enrolled in the REACH Forgiveness intervention or those who might not have participated in the awareness-raising because no random assignment was employed. Nonetheless, as compared to students who chose only to participate in the forgiveness campaign, each study found that the benefits of the forgiveness campaign tended to be stronger among those who were also enrolled in the REACH Forgiveness psychoeducational intervention. These studies provided preliminary, albeit weak, evidence that community-based interventions can have favorable effects on forgiveness.

The third community-based intervention study to promote forgiveness enrolled nearly 1,200 college students (about 50% of the student body), exposed students to a two-week forgiveness awareness-raising campaign, and utilized an uncontrolled, single-group, triple pre-test and single post-test design (Griffin et al., 2019). Measurement included the trait of forgivingness and ratings of relationships with friends, roommates, teachers, and parents on dimensions of forgiveness, love, and conflict. The community-based forgiveness intervention used by Griffin et al. (2019) was a multi-pronged "community forgiveness blitz" that engaged students, student life and counseling staff, and faculty. The aim of the action-research-based approach was to saturate the campus with education about forgiveness and its associated benefits for a period of two weeks. The education involved both passive and active programming. Passive programming involved things that educated the campus about forgiveness but did not require participation in a formal event at a specific place and time, such as flyers, infographics on cafeteria tabletops, social media groups, closed-captioned campus television spots, and bulletin boards. A range of active programming was also provided, including lectures, forgiveness-focused chapel services, movie nights, and inclusion of forgiveness elements into the annual ethnic arts festival, among others. Based on responses to post-campaign questionnaires, it was estimated that students were exposed to approximately 2.5 hours of community forgiveness education. This education resulted in significant improvements in trait forgiveness, as well as more feelings of love and forgiveness and less conflict with teachers, more forgiveness and less conflict with parents, and more love toward friends.

The fourth community-based forgiveness intervention study enrolled almost 2900 students at a private, nonreligious university in Colombia (Ortega Bechara et al., 2024). This study engaged students in a four-week forgiveness awareness-raising campaign and utilized an uncontrolled, single-group, pre-test post-test design. Measurement included several assessments of forgiveness, depression and anxiety symptoms, and individual flourishing. The community-based forgiveness intervention used by Ortega Bechara et al. (2024) shared some similarities (about 33%) with the approach used by Griffin et al. (2019) and was a multi-pronged "community forgiveness blitz" that engaged students in 16 forgiveness-promoting activities. The aim of the action-research-based approach was to saturate the campus with education about forgiveness and its associated benefits for a period of four weeks. The education involved knowledge-based training (mastery-based forgiveness knowledge test and REACH Forgiveness workbooks), online written-discussion entries (personal journals, online discussion site, and video club that watched and discussed forgiveness videos), forgiveness videos (movies and expert talks), and online forgiveness webinars (20 webinars were offered).

Results of the community-based forgiveness intervention showed improvements in forgiveness ($d = .36$), depression ($d = .18$) and anxiety symptoms ($d = .10$), and individual flourishing ($d = .24$). Nearly every student (94%) engaged in at least one activity during the campaign, with an average student engaging in about seven activities. Results also showed that a minimum of five activities was needed to produce meaningful changes in forgiveness.

The community forgiveness intervention was effective, and the most impactful activities required moderate amounts of time, were engaging, emphasized learning and motivation as well as aspects of application, and provided feedback about learning.

Community forgiveness interventions are new, but initial studies point to the potential of these types of approaches for providing forgiveness and health-enhancing training to large swaths of a population in a relatively short period of time. Of course, four studies are not sufficient to draw firm conclusions, but early results appear promising.

Limits to What We Know and Future Directions

There are important limits to what we know about how to help people forgive in educational, psychoeducational, and community settings. First, although there are now numerous randomized-controlled trials showing the efficacy of psychoeducational methods for educating people about forgiveness, most have been conducted with samples from Western, educated, industrialized, rich, and democratic countries (Henrich et al., 2010). Thus, evidence concerning the generalizability of these findings to diverse peoples and cultures is limited. This is also true even within just the United States. Most of the randomized-controlled trials in the United States have been conducted with White, middle-upper-class, educated college students in the Southeast or Midwest (cf. Enright's work with various clinical populations). Very little is known about how forgiveness psychoeducational methods would apply in exclusively Black, Latine, or Asian-American communities. It is also unclear how well these methods translate to impoverished segments of the population living in rural or urban areas.

A second key limitation in our understanding of methods to promote forgiveness is that most of the work has been done in the United States. This is not surprising, as the authors of the most widely used and tested approaches are academicians based in the United States. However, a disproportionate emphasis on specific populations limits our ability to understand cultural dimensions of forgiveness education, and it interferes with the ability to help others who might be hurting in different parts of the world. For instance, as we mentioned earlier, Africa is one place that has a particularly difficult past with much conflict, violence, and war. There are several countries in Africa that have experienced historical or present-day violence and war that might be especially open to or in need of learning how to forgive, but at present, there is little guidance from the research on how to help promote forgiveness in Africa. We identified only two such studies – from Sierra Leone and Ghana – in our review. Of course, forgiveness and reconciliation have been salient topics and part of national and international rhetoric for decades in Africa (for a review of almost 100 studies, see Worthington et al., 2020), perhaps most notably in South Africa (for a review, see Worthington & Cowden, 2017). However, focused approaches to educating children and adults, families and communities, and even economic and political leaders about forgiveness have been limited.

Greater emphasis on forgiveness education and dedication of resources to promote forgiveness in Africa could also be a useful stepping-stone for developing other character strengths and virtues more broadly, particularly among children and young adults. Many African countries continue to experience pervasive social-structural issues (e.g., gender inequality and poverty) that pose significant challenges to young people as they transition from childhood to adulthood (Cowden, Tucker, et al., 2020a). Emphasizing forgiveness education and promoting forgiveness in schools and local communities could offer children and adolescents valuable opportunities to learn lessons about other character strengths and virtuous acts that will be beneficial to their lives as they are confronted with context-specific problems rooted in the social-structural issues that exist. For example, forgiveness engages and can foster several other character strengths, such as self-regulation, gratitude, courage, kindness, perspective-taking, and perseverance (among others) (Enright, 2001; Luskin, 2002; Worthington, 2008, 2022). These kinds of character strengths could serve as important protective resources that contribute to positive adjustment among young people living on the African continent, including being able to persevere through the hardship of unemployment and financial insecurity, having the courage to end an abusive and exploitative romantic relationship, or choosing to avoid risky sexual practices that could have devastating consequences for one's physical health. Although historical injustices, intergroup resentment, and ongoing conflicts within parts of Africa underscore the need to prioritize forgiveness education and promotion on the continent, forgiveness could also function as a "gateway" topic that lays the groundwork for broader interventions and campaign initiatives in African schools or communities that aim to cultivate character strengths and virtue more holistically among young people.

A third limitation regards the size, scope, and durability of forgiveness education efforts. The work in the Sierra Leone Forgiveness project (Toussaint et al., 2009) began in 2007 and has continued in various different forms until the present. Over the 15 years of this project, however, it has been difficult to ensure consistency in training, recruitment, measurement, and follow-up. In many cases, there have been seasonal/climate, public health (i.e., Ebola), infrastructure, and political obstacles. These challenges often have to be met in new and innovative ways (Tribe & Tunariu, 2018). Further, consider that we are simply using the work done in Africa as one poignant example. Limitations to collective work in forgiveness education exist in all corners of the world, while the need for forgiveness appears to be growing globally.

As a final limitation, it is important to note that there are just two pilot studies (Lampton et al., 2005; Stratton et al., 2008) and two larger studies (Griffin et al., 2019; Ortega Bechara et al., 2024) of community forgiveness interventions. Key limitations to our understanding of community-level forgiveness interventions are quite evident. All four studies involved college campus communities. All studies used relatively short interventions. All studies used individual self-reported measurements of forgiveness and related psychosocial variables. Community forgiveness interventions need to move off campus and be developed and tested in the community. A community participatory-action research model is likely necessary. What works in and for a community needs to be prioritized above what traditional research design and analyses might mandate (Tribe & Tunariu, 2018; Trickett, 2009). This applies to engagement, recruitment, and, importantly, measurement. Measures of success might need to involve simple assessment of individual-level satisfaction, community-level markers of change (e.g., objective data on conflict, violence, and crime), and reports of intervention uptake by community leaders and key stakeholders in healthcare, education, and government. Most importantly, work needs to be suited to the particular demographics and lifestyles of the individuals in the community, and this is especially important as community-level interventions are being developed for minority groups and communities in the United States and abroad. For instance, the norms and mores of a US Latine community are likely to be quite different from a tribal community in the remote areas of (for example) Sierra Leone, Colombia, Afghanistan, or China.

Conclusions

Psychoeducational approaches to helping people forgive have been developed and shown to be quite effective in improving forgiveness and many different facets of well-being (e.g., mental health and social relationships). We know considerably less about promoting forgiveness on the community level. Engagement of a diverse array of community organizers, community leaders, government and economic leaders, and applied scientists will be necessary to strengthen and build more knowledge in this area. Both areas are critical for the promotion of forgiveness, as there will remain a need for individual and smaller group forgiveness education, and our communities will no doubt continue to need to foster forgiveness as many communities, societies, and nations continue to struggle with injustice, conflict, and war and their ramifications. If the 2022 war in Ukraine, the 2023 Israel-Hamas war, and numerous within-country conflicts around the globe are harbingers, continued conflict and worldwide dissension will remain in the forefront for the foreseeable future. In the wake of these world-changing events, the pursuit of justice will likely remain a high priority. However, serving the needs of those most affected, not only in terms of necessities such as safety, security, and justice, but also in terms of psychosocial adjustment and the promotion of happiness and quality of life, should also remain a top priority. Consequently, our continued investment in the development and refinement of methods to help individuals, families, communities, and entire nations forgive may be one of the most important objectives for human flourishing for many years to come.

References

Akhtar, S., & Barlow, J. (2018). Forgiveness therapy for the promotion of mental well-being: A systematic review and meta-analysis. *Trauma, Violence, & Abuse*, *19*(1), 107–122. https://doi.org/10.1177/1524838016637079

Baethge, C., Goldbeck-Wood, S., & Mertens, S. (2019). SANRA—a scale for the quality assessment of narrative review articles. *Research Integrity and Peer Review*, *4*(1), 5. https://doi.org/10.1186/s41073-019-0064-8

Baskin, T. W., & Enright, R. D. (2004). Intervention studies on forgiveness: A meta-analysis. *Journal of Counseling & Development*, *82*(1), 79–90. https://doi.org/10.1002/j.1556-6678.2004.tb00288.x

Cavalcanti, T. M., de Holanda Coelho, G. L., Rezende, A. T., Vione, K. C., & Gouveia, V. V. (2019). Decisional and emotional forgiveness scales: Psychometric validity and correlates with personality and vengeance. *Applied Research in Quality of Life*, *14*(5), 1247–1264. https://doi.org/10.1007/s11482-018-9653-9

Cook, K. V., Kurniati, N. M. T., Suwartono, C., Widyarini, N., Worthington Jr, E. L., & Cowden, R. G. (2022). Differential effects of decisional and emotional forgiveness on distress and well-being: A three-wave study of Indonesian adults. *Frontiers in Psychology*, *13*, 918045. https://doi.org/10.3389/fpsyg.2022.918045

Cowden, R. G., Tucker, L. A., & Govender, K. (2020a). Conceptual pathways to HIV risk in Eastern and Southern Africa: An integrative perspective on the development of young people in contexts of social-structural vulnerability. In K. Govender & N. K. Poku (Eds.), *Preventing HIV Among Young People in Southern and Eastern Africa: Emerging Evidence and Intervention Strategies* (pp. 31–47). Routledge.

Cowden, R. G., Worthington, E. L., Jr., Griffin, B. J., Davis, D. E., & Grubbs, J. B. (2020b). Trait tendencies to forgive, punish, and exonerate oneself: A multi-study investigation. *Journal of Research in Personality*, *86*, 103934. https://doi.org/10.1016/j.jrp.2020.103934

Cowden, R. G., Worthington, E. L., Jr., Nonterah, C. W., Cairo, A. H., Griffin, B. J., & Hook, J. N. (2019). Development of the collectivist-sensitive trait forgivingness scale. *Scandinavian journal of psychology*, *60*(2), 169–180. https://doi.org/10.1111/sjop.12519

Demiris, G., Oliver, D. P., & Washington, K. T. (2019). Chapter 3 - Defining and Analyzing the Problem. In G. Demiris, D. P. Oliver, & K. T. Washington (Eds.), *Behavioral Intervention Research in Hospice and Palliative Care* (pp. 27–39). Academic Press. https://doi.org/10.1016/B978-0-12-814449-7.00003-X

Enright, R. D. (2001). *Forgiveness is a choice: A step-by-step process for resolving anger and restoring hope*. American Psychological Association.

Enright, R. D., Knutson, J. A., Holter, A. C., Baskin, T., & Knutson, C. (2007). Waging peace through forgiveness in Belfast, Northern Ireland II: Educational programs for mental health improvement of children. *Journal of Research in Education, Fall, 17*(1), 63–78.

Enright, R. D., & North, J. (1998). *Exploring forgiveness*. University of Wisconsin Press.

Freedman, S. (2018). Forgiveness as an educational goal with at-risk adolescents. *Journal of Moral Education, 47*(4), 415–431. https://doi.org/10.1080/03057240.2017.1399869

Freedman, S. R., & Enright, R. D. (1996). Forgiveness as an intervention goal with incest survivors. *Journal of Consulting & Clinical Psychology, 64*(5), 983–992. https://doi.org/10.1037/0022-006X.64.5.983

Freedman, S. R., & Enright, R. D. (2020). A review of the empirical research using Enright's process model of interpersonal forgiveness. In E. L. Worthington, Jr. & N. G. Wade (Eds.), *Handbook of forgiveness* (2nd ed., pp. 266–276). Routledge/Taylor & Francis Group.

Griffin, B. J., Toussaint, L. L., Zoelzer, M., Worthington, E. L., Jr., Coleman, J. A., Lavelock, C. R., McElroy, A., Hook, J. N., Wade, N. G., & Sandage, S. J. (2019). Evaluating the effectiveness of a community-based forgiveness campaign. *The Journal of Positive Psychology, 14*(3), 354–361. https://doi.org/10.1080/17439760.2018.1437464

Griffin, B. J., Worthington, E. L., Jr., Davis, D. E., Hook, J. N., & Maguen, S. (2018). Development of the Self-Forgiveness Dual-Process Scale. *Journal of Counseling Psychology, 65*(6), 715–726. https://doi.org/10.1037/cou0000293

Hansen, M. J., Enright, R. D., Baskin, T. W., & Klatt, J. (2009). A palliative care intervention in forgiveness therapy for elderly terminally ill cancer patients. *Journal of Palliative Care, 25*(1), 51–60. https://doi.org/10.1177/082585970902500106

Hebl, J., & Enright, R. D. (1993). Forgiveness as a psychotherapeutic goal with elderly females. *Psychotherapy: Theory, Research, Practice, Training, 30*(4), 658–667.

Henrich, J., Heine, S. J., & Norenzayan, A. (2010). The weirdest people in the world? *Behavioral and Brain Sciences, 33*(2–3), 61–83. https://doi.org/10.1017/S0140525X0999152X

Ho, M. Y., Worthington, E. L., Jr., Cowden, R. G., Bechara, A. O., Chen, Z. J., Gunatirin, E. Y., Joynt, S., Khalanskyi, V. V., Korzhov, H., Kurniati, N. M. T., Rodriguez, N., Salnykova, A., Shtanko, L., Tymchenko, S., Voytenko, V. L., Zulkaida, A., Mathur, M. B., & VanderWeele, T. J. (2024). International REACH forgiveness intervention: A multisite randomised controlled trial. *BMJ Public Health, 2*(1), e000072. https://doi.org/10.1136/bmjph-2023-000072

Hook, J. N., Worthington, E. L., Jr., Utsey, S. O., Davis, D. E., & Burnette, J. L. (2012). Collectivistic self-construal and forgiveness. *Counseling and Values, 57*(1), 109–124. https://doi.org/10.1002/j.2161-007X.2012.00012.x

Kurniati, N. M. T., Dwiwardani, C., Worthington, E. L., Jr., Widyarini, N., Citra, A. F., & Widhiarso, W. (2020). Does forgiving in a collectivistic culture affect only decisions to forgive and not emotions? REACH Forgiveness Collectivistic (REACH-FC) in Indonesia. *International Journal of Psychology, 55*(5), 861–870. https://doi.org/10.1002/ijop.12648

Lampton, C., Oliver, G. J., Worthington, E. L., Jr., & Berry, J. W. (2005). Helping Christian college students become more forgiving: An intervention study to promote forgiveness as part of a program to shape Christian character. *Journal of Psychology and Theology, 33*(4), 278–290. https://doi.org/10.1177/009164710503300404

Lin, W.-F., Mack, D., Enright, R. D., Krahn, D., & Baskin, T. W. (2004). Effects of forgiveness therapy on anger, mood, and vulnerability to substance use among inpatient substance-dependent clients. *Journal of Consulting and Clinical Psychology, 72*(6), 1114–1121. https://doi.org/10.1037/0022-006X.72.6.1114

Luskin, F. (2002). *Forgive for Good: A Proven Prescription for Health and Happiness*. HarperCollins.

Luskin, F. (2007). *Forgive For Love: The Missing Ingredient For A Healthy And Lasting Relationship*. HarperOne/HarperCollins.

Luskin, F., & Bland, B. (2000). Stanford-Northern Ireland hope 1 project. learningtoforgive.com

Luskin, F., & Bland, B. (2001). Stanford-Northern Ireland hope 2 project. learningtoforgive.com

Luskin, F. M. (1999). The effect of forgiveness training on psychosocial factors in college-age adults. *Dissertation Abstracts International Section A: Humanities & Social Sciences, 60*(4), 1026.

McCullough, M. (2008). *Beyond revenge: The evolution of the forgiveness instinct.* John Wiley & Sons.

McCullough, M. E., Rachal, K. C., Sandage, S. J., Worthington, E. L., Jr., Brown, S. W., & Hight, T. L. (1998). Interpersonal forgiving in close relationships: II. Theoretical elaboration and measurement. *Journal of Personality and Social Psychology, 75*(6), 1586–1603. https://doi.org/10.1037/0022-3514.75.6.1586

Murphy, J. G. (2003). Self forgiveness. In *Getting even: Forgiveness and its limits.* Oxford University Press.

Nation, J. A., Wertheim, E. H., & Worthington, E. L., Jr. (2018). Evaluation of an online self-help version of the *REACH forgiveness* program: Outcomes and predictors of persistence in a community sample. *Journal of Clinical Psychology, 74*(6), 819–838. https://doi.org/10.1002/jclp.22557

Ortega Bechara, A., Chen, Z. J., Cowden, R. G., Worthington, E. L., Jr., Toussaint, L., Rodriguez, N., Guzman Murillo, H., Ho, M. Y., Mathur, M. B., & VanderWeele, T. J. (2024). Do forgiveness campaign activities improve forgiveness, mental health, and flourishing? *International Journal of Public Health, 69*, 1605341. https://doi.org/10.3389/ijph.2024.1605341

Osei-Tutu, A., Osafo, J., Anum, A., Appiah-Danquah, R., Worthington, E. L., Jr., Chen, Z. J., Cowden, R. G., & Nonterah, C. W. (2020). Is cultural adaptation needed beyond using Christian-accommodated REACH Forgiveness psychoeducational group intervention in Ghana? An efficacy study comparing a Christian-accommodated version against a version accommodated by Christian and cultural adaptations. *Spirituality in Clinical Practice, 7*(2), 73–88. https://doi.org/10.1037/scp0000215

Park, J.-H., Enright, R. D., Essex, M. J., Zahn-Waxler, C., & Klatt, J. S. (2013). Forgiveness intervention for female South Korean adolescent aggressive victims. *Journal of Applied Developmental Psychology, 34*(6), 268–276. https://doi.org/10.1016/j.appdev.2013.06.001

Rahman, A., Iftikhar, R., Kim, J. J., & Enright, R. D. (2018). Pilot study: Evaluating the effectiveness of forgiveness therapy with abused early adolescent females in Pakistan. *Spirituality in Clinical Practice, 5*(2), 75–87. https://doi.org/10.1037/scp0000160

Reed, G. L., & Enright, R. D. (2006). The effects of forgiveness therapy on depression, anxiety, and posttraumatic stress for women after spousal emotional abuse. *Journal of Consulting and Clinical Psychology, 74*(5), 920–929. https://doi.org/10.1037/0022-006X.74.5.920

Ripley, J. S., Leon, C., Worthington, E. L., Jr., Berry, J. W., Davis, E. B., Smith, A., Atkinson, A., & Sierra, T. (2014). Efficacy of religion-accommodative strategic hope-focused theory applied to couples therapy. *Couple and Family Psychology: Research and Practice, 3*(2), 83–98. https://doi.org/10.1037/cfp0000019

Sandage, S. J., Long, B., Moen, R., Jankowski, P. J., Worthington, E. L., Jr., Wade, N. G., & Rye, M. S. (2015). Forgiveness in the treatment of borderline personality disorder: A quasi-experimental study. *Journal of Clinical Psychology, 71*(7), 625–640. https://doi.org/10.1002/jclp.22185

Stratton, S. P., Dean, J. B., Nonneman, A. J., Bode, R. A., & Worthington, E. L., Jr. (2008). Forgiveness interventions as spiritual development strategies: Comparing forgiveness workshop training, expressive writing about forgiveness, and retested controls. *Journal of Psychology and Christianity, 27*(4), 347–357.

Strelan, P. (2020). The stress-and-coping model of forgiveness: Theory, research, and the potential of dyadic coping. In E. L. Worthington, Jr. & N. G. Wade (Eds.), *Handbook of forgiveness* (2 ed., pp. 63–73). Routledge/Taylor & Francis Group.

Sukhera, J. (2022). Narrative Reviews: Flexible, Rigorous, and Practical. *Journal of Graduate Medical Education, 14*(4), 414–417. https://doi.org/10.4300/jgme-d-22-00480.1

Taysi, E., & Vural, D. (2016). Forgiveness education for fourth grade students in Turkey. *Child Indicators Research, 9*(4), 1095–1115. https://doi.org/10.1007/s12187-015-9364-9

Tibbits, D., Ellis, G., Piramelli, C., Luskin, F., & Lukman, R. (2006). Hypertension reduction through forgiveness training. *The Journal of Pastoral Care & Counseling, 60*(1–2), 27–34. https://doi.org/10.1177/154230500606000104

Toussaint, L., Luskin, F., Aberman, R., & DeLorenzo, A. (2019). Is forgiveness one of the secrets to success? Considering the costs of workplace disharmony and the benefits of teaching employees to forgive. *American Journal of Health Promotion, 33*(7), 1090–1093. https://doi.org/10.1177/0890117119866957e

Toussaint, L., Peddle, N., Cheadle, A., Sellu, A., & Luskin, F. (2009). Striving for peace through forgiveness in Sierra Leone: Effectiveness of a psycho-educational forgiveness intervention. In A. Kalayjian & D. Eugene (Eds.), *Mass trauma and emotional healing around the world: Rituals and practices for resilience* (Vol. 2, pp. 251–267). Greenwood Publishing Group.

Toussaint, L., & Webb, J. R. (2005). Theoretical and empirical connections between forgiveness and mental health and well-being. In E. L. Worthington, Jr. (Ed.), *Handbook of forgiveness* (pp. 349–362). Routledge.

Toussaint, L., Worthington, E. L., Jr., Cheadle, A., Marigoudar, S., Kamble, S., & Büssing, A. (2020b). Efficacy of the REACH Forgiveness intervention in Indian college students. *Frontiers in Psychology*, *11*, 671. https://doi.org/10.3389/fpsyg.2020.00671

Toussaint, L. L., Griffin, B. J., Worthington, E. L., Jr., Zoelzer, M., & Luskin, F. (2020a). Promoting forgiveness at a Christian college: A comparison of the REACH Forgiveness and Forgive for Good methods. *Journal of Psychology and Theology*, *48*(2), 154–165. https://doi.org/10.1177/0091647120911109

Toussaint, L. L., Worthington, E. L., Jr., & Williams, D. R. (2015). *Forgiveness and health: Scientific evidence and theories relating forgiveness to better health*. Springer Science + Business Media. https://doi.org/10.1007/978-94-017-9993-5

Tribe, R., & Tunariu, A. (2018). Psychological interventions. In D. Bhugra & K. Buhi (Eds.), *Textbook of cultural psychiatry* (pp. 458–471). Cambridge University Press.

Trickett, E. (2009). Community psychology: Individuals and interventions in community context. *Annual Review of Psychology*, *60*, 395–419. https://doi.org/10.1146/annurev.psych.60.110707.163517

Wade, N. G., Hoyt, W. T., Kidwell, J. E., & Worthington, E. L. (2014). Efficacy of psychotherapeutic interventions to promote forgiveness: a meta-analysis. *Journal of consulting and clinical psychology*, *82*(1), 154–170. https://doi.org/10.1037/a0035268

Waltman, M. A., Russell, D. C., Coyle, C. T., Enright, R. D., Holter, A. C., & Swoboda, C. M. (2009). The effects of a forgiveness intervention on patients with coronary artery disease. *Psychology & Health*, *24*(1), 11–27. https://doi.org/10.1080/08870440801975127

Webb, J. R. (2021). *Understanding forgiveness and addiction: Theory, research, and clinical application*. Routledge.

Webb, J. R., Bumgarner, D. J., Conway-Williams, E., Dangel, T., & Hall, B. B. (2017). A consensus definition of self-forgiveness: Implications for assessment and treatment. *Spirituality in Clinical Practice*, *4*(3), 216–227. https://doi.org/10.1037/scp0000138

Wenzel, M., Woodyatt, L., & Hedrick, K. (2012). No genuine self-forgiveness without accepting responsibility: Value reaffirmation as a key to maintaining positive self-regard. *European Journal of Social Psychology*, *42*(5), 617–627. https://doi.org/10.1002/ejsp.1873

Woodyatt, L., Worthington, E. L., Jr., Wenzel, M., & Griffin, B. J. (Eds.). (2017). *Handbook of the psychology of self-forgiveness*. Springer Nature.

Worthington, E. L., Jr. (2008). *Steps to REACH forgiveness and to reconcile*. Pearson.

Worthington, E. L., Jr. (2013). *Moving forward: Six steps to forgiving yourself and breaking free from the past*. WaterBrook.

Worthington, E. L., Jr. (2020a). Understanding forgiveness of other people: Definitions, theories, and processes. In E. L. Worthington, Jr. & N. G. Wade (Eds.), *Handbook of forgiveness* (2nd ed., pp. 11–21). Routledge/Taylor & Francis Group.

Worthington, E. L., Jr. (2020b). An update of the REACH Forgiveness model: Psychoeducation in groups, do-it-yourself formats, couple enrichment, religious congregations, and as an adjunct to psychotherapy. In E. L. Worthington, Jr. & N. G. Wade (Eds.), *Handbook of forgiveness* (2nd ed., pp. 277–287). Routledge/Taylor & Francis Group.

Worthington, E. L., Jr. (2022). Forgiveness. In J. R. Peteet (Ed.), *The virtues in psychiatric practice* (pp. 87–108). Oxford University Press.

Worthington, E. L., Jr., Berry, J. W., Hook, J. N., Davis, D. E., Scherer, M., Griffin, B. J., Wade, N. G., Yarhouse, M., Ripley, J. S., Miller, A. J., Sharp, C. B., Canter, D. E., & Campana, K. L. (2015). Forgiveness-reconciliation and communication-conflict-resolution interventions versus retested controls in early married couples. *Journal of Counseling Psychology*, *62*(1), 14–27. https://doi.org/10.1037/cou0000045

Worthington, E. L., Jr., Berry, J. W., & Parrott, L., III. (2001). Unforgiveness, forgiveness, religion, and health. In T. G. S. Plante, Allen C. (Ed.), *Faith and health: Psychological perspectives*. (pp. 107–138). Guilford Press.

Worthington, E. L., Jr., & Cowden, R. G. (2017). The psychology of forgiveness and its importance in South Africa. *South African Journal of Psychology*, *47*(3), 292–304. https://doi.org/10.1177/0081246316685074

Worthington, E. L., Jr., Hunter, J. L., Sharp, C. B., Hook, J. N., Van Tongeren, D. R., Davis, D. E., Miller, A. J., Gingrich, F. C., Sandage, S. J., Lao, E., Bubod, L., & Monforte-Milton, M. (2010). A psychoeducational intervention to promote forgiveness in Christians in the Philippines. *Journal of Mental Health Counseling*, *32*(1), 75–93. https://doi.org/10.17744/mehc.32.1.t3677072811lj864

Worthington, E. L., Jr.,, Nonterah, C. W., Utsey, S. O., Griffin, B. J., Carneal, C. C., Osei-Tutu, A., Cowden, R. G., Cairo, A. H., Pillay, B. J., Kulick, K., & Germer, L. S. (2020). Forgiveness research in Africa: The present status and future prospects. In E. L. Worthington, Jr. & N. G. Wade (Eds.), *Handbook of forgiveness* (2 ed., pp. 223–233). Routledge/Taylor & Francis Group.

Worthington, E. L., Jr., & Sandage, S. J. (2016). *Forgiveness and spirituality in psychotherapy: A relational approach*. American Psychological Association.

Worthington, E. L., Jr., & Wade, N. G. (2020). *Handbook of forgiveness*. Routledge/Taylor & Francis Group.

Part VII

Conclusion

Chapter 44

Moving the Psychological Science of Spirituality, Health, and Well-Being Forward

*Jon R. Webb**

At the beginning of the introductory chapter to this edited volume, I shared two statements made by Albert Einstein. The first, "I want to know [God's] thoughts, the rest are details" (Salaman, 1955, p. 371), caught my attention nearly 25 years ago when I met my friend and colleague, Loren Toussaint. We were both postdoctoral fellows at the University of Michigan – he at the Institute for Social Research under the mentorship of David R. Williams, PhD, and I in the Department of Physical Medicine and Rehabilitation under the mentorship of Denise G. Tate, PhD.[1] Loren was near the end of his fellowship, and I was near the beginning of mine. Although we were both interested in forgiveness and health, we only discovered it when he was presenting on forgiveness at a seminar on campus that I was attending. In the days after that chance meeting, I went over to the other side of campus and visited Loren in his office to begin what has become a fruitful and rewarding professional and personal relationship. One of the first things I noticed was a poster on his wall with this quote from Einstein. Needless to say, the sentiment expressed by Albert Einstein strongly resonated with me then and continues to do so to this day. I am tempted to use it as my "elevator speech," as it perfectly sums up – in 10 words – not only my research interests, but also my personal interests as well.

Another experience just came to mind. Shortly after starting my first academic position at East Tennessee State University about 20 years ago (i.e., fall semester, 2005), I had a discussion with one of my colleagues, who suggested that another colleague in our department and I should publish on how we have been able to apply the scientific method to the psychological study of religious topics. In the sense that – at least in this person's view – it is not an easy thing to do, and it might be instructive for others with similar interests, but who are unsure of how to go about it. The way I interpreted this discussion was not that the person was being critical of my work, but that they were impressed that the other colleague and I (separately) were able to bridge the incompatibility gap between science and religion. Which brings me to the second statement of Albert Einstein (1954) that I shared in the introductory chapter; that is, "science without religion is lame, religion without science is blind" (p. 49). In 1941, Einstein viewed science and religion as compatible; in the mid-2000s, my former colleague viewed science and religion, presumably, as largely incompatible. These opinions were expressed by two highly intelligent and thoughtful people. Indeed, both of these opinions have been commonly held throughout history (likely since day one, so to speak), are commonly held today, and, arguably, will be commonly held for the foreseeable future, and beyond.

What is my point? It seems likely that the debate regarding the compatibility of science and religion is fundamentally tied to the question of the existence of a transcendent reality, if not

* Corresponding Author: jon.r.webb@ttu.edu.

DOI: 10.4324/9781003440048-51

deity. Although this question is valid and sensibly of ontological,[2] teleological,[3] and existential[4] interest (cf. Existangst; Webb, 2021; Webb et al., 2015) to many humans (perhaps nearly all; see Chapter 5 of this volume), it is not an empirical question (i.e., it is not conducive to the scientific method) and is, therefore, unknowable.[5] As such, the debate will continue. Some argue that *skepticism* is healthy and constructive. I would argue that *healthy* skepticism is constructive. This brings me to one of my two favorite, otherwise secular quotes.[6] The 35th President of the United States, John F. Kennedy (1963), during remarks made to the Irish Parliament, stated that "The problems of the world cannot possibly be solved by skeptics or cynics whose horizons are limited by the obvious realities" (p. 1). Which brings us full circle to the World Health Organization's definition of health as "a state of complete physical, mental and social well-being and not merely the absence of disease or infirmity" (WHO, 2025, p. 1). Indeed, the JFK quote is consistent with the WHO's definition of health. That is, although symptoms and diagnoses are incredibly important – indeed, critical – so too is the importance of looking beyond the otherwise obvious and acknowledging, examining, and adjusting for both the largely salubrious and also deleterious effects of spirituality on health and well-being.

The remainder of this concluding chapter will review important issues and themes distilled from this volume regarding spirituality, including (a) its definition and (b) leveraging its wide-ranging evidence base in association with health and well-being toward active dissemination and implementation of its largely salubrious effects – whether in the context of prevention or intervention. Importantly, themes apparent with regard to limitations and needed future directions will also be discussed, as is needed in order to truly move forward the science of spirituality, health, and well-being.

Defining and Approaching Spirituality

As discussed in some detail in Chapter 3 of this volume and briefly touched upon in Chapters 1 and 7, there are many definitions of religion (cf. religiousness) and spirituality. Indeed, there are likely nearly as many definitions as persons thinking on the matter, whether from a scientific perspective or a lay perspective. As mentioned immediately above, consistent with the difficulties associated with coming to an agreement regarding the compatibility of science and religion, due to its unknowable and therefore subjective nature, so too is arriving at a consensus definition of religion/spirituality difficult and likely a perpetual struggle/endeavor.

One of my original plans for this volume with respect to defining spirituality was to have the author(s) of each chapter briefly (1) provide their working definition of spirituality and (2) contrast their working definition with the RiTE Model's definition of spirituality (see below). My plan in this regard was to distill a consensus-oriented definition that could inform and thus move the psychological science of religion and spirituality forward, not only in the particular context of health and well-being, but more broadly as well. However, as one reads through each chapter, there is still meaningful variation, from no definition and contrast (whether inadvertent or intentional) to brief discussions (as requested) to detailed discussions (including from scientific perspectives and personal perspectives; not necessarily discouraged).

Why is this the case? Consistent with the *subjective* nature of (1) the debate regarding the compatibility of science and religion and (2) the definition of religion/spirituality, these topics are very much *personal* issues as well, whether at the individual, communal, cultural, or societal levels. That is, given their subjective and empirically unknowable nature, and with all of their ontological, teleological, and existential implications, these issues and the conclusions individuals and/or groups draw become very personal (and passion-filled). And, just as clinicians and healthcare providers are not to impose their beliefs (and values) on their clients and patients for *or* against religion/spirituality (see Chapter 20; see also, Toussaint et al., 2012), so too is it largely counterproductive for the practitioners of science (i.e., scientists) to impose definitions of religion/spirituality on any given scientific field or the consumers thereof (i.e., the general public).

Does this mean that there is no need for or value to bringing consensus or objectivity to our understanding of the definition of religion/spirituality, or what is meant by these constructs, and the implications and outcomes thereof? In my view, only through attempting to understand the definition and nature of religion/spirituality will we be able to better disseminate and implement their largely salubrious effects on health and well-being, both at the individual[7] and public levels and whether in terms of prevention or intervention. How do we approach understanding the subjective and personal nature of religion/spirituality? Do we focus on the nomothetic and ignore the idiographic? Do we focus on the idiographic and ignore the nomothetic? The question of where our focus should be is not unlike the question of whether scientists should focus on avoiding Type I error (i.e., in lay terms, determining a conclusion is accurate, when it is inaccurate) versus avoiding Type II error (i.e., in lay terms, determining a conclusion is inaccurate, when it is accurate (see American Psychological Association, 2015, p. 1115). As an example, is it better to make the mistake of concluding that God exists, when in reality God does not exist (Type I error)? Or, is it better to make the mistake of concluding that God does not exist, when in reality God does exist (Type II error)? Whether in the context of nomothetic/idiographic or Type I/Type II error, perhaps approaching the issue as one of *versus* rather than *and* is problematic. Indeed, *versus* implies that it can only be one or the other; whereas, *and* implies that it can be both.[8] Or, in the case of something that is empirically unknowable (e.g., the existence of deity), acknowledging a false dichotomy.[9] In the context of religion/spirituality, we can increase our understanding of *both* nomothetic *and* idiographic manifestations of religion/spirituality. This allows for recognizing similarities and acknowledging the unifying implications thereof. Of equal importance, it allows for honoring the singular existence and relevance of each variant of religion/spirituality. In sum, understanding both the nomothetic and the idiographic allows for both diversity and inclusivity.

How do we go about this? Indeed, as also discussed in Chapter 1, how do we refine – without constricting – our definition and conceptualization of spirituality? In my view, we can "acknowledge and provide a sufficiently distinct, yet broad and overlapping categorization of the myriad possibilities of the human capacity and drive for seeking and experiencing the transcendent aspect of what it means to be human" (Chapter 1, p. 15, this volume). In this regard, Pargament (2013) has provided a seminal foundation on which to build our understanding of the non-reductionistic nature of spirituality, such that it "reflects a distinctive, in some ways irreducible, human motivation, a yearning [cf. search] for the sacred" (p. 257). Likewise, Piedmont (Chapter 5 of this volume) makes a compelling, data-driven case for the presence of a sixth personality trait, termed *the Numinous*. Akin to the so-called Big 5 personality traits of openness, conscientiousness, extraversion, agreeableness, and neuroticism, or emotional (in)stability (see Allik et al., 2013; McCrae & Costa, 2013), this sixth trait is observed across the globe; that is, the Numinous trait is not restricted by culture or geography, nor by theistic or non-theistic beliefs or value systems. Consistent with Piedmont's work, and derived in part from Pargament's work, the RiTE Model defines *Spirituality* as "the salient, searching pursuit of the transcendently sacred ritualistic, theistic, and/or existential aspects of the human condition" (Webb et al., 2014, p. 974; see Figure 44.1). Of note, the RiTE Model and definition of spirituality allows us to move away from the notion of religion *versus* spirituality and toward the notion of religion *and* spirituality (see above). Moreover, it allows us to discuss the matter in terms of *Spirituality* as the whole construct; that is, incorporating its ritualistic (structured), theistic (non-structured), and existential (meaning and purpose) transcendent-level dimensions or facets, whether theistic or non-theistic in nature (i.e., the otherwise balanced nature of healthy or constructive spirituality). And, not artificially trichotomizing the three inter-related subsets of the whole. One of the very practical implications of this conceptualization is that, rather than using the potentially confusing term *religion/spirituality* to otherwise *emphasize* their meaningful difference, we can use the redefined term *spirituality* to *reflect* their meaningful similarity. Also, recognizing the overarching quality of the larger construct of spirituality with its attendant sub-constructs of ritualistic, theistic, and existential spirituality allows for honoring both diversity and inclusivity as important

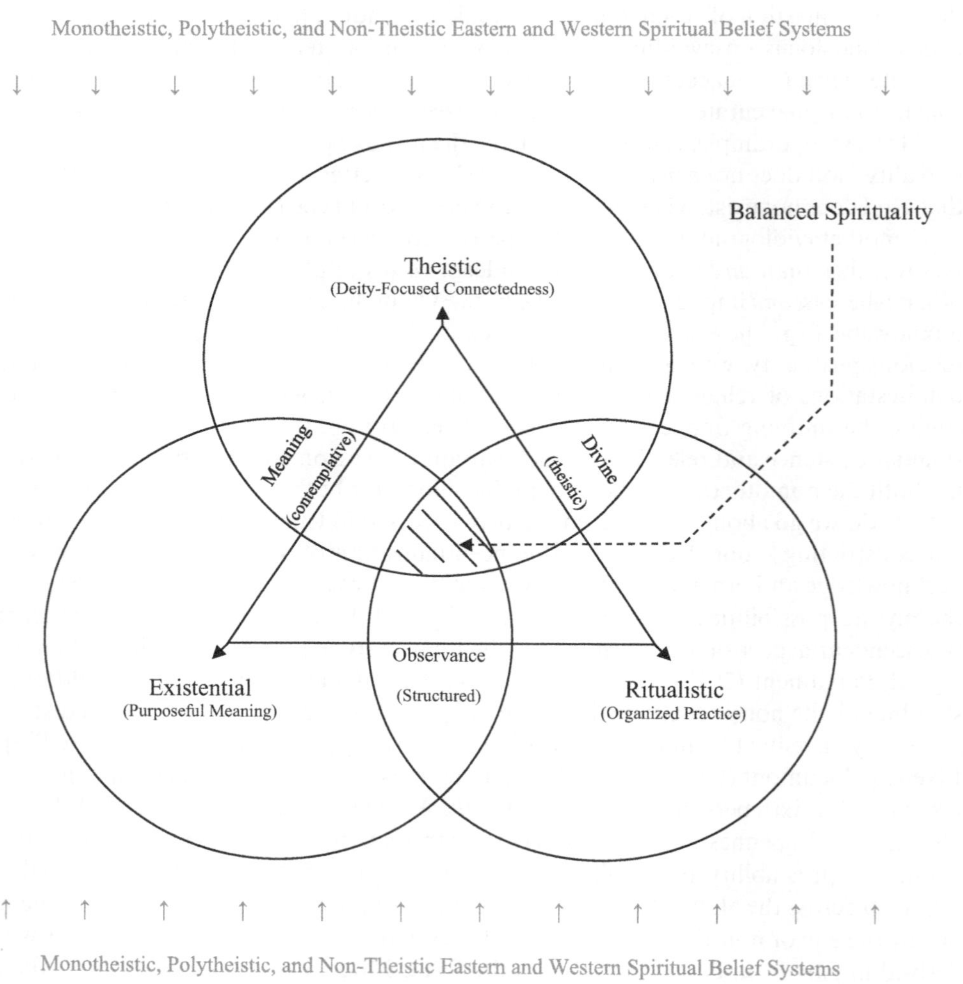

Figure 44.1 The RiTE Model of Spirituality. Adapted from Webb (2021). See also Webb et al. (2014) and Webb (2007/2003).

values and organizing principles. See Chapter 1 for more discussion regarding the RiTE Model of Spirituality.

In sum, although there are meaningful differences (e.g., conception of the self), there are meaningful similarities comprising a "coherent resemblance" (Peterson & Seligman, 2004, p. 35) across the major religious/spiritual belief systems of the world (see Chapter 7), such that it is fair to conclude that there is a *transcendent thread* serving to unify humanity (see Webb, 2021; i.e., pp. 60–61, 66). Indeed, to tie together all human beings both in spiritual terms as well as in practical terms. Importantly, in the specific – but not only – context of health and well-being, understanding the nature and function of spirituality stands to benefit humanity as a whole.

Spirituality, Health, and Well-Being

This volume provides several lines of evidence to justify and advocate for the active, explicit, and deliberate incorporation of spirituality into the provision of healthcare and the promotion of well-being at all levels, whether individual-level healthcare,[7] public health initiatives, prevention, or intervention. First, the ubiquitous presence and valuation of spirituality in the world (see Chapter 1). Second, spirituality as a manifestation of culture and diversity (Chapter 2). Third, the reality of the Numinous as a personality trait, not restricted by Eastern versus Western culture or geographic locale (Chapter 5), nor secular worldviews (Chapter 6). Fourth, the parallels between the major spiritual belief systems of the world (i.e., Judaism, Christianity, Islam, Hinduism, and Buddhism) and positive psychology (Chapter 7). Fifth, the neurological correlates of spirituality (Chapter 8). And, perhaps most importantly, the common, though varied, empirical association of spirituality with health and well-being as reflected in Chapters 10 through 43 (whether based on many aspects of spirituality as predictors or many aspects of health and well-being as outcomes), and the comprehensive modeling described in Chapter 9, explaining the mechanisms of the association of spirituality with health and well-being derived from theory and increasingly supported by said empirical evidence. Indeed, this volume, providing an expanded perspective regarding (1) specific principles and practices of spirituality and (2) health and well-being more broadly construed (i.e., the physical, mental, and social aspects thereof), *together* with previous compendiums largely focused on basic religiousness (i.e., activity and commitment) and medical diagnosis (see Koenig et al., 2024; Rosmarin & Koenig, 2020),[10] allows us to move forward. That is, beyond the self-imposed limitations of the obvious realities arising from the otherwise *excessive* skepticism and cynicism that can (and likely often does) result from the largely unnecessary, too-often contentious debate regarding the (in)compatibility of science and religion.

Given the reality of the largely salubrious association of spirituality with health and well-being, though continual examination, elucidation, and clarification are needed and necessary (including the use of more sophisticated methods; see below), intentional, deliberate, and explicit dissemination and implementation of such principles and practices are warranted in practical terms, and called for in ethical terms. Indeed, in order to *follow through* with the internationally affirmed definition, value, and approach to comprehensive and inclusive healthcare, as enshrined in the preamble and first two principles of the World Health Organization's Constitution. That is,

> THE STATES Parties to this Constitution declare, in conformity with the Charter of the United Nations, that the following principles are basic to the happiness, harmonious relations and security of all peoples: [1] Health is a state of complete physical, mental and

> social well-being and not merely the absence of disease or infirmity. [2] The enjoyment of the highest attainable standard of health is one of the fundamental rights of every human being without distinction of race, religion, political belief, economic or social condition.[11]
>
> (WHO, 2025, p. 1)

Related to this, public and private funding entities, policymakers, and legislative bodies are called upon – indeed, it is imperative – to continually, consistently, and comprehensively fund not only focused, but also broad-scoped basic-, applied-, clinical-, individual-, and public-level health and well-being initiatives grounded in the scientific study of spirituality as related to prevention, intervention, postvention (broadly construed; see Ramamurthy et al., 2025), and aftercare.

Limitations and Future Directions

As always, there are limitations to the data-driven, quantitative, and qualitative empirical evidence regarding the association of spirituality with health and well-being described in this volume. This is the nature of empiricism and the scientific method. Indeed, this is why scientific theories and explanations of mechanisms evolve. Science, by definition, is and must always be open to additional, sometimes revolutionary, evidence. Theory and/or previous evidence inform testable hypotheses, the results of which modify understanding, which involves adjusting the theory from which arise improved testable hypotheses, and so on. Thereby, allowing for continual refinement of knowledge and its efficient and effective application to the betterment of the human condition, which sometimes leads to the abandonment of particular ideas and practices due to a lack of empirical support and/or contradictory evidence.[12] Without this process, the promotion and realization of health and well-being (or any advancement in the human condition) is stagnant at best and extinction-enabling at worst.

What are the limitations of the psychological science of spirituality, health, and well-being, which, by definition, are the future directions in need of attention? Of note, not only by addressing its known limitations does a field move forward, but the process of addressing them (cf. empiricism and the scientific method) itself will also help us understand better the limitations to our knowledge that we are not currently aware of.

The limitations most frequently encountered in the empirical examination of spirituality with health and well-being are those typically – unfortunately – associated with psychological science. These include the too-frequent use of cross-sectional data, lack of diversity, self-selection bias, and researcher bias (also, see each chapter for more topic-specific limitations and recommendations). As cross-sectional data is information gathered at one point in time and limited to descriptive and correlational analyses, though critically important in its own right (see Cronbach, 1957), it is impossible to examine associations over time, thereby precluding definitive statements of causality. Moreover, with particular spiritual topics, it can be difficult to draw causal conclusions even with more sophisticated research designs and statistical methods enabled by the use of, for example, longitudinal and/or intervention-based data. For example, consider prayer. Though much evidence suggests a salubrious effect is likely, effect sizes are often small and derived from large samples and third variables are difficult to rule out, as is causality to rule in (see Spilka & Ladd, 2013). Likewise, (quasi)experimental designs may not be possible. Manipulation based on real or deceptive experiences may be otherwise unethical at best and traumatic at worst. As another example, consider faith-oriented healing. Assigning otherwise suffering, ill, diagnosed, or disabled persons into separate groups based on receiving standard healthcare compared to relying on one's belief in a transcendent enabling power for healing can have negative consequences ranging from inconvenience to death, with an attendant potential for traumatic experiences for the participants and their loved ones alike.

A variant of the nomothetic/idiographic issue (see above) is also present in the context of the diversity of participant samples used in research (which are intended to represent the larger population they are drawn from). One topic I often try to help students understand better is the value and necessity of representative samples in the context of any research. An example I typically use is polling conducted during election seasons. The question being, how does a typical sample size being reported of about 1000 participants accurately reflect the country's (1) views of a politician or political issue or (2) likely voting behavior? I then discuss representative sampling. As a way to solidify students' understanding of this concept, I ask if the polling was conducted in Lubbock, Texas (the location of Texas Tech University, where I serve as faculty in the Department of Community, Family, and Addiction Sciences), would it likely reflect the views of the United States as a whole? Most students seem to readily understand that Lubbock (or any other given locale) likely does not reflect the larger whole. And, thus, to understand the larger whole, whatever it may be, meaningful subsets of the whole need to be included. The relevance of the nomothetic/idiographic issue here is that, in some respects, all humans are the same, and in others, they are not. Therefore, we cannot assume sameness and must also account for differentness in understanding the whole. Similarly, there is a critical necessity in gathering diverse perspectives if seeking to understand spirituality as a whole construct in its association with health and well-being.

In short, much of the research examining relationships among spirituality, health, and well-being is in the context of White, Western, and Christian samples. Said another way, much of our understanding of the association of spirituality with health and well-being comes from the United States and Western Europe, and does not include sufficient data (whether quantitative or qualitative) drawn from (1) (a) the other major world spiritual belief systems (i.e., Judaism, Islam, Hinduism, and Buddhism), (b) minority spiritual belief systems (e.g., Wicca), (c) the so-called "nones" and "dones" - those that no longer affiliate or believe (for various reasons), (d) the "nevers" – those that decline to consider spiritual topics, or (e) secular spirituality (not necessarily "nones", "dones", or "nevers"), (2) ethnic and racial minorities, (3) persons from or living in other parts of the world (especially with respect to Eastern and/or collectivist cultures), and/or (4) gender and sexual minorities. In short, there are many differences between groups to consider, while also remembering that there are many differences within groups, and these differences may be profound (e.g., conceptualization of the self[13]) or nuanced.[14]

Lastly, with regard to outlining *broad* issues related to limitations and future directions, there are concerns related to self-selection bias and researcher bias. Regarding self-selection bias, although a potential problem for any research (i.e., participants volunteering to participate in a project that they are interested in), it seems likely that it could be more problematic for research conducted in the context of spirituality. Given the personal nature of spirituality (see above), it seems likely that prospective participants are less likely to have neutral or otherwise dispassionate views about spirituality, which may influence their pursuit of such research, for or against. Whereas, self-selection bias may play less of a role in research regarding sensation and perception (e.g., olfactory and gustatory research), behavior related to driving a vehicle,[15] or decision-making, to name a few examples. In this regard, though it is a simplified illustration, when discussing with students the notion of self-selection bias in the context of research focused on spirituality, I emphasize that we are not simply interested in conducting the research among believers. Indeed, belief is not a prerequisite for participating in a study. We need believers, former believers, disbelievers, and non-believers alike so as to be able to more accurately assess the data. Indeed, to make better decisions about whether or not our hypotheses are supported.

Researcher bias is another fundamental limitation to the psychological science of spirituality, health, and well-being. Researcher bias limits findings based on a constricted perspective on both conceptualizing and interpreting research (see Chapter 4). That is, just as self-selection bias influences whether a prospective participant is interested in and makes a choice to voluntarily participate (or not), so too does researcher bias influence how to approach research and how to interpret findings. For example, the measures used are not only chosen, but were developed with a particular perspective and set of assumptions. Likewise, the data drawn from said research is analyzed with the same worldview. Granted, the philosophy of science dictates objectivity. Yet, scientists (i.e., the practitioners of science) are fallible human beings, and susceptible to personal perspectives and values. There has been much debate regarding whether psychological science is value-free or value-laden (e.g., Bergin, 1980a; Bergin, 1980b; Ellis, 1980). Which, arguably, has led to the common realization that psychological scientists have personal biases and must strive to recognize, acknowledge, and manage their impact on our work. One way to go about this is to engage in community-based participatory research (Wallerstein et al., 2018). Another way to approach this, particularly in the context of clinical work, is to avoid the Procrustean approach to counseling and psychotherapy (Hoffman, 1992).

The Bottom Line

As outlined in Chapter 1, the valued presence of spiritual beliefs and practices in the world is ubiquitous (e.g., belief in God or a higher power of some sort, and the importance of religion; see also associated Tables 1.1 through 1.8 and Figures 1.1 through 1.4). Related to this, the search for transcendent meaning and purpose is inherent to the human condition (Chapter 5), such that spirituality is a manifestation of culture and, therefore, diversity (Chapter 2). Moreover, the major spiritual belief systems of the world (i.e., Judaism, Christianity, Islam, Hinduism, and Buddhism) share many fundamental principles and practices, though important differences are present as well, some profound (e.g., conceptualization of the self) and some nuanced (see Chapter 7). This, together with much supportive empirical evidence (see Chapters 10 through 43), notwithstanding important limitations to address moving forward, suggests that the association of spirituality with health and well-being is not only robust (and, perhaps, causal; see Chapters 3 and 21), but also important to incorporate into the ethical provision of comprehensive healthcare. Indeed, "the pathway from spirituality to [health and well-being] is likely complex, yet comprised of much and varied opportunity for success" (Webb, in press, p. 4).

Notes

1 While at the University of Michigan Medical School (UM), I subsequently completed another postdoctoral fellowship in the Department of Psychiatry, Substance Abuse Section, Addiction Research Center, under the mentorship and training of Kirk J. Brower, M.D., Elizabeth A. R. Robinson, Ph.D., and Robert A. Zucker, Ph.D. Each of my mentors – at UM and elsewhere – have played an important role in my professional development and career. For which, I am truly grateful.

2 Merriam-Webster (online) defines *ontology* as: "1. a branch of metaphysics concerned with the nature and relations of being. 2. a particular theory about the nature of being or the kinds of things that have existence" (see https://www.merriam-webster.com/dictionary/ontology).

3 Merriam-Webster (online) defines *teleology* as: "2. the fact or character attributed to nature or natural processes of being directed toward an end or shaped by a purpose" (see https://www.merriam-webster.com/dictionary/teleology).

4 Merriam-Webster (online) defines *existentialism* as: "a chiefly 20th century philosophical movement embracing diverse doctrines but centering on analysis of individual existence in an unfathomable universe and the plight of the individual who must assume ultimate responsibility for acts of free will without any certain knowledge of what is right or wrong or good or bad" (see https://www.merriam-webster.com/dictionary/existentialism).

5 In Chapter 1 of this volume, I included two endnotes related to the question of the existence of deity, the scientific method, and empiricism. They are reproduced here as they are once again relevant.

[Chapter 1, Endnote 7: Related questions include: Does empirical evidence of an association between religiousness/spirituality and health and well-being provide support for the veracity claims of any given religious/spiritual belief system? Or, more broadly, the existence of deity, or an existence (a) before this life or (b) after death? The short answer to all of these types of questions is a friendly, but resounding, No, of course not! Nor are these questions included in the aims of this edited volume. Why? Because these are not scientific questions. That is, these questions are not conducive to the scientific method.* Does this mean that questions not conducive to the scientific method are not important? Again, the answer is a friendly, No. Fortunately, we *can* ask empirical questions about how religious and spiritual principles and activities may or may not be related to better health and well-being. An example empirical question in this regard is: Are higher levels of forgiveness associated with lower levels of depression? The short answer is, Yes (see Chapters 23 and 43). Why is this an empirical question? Because forgiveness can be measured, as can depression.

* The American Psychological Association (APA, 2015, p. 941) defines the *scientific method* as: "a set of procedures, guidelines, assumptions, and attitudes required for the organized and systematic collection, interpretation, and verification of data and the discovery of reproducible evidence, enabling laws and principles to be stated or modified. See also science; scientific explanation." See Chapter 4 for more discussion of the philosophy of science and its interface with the psychology of faith and spirituality.

Chapter 1, Endnote 12: Aside from any/all theological-level claims of any/all past, current, or future religious/spiritual belief systems (and persons) in the world, in my view, all human beings have been, are, and forever will be agnostic,** or as literally translated from Greek, *without knowledge*; in *this* case, regarding the existence of deity, and related potentialities. That is, and more precisely, without *empirical* knowledge of such matters. No doubt there are other ways of knowing (cf. epistemology), but such ways are not necessarily conducive to empiricism and the scientific method (see above). The APA (2015, p. 366) defines *empiricism* as: "1. an approach to epistemology holding that all knowledge of matters of fact either arises from experience or requires experience for its validation. In particular, empiricism denies the possibility of innate ideas, arguing that the mind at birth is like a blank sheet of paper (see tabula rasa). .... 2. the view that experimentation is the most important, if not the only, foundation of scientific knowledge and the means by which individuals evaluate truth claims or the adequacy of theories and models. 3. in philosophy, the position that all linguistic expressions that are not tautologous must be empirically verifiable if they are to be deemed valid or meaningful. This principle was essential to the philosophy of logical positivism. See also positivism." Hence, my use of the phrase *formally agnostic* in reference to those who otherwise select agnostic when presented with the question of whether to identify as religious, spiritual, agnostic, or atheist. See Chapter 4 for more discussion of the philosophy of science and its interface with the psychology of faith and spirituality.

** That is, unless and until empirical (experiential) evidence is discovered (gained). Which evidence ostensibly will only come in some other realm of existence, if there is such a thing. As noted above, I am a believer, but only because I am without *empirical* knowledge.].

6 My other favorite, otherwise secular quote (also with spiritual implications) is from Sir Arthur C. Clarke (1917–2008), a notable figure during his lifetime, including as a prolific author of science fiction (see Clarke, 2000). Sir Arthur surmised that "Two possibilities exist: Either we are alone in the Universe or we are not. Both are equally terrifying" (Clarke, 2025).

7 In this context, individual-level healthcare includes individual persons, couples, families, and groups (in terms of group-level therapy, psychoeducation, etc.). That is, an otherwise circumscribed set of one or more humans in the same room, so to speak, with the healthcare provider(s).

8 This same discussion applies to the debate regarding the (in)compatibility of science and religion. However, in this case *versus* equates with the phrasing of the (in)compatibility of science *with* religion, whereas the implication of using *and* remains the same.

9 In the case of the existence versus non-existence of deity, being empirically unknowable, the dichotomy is false. Thus, both options are subjective and, arguably, qualitatively equal; such that, one is not necessarily "better" or more reasonable than the other. No doubt there will be debate about their qualitative equivalence, but given the subjective nature of the question, the conclusion will be based in personal preference, rather than objectivity. Some may argue that (1) requiring proof from those making a claim that is unknowable is a reasonable burden and/or (2) requiring proof of a negative is an unreasonable burden. I would argue that requiring proof for or against something not conducive to empiricism and the scientific method (cf. personal preference) is another false dichotomy. Put another way, with regard to the question of the existence of deity, some say that there is enough reason/proof (cf. epistemology) for one to (1) believe or (2) disbelieve. Such that, the burden of *choice* is on the individual pondering the question.

10 To be clear, my intention is not to disparage or minimize said previous compendium-based work, which provides extensive empirical evidence in support of the association of ritualistic spirituality with health (cf. the RiTE Model of Spirituality, as described in Chapter 1 of this volume, and briefly expanded upon in this chapter). Rather, quite the contrary, to emphasize that the additional needed information elucidated by the focus of this volume on (1) specific spiritual principles and practices and (2) health and well-being more broadly construed, *together* with said previous foundational work, provides considerable additive, indeed, compounding strength to the argument for recognizing, disseminating, and implementing the science of spirituality, health, and well-being.

11 This is the second time I have included this quote in this chapter, though this time it is in an expanded form. In my view, the definition of health provided by the World Health Organization and its critical importance, cannot be overemphasized.

12 Some might say that given the lack of empirical evidence for deity (etc.), we should therefore abandon religious/spiritual topics, whether scientifically, or altogether. This may be a variant of Type III error,*** or interpreting data as an answer to the wrong question. Remember, the question of the existence of deity and/or a transcendent realm is not conducive to the scientific method and thus, is not an empirical question. Which begs the question of whether non-empirical questions are therefore not important? However, many religious/spiritual topics are conducive to the scientific method and thus, are empirical questions, especially principles and practices as related to health and well-being.

*** The APA (2015, p. 1115) defines *Type III error* as: "1. the error that occurs when there is a discrepancy between the research focus and the hypothesis actually tested." See [https://dictionary.apa.org/type-iii-error].

13 Though this particular difference is profound, there may yet be a thread of similarity here, too. That is, at least in one sense, the basic differences are related to finding an otherwise higher or transcendent-level enabling power (1) external to the self, (2) within the self, or (3) aside from the self (see Chapters 1 and 7). The thread of similarity – and thus, contributing to the earlier discussion of a transcendent thread tying humanity together – is that access to said enabling power is a function of the self. This is not to say that I, myself, directly have the power, but that through the relationship that I have with my *self*, I can access said enabling power.

14 Another way to describe these limitations is with a term coined by Henrich et al. (2010); that is, much of psychological/behavioral science is derived from samples comprised of persons "from Western, Educated, Industrialized, Rich, and Democratic (WEIRD)[1] societies" (p. 61; see also, Arnett, 2008; Thalmayer et al., 2021). In the second paragraph of their paper when introducing the term, Henrich et al. are careful to include an endnote pointing also to "the exceptional nature of this sample, and [that they] do not intend any negative connotations or moral judgments by the acronym" (p. 83).

15 This example is in honor of my friend Christopher S. Dula, Ph.D. (1969-2019). See: https://www.johnsoncitypress.com/news/beloved-etsu-professor-musician-chris-dula-dies/article_1e3d11f4-cf4c-57d9-a847-9553463dbb2b.html

See also: Bumgarner, Webb, and Dula (2016), Webb, Toussaint, and Dula (2014), and Webb, Dula, and Brewer (2012).

References

Allik, J., Realo, A., & McCrae, R. R. (2013). Universality of the five-factor model of personality. In T. A. Widiger & P. T. Costa, Jr. (Eds.), *Personality disorders and the five-factor model of personality*. (pp. 61–74). American Psychological Association. https://doi.org/10.1037/13939-005

American Psychological Association. (2015). *APA dictionary of psychology* (Second ed.). Author.

Arnett, J. J. (2008). The neglected 95%: Why American psychology needs to become less American. *American Psychologist*, *63*(7), 602–614. https://doi.org/10.1037/0003-066X.63.7.602

Bergin, A. E. (1980a). Psychotherapy and religious values. *Journal of Consulting and Clinical Psychology*, *48*(1), 95–105. https://doi.org/10.1037/0022-006X.48.1.95

Bergin, A. E. (1980b). Religious and humanistic values: A reply to Ellis and Walls. *Journal of Consulting and Clinical Psychology*, *48*(5), 642–645. https://doi.org/10.1037/0022-006X.48.5.642

Bumgarner, D. J., Webb, J. R., & Dula, C. S. (2016). Forgiveness and adverse driving outcomes within the past five years: Driving anger, driving anger expression, and aggressive driving behaviors as mediators. *Transportation Research Part F: Traffic Psychology and Behaviour*, *42*, 317–331. https://doi.org/10.1016/j.trf.2016.07.017

Clarke, A. C. (2000). *The collected stories of Arthur C. Clarke*. Tom Doherty Associates, LLC.

Clarke, A. C. (2025). Aurthur C. Clarke: Biography: Quotes. Retrieved May 11, 2025, from https://clarkefoundation.org/arthur-c-clarke-biography/

Cronbach, L. J. (1957). The two disciplines of scientific psychology. *American Psychologist*, *12*(11), 671–684. https://doi.org/10.1037/h0043943

Einstein, A. (1954). *Ideas and opinions* (1994 Modern Library ed.). Random House, Inc.

Ellis, A. (1980). Psychotherapy and atheistic values: A response to A. E. Bergin's 'Psychotherapy and religious values.'. *Journal of Consulting and Clinical Psychology*, *48*(5), 635–639. https://doi.org/10.1037/0022-006X.48.5.635

Henrich, J., Heine, S. J., & Norenzayan, A. (2010). The weirdest people in the world? *Behavioral and Brain Sciences*, *33*(2–3), 61–83. https://doi.org/10.1017/S0140525X0999152X

Hoffman, S. (1992). Procrustean psychotherapy. *Journal of Integrative and Eclectic Psychotherapy*, *11*(1), 5–7.

Kennedy, J. F. (1963). A journey home: John F. Kennedy in Ireland. Retrieved May 11, 2025, from https://www.jfklibrary.org/visit-museum/exhibits/past-exhibits/a-journey-home-john-f-kennedy-in-ireland

Koenig, H. G., VanderWeele, T. J., & Peteet, J. R. (2024). *Handbook of religion and health* (3rd ed.). Oxford University Press.

McCrae, R. R., & Costa, P. T., Jr. (2013). Introduction to the empirical and theoretical status of the five-factor model of personality traits. In T. A. Widiger & P. T. Costa, Jr. (Eds.), *Personality disorders and the five-factor model of personality*. (Third ed., pp. 15–27). American Psychological Association. https://doi.org/10.1037/13939-002

Pargament, K. I. (2013). Searching for the sacred: Toward a nonreductionistic theory of spirituality. In K. I. Pargament, J. J. Exline, & J. W. Jones (Eds.), *APA handbook of psychology, religion, and spirituality (Vol 1): Context, theory, and research*. (pp. 257–273). American Psychological Association. https://doi.org/10.1037/14045-014

Peterson, C., & Seligman, M. E. P. (2004). *Character strengths and virtues: A handbook and classification*. American Psychological Association / Oxford University Press.

Ramamurthy, C., Fraser, T., Krysinska, K., Hawgood, J., Kõlves, K., Reifels, L., Reavley, N., & Andriessen, K. (2025). Effectiveness of suicide postvention service models and guidelines 2014–2024: A scoping review. *Preventive Medicine: An International Journal Devoted to Practice and Theory*, *195*, 1–8. https://doi.org/10.1016/j.ypmed.2025.108279

Rosmarin, D. H., & Koenig, H. G. (Eds.). (2020). *Handbook of spirituality, religion, and mental health* (2nd ed.). Elsevier Academic Press.

Salaman, E. (1955). A talk with Einstein. *The Listener*, *54*(1384), 370–371.

Spilka, B., & Ladd, K. L. (2013). *The psychology of prayer: A scientific approach*. The Guilford Press. http://search.ebscohost.com/login.aspx?direct=true&db=psyh&AN=2012-26099-000&site=ehost-live

Thalmayer, A. G., Toscanelli, C., & Arnett, J. J. (2021). The neglected 95% revisited: Is American psychology becoming less American? *American Psychologist*, *76*(1), 116–129. https://doi.org/10.1037/amp0000622

Toussaint, L. L., Webb, J. R., & Keltner, W. (2012). Religion, spirituality, and mental health. In J. D. Aten, K. A. O'Grady, & E. L. Worthington, Jr. (Eds.), *The psychology of religion and spirituality for clinicians: Using research in your practice* (pp. 331–356). Routledge.

Wallerstein, N., Duran, B., Oetzel, J. G., & Minkler, M. (Eds.). (2018). *Community-based participatory research for health: Advancing social and health equity* (third ed.). Jossey-Bass.

Webb, J. R. (2007/2003). Spiritual factors and adjustment in medical rehabilitation: Understanding forgiveness as a means of coping. In A. E. DellOrto & P. W. Power (Eds.), *The psychological and social impact of illness and disability* (5th ed., pp. 455–471). Springer. (Reprinted from *Journal of Applied Rehabilitation Counseling*, 34(3), 16–24: 2003.)

Webb, J. R. (2021). *Understanding forgiveness and addiction: Theory, research, and clinical application*. Routledge.

Webb, J. R. (in press). Spirituality and addictions. In J. M. Currier, J. Fox, & C. Vieten (Eds.), *Handbook of training in spiritual and religious competencies in mental health professions*. Oxford University Press.

Webb, J. R., Dula, C. S., & Brewer, K. (2012). Forgiveness and aggression among college students. *Journal of Spirituality in Mental Health*, *14*(1), 38–58. https://doi.org/10.1080/19349637.2012.642669

Webb, J. R., Hirsch, J. K., & Toussaint, L. L. (2015). Forgiveness as a positive psychotherapy for addiction and suicide: Theory, research, and practice. *Spirituality in Clinical Practice*, *2*(1), 48–60. https://doi.org/10.1037/scp0000054 (Suicide and Spirituality in the Military)

Webb, J. R., Toussaint, L., & Dula, C. S. (2014). Ritualistic, theistic, and existential spirituality: Initial psychometric qualities of the RiTE measure of spirituality. *Journal of Religion and Health*, *53*(4), 972–985. https://doi.org/10.1007/s10943-013-9697-y

World Health Organization. (2025). *Constitution of the World Health Organization*. Author. Retrieved April 29, 2025, from https://www.who.int/about/governance/constitution

Index

bolded page numbers (e.g., **10**): text within tables
italicized page numbers (e.g., *404*): text within figures
#n# (e.g., 137n4): page number of text within a chapter note

Note: This is a non-exhaustive list; both for possible terms included, and of the page numbers for the terms included. Many entries have multiple occurrences in this volume, which are not listed here. For example, regarding the Index term "belief systems," there are many references to the mainstream religious/spiritual traditions of the world (i.e., Judaism, Christianity, Islam, Hinduism, and Buddhism) in many and varied chapters. However, simply put, many otherwise important topics are not listed in the Index, and for many of the Index terms featured there are too many occurrences to include. If a term and occurrence for any particular topic is provided, it is likely one of the first (if not the only) occurrence(s) in any given chapter.

For Product Safety Concerns and Information please contact our
EU representative GPSR@taylorandfrancis.com Taylor & Francis
Verlag GmbH, Kaufingerstraße 24, 80331 München, Germany